The Jerusalem Talmud
Second Order: Mo'ed
Tractates *Pesaḥim* and *Yoma*

Studia Judaica

Forschungen zur Wissenschaft des Judentums

Begründet von
Ernst Ludwig Ehrlich

Herausgegeben von
Günter Stemberger,
Charlotte Fonrobert und
Alexander Samely

Band 74

De Gruyter

The Jerusalem Talmud
תלמוד ירושלמי

Second Order: Moʻed
סדר מועד
Tractates *Pesaḥim* and *Yoma*
מסכתות פסחים ויומא

Edition, Translation, and Commentary

by
Heinrich W. Guggenheimer

De Gruyter

ISBN 978-3-11-068124-6
e-ISBN (PDF) 978-3-11-031598-1

This volume is text- and page-identical with the hardback published in 2013.

Library of Congress Control Number: 2020943229

Bibliographic information published by the Deutsche Nationalbibliothek
The Deutsche Nationalbibliothek lists this publication in the
Deutsche Nationalbibliografie;
detailed bibliographic data are available on the Internet at http://dnb.dnb.de.

© 2020 Walter de Gruyter GmbH, Berlin/Boston

Printing and binding: CPI books GmbH, Leck

www.degruyter.com

Preface

The present volume is the Fifteenth in this series of the Jerusalem Talmud, the second in a four-volume edition, translation, and Commentary of the Second Order of this Talmud. The principles of the edition regarding text, vocalization, and Commentary have been spelled out in detail in the Introduction to the first volume. The text in this volume is based on the manuscript text of the Yerushalmi edited by J. Sussman for the Academy of the Hebrew Language, Jerusalem 2001. The text essentially represents an outline, to be fleshed out by a teacher's explanation. The translation should mirror this slant; it should not endow the text with literary qualities which the original does not possess. In particular, the translation is not intended to stand separate from the Commentary. In one respect the principles of edition have been changed from the previous volumes. Instead of occasionally remarking about questionable changes of the text by the corrector preparing the Venice *editio princeps,* in all cases where the corrector changed the text, the scribe's version is given in (parentheses), the corrector's in [brackets]. Naturally, usually the corrector rectifies spelling errors and omissions, mostly sentences left out because of homeoteleuton; but in many cases the corrector's additions are questionable, as indicated in the Commentary. The full text will permit every reader to form his own judgment. Translator's additions in the English text are put in {braces}.

As in the preceding volumes, for each paragraph the folio and line numbers of the Krotoschin edition are added. It should be remembered that these numbers may differ from the *editio princeps* by up to three lines. It seems to be important that a translation of the Yerushalmi be accompanied by the text, to enable the reader to compare the interpretation with other translations.

Biblical quotations are given with the masoretic accents, except for words which differ (usually by *plene* spelling) from the masoretic texts. Since the quotes are part of oral tradition, the deviations in spelling are examples of substandard spelling, rather than changes in the text.

Again, I wish to thank my wife, Dr. Eva Guggenheimer, who acted as critic, style editor, proof reader, and expert on the Latin and Greek vocabulary. Her own notes on some possible Latin and Greek etymologies are identified by (E. G.).

Contents

Introduction to Tractate Pesaḥim   1

Pesaḥim Chapter 1, אור לארבעה עשר

    Halakhah 1   3
    Halakhah 2   15
    Halakhah 3   16
    Halakhah 4   20
    Halakhah 5   25
    Halakhah 6   28
    Halakhah 7   29
    Halakhah 8   35

Pesaḥim Chapter 2, כל שעה

    Halakhah 1   49
    Halakhah 2   63
    Halakhah 3   73
    Halakhah 4   78
    Halakhah 5   88
    Halakhah 6   91
    Halakhah 7   92

Pesaḥim Chapter 3, ואלו עוברין

    Halakhah 1   97
    Halakhah 2   103
    Halakhah 3   107
    Halakhah 4   113
    Halakhah 5   115
    Halakhah 6   116
    Halakhah 7   118
    Halakhah 8   121

Pesaḥim Chapter 4 מקום שנהגו

    Halakhah 1   124
    Halakhah 2   134
    Halakhah 3   135

Halakhah 4	141
Halakhah 5	146
Halakhah 6	146
Halakhah 7	147
Halakhah 8	149
Halakhah 9	150

Pesaḥim Chapter 5 תמיד נשחט

Halakhah 1	160
Halakhah 2	167
Halakhah 3	178
Halakhah 4	184
Halakhah 5	195
Halakhah 6	197
Halakhah 7	198
Halakhah 8	200
Halakhah 9	202
Halakhah 10	203

Pesaḥim Chapter 6 אילו דברים

Halakhah 1	205
Halakhah 2	216
Halakhah 3	220
Halakhah 4	222
Halakhah 5	225
Halakhah 6	226
Halakhah 7	229
Halakhah 8	234

Pesaḥim Chapter 7 כיצד צולין

Halakhah 1	239
Halakhah 2	244
Halakhah 3	248
Halakhah 4	249
Halakhah 5	251
Halakhah 6	259
Halakhah 7	265
Halakhah 8	276
Halakhah 9	277
Halakhah 10	285

Halakhah 11	289
Halakhah 12	293

Pesaḥim Chapter 8 האשה

Halakhah 1	299
Halakhah 2	306
Halakhah 3	310
Halakhah 4	314
Halakhah 5	317
Halakhah 6	318
Halakhah 7	320
Halakhah 8	321

Pesaḥim Chapter 9 מי שהיה טמא

Halakhah 1	329
Halakhah 2	334
Halakhah 3	336
Halakhah 4	338
Halakhah 5	343
Halakhah 6	348
Halakhah 7	349
Halakhah 8	350
Halakhah 9	351
Halakhah 10	353

Pesaḥim Chapter 10 ערב פסחים

Halakhah 1	355
Halakhah 2	363
Halakhah 3	365
Halakhah 4	368
Halakhah 5	370
Halakhah 6	370
Halakhah 7	373
Halakhah 8	374
Halakhah 9	375

Introduction to Tractate Yoma — 379

Yoma Chapter 1 שבעת ימים

Halakhah 1	380

Halakhah 2	407
Halakhah 3	411
Halakhah 4	413
Halakhah 5	414
Halakhah 6	419
Halakhah 7	419
Halakhah 8	420

Yoma Chapter 2 בראשונה

Halakhah 1	422
Halakhah 2	431
Halakhah 3	434
Halakhah 4	441
Halakhah 5	442
Halakhah 6	445

Yoma Chapter 3 אמר להם הממונה

Halakhah 1	447
Halakhah 2	449
Halakhah 3	452
Halakhah 4	454
Halakhah 5	456
Halakhah 6	461
Halakhah 7	469
Halakhah 8	475
Halakhah 9	480

Yoma Chapter 4 טרף בקלפי

Halakhah 1	485
Halakhah 2	494
Halakhah 3	495
Halakhah 4	499
Halakhah 5	500
Halakhah 6	506

Yoma Chapter 5 הוציאו לו את הכף

Halakhah 1	510
Halakhah 2	514
Halakhah 3	519
Halakhah 4	523
Halakhah 5	525

Halakhah 6	534
Halakhah 7	536
Halakhah 6	545

Yoma Chapter 6 שני שעירי

Halakhah 1	550
Halakhah 2	556
Halakhah 3	558
Halakhah 4	562
Halakhah 5	565

Yoma Chapter 7 בא לו כהן גדול

Halakhah 1	576
Halakhah 2	580
Halakhah 3	585
Halakhah 5	587

Yoma Chapter 8 יום הכיפורים

Halakhah 1	592
Halakhah 2	599
Halakhah 3	601
Halakhah 4	609
Halakhah 5	611
Halakhah 6	615
Halakhah 8	620
Halakhah 9	623

Addenda and Corrigenda to prior volumes	627

Indices

Sigla	629
Index of Biblical quotations	629
Index of Talmudical quotations	
Babylonian Talmud	632
Jerusalem Talmud	634
Mishnah	635
Tosephta	636
Midrashim and Related Texts	637
Rabbinic and Modern Authors	637

Index of Greek, Latin, Arabic, and Hebrew Words 638
Subject Index 639

Introduction to Tractate Pesaḥim

The Tractate deals with all aspects of the Passover celebration, from the removal of leavened matter before the Fourteenth of Nisan (*Ex.* 12:15; 13:7), the rules of the *Pesaḥ* sacrifice on the Fourteenth and its consumption in the following night (*Ex.* 12:43-50) with unleavened bread and bitter herbs (*Ex.* 12:8-9), followed by the seven days of the Holiday of Unleavened Bread (*Ex.*12:14-20), with the Temple ritual of the Second *Pesaḥ* on the Fourteenth of the following month for individuals impure or absent at the time of the original *Pesaḥ* (*Num.* 9:9-14). It is this Second *Pesaḥ* which explains the plural in the title of the Tractate.

The rules of removal of leavened matter on the Thirteenth of Nisan are the topic of Chapter One. Chapter Two is dedicated to the rules of preparing the flour for the unleavened breads, *mazzot*, together with the list of herbs classified as bitter for consumption with the sacrifice in Temple times, or in later times separately as a rabbinic ordinance in remembrance of the Temple service. The rules of actually baking the *mazzot* are the topic of Chapter Three. Since as a general rabbinic rule work is forbidden for any person offering a sacrifice during the time his sacrifice is dealt with in the Temple, people present in Jerusalem in the afternoon of the Fourteenth of Nisan automatically are prevented from working anytime during that period. Chapter Four deals with the extension of this rule to the entire afternoon of the Fourteenth and possibly to the entire daylight part of that day. Chapters Five and Six treat the Temple ritual of the *Pesaḥ* sacrifice while Chapter Seven first gives the rules for roasting the lamb outside the Temple. Since the rules for the Second *Pesaḥ* clearly are formulated for individuals it is concluded that the original *Pesaḥ*, while a family affair, has the status of a public sacrifice and therefore is to be brought in impurity if a majority of the people are impure. The delicate rules in this case form the second topic of Chapter Seven. By biblical decree the *Pesaḥ* is available only to members of a well-defined group. Chapter Eight gives the rules of membership, adding and subtracting to it, and complications arising from competing sacrifices. Chapter Nine gives the rules of the Second *Pesaḥ* which in contrast to the First is not a family affair but is only required for and available to adult males. Finally Chapter Ten gives the rules of the *Seder* celebration in the night of the Fifteenth of Nisan which is the essence of the modern observation of Passover[1].

Both in *Pesaḥim* and in *Yoma* the count of Mishnaiot, taken from the *editio princeps*, and that of Halakhot in the manuscript frequently do not correspond to one another.

---

1. This celebration is commented on in detail in the author's *The Scholar's Haggadah*, Northvale NJ 1995 (xi + 418 pp.)

אור לארבעה עשר פרק ראשון

(fol.27a) **משנה א**׃ אוֹר לְאַרְבָּעָה עָשָׂר בּוֹדְקִין אֶת הֶחָמֵץ לְאוֹר הַנֵּר. כָּל־מָקוֹם שֶׁאֵין מַכְנִיסִין בּוֹ חָמֵץ אֵינוֹ צָרִיךְ בְּדִיקָה. וּבְמָה אָמְרוּ שְׁתֵּי שׁוּרוֹת בַּמַּרְתֵּף מָקוֹם שֶׁמַּכְנִיסִין בּוֹ חָמֵץ. בֵּית שַׁמַּאי אוֹמְרִים שְׁתֵּי שׁוּרוֹת עַל פְּנֵי כָל־הַמַּרְתֵּף וּבֵית הִלֵּל אוֹמְרִים שְׁתֵּי שׁוּרוֹת הַחִיצוֹנוֹת שֶׁהֵן הָעֶלְיוֹנוֹת׃

Mishnah 1: At nightfall of the Fourteenth one checks leavened matter by candle light. A place into which no leavened matter is introduced does not need checking. And where[1] did they say two rows in the cellar[2]? A place where one introduces leavened matter. The House of Shammai are saying two rows in the front of the entire cellar[3], but the House of Hillel are saying the outermost two rows which are the uppermost[4].

1 The Babli and Maimonides read ולמה "why" instead of ובמה "where".

2 The storage place for wine or oil amphoras. While this is not a place where one usually stores leavened matter it is possible that the person who is asked to bring a barrel of wine or oil for household use is eating some bread and deposits it temporarily near the entrance door. Therefore it needs checking except for a wholesaler's cellar.

3 The amphoras are arranged in a rectangular pattern. The House of Shammai requires checking of two rows in all directions accessible from the door. Since usually one starts arranging the amphoras starting at two walls meeting at an angle, the outer rows at the other two sides of the rectangular arrangement have to be checked.

4 Only the rows facing the door have to be checked. If the amphoras also are stacked on top of one another, the two top rows facing the door have to be checked.

(27a line 47) **הלכה א**׃ אוֹר לְאַרְבָּעָה עָשָׂר כול׳. כָּתוּב וּשְׁמַרְתֶּם אֶת־הַמַּצּוֹת כִּי בְּעֶצֶם הַיּוֹם הַזֶּה הוֹצֵאתִי אֶת־צִבְאוֹתֵיכֶם מֵאֶרֶץ מִצְרָיִם. בָּרִאשֹׁן בְּאַרְבָּעָה עָשָׂר יוֹם לַחוֹדֶשׁ בָּעֶרֶב תֹּאכְלוּ מַצּוֹת וגו׳. מָה אֲנָן קַיָּימִין. אִם לַאֲכִילַת מַצָּה. כְּבָר כָּתוּב שִׁבְעַת יָמִים מַצּוֹת תֹּאכֵלוּ. וְאִם לוֹמַר שֶׁמַּתְחִיל בְּאַרְבָּעָה עָשָׂר. וְהָכְתִיב עַד יוֹם הָאֶחָד וְעֶשְׂרִים לַחוֹדֶשׁ. אֶלָּא אִם אֵינוֹ עִנְיָן לַאֲכִילַת מַצָּה תְּנֵיהוּ עִנְיָן לְבִיעוּר חָמֵץ.

Halakhah 1: "At nightfall of the fourteenth," etc. It is written[5]: *You shall guard the mazzot, because on this same day I took out your multitudes from* *the Land of Egypt. On the first, on the fourteenth of the month, in the evening, you shall eat mazzot*, etc. Where do we hold[6]? If for eating *mazzah*, is it not already written, *seven days you shall eat mazzot*[7]? Or if to say that one starts on the Fourteenth, is it not written, *until the twenty-first of the month*[5]? But if it is not needed as a reference to the eating of *mazzah*, take it as a reference to the elimination of leavened matter[8].

5   Ex. 12:17-18.
6   What means *on the first*? Does it mean on the first month, or on the first day of the holidays?
7   Ex. 12:15.
8   As usual, the argument partially refers to parts of the verse which are not quoted in the text. It says in 12:15, *seven days you shall eat mazzot, only on the first day you shall eliminate sour dough from your houses*. No calendar date has been given. One could read v. 17 to state that *mazzot* have to be eaten and leavened matter eliminated on the 14th. This is impossible since the same verse states that the seventh day is the 21st. Therefore the obligation to eat *mazzot* starts in the evening preceding the 15th. Since it is accepted doctrine that the calendar day starts at nightfall of the preceding night, the reference to the 14th cannot possibly refer to eating, but must give the date of the elimination of leavened matter for which the search in the preceding night is a preparation.

(27a line 52) לָמָה לְאוֹר הַנֵּר. אָמַר רִבִּי שְׁמוּאֵל בַּר רַב יִצְחָק. מִפְּנֵי שֶׁהַנֵּר בּוֹדֵק כָּל־שֶׁהוּא. לָמָה בַלַּיְלָה. אָמַר רִבִּי יוֹסֵה. שֶׁאֵין בְּדִיקַת הַנֵּר יָפָה אֶלָּא בַלַּיְלָה. רִבִּי מָנָא לֹא אָמַר כֵּן. וּשְׁמַרְתֶּם אֶת־הַיּוֹם הַזֶּה לְדֹרֹתֵיכֶם לְחוּקַּת עוֹלָם: עֲשֵׂה שֶׁיְהֵא הַיּוֹם וְהַלַּיְלָה מְשׁוּמָּרִין. וְיַתְחִיל בִּשְׁלֹשָׁה עָשָׂר וִיהֵא הַיּוֹם וְהַלַּיְלָה מְשׁוּמָּרִין. אַף אִית לֵיהּ כַּיי דָמַר רִבִּי יוֹסֵי. וְיַתְחִיל אוֹר לִשְׁלֹשָׁה עָשָׂר. אִין כֵּינִי יִבְדּוֹק אֲפִילוּ מֵרֹאשׁ חוֹדֶשׁ.

Why by candlelight? Rebbi Samuel bar Rav Isaac said, because a candle permits checking everywhere[9]. Why in the night? Rebbi Yose said, because checking with a candle is exact only during night time[10]. Rebbi Mana did not say so: *And guard this day for your generations as an eternal law*[5], see to it that day and night be guarded[11]. Then should one not start on the Thirteenth that day and night be guarded? He also agrees with the statement of Rebbi Yose[12]. Then should one start in the evening of the Thirteenth? If so, he could even check on the beginning of the month[13].

9   In holes and crevices which are dark in daytime (Babli 8a). The "candle" mentioned here is a small clay vessel filled with oil.

10   As stated later, candle light is not effective during daytime.
11   The entire day should be dedicated to the elimination of leavened matter.
12   One cannot say that R. Mana disagrees with R. Yose; he adds to his statement.
13   Since checking two weeks in advance would be useless, so is checking a full day in advance. Since checking should be done at nighttime, the only remaining date is the evening of the 14th of Nisan (preceding the day).

(27a line 58) רִבִּי יִרְמְיָה אָמַר רִבִּי שְׁמוּאֵל בַּר רַב יִצְחָק בָּעֵי. מָהוּ לִבְדּוֹק לְאוֹר הָאֲבוּקוֹת. מַה צְּרִיכָה לֵיהּ. מִפְּנֵי שֶׁאוֹרָן מַבְלִיחַ. רִבִּי שְׁמוּאֵל בַּר רַב יִצְחָק כְּדַעְתֵּיהּ. דְּרִבִּי שְׁמוּאֵל בַּר רַב יִצְחָק אָמַר. מִפְּנֵי שֶׁהַנֵּר בּוֹדֵק כָּל־שֶׁהוּא. אַף עַל פִּי שֶׁאֵין רְעָיָה לַדָּבָר זֵכֶר לַדָּבָר. וְהָיָה ׄ בַּיּוֹם הַהוּא אֲחַפֵּשׂ אֶת־יְרוּשָׁלַם בַּנֵּרוֹת. וְאִית דְּבָעֵי אֵימַר. נִישְׁמַעִינָהּ מִן הָדָא. נֵר יְיָ נִשְׁמַת אָדָם חֹפֵשׂ כָּל־חַדְרֵי־בָטֶן׃

Rebbi Jeremiah said that Rebbi Samuel bar Rav Isaac asked: May one check by the light of torches? What is his problem? Because their light is unsteady[14]. Rebbi Samuel bar Rav Isaac is consistent since Rebbi Samuel bar Rav Isaac said, because a candle permits checking everywhere[15].   [[16]Even though it is not proof of the matter, it is an allusion to the matter: *It shall be on that day*[17] *that I shall search Jerusalem by candles*[18]. But some want to say,] one can understand it from the following: *A candle of the Eternal is a person's soul, it searches all rooms of the body*[19].

14   Since the light is unsteady, it does not serve in searching nooks and crannies.
15   The scribe wrote בודק כל שהוא כל שהוא "checking extremely well everywhere." The second כל שהוא was deleted by the corrector; probably incorrectly.
16   Tosephta *Pisha* 1:1; corrector's addition.
17   Misquote from memory.
18   *Zeph.* 1:12, Babli 7b-8a.
19   *Prov.* 20:27, Babli 7b-8a.

(27a line 63) אָמַר רִבִּי יוֹסֵה. מַתְנִיתָא אָמְרָה שֶׁבְּדִיקַת הַיּוֹם בְּדִיקָה. דְּתַנִּינָן. רִבִּי יוּדָה אוֹמֵר. בּוֹדְקִין אוֹר לְאַרְבָּעָה עָשָׂר וּבְאַרְבָּעָה עָשָׂר שַׁחֲרִית וּבִשְׁעַת הַבִּיעוּר. לֹא סוֹף דָּבָר רִבִּי יוּדָה אֶלָּא אֲפִילוּ דְרַבָּנִין. דְּתַנִינָן. וַחֲכָמִים אוֹמְרִים אִם לֹא בָדַק אוֹר אַרְבָּעָה עָשָׂר יִבְדּוֹק בְּאַרְבָּעָה עָשָׂר. וְצָרִיךְ לִבְדּוֹק לְאוֹר הַנֵּר. נִישְׁמַעִינָהּ מִן הָדָא. אֵין בּוֹדְקִין לֹא לְאוֹר הַחַמָּה וְלֹא לְאוֹר הַלְּבָנָה וְלֹא לְאוֹר הַכּוֹכָבִים אֶלָּא לְאוֹר הַנֵּר. נִיחָא לֹא לְאוֹר הַלְּבָנָה וְלֹא לְאוֹר הַכּוֹכָבִים (אלא) [וְלֹא] לְאוֹר הַחַמָּה. וְכִי יֵשׁ חַמָּה בַּלַּיְלָה. הָדָא אָמְרָה. אֲפִילוּ בַּיּוֹם צָרִיךְ לִבְדּוֹק לְאוֹר הַנֵּר. לֹא

סוֹף דָּבָר בַּיִת שֶׁאֵין בּוֹ אוֹרָה. אֶלָּא אֲפִילוּ בַּיִת שֶׁיֵּשׁ בּוֹ אוֹרָה אֲפִילוּ בְיוֹם צָרִיךְ לִבְדּוֹק לְאוֹר הַנֵּר.

Rebbi Yose said, the Mishnah implies that checking during daytime is called checking, as we have stated[20]: "Rebbi Jehudah says, one checks at nightfall of the Fourteenth, and on the Fourteenth, and at the moment of elimination." Not only Rebbi Jehudah but even the rabbis, as we have stated: "If he did not check at nightfall of the Fourteenth he shall check on the Fourteenth."

Is it obligatory to check by candlelight[21]? Let us hear from the following[22] "One checks neither by sunlight, nor by moonlight, nor by starlight, but by candlelight." One understands "neither by moonlight, nor by starlight," but "neither by sunlight"? Is there any sun in the night? This implies, even during daytime one has to check by candlelight; not only in a house without light, but even in a house which has light, even during daytime, it is necessary to check by candlelight.

20 Mishnah 3.
21 When checking during daytime, even following the rabbis.
22 Tosephta 1:1, Babli 7b.

(27a line 72) מְבוֹאוֹת הָאֲפֵלִין מָהוּ שֶׁיְּהֵא צָרִיךְ לְבוֹדְקָן כַּתְּחִילָּה לְאוֹר הַנֵּר. מִילֵּיהוֹן דְּרַבָּנִין אֱמְרִין. לֹא כְמָה דְהוּא מְנָהַר בַּלַּיְלִיָא הוּא מְנָהַר בַּיוֹמָמָא. דְּאָמַר רַב הוּנָא. כַּד הֲוִינָן עֲרָקִין בְּאִילֵּין בּוֹטִיתָא דְּסִדְרָא רַבָּא הָיוּ מַדְלִיקִין עָלֵינוּ נֵירוֹת. בְּשָׁעָה שֶׁהָיוּ כֵּיהִים הָיִינוּ יוֹדְעִין שֶׁהוּא יוֹם. וּבְשָׁעָה שֶׁהָיוּ מַבְהִיקִין הָיִינוּ יוֹדְעִין שֶׁהוּא לַיְלָה. וַתְּיָא כַיי דְּאָמַר רִבִּי אֲחַוָוא בַּר זְעִירָא. נֹחַ בִּכְנִיסָתוֹ לַתֵּיבָה הִכְנִיס עִמּוֹ אֲבָנִים טוֹבוֹת וּמַרְגָּלִיּוֹת. בְּשָׁעָה שֶׁהָיוּ כֵּיהוֹת הָיָה יוֹדֵעַ שֶׁהוּא יוֹם. וּבְשָׁעָה שֶׁהָיוּ מַבְהִיקוֹת הָיָה יוֹדֵעַ שֶׁהוּא לַיְלָה. לָמָה. יֵשׁ חַיָּה אוֹכֶלֶת בַּיּוֹם וְיֵשׁ חַיָּה אוֹכֶלֶת בַּלַּיְלָה. וְהָא כְתִיב צוֹהַר תַּעֲשֶׂה לַתֵּיבָה. כְּמָאן דְּאָמַר. לֹא שִׁימְּשׁוּ הַמַּזָּלוֹת בִּשְׁנַת הַמַּבּוּל.

May one[23] check dark passages[24] purposely[25] by candlelight? The words of the rabbis imply that not as it radiates at night it radiates during the day, [26]as Rav Huna said, when we were fleeing to these catacombs of the great assembly they were lighting candles for us. When they were faint, we knew that it was day; when they were bright we knew that it was night. This parallels what Rebbi Ahawa bar Ze`ira[27] said, when Noah entered the Ark he brought with him precious stones and pearls. When they were dull, he knew that it was daytime; when they were shiny he knew that it was nighttime.

Why? There are animals eating at daytime and there are animals eating at nighttime. But is there not written, *make a skylight to the ark*[28]? Following him who said that the stars were not operative in the year of the flood[29].

23 This translation of צריך follows S. Liebermann.
24 Roofed public spaces.
25 As the parallel expression in the next paragraph shows, a word "during daytime" is missing here.
26 *Gen. r.* 31:12, a much better text. As given here, the story is Babylonian and there is no reason why they should be fleeing, and why the earth under the place (under the open sky) where the twice-yearly assembly of scholars was held should have been tunnelled. In *Gen. rabba* the name is *Rebbi Huna*, the place is Tiberias, and they were hiding from soldiers.
27 The son of R. Ze`ira. In *Gen. r.* "R. Phineas in the name of R. Ze`ira". In the Babli *Sanhedrin* 108b is a similar statement of R. Johanan.
28 *Gen.* 6:16.
29 *Gen. r.* 25:2, interpretation of *Gen.* 8:22.

(27b line 7) רִבִּי יִרְמְיָה בָעֵי. בָּתֵּי כְנֵיסִיּוֹת וּבָתֵּי מִדְרָשׁוֹת מָהוּ שֶׁיִּהוּ צְרִיכִין בְּדִיקָה. מַה צְרִיכָה לֵיהּ. שֶׁכֵּן מַכְנִיסִין לְשָׁם בְּאִבָּרַיּוּת וּבְרָאשֵׁי חֲדָשִׁים. וַתֵּי פְּשִׁיטָא לֵיהּ וְהָכֵן צְרִיכָה לֵיהּ. הוֹאִיל וְאוֹרָן מְרוּבֶּה. מָהוּ שֶׁיְּהֵא צָרִיךְ לְבוֹדְקָן כַּתְּחִילָּה בַּיּוֹם לְאוֹר הַנֵּר.

רִבִּי יוֹסֵה בָעֵי. חֲצֵירוֹת שֶׁבִּירוּשָׁלִַם שֶׁאוֹכְלִין שָׁם חַלּוֹת תּוֹדָה וּרְקִיקֵי נָזִיר. מָהוּ שֶׁיִּהוּ צְרִיכִין בְּדִיקָה. בְּלֹא כֵן אֵיכֵן בְּדוּקוֹת מִן הַנּוֹתָר. יָבֹא כְהָדָא תַּנָּא רִבִּי זְכַרְיָה חַתְנֵי דְרִבִּי לֵוִי. נִידָּה חוֹפֶפֶת וְסוֹרֶקֶת. [כֹּהֶנֶת אֵינָהּ חוֹפֶפֶת וְסוֹרֶקֶת. נִידָה כֹּהֶנֶת חוֹפֶפֶת וְסוֹרֶקֶת.] שֶׁלֹּא תַחֲלוֹק בֵּין נִידָּה לִנְידָה. אוֹף הָכָא שֶׁלֹּא תַחֲלוֹק בֵּין בִּיעוּר לְבִיעוּר. תַּנֵּי רִבִּי גַמְלִיאֵל בַּר אִינְיָינֵי קוֹמֵי רִבִּי מָנָא. נִידָּה שֶׁהִיא מַפְסֶקֶת כָּל־שִׁבְעָה חוֹפֶפֶת וְסוֹרֶקֶת. כֹּהֶנֶת שֶׁהִיא טוֹבֶלֶת בְּכָל־יוֹם אֵינָהּ חוֹפֶפֶת וְאֵינָהּ סוֹרֶקֶת. אָמַר לֵיהּ. לְשׁוֹמֶרֶת יוֹם כְּנֶגֶד יוֹם נִצְרְכָה.

Rebbi Jeremiah asked: Do synagogues and houses of study need checking? What is his problem? Since one brings[30] there for intercalations[31] and on the days of the New Moon. It should be obvious for him[32], but what really is his problem? Since they are very well illuminated, may one check them purposely during daytime by candlelight[33]?

Rebbi Yose asked: The courtyards in Jerusalem where one eats the bread of thanksgiving offerings[34] and the wafers of a *nazir*[35], do they need checking? Are they not checked anyhow for leftovers[36]? It should be parallel to what Rebbi Zachariah the son-in-law of Rebbi Levi stated: A menstruating woman washes her hair and combs[37]. A priestly woman does not wash her hair and comb[38]. A menstruating priestly woman washes her hair and combs, not to differentiate between one menstruating woman and another. So also here, not to differentiate between elimination and elimination. Rabbi Gamliel bar Inyany stated before Rebbi Mana: A menstruating woman who interrupts for seven days washes her hair and combs. A priestly woman who immerses herself every day does not wash her hair and comb[39]. He told him, it is necessary for one who watches one day for a day[40].

30 In general it is forbidden to bring food into a synagogue or study hall proper, but for a meal accompanying the public declaration of the new month or the additional month one brought food there, bread and vegetables (Babli *Sanhedrin* 70b) or grapes and bread (Yerushalmi *Berakhot* 6:4, Note 149).

31 In a responsum of R. Nissim of Kairawan (*Teshuvot Hegaonim Lyck*, #105) and the Frankfurt ms. of *Or zarua* II §453, עיבריות. Even the word spelled with א is interpreted as if written with ע, "intercalations"; J. N. Epstein, *Tarbiz* 5 (1933-34) p. 263. In the printed editions of the Yerushalmi, following a correction on the margin of the ms., "on Sabbaths" (cf. R. Nissim *loc. cit.*, p. 34).

32 That one has to check, even if the place was not usually used for public meals.

33 And not in the evening of the 14th, when people are occupied in their own houses. Since no answer is given, the answer is negative.

34 Which have an obligatory component of leavened bread, *Lev.* 7:13.

35 Part of the offering of the *nazir* at the fulfillment of his vow, *Num.* 6:15. These are unleavened.

36 Since any leftovers from any well-being offering, including the thanksgiving offering, must be burned (*Lev.* 7:17), every day of the year these localities are treated the way every other dwelling is treated on Passover Eve.

37 She becomes pure by immersing *all* her body in water. Therefore it is imperative that not two hairs cling together; before immersion she has to make sure that this does not happen.

38 The wife, unmarried daughter, or slave of a Cohen who participate with the Cohen in eating heave and other sancta. As long as the rules of purity could be kept, these women, together with the Cohen, have to immerse themselves every day close to sundown (cf. Mishnah *Berakhot* 1:1, Note 3). Therefore washing the hair is not necessary. Quoted Tosaphot *Niddah* 66b.

39 From the comparison of the menstruating and the priestly women one cannot infer anything since the menstruating priestly woman is excluded from the common meal of *sancta* for the period of her impurity. The statement which exempts her from washing her hair applies only to pure priestly women.

40 As long as the rules of purity could be observed, a woman in the household of a Cohen was obligated to reduce the period of

her impurity to a minimum. The method by which any other woman could avoid showing her blood to a rabbinic authority to ascertain the status of her impurity (cf. *Niddah* 4:1 Note 3) is not available to the priestly woman. It is rabbinic doctrine that after one menstruation, the next is possible only after 11 days.(Mishnah *Niddah* 4:7). If she loses blood on one of these days, she does not follow the rules of *niddah* but those of *zavah*. For the first two occurrences in one period she is impure only for 24 hours. The statement about the impure priestly woman is needed to decree that even an interruption of one day without immersion triggers the obligation of washing the hair.

(27b line 14) חוֹרֵי הַבַּיִת הָעֶלְיוֹנִים וְהַתַּחְתּוֹנִים וְהַיָּצִיעַ וְהַחֲדוּת וְהָעֲלִיָּה וְנַג הַבַּד וְנַג הַמִּגְדָּל בֵּית הַתֶּבֶן וּבֵית הַבָּקָר וּבֵית הָעֵצִים וּבֵית הָאוֹצָרוֹת אוֹצָרוֹת הַיַּיִן וְאוֹצָרוֹת הַשֶּׁמֶן וְאוֹצָרוֹת הַפֵּירוֹת אֵינָן צְרִיכִין בְּדִיקָה. נִיחָא הָעֶלְיוֹנִים. וְהַתַּחְתּוֹנִים. הָדָא אָמְרָה. לֹא חָשׁוּ לִנְפִילָה. אָמַר רִבִּי יוֹסֵה. תִּיפְתָּר שֶׁהָיוּ שְׁנֵיהֶן סְמוּכִין לַכּוֹתֶל. אֶחָד לְמַעְלָה מֵעֲשָׂרָה וְאֶחָד לְמַטָּה מֵעֲשָׂרָה. וְהָא תַנִּינָן חֲדוּת. הָדָא אָמְרָה שֶׁלֹּא חָשׁוּ לִנְפִילָה. מִתְיָירֵא הוּא הַתִּינוֹק לֵילֶךְ לְשָׁם. וְחָשׁ לוֹמַר. שֶׁמָּא נִתְגַּלְגֵּל חָמֵץ לְשָׁם. תִּיפְתָּר בְּחָדוּת שֶׁיֵּשׁ לָהּ לִיזְבִּיז. וְנַג הַבַּד וְנַג הַמִּגְדָּל. הָדָא דְתֵימַר. בִּגְבוֹהִין שְׁלֹשָׁה טְפָחִים. אֲבָל אִם אֵינָן גְּבוֹהִין שְׁלֹשָׁה טְפָחִים כָּאֶרֶץ הֵם. וּבְאוֹתוֹ שֶׁלֹּא נִשְׁתַּמֵּשׁ בּוֹ חָמֵץ. אֲבָל בְּאוֹתוֹ שֶׁנִּשְׁתַּמֵּשׁ בּוֹ חָמֵץ אֲפִילוּ גָבוֹהּ כַּמָּה צָרִיךְ בְּדִיקָה. אָמַר רִבִּי מָנָא. וְיֵאוּת. כֵּן אֲנָן אָמְרִין. הָדָא פִּיפְיָארוֹת אֲפִילוּ גָבוֹהּ כַּמָּה לֹא תְהֵא צְרִיכָה בְּדִיקָה.

[41]"Holes in the house, the upper and the lower ones, and the veranda[42], and the ditch[43], and the upper floor[44], and the roof of the olive press[45], and the roof of the tower[46], the storage room of straw, and the cattle stable, and the storage room of wood, and the storage room of provisions, wine storage, and oil storage, and produce storage, do not need checking." One understands the upper ones[47]. The lower ones? Does this mean that they did not worry about things falling down? Rebbi Yose said, explain it if both were close to the wall[48], whether higher than ten or lower than ten [hand-breadths][49]. Did we not state "the ditch"? Does this not mean that they did not worry about things falling down? The toddler is afraid to go there. But should one not be afraid that leavened matter rolled there? Explain it by a ditch which has a rim. "And the roof of the olive press, and the roof of the tower." That is, if they are three hand-breadths high; but if they are not three hand-breadths high they are like ground. And if they were not used for leavened matter, but if they were used for leavened matter even if it is very high it needs checking. Rebbi

Mana said, this is correct. Would we say that this papyrus scaffold which is very high should not need checking[50]?

41 Tosephta 1:3, Babli 8a.
42 Any additional structure having a sloping roof.
43 חדות is the same as דות in the Tosephta.
44 Used only for storage but not as dwelling.
45 It seems that the reading of the Tosephta, גג הבית "the roof of the house" is the correct one (as it is quoted as reading of the Yerushalmi by R. Isaac Ibn Ghiat). A flat roof is exposed to the wind and to foraging birds; one may assume that no leavened matter stays there for long.
46 This has a sloping roof on which nothing stays.

46 If "upper" means "higher than the reach of a person", one need not expect that leavened matter was deposited there. But very low lying holes are at the reach of children.
47 Holes at the outside of the wall.
48 The text is confirmed by a quote in *Tur Orah Hayyim* §433; it does not make any sense since 10 hand-breadths is a height very accessible to all uses. The statement is rejected by all authorities who quote it.
49 Tosephta *Šabbat* 14(15):3 mentions an instrument used to remove bread from the papyrus scaffold where it is stored. Cf. *Kilaim* 6:3 Note 38.

(27b line 32) תַּנֵּי. רַבָּן שִׁמְעוֹן בֶּן גַּמְלִיאֵל אוֹמֵר. מִטָּה שֶׁהִיא חוֹצֶצֶת בְּתוֹךְ הַבַּיִת וְעֵצִים וַאֲבָנִים מוּנָחִין תַּחְתֶּיהָ. בּוֹדֵק צַד הַחִיצוֹן וְאֵינוֹ בּוֹדֵק צַד הַפְּנִימִי. מִפְּנֵי שֶׁעֵצִים וַאֲבָנִים מוּנָחִין תַּחְתֶּיהָ. הָא אִם אֵין עֵצִים וַאֲבָנִים מוּנָחִין תַּחְתֶּיהָ צָרִיךְ לִבְדּוֹק צַד הַפְּנִימִי. הָדָא אָמְרָה (שֶׁלֹּא) חָשׁוּ לִנְפִילָה. אֲנִי אוֹמֵר. תִּינוֹק (יָגַע) [רָגַע] וְהִכְנִיס שָׁם חָמֵץ.

It was stated: [41]"Rabban Simeon ben Gamliel says, a couch which was separated[52] in the house but wood and stones are stored under it, one checks at the outside but does not have to check on the inside." Because wood and stones are stored under it, but if no wood and stones are stored under it, one has to check on the inside. Does this mean that they did (not)[53] worry about things falling down? I am saying that (a child exerted himself and) [an unruly child][53*] brought leavened matter there[54].

52 The couch was separated from the floor, i. e., it was on high legs which left room for storage under the bed.
53 The word was written by the scribe but correctly deleted by the corrector.

53* Versions of (scribe) and [corrector.]
54 Just as the first part of the Tosephta, quoted in the preceding paragraph, does not prove that the earlier generations were not afraid of bread accidentally falling down

without being picked up, so this part does
not prove the opposite conclusion.

(27b line 36) מַרְתֵּף שֶׁלְיַיִן צָרִיךְ בְּדִיקָה. מַרְתֵּף שֶׁלְשֶׁמֶן אֵינוֹ צָרִיךְ בְּדִיקָה. מַה בֵּין יַיִן וּמַה בֵּין שֶׁמֶן. יַיִן אֵין לוֹ קֶבַע. שֶׁמֶן יֵשׁ לוֹ קֶבַע. אוֹצָר בֵּין שֶׁלְיַיִן בֵּין שֶׁלְשֶׁמֶן אֵינוֹ צָרִיךְ בְּדִיקָה. אֵיזֶהוּ מַרְתֵּף. כָּל־שֶׁנָּתְנוּ עִם הַלֶּחֶם בֶּחָצֵר. יֵשׁ מַרְתֵּף שֶׁהוּא כָאוֹצָר וְאוֹצָר שֶׁהוּא כְמַרְתֵּף. מַרְתֵּף שֶׁהוּא בוֹשׁ לוֹכַל בְּתוֹכוֹ הֲרֵי הוּא כָאוֹצָר. וְאוֹצָר שֶׁאֵינוֹ בוֹשׁ לוֹכַל בְּתוֹכוֹ הֲרֵי הוּא כְמַרְתֵּף. יֵשׁ חָצֵר שֶׁהוּא כְמָבוֹי וּמָבוֹי שֶׁהוּא כְחָצֵר. חָצֵר שֶׁהָרַבִּים בּוֹקְעִין בְּתוֹכָהּ הֲרֵי הוּא כְמָבוֹי. וּמָבוֹי שֶׁאֵין הָרַבִּים בּוֹקְעִין בְּתוֹכוֹ הֲרֵי הוּא כְחָצֵר. וְחָשׁ לוֹמַר. שֶׁמָּא הַבַּהֲמִים מַכְנִיסִין לְתוֹכוֹ חָמֵץ. אֵין דֶּרֶךְ הַבַּהֲמִים לִהְיוֹת מַכְנִיסִין לְתוֹכוֹ חָמֵץ אֶלָּא מִינֵי מְתִיקָה. שֶׁהֵן בּוֹדְקִין הַיַּיִן יָפֶה.

A wine cellar needs checking, an oil cellar does not need checking[55]. What is the difference between wine and oil? Wine has no staying power, oil has staying power[56]. Storage[57], whether of wine or oil, does not need checking. What is a cellar? Anything used with bread in the courtyard[58]. There exists a cellar which is like storage and storage which is like a cellar. A cellar in which he is ashamed to eat is like storage; storage where he is not ashamed to eat is like a cellar. [59]There is a courtyard which is like an alley and an alley which is like a courtyard. A courtyard which is used by the public is like an alley, and an alley which is not used by the public is like a courtyard. But should one not be afraid that animal drivers introduce leavened matter into it[60]? Animal drivers usually do not introduce leavened matter into it but sweets since they help in checking the quality of the wine[61].

55 Babli 8a.
56 Wine is drawn from the amphora at least once a day; fresh oil is needed only from time to time.
57 Wholesale storage for commercial purposes.
58 Any place where bread is introduced during the year needs checking. Some Medieval authors, e.g. Meïri (ed. J. Klein, Jerusalem 1964, p. 39, Notes 468-469) read here an additional sentence: "Storage is what is not used with bread in the courtyard."

59 This does not belong here; because of the similarity in language it is copied from *Ketubot* 7:7, Notes 71-72.
60 This refers back to storage areas. While the producer of the wine will not introduce bread into his storage area, what can be said about the teamster who will transport the wine for sale at other places?
61 If the teamster is transporting for his own account, he will want to check the quality of the wine he is buying; for that he eats taste enhancing candy, not taste dulling bread.

(27b line 46) הַיּוֹצֵא לְפָרֵשׁ קוֹדֶם שְׁלֹשִׁים יוֹם אֵינוֹ צָרִיךְ לִבְדּוֹק. בְּתוֹךְ שְׁלֹשִׁים צָרִיךְ לִבְדּוֹק. הָדָא דְתֵימַר בְּשֶׁיֵּשׁ בְּדַעְתּוֹ לַחֲזוֹר. אֲבָל אֵין בְּדַעְתּוֹ לַחֲזוֹר אֲפִילוּ קוֹדֶם שְׁלֹשִׁים יוֹם צָרִיךְ לִבְדּוֹק. וּבְסָפֵק. אֲבָל בְּוַדַּאי אֲפִילוּ מֵרֹאשׁ הַשָּׁנָה. אָמַר רִבִּי בָּא. וַאֲפִילוּ יֵשׁ בְּדַעְתּוֹ לַחֲזוֹר צָרִיךְ לִבְדּוֹק. שֶׁמָּא יִמָּלֵךְ וְלֹא יַחֲזוֹר.

"If somebody leaves to travel by sea, before thirty days he does not have to check; within thirty [days] he has to check"[62]. [63]That is to say, if he intends to return. But if he does not intend to return, even before thirty days he has to check. If there is a doubt; but if it is certain then even from New Year's Day. Rebbi Abba said, but even if he intends to return he has to check, maybe he will change his mind and not return.

62 Tosephta 1:4 (in the formulation of the Babli 6a).
63 The Babli 6a rules in everything the exact opposite of the Yerushalmi, which holds that everybody is obligated at all times to see to it that his property contains no leavened matter on Passover, wherever it be situated and wherever he spends the holiday.

(27b line 51) הַכֹּל נֶאֱמָנִין עַל בִּיעוּר חָמֵץ. אֲפִילוּ נָשִׁים אֲפִילוּ עֲבָדִים. רִבִּי יִרְמְיָה בְּשֵׁם רִבִּי זְעִירָה. לֵית כָּאן אֲפִילוּ נָשִׁים. נָשִׁים עַצְמָן הֵן נֶאֱמָנוֹת. מִפְּנֵי שֶׁהֵן עֲצֵילוֹת וְהֵן בּוֹדְקוֹת כָּל־שֶׁהוּא כָּל־שֶׁהוּא. כּוּתִים כָּל־זְמַן שֶׁעוֹשִׂין מַצָּתָן עִם יִשְׂרָאֵל נֶאֱמָנִין הֵן עַל בִּיעוּר חָמֵץ. אִם אֵינָן עוֹשִׁין מַצָּתָן עִם יִשְׂרָאֵל אֵינָן נֶאֱמָנִים עַל בִּיעוּר חָמֵץ. אָמַר רִבִּי יוֹסֵה. הָדָא דְתֵימַר בַּבָּתִּים. אֲבָל בַּחֲצֵירוֹת חֲשׁוּדִין הֵן. דְּאִינּוּן דָּרְשִׁין לֹא יִמָּצֵא בְּבָתֵּיכֶם. לֹא בַחֲצֵירוֹתֵיכֶם.
תַּנֵּי. רַבָּן שִׁמְעוֹן בֶּן גַּמְלִיאֵל אוֹמֵר. כָּל־מִצְוָה שֶׁהַכּוּתִים נוֹהֲגִין בָּהּ הֵם מְדַקְדְּקִין בָּהּ יָתֵיר מִיִּשְׂרָאֵל. אָמַר רִבִּי שִׁמְעוֹן. הָדָא דְתֵימַר בָּרִאשׁוֹנָה שֶׁהָיוּ מְשׁוּקָעִין בְּכוּפְרֵנֵיהֶן. אֲבָל עַכְשָׁיו שֶׁאֵין לָהֶן לֹא מִצְוָה וְלֹא שְׁיָרֵי מִצְוָה חֲשׁוּדִין הֵן וּמְקוּלְקָלִין הֵן.

Everybody is trustworthy about elimination of leavened matter, even women, even slaves. Rebbi Jeremiah in the name of Rebbi Ze`ira: There is no "even" women. Women intrinsically are trustworthy; since they are slow they check everything very carefully. Samaritans any time when they prepare their *mazzah* with Jews[64] are trustworthy about checking for leavened matter; if they do not prepare their *mazzah* with Jews they are not trustworthy about checking for leavened matter. Rebbi Yose said, this means in the houses, but they are suspect in courtyards since they explain that *it should not be found in your houses*,[65] does not apply to your courtyards.

It was stated: [66]Rabban Simeon ben Gamliel says, any commandment which the Samaritans keep they are much more exact with them than Jews. Rebbi Simeon[67] said, that means earlier when they were concentrated in their villages. But today, when they have no commandments nor remainders of commandments they are suspect and degenerate.

64	If the Samaritan calendar has Passover on the same day as the rabbinic one.	*Qiddushin* 76a, *Ḥulin* 4a.
65	*Ex.* 12:19.	67 This author cannot be R. Simeon ben Yoḥai, but he might be R. Simeon ben Eleazar (*Avodah zarah* 5:4, p. 447).
66	Tosephta 2:3, Babli *Gittin* 10a,	

(27b line 62) שׁוֹאֲלִין בְּהִילְכוֹת הַפֶּסַח בְּפֶסַח. הִילְכוֹת עֲצֶרֶת בָּעֲצֶרֶת. הִילְכוֹת חַג בְּחַג. בְּבֵית וַעַד שׁוֹאֲלִין קוֹדֶם לִשְׁלֹשִׁים יוֹם. רַבָּן שִׁמְעוֹן בֶּן גַּמְלִיאֵל אוֹמֵר. שְׁתֵּי שָׁבוּעוֹת. אַתְיָיא דְרַבִּי יוֹחָנָן כְּרַבָּנָן. וְדַחֲבֵרַיָּיא כְּרַבָּן שִׁמְעוֹן בֶּן גַּמְלִיאֵל. אָמַר רִבִּי יוֹחָנָן. טַעֲמוֹן דְּרַבָּנָן. שֶׁכֵּן מֹשֶׁה עוֹמֵד בַּפֶּסַח רִאשׁוֹן וְאוֹמֵר לָהֶן הִילְכוֹת הַפֶּסַח הַשֵּׁנִי. וְדַחֲבֵרַיָּיא כְּרַבָּן שִׁמְעוֹן בֶּן גַּמְלִיאֵל. שֶׁכֵּן מֹשֶׁה עוֹמֵד בְּרֹאשׁ חוֹדֶשׁ וְאוֹמֵר לָהֶם הִילְכוֹת הַפֶּסַח.

One asks about practices of Passover at Passover, practices of Pentecost at Pentecost, practices of Tabernacles at Tabernacles[68]. In the House of Assembly one asks thirty days in advance; Rabban Simeon ben Gamliel says, two weeks[69]. The statement of Rebbi Joḥanan follows the rabbis, that of the colleagues Rabban Simeon ben Gamliel. Rebbi Joḥanan said, the reason of the rabbis, because Moses stands on the First Passover and explains to them the rules of Second Passover[70]. That of the colleagues follows Rabban Simeon ben Gamliel, because Moses stands on the day of the New Moon and explains to them the rules of Passover[71].

68	Babli *Megillah* 4a. *Sifry Num.* 66.	impure on the 14th of Nisan were promulgated on the 13th of Nisan, *Num.* 9:9-14.
69	Babli *Pesaḥim* 6a.	
70	The rules of the Second Passover to be celebrated on the 14th of Iyar by people	71 *Num.* 9:1-4.

(27b line 68) כַּמָּה אֲמָרוּ שְׁתֵּי שׁוּרוֹת בַּמַּרְתֵּף וכו'. רַב חוּנָה בְּשֵׁם רַב. קוֹלְפוֹ כְּמִין גַּם. תַּנִּי בַּר קַפָּרָא. קוֹלְפוֹ כְּמִין שְׁנֵי גַּמִּין. הָיָה נָתוּן בְּאֶמְצַע הַבַּיִת. עַל דַּעְתֵּיהּ דְּרַב חוּנָא מַפְשִׁיטוֹ חָלוּק אֶחָד. עַל דַּעְתֵּיהּ דְּבַר קַפָּרָא מַפְשִׁיטוֹ שְׁנֵי חֲלָקוֹת. הָיָה עָשׂוּי מַדְרֵיגוֹת מַדְרֵיגוֹת. קוֹלְפוֹ גַּמִּים גַּמִּים. רִבִּי יַעֲקֹב בַּר אָחָא בְּשֵׁם חִזְקִיָּה. שִׁמְעוֹן בַּר בָּא בְּשֵׁם רִבִּי יוֹחָנָן. שׁוּרָה הַחִיצוֹנָה הִיא

הָעֶלְיוֹנָה הָרוֹאָה אֶת הַפֶּתַח וְאֶת הַקּוֹרָה. שֶׁלְּפָנִים מִמֶּנָּה. תַּנֵּי. שֶׁלְּמַטָּה מִמֶּנָּה. הָווֹן בָּעֵי מֵימַר. מָאן דְּאָמַר. שֶׁלְּפָנִים הֵימֶינָּה. כָּל־שֶׁכֵּן שֶׁלְּמַטָּה הֵימֶינָּה. מָאן דָּמַר. שֶׁלְּמַטָּה הֵימֶינָּה. הָא לִפְנִים הֵימֶינָּה לֹא. נִשְׁתַּמֵּשׁ בַּחֲצִי שׁוּרָה. פְּשִׁיטָא. אוֹתָהּ שֶׁנִּשְׁתַּמֵּשׁ יֵשׁ לָהּ שֶׁלְּפָנִים מִמֶּנָּה וְשֶׁלְּמַטָּה מִמֶּנָּה. אוֹתָהּ שֶׁלֹּא נִשְׁתַּמֵּשׁ בָּהּ יֵשׁ לָהּ שֶׁלְּפָנִים מִמֶּנָּה וְשֶׁלְּמַטָּה מִמֶּנָּה. הָדָא דְתֵימַר. בִּמְחוֹלְלוֹת. אֲבָל בְּאֲפוּצוֹת מַעֲבִיר עֲלֵיהֶן אֶת [הַנֵּר וְדַיּוֹ.] הָדָא אֲמָרָה שֶׁחָשׁוּ לִנְפִילָה. אָמַר רִבִּי פִינְחָס דָּיָפוֹ. אֲנִי אוֹמֵר. בְּשָׁעָה שֶׁסִּידְּרָן הִכְנִיס שָׁם חָמֵץ.

"Where[1] did they say two rows in the cellar[2]," etc. Rav Huna in the name of Rav: He peels it[72] like a Gamma. Bar Qappara stated, he peels it like two Gamma[73]. If it was situated in the middle of the room. In the opinion of Rav Huna he strips it of one garment, in the opinion of Bar Qappara he strips it of two garments[74]. If it[75] was built in steps, he strips it by many Gamma. Rebbi Jacob bar Aḥa in the name of Ḥizqiah: Simeon bar Abba in the name of Rebbi Joḥanan. The outermost row which is the uppermost which sees both door and beam of the roof, [and] the one inside of it[76]. It was stated: the one below it. They wanted to say that he who says, the one inside of it, so much more that one below it. He who says, the one below it, therefore not the one inside of it[77]. If half a row was used, it is obvious that what was used has inside of it and below it. That which was not used has inside of it and below it[78]. That is to say, if they are spaced[79]. But if they are tightly packed he passes the light over them[80] and it is enough. Does this mean that they did worry about things falling down? Rebbi Phineas from Yafo[80*] said, I am saying that the servant introduced leavened matter when he placed them.

73   He checks the outer rows in the cellar in two directions orthogonal to one another, in the shape of Ã. Babli 8b in the name of R. Joḥanan.

74   He has to check the lower row and one vertical row and the upper row and, depending on the interpretation given later, either another vertical row or a horizontal row inwards.

75   The storage room. Each step defines a new front row.

76   If the amphoras are stored at least two layers high, one has to check the two rows close to the entrance of the top layer.

77   Only the front rows in all layers have to be checked.

78   Even if during the year wine was taken only from one side of one row, once part of a row must be checked, the entire row must be checked.

79   According to Tosephta *Ahilut* 10:5, amphoras are spaced if on two opposite sides there is one hand-breadth of free space.

80   Corrector's text. The scribe's הנייר ולווי "the paper and appurtenances" is unin-

telligible.

80* Nothing more is known about him.

(fol. 27a) **משנה ב**: אֵין חוֹשְׁשִׁין שֶׁמָּא גְרָרָה חוּלְדָּה מִבַּיִת לְבַיִת וּמִמָּקוֹם לְמָקוֹם אִם כֵּן מֵחָצֵר לְחָצֵר וּמֵעִיר לְעִיר אֵין לַדָּבָר סוֹף:

Mishnah 2: One does not suspect[81] that a mole dragged it from room to room or from place to place[82]; if that were the case, also from courtyard to courtyard[83] and from town to town without end.

81 After a room has been searched for leavened matter, one does not fear that an animal brought such matter back into the room; no place has to be searched more than once.

82 In one courtyard.

83 Since not all people search their property at the same time, animals could find leavened matter somewhere at all times and no search could ever be completed.

(27c line 5) **הלכה ב**: אֵין חוֹשְׁשִׁין כול'. אָמַר רִבִּי יוֹנָה. הָכֵין צוֹרְכָה מַתְנֵי. מֵעִיר לְעִיר וּמֵחָצֵר לְחָצֵר מִמָּקוֹם לְמָקוֹם וּמִבַּיִת לְבַיִת. אִם חוֹשֵׁשׁ אַתְּ מֵעִיר לְעִיר חוֹשֵׁשׁ אַתְּ מֵחָצֵר לְחָצֵר. אִם חוֹשֵׁשׁ אַתְּ מֵחָצֵר לְחָצֵר חוֹשֵׁשׁ אַתְּ מִמָּקוֹם לְמָקוֹם. אִם חוֹשֵׁשׁ אַתְּ מִמָּקוֹם לְמָקוֹם אַתְּ חוֹשֵׁשׁ מִבַּיִת לְבַיִת. אָמַר רִבִּי יוֹסֵה. אֲפִילוּ כְּמַתְנִיתָא אַתְיָא הִיא. אֵין חוֹשְׁשִׁין שֶׁמָּא גְרָרָה חוּלְדָּה מִבַּיִת לְבַיִת וּמִמָּקוֹם לְמָקוֹם אִם כֵּן מֵחָצֵר לְחָצֵר וּמֵעִיר לְעִיר אֵין לַדָּבָר סוֹף. שֶׁאִם מִבַּיִת לְבַיִת אֵי אַתָּה חוֹשֵׁשׁ אַתְּ כָּל־שֶׁכֵּן מִמָּקוֹם לְמָקוֹם. אִם מִמָּקוֹם לְמָקוֹם אֵי אַתְּ חוֹשֵׁשׁ לֹא כָּל־שֶׁכֵּן מֵחָצֵר לְחָצֵר. אִם מֵחָצֵר לְחָצֵר אֵי אַתְּ חוֹשֵׁשׁ לֹא כָּל־שֶׁכֵּן מֵעִיר לְעִיר. יְכוֹלִין הֵן כָּל־יִשְׂרָאֵל לִבְדּוֹק חֲמֵיצָן כְּאַחַת.

Halakhah 2: "One does not suspect," etc. Rebbi Jonah said, so the Mishnah should have been stated: From town to town and from courtyard to courtyard, from place to place and from room to room. If you suspect from town to town, you will suspect from courtyard to courtyard. If you suspect from courtyard to courtyard, you will suspect from place to place. If you suspect from place to place, you will suspect from room to room. Rebbi Yose said, even following the Mishnah it is correct. "One does not suspect that a mole pulled it from room to room or from place to place; if that were the case, also from courtyard to courtyard and from town to town without end." For if you do not suspect from room to room, not so much more you suspect from place to place? If you do not suspect from place to place, not so much more from courtyard to courtyard? If you do not suspect from courtyard to courtyard, not so much more from town to town? All of Israel can check their leavened matter together[84].

84 Mishnah 2 is a consequence of Mishnah 1. One really should be worried that animals could transport food from one place to another. But since everybody checks at the same time, after sundown of the 13ᵗʰ of Nisan, there is no danger of later contamination.
This paragraph is the corrector's text; the scribe's text "if you do not suspect from town to town you certainly do mot worry from courtyard to courtyard , etc." has all arguments the wrong way.

(fol. 27a) **משנה ג** רִבִּי יְהוּדָה אוֹמֵר בּוֹדְקִין אוֹר אַרְבָּעָה עָשָׂר וְאַרְבָּעָה עָשָׂר בְּשַׁחֲרִית וּבִשְׁעַת הַבִּעוּר. וַחֲכָמִים אוֹמְרִים לֹא בָדַק אוֹר אַרְבָּעָה עָשָׂר יִבְדּוֹק בְּאַרְבָּעָה עָשָׂר. אִם לֹא בָדַק בְּאַרְבָּעָה עָשָׂר יִבְדּוֹק בְּתוֹךְ הַמּוֹעֵד. לֹא בָדַק בְּתוֹךְ הַמּוֹעֵד יִבְדּוֹק לְאַחַר הַמּוֹעֵד. וּמַה שֶׁהוּא מְשַׁיֵּיר יַנִּיחֶנּוּ בְּצִינְעָא כְּדֵי שֶׁלֹּא יְהֵא צָרִיךְ בְּדִיקָה אַחֲרָיו:

Mishnah 3: Rebbi Jehudah says, one checks at nightfall of the Fourteenth, and on the mourning of the Fourteenth, and at the time of elimination[85]. But the Sages say, he who did not check at nightfall of the Fourteenth has to check on the Fourteenth; he who did not check on the Fourteenth has to check on the holiday. He who did not check on the holiday has to check after the holiday[86]. And what he leaves he should deposit at a guarded place so that he would not be obligated to repeat checking[87].

85 In the interpretation of the Yerushalmi, R. Jehudah requires three checks for every place. Rav Joseph in the Babli (10b) reads the conjunctions in R. Jehudah's statement as "or". The time of elimination is given in Mishnah 4.
86 Since leavened matter which was in the possession of a Jew during Passover is forbidden for all usufruct (Mishnah 2:2), such matter if it was not eliminated before the holiday must be eliminated afterwards.
87 Any bread and leavened matter to be used on the morning of the Fourteenth must be secured after the checking in the evening since if some of it would be missing in the morning the entire checking procedure would have to be repeated.

(27c line 16) **הלכה ג:** רִבִּי יְהוּדָה אוֹמֵר כול'. אָמַר רִבִּי יוֹחָנָן. טַעֲמֵיהּ דְּרִבִּי יוּדָה כְּנֶגֶד שְׁלֹשָׁה פְּעָמִים שֶׁכָּתוּב בַּתּוֹרָה לֹא יֵרָאֶה לְךָ שְׂאוֹר. וְהָכְתִיב תַּשְׁבִּיתוּ שְׂאוֹר מִבָּתֵּיכֶם. בַּעֲשֵׂה הוּא. וְהָא כְתִיב שִׁבְעַת יָמִים שְׂאוֹר לֹא יִמָּצֵא בְּבָתֵּיכֶם. אָמַר רִבִּי יוֹסֵה. מִכֵּיוָן שֶׁזֶּה צָרִיךְ לָזֶה וְזֶה צָרִיךְ לָזֶה כְּמִי שֶׁכּוּלָּן אֶחָד. לֹא יֵרָאֶה לְךָ. הָיִיתִי אוֹמֵר. הִפְקִיד אֶצְלוֹ יְהֵא מוּתָּר. תַּלְמוּד לוֹמַר לֹא יִמָּצֵא בְּבָתֵּיכֶם. אִי לֹא יִמָּצֵא בְּבָתֵּיכֶם הָיִיתִי אוֹמֵר. יִחֵד לוֹ בַיִת יְהֵא אָסוּר. תַּלְמוּד לוֹמַר לֹא יֵרָאֶה לְךָ. הָא כֵיצַד. הִפְקִיד אֶצְלוֹ אָסוּר. יִחֵד לוֹ בַיִת מוּתָּר.

מַחְלְפָה שִׁיטָתֵיהּ דְּרִבִּי יוּדָה. דְּתַנֵּי. רִבִּי יוּדָה אוֹמֵר. בּוֹדְקִין אוֹר לְאַרְבָּעָה עָשָׂר. וּבְאַרְבָּעָה עָשָׂר בְּשַׁחֲרִית. וּבִשְׁעַת הַבִּעוּר. וַחֲכָמִים אוֹמְרִים. אִם לֹא בָדַק אוֹר לְאַרְבָּעָה עָשָׂר יִבְדּוֹק בְּאַרְבָּעָה עָשָׂר. צָרִיךְ לִבְדּוֹק שְׁלֹשָׁה פְעָמִים. מָה אִם בְּשָׁעָה שֶׁלֹּא הִגִּיעַ זְמַן בִּעוּרוֹ אַתְּ אָמַר. צָרִיךְ לִבְדּוֹק שְׁלֹשָׁה פְעָמִים. בְּשָׁעָה שֶׁהִגִּיעַ זְמַן בִּעוּרוֹ לֹא כָל־שֶׁכֵּן. (לֹא צוֹרְכָה דְלֹא. לֹא בָדַק בְּאַרְבָּעָה עָשָׂר יִבְדּוֹק בְּמוֹעֵד. צָרִיךְ לִבְדּוֹק שְׁלֹשָׁה פְעָמִים. מָה אִם בְּשָׁעָה שֶׁלֹּא הִגִּיעַ זְמַן בִּעוּרוֹ אַתְּ אָמַר. צָרִיךְ לִבְדּוֹק שְׁלֹשָׁה פְעָמִים. בְּשָׁעָה שֶׁהִגִּיעַ זְמַן בִּעוּרוֹ לֹא כָל־שֶׁכֵּן.) לֹא צוֹרְכָה דְלֹא. אִם לֹא בָדַק בְּתוֹךְ הַמּוֹעֵד יִבְדּוֹק לְאַחַר הַמּוֹעֵד.

Halakhah 3: "Rebbi Jehudah says," etc. Rebbi Johanan said, the reason of Rebbi Jehudah, corresponding to the three times that in the Torah is written, *leavening shall not be seen as yours*[88]. But is it not written[89], *you shall remove leavening from your houses*? That is a positive commandment. But is it not written[90], *for seven days leavening shall not be found in your houses*? Rebbi Yose said, since they are mutually needed[91], they are as one. *It should not be seen as yours*, I would have said, if somebody[92] deposited with him it should be permitted. The verse says, *it shall not be found in your houses*. If *it shall not be found in your houses*, if he gave him a separate place[93] it should be forbidden. The verse says, *it shall not be seen as yours*. How is this? If he deposited with him it is forbidden; if he gave him a separate place it is permitted.

The argument of Rebbi Jehudah seems inverted[94]. As we have stated, "Rebbi Jehudah says, one checks at nightfall of the Fourteenth, and on the mourning of the Fourteenth, and at the time of elimination[5]. But the Sages say, if he did not check at nightfall of the Fourteenth, he has to check on the Fourteenth." Does he have to check three times? Since at a time before its term of elimination you are saying that he has to check three times, at the moment of the term of elimination not so much more? [95](No, it need not be so. If he did not check on the Fourteenth, he has to check on the holiday.

Does he have to check three times? Since at a time before its term of elimination you are saying that he has to check three times, at the moment of the term of elimination not so much more?) No, it need not be so. If he did not check on the holiday, he has to check after the holiday[96].

88 Twice in *Ex.* 13:7, once in *Deut.* 16:4.
89 *Ex.* 12:15.
90 *Ex.* 12:19.
91 As explained in the sequel.
92 A Gentile's leavened matter, which is exempt from Jewish law. But if it is a deposit, i. e., that the Jew is responsible for damages, it becomes the Jew's property for the rules of Passover.
93 A Gentile's leavened matter stored at a separate place for which the Jewish owner of the place accepts no responsibility may stay there over Passover. Babli 6a.
94 It is not spelled out what other opinion of R. Jehudah is in conflict with his statement in the Mishnah. It seems that while he is stringent in the requirement of triple checking before the holiday he is lenient in not requiring anything afterwards if checking was not done by the time of elimination.
95 The text in parentheses was deleted by the corrector and therefore is not found in the printed texts. It is a necessary component of the argument.
96 The answer to the question was that certainly R. Jehudah would agree with the Sages that checking during or after the holidays is required if it was not done beforehand (a position rejected by the Babli 10b-11a.) The only question is whether in these cases also R. Jehudah requires triple checking. Since he does not spell out his position, an attempt to determine this by inferences is unsuccessful. Since practice does not follow R. Jehudah, a final answer is not given.

(27c line 30) וּמַה שֶׁהוּא מְשַׁיֵּיר יַנִּיחֶנּוּ בְצִינְעָא כְּדֵי שֶׁלֹא יְהֵא צָרִיךְ בְּדִיקָה אַחֲרָיו. כֵּיצַד הוּא עוֹשֶׂה. כּוֹפָה עָלָיו כְּלִי. כָּפָה עָלָיו כְּלִי וְלֹא מְצָאוֹ. אֲנִי אוֹמֵר יָד נְטָלַתּוֹ. לֹא כָפָה עָלָיו כְּלִי וְלֹא מְצָאוֹ. אוֹתוֹ הַבַּיִת צָרִיךְ בְּדִיקָה. אוֹ שְׁאָר הַבָּתִּים לֹא יְהוּ צְרִיכִין בְּדִיקָה. נִשְׁמְעִינָהּ מִן הָדָא. אָבַד כְּזַיִת מִן הַמֵּת בַּבַּיִת. בִּקְשׁוֹ וְלֹא מְצָאוֹ. הַבַּיִת טָהוֹר. לִכְשֶׁיִּימָּצֵא. הַבַּיִת טָמֵא לְמַפְרֵעַ. הָדָא יְלֵפָה מִן הַהִיא. וְהַהִיא יְלֵפָה מִן הָדָא. הָדָא יְלֵפָה מִן הַהִיא. הִיא אִיבֵּד הִיא הִינִּיחַ. וְהַהִיא יְלֵפָה מִן הָדָא. אֵין לָךְ צָרִיךְ בְּדִיקָה אֶלָּא אוֹתוֹ הַבַּיִת בִּלְבָד. וּכְרַבִּי יוּדָה אֲפִילוּ אוֹתוֹ הַבַּיִת לֹא יְהֵא צָרִיךְ בְּדִיקָה. נִשְׁמְעִינָהּ מִן הָדָא. אָמַר רַבִּי יוּדָה. מַעֲשֶׂה בְשִׁפְחָתוֹ שֶׁלְּמַסִּיק אֶחָד בְּרִימּוֹן שֶׁהִשְׁלִיכָה נֶפֶל אֶחָד לַבּוֹר. וּבָא כֹהֵן אֶחָד וְהֵצִיץ לֵידַע מַה שֶׁהִשְׁלִיכָה. וּבָא מַעֲשֶׂה לִפְנֵי חֲכָמִים וְטִיהֲרוּ. שֶׁדֶּרֶךְ חוּלְדָּה וּבַרְדְּלִיס לִהְיוֹת גּוֹרְרִין אוֹתוֹ. רָצָה הִיא אַחַר הַבָּשָׂר. וְאֵינָהּ רָצָה אַחַר הַפַּת. וַאֲפִילוּ תֵימַר. רָצָה הִיא אַחַר הַבָּשָׂר וְאַחַר הַפַּת. בָּשָׂר גּוֹרֶרֶת וְאוֹכָלֶת. פַּת גּוֹרֶרֶת וּמַנַּחַת. רַבָּנִין דְּקַיְסָרִין בְּשֵׁם רִבִּי אַבָּהוּ. אֵין חוֹשְׁשִׁין שֶׁמָּא גְרָרָה חוּלְדָּה. וּכְרַבִּי יוּדָה חוֹשְׁשִׁין.

"And what he leaves he should deposit at a guarded place so that he would not be obligated to repeat checking[87]." What does he do? He covers it with a vessel. If he covered it with a vessel but did not find it[97]. I am saying that a hand took it. If he did not cover it with a vessel and did not find it, this house[98] needs checking. Or the other houses would not need checking? Let us hear from the following[99]: "If the volume of an olive from a cadaver was lost in a house; it was searched but not found. The house is pure; if it will be found, the house is retroactively impure." This can teach about that and that can teach about this. This can teach about that, there is no difference between "was lost" and "what he leaves"[100]. And that can teach about this, only this house needs to be checked. Following Rebbi Jehudah even this house should not need to be checked, as we may hear from the following:[101] "Rebbi Jehudah said, it happened that the slave girl of a discharged veteran[102] at Rimmon threw a still birth into a cistern. A Cohen came and looked to know what she had thrown down. The case came before the Sages and they declared him pure[103] for moles and martens usually drag it away." It runs after flesh, it does not run after bread[104]. And even if you are saying that it runs after flesh and bread, it drags away flesh and eats it; it drags away bread and stores it. The rabbis of Caesarea in the name of Rebbi Abbahu: One does not suspect that a mole dragged it, but following Rebbi Jehudah one suspects it[105].

97 If the bread was covered, we assume that a human took it. If it was uncovered, one assumes that an animal took it. In the Babli 9b one supposes in both cases that an animal took it; this also seems to be the underlying hypothesis in the Yerushalmi. Rabbenu Yeruham (Part 1, Path 5, 39a) reads in the first case אימא שד נטלתו "I would say, a spirit took it" but from Ravia §444 (vol. 2, p.68) it seems that for שד "spirit" one should read שיד "that a hand", meaning a human hand. Raviah notes that his own copy of the Yerushalmi does not contain the passage. In any case the reading of R. Yeruham is suspect since אימא is

Babylonian Aramaic based on Accadic, for standard אימר, תימר.

98 Since a standard house had one room, it might be better to translate "a room".

99 Tosephta *Tahorot* 3:5.

100 This is the original assertion that the rules of Passover Eve can be compared to the rules of impurity.

101 Babli 9a, Tosephta *Ahilut* 16:13.

102 Latin *missicus*, cf. *Bava qamma* 10:6, Notes 60.

103 By bending over the opening of the cistern the Cohen would become impure by "tent impurity" if the body still was there.

104 Babli 9a.

105 R. Jehudah cannot accept Mishnah 2, otherwise he would accept single checking.

(fol. 17a) **משנה ד**: רִבִּי מֵאִיר אוֹמֵר אוֹכְלִין כָּל־חָמֵשׁ וְשׂוֹרְפִין בִּתְחִילַת שֵׁשׁ. רִבִּי יְהוּדָה אוֹמֵר אוֹכְלִין כָּל־אַרְבַּע וְתוֹלִין כָּל־חָמֵשׁ וְשׂוֹרְפִין בִּתְחִילַת שֵׁשׁ:

Mishnah 4: Rebbi Meïr says, one eats[106] all during the fifth [hour][107] and burns at the start of the sixth. Rebbi Jehudah says, one eats the entire fourth [hour], suspends[108] during the fifths, and burns at the start of the sixth.

106 Leavened food on the 14th of Nisan.
107 According to most opinions. the standard day is counted from sunrise to sundown and is divided into 12 hours. At the spring equinox the day starts at 6 am local time; then the fourth hour is 9-10 am, the fifth 10-11 am and the start of the sixth is 11 am.
108 One neither eats nor burns.

(27c line 46) **הלכה ד**: רִבִּי מֵאִיר אוֹמֵר אוֹכְלִין כָּל־חָמֵשׁ כול׳. רִבִּי מֵאִיר אוֹמֵר. מְשֵׁשׁ שָׁעוֹת וּלְמַעְלָן מִדְּבְרֵיהֶן. רִבִּי יוּדָה אוֹמֵר. מְשֵׁשׁ שָׁעוֹת וּלְמַעְלָן מִדְּבְרֵי תוֹרָה. מַה טַעֲמָא דְרִבִּי מֵאִיר. אַךְ בַּיּוֹם הָרִאשׁוֹן. זֶה חֲמִשָּׁה עָשָׂר. יָכוֹל מִשֶּׁתְּחְשַׁךְ. תַּלְמוּד לוֹמַר אַךְ. הָא כֵיצַד. תֶּן לוֹ לִפְנֵי שְׁקִיעַת הַחַמָּה שָׁעָה אַחַת. מַה טַעֲמָא דְרִבִּי יוּדָה. אַךְ בַּיּוֹם הָרִאשׁוֹן. זֶה אַרְבָּעָה עָשָׂר. יָכוֹל כָּל־הַיּוֹם כּוּלּוֹ. תַּלְמוּד לוֹמַר אַךְ. הָא כֵיצַד. חֲלוֹק אֶת הַיּוֹם חֶצְיוֹ לְחָמֵץ וְחֶצְיוֹ לְמַצָּה. מַחְלֶפֶת שִׁיטָתֵיהּ דְּרִבִּי מֵאִיר. תַּמָּן הוּא אָמַר. אַךְ לְרַבּוֹת. וְהָכָא הוּא אָמַר. אַךְ לְמַעֵט. אָמַר רִבִּי שְׁמוּאֵל בַּר אֲבִידּוּמָא. מִיעֲטוֹ שֶׁאֵינוֹ בְחָמֵץ. רִבִּי מֵאִיר אוֹמֵר. לֹא־תֹאכַל עָלָיו חָמֵץ. עַל אֲכִילָתוֹ. רִבִּי יוּדָה אוֹמֵר. לֹא־תֹאכַל עָלָיו חָמֵץ. עַל עֲשִׂייָתוֹ.

רִבִּי יוּדָה עֲבַד לֵיהּ וְעָשָׂה וְלֹא תַעֲשֶׂה עַל אֲכִילָתוֹ. עָשָׂה וְלֹא תַעֲשֶׂה עַל בִּיעוּרוֹ. עָשָׂה עַל אֲכִילָתוֹ. שִׁבְעַת יָמִים תֹּאכַל־עָלָיו מַצּוֹת. וְלֹא חָמֵץ. כָּל־לֹא תַעֲשֶׂה שֶׁהוּא בָא מִכֹּחַ עֲשֵׂה. עֲשֵׂה. לֹא תַעֲשֶׂה עַל אֲכִילָתוֹ. לֹא־תֹאכַל עָלָיו חָמֵץ. עָשָׂה עַל בִּיעוּרוֹ. תַּשְׁבִּיתוּ שְׂאֹר. לֹא תַעֲשֶׂה עַל בִּיעוּרוֹ. שִׁבְעַת יָמִים שְׂאֹר לֹא יִמָּצֵא בְּבָתֵּיכֶם.

הָא רִבִּי מֵאִיר אוֹמֵר. מְשֵׁשׁ שָׁעוֹת וּלְמַעְלָה מִדְּבְרֵיהֶן. שְׁבִיעִית אֲסוּרָה מִשּׁוּם גֶּדֶר. שְׁשִׁית לָמָּה. מִשּׁוּם גֶּדֶר. וְיֵשׁ גֶּדֶר לְגֶדֶר. אֶלָּא שָׁעָה שְׁשִׁית מִתְחַלֶּפֶת בַּשְּׁבִיעִית. הָא רִבִּי יְהוּדָה אוֹמֵר. מֵחָמֵשׁ וּלְמַעְלָה מִדְּבְרֵיהֶן שְׁשִׁית אֲסוּרָה מִשּׁוּם גֶּדֶר. חֲמִישִׁית לָמָּה. מִשּׁוּם גֶּדֶר. וְיֵשׁ גֶּדֶר לְגֶדֶר. אֶלָּא שֶׁחֲמִישִׁית מִתְחַלֶּפֶת בַּשְּׁבִיעִית.

מַחְלָפָה שִׁיטָתֵיהּ דְּרִבִּי יְהוּדָה. תַּמָּן הוּא אָמַר. אֵין חֲמִישִׁית מִתְחַלֶּפֶת בַּשְּׁבִיעִית. אָמַר רִבִּי יוֹסֵי. תַּמָּן הַדָּבָר מָסוּר לְבֵית דִּין. וּבֵית דִּין זְרִיזִין הֵן. בְּרַם הָכָא הַדָּבָר מָסוּר לַנָּשִׁים. וְהַנָּשִׁים עֲצֵילוֹת הֵן. אָמַר רִבִּי יוֹסֵי בֶּרִבִּי בּוּן. תַּמָּן תְּחִילַת חֲמִישִׁית סוֹף שְׁבִיעִית. בְּרַם הָכָא

סוֹף חֲמִישִׁית תְּחִילַּת שְׁבִיעִית. וְתַנֵּי כֵן. שֶׁבַּתְּחִילַּת חָמֵשׁ חַמָּה בַּמִּזְרָח וְסוֹף שָׁעָה חַמָּה בַּמַּעֲרָב.
לְעוֹלָם אֵין הַחַמָּה נוֹטָה לַמַּעֲרָב אֶלָּא בְסוֹף שֶׁבַע.]

Halakhah 4: "Rebbi Meïr says, one eats all during the fifth [hour]," etc. [109]Rebbi Meïr says, from noontime on it[110] is from their words; Rebbi Jehudah says, from noontime on it is biblical. What is Rebbi Meïr's reason? *Only on the first day*[111], that is the fifteenth[112]. I could think at nightfall; the verse says *only*,[113]. How is this? Give it one hour before sundown[114]. What is Rebbi Jehudah's reason? *Only on the first day*, that is the fourteenth. I could think the entire day; the verse says *only*. How is that? Split the day, half for leavened matter, half for *mazzah*. Rebbi Meïr's argument seems inverted. There, he said *only* to add; here he said *only* to diminish[115]. Rebbi Samuel bar Eudaimon said, he diminished, he excludes leavened matter. Rebbi Meïr says, *do not eat leavened matter with it*[116], while it is eaten. Rebbi Jehudah says, *do not eat leavened matter with it*, while it is prepared[117].

Rebbi Jehudah has [both a positive and a negative commandment concerning its eating[118], a positive and a negative commandment concerning its[119] removal. A positive commandment concerning its eating, *seven days you shall eat unleavened bread with it*, but not leavened. Any prohibition which is implied by a positive commandment has the status of positive commandment[120]. A negative commandment concerning its eating, *do not eat leavened for it*. A positive commandment concerning its removal, *you shall remove sour dough*[111]. A negative commandment concerning its removal, *for seven days sour dough shall not be found in your houses*[121].

Now Rebbi Meïr says, after noontime it is forbidden because of their words. The seventh hour is forbidden because of a fence. Why the sixth? Because of a fence[122]. Is there a fence around a fence? But the sixth hour may be confounded with the seventh[123]. [124]Now Rebbi Jehudah says, after the fifth hour it is forbidden because of their words; the sixth hour is forbidden because of a fence. Why the fifth? Because of a fence. Is there a fence around a fence? But the fifth hour may be confounded with the seventh.

Rebbi Jehudah's argument seems inverted. There[125], he says that the fifth cannot be confounded with the seventh. Rebbi Yose said, there the matter is given over to the court, and the court is diligent. But here the matter is given over to women who are slow. Rebbi Yose ben Rebbi Abun said, there[126] it is a matter between the beginning of the fifth and the end of the seventh hour. Here it is between the end of the fifth and the start of the seventh[127]. It also was stated thus[128]: At the start of the fifth hour the sun is in the East, and at the end of the [seventh] hour the sun is in the West. The sun never starts setting before the end of the seventh hour.]

109 The text is copied from *Sanhedrin* 5:3 where in general it is agreed that in a criminal case where it is necessary to determine the time of an alleged crime a difference of two hours in the testimony of different witnesses invalidates the testimonies; R. Jehudah applies this also to noontime but the anonymous Tanna (supposed to be R. Meïr) disagrees and allows discrepancies up to two hours in this case.

The scribe of the Leiden ms., after the text translated here in the first 5 sentences, wrote: "one repeats from *Sanhedrin* until 'the sun never starts setting'." The corrector who prepared the ms. for the Venice printer added the omitted portion; his text differs from *Sanhedrin* by both an addition and a lacuna. It is impossible to decide whether the corrector's text be copied from a different ms. or represents the corrector's emendations of the *Sanhedrin* text. In neither text is the use of references "here" and "there" (either *Pesaḥim* or *Sanhedrin*) completely consistent.

110 The prohibition of leavened matter on Passover Eve.

111 *Ex.* 12:15: *Seven days you shall eat mazzot; only on the first day you shall eliminate sour dough from your houses . . .* אך might also be translated as "certainly".

112 *Ex.* 12:14 states: *This day shall be a remembrance for you; you shall keep it as a holiday of pilgrimage for the Eternal . . . Num.* 28:15-16 require that the 14th of Nisan be *pesaḥ* for the Eternal; starting from the 15th for seven days it is the holiday of *mazzot*. Since *pesaḥ* (i. e., the day of the slaughter of the *pesaḥ* sacrifice) is connected inextricably with the holiday of *mazzot*, the reference in v. 14 to the "first day" is intrinsically ambiguous, whether it refer to *pesaḥ* or to the holiday.

113 A similar argument is in the Babli, 4b, *Mekhilta dR. Ismael* (ed. Horovitz-Rabin p. 28), *Mekhilta dR. Simeon b. Iohai* (ed. Epstein-Melamed p. 17).

114 I. e., the only biblical requirement is that all leavened matter be completely disposed of before the holiday at sundown.

115 It seems that this refers to *Ex.* 12:16: *. . . no work shall be done [on the holidays], only what may be eaten by any soul, it alone may be made by you.* Everybody agrees that food may be prepared on a holiday. According to R. Meïr (i. e., the anonymous opinion in Mishnah *Megillah* 1:8) *only* food may be prepared, not preparations necessary for the preparation of food. According to R. Jehudah (*Megillah* 1:8), anything that in the end leads to preparation of food is permitted on a holiday. R. Meïr reads *only* as a

HALAKHAH FOUR

restriction in v. 16 and as an addition in v. 15!

116 *Deut.* 16:3, referring to the *pesah* sacrifice which is slaughtered on the afternoon of the 14th and eaten in the night of the 15th.

117 In the afternoon of the 14th. This supports R. Jehudah's contention that leavened matter is biblically forbidden in the afternoon of the 14th; *Sifry Deut.* 130.

118 "It" here refers to *mazzah*.

119 "It" here refers to leavened matter.

120 It is not an indictable offense; cf. *Bikkurim* 1:5, Note 103. If a positive commandment is in conflict with a negative one (a prohibition), the positive is stronger. But an obligation which is both positive and negative is stronger than anything else.

121 *Ex.* 12:19.

122 For R. Meïr, the biblical prohibition of leavened matter starts at the 11th hour (5 pm local time). The earlier afternoon hours, including the 7th, are rabbinically forbidden as a "fence around the law". Then it is difficult to understand why leavened matter has to be burned *at the start* of the 6th, extending the rabbinic prohibition for another hour as a fence around the fence, a practice generally rejected.

123 It is not a fence around a fence but consistent with the opinion of the Sages (R. Meïr) in *Sanhedrin* 5:3. In a society without watches the difference between 11am and 12am is not generally recognized; a prohibition enforced after noontime must practically be enforced starting from 11am.

124 The remainder of the paragraph is missing in *Sanhedrin*.

125 Referring to *Sanhedrin*. R. Jehudah agrees that while without watches people cannot distinguish between two morning or two afternoon hours, he explicitly agrees that people distinguish between fifth (10-11am) and seventh (12am-1pm).

126 In *Sanhedrin* the Mishnah does not require the court to accept any testimonies where the witnesses differ widely in determining the time of a crime; R. Jehudah admonishes the court under certain circumstances to investigate whether the witnesses do not in reality testify about the same time; Babli *Pesahim* 12b.

127 In *Pesahim* the period of doubt is little more than 60 min., in *Sanhedrin* close to 180 min. The apparent inconsistency is due to the informal use of "hour."

128 Babli 12b.

(27b line 72) רַב אָמַר. דִּבְרֵי רִבִּי מֵאִיר. הַמְקַדֵּשׁ בְּחָמֵץ מִשֵּׁשׁ שָׁעוֹת וּלְמַעְלָן לֹא עָשָׂה כְלוּם. אָמַר רִבִּי חוּנָה. וְיֵאוּת. אִילוּ חִטִּים קוּרְטַבָּנִיּוֹת בַּמִּדְבָּר דִּילְמָא טָבָן אִינּוּן בְּמוֹעֲדָא כְלוּם. חַד בַּר נַשׁ אַפְקִיד דִּיסִיקְיָא דְּפִיסְתָּא גַּבֵּי רִבִּי חִיָּיה רוּבָה. אָמַר רִבִּי יוֹסֵי בֵּירִבִּי בּוּן. יוֹחָנָן חִיקוֹקְיָא הֲוָה. אֲתָא שְׁאַל לְרִבִּי. אֲמַר לֵיהּ. תִּימָכֵר עַל פִּי בֵּית דִּין בִּשְׁעַת הַבִּיעוּר. חַד בַּר נַשׁ אַפְקִיד גַּרְבָּא דְּכוּתְחָא גַּבֵּי רַב חִיָּיה בַּר אַשִׁי. אֲתָא שְׁאַל לְרַב. אֲמַר לֵיהּ. יִמָּכֵר עַל פִּי בֵּית דִּין בִּשְׁעַת הַבִּיעוּר. הֵיי דָּנוּ שְׁעַת הַבִּיעוּר. רִבִּי יִרְמְיָה אָמַר. בְּשַׁחֲרִית. רִבִּי בָּא אָמַר. חֲמִישִׁית כְּרִבִּי יוּדָה. אָמַר רִבִּי יוֹסֵה. יָאוּת אָמַר רִבִּי יִרְמְיָה. כְּלוּם אָמְרוּ לִיגַּע בָּהֶן לְמוֹכְרָן לֹא מִפְּנֵי הָשֵׁב אֲבֵידָה לַבְּעָלִים. חֲמִישִׁית כְּרִבִּי יוּדָה לֹא טָבָה כְלוּם.

חֲבֵרַיָּא אָמְרִין. חֲמִישִׁית כְּרִבִּי יוּדָה הִקְדִּישׁוֹ מוּקְדָּשׁ. עֲשָׂאוֹ תְרוּמָה אֵינָהּ תְּרוּמָה. הִקְדִּישׁוֹ מוּקְדָּשׁ. הֶקְדֵּשׁ דָּמִים. עֲשָׂאוֹ תְרוּמָה אֵינָהּ תְּרוּמָה. שֶׁלֹּא נִיתְּנָה תְרוּמָה אֶלָּא לַאֲכִילָה בִּלְבָד. אָמַר לוֹן רִבִּי יוֹסֵי. לָא מִסְתַּבְּרָא דְלָא חִילּוּפִין. הִקְדִּישׁוֹ אֵימוֹ מוּקְדָּשׁ. עֲשָׂאוֹ תְרוּמָה הֲרֵי זָה תְּרוּמָה. הִקְדִּישׁוֹ אֵינוֹ מוּקְדָּשׁ. שֶׁאֵין פּוֹדִין אֶת הַקֳּדָשִׁים לְהַאֲכִילָן לִכְלָבִים. עֲשָׂאוֹ תְרוּמָה הֲרֵי זָה תְּרוּמָה. טְהוֹרָה הִיא דְּבַר תּוֹרָה. אַתְּ הוּא שֶׁגָּזַרְתָּה עָלֶיהָ שְׂרִיפָה.

Rav said, the words of Rebbi Meïr: He who preliminarily marries with leavened matter starting from the sixth hour did not do anything[129]. Rebbi Huna said, this is correct. Would Cordovanian[130] wheat in the desert be any good on the holiday? A person deposited a double sack[131] of bread with the Elder Rebbi Ḥiyya. Rebbi Yose ben Rabbi Abun said, he was Joḥanan from Ḥiqoq. He went and asked Rebbi who told him, it should be sold under judicial supervision at the time of elimination[132]. A person deposited a jar of *kutah*[133] with Rav Ḥiyya bar Ashi. He went and asked Rav who told him, it should be sold under judicial supervision at the time of elimination. What is the time of elimination[134]? Rebbi Jeremiah said, in the morning[135]. Rebbi Aḥa said, the fifth [hour] following Rebbi Jehudah[136]. Rebbi Yose said, Rebbi Jeremiah said it correctly. Did they not say to touch them in order to sell them only to return a lost article to its owner[137]? In the fifth [hour] following Rebbi Jehudah it is not worth anything.

The colleagues said, in the fifth [hour] following Rebbi Jehudah if he dedicated it it is dedicated[138]; if he designated it as heave it is no heave. If he dedicated it it is dedicated, dedication of money's worth[139]. If he designated it as heave it is no heave, since heave was given only to be consumed[140]. Rebbi Yose told them, the opposite is reasonable. If he dedicated it it is not dedicated; if he designated it as heave it is heave. If he dedicated it it is not dedicated, since one does not redeem *sancta* to feed to the dogs[141]. If he designated it as heave it is heave, since it is pure by the words of the Torah[142]. You are the one who decided that it has to be burned.

129 *Qiddušin* 1:1, Note 73. A preliminary marriage can be contracted in different ways; one of them is delivering something of value to the bride. While leavened matter for R. Jehudah is prohibited only after noontime of the 14ᵗʰ of Nisan, since it is rabbinically forbidden after the start of the fifth hour it no longer has any monetary value. Babli 7a.

130 In the Babli, *loc. cit.*, קורדנייתא

"Kurdish". According to Rashi and R. Hananel they are very hard; to be used they have to be soaked in water and then are considered leavened and forbidden for ususfruct on Passover.

131 Greek δισάκκιον, τό. A different version is in the Babli 13a.

132 The owner did not collect his property before Passover Eve. To avoid it becoming worthless, it has to be sold to Gentiles and the proceeds kept in trust for the owner.

133 A kind of yogurt made in Babylonia from milk, salt, and mouldy bread as source of the bacteria. This is leavened matter.

134 When is the time to sell leavened matter whose owner did not collect it in time?

135 The entire morning of the 14th of Nisan.

136 This is the Babli's decision in the name of Rebbi, 13a.

137 In general, an unpaid keeper is not responsible for losses unless he manipulates the deposit without authorization. Without incurring financial responsibility he only can sell by direction of the court in order to avoid major financial loss to the depositor.

138 In order to avoid having to burn the leavened matter, he dedicates it to the Temple to be sold and the proceeds used for the Temple's needs. Temple property is not subject to the prohibition of leavened matter since it is not *yours* as mentioned in *Ex.* 13:7.

139 Even for R. Jehudah the biblical prohibition of usufruct only starts on midday of the 14th; during the fifth hour the matter is worth money even for Jews, since it may be used as cattle feed.

140 Heave is a *sanctum* to be given to the Cohen to be consumed in purity; nothing pure that cannot be consumed may become heave.

141 Babli 29a, *Ševuot* 11b, *Bekhorot* 15a, *Temurah* 17a,30b,31a; Yerushalmi *Ma`aser Šeni* 2:5 Note 82.

142 Since by biblical standards it is food until 12 am, a rabbinic prohibition cannot invalidate a biblically valid dedication. This cannot be compared with the case of preliminary marriage since there money's worth is required, which was eliminated by rabbinic usage.

(fol. 27a) **משנה ה**: וְעוֹד אָמַר רבִּי יְהוּדָה שְׁתֵּי חַלּוֹת שֶׁל תּוֹדָה פְּסוּלוֹת וּמוּנָּחוֹת עַל גַּג הָאִיצְטֶבָא. כָּל־זְמַן שֶׁהֵן מוּנָּחוֹת כָּל־הָעָם אוֹכְלִין. נִיטְלָה אַחַת תּוֹלִין לֹא אוֹכְלִין וְלֹא שׂוֹרְפִין. נִיטְלוּ שְׁתֵּיהֶן הִתְחִילוּ כָּל־הָעָם שׂוֹרְפִין.

Mishnah 5: In addition, Rebbi Jehudah said, two disqualified loaves of thanksgiving offering[143] were lying on the roof of the stoa[144]. As long as they were lying there, everybody was eating. If one was removed one suspends, neither does one eat nor burn. If both were removed, everybody started to burn.

143 At Jerusalem in Temple times, the Temple was the timekeeper and signalled to the people the times to dispose of leavened matter. A thanksgiving offering requires the addition of leavened bread (*Lev.* 7:13). Since the bread was kept until the time its consumption was forbidden, one used loaves which could not be eaten, either because they were impure or because they were from the preceding day's offering. A thanksgiving offering must be consumed on the day it is offered (*Lev.* 7:15), this applies not only to the meat but also to the accompanying cereal.

144 The stoa surrounding the Temple Mount. Babli 13b

(27d line 13) **הלכה ה**: רִבִּי שִׁמְעוֹן בֶּן לָקִישׁ אָמַר בְּשֵׁם רִבִּי יַנַּאי. כְּשֵׁירוֹת הָיוּ. מִשּׁוּם מַאי הוּא פוֹסְלָן. שֶׁלֹּא לִשְׁחוֹט עֲלֵיהֶן אֶת הַזֶּבַח. וְלֹא בִשְׁחִיטָה הֵן קְדִישׁוֹת. וְיִפָּדֶה וְיֵאָכֵל. אָמַר רִבִּי חֲנַנְיָה. חוּלְיָיא קוֹמוֹי לֹא אָכַל. וְאַתְּ אָמַרְתְּ. יִפָּדֶה וְיֵאָכֵל. רִבִּי [חֲנִינָא] אָמַר. פְּסוּלוֹת הָיוּ. מִפְּנֵי שֶׁהָיוּ מְמַהֲרִין לְהָבִיא תּוֹדוֹתֵיהֶן מִפְּנֵי חָמֵץ שֶׁבַּתּוֹדָה. וְאִי אֶיפְשַׁר שֶׁלֹּא יִשָּׁפֵךְ דָּמָהּ שֶׁלְּאַחַד וְהִיא נִפְסֶלֶת.

תַּנֵּי. שְׁתֵּי פָרוֹת חוֹרְשׁוֹת [בִּירוּשָׁלַם.] וִירוּשָׁלַם לֹא בְמָקוֹם שֶׁנָּהֲגוּ שֶׁלֹּא לַעֲשׂוֹת מְלָאכָה בָּאַרְבָּעָה עָשָׂר הִיא. נְרָאִית כְּחוֹרְשׁוֹת. אִית תַּנָּיֵי תַנֵּי. שְׁתֵּי נֵירוֹת דּוֹלְקִין. אִית תַּנָּיֵי תַנֵּי. שְׁנֵי סַדִּינִין. אָמַר רִבִּי פִינְחָס. וְלֹא פְלִיגִין. מָאן דְּאָמַר. שְׁתֵּי פָרוֹת שְׁתֵּי נֵירוֹת. בַּחוֹל. מָאן דָּמַר. שְׁנֵי סַדִּינִין. בַּשַּׁבָּת.

רִבִּי חֲנַנְיָה בְּעָא קוֹמֵי רִבִּי מָנָא. וְיִקְבְּעוּ לָהּ תְּקִיעָה. אָמַר לֵיהּ. אִם אוֹמֵר אַתְּ כֵּן נִמְצֵאתָה [אוֹמֵר. שֶׁמָּא] לְתָמִיד הֵן תּוֹקְעִין [וְהֵן מִתְקַלְקְלִין]. אָמַר לֵיהּ. וְהָא תַנִּינָן. שָׁלֹשׁ לְהַבְטִיל הָעָם מִן הַמְּלָאכָה. וְשָׁלֹשׁ לְהַבְדִּיל בֵּין קוֹדֶשׁ לְחוֹל. אָמַר לֵיהּ. תַּמָּן כָּל־עֶרֶב שַׁבָּת וְעֶרֶב שַׁבָּת הֵן תּוֹקְעִין וְאֵינָן טוֹעִין. בְּרַם הָכָא אַחַת לְקִיצִּין הֵן. אִם אוֹמֵר אַתְּ כֵּן. אַף הֵן סְבוּרִין שֶׁמָּא לְתָמִיד הֵן תּוֹקְעִין וְהֵן מִתְקַלְקְלִין.

Halakhah 5: Rebbi Simeon ben Laqish said in the name of Rebbi Yannai: They were qualified[145]. And why does he treat them as disqualified? Not to slaughter the sacrifice for them[6]. But do they not become *sancta* only by the slaughter? They should be redeemed and be eaten[146]! Rebbi Hanania said, he has profane [bread] before him which he could not eat and you are saying, they should be redeemed and be eaten? Rebbi [Hanina][147] said, they were disqualified. Since they are in a hurry to bring their thanksgiving sacrifices because of the leavened bread with the sacrifice[148], it is impossible that not the blood of one of them be spilled[149] and it becomes disqualified.

It was stated: Two cows were ploughing [in Jerusalem][150]. But is Jerusalem not a place where they used not to work on the Fourteenth[151]? They were looking as if ploughing. There are Tannaim who stated: Two lights were burning. There are Tannaim who stated: Two sheets[152]. Rebbi Phineas said, they do not disagree. He who said, two cows, two lights, on a weekday. He who said, two sheets, on the Sabbath.

Rebbi Hananiah asked before Rebbi Mana, should they not insitute trumpet blowing? If you say so, it would turn out that [they would say, maybe] they blow for the daily sacrifice[153][, and they would be led astray]. He retorted, but did we not state: "Three to separate people from work, and three to separate between weekday and holiness"[154]? He answered him, there every single Friday they are blowing, one will not err. But here it is once in a long time; if you say so, it would turn out that they would say, maybe they blow for the daily sacrifice, and they would be led astray.

145 The breads exhibited as a sign. Babli 13b.

146 They were dedicated as bread accompanying a thanksgiving sacrifice; their holiness is that of a gift to the Temple, not that of a sacrifice. Once the sacrifice was slaughtered and the blood sprinkled on the altar, the bread becomes intrinsically holy and its status equals that of sacrificial meat which cannot be redeemed. This implies that any time before the slaughter, the bread can be redeemed to regain profane status and other bread dedicated in its stead. The bread cannot become disqualified if the corresponding sacrifice is not slaughtered.

147 The name is missing in the ms. and the printed editions but retained in the quote of this passage by Tosaphot (13b s.v. אלא).

148 The Yerushalmi assumes that thanksgiving sacrifices may be offered on the 14th. These are family sacrifices and in this case must be eaten as long as the bread may be eaten. Since no sacrifices may be offered before the daily morning sacrifice, the time to consume an entire animal is very short.

The Babli 13b holds that no thanksgiving sacrifice is accepted on the 14th and refers R. Yannai's statement to bread dedicated for such a sacrifice which then cannot be used for sacrificial purposes.

149 An argument accepted in the Babli 13b as minority opinion of R. Simeon ben Eleazar.

150 Babli 14a. In this version they were ploughing on Mount Olivet and could be seen everywhere in Jerusalem. One had to stop eating leavened bread when only one cow was seen.

151 The 14th is a semi-holiday. As noted in Mishnah 4:1, whether work in the morning was permitted or forbidden was a matter of local custom.

152 Two large linen sheets displayed as flags.

153 As required by *Num.* 10:10.

154 Mishnah *Sukkah* 5:5. Every Friday afternoon after the daily sacrifice trumpets were blown to announce the coming of the Sabbath.

(27d line 30) לָמָּה. מִפְּנֵי קְדוּשָׁתָהּ. אוֹ מִשּׁוּם שֶׁאֵין אוֹכְלֶיהָ מְצוּיִין. מַה נָּפִיק מִבֵּינֵיהוֹן. חַלּוֹת תּוֹדָה. אִין תֵּימַר מִשּׁוּם שֶׁאֵין אוֹכְלֶיהָ מְצוּיִין. אֵילּוּ אוֹכְלֶיהָ מְצוּיִין. אִין תֵּימַר מִפְּנֵי קְדוּשָׁתָהּ. אֵילּוּ יֵשׁ לָהֶן קְדוּשָׁה. רִבִּי נָתָן אוֹמֵר. כְּשֵׁירוֹת נִיטְלוּ (שֶׁיְּהוּ) [שׁוֹהִין] לָהֶן שָׁעָה אַחַת לַאֲכִילָתָן וְתוֹלִין אֲבָל לֹא שׂוֹרְפִין. אִית לָךְ מֵימַר מִשּׁוּם שֶׁאֵין אוֹכְלֶיהָ מְצוּיִין. לֹא מִפְּנֵי קְדוּשָׁתָהּ. אוֹף הָכָא מִפְּנֵי קְדוּשָׁתָהּ.

Why[155]? Because of its holiness or because its eaters are few? What is the difference between them? The breads of the thanksgiving sacrifice. If you are saying because its eaters are few, the eaters of these are many[156]. If you are saying because of its holiness, these are holy. Rebbi Nathan says, they[157] were taken when qualified, (that there be) [one waits][158] one hour when they can be eaten, one suspends but does not burn. Could you say because its eaters are few[159]? No, because of its holiness; here also because of its holiness.

155 Why may heave, which is a *sanctum* and may be eaten only by pure Cohanim, be eaten an additional hour?
156 Of the 10 breads accompanying a thanksgiving sacrifice, 9 are eaten by the offerer and his family, only one by a Cohen.
157 He agrees with R. Jehudah that two breads were displayed as a sign that leavened matter may be eaten. He disagrees with him on two points. First, that the breads were pure *sancta*, and that they were lifted together and eaten, exactly one hour before leavening had to be burned.
158 The scribe's text (in parentheses) is as good as the corrector's [in brackets]/
159 Since they are only two, they could be eaten by the person lifting them.

(fol. 27a) **משנה ו**: רַבָּן גַּמְלִיאֵל אוֹמֵר חוּלִין נֶאֱכָלִין כָּל־אַרְבַּע וּתְרוּמָה כָּל־חָמֵשׁ וְשׂוֹרְפִין בִּתְחִלַּת שֵׁשׁ:

Mishnah 6: Rabban Gamliel says, profane food is eaten the entire fourth [hour] and heave the entire fifth; and one burns at the start of the sixth.

(27d line 35) **הלכה ו**: אָמַר רִבִּי יוּדָה בֶּן פָּזִי. נִרְאִין דְּבָרִים שֶׁתְּהֵא הֲלָכָה כְּרַבָּן גַּמְלִיאֵל. שֶׁהוּא אוֹמֵר מֵעֵין שְׁנֵיהֶן. אֲתָא רִבִּי אָבוּן רִבִּי יוֹחָנָן בְּשֵׁם רִבִּי שִׁמְעוֹן בֶּן יוֹצָדָק. הֲלָכָה כְּרַבָּן גַּמְלִיאֵל. שֶׁהוּא אוֹמֵר מֵעֵין שְׁנֵיהֶן.

Halakhah 6. Rebbi Jehudah ben Pazi said, it seems that practice has to follow Rabban Gamliel since he says it similar to both of them[160] There came

Rebbi Abun, Rebbi Joḥanan in the name of Rebbi Simeon ben Joṣadaq: practice follows Rabban Gamliel since what he says is similar to both of them.

160 R. Meïr and R. Jehudah in Mishnah 4.

(fol. 27a) **משנה ז**: רִבִּי חֲנַנְיָה סְגָן הַכֹּהֲנִים אוֹמֵר מִיְּמֵיהֶן שֶׁל כֹּהֲנִים לֹא נִמְנְעוּ מִלִּשְׂרוֹף אֶת הַבָּשָׂר שֶׁנִּטְמָא בִוְולַד הַטּוּמְאָה עִם בָּשָׂר שֶׁנִּטְמָא בְאַב הַטּוּמְאָה אַף עַל פִּי שֶׁמּוֹסִיפִין לוֹ טוּמְאָה עַל טוּמְאָתוֹ. הוֹסִיף רִבִּי עֲקִיבָה מִיְּמֵיהֶן שֶׁל כֹּהֲנִים לֹא נִמְנְעוּ מִלְּהַדְלִיק אֶת הַשֶּׁמֶן שֶׁנִּפְסַל בִּטְבוּל יוֹם בְּנֵר שֶׁנִּטְמָא בְטָמֵא מֵת אַף עַל פִּי שֶׁמּוֹסִיפִין לוֹ טוּמְאָה עַל טוּמְאָתוֹ:

Mishnah 7: Rebbi Ḥananiah, the executive officer of the Cohanim[161], says, the Cohanim never refrained from burning meat which became impure by derivative impurity[162] with meat which became impure by original impurity even though they added impurity to it. Rebbi Aqiba added and said, the Cohanim never refrained from burning oil which became disqualified by a *tevul-yom*[163] in a lamp impure by the impurity of the dead even though they added impurity to it[164].

161 The organizer of the Temple service; one of the few permanent positions in the Temple service.

162 Since it is written (*Num.* 19:22) *anything an impure person touches will become impure*, it is clear that biblical original impurity induces biblical derivative impurity. In both cases, sacrificial meat which became impure must be burned. The question is raised in the Halakhah, how many stages of derivative impurity are implied by biblical law and how many are purely rabbinical. If biblically impure meat would be burned together with rabbinically impure (but biblically pure) meat, the latter could become more impure before being destroyed.

163 A person who is cleansed from impurity by immersion in a *miqweh*, who is no longer impure but prevented from touching *sancta* before the sundown following his immersion (*Lev.* 22:7).

164 The oil was heave which became disqualified from being consumed by the touch of a *tevul-yom* but is biblically pure. By being filled into an impure lamp it becomes biblically impure.

(27d line 38) בַּר קַפָּרָא אָמַר. אַב הַטּוּמְאָה דְּבַר תּוֹרָה. וְולַד טוּמְאָה מִדִּבְרֵיהֶן. רִבִּי יוֹחָנָן אָמַר. בֵּין זֶה בֵּין זֶה דְּבַר תּוֹרָה. עַל דַּעְתֵּיהּ דְּבַר קַפָּרָא נִיחָא. עַל דַּעְתֵּיהּ דְּרִבִּי יוֹחָנָן אַב

הַטוּמְאָה עוֹשָׂה רִאשׁוֹן. וְלַד הַטּוּמְאָה עוֹשָׂה שֵׁנִי. שֵׁינִי שֶׁנָּגַע בְּרִאשׁוֹן הֲרֵי הוּא בִּמְקוֹמוֹ שֵׁינִי. שֶׁהַשְּׁלִישִׁי שֶׁנָּגַע בְּרִאשׁוֹן נַעֲשָׂה שֵׁינִי.

תַּנֵּי. בֵּית שַׁמַּי אוֹמְרִין. אֵין שׂוֹרְפִין בָּשָׂר טָהוֹר עִם בָּשָׂר טָמֵא. וּבֵית הִלֵּל מַתִּירִין. עַל דַּעְתֵּיהּ דְּבַר קַפָּרָא נִיחָא. שׂוֹרְפִין פְּסוּל תּוֹרָה עִם פְּסוּל טוּמְאַת תּוֹרָה. וּצְרִיכִינָן מַשְׁמַע. טוּמְאַת דִּבְרֵיהֶן עִם טוּמְאַת תּוֹרָה. עַל דַּעְתֵּיהּ דְּרִבִּי יוֹחָנָן אִם פְּסוּל תּוֹרָה עִם טוּמְאַת תּוֹרָה שׂוֹרְפִין. כָּל־שֶׁכֵּן טוּמְאַת תּוֹרָה עִם טוּמְאַת תּוֹרָה. רִבִּי חֲנַנְיָה סְגַן הַכֹּהֲנִים שְׁנֵיָּיהּ מִשֵּׁם בֵּית שַׁמַּי וּבֵית הִלֵּל. אָמַר רִבִּי מָנָא קוֹמֵי רִבִּי יוֹסֵה. עַל דַּעְתֵּיהּ דְּרִבִּי יוֹחָנָן נִיחָא. דְּמַר רִבִּי יוֹחָנָן שֵׁשָׁה סְפֵיקוֹת הָיוּ תוֹלִין עֲלֵיהֶן וּבָאִין. וּבְאוּשָׁא גָּזְרוּ עֲלֵיהֶן שְׂרֵיפָה. רִבִּי חֲנַנְיָה סְגַן הַכֹּהֲנִים לֹא לְקוֹדֶם לְאוּשָׁא הָיָה. וְקוֹדֶם לְאוּשָׁא לֹא הָיְתָה שְׂרֵיפָה לְדִבְרֵיהֶן. אָמַר לֵיהּ. תִּיפְתָּר שֶׁנִּיטְמָא בִּכְלֵי זְכוּכִית. אָמַר לֵיהּ. אֲפִילּוּ תֵימַר. נִיטְמָא בִּכְלִי זְכוּכִית. לֹא כֵן אָמַר רִבִּי זְעוּרָא רִבִּי אָבוּנָה בְשֵׁם רִבִּי יִרְמְיָה. יוֹסֵי בֶּן יוֹעֶזֶר אִישׁ צְרִידָה וְיוֹסֵי בֶּן יוֹחָנָן אִישׁ יְרוּשָׁלַיִם גָּזְרוּ טוּמְאָה עַל אֶרֶץ הָעַמִּים וְעַל כְּלֵי זְכוּכִית. [רִבִּי יוּדָא אָמַר. יְהוּדָה בֶּן טַבַּאי וְשִׁמְעוֹן בֶּן שָׁטַח גָּזְרוּ עַל כְּלֵי מַתָּכוֹת. הִלֵּל וְשַׁמַּאי גָּשְׂרוּ עַל טָהֳרַת יָדַיִם.] רִבִּי יִרְמְיָה סָבַר מֵימַר. אֶרֶץ הָעַמִּים וּכְלֵי זְכוּכִית תְּלוּיָה. רִבִּי יוֹסֵי סָבַר מֵימַר. אֶרֶץ הָעַמִּים תְּלוּיָה וּכְלֵי זְכוּכִית שְׂרֵיפָה. אֵלּוּ הֵן שֵׁשָׁה סְפֵיקוֹת. עַל סְפֵק בֵּית הַפְּרָס. עַל סְפֵק אֶרֶץ הָעַמִּים. עַל סְפֵק בִּגְדֵי עַם הָאָרֶץ. עַל סְפֵק הָרוֹקִין. עַל סְפֵק מֵי רַגְלֵי אָדָם שֶׁהוּא כְּנֶגֶד מֵי רַגְלֵי בְהֵמָה. עַל וַדַּאי מַגָּעָן שֶׁהִיא סְפֵק טוּמְאָתָן. עַל אֵלּוּ שׂוֹרְפִין תְּרוּמָה.

[165]Bar Qappara said, original impurity is a word from the Torah, derivative impurity is of their words[166]. Rebbi Joḥanan said, both these and those are word of the Torah[167]. In the opinion of Bar Qappara it is understandable[168]. In the opinion of Rebbi Joḥanan, original impurity induces first degree derivative. Derivative impurity[169] induces second degree derivative. Second degree impurity which touched first degree one remains in its place, second degree, since third degree which touches first degree becomes second degree[170].

It was stated[171]: "The House of Shammai say, one does not burn pure meat with impure meat, but the House of Hillel permit." In the opinion of Bar Qappara it is understandable. One burns what is disqualified[172] by the Torah with what is disqualified as impure[173] by the Torah. And it was necessary to let hear, impurity by their words with impurity by the Torah[166]. In the opinion of Rebbi Joḥanan, if one burns disqualified by the Torah together with impurity by the Torah, so much more impurity by the Torah together with impurity by the Torah. Rebbi Ḥananiah, the executive officer of the Cohanim, did state it in the name of the House of Shammai and the House of Hillel[174]. Rebbi Mana said before Rebbi Yose: The opinion of Rebbi Johanan is understandable, for Rebbi Johanan said, for six doubts one was permanently suspending, but in Usha they decided burning for them[175]. Was Rebbi Hananiah, the executive officer of the Cohanim, not before Usha[176]? Before Usha there was no burning for their words[177]. He told him, explain it if it became impure in a glass vessel[178]. He retorted, even if you are saying that it became impure in a glass vessel, did not Rebbi Ze'ira, Rebbi Abuna say in the name of Rebbi Jeremiah[179], Yose ben Yo'ezer from Sereda and Yose ben Johanan from Jerusalem decided impurity for Gentile land and glass ware[180]. [Rebbi Jehuda said, Jehudah ben Tabbai and Simeon ben Šetah decided on metal vessels[181]. Hillel and Shammai decided on purity of hands[182].] Rebbi Jeremiah[179] was of the opinion that for Gentile land there is suspension and for glass ware there is suspension. Rebbi Yose was of the opinion that for Gentile lands there is suspension, for glassware burning[183]. The following are the six doubts[184]: "On the doubt of a *bet happeras*[185], on the doubt of Gentile land, on the doubt of clothing of the vulgar[186], on the doubt of spittle[187], on the doubt of human urine which is separate from animal urine[188], on certain touch which is a doubt of impurity[189] on these one burns heave.

165 Here starts the discussion of Mishnah 7, even though this is noted only later.
166 This refers to the terms used by R. Hananiah in the Mishnah. In the Babli, 15a/15b, the attributions are switched. In the Yerushalmi the attributions are confirmed in *Šeqalim* 8:5.
167 In his opinion, biblically pure food, even if it may no longer be eaten or sacrificed, may not be destroyed.
168 The statement of R. Hananiah contains essential information, that one may cause impurity to food which is biblically pure in order to burn it together with biblically impure food. While it is a matter of dispute whether this applies to food in a profane setting, it is agreed that it is prohibited to increase impurity in a sacral setting.
169 Derivative impurity in the first degree such as described in *Num.* 19:22. The biblical rule that for material susceptible to impurity contact with derivative impurity in the first degree induces derivative impurity in the second degree is derived from *Lev.* 7:19. Since there is no verse which implies the possibility of biblical derivative impurity in the third degree, derivative impurity in the second degree biblically should be characterized as *disqualified for sacral use* rather than *impure*.
170 Babli 14a. Then R. Hananiah's statement is trivial and unnecessary.

171 Tosephta 1:6.

172 Derivative impurity in the second degree.

173 Original impurity or derivative impurity in the first degree.

174 For R. Joḥanan, while the statement of R. Ḥananiah is trivial, it is important as summarizing the consensus of the Houses of Shammai and Hillel.

175 Babli *Šabbat* 15b.

176 In Usha, the place of R. Jehudah, a loyal supporter of the Roman government, the Rabbinate was reconstituted by the third generation Tannaim after the death of Hadrian and the suspension of the latter's anti-Jewish decrees. The executive officer of the Cohanim must have served in the Temple; he therefore belongs to the first generation of Tannaim.

177 Rabbinically impure *sancta* neither could be used nor destroyed.

178 Biblical impurity applies only to kinds of vessels and implements mentioned in the rules of impurity: earthenware and metal (*Lev.* 6:21), leather and textiles (*Lev.* 13:49), bone and wood (*Num.* 31:20). Other vessels cannot become impure; to this fact one attributes the great number of stone vessels found on archeological sites of the Second Temple period. (Similarly intrinsically pure vessels made of cow dung have not survived for the archeological record.) The impurity of glass vessels, unknown to Moses, is purely rabbinical. One has to take the information that the impurity of glass ware "was decided" by the heads of the Synhedrion to mean that they codified the rules which were popularly observed before. Glass vessels are compared to earthenware vessels since the former are made from sand, the latter from clay. They are also compared to metal vessels since if broken they can be melted down and made into new vessels.

179 Rebbi or Rav Jeremiah bar Abba, the first generation Babylonian Amora. The main place of the statement is *Ketubot* 8:11, Notes 98-105; Babli *Šabbat* 14b.

180 The land outside the Holy Land was always being considered impure (cf. *Am.* 7:17). What they decided was that earth of Gentile places, within or outside the Holy Land, is considered infected with the impurity of rotting human bodies. While it is in dispute whether Gentile corpses induce tent impurity, it is universally accepted that they transmit impurity by touching.

181 The possible impurity of metal vessels is biblical (Note 178). Following the Babli *Šabbat* 16b, what they decreed was that metal impure by the impurity of the dead should not become pure by being melted down, but only by sprinkling with water containing ashes of the Red Cow.

182 They codified the rules that hands which were not all the time consciously guarded from impurity after being washed are impure in the second degree and, therefore, impart impurity to fluids, heave, and sacrifices but not to solid profane food (cf. *Demay* 2:3, Notes 136-137; Babli *Šabbat* 14b). Corrector's addition from *Ketubot*.

183 That it was decided that glassware has the biblical status of metalware.

184 Mishnah *Ṭaharot* 4:5.

185 A place known to contain a grave whose position is no longer known or ascertainable. If heave was transported over this place, it might have become impure by tent

impurity.

186 A person not known to observe the rules of impurity. His clothing may be impure either by contact with his impure wife in her period or because he suffers from gonorrhea.

The quote here is lacunary; there is missing the possible impurity of vessels found in the public domain.

187 Which might be the source of biblical original impurity as body fluid of a woman menstruating or suffering from flux or a male sufferer from gonorrhea.

188 Urine was used industrially and as a household chemical. Animal urine is pure; human urine may be a source of biblical original impurity as body fluid of a person whose impurity is caused by his own body (Note 187).

189 If the fact that it touched the object in question is not in doubt; the only doubt is whether that object transmits impurity or not.

(27d line 63) **הלכה ז:** עַל דַּעְתֵּיהּ דְּרִבִּי יוֹחָנָן תַּמָּן שׂוֹרְפִין טוּמְאַת תּוֹרָה עִם טוּמְאַת תּוֹרָה. וּבָא לְהוֹסִיף פְּסוּל תּוֹרָה עִם טוּמְאַת תּוֹרָה. עַל דַּעְתֵּיהּ דְּבַר קַפָּרָה תַּמָּן שׂוֹרְפִין טוּמְאַת דִּבְרֵיהֶן עִם טוּמְאַת תּוֹרָה. וְהָכָא פְּסוּל תּוֹרָה עִם טוּמְאַת תּוֹרָה לֹא בָא אֶלָּא לְפָחוֹת. תִּיפְתָּר בִּטְבוּל יוֹם מִבֵּית פְּרָס. שֶׁהוּא מִדִּבְרֵיהֶן. רִבִּי חֲנַנְיָה סְגַן הַכֹּהֲנִים שְׁנִייָהּ מִשֵּׁם בֵּית שַׁמַּי וּבֵית הִלֵּל.

אָמַר רִבִּי מָנָא קוֹמֵי רִבִּי יוֹסֵי. רִבִּי עֲקִיבָה כְּדַעְתֵּיהּ. דְּרִבִּי עֲקִיבָה אָמַר. יְטַמָא יְטַמָא דְּבַר תּוֹרָה. אָמַר רִבִּי יוֹסֵי בֵּירִבִּי בּוּן. אַף עַל גַּב דְּלֵית לֵיהּ לְרִבִּי יִשְׁמָעֵאל יְטַמָא יְטַמָא בְּאוֹכָלִים. אִית לֵיהּ יְטַמָא יְטַמָא בְּכֵלִים.

אִית תַּנָּיֵי תַנֵּי. טָמֵא מֵת. אִית תַּנָּיֵי תַנֵּי. בִּטְמֵא מֵת. מָאן דְּאָמַר. טָמֵא מֵת. בִּכְלֵי שָׁטֵף. מָאן דְּאָמַר. בִּטְמֵא מֵת. בִּכְלֵי מַתָּכוֹת. מַה טַעֲמָא. כֹּל כְּלִי פָתוּחַ וגו' טָמֵא הוּא: [הוּא] טָמֵא [וְ]אֵינוֹ נַעֲשֶׂה אַב הַטּוּמְאָה לְטַמֵּא.

Halakhah 7[190]: In the opinion of Rebbi Johanan there[191] one burns biblical impurity with biblical impurity. He[192] comes to add biblical disqualification with biblical impurity. In the opinion of Bar Qappara there[191] one burns rabbinical impurity with biblical impurity. Here, biblical disqualification with biblical impurity only comes to diminish[193]. Explain it if he was *tevul yom* from a *bet happeras* which is rabbinical[194]. Rebbi Ḥananiah, the executive officer of the Cohanim, did state it in the name of the House of Shammai and the House of Hillel[174].

Rebbi Mana said before Rebbi Yose: Rebbi Aqiba follows his opinion, since Rebbi Aqiba said, *shall be impure*, shall make impure by word of the Torah[195]. Rebbi Yose ben Rebbi Abun said, even though Rebbi Ismael[196] does not accept *shall be impure*, shall make impure, for foodstuffs, he accepts *shall be impure*, shall make impure, for implements.

There are Tannaim who state "impurity of the dead". There are Tannaim who state "by the impurity of the dead"[197]. He who said "impurity of the dead", about vessels that have to be rinsed[198]. He who said "by the impurity of the dead", about metal vessels. What is the reason? *Any open vessel* etc. *is impure*[199]. [It is] impure but does not become a source of impurity to transmit impurity[195].

190 It seems that in this tradition the statement of R. Aqiba in Mishnah 7 was a separate Mishnah.

191 "Here" refers to the statement of R. Aqiba, "there" to that of R. Hananiah, the executive officer of the Cohanim (Notes 166,167).

192 R. Aqiba compared to R. Hananiah.

193 This is unlikely.

194 In the interpretation of Bar Qappara, the rabbinic impurity mentioned by R. Hananiah is secondary or tertiary impurity derived from biblical original impurity whereas R. Aqiba adds rabbinic impurity which has no biblical source.

195 As explained in *Soṭah* 5:2, R. Aqiba takes טמא as a transitive verb. Therefore he reads the expression יטמא as "will transmit impurity", in contrast to טָמֵא "is passively impure." This applies not only to *Num.* 19:22 but also to *Lev.* 11:32-35.

196 *Soṭah* 5:2 Notes 103-106. The position of R. Ismael on *Num.* 19:22 is not known from other sources.

197 This is about the wording of R. Aqiba's statement. A dead human body is the source of original impurity. A person or vessel touching the dead becomes originally impure, carrying "the impurity of the dead". A vessel touching such a person or vessel becomes impure in the first derivative degree "by the impurity of the dead".

198 Impure clay vessels cannot be purified, but become pure only as potsherds or otherwise impossible to use as containers. The expression "vessels to be rinsed" comes from *Lev.* 6:21 where it characterized metal pots. In rabbinic usage, the expression is applied to all vessels that can be purified; here it applies to wooden vessels since metal vessels are excluded in the next sentence.

The separate treatment of metal in cases of impurity of the dead is based on *Num.* 19:16 where in the expression "slain by the sword" the mention of "sword" seems to be superfluous in the context and therefore one concludes that the sword, and by extension any metal, acquires the super-impurity of the dead to impart original impurity to its contents and anything it comes in contact with (*Sifry Num.* 127). The contents of the wooden vessel are impure in the second degree but those in the metal vessel in the first.

199 *Num.* 19:15, referring mainly to clay vessels but also to all other non-metallic containers (*Sifry Num.* 126).

(fol. 17a) **משנה ח**: אָמַר רִבִּי מֵאִיר מִדִּבְרֵיהֶן לָמַדְנוּ שֶׁשּׂוֹרְפִין תְּרוּמָה טְהוֹרָה עִם הַטְּמֵאָה בְּפֶסַח. אָמַר לוֹ רִבִּי יוֹסֵה אֵינָהּ הִיא הַמִּידָה. מוֹדִין רִבִּי אֱלִיעֶזֶר וְרִבִּי יְהוֹשֻׁעַ שֶׁשּׂוֹרְפִין זוֹ לְעַצְמָהּ וְזוֹ לְעַצְמָהּ. וְעַל מַה נֶחְלָקוּ עַל הַתְּלוּיָה וְעַל הַטְּמֵאָה שֶׁרִבִּי אֱלִיעֶזֶר אוֹמֵר תִּישָּׂרֵף זוֹ לְעַצְמָהּ וְזוֹ לְעַצְמָהּ וְרִבִּי יְהוֹשֻׁעַ אוֹמֵר שְׁתֵּיהֶן כְּאֶחָת:

Mishnah 8: Rebbi Meïr said, from their words we learned that one burns pure heave together with impure on Pesaḥ[200]. Rebbi Yose said to him, this is not the implication[201]. Rebbi Eliezer and Rebbi Joshua agree that each of these is burned separately. Where did they disagree? On the suspended[202] and impure ones, where Rebbi Eliezer says each one should be burned separately while Rebbi Joshua said, both together.

200 The 14th of Nisan where pure leavened heave becomes rabbinically forbidden as food at the start of the sixth hour and must be disposed of before its possession becomes biblically (for the majority) or rabbinically (for R. Meïr) forbidden at noontime.

201 R. Ḥananiah and R. Aqiba stated their positions only about (biblically or rabbinically) impure food, not about pure heave which becomes forbidden for an unrelated reason.

202 Heave whose status of purity is in doubt, which cannot be used either as pure or impure (Mishnah *Terumot* 8:7, Note 180).

(27d line 75) **הלכה ח**: מַהוּ בַּפֶּסַח. בְּאַרְבָּעָה עָשָׂר. אָמַר רִבִּי יוֹחָנָן. מִדִּבְרֵי רִבִּי עֲקִיבָה מִדִּבְרֵי רִבִּי חֲנַנְיָה סְגַן הַכֹּהֲנִים. רִבִּי שִׁמְעוֹן בֶּן לָקִישׁ אָמַר. מִדִּבְרֵי רִבִּי אֱלִיעֶזֶר וּמִדִּבְרֵי רִבִּי יְהוֹשֻׁעַ. אָמַר רִבִּי זְעִירָא קוֹמֵי רִבִּי יָסֵי. עַל דַּעְתֵּיהּ דְּרִבִּי יוֹחָנָן נִיחָא. עַל דַּעְתֵּיהּ דְּרִבִּי שִׁמְעוֹן בֶּן לָקִישׁ מַה בָּא רִבִּי לִיעֶזֶר וְרִבִּי יוֹשֻׁעַ לְכָאן. אָמַר לֵיהּ. תַּנָּיִין אִינּוּן. רִבִּי יָסֵי בְּשֵׁם רִבִּי יוֹחָנָן. הַכֹּל מוֹדִין בְּשִׁשָּׁה עָשָׂר שֶׁשּׂוֹרְפִין תְּרוּמָה טְהוֹרָה וּטְמֵיאָה.

Halakhah 8: What is "on Pesaḥ"? On the Fourteenth[203]. Rebbi Joḥanan said, from the words[204] of Rebbi Aqiba and Rebbi Ḥananiah the executive officer of the Cohanim. Rebbi Simeon ben Laqish said, from the words of Rebbi Eliezer and the words of Rebbi Joshua. Rebbi Ze`ira said before Rebbi Yasa: The opinion of Rebbi Joḥanan is understandable[205]. In the opinion of Rebbi Simeon ben Laqish, where enter Rebbi Eliezer and Rebbi Joshua in the discussion? He told him, there are [different] Tannaim[206]. Rebbi Yasa in the name of Rebbi Joḥanan: Everybody agrees that on the Sixteenth one burns pure and impure heave [together][207].

203 In biblical Hebrew "*Pesaḥ*" denotes the 14th of Nisan, the day of the *Pesaḥ* sacrifice (*Lev.* 23:5, *Deut.* 28:16). In popular language "*Pesaḥ*" denotes the festival of unleavened bread, the 15th-21st. The Mishnah uses the biblical expression.

204 Explaining what R. Meïr in the Mishnah is referring to.

205 S. Liebermann here endorses the opinion of earlier commentators who want to emend the text and switch the names of RR. Johanan and Simeon ben Laqish, since otherwise how could the latter ask where RR. Eliezer and Joshua enter the discussion? But it seems that with the two classical commentaries one may explain the text as it stands. According to R. Johanan, R. Meïr refers to Mishnsh 7. Since RR. Eliezer and Joshua are mentioned only in the argument of R. Yose, the statement quoted at the end of Mishnah 8 cannot be the one to which R. Meïr refers; it must be Mishnah *Terumot* 8:7, quoted later in the Halakhah, which on the face of it deals with an unrelated subject, whether it is better to keep heave from becoming certainly impure or see to it that it be usable in conformity with the rules (Notes 216 ff.).

206 There are Tannaim who state Mishnah 7 in the name of R. Eliezer and R. Joshua.

207 If leavened heave was discovered during the holiday it must be burned. If unleavened heave became impure during the holiday, it must be burned, in both cases by biblical decree. But *sancta* other than Temple sacrifices may not be burned on the holiday; the burning must be on the first of the intermediate days where work is permitted.

(28a line 5) רִבִּי יָסֵי מַקְשֵׁי. לָמָּה רִבִּי יֹסֵי אוֹמֵר. אֵינָהּ הַמִּידָה. רִבִּי יָסֵי דּוּ שָׁמַע דְּאָמַר רִבִּי יוֹחָנָן. מִדְּבְרֵי רִבִּי עֲקִיבָה מִדְּבְרֵי רִבִּי חֲנִינָא סְגַן הַכֹּהֲנִים. וְהוּא שָׁמַע דְּבַר קַפָּרָא אָמַר. אַב הַטּוּמְאָה דְּבַר תּוֹרָה. וְלַד הַטּוּמְאָה מִדִּבְרֵיהֶן. וְלֹא שָׁמַע דָּמַר רִבִּי יוֹחָנָן. בֵּין זֶה בֵּין זֶה דְּבַר תּוֹרָה. וְהוּא מַקְשֵׁי. כְּשֵׁם שֶׁמּוּתָּר לִשְׂרוֹף אִיסּוּר (דִּבְרֵיהֶן) [תּוֹרָה] עִם טוּמְאַת תּוֹרָה. שֶׁכֵּן שׂוֹרְפִין טוּמְאַת (דִּבְרֵיהֶן) [תּוֹרָה] עִם טוּמְאַת תּוֹרָה. כָּךְ יְהֵא מוּתָּר לִשְׂרוֹף אִיסּוּר (תּוֹרָה) [דִּבְרֵיהֶן] עִם טוּמְאַת תּוֹרָה. שֶׁכֵּן שׂוֹרְפִין טוּמְאַת (תּוֹרָה) [דִּבְרֵיהֶן] עִם טוּמְאַת תּוֹרָה. אֶלָּא שְׁנִיָּיה הִיא אִיסּוּר שְׁנִיָּיה הִיא טוּמְאָה. וְאָמַר רִבִּי יָסֵי בְּשֵׁם רִבִּי יוֹחָנָן. הַכֹּל מוֹדִין בְּשִׁשָּׁה עָשָׂר שֶׁשּׂוֹרְפִין תְּרוּמָה טְהוֹרָה וּטְמֵיאָה. כְּשֵׁם שֶׁלֹּא חָלַקְתָּ לָנוּ בֵּין אִיסּוּר תּוֹרָה לְטוּמְאַת תּוֹרָה. שֶׁכֵּן שׂוֹרְפִין טוּמְאַת תּוֹרָה עִם טוּמְאַת תּוֹרָה. כָּךְ לֹא תַחֲלוֹק לָנוּ בֵּין אִיסּוּר דִּבְרֵיהֶן לְטוּמְאַת תּוֹרָה. שֶׁכֵּן שׂוֹרְפִין טוּמְאַת דִּבְרֵיהֶן עִם טוּמְאַת תּוֹרָה. אֶלָּא בֵּין זֶה וּבֵין זֶה דְּבַר תּוֹרָה. אֲתָא רִבִּי חִייָה בַּר בָּא מִן צוֹר וְאָמַר מִן שְׁמֵיהּ דְּרִבִּי יוֹחָנָן. בֵּין זֶה וּבֵין זֶה דְּבַר תּוֹרָה. וַאֲמָרִית. יָאוּת. תַּמָּן טוּמְאַת (דִּבְרֵיהֶן) [תּוֹרָה] עִם טוּמְאַת תּוֹרָה. בְּרַם הָכָא פְּסוּל תּוֹרָה עִם טוּמְאַת תּוֹרָה. בְּגִין כָּךְ רִבִּי יֹסֵי אָמַר. אֵינָהּ הִיא הַמִּידָה. וְקַשְׁיָא דְּרִבִּי יוֹחָנָן עַל דְּרִבִּי מֵאִיר. וְהָדָא דְּרִבִּי יוֹסֵי אָמַר. אֵינָהּ הִיא הַמִּידָה. סָבַר בַּר קַפָּרָא כְּרִבִּי שִׁמְעוֹן בֶּן לָקִישׁ. דְּרִבִּי שִׁמְעוֹן בֶּן לָקִישׁ אָמַר. מִדְּבְרֵי רִבִּי אֱלִיעֶזֶר וְרִבִּי יְהוֹשֻׁעַ. וְקַשְׁיָא דְּבַר קַפָּרָא עַל דְּרִבִּי יוֹסֵי. וְהָדָא דְּרִבִּי מֵאִיר אָמַר. מִדְּבְרֵיהֶם לָמַדְנוּ. אָמַר רִבִּי אַבִּין. רִבִּי נֵאֲיֵי כְּדַעְתֵּיהּ. דְּרִבִּי מֵאִיר מַחֲמִיר בְּדִבְרֵיהֶם כְּדִבְרֵי

HALAKHAH EIGHT

תּוֹרָה. אָן אַשְׁכְּחָן דְּרִבִּי מֵאִיר מַחְמִיר בְּדִבְרֵיהֶן כְּדִבְרֵי תוֹרָה. אָמַר רִבִּי חִינְנָה. כַּיי דְתַנִּינָן תַּמָּן. הָרוֹאָה כֶּתֶם הֲרֵי זוֹ מְקוּלְקֶלֶת וְחוֹשֶׁשֶׁת מִשּׁוּם זוֹב [דִבְרֵי רִבִּי מֵאִיר. וַחֲכָמִים אוֹמְרִים אֵין בַּכְּתָמִים מִשּׁוּם זוֹב:]

Rebbi Yasa asked: Why does Rebbi Yose say, this is not the implication? Rebbi Yasa had heard that Rebbi Johanan said, "from the words of Rebbi Aqiba and Rebbi Hananiah the executive officer of the Cohanim," and he had heard that Bar Qappara said, "original impurity is a word from the Torah, derivative impurity is of their words[166]." But he had not heard that Rebbi Johanan had said, "both these and those are words of the Torah[167]." Therefore, he was asking: Just as it is permitted to burn what is (rabbinically) [biblically] forbidden with what is biblically impure, since one burns what is (rabbinically) [biblically] impure with what is biblically impure, so it should be permitted to burn what is (biblically) [rabbinically] forbidden with what is biblically impure since one burns what is (biblically) [rabbinically] impure with what is biblically impure. But there must be a difference between prohibition and impurity. And Rebbi Yasa said in the name of Rebbi Johanan: Everybody agrees that on the Sixteenth one burns pure and impure heave [together][207]. Just as you did not make a difference for us between biblical prohibition and biblical impurity since one burns what is biblically impure with what is biblically impure, so you should not make a difference for us between what is rabbinically forbidden with what is biblically impure since one burns what is rabbinically impure with what is biblically impure. But it must be that both these and those are words of the Torah[208]. There came Rebbi Hiyya bar Abba from Tyre and said in the name of Rebbi Johanan: both these and those are words of the Torah, and I[209] said, it is correct. There[191] (rabbinic) [biblical] impurity with biblical impurity but here[192] biblical disqualification with biblical impurity. Therefore Rebbi Yose said, this is not the implication[210]. The position of Rebbi Johanan is difficult for Rebbi Meïr[211]; therefore Rebbi Yose said, this is not the implication. Bar Qappara must argue like Rebbi Simeon ben Laqish, as Rebbi Simeon ben Laqish said, from the words of Rebbi Eliezer and the words of Rebbi Joshua. Then the opinion of Bar Qappara is difficult for Rebbi Yose[212] based on what Rebbi Meïr said, "from their words we learned." Rebbi Abbin said, Rebbi

Meïr is consistent[213] since Rebbi Meïr is restrictive in their words as in words of the Torah. Where do we find that Rebbi Meïr is restrictive in their words as in words of the Torah? Rebbi Hinena said, as we have stated there[214]: "A woman who sees a stain is out of order and worries because of flux[, the words of Rebbi Meïr. But the Sages say, nothing in stains implies flux[215]]."

208 Since the statement of R. Johanan about the 16th implies that it does not apply on the 14th, it is inconsistent with the statement of Bar Qappara. R. Yasa concluded that R. Johanan must disagree with Bar Qappara without having heard his statement. Then the correct text is the scribe's (in parentheses), not the corrector's the the printed texts' [in brackets] since for R. Johanan Mishnah 7 refers to biblical impurities.

209 R. Yasa.

210 In addition to the reason given in Note 201, if R. Johanan's statement about the 16th is correct, R. Yose will not accept R. Meïr's treatment of rabbinic and biblical impurity as equivalent.

211 Since R. Johanan is an Amora and R. Meïr a Tanna, the statement rather should be that R. Johanan's position is inconsistent with R. Meïr's.

212 Bar Qappara allows burning of rabbinically impure sacrificial meat with biblically impure even though momentarily the rabbinically impure will become biblically impure. In Mishnah *Terumot* 8:7, discussed in the next paragraph, R. Joshua prescribes making possibly rabbinically impure heave biblically impure. Since the first generation R. Joshua is an overriding authority, it is difficult to see how the third generation R. Yose could disagree.

213 For R. Meïr the disputes between Bar Qappara and R. Johanan and R. Johanan and R. Simeon ben Laqish are irrelevant. Even if R. Hananiah speaks only about biblical impurities, it makes no difference for R. Meïr who applies all biblical stringencies to rabbinic prohibitions.

214 Mishnah *Niddah* 6:13.

215 In biblical rules (which are difficult for rabbinic women to follow, cf. *Niddah* Chapter 4, Note 3) there is a big difference between menstrual discharges (*Lev.* 19:15-24) and non-menstrual flux (*Lev.* 19:25-30). In rabbinic theory, there are 11 days after the end of a menstrual period in which no discharges are menstrual. If a woman discovers a stain on an undergarment, it is rabbinically considered evidence of a discharge. Since this is a purely rabbinic rule, she is "out of order" in that the 11 day rule cannot be applied. In addition, if the undergarment was worn for three days and the stain is large enough to possibly be the result of three discharges, for R. Meïr all rules spelled out in *vv.* 19:28-30 do apply even though there is no biblical impurity.

(28a line 29) תַּמָּן תַּנֵּינָן. חָבִית שֶׁלִּתְרוּמָה שֶׁנּוֹלַד בָּהּ סְפֵק טוּמְאָה. רִבִּי אֱלִיעֶזֶר אוֹמֵר. אִם הָיְתָה מוּנַּחַת בְּמָקוֹם תּוּרְפָּה יַנִּיחֶינָה בְּמָקוֹם מוּצְנָע. וְאִם הָיְתָה מְגוּלָה יְכַסֶּנָּה. רִבִּי יֹשוּעַ

HALAKHAH EIGHT

אוֹמֵר אִם הָיְתָה מוּנַחַת בְּמָקוֹם הַמּוּצְנָע יַנִּיחֶנָּה בְּמָקוֹם תּוּרְפָה. וְאִם הָיְתָה מְכוּסָּה יְגַלֶּנָּה. רַבָּן גַּמְלִיאֵל אוֹמֵר אַל יְחַדֵּשׁ בָּהּ דָּבָר:

There[216], we have stated: An amphora of heave about which a doubt of impurity arose, Rebbi Eliezer says, if it was at a vulnerable place, he should move it to a hidden place. If it was uncovered, he should cover it. Rebbi Joshua says, if it was at a hidden place, he should move it to a vulnerable place. If it was covered, he should uncover it. Rabban Gamliel says, he should not change anything[217].

216 Mishnah *Terumot* 8:7. The text from here to the end of the Chapter is from *Terumot* 8:8-9 (Notes 180-235,ת); it cannot be understood without Mishnaiot 8:8-9 which are not reproduced here.

217 If it were certainly impure, heave wine could be used to settle dust on dirt floors, heave oil or grain as fuel. If there only is a doubt, the heave is called "suspended". It cannot be used as impure since it might be pure, nor as pure since it might be impure. R. Eliezer holds that one has to treat this heave according to all rules of holiness. R. Joshua holds that one has to make sure that the heave be used somehow. Since it never will be usable as pure heave, one has to make sure it will be usable impure (Rashi in *Bekhorot* 33b).

(28a line 33) אָמַר רִבִּי יוֹסֵה בֵּירִבִּי בּוּן מִדִּבְרֵי שְׁלָשְׁתָּן תְּלוּיָה אָסוּר לְשׂוֹרְפָהּ.
תלויה | ת תלוייה

חֲבֵרַיָּיא בְּשֵׁם רִבִּי אֶלְעָזָר. חָבִית הָרִאשׁוֹנָה כְּרִבִּי יוֹסֵי. הַשְּׁנִיָּיה כְּרִבִּי מֵאִיר. חֲבֵרַיָּא אָמְרִין. חָבִית הָרִאשׁוֹנָה כְּרִבִּי יוֹסֵי. וְלֵית רִבִּי מֵאִיר מוֹדֶה בָהּ. חָבִית הַשְּׁנִיָּיה כְּרִבִּי מֵאִיר. וְלֵית רִבִּי יוֹסֵי מוֹדֶה בָהּ. אָמַר לוֹן רִבִּי יוֹסֵי. חֲמוּן מַה אַתּוּן אֲמְרִין. חָבִית הָרִאשׁוֹנָה כְּרִבִּי יוֹסֵי. בְּרַם כְּרִבִּי מֵאִיר שׂוֹרְפִין וּכְרִבִּי שִׁמְעוֹן שׂוֹרְפִין. וְיַרְבּוּ רִבִּי מֵאִיר וְרִבִּי שִׁמְעוֹן עַל רִבִּי יוֹסֵה וְיִשְׂרוֹף. וְעוֹד [שָׁמְעִינָן] מִן הָדָא. מִן מַה דַּאֲנָן חַמְיִין רַבָּנִין עוֹבְדָא אָתֵי קוֹמֵיהוֹן וְאֵינוּן אֲמְרִין. אֵיזִיל תְּלִי. הֵן אַשְׁכַּחְנָן דְּרִבִּי שִׁמְעוֹן אוֹמֵר. שׂוֹרְפִין. הָדָא דְתַנִּינָן. מוֹדֶה רִבִּי לִיעֶזֶר לְרִבִּי יֹשׁוּעַ שֶׁשּׂוֹרְפִין זוֹ לְעַצְמָהּ וְזוֹ לְעַצְמָהּ. אָמַר רִבִּי יוֹחָנָן. רִבִּי שִׁמְעוֹן שְׁנַיָּיא. אֵין תֵּימַר לֵית לְרִבִּי מֵאִיר תְּלוּיָה. וְהָא תַּנֵּי. תְּרוּמָה תְלוּיָה טְהוֹרָה שׂוֹרְפִין אוֹתָהּ עֶרֶב שַׁבָּת עִם חֲשֵׁיכָה. דִּבְרֵי רִבִּי מֵאִיר. וַחֲכָמִים אוֹמְרִים. בִּזְמַנָּהּ. אָמַר רִבִּי עֶזְרָא קוֹמֵי רִבִּי מָנָא. תִּיפְתָּר בִּתְלוּיָה שֶׁאֵין דַּעְתּוֹ לְהַשְׁאִיל עָלֶיהָ. אָמַר לֵיהּ. וְכֵן אָמַר רִבִּי יוֹסֵי. כָּל־מַה דַּאֲנָן קַיָּימִין הָכָא בִּתְלוּיָה שֶׁאֵין דַּעְתּוֹ לְהַשְׁאִיל עָלֶיהָ. אֲבָל בִּתְלוּיָה שֶׁדַּעְתּוֹ לְהַשְׁאִיל עָלֶיהָ הֲרֵי זוֹ טְהוֹרָה. וְתַנֵּי כֵן. תְּרוּמָה תְלוּיָה שֶׁאָמְרוּ. טְהוֹרָה הִיא. הֲרֵי זוֹ טְמֵאָה. אִם אָמַר. הֲרֵי אֲנִי מַנִּיחָהּ עַל מְנָת לְהַשְׁאִיל עָלֶיהָ. הֲרֵי זוֹ טְהוֹרָה. אָמַר רִבִּי יוֹסֵי בֵּירִבִּי בּוּן. תִּיפְתָּר שֶׁנּוֹלַד לָהּ סְפֵק טוּמְאָה עִם דִּימְדּוּמֵי חַמָּה. וְלֵית שְׁמַע מִינָהּ כְּלוּם.

1 אלעזר | ת לעזר השנייה | ת והשנייה חבריא | ת חברייא אמרין | ת אמרי   2 חבית השנייה | ת והשנייה   3 אמרין | ת מרין ברם | ת הא   4 יוסה | ת יוסי וישרוף | ת וישרופו   5 [שמעינן] | ת - מן מה דאנן חמיין | ת ואנא חמי עובדא אתי | ת אתא עובדא ואינון אמרין | ת ואמרין הן | ת והא   6 אשכחנן | ת אשכחן דר' שמעון

או' | ת דאמ' ר' שמעון הדא | ת - מודה | ת מודי לר' יושוע | ת ור' יהושע   7 אמ' | ת ואמ'   שנייא | ת שנייה
תימר | ת תימרון והא | ת הא   8 טהורה | ת וטמיאה   9 עזרא | ת זעירא שאין | ת - להשאיל | ת להישאל
10 וכן | ת כן יוסי | ת יוסי רבו מה | ת תלויה קיימין | ת אמרין להשאיל | ת להישאל   11 בתלויה | ת -
שדעתו | ת דעתו להשאיל | ת להישאל הרי זו טהורה | ת טהורה היא ותני כן | ת דתני תרומה | ת -   12 -|
ת טמיאה היא טמאה | ת טמיאה אני | ת - להשאיל | ת להישאל הרי זו | ת -   13 שנולד | ת שנולדה

Rebbi Yose ben Rebbi Abun said, from the opinion of all three of them: It is forbidden to burn suspended [heave][218].

The colleagues in the name of Rebbi Eleazar: The first amphora[219] following Rebbi Yose, the second[220] following Rebbi Meïr. The colleagues say, the first amphora following Rebbi Yose but Rebbi Meïr will not agree; the second following Rebbi Meïr but Rebbi Yose will not agree. Rebbi Yose told them, be careful what you are saying. The first amphora following Rebbi Yose, but following Rebbi Meïr one burns and following Rebbi Simeon one burns. Then Rebbi Meïr and Rebbi Simeon should form a majority against Rebbi Yose[221] and one should burn. In addition, we understand from the following: we see the rabbis, if a case comes before them, they say, go and suspend[222]. Where do we find that Rebbi Simeon says, one burns? It is what we have stated: "Rebbi Eliezer and Rebbi Joshua agree that each of these is burned separately." Rebbi Johanan said, Rebbi Simeon stated this[223]. If you want to say that Rebbi Meïr does not recognize suspension[224], have we not stated[225]: "Suspended (pure)[226] heave is burned on Sabbath eve when it gets dark, the words of Rebbi Meïr; but the Sages say, at its appointed time[227]." Rebbi Ezra[228] said before Rebbi Mana, explain it that it is suspended because he does not intend to ask about it. He said to him, so also said Rebbi Yose[229]: All we are occupied with here is with suspended [heave] about which he does not intend to ask[230]; but suspended [heave] about which he intends to ask is pure. It was stated thus[231]: "Suspended heave about which they said, is it pure? It is impure. If he said, I am keeping it in order to ask about it, it is pure." What about it? Rebbi Yose ben Rebbi Abun said, explain it if the doubt arose at sundown. Then one cannot infer anything[232].

218 Since neither of them proposes burning the heave as an alternative.
219 Mishnah *Terumot* 8:7 is consistent with the position of R. Yose in *Pesahim* 1:8. Since R. Joshua only permits to put suspended heave in a situation where there is great probability that it accidentally will become impure but does not allow actively to make it impure, it follows that he will not allow pure heave to be made impure in the

process of burning, as prescribed by R. Meïr.

220 The amphora which is the topic of Mishnah *Terumot* 8:10. If there is a choice of either making heave impure or letting it go to waste, R. Joshua permits to make it impure. This parallels the position of R. Meïr in *Pesahim* 1:8, who permits making heave impure in the process of required destruction. Since that Mishnah is not quoted here, it is clear that the origin of the text is in *Terumot*.

221 Even though R. Yose (ben Ḥalafta) is a greater authority than either R. Meïr or R. Simeon, they together should be a majority to determine practice.

222 In the last generation of Amoraim practice still followed R. Yose.

223 Tosefta 1:5. While this does not prove that R. Simeon agrees with the position of R. Meïr about *sancta*, it establishes that he agrees with him about heave. The translation follows the spelling in *Terumot*, שנייה.

224 But treats heave of doubtful status as impure.

225 Tosephta 3:10, about leavened heave to be disposed of if the 14th of Nisan is a Sabbath.

226 With the text in a later paragraph and in *Terumot* one has to read: "or impure".

227 The 14th of Nisan.

228 This reading, R. Ezra (fifth generation) sitting before R. Mana II, is preferable to that of *Terumot*, R. Ze`ira (third generation) before R. Mana I (early second generation).

229 Fifth generation, the teacher of R. Mana II.

230 Since designating any produce as heave is a dedication, it has the status of a vow and as such is subject to annulment by an ordained rabbi or a court. If the vow is annulled, the original produce reverts to profane status where secondary impurity is excluded; in most cases this means that it will automatically revert to purity. Then heave must be given from some other produce of the same harvest. Since all problems arising for suspended heave can be easily resolved by asking for annulment, it is clear that the Mishnah must assume that this way out is not chosen.

231 A related text is Tosephta *Terumot* 7:18.

232 Since there is no time to burn anything, the opinion of the Sages must be followed even by their opponents. This does not prove anything about the position of R. Meïr if the heave already was suspended in the morning.

A different treatment in the Babli, 20b.

(28a line 52) וְאַתּוּן אֲמְרִין. חָבִית הָרִאשׁוֹנָה כְּרַבִּי יוֹסֵי. וְלֵית רִבִּי מֵאִיר מוֹדֶה בָהּ. וְהָתַנֵּי. בַּמֶּה דְבָרִים אֲמוּרִים. בְּבוֹר שֶׁיֵּשׁ בּוֹ כְּדֵי לְהַעֲלוֹת. אֲבָל בְּבוֹר שֶׁאֵין בּוֹ כְּדֵי לְהַעֲלוֹת אֲפִילוּ כָּל־שֶׁהוּא אָסוּר לְטַמְאוֹת. וְאֵין כְּרַבִּי מֵאִיר. הִיא בוֹר שֶׁיֵּשׁ בּוֹ כְּדֵי לְהַעֲלוֹת וְהִיא בוֹר שֶׁאֵין בּוֹ כְּדֵי לְהַעֲלוֹת. אֲפִילוּ כָּל־שֶׁהוּא אָסוּר לְטַמּוֹת. וְעוֹד מִן הָדָא דְתַנִּינָן. אָמַר לוֹ רִבִּי יוֹסֵי. אֵינָהּ הִיא הַמִּידָה. לֵית בַּר נַשׁ אָמַר. אֵינָהּ הִיא מִכְּלָל דּוּ מוֹדֶה עַל קַדְמַיְיתָא. מַיי כְּדוֹן. אָמַר רִבִּי יוֹסֵי בֵּירִבִּי בּוּן. תַּמָּן כְּדֵי לָחוּס עַל נִכְסֵיהוֹן שֶׁלְיִשְׂרָאֵל. וְהָכָא מָה אִית לָךְ. אֲפִילוּ הָכָא אֵינוֹ מַפְסִיד

לְיִשְׂרָאֵל מָמוֹן. שֶׁהוּא צָרִיךְ לִשְׂרוֹף עֵצִים בִּפְנֵי עַצְמָן וְזוֹ בִּפְנֵי עַצְמָהּ. לְהֶפְסֵד מְרוּבֶּה חָשׁוּ. לְהֶפְסֵד מָמוּעָט לֹא חָשְׁשׁוּ. אָמַר רִבִּי חֲנַנְיָה קוֹמֵי רִבִּי מָנָא. תִּיפְתָּר כְּמָאן דְּאָמַר. מִדִּבְרֵי רִבִּי עֲקִיבָה וּמִדִּבְרֵי רִבִּי חֲנִינָה סְגַן הַכֹּהֲנִים. וְלֵית שְׁמַע מִינָּהּ כְּלוּם.

2 בו (first occurrence) | ת בהן | 3 שהוא | ת שהיא היא בור | ת הא שיש בו | ת יש בה והיא בור שאין | ת הא אין | 4 שהוא | ת שהיא לו | ת - 5 לית | ת וליח היא מכלל | ת אלא דו | ת דהוא מודה | ת מודי אמ' ר' יוסי | ת - 6 ביר' בון | ת - 6 תמן כדי לחוח | ת תמן התורה חסה ממון נכסיהון | ת ממונן והכא | ת הכא לך | ת לך מימר אפילו הכא | ת ו הכא מפסיד ליש' 7 לשרוף עצים | ת עצים לשרפו בפני עצמן | ת זה לעצמו וזו בפני עצמה | ת וזה לעצמו 8 חששו | ת חשו חנניה קומי ר' מנא | ת יוסי ביר' בון

And you[233] are saying, the first amphora following Rebbi Yose and Rebbi Meïr will not agree[234]? But did we not state:[235] When has this been said? Regarding a vat which contains enough to lift it. But for a vat which does not contain enough to lift it, it is forbidden to make any amount impure. And if it follows Rebbi Meïr, whether it is a vat which contains enough to lift it or a vat which does not contain enough to lift it, is it forbidden to make any amount impure?[236] In addition, from what we have stated: "Rebbi Yose said, this is not the implication," nobody says "this is not" unless he agrees with the premise. How is that? Rebbi Yose ben Rebbi Abun said, there in order to care for the property of Jews[237]; here what do you have? Does the Jew not lose money even here? For he needs to burn wood separately[238] and this separately? They worried about a big loss, they did not worry about a small loss. Rebbi Ḥananiah said before Rebbi Mana[239], explain it following him who said, from the words of Rebbi Aqiba and Rebbi Ḥanina the executive officer of the Cohanim; and one cannot infer anything[240].

233 Continuation of the attack of R. Yose the Amora against the statement of the colleagues.

234 While this R. Yose's argument in both texts it is clear from the following that the discussion is about the second of their statements, that R. Yose cannot agree with the ruling of Mishnah *Terumot* 8:8 and 8:10 about a barrel of pure heave wine which is breaking on top of a container of impure wine.

235 "Lifting" is explained in *Terumot* Chapter 5. If heave falls into a container of profane produce of the same kind as the heave and the volume of the profane matter is less than 101 times that of the heave, the entire matter is forbidden to non-Cohanim. But if it is at least that amount, a volume equal to that of the heave which was lost can be lifted from the mixture and declared as replacement heave. Then the particles of the original heave in the mixture revert to profane status and become permitted to lay persons.

Mishnaiot *Terumot* 8:8,10: "If an amphora broke in the upper part of a wine press whose lower part was impure, R. Eliezer and R. Joshua agree that if one can save a *quartarius* from it, he shall save that in purity.... Rebbi Joshua said, this is not a case for which I have been warned not to make it impure ..."

236 Since R. Meïr permits to bring impurity to anything that later automatically would become impure. Babli 21a.

237 Mishnah *Nega`im* 12:5. Babli 20b.

238 This text is corrupt. The correct version is in *Terumot*: For he needs wood to burn each lot separately.

239 In *Terumot*: R. Yose ben R. Abun said.

240 There is no inference to be drawn from the Mishnah in *Pesahim* which according to R. Meïr speaks about impurity and disqualification and in *Terumot* dealing with impurity and purity. R. Yose's second objection to the colleagues is not proven.

(28a line 64) רִבִּי זְעוּרָה רִבִּי אִילָא תְּרֵיהוֹן בְּשֵׁם רִבִּי אֶלְעָזָר. חָבִית הָרִאשׁוֹנָה כְּרִבִּי יוֹסֵי. וְהַשְּׁנִייָה בֵּין כְּרִבִּי מֵאִיר בֵּין כְּרִבִּי יוֹסֵי. אָמַר רִבִּי עֶזְרָא קוֹמֵי רִבִּי מָנָא. לֵית הָדָא פְלִיגָא עַל רִבִּי יוֹסֵי. אָמַר לֵיהּ. וּדְלָא כְרִבִּי יוֹסֵי נֵימַר וּדְלָא כְרִבִּי מֵאִיר. לְפִי שֶׁמָּצִינוּ רִבִּי יוֹסֵי שׂוֹרֵף תְּלוּיָה בְּכָל־מָקוֹם. אָמַר רִבִּי מָנָא. אֲזָלִית לְקֵיסָרִין וּשְׁמָעִית רִבִּי זְרִיקָן בְּשֵׁם רִבִּי זְעוּרָה. רִבִּי מֵאִיר שׂוֹרֵף תְּלוּיָה בְּכָל־מָקוֹם. וְאָמְרִית לֵיהּ. אֲפִילוּ כְגוֹן הַהִיא שֶׁהִיא תְלוּיָה דְּבַר תּוֹרָה. וְאָמַר לִי. אִין. אֲנָא פָתַר לָהּ שֶׁנִּיטְמֵאת מָדוֹר גּוֹיִם. מַה בְיָדָךְ. תַּנֵּי. מָדוֹר גּוֹיִם תּוֹלִין. רִבִּי יוֹסֵה בֵירִבִּי יוּדָה אוֹמֵר. שׂוֹרְפִין. רִבִּי חוּנָה בְּשֵׁם רִבִּי זְעוּרָא. רִבִּי מֵאִיר שׂוֹרֵף תְּלוּיָה בִּשְׁאַר יְמוֹת הַשָּׁנָה. וְהָא תַנֵּי כֵן. תְּרוּמָה תְלוּיָה טְמֵיאָה שׂוֹרְפִין אוֹתָהּ עֶרֶב שַׁבָּת עִם חֲשֵׁיכָה. דִּבְרֵי רִבִּי מֵאִיר. וַחֲכָמִים אוֹמְרִים. בִּזְמַנָּהּ. וְיִשְׂרוֹף בְּשַׁחֲרִית. תִּיפְתָּר שֶׁנִּתְעַצֵּל וְלֹא שָׂרַף. תֵּדַע לָךְ שֶׁהוּא כֵן. דְּתַנֵּי טְמֵיאָה. לֹא מִשֶּׁנִּתְעַצֵּל וְלֹא שָׂרַף. אָמַר רִבִּי אַבָּא מָרִי אֲחוּהָ דְּרִבִּי יוֹסֵי. תִּיפְתָּר שֶׁנּוֹלַד לָהּ טוּמְאָה בְּאוֹתָהּ שָׁעָה. וְלֵית שְׁמַע מִינָהּ כְּלוּם.

1 ר' זעורה ר' אילא | ת ר' אילאר' זעירא אלעזר | ת יוחנן   2 עזרא | ת זעירא לית | ת ולית   3 יוסי | ת מאיר ודלא | ת נאמ' ודלא יוסי | ת מאיר ונאמ' מאיר | ת יוסי ודלא | ת דלא יוסי | ת מאיר   4 ושמעית | ת שמעינא ר' זריקן בשם ר' זעורה | ת חזקיה בשם ר' ירמיה   5 תלויה | ת - מקום | ת מקום תלויה אפי' כגון | ת בגין ואמ' לי ת אמ' לו   6 מדור גויים | ת במדור שלגוים בידך | ת אית לך תני | ת דתני גוים | ת שלגוים   7 יודה | ת יהודה חונה | ת הונא זעורא | ת ירמיה   8 והא תני כן | ת דתני טמיאה | ת וטמיאה   10 דתני טמיאה | ת דלא תנינן שחרית לא | ת ולא אחוה | ת אחוי

Rebbi Ze`ira, Rebbi Ila, both in the name of Rebbi Eleazar. The first amphora following Rebbi Yose, but the second both following Rebbi Meïr and Rebbi Yose. Rebbi Ezra said before Rebbi Mana[228]: Does this not disagree with Rebbi Yose? He told him, if not following Rebbi Yose[241], we may say not following Rebbi Meïr since we find that Rebbi Yose is burning suspended [heave] in all cases. Rebbi Mana said, I went to Caesarea and heard Rebbi Zeriqan in the name of Rebbi Ze`ira: Rebbi Meïr is burning suspended [heave] in all cases. I asked him, even in a case where it is suspended by word of the Torah[242]? He told me, if I explain it that it became impure in Gentiles' dwelling[243], what do you have in your hand? It was stated[244]: "For Gentiles' dwelling one suspends, Rebbi Yose ben Rebbi Jehudah says, one burns." Rebbi Huna in the name of Rebbi Ze`ura: Rebbi Meïr burns suspended [heave] any day of the year, and so it was stated: "Suspended [and][245] impure heave are burned on Sabbath eve when it gets dark, the words of Rebbi Meïr; but the Sages say, at its appointed time[227]." Should he not burn in the morning? Explain it that he was lazy and did not burn. You should know that this is so, since it was stated "impure"[246]. Not because he was lazy and did not burn? Rebbi Abba Mari the brother of Rebbi Yose said, explain it that the impurity came to it at that moment and one cannot infer anything.

241 In *Terumot* the names Yose and Meïr are systematically switched. For the interpretation there is no difference since, as stated in the next sentence, the two rabbis agree in this matter. Nevertheless it seems that the text in *Terumot* is more reliable since the remainder of the discussion concentrates on determining R. Meïr's position.
242 If we hold that the rule which states that doubts in cases of biblical commandments have to be decided restrictively is itself biblical, then suspended heave would have to be considered impure by biblical standards and immediately used as fuel.
243 Since Gentiles are suspected of burying their stillbirths in the dirt floors of their houses, their dwellings in the Holy Land are considered possibly impure by "tent impurity" (*Kilaim* Chapter 6 Note 25). Practice disregards the opinion of R. Simeon who denied the possibility of "tent impurity" for Gentiles.
244 Tosephta *Ahilut* 18:7.
245 Added from the text in *Terumot*, necessary by the context.
246 Since impure heave is used as fuel, there is no reason why it should not be used to burn leavened matter in the morning. Since in most years Passover Eve is not a Sabbath and one is obligated to burn in the morning, if Friday is the 13th of Nisan the rule is that in this case also one burns in the morning.

(28b line 3) אָמַר רבִּי יוֹחָנָן. רִבִּי שִׁמְעוֹן וְרִבִּי יְשׁוּעַ שְׁנֵיהֶן אָמְרוּ דָבָר אֶחָד. אָמַר רבִּי אִילָא. רִבִּי שִׁמְעוֹן דִּבְכוֹרוֹת וְרִבִּי יְשׁוּעַ דִּתְרוּמוֹת לֹא דֵין מוֹדֶה לְדֵין וְלֹא דֵין מוֹדֶה לְדֵין. אָמַר רבִּי זְעִירָא. מִסְתַּבְרָא רִבִּי שִׁמְעוֹן מוֹדֶה לְרִבִּי יְשׁוּעַ. [וְאָמַר רבִּי בּוּן בַּר חִייָא לְרבִּי זְעִירָא. עַל דַּעְתָּךְ דְּתֵימַר. רִבִּי שִׁמְעוֹן מוֹדֶה לְרִבִּי יְהוֹשֻׁעַ. וְהָא תַנִּינָן. אֲבָל הֵיאַךְ נִשְׂרָף תְּלוּיָה עִם הַטְּמֵאָה.] מוֹדֶה רבִּי לִיעֶזֶר לְרבִּי יְשׁוּעַ שֶׁשּׂוֹרְפִין זוֹ לְעַצְמָהּ וְזוֹ לְעַצְמָהּ. וְיִשְׂרוֹף שְׁתֵּיהֶן כְּאַחַת. טְהוֹרָה

HALAKHAH EIGHT

הִיא דְּבַר תּוֹרָה. אַתְּ הוּא שֶׁגָּזַרְתָּה עָלֶיהָ שְׂרֵיפָה. מִכָּל־מָקוֹם לֹא נִפְסְלָה בְהֶיסַח הַדַּעַת. לֹא כֵן אָמַר רִבִּי יוֹחָנָן. הֶסֵּיעַ דְּבַר תּוֹרָה. אֲחִוַּת דָּם כְּרִבִּי שִׁמְעוֹן תּוֹרָה. חָבִית הַשְּׁנִיָּיה כְּרִבִּי מֵאִיר תּוֹרָה. אֵינָהּ כֵּן. אֶלָּא מְשַׁמְּרָהּ הוּא שֶׁלֹּא תִגַּע בְּטָהֳרוֹת אֲחֵרוֹת. הָתִיב רִבִּי יִצְחָק בְּרֵיהּ דְּרִבִּי חִייָא כְּתוֹבָה. הַגַּע עַצְמָךְ שֶׁהָיְתָה נְתוּנָה עַל גַּבֵּי הַגֶּחָלִים. אָמַר לֵיהּ. לִכְשֶׁיִּיתְּנֶנָּה. אָמַר רִבִּי מָנָא לְרִבִּי שַׁמַּי. אַתּוּן אָמְרִין. רִבִּי שִׁמְעוֹן יוֹדֶה לְרִבִּי יוֹשֻׁעַ. אֲפִילוּ רִבִּי יוֹשֻׁעַ לֵית הוּא רִבִּי יוֹשֻׁעַ. אָמַר לֵיהּ. תַּנָּיִין אִינּוּן. תַּמָּן רִבִּי מֵאִיר בְּשֵׁם רִבִּי יוֹשֻׁעַ. בְּרַם הָכָא רִבִּי שִׁמְעוֹן בְּשֵׁם רִבִּי יוֹשֻׁעַ.

1 ר' שמעון ור' יושוע | **ת** ר' יהושע ור' שמעון   2 יושוע | **ת** יהושע   דין | **ת** הדין (2)   3 יודה | **ת** מודי - | **ת** ור' יהושע לא מודי לר' שמעון אמ' לר' | **ת** קומי ר'   4 יודה | **ת** יודי יושוע | **ת** יהושע והא תנינן | **ת** והתנינן אבל היאך נשרף תלויו עם הטמיאה | **ת** -   מודה ר' ליעזר לר' יושוע | **ת** מודין ר' ליעזר ור' יהושע   5 טהורה | **ת** אמ' ליה. תמן טהורה   6 את | **ת** תרומה בעיינה היא. אתה עליה שריפה | **ת** לשורפה מכל | **ת** בכל   7 הסיע | **ת** היסח הדעת אחוות . . . אחיות | **ת** חבית | **ת** חבית . . . אחיות   8 אינה כן. אלא | **ת** אמ' ליה. שהוא הוא | **ת** - 9 שהיתה | **ת** שהיא הגחלים | **ת** גחלים   10 ר' שמעון יודי | **ת** יודי ר' ליעזר יושוע | **ת** יהושע אפי' | **ת** ואפילו יושוע | **ת** יהושע   11 הוא ר' יושוע | **ת** היא ר' יהושע יושוע יושוע | **ת** יהושע   12 יושוע | **ת** יהושע

Rebbi Johanan said, Rebbi Simeon and Rebbi Joshua[247] both said the same thing. Rebbi Ila said, Rebbi Simeon in *Bekhorot*[248] and Rebbi Joshua in *Terumot*, neither of them will agree with the other. Rebbi Ze'ira said, it is reasonable that Rebbi Simeon agrees with Rebbi Joshua[249]. [Rebbi Abun bar Hiyya said to Rebbi Ze'ira: In your opinion, since you say that Rebbi Simeon agrees with Rebbi Joshua, did we not state: How may one burn suspended [heave] with impure one][250]? "Rebbi Eliezer agrees with Rebbi Joshua[251] that each of these is burned separately." Should one not burn both together? It is pure by words of the Torah. You are the one who decided on burning. In any case, would it not become disqualified by inattention[252]? Did nor Rebbi Johanan say, inattention is a word of the Torah; blood affliction following Rebbi Simeon is Torah, the second amphora following Rebbi Meïr is Torah? It is not so[253]; but he watches it that it should not come in contact with other pure things. Rebbi Isaac, the son of Rebbi Hiyya the scribe, objected: Think of it, if it was put on coals[254]. He told him, after it was put there[254]. Rebbi Mana said to Rebbi Shammai: You are saying that Rebbi Simeon agrees with Rebbi Joshua. Even Rebbi Joshua does not agree with Rebbi Joshua[255]. He told him, these are Tannaim. There Rebbi Meïr in the name of Rebbi Joshua, here Rebbi Simeon in the name of Rebbi Joshua[256].

247 The order appearing in the text of *Terumot*, R. Joshua (first generation), R. Simeon (third generation) is preferable.

248 Mishnah *Bekhorot* 5:2, quoted in the next paragraph. While a firstling calf or lamb has to be treated as a sacrifice, R. Simeon permits any surgical operation if the health of the animal requires it, even if it is

clear that by the operation the animal will become disqualified as sacrifice.

249 Talmudic style requires the addition found in *Terumot*: "But R. Joshua will not agree with R. Simeon". R. Joshua (*Terumot* 8:8-10) permits to cause impurity to heave in order to save food; R. Simeon permits to make a blemish on a firstling in order to save its life. But the Mishnah in *Bekhorot* states that a firstling with this intentionally induced blemish may not be slaughtered; it cannot become food for anybody. Therefore it is not necessary to conclude that R. Joshua agrees with R. Simeon. Babli *Bekhorot* 33b.

250 This sentence is neither in the Mishnah nor in *Terumot*; the question is correct as objection of R. Eliezer to R. Joshua.

251 While the Mishnah states, "R. Eliezer and R. Joshua agree", the formulation here is more to the point.

252 Heave must be eaten in purity, which can be guaranteed only if the heave is guarded at all times or at least kept at a place locked away from possible impurities (Babli 34a, *Šeqalim* 7:2). Since on the 14th of Nisan heave cannot be eaten after 10 a.m., there is no need to watch it any longer and, by being released from supervision, it should become disqualified immediately even by biblical standards.

253 Even if disqualified for other reasons, it still has to be watched; the prior objection is baseless.

254 If one starts the fire to burn the leavened matter, guarding against impurity certainly is unnecessary. The answer is that this argument is irrelevant since we are dealing with the time before the fire was started.

255 The positions of R. Joshua in *Pesahim* 1:7 and *Terumot* 8:8-10 do not necessarily coincide.

256 It is impossible to fully reconstruct the original position of R. Joshua since the only knowledge we have of his statements is through the interpretation of third generation Amoraim.

(28b line 19) תַּמָּן תַּנִּינָן. בְּכוֹר שֶׁאֲחָזוֹ דָם. אֲפִילוּ מֵת מַקִּיזִין לוֹ אֶת הדָּם. דִּבְרֵי רִבִּי יְהוּדָה. וַחֲכָמִים אוֹמְרִים. יַקִּיז וּבִלְבַד שֶׁלֹּא יַעֲשֶׂה בּוֹ מוּם. אִם עָשָׂה בּוֹ מוּם הֲרֵי זֶה לֹא יִשְׁחוֹט עָלָיו. רִבִּי שִׁמְעוֹן אוֹמֵר. יַקִּיז אַף עַל פִּי שֶׁהוּא עוֹשֶׂה בּוֹ מוּם:

2 יהודה | **ת** יודה   ובלבד שלא יעשה | **ת** ואע"פ שעשה אם | **ת** ואם   3 אע"פ | **ת** ואע"פ

רִבִּי אַבָּהוּ בְשֵׁם רִבִּי לְעָזָר. אַתְיָא דְּרִבִּי יוּדָה כְּרַבָּן גַּמְלִיאֵל. וּדְרַבָּנִין כְּרִבִּי אֱלִיעֶזֶר. וּדְרִבִּי שִׁמְעוֹן כְּרִבִּי יוֹשֻׁעַ. תַּנֵּי בְשֵׁם רִבִּי שִׁמְעוֹן. יַקִּיז אַף עַל פִּי שֶׁהוּא מִתְכַּוֵּין לַעֲשׂוֹת בּוֹ מוּם. וְאַתְיָא כְּרִבִּי יוֹשֻׁעַ אַחֲרַיָּיא. אָמַר רִבִּי בּוּן בַּר חִייָה קוֹמֵי רִבִּי זְעִירָא. תִּיפְתָּר בְּקֳדָשִׁים שֶׁהוּא חַייָב בְּאַחֲרָיוּתָן כְּרִבִּי שִׁמְעוֹן.

1 אתיא | **ת** אתייא   ודרבנין | **ת** ודרבנן   אליעזר | **ת** ליעזר   2 יושוע | **ת** יהושע תני | **ת** ותני   אע"פ | **ת** ואע"פ
3 ואתיא | **ת** ואתייא   יושוע | **ת** יהושע   אחרייא | **ת** אחרייה   אמ' ר' בון . . . כר' שמעון | **ת** -

רִבִּי אַבָּהוּ בְשֵׁם רִבִּי שִׁמְעוֹן בֶּן לָקִישׁ. טַעֲמֵיהּ דְּרִבִּי יוּדָה. לֹא תֹאכְלֻנּוּ עַל־הָאָרֶץ תִּשְׁפְּכֶנּוּ כַּמָּיִם: לֹא הִיתַּרְתִּי לָךְ אֶת דָּמוֹ אֶלָּא בִשְׁפִיכָה. הָתִיב רִבִּי אַבָּא מָרִי אֲחוּהָ דְּרִבִּי יוֹסֵה. וְהָכְתִיב

אַף בִּפְסוּלֵי הַמּוּקְדָּשִׁין כֵּן. לֹא תֹאכְלֶנּוּ עַל־הָאָרֶץ תִּשְׁפְּכֶנּוּ כַּמָּיִם: אָמַר רִבִּי חִיָּיה בַּר אָדָא. לְהַכְשִׁיר אִתְאָמָרַת. מָה הַמַּיִם מַכְשִׁירִין אַף הַדָּם יְהֵא מַכְשִׁיר.

2 היתרתי | ת התירתי את | ת - בשפיכה | ת לשפכים התיב | ת מתיב | ת אחוי יוסה | ת יוסי והכת' | ת והא   3 אף בפסולי | ת פסולי | ת כת' אדא | ת כת | ת אבא   4 הדם יהא | ת דם

רִבִּי אַבָּהוּ בְשֵׁם רִבִּי יוֹחָנָן. שְׁנֵיהֶן מִקְרָא אֶחָד הֵן דּוֹרְשִׁין. תָּמִים יִהְיֶה לְרָצוֹן כָּל־מוּם לֹא יִהְיֶה־בּוֹ: רִבִּי שִׁמְעוֹן אוֹמֵר. בְּשָׁעָה שֶׁהוּא לְרָצוֹן אֵין אַתְּ רַשַּׁאי לִיתֵּן בּוֹ מוּם. [וּבְשָׁעָה שֶׁאֵינוֹ לְרָצוֹן אַתָּה רַשַּׁאי לִיתֵּן בּוֹ מוּם.] וַחֲכָמִים אוֹמְרִים. אֲפִילוּ כּוּלּוֹ מוּמִין אֵין אַתְּ רַשַּׁאי לִיתֵּן בּוֹ מוּם.

1 שניהן | ת ושניהם   2 או' | ת דרש ובשעה | ת בשעה

There, we have stated[257]: "A firstling afflicted by blood, even if it is going to die, cannot be bled, the words of Rebbi Jehudah. But the Sages say, it should be bled, only he should not intend to cause a blemish. If it did cause a blemish, it may not be slaughtered because of it. Rebbi Simeon says, he should bleed it even if he makes a blemish."

Rebbi Abbahu in the name of Rebbi Eleazar: Rebbi Jehudah parallels Rabban Gamliel, the rabbis parallel Rebbi Eliezer, Rebbi Simeon parallels Rebbi Joshua[258]. It was stated in the name of Rebbi Simeon: "He should bleed it even if he intends to make a blemish." This parallels another opinion of Rebbi Joshua[259]. Rebbi Abun bar Ḥiyya said before Rebbi Ze`ira: Explain about *sancta* for which he is liable following Rebbi Simeon[260].

Rebbi Abbahu in the name of Rebbi Simeon ben Laqish. The reason of Rebbi Jehudah: *You shall not eat it, on the earth you shall you shall spill it like water*[261]. I did permit you its blood only for spilling. Rebbi Abba Mari the brother of Rebbi Yose said, is not about disqualified sancta written so, *you shall not eat it, on the earth you shall spill it like water*[262]? Rebbi Ḥiyya bar Ada said, it was said for preparation[263]. Just as the water prepares, so the blood shall prepare.

Rebbi Abbahu in the name of Rebbi Joḥanan, both of them explain the same verse[264]: *Perfect it*[265] *shall be for goodwill; any blemish shall not be on it*. Rebbi Simeon explains: As long as it is for goodwill, you may not induce a blemish. If it is no longer for goodwill, you may induce a blemish. But the Sages say, even if it is all blemishes, you may not add a blemish[266].

257 Mishnah *Bekhorot* 5:2 [*Sifra Emor Parashah* 7(10)]. Since a firstling is a sacrifice by birth, it has to be treated according to the rules of sacrifices. The

only difference is that a dedicated sacrifice which develops a blemish must be redeemed to become profane whereas a firstling in the hands of a Cohen which develops a blemish automatically becomes profane and may be eaten by everybody and in impurity. Therefore, Cohanim are suspected to induce blemishes on the firstlings in their possession.

258 The opinions stated in Mishnah *Terumot* 8:7 ("the first amphora.") The Babli *Bekhorot* 35b identifies the position of the Sages with that of R. Joshua (i. e., the operative opinion in *Bekhorot* with that in *Terumot*) while the Yerushalmi implies that practice should follow R. Simeon.

259 His opinion about the "second amphora" where he permits to induce impurity on most of the heave in order to save a small portion in purity.

260 This sentence is missing in *Terumot*. The verse is formulated for all sacrifices which develop a blemish; it is more reasonable to apply it to the vast majority of dedicated sacrifices which have to be redeemed rather than to firstlings for which change to semi-profane status is automatic.

If somebody dedicates a specific animal and it later develops a blemish, there is no sacrifice. But if he vows "a sacrifice" and then dedicates a particular animal which later develops a blemish, he has to redeem the animal by an unblemished replacement.

261 *Deut.* 12:24.

262 One would have expected R. Jehudah to use *Deut.* 15:23, speaking of the firstling: *Only its blood you shall not eat, spill it onto the ground like water.* The verse used gives the rules for animals which develop blemishes after being dedicated. This also includes firstlings.

263 Produce in the ground is impervious to impurity. It remains so after harvesting as long as it stays completely dry. Blood is one of the fluids that prepare dry food to accept impurity (cf. *Demay* Chapter 2, Notes 136,141). Since the rules for preparation are spelled out for water (*Lev.* 11:38), other fluids have this property of water only if there is a biblical verse which compares them to water. *Sifry Deut.* #71.

264 *Lev.* 22:21.

265 Any animal sacrifice.

266 As Rashi explains in *Bekhorot* 35b, the Sages hold that R. Simeon would be justified if the verse read "*no blemish* shall be on it." But the involved language, *any blemish*, forbids the imposition of a new blemish on existing blemishes.

כל שעה פרק שני

(fol.28b) **משנה א**: כָּל־שָׁעָה שֶׁהוּא מוּתָּר לוֹכַל מַאֲכִיל לַבְּהֵמָה לַחַיָּה וְלָעוֹפוֹת וּמוֹכְרוֹ לַנָּכְרִי וּמוּתָּר בַּהֲנָאָתוֹ. עָבַר זְמַנּוּ אָסוּר בַּהֲנָאָתוֹ. לֹא יַסִּיק בּוֹ תַּנּוּר וְכִירַיִם. רִבִּי יוּדָה אוֹמֵר אֵין בִּיעוּר חָמֵץ אֶלָּא שְׂרֵיפָה. וַחֲכָמִים אוֹמְרִים מְפָרֵר וְזוֹרֶה לָרוּחַ אוֹ מַטִּיל לַיָּם:

Mishnah 1: Any time one is permitted to eat one feeds it[1] to domestic or wild animals or birds, or sells it to a Non-Jew[2], and one may have usufruct from it[3]. If its time has passed[4] one may not have usufruct from it, nor use it to heat an oven or a cooking stove. Rebbi Jehudah says, leavened matter may only be eliminated by burning. But the Sages say, he makes crumbs and scatters them in the wind or throws it into the Sea[5].

1 Leavened matter on the 14th of Nisan which has to be eliminated before noontime.
2 Since only leavened matter in the possession of a Jew has to be eliminated, the Gentile may keep the leavened matter bought from the Jew and also use it during Passover time.
3 For example one may use the matter as fuel and its ashes as fertilizer.
4 After noontime on the 14th, even though according to the majority opinion the biblical prohibition of usufruct only starts shortly before sundown, there is a rabbinic prohibition of usufruct for the entire afternoon.
5 In this version, which also is the reading of the Munich ms. of the Babli, R. Hananel, some texts of Alfasi, and Maimonides's autograph Mishnah, the Sages disagree with R. Jehudah. The Mishnah in the printed Babli, starting with the *editio princeps*, reads "But the Sages say, he *also* may make crumbs and . . ." This determines current practice following R. Jehudah, even though *also* is missing in the Mishnah quote in the Babli Halakhah (28a). Cf. *Diqduqe Soferim Pesahim* p. 28a Note 1.

(18c line 3) **הלכה א**: כָּל־שָׁעָה כול'. אָמַר רִבִּי אִימִּי. מָאן תַּנָּא כָּל־שָׁעָה שֶׁהוּא מוּתָּר לוֹכַל מוּתָּר לְהַאֲכִיל. אָסוּר לָאוֹכַל אָסוּר לְהַאֲכִיל. רִבִּי מֵאִיר. בְּרַם כְּרִבִּי יוּדָה. חֲמִישִׁית אַף עַל פִּי שֶׁהוּא אָסוּר לוֹכַל מוּתָּר לְהַאֲכִיל. וְהָתַנִּינָן. הֵתִיב רִבִּי בָא. סִיעוּר יִשְׂרָף וְהָאוֹכְלוֹ פָּטוּר. וְאָמַר רַב חוּנָה בְשָׁם רִבִּי. מוּתָּר לְהַאֲכִילוֹ לַכְּלָבִים. אָמַר רִבִּי יוֹסֵה. מָה אֲתִינָן מִיתְנֵי כָּל־חָמֵץ. לֹא שָׁעוֹת. מָאן תַּנָּא שָׁעוֹת. רִבִּי מֵאִיר.

Halakhah 1: "Any time" etc. Rebbi Immi said, who is the Tanna of "any time when he is permitted to eat he is permitted to feed, when it is forbidden to the eater he is forbidden to feed"? Rebbi Meïr[6]. But following Rebbi Jehudah, in the fifth hour even though he is forbidden to eat he is permitted to feed. Rebbi Abba objected: Did we not state[7], "sour dough has to be burned but one who eats it is not liable[8]," and did not Rav Huna say in the name of Rebbi, one may feed it to the dogs[9]? Rebbi Yose said, did we state "any leavened matter", not "time[10]"? Who is the Tanna of "time", Rebbi Meïr.

6   Babli 21a. In Mishnah 1:4 R. Meïr permits to eat up to the time one has to dispose of the leftovers, in contrast to R. Jehudah who forbids to eat starting one hour before the leavened matter will be forbidden. The latter could not have formulated "any time".
7   Mishnah 3:5, presumed to be R. Meïr's.
8   *Ex.* 12:19 contains two statements. 1° leavened matter may not be in a Jew's possession on Passover, and 2°, it is a deadly sin, punishable by extirpation, to eat leavened matter during the holiday. The Tanna of the Mishnah holds that the second statement is not applicable to matters commonly considered to be inedible.
9   Mishnah 1 excludes feeding to animals.
10   Mishnah 2:1 is formulated to apply only to the 14th of Nisan. Mishnah 3:5, referring to Nisan 15-21, does not contradict the earlier Mishnah.

(8 line 28c) אָמַר רִבִּי בּוּן בַּר חִיָּיה קוֹמֵי רִבִּי זְעִירָא. זֹאת אוֹמֶרֶת שֶׁמּוּתָּר לְהַאֲכִילוֹ לְבֶהֱמַת הֶבְקֵר. הָתִיב רִבִּי יִרְמְיָה. וְהָתַנִּינָן. מְפָרֵר. סָבַר רִבִּי יִרְמְיָה כִּפָּרוֹת. אָמַר לֵיהּ רִבִּי יוֹסֵה. לֹא אָמַר אֶלָּא מְפָרֵר. מִכֵּיוָן שֶׁפֵּיְרְרוֹ בָטֵל. וְאַיְיִדָא אָמַר דָא. לֹא יֵאָכֵל חָמֵץ הַיּוֹם. אֲפִילוּ לַכְּלָבִים. הֲרֵי זֶה בָא לְאוֹסְרוֹ בַּהֲנָיָיה. מָה אֲנָן קַיָּימִין. אִם לְכַלְבּוֹ. הֲתַנֵּי אִיסּוּר הֲנָיָיה. אֶלָּא כִּי נָן קַיָּימִין. אֲפִילוּ לְכֶלֶב [אֲחֵרִים]. זֹאת אוֹמֶרֶת. שֶׁאָסוּר לְהַאֲכִילוֹ לְבֶהֱמַת הֶבְקֵר.

Rebbi Bun bar Hiyya said before Rebbi Ze`ira: This[11] implies that one is permitted to feed it to ownerless animals. Rebbi Jeremiah objected, did we not state "he crumbles it"? Rebbi Jeremiah was of the opinion, loaf sized[12]. Rebbi Yose said to him, it only mentioned "he crumbles it", that when he crumbled it it was nullified[13]. But the following says it, *leavend matter may not be eaten today*[14], even by the dogs. This includes to forbid it for usufruct. Where do we hold? If for his own dog, the prohibition of usufruct had been stated[15]. But we must hold for the dog [of others]. This implies that one is prohibited from feeding it to ownerless animals.

11 The statement of the Mishnah, "if its time has passed one may not have usufruct from it," seems to imply that any use from which the owner does not derive usufruct is permitted.

12 He reads the Mishnah as requiring only that loaves should not be disposed of whole, but may be disposed of in sizeable pieces. If these are thrown to the wind, the probability is great that a bird or a squirrel will pick them up; the reference to *his* usufruct seems to be unnecessary.

13 The Mishnah requires that any leftovers be reduced to tiny crumbs which are of no use. These crumbs do no longer qualify as food; the leavened matter is considered disposed off even if not thrown to the wind.

14 *Ex.* 13:3-4: *Moses said to the people, remember this day on which you left Egypt, the House of Slavery, for with a strong hand did the Eternal remove you from there, and leavened matter shall not be eaten. Today you are leaving, in the Spring month.* Since the text is written without commas and periods, the period implied by the oral tradition of separation of verses may be disregarded. A different interpretation of the same reading is in *Mekhilta dR. Ismael ad loc.* (ed. Horovitz-Rabin p. 62 line 2), Babli 28b.

15 The passive voice in *Ex.* 13:3 implies that the identity of the eater is irrelevant, against the argument of Note 11.

(28c line 14) רִבִּי אַבָּהוּ בְשֵׁם רִבִּי אֶלְעָזָר. כָּל־מָקוֹם שֶׁנֶּאֱמַר לֹא תֹאכַל לֹא תֹאכְלוּ לֹא יֵאָכְלוּ אַתְּ תּוֹפֵשׂ אִיסּוּר הֲנָייָה כְּאִיסּוּר אֲכִילָה. עַד שֶׁיָּבוֹא הַכָּתוּב וִיפָרוֹשׁ לָךְ כְּשֵׁם שֶׁפֵּירֵשׁ לָךְ בְּאֶבֶר מִן הַחַי וּבִנְבֵילָה. וְכִי מַה פֵּירֵשׁ לָנוּ בְּאֶבֶר מִן הַחַי. וּבָשָׂר בַּשָּׂדֶה טְרֵיפָה לֹא תֹאכֵלוּ לַכֶּלֶב תַּשְׁלִיכוּן אוֹתוֹ. וְכִי מַה פֵּירֵשׁ לָנוּ בִּנְבֵילָה. כֹא לֹא־תֹאכְלוּ כָל־נְבֵילָה לַגֵּר אֲשֶׁר־בִּשְׁעָרֶיךָ תִּתְּנֶנָּה וַאֲכָלָהּ אוֹ מָכוֹר לְנָכְרִי. תַּנֵּי חִזְקִיָה וּפְלִיג. וְכִי מִי אֲסָרוֹ לַכֶּלֶב.

1 אלעזר | ע לעזר   2 תופש | ע תופס כאיסור | ע באיסור   3 וכי | ע - לנו | ע לך לכלב תשליכון אותו | ע - 4 וכי | ע - לנו | ע לך   5 או מגור לנכרי | ע -

[16]Rebbi Abbahu in the name of Rebbi Eleazar[17]: Everywhere it is written *do not eat, do not eat*[18], *it shall not be eaten*, you understand a prohibition of usufruct included in the prohibition of eating unless the verse is explicit and explains to you as it did explain about limbs of a living animal and a carcass. What did it explain about limbs of a living animal? *Flesh torn in the field you shall not eat; throw it to the dog*[19]. And what did it explain about a carcass? *Do not eat any carcass; to the sojourner in your gates you shall give it and he may eat it, or sell to the stranger.*[20] Hizqiah stated a disagreement[21]. What does one forbid to the dog[22]?

16 The text from here to Note 64 also is in *Orlah* 3:1, Notes 10-44, ע. It seems that the origin of the text is in *Pesahim* since only here the verses are quoted in full and an

important sentence is missing in **ע**. In the Babli, the parallel is 21b-23a.

17   In the printed editions of the Babli, R. Eleazar is not mentioned, but his name appears in the Munich ms.

18   Plural.

19   *Ex.* 22:30. Why is it necessary to permit torn limbs as dog food? R. Eleazar argues that this shows that without such permission the limb would be forbidden for all usufruct.

20   *Deut.* 14:21.

21   In the Babli 21b, Hizqiah accepts the statement of R. Eleazar only for the passive formulation; later (Note 48) this is clarified to be the position of Hizqiah and R. Johanan in a second version. In this first version, Hizqiah must hold that an inference from a verse is only valid if there is no second verse leading to the same result. The theoretical basis is the recognition that the legal texts in the Torah are incomplete and sometimes contradictory as a system. In addition, it is held that words do not change their meaning in legal contexts. Therefore, a mechanism of translation of the Torah text into a coherent and reasonably complete system must exist. The rule quoted by Hizqiah is one of the translation rules; cf. H. Guggenheimer, Logical Problems in Jewish Tradition, in: Ph. Longworth (ed.), *Confrontations with Judaism (*London 1966) pp. 171-196.

Since here the mention of the torn limb and the carcass both lead to the same argument, either one of them would be superfluous and, therefore, both must be needed for other inferences. The argument of R. Eleazar is refuted.

22   The dog is not a human and is not obliged by any rules.

(28c line 20) וְהָא כְתִיב. כָּל־חֵלֶב שׁוֹר וְכֶשֶׂב וָעֵז לֹא תֹאכֵלוּ. מֵעַתָּה אַתְּ תּוֹפֵשׂ אִיסּוּר הֲנָיָיה כְּאִיסּוּר אֲכִילָה. שַׁנְיָיא הִיא דִכְתִיב וְחֵלֶב נְבֵילָה וְחֵלֶב טְרֵיפָה יֵעָשֶׂה לְכָל־מְלָאכָה וְאָכֹל לֹא תֹאכְלוּהוּ: וְהָכְתִיב רַק הַדָּם לֹא תֹאכֵלוּ. מֵעַתָּה אַתְּ תּוֹפֵשׂ אִיסּוּר הֲנָיָיה כְּאִיסּוּר אֲכִילָה. שַׁנְיָיא הִיא דִכְתִיב עַל־הָאָרֶץ תִּשְׁפְּכֶנּוּ כַּמָּיִם: מָה הַמַּיִם מוּתָּרִין בַּהֲנָיָיה אַף הַדָּם יְהֵא מוּתָּר בַּהֲנָיָיה. וְהָכְתִיב עַל־כֵּן לֹא־יֹאכְלוּ בְנֵי־יִשְׂרָאֵל אֶת־גִּיד הַנָּשֶׁה. אָמַר רִבִּי אַבָּהוּ. קִיַּימְתֵּיהּ בְּגִיד הַנָּשֶׁה שֶׁבַּנְּבֵילוֹת. וְהָא כְתִיב וְלֶחֶם וְקָלִי וְכַרְמֶל לֹא תֹאכְלוּ עַד־עֶצֶם הַיּוֹם הַזֶּה. אָמַר רִבִּי אַבָּא מָרִי אֲחוּי דְרִבִּי יוֹסֵי. שַׁנְיָיה הִיא. שֶׁקָּבַע הַכָּתוּב זְמָן. וְהָא כְתִיב לֹא תֹאכְלוּם כִּי־שֶׁקֶץ הֵם: אָמַר רִבִּי. מִיעֵט אִיסּוּר הֲנָיָיה שֶׁבּוֹ.

1 את | ע אתה   2 באיסור | ע לאיסור   יעשה לכל מלאכה ואבל לא תאכלוהו | ע -   3 הדם לא תאכלו | ע את הדם שנייה | ע שנייא   4 המים | ע מים יהא | ע -   6 שבנבילות | ע שלנבילה   והא בת' | ע והכת'   עד עצם היום הזה | ע -   7 אחוי | ע אחוה   שקבע | ע שקבע לו   8 ר' | ע ר' מנא

But is it not written[23]: *Any fat of cattle, sheep, or goats you shall not eat?* Do you not have to understand the prohibition of usufruct from the prohibition of eating? There is a difference, for it is written[24]: *But fat of a carcass and fat of a torn animal may be used for any work, only it may not be eaten.* But is it not written[25]: *Only the blood you may not eat?* Do you not have to understand the prohibition of usufruct from the prohibition of eating? There is a difference, for it is written: *You shall pour it on the ground like water*[26]. Since water is permitted for use, so blood shall be permitted for use. But is it not written[27]: *Therefore, the Children of Israel do not eat the sinew of the sciatic nerve?* Rebbi Abbahu said, I explained it by the sinew of a carcass[28]. But is it not written[29]: *Bread, parched or fresh grains you shall not eat until this very day?* Rebbi Abba Mari, the brother of Rebbi Yose, said there is a difference since the verse fixed a time for it. But is it not written[30]: *Do not eat them for they are abominations?* Rebbi [Mana][31] said, that excludes their prohibition of usufruct[33].

23 Lev. 7:23. This paragraph discusses verses which present difficulties for R. Eleazar.

24 Lev. 7:23. In the opinion of the Babli 23a, the verse is needed to permit any use of profane fat since otherwise one would argue that since fat is forbidden for humans but required for the altar, fat of animals unfit for the altar should be permitted for use in the Temple but forbidden for profane use. In the *Sifra Saw* (*Parasha* 10), the argument of the Babli is attributed to R. Yose the Galilean; R. Aqiba concludes that fat of domesticated animals is not food nor subject to the impurity of food.

In the opinion of the Yerushalmi, since some fat is permitted for unrestricted use, no fat can be forbidden for usufruct in the absence of an explicit verse. For Hizqiah, this is a third verse that could be used for R. Eleazar's argument; nobody will contest that three parallel verses invalidate the argument. In the second version of Hizqiah's position (below, after Note 49), he needs the verse to permit use of fat for work on Temple property.

25 Deut. 12:16.

26 The Babli 22b deduces from here that animal blood is a fluid which prepares for impurity only if it is spilled on the ground (cf. *Demay* 2:3, Note 136). The argument of the Yerushalmi, and an argument that animal blood prepares for impurity in all cases, is in *Sifry Deut.* 73 and later here, in the second version of Hizqiah. (Preparation for impurity is explained in *Demay* 2:3, Notes 136-141.)

27 Gen. 32:33.

28 The argument is more explicit in the Babli 22a. R. Abbahu holds that when carcass and torn meat was permitted for the sojourner (Note 53) and the pagan, the entire animal was permitted, including the fat. Then the last paragraph of Note 24 establishes that the schiatic sinew cannot be forbidden for usufruct.

29 Lev. 23:14.

30 Lev. 11:42.

31 Added from *Orlah*, missing here.

32 The argument seems to be that the verse has to be read: "For *they* are abominations", they (snakes and centipedes) are abominations but not anything manufactured from them.

(28c line 30) רִבִּי אַבָּהוּ בְשֵׁם רִבִּי יוֹחָנָן. הָעוֹשֶׂה אִיסְפְּלָנִית מִשּׁוֹר הַנִּסְקָל וּמֵחָמֵץ שֶׁעָבַר עָלָיו הַפֶּסַח אֵינוֹ לוֹקֶה. שֶׁאֵין לֹא תַעֲשֶׂה שֶׁבּוֹ מְחוּוָר. מִכִּלְאֵי הַכֶּרֶם לוֹקֶה. אָמַר רִבִּי חֲנִינָה. פֶּן־תִּקְדָּשׁ. פֶּן תּוּקַד אֵשׁ. מֵעָרְלָה צְרִיכָה. עֲשֵׂה לְרָחֲקוֹ כָּתוּב. לֹא תֵיעָשֶׂה לְאוֹכְלוֹ כָּתוּב לֹא תֹאכְלוּ כָּתוּב. לֹא תֵיעָשֶׂה לְרָחֲקוֹ לֹא כָתוּב.

2 שבו | ע שלו אמ' | ע דאמ' חנינה | ע חנינא 3-4 לא תאכלו כת' | ע -

מַתְנִיתָא פְלִיגָא עַל רִבִּי יוֹחָנָן. מִמַּשְׁמַע שֶׁנֶּאֱמַר סָקוֹל יִסָּקֵל הַשּׁוֹר. וְכִי אֵין אָנוּ יוֹדְעִין שֶׁבְּשָׂרוֹ אָסוּר בַּאֲכִילָה. מַה תַּלְמוּד לוֹמַר לֹא יֵאָכֵל אֶת־בְּשָׂרוֹ. בָּא לְהוֹדִיעֲךָ. שֶׁכְּשֵׁם שֶׁהוּא אָסוּר בַּאֲכִילָה כָּךְ הוּא אָסוּר בַּהֲנָיָיה. מַה עֲבַד לָהּ רִבִּי יוֹחָנָן. פָּתַר לָהּ בְּשֶׁקְּדָמוּ הַבְּעָלִים וּשְׁחָטוּהוּ עַד שֶׁלֹּא נִגְמַר דִּינוֹ.

2 מה ן | ע ומה בא | ע -

רִבִּי זְעִירָא בְעָא קוֹמֵי רִבִּי אַבָּהוּ. הָכָא תֵימַר הָכִין וְהָכָא תֵימַר הָכֵין. אָמַר לֵיהּ. הָדָא בְשֵׁם רִבִּי לְעָזָר וְהָדָא בְשֵׁם רִבִּי יוֹחָנָן.

1 זעירא | ע זעירה תימר | ע את אמר (2) הדא | ע חדא בשם | ע משמיה 2 הדא | ע חדא בשם ר' | ע משמיה דר'

Rebbi Abbahu in the name of Rebbi Johanan: He who makes a wound dressing[33] from a stoned ox[34] or from leftover sour matter after Passover[35] cannot be whipped since its prohibition is not clear. For vineyard *kilaim* he is whipped since Rebbi Hanina said[36]: *Lest it be sanctified*, lest fire should be kindled. For *'orlah* it is problematic. A prescriptive commandment to removal is written[37], a prohibition to eat is written[38], ["do not eat"][39], a prohibition to remove it is not written[40].

In a *baraita*[41] one disagrees with Rebbi Johanan: What does one understand from what has been said[42]: *the ox shall certainly be stoned*? Do we not know that its meat is forbidden as food[43]? Then why does the verse say, *its meat shall not be eaten*? To tell you that just as it is forbidden as food so it is forbidden for usufruct. What does Rebbi Johanan do with this? He explained it if the owners slaughtered it before sentence was pronounced[44].

Rebbi Ze'ira asked before Rebbi Abbahu: Here you say so, there you say so[45]? He said to him, here in the name of Rebbi Eleazar, there in the name of Rebbi Johanan.

33 Latin *splenium*, Greek σπληνίον, τό, "pad, wound dressing."
34 The Babli 24b explains that one might use fat from the stoned ox to cover a wound.

The ox was stoned by order of the court because it killed humans (*Ex.* 21:28-29). Its meat is forbidden for usufruct as explained in the sequel. Cf. *Mekhilta dR.*

Ismael Mišpatim 10 (p. 282).

35 Since the Mishnah had stated that leavened matter becomes prohibited for all usufruct in the afternoon of the 14th of Nisan, after the holiday it cannot become permitted again.

36 *Deut.* 22:9. For this derivation, cf. *Kilaim* 8:1, Note 6.

37 Since Lev. 19:23 requires that the (budding) fruit is treated as "foreskin" and the foreskin has to be removed, one may take the verse as prescribing the removal of any *'orlah* fruit.

38 Last two words of *Lev.* 19:23. Since R. Johanan reads לֹא יֵאָכֵל as prohibition of eating, not of usufruct, he follows his teacher Hizqiah in rejecting the argument of R. Eleazar.

39 An incorrect and unnecessary addition by the corrector, not part of the original ms.

40 Non-fulfillment of a prescriptive commandment is not prosecutable.

41 The *baraita* as stated here is not found in any other source except the Yerushalmi parallels in *Orlah* and *Avodah Zarah* 5:12

(Note 155). In *Mekhilta Mišpatim* 19; quoted in Babli 22b, *Qiddušin* 56b, *Bava Qamma* 41a the text explicitly notes that, since "its meat shall not be eaten" is included in the statement of the sentence to be passed by the court, only after judgment is rendered does slaughter become ineffective. This may also be he rule implied by the Yerushalmi Targum to *Ex.* 21:28: וְלָא יִתְנְכַס לְמֵיכוֹל יַת בִּשְׂרֵיהּ "it should not be slaughtered to make its flesh edible." Since the Babli follows R. Eleazar, no discussion of the prohibition of usufruct is necessary.

42 *Ex.* 21:28.

43 As carcass meat.

44 This statement directly contradicts the position of the Babli. R. Johanan will hold that the prescriptive commandment to stone the ox after judgment has been passed automatically makes any slaughter invalid; that would not need a proof from the verse.

45 He states contradictory theses, whether or not prohibition as food implies prohibition of usufruct.

(28c line 40) רַבָּנָן דְּקֵיסָרִין רַבִּי אַבָּהוּ בְּשֵׁם רַבִּי יוֹחָנָן. כָּל־מָקוֹם שֶׁנֶּאֱמַר לֹא תֹאכַל לֹא תֹאכְלוּ אֵין אַתְּ תּוֹפֵשׂ אִיסוּר הֲנָייָה כְּאִיסוּר אֲכִילָה. לֹא תֹאכֵל לֹא יֵאָכֵל אַתְּ תּוֹפֵשׂ אִיסוּר הֲנָייָה כְּאִיסוּר אֲכִילָה. בִּנְיָין אָב שֶׁבְּכוּלָם. וְכָל־חַטָּאת אֲשֶׁר יוּבָא מִדָּמָהּ אֶל אֹהֶל מוֹעֵד לְכַפֵּר בַּקֹּדֶשׁ לֹא תֵאָכֵל בָּאֵשׁ תִּשָּׂרֵף. תַּנֵּי חִזְקִיָּה מְסַיֵּיעַ לְרַבִּי יוֹחָנָן. מִמַּשְׁמַע שֶׁנֶּאֱמַר חֵלֶב שׁוֹר וְכֶשֶׂב וָעֵז לֹא תֹאכֵלוּ: לְאֵי זֶה דָבָר נֶאֱמַר וְחֵלֶב נְבֵילָה וְחֵלֶב טְרֵיפָה יֵעָשֶׂה לְכָל־מְלָאכָה. אֲפִילוּ לִמְלֶאכֶת גָּבוֹהַּ. מִמַּשְׁמַע שֶׁנֶּאֱמַר רַק הַדָּם לֹא תֹאכֵלוּ. לְאֵי זֶה דָבָר נֶאֱמַר עַל־הָאָרֶץ תִּשְׁפְּכֶנּוּ כַּמָּיִם: מָה הַמַּיִם מַכְשִׁירִין. אַף הַדָּם יְהֵא מַכְשִׁיר. מִמַּשְׁמַע שֶׁנֶּאֱמַר לֹא־תֹאכְלוּ כָל־נְבֵילָה. לְאֵי זֶה דָבָר נֶאֱמַר לַגֵּר אֲשֶׁר־בִּשְׁעָרֶיךָ תִּתְּנֶנָּה וַאֲכָלָהּ. בָּא לְהוֹדִיעֲךָ. גֵּר תּוֹשָׁב אוֹכֵל בִּנְבֵילוֹת. מִמַּשְׁמַע שֶׁנֶּאֱמַר וּבָשָׂר בַּשָּׂדֶה טְרֵיפָה לֹא תֹאכֵלוּ. מַה תַּלְמוּד לוֹמַר לַכֶּלֶב תַּשְׁלִכוּן אֹתוֹ: אוֹתוֹ אַתָּה מַשְׁלִיךְ לַכֶּלֶב וְאֵין אַתְּ מַשְׁלִיךְ לַכֶּלֶב חוּלִין שֶׁנִּשְׁחֲטוּ בָעֲזָרָה.

1 לא תאכל | ע - 2 תופש | ע תופס   לא תאכל לא יאכל את תופש איסור הנייה כאיסור אכילה | ע - 3 שבכולם ע שבכולן   אוהל | ע אהל   4 תשרף | ע ישרף   חלב | ע כל חלב   5 אפי' | ע בא להודיעך אפילו   6

גבוה | ע הגבוה   7 מה | ע בא להודיעך מה יהא | ע -   8 גר | ע שגר | ע בנבילות | ע נבילות   9 מה ת"ל | ע לאי זה דבר נאמ'   10 את | ע אתה לכלב | ע -

The rabbis of Caesarea, Rabbi Abbahu in the name of Rebbi Joḥanan: Nowhere do you understand a prohibition of usufruct included in the prohibition of eating if it is written *do not eat, do not eat. It may not be eaten (f.). it may not be eaten (m.)*, you understand a prohibition of usufruct included in the prohibition of eating[46]. The paradigm for all cases is[47]: *Any purification offering of whose blood was brought into the Tent of Meeting to purify the sanctuary shall not be eaten, in fire it shall be burned*[48]. Hizqiah stated support for Rebbi Joḥanan: If one understands what has been said[49]: *Any fat of cattle, sheep, or goats you shall not eat*, why has it been said: *but fat of a carcass and fat of a torn animal may be used for any work*? Even for the work of Heaven[24]. If one understands what has been said[50]: *But the blood you shall not eat*, why has it been said, *you shall pour it on the ground like water*? As water prepares[51], so blood prepares. If one understands what has been said[52]: *Do not eat any carcass*; why has it been said, *to the sojourner in your gates you shall give it and he may eat it*? It serves to tell you that the resident sojourner may eat carcass meat[53]. If one understands what has been said[54]: *Flesh torn in the field you shall not eat*, why does the verse say, *throw it to the dog*? This you throw to the dog but you do not throw profane meat slaughtered in the Temple precinct[55].

46 In contrast to the statement of R. Eleazar (Note 17) it is asserted that if the prohibition of food is in the active voice it does not imply prohibition of usufruct. Still the passive voice does imply prohibition of usufruct.

47 Lev. 6:23.

48 It is shown that the passive voice implies prohibition of usufruct, since it is the only such case where the inference is valid according to everybody. The verse is understood (*Sifra Saw Pereq* 8(5), quoted in Babli *Zebahim* 82a, Yerushalmi *Pesahim* 7:9, fol. 35a] following a punctuation which differs from the masoretic one: *Any purification offering, some of whose blood was brought into the Tent of Meeting to purify, in the Sanctuary it shall not be eaten, in fire it shall be burned*. This is a possible reading since purification offerings may be eaten only in the Sanctuary. Then "Sanctuary" is taken also to refer to the last clause, (in the sanctuary) *in fire it shall be burned*. This excludes all sacred and profane usufruct after purification.

49 Lev. 7:23.

50 Deut. 12:16.

51 Preparation for impurity is explained

in *Demay* 2:3, Notes 136-141.

52 *Deut.* 14:21.

53 The resident sojourner, in order to receive the full protection of the law, only has to follow the "precepts of the descendants of Noe", to abstain from idolatry, murder, incest and adultery, eating limbs torn from a living animal, blasphemy, robbery, and anarchy.

54 *Ex.* 22:30.

55 In the Babli 22a this is quoted as the opinion of R. Meïr. It is forbidden to slaughter anything but sacrifices in the Temple precinct, *Lev.*17:4.

(28c line 52) מַתְנִיתָא מְסַיְּיעָא לְדֵין וּמַתְנִיתָא מְסַיְּיעָא לְדֵין. מַתְנִיתָא מְסַיְּיעָא לְרִבִּי אֶלְעָזָר. לֹא יֵאָכֵל חָמֵץ. לַעֲשׂוֹת אֶת הַמַּאֲכִיל כְּאוֹכֵל. וְאַתָּה אוֹמֵר. לַעֲשׂוֹת הַמַּאֲכִיל כְּאוֹכֵל. אוֹ אֵינוֹ אֶלָּא לְאוֹסְרוֹ בַּהֲנָיָיה. וּכְשֶׁהוּא אוֹמֵר לֹא־תֹאכַל עָלָיו חָמֵץ. הָא לָמַדְנוּ שֶׁהוּא אָסוּר בַּהֲנָיָה. מַה תַּלְמוּד לוֹמַר לֹא יֵאָכֵל חָמֵץ. לַעֲשׂוֹת הַמַּאֲכִיל כְּאוֹכֵל. דִּבְרֵי רִבִּי יֹאשִׁיָּה. רִבִּי יִצְחָק אוֹמֵר. אֵינוֹ צָרִיךְ. וּמַה שְׁרָצִים קַלִּים עָשָׂה בָּהֶם אֶת הַמַּאֲכִיל כְּאוֹכֵל. חָמֵץ הֶחָמוּר אֵינוֹ דִין שֶׁנַּעֲשֶׂה בּוֹ אֶת הַמַּאֲכִיל כְּאוֹכֵל. וּמַה תַּלְמוּד לוֹמַר לֹא יֵאָכֵל חָמֵץ. לֹא בָא הַכָּתוּב אֶלָּא לְאוֹסְרוֹ בַּהֲנָיָיה. בְּגִין כָּךְ כָּתוּב לֹא יֵאָכֵל. הָא מִלָּא תֹאכַל לֵית שְׁמַע מִינָּהּ כְּלוּם. וְהָדָא מְסַיְּיעָא לְרִבִּי יוֹחָנָן.

1 אלעזר | ע יוחנן   2 ואתה | ע אתה   לכך | ע לעשות המאכיל כאוכל | ע לכך   3 וכשהוא | ע כשהוא   הא | ע - מה | ע הא מה   4 לא | ע ולא   המאכיל | ע את המאכיל   אינו צריך | ע -   5 ומה | ע מה   קלים | ע קלין   בהם | ע בהן   את | ע - (2)   6 ומה | ע הא מה   7 כך כת' | ע דכת'

A *baraita*[56] supports both of them. The *baraita* supports Rebbi Eleazar[57]. *Sour bread shall not be eaten*[58], to make the feeder equal to the eater[59]. And you say for this, or is it only to forbid its usufruct? Since it says:[60] *You shall not eat sour bread with it*, we learned that usufruct is forbidden[61]. Therefore, why does the verse say, *sour bread shall not be eaten*? To make the feeder equal to the eater, the words of Rebbi Josia. Rebbi Isaac says, this is unnecessary. Since for crawling things, a minor prohibition[62], He made the feeder equal to the eater[63]; regarding sour bread which is a major prohibition it should only be logical that we consider the feeder to be equal to the eater. Therefore, why does the verse say, sour bread shall not be eaten? The verse serves only to forbid its usufruct. Since it is written, *sour bread shall not be eaten*, therefore from *you shall not eat* one cannot infer anything. This supports Rebbi Johanan[64].

56 *Mekhilta dR. Ismael, Bo* 16, p. 51. *Tanhuma Bo* 11

57 The disagreement between R. Eleazar and R. Johanan is an old tannaitic disagreement between Rabbis Josia and Isaac of the fourth tannaitic generation.

58 *Ex.* 13:3.

59 The person who serves sour matter to a Jew on Passover is guilty as if he ate it, to be

punished by extirpation. If the server acts intentionally and the eater unintentionally, the server alone is punishable.
60   Deut. 16:3.
61   This is the position of R. Eleazar.
62   Eating forbidden living things is punished by whipping by the earthly court; but eating sour matter on Passover is punished by Heaven with extirpation.
63   *Sifra Šemini Pereq* 5(1). R. Abraham ben David in his commentary notes that this is not the position of the Babli; he does not refer to the Yerushalmi.
64   Here ends the parallel with `Orlah 3:1.

(28c line 61) לֹא יַסִּיק בּוֹ תַּנּוּר וְכִירַיִם. עָבַר וְהִסִּיק. יָיבָא כְהָדָא. אִם חָדָא יוּתָּץ. אִם יָשָׁן יוּצַן.

"Nor use it to heat an oven or a cooking stove." If he transgressed and heated, it shall come like the following[65]: "If it was new it must be destroyed[270], if it was old it must be cooled down."

65   Mishnah *Avodah zarah* 3:14, dealing with using wood from an *Asherah* to heat a clay stove which was not finished in a kiln. It would become hardened by being exposed to the fire kindled in them. Therefore a new oven would be finished by the *Ashera* wood; it must be destroyed. The text might be a quote not of this Mishnah but of Tosephta *Orlah* 7 dealing with the same situation if the fuel is *orlah* fruit (*Orlah* 3:3 Note 114) which is quoted *in extenso* in the Babli 26b.

(28c line 62) תַּנֵּי. רְבִּי יוּדָה אוֹמֵר. אֵין בִּיעוּר חָמֵץ אֶלָּא בִשְׂרֵיפָה. דִּין הוּא. מַה אִם פִּיגּוּל וְנוֹתָר שֶׁאֵינוֹ בַּל יֵרָאֶה וּבַל יִמָּצֵא אֵינוֹ אֶלָּא בִשְׂרֵיפָה. חָמֵץ שֶׁהוּא בְּבַל יֵרָאֶה וּבַל יִמָּצֵא אֵינוֹ דִין שֶׁלֹּא יְהֵא אֶלָּא בִשְׂרֵיפָה. אָמְרוּ לוֹ לְרִבִּי יוּדָה. כָּל־דִּין שֶׁאַתָּה דָן תְּחִילָּתוֹ לְהַחֲמִיר וְסוֹפוֹ לְהָקֵל אֵינוֹ דִין. הָא אִם לֹא נִתְמַנָּה לוֹ אוּר יֵשֵׁב לוֹ וְלֹא יַבְעִיר. אָמְרָה תוֹרָה תַּשְׁבִּיתוּ שְׂאוֹר מִבָּתֵּיכֶם.

It was stated: Rebbi Jehudah says, leavened matter may only be eliminated by burning. [66]It is an argument *de minore ad majus*. Since *piggul*[67] and leftover[68], which are not under an injunction not to be seen and not to be found, only may be disposed of by burning, for leavened matter which is under an injunction not to be seen and not to be found, it is only logical that it only may be disposed by burning. They told Rebbi Jehudah, any argument *de minore ad majus* which you argue in the beginning as a restriction but it turns out in the end to be a leniency, is no argument *de minore ad majus*[69]. It would imply that if he does not find fire he could sit and not dispose of it. The Torah said[70], *eliminate sour dough from your houses*.

כְּיוֹצֵא בוֹ. אָמַר רִבִּי יוּדָה. אִשָּׁה כִּי תַזְרִיעַ וְיָלְדָה זָכָר. מַה תַלְמוּד לוֹמַר. לְפִי שֶׁנֶּאֱמַר וְטָמְאָה שִׁבְעַת יָמִים וּבַיּוֹם הַשְּׁמִינִי יִמּוֹל. שׁוֹמֵעַ אֲנִי בְיוֹצֵא חַי שֶׁהוּא מְטַמֵּא אֶת אִמּוֹ טוּמְאַת לֵידָה. מִנַּייִן לְיוֹצֵא מֵת שֶׁהוּא מְטַמֵּא אֶת אִמּוֹ טוּמְאַת לֵידָה. אָמַר רִבִּי יוּדָה. הֲרֵי אֲנִי דָן. מָה אִם בְּיוֹצֵא חַי. שֶׁאֵינוֹ מְטַמֵּא אֶת אִמּוֹ וְאֶת הַבָּאִין עִמּוֹ [וְאֶת הַבָּא עִם אִמּוֹ] לְאוֹהֶל טוּמְאַת שִׁבְעָה. מְטַמֵּא אֶת אִמּוֹ טוּמְאַת לֵידָה. הַיּוֹצֵא מֵת. שֶׁהוּא מְטַמֵּא אֶת אִמּוֹ וְאֶת הַבָּאִין עִמּוֹ [וְאֶת הַבָּא עִם אִמּוֹ] לְאוֹהֶל טוּמְאַת שִׁבְעָה. אֵינוֹ דִין שֶׁיְטַמֵּא אֶת אִמּוֹ טוּמְאַת לֵידָה. אָמְרוּ לוֹ לְרִבִּי יוּדָה. כָּל־דִּין שֶׁתְּחִילָּתוֹ אַתָּה דָן לְהַחֲמִיר וְסוֹפוֹ לְהָקֵל אֵינוֹ דִין. הָא אִם טִיהֵר הַחַי אֶת אִמּוֹ יְטַהֵר אַף הַמֵּת אֶת אִמּוֹ. אִם לֹא זָכִיתִי מִן הַדִּין. [לְפִיכָךְ] אָמְרָה תוֹרָה זָכָר. לְרַבּוֹת אֶת הַמֵּת.

Similarly said Rebbi Jehudah, *if a woman carries seed and gives birth to a male*[71]. What does the verse imply? Since it is said, *she shall be impure for seven days,* [72]*and on the eighth day one shall circumcise,* I understand that a live birth makes his mother impure by the impurity of birth. From where that a stillbirth makes his mother impure by the impurity of birth? Rebbi Jehudah said, I am presenting an argument *de minore ad majus*. Since a live birth, who does not make impure for seven days his mother, and those who come with him[73], [or who comes with his mother,][74] into a tent[75], the stillbirth who makes impure for seven days his mother, and those who come with him, [or who comes with his mother,][74] into a tent, it is only logical that he should make his mother impure by the impurity of birth. They told Rebbi Jehudah, any argument *de minore ad majus* which you argue in the beginning as a restriction but it turns out in the end to be a leniency is no argument *de minore ad majus*. As a consequence, since a live birth purifies his mother[76], also the stillbirth should purify his mother? Since I cannot prove it by an argument *de minore ad majus,* [therefore} the Torah said *a male*, to include the stillbirth[77].

כְּיוֹצֵא בוֹ. אָמַר רִבִּי יוּדָה. תֵּשְׁבוּ בַּסּוּכוֹת. סוּכָּה שֶׁלְּכָל־דָּבָר. שֶׁהָיָה רִבִּי יוּדָה אוֹמֵר. הַדִּין נוֹתֵן שֶׁלֹּא תְהֵא הַסּוּכָּה בָאָה אֶלָּא מֵאַרְבַּעַת הַמִּינִין. מָה אִם לוּלָב שֶׁאֵינוֹ נוֹהֵג בַּלֵּילוֹת כְּבַיָּמִים אֵינוֹ בָא אֶלָּא מֵאַרְבַּעַת הַמִּינִין. סוּכָּה שֶׁהִיא נוֹהֶגֶת בַּלֵּילוֹת כְּבַיָּמִים אֵינוֹ דִין שֶׁלֹּא תָבוֹא אֶלָּא מֵאַרְבַּעַת הַמִּינִין. אָמְרוּ לוֹ לְרִבִּי יוּדָה. כָּל־דִּין שֶׁאַתָּה דָן תְּחִילָּתוֹ לְהַחֲמִיר וְסוֹפוֹ לְהָקֵל אֵינוֹ דִין. הָא לֹא מָצָא מֵאַרְבַּעַת הַמִּינִין יֵשֵׁב לוֹ בְלֹא סוּכָּה. וְאָמְרָה תוֹרָה תֵּשְׁבוּ בַּסּוּכוֹת. סוּכָּה שֶׁלְּכָל־דָּבָר. [וְכֵן עֶזְרָא אָמַר וַאֲשֶׁר יַשְׁמִיעוּ וְיַעֲבִירוּ קוֹל בְּכָל־עָרֵיהֶם וּבִירוּשָׁלַםִ לֵאמֹר צְאוּ הָהָר וְגוֹ'.]

Similarly said Rebbi Jehudah, "you should dwell in huts[78]," a hut made of anything. For Rebbi Jehudah was saying, it is an argument *de minore ad majus* that the hut should come only from the Four Kinds[79]. Since the *lulav* which is not used in nights as in days may come only from the Four Kinds, it is only logical that a hut which is used by nights as well as by days should come only from the Four Kinds. They told Rebbi Jehudah, any argument *de minore ad majus* which you argue in the beginning as a restriction but it turns out in the end to be a leniency is no argument *de minore ad majus*. As a consequence, if he did not find of the Four Kinds, should he sit without a hut? But the Torah said, "you should dwell in huts," a hut made of anything. [And so Ezra said[80], *they informed and did proclaim in all cities and in Jerusalem, go to the mountain, etc.*]

חָזַר רִבִּי יוּדָה וְדָנוּ דִּין אַחֵר. חָמֵץ אָסוּר בַּאֲכִילָה וְנוֹתָר אָסוּר בַּאֲכִילָה. מַה זֶּה בִּשְׂרֵיפָה אַף זֶה בִּשְׂרֵיפָה. אָמְרוּ לוֹ. נְבֵילָה תּוֹכִיחַ. שֶׁהִיא אֲסוּרָה בַּאֲכִילָה וְאֵינָהּ בִּשְׂרֵיפָה. אָמַר לָהֶן. חָמֵץ אָסוּר בַּאֲכִילָה וּבַהֲנָייָה וְנוֹתָר אָסוּר בַּאֲכִילָה וּבַהֲנָייָה. אַל תּוֹכִיחַ נְבֵילָה שֶׁאֵינָהּ אֲסוּרָה בַּהֲנָייָה. אָמְרוּ לוֹ. וַהֲרֵי שׁוֹר הַנִּסְקָל יוֹכִיחַ. שֶׁהוּא אָסוּר בַּאֲכִילָה וּבַהֲנָייָה וְאֵינוֹ בִּשְׂרֵיפָה. אָמַר לָהֶן. חָמֵץ אָסוּר בַּאֲכִילָה וּבַהֲנָייָה וְחַייָבִין עָלָיו כָּרֵת [וְנוֹתָר אָסוּר בַּאֲכִילָה וּבַהֲנָייָה וְחַייָבִין עָלָיו כָּרֵת]. אַל יוֹכִיחַ שׁוֹר הַנִּסְקָל שֶׁאֵין חַייָבִין עָלָיו כָּרֵת. אָמְרוּ לוֹ. וַהֲרֵי חֵלֶב שׁוֹר הַנִּסְקָל יוֹכִיחַ. שֶׁהוּא אָסוּר בַּאֲכִילָה וּבַהֲנָייָה וְחַייָבִין עָלָיו כָּרֵת וְאֵינוֹ בִּשְׂרֵיפָה. אָמַר לָהֶן. חָמֵץ אָסוּר בַּאֲכִילָה וּבַהֲנָייָה וְחַייָבִין עָלָיו כָּרֵת וְיֵשׁ לוֹ זְמָן וְנוֹתָר אָסוּר בַּאֲכִילָה וּבַהֲנָייָה וְחַייָבִין עָלָיו כָּרֵת וְיֵשׁ לוֹ זְמָן. אַל יוֹכִיחַ חֵלֶב שׁוֹר הַנִּסְקָל שֶׁאֵין לוֹ זְמָן. אָמְרוּ לוֹ. וַהֲרֵי אָשָׁם תָּלוּי כְּשִׁיטָתָךְ יוֹכִיחַ. שֶׁהוּא אָסוּר בַּאֲכִילָה וּבַהֲנָייָה וְחַייָבִין עָלָיו כָּרֵת וְיֵשׁ לוֹ זְמָן [וְאֵינוֹ בִּשְׂרֵיפָה]. וְשָׁתַק רִבִּי יוּדָה.

Rebbi Jehudah came back and presented another argument: Leavened matter is forbidden as food and leftover[68] is forbidden as food. Since the latter is to be burned[81], the former is to be burned. They told him, carcass meat disproves since it is forbidden as food and is not to be burned[20]. He said to them, leavened matter is forbidden as food and for usufruct and leftover is forbidden as food and for usufruct; carcass meat does not disprove since it is not forbidden for usufruct. They told him, the stoned ox[34] disproves which is forbidden as food and for usufruct[82] and is not to be burned. He said to them, leavened matter is forbidden as food, and for usufruct, and makes liable for extirpation[83], [and leftover is forbidden as food, and for usufruct, and makes liable for extirpation][84]; the stoned ox does not disprove since it does not make liable for extirpation. They told him, the fat[85] of the stoned ox disproves which is forbidden as food, and for usufruct, and makes liable for extirpation, and is not to be burned. He said to them, leavened matter is forbidden as food, and for usufruct, and makes liable for extirpation, and is dependent on time, and leftover is forbidden as food, and for usufruct, and makes liable for extirpation, and is dependent on time; the fat of the stoned ox does not disprove since it does not depend on time. They told him, a suspended sacrifice[86] following your opinion[87] does disprove since it is forbidden as food, and for usufruct, and makes liable for extirpation, and is dependent on time, [but is not to be burned]. Rebbi Jehudah remained silent[88].

66 The first and last paragraphs in this section are also quoted in the Babli, 27b-28a; *Mekhilta dR. Simeon ben Yohay ad Ex.* 12:15, pp. 17-18..

67 Sacrifices which were offered with the intention that the meat be eaten out of place or time; *Lev.* 19:7.

68 Sacrificial meat left over after the time allotted for its consumption, depending on the kind of sacrifice either day and night or two daytimes with the night in between.

69 The premise that there be a case of major and minor is disproved. Cf. H. Guggenheimer, *Logical Problems in Jewish Tradition*, in: *Confrontations with Judaism*, Ph. Longworth, ed., London 1966, pp. 171-196.

70 *Ex.* 12:15.

71 *Lev.* 13:1. *Sifra Tazria' Introduction* (5); another version of *Sifra* in *Midrash Haggadol Lev.*, ed A. Steinsalz, Jerusalem 1976, pp. 313-314.

72 *Lev.* 13:2.

73 According to *Pene Mosheh*, this refers to multiple births if one of the fetuses is dead.

74 Unnecessary addition by the corrector.

75 A live birth causes his mother to be impure for seven days; after this time she may remove her impurity at any time by immersion in a *miqweh*. A stillbirth causes impurity of the dead not only by touch but also by being under the same "tent" and requires the purification rite of the ashes of the Red Cow described in *Num.* 19.

76 After the impurity of the first 7 days, the next 33 days for a male or 66 days for a female no genital discharge of the mother induces biblical impurity.

77 Since the mention of a female in v. 5 implies that the preceding verses refer to a male, the explicit mention of "male" is unnecessary. It is concluded that the verses refer to *any* fetus recognizably male.

78 The reference obviously is to *Lev.* 23:42 where the text reads either בַּסֻּכֹּת תֵּשְׁבוּ or יֵשְׁבוּ בַּסֻּכֹּת. The quote is correct in *Sifra Emor Pereq* 17(10) but incorrect in *Midrash Haggadol* (Note 71) p. 763. The reference is to the holiday of Tabernacles.

79 This can only mean that the thatched roof of the hut, which must be of vegetal material, should be composed of willow, myrrh, or palm branches. The fourth kind,

the fruit of the *hadar* tree (*Lev.* 23:40), probably cannot be used for this purpose. [In medieval Germany the roof of the festival hut usually was covered with willow branches, *Sefer Maharil* (ed. S. J. Spitzer, Jerusalem 1989, p. 363)].

80 *Neh.* 8:15. The proof is from the continuation of the verse, not quoted in the text: *Bring olive leaves, and oil-wood leaves, and myrrh leaves, and palm leaves, and `avot-tree leaves, to make huts as it is written.* Corrector's addition from the parallel sources.

81 *Lev.* 19:8.

82 Since it says, *its meat may not be eaten* (*Ex.* 21:18) in the passive voice, according to everybody this implies prohibition of usufruct.

83 *Ex.* 12:19.

84 *Lev.* 19:8.

85 *Lev.* 7:25.

86 The sacrifice by a person who suspects that he inadvertently committed a deadly sin. He may not bring a purification sacrifice since that is possible only if there is proof of inadvertent sin; *Lev.* 5:17-19.

87 In Mishnah *Temurah* 7:6 it is stated that Sages hold that the body of an animal dedicated as a hung sacrifice which was wrongly slaughtered has to be burned, but R. Jehudah requires that it be buried.

88 And practice does not follow him.

(28d line 26) תַּנֵּי. עַד שֶׁלֹּא הִגִּיעַ זְמַן בִּיעוּרוֹ אַתְּ מְבַעֲרוֹ בְּכָל־דָּבָר. מִשֶּׁהִגִּיעַ זְמַן בִּיעוּרוֹ אַתְּ מְבַעֲרוֹ בִשְׂרֵיפָה. וְאַתְיָא כְרַבִּי יוּדָה. אִית תַּנָּיֵי תַּנֵּי. עַד שֶׁלֹּא הִגִּיעַ זְמַן בִּיעוּרוֹ אַתְּ מְבַעֲרוֹ בִשְׂרֵיפָה. מִשֶּׁהִגִּיעַ זְמַן בִּיעוּרוֹ אַתְּ מְבַעֲרוֹ בְּכָל־דָּבָר. וְאַתְיָא כְרַבָּנִין. רַבִּי אוֹמֵר. תַּשְׁבִּיתוּ שְׂאוֹר מִבָּתֵּיכֶם. דָּבָר שֶׁהוּא בַּל יֵרָאֶה וּבַל יִמָּצֵא. וְאֵי זֶה. זֶה בִשְׂרֵיפָה. רַבִּי יִרְמְיָה בָּעֵי. פֶּטֶר חֲמוֹר שֶׁהֵמִית בַּמֶּה הִיא מִיתָתוֹ. בָּעֲרִיפָה [אוֹ] בִסְקִילָה. רַבִּי בִּנְיָמִן בַּר לֵוִי שָׁאַל. חַלּוֹת תּוֹדָה שֶׁנַּעֲשׂוּ נוֹתָר. נֵימַר. אִם נַעֲשׂוּ נוֹתָר עַד שֶׁלֹּא הִגִּיעַ זְמַן בִּיעוּרָן. אַתְּ מְבַעֲרָן בְּכָל־דָּבָר. מִשֶּׁהִגִּיעַ זְמַן בִּיעוּרָן אַתְּ מְבַעֲרָן בִשְׂרֵיפָה.

It was stated: Before the time of its elimination you eliminate it in any way you wish; at the time of its elimination you eliminate it by burning. This follows Rebbi Jehudah. There are Tannaim who state, before the time of its elimination you eliminate it by burning; at the time of its elimination you eliminate it in any way you wish[89]. This follows the rabbis. Rebbi says, *remove sour dough from your houses*, anything which may not be seen nor found[90]. How is this? By burning. Rebbi Jeremiah asked, if the firstling of a donkey killed, what is the form of his execution? By breaking the neck or by stoning[90a]? Rebbi Benjamin bar Levi asked about leftover flat-bread from a thanksgiving sacrifice, should we say that if they were left before the time of elimination you may eliminate it in any way you wish; at the time of its elimination you have to eliminate it by burning[91]?

89 The Babli disagrees, 12b.
90 *Ex.* 12:15. Rebbi disagrees with both the preceding *baraitot*. Since it is spelled out in Chapter 13 that on Passover sour matter may neither be seen nor found, the only acceptable form of removal both before noontime of the 14th or at noontime is by burning which transforms everything into ashes. If one would bury the leavened matter or crumble it and scatter it in the wind, it still would exist and could be found.
90a The firstling of a donkey which was not redeemed by a lamb given to a Cohen must be killed by breaking its neck (*Ex.* 13:13). An animal which killed a human must be stoned (*Ex.* 21:28). If both conditions apply there are no rules to decide which precept to apply.
91 A thanksgiving offering must be accompanied by leavened bread (Chapter 1, Notes 34, 143). The argument is that if the offering was brought on the 14th of Nisan (cf. Chapter 1, Note 148) and there was no time to eat the bread, it is not biblical leftover; before noontime any elimination is purely rabbinical and can be done in any way. At noontime it no longer can be eaten by biblical standards, it becomes biblical leftover before its time and has to be burned. That latter statement is independent of the disagreements between R. Jehudah, Rebbi, and the Sages.

(fol. 28b) **משנה ב**: חָמֵץ שֶׁל נָכְרִי שֶׁעָבַר עָלָיו הַפֶּסַח מוּתָּר בַּהֲנָאָה וְשֶׁל יִשְׂרָאֵל אָסוּר בַּהֲנָאָה שֶׁנֶּאֱמַר לֹא יֵרָאֶה לָךְ: נָכְרִי שֶׁהִלְוָה אֶת יִשְׂרָאֵל עַל חֲמֵיצוֹ לְאַחַר הַפֶּסַח מוּתָּר בַּהֲנָאָה וְיִשְׂרָאֵל שֶׁהִלְוָה אֶת הַנָּכְרִי עַל חֲמֵיצוֹ לְאַחַר הַפֶּסַח אָסוּר בַּהֲנָאָה. חָמֵץ שֶׁנָּפְלָה עָלָיו מַפּוֹלֶת הֲרֵי הוּא כִמְבוֹעָר. רַבָּן שִׁמְעוֹן בֶּן גַּמְלִיאֵל אוֹמֵר כָּל־שֶׁאֵין הַכֶּלֶב יָכוֹל לְחַפֵּשׂ אַחֲרָיו:

Mishnah 2: A Non-Jew's leavened matter which existed during Passover is permitted for usufruct but a Jew's is forbidden for usufruct since it is said[92], *it should not be seen in your possession*. If a Non-Jew gave a loan to a Jew secured by leavened matter, after Passover it is permitted for usufruct[93] but if a Jew gave a loan to a Non-Jew secured by leavened matter, after Passover it is forbidden for usufruct. Leavened matter on which debris fell[94] is as if eliminated; Rabban Simeon ben Gamliel says, only one which cannot be dug out by a dog.

92 *Ex.* 13:7.
93 If the leavened matter is mortgaged, the Jew may not sell or destroy it; therefore it is considered the creditor's property. The Babli disagrees and restricts the Mishnah to the case that the Non-Jew has custody of the material.
94 When a wall or a house collapsed.

(28d line 35) **הלכה ב**: הָא בָּאֲכִילָה אָסוּר. מַתְנִיתָא בְּמָקוֹם שֶׁלֹא נָהֲגוּ לוֹכַל פַּת גּוֹיִם.] אֲבָל בְּמָקוֹם שֶׁנָּהֲגוּ לוֹכַל פַּת גּוֹיִם[מוּתָּר אֲפִילוּ בַּאֲכִילָה.

Halakhah 2: Therefore it is forbidden for eating[95]? The Mishnah refers to a place where they used not to eat Gentile bread; [but at a place where they used to eat Gentile bread] it is permitted even for eating.

בְּתוֹךְ הַפֶּסַח מָהוּ. רִבִּי יִרְמְיָה אָמַר. מוּתָּר. רִבִּי יוֹסֵה אָמַר. אָסוּר. הָתִיב רִבִּי יוֹסֵה. וְהָתַנֵּי. לֹא יַשְׂכִּיר יִשְׂרָאֵל אֶת בְּהֶמְתּוֹ לְגוֹי לְהָבִיא עָלֶיהָ חָמֵץ. פָּתַר לָהּ. בְּבָא עִמּוֹ. וְהָתַנֵּי. לֹא יַשְׂכִּיר יִשְׂרָאֵל אֶת סְפִינָתוֹ לְגוֹי לְהָבִיא עָלֶיהָ חָמֵץ. פָּתַר לָהּ. בְּבָא עִמּוֹ. וְהָא תַנֵּי. לֹא יַשְׂכִּיר יִשְׂרָאֵל אֶת בֵּיתוֹ לְגוֹי לִיתֵּן בְּתוֹכוֹ חָמֵץ. אִית לָךְ מֵימַר. בְּדָר עִמּוֹ.

What is it during Passover[96]? Rebbi Jeremiah said, it is permitted. Rebbi Yose said, it is forbidden. Rebbi Yose objected: but was it not stated: An Israel may not lease his animal to a Gentile to use it to transport leavened matter? He[97] explains it, if he comes with him. But was it not stated: An Israel may not lease his ship to a Gentile to use it to transport leavened matter? He explains it, if he comes with him. But was it not stated: An Israel may not lease his house to a Gentile to store leavened matter in it. Can you say, if he dwells with him[98]?

95 Since the Mishnah is formulated "is permitted for usufruct" and not simply "is permitted", it appears that the addition "for usufruct" is a restriction, excluding the use as kosher food.
96 May the Jew use the Gentile's leavened matter for industrial purposes on Passover?
97 R. Jeremiah.
98 Therefore practice has to follow R. Yose. However, since the Tosephta 2:14 states: "An Israel may lease his animal to a Gentile to transport leavened matter from place to place", Raviah (§449) reads the quotes as declarative sentences supporting R. Jeremiah, that leasing animal or ship to a Gentile is forbidden only if the Jew drives the animal or steers the ship. Then the last question is not rhetorical and is left without answer.

(28d line 42) גַּגּוֹ שֶׁלְּגוֹי שֶׁהָיָה סָמוּךְ לְגַגּוֹ שֶׁלְּיִשְׂרָאֵל. וְנִתְגַּלְגֵּל חָמֵץ מִגַּגּוֹ שֶׁלְּגוֹי לְגַגּוֹ שֶׁלְּיִשְׂרָאֵל. הֲרֵי זֶה דּוֹחֲפוֹ בְקָנֶה. אִם הָיְתָה שַׁבָּת אוֹ יוֹם טוֹב. רַב אָמַר. כּוֹפֶה עָלָיו כְּלִי.

HALAKHAH TWO

רַב אָמַר. צָרִיךְ לוֹמַר. כָּל־חָמֵץ שֶׁיֵּשׁ לִי בְתוֹךְ בֵּיתִי וְאֵינִי יוֹדֵעַ בּוֹ יִבָּטֵל.

רַב אָמַר. צָרִיךְ לוֹמַר. אֲשֶׁר קִידְּשָׁנוּ בְמִצְוֹתָיו וְצִיוָּנוּ עַל מִצְוַת בִּיעוּר חָמֵץ.

רַב אָמַר. הַטָּח בֵּיתוֹ חָמֵץ צָרִיךְ לְבָעֵר. תַּנֵּי. אָמַר רִבִּי שִׁמְעוֹן בֶּן אֶלְעָזָר. בָּצֵק שֶׁעֲשָׂאוֹ כוּפָת בָּטֵל. פָּתַר לָהּ. אוֹ חֲלוּקִין עַל רִבִּי שִׁמְעוֹן בֶּן אֶלְעָזָר. אוֹ אֲהֵן כּוּפָת מָאִיס הוּא.

If the roof of a Gentile was adjacent to a Jew's roof and leavened matter rolled from the Gentile's roof to the Jew's roof, he pushes it away with a stick[99]. If it was Sabbath or holiday[100], Rav said, he covers it with a vessel.

Rav said, one has to say "any leavened matter which I have in my house unknown to me shall be nullified.[101]"

Rav said, one has to say "Who sanctified us by His Commandments and commanded us about the precept of eliminating leavened matter.[102]"

Rav said, he who affixes leavened matter to his house has to eliminate[103]. It was stated: Rebbi Simeon ben Eleazar said, if one turns dough into a clump, it is nullified[104] He[105] explains it, either that one disagrees with Rebbi Simeon ben Eleazar or that this clump is repugnant.

99 But he may not touch leavened matter on Passover.

100 Since leavened matter is forbidden, it is *muqseh* on Sabbath or holiday and may not be moved. A similar statement appears in the Babli 6a.

101 Babli 6b. While the Babli does not mention "unknown to me", the discussion there implies that this is understood.

102 Babli 7a (bottom) in the name of later Amoraim. The benediction has to be introduced by the formula: "Praise to You, Eternal, our God, King of the universe". Cf. H. Guggenheimer, *The Scholar's Haggadah*, Northvale 1995, p.194.

103 Ravan (ed. S. Albeck, Warsaw 1904) §7: "For what is customary to rub off walls which were touched by leavened matter before Passover and also to wash the chairs, I found support in the Yerushalmi: Rav said, he who affixes leavened matter to his house has to eliminate." Copied by Raviah (§451) and later authors.

104 Babli 45b, *Hulin* 129a. In the Babli: "A clump used to sit on it." The leavened matter no longer is food.

105 Rav, who requires that leavened matter on walls be eliminated.

(28d line 50) יִשְׂרָאֵל וְגוֹי שֶׁהָיוּ בָאִין בִּסְפִינָה וְחָמֵץ בְּיַד יִשְׂרָאֵל. הֲרֵי זֶה מוֹכְרוֹ לְגוֹי אוֹ נוֹתְנוֹ לוֹ בְמַתָּנָה. וְחוֹזֵר וְלוֹקְחוֹ מִמֶּנּוּ לְאַחַר הַפֶּסַח. וּבִלְבָד שֶׁיִּתְּנוֹ לוֹ מַתָּנָה גְמוּרָה. אוֹמֵר הוּא יִשְׂרָאֵל לְגוֹי. עַד שֶׁאַתְּ לוֹקֵחַ בְּמָנֶה. בּוֹא וְקַח לְךָ בְּמָאתַיִם. עַד שֶׁאַתְּ לוֹקֵחַ לְךָ מִגּוֹי. בּוֹא וְקַח לְךָ מִיִּשְׂרָאֵל. שֶׁמָּא אֶצְטָרֵךְ וְאֶקַּח מִמָּךְ אַחַר הַפֶּסַח.

[106]"If a Jew and a Gentile were travelling by ship[107] and leavened matter was in the Jew's hand, he sells it to the Gentile or gives it to him as a gift; then he reverts and buys it from him after Passover[108], on condition that it was an unconditional gift[109]. The Jew may say to the Gentile, instead of buying it for a mina, come and buy it for 200 [denar][110]. Instead that you buy from a Gentile, come and buy it from a Jew, maybe I shall have need, then I shall buy from you after Passover[111]."

106 Tosephta 2:13-14.
107 On the 14th of Nisan.
108 Since the leavened matter was the Gentile's property on Passover, it is permitted for the Jew after the holiday, as stated in the Mishnah.
109 It may not be given on condition that the Gentile return it after the holiday. It is necessary that the entire transaction result in some monetary reward for the Gentile.
110 While this cannot refer to dough (except in times of hyperinflation), it is common practice at the least to double the price in the sale for Passover of valuable enterprises engaged in processing leavened matter (e. g., a beer brewery), in order to guard against the Gentile selling the enterprise to an outsider.
111 While the Jew cannot sign a contract requiring him to buy back the items after Passover, he can use language which the Gentile will interpret to that effect.

(28d line 54) הַמַּשְׂכִּיר בַּיִת לַחֲבֵירוֹ. עַד שֶׁלֹּא יִכָּנֵס לְתוֹכוֹ. הַמַּשְׂכִּיר צָרִיךְ לְבָעֵר. מִשֶּׁיִּכָּנֵס לְתוֹכוֹ. הַשּׂוֹכֵר צָרִיךְ לְבָעֵר. אָמַר רִבִּי שִׁמְעוֹן. אֵימָתַי. בִּזְמַן שֶׁמָּסַר לוֹ אֶת הַמַּפְתֵּחַ. אֲבָל בִּזְמַן שֶׁלֹּא מָסַר לוֹ אֶת הַמַּפְתֵּחַ אֵינוֹ צָרִיךְ לְבָעֵר.

אָמַר רִבִּי יוּדָה בַּר פָּזִי בְּעִי. מָסַר לוֹ אֶת הַמַּפְתֵּחַ מָהוּ. אָמַר רִבִּי זְכַרְיָה חַתְנִיהּ דְּרִבִּי לֵוִי. מַחֲלוֹקֶת רִבִּי שִׁמְעוֹן וַחֲכָמִים. דִּתְנִינָן תַּמָּן. הַמּוֹסֵר מַפְתֵּיחוֹ לְעַם הָאָרֶץ הַבַּיִת טָהוֹר. שֶׁלֹּא מָסַר לוֹ אֶלָּא שְׁמִירַת הַמַּפְתֵּחַ: תַּנֵּי. רִבִּי שִׁמְעוֹן מְטַמֵּא.

If somebody rents out his house to another, as long as this one does not enter into it[112], the lessor has to eliminate; after this one entered into it, the lessee has to eliminate. Rebbi Simeon said, when? If he handed him the key, but as long as he did not hand him the key, he does not have to eliminate[113].

[114]Rebbi Jehudah bar Pazi said, I asked: What if he handed him the key[115]? Rebbi Zachariah the son-in-law of Rebbi Levi said, this is the disagreement between Rebbi Simeon and the Sages, as we have stated there[116]: "If somebody hands over his key to a vulgar person, the house remains pure since

he only entrusted him with safekeeping the key." It was stated: Rebbi Simeon declares it impure[117].

112 As the following remark of R. Simeon shows, this cannot mean that the lessee actually started using the house, but it must mean that the contract entered into effect on the 13th of Nisan. Babli 4a.

113 As long as the lessor controls the access to the house, even though the lessee has the right of use, the lessor is required to eliminate.

114 *Qiddušin* 1:4, Notes 435-438.

115 S. Liebermann points out that this cannot mean that the key was handed over after a contract for lease or sale was signed, since for a lease the matter was settled in the preceding paragraph and for a sale it is stated that transfer of the key is transfer of the property (*Bava batra* 3:1, Note 12). Nevertheless *Sefer Ha`ittur* (vol. 2, p. 121a, Note 17) reads the question as complement of the preceding statement.

116 Mishnah *Tahorot* 7:1. The vulgar person is one who does not observe the rules of purity. He is considered a source of original impurity; cf. *Introduction to Tractate Demay*.

117 Tosephta *Tahorot* 8:1. He holds that handing over the key implies authorization for unlimited entry into the premises.

(28d line 61) גּוֹי שֶׁבָּא אֵצֶל יִשְׂרָאֵל וּבְיָדוֹ חָמֵץ אֵינוֹ צָרִיךְ לְבָעֵר. הִפְקִיד אֶצְלוֹ צָרִיךְ לְבָעֵר. יִיחַד לוֹ בַּיִת אֵינוֹ צָרִיךְ לְבָעֵר. לֹא בִיעֵר לְאַחַר הַפֶּסַח מָהוּ. רִבִּי יוֹנָה אָמַר. מוּתָּר. רִבִּי יוֹסֵה אָמַר. אָסוּר. אָמַר רִבִּי יוֹסֵה. חֲמֵיצוֹ שֶׁלְגּוֹי הוּא. יִשְׂרָאֵל הוּא שֶׁעָבַר עָלָיו וְלֹא בִיעֲרוֹ.

[118]"If a Gentile comes to a Jew with leavened matter in his hand, one does not need to eliminate. If he deposited with him, he has to eliminate[119]. If he gave him a separate room[120] he does not need to eliminate." If he did not eliminate[121], what is its status after Passover? Rebbi Jonah said, it is permitted; Rebbi Yose said, it is forbidden. Rebbi Yose said, it is the Gentile's leavened matter [but] the Jew acted wrongly and did not eliminate[122].

118 Babli 6a; Tosephta 2:11; *Mekhilta dR. Simeon ben Yohay Ba* (p. 23 l.16).
119 If the Jew is responsible for loss.
120 Which is not used for the Jew's property during Passover.
121 The Gentile's leavened matter for which the Jew is responsible.
122 While it is not the Jew's property, it is his responsibility. Rabbinically one forces the Jew to destroy the leavened matter and to indemnify the Gentile. There is no need to emend the text.

(28d line 65) מָאן תַּנָּא לֹא יֵרָאֶה לְךָ. רְבִּי יוּדָה. דְּתַנֵּי. הָאוֹכֵל חָמֵץ מִשֵּׁשׁ שָׁעוֹת וּלְמַעֲלָה. וְכֵן חָמֵץ שֶׁעָבַר עָלָיו הַפֶּסַח. הֲרֵי זֶה בְּלֹא תַעֲשֶׂה וְאֵין בּוֹ כָרֵת. דִּבְרֵי רְבִּי יוּדָה. רְבִּי שִׁמְעוֹן אוֹמֵר. כָּל־שֶׁאֵין בּוֹ כָרֵת אֵין בּוֹ בְלֹא תַעֲשֶׂה. מוֹדֶה רְבִּי שִׁמְעוֹן בְּאִיסּוּר שֶׁהוּא אָסוּר. אִיסּוּרוֹ מָהוּ. רְבִּי יִרְמְיָה אָמַר. אִיסּוּרוֹ דְּבַר תּוֹרָה. רְבִּי יוֹנָה וְרְבִּי יוֹסֵה תְּרֵיהוֹן אָמְרִין. אִיסּוּרוֹ מִדִּבְרֵיהֶן. מַה טַעֲמֵיהּ דְּרְבִּי יוּדָה. לֹא יֵאָכֵל חָמֵץ. הַיּוֹם. מָה אֲנַן קַיָּימִין. אִם בְּתוֹךְ הַמּוֹעֵד. כְּבָר כָּתוּב [לֹא־תֹאכַל עָלָיו חָמֵץ]. אֶלָּא אִם אֵינוֹ עִנְיָין בְּתוֹךְ הַמּוֹעֵד תְּנֵיהוּ לְאַחַר הַמּוֹעֵד. מַה מְקַיֵּים רְבִּי שִׁמְעוֹן טַעֲמֵיהּ דְּרְבִּי יוּדָה. לֹא יֵאָכֵל חָמֵץ. הַיּוֹם. אָמַר רְבִּי בּוּן בַּר חִיָּיה. פָּתַר לָהּ כְּרְבִּי יוֹסֵי הַגְּלִילִי. דְּתַנֵּי. רְבִּי יוֹסֵי הַגְּלִילִי אוֹמֵר. אוֹמֵר אֲנִי שֶׁלֹּא הָיָה פֶּסַח בְּמִצְרַיִם אֶלָּא יוֹם אֶחָד בִּלְבַד. שֶׁנֶּאֱמַר לֹא יֵאָכֵל חָמֵץ. הַיּוֹם.

Who is the Tanna of *it should not be seen in your possession*[123]? Rebbi Jehudah, as it was stated[124]: He who eats leavened matter after the sixth hour[125], as well as leavened matter which was in existence during Passover violates a biblical prohibition but there is no extirpation, the words of Rebbi Jehudah. Rebbi Simeon says, anything for which there is no extirpation there is no biblical prohibition. Rebbi Simeon agrees about the prohibition that it is prohibited. What is its prohibition[126]? Rebbi Jeremiah said, its prohibition is a word of the Torah. Rebbi Jonah and Rebbi Yose both say, its prohibition is from their words. What is Rebbi Jehudah's reason? *No leavened matter may be eaten, today*[127]. Where do we hold? If during the holiday, it already is written, *you may not eat leavened matter with it*[128]. But if it does not refer to the time during the holiday, transfer it to the time after the holiday. How does Rebbi Simeon explain Rebbi Jehudah's reason, *no leavened matter may be eaten, today*? Rebbi Abun bar Ḥiyya said, he will explain if following Rebbi Yose the Galilean, as it was stated: [129]Rebbi Yose the Galilean says, I am saying that in Egypt the Passover was only one day as it was said, *no leavened matter may be eaten, today*.

123 The first part of Mishnah 2, which requires elimination of the Gentile's leavened matter for which the Jew is responsible.
124 Somewhat differently quoted in the Babli, 28a/b.
125 On the 14th of Nisan.
126 This is asked for R. Simeon. It is clear that R. Jehudah holds that the prohibition is biblical since he forbids leavened matter one hour before it becomes biblically forbidden.
127 *Ex.* 13:4-5. "Today" belongs to the next sentence.
128 *Deut* 16:3.
129 Tosephta 8:21, cf. Mishnah 9:4. Babli 28b; *Tanhuma Bo* 11; *Mekhilta dR. Ismael*

Bo 16 (p. 62), *dR. Simeon Bar Yohay, Bo* (p. 38 l. 15).

(29a line 1) לֹא יֵרָאֶה לְךָ. אִית תַּנָּיֵי תַנֵּי. לֹא יֵרָאֶה לְךָ. לְךָ אֵין אַתְּ רוֹאֶה. [אֲבָל] רוֹאֶה אַתְּ לַגָּבוֹהַּ. אִית תַּנָּיֵי תַנֵּי. אֲפִילוּ לַגָּבוֹהַּ. מָאן דְּאָמַר. לְךָ אֵין אַתְּ רוֹאֶה רוֹאֶה אַתְּ לַגָּבוֹהַּ. בְּשֶׁהֶקְדֵּישׁוֹ קוֹדֶם לְבִיעוּרוֹ. מָאן דְּאָמַר. אֲפִילוּ לַגָּבוֹהַּ. כְּשֶׁהֶקְדֵּישׁוֹ לְאַחַר בִּיעוּרוֹ. אָמַר רִבִּי בּוּן בַּר חִיָּיה קוֹמֵי רִבִּי זְעוּרָא. תִּיפְתָּר בַּקֳּדָשִׁים שֶׁהוּא חַיָּיב בַּאֲחֲרָיוּתָן כְּרִבִּי שִׁמְעוֹן.

לֹא יֵרָאֶה לְךָ. [אִית תַּנָּיֵי תַנֵּי.] לְךָ אֵין אַתְּ רוֹאֶה. רוֹאֶה אַתְּ בִּפְלַטְיָא. אִית תַּנָּיֵי תַנֵּי. אֲפִילוּ בִּפְלַטְיָא. מָאן דְּאָמַר. לְךָ אֵין אַתְּ רוֹאֶה רוֹאֶה אַתְּ בִּפְלַטְיָא. בְּשֶׁהִבְקִירוֹ קוֹדֶם לְבִיעוּרוֹ. מָאן דְּאָמַר. אֲפִילוּ בְּפַלַטְיָא. בְּשֶׁהִבְקִירוֹ לְאַחַר בִּיעוּרוֹ. אָמַר רִבִּי בּוּן בַּר חִיָּיה.. תִּיפְתָּר בַּקֳּדָשִׁים וגו'.

הִבְקִיר חֲמֵצוֹ בִּשְׁלֹשָׁה עָשָׂר לְאַחַר הַפֶּסַח מַהוּ. רִבִּי יוֹחָנָן אָמַר. אָסוּר. רִבִּי שִׁמְעוֹן בֶּן לָקִישׁ אָמַר. מוּתָּר. מָתִיב רִבִּי יוֹחָנָן לְרִבִּי שִׁמְעוֹן בֶּן לָקִישׁ. אֵין אַתְּ מוֹדֶה לִי מִשֵּׁשׁ שָׁעוֹת וּלְמַעְלָן שֶׁהוּא אָסוּר. אָמַר לֵיהּ. תַּמָּן אִיסּוּרוֹ גָרַם לוֹ. הָכָא מַה אִית לָךְ [לְמֵימַר]. אָמַר רִבִּי יוֹסֵה לְרִבִּי פִּינְחָס. נְהִיר אַתְּ כַּד הֲוֵינָן אֲמָרִין. אַתְיָיא לְרִבִּי יוֹחָנָן כְּרִבִּי יוֹסֵה. וּדְרִבִּי שִׁמְעוֹן בֶּן לָקִישׁ כְּרִבִּי מֵאִיר. אֵינָהּ כֵּן. אֶלָּא רִבִּי יוֹחָנָן חֲשַׁשׁ לְהַעֲרָמָה. וְרִבִּי שִׁמְעוֹן בֶּן לָקִישׁ לֹא חֲשַׁשׁ לְהַעֲרָמָה. מַה נָפַק מִבֵּינֵיהוֹן. נָפְלָה עָלָיו מַפּוֹלֶת. מָאן דְּאָמַר. הַעֲרָמָה. לֵית כָּאן הַעֲרָמָה. וְהוּא מוּתָּר. מָאן דְּאָמַר. זְכִיָּה. לֵית כָּאן זְכִיָּה. וְהוּא אָסוּר. הַכֹּל מוֹדִין כְּגַר שֶׁמֵּת וּבִיזְבְּזוּ יִשְׂרָאֵל אֶת נְכָסָיו. מָאן דְּאָמַר. הַעֲרָמָה. מוּתָּר. וּמָאן דְּאָמַר. זְכִיָּה. מוּתָּר.

It should not be seen in your possession[92]. There are Tannaim who state, *it should not be seen in your possession*, yours you may not see, [but][130] you may see Heaven's. There are Tannaim who state, not even Heaven's. He who said, yours you may not see, you may see Heaven's, if its dedication precedes its elimination[131]. He who said, not even Heaven's, if its dedication is after its elimination. Rebbi Abun bar Ḥiyya said before Rebbi Ze`ira: Explain it about *sancta* for which he is responsible in case of alienation following Rebbi Simeon[132].

It should not be seen in your possession. There are Tannaim who state, *it should not be seen in your possession*, yours you may not see; you may see it in the street[133]; there are Tannaim who state, not even if in the street;. He who says, yours you may not see, you may see it in the street, if his renunciation of ownership precedes its elimination[134]; he who said, not even in the street, if his renunciation of ownership follows its elimination. Rebbi Abun bar Ḥiyya said, explain it for *sancta*[135], etc.

If he declared his leavened matter ownerless on the thirteenth; what is its status after Passover[136]? Rebbi Johanan said, it is forbidden; Rebbi Simeon ben Laqish said, it is permitted. Rebbi Johanan objected to Rebbi Simeon ben Laqish. Do you not agree with me that it is forbidden after noontime[137]? He answered, there its prohibition caused it; here what can you say[138]? Rebbi Yose said to Rebbi Phineas, do you remember that we said, Rebbi Johanan follows Rebbi Yose, and Rebbi Simeon ben Laqish Rebbi Meïr[139]? It is not so. Only Rebbi Johanan is concerned about cunning[140], but Rebbi Simeon ben Laqish is not concerned about cunning. What is the difference? If debris fell on it. He who says cunning, there is no cunning and it is permitted. He who said acquisition[141], there is no acquisition and it is prohibited. Everybody agrees about a proselyte who died[142] and the Jews plundered his property. For him who says cunning, it is permitted, and for him who says acquisition, it is permitted[142*].

130 Corrector's addition. As the sentence after the next shows, the addition is unnecessary.

131 Everybody agrees that Temple property is exempt from elimination. A person may dedicate his leavened matter to the Temple, to be sold and the proceeds used for the service. If he did this before noontime on the 14th, the dedication is valid. But if it was done on or after noontime, the matter already is (rabbinically) forbidden for usufruct, it is worthless, and nothing worthless can be dedicated to the Temple. The dedication is invalid and he is guilty of disregarding the obligation to eliminate leavened matter in a timely fashion.

132 It seems that here also one refers to matters dedicated to the Temple, which are *sancta* as long as they are not redeemed for the benefit of the Temple. It is assumed that the dedication was not "this is given to the Temple" but "I will give a certain value to the Temple". In the latter case only actual delivery fulfills the vow and according to R. Simeon [Mishnah *Bava qamma* 7:5 (Note 56)] even after dedication it remains the votary's personal property until delivered.

133 Greek πλατεῖα (sc., ὁδός) "a wide (road)", equivalent of Hebrew רחוב.

134 If the leavened matter was abandoned in the street and declared ownerless before noontime of the 14th. However, this statement has to be qualified, cf. Note 139.

135 This sentence is a mindless copy from the preceding paragraph and is to be deleted.

136 It is clear that it is forbidden during Passover (unless picked up by a Gentile before the holiday). May the original owner go back and pick it up again after the holiday?

137 How can the prohibition be removed automatically?

138 Even on the afternoon of the 14th it only is forbidden if no Gentile picked it up;

it never was intrinsically forbidden; if the outside cause disappeared, the prohibition disappeared.

139 The disagreement of RR. Yose (ben Halaphta) and Meïr is in *Peah* 6:1 (Notes 18,19) where R. Meïr holds that an object becomes ownerless as soon as it is abandoned in a public place and declared to be ownerless, whereas for R. Yose it remains the original owner's property until picked up by another person.

140 The owner might circumvent the obligation of elimination by declaring it ownerless but from the start intend to take it back after the holiday.

141 For R. Yose the leavened matter remains the owner's property. He does not have to dig it out to burn since it is neither visible nor can it be used, but it remains permanently prohibited if it would be dug out afterwards.

142 If he failed to contract a Jewish marriage and start a Jewish family, his estate has no heirs and has the status of abandoned property. Cf. *Bava qamma* 9:15 Notes 111,121.

142* If the proselyte died before Passover and Jews took possession of his estate with leavened matter after Passover, the estate became ownerless by itself. The suspicion of cunning does not apply. Since a dead person cannot own anything, even R. Yose must agree that it was not property of a Jew during Passover; it is permitted.

(29a line 21) תַּמָּן תַּנִּינָן. עֶבֶד שֶׁעֲשָׂאוֹ רַבּוֹ אַפּוֹתֵיקִי לַאֲחֵרִים וְשִׁיחְרְרוֹ. [שׁוּרַת הַדִּין אֵין הָעֶבֶד חַיָּיב כְּלוּם. אֶלָּא מִפְּנֵי תִקּוּן הָעוֹלָם כּוֹפִין אֶת רַבּוֹ וְעוֹשֶׂה אוֹתוֹ בֶּן חוֹרִין וְכוֹתֵב שְׁטָר עַל דָּמָיו. רַבָּן שִׁמְעוֹן בֶּן גַּמְלִיאֵל אוֹמֵר. אֵינוֹ כוֹתֵב אֶלָּא מְשַׁחְרֵר:] מִי מְשַׁחְרֵר. רַב אָמַר. בֵּין רַבּוֹ רִאשׁוֹן בֵּין רַבּוֹ אַחֲרוֹן. אָמַר רִבִּי יוֹחָנָן. אֵין לָךְ מְשַׁחְרֵר אֶלָּא רַבּוֹ רִאשׁוֹן בִּלְבָד. הָתִיב רִבִּי חַגַּי קוֹמֵי רִבִּי יוֹסֵה. מַתְנִיתָא פְּלִיגָא עַל רַב. יִשְׂרָאֵל שֶׁהִלְוָה אֶת הַנָּכְרִי עַל חֲמֵיצוֹ לְאַחַר הַפֶּסַח מוּתָּר בַּהֲנָייָה. אִין תֵּימַר. בִּרְשׁוּת יִשְׂרָאֵל הוּא. יְהֵא אָסוּר. מַה עָבַד לָהּ רַב. אָמַר רִבִּי יוּדָן. קַל הוּא בְשִׁיחְרוּר. כְּהָדָא דְתַנֵּי. הָעוֹשֶׂה עַבְדּוֹ אַפּוֹתֵיקִי. מְכָרוֹ אֵינוֹ מָכוּר. שִׁיחְרְרוֹ הֲרֵי זֶה מְשׁוּחְרָר. חֵיילֵיהּ דְּרִבִּי יוֹחָנָן מִן הָדָא. רַבָּן שִׁמְעוֹן בֶּן גַּמְלִיאֵל אוֹמֵר: אֵינוֹ כוֹתֵב אֶלָּא מְשַׁחְרֵר: אִילּוּ הַמַּשְׁעֲבֵּד שָׂדֶה לַחֲבֵירוֹ וְהָלַךְ וּמְכָרָהּ. שֶׁמָּא אֵין בַּעַל חוֹב בָּא וְטוֹרֵף. אָמַר רִבִּי אַבָּהוּ. פָּתַח לָנוּ רִבִּי יוֹחָנָן פֶּתַח מֵאִיר כְּאוֹרָה. לֹא מָצִינוּ עֶבֶד מִשְׁתַּחְרֵר וְחוֹזֵר וּמִשְׁתַּבֵּד. מֵעַתָּה לֹא יִכְתּוֹב שְׁטָר עַל דָּמָיו. אָמַר רִבִּי אִילָא. מוּטָב שֶׁיֹּאמַר לוֹ. תֵּן לִי מָאתַיִם זוּז שֶׁיֵּשׁ לִי בְיָדָךְ. וְעַל יֹאמַר לוֹ. עַבְדִּי אַתָּה. רַבָּנִין דְּקַיְסָרִין בְּשֵׁם רִבִּי נַסָא. אַתְיָא דְּרַבָּן שִׁמְעוֹן בֶּן גַּמְלִיאֵל כְּרִבִּי מֵאִיר. כְּמָה דְרִבִּי מֵאִיר קוֹנֵס בִּדְבָרִים. כֵּן רַבָּן שִׁמְעוֹן בֶּן גַּמְלִיאֵל קוֹנֵס בִּדְבָרִים. דְּתַנֵּי. [שְׁטָר] יֵשׁ בּוֹ רִבִּית קוֹנְסִין אוֹתוֹ וְאֵינוֹ גוֹבֶה לֹא אֶת הַקֶּרֶן וְלֹא אֶת הָרִיבִּית. דִּבְרֵי רִבִּי מֵאִיר. וַחֲכָמִים אוֹמְרִים. גּוֹבֶה אֶת הַקֶּרֶן וְאֵינוֹ גוֹבֶה אֶת הָרִבִּית.

There, we have stated: [143]"A slave whom his master gave as mortgage[144] to others and then freed him [in strict law does not owe anything, but for the public good one forces the master to formally manumit him and he writes a bond for his own value. Rabban Simeon ben Gamliel says, only the one who manumits writes.] Who frees? Rav says, either his first or his second master. Rebbi Joḥanan says, only his first master alone is able to free. Rebbi Ḥaggai objected before Rebbi Yose: Does not a *baraita* disagree with Rav? If a Jew gave a loan to a Gentile on the latter's leavened matter, it is permitted after Passover. If you say that the Jew has property rights in it, it would be forbidden. What does Rav do with this? Rebbi Yudan said, manumission is made easy, as it was stated: If somebody gives his slave as mortgage[144], if he sold him, he is not sold; if he freed him, he is freed. The strength of Rebbi Joḥanan is from the following: Rabban Simeon ben Gamliel says, only the manumittor writes. If somebody mortgaged his field to another, then went and sold it, can the creditor not come and foreclose? Rebbi Abbahu said, in this matter Rebbi Joḥanan opened for us a door to illuminate. We do not find that a slave can again be enslaved after having been freed. If that is so, he should not have to write a bond for his value! Rebbi Ila said, it is better that a person say to him, give me the 200 *zuz* which you owe me than say to him, you are my slave! The rabbis of Caesarea say in Rebbi Nasa's name: Rabban Simeon ben Gamliel follows Rebbi Meïr. Just as Rebbi Meïr imposes a fine for words, so Rabban Simeon ben Gamliel imposes a fine for words. As it was stated: With a bond documenting both principal and interest one can collect neither principal nor interest, the words of Rebbi Meïr. But the Sages say, one collects the principal but not the interest.

143 This paragraph is from *Gittin* 4:4 where the few differences in spelling are noted and which is explained there in Notes 75-78, 120-130.

144 Greek ὑποθήκη.

(29a line 40) רַבָּן שִׁמְעוֹן בֶּן גַּמְלִיאֵל אוֹמֵר כָּל־שֶׁאֵין הַכֶּלֶב יָכוֹל לַחֲפֵשׂ אַחֲרָיו: עַד אֵיכָן. רִבִּי אָבוּן רִבִּי יוֹחָנָן בְּשֵׁם רִבִּי שִׁמְעוֹן בֶּן יוֹצָדָק. עַד שְׁלֹשָׁה טְפָחִים.

"Rabban Simeon ben Gamliel says, only one which cannot be dug out by a dog.." How far[145]? Rebbi Abun, Rebbi Joḥanan in the name of Rebbi Simeon ben Joṣadaq: Up to three hand-breadths.

145 How far must one presume that a dog may dig?

(fol. 28b) **משנה ג**: הָאוֹכֵל תְּרוּמַת חָמֵץ בַּפֶּסַח בְּשׁוֹגֵג מְשַׁלֵּם קֶרֶן וָחֹמֶשׁ. בְּמֵזִיד פָּטוּר מִתַּשְׁלוּמִים וּמִדְּמֵי עֵצִים:

Mishnah 3: Somebody who eats leavened heave on Passover, if in error pays its value and a fifth[146], if intentionally is not liable for restitution even as value of wood[147].

146 A Non-Cohen who eats sanctified heave (which either was dedicated leavened before Passover or was dedicated unleavened but became leavened by itself on Passover) has to pay restitution to the priests together with a biblically ordained surcharge; Mishnah *Terumot* 6:1 Note 1.

147 Intentional desecration of heave (e. g., used as food by a Non-Cohen) is too great a sin to be forgiven for just a monetary fine (Mishnah *Terumot* 7:1 Note 2). Also, while the restitution money and the fine for inadvertent consumption are *sancta*, the restitution for intentionally consumed heave is profane (*loc. cit.*) and therefore has to follow the rules of civil debts. Since leavened matter on Passover is forbidden for usufruct, it has no monetary value, not even as fuel to be burned.

(29a line 42) **הלכה ג**: תַּנֵּי. רִבִּי שִׁמְעוֹן בֶּן אֶלְעָזָר אוֹמֵר מִשּׁוּם רִבִּי שִׁמְעוֹן בֶּן יוֹצָדָק. מַתְנִיתָא בְּשֶׁהִפְרִישָׁהּ מַצָּה וְנִתְחַמְּצָה. אֲבָל אִם הִפְרִישָׁהּ חָמֵץ לֹא בְדָא. הִפְרִישׁ מַצָּה עַל חָמֵץ. אָמַר רִבִּי זְעוּרָה. כָּל־תְּרוּמָה שֶׁאֵינָהּ מַתֶּרֶת אֶת הַשְּׁיָרִים לַאֲכִילָה אֵינָהּ תְּרוּמָה. [אֲפִילוּ] הִפְרִישׁ חָמֵץ עַל מַצָּה. אָמַר רִבִּי זְעוּרָה. מֵאַחַר שֶׁאִילוּ מִינָהּ עָלֶיהָ אֵינָהּ תְּרוּמָה. וַאֲפִילוּ הֵימִינָהּ לְמָקוֹם אַחֵר אֵינָהּ תְּרוּמָה.

Halakhah 3: It was stated: Rebbi Simeon ben Eleazar[148] says in the name of Rebbi Simeon ben Joṣadaq: Our Mishnah if he separated it as unleavened and it became leavened[149]. But if he separated it leavened, it does not apply[150]. If he separated unleavened for leavened? Rebbi Ze`ira said, any heave which does not permit the remainder as food is no heave[151]. [Even][152] if he separated leavened for unleavened? Rebbi Ze`ira said, since if he gave from its kind it would not be heave, and even if he gives from this kind for another place it is not heave[153].

148 This name tradition raises serious questions. While it is likely that the young R. Simeon ben Joṣadaq (of the generation of transition from Tannaim to Amoraim) knew the very old R. Simeon ben Eleazar (a 5th generation Tanna), it is most unlikely that the latter would formulate a tradition in the former's name. Also this would be the only statement of R. Simeon ben Joṣadaq in the Talmudim not transmitted by his student R.

Johanan.

149 On Passover (Babli 32a). It seems that the Yerushalmi agrees with the Babli that leavened heave dedicated before Passover is included though it should have been burned if not consumed by the 14th of Nisan.

150 Giving leavened heave on Passover is impossible. Since leavened matter is forbidden for usufruct, giving leavened heave is giving nothing; nothing cannot be heave.

151 Since leavened matter may not be eaten on Passover, and is worthless; giving heave for it does not change its status. But heave is given in order to make the remainder of the food available for profane use.

152 Unnecessary addition by the corrector.

153 Since leavened matter cannot be used for leavened matter (Note 150) it cannot be used in this capacity for any other matter.

(29 line 47) (עירס) אַרְבַּעַת רְבָעִים בִּפְנֵי עַצְמָן וְחִימְּצָן. וְאַרְבַּעַת רְבָעִים בִּפְנֵי עַצְמָן וְעִירְבָן. אִם הִתְרוּ בוֹ מִשּׁוּם אוֹכֵל טֶבֶל. אֵינוֹ לוֹקֶה. מִשּׁוּם הָאוֹכֵל חָמֵץ בַּפֶּסַח. לוֹקֶה. אִיסּוּר חָמוּר חָל עַל אִיסּוּר קַל. וְאֵין אִיסּוּר קַל חָל עַל אִיסּוּר חָמוּר. אֲבָל אִם עִירְבָן וְאַחַר כָּךְ חִימְּצָן. אִם הִתְרוּ בוֹ מִשּׁוּם הָאוֹכֵל טֶבֶל. לוֹקֶה. מִשּׁוּם הָאוֹכֵל חָמֵץ בַּפֶּסַח. לוֹקֶה. אִיסּוּר חָמוּר חָל עַל אִיסּוּר קַל. וְאֵין אִיסּוּר קַל חָל עַל אִיסּוּר חָמוּר.

עָשָׂה כְרִי וְהִשְׁתַּחֲוָה לוֹ וּמֵירְחוֹ וְאַחַר כָּךְ אֲכָלוֹ. אִם הִתְרוּ בוֹ מִשּׁוּם אוֹכֵל טֶבֶל. אֵינוֹ לוֹקֶה. מִשּׁוּם הָאוֹכֵל עֲבוֹדָה זָרָה. לוֹקֶה. אִיסּוּר חָמוּר חָל עַל אִיסּוּר קַל. וְאֵין אִיסּוּר קַל חָל עַל אִיסּוּר חָמוּר. [אֲבָל אִם מֵירְחוֹ וְאַחַר כָּךְ הִשְׁתַּחֲוָה לוֹ. אִם הִתְרוּ בוֹ מִשּׁוּם אוֹכֵל טֶבֶל. לוֹקֶה. מִשּׁוּם עֲבוֹדָה זָרָה. לוֹקֶה. אִיסּוּר חָמוּר חָל עַל אִיסּוּר קַל. וְאֵין אִיסּוּר קַל חָל עַל אִיסּוּר חָמוּר.]

(If he beat)[154] four quarters for themselves and made them leavened, and another four quarters for themselves, and mixed them[155]. If one warned him[156] because of eating *tevel*, he is not flogged, because of one who eats leavened matter on Passover, he is flogged. A severe prohibition falls upon a minor prohibition but a minor prohibition does not fall on a severe prohibition[157]. But if he mixed them[158] and afterwards made them leavened, if one warned him because of eating *tevel*, he is flogged, because of one who eats leavened matter on Passover, he is flogged. A severe prohibition falls upon a minor prohibition but a minor prohibition does not fall on a severe prohibition.

If he made a grain heap and worshipped it[159], then smoothed it[160], and then ate from it: if one warned him because of eating *tevel*, he is not flogged, because of one who eats idolatrical food, he is flogged. A severe prohibition falls upon a minor prohibition but a minor prohibition does not fall on a

HALAKHAH THREE

severe prohibition. [But if he smoothed it[161] and then worshipped it, if one warned him because of eating *tevel*, he is flogged, because of idolatrical food, he is flogged. A severe prohibition falls upon a minor prohibition but a minor prohibition does not fall on a severe prohibition.]

154 The word was unnecessarily deleted by the corrector, who apparently did not understand it although it appears in both Talmudim.

155 A dough made of at least ⁵/₄ *qab* of flour (of the kinds enumerated in Mishnah 4) is subject to *hallah* (cf. Introduction to Tractate *Hallah*). Before *hallah* is removed, bread baked from the dough is *tevel* and forbidden as food. If the dough becomes leavened on Passover it becomes forbidden for usufruct and its consumption is a deadly sin. Therefore even if later it is mixed with another *qab* of new flour, there is no *tevel* since the first *qab* forbidden for usufruct cannot become *tevel*, and the second *qab* is less than the minimum quantity triggering the obligation of *hallah*. Clearly the mixture if forbidden as food and for usufruct because of the laws of Passover.

156 No criminal prosecution is possible unless the perpetrator was warned by two witnesses that his intended act would be criminal, and only if the nature of the crime was spelled out.

157 Cf. Babli 35b (last line), *Hulin* 101a.

158 Then the mixture is forbidden as *tevel*; if later it also becomes forbidden both as food and for usufruct as leavened on Passover, the prohibition of *tevel* is not removed.

159 It becomes forbidden for usufruct as object of pagan worship (*Deut.* 7:26).

160 If it were not forbidden as object of pagan worship, the completion of threshing by storage of the grain in a smooth heap causes the obligation of tithes; the heave of the tithe included in the tithe would make the entire heap *tevel* (Mishnah *Ma`serot* 1:6). But since worshipped grain is not food, it cannot become subject to tithe.

161 And now it becomes *tevel* as food. (Corrector's addition.)

(29a line 59) רִבִּי בּוּן בַּר חִייָה בָּעֵי. הָאוֹכֵל תְּרוּמַת חָמֵץ בַּפֶּסַח לְמִי הוּא מְשַׁלֵּם. תַּפְלוּגְתָּא דְרִבִּי יוֹחָנָן וּדְרִבִּי שִׁמְעוֹן בֶּן לָקִישׁ. דְּאִיתְפַּלְגוּן. הַגּוֹזֵל תְּרוּמָה מֵאֲבִי אִמּוֹ כֹהֵן. רִבִּי יוֹחָנָן אָמַר. מְשַׁלֵּם לַשֵּׁבֶט. רִבִּי שִׁמְעוֹן בֶּן לָקִישׁ אָמַר. מְשַׁלֵּם לְעַצְמוֹ. אָמַר רִבִּי מָנָא קוֹמֵי רִבִּי יוֹסֵה. מִסְתַּבְּרָא יוֹדֶה רִבִּי שִׁמְעוֹן בֶּן לָקִישׁ לְרִבִּי יוֹחָנָן בַּחוֹמֶשׁ שֶׁהוּא מְשַׁלֵּם לַשֵּׁבֶט. אָמַר לֵיהּ. אוֹף אֲנִי סוֹבֵר כֵּן. שֶׁכֵּן תְּרוּמָה טְמֵיאָה אֲסוּרָה לַשֵּׁבֶט. אָתָא רִבִּי יוֹסֵי בֵּירִבִּי בּוּן בְּשֵׁם רִבִּי אָחָא. אֲפִילוּ עָלֶיהָ פְּלִיגִין.

Rebbi Abun bar Hiyya asked: He who eats leavened heave on Passover[162], to whom does he pay? It is a disagreement between Rebbi Johanan and Rebbi Simeon ben Laqish, since the disagreed: One who robbed heave from his mother's father who was a Cohen[163], Rebbi Joḥanan said, he pays to the tribe[164]; Rebbi Simeon ben Laqish said, he pays to himself[165]. Rebbi Mana said before Rebbi Yose: It is reasonable that Rebbi Simeon ben Laqish agree with Rebbi Joḥanan about the fifth that he has to pay it to the tribe[166]. He told him, I also do agree with this, since impure heave is forbidden to the tribe[167]. There came Rebbi Yose ben Rebbi Abun in the name of Rebbi Aḥa: Even in this case they disagree[167*].

162 Where the Mishnah requires restitution even though it is prohibited for usufruct.

163 When the grandfather dies and the grandson from an Israel father is the only heir.

164 Even though he is the legal heir of the Cohen, and if he had not stolen the heave he would have inherited it and could sell to a Cohen, he is forced to give it away but he has the right to choose the recipient.

165 He must separate heave, which becomes a *sanctum* and is forbidden to any layman, including himself. He may then sell the heave to a Cohen who will offer little money since there are very few competitors for heave food.

166 Since the additional fifth is a fine, it is unreasonable to assume that he may have usufruct from it other than the goodwill which he gets from the recipient of his heave.

167 Since impure heave may only be used as fuel it is of little value; nevertheless illegitimate use triggers the obligation of paying the fine.

167* Since for R. Simeon ben Laqish the Mishnah is purely rabbinic.

(29a line 65) רִבִּי יוֹסֵה בָּעֵי. הַנֶּהֱנֶה מִן הַהֶקְדֵּשׁ פָּחוּת מִשְׁוֵה פְרוּטָה. [מַהוּ שֶׁיְהֵא חַיָּיב בַּתַּשְׁלוּמִין. (אָמַר לֵיהּ.) נִשְׁמְעִינַהּ מִן הָדָא. וְאֵת אֲשֶׁר חָטָא מִן־הַקּוֹדֶשׁ יְשַׁלֵּם. פְּרָט לְפָחוּת מִשְׁוֵה פְרוּטָה. אִית תַּנָּיֵי תַנֵּי. לְרַבּוֹת. (מָאן דְּאָמַר פְּרָט) [לַתַּשְׁלוּמִין. מָאן דְּאָמַר. פְּרָט. לְפָחוּת מִשְׁוֵה פְרוּטָה לַתַּשְׁלוּמִין] לְקָרְבָּן. מָאן דְּאָמַר. לְרַבּוֹת. בַּתַּשְׁלוּמִין. כְּנָה דְּתֵימַר תַּמָּן. פָּחוּת מִשְׁוֵה פְרוּטָה מֵזִיד. אַף עַל פִּי שֶׁאֵינוֹ מְשַׁלֵּם חוֹמֶשׁ וְאָשָׁם יְשַׁלֵּם לַשֵּׁבֶט. וְאָמַר אוֹף הָכָא כֵן. אָמְרִין חֲבֵרַיָּא קוֹמֵי רִבִּי יוֹסֵה. וְלָאו מַתְנִיתָא הִיא. הָאוֹכֵל תְּרוּמַת חָמֵץ בַּפֶּסַח. שׁוֹגֵג מְשַׁלֵּם קֶרֶן וָחוֹמֶשׁ. מֵזִיד פָּטוּר מִתַּשְׁלוּמִים וּמִדְּמֵי הָעֵצִים: אָמַר לוֹן. תַּמָּן אֵינוֹ רָאוּי לְהַשְׁלִים עָלֶיהָ. בְּרַם הָכָא הוּא רָאוּי לְהַשְׁלִים עָלֶיהָ.

Rebbi Yose asked, if somebody benefited from Temple property less than the value of a *peruṭah*[168], is he liable for reimbursement? (He said to him.)[169] Let us hear from the following: *What he appropriated from sancta he has to repay*[170], except what is less than the value of a *peruṭah*. There are Tannaim who state, to add. (He who said except, for) [he who said "except what is less than the value of a *perutah*" for reimbursement¹⁷¹ and] sacrifice. He who said "to add", for reimbursement¹⁷². As you are saying there¹⁷²*, intentionally less than the value of a *perutah*, even though he does not pay the fifth and a reparation sacrifice he has to pay to the tribe, one says the same here. The colleagues said before Rebbi Yose, is that not a Mishnah? "Somebody who eats leavened heave on Passover, if in error pays its value and a fifth¹⁴⁶, if intentionally he is not liable for restitution even as value of wood¹⁴⁷"? He told them, there it is impossible to complete¹⁷³, but here it is possible to complete.

168 Which therefore cannot be claimed in court and there is no coin with which to pay.
169 Addition by the corrector; to be deleted.
170 *Lev.* 5:16. This seems to exclude amounts smaller than the smallest coin in circulation since such an amount cannot be paid.
171 *Sifra Hovah (Wayyiqra II) Parashah* 11(7). The argument there is based on the expression *from sancta*, even a minute part.
172 While is cannot be paid for in coin, it can be restituted in kind. Everybody agrees that no sacrifice as prescribed in 5:15 is due in this case. (The scribe's text, in parentheses, is preferable.)
172* Appropriating less than the value of a *perutah* from *sancta* does not trigger the obligation to pay an additional fifth since no amount less that a *perutah* can be invoiced.
173 Since leavened matter on Passover is worthless, rules about it cannot be invoked in discussions about money's worth.

(29d line 75) שׁוֹגֵג בִּתְרוּמָה וּמֵזִיד בְּחָמֵץ. שׁוֹגֵג בִּתְרוּמָה וּמֵזִיד בְּנָזִיר. שׁוֹגֵג בִּתְרוּמָה וּמֵזִיד בְּיוֹם הַכִּיפּוּרִים. אִין תִּפְתְּרִינָהּ לִשְׁנֵי דְבָרִים. נִיחָא. וְאִין תִּפְתְּרִינָהּ לְדָבָר אֶחָד. מַחֲלוֹקֶת רִבִּי יוֹחָנָן וְרִבִּי שִׁמְעוֹן בֶּן לָקִישׁ.

In error for heave and intentional for leavened matter, in error for heave and intentional for nazir, in error for heave and intentional for the Day of Atonement. If one explains it with two things, it is fine. If one explains it for one, this is the disagreement of Rebbi Johanan and Rebbi Simeon ben Laqish¹⁷⁴.

174 This text is copied from *Ketubot* 3:1 (after Note 33); there is a somewhat defective copy in *Terumot* 7:1, Notes 47-51.

The disagreement between R. Johanan and R. Simeon ben Laqish referred to here is not the one quoted earlier, but the one discussed in *Ketubot* and *Terumot*, whether a criminal conviction precludes monetary claims arising from the same case or not. If one holds that with one action two different laws have been broken, each infraction is punished according to its separate rules and everybody agrees that for heave he has to pay. But if one holds that for one action there can be only one punishment, he has to pay only following R. Johanan.

(fol. 28b) **משנה ד**: אֵילוּ דְבָרִים שֶׁאָדָם יוֹצֵא בָהֶן יְדֵי חוֹבָתוֹ בַפֶּסַח. בַּחִטִּים וּבַשְּׂעוֹרִים וּבַכּוּסְמִין וּבְשִׁיבֹּלֶת שׁוּעָל וּבְשִׁיפוֹן וּבַדְּמַאי וּבְמַעֲשֵׂר רִאשׁוֹן שֶׁנִּיטְּלָה תְרוּמָתוֹ וּבְמַעֲשֵׂר שֵׁנִי וְהֶקְדֵּשׁ שֶׁנִּפְדּוּ וְהַכֹּהֲנִים בַּחַלָּה וּבַתְּרוּמָה. אֲבָל לֹא בַטֶּבֶל וְלֹא בְמַעֲשֵׂר רִאשׁוֹן שֶׁלֹּא נִיטְּלָה תְרוּמָתוֹ וְלֹא בְמַעֲשֵׂר שֵׁנִי וְהֶקְדֵּשׁ שֶׁלֹּא נִפְדּוּ. חַלּוֹת תּוֹדָה וּרְקִיקֵי נָזִיר עֲשָׂאָן לְעַצְמוֹ אֵין יוֹצֵא בָהֶן. עֲשָׂאָן לִמְכּוֹר לַשּׁוּק יוֹצֵא בָהֶן:

Mishnah 4: With the following one fulfills his obligation[175] on Passover: With wheat, and with barley, and with spelt, and with rye, and with fox grain[176], and with *demay*[177], and with First Tithe whose heave was removed[178], and with Second Tithe or *sancta* which were redeemed[179], and the Cohanim with *hallah* and heave[180]. But not with *tevel*[181], nor with First Tithe whose heave was not removed[182], nor with Second tithe or *sancta* which were not redeemed[183]. Flat cakes for a thanksgiving offering and wafers of a *nazir*[184], if he made them for himself one cannot fulfill his obligation[185]; if he made them to sell on the market one fulfills his obligation[186].

175 While on the holiday of Passover there only is a prohibition of leavened matter, on the first night there is a positive commandment (*Ex.* 12:18) to consume azyme bread (cf. the author's *The Scholar's Haggadah*, Northvale NJ 1995, p. 329). Only bread made from cereal which can become leavened is admitted; by tradition only the grains enumerated in the sequel qualify in this respect.

176 According to Rashi, oats. Maimonides in his Commentary to *Kilaim* 1:1: prairie barley.

177 Grain of which it is not known whether tithe was removed. Since one is permitted to feed *demay* to the poor and passing travellers, it is profane food by biblical standards.

178 This is totally profane in the hand of the Levite.

179 Once redeemed all sanctity is transferred to the redemption money; the produce reverts to profane status.

180 These are *sancta*, but since the Cohanim are obliged to consume them, they may consume them to fulfill their obligation.

181 Grain after threshing and storage, before heave and tithe was taken. It is forbidden as food; it would be sinful to use it for the biblical obligation.

182 This statement is not really necessary since it is *tevel*.

183 They have to be consumed in purity in Jerusalem; one actlon cannot be used to satisfy two distinct biblical obligations.

184 These are obligatory additions to the

sacrifices; *Lev.* 7:12, *Num.* 6:15.
185 Since then they are *sancta*.

186 They are profane; only dedication by the buyer might make them *sancta*.

(29b line 2) **הלכה ד**: כְּתִיב וְהָיָה בַּאֲכָלְכֶם מִלֶּחֶם הָאָרֶץ תָּרִימוּ תְרוּמָה לַיָי. הָיִיתִי אוֹמֵר. יְהוּ כָל־הַדְּבָרִים חַיָּיבִין בַּחַלָּה. תַּלְמוּד לוֹמַר מִלֶּחֶם. וְלֹא כָל־לֶחֶם. אִם מִלֶּחֶם לֹא כָל־לֶחֶם. אֵין לִי אֶלָּא לְחִטִּים וְלִשְׂעוֹרִים בִּלְבָד. [שְׁאָר מִינִין מְנַיִין.] תַּלְמוּד לוֹמַר רֵאשִׁית עֲרִסוֹתֵיכֶם רִיבָה. וְרִיבָה אֶת הַכֹּל. רִבִּי יוֹסֵה בְשֵׁם רִבִּי שִׁמְעוֹן תַּנֵּי רִבִּי יִשְׁמָעֵאל כֵּן. רִבִּי יוֹנָה רִבִּי זְעוּרָא רִבִּי שִׁמְעוֹן בֶּן לָקִישׁ בְּשֵׁם רִבִּי יִשְׁמָעֵאל.

1 הייתי אומר | **ח** יכול   2 לא **ח** ולא   3 לחטים ולשעורים | **ח** חטין ושעורין   שאר מינין | **ח** כוסמין שיבולת שועל ושיפון   4 את **ח** - יוסה | **ח** יוסי   זעורא | **ח** זעירא

Halakhah 4: [187]It is written[188]: *It shall be when you eat of the bread of the Land you shall lift a heave*[189] *for the Eternal.* I could think that everything[190] is subject to *hallah*; the verse says *of the bread* but not all bread[191]. If *of the bread* and not all bread, that might be only wheat and barley[192]? From where the other kinds? The verse says *the first of your dough*[192], this includes[193]. Does it include everything? Rebbi Yose in the name of Rebbi Simeon:[194] Rebbi Ismael stated this. Rebbi Jonah, Rebbi Ze`ira, Rebbi Simeon ben Laqish, in the name of Rebbi Ismael[195].

187 This and the the following paragraphs up to Note 207 are also in *Ḥallah* 1:1, Notes 6-21, **ח**.
188 *Num.* 15:19.
189 This is *hallah* which follows the rules of heave.
190 Since לֶחֶם also means food in general.
191 Which are the main bread grains.
192 *Num.* 15:20,21.

193 Not only rye, spelt, and fox grain but also rice and millet would be included.
194 This must be R. Simeon ben Laqish. R. Yose asserts that R. Ismael accepted the inference as valid; "dough" includes every bread-dough made from grains similar to wheat and barley. R. Aqiba's interpretation of these verses is reported in *Sifry Num.* 110.
195 Confirmed this tradition.

(29b line 8) אָמַר רִבִּי מָנָא. אֲזָלִית לְקַיְסָרִין וּשְׁמָעִית רִבִּי אֲחַוְנָא בַּר זְעוּרָא (אָמַר וַאֲנָא) [אַבָּא] הֲוָה אָמַר לָהּ בְּשֵׁם רִבִּי יִשְׁמָעֵאל. נֶאֱמַר לֶחֶם בַּפֶּסַח וְנֶאֱמַר לֶחֶם בַּחַלָּה. מַה לֶּחֶם שֶׁנֶּאֱמַר בַּפֶּסַח דָּבָר שֶׁהוּא בָא לִידֵי מַצָּה וְחָמֵץ. אַף לֶחֶם שֶׁנֶּאֱמַר בַּחַלָּה דָּבָר שֶׁהוּא בָא לִידֵי מַצָּה וְחָמֵץ. וּבֶדְקוּ וּמָצְאוּ שֶׁאֵין לָךְ בָּא לִידֵי מַצָּה וְחָמֵץ אֶלָּא חֲמֵשֶׁת הַמִּינִין בִּלְבָד. וּשְׁאָר כָּל־הַמִּינִין אֵינָן בָּאִין לִידֵי מַצָּה וְחָמֵץ אֶלָּא לִיגֵי סֵירָחוֹן.

1 אחווא בר | **ח** אחווה ור' [אבא] | **ח** ואבא   לה **ח** ליה   4 המינין | **ח** הדברים

Rebbi Mana said, I went to Caesarea and heard Rebbi Ahava ben Rebbi Ze`ira[196] (who said, I) [my father] said in the name of Rebbi Ismael[197]: "Bread" is mentioned for Passover[198] and "bread" is mentioned for *hallah*[199]. Since bread mentioned in a discussion of Passover is something that can be either *mazzah* or leavened, bread mentioned for *hallah* must be something that can be either *mazzah* or leavened. They checked and found that only the five kinds can be either *mazzah* or leavened; all others cannot be *mazzah*[200] or leavened but would spoil.

196 The son of R. Ze`ira who had been a *baraita* teacher in his father's academy.

197 A similar text *Sifry Num.* 110. As regards Passover only, Babli *Pesahim* 35a, *Mekhilta deR. Ismael Bo* Chap. 8, 17; *Sifry Num.* 146.

198 *Deut.* 16:2.

199 *Num.* 15:19.

200 Rice cakes, while unleavened, cannot be called *mazzah* since rice bread (not containing gluten) does not qualify as leavened bread. If left standing with leavening it will not rise but spoil.

(20b line 15) רִבִּי יוֹחָנָן בֶּן נוּרִי אָמַר. קְרָמִית חַיֶּיבֶת בַּחַלָּה. שֶׁהִיא בָאָה לִידֵי מַצָּה וְחָמֵץ. וְרַבָּנִין אֲמְרִי. אֵינָהּ בָאָה לִידֵי מַצָּה וְחָמֵץ. וְיִבְדְּקוּהָ. עַל עִיקַר בְּדִיקָתָהּ הֵן חוֹלְקִין. רִבִּי יוֹחָנָן בֶּן נוּרִי אָמַר. בְּדָקוּהָ וּמָצְאוּ אוֹתָהּ שֶׁהִיא בָאָה לִידֵי מַצָּה וְחָמֵץ. וְרַבָּנִין אֲמְרִין. בְּדָקוּהָ וְלֹא מָצְאוּ אוֹתָהּ שֶׁהִיא בָאָה לִידֵי מַצָּה וְחָמֵץ.

1 ר' | ח תני. אמר ר' | ח אמר | ח ר' - שהיא באה | ח ר' יוחנן בן נורי אמר. באה היא 2 ורבניין | G ורבנן אמרי | Gח אמרין ויבדקוה | G ויבדקוהא הן חולקין | G חלוקין 3 ומצאו אותה | Gח ומצאוה ורבניין | G ורבנן אמרין | Gח אמרי בדקוה | G בדקוהא מצאו אותה | G מצאוה

תַּמָּן תַּנֵּינָן. תַּפּוּחַ שֶׁרִיסְּקוֹ וּנְתָנוֹ לְתוֹךְ עִיסָה וְחִימְּצָה. הֲרֵי זוֹ אֲסוּרָה. [שְׂעוֹרִין שֶׁנָּפְלוּ לְתוֹךְ הַבּוֹר שֶׁל מַיִם. אַף עַל פִּי שֶׁהִבְאִישׁוּ מֵימָיו. מוּתָּרִין:] רִבִּי יוֹסֵי אוֹמֵר. מוּתָּר. רִבִּי אָחָא רִבִּי אַבָהוּ בְּשֵׁם רִבִּי יוֹסֵה בַּר חֲנִינָה. מַה פְּלִיגִין. בְּמַחֲמֵץ בְּמֵימָיו. אֲבָל בִּמְחַמֵּץ בְּגוּפוֹ דִּבְרֵי הַכֹּל מוּתָּר. רִבִּי יוֹסֵי כְּדַעְתֵּיהּ. כַּמָּה דוּ אָמַר תַּמָּן. אֵין תַּבְשִׁילוֹ תַבְשִׁיל בָּרוּר. כָּךְ הוּא אָמַר הָכָא. אֵין חִמּוּצוֹ חָמֵץ בָּרוּר.

1 תפוח | G תפס' וחימצה | ח וחימיצה שעורין ... מוותרין | Gח - יוסי או' מותר | G יוסה מתיר אחא | G אחה 3 יוסה | ח יוסי בר | Gח בן מה פליגין | ח מפליגין במחמץ | G במחמיץ (2) 4 יוסי | G יוסה כמה | ח - דו | G דהוא כך | ח וכן אמ' | ח או' 5 הכא | G הכה חמוצו | Gח חימוצו[201] חמץ | G חימוץ

It was stated[202]: "Rebbi Johanan ben Nuri said, *qeramit*[203] is obligated for *hallah*." Rebbi Johanan ben Nuri said, [204]it can be either *mazzah* or leavened., but the rabbis say, it cannot be either *mazzah* or leavened. Let them check! They disagree about the outcome of the checking. Rebbi Johanan ben Nuri said, they checked and found that it can be either *mazzah* or leavened., but the rabbis say, they checked and did not find that it can be either *mazzah* or leavened.

There[205], we have stated: "If a mashed apple is added to dough which soured, [the dough] is forbidden. But if barley grains fell into a cistern of water, even though they made it stink, [the water] is permitted[206]. It was stated: Rebbi Yose says, it is permitted. Rebbi Aḥa, Rebbi Abbahu in the name of Rebbi Yose ben Ḥanina: They disagree when it becomes sour from the juice [of the apple]. But if it becomes sour from its solid substance it is permitted according to everybody[207]. Rebbi Yose stays with his opinion; just as he says there, its cooking is not clearly cooking[208], so he says here, its souring is not clearly souring.

---

201 The word was added by the corrector; one may assume that the scribe would have adopted the Yerushalmi spelling of the *Hallah* text.

202 Tosephta 2:17, *Hallah* 1:1; Babli 35a.

203 According to the Geonim (*Ozar Hageonim Pesahim* p. 33) a grain growing wild among reeds in swamps, used as human food in times of famine. In the opinion of I. Löw, (*Flora der Juden* 1, p. 703) *Glyceria fluitans*, a grain preferring swampy ground, frequently used for animal feed, also for soups and flour. {Also cf. Latin *gramen, -inis, n.* "grass, dog's grass" (*Plin. Hist. Nat.* 24,19,118, §178) (E. G.)}.

204 Here starts a Genizah text edited by L Ginzberg (*Yerushalmi Fragments from the Genizah*, New York 1909, pp. 102-115.)

205 Mishnah *Terumot* 10:2. The paragraph also appears there, Notes 15-19, as well as in *Šabbat* 3, Notes 67-70 with the mention of "cooking" and "souring" switched correctly.

206 Sentence added unnecessarily by the corrector from the Mishnah in *Terumot*. The discussion only refers to the first sentence.

207 Even the anonymous Sages admit that dry mixing of a mashed apple with flour will not induce souring.

208 R. Yose permits to use the sun's rays to make poached eggs on the Sabbath. Mishnah *Šabbat* 3:3.

(29b line 25) תַּנֵּי. פַּגָּה שֶׁטְּמָנָהּ בְּתֶבֶן וַחֲרָרָה שֶׁטְּמָנָהּ בְּגֶחָלִים. אִם הָיוּ מִקְצָתָן מְגוּלִּין נִיטָּלִין בַּשַּׁבָּת. וְאִם לָאו אֵין נִיטָּלִין.

1 בתבן | S בגפן G בטבל בגחלים | G בגחלין   2 אין | G אינן

²¹⁰It was stated: "An unripe fig which he hid in straw or a flat pita which he hid in coals may be taken on the Sabbath if they were partially uncovered, otherwise they may not be taken."

209 This paragraph does not belong here; it is copied from *Šabbat* 3 immediately following the text of the preceding paragraph (Note 71). *Kilaim* 1:9 (Note 167); Babli *Šabbat* 123a, *Eruvin* 77a.

(29b line 27) מְנַיִין שֶׁהַכֹּהֲנִים יוֹצְאִין יְדֵי חוֹבָתָן בַּחַלָּה וּבַתְּרוּמָה וְיִשְׂרָאֵל בְּמַעֲשֵׂר שֵׁינִי בְּפֶסַח. תַּלְמוּד לוֹמַר תֹּאכְלוּ מַצּוֹת. רִיבָה.

1 מניין G ומניין

יָכוֹל יֵצְאוּ חוֹבָתָן בַּבִּיכּוּרִים. תַּלְמוּד לוֹמַר בְּכֹל מוֹשְׁבוֹתֵיכֶם תֹּאכְלוּ מַצּוֹת׃ מַצָּה הַנֶּאֱכֶלֶת בְּכָל־מוֹשָׁב. יֵצְאוּ הַבִּיכּוּרִים שֶׁאֵינָן נֶאֱכָלִין בְּכָל־מוֹשָׁב. הֲתִיבוּן. הֲרֵי מַעֲשֵׂר שֵׁינִי הֲרֵי אֵינוֹ נֶאֱכָל בְּכָל־מוֹשָׁב. רָאוּי הוּא לְהִיפָּדוֹת וּלְהֵיאָכֵל בְּכָל־מוֹשָׁב. רִבִּי בּוּן בַּר חִייָה בָּעֵי. (מֵעַתָּה) הַלָּקוּחַ בְּכֶסֶף מַעֲשֵׂר שֶׁנִּיטְמָא כְרִבִּי יוּדָה [מָהוּ. דְּתַנֵּי. לָקוּחַ בְּכֶסֶף מַעֲשֵׂר שֶׁנִּיטְמָא יִפָּדֶה. רִבִּי יְהוּדָה אוֹמֵר. יִקָּבֵר. אָמְרוּ לוֹ לְרִבִּי יוּדָא. מָה אִם מַעֲשֵׂר שֵׁנִי עַצְמוֹ שֶׁנִּיטְמָא הֲרֵי הוּא נִפְדָּה. הַלָּקוּחַ בְּכֶסֶף מַעֲשֵׂר שֶׁנִּיטְמָא אֵינוֹ דִין שֶׁיִפָּדֶה. אָמַר לָהֶן. לֹא. אִם אֲמַרְתֶּם בְּמַעֲשֵׂר שֵׁנִי. שֶׁכֵּן הוּא נִפְדֶּה טָהוֹר בְּרִיחוּק מָקוֹם. תֹּאמְרוּ בַּלָּקוּחַ בְּכֶסֶף מַעֲשֵׂר. שֶׁאֵינוֹ נִפְדֶּה טָהוֹר בְּרִיחוּק מָקוֹם:] הוֹאִיל וְאֵינוֹ רָאוּי לְהִיפָּדוֹת וְלֵיאָכֵל בְּכָל־מוֹשָׁב אֵין יוֹצְאִין בּוֹ. רִבִּי שִׁמְעוֹן בֶּן לָקִישׁ בָּעֵי. מֵעַתָּה חַלַּת עִיסַת מַעֲשֵׂר שֵׁינִי בִּירוּשָׁלַם. הוֹאִיל וְאֵינָהּ רְאוּיָה לְהִיפָּדוֹת וּלְהֵיאָכֵל בְּכָל־מוֹשָׁב אֵין יוֹצְאִין בָּהּ.

2 שיני G | שני 3 להיפדות G | לפדות ולהיאכל G | ולאכל 4 כר' C | לר' C | - SG 8-4 [entire text] C } 8 ולאכל G | בכל מושב 9 ולהיאכל G | ולאכל

יָכוֹל יֵצְאוּ יְדֵי חוֹבָתָן בַּחַלּוֹת תּוֹדָה וּרְקִיקֵי נָזִיר. תַּלְמוּד לוֹמַר שִׁבְעַת יָמִים מַצּוֹת תֹּאכֵלוּ. מַצָּה הַנֶּאֱכֶלֶת כָּל־שִׁבְעָה. וְאֵין חַלּוֹת תּוֹדָה וּרְקִיקֵי נָזִיר נֶאֱכָלִין כָּל־שִׁבְעָה. רִבִּי יוֹנָה בְּשֵׁם רִבִּי שִׁמְעוֹן בֶּן לָקִישׁ. מִמָּה שֶׁנֶּאֱכָלוּ חַלּוֹת תּוֹדָה וּרְקִיקֵי נָזִיר בְּכָל־גְּבוּל אֶרֶץ יִשְׂרָאֵל לֹא צָרַךְ הַשּׁוֹנֶה לְהוֹצִיאָן מִמּוֹשָׁב. רִבִּי יוֹסֵה בְּשֵׁם רִבִּי שִׁמְעוֹן בֶּן לָקִישׁ. זֹאת אוֹמֶרֶת שֶׁנֶּאֱכָלוּ חַלּוֹת תּוֹדָה וּרְקִיקֵי נָזִיר בְּכָל־עָרֵי יִשְׂרָאֵל. לְפִיכָךְ לֹא צָרַךְ הַשּׁוֹנֶה לְהוֹצִיאָן מִמּוֹשָׁב. נִיחָא חַלּוֹת תּוֹדָה. וּרְקִיקֵי נָזִיר אֵינוֹ כֵן. אָמַר רִבִּי יוֹחָנָן. לֵית כָּאן נְזִירוּת. נְזִירוּת חוֹבָה הִיא. אָמַר רִבִּי בּוּן בַּר כָּהֲנָא. תִּיפְתָּר שֶׁקָּרְבָה חַטָּאתוֹ בְּשִׁילֹה. וְעוֹלָתוֹ וּשְׁלָמָיו בְּנוֹב וְגִבְעוֹן. רִבִּי חֲנַנְיָה רִבִּי עֶזְרָה בְּעוֹן קוֹמֵי רִבִּי מָנָא. לֹא כֵן אָמַר רִבִּי בְּשֵׁם רִבִּי יוֹסֵה. שַׁלְמֵי חֲגִיגָה הַבָּאִים בְּבָמָה כְּשֵׁירִים אֶלָּא שֶׁלֹּא עָלוּ לַבְּעָלִים לְשֵׁם חוֹבָה. אֶלָּא כְרִבִּי יְהוּדָה. דְּרִבִּי יְהוּדָה אָמַר. חַטָּאת וּפֶסַח לְיָחִיד בְּבָמָה גְדוֹלָה. אֵין חַטָּאת וּפֶסַח לְיָחִיד בְּבָמָה קְטַנָּה. לֹא אַתְיָא אֶלָּא כְרִבִּי שִׁמְעוֹן. דְּרִבִּי שִׁמְעוֹן אָמַר. כֵּיוָן שֶׁנִּזְרַק עָלָיו אֶחָד מִן הַדָּמִים הוּתַּר הַנָּזִיר לִשְׁתּוֹת בַּיַּיִן וְלִיטַּמֵּא לַמֵּתִים:

6 אינו G | ולא 7 תיפתר G | תפתר עזרה G | עזריה בעון G | בעה 8 הבאים G | הבאין כשירים G | כשירין 9 לשם G | משם יהודה G | יודה (2) 10 אתיא G | אתייה 11 הדמים G | הדמיו

From where that the Cohanim may fulfill their obligation with *hallah* or heave, and Israel with Second Tithe on Passover? The verse says, *you shall eat mazzot*[210]; this adds.

Could I think that they may fulfill their obligation with First Fruits? The verse says, *in **all** your dwelling places you shall eat mazzot*[211], *mazzah* which may be eaten at any dwelling place; this excludes First Fruits which are not eaten at any dwelling place[212]. They objected, but Second Tithe may not be eaten at any dwelling place[213]! It may be redeemed and be eaten at any dwelling place[214]. Rebbi Abun bar Ḥiyya asked: What was bought with tithe money and became impure, following Rebbi Jehudah, [215][what is its status? As it was stated: "If what was bought with tithe money became impure, it should be redeemed. Rebbi Jehudah says, it should be buried[115]. They said to Rebbi Jehudah, if original Second Tithe which became impure is redeemed, what was bought with tithe money and became impure certainly should be redeemed. He said to them, no! If you referred to original Second Tithe, which can be redeemed when it is pure and far from the Place, can you say the same about what was bought with tithe money which cannot be redeemed when it is pure and far from the Place?[216"]] since it is not subject to being redeemed and eaten at any dwelling place, one may not fulfill one's obligation with it. Rebbi Simeon ben Laqish asked: *Hallah* from dough made from Second Tithe in Jerusalem, since it is not subject to being redeemed and eaten at any dwelling place, one may not fulfill one's obligation with it[217].

I could think that they may fulfill their obligation with flat cakes for a thanksgiving offering and wafers of a *nazir*[218]. The verse says, *seven days you shall eat mazzot*[219]; *mazzah* which may be eaten all seven days. But flat cakes for a thanksgiving offering and wafers of a *nazir* may not be eaten all seven days[220]. Rebbi Jonah in the name of Rebbi Simeon ben Laqish: since flat cakes for a thanksgiving offering and wafers of a *nazir* may be eaten in the entire domain of the Land of Israel, the presenter could not exclude because of "dwelling place"[221]. Rebbi Yose in the name of Rebbi Simeon ben Laqish: this implies that wafers of a *nazir* may be eaten in the entire domain of the Land of Israel, the presenter could not exclude because of "dwelling place". One understands about flat cakes for a thanksgiving offering. But it is not so for wafers of a *nazir*[222]. Rebbi Joḥanan said, there is no *nazir* here; *nezirut* is an obligation. Rebbi Abun bar Cahana said, explain it if his purification offering was presented in Shiloh but his elevation and well-being offerings in Nob or Gibeon[223]. Rebbi Hananiah, Rebbi [Azariah][224] asked before Rebbi Mana: Did not the teacher say in the name of Rebbi Yose: Holiday well-being offerings brought at an elevated place are qualified but they are not counted against an obligation of the owner[225]? But it must be for Rebbi Jehudah, as Rebbi Jehudah said, purification and Passover offerings of individuals at a principal elevated place, but no purification and Passover offerings of individuals at a minor elevated place[226]. It only follows Rebbi Simeon, since "Rebbi Simeon said, when one of the bloods was sprinkled, the *nazir* is permitted to drink wine and to defile himself for the dead.[227]"

210 *Ex.* 12:18,20. *Mekhilta dR. Simeon ben Yohay* 12:20 (p. 24).
211 *Ex.* 12:20.
212 First Fruits are *sancta* presented to the priest in the Temple and consumed in Jerusalem only (Mishnah *Bikkurim* 2:2). Babli 39a, *Mekhilta dR. Ismael Ba* 10, dR. *Simeon ben Yohay* 12:20 (p. 24).
213 It may be eaten only in Jerusalem, Mishnah *Bikkurim* 2:2, *Deut.* 14:23.
214 *Deut.* 14:24. Redemption of pure Second Tithe is possible only outside of Jerusalem.
215 The text in brackets is an addition from the corrector who was misled by the expression "asked" because the statement of R. Abun bar Hiyya is a straight declarative sentence: "What was bought with tithe money which became impure, following Rebbi Jehudah since it is not subject to being redeemed and eaten at any dwelling place, one may not fulfill one's obligation with it." The question here and in the next sentence is whether there is any objection to the inference drawn. Since the scribe's text is confirmed by G, the addition should be deleted.

216 Mishnah *Ma`aser šeni* 3:11 (p. 111).
217 Since *hallah* is heave and if impure must be burned, even for the majority which disagrees with R. Jehudah it cannot be used for the Passover obligation. Since no objection is raised, this is accepted doctrine in the Yerushalmi, rejected in the Babli 38a.
218 The question is raised about *mazzot* which were baked to be used with a thanksgiving offering (*Lev.* 7:12) or with the offerings required at the end of a vow of *nazir* (*Num.* 6:15) but were not used for that purpose, as implied by the text of the Mishnah. Babli 38a as Amoraic statement.
219 *Ex.* 12:15.
220 Both kinds of bread may be eaten only on the day of the sacrifice and the following night; if it was intended not to be eaten for a longer period it may not be used even if it was not used for the original purpose.
221 The argument really goes the other way. Since the statement at the start of the paragraph (which also in the Yerushalmi seems to be Amoraic as shown by the expression שׁוֹנֶה instead of תֵּנֵי) uses a verse different from the one quoted in the preceding Tannaitic source, it follows that

the verse quoted earlier is not applicable. The bread accompanying the animal sacrifices must be consumed at the place prescribed for consumption of the meat.

222 While during the existence of the Sanctuary at Shilo or after the building of the Temple all sacrifices had to be offered at the place of the Sanctuary, before the building of the Sanctuary at Shiloh and after its destruction voluntary offerings could be given at private altars ("minor elevated places") whereas obligatory offerings were restricted to altars erected at the place of the Tabernacle or the Ark of Covenant ("principal elevated places", Gilgal, Nob, and Gibeon); Mishnah *Megillah* 1:13. Therefore there were times when thanksgiving offerings could be presented anywhere in the Land, but while making a vow of *nazir* was voluntary, once it was made the sacrifices of *nezirut* became mandatory.

223 Not that they were sacrificed at Nob or Gibeon, but they were sacrificed at the time when Nob or Gibeon were principal elevated places, i. e., the sanctuary at Shiloh was presumed destroyed immediately after the purification sacrifice was offered. Since elevation and well-being offerings are by their nature voluntary (even though in this case they are obligatory), they can be offered at a local sanctuary and the accompanying bread eaten anywhere in the Land.

224 It seems that this was his name; the spelling עֶזְרָה in the Leiden text is irregular since *Ezra* should be spelled with א.

225 Well-being sacrifices mostly are voluntary; they can be offered at a local shrine according to all the rules spelled out in *Lev.* 3. But the holiday offering is obligatory; at a local shrine they cannot satisfy an obligation. Therefore the accompanying bread cannot be eaten at all places.

226 But all other obligatory sacrifices can be brought locally, including two of the three sacrifices of the *nazir*.

227 Mishnah *Nazir* 6:11 (Note 224). Therefore only the first sacrifice of the *nazir* is obligatory, the others together with the bread may be offered locally.

(29b line 57) רִבִּי סִימוֹן בְּשֵׁם רִבִּי יוֹשֻׁעַ בֶּן לֵוִי. אוֹתוֹ כְזַיִת שֶׁאָדָם יוֹצֵא בוֹ יְדֵי חוֹבָתוֹ בַּפֶּסַח צָרִיךְ שֶׁלֹּא יְהֵא בּוֹ מַשְׁקִין. רִבִּי יִרְמְיָה אָמַר. לְמִצְוָה אִיתְאֲמָרַת. רִבִּי בָּא אָמַר. לְמִצְוָה אִיתְאֲמָרַת. רִבִּי יוּדָה בַּר פָּזִי אָמַר. לְעִיכּוּב אִיתְאֲמָרַת. מִילְתֵיהּ דְּרִבִּי בּוּן בַּר חִייָה אָמְרָה. לְעִיכּוּב אִיתְאֲמָרַת. הֲתִיב רִבִּי בּוּן בַּר חִייָה. וְהָתַנִּינָן. חַלּוֹת תּוֹדָה. אִית לָךְ מֵימַר. חַלּוֹת תּוֹדָה שֶׁאֵין בָּהֶן מַשְׁקִין. אָמַר רִבִּי יוֹסֵה. תַּמָּן רְבִיעִית הִיא. וּרְבִיעִית מִתְחַלֶּקֶת לְכַמָּה מִינִין. וְהַיי דָא אָמְרָה דָא. יָכוֹל יֵצֵא חוֹבָתוֹ בִּרְבִיכָה. תַּלְמוּד לוֹמַר. וּשְׁמַרְתֶּם אֶת־הַמַּצּוֹת. מַצָּה שֶׁצְּרִיכָה שִׁימוּר. יָצְאַת זוֹ שֶׁאֵינָהּ צְרִיכָה שִׁימוּר. מִפְּנֵי שֶׁאֵינָהּ צְרִיכָה שִׁימוּר. הָא אִם הָיְתָה צְרִיכָה שִׁימוּר יוֹצְאִין בָּהּ. וְהָא תַנֵּי. יוֹצְאִין בְּמַצָּה מְתוּבֶּלֶת אַף עַל פִּי שֶׁאֵין בָּהּ טַעַם דָּגָן. וְהִיא שֶׁיְּהֵא רוּבָּהּ דָּגָן. סָבְרִין מֵימַר. מְתוּבֶּלֶת מַשְׁקִין. נֵאמַר. מְתוּבֶּלֶת שׁוּמְשְׁמִין. מְתוּבֶּלֶת אֱגוֹזִים. וְהֵיי דָא אָמְרָה דָא. יָכוֹל שֶׁאֵינוֹ יוֹצֵא בַּפֶּסַח אֶלָּא בְפַת (חֲרֵרָה) [הֲדָרָאָה]. מְנַיִין אֲפִילוּ בְמַצַּת

שְׁלֹמֹה. תַּלְמוּד לוֹמַר. תְּאכְלוּ מַצּוֹת: רִיבָּה. אִם כֵּן מַה תַּלְמוּד לוֹמַר. לֶחֶם עוֹנִי. פְּרָט לְסוּרְסִין וּלְחַלַּת הַמַּסְרֵת וְלַאֲשִׁישָׁה.

1 יושוע G | יהושע   2 יהא G | יהיה   איתאמרת G | אתאמ[רת] | אתאמרת G | בא - G | 3 איתאמרת G | אתאמרת   5 שאין G | אין   מינין G | מינים   והיי דא G | וידא   9 מתובלת G | מתובללת   משקין G | במשקין   מתובלת | G מתובללת   שומשמין G | שמשמין   אגוזין G | אגוזים   10 והידא G | והדה   S חרה C | הדראה   11 שלמה G | שלימה

Rebbi Simon in the name of Rebbi Joshua ben Levi: The olive-sized piece of *mazzah* with which a person fulfills his obligation on Passover must be without fluid[228]. Rebbi Jeremiah said, this was said for a meritorious deed[229]. Rebbi Abba said, this was said for a meritorious deed. Rebbi Jehudah bar Pazi said, this was said as a necessary condition. The word of Rebbi Abun bar Hiyya implies that this was said as a necessary condition. Rebbi Abun bar Hiyya objected, did we not state: "flat cakes for a thanksgiving offering"? Are there flat cakes for a thanksgiving offering without fluids[230]? Rebbi Yose said, there it is a *quartarius*; one *quartarius* splits into many kinds[231]. But what implies this? "One might think and a person could satisfy his obligation with pancake, the verse says, *guard the mazzot*[232], a *mazzah* which needs guarding, excluding this one which does not need guarding." Because it does not need guarding; therefore if it would need guarding one would satisfy his obligation with it. And so we stated: "One fulfills his obligation with spiced *mazzah*, even if it does not taste of grain, on condition that it be mostly grain"[233]. They thought to say, spiced by fluids. We may say, spiced by sesame, spiced by nuts. But the following says it: One might think that a person only could satisfy his obligation on Passover with (roasted) [whole grain][234] bread? From where even with Solomon's *mazzah*[235]? The verse says, *you shall eat mazzot*, it included. If it is so, why does it say *bread of affliction*[236]? To exclude *sursīn*[237], and pancake, and cake.

228 The dough must be made with water to the exclusion of any other fluid. Cf. Babli 36a.

229 In this opinion the *mazzah* which either was made from dough containing other fluids or where fluid was rubbed into it after baking is undesirable but not forbidden.

230 Lev. 7:12 prescribes "flat cakes mixed with oil". If the Mishnah permits such cakes when commercially made, it must permit all *mazzah* kneaded with a mixture of oil and water.

231 Mishnah *Menahot* 9:3 specifies that half a *log* (2 *quartarii*, slightly more than ¼ liter) was used to bake the bread required for

a thanksgiving offering, 10 flat cakes, 10 wafers, and flour mixed with oil. The amount used for a single flat cake was negligible. Babli 38b.

232 Ex. 12:17; a similar *baraita* is quoted in *Midrash Haggadol Ba* 12:17; where it is spelled out that a pancake made from flour fried in oil is unacceptable since it never can become leavened.

233 Tosephta 2:21.

234 The scribe wrote "roasted bread", i. e., baked on the open fire (parallel to the roasting prescribed for the Passover sacrifice.). The corrector changed this to "bread from the second milling", i. e., from non-white flour. This correction is induced from the Babli 36b and should be disregarded.

235 Which certainly was made from pure white flour. *Sifry Deut.* 130.

236 Deut. 16:3.

237 This word is unexplained. סוּרְסִי is the name of the Syriac language. We do not know what "Syriac cakes" are. *Sifry* only mentions חָלוּט "pancake fried in oil" and cake. The rule is mentioned in the Tosephta 2:20, Babli 119b; the Babli version also in *Mekhilta dR. Ismael Ba* 10 (end).

(29b line 72) יוֹצְאִין בְּמַצָּה עָבָה עַד טֶפַח כְּלֶחֶם הַפָּנִים. יוֹצְאִין בְּמַצָּה נָא כְּדֵי שֶׁתִּיפָּרֵס וְלֹא תֵיעָשֶׂה גִידִין. מַצָּה הַיְשָׁנָה תַּפְלוּגְתָּא דְּבֵית שַׁמַּי וּבֵית הִלֵּל. אָמַר רִבִּי יוֹסֵה. דִּבְרֵי הַכֹּל הִיא. מִכֵּיוָן שֶׁלֹּא עֲשָׂאָהּ לְשֵׁם פֶּסַח דָּבָר בָּרִיא שֶׁלֹּא דִיקְדֵּק בָּהּ. יוֹצְאִין בִּסְרוּקִין בֵּין מְצוּיָּירִין בֵּין שֶׁאֵינָן מְצוּיָּירִין. אַף עַל פִּי שֶׁאָמְרוּ. אֵין עוֹשִׂין סְרִיקִין מְצוּיָּירִין בַּפֶּסַח.

One may fulfill his obligation with *mazzah* thick up to one hand-width like the shew bread[238]. One may fulfill his obligation with raw *mazzah* if only it does not draw fibers when broken[239]. An old *mazzah* is subject of a disagreement between the House of Shammai and the House of Hillel. Rebbi Yose said, it is everybody's opinion; since he did not make it for Passover it is certain that he did not care to make it accurately[240]. One may fulfill his obligation with *seriqin*[241] both with figures or without figures, even though they said, one does not make painted *seriqin* on Passover.

238 Rejected in the Babli, 37a.

239 Babli 37a, bottom. It does not really mean raw but lightly baked so that the *mazzah* is not dark like a bread crust. The Babli's expression is הינא (הנן "easily digested"). A *mazzah* is fully baked if it breaks cleanly.

240 An old *mazzah* is one baked before Passover. Tosephta 2:21 permits the use of old *mazzah* if it was baked for Passover use.

241 Tosephta 2:19, Babli 37a. It seems that *seriqin* are today's common *mazzot*: flat bread grated with a comb (מָסָרֵק) exhibiting an orderly pattern of tiny holes (*Orhot Hayyim* I, *Hilkhot Hamez Umazzah* 103, p. 75d ed. Firenze 1734.)

(29c line 1) תַּנֵי. אָמַר רִבִּי יוּדָה. שָׁאַל בַּיְיתוֹס בֶּן זוֹנִין אֶת רַבָּן גַּמְלִיאֵל וַחֲכָמִים בְּיַבְנֶה. מַהוּ לַעֲשׂוֹת סְרִיקִין הַמְצוּיָּירִין בַּפֶּסַח. אָמְרוּ לוֹ. אָסוּר. מִפְּנֵי שֶׁהָאִשָּׁה מִשְׁתָּהָא בָּהֶן וְהֵן בָּאִין לִידֵי חָמֵץ. אָמַר לָהֶן. אִם כֵּן יַעֲשׂוּ אוֹתָן בְּטִפּוּס. אָמְרוּ לוֹ. יְהוּ אוֹמְרִים. כָּל־הַסְּרִיקִין אֲסוּרִין וּסְרִיקֵי בַּיְיתוֹס בֶּן זוֹנִין מוּתָּרִין. תַּנֵי. רִבִּי יוֹסֵה אוֹמֵר. עוֹשִׂין סְרִיקִין כִּרְקִיקִין. וְאֵין עוֹשִׂין רְקִיקִין כְּקלוּסְקָאוֹת.

1 בייתוס G | בויתס   מהו G | מבוא   2 מצויירין G | המצויירין   3 להן | לחם   אותן G | אותם   בטפוס |
G בטפס   יהו G | יהוא   4 בייתוס G | בויתס   5 רקיקין G | סריקין   כקלוסקאות G | כגלוסקאות

It was stated[242] "Boethos ben Zenon asked Rabban Gamliel and the Sages at Jabneh: May one make *seriqin* with figures on Passover? They told him, no, because a woman would spend time with it and it would become leavened. He said to them, then one should make it in a form[243]. They told him, one would say, all *seriqin* are forbidden but the *seriqin* of Boethos ben Zenon are permitted. Rebbi Yose said, one may make *seriqin* like wafers; one does not make (wafers) [*seriqin*][244] as loaves[245]."

242 Tosephta 2:19, Babli 37a (without the last statement.)
243 Greek τύπος, ὁ, "figure, form".
244 The reading of G [in brackets] is confirmed by the Tosephta.
245 Greek κόλλιξ; S. Fraenkel conjectures a diminutive κολλίσκιον, τό.

(fol. 28b) **מִשְׁנָה ח**: וְאֵילּוּ יְרָקוֹת שֶׁאָדָם יוֹצֵא בָהֶן יְדֵי חוֹבָתוֹ בַּפֶּסַח בַּחֲזֶרֶת וּבְעוּלְשִׁין וּבְתַמְכָה וּבְחַרְחֲבִינָה וּבַמָּרוֹר. יוֹצְאִין בָּהֶן בֵּין לַחִין בֵּין כְּמוּשִׁין. אֲבָל לֹא כְבוּשִׁים וְלֹא שְׁלוּקִין וְלֹא מְבוּשָּׁלִין. וּמִצְטָרְפִין בְּכַזַּיִת. וְיוֹצְאִין בַּקֶּלַח שֶׁלָּהֶן וּבְדִמַאי וּבְמַעֲשֵׂר רִאשׁוֹן שֶׁנִּיטְּלָה תְרוּמָתוֹ וּבְמַעֲשֵׂר שֵׁנִי וְהֶקְדֵּשׁ שֶׁנִּפְדּוּ:

Mishnah 5: And with the following vegetables[246] a person can fulfill his obligation on Passover: With Romaine lettuce, with endives, with *gingidium*, *harhabina* and bitter herb. One fulfills his obligation with both fresh and wilted, but not marinated or cooked in water or cooked in broth; and they may be combined for the volume of an olive. One fulfills his obligation with their stalk, and with *demay*[177], and with First Tithe whose heave was removed[178], and with Second Tithe or *sancta* which were redeemed[179].

246 For the bitter herbs accompanying the *mazzah* or the Passover sacrifice. The names of the plants are described in the Halakhah; for a comparison with the

somewhat different explanations of the Babli (39a) and their Medieval interpretations cf. the author's *The Scholar's Haggadah*, Northvale 1995, p.333.

(29c line 6) **הלכה ה:** בַּחֲזֶרֶת. חַסִּין. בָּעוּלְשִׁין. טְרוֹקְסִימוֹן. וּבַתַּמְכָה. גִּנְגִּידִין. בַּחַרְחֲבִינָה. רִבִּי יוֹסֵה בֵּירִבִּי בּוּן אָמַר. יסי חלי. וּבַמָּרוֹר. יָרָק מַר וּפָנָיו מַכְסִיפִין וְיֵשׁ לוֹ שָׂרָף. הֵתִיבוּן. הֲרֵי חֲזֶרֶת מָתוֹק. הֲרֵי אֵינוֹ קָרוּי חֲזֶרֶת אֶלָּא מָתוֹק. רִבִּי חִיָּיה בְשֵׁם רִבִּי הוֹשַׁעְיָה. כָּל־עַצְמָן אֵין הַדָּבָר תָּלוּי אֶלָּא בַחֲזֶרֶת. מַה חֲזֶרֶת תְּחִילָתָהּ מָתוֹק וְסוֹפָהּ מָר. כָּךְ עָשׂוּ הַמִּצְרִיִּים לַאֲבוֹתֵינוּ בְמִצְרַיִם. בַּתְּחִילָה בְּמֵיטַב הָאָרֶץ הוֹשֵׁב אֶת־אָבִיךָ וְאֶת־אַחֶיךָ. וְאַחַר כָּךְ וַיְמָרֲרוּ אֶת־חַיֵּיהֶם בַּעֲבוֹדָה קָשָׁה בְּחוֹמֶר וּבִלְבֵנִים.

1 טרוקסימון G | טרוכסימון ובתמכה G | בתמכה גנגידין | גינגיבין 2 יסי חלי G | יסא חלי ובמרור G | במרור מר G | ומר מכסיפין G | מכסיפות שרף G | סריף הרי G | - 3 חזרת מתוק G | מתוקה חזרת ר' חייה בשם ר' הושעיה G | ... G | אינו קרוי חזרת 4 כל עצמן אין הדבר תלוי אלא בחזרת. מה חזרת ר' המצריים G | המצרים 6 בחומר ובלבינים G | -

Halakhah 5: "With *ḥazeret*", lettuce[247]. "With *ʿulšin*", τρώξιμον[248]. "And with *tamka*", γιγγίδιον[249] "With *ḥarḥabina*". Rebbi Yose ben Rebbi Abun said, [250]יסי חלי. "And with *maror*". A bitter vegetable turning grey and containing sap. They objected, is not lettuce sweet? Is it not called "lettuce" only if it be sweet? Rebbi Ḥiyya in the name of Rebbi Hoshaya: (Itself it depends only on change) [Itself it is only called "change"][251]. (As) *ḥazeret* is sweet at the beginning and bitter at the end, so did the Egyptians behave towards our forefathers in Egypt. At the start, *in the best part of the land settle your father and your brothers*[252], and after that *they embittered their lives with hard labor, with mortar and bricks*[253].

247 Arabic خس.
248 Greek τρώξιμος, -ον, "edible"; τά τρώξιμα "vegetables eaten raw", in rabbinic sources traditionally used for endives.
249 A plant of the family of carrots.
250 This is the reading of the Rome ms. of the Yerushalmi *Zeraʿim* for the explanation of *Kilaim* 1:2 חזרת גלין which Maimonides in his Mishnah Commentary explains as "wild growing lettuce" (*Kilaim* Chapter 1, Notes 37, 51,52.)
251 A play on words from the Hebrew root חזר "to return" which in Rabbinic Hebrew is used in the combination חזר בו "he changed his mind". The text of G [in brackets] is preferable.

The same homily but without the play on words is in the Babli 39a.
252 *Gen.* 47:6.
253 *Ex.* 1:6.

(29c line 14) בֵּין כְּמוּשִׁין. אִית תַּנָּיֵי תַנֵּי. אֲבָל לֹא כְמוּשִׁין. אָמַר רַב חִסְדָּא. מָאן דְּאָמַר. כְּמוּשִׁין. בְּקֶלַח. מָאן דְּאָמַר. אֲבָל לֹא כְמוּשִׁין. בָּעָלִין.

1 כמושין G | כמושין (2) | דאמ' G | דמר G | דאמ' 2 דמר G | כמושין G | כמושין העלין G | בעלים

"And wilted". There are Tannaim who state, "but not wilted". Rav Hisda said, he who said "and wilted", about a stalk. He who said, "but not wilted", about leaves[254].

254 Babli 39b.

(29c line 16) רִבִּי חִיָּיה בְשֵׁם רִבִּי יוֹחָנָן. זַיִת כָּבוּשׁ אוֹמֵר עָלָיו. בּוֹרֵא פְּרִי הָעֵץ. רִבִּי בִּנְיָמִין בַּר יֶפֶת בְּשֵׁם רִבִּי יוֹחָנָן. יָרָק שָׁלוּק אוֹמֵר עָלָיו. שֶׁהַכֹּל נִהְיָה בִדְבָרוֹ. אָמַר רִבִּי שְׁמוּאֵל בַּר רַב יִצְחָק. מַתְנִיתָהּ מְסַייְעָה לְרִבִּי בִּנְיָמִין בַּר יֶפֶת. אֲבָל לֹא כְבוּשִׁין וְלֹא שְׁלוּקִין וְלֹא מְבוּשָּׁלִין. אִם בְּעֵינָן הֵם יָצֵא בָהֶם יְדֵי חוֹבָתוֹ בַּפֶּסַח. אָמַר רִבִּי זְעוּרָה. מָאן יָדַע מִשְׁמַע מִן רִבִּי יוֹחָנָן יָאוּת. רִבִּי חִיָּיה בַּר בָּא אוֹ רִבִּי בִּנְיָמִין. לָא רִבִּי חִיָּיה בַּר בָּא. וְעוֹד מִן הָדָא. מִן מַה דַּאֲנַן חַמְיִין רַבָּנִין עָלִין לַבְרַייְתָה וְנָסְבִין תּוּרְמוּסִין וּמְבָרְכִין עֲלֵיהוֹן. בּוֹרֵא פְּרִי הָאֲדָמָה. וְתוּרְמוּסִין לֹא שְׁלוּקִין הֵן. אִין תֵּימַר. שַׁנְיָא הִיא. שֶׁאָמְרָה תוֹרָה מְרוֹרִים. תּוּרְמוּסִין כֵּיוָן שֶׁשְּׁלָקָן בָּטְלָה מָרָתָן. אָמַר רִבִּי יוֹסֵה בֵּירִבִּי בּוּן. וְלֹא פְּלִיגִין. זַיִת עַל יְדֵי שֶׁדַּרְכּוֹ לֵיאָכֵל חַי. אֲפִילוּ כָּבוּשׁ בְּעֵינוֹ הוּא. יָרָק כֵּיוָן שֶׁשְּׁלָקוֹ נִשְׁתַּנָּה.

1 חייה | ב חייא בר ווא בר | G בן 2 בר | G בן 3 מסייעה | ב מסייעא 4 בעיינן | G בעינן הם | ב הן יצא בהם ידי חובתו G יוצאין בהן ידי חובתן | ב אדם יוצא בהן ידי חובתו זעורה | Ga זעורא מאן ידע | G מן חכם 5 חייה | Ga חייא בא | ב ווא בנימין | Ga במינימן בר יפת חייה בר בא | ב חייא בר ווא הדא | G הדא | ב רבנן רברביא 6 עלין | G עללין | ב עלון לבריתה | G לאבריתה ב לאבריתא עליהון | ב עליהו 7 שנייא | G שנייה תורה | ב התורה מרורים | Ga מרורין כיון | G מכיון 8 בון | ב אבון ליאכל | Ga לאכל

[255]Rebbi Hiyya bar Abba in the name of Rebbi Yohanan: One says "Creator of the fruit of the tree" on marinated olives[256]. Rebbi Benjamin bar Jephet in the name of Rebbi Yohanan: One says "By Whose word everything was created" on water-cooked vegetables[257]. Rebbi Samuel bar Rav Isaac said: a Mishnah supports Rebbi Benjamin bar Yephet: "but not marinated or cooked in water or cooked in broth"; if they were recognizable in their state one could fulfill his duty with them on Passover. Rebbi Ze`ira said, who understands well what Rebbi Yohanan said, Rebbi Hiyya bar Abba or Rebbi Benjamin? Not Rebbi Hiyya bar Abba? And in addition from the fact that we see great rabbis going to a mourner's meal, eat lupines[258] and recite on them "Creator of the fruit of the earth;" Are not lupines certainly cooked? If you wish, you may say there is a difference, since the Torah said *bitter herbs*, and

cooked lupines have lost their bitterness. Rebbi Yose ben Rebbi Abun said, they have no disagreement. Since olives usually are eaten fresh, they are recognizable in their state even if they are marinated. Vegetables are changed once they are cooked[259].

255 This paragraph is copied from *Berakhot* 6:1 (Notes 34-41,ב).

256 The required benediction before the consumption of raw fruits growing on a tree. He seems to hold that marinating does not change the nature of the fruit; then it is difficult to understand why marinated bitter herbs cannot be used on Passover.

257 The benediction for anything that cannot be classified as agricultural produce. He is supported by the Mishnah here which seems to indicate that once processed, vegetables are no longer counted as agricultural produce.

258 Greek θέρμος, ὁ. Raw lupines are cattle feed, too bitter for human consumption. They become edible only after long cooking. This statement seems to supprt R. Hiyya bar Abba.

259 One must assume that roots of lupine keep their shape and general appearance in cooking. The rule that vegetables which are inedible unless cooked require the blessing "Creator of the fruit of the earth" is the opinion of Rav Ḥisda in the Babli *Berakhot* 38b.

(fol. 28b) **משנה ו**: אֵין שׁוֹרִין אֶת הַמּוּרְסָן לַתַּרְנְגוֹלִים אֲבָל חוֹלְטִין. הָאִשָּׁה לֹא תִשְׁרֶה אֶת הַמּוּרְסָן שֶׁתּוֹלִיךְ בְּיָדָהּ לַמֶּרְחָץ אֲבָל שָׁפָה הִיא בִּבְשָׂרָהּ יָבֵשׁ. לֹא יִלְעוֹס אָדָם חִטִּים וְיִתֵּן עַל גַּבֵּי מַכָּתוֹ בַּפֶּסַח מִפְּנֵי שֶׁהֵן מַחְמִיצוֹת:

Mishnah 6: One may not soak bran as chicken feed but one may parboil[260]. A woman may not soak bran to take it in her hand to the bath house but she may rub it dry on her skin[261]. A person may not chew wheat kernels to put on his wound since they become leavened[262].

260 Bran, the outer shell of wheat kernels, also may become leavened. Since leavened matter is forbidden for usufruct, it also is forbidden as animal feed. It is assumed that the bran becomes inert if parboiled in boiling water.

261 To be used as cleansing powder, even if applied to her wet body, since it will be washed off before it can become leavened.

262 By the spittle.

(29c line 27) **הלכה ו**: תַּנֵּי. רִבִּי יִשְׁמָעֵאל בֵּירְבִּי יוֹסֵי אָמַר מִשּׁוּם אָבִיו. אֵי זוֹ הִיא הַמְּעִיסָה. הַנּוֹתֵן חַמִּין לְתוֹךְ קֶמַח. חֲלִיטָה. קֶמַח לְתוֹךְ חַמִּין. וְהָכָא בֵּין מַיִם לְתוֹךְ מוּרְסָן בֵּין מוּרְסָן לְתוֹךְ חַמִּין.

1 יוסי G | יוסה   המעיסה G | מעיסה   2 הנותן G | נותן   חמין G | חמים (2)   3 חמין G | חמים

Halakhah 6: It was stated[263]: "Rebbi Ismael ben Rebbi Yose said in his father's name: What is parboiled? If one adds hot water to flour. Dumpling, flour into hot water." But here either water into bran or bran into water[264].

263 Tosephta *Hallah* 1:1; Yerushalmi *Hallah* 1:5 (Note 189). In Babli *Pesahim* 37b, the definitions are switched.
264 In all cases it is forbidden.

(29c line 30) בְּשֵׁישׁ בָּהֶן שַׁמְנוּנִית. מָלוּגְמָא שֶׁנִּסְרְחָה. אִית תַּנָּיֵי תַנֵּי. זָקוּק לְבַעֵר. וְאִית תַּנָּיֵי תַנֵּי. אֵין זָקוּק לְבַעֵר. מָאן דְּאָמַר. זָקוּק לְבַעֵר. בְּשֶׁנִּתְחַמְּצָה וְאַחַר כָּךְ נִסְרְחָה. וּמָאן דְּאָמַר. אֵינוֹ זָקוּק לְבַעֵר. בְּשֶׁנִּסְרְחָה וְאַחַר כָּךְ נִתְחַמְּצָה.

1 שנסרחה G | ש[נ]סרסה   2 מאן דאמ' G | מן דמר   בשנתחמצה G | בשניחמצה   נסרחה G | ניסרחה   ומאן דאמ' G | מן דמר   3 נתחמצה G | ניחמצה

If there is any fat in them[266]. Unguent[267] which became putrid, there are Tannaim who state, he is required to eliminate; and there are Tannaim who state, he is not required to eliminate. He who said, he is required to eliminate, if it became leavened before becoming putrid; he who said, he is not required to eliminate, if it became putrid before becoming leavened[268].

266 One is forbidden to chew wheat kernels for medical use if there is any moisture left in them, the moisture being called "fat" in *Deut.* 32:14. If the kernels are completely devoid of moisture, they are inert and may be chewed.
267 Greek μάλαγμα. The base of the unguent contains flour.
268 If the unguent becomes unusable and worthless before Passover, or even on Passover but it was spoiled before showing signs of leavening, it is neither food nor valuable and not subject to the Passover prohibition.

(fol. 28c) **משנה ז**: אֵין נוֹתְנִין אֶת הַקֶּמַח לֹא לְתוֹךְ חֲרוֹסֶת וְלֹא לְתוֹךְ חַרְדָּל אִם נָתַן יֹאכַל מִיָּד וְרִבִּי מֵאִיר אוֹסֵר. אֵין מְבַשְּׁלִין אֶת הַפֶּסַח לֹא בְּמַשְׁקִין וְלֹא בְּמֵי פֵּרוֹת אֲבָל סָכִין וּמַטְבִּילִין אוֹתוֹ בָּהֶן. מֵי תַשְׁמִישָׁיו שֶׁל נַחְתּוֹם יִשָּׁפְכוּ מִפְּנֵי שֶׁהֵן מַחְמִיצִין:

Mishnah 7: One adds flour neither to *haroset*[269] nor to mustard[270]. If one did add, he has to eat it immediately, but Rebbi Meïr forbids[271]. One may not cook the Passover sacrifice either in fluid[272] or in fruit juice, but one may rub it or immerse it in them[273]. Water used by a baker[274] has to be poured out because it causes leavening.

269 The sauce in which the bitter herbs are dipped, cf. Mishnah 10:3; *The Scholar's Haggadah* pp. 333-334.
270 Prepared to be used with the meat. Since both this and *haroset* are moist, leavening would be caused by the addition of flour.
271 As explained in the Halakhah, he does not believe that it will be eaten quickly enough.
272 Neither water (which is explicitly forbidden by the verse) nor fruit juice.
273 Before the Passover lamb is roasted over the open fire, it may be basted with fluids as taste enhancers.
274 Water in which he dips his hands while kneading the dough. This water will contain flour particles.

(29c line 34) **הלכה ז׃** [תַּנֵּי.] אֵין נוֹתְנִין אֶת הַקֶּמַח לֹא לְתוֹךְ חֲרוֹסֶת אוֹ לְתוֹךְ חַרְדָּל. אִם נָתַן יֹאכַל מִיָּד וּבִלְבַד שֶׁלֹּא יִשְׁהֶא. רִבִּי מֵאִיר אוֹסֵר. מִפְּנֵי שֶׁהוּא מַשְׁהֵא.

C תני | SG - | חרדל G | החרדל

Halakhah 7: It was stated: "One adds flour neither to *haroset*[269] nor to mustard[270]; it one did add, he has to eat it immediately, on condition that he not tarry. Rebbi Meïr forbids since he tarries.[275]"

כָּתוּב וּבָשֵׁל מְבוּשָּׁל בַּמַּיִם. אֵין לִי אֶלָּא מַיִם. מִנַּיִין לְרַבּוֹת שְׁאָר מַשְׁקִין. תַּלְמוּד לוֹמַר וּבָשֵׁל מְבוּשָּׁל [מִכָּל־מָקוֹם.] עַד כְּדוֹן כְּרִבִּי עֲקִיבָה. כְּרִבִּי יִשְׁמָעֵאל. תַּנֵּי רִבִּי יִשְׁמָעֵאל. קַל וְחוֹמֶר. מָה אִם מַיִם שֶׁאֵינָן מִפִּיגִין טַעֲמָן אַתְּ אָמַר. אָסוּר. שְׁאָר מַשְׁקִין שֶׁמְּפִיגִין טַעֲמָן לֹא כָל־שֶׁכֵּן.

1 משקין G | המשקין   2 מכל מקום GS - | קל G | - 3 וחומר G | - מים G | המים שאינן G | שאין משקין G | המשקין שמפיגין G | שאינן מפיגין את

It is written: *or cooking cooked in water*[276]. I not only have water, from where other fluids? The verse says, *cooking cooked*, in any way. So far following Rebbi Aqiba; following Rebbi Ismael[277]? An argument *de minore ad majus*. Since for water which does not mask its taste you are saying it is forbidden, other fluids which mask its taste not so much more[278]?

275 The Babli 40b restricts this argument to mustard, requires *haroset* to be burned.
276 *Ex.* 12:9.
277 Who considers the combination of infinitive and perfect a form of common speech, not a duplication.
278 Babli 41a; *Mekhilta dR. Ismael Ba, Parašah* 6, pp. 20=-21/

(29 line 40) אֵין לָשִׁין מַצָּה בְמַשְׁקִין אֲבָל מְקַטְּפִין אוֹתָהּ בְּמַשְׁקִין. אָמַר רִבִּי עֲקִיבָה. אֲנִי הָיִיתִי עִם רִבִּי אֱלִיעֶזֶר וְרִבִּי יְהוֹשֻׁעַ בִּסְפִינָה וְלַשְׁתִּי מַצָּתָן בְּמַשְׁקִין. אֵין לָשִׁין מַצָּה בְרוֹתְחִין מִפְּנֵי שֶׁהֵן חוֹלְטִין. וְלֹא בְפוֹשְׁרִין מִפְּנֵי שֶׁהֵן מַחְמִיצִין. אֲבָל לָשִׁין אוֹתָן בְּצוֹנִין. וְהָא תַנִּינָן. כָּל־הַמְּנָחוֹת נִילוֹשׁוֹת בְּפוֹשְׁרִין [וּמְשַׁמְּרָן שֶׁלֹּא יַחֲמִיצוּ]. רִבִּי אַמִּי בְשֵׁם רִבִּי שִׁמְעוֹן בֶּן לָקִישׁ. תַּמָּן הַדָּבָר מָסוּר לַכֹּהֲנִים וְהַכֹּהֲנִים זְרִיזִין הֵן. וְהָכָא הַדָּבָר מָסוּר לַנָּשִׁים וְהַנָּשִׁים עֲצֵילוֹת הֵן. לֹא צוּרְכָה דְלֹא. הַכֹּהֲנִים עַצְמָן מָהוּ שֶׁיִּלוֹשׁוּ מַצָּתָן בְּפוֹשְׁרִין. יָבֹא כְהָדָא תַנָּא. רִבִּי זְכַרְיָה חַתְנֵיהּ דְּרִבִּי לֵוִי. נִידָה חוֹפֶפֶת וְסוֹרֶקֶת. [כֹּהֶנֶת אֵינָהּ חוֹפֶפֶת וְסוֹרֶקֶת. נִידָה כֹהֶנֶת חוֹפֶפֶת וְסוֹרֶקֶת.] שֶׁלֹּא תַחֲלוֹק בֵּין נִידָה לְנִידָה. אוֹף הָכָא שֶׁלֹּא תַחֲלוֹק בֵּין מַצָּה לְמַצָּה.

1 - | תני אני G | מעשה 2 | הייתי G שהייתי | אליעזר G ליעזר | לשין G לשים | אבל G | אבל מקטפין אותה במשקין. 4 | [ומשמרן G ומשמרין | תמן G | - 5 | מסור G אסור | והכא G | ברם הכה 6 | דלא G אלא | הכהנים G לכהנים | מהו G מהו | בפושרין G ברותחין מהוא שילושו מצתן ברותחין מהוא שילושו בפושרין | ייבא G ייבה | כהדא G כהדה | תנא G דתנה 7 | נידה G נידה 8 | נידה לנידה G נדה לנדה אוף הכא G והכה

[279]"One does not knead *mazzah* with fluids[272] but one may rub it with them. Rebbi Aqiba said, I was with Rebbi Eliezer and Rebbi Joshua on a ship and kneaded their *mazzah* with fluids. One may not knead *mazzah* with boiling water since it parboils[260], nor with lukewarm water because this makes leavened, but one kneads with cold water." But did we not state[280]: "All flour offerings are kneaded with lukewarm water and one guards them lest they become leavened"? Rebbi Immi in the name of Rebbi Simeon ben Laqish: There the matter is in the hands of the Cohanim and Cohanim are quick; here it is in the hands of women and women are slow. Then it is a problem about Cohanim themselves, may they knead their *mazzah* with lukewarm water? [281]It should be parallel to what Rebbi Zachariah the son-in-law of Rebbi Levi stated: A menstruating woman washes her hair and combs. A priestly woman does not wash her hair and combs. A menstruating priestly woman washes her' hair and combs, not to differentiate between one menstruating woman and another. So also here, not to differentiate between *mazzah* and *mazzah*.

279 Tosephta 3:5; Babli 36a, *Menahot* 52a.
280 Mishnah *Menahot* 5:2, speaking of the flour offerings in the Temple where leavening is forbidden (*Lev.* 2:11).
281 Chapter 1:1, Notes 37-38. Here the corrector's additions are justified by G.

(29c line 50) מֵי תַשְׁמִישָׁיו שֶׁל נַחְתּוֹם יִשָּׁפְכוּ. מִפְּנֵי שֶׁהֵן מַחְמִיצִין. אִית תַּנָּיֵי תַנֵּי. שׁוֹפְכָן בְּמָקוֹם אַשְׁבּוֹרֶן. אִית תַּנָּיֵי תַנֵּי. שׁוֹפְכָן בְּמָקוֹם קַטְפֶּרֶס. אָמַר רִבִּי יוֹסֵה. מָאן דְּאָמַר. שׁוֹפְכָן בְּמָקוֹם אַשְׁבּוֹרֶן. כְּשֶׁהָיָה אַשְׁבּוֹרֶן גָּדוֹל. מָאן דְּאָמַר. בְּמָקוֹם קַטְפֶּרֶס. כְּשֶׁהָיָה קַטְפֶּרֶס גָּבוֹהַּ. אָמַר

לֵיהּ רִבִּי פִּינְחָס בְּשֵׁם רִבִּי אִילָא. הָכֵין הֲוָה הֲוִי בָהּ. שָׁרָה חִיטִין וּשְׂעוֹרִים בַּמַּיִם. נִתְחַמְּצוּ אֲסוּרוֹת. לֹא נִתְחַמְּצוּ מוּתָּרוֹת. רִבִּי יוֹסֵה אָמַר. שָׁרָה וּשְׂעוֹרִים בַּמַּיִם. נִתְבַּקְעוּ הֲרֵי אֵילוּ אֲסוּרוֹת. שְׁרָיָין בַּחוֹמֶץ מוּתָּר מִפְּנֵי שֶׁהַחוֹמֶץ צוֹפְדָן.

1 תשמישיו | G תשמישו ישפכו | G ישפיכו   2 קטפרס | G קטפריס   3 קטפרס | G קטפריס   קטפריס | G מאן דאמ'| G מן דמר   קטפרס | G קטפריס   4 הוה הוי | G רבי הוה   חיטין | G חטי ושעורים | G ושעורין   5 לא נתחמצו | G ואם לאו

"Water used by a baker[274] has to be poured out because it makes leavened." There are Tannaim who state, he pours it into a depression[282]. There are Tannaim who state, he pours it into a declivity[283]. Rebbi Yose said, he who said, he pours it into a depression, if the depression was large. He who said, he pours it into a declivity, if the declivity was consierable. Rebbi Phineas said to him in the name of Rebbi Ila: So was he[284] discussing it: If he soaked wheat or barley grains in water, if they became leavened, they are forbidden; if they did not become leavened, they are permitted. Rebbi Yose said, if he soaked barley in water, if they split they are forbidden[285]. If he soaked them in vinegar they are permitted since the vinegar contracts them.

282 It is presumed that the water will be absorbed into the ground.
283 Greek adjective καταφερές, "inclined".
284 In G: "so was my teacher . . .".
285 Babli 40a.

(29d line 58) רִבִּי שְׁמוּאֵל בַּר רַב יִצְחָק הָיָה לוֹ יַיִן קוֹסֵס. יָהַב בְּגַוֵּיהּ שְׂעָרִין בְּגִין דְּיִתְמַע. שָׁאַל לְרִבִּי אִימִּי. אָמַר לֵיהּ. צָרִיךְ אַתְּ לְבָעֵר. [וְרִבִּי חֲנִינָה בְּרֵיהּ דְּרִבִּי כָּהַיי הֲוָה לֵיהּ דְּבַשׁ מְזוּיָּף בְּסוֹלֶת. שָׁאַל לְרִבִּי מָנָא. אָמַר לֵיהּ. צָרִיךְ אַתְּ לְבָעֵר.] חַד מִן אִילֵּין דְּרִבִּי כִּיָרַיי הֲוָה לֵיהּ גַּרְבִּין דְּמִשַׁח בְּגוֹ אוֹצְרֵהּ דְּחִיטַיָּא. שָׁאַל לְרַבָּנִין. אָמְרִין לֵיהּ. אֵיזִיל גְּרוֹף תּוֹחְתֵּיהֶן. הוֹרֵי רִבִּי אִימִּי בְּאִילֵּין גַּרְבַּיָּיא דְּכוּתָחָא. מְמַלֵּא אוֹתָן מַיִם שְׁלֹשָׁה יָמִים מֵעֵת לָעֵת.

1 יהב | G ויהב   שאל | G אתא שאל   2 חנינה | G חנה   כהיי | G כירריי היה | G הוה   3 בסולת | G בסלת   שאל | G אתא שאל   דר' | G דבית ר'   4 אוצרה | G אוצריה   דחיטיא | G דחיטייא   שאל לרבנין | G אזא שאל לרבננן   אמרין | G אמרון   איזיל | G אזיל   תוחתיהון | G כל מה דתוחתיהון   הורי ר' אמי | G ר' אמי הורי   5 גרבייא דכותחא | G גרבייה דכותחה   שלשה | G שלושה   מעת | G ומערן מעת

Rebbi Samuel ben Rav Isaac had wine which was getting sour. He added barley to it that it should become vinegar[286]. He asked Rebbi Immi, who told him, you have to eliminate[287]. [Rebbi Hanina the son of Rebbi Kihai {Kirai}[288] had honey adulterated with flour. He asked Rebbi Mana who told him, you have to eliminate. One of the people of [the house of][289] Rebbi Kirai had leather sacks of oil in the storage room of wheat. He asked the rabbis, who told him, go and clean out from under them[290]. Rebbi Immi instructed about those leather sacks of *kutah*[291], one fills them with water for three days [and empties them][289] every 24 hours.

286 In G (confirmed by quotes in Raviah and Meïri): That it certainly should become vinegar. Wine which starts to get sour can be sold neither as wine nor as vinegar; it is better to turn it into vinegar as quickly as possible.

287 Since the barley grains became leavened matter in the wine, in contrast to barley preserved in fully sour vinegar.

It seems that the Yerushalmi implies from the linguistic relation between חָמֵץ "leavened matter" and חוֹמֶץ "vinegar" that the processes which turn dough into leavened bread and wine into vinegar are essentially the same. Rabbenu Tam, in a ms. of his Pentateuch Commentary edited by S. E. Stern (קובץ המיעדים פסח vol. 1, p. 16, Moriah, Jerusalem 2005), notes that this and the following example imply that all fluids except vinegar may cause grain to become leavened, in contrast to the Babli (35b) who states categorically that fruit juices (with no water added) cannot cause leavening.

288 Reading of G. The text added by the corrector is confirmed by G.

289 Added from G.

290 The wheat kernels on the flour have to be removed before Passover since they may have become wet during the rainy season.

291 Yogurt for which the source of the bacteria is mouldy bread, which is certainly leavened matter. But since the contents of the leather sacks always were cold, three days of leaching by water is enough.

ואלו עוברין פרק שלישי

(fol.29c) **משנה א**: וְאֵילּוּ עוֹבְרִין בַּפֶּסַח כּוּתָּח הַבַּבְלִי וְשֵׁכָר הַמָּדִי וְחוֹמֶץ הָאֲדוֹמִי וְזִיתוֹם הַמִּצְרִי וְזוֹמָן שֶׁל צַבָּעִין וַעֲמִילָן שֶׁל טַבָּחִין וְקוֹלָן שֶׁל סוֹפְרִים. רִבִּי אֱלִיעֶזֶר אוֹמֵר אַף תַּכְשִׁיטֵי נָשִׁים. זֶה הַכְּלָל כָּל־שֶׁהוּא מִין דָּגָן הֲרֵי זֶה עוֹבֵר בַּפֶּסַח הֲרֵי אֵילּוּ בְּאַזְהָרָה וְאֵין בָּהֶן מִשּׁוּם כָּרֵת:

Mishnah 1: And the following are removed on Passover: Babylonian *kutah*[1], and Median beer[2], and Edomite vinegar[3], and Egyptian *zythum*[4], and dyers' gravy[5], and cooks' starch, and scribes' glue[6]; Rebbi Eliezer says, also women's make-up[7] This is the principle: Anything made from grain one removes on Passover; these are included in the warning[8] but they are not cause for extirpation[9].

1 Cf. Chapter 2, Note 290.
2 Made from barley.
3 Made with barley; cf. Chapter 2, Note 286.
4 Greek ζῦθος, ὁ, a kind of beer.
5 Greek ζῶμα, ἡ.
6 Greek κόλλα, -ης, ἡ, "flour paste".
7 If the base contains flour.
8 They are biblically forbidden.
9 If edible, the grain is no longer visible. If not edible, consumption is not punishable.

(29d line 40) וְאֵילּוּ עוֹבְרִין בַּפֶּסַח כּוּל׳. אָמַר רִבִּי מָנָא. וְכוּלְּהוֹן עַל יְדֵי מוֹי.
כּוּתָּח הַבַּבְלִי. דּוּ יָהִיב בֵּיהּ מַלְמוֹלִין דְּלִישׁ.
שֵׁכָר הַמָּדִי. דּוּ יָהִיב בֵּיהּ קֶמַח דִּשְׂעָרִין.
חוֹמֶץ הָאֲדוֹמִי. בְּסִימָא דְרוֹמָיָא. בָּרִאשׁוֹנָה שֶׁהָיוּ עוֹשִׂין יַיִן בְּטָהֳרָה לַנְּסָכִים לֹא הָיָה יַיִן מַחְמִיץ. וַהֲווֹן יָהֲבִין בְּגַוֵּיהּ שְׂעָרִין בְּגִין דְּיַחְמַע. וַהֲווֹן צָוְחִין לֵיהּ בְּסִימָא דְרוֹמָיָה.
זִיתוֹס הַמִּצְרִי. זַייְתַיָּה.
וְזִימֵי שֶׁלְצַבָּעִין. דּוּ יָהַב בְּגַוֵּיהּ קוּצָם בְּגִין דִּיקְלוֹט צִיבְעָא.
עֲמִילָן שֶׁל טַבָּחִין. אָמַר רִבִּי חִיָּיא בַּר בָּא. מֵבִיא מְלִילוֹת שֶׁלֹּא הֵבִיאוּ שְׁלִישׁ וְכוֹתְשָׁן וְעוֹשֶׂה אוֹתָן כְּחַלּוֹת חָרִיעַ. וְנוֹתֵן בַּקְּדֵירָה. וְהוּא עָבֵד כִּילְדִין.
וְקוֹלָן שֶׁל סוֹפְרִין. בְּאַלְכְּסַנְדְּרִיאָה עָבְדִין אַמְבַּטִיּוֹת שֶׁל בָּצֵק.

1 מוי G | מים 2 דו G | דהוא ביה 3 דו G | דהוא ביה בגויה 4 יין G | את יין לנסכים | לנסכין לא G | ולא היין G - | 5 והוון G | הוון 6 זיתוס G | זיתים זייתיה | זיתיה G | זותאיה 7 וזימי G | זומי שלצבעין G | שלצבעים דו יהב G | דיהב קוצם G | קוצים בגין G | בגון 8 עמילן G | אמילן שלטבחין G | שלטבהים 9 כחלות G | כמין חלות ומותן בקדירה G | ומותנן לתוך קדירה כילדין G | כלרין

10 שלסופרין G | שלסופרים באלכסנדריאה G | באלכסנדריה עבדין | G היו עושין

"And the following are removed on Passover," etc. Rebbi Mana said, all by the action of water[10].

"Babylonian *kutah*", for he puts in crumbs of dough.

"Median beer[2]," for he puts in barley flour.

"Edomite vinegar[3]," Southern aromatic. In earlier times, when one made wine in purity for libations, wine did not turn sour[11]. One had to spike it with barley to make it sour; one did call it "Southern aromatic."

"Egyptian *zythum*[4]," ζύθος.

"Dyers' gravy[5]," for he puts in *qussam*[12] so the dye should be absorbed.

"Cooks' starch." Rebbi Ḥitta bar Abba said, one brings ears of grain which are less than one-third ripe, pounds them, forms them like loaves of saffron, and puts them in the pot, so they should absorb the impurities[13].

"Scribes' glue[6]." In Alexandria they make tubs of dough[14].

10 He agrees with the Babli and disagrees with the opinion expressed in Chapter 2, Note 287, that fluids other than water can induce fermentation leading to leavening of grains.

11 But in later Talmudic times, at the beginning of the global cooling characterizing the time of migration of the nations, in many years sour wine naturally turned into vinegar. Babli 42b.

12 As S. Liebermann points out (*Tosephta kiFshutah* 3, *Šabbat* 8, pp. 111-112) if one adopts the reading of the text, the word is Syriac "barley flower" (as pointed out by E. S. Rosenthal), but the reading of G has to be explained as plural of קצי "morsel of bread". There remains the difficulty that in the preceding lines both "barley flour" and "bread crumbs" appear in their Hebrew forms. {Perhaps cf. Latin *quasso* "to shake, toss" (E. G.).}

13 Greek χλῆδος, ὁ, "dirt, slime".

14 The glue used in the manufacture of papyrus was grain-based.

(29d line 49) רִבִּי אֱלִיעֶזֶר אוֹמֵר. אַף תַּכְשִׁיטֵי נָשִׁים. אִית תַּנָּיֵי תַנֵּי. תַּכְשִׁיטֵי. וְאִית תַּנָּיֵי תַנֵּי. טִיפּוּלֵי. מָאן דְּאָמַר. טִיפּוּלֵי. כָּל־שֶׁכֵּן תַּכְשִׁיטֵי. מָאן דְּאָמַר. תַּכְשִׁיטֵי. הָא טִיפּוּלֵי לֹא.

1 אליעזר G | ליעזר   תכשיטי G טיפולי | תכשיטי G תכשיטין ואית תניי תני. טיפולי | G - 2 מאן דאמ' | G הוון בעיי מימר מן דמר   תכשיטי G טקשיטי וכל G | מאן דאמ' G | מן דמר   תכשיטי G טקשיטי

"Rebbi Eliezer says, also women's make-up." There are Tannaim who state "make-up"; and there are Tannaim who state "treatments". He who says "treatments", so much more "make-up"; he who says "make-up", but not "treatments"¹⁵.

15 The Babli 42b-43a explains that 'treatments" are depilatories used on a woman's body whereas make-up is used on her face. According to the second opinion, depilatories are so far removed from edibles that they need not be removed for Passover even if grain-based.

In G, the statement is quoted as a non-authoritative opinion: "they wanted to say that he who said ...".

(29d line 51) כָּתוּב כָּל־מַחְמֶצֶת לֹא תֹאכֵלוּ. לְרַבּוֹת כּוּתָּח הַבַּבְלִי וְשֵׁכָר הַמָּדִי וְחוֹמֶץ הָאֲדוֹמִי שֶׁיְּהוּ בָאַזְהָרָה. יָכוֹל יְהוּ בְהִכָּרֵת. תַּלְמוּד לוֹמַר כִּי. כָּל־אֹכֵל חָמֵץ וְנִכְרְתָה. חֲבֵרַייָא בְעוֹן קוֹמֵי רִבִּי יוֹנָה. הָכָא כְתִיב כָּל וְהָכָא כְתִיב כָּל. הָכָא אַתְּ מַרְבֶּה וְהָכָא אַתְּ מְמַעֵט. אָמַר לוֹן. כָּאן רִיבָּה בָאוֹכְלִין וְכָאן רִיבָּה בַנֶּאֱכָלִין. הֲתִיבוּן. וְהָתַנֵּי. יוֹצְאִין בְּמַצָּה מְתוּבֶּלֶת אַף עַל פִּי שֶׁאֵין בָּהּ טַעַם דָּגָן. וְהִיא שֶׁיְּהֵא רוּבָּהּ דָּגָן. וְאִילּוּ הוֹאִיל וְרוּבָּן חָמֵץ יְהֵא חַיָּיב. אֲמַר לוֹן. שַׁנְיָיא הִיא. דִּכְתִיב לֶחֶם. וְאִילּוּ אֵינָן לֶחֶם. הָתִיב רִבִּי יוֹסֵה. וְהָתַנֵּי. כָּל־עַצְמוֹ אֵינוֹ קָרוּי לֶחֶם אֶלָּא מַצָּה. שִׁבְעַת יָמִים תֹּאכַל־עָלָיו מַצּוֹת לֶחֶם עֹנִי. וְהָכָא אַתְּ יָלֵיף מַצָּה מֵחָמֵץ. וְעוֹד מִן הָדָא דְתַנֵּי. יוֹצֵא הוּא אָדָם יַד חוֹבָתוֹ בִּרְקִיק שָׂרוּי וּבִרְקִיק מְבוּשָּׁל שֶׁלֹּא נִמְחָה. לֹא אָמַר אֶלָּא שֶׁלֹּא נִמְחָה. הָא אִם נִמְחָה לֹא. וּלְעִנְיַין חָמֵץ אַתְּ אָמַר. הַמְחָה אֶת הֶחָמֵץ וּגְמָעוֹ חַיָּיב. מַאי כְדוֹן. רִבִּי יוֹסֵי בְשֵׁם רִבִּי אִידִי. אֵין חִימּוּצוֹ חִימּוּץ בָּרוּר. מָהוּ שֶׁיִּלְקֶה. רִבִּי יִרְמְיָה בְשֵׁם רִבִּי לְעָזָר. רִבִּי לָא בְשֵׁם רִבִּי שִׁמְעוֹן בֶּן לָקִישׁ. אַף לְלָקוֹת אֵין לוֹקֶה. דְּתַנֵּי. עַל חָמֵץ בָּרוּר חַיָּיב כָּרֵת וְעַל עֵירוּבוֹ סוֹפָג אַרְבָּעִים. רַב אָמַר. זֶה סִיעוֹר. וְאָמַר. זֶה כּוּתָּח הַבַּבְלִי וְשֵׁכָר הַמָּדִי. אָמַר רִבִּי בּוּן בַּר כַּהֲנָא קוֹמֵי רִבִּי לָא. תִּיפְתָּר בְּחָמֵץ וּמַצָּה שֶׁנִּתְעָרְבוּ. אָמַר רִבִּי יוֹסֵה. קַשְׁיָיתָהּ עַל הָדָא דְרִבִּי בּוּן בַּר כַּהֲנָא. מָה נָן קַיָּימִין. אִם בְּשֵׁרוּבּוֹ חָמֵץ. חַיָּיב כָּרֵת. אִם בְּשֵׁרוּבּוֹ מַצָּה. יוֹצֵא בָהֶן יְדֵי חוֹבָתוֹ בַּפֶּסַח. אֲמַר רִבִּי שְׁמוּאֵל בַּר רַב יִצְחָק. תִּיפְתָּר שֶׁיֵּשׁ בּוֹ חָמֵץ וְאֵין בּוֹ כַּזַּיִת. כְּרִבִּי שִׁמְעוֹן. דְּרִבִּי שִׁמְעוֹן אָמַר. כָּל־שֶׁהוּא לְמַכּוֹת.

2 שיהו | G שהוא יהו | G יהוא חבריא | G חברייא 3 הכא | G הכה והכא | G והכה הכא | G הכא והכא | G הכה והכה G| והכה 4 והתני | G והא תני מתובלת | G מתובבלת 5 ורובן | G ורובו שנייא | G שנייה 6 ואילו | G אילו והתני | G והא תני 7 והכא | G הכא הדא | G הדה 8 הוא - | G שרוי | G השרוי לא אמ' אלא שלא נמחה | G - 9 המחה את החמץ | G הימחה את החלב חייב | G הרי זה חייב מאי | G מאי יוסי G יוסה 10-11 בשם ר' אידי. אין חימוצו חימוץ ברור. מהו שילקה. ר' ירמיה בשם ר' לעזר. ר' לא | G - 11 דתני G | מילתיה דר' אמרה אף ללקות אינו לוקה. דתני חמץ | G החמץ חייב | G ענוש 12 ואמ'| G ומר 13 לא G | אילא קשייתה | G קשייתא הדא | G הדה 14 בשרובו | G בשרובן 15 תנא | G תנה יושע | G יהוש' תיפתר | G תפתר

"It is written: *Any leavened matter you shall not eat*¹⁶, to include Babylonian *kutah*, and Median beer, and Edomite vinegar, in the admonition. I might think that these are subject to extirpation, the verse says, *for anybody who eats leavened bread will be extirpated*¹⁷." The colleagues asked before

Rebbi Jonah: Here it is written *any*, and there it is written *any*. Here you are adding but there you are excluding[18]. He told them, there He added eaters but there He added edibles[19]. They objected, was it not stated: "One fulfills his obligation with spiced *mazzah*, even if it does not taste of grain, on condition that it be mostly grain"[20]. And for these[21], because they are mostly grain, he should be liable. He told them, there is a difference, for it is written *bread*, and these are not bread. Rebbi Yose objected, was it not stated that only *mazzah* is called bread, *seven days you shall eat mazzot, the bread of deprivation*[22]? But here you infer *mazzah* from leavened bread? In addition, from the following which was stated: "A person may acquit himself of his obligation with a soaked wafer, or a cooked wafer, as long as it did not lose its shape.[23]" It only says, "as long as it did not lose its shape," therefore not if it lost its shape. But in the matter of leavened bread you are saying, if he mashed leavened bread and slurped it, he is liable[24]. How is this? Rebbi Yose in the name of Rebbi Idi: Their[25] leavening is not clear leavening. Should he be flogged? Rebbi Jeremiah in the name of Rebbi Eleazar, Rebbi La in the name of Rebbi Simeon ben Laqish: Concerning flogging, he cannot be flogged, as it was stated: On certain leavened bread he is subject to extirpation, for its admixture he receives forty [lashes][26]. Rav said, that is sour dough. He could have said, that is Babylonian *kutah*, and Median beer[27]. Rebbi Abun bar Cahana said before Rebbi La: Explain it if leavened bread and *mazzah* were mixed[28]. Rebbi Yose said, I pointed out a difficulty for Rebbi Abun bar Cahana: Where do we hold? If most of it was leavened bread, he is subject to extirpation. If most of it is *mazzah*, he could use it to fulfill his obligation on Passover[29]. Rebbi Samuel bar Rav Isaac said, Rebbi Joshua from Ono stated: Explain it if the amount of leavened bread was less than the volume of an olive, following Rebbi Simeon, since Rebbi Simeon said, the most minute amount for flogging[30].

16   Ex. 12:20.
17   Ex. 12:15. Babli 33a, *Mekhilta dR. Ismael Ba* 10 (p. 35), *dR. Simeon ben Yohay* 12:20 (p.24).
18   Both in v. 15 and in v. 20 is written *any*. Why in matters of the prohibition one includes admixture of leavening but in matters of extirpation one excludes it?
19   In both cases, "any" implies addition and extension. In v. 15, *any who eats,*

includes women who are obligated to eat *mazzah* even though this is a positive commandment activated at a fixed date from which in general women are exempted (Mishnah *Qiddušin* 1:7). V. 20 *any leavened matter* includes admixture of leavening to edibles.

20 Cf. Chapter 2, Note 233.

21 Median beer. One agrees that Babylonian *kutah* might not trigger extirpation since the amount of leavened matter is small, but why should beer, which essentially is water and malt, be treated differently from bread which is water and flour?

22 *Deut.* 16:3. Since *mazzah* is called bread, it is clear that the positive commandment to eat *mazzah* can only be fulfilled by eating azyme bread. But leavened matter is always called חָמֵץ, and never is explicitly called "bread"; there seems to be no reason why extirpation should be restricted to those who eat bread.

23 Babli 41a, *Berakhot* 38b.

24 It is true that the positive commandment can be fulfilled only with bread but the prohibition extends to anything produced from leavened flour.

25 The items enumerated in the Mishnah.

26 Since *Ex.* 12:20 states a general prohibition for food with an admixture of leavened matter, transgression has to be punished by the generic punishment prescribed for all prohibitions for which no particular punishment is specified.

G has an additional sentence: "The word of Rebbi (probably meaning *Rabbenu*, i. e., Rav) implies that he is not flogged." On the other hand, a sentence of the ms. text is missing in G because of homoioteleuton.

27 Since Rav explains that one is flogged for consuming something containing an admixture of sour dough but not the items enumerated in the Mishnah, one may conclude that only active souring agent exposes one to flogging.

28 The preceding argument may be irrelevant since the *baraita* can be explained as referring directly to bread, eaten alone or with other edibles.

29 Since by biblical standards, anything greater than 50% is counted as whole. Since the mixture still is forbidden, the argument is possible only for R. Yose (cf. *Šabbat* 13, Note 56), but nobody else.

30 Babli *Makkot* 17a, *Ševuot* 21a, 24b, .*Menahot* 4a, *Me`ilah* 18a. R. Simeon restricts the possibility of a purification sacrifice to the case that a person ingested at least the volume of an olive of food forbidden under punishment of extirpation (such as forbidden fat or leavened matter on Passover) but admits the possibility of criminal prosecution for the most minute amount.

(29d line 72) רִבִּי יִרְמְיָה רִבִּי שְׁמוּאֵל בַּר רַב יִצְחָק בְּשֵׁם רַב. קְדֵירָה שֶׁבִּישֵּׁל בָּהּ [מוּדָה] לֹא יְבַשֵּׁל בָּהּ מֵאוֹתוֹ הַמִּין אֶלָּא לְאַחַר הַפֶּסַח. הָא מִמִּין אַחֵר מוּתָּר וּבִלְבַד לְאַחַר שְׁלֹשָׁה תַבְשִׁילָיו. כְּשֵׁם שֶׁהוּא בָטֵל עַל שֶׁאֵינוֹ מִינוֹ כָּךְ יְבָטֵל עַל מִינוֹ. מִין מְעוֹרֵר עַל מִינוֹ לֵיאָסֵר. אָמַר רִבִּי יַעֲקֹב בַּר זַבְדִּי. רִבִּי אַבָּהוּ מְפַקֵּד לְטוֹחֲנַיָּיא דְּלָא מִיתָּן קוּפַּיָּיא עַל אִילֵּין דְּלָא יְרַתְחָן וְיַחְמְעָן. רִבִּי חִינָּנָא בַּר פַּפָּא אָזַל לֵיהּ גַּבֵּי טוֹחֲנַיָּיא. רִבִּי יוֹסֵי בֵּירִבִּי בּוּן טָחַן לֵיהּ צְרָף. רִבִּי אָבוּן הוֹרֵי

לְטוּחֲנַיָּיא מִיתֵּן טַרְטוֹן דְּמֵיי בְּגִין מוֹדִיָּיה וּמְתַלְנָה אַרְבָּעָה זִימְנִין. רִבִּי חֲנַנְיָה וְרִבִּי מָנָא. חַד אָמַר. בָּעֲשָׂבִין שָׁרֵי. מְטַנְּנָה אֲסִיר. וְתָרָנָה מִיחְלַף. אָמַר רִבִּי חֲנַנְיָה בְּרֵיהּ דְּרִבִּי הִלֵּל. וְאַפִילוּ כְּמָאן דְּאָמַר. בָּעֲשָׂבִין שָׁרֵי. בְּלוֹקְטָן מִשֵּׁשׁ שָׁעוֹת וּלְמַעֲלָן. מָה. דְּטַלָּא פִּינָא מִינֵּיהּוֹן.

1 לא G | אל G | 3 על C | SG את ליאסר | G לוסר 4 אבהו G | אבהוא לטוחנייא G | לטוחנה קופייא G | קופיה אילין G | אלין (2) 5 חיננה G | חננה טוחנייא G | טוחנה יוסי G | יוסה טחן G | טחין צרף G | צריף 6 לטוחנייא G | לטוחנה טרטין G | טטרטון בגין G | גו ומתלנה G | ומתנונה 8 כמאן דאמ' G | כמן דמר

Rebbi Jeremiah, Rebbi Samuel bar Rav Isaac in the name of Rav: In a pot in which one cooked with water[31] one may cook the same kind only after Passover. Therefore another kind is permitted although only after three dishes[32]. If it becomes insignificant by other kinds, should it not become insignificant also by its own kind[33]? A kind awakes its own kind to prohibit[34]. Rebbi Jacob bar Zavdi said, Rebbi Abbahu ordered the millers[35] not to put boxes one on top of the other lest they heated up and became leavened. Rebbi Hinena bar Pappos went to the millers[36]. Rebbi Yose ben Rebbi Abun milled himself as guest[37]. Rebbi Abun instructed the millers to fill a *quartarius*[38] of water in the *modii* and moisten it four times. Rebbi Hananiah and Rebbi Mana, one said, grasses are permitted, moistened it is forbidden[39], but the other one switches. Rebbi Hananiah the son of Rebbi Hillel said, even the one who permits grasses, if he collected them in the afternoon. Why? For dew faded away from it[40].

31 מודה, a reading confirmed by G, cannot have the usual meaning "to agree". The unique meaning here is derived from Arabic مذى "mix with much water". If leavening was cooked with little water in a clay pot, everybody agrees that it cannot be completely cleaned for Passover use. Even if it was cooked with much water, Rav prohibits the use on Passover.

32 If the pot was used before Passover three times with water but no leavened matter, one assumes that the leavened matter absorbed in the walls was leached out and the pots may be used on Passover.

33 Where one assumes that no leavened matter was used.

34 A general principle recognized in the Babli (*Eruvin* 9a, *Avodah zarah* 73a, *Bekhorot* 22a, 33a).

35 In this version, this is a general instruction to the millers preparing Passover flour. In G the singular is used, "the miller", referring to the one who delivered to his household.

36 He personally supervised the milling for Passover.

37 Guest of the miller's. Reading צרף as ضرف, "to somebody's guest".

38 Following the reading of G; τέταρτον is the Greek equivalent of the Roman *quar-*

tarius, "a quarter"..

39 Grain silos used to be padded with grasses, Mishnah *Makhshirin* 3:5. It is difficult to understand how anybody could permit storing grain on moist grasses. S.

Liebermann conjectures that instead of מטוננה one has to read בטיט הגוב "in dried clay". But since the text is confirmed by G, emendation is problematic.

40 Here ends this fragment from G.

(fol. 29d) **משנה ב**: בָּצֵק שֶׁבְּסִדְקֵי הָעֲרֵיבָה אִם יֵשׁ כַּזַּיִת בְּמָקוֹם אֶחָד חַיָּב לְבָעֵר פָּחוֹת מִכֵּן בָּטֵל בְּמִיעוּטוֹ. וְכֵן לְעִנְיַן הַטּוּמְאָה אִם הִקְפִּיד עָלָיו חוֹצֵץ אִם רוֹצָה הוּא בְּקִיּוּמוֹ הֲרֵי הוּא כָּעֲרֵיבָה. בָּצֵק הַחֵרֵשׁ אִם יֵשׁ כַּיּוֹצֵא בוֹ שֶׁהֶחֱמִיץ הֲרֵי זֶה אָסוּר:

Mishnah 2: Dough in crannies of the baking trough: if there is the volume of an olive at one place one is obligated to eliminate; less than this becomes insignificant. Similarly in matters of impurity, if he is bothered by it it separates; if he desires its existence it is like the baking trough[41]. Deaf dough[42] is forbidden if a similar kind became sour.

41 Since for cleansing from impurity the verse requires that one immerse "all his flesh" in water, any dirt on the skin prevents the water to touch the skin and invalidates the immersion. The Mishnah restricts that to unwanted dirt; wanted adhesions separate only in the volume of an olive. Dry dough which acts as glue becomes part of the trough.

42 As explained in the Halakhah, dough refrigerated immediately after kneading.

(30a line 7) **הלכה ב**: חַבְרַיָּיא בְּשֵׁם רִבִּי יוֹחָנָן. רִבִּי סִימוֹן בְּשֵׁם רִבִּי יְהוֹשֻׁעַ בֶּן לֵוִי. בְּנִקְלַף כּוּלוֹ כְּאַחַת. עַד כְּדוֹן לַח. יָבֵשׁ. מֵאַחַר שֶׁאִילּוּ הָיָה לַח הָיָה נִקְלַף כּוּלוֹ כְּאַחַת. וַאֲפִילוּ יָבֵשׁ כְּסֵדֶר הַזֶּה.

Halakhah 2: The colleagues in the name of Rebbi Joḥanan, Rebbi Simon in the name of Rebbi Joshua ben Levi: If it could be scraped off together[43]. So far moist; dry? Since if it were moist it could be scraped together, even if dry the same applies.

43 "At one place" mentioned in the Mishnah does not mean that the leavened matter must be in one lump, only that the dough somehow must be connected (Babli 45b). If it is moist, it can be scraped off and remain connected; it dry, it will break when being scraped off. Nevertheless, since it was connected before being scraped off, the

rule of the Mishnah applies.

(30a line 10) רִבִּי יִרְמְיָה בְּשֵׁם רִבִּי זְעִירָה. שְׁנֵי חֲצָאֵי זֵיתִים בְּתוֹךְ הַבַּיִת. אֵין הַבַּיִת מְצָרֵף. בְּתוֹךְ הַכְּלִי. הַכְּלִי מְצָרֵף. וְהָא תַנִּינָן. פָּחוּת מִכֵּן בָּטֵל בְּמִיעוּטוֹ. כָּאן בְּתָלוּשׁ וְכָאן בִּמְחוּבָּר. מַהוּ. מִיעֲטוֹ בָטֵל. אוֹ מִכֵּיוָן שֶׁנִּרְאָה לְבַעֵר צָרִיךְ לְבַעֵר אֶת כּוּלּוֹ. עַד אֵיכָן. סָבְרִין מֵימַר. עַד רוּבָּהּ שֶׁלָּעֲרֵיבָה. מָה. מִיעֵט רוּבָּהּ שֶׁלָּעֲרֵיבָה בָּטֵל. אוֹ אוֹ מִכֵּיוָן שֶׁנִּרְאָה לְבַעֵר צָרִיךְ לְבַעֵר אֶת כּוּלּוֹ. (וְתַמָּן אָמַר רִבִּי יִרְמְיָה בְּשֵׁם רִבִּי זְעִירָה. שְׁנֵי חֲצָיֵי זֵיתִים בְּתוֹךְ הַבַּיִת. אֵין הַבַּיִת מְצָרֵף. בְּתוֹךְ הַכְּלִי. הַכְּלִי מְצָרֵף. וְהָכָא הוּא אָמַר הָכֵין.)

Rebbi Jeremiah in the name of Rebbi Ze`ira: Two volumes of half an olive in one house, the house does not combine them; in one vessel, the vessel does combine them. But did we not state, "less than this becomes insignificant"? One if plucked, one if connected[44]. If he reduced it, did it become insignificant, or since it was to be eliminated it has to be completely eliminated? How much? They wanted to say, up to most of the trough. How is this? If he reduced most of the trough, the remainder becomes insignificant, or since it was to be eliminated it has to be completely eliminated[45]? (There, Rebbi Jeremiah said in the name of Rebbi Ze`ira: Two volumes of half an olive in one house, the house does not combine them; in one vessel, the vessel does combine them; and here he says so?[46]).

44 The Mishnah states that leavened matter less than the volume of an olive is insignificant; R. Ze`ira states that several insignificant pieces in one vessel combine to be significant. Since the Amora R. Ze`ira cannot disagree with the Mishnah, how can his statement be interpreted? The Mishnah deals with specks of חָמֵץ material embedded in the walls of the vessel; they are permanently separate. R. Ze`ira speaks of movable specks; they combine since they can be assembled at one place (Babli 45b in the name of Ulla.).

45 If the walls of the trough were covered with a thin film of חָמֵץ, is it enough to clean the walls so that the remainder be less than the volume of an olive or must it be thoroughly cleaned? No answer is given; since the obligation of elimination is biblical, the automatic answer is that it must be thoroughly cleaned.

46 The text in parentheses does not belong here, it is from Halakhah 3, Note 87.

(30a line 17) אִם הִקְפִּיד עָלָיו חוֹצֵץ הוּא לִטְבִילָה. וְאִם לָאו אֵינוֹ חוֹצֵץ לִטְבִילָה הִיא טְבִילָה הִיא הַזָּיָיה. אֵינוֹ חִיבּוּר לְטוּמְאָה. מִן הָדָא. אִם רוֹצֶה הוּא בְקִיּוּמוֹ הֲרֵי הוּא כָעֲרֵיבָה. וְאִם לָאו כְּגוּפָהּ שֶׁלָּעֲרֵיבָה. רִבִּי שִׁמְעוֹן בֶּן לָקִישׁ אָמַר. כָּךְ שָׁנָה רִבִּי. צוֹאָה שֶׁתַּחַת הַכַּסֵּא חִיבּוּר

לְטוּמְאָה וְאֵינוֹ חִיבּוּר לַהַזָּיָיה. רִבִּי שִׁמְעוֹן בֶּן לָקִישׁ בְּשֵׁם רִבִּי שִׁמְעוֹן בַּר כַּהֲנָא. אֵבָר מְדוּלְדָּל צִפּוֹרֶן מְדוּלְדֶּלֶת וְצוֹאָה שֶׁתַּחַת הַכִּסֵּא וְהִידּוּק קֵירוּיָה וְכִרְוָיָה. רִבִּי יוֹסֵי בֵּירִבִּי בּוּן אָמַר. אַף כְּשׁוּת שֶׁלִּיקְטוֹ חִיבּוּר לְטוּמְאָה וְאֵינוֹ חִיבּוּר לַהַזָּיָיה. מַה בֵּין טוּמְאָה מַה בֵּין הַזָּיָיה. אָמַר רִבִּי לָא. בַּהַזָּיָיה כָּתוּב וְהִזָּה עַל־הָאֹהֶל וְעַל־כָּל־הַכֵּלִים. וְעַל כָּל הַמְקוּיָימִין שֶׁבַּכֵּלִי. בְּרַם הָכָא לָכֶם. כָּל־ שֶׁהוּא לְצוֹרֶךְ לָכֶם.

"If he is bothered by it it separates" for immersion; so if he is not bothered it does not separate for immersion[41]. The same is true for immersion and for sprinkling[47]. It[48] is not a connection for impurity, from the following: "if he desires its existence it is like the baking trough," otherwise it is not really[49] like the trough. Rebbi Simeon ben Laqish said, so did Rebbi formulate: Dirt under the chair[50] is connection for impurity, but no connection for sprinkling[51]. Rebbi Simeon ben Laqish in the name of Rebbi Simeon bar Cahana: An atrophied limb, an atrophied nail[52], the ballast of a pumpkin and its hollow[53]. Rebbi Yose ben Rebbi Abun said, also down which he plucked[54] is connection for impurity but no connection for sprinkling. What is the difference between impurity and sprinkling? Rebbi La said, about sprinkling it is written, *he shall sprinkle on the tent and on all vessels*[55]. But here, *for you*[56], all you have use for.

47 For the ritual of cleansing from the impurity of the dead, sprinkling with water containing ashes of the Red Cow (*Num.* 19). If the water only is sprinkled on dirt which would invalidate immersion, the implement is purified.

48 The dough in the volume of an olive sticking to the trough, as described in the Mishnah.

49 S. Liebermann points to *Yoma* 6:4 (Note 83), where גופו "its body" is used as *opposite* of מַמָּשׁ "really it".

50 Used as glue.

51 The two statements are not quite parallel. Immersion requires that the object to be purified be completely immersed; "connection" then means that if the glue is wetted, the wood below also is purified. In sprinkling, only drops are used; if a drop falls on the glue, the object is not purified.

52 Inoperative but still connected to the body.

53 A hollowed-out pumpkin used as a bottle. Since it is lighter than water, it cannot be immersed and filled with water without a ballast, usually a stone. While it is not part of the pumpkin, it is an intrinsic part of the bottle, as much as its hollow. All these are included in "connection for impurity, but no connection for sprinkling."

54 Downy facial hair. If a woman insists on removing it it acquires the status of unwanted dirt described in the Mishnah, being an obstacle to immersion and no

receptor of sprinkling drops.
55 *Num.* 19:18.
56 Many occurrences in the rules of impurity in *Lev.* 11: Babli *Hulin* 118a, a discussion of people having different needs at different times in *Šabbat* 48b.

(30a line 27) תַּמָּן אָמְרִין. טְרַקְטָא. הוֹרֵי רִבִּי יִצְחָק מֵיעֲבַד חַד. תְּרֵיי תְלָתָא אָסוּר. אֶלָּא אִין שָׁזַג יָדוֹי בְּמַיָּא. תַּנֵּי. קוּבָּטִיּוֹת בִּירָתִיּוֹת צָרִיךְ לְבָעֵר. הוֹרֵי רִבִּי יַסִּי בְּאִילֵּין פְּלוֹלֵינָא צָרִיךְ לְבָעֵר.

There, they are saying, *tracta*[57], Rebbi Isaac instructed that one may make one; two or three are forbidden unless one cleans his hands with water[58]. It was stated: Bireh boxes[59] have to be eliminated. Rebbi Yasa instructed that the surroundings of baking troughs[60] have to be eliminated.

57 Latin *tractum, tracta*, Greek τρακτόν, τό "long piece of dough drawn out in making pastry". Mentioned in Apicius (*De re coquinaria*, Ed. M. E. Milham, Leipzig 1969 Bk. IV iii) as used in serving fish, Bk. VII using "three small *tracta* balls" for *pultes tractogalatae*.
58 Since preparation of *tracta* takes time, one may bake these for Passover use only if one thoroughly cleanses his hands between any two of these, to avoid fermentation of the dough on the pastry cook's hands.

59 Greek κιβωτός "box, chest" (in LXX used to translate תֵּיבָה). Obviously not the boxes have to be eliminated but their contents have to be cleaned out. It seems that the boxes made in Bireh were used to store pastry. (S. Liebermann).
60 Liebermann reads προλήνια, places surrounding the ληνός, "kneading trough." Not only the implement where one makes dough has to be cleaned, but also its surroundings.

(30a line 30) רִבִּי אַבָּהוּ בְּשֵׁם רִבִּי יוֹחָנָן. בָּצֵק שֶׁצִּינָּנוּ. לֹא הָיָה שָׁם אַחֵר כְּיוֹצֵא בוֹ שֶׁהֶחֱמִיץ עַד אֵיכָן. רִבִּי יַעֲקֹב בַּר אָחָא רִבִּי עוּלָּא דְקַיְסָרִין בְּשֵׁם רִבִּי חֲנִינָה. עַד כְּדֵי הִילּוּךְ אַרְבָּעַת מִיל.

Rebbi Abbahu in the name of Rebbi Johanan: Cooled dough[42]. If there was not other dough like it, how long[61]? Rebbi Jacon bar Aha, Rebbi Ulla of Caesarea: Up to four *mil*'s walk[62].

61 How long is it permitted to keep cooled dough in preparation for Passover, without risk of fermentation.
62 Slightly more than one standard hour.

(fol. 29d) **משנה ג**: כֵּיצַד מַפְרִישִׁין חַלַּת טוּמְאָה בְּיוֹם טוֹב. רִבִּי אֱלִיעֶזֶר אוֹמֵר לֹא תִקְרָא לָהּ שֵׁם עַד שֶׁתֵּאָפֶה. בֶּן בְּתֵירָא אוֹמֵר תַּטִּיל לַצּוֹנֵן. אָמַר רִבִּי יְהוֹשֻׁעַ לֹא זֶהוּ חָמֵץ שֶׁמּוּזְהָרִין עָלָיו בְּבַל יֵרָאֶה וּבְבַל יִמָּצֵא אֶלָּא מַפְרִשְׁתָּהּ וּמַנַּחְתָּהּ עַד הָעֶרֶב וְאִם הֶחֱמִיצָה הֶחֱמִיצָה:

Mishnah 3: How does one separate *hallah* in impurity on the holiday[63]? Rebbi Eliezer says, it should not be given a name until after it is baked[64]. Ben Bathyra[65] says, one should keep it in cold water. Rebbi Joshua said, this is not leavening where one is warned that it should not be seen nor found, but one separates it and leaves it until the evening, and if it fermented, it fermented[66].

63 The problem is mainly for the holiday of Passover. Since *hallah* is a kind of heave, it must be consumed by a Cohen in purity. Dough of a minimum volume (cf. Introduction to Tractate *Hallah*) is forbidden as food as long as its heave was not taken. It is permitted to bake bread on a holiday which is not a Sabbath. If the dough is impure (e. g., if the person kneading the dough is impure, as is everybody today), the *hallah* is impure and has to be burned as impure heave. But since *sancta* other than Temple sacrifices may not be burned on any holiday, the impure *hallah* may not be burned immediately and, therefore, can be expected to become fermented. (In the talmudic languages, *hallah* never means "Sabbath bread" as in Eastern European Yiddish.)

64 He permits to bake the bread without *hallah* being taken from the dough (even though in this case the bread in the oven is forbidden as food) and to remove *hallah* (preferably a small loaf intended as *hallah* from the start) and declare it as such, which then releases the remainder of the bread for human consumption and retroactively justifies baking it on the holiday.

65 R. Jehudah ben Bathyra of Nisibis on the upper Tigris. In the interpretation of the Halakhah, he requires that the dough be kneaded continuously with cold water until the end of the holiday.

66 Since *hallah* is for Cohanim, it is not property of the maker of the dough and since the prohibition is that *yours shall not be seen, yours shall not be found*, it does not apply in this case and it is preferable to bake the dough into bread when clearly permitted as food.

(30a line 33) **הלכה ג**: מַתְנִיתָא בְּשֶׁנִּטְמֵאת לְאַחַר גִּילְגּוּלָהּ. אֲבָל אִם נִטְמֵאת קוֹדֶם לְגִילְגּוּלָהּ יַעֲשֶׂנָּה קַבִּין. בְּלָשָׁהּ בְּיוֹם טוֹב. אֲבָל לָשָׁהּ מֵעֶרֶב יוֹם טוֹב כְּהָנָא דְּתַנֵּי. הַלָּשׁ עִיסָּה בְּיוֹם טוֹב מַפְרִישׁ חַלָּתָהּ בְּיוֹם טוֹב. לָשָׁהּ מֵעֶרֶב יוֹם טוֹב וְשָׁכַח לְהַפְרִישׁ חַלָּתָהּ. אָסוּר לְטַלְטְלָהּ. אֵין צָרִיךְ לוֹמַר. לִיטּוֹל מִמֶּנָּה. עֵירָס. לֹא אָמַר אֶלָּא לָשׁ. הָא עֵירָס לֹא. אָמַר רִבִּי שְׁמוּאֵל אֲחוֹי דְּרִבִּי בְּרֶכְיָה. תִּיפְתָּר בְּעִיסָּה טְמֵיאָה שֶׁאֵינוֹ מַפְרִישׁ חַלָּתָהּ אֶלָּא בַּסּוֹף. אָמַר רִבִּי יוֹסֵה בֵּירִבִּי בּוּן. בְּדִין הָיָה בְעִיסָּה טְהוֹרָה שֶׁלֹּא יַפְרִישׁ חַלָּתָהּ אֶלָּא בַּסּוֹף. תַּקָּנָה תִקְנוּ בָהּ שֶׁיַּפְרִישֶׁנָּה תְחִילָּה. שֶׁלֹּא תִטָּמֵא אֶת הָעִיסָּה. מַתְנִיתָא בְּיוֹם טוֹב שֶׁלַּפֶּסַח. הָא בָּעֲצֶרֶת וּבַחַג מוּתָּר. רִבִּי

יוֹסֵה בֵּירְבִּי בּוּן רִבִּי חוּנָא בְשֵׁם רִבִּי אֲחָא. אֲפִילוּ בָעֲצֶרֶת וּבֶחָג אָסוּר. עַל שֵׁם כָּל־מְלָאכָה לֹא־יֵעָשֶׂה בָהֶם.

3 אין | צ ואין   8 תטמא | צ תיטמא   9 חונא | צ חונה

Halakhah 3: The Mishnah if it became impure after rolling. But if it became impure before rolling, he should make them into pieces of single *qab*[67]. If it was kneaded on the holiday. But if it was kneaded before the holiday, it is as it was stated:[68] "if one kneads dough on a holiday, he separates its *hallah* on the holiday. If he kneaded it before the holiday but forgot to take its *hallah*, it is forbidden to move it; it is unnecessary to say, to take *hallah* from it." If he mixed water and flour? He only mentioned "kneaded", so not when he mixed[69]? Rebbi Samuel, brother of Rebbi Berekhiah, said: explain it if the dough was impure where he takes *hallah* only at the end. Rebbi Yose ben Rebbi Abun said, it should have been the rule that for pure dough one should take *hallah* only at the end. They instituted that one should take it at the start, lest the dough become impure[70]. The Mishnah is about the holiday of Passover; therefore on Pentecost and Tabernacles it is permitted[71]. Rebbi Yose ben Rebbi Abun, Rebbi Huna in the name of Rebbi Aha, even on Pentecost and Tabernacles it is prohibited, because of *no work shall be done on them*[72].

67 After kneading the dough was shaped ready to be baked. This is the end of preparation of dough and, as for all heave, the completion of processing induces the obligation of heave. While the obligation of *hallah* starts only with completion of the dough, the possibility of giving *hallah* legally exists from the moment the preparation of the dough has begun. Later in this paragraph R. Yose ben R. Abun notes that it became customary to give *hallah* from pure dough at the earliest possible moment, to protect it from possible impurity during processing. Mishnah *Hallah* 3:1 states that the obligation of *hallah* exists only for a dough of ⁵/₄ *qab* of flour. Using impure flour on a holiday one is required to make loaves not larger than 1 *qab* (of 4 *log* of 4 *quartarii*); then the dough is never obligated for *hallah* and the problem of the Mishnah does not even start.

68 Tosephta *Yom Tov* 1:14. The text from here to the end of the paragraph is repeated in *Besah* 1:7 (צ).

69 Even though Mishnah *Hallah* 3:1 permits separating *hallah* immediately after mixing the flour with water.

70 Since then only the *hallah* has to be guarded from impurity but not the dough itself.

71 The remark applies both to Mishnah *Pesahim* 3:3 and Tosephta *Yom Tov* 1:14.

72 *Ex.* 12:16. Since impure *hallah* may not be eaten, it may not be baked on a holi- day.

(30a line 44) מַה בֵּינָהּ לִקְנִיבַת יָרָק שֶׁלִּתְרוּמָה. זוֹ רְאוּיָה לַאֲכִילָה. וְזוֹ אֵינָהּ רְאוּיָה לַאֲכִילָה. רַבָּנִין דְּקַיְסָרִין בְּעָיָן. מַה בֵּינָהּ לְבוֹרֵר קִטְנִית בְּיוֹם טוֹב.

What is the difference between this and cleansing heave vegetables[73]? The latter is possible food, the former is not possible food. The rabbis of Caesarea asked, what is the difference between this and picking out legumes on a holiday[74]?

73 It is permitted to trim heave vegetables on a holiday; the parts eliminated are no longer human food but as coming from *sancta* may not be used as animal feed. Cleansing vegetables as a regular component of preparing food is permitted on a holiday.

74 This question is similar to the preceding one, therefore the answer given to the first also applies here. The assumption here is that the chaff eliminated when picking out the edible parts is not even animal feed.

(30a line 46) כֵּיצַד יַעֲשֶׂה עַל דְּרַבִּי אֱלִיעֶזֶר. מַעֲרִים וְאוֹמֵר. זוֹ אֲנִי רוֹצֶה לוֹכַל [וְזוֹ אֲנִי רוֹצֶה לֶאֱכוֹל.] וְאוֹפֶה אֶת כּוּלָּהּ. וּכְשֶׁהוּא רוֹדֶה מַעֲרִים וְאוֹמֵר. זוֹ אֲנִי רוֹצֶה לְיַישֵׁן. זוֹ אֲנִי רוֹצֶה לְיַישֵׁן. וּמְשַׁיֵּיר אַחַת.

אָמַר לוֹ רִבִּי יוֹשׁוּעַ. לֹא נִמְצֵאתָהּ כְּשׂוֹרֵף קֳדָשִׁים בְּיוֹם טוֹב. אָמַר לוֹ רִבִּי אֱלִיעֶזֶר. מֵאֵילֵיהֶן הֵן נִשְׂרָפִין. אָמַר לוֹ רִבִּי יוֹשׁוּעַ. לֹא נִמְצֵאת עוֹבֵר עַל בַּל יֵרָאֶה וּבַל יִמָּצֵא. אָמַר לוֹ. מוּטָב לַעֲבוֹר מִצְוָה בְלֹא תַעֲשֶׂה שֶׁלֹּא בָאת לְפָנָיו מִמִּצְוָה בְלֹא תַעֲשֶׂה שֶׁבָּאת לְפָנָיו. [אָמַר רִבִּי פִּינְחָס. אַתְיָין אִילֵּין פְּלוּגָתָא כְּאִילֵּין פְּלוּגָתָא.

דְּתַנִּינָן תַּמָּן. הִנִּיתָנִין בְּמַתָּנָה אַחַת וכו׳. אָמַר לוֹ רִבִּי אֱלִיעֶזֶר. לֹא נִמְצֵאתָ עוֹבֵר עַל בַּל תִּגְרַע. אָמַר לוֹ רִבִּי יְהוֹשֻׁעַ. לֹא נִמְצֵאתָ עוֹבֵר עַל בַּל תּוֹסִף. אָמַר לוֹ. מוּטָב לַעֲבוֹר מִצְוָה בְלֹא תַעֲשֶׂה שֶׁלֹּא בָאת לְפָנָיו מִמִּצְוָה בְלֹא תַעֲשֶׂה שֶׁבָּאת לְפָנָיו.]

What should he do in Rebbi Eliezer's opinion? He is cunning and says, this I want to eat[and this I want to eat], and bakes all of them. When he removes the loaves, he is cunning and says, this I want to leave for later, and this I want to leave for later, and leaves one as remainder[75].

[76]Rebbi Joshua said to him, are you not like one who burns *sancta* on a holiday? Rebbi Eliezer told him, it is burned automatically. Rebbi Joshua said to him, are you not transgressing *it should not be seen, and it should not*

be found[77]? He told him, it is better to violate a prohibition that was not caused by you than a prohibition which will come before you.

[Rebbi Phineas said, this disagreement is parallel to other disagreements.

As we have stated there[78]: "[Blood] to be given in one batch etc. Rebbi Eliezer said to him, would you not transgress *do not diminish*? Rebbi Joshua answered him, would you not transgress *do not add*?[79]" He said to him, it is better to violate a prohibition that was not caused by me than a prohibition which will come before me.]

75   While he forms a small loaf that in the end will be impure *hallah*, he treats it as if he wanted to eat it while it is being baked, and only at the end, before he takes the first bite of the bread, declares it to be *hallah*. Then he leaves it in the oven where eventually it will be burned and turned into coal.

76   The following is a much shortened version, mostly by the corrector, of a text in *Eruvin* 10, Notes 165-175.
77   *Ex.* 13:7.
78   Mishnah *Zevahim* 8:10.
79   *Deut.* 4:2, 13:1.

(30a line 52) עַל דַּעְתֵּיהּ דְּרִבִּי אֱלִיעֶזֶר. יִקְרָא לָהּ שֵׁם וְיִרְדֶּנָּה. אֲסוּרָה לְטַלְטֵל. וְיִרְדֶּנָּה וְיִקְרָא לָהּ שֵׁם. שֶׁמָּא יִשְׁכַּח וְיֹאכַל. וְיִרְדֶּנָּה וְיִקְרָא לָהּ שֵׁם וְיוֹלִיךְ עִמָּהּ אַחֶרֶת לְקֶרֶן זָוִית. כַּהִיא דְתַנִּינָן תַּמָּן. מְטַלְטְלִין תְּרוּמָה טְהוֹרָה עִם הַטְּמֵיאָה עִם הַחוּלִין. וְלָא דָמְיָא. תַּמָּן טְמֵיאָה לְצוֹרֶךְ טְהוֹרָה. בְּרַם הָכָא חוּלִין לְצוֹרֶךְ טְמֵאָה. חַבְרַיָּיא בָעֵי. וְיַשְׁלִיכֶנָּה לָאַשְׁפָּה וְיַקְדִּישֶׁנָּה. וְיֵשׁ אָדָם מַקְדִּישׁ דָּבָר שֶׁאֵינוֹ שֶׁלּוֹ. וְיַקְדִּישֶׁנָּה וְיַשְׁלִיכֶנָּה לָאַשְׁפָּה. וְיֵשׁ אָדָם מַבְקִיר דָּבָר שֶׁאֵינוֹ שֶׁלּוֹ. רִבִּי יִרְמְיָה בָעֵי. וְיַפְרִידֶינָה וְיַשְׁלִיכֶינָה לַאֲוֵיר הַבַּיִת וְיִקְרָא לָהּ שֵׁם. תַּמָּן אָמַר רִבִּי יִרְמְיָה בְשֵׁם רִבִּי זְעוּרָה. שְׁנֵי חֲצָיֵי זֵיתִים בְּתוֹךְ הַבַּיִת. אֵין הַבַּיִת מְצָרֵף. בִּכְלִי הַבֵּלִי מְצָרֵף. וְהָכָא הוּא אָמַר (אָכֵן) [הָכֵן]. אָמַר רִבִּי יוֹסֵה. עַד שֶׁהוּא בַאֲוֵיר הַבַּיִת יִקְרָא לָהּ שֵׁם. אֲוֵיר הַבַּיִת מְצָרֵף לְחַלָּה. אֵין קַרְקַע הַבַּיִת מְצָרֵף לְחָמֵץ.

In Rebbi Eliezer's opinion, should he not give it its name and then take it down[80]? It will be forbidden to move it[81]. Then should he not take it down and then give it its name? Maybe he would forget and eat it. Should he not take it down, then give it its name, and with another piece put it in an isolated corner, following what we did state there, "one may move impure heave together with pure one or with profane food[82]"? It cannot be compared; there impure for the needs of pure[83], but here profane for the needs of impure. The colleagues asked, could he not throw it onto the garbage heap and then dedicate it[84]? May a person dedicate what is not his[85]? Then could he not dedicate it and throw it on the garbage heap? Can a person declare ownerless something that is not his[86]?

Rebbi Jeremiah asked: Could he not separate it, throw it in the air in the house[87] and then give it its name[88]? There[44], Rebbi Jeremiah said in the name of Rebbi Ze'ira: Two volumes of half an olive in one house, the house does not combine them; in one vessel, the vessel does combine them; and here he says so? Rebbi Yose said, when it still is in the air of the house he gives it its name. Does the air of the house combine for *hallah* but the ground of the house does not combine for leavening[89]?

80 Why does R. Eliezer require that the *hallah* remain in the oven (Note 67)?

81 Since it is neither food nor implement, it is *muqseh*.

82 Mishnah *Šabbat* 21:1.

83 It is permitted to move impure heave on the Sabbath only if this is needed to allow access to permitted items (Babli *Šabbat* 142a.)

84 Could one not remove some raw dough, throw in on the garbage heap (where it is abandoned and may be taken by scavengers). Since it no longer is his possession, he should not be concerned about it fermenting.

85 If it is abandoned and no longer his property, it is not his dough anymore and cannot be declared as *hallah*.

86 Since *hallah* is the Cohen's property, he cannot declare it ownerless; even on the garbage heap it remains his property and he has sinned if it ferments there.

87 Take the piece of raw dough reserved for *hallah*, separate it into minuscule parts, throw them into the air in the house, and only then declare them to be *hallah*. By Mishnah 3:2 he would not be liable if some of the flakes fermented, and in any case these would soon be swept away if the house is cleaned.

88 Declare it to be *hallah*.

89 The question of R. Jeremiah rests on an unproven and unreasonable hypothesis. For R. Eliezer there is no way to give *hallah* for impure dough easier than the complicated procedure explained earlier.

(30a line 68) אוֹתוֹ וְאֶת־בְּנוֹ שֶׁנָּפְלוּ לַבּוֹר. רִבִּי אֱלִיעֶזֶר אוֹמֵר. יַעֲלֶה אֶת הָרִאשׁוֹן עַל מְנָת לִשְׁחוֹט וְיִשְׁחוֹט. וְהַשֵּׁינִי עוֹשִׂין לוֹ פַּרְנָסָה שֶׁלֹּא יָמוּת. רִבִּי יוֹשֻׁעַ אוֹמֵר. יַעֲלֶה אֶת הָרִאשׁוֹן עַל מְנָת לִשְׁחוֹט וְלֹא יִשְׁחוֹט וְיַעֲרִים וְיַעֲלֶה אֶת הַשֵּׁינִי. אַף עַל פִּי שֶׁחִישֵּׁב שֶׁלֹּא לִשְׁחוֹט אֶחָד מֵהֶן מוּתָּר. רִבִּי בּוּן בַּר חִייָה בָעֵי. מְחִלְפָה שִׁיטָתֵיהּ דְּרִבִּי אֱלִיעֶזֶר. תַּמָּן הוּא אָמַר. אָסוּר לְהַעֲרִים. וְהָכָא הוּא אָמַר. מוּתָּר לְהַעֲרִים. הָכָא מְשׁוּם בַּל יֵרָאֶה וּבַל יִמָּצֵא. תַּמָּן מָה אִית לָךְ. מְחִלְפָה שִׁיטָתֵיהּ דְּרִבִּי יְהוֹשֻׁעַ. תַּמָּן הוּא אָמַר. מוּתָּר לְהַעֲרִים. וְהָכָא הוּא אָמַר. אָסוּר לְהַעֲרִים. אָמַר

רִבִּי אִידִי. כָּאן שְׁבוּת. וְכָאן חִיּוּב חַטָּאת. אָמַר רִבִּי יוֹסֵי בֵּירִבִּי בּוּן. תַּמָּן כְּדֵי לָחוּס עַל נִכְסֵיהֶן שֶׁל יִשְׂרָאֵל. הָכָא מָה אִית לָךְ.

It and its young[90] fell into a cistern. Rebbi Eliezer said, he should lift the first one for the purpose of slaughtering it and slaughter it. The second one has to be provided for so it should not die. Rebbi Joshua says, he should lift the first one for the purpose of slaughtering it and not slaughter it, and be cunning and lift the second one[91]. Even though he had no intention of slaughtering either of them, he is permitted[92]. Rebbi Abun bar Hiyya asked: Is the argument of Rebbi Eliezer not inverted? There he says, one is prohibited from cunning but here he says, one is permitted to be cunning[93]. Here it is because "not to be seen nor found"; there, what do you have[94]? Is the argument of Rebbi Joshua not inverted? There he says, one is permitted to be cunning, but here, he says, one is prohibited from cunning[95]. Rebbi Idi said, there it is a rabbinic Sabbath prohibition, but here liability for a purification offering[96]. Rebbi Yose ben Rebbi Bun said, there it is to protect Jews' money; here what do you have[97]?

רִבִּי יִצְחָק וְרִבִּי יֹאשִׁיָּה. חַד כְּהָדֵין וְחַד כְּהָדֵין. דָּרַשׁ רִבִּי בֶּרֶכְיָה כְּהָדָא דְבֶן בְּתֵירָה. מַתְנִיתָא אָמְרָה כֵן. תִּפָּח תִּלְטוֹשׁ בְּצוֹנֵין. מִילֵּיהוֹן דְּרַבָּנִין פְּלִיגִין. דָּמַר רִבִּי חִזְקִיָּה רִבִּי אַבָּהוּ בְשֵׁם רִבִּי לָעֲזָר. כָּל־מָקוֹם שֶׁשָּׁנָה רִבִּי מַחֲלוֹקֶת וְחָזַר וְשָׁנָה סְתָם. הֲלָכָה כִסְתָם.

Rebbi Isaac and Rebbi Joshia, one like one of them, the other like the other[98]. Rebbi Berekhiah preached following Ben Bathyra[99], the Mishnah says so: "she shall beat it and wet it with cold water.[100]" The words of the rabbis disagree[101], but Rebbi Ḥizqiah, Rebbi Abbahu said in the name of Rebbi Eleazar: In every instance where Rebbi formulated a disagreement and later formulated it anonymously, practice follows the anonymous statement[101].

90 *Lev.* 22:28. It is prohibited to slaughter an animal and its young on the same day. Therefore, if both an animal and its young fell into a cistern on a holiday, only one of them can be potential food. The other one is *muqseh* and cannot be moved by humans. Babli 117b, *Beṣah* 37a, Tosephta *Yom Tov* 3:2.. The paragraph also appears as Halakhah *Beṣah* 3:5 with the references to "here" and "there" switched correctly.

91 As long as it is not determined which animal is to be turned into food, both are potential food and can be moved.

92 He is permitted to declare both animals as potential food even though he had no intention of slaughtering either one.

93 In the matter of an animal and its

young he requires strict adherence to the rules; in the matter of impure *hallah* he permits bending them.

94 In matters of dough on Passover there is no other way out (short of not making food on the holiday); in the matters of the animals it is possible to follow all the rules.

95 For the animals in the cistern he allows a fake declaration which permits their rescue; for impure *hallah* he removes the prohibition by declaring it inapplicable.

96 *Muqseh* is rabbinic; eating bread without taking *hallah* is a deadly sin.

97 The animals in the cistern are valuable; impure *hallah* is worthless.

98 Since R. Isaac and R. Josia are last generation Tannaim, their disagreement must refer to the difference between the first generation RR. Eliezer and Joshua.

The sentence is copied in *Beṣah*.

99 He decided that practice has to follow Ben Bathyra.

100 Mishnah 3:4. Vocalization and translation follow Maimonides in his Mishnah Commentary (cf. Note 17 in the edition by R. Y. Qafeh). Dough is not fermenting only as long as it is worked on with cold water.

101 RR. Isaac and Josia disagree but by the rule formulated by the Amoraim one has to accept R. Berekhia's determination. The rule is affirmed *Orlah* 2:1 (Note 30), *Ta'aniot* 2:14, Babli *Yebamot* 42b, *Avodah zarah* 7a.

(fol. 29d) **משנה ד**: רַבָּן גַּמְלִיאֵל אוֹמֵר שָׁלֹשׁ נָשִׁים לָשׁוֹת כְּאַחַת וְאוֹפוֹת בְּתַנּוּר אֶחָד זוֹ אַחַר זוֹ. וַחֲכָמִים אוֹמְרִים שָׁלֹשׁ נָשִׁים עוֹסְקוֹת בַּבָּצֵק אַחַת לָשָׁה וְאַחַת עוֹרֶכֶת וְאַחַת אוֹפָה. רְבִּי עֲקִיבָה אוֹמֵר לֹא כָל־הַנָּשִׁים וְלֹא כָל־הָעֵצִים וְלֹא כָל־הַתַּנּוּרִים שָׁוִין. זֶה הַכְּלָל תְּפַח תִּלְטוֹשׁ בְּצוֹנֵן:

Mishnah 4: Rabban Gamliel says, three women knead dough simultaneously and bake in one oven one after the other, but the Sages say, three women are occupied with dough; one is kneading, one is forming, and one is baking[102]. Rebbi Aqiba says, neither all women nor all wood nor all ovens are equal. This is the principle, she shall beat it and wet it with cold water[100,103].

102 This determines the time from the start of making dough to baking when no fermenting is occurring. The details are described in the Halakhah.

103 The preceding paragraph makes it clear that this sentence is accepted by everybody; it is not part of R. Aqiba's dissent.

(30b line 8) **הלכה ד**: תָּנֵי. הָרִאשׁוֹנָה כְדֵי שֶׁיְהֵא כְדֵי הַסִּיקָה. וְהַשְּׁנִיָּה כְדֵי שְׁנֵי הַסִּיקִין וַאֲפִיָּה אַחַת. וְהַשְּׁלִישִׁית כְדֵי שְׁלֹשָׁה הַסִּיקִין וּשְׁתֵּי אֲפִיּוֹת. אִם עָשָׂת כִּכַּר רִאשׁוֹן אַחֲרוֹן כְּדֵי שְׁלֹשָׁה הַסִּיקִין וְשָׁלֹשׁ אֲפִיּוֹת.

תָּנֵי. גָּמְרָה זֶה לִישָׁתָהּ וְגָמְרָה זֶה קִיטּוּפָהּ וְגָמְרָה זֶה הַסִּיקָהּ. הָרִאשׁוֹנָה שׁוֹהָא כְּדֵי הַסִּיקָה. וְהַשְּׁנִיָּה כְּדֵי הַסִּיקָה וַאֲפִיַּת חֲבֶירְתָהּ. וְהַשְּׁלִישִׁית כְּדֵי שְׁנֵי הַסִּיקִין וַאֲפִיָּה אַחַת. אִם עָשָׂת כִּכַּר רִאשׁוֹן אַחֲרוֹן כְּדֵי שְׁנֵי הַסִּיקִין וּשְׁתֵּי אֲפִיּוֹת.

Halakhah 4: It was stated: The first one waits for heating, the second for two heatings and one baking, and the third for three heatings and two bakings. If she made one of the first loaves last, for three heatings and three bakings[104].

It was stated: If one finished kneading, one finished forming, and one finished baking. The first one waits for heating, the second for her colleague's heating and baking, and the third for two heatings and one baking. If she made one of the first loaves last, for two heatings and two bakings[105].

104 This follows Rabban Gamliel. If three women finish kneading the dough and forming the loaves all at the same time and the first to use the oven bakes only part of it the first time and for the remainder she waits until after the other two are finished with theirs, she will use the oven again after three baking runs. The ovens are small and have to be refuelled for each run. This is purely as explanation of the Mishnah since the last sentence of the Mishnah explains, in the words of Maimonides, "know that all the time the hand is working on the dough it does not start to ferment even if this takes an entire day".

105 This follows the Sages, for whom one starts baking while the second one is still forming loaves and the third kneading dough. Since the first baking run is made while the second and third batches are not ready, it is not counted.

(30b line 15) רַבָּן גַּמְלִיאֵל אוֹמֵר שָׁלֹשׁ נָשִׁים לָשׁוֹת כְּאַחַת וְאוֹפוֹת בְּתַנּוּר אֶחָד זוֹ אַחַר זוֹ. וַחֲכָמִים אוֹמְרִים שָׁלֹשׁ נָשִׁים עוֹסְקוֹת בַּבָּצֵק. אַחַת לָשָׁה וְאַחַת עוֹרֶכֶת וְאַחַת אוֹפָה. תָּנֵי רִבִּי הוֹשַׁעְיָה. וְאַחֶרֶת בָּאָה וְלָשָׁה וְלָשָׁה תַחְתֵּיהֶן. אִית תַּנָּיֵי תַנֵּי. בַּחִיטִּין שְׁלֹשָׁה קַבִּין. וּבַשְּׂעוֹרִין אַרְבָּעַת קַבִּין. אִית תַּנָּיֵי תַנֵּי. בַּחִיטִּין אַרְבָּעַת קַבִּין. וּבַשְּׂעוֹרִין שְׁלֹשָׁה קַבִּין. מָאן דְּאָמַר. בַּחִיטִּין שְׁלֹשָׁה קַבִּין. בְּשֶׁיֵּשׁ בָּהֶן שְׁמַנּוּנִית. בַּשְּׂעוֹרִין אַרְבָּעַת קַבִּין. בְּשֶׁאֵין בָּהֶן שְׁמַנּוּנִית. מָאן דְּאָמַר. בַּחִיטִּין אַרְבָּעַת קַבִּין. וּבַשְּׂעוֹרִין שְׁלֹשָׁה קַבִּין. דְּאִינּוּן רְטִישִׁין.

"Rabban Gamliel says, three women knead dough simultaneously and bake in one oven one after the other, but the Sages say, three women are occupied with dough; one is kneading, one is forming, and one is baking."

Rebbi Hoshaia stated: And another one comes and kneads in their stead[106]. There are Tannaim who state: Three *qab* wheat or four *qab* barley[107]. There are Tannaim who state: Four *qab* wheat or three *qab* barley. He who said, three *qab* wheat, if they have fat, or four *qab* barley, if they have no fat. He who said, four *qab* wheat, if they are soft, or three *qab* barley, if they are hard[108].

106 To work on the dough during the waiting period as required.
107 These are maximal quantities permitted to be worked on in one batch without fear of fermentation. Cf. Babli 48a.
108 "Fat" grain produces flour which easily ferments; soft grain needs little water and therefore is not prone to quick fermentation, hard grain has to be soaked.
The translation of רטש as "hard" presumes a metathesis and reads the word as טרש.

(fol. 29d) **משנה ה**: שִׂיאוּר יִשָּׂרֵף וְהָאוֹכְלוֹ פָּטוּר. סִידּוּק יִשָּׂרֵף וְהָאוֹכְלוֹ חַיָּב כָּרֵת. אֵיזֶהוּ שִׂיאוּר כְּקַרְנֵי חֲגָבִים. סִידּוּק שֶׁנִּתְעָרְבוּ סְדָקָיו זֶה בָזֶה דִּבְרֵי רִבִּי יְהוּדָה. וַחֲכָמִים אוֹמְרִים זֶה וָזֶה הָאוֹכְלוֹ חַיָּב כָּרֵת. אֵי זֶהוּ שִׂיאוּר כָּל־שֶׁהִכְסִיפוּ פָנָיו כְּאָדָם שֶׁעָמְדוּ שַׂעֲרוֹתָיו:

Mishnah 5: Sour dough[109] is to be burned but a person who eats it is not liable; cracked dough[110] is to be burned and a person who eats it is liable for extirpation. What is sour dough? Like locusts' antlers[111]; cracked if its fissures joined one another, the words of Rebbi Jehudah, but the Sages say, in both cases one who eats it is liable. What is sour dough? Any which is pale like a man whose hair is standing up[112].

109 Dough in the process of fermentation which is not edible for most people. Extirpation is decreed only for people eating leavened food on Passover.
110 Not fully fermented but edible dough.
111 The CO_2 created in the fermentation process causes small fissures the size of locusts' antlers.
112 In fear.

(30b line 22) **הלכה ה**: רַב הוּנָא בְּשֵׁם רַב. מוּתָּר לְהַאֲכִילוֹ [לְכַלְבּוֹ]. תַּנֵּי בַּר קַפָּרָא. אֵין לְךָ סֶדֶק מִלְּמַעְלָן שֶׁאֵין תַּחְתָּיו כַּמָּה סְדָקִין.

Halakhah 5: Rav Huna in the name of Rav: One is permitted to feed it [to his dog][113]. Bar Qappara stated: There is no fissure on top which does not have several fissures below[114].

113 Since it is inedible, the prohibition of eating cannot imply prohibition of usufruct; cf. Chapter 2, Notes 9,14.

114 He gives the reason why the Sages reject the definition of R. Jehudah. Even if only one fissure the size of a locust antler is visible, it is a confluence of a number of interior bubbles. Babli 48b.

(fol. 29d) **משנה ו:** אַרְבָּעָה עָשָׂר שֶׁחָל לִהְיוֹת בַּשַּׁבָּת מְבַעֲרִין אֶת הַכֹּל מִלִּפְנֵי הַשַּׁבָּת דִּבְרֵי רִבִּי מֵאִיר. וַחֲכָמִים אוֹמְרִים בִּזְמַנָּן. רִבִּי אֶלְעָזָר בַּר צָדוֹק אוֹמֵר תְּרוּמָה מִלִּפְנֵי הַשַּׁבָּת וְחוּלִין בִּזְמַנָּן:

Mishnah 6: If the Fourteenth falls on a Sabbath one eliminates everything before the Sabbath[115], the words of Rebbi Meïr, but the Sages say, on their time[116]. Rebbi Eleazar bar Sadoq says, heave before the Sabbath[117] and profane on their time.

115 By burning on Friday.

116 Since the remaining leavened matter cannot be burned on the Sabbath, if not eaten by that time it either has to be given to Gentiles or it has to be crumbled into minute pieces which are strewn to the wind, the preferred method of disposal of the Sages

(Mishnah 2:1)..

117 Since heave must be consumed by Cohanim, who are few, the ways of disposal on the Sabbath are not available; it must be disposed of on Friday. But profane matter may be disposed of following the Sages.

(30b line 25) **הלכה ו:** אַתְיָא דְּרִבִּי מֵאִיר כְּרִבִּי לִיעֶזֶר וְרוּבָה מִן דְּרִבִּי אֱלִיעֶזֶר. דְּרִבִּי לִיעֶזֶר אוֹמֵר. שֶׁלֹּא יָבוֹא לִידֵי בַּל יֵרָאֶה וּבַל יִמָּצֵא. רִבִּי מֵאִיר אוֹמֵר. שֶׁלֹּא יָבוֹא לְסָפֵק בַּל יֵרָאֶה וּבַל יִמָּצֵא. אַתְיָא דְּרַבָּנִין כְּרִבִּי יוֹשׁוּעַ וְרוּבָה מֵרִבִּי יוֹשׁוּעַ. דְּרִבִּי יושוע אוֹמֵר. אֵין שׂוֹרְפִין אֶת הַקֳּדָשִׁים בְּיוֹם טוֹב. וְרַבָּנִין אֲמָרִין. אֲפִילוּ בַחוֹל אֵין שׂוֹרְפִין אֶת הַקֳּדָשִׁים.

Halakhah 6: It turns out that Rebbi Meïr parallels Rebbi Eliezer but is more stringent than Rebbi Eliezer. For Rebbi Eliezer says "that he not transgress *not to be seen nor be found*." Rebbi Meïr says, that he not possibly transgress *not to be seen nor be found*[118]. It turns out that the rabbis parallel Rebbi Joshua but are more stringent than Rebbi Joshua. For Rebbi Joshua says that one does not burn *sancta* on a holiday, and the rabbis say, even on weekdays one does not burn *sancta*[119].

118 In Halakhah 3, R. Eliezer requires that the rules of *hallah* be bent to avoid the *hallah* dough becoming fermented. Here R. Meïr requires that heave be eliminated early even though it is a biblical requirement that it be treated as *sanctum* (*Num.* 18:8) and be consumed by the priests and their families (v. 13).

119 Since profane food may be disposed of at any time (Halakhah 2:1), it is clear that the Sages only insist that heave may not be destroyed before its time. This parallels the opinion of R. Joshua who in Halakhah 3 insists that *hallah* dough may not be touched.

(30b line 31) תָּנֵי. אָמַר רִבִּי יוּדָה. לֹא נֶחְלְקוּ בֵית שַׁמַּי וּבֵית הֵלֵּל עַל תְּרוּמָה טְהוֹרָה שֶׁאָסוּר לְשׁוֹרְפָהּ וְעַל תְּרוּמָה טְמֵיאָה שֶׁמּוּתָּר לְשׁוֹרְפָהּ. עַל מַה נֶחְלְקוּ. עַל הַתְּלוּיָה. שֶׁבֵּית [שַׁמַּאי] אוֹמְרִין. אֵין שׂוֹרְפִין. וּבֵית הֵלֵּל אוֹמְרִין. שׂוֹרְפִין. אָמְרוּ בֵית שַׁמַּי לְבֵית הֵלֵּל. כְּלוּם אַתֶּם אוֹמְרִין בִּטְהוֹרָה שֶׁלֹּא תִישָּׂרֵף. אֶלָּא שֶׁאֲנִי אוֹמֵר. שֶׁמָּא כֹהֵן אֶחָד שָׁבַת בְּתוֹךְ הַתְּחוּם וְהוּא בָא וְאוֹכְלָהּ בַּשַּׁבָּת. אַף תְּלוּיָה לֹא תִישָּׂרֵף. שֶׁאֲנִי אוֹמֵר. שֶׁמָּא אֵלִיָּהוּ שָׁבַת בְּהַר הַכַּרְמֶל וְהוּא בָא וּמֵעִיד עָלֶיהָ בַּשַּׁבָּת שֶׁהִיא טְהוֹרָה. אָמְרוּ לָהֶן בֵּית הֵלֵּל. מוּבְטָחִין אָנוּ שֶׁאֵין אֵלִיָּהוּ בָא לֹא בַשַּׁבָּתוֹת וְלֹא בַיָּמִים טוֹבִים.

2 על G |ועל שמאי| שמיי G| שמיי 3 |שמיי G |שני 4 שאני| G |תליה 5 תלוייה| שאני| G |שני בהר ראש| G

It was stated: "Rebbi Jehudah said, the House of Shammai and the House of Hillel did not disagree [120]about pure heave that it is forbidden to burn it[121], and about impure heave that one is permitted to burn it[121]; about what did they disagree? About the suspended[122] one, about which the House of Shammai[123] say, one may not burn it, but the House of Hillel say, one burns it. The House of Shammai said to the House of Hillel: Do you not say that the pure one may not be burned because I am saying that maybe a Cohen was keeping the Sabbath within the domain and he might come and eat in on the Sabbath, so also the suspended one may not be burned because I am saying that maybe Elijah[125] was keeping the Sabbath on Mount Carmel and he might come and testify on the Sabbath that it is pure. The House of Hillel told them, we are sure that Elijah will come neither on a Sabbath nor on a holiday[126]."

120 Here starts a new Genizah fragment (G).

121 On a Friday the 13th of Nisan.

122 Heave whose purity is in question. It

may not be eaten since it may be impure; it may not be disposed of since it may be pure.
123 The spelling is the Babylonian one of the corrector; it should be disregarded.
125 He may appear anywhere and as a member of the Divine Court he knows the true facts about everything.
126 In the Babli 13a in a related *baraita*: "neither on a Friday nor on the day preceding a holiday because of the trouble [this would cause.]"

(30b line 40); רִבִּי אַבָּהוּ בְשֵׁם רִבִּי יוֹחָנָן. אַתְיָא דְרִבִּי אֶלְעָזָר בֵּירִבִּי צָדוֹק כְּרַבָּן גַּמְלִיאֵל. כְּמָה דְרַבָּן גַּמְלִיאֵל אָמַר מַה שָׁנֵי בֵּין חוּלִין לִתְרוּמָה. כֵּן רִבִּי אֶלְעָזָר בֵּירִבִּי צָדוֹק טָמַר מַה שָׁנוּ בֵּין חוּלִין לִתְרוּמָה. כָּמָה דְתֵימַר. הֲלָכָה כְּרַבָּן גַּמְלִיאֵל. וְדִכְוָותָהּ. הֲלָכָה כְּרִבִּי אֶלְעָזָר בֵּירִבִּי צָדוֹק.

1 אבהו G | אבהוא אתיא G | אתייה אלעזר | G לעזר   2 אמ' | G - (2) | G - | אלעזר ביר' | G לעזר בר'   אמ' | G -
3 כמה דתימר | G וכמה דתמר אלעזר | G לעזר

Rebbi Abbahu in the name of Rebbi Johanan: It turns out that Rebbi Eleazar ben Rebbi Ṣadoq parallels Rabban Gamliel[127]. Just as Rabban Gamliel (said)[128] distinguishes between profane and heave, so Rebbi Eleazar ben Rebbi Ṣadoq (said)[128] distinguishes between profane and heave. Since you say that practice follows Rabban Gamliel, similarly practice has to follow Rebbi Eleazar ben Rebbi Ṣadoq[129].

127 Who in Mishnah 1:6 allows more time to consume leavened heave than leavened profane food.
128 Omit with G.
129 Cf. Chpater 1, Halakhah 6, Note 160; Maimonides *Hames umazzah* 3:3, Note by Ravad.

(fol. 29d) **משנה ז:** הַהוֹלֵךְ לִשְׁחוֹט אֶת פִּסְחוֹ וְלָמוּל אֶת בְּנוֹ וְלֶאֱכוֹל סְעוּדַת אֵירוּסִין בְּבֵית חָמִיו וְנִזְכַּר שֶׁיֵּשׁ לוֹ חָמֵץ בְּתוֹךְ בֵּיתוֹ אִם יָכוֹל לַחֲזוֹר וּלְבַעֵר וְלַחֲזוֹר לְמִצְוָתוֹ יַחֲזוֹר. וְאִם לָאו יְבַטֵּל בְּלִבּוֹ. לְהַצִּיל מִיַּד הַגַּיִיס וּמִיַּד הַנָּהָר וּמִן הַדְּלֵיקָה וּמִן הַמַּפּוֹלֶת יְבַטֵּל בְּלִבּוֹ. וְלִשְׁבּוֹת שְׁבִיתַת הָרְשׁוּת יַחֲזוֹר מִיָּד:

Mishnah 7: A person who goes to slaughter his Passover sacrifice, or to circumcise his son, or to eat the betrothal meal at his father-in-law's house[130], and remembers that he has leavened matter in his house, if he can return, eliminate it, and return to his meritorious deed, he shall return and eliminate; otherwise, he has to nullify it in his thought[131]. To save from the army[132], or from a river[133], or from a conflagration, or from a house collapse, he has to nullify it in his thought[134]. To celebrate the holiday according to his wishes[135], he has to return immediately.

130 On the 14th of Nisan.
131 While the condition given in Chapter 2, Note 101, is not strictly satisfied, in an emergency situation mental annulment is sufficient as legal abandonment to satisfy the biblical requirement not to have one's own leavened matter in his possession.
132 The Roman army on the march in the Roman empire. Since the soldiers will steal anything not hidden, this is an emergency.
133 A flood.
134 These are real emergency situations.
135 He goes to celebrate the holiday at another place of his choosing, not to fulfill a religious precept.

(30d line 45) **הלכה ז:** אָמַר רִבִּי יוֹסֵה בֵּירִבִּי בּוּן. בּוֹא וּרְאֵה מַה גָּדוֹל הוּא הַשָּׁלוֹם שֶׁהוּקַשׁ לִשְׁנֵי דְבָרִים שֶׁחַיָּיבִין עֲלֵיהֶן כָּרֵת.

Halakhah 7: Rebbi Yose ben Rebbi Abun said, come and see how great is peace that it is bundled with two things about whom one is liable to extirpation[136].

136 In the Mishnah, a meal with his future in-laws is put on the same level as the Passover sacrifice and circumcision; two commandments whose omission is punished by Divine extirpation (*Gen.* 17:14, *Num.* 9:13).

(30b line 46) מִילַת בְּנוֹ וּשְׁחִיטַת פִּסְחוֹ מִי קוֹדֵם. אָמַר רִבִּי פִּינְחָס. מִן מַה דִכְתִיב הִמּוֹל לוֹ כָל־זָכָר וְאָז יִקְרַב לַעֲשׂוֹתוֹ. הָדָא אָמְרָה שֶׁמִּילַת בְּנוֹ קוֹדֶמֶת לִשְׁחִיטַת פִּסְחוֹ.

2 הדא | הדא G
אפילו יָכוֹל לַחֲזוֹר וּלְבָעֵר וְלֵילֵךְ וּלְהַצִּיל. אפילו יָכוֹל לֵילֵךְ וְלָשׁוּב לַחֲזוֹר וּלְבַטֵּל.
1 ולהציל G | להציל   יכול | G - לחזור ולבטל | G ולחזור לבער

His son's circumcision and the slaughter of his Passover sacrifice. what has precedence? Rebbi Phineas said, since it is written, *all his males have to be circumcided, then he will be admitted to nake it*, this implies that his sons' circumcisions has priority over the slaughter of his Passover sacrifice.

Even if he could return and eliminate, or go and save[137]. Even if he could go and acquire rest status, return and (nullify) [eliminate][138].

137 Since the second series of cases in the Mishnah is formulated as apodictic rule, not subject to a condition as in the first series, it follows that a person starting to save from soldiers, flood, fire, and collapse, is not permitted to return and eliminate but forced

to annul mentally.
138 In the last case, if he leaves his place but not to go to Jerusalem, he is required to return immediately even if he could go to the place of his destination, deposit some food there to symbolically move his dwelling to that place, then return to his own house, eliminate the leavened matter, and return to his place of holiday rest

(29d line 50) מַהוּ [שֶׁאֵין] שְׁבִיתַת הָרְשׁוּת. אֵצֶל רַבּוֹ אוֹ אֵצֶל מִי שֶׁהוּא גָדוֹל מִמֶּנּוּ בְחָכְמָה. כָּךְ שָׁנָה רִבִּי. הַמַּעֲשֶׂה קוֹדֵם לַתַּלְמוּד. נִמְנוּ בַּעֲלִיַּת בֵּית אָרוֹס בְּלוֹד. הַתַּלְמוּד קוֹדֵם לַמַּעֲשֶׂה.

1 מהו G מהוא שאין | - G | בכחמה G בתורה   2 בעלית G בעליית ארוס G אריס

[What is][139] (no)[140] to celebrate the holiday according to his wishes? At his teacher's or at somebody greater than he in wisdom. Here did Rebbi state that action precedes study[141]. They voted in the upper floor of the house of Arius in Lydda that study precedes action[142].

139 This was written by the scribe and then erased by him; it should be read following G..
140 Addition of the corrector; to be deleted with G.
141 Since the action of eliminating leavened matter, even though it could have been replaced by a declaration of nullification, has precedence over a possibility of further study.
142 According to the Babli, *Qiddušin* 40b, this was an early Tannaitic decision following R. Aqiba against R. Tarphon. *Hagigah* 1:7.

(30b line 53) רִבִּי אַבָּהוּ שָׁלַח לְרִבִּי חֲנִינָה בְּרֵיהּ יִזְכֵּי בְטִיבֶּרְיָה. אָתוֹן וְאָמְרוֹן לֵיהּ. גְּמַל הוּא חֶסֶד. שָׁלַח וַאֲמַר לֵיהּ. הֲמִבְּלִי אֵין קְבָרִים בְּקֵיסָרִין שְׁלַחְתִּיךָ לִטְבֶרְיָא. שֶׁכְּבָר נִמְנוּ וְגָמְרוּ בַּעֲלִיַּת בֵּית אָרוֹס בְּלוֹד שֶׁהַתַּלְמוּד קוֹדֵם לַמַּעֲשֶׂה. רַבָּנִן דְּקֵיסָרִין אָמְרִין. הָדָא דְתֵימַר. כְּשֶׁיֵּשׁ שָׁם מִי שֶׁיַּעֲשֶׂה. אֲבָל אִם אֵין שָׁם מִי שֶׁיַּעֲשֶׂה הַמַּעֲשֶׂה קוֹדֵם. דִּלְמָא. רִבִּי חִייָה רִבִּי יַסִי רִבִּי אִימִי עָנוֹן לְמֵיתֵי גַּבֵּי רִבִּי אֶלְעָזָר. אָמַר לוֹן. אָן הֲוֵיתוֹן. אָמְרִין לֵיהּ. גְּמַל חֶסֶד. אָמַר לוֹן. וְלֹא הֲוָה תַּמָּן חוֹרָנִין. אָמְרִין לֵיהּ. מָגוֹר הֲוָה.

1 חנינה G חנניה יזכי G למיתב אתון G שלחון ואמרון G אמרון   2 ואמ' G אמ' | לטבריא G לטבריה שכבר G כבר וגמרו G -   3 ארוס G אריס שהתלמוד G התלמוד רבנין G רבנן הדא דתימר G הדה דתמר   4 קודם G קודם לתלמוד דלמא G דלמה ר' יסי G ור' יוסי   5 ר' אימי G ור' אמי למיתי G מאתי אלעזר G אלעזר לעזר אן הויתון G הין הוויתון אמרין G אמרון גמל G גמלון   6 הוה G הווה חורנין G אוחרנין אמרין ליה G אמרון מגור G מעיר

Rebbi Abbahu sent his son Rebbi Hanina to acquire merit in Tiberias. They came and said to him, he does works of charity[143]. He sent to tell him, are there no graves in Caesarea[144] that I sent you to Tiberias? For they already voted and decided[145] in the upper floor of the house of Arius in Lydda that study precedes action[146]. The rabbis of Caesaria say, that is, if there is somebody there who will do it. But if nobody is there who will do it, the action has precedence[147]. Example. Rebbi Ḥiyya, Rebbi Yasa, Rebbi Immi, were late in coming to Rebbi Eleazar. He asked them, where have you been? They told him, performing an act of charity. He asked them, where there no others? They answered him, it was a neighbor[148].

143 Burying the dead.
144 A reference to *Ex.* 14:11.
145 Delete with G.
146 Therefore he has to spend his time studying in the Academy there.

147 In particular, religious obligations of a personal nature, which cannot be delegated, have precedence over study.
148 It was an obligation irrespective of the number of attendees at the funeral.

(fol. 29d) **משנה ח**: וְכֵן מִי שֶׁיָּצָא מִירוּשָׁלַם וְנִזְכַּר שֶׁיֵּשׁ בְּיָדוֹ בְּשַׂר קוֹדֶשׁ אִם עָבַר הַצּוֹפִים יִשָּׂרְפוּ בִּמְקוֹמוֹ. וְאִם לָאו חוֹזֵר וְשׂוֹרְפוֹ לִפְנֵי הַבִּירָה מֵעֲצֵי הַמַּעֲרָכָה. עַד כַּמָּה הֵן חוֹזְרִין רַבִּי מֵאִיר אוֹמֵר זֶה וָזֶה בְּכַזַּיִת. רִבִּי יְהוּדָה אוֹמֵר זֶה וָזֶה בְּכַבֵּיצָה. וַחֲכָמִים אוֹמְרִים בְּשַׂר קוֹדֶשׁ בְּכַזַּיִת וְחָמֵץ בְּכַבֵּיצָה:

Mishnah 8: Similarly, somebody who left Jerusalem and remembers that he has with him sacrificial meat[149], if he passed Mount Scopus[150] he burns it on the spot, otherwise he returns and burns it before the citadel on altar wood. Up to what[151] do they return? Rebbi Meïr says, in both cases the size of an olive; Rebbi Jehudah says, in both cases the size of an egg[152]. But the Sages say, sacrificial meat in the volume of an olive, but leavened matter in that of an egg.

149 Family sacrifices which can be eaten anywhere within the walls of Jerusalem but become invalid and impure the moment they are taken outside.
150 When he no longer can see the walls of the city. For "citadel" see Halakhah 7:8.
151 What is the minimal volume for which one has to return, either to eliminate leavened matter or to burn *sancta*.
152 Slightly more than three olives.

(30d line 61) **הלכה ח**: רִבִּי סִימוֹן בְּשֵׁם רִבִּי יֹושֻׁעַ בֶּן לֵוִי. כָּתוּב בַּיּוֹם הַהוּא יִהְיֶה (עַל) כָּל־מְצִילּוֹת הַסּוּס קוֹדֶשׁ וגו'. עַד מָקוֹם שֶׁהַסּוּס רָץ וְאֵינוֹ עוֹשֶׂה צֵל.

1 יושוע G | יהוש' G   2 כל G | וגו' G | לוי

רִבִּי שְׁמוּאֵל בַּר רַב יִצְחָק בָּעֵי. אִם קוֹדֶשׁ הוּא יִשְׂרְפֶנּוּ בִמְקוֹמוֹ. שֶׁכֵּן אֲפִילוּ בִירוּשָׁלַיִם שׂוֹרְפִין אוֹתוֹ לִפְנֵי הַבִּירָה מֵעֲצֵי הַמַּעֲרָכָה. הָהֵן יוֹצֵא מָה אַתְּ עָבַד לֵיהּ. כִּי מִטַּמֵּא בַחוּץ אוֹ כִי מִטַּמֵּא בִפְנִים. אָמַר רִבִּי יוֹסֵה. מִכֵּיוָן שֶׁנִּמְצָא פָסוּל מַחְמַת מְקוֹמוֹ נַעֲשָׂה כְמִטַּמֵּא בַחוּץ. אָמַר רִבִּי יוֹסֵה בֵּירִבִּי בּוּן. טָהוֹר הוּא דְּבַר תּוֹרָה. אַתְּ הוּא שֶׁגָּזַרְתָּ עָלָיו טוּמְאָה. לֹא דַיֵּיךְ שֶׁגָּזַרְתָּ עָלָיו טוּמְאָה אֶלָּא שֶׁאַתְּ מְבַקֵּשׁ לַעֲשׂוֹתוֹ כְמִטַּמֵּא בַחוּץ. אֶלָּא כְמִטַּמֵּא בִפְנִים.

2 כי מטמא G | כניטמא   3 כי מטמא G | כניטמא   כמטמא G | כניטמא   4 שגזרת G | שגזרתה (2)   5 טומאה G | את הטומאה   אלא G | אינו אלא   כמטמא G | כניטמא (2)

אִית תַּנָּיֵי תַנֵּי וּמַחֲלִף. רִבִּי יַעֲקֹב בַּר אָחָא בְּשֵׁם רִבִּי יַסָּי כְּמַתְנִיתִין. אָמַר רִבִּי יוּדָן. סִימָנָא מִן הַהִיא דִבְרָכוֹת. עַד כַּמָּה מְזַמְּנִין. עַד כַּזַּיִת. רִבִּי יְהוּדָה אוֹמֵר. עַד כַּבֵּיצָה: תַּנֵּי. פָּחוּת מִכֵּן אֵין מַטְרִיחִין עָלָיו שֶׁיַּחֲזוֹר. מַה בֵין זֶה לָזֶה. זֶה יֵשׁ לוֹ בִיטוּל. וְזֶה אֵין לוֹ בִיטוּל. עַד כְּדוֹן בְּשַׂר קוֹדֶשׁ. חָמֵץ מְנַיִין. אָמַר רִבִּי יוֹסֵה בֵּירִבִּי בּוּן. מִן מַה דְּתַנִּינָן. וְכֵן מִי שֶׁיָּצָא מִירוּשָׁלַם. הָדָא אֲמָרָה. מַה דִּנְפַל לְדֵין נְפַל לְדֵין.

1 סימנא G | וסימנה   4 הדא G | הדה   5 לדין G | לדן (2)

Halakhah 8: Rebbi Simon in the name of Rebbi Joshua ben Levi: It is written, *on that day will all shadow of horses be holy*[153] etc.; to the place where the horse runs without having a shadow[154].

Rebbi Samuel bar Rav Isaac asked, if it is a *sanctum* should he burn it on the spot? Since even in Jerusalem one burns it before the Temple on altar wood[155]. This one outside, how do you treat it? As having become impure outside or having become impure inside[156]? Rebbi Yose said, since it is disqualified because of its place it becomes as if having become impure outside. Rebbi Yose ben Rebbi Abun said, it is pure by the words of the Torah. You have decided that it be impure. It is not enough that you decided that it be impure, but you also want to make it as if having become impure outside? It [only][157] is like having become impure inside.

Some Tannaim state it switched[158]. Rebbi Jacob bar Aha in the name of Rebbi Yasa following our Mishnah[159]. Rebbi Yudan said, an indication is that of *Berakhot*[160]: "What is the minimum to 'invite'? Down to the size of an olive, Rebbi Jehudah says to the size of an egg." Less than that[161] one does not importune him to return. What is the difference between one and the other[162]? One can be declared insignificant, the other cannot be declared insignificant. So far sacrificial meat; leavened matter from where? Rebbi Yose ben Rebbi Abun said, from what we have stated, "*similarly*, somebody who left Jerusalem", this implies that what is incident to one is incident to the other[163].

153 *Zach.* 14:20. Cf. Babli 50a.

154 The future size of the suburbs of Jerusalem will be as far as a horse can run outside the walls of Jerusalem during noontime at the summer solstice when it casts no shadow (Rashi in the Babli, explanation by R. Makhir.)

155 He asks why outside of sight of Jerusalem one burns it on the spot where one realizes that one has impure sacrificial meat when in Jerusalem itself in such a case one cannot burn it on the spot but has to bring it to a central place on the Temple Mount outside the Temple enclosure.

156 To answer R. Samuel bar Rav Isaac's question one first has to determine the status of impurity of the meat. It is accepted by everybody (and discussed in the last paragraph of this Tractate) that sacrificial meat outside the place appropriate for its consumption is biblically disqualified and rabbinically impure. The modalities of burning depending on the status of the impurity are in dispute in Mishnah *Šeqalim* 8:6-7.

157 Added from G.

158 They state the Babylonian tradition that R. Meïr states "egg" and R. Jehudah "olive".

159 He confirms the attributions as quoted in the Mishnah.

160 Mishnah *Berakhot* 7:2. "Inviting" is the exhortation for groups of at least 3 people who ate together to say Grace together aloud, with the appropriate introduction.

161 The size of an olive for R. Meïr, of an egg for R. Jehudah, or depending on the case an egg or an olive for the Sages.

162 This is a question for the Sages: why are they more restrictive for sacrificial meat than for leavened matter?

163 Since the rules of sacrificial meat are appended to those of leavened matter, they must follow the same pattern.

מקום שנהגו פרק רביעי

(fol.30c) **משנה א**: מְקוֹם שֶׁנָּהֲגוּ לַעֲשׂוֹת מְלָאכָה בְּעַרְבֵי פְסָחִים עַד חֲצוֹת עוֹשִׂין. מְקוֹם שֶׁנָּהֲגוּ שֶׁלֹּא לַעֲשׂוֹת אֵין עוֹשִׂין. הַהוֹלֵךְ מִמָּקוֹם שֶׁעוֹשִׂין לְמָקוֹם שֶׁאֵינָן עוֹשִׂין אוֹ מִמָּקוֹם שֶׁאֵינָן עוֹשִׂין לְמָקוֹם שֶׁעוֹשִׂין נוֹתְנִין עָלָיו חוּמְרֵי הַמָּקוֹם שֶׁיָּצָא מִשָּׁם וְחוּמְרֵי הַמָּקוֹם שֶׁהָלַךְ לְשָׁם. וְאַל יְשַׁנֶּה אָדָם מִפְּנֵי הַמַּחֲלוֹקֶת:

Mishnah 1: In a place where one was used to work on Passover Eve before noon one works; in a place where one was used not to work on Passover Eve before noon one does not work[1]. If one goes from a place where he works to one where he does not work, or from a place where he does not work to one where he works, one puts on him the restrictions of the place he left and the restrictions of the place to which he comes, but a person should not change because of the controversy[2].

1 Since on Passover Eve one has to eliminate leavening, bake *mazzot*, prepare for the evening celebration, and in Jerusalem slaughter the *Pesaḥ* sacrifice, there were places where the day was considered a kind of holiday. "Work" here is not to be understood in the technical sense of the rules of Sabbath and holidays but as "gainful employment".

2 As a matter of principle one should not use the leniencies of one place to avoid stringencies of another, but if this would lead people to question the person's behavior or their own usage, one has to refrain from stringencies which are not based on well-founded practice. The Babli reads this Mishnah differently and takes "one puts on him the restrictions of the place he left and the restrictions of the place to which he comes" as absolute rule.

(30c line 42) **הלכה א**: מְקוֹם שֶׁנָּהֲגוּ לַעֲשׂוֹת מְלָאכָה כול׳. כְּתִיב שָׁם תִּזְבַּח אֶת־הַפֶּסַח בָּעֶרֶב. אֵין לִי אֶלָּא הוּא. שְׁלוּחוֹ מְנַיִן. תַּלְמוּד לוֹמַר וּבִשַּׁלְתָּ וְאָכַלְתָּ. מַה תַּלְמוּד לוֹמַר שָׁם תִּזְבַּח אֶת־הַפֶּסַח בָּעֶרֶב. אֵינוֹ בְדִין שֶׁתְּהֵא עָסוּק בִּמְלַאכְתָּךְ וְקָרְבָּנְךָ קָרֵב. אֲבָל אָסְרוּ מִלַּעֲשׂוֹת מְלָאכָה. כְּהָדָא דְתַנֵּי. לְהֶן כָּל־אֵינַשׁ דִּיהֲוֵי עֲלוֹהִי אָעִין וּבִיכּוּרִין. הָאוֹמֵר. הֲרֵי עָלַי עֵצִים לַמִּזְבֵּחַ וְגִיזִירִים לַמַּעֲרָכָה. אָסוּר בְּהֶסְפֵּד וְתַעֲנִית וּמִלַּעֲשׂוֹת מְלָאכָה בּוֹ בַיּוֹם.

1 כול׳ | G בע׳ פס׳ וגו׳   4 כהדא | G כחדה כל | G - | דיהוי | G דיחוי עלוהי | G עלוי   5 C בהספד | GS בספד   ותענית | G ובתענית

Halakhah 1: "In a place where one was used to work," etc. It is written, *there you shall slaughter the Pesaḥ in the evening*[3]. Not only he, from where his agent? The verse says, *and you shall cook and you shall eat*[4]. Why does the verse say, *there you shall slaughter the Pesah in the evening*? It is not in order that he should be occupied by his work while his sacrifice is offered[5]. As what was stated[6], "therefore anybody who has an obligation for wood and first fruits. He who says, I am taking upon me [to bring] wood for the altar and logs for the arrangement[7] on that day is forbidden funeral orations, and fasting, and working."

3 *Deut.* 16:6.
4 *Deut.* 16:7. Since the *Pesah* sacrifice *must* be eaten in a group (*Ex.* 12:3-4), the singular in these verses cannot mean that the slaughter has to be done by the eater; this is proof that it may be delegated.
5 The singular is interpreted that even if the sacrifice is presented by an agent, the owner still has to behave as if he himself were present.
6 The first sentence is a quote from *Megillat Ta`anit*. The entire text is copied in *Hagigah* 2:4.
7 The arrangement of the firewood on the altar.

(30c line 48) אָמַר רִבִּי יוֹנָה. אִילֵּין תְּמִידִין קָרְבְּנוֹתֵיהֶן שֶׁלְּכָל־יִשְׂרָאֵל אִינּוּן. אִם יִהְיוּ כָל־יִשְׂרָאֵל עוֹלִין לִירוּשָׁלַם. לֵית כְּתִיב אֶלָּא שָׁלוֹשׁ פְּעָמִים | בַּשָּׁנָה יֵרָאֶה כָל־זְכוּרְךָ. אִם יִהְיוּ כָל־יִשְׂרָאֵל יוֹשְׁבִין וּבְטֵילִין. וְהָכְתִיב וְאָסַפְתָּ דְגָנֶךָ. מִי אוֹסֵף לָהֶן אֶת הַדָּגָן. אֶלָּא שֶׁהִתְקִינוּ הַנְּבִיאִים הָרִאשׁוֹנִים עֶשְׂרִים וְאַרְבַּע מִשְׁמָרוֹת. עַל כָּל־מִשְׁמָר וּמִשְׁמָר הָיָה עוֹמֵד בִּירוּשָׁלַם [שֶׁל כֹּהֲנִים וְשֶׁל לְוִיִּם וְשֶׁל יִשְׂרְאֵלִים]. תַּנֵּי. עֶשְׂרִים וְאַרְבָּעָה אֶלֶף. עַמּוּד מִירוּשָׁלַם וַחֲצִי עַמּוּד מִיִּרִיחוֹ. אַף יְרִיחוֹ הָיְתָה יְכוֹלָה לְהוֹצִיא עַמּוּד שָׁלֵם. אֶלָּא בִּשְׁבִיל לַחֲלוֹק כָּבוֹד לִירוּשָׁלַם הָיְתָה מוֹצִיאָה חֲצִי עַמּוּד. הַכֹּהֲנִים לַעֲבוֹדָה וְהַלְוִיִּם לַדּוּכָן וְיִשְׂרָאֵל מוֹכִיחִין עַל עַצְמָן שֶׁהֵן שְׁלוּחֵיהֶן שֶׁלְּכָל־יִשְׂרָאֵל.

2 לירושלם G | לירושלים לית G | לא פעמים בשנה יראה כל זכורך G | רגלים תחוג לי בשנה 3 והכת' G | והא כתיב להן | נ להם 4 על | נ ועל הנביאים הראשונים G | הנביאין הראשונין עשרים G | עשרין עומד | נ עמוד C 5 ושל ישראלים G | נ ושלישראל מירושלם G | מירושלים 6 לירושלם G | לירושלים

[8]Rebbi Jonah said, these daily sacrifices are the offerings of all of Israel[9]. Could all of Israel ascend to Jerusalem? Is it not written[10], *three times a year all your males shall be seen*? If all of Israel would sit there and do nothing, is there not written[11], *you shall harvest your grain*? Who would harvest their grain? But the early prophets[12] instituted 24 watches; from each watch there were [Cohanim, Levites, and Israel] present in Jerusalem. It was stated, *twenty-four thousand*[13]. A stand-by group[14] from Jerusalem, and half a stand-by group from Jericho. Jericho also could have produced a full

stand-by group, but to give precedence to Jerusalem it only produced half a stand-by group. The Cohanim for service, the Levites for the podium[15], and the Israel as proof that they are the agents for all of Israel[16].

8   From here on there also is a parallel in *Ta`aniot* 4:2 (נ).

9   By the statement of the preceding paragraph, no man in Israel would be permitted to work both in the morning and in the evening.

10   *Deut*. 16:16. G instead quotes *Ex*. 23:14.

11   *Deut*. 11:14.

12   David, Asaph, Heman, and Yedutun, *1Chr*. 25:1.

13   *1Chr*. 27:1. The verse is read as meaning that every month there were 24'000 representatives of the people at the Temple.

14   Since the Cohanim were changed every week, the people's representatives also were changed every week; only one quarter of the 24'000 on stand-by were actually needed for one week. The Babylonian term for עמוד is מֲעֲמָד (*Ta`anit* 27a). The actual numbers in Second Temple times were small.

15   For the musical accompaniment of the Temple service.

16   These are forbidden any work while the Daily Sacrifice is offered but everybody else may work.

(30c line 58) תָּנֵי רִבִּי שִׁמְעוֹן בֶּן אֶלְעָזָר אוֹמֵר. כֹּהֲנִים וּלְוִיִּים וְיִשְׂרָאֵל וְשִׁיר מְעַכְּבִין אֶת הַקָּרְבָּן. רִבִּי אַבִּין בְּשֵׁם רִבִּי אֶלְעָזָר. טַעֲמֵהּ דְּרִבִּי שִׁמְעוֹן בֶּן אֶלְעָזָר. כָּל הַקָּהָל מִשְׁתַּחֲוִים. אֵילוּ יִשְׂרָאֵל. וְהַשִּׁיר מְשׁוֹרֵר אֵילוּ הַלְוִיִּם. וְהַחֲצֹצְרוֹת מַחְצְרִים אֵילוּ הַכֹּהֲנִים. הַכֹּל עַד לִכְלוֹת הָעֹלָה. הַכֹּל מְעַכְּבִין אֶת הַקָּרְבָּן. רִבִּי תַּנְחוּמָא בְּשֵׁם רִבִּי לְעָזָר שָׁמַע לָהּ מִן הָדָא. וְאֶתְּנָה אֶת־הַלְוִיִּם נְתֻנִים | לְאַהֲרֹן וּלְבָנָיו מִתּוֹךְ | בְּנֵי יִשְׂרָאֵל. לַעֲבֹד אֶת־עֲבֹדַת בְּנֵי־יִשְׂרָאֵל בְּאֹהֶל מוֹעֵד. אֵילוּ הַכֹּהֲנִים. וּלְכַפֵּר עַל־בְּנֵי יִשְׂרָאֵל. אֵילוּ הַלְוִיִּם. וְלֹא יִהְיֶה בִּבְנֵי יִשְׂרָאֵל נֶגֶף בְּגֶשֶׁת בְּנֵי־יִשְׂרָאֵל אֶל־הַקֹּדֶשׁ. אֵילוּ יִשְׂרָאֵל.

מִנַיִין שֶׁהַשִּׁיר קָרוּי כַּפָּרָה. חִינָּנָא אָבוֹי דְּרַב יַנְטָה בְּשֵׁם רִבִּי בְּנָיָה. וּלְכַפֵּר עַל־בְּנֵי יִשְׂרָאֵל. זֶה הַשִּׁיר. מִנַיִין שֶׁהַשִּׁיר מְעַכֵּב. רִבִּי יַעֲקֹב בַּר אָחָא רִבִּי שִׁמְעוֹן בּוּלְווֹטָה בְּשֵׁם רִבִּי חֲנִינָא. וּלְכַפֵּר עַל־בְּנֵי יִשְׂרָאֵל. זֶה הַשִּׁיר.

1 בן אלעזר אומר | נ - אלעזר | G לעזר הכהנים | G כהנים ולויים | G ולוים נר והלוים ושיר | ר וכלי שיר   2 אבין | Gנ אבון אלעזר | Gנ לעזר (2) | בן אלעזר אומר | נ - כל | G וכל אילו | G אלו 3 אילו G אלו מחצרים | G מחצרים אילו | G אלו הכל | נ - 4 מעכבין | G שמעכבין תנחומא | G תנחומה הדא | G הכה 5 אילו | G אלו לעבד | נ לעבוד 6 באהל מועד | Gנ - אילו | G אלו 7 אילו | G אלו 8 חיננה | G חננה דרב ינטה | G דברנטי נ דבר נטה 9 ר | G - אחא | G אחה חנינה | G חנינה

[17]It was stated: "Rebbi Simeon ben Eleazar said, Cohanim, Levites, Israel, and song invalidate the sacrifice[18]." Rebbi Abbin[19] in the name of Rebbi Eleazar, the reason of Rebbi Simeon ben Eleazar: [20]*The entire congregation*

were bowing down, these are Israel, *and the song was sung*, these are the Levites, *and the trumpets were trumpeting*, these are the Cohanim, *everything up to the end of the elevation offering*, all are indispensable for the sacrifice. Rebbi Tanḥuma in the name of Rebbi Eleazar understood it from here[21]: *And I gave the Levites to Aaron and his sons from the midst of the Children of Israel*, these are the Levites, *to work the service of the Children of Israel in the Tent of Meeting*, these are the Cohanim, *and to atone for the Children of Israel*, that is the song[22], *so there shall be no plague when the Children of Israel approach the Sanctuary*, these are Israel.

From where that the song is called atonement? Ḥinena the father of (Rav Yanta) [Bar Nata][23] in the name of Rebbi Banaia: *and to atone for the Children of Israel*, that is the song. From where that the song invalidates? Rebbi Jacob bar Aha, Rebbi Simeon βουλευτής[24], in the name of Rebbi Ḥanina, *and to atone for the Children of Israel*, that is the song.

17 The first sentence is also in *Eruvin* 10 (Note 141,ו). The text there reads "musical instruments", which is required by the context there and must be understood here also since the choir is subsumed under "Levites".

18 A sacrifice requiring a wine offering is invalid if not accompanied by the Levite's song.

19 In the other sources: Abun.

20 *2Chr.* 29:28. Since this is not a pentateuchal verse it only can prove what people did or, as explained there in v. 25, what was prophetic instruction.

21 *Num.* 8:19.

22 In this version the implication is incomprehensible. It is understandable in the Babli, *Arakhin* 11a, where it is a tannaitic statement: "Song invalidates the sacrifice, the words of R. Meïr, but the Sages say, it does not invalidate. What is R. Meïr's reason? The verse says, *and I gave the Levites to Aaron and his sons from the midst of the Children of Israel, to work the service of the Children of Israel in the Tent of Meeting, and to atone for the Children of Israel*." Since the Levites had three biblical obligations in the Sanctuary, *viz.*, to carry the Tent, to be its watchmen, and to sing. Since only the third can be classified as ritual service, it must be what is referred to as atoning.

23 The version of G and *Ta'aniot* in brackets must be preferred over that of the text here in parentheses since a Galilean cannot carry the title "Rav".

24 "The city councillor".

(30c line 70) הֲרֵי פֶסַח הֲרֵי קָרְבָּנָן שֶׁלְּכָל יִשְׂרָאֵל הוּא וְתָלוּ אוֹתוֹ מִנְהָג. אָמַר רִבִּי אַבָּהוּ. שַׁנְיָא הִיא. שֶׁאֵין הַפֶּסַח קָרֵב אֶלָּא מִשֵּׁשׁ שָׁעוֹת וּלְמַעֲלָן. רִבִּי אַבָּהוּ בָּעֵי. אָמַר. הֲרֵי עָלַי עוֹלָה מִשֵּׁשׁ שָׁעוֹת וּלְמַעֲלָן. מוּתָּר לַעֲשׂוֹת מְלָאכָה מִשֵּׁשׁ שָׁעוֹת וּלְמַטָּן. אָמַר רִבִּי יוֹסֵה. פֶּסַח שֶׁהִקְרִיבוֹ בַּשַּׁחֲרִית אֵינוֹ פָסַח. עוֹלָה שֶׁהִקְרִיבוּהָ בַּשַּׁחֲרִית עוֹלָה הִיא.

1 קרבנן G קרבניי מנהג G במנהג אבהו G אבהוא שנייא G שנייא 2 אבהו G אבהוא עלי G עליו
4 שהקריבוה G שהקריבה

Is not *Pesaḥ* a sacrifice of all of Israel and they made it dependent on usage[25]? Rebbi Abbahu said, there is a difference, since the *Pesaḥ* cannot be offered before noontime. Rebbi Abbahu asked, if one said, I have the obligation to bring an elevation offering in the afternoon, is he permitted to work in the morning[26]? Rebbi Yose said, a *Pesaḥ* which he brought in the morning is no *Pesaḥ*; an elevation offering which he brought in the morning is an elevation offering[27].

25 Work should be biblically forbidden.
26 As stated earlier (Note 7), the entire day he is forbidden gainful work until he has discharged his obligation.
27 The sacrifice is valid even though he has to bring another one to fulfill his vow.

(30c line 76) כָּל־הַדְּבָרִים תָּלוּ אוֹתָן בַּמִּנְהָג. נַשַּׁיָּיא דְּנָהֲגִין דְּלָא לְמֵיעֲבַד עוֹבְדָא בָּאַפּוֹקֵי שׁוּבְתָא אֵינוֹ [מִנְהָג]. עַד יַפְנֵי סִדְרָא [מִנְהָג]. בַּתְרַיָּיא וּבַחֲמִישְׁתָּא [אֵינוֹ מִנְהָג]ג. עַד יִתְפְּנֵי תַעֲנִיתָא מִנְהָג. יוֹמָא דַעֲרוּבְתָא אֵינוֹ מִנְהָג. מִן מִנְחָתָא וּלְעֵיל מִנְהָג. יוֹמָא דְיַרְחָא מִנְהָג. אָמַר רִבִּי זְעוּרָה. נַשַּׁיָּיא דְּנָהֲגִין דְּלָא לְמִשְׁתַּיָּיא מִן דְּאָב עָלִיל מִנְהָג. שָׁבוּ פַּסְקָה אֲבֶן שְׁתִיָּיה. מַה טַּעֲמָא כִּי־הַשָּׁתוֹת יֵהָרֵסוּן.

1 אותן G אותם נשייא G נשייא דנהידין G דנהגן למיעבד G מעבד עובדא G עבידתא באפוקי G
בפקי נ בפוקי   2 שובתא G שבתה יפני סדרא G דיפנה סידרה נ דיתפני סידרא נתרייא ובחמשתא G
בתרייה ובחמשתה יתפני G דיתפנה נ דיתפני תעניתא G תעניתה   3 יומא G נ ביומא דערובתא G
דערובתה מנחתא נ מנחה יומא נG ביומא דירחא G דירחה   4 זעורה G זעירא נשייא G נשייה
דנהידין נ דנהגן למשתייא G למשתייה שנו פסקא G שפסקה   5 יהרסון G וגו'

אָמַר רִבִּי חִינָנָא. כָּל־הַדְּבָרִים מִנְהָג. אָעִין דְּשִׁיטִין הֲוֵי בְּמִגְדַּל צְבָעַיָּיה. אָתוּן וּשְׁאָלוֹן לְרִבִּי חֲנַנְיָה חֲבֵרְהוֹן [דְּרַבָּנִין]. מָהוּ מֵיעֲבַד בָּהֶן עֲבוֹדָה]. אָמַר לְהֶן. מִכֵּיוָן שֶׁנָּהֲגוּ בָּהֶן אֲבוֹתֵיכֶם בְּאִיסּוּר אַל תְּשַׁנּוּ מִנְהַג אֲבוֹתֵיכֶם נוּחֵי נֶפֶשׁ. רִבִּי אֶלְעָזָר בָּשֵׁם רִבִּי אַבִּין. כָּל־דָּבָר שֶׁאֵינוֹ יוֹדֵעַ שֶׁהוּא מוּתָּר וְטוֹעֶה בּוֹ בְּאִיסּוּר נִשְׁאָל וְהֵן מַתִּירִין לוֹ. וְכָל־דָּבָר שֶׁהוּא יוֹדֵעַ בּוֹ שֶׁהוּא מוּתָּר וְהוּא נוֹהֵג בּוֹ בְּאִיסּוּר נִשְׁאָל וְאֵין מַתִּירִין לוֹ.

1 חיננא G חנינה הוו G הוון צבעייה G צבעייא נ צבעיה ושאלון G שאלון   2 דרבנין נG דרבנן
מיעבד G מעבד בהן G בון נ בהון עבודה נG עבידא להן G להו   3 אלעזר נG לעזר אבין נG אבון
4 שהוא G בו שהוא   וטועה G והוא נוהג נ והוא טועה   והן מתירין G נG ומתירין

[28]Everything they made dependent on usage. If women use not to work after the end of the Sabbath, it is no [{legitimate} usage]; until the end of the *seder*[29] it is [{legitimate} usage]. On Monday and Thursday[30], it is no [{legitimate} usage], to the end of the fast-day prayers it is [legitimate] usage. On the day of the willow twigs[31] it is not {legitimate} usage, after afternoon prayers it is {legitimate} usage. On the day of the New Moon it is {legitimate} usage. Rebbi Ze'ira said, if women use not to weave[32] from the start of Av it is {legitimate} usage, for the *šetiah* stone stopped to exist[33]. What is the reason? *For the woofs will be torn down*[34].

Rebbi Hinena said, everything they made dependent on usage. There were acacia trees in Migdal Sevaya[35]. They came and asked Rebbi Hanania, the colleague of the rabbis, may one use them for work? He told them, since your ancestors used to treat them as forbidden, do not change the usage of your deceased ancestors. Rebbi Eleazar in the name of Rebbi Abbin[19,36]. In any case which is permitted but in error he treats it as forbidden, if he asks they will permit him. But in any case where he knows that it is permitted but he has the usage to treat it as forbidden, if he asks they will not permit him[37].

28 The following two paragraphs are also in *Ta'aniot* 1:6 (ג); in a slightly different order it is copied in *Raviah* §495 (vol. 2, p. 119).

29 The additional prayer at the end of the evening service at the end of the Sabbath.

30 Which were common fast-days of the pious in Palestine (cf. L. Ginzberg, *Genizah Studies in Memory of Doctor Solomon Schechter*, vol. 1, p. 483, §6.)

31 The Seventh Day of Tabernacles. Since the following day is a holiday, it is appropriate that the preparations be finished by the time of the afternoon prayers.

32 Between the first and the tenth of Av.

33 The stone in the Holiest of Holies in the Temple.

34 *Ps.* 11:3. If read as *the foundations will be torn down* it is appropriate for the anniversary of the destruction of the Temple.

35 Since by a Galilean tradition the Tabernacle was built in the desert from perfect logs of acacia wood (*Mimosa nilotica L.*) cut for this purpose by Jacob and his sons when they travelled to Egypt [*Gen. rabba* 94(4).]

36 Even though all three sources have R. Eleazar in the name of . . ., it must be . . . in the name of R. Eleazar.

37 Since he intentionally accepted an unnecessary stringency, it has the status of a vow.

(30d line 11) יוֹשְׁבִין עַל סַפְסְלוֹ שֶׁלְּגוֹי בַּשַּׁבָּת. מַעֲשֶׂה בְרַבָּן גַּמְלִיאֵל שֶׁיָּשַׁב לוֹ עַל סַפְסִילוֹ שֶׁלְּגוֹי בַּשַּׁבָּת בְּעַכּוֹ. אָמְרוּ לוֹ. לֹא הָיוּ נוֹהֲגִין כֵּן לִהְיוֹת יוֹשְׁבִין עַל סַפְסִילוֹ שֶׁלְּגוֹי בַּשַּׁבָּת. וְלֹא רָצָה לוֹמַר לָהֶן. מוּתָּר לַעֲשׂוֹת כֵּן. אֶלָּא עָמַד וְהָלַךְ לוֹ.

2 בשבת G - | אמרו G - | ואמרו היו נוהגין G | נהגו 3 | להן G | להם לעשות G -

מַעֲשֶׂה בִיהוּדָה וּבְהִלֵּל בָּנָיו שֶׁלְּרַבָּן גַּמְלִיאֵל שֶׁנִּכְנְסוּ לִרְחוֹץ בַּמֶּרְחָץ בְּכָבוּל. אָמְרוּ לָהֶן. לֹא נָהֲגוּ כֵן לִהְיוֹת רוֹחֲצִין שְׁנֵי אַחִים כְּאַחַת. וְלֹא רָצוּ לוֹמַר. מוּתָּר כֵּן. אֶלָּא נִכְנְסוּ זֶה אַחַר זֶה. וְעוֹד שֶׁיָּצְאוּ לְטַיֵּיל בְּקוֹרְדְקָיוֹת שֶׁלְּזָהָב בְּלֵילֵי שַׁבָּת בְּבִירוֹ. אָמְרוּ לָהֶן. לֹא נָהֲגוּ לִהְיוֹת מְטַיְּילִין בְּקוֹרְדְקָיוֹת שֶׁלְּזָהָב בַּשַּׁבָּת. וְלֹא רָצוּ לוֹמַר לָהֶן. מוּתָּר כֵּן. אֶלָּא שִׁילְחוּ בְּיַד עַבְדֵיהֶן.

2 אחים G | אחין לומר G | לומר לחן G | מותר מותרין G | יצאו 3 | שיצאו בקורדקיות G | הקורדקייות 4 בקורדקיות G | הקורדקייות בשבת G | בלילי שבת לחן G | להם מותר G | מותרין שילחו G | שילחום

[38]One may sit on a Gentile's bench on the Sabbath. It happened that Rabban Gamliel[39] was sitting on a Gentile's bench at Acco on a Sabbath. They said to him, it is not our usage to sit on a Gentile's bench on a Sabbath. He did not want to tell them that it is permitted to do this but got up and went away.

It happened that Jehudah and Hillel, Rabban Gamliel's[39] sons, went to bathe in the bathhouse of Kabul[40]. They said to them, it is not our usage that two brothers should be bathing together. They did not want to tell them, so it is permitted, but entered one after the other. Also they went to promenade in gilded bark sandals[40a] at Biro[41] in the night of the Sabbath. They said to them, it is not our usage to promenade in gilded bark sandals on the Sabbath. They did not want to tell them, so it is permitted, but sent them by their slaves.

38 Babli 51a.
39 Gamliel III, son of Rebbi.
40 *Jos.* 19:27.
40a Latin *corticea*.
41 In Upper Galilee.

(39d line 20) וְלֹא סוֹף דָּבָר פֶּסַח. אֶלָּא אֲפִילוּ מִנְהָג קִיבְּלוּ עֲלֵיהֶן חַרְמֵי טִיבֶּרְיָה וּגְרוֹסֵי צִיפּוֹרִי דְשׁוּשֵׁי עַכּוֹ. שֶׁלֹּא לַעֲשׂוֹת מְלָאכָה בְחוּלּוֹ שֶׁלְּמוֹעֵד. נִיחָא גְרוֹסֵי צִיפּוֹרִין דְּשׁוּשֵׁי עַכּוֹ. חַרְמֵי טִיבֶּרְיָה וְאֵינָן מְמַעֲטִין בְּשִׂמְחַת הָרֶגֶל. צַד הוּא בְחַכָּה צַד הוּא בְמִכְמוֹרֶת. אֲפִילוּ כֵן אֵינָן מְמַעֲטִין בְּשִׂמְחַת הָרֶגֶל. שֶׁהֵן מְמַעֲטִין בְּשִׂמְחַת הָרֶגֶל. רִבִּי אִימִּי מֵיקַל לוֹן.

1 ולא G | לא עליהן G | עליהם 1-2 וגרוסי ציפורי דשושי עכו G | ורשושי עכו וגרוסי ציפורין מ ודשושי עכו וגרוסי ציפורין g גרוסי ציפורין ורשושי עכו 2 ניחא gG | ניחה גרוסי ציפורין דשושי עכו G | רשושי עכו וגרוסי ציפורין g גרוס' דציפורין ורשושי עכו 3 ממעטין g ממעטים 4 ממעטין g ממעטים (2) | אימי Gמ אמי g מא שהן G | שהם

Not only the *Pesah* but also usage⁴². The net-fishermen⁴³ of Tiberias, and the farina millers of Sepphoris, and the grain splitters⁴⁴ of Acco, accepted not to work on the intermediate days of a holiday⁴⁵. One understands the farina millers of Sepphoris, and the grain splitters of Acco. The net-fishers of Tiberias, do they not diminish the enjoyment of the holiday⁴⁶? He may fish with a hook; he may fish with a stationary net. Even so, do they not diminish the enjoyment of the holiday? Rebbi Immi cursed them because they diminish the enjoyment of the holiday⁴⁷.

42 Religious observances which have no basis in codified practice.

43 They fish with boats on Lake Genezareth. The following also is in *Mo`ed qatan* 2:5 (ס, Genizah text g)..

44 They pound grain to split it into two or three parts for the preparation of cereal.

45 When preparation of food and provisions is permitted without restriction.

46 Since they leave the people of Tiberias without fish for the latter parts of the holiday week.

47 Baseless religious observances of private groups are to be rejected if they interfere with public needs. The Babli *Mo`ed qatan* 13b approves of the action of the fishermen's guild which they base at Acco.

(30d line 25) גָּלוּ מִמָּקוֹם לְמָקוֹם וּבִיקְשׁוּ לַחֲזוֹר בָּהֶן. יָבֹא כְהָדָא דְאָמַר רִבִּי בָּא. בְּנֵי מֵישָׁא קִיבְּלוּ עֲלֵיהֶן שֶׁלֹּא לְפָרֵשׁ בַּיָּם הַגָּדוֹל. אָתוֹן שָׁאֲלוֹן לְרִבִּי. אָמְרִין לֵיהּ. אֲבוֹתֵינוּ נָהֲגוּ שֶׁלֹּא לְפָרֵשׁ בַּיָּם הַגָּדוֹל. אָנוּ מַה אָנוּ. אָמַר לָהֶן. מִכֵּיוָן שֶׁנָּהֲגוּ בָהֶן אֲבוֹתֵיכֶם בְּאִיסּוּר אַל תְּשַׁנּוּ מִנְהַג אֲבוֹתֵיכֶם נוֹחֵי נֶפֶשׁ. וְאֵין אָדָם נִשְׁאָל עַל נִדְרוֹ. תַּמָּן מְשֻׁנָּדָּר נִשְׁאָל. בְּרַם הָכָא אֲבוֹתֵיכֶם נָדְרוּ. כָּל־שֶׁכֵּן יְהוּ מוּתָּרִין. אָמַר רִבִּי חֲנַנְיָה. לֹא מָן הָדָא אֶלָּא מָן הָדָא. רִבִּי תַּלְמִידֵי דְרִבִּי יוּדָה הֲוָה. דְּרִבִּי יוּדָה אָמַר. אָסוּר לְפָרֵשׁ בַּיָּם הַגָּדוֹל.

1 בהן | G בהם יבא | G ייבה מישא | G מיישא | G ייבה אמרין | G אמרון 3 לפרש | G ליפרש להן | G להם 4 נשאל | G נישאל נדרו | G נידרו משנדר | G מישנדר הכא | G הכה 5 יהו | G יהוא הדא | G הדה (2) 6 לפרש | G ליפרש

If they were exiled from one place to another and wanted to change their ways⁴⁸? Would it be as Rebbi Abba said, the people of Mesha⁴⁹ took it upon themselves not to travel on the ocean. They came, asked Rebbi, and said to him, our forefathers used not to travel by sea; what is our situation? He said to them, since your forefathers treated it as a prohibition, do not change the usage of your deceased ancestors. May a person not ask about his vow⁵⁰? There he asks when he made the vow, but here their ancestors made the vow. Then they should be permitted *a fortiori*⁵¹. Rebbi Ḥanania said, it is not because of this but because of the following. Rebbi was the student of Rebbi Jehudah, and Rebbi Jehudah said, one is forbidden to travel by sea[52].

48 If the certain restriction is particular to a place and the people from this place migrate to another where there is no established usage, are they bound by their prior usage?

49 From the context it seems that this place was in Palestine on the coast and the question is whether they are permitted to go by sea to another port on the coast when they could go by land (in a more laborious way) without leaving the Land.

50 Most of Tractate *Nedarim* deals with the modalities of rabbinic annulment of vows.

51 If restrictive usage is considered a vow then automatically it cannot oblige people who were not present when the vow was made.

52 In order to avoid leaving the Land (*Mo'ed qatan* 3:1). R. Jehudah forbids leaving the rabbinic Land of Israel even though he defines the biblical land of Canaan as including most islands of the Mediterranean (*Ševi'it* 6:1 Note 93, *Hallah* 4:8 Note 99, Babli *Gittin* 8a.)

(30d line 33) רִבִּי שִׁמְעוֹן בֶּן לָקִישׁ שָׁאַל לְרִבִּי יוֹחָנָן. וְאֵינוֹ אָסוּר מִשּׁוּם בַּל תִּתְגּוֹדְדוּ. אָמַר לֵיהּ. בְּשָׁעָה שֶׁאֵילּוּ עוֹשִׂין כְּבֵית שַׁמַּי וְאֵילּוּ עוֹשִׂין כְּבֵית הִלֵּל. בֵּית שַׁמַּי וּבֵית הִלֵּל אֵין הֲלָכָה כְּבֵית הִלֵּל. אָמַר לֵיהּ. בְּשָׁעָה שֶׁאֵילּוּ עוֹשִׂין כְּרִבִּי מֵאִיר וְאֵילּוּ עוֹשִׂין כְּרִבִּי יוֹסֵי. רִבִּי מֵאִיר וְרִבִּי יוֹסֵי אֵין הֲלָכָה כְּרִבִּי יוֹסֵי. אָמַר לֵיהּ. תְּרֵי תַנָּיִין אִינּוּן עַל דְּרִבִּי מֵאִיר וּתְרֵין תַּנָּיִין אִינּוּן עַל דְּרִבִּי יוֹסֵי. אָמַר לֵיהּ. הֲרֵי רֹאשׁ הַשָּׁנָה וְיוֹם הַכִּיפּוּרִים בִּיהוּדָה נָהֲגוּ כְּרִבִּי עֲקִיבָה. וּבַגָּלִיל נָהֲגוּ כְּרִבִּי יוֹחָנָן בֶּן נוּרִי. אָמַר לֵיהּ. שַׁנְיָיה הִיא. שֶׁאִם עָבַר וְעָשָׂה בִּיהוּדָה כְּגָלִיל וּבַגָּלִיל כִּיהוּדָה יָצָא. הֲרֵי פּוּרִים. הֲרֵי אֵילּוּ קוֹרִין בְּאַרְבָּעָה עָשָׂא וְאֵילּוּ קוֹרִין בַּחֲמִשָּׁה עָשָׂר. אָמַר לֵיהּ. מִי שֶׁסִּידֵּר אֶת הַמִּשְׁנָה סָמְכָהּ לַמִּקְרָא. מִשְׁפָּחָה וּמִשְׁפָּחָה מְדִינָה וּמְדִינָה וָעִיר וָעִיר.

1 שאל לר׳ | G בעה קומי ר׳   2 בית | G ובית   5 ר׳ | G ור׳   4 תרי | G תרין   6 שאם עבר ועשה | G שכן אם עשה   8 שסידר | G שסדר

Rebbi Simeon ben Laqish asked Rebbi Joḥanan: Is it not forbidden because of "do not split into sects"[53]? He said to him[54], in case these follow the House of Shammai and those the House of Hillel. But between the House of Shammai and the House of Hillel does practice not follow the House of Hillel[55]? He said to him, in case these follow Rebbi Meïr and those follow Rebbi Yose. But between Rebbi Meïr and Rebbi Yose, does practice not follow Rebbi Yose? He answered him, there are two Tannaim regarding Rebbi Meïr and two Tannaim regarding Rebbi Yose[56]. He said to him, is there not New Year's Day and the Day of Atonement, where in Judea one used to follow Rebbi Aqiba and in Galilee Rebbi Johanan ben Nuri[57]. He told him, there is a difference since if he changed and in Judea acted as in Galilee or in Galilee as in Judea he discharged his obligation[58]. But is there not Purim, where these read on the fourteenth and those on the fifteenth[59]? He told him, he who edited the Mishnah based it on Scripture[60]: *Family and family, country and country, and town and town.*

53 How can the Mishnah require people who move from place to place to follow the more restrictive practice? Does this not violate the basic principle of uniform practice based on an aggadic interpretation of *Deut.* 14:1. Babli *Yebamot* 13b.

54 He wants to restrict the prohibition of concurrent different practices to cases of fundamental differences in the formulation of rules, not to differing interpretations of existing rules.

55 The answer is unsatisfactory since in post-Jabneh Judaism, practices of the House of Shammai are not recognized anyhow.

56 While it is agreed as general rule that between R. Meïr and R. Yose practice follows R. Yose (*Ma`serot* 1:7 Note 200; Babli *Eruvin* 46b), this is only a general rule, not an invariable principle. There are many examples where other Tannaim follow the lines of argument of R. Meïr and R. Yose and practice was decided only in later generations.

57 Mishnah *Roš Haššanah* 4:6,7 explains their differences in the way prayers and *shofar* blowings are combined on New Year's day and the Day of Atonement in a *Yovel* year.

58 Everybody will agree that either way fulfills the biblical requirement.

59 Days of reading of the Esther scroll in the month of Adar. Since the date of reading is determined by the place of reading, it is obvious that a visitor has to read with the local people.

60 *Esth.* 9:28. Since the differences are of biblical origin, the example is irrelevant for the rabbinic prohibition.

(30d line 42) נִיחָא מִמְּקוֹם שֶׁעוֹשִׂין לְמָקוֹם שֶׁאֵינָן עוֹשִׂין. מִמְּקוֹם שֶׁאֵין עוֹשִׂין לְמָקוֹם שֶׁעוֹשִׂין.
וִיבַטֵּל. שֶׁהֲרֵי כַּמָּה בְטֵילִין יֵשׁ לוֹ בְאוֹתוֹ מָקוֹם. רִבִּי סִימוֹן בְּשֵׁם רִבִּי יוֹחָנָן. בְּמַתְמִיהַּ.

One understands "one goes from a place where he works to one where he does not work." "From a place where he does not work to one where he works," why should he not be idle? Are there not may idlers at that place? Rebbi Simon in the name of Rebbi Johanan: If he causes to wonder[61].

61 The question is about the last sentence in Mishnah 1, "but a person should not change because of the controversy." It is clear that when one comes to a place where nobody works, he cannot work there, and "one puts on him the restrictions of the place he left and the restrictions of the place to which he comes." But if he comes to a

place where one works, why should he not be required to be idle? If he is required to be idle in all circumstances then the last clause, "but a person should not change because of the controversy" would be pointless. The answer is that the person who comes from a place where he does not work should not work at the other place if he might appear as an idler; he may not stay idle if he would have to declare this as a religious principle. The Babli 51b disagrees.

(fol. 30c) **משנה ב**: כַּיּוֹצֵא בּוֹ הַמּוֹלִיךְ פֵּירוֹת שְׁבִיעִית מִמָּקוֹם שֶׁכָּלוּ לְמָקוֹם שֶׁלֹּא כָלוּ אוֹ מִמָּקוֹם שֶׁלֹּא כָלוּ לְמָקוֹם שֶׁכָּלוּ חַיָּיב לְבָעֵר. רִבִּי יְהוּדָה אוֹמֵר צֵא וְהָבֵא לָךְ אַף אָתָּה:

Mishnah 2: Similarly, he who brings Sabbatical produce from a place where it was exhausted[62] to one where it was not exhausted or from a place where it was not exhausted to one where it was exhausted is obligated to eliminate. Rebbi Jehudah says, go and get it for yourself[63].

62 Since the laws of the Sabbatical state (*Lev.* 25:6-7) that Sabbatical produce be food for "you, . . . , your domestic animals, and the wild animals on your fields" it is inferred that Sabbatical produce stored in one's house must be eliminated (by being eaten or given to the poor) when nothing is left of the same kind on the fields for wildlife. According to Mishnah *Ševi`it* 9:2 the dates are determined separately for each region where in particular Galilee is divided into three, Upper Galilee, Lower Galilee with Sepphoris, and the Jordan valley with Tiberias. For the anonymous majority it is not possible to keep produce by moving it to another region where it still is in abundance.

63 He denies that Galilee is split into three different regions in this respect (an opinion attributed to R. Simeon in Mishnah *Ševi`it* 9:3) and in general that artificial boundaries are to be disregarded between places of easy commerce.

(30d line 45) **הלכה ב**: כָּלוּ מִטְיבֶּרְיָה וְלֹא כָלוּ מִצִּיפּוֹרִין. אָמַר לוֹ. מִצִּיפּוֹרִין הֲבֵאתִים. אִם אֵין אַתְּ מַאֲמִינִי צֵא וְהָבֵא לָךְ אַף אָתָּה. רִבִּי חֲנַנְיָה וְרִבִּי פִּינְחָס. רִבִּי יוּדָה וְרִבִּי יוֹסֵה שְׁנֵיהֶן אָמְרוּ דָבָר אֶחָד. דְּתַנִּינָן תַּמָּן. אוֹכְלִין עַל הַמּוּבְקָר אֲבָל לֹא עַל הַשָּׁמוּר. רִבִּי יוֹסֵי אוֹמֵר. אַף עַל הַשָּׁמוּר. אָמַר לוֹן. מָן הַשָּׁמוּר הֲבֵאתִים. וְאִם אֵין אַתְּ מַאֲמִינִי הֲרֵי שָׂדֶה פְּלוֹנִית מְשׁוּמֶּרֶת לְפָנֶיךָ. צֵא וְהָבֵא לָךְ אַף אָתָּה.

1 מציפורין הבאתים | G מצפרין הביאתין   2 ור' פינחס | G בשם[ם] ר' פינחס   3 יוסי | G יֹוסה   4 לון | G ליה מאמיני | G מאמיניני

Halakhah 2: If they run out in Tiberias but did not run out in Sepphoris[64]. He says to him[65], I brought it from Sepphoris; if you do not believe me, go and bring for yourself. Rebbi Hanania and[66] Rebbi Phineas: Rebbi Jehudah and Rebbi Yose both said the same, as we have stated there[67]: "One eats based on what is abandoned but not on what is guarded[68]. Rebbi Yose says, also on what is guarded." He says to him[69], I brought it from what is guarded; if you do not believe me, there is field *x* guarded before you, go and bring for yourself.

64 One explains the argument of R. Jehudah; the implication being that practice follows him. The Babli disagrees, 52a.
65 These words are part of the Babli Mishnah.
66 G: In the name of.
67 Mishnah Ševiʿit 9:4.
68 "One eats" means "one does not have to eliminate". "Guarded" according to Maimonides means that it grows in a fenced-in field, whose Sabbatical produce is not private property and available to all comers.
69 Text of G; text here "them". The reasoning of R. Yose is parallel to that of R. Jehudah. Since R. Yose is the preeminent authority in the generation after R. Aqiba, practice follows him.

(fol. 30d) **משנה ג:** מָקוֹם שֶׁנָּהֲגוּ לִמְכּוֹר בְּהֵמָה דַקָּה לַגּוֹיִם מוֹכְרִין. מָקוֹם שֶׁנָּהֲגוּ שֶׁלֹּא לִמְכּוֹר אֵין מוֹכְרִין. וְאַל יְשַׁנֶּה אָדָם מִפְּנֵי הַמַּחֲלוֹקֶת. וּבְכָל־מָקוֹם אֵין מוֹכְרִין לָהֶם בְּהֵמָה גַסָּה עֲגָלִים וּסְיָחִים שְׁלֵימִין וּשְׁבוּרִין. רִבִּי יְהוּדָה מַתִּיר בַּשְּׁבוּרָה. בֶּן בְּתֵירָה מַתִּיר בַּסּוּס:

Mishnah 4: At a place where they used to sell small cattle to Gentiles one sells[70]; at a place where they used not to sell one does not sell; nobody should change this because of controversy[71]. Nowhere does one sell to them large animals, calves, and donkey foals, whole or damaged[72]. Rebbi Jehudah permits damaged ones; Ben Bathyra permits horses[73].

70 At places where sheep and goats are not sacrificed in pagan rites.
71 Even if the situation changes one should not change old usage since this will destroy communal peace.
72 Cattle and donkeys were used as animals for work and beasts of burden. Belonging to Jews, these animals have a right to rest on the Sabbath. If they are sold to Gentiles, the seller deprives them of this right; depending on circumstances this might be counted as violation of the Sabbath by the seller. Calves and foals do not work but are raised for work.
73 In antiquity horses were used only for riding, not for work. Even if the horse is used for hunting, he holds that transporting

live animals or birds is not a breach of biblical Sabbath law.

Mishnah and Halakhah are also in *Avodah zarah* 1:6, where the different readings are noted. It is difficult to determine which text is original.

(30d line 51) **הלכה ג:** מוּתָּר לְגַדֵּל. אָמַר רִבִּי בָא. כְּגוֹן מָהִיר שֶׁהוּא שִׁשָּׁה עָשָׂר מִיל עַל שִׁשָּׁה עָשָׂר מִיל. הֲווֹן בָּעֲיֵי מֵמַר. מָאן דְּאָמַר. מוּתָּר לִמְכּוֹר. מוּתָּר לְיַיחֵד. וּמָאן דָּמַר. אָסוּר לִמְכּוֹר אָסוּר לְיַיחֵד. רִבִּי יוֹנָה רִבִּי לְעָזָר בְּשֵׁם רַב. וַאֲפִילוּ כְּמָאן דְּאָמַר. מוּתָּר לִמְכּוֹר. אָסוּר לְיַיחֵד. מַה בֵין לִמְכּוֹר מַה בֵין לְיַיחֵד. תַּמָּן מִכֵּיוָן שֶׁהוּא מוֹכְרָהּ לוֹ כִּבְהֶמְתּוֹ שֶׁלְּגוֹי הִיא. בְּרַם הָכָא בְּהֶמְתּוּ שֶׁלְּיִשְׂרָאֵל הִיא וְהוּא חָשׂוּד עָלֶיהָ.

Halakhah 3: Is it permitted to raise them[74]? Rebbi Abba said, for example Mahir which is sixteen by sixteen *mil*[75]. They wanted to say, he who said it is permitted to sell [says] it is permitted to leave it alone. But he who says, it is forbidden to sell [says] it is forbidden to leave it alone[76]. Rebbi Jonah, Rebbi Eleazar in the name of Rav[77]: Even one who says it is permitted to sell it [says] it is forbidden to leave it alone. What is the difference between selling and leaving alone? There, because he intends to sell it to him it is like the Gentile's animal. But here it is the Jew's animal and he is suspected about it.

74 Since it is forbidden to raise sheep and goats in the Land of Israel (Mishnah *Bava qamma* 7:10, Note 97), from where does one get them to sell them to a Gentile?

75 The Mishnah permits to raise goats and sheep in places unfit for agriculture. *Mahir* is described in *Eccl. rabba* 1(34) as situated in the domain of the tribe of Reuben in Transjordan, a country of sheep and goats (*Num.* 32:4). B. Z. Lurie (*Sinai* 83, 1978, pp. 24-29 finds *Mahir* in the Syrian village of *Mahin*, on the *via Diocletiana* from Syria to Iraq, on the border of the desert.

76 Gentiles are suspected of bestiality (Mishnah *Avodah zarah* 2:1).

77 In the Babli, *Avodah zarah* 14b/15a, this is R. Eleazar's statement opposing Rav.

(30d line 57) מָקוֹם שֶׁנָּהֲגוּ שֶׁלֹּא לִמְכּוֹר אֵין מוֹכְרִין. לָמָּה. שֶׁהוּא מוֹצִיאָהּ מִידֵי גִיזָה. הַגַּע עַצְמָךְ שֶׁהָיְיתָה עֵז. שֶׁהוּא מוֹצִיאָהּ מִידֵי בְכוֹרָה. הַגַּע עַצְמָךְ שֶׁהָיָה זָכָר. שֶׁהוּא מוֹצִיאוֹ מִידֵי מַתָּנוֹת. מֵעַתָּה חִיטִּין אַל יִמְכּוֹר לוֹ. שֶׁהוּא מוֹצִיאָן מִידֵי חַלָּה. יַיִן וְשֶׁמֶן אַל יִמְכּוֹר לוֹ. שֶׁהוּא שֶׁמּוֹצִיאָן מִידֵי בְרָכָה.

"At a place where they used not to sell one does not sell." Why? Because he eliminates the duty of shearing[78]. Think of it, if it was a goat! Because he eliminates the duty of the first-born[79]. Think of it, if it was a male! Because he eliminates the gifts[80]. Then one should not sell wheat to him because he eliminates the duty of *hallah*; then one should not sell wine and oil to him because he eliminates the duty of benedictions[81].

78 The first wool of shearing sheep should be given to a Cohen, *Deut.* 18:4. But goats are not raised for wool and are included in the prohibition.

79 Which must be given to a Cohen, *Deut.* 15:19. But a male animal does not bear lambs and also is included in the prohibition.

80 The parts of the animal to be given to a Cohen, *Deut.* 18:3.

81 Which are pronounced before and after food, as described in the later Chapters of Tractate *Berakhot*.

The problem treated here is that in the next paragraph it is stated that one does not sell large animals to Gentiles because of problems with the laws of the Sabbath. Therefore one is inclined to say that the prohibitions of Mishnah *Avodah zarah* 1:5 are because of pagan worship and those of our Mishnah, which also is Mishnah *Avodah zarah* 1:6, because of Jewish worship. It is shown that this does not hold; the first part of the Mishnah is about pagan worship, about places where sheep or goats are sacrificed by pagans; only the second part is about Jewish matters.

(30d line 61) בְּכָל מָקוֹם אֵין מוֹכְרִין לָהֶם בְּהֵמָה גַסָה. מַה בֵין גַּסָה מַה בֵין בְּהֵמָה דַקָה. בְּהֵמָה גָסָה יֵש בָּה חִיוּב חַטָּאת. בְּהֵמָה דַקָה אֵין בָּה חִיוּב חַטָּאת. וְאֵינוֹ חוֹלֵב וְאֵינוּ גוֹזֵז. תַּמָּן הוּא מִתְחַיֵיב. בְּרַם הָכָא הִיא מִתְחַיֶיבֶת. וְכֵיוָן שֶׁהוּא מוֹכְרָהּ לוֹ לֹא בְּהֶמְתּוֹ שֶׁלְגוֹי הִיא. אָמַר רִבִּי אִימִי בַּבֵּלְיָיא בְשֵׁם רַבָּנִין דְּתַמָּן. פְּעָמִים שֶׁהוּא מוֹכְרָהּ לוֹ לְנִיסָיוֹן. וְהוּא מַחֲזִירָהּ לוֹ לְאַחַר ג' יָמִים. וְנִמְצָא עוֹבֵר עֲבֵירָה בִּבְהֶמְתּוֹ שֶׁלְיִשְׂרָאֵל. מֵעַתָּה לְנִיסָיוֹן אָסוּר. שֶׁלֹא לְנִיסָיוֹן מוּתָּר. זוֹ מִפְּנֵי זוֹ.

עָבַר וּמָכַר קוֹנְסִין בּוֹ. כְּשֵׁם שֶׁקוֹנְסִין לַהֲלָכָה כָּךְ קוֹנְסִין לַמִּנְהָג. מְנַיִין שֶׁקוֹנְסִין בּוֹ לַמִּנְהָג. חַד בַּר נַש זְבִין גְּמָלָא לְחַד אֲרָמַאי. אֲתָא עוֹבְדָא קוֹמֵי רִבִּי שִׁמְעוֹן בֶּן לָקִישׁ וּקְנָסֵי בְּכִיפְלֵה בְּגִין דְּיֵיחֲזוֹר לֵיהּ גְּמָלָא. אָמַר רִבִּי יוֹסֵה בֵּירִבִּי בּוּן. לְסַרְסוּר קָנְסוּ וַהֲווֹן צָוְוחִין לֵיהּ בְּרָא דִמְסַרְסֵר לַאֲרָמָאָה. מַה. רִבִּי שִׁמְעוֹן בֶּן לָקִישׁ כְּרִבִּי יוּדָה. דְּתַנֵּי בְשֵׁם רִבִּי יוּדָה. הַלוֹקֵחַ בְּהֵמָה מִן הַגוֹי וְיָלְדָה בְכוֹר. מַעֲלֶה עִמּוֹ בְשָׁוֶה וְנוֹתֵן חֲצִי דָמִים לַכֹּהֵן. נְתָנָהּ לוֹ בְקַבָּלָה. מַעֲלֶה עִמּוֹ אֲפִילוּ עֶשֶׂר דָמִים בְּשָׁוֶה וְנוֹתֵן כָּל־הַדָמִים לַכֹּהֵן. וַחֲכָמִים אוֹמְרִים. הוֹאִיל וְאֶצְבַּע הַגוֹי בָּאֶמְצַע נִפְטְרָה מִן הַבְּכוֹרָה. רִבִּי שִׁמְעוֹן בֶּן לָקִישׁ כְּרִבִּי יוּדָה. וְרָבָה מִן דְּרִבִּי יוּדָה. מַה דְּאָמַר רִבִּי יוּדָה מִשּׁוּם הִילְכוֹת בְּכוֹרָה. מַה דְּאָמַר רִבִּי שִׁמְעוֹן בֶּן לָקִישׁ מִשּׁוּם הִילְכוֹת בְּהֵמָה גַסָה.

"Nowhere does one sell large animals to them." What is the difference between large and small animals? For a large animal there might be an obligation for a purification offering[82]; for a small animal there can be no obligation for a purification offering. But does he not shear, does he not milk? There he is liable; here would it be liable[83]? But if it is sold, is it not the Gentile's animal? The Babylonian Rebbi Immi[84] in the name of the rabbis there: Sometimes he sells it on trial and returns it after three days, then it turns out that he did forbidden work with the Jew's animal[85]. Then on trial it should be forbidden, not on trial permitted. One is because of the other[86].

If he transgressed and sold one fines him. Just as one fines for practice so one fines for custom. From where that one fines for custom? A person sold his camel to an Aramean[87]. The case came before Rebbi Simeon ben Laqish who fined him double to make him take back the camel. Rebbi Yose ben Rebbi Abun said, they fined the broker and called him son who brokers to an Aramean. Does Rebbi Simeon ben Laqish follow Rebbi Jehudah[88]? As it was stated in the name of Rebbi Jehudah[89]: "If somebody buys an animal from a Gentile and it gave birth to a firstling, he buys it up to its worth and gives half of its worth to a Cohen. If it was given to him as contractor, he has to pay for up to ten times its worth and gives all of its worth to the Cohen. But the Sages say, since the finger of the Gentile in involved it is no longer liable as firstling[90]." Rebbi Simeon ben Laqish follows Rebbi Jehudah and says more than Rebbi Jehudah. What Rebbi Jehudah said because of the practice of firstlings; but what Rebbi Simeon ben Laqish said because of practice regarding a large animal[91].

82 If the Gentile does work with the Jew's animal on the Sabbath, it is a violation of the Sabbath by biblical standards.

83 It is clear that shearing a sheep on the Sabbath is a violation of biblical law (Mishnah *Šabbat* 7:2). The Yerushalmi holds that milking a goat also is a biblical prohibition. But giving the animal rest on the Sabbath is an obligation of the owner; he is liable even if another person does the work with his consent. But the Gentile who shears or milks the animal violates no prohibition; since the animal is passive the owner also does not violate any biblical statute.

84 A Babylonian who immigrated to Galilee in the generation after R. Immi the Galilean. In the Babli *Avodah zarah* 15a he is called Rami ben Rebbi Yeva.

85 If the Gentile takes the animal on Friday and returns it on Sunday he will have worked with it on the Sabbath with the agreement of the Jew who it turns out still is the owner.

86 This is a rabbinic "fence around the law," far from biblical prohibitions.
87 A Gentile. While "Gentile" is used to emphasize the pagan character of a person, "Aramean" simply characterizes him as Non-Jew.
88 Could R. Simeon ben Laqish act against accepted practice in this case?
89 Tosephta *Bekhorot* 2:1, Babli *Bekhorot* 2b.
90 Undisputed practice follows the Sages, cf. Note 94.
91 The two cases have nothing in common.

(31a line 4) רִבִּי יוּדָה מַתִּיר בַּשְׁבוּרָה. לֹא אָמַר רִבִּי יוּדָה אֶלָּא בַּשְׁבוּרָה שֶׁאֵינָהּ יְכוֹלָה לְהִתְרַפְּאוֹת. אָמְרוּ לוֹ. וַהֲרֵי מְבִיאִין לָהּ זָכָר וְנִרְבַּעַת מִמֶּנּוּ. אָמַר לָהֶן. אַף אֲנִי לֹא אָמַרְתִּי אֶלָּא בְּשָׁבוּר [זָכָר שֶׁאֵינוֹ יָכוֹל לְהִתְרַפְּאוֹת]. אָמְרוּ לוֹ. וַהֲלֹא מְבִיאִין לוֹ נְקֵיבָה וְהוּא רוֹבְעָהּ וְהִיא יוֹלֶדֶת. רַב אָבוּן בְּשֵׁם רַבָּנִין דְּתַמָּן. זֹאת אוֹמֶרֶת שֶׁאָסוּר לְהַמְצִיא לָהֶן זֶרַע. תַּמָּן תַּנִּינָן. הַלּוֹקֵחַ עוּבַּר חֲמוֹרוֹ שֶׁלְּנָכְרִי. הַמּוֹכֵר לוֹ אַף עַל פִּי שֶׁאֵינוֹ רַשַּׁאי. הַמִּשְׁתַּתֵּף לוֹ. וְהַמְקַבֵּל מִמֶּנּוּ. וְהַנּוֹתֵן לוֹ בְקַבָּלָה פָּטוּר מִן הַבְּכוֹרָה. רִבִּי חַגַּיי בְּעָא קוֹמֵי רִבִּי יוֹסֵי. לֵית הָדָא אָמְרָה שֶׁאָסוּר לְהַמְצִיא לָהֶן עבדים. אָמַר לֵיהּ. כְּבָר קְדָמָךְ רִבִּי אָבוּן בְּשֵׁם רַבָּנִין דְּתַמָּן. דָּמַר רִבִּי אָבוּן בְּשֵׁם רַבָּנִין דְּתַמָּן. זֹאת אוֹמֶרֶת שֶׁאָסוּר לְהַמְצִיא לָהֶן זֶרַע.

6 בעא G | בעה הדא G | הדה 7 עבדים G | עוברין

"Rebbi Jehudah permits damaged ones." Rebbi Jehudah said this only for a damaged one which cannot be healed[92]. They told him, may they not bring a male to her, she is fertilized and gives birth? He said to them, I also said this only about a male damaged one which cannot be healed. They told him, may they not bring a female to him, he fertilizes her and she gives birth? Rav Abun in the name of the rabbis there: This implies that one is forbidden to provide them with semen[93]. There[94], we have stated: "If somebody buys a Non-Jew's donkey fetus or who sells one to him even though he is not authorized, or one who enters into partnership, or accepts from him as contractor, or lets it in contract, is not liable for firstling." Rebbi Ḥaggai asked before Rebbi Yose, does this[95] not imply that one is forbidden to provide them with (slaves) [fetuses][96]? He said to them, Rebbi Abun in the name of the rabbis there already preceded you, since Rebbi Abun said in the name of the rabbis there, this implies that one is forbidden to provide them with semen.

92 To ever work again.
93 Since the argument of the rabbis has nothing to do with Sabbath prohibitions. The Babli, *Avodah zarah* 16a and *Bekhorot*

2b, disagrees and reports that R. Jehudah denies that a disabled cow will accept a male.

94   Mishnah *Bekhorot* 1:1.

95   The note that one is not authorized to sell a pregnant animal to a Gentile.

96   The word עבדים "slaves" in the Leiden ms. is a scribal error for עוּבָּרִין "fetuses" in G and *Avodah zarah*.

(31a line 14) בֶּן בְּתֵירָה מַתִּיר בַּסּוּס: לֹא אָמַר רִבִּי יוּדָה אֶלָּא בְּסוּס זָכָר שֶׁהוּא הוֹרֵג [בְּעָלָיו] בַּמִּלְחָמָה. יֵשׁ אוֹמְרִים. שָׁרָץ אַחַר נְקֵיבָה. וְיֵשׁ אוֹמְרִים. שֶׁהוּא עוֹמֵד וּמַשְׁתִּין. מַה נָפֵק בֵּינֵיהוֹן. הַסְרִיס. מָאן דְּאָמַר. שֶׁהוּא רָץ אַחַר הַנְּקֵיבָה. [זֶה] אֵינוּ רָץ אַחַר נְקֵיבָה. מָאן דָּמַר. שֶׁהוּא עוֹמֵד וּמַשְׁתִּין. אַף הוּא עוֹמֵד וּמַשְׁתִּין. דִּבְרֵי חֲכָמִים. רִבִּי אָחָא בְּשֵׁם רִבִּי תַּנְחוּם בַּר חִייָה. לִכְשֶׁיַּזְקִין הוּא כּוֹדְנוֹ בָּרֵיחַיִים. רִבִּי יוֹסֵה בֵּירִבִּי בּוּן בְּשֵׁם רִבִּי חוּנָה. בֶּן בְּתֵירָה וְרִבִּי נָתָן אָמְרוּ דָּבָר אֶחָד. דְּתַנֵּי. הוֹצִיא בְּהֵמָה וְחַיָּה וְעוֹפוֹת. בֵּין חַיִּים בֵּין מֵתִים חַיָּיב. רִבִּי נָתָן אוֹמֵר. מֵתִים חַיָּיב. חַיִּין פָּטוּר. רַבָּנִין אִית לְהוֹן מִשּׁוּם חִיּוּב חַטָּאת. וְאִינּוּן מְתִיבִין לֵיהּ הָכֵין. כְּשִׁיטָתוֹ הֱשִׁיבוּהוּ. כְּשִׁיטָתְךָ שֶׁאַתְּ אוֹמֵר. מִשּׁוּם הִילְכוֹת בְּהֵמָה גַסָּה. אוֹף אֲנָן אִית לָן. לִכְשֶׁיַּזְקִין הוּא כּוֹדְנוֹ בָּרֵיחַיִים. רִבִּי אוֹמֵר. אוֹמֵר אֲנִי שֶׁהוּא אָסוּר מִשּׁוּם שְׁנֵי דְבָרִים. מִשּׁוּם כְּלִי זַיִין וּמִשּׁוּם הִילְכוֹת בְּהֵמָה גַסָּה. וְתַנֵּי כֵן. חַיָּה גַסָּה כִּבְהֵמָה גַסָּה. מָאן תַּנִּיתָהּ. רִבִּי. דִּבְרֵי חֲכָמִים. רִבִּי בִּיסְנָא חָנִין בַּר בָּא בְּשֵׁם רַב. חַיָּה גַסָּה כִּבְהֵמָה דַקָּה.

"Ben Bathyra permits horses." Rebbi Jehudah[97] said this only about a male horse because it kills [its owner] in war. Some say, because it runs after a female, and some say, because it stands still to urinate[98]. What is between them? A gelding. He who says because it runs after a female, [this one] does not run after a female. He who says because it stands still to urinate, this one also stands still to urinate. Rebbi Aha in the name of Rebbi Tanhum bar Hiyya: If it gets old he binds it to the grindstone[99]. Rebbi Yose ben Rebbi Abun in the name of Rebbi Huna: Ben Bathyra and Rebbi Nathan both said the same[100], as it was stated[101]: "If he carried domestic animals, wild animals, or birds, whether alive or dead, he is liable. Rebbi Nathan says, dead he is liable, alive he is not liable." The rabbis hold that he is liable for a purification sacrifice and they answer him so[102]? They answer following his own argument. Following your argument, since you are saying because of rabbinic Sabbath prohibition, also we hold that if it gets old he binds it to the grindstone. Rebbi says, I am saying that it is forbidden for two reasons, as a weapon[103] and as a large animal. It was stated so: A large wild animal is like a large domestic animal[104]. Who stated this? Rebbi. The words of the Sages:

Rebbi Bisna, Ḥanin bar Abba in the name of Rav[105]: A wild animal is like a small[105] domestic animal.

97 R. Jehudah ben Bathyra.
98 At this moment the horse will not obey its master and therefore be dangerous.
99 Then it is used like a beast of burden and the same restriction may apply as to the sale of cattle. Babli *Avodah zarah* 16a.
100 For the laws of Sabbath. Everybody agrees that "a living person carries himself"; it is permitted to carry a human baby from private to public domains. The rabbis restrict this to humans; R. Nathan explicitly and Ben Bathyra implicitly (Note 73) extend the rule to animals. Babli *Šabbat* 94a.
101 Tosephta *Šabbat* 8:34 Babli *Šabbat* 94a.
102 Why do they object because of the use of old horses which only implies a violation of rabbinic rules but not to the possible use of a younger horse in hunting, which would violate biblical rules? It seems clear that in contrast to the Babli, the Yerushalmi does not consider riding on a horse on a Sabbath or a holiday as a violation.
103 Which makes the seller of the weapon an accessory to murder before the fact. Babli 16a.
104 A horse is considered a tamed wild animal, not domesticated by nature.
105 The Genizah text has the statement in the name of Rebbi Hiyya, Rav's uncle and foremost teacher.

(fol. 30c) **משנה ד**: מָקוֹם שֶׁנָּהֲגוּ לוֹכַל צָלִי בְּלֵילֵי פְסָחִים אוֹכְלִין. מָקוֹם שֶׁנָּהֲגוּ שֶׁלֹּא לוֹכַל אֵינָן אוֹכְלִין. מָקוֹם שֶׁנָּהֲגוּ לְהַדְלִיק אֶת הַנֵּר בְּלֵילֵי יוֹם הַכִּיפּוּרִים מַדְלִיקִין. מָקוֹם שֶׁנָּהֲגוּ שֶׁלֹּא לְהַדְלִיק אֵין מַדְלִיקִין. מַדְלִיקִין בְּבָתֵּי כְנֵסִיּוֹת וּבְבָתֵּי מִדְרָשׁוֹת וּבִמְבוֹאוֹת אֲפֵילִין וְעַל גַּבֵּי הַחוֹלִין:

Mishnah 4: In a place where usually one eats roast meat in the Passover nights one eats; in a place where one does not usually eat[106] one does not eat. In a place where one is used to ignite a candle in the night of the Day of Atonement[107] one ignites, in a place where one is used not to ignite one does not ignite. One ignites in synagogues, and in houses of study[108], and in dark passages[109], and near sick persons.

106 Since this would suggest eating the *Pesah* sacrifice outside the sacred precinct, a deadly sin.
107 The Day of Atonement follows the rules of the Sabbath, but the reasons for illuminating the house for the festive Friday evening meal do not apply to the fast day.
108 Since on the day of Atonement long

evening prayers are conducted in synagogues and houses of study, these have to be illuminated.

109 Since late in the night people will return to their houses from the synagogue.

(31a line 29) **הלכה ד**: רִבִּי בָּא בְעָא קוֹמֵי רִבִּי אִימִּי. אֲפִילוּ בְשַׂר עֵגֶל. אָמַר לֵיהּ. אֲפִילוּ בְשַׂר עֵגֶל. אֲפִילוּ בְשַׂר עוֹף. אָמַר לֵיהּ. אֲפִילוּ בְשַׂר עוֹף. סָבְרִין מֵימַר. אֲפִילוּ בֵיצָה. אֲפִילוּ קוֹלָקָס. אָמַר רִבִּי יוּדָן בֵּירִבִּי חָנִין. וּבִלְבַד מִן הַשְּׁחִיטָה.

1 בעא G | בעה אפי' G | ואפילו (2) 2 אפי' G | ואפילו (2) 3 חנין G | חנן מן השחיטה | G מין שחיטה

Halakhah 4: Rebbi Abba asked before Rebbi Immi: Even calf meat? He said to him, even calf meat[110]. Even fowl meat? He said to him, even fowl meat. They wanted to say, even an egg, even colocasia[111]. Rebbi Yudan ben Rebbi Ḥanin said, but only what needs slaughter[112].

110 Since already in his time nowhere was roast meat eaten in the Passover night, the question is whether the customary prohibition is restricted to lambs' or kid goats' meat, which would imitate the *Pesaḥ* sacrifice, or applies to meat in general.

111 *Colocasia antiquorum Schott.*, an edible fruit.

112 Only roast meat is forbidden. In fact, on modern *seder* plates, many communities use roasted egg.

(31a line 32) תַּנֵּי. רִבִּי שִׁמְעוֹן בֶּן אֶלְעָזָר אוֹמֵר. יוֹם הַכִּיפּוּרִים שֶׁחָל לִהְיוֹת בַּשַּׁבָּת. אֲפִילוּ בִּמְקוֹם שֶׁלֹּא נָהֲגוּ לְהַדְלִיק מַדְלִיקִין. רִבִּי סִימוֹן בְּשֵׁם רִבִּי יְהוֹשֻׁעַ בֶּן לֵוִי רִבִּי יוֹסֵי בֶּן שָׁאוּל בְּשֵׁם רִבִּי. הֲלָכָה כְּרִבִּי שִׁמְעוֹן בֶּן אֶלְעָזָר. דָּרַשׁ רִבִּי חִיָּיה בַּר בָּא לְטִיבֶּרְיָא כְּהָדָא דְּרִבִּי שִׁמְעוֹן בֶּן אֶלְעָזָר. רִבִּי יוֹסֵה אָמַר לָהּ רִבִּי שְׁמוּאֵל בַּר נַחְמָן בְּשֵׁם רִבִּי יוֹנָתָן רִבִּי חִזְקִיָּה וְאָמְרִי לָהּ רִבִּי יַעֲקֹב בַּר אָחָא בְּשֵׁם רִבִּי שְׁמוּאֵל בַּר נַחְמָן. מְקוֹם שֶׁנָּהֲגוּ לְהַדְלִיק מְשׁוּבָּח מִמָּקוֹם שֶׁנָּהֲגוּ שֶׁלֹּא לְהַדְלִיק. אָמַר רִבִּי יִרְמְיָה. תֵּדַע לָךְ שֶׁהוּא כֵן. שֶׁהֲרֵי יוֹם הַכִּיפּוּרִים שֶׁחָל לִהְיוֹת בַּשַּׁבָּת אֲפִילוּ מְקוֹם שֶׁנָּהֲגוּ שֶׁלֹּא לְהַדְלִיק מַדְלִיקִין. רִבִּי בָּא וְרִבִּי סִימוֹן תְּרֵיהוֹן אָמְרִין. תֵּדַע לָךְ שֶׁהוּא כֵן. שֶׁהֲרֵי הָאִישׁ הַזֶּה צָנוּעַ וְאֵינוֹ מְשַׁמֵּשׁ מִיטָּתוֹ לְאוֹר הַנֵּר. בֵּין כְּמַאן דְּאָמַר. מַדְלִיקִין. בֵּין כְּמַאן דְּאָמַר. אֵין מַדְלִיקִין. מִפְּנֵי הֶרְגֵּל עֲבֵירָה. מָאן דְּאָמַר. מַדְלִיקִין. שֶׁהוּא רוֹאֶה וּמִתְבַּיֵּישׁ. וּמָאן דְּאָמַר. אֵין מַדְלִיקִין. שֶׁלֹּא יִרְאֶה וְיִתְאַוֶּה. תַּנֵּי. בָּתֵּי כְּנֵסִיּוֹת וּבָתֵּי מֶרְחֲצָיוֹת. לָכֵן צְרִיכָה. אֲפִילוּ מְקוֹם שֶׁלֹּא נָהֲגוּ לְהַדְלִיק מַדְלִיקִין.

1 אלעזר G | לעזר 2 שלא נהגו G | שנהגו שלא יהוש' G | יהושע 3 אלעזר G | לעזר בר בא G | רובה לטיבריא G | לטיבראי כהדא G | כהדה 4 אלעזר G | לעזר בר נחמן G | בר רב נחמן ואמרי G | אמ' 5 אחא G | אחה 6 תדע G | תידע תדע G | תידע במקום G | מקום 7 מקום G | שהיא שהוא G | מיטתו G | את מיטתו 8 דאמ' G | דאמר (2) כמן דמר G | כמאן דאמ' 9 מאן דאמ' G | מן דמר ומתבייש G | ומיתבייש ומאן G | מן 10 בתי כניסיות G | בבתי כיסאיות ובתי G | ובבתי - G | כן 11 מקום G | במקום שלא נהגו G | שנהגו

HALAKHAH FOUR 143

It was stated: Rebbi Simeon ben Eleazar says, on a Day of Atonement which falls on a Sabbath, even in a place where one is not used to ignite one ignites. Rebbi Simon in the name of Rebbi Joshua ben Levi, Rebbi Yose ben Saul in the name of Rebbi: Practice follows Rebbi Simeon ben Eleazar[113]. Rebbi Hiyya bar Abba[114] preached to the Tiberians following Rebbi Simeon ben Eleazar. Rebbi Yose said it in the name of Rebbi Samuel bar Nahman in the name of Rebbi Jonathan, Rebbi Hizqiah, but some say Rebbi Jacob bar Aha, in the name of Rebbi Samuel bar Nahman: A place where one is used to ignite is better than a place where one is used not to ignite. Rebbi Jeremiah said, you should know that this is so since on a Day of Atonement which falls on a Sabbath, even in a place where one is not used to ignite one ignites. Rebbi Abba and Rebbi Simon both are saying, you should know that this is so since a man is modest and will not engage in sexual activity when a light is burning[115]. Both he who said, one lights, as he who said, one does not light, because of leading into sin[116]. He who said that one lights, because he will see and be ashamed. But he who said that one does not light, that he should not see and become desirous. It was stated: Even in (synagogues) [privies][117] and wash rooms. For that it is necessary: One ignites even in a place where one is not used to ignite[118].

113 In the Babli 53b R. Johanan disagrees.
114 In G, "R. Hiyya the Elder", a most unlikely reading.
115 Sexual activity is forbidden on the Day of Atonement. It is presumed that the light is burning the entire night in the one-room house, or in the bedroom in a multi-room apartment. Babli 53b.
116 Tosephta 3:16, Babli 53b.
117 The reading of G [in brackets] is preferable to that of the Leiden ms. (in parentheses). A related text in Tosephta 3:16.
118 The reason here is the same as for illuminating dark passages. The statement applies to all Days of Atonement, not only on a Sabbath.

(31a line 46) יוֹם הַכִּיפּוּרִים שֶׁחָל לִהְיוֹת בַּשַּׁבָּת. מַהוּ לְהַדִּיחַ כְּבָשִׁין וּשְׁלָקוֹת מִן הַמִּנְחָה וּלְמַעְלָן. רַב אָמַר. אָסוּר. רִבִּי לָעְזָר אָמַר. מוּתָּר. רִבִּי יַעֲקֹב בַּר אָחָא בְשֵׁם רִבִּי אֶלְעָזָר. מַה טַעַם אָמְרוּ. מַדִּיחִין כְּבָשִׁים וּשְׁלָקוֹת מִן הַמִּנְחָה וּלְמַעְלָן. מִפְּנֵי סַכָּנָה. שַׁנְיָיא הִיא סַכָּנַת יוֹם הַכִּיפּוּרִים שֶׁחָל לִהְיוֹת בַּשַּׁבָּת. שַׁנְיָיא הִיא יוֹם הַכִּיפּוּרִים שֶׁחָל לִהְיוֹת בַּחוֹל. הָתִיב רִבִּי חֲנַנְיָה חֲבֵרוֹן דְּרַבָּנִין. מַתְנִיתָא פְּלִיגָא עַל רִבִּי אֶלְעָזָר. יוֹם הַכִּפּוּרִים שֶׁחָל לִהְיוֹת בַּשַּׁבָּת חַלּוֹת

מִתְחַלְּקוֹת לָעֶרֶב. שְׁנִיָּיא הִיא. שֶׁעַל יְדֵי שֶׁהוּא דָבָר קַל שֶׁמָּא יִשְׁכַּח וְיֹאכַל. הָתִיב רִבִּי פִּינְחָס. מַתְנִיתָא דְּרִבִּי לַעֲזָר פְּלִיגָא עָלוֹי. יוֹם הַכִּיפּוּרִים שֶׁחָל לִהְיוֹת בַּשַׁבָּת שְׁבוּת וּבַחוֹל שַׁבָּתוֹן שְׁבוּת. אִם בַּחוֹל אַתְּ שׁוֹבֵת לֹא עַל־שָׁכֵּן בַּשַׁבָּת. לֹא צוֹרְכָה דְּלֹא [אֲפִילוּ] דְּבָרִים שֶׁאַתְּ מוּתָּר לַעֲשׂוֹתָן בַּחוֹל אַתְּ שׁוֹבֵת עֲלֵיהֶן בַּשַׁבָּת. וְאֵי זוֹ זוֹ. זוֹ הֲדָחַת כְּבָשִׁים וּשְׁלָקוֹת. רִבִּי יַעֲקֹב בַּר זַבְדִּי בְשֵׁם רִבִּי אַבָּהוּ. נִרְאִין דְּבָרִים בְּדָבָר שֶׁדַּרְכּוֹ לָבוֹא בְצוֹנִין. אֲבָל דָּבָר שֶׁדַּרְכּוֹ לָבוֹא בְרוֹתְחִין עַד דְּיָיְדַע גְּלָשָׁה הוּא מְקַנֵּב. אָמַר רִבִּי מָנָא. אִם אוֹמֵר אַתְּ כֵּן. אַף מִתְבַּיֵּישׁ וְלֹא מְקַנֵּב. וְנִמְצָא בָא לִידֵי סַכָּנָה. רִבִּי בָּא בְעָא קוֹמֵי רִבִּי אִימִּי. מָהוּ לְהַדִּיחַ כְּבָשִׁים וּשְׁלָקוֹת מִן הַמִּנְחָה וּלְמַעֲלָן. אָמַר לֵיהּ. שָׁרֵי. רִבִּי יַעֲקֹב בַּר אָחָא שָׁאַל לְרִבִּי חִייָה וּלְרִבִּי יָסָה. מָהוּ לְהַדִּיחַ כְּבָשִׁים וּשְׁלָקוֹת [מִן הַמִּנְחָה וּלְמַעֲלָן]. אָמְרֵי לֵיהּ. שָׁרֵי. רִבִּי זְעוּרָה בָעָא קוֹמֵי רִבִּי אִימִּי. מָהוּ מֵימַר לַחֲלִיטָה. עֲבַד לִי חֲלִיטָה. אָמַר לֵיהּ. שָׁרֵי. עֲבַד לִי תוֹפִין. שָׁרֵי. עֲבַד לִי פְתִילָה. אָמַר לֵיהּ. לֹא. מַה בֵּין זֶה לָזֶה. זֶה אוֹכֵל נֶפֶשׁ. וְזֶה אֵינוֹ אוֹכֵל נֶפֶשׁ.

1 יום | G ביום מהו | G מהוא 2 אלעזר | G לעזר 3 מדיחין | G הדיחין כבשים | G כבשין ולמעלן | G ולמעלה סכנה | G הסכנה שנייא | G שנייה 4 שנייא | G שנייה היא | G היא סכנ[ה] חנניה חברון דרבנין | G פינחס 5 פליגא | G פליגה אלעזר | G לעזר יום הכיפורים שחל | G חל יום הכיפורים חלות | G החלות 6 שנייא | G שנייה שהוא | G שהיא פינחס | G חנניה חברהון דרבנן 7 אלעזר | G לעזר פליגא | G פליגה 8 דלא | G דילא 9 כבשים | G כבשין 10 אבהו | G אבהוא דברים | G הדבריו בצונין | G ברותחין 11 ברותחיון | G בצוניי עד דיידא | G מן דאמרה מתבייש | G משתבש

On a Day of Atonemement which falls on a Sabbath may one soak pickles[119] and preserves[120] starting from the time of afternoon prayers[121]? Rav said, it is forbidden[122]; Rebbi Eleazar said, it is permitted. Rebbi Jacob bar Aha in the name of Rebbi Eleazar, why did they say, one may soak pickles and preserves starting from the time of afternoon prayers? Because of danger. Is there a difference between the danger on a Day of Atonement which falls on a Sabbath and a Day of Atonement which falls on a weekday[123]? Rebbi Hanania the colleague of the rabbis[124] objected, a Mishnah disagrees with Rebbi Eleazar: "On a Day of Atonemement which falls on a Sabbath, the shew-breads are distributed in the evening.[125]" There is a difference. Since this is a small matter, he might forget and eat. Rebbi Phineas objected:: A *baraita* of Rebbi Eleazar disagrees with him. The Day of Atonemement which falls on a Sabbath is a day of rest; on a weekday it is a day of rest[126]. If one is resting on a weekday, not so much more on a Sabbath? Is it not necessary that even things which you are permitted to do on a weekday you have to refrain from on a Sabbath? What would this be? This is soaking pickles and preserves[127]. Rebbi Jacob bar Zavdi in the name of Rebbi Abbahu. The matter is evident for anything which is served with cold food but for anything which is served with hot food while it is heated he can trim it[128]. Rebbi Mana said, if you are saying so, also he will be embarrassed and will not trim; it will turn out that he will become endangered[129]. Rebbi Abba asked before Rebbi Immi: May one soak pickles and preserves starting from the time of afternoon prayers? He said to him, it is permitted. Rebbi Jacob bar Aḥa asked Rebbi Ḥiyya and Rebbi Yasa, may one soak pickles and preserves starting from the time of afternoon prayers? They said to him, it is permitted. Rebbi Ze`ira asked before Rebbi Immi, may one say to the maker of fried food[130] make me some fried food? He said to him, it is permitted. Make me baked goods? Permitted. Prepare me a wick? No. What is the difference between one and the other? This is food, the other is not food[131].

119 Any food preserved in vinegar.
120 Food preserved in water after extensive cooking.
121 On a regular Sabbath or holiday it is forbidden to prepare food for use after the end of the day. The exception is the Day of Atonement where one is encouraged to start preparing for the end of the fast in the late afternoon in order to minimize the time between nightfall and the evening meal, the "danger" from an extension of the fast.
122 Babli Šabbat 114b.
123 There is no reason to distinguish between Sabbath and weekday in this respect.
124 G switches the attributions between him and R. Phineas.
125 Mishnah Menahot 11:7. The shew-breads are changed every Sabbath (Lev. 24:8); the previous week's bread must be eaten by the Cohanim in the Temple precinct. Since the consumption of the bread is part of the Temple service (v. 9), if this cannot be prepared before the end of the Day of Atonement then certainly profane food cannot be prepared.

126 Sifra Emor Pereq 14(4); Babli Šabbat 114b. The Day of Atonement is called שַׁבָּת שַׁבָּתוֹן. The expression Šabbat refers to all activity biblically forbidden on the Sabbath; שַׁבָּתוֹן therefore must refer to additional restraint from permitted activity incompatible with the nature of the day. The verse does not distinguish between a Day of Atonement on a Sabbath or on a weekday.
127 This implies that according to everybody on a Day of Atonement on a weekday one prepares for the end of the fast before the end of the day.
128 Since cooking is biblically forbidden on the Sabbath and on the Day of Atonement, hot food never can be prepared before the end of the day.
   The translation follows G; the text of the Leiden ms. is rather unintelligible.
129 Here ends G.
130 A Gentile. It is obvious that on a regular Sabbath this is forbidden.
131 In all matters not pertaining to the preparation of food, the regular Sabbath

(fol. 30c) **משנה ה**: מָקוֹם שֶׁנָּהֲגוּ לַעֲשׂוֹת מְלָאכָה בְּתִשְׁעָה בְאָב עוֹשִׂין. מָקוֹם שֶׁנָּהֲגוּ שֶׁלֹּא לַעֲשׂוֹת אֵין עוֹשִׂין. וּבְכָל־מָקוֹם תַּלְמִידֵי חֲכָמִים בְּטֵלִין. רַבָּן שִׁמְעוֹן בֶּן גַּמְלִיאֵל אוֹמֵר יַעֲשׂוּ כָל־אָדָם עַצְמָן כְּתַלְמִידֵי חֲכָמִים.

Mishnah 5: In a place where usually one works on the Ninth of Av, one works. In a place where usually one refrains one does not work, but everywhere the scholars are idle. Rabban Simeon ben Gamliel says, should everybody make himself a scholar?

(31a line 68) **הלכה ה**: רִבִּי אָבוּן רִבִּי שִׁמְעוֹן בֶּן לָקִישׁ בְּשֵׁם רִבִּי יוּדָן נְשִׂיָּא. כְּמַתְמִיהַּ. יַעֲשׂוּ כָל־אָדָם עַצְמָן תַּלְמִידֵי חֲכָמִים. כָּל־עַצְמָן לֹא גָזְרוּ חֲכָמִים בְּטִילָה בְּתִשְׁעָה בְאָב.

Halakhah 5: Rebbi Abun, Rebbi Simeon ben Laqish in the name of Rebbi Yudan the Prince: With a question mark, "should everybody make himself a scholar?" The Sages themselves did not decree idleness[132].

132 Since according to the anonymous majority, it is recommended that everybody be idle on the Ninth of Av, the day of mourning for the destruction of the Temple, the original intent of the Mishnah, that this be a matter of local custom, would be contradicted. Therefore he requires that scholars do not behave differently from anybody else.

R. Salomon Adani in his Mishnah Commentary מלאכת שלמה quotes a reading במתמיה "if he causes people to wonder" (cf. Note 61); in this version Rabban Simeon ben Gamliel only forbids idleness if it is noticed in public.

The Babli 54b-55a has a slightly different reading in Rabban Simeon ben Gamliel's text and reads it as a straight declarative sentence.

(fol. 30c) **משנה ו**: וַחֲכָמִים אוֹמְרִים בִּיהוּדָה הָיוּ עוֹשִׂין מְלָאכָה בְּעַרְבֵי פְסָחִים עַד חֲצוֹת. וּבַגָּלִיל לֹא הָיוּ עוֹשִׂין כָּל עִקָּר. הַלַּיְלָה בֵּית שַׁמַּאי אוֹסְרִין וּבֵית הִלֵּל מַתִּירִין עַד שֶׁתֵּנֵץ הַחַמָּה:

Mishnah 6: Also the Sages say, in Judea one did work on Passover Eve until noon, but in Galilee one did not work at all. In the night, the House of Shammai forbid, but the House of Hillel permit until sunrise[133].

133 Since the Mishnah is formulated in the past tense, it must refer to the time of the Temple, where the afternoon of the 14th of Nisan was the time of slaughter of the Passover lamb, which was slaughtered for everybody, and where nobody could work (Note 5). Then the question remains whether the difference in pharisaic practice between Judea and Galilee has to be considered a difference in the interpretation of the law by different schools or a matter of popular usage.

(31a line 70) **הלכה ו:** הָא יוֹם אָסוּר. רִבִּי לְעָזָר בְּשֵׁם רִבִּי הוֹשַׁעְיָה. יוֹם פֶּסַח הוּא לַיי. רִבִּי יַעֲקֹב בַּר אֲחָא בְשֵׁם רִבִּי יוֹחָנָן רִבִּי לָא בְשֵׁם רִבִּי לְעָזָר. שְׁנֵי תַלְמִידִים שָׁנוּ אוֹתָהּ. אָמַר רִבִּי זְעוּרָה. אַשְׁכְּחִית אֲמַר. תְּלָתָא אִינּוּן. חַד אֲמַר. אָסוּר. וְחַד אֲמַר. מוּתָּר. וְחַד אֲמַר. מִנְהָג.

Halakhah 6: Therefore, the day is forbidden[134]. Rebbi Eleazar in the name of Rebbi Hoshaia: "*A day of Pesah it is for the Eternal.*[135]" Rebbi Jacob bar Aḥa in the name of Rebbi Joḥanan, Rebbi La in the name of Rebbi Eleazar: Two students formulated it. Rebbi Ze`ira said, I found to say that they are three. One said, it is forbidden, another said, it is permitted, and another said it is a matter of usage[136].

134 The Mishnah contradicts itself. If even the House of Hillel permit work only until sunrise, then nobody should be allowed to work in the morning of the 14th. There should be some biblical support for this conclusion.

135 Such a verse does not exist; it is a combination of *Num.* 28:16, (*In the first month, on the fourteenth*) *day* (*of the month,*) *a Pesah for the Eternal,* and *Ex.* 12:27: (*And you shall say, a sacrifice*) of *Pesah it is for the Eternal.* This kind of scriptural argument is not proof; it is a hint to support popular usage.

136 The Babli 55a identified R. Meïr as the one who holds that it is a matter of usage but keeps open the possibility of reading R. Jehudah's opinion either following the action in Judea or that in Galilee.

(fol. 30c) **משנה ז:** רִבִּי מֵאִיר אוֹמֵר כָּל־מְלָאכָה שֶׁהִתְחִיל בָּהּ קוֹדֶם לְאַרְבָּעָה עָשָׂר גּוֹמְרָהּ בְּאַרְבָּעָה עָשָׂר. אֲבָל לֹא יַתְחִיל בָּהּ בַּתְּחִלָּה בְּאַרְבָּעָה עָשָׂר אַף עַל פִּי שֶׁיָּכוֹל לְגוֹמְרָהּ. וַחֲכָמִים אוֹמְרִים שָׁלֹשׁ אוּמָּנִיּוֹת עוֹשִׂין מְלָאכָה בְּעַרְבֵי פְסָחִים הַחַיָּטִים וְהַסַּפָּרִים וְהַכּוֹבְסִין. רִבִּי יוֹסֵי בֵּי רִבִּי יְהוּדָה אוֹמֵר אַף הָרוֹצְעָנִים:

Mishnah 7: Rebbi Meïr says, any work which one started before the Fourteenth he may finish on the Fourteenth. But he may not start one on the

Fourteenth even if he can finish it. But the Sages say, three trades are permitted working on Passover Eve, the tailors, and the barbers, and the laundrymen. Rebbi Yose ben Rebbi Jehudah says, also the cobblers.

(31a line75) **הלכה ז׃** רִבִּי מֵאִיר אוֹמֵר. כָּל־מְלָאכָה שֶׁהִתְחִיל בָּהּ קוֹדֶם לְאַרְבָּעָה עָשָׂר גּוֹמְרָהּ בְּאַרְבָּעָה עָשָׂר. וּבִלְבַד דָּבָר שֶׁהוּא לְצוֹרֶךְ הַמּוֹעֵד. אֲבָל לֹא יַתְחִיל בָּהּ בַּתְּחִלָּה בְּאַרְבָּעָה עָשָׂר. אֲפִילוּ דָּבָר שֶׁהוּא לְצוֹרֶךְ הַמּוֹעֵד. וַחֲכָמִים אוֹמְרִים. שָׁלֹשׁ אוּמָנִיּוֹת עוֹשִׂין מְלָאכָה בְּעַרְבֵי פְסָחִים. הַחַיָּיטִין. שֶׁכֵּן הֶדְיוֹט תּוֹפֵר כְּדַרְכּוֹ בְחוֹלוֹ שֶׁלְּמוֹעֵד. הַסַּפָּרִין. שֶׁכֵּן נְזִירִין וּמְצוֹרָעִין מְגַלְּחִין בַּמּוֹעֵד. הַכּוֹבְסִין. שֶׁכֵּן דֶּרֶךְ הָעוֹלִים מִטּוּמְאָה לְטַהֲרָה לִהְיוֹת מְכַבְּסִין בַּמּוֹעֵד. רִבִּי יוֹסֵי בֵּירִבִּי יְהוּדָה אוֹמֵר אַף הָרוֹצְעָנִים: שֶׁכֵּן דֶּרֶךְ עוֹלֵי רְגָלִים לִהְיוֹת מְתַקְּנִין מִנְעָלֵיהֶן וְסַנְדְּלֵיהֶן בַּמּוֹעֵד. וְרַבָּנִין אֲמְרִין. עֲשִׁירִים הָיוּ וּבַבְּהֵמָה הָיוּ עוֹלִין.

Halakhah 7: [137]"Rebbi Meïr says, any work which one started before the Fourteenth he may finish on the Fourteenth," but only what is needed on the holiday. "But he may not start one on the Fourteenth," even something needed for the holiday. "But the Sages say, three trades are working on Passover Eve, the tailors," since a non-professional[138] may sew normally on the intermediate days of the holiday[139]. "The barbers," since *nezirim*[140] and lepers[141] shave on the holiday. "The laundrymen," since usually people who ascend from impurity to purity launder on the holiday[142]. "Rebbi Yose ben Rebbi Jehudah says, also the cobblers," since the pilgrims are used to repair their boots and sandals on the holiday. But the rabbis say, they were rich and made the pilgrimage on animals[143].

137 Babli 55a/b, slightly different.
138 Greek ἰδιώτης, ὁ.
139 When necessary non-agricultural work is permitted. In the following, "holiday" always implies "intermediate days of".
140 If the vow of a *nazir* expires during the holiday, his shaving is part of the required ceremony.
141 If a sufferer from skin disease is healed during the holiday, his shaving is part of the required ceremony of purification (*Lev.* 14:8).
142 Since in most cases, the impure person makes his garments impure, the garments also have to be immersed in a *miqweh* and have to be washed to be free of dirt.
143 This argument also restricts the Mishnah to Temple times.

(fol. 30c) **משנה ח**: מוֹשִׁיבִין שׁוֹבָכִין לַתַּרְנְגוֹלִין בְּאַרְבָּעָה עָשָׂר. וְתַרְנְגוֹלֶת שֶׁבָּרְחָה מַחֲזִירִין אוֹתָהּ לִמְקוֹמָהּ. וְאִם מֵתָה מוֹשִׁיבִין אַחֶרֶת תַּחְתֶּיהָ. גּוֹרְפִין מִתַּחַת רַגְלֵי בְהֵמָה בְּאַרְבָּעָה עָשָׂר וּבַמּוֹעֵד מְסַלְּקִין לַצְּדָדִין. מוֹלִיכִין וּמְבִיאִין כֵּלִים מִבֵּית הָאוּמָּן אַף עַל פִּי שֶׁאֵינָם לְצוֹרֶךְ הַמּוֹעֵד:

Mishnah 8: One sets hens on brooding stalls on the Fourteenth[144]; and a hen which fled one returns to its place, or if it died one installs another in its place. One cleans under the feet of animals on the Fourteenth; on the holiday one sweeps to the side[145]. Vessels one delivers to and brings from the artisan's house[146] even though they are not needed on the holiday.

144 But not during the intermediate days of the holiday.
145 One sweeps the manure away but one may not transport it to the dungheap.
146 The entire day of Passover Eve, even in the afternoon.

(31b line 8) **הלכה ח**: מוֹשִׁיבִין שׁוֹבָכִין לַתַּרְנְגוֹלִין בְּאַרְבָּעָה עָשָׂר. הָא בַּמּוֹעֵד אָסוּר. אֵין מַרְבִּיעִין אֶת הַבְּהֵמָה בְמוֹעֵד. אֲבָל מוֹלִיכִין אוֹתָהּ לַבִּקּוֹרֶת. רִבִּי יוּדָה אוֹמֵר. חֲמוֹרָה שֶׁהִיא תּוֹבַעַת זָכָר מַרְבִּיעִין אוֹתָהּ שֶׁלֹּא תֵיצַן. וּשְׁאָר כָּל־הַבְּהֵמָה מוֹלִיכִין אוֹתָהּ לַבִּקּוֹרֶת. וּמַקִּיזִין דָּם לְאָדָם וְלַבְּהֵמָה בְמוֹעֵד. וְאֵין מוֹנְעִין רְפוּאָה מֵאָדָם וּמִבְּהֵמָה בְמוֹעֵד.

Halakhah 8: "One installs hens on brooding stalls on the Fourteenth," therefore not during the holiday[147]. One does not breed an animal on the holiday but may lead it to the corral[148]. Rebbi Jehudah says, one breeds a female donkey in heat on the holiday, lest it cool down; all other animals one leads to the corral. One bleeds humans and animals on the holiday[147], and does not refrain from any medical procedure for humans or animals on the holiday.

147 "Holiday" always implies "intermediate days of the holiday".
148 One may not bring the male on the female but one may bring an animal in heat to a corral where there are many males and it can find a mate on its own. Babli *Mo`ed qatan* 12a.
149 This includes all surgical procedures. Babli *Mo`ed qatan* 10b.

(31b line 13) תַּרְנְגוֹלֶת שֶׁבָּרְחָה מַחֲזִירִין אוֹתָהּ לִמְקוֹמָהּ. וְהֵן שֶׁיַּחֲזִירוּהָ שְׁלֹשָׁה יָמִים לַמְּדוּרָה. וְאִם מֵתָה מוֹשִׁיבִין אַחֶרֶת תַּחְתֶּיהָ. וְהִיא שֶׁיָּשְׁבָה עַל בֵּיצֶיהָ שְׁלֹשָׁה יָמִים מֵעֵת לָעֵת. אָמַר רִבִּי

מָנָא. מַתְנִיתָא אֲמָרָה כֵן. שְׁלֹשָׁה עָשָׂר אַרְבָּעָה עָשָׂר חֲמִשָּׁה עָשָׂר. וּמִקְצָת הַיּוֹם כְּכוּלּוֹ. אָמַר רִבִּי אָבוּן. תִּיפְתָּר שֶׁיָּשְׁבָה מֵאֵילֶיהָ. וְלֵית שְׁמַע מִינָהּ כְּלוּם.

זֶבֶל שֶׁבַּמָּבוֹי מְסַלְּקוֹ לַצַּד. שֶׁבָּרֶפֶת וְשֶׁבֶּחָצֵר מוֹצִיאוֹ לָאַשְׁפָּה. אָמַר רִבִּי בָא. הָדָא דְתֵימַר. בְּחָצֵר קְטַנָּה. אֲבָל בְּחָצֵר גְּדוֹלָה מְסַלְּקוֹ לַצַּד. הָרֶפֶת בֵּין גְּדוֹלָה בֵּין קְטַנָּה מוֹצִיאוֹ לָאַשְׁפָּה. אָמַר רִבִּי בָא. מִפְּנֵי שֶׁנִּיוּוּלָהּ קָשָׁה.

"A hen which fled one returns to its place[150]," only if one returns it within three days of its escape[151]. "Or if it died one installs another in its place," only it sat on its eggs three days of 24 hours. Rebbi Mana said, the Mishnah implies this, the 13th, 14th, 15th, and part of a day is counted as a whole day[152]. Rebbi Abun said, explain it if it sat down by itself and it implies nothing[153].

[154]Manure in an alley one sweeps aside, in a cowshed and a courtyard one takes it out to the dungheap. Rebbi Abba said, this is for a small courtyard, but in a large courtyard one sweeps it aside. In a cowshed, whether large or small, one takes out to the dungheap. Rebbi Abba said, because its ugliness is dangerous.

150 The hen left the eggs on which it was sitting.
151 Reading with the Babli 55b מֶרְדָּהּ instead of the text מדורה "dwelling".
152 The argument is reasonable but the numbers are wrong. If the eggs were laid on the 14th, and the hen sat on it on the 14th, on the full holiday the 15th, and ran away the first of the intermediate days, the 16th, it is the third day of breeding. The requirement of 3 times 24 hrs. is not proven.
153 The chicken could have started in the morning of the day on which it ran away.
154 Babli 55b.

(fol. 30c) **משנה ט**: שִׁשָּׁה דְבָרִים עָשׂוּ אַנְשֵׁי יְרִיחוֹ עַל שְׁלֹשָׁה מִיחוּ בְיָדָן וְעַל שְׁלֹשָׁה לֹא מִיחוּ בְיָדָן. אֵילּוּ שֶׁלֹּא מִיחוּ בְיָדָן מַרְכִּיבִין דְּקָלִים כָּל־הַיּוֹם וְכוֹרְכִין אֶת שְׁמַע וְקוֹצְרִין וְגוֹדְשִׁין לִפְנֵי הָעֹמֶר וְלֹא מִיחוּ בְיָדָן. אֵילּוּ שֶׁמִּיחוּ בְיָדָן מַתִּירִין בְּגִמְזִיּוֹת שֶׁל הֶקְדֵּשׁ וְאוֹכְלִין מִתַּחַת הַנְּשָׁרִים בַּשַּׁבָּת וְנוֹתְנִין פֵּיאָה לַיָּרָק וּמִיחוּ בְיָדָן חֲכָמִים:

Mishnah 9: Six things used the people of Jericho to do; on three of them they[155] interfered, about three they did not interfere. The following are where they did not interfere: They grafted date palms during the entire day[156], and they bundled the *šema*'[157] and they cut grain and tied it into sheaves before the '*omer*[158]; they did not interfere. The following are where they did interfere: They permitted sycamore figs[159] of dedicated trees[160], and they ate wind-fall on the Sabbath[161], and they gave *peah* from vegetables[162]; here they did interfere.

155 The rabbinic authorities of the day did not interfere even though the actions were somewhat against the rules. The Jewish settlement of Jericho came to an end at the latest in the aftermath of the war of Bar Kokhba.

156 The 14th of Nisan. "Grafting" here means cutting male flowers and hanging them in female trees for pollination by the wind. This operation has to be done in a very narrow time frame in the spring.

157 Different opinions about this are given in the Halakhah.

158 The start of the barley harvest. Consumption of new barley is strictly forbidden before the ceremony (*Lev.* 23:14).

159 Arabic جمّيز, in modern Hebrew also the ג is pronounced "j". Cf. *Peah* Chapter 7, Note 159.

160 Old sycamores whose trunks were dedicated to the Temple; they were of the opinion that it was possible to dedicate a trunk while excepting new shoots from the dedication.

161 Fruit still on the tree at sundown is *muqseh* the entire Sabbath (or holiday) even after it fell from the tree.

162 It is obligatory to leave the last corner of a field unharvested for the poor to collect only for produce that is similar to grain in that it is harvested all at once and is stored for use during the year (Mishnah *Peah* 1:4). Legal *peah* is freed from the obligation of heave and tithes; illegitimate *peah* is not. People giving illegal *peah* lead the poor into deadly sin by making them eat *tevel* produce.

(31b line 21) **הלכה ט**: מָאן תַּנָּא. קוֹצְרִין. רִבִּי מֵאִיר. מָאן תַּנָּא. גּוֹדְשִׁין. רִבִּי יוּדָה. אָמַר רִבִּי יַעֲקֹב בְּרִבִּי סוֹסַיי קוֹמֵי רִבִּי יוֹסֵי. כָּל־עַמָּא מוֹדַיי שֶׁקּוֹצְרִין וְכָל־עַמָּא מוֹדַיי שֶׁאֵין גּוֹדְשִׁין. מַפְלִיגִין. בְּהֶרְכֵּב דְּקָלִים. רִבִּי מֵאִיר אוֹמֵר. מַרְכִּיבִין דְּקָלִים כָּל־הַיּוֹם וְכִרְצוֹן חֲכָמִים הָיוּ עוֹשִׂין. רִבִּי יוּדָה אוֹמֵר. לֹא הָיוּ עוֹשִׂין כִּרְצוֹן חֲכָמִים.

Halakhah 9: Who is the Tanna of "cutting"? Rebbi Meïr. Who is the Tanna of "binding into sheaves"? Rebbi Jehudah. Rebbi Jacob ben Rebbi Sosai said before Rebbi Yose: Everybody agrees that one may cut[163], and everybody agrees that one may not tie into sheaves[164]. Where did they disagree? About grafting of date palms. Rebbi Meïr says, one grafts date entire day, and they acted following the will of the rabbis. Rebbi Judah says, they were not acting following the will of the rabbis[165].

163 The verse *Lev. 23:9: the beginning of your harvest for the Cohen* is interpreted (*Sifra Emor Parašah* 10(2)) that cutting grain before the `omer is forbidden only in places whose grain is acceptable in the Temple, which excluded grain grown in irrigated fields (including those of Jericho).

Therefore cutting the grain these could not have been a problem. Mishnah *Menahot* 10:8; Babli 56a, *Menahot* 71a.
164 Only the offense did not warrant interference.
165 Tosephta 3:19.

(31b line 25) כֵּיצַד הָיוּ כּוֹרְכִין אֶת שְׁמַע. אָמַר רִבִּי אָחָא אָמַר רִבִּי זְעוּרָה אָמַר רִבִּי לָא. שְׁמַע יִשְׂרָאֵל יי אֱלֹהֵינוּ יי אֶחָד. אֶלָּא שֶׁלֹּא הָיוּ מַפְסִיקִין בֵּין תֵּיבָה לְתֵיבָה. דִּבְרֵי רִבִּי מֵאִיר. רִבִּי יוּדָה אוֹמֵר. מַפְסִיקִין הָיוּ. אֶלָּא שֶׁלֹּא הָיוּ אוֹמְרִים. בָּרוּךְ שֵׁם כְּבוֹד מַלְכוּתוֹ לְעוֹלָם וָעֶד. רִבִּי יוֹסֵה אָמַר רִבִּי זְעוּרָה רִבִּי לָא. שְׁמַע יִשְׂרָאֵל יי וגו' אֶלָּא שֶׁלֹּא הָיוּ מַפְסִיקִין בֵּין אֶחָד לְבָרוּךְ דִּבְרֵי רִבִּי מֵאִיר. רִבִּי יוּדָה אוֹמֵר. מַפְסִיקִין הָיוּ אֶלָּא שֶׁלֹּא הָיוּ אוֹמְרִים. בָּרוּךְ שֵׁם כְּבוֹד מַלְכוּתוֹ לְעוֹלָם וָעֶד.

How did they bundle the *šema`*? Rebbi Aha said, Rebbi Ze`ira said, Rebbi La said[166]: *Hear, o Israel, the Eternal, our God, the Eternal is One*[167], only they did not stop between words, the words of Rebbi Meïr. Rebbi Jehudah said, they did stop but they did not say "Praised be the Name of the Glory of His Kingdom for ever and ever.[168]"

Rebbi Yose said, Rebbi Ze`ira, Rebbi La said: *Hear, o Israel, the Eternal,* etc., only they did not stop between *One* and "Praised", the words of Rebbi Meïr. Rebbi Jehudah said, they did stop but they did not say "Praised be the Name of the Glory of His Kingdom for ever and ever."

166 The discussion is about the formulation of a text close to Tosephta 3:19; cf. Babli 56a. The sequence of three "said" is Babli style.

167 *Deut.* 6:4.
168 The customary insert between the recitation of v. 4 and vv. 5-9.

(31b line 32) כֵּיצַד הָיוּ מַתִּירִין בְּגֵמְזִיּוֹת שֶׁלְּהֶקְדֵּשׁ. אָמְרוּ לָהֶן חֲכָמִים. אֵין אַתֶּם מוֹדִין לָנוּ בְּגִידּוּלֵי הֶקְדֵּשׁ שֶׁהֵן אֲסוּרִין. אָמְרוּ לָהֶן. אֲבוֹתֵינוּ כְּשֶׁהִקְדִּישׁוּ לֹא הִקְדִּישׁוּ אֶלָּא קוֹרוֹת מִפְּנֵי בַעֲלֵי אֶגְרוֹף. שֶׁהָיוּ בָאִין וְנוֹטְלִין אוֹתָן בִּזְרוֹעַ. מָה רַבָּנָן סָבְרִין מֵימַר. קוֹרוֹת וּפֵירוֹת הִקְדִּישׁוּ. אֲפִילוּ תֵּימַר. קוֹרוֹת

הִקְדִּישׁוּ וּפֵירוֹת לֹא הִקְדִּישׁוּ. צְרִיכָה לְרַבָּנִין. הַמַּקְדִּישׁ שְׂדֵי אִילָן מָהוּ שֶׁיְּשַׁיֵּיר לוֹ מִן הַגִּידוּלִין. נִשְׁמְעִינָהּ מִן הָדָא. מִשֶּׁנּוֹדְעוּ הָעוֹלֵלוֹת. הָעוֹלֵלוֹת לָעֲנִיִּים. שַׁנְיָא הִיא שֶׁאֵין אָדָם מַקְדִּישׁ דָּבָר שֶׁאֵינוֹ שֶׁלּוֹ. מֵעַתָּה אֲפִילוּ לֹא נוֹדְעוּ הָעוֹלֵלוֹת יְהוּ הָעוֹלֵלוֹת לָעֲנִיִּים. שַׁנְיָא הִיא שֶׁהוּא כֶּרֶם לְהֶקְדֵּשׁ. כְּהָדָא דְּתָנֵי. הַנּוֹטֵעַ כֶּרֶם לַהֶקְדֵּשׁ פָּטוּר [מִן הַפֶּרֶט] מִן הָעוֹרְלָה וּמִן הָרְבָעִי וּמִן הָעוֹלֵלוֹת וְחַיָּיב בַּשְּׁבִיעִית. רִבִּי זְעוּרָה בְּשֵׁם רִבִּי יוֹחָנָן. וְשָׁבְתָה הָאָרֶץ שַׁבָּת לַיי. אֲפִילוּ דָּבָר שֶׁהוּא לַיי קְדוּשַּׁת שְׁבִיעִית חָלָה עָלָיו.

3 הקדישו | פ לא הקדישו   קורות | פ קורות ופירות קורות   4 מן הגידולין | פ בגידולין   6 שהוא | פ שהיא
7 להקדש | פ הקדש   כהדא דתני | ג כהדה דתנה   C מן הפרט | Sפ -   העוללות | ג העוליליות   8 זעורה | פ
זעירא   אפי׳ | פ -

[169]"How did they permit sycamore figs of dedicated trees? The Sages said to them, do you not agree with us that growth of dedicated [plants] is forbidden? They told them, when our forefathers dedicated them, they dedicated only the tree stems because of the strong men who came and took them by force.[170]" Do the rabbis mean to say that they dedicated tree stems and fruits? Even if you say that they dedicated the tree stems but not the fruits, the rabbis wonder if somebody dedicates an orchard, may he reserve the growth for himself[171]? Let us hear from the following[172]: "After the gleanings are recognizable, the gleanings belong to the poor." That is different because nobody may dedicate anything that is not his own[173]. Does that not mean that even if the gleanings were not yet recognizable, they should belong to the poor? This is different, because it is a vineyard for the Temple, as it was stated[174]: "It somebody plants a vineyard for the Temple, it is exempt from single berries[175], and from *orlah*[176], and from the Fourth Year[177], but it is subject to the Sabbatical year." Rebbi Ze`ira in the name of Rebbi Johanan: *The land shall observe a Sabbath for the Eternal*[178]. The sanctity of the Sabbatical falls even on anything that is the Eternal's.

169 From here on, the Halakhah also is *Peah* 7:8 (פ).

170 Tosephta 3:22 (Babli 56b). Sycamores produce inferior fruits but superior building material. The "strong men" are probably the Hasmonean rulers or Herod. The people protected their sycamore groves by putting them out of bounds of any human government.

171 In Mishnah *Me`ilah* 3:6 the anonymous Tanna declares that taking the fruits of a Temple tree does not constitute the crime of *me`ilah*, larceny committed on Temple property. But R. Yose declares the fruits to be covered by *me`ilah*. The Babli 56b points out that the Sages of the Tosephta, while agreeing that no felony is committed by taking the sycamore figs,

nevertheless must assume that taking them means overstepping a prohibition. No such prohibition is written in the Torah. While any stipulation contradicting a commandment of the Torah is invalid (*Peah* 6:9), one violating a rabbinic prohibition may be valid. It remains unresolved whether the people of Jericho had permission to reserve the right to use the *jummiz*.

172 Mishnah *Peah* 7:8, about a vineyard dedicated to the Temple (i. e., its fruits to be sold by the Temple and the proceeds to be given to the Temple treasury).

173 Since gleanings on vines belong to the poor by Divine decree (*Deut.* 24:21).

174 Tosephta *Peah* 3:15. Here starts a Genizah fragment, edited by L. Ginzberg in *Ginze Schechter*, vol. 1, New York 1928, pp. 442-448 (ג).

175 Which in secular growth belong to the poor (*Lev.* 19:10). Addition by the corrector, supported by a lacuna in ג.

176 The fruits growing in the first three years after planting, forbidden for use (*Lev.* 19:23).

177 Where the fruit has to be redeemed (*Lev.* 19:24).

178 *Lev.* 25:2.

(31b line 44) רִבִּי חִיָּיה בַּר אַבָּא בְּעָא קוֹמֵי [דְרִבִּי מָנָא]. לְאוֹכְלוֹ בְּלִי פִּדְיוֹן [אִי] אֶיפְשָׁר. [שֶׁאִי] (שֶׁ)אֶיפְשָׁר לְהֶקְדֵּשׁ לָצֵאת בְּלֹא פִּדְיוֹן. לִפְדּוֹתוֹ וּלְאָכְלוֹ נִמְצָא לוֹקֵחַ לוֹ קוּרְדּוֹם מִדְּמֵי שְׁבִיעִית. אָמַר לֵיהּ. הַגִּיזְבָּר הָיָה מַחֲלִפָן בְּיַד אַחֵר. אָמַר רִבִּי מַתַּנְיָה. לָמָּה לִי נָן פֶּתְרִין לָהּ דִּבְרֵי הַכֹּל כְּהַהִיא דָמַר רִבִּי יוֹחָנָן. דִּבְרֵי רִבִּי יוֹסֵה מִפְּנֵי שֶׁקְּדָמָם נִדְרוֹ לְהֶבְקֵירוֹ. וְהָכָא מִפְּנֵי שֶׁקְּדָם הֶבְקֵר נִדְרוֹ לְהֶקְדֵּישׁוֹ. אָמַר רִבִּי יוֹחָנָן. מַעֲשֶׂה הָיָה וְהוֹרוּן כְּרִבִּי יוֹסֵה.

1 חייה | פ חייא   אבא | ג אדה   C דרבי מנא | S - גר' מ' פ ר' מנא   בלי | פ בלא   C אי | S גפ - C שאי | S גפ -
2 איפשר | S גפ שאיפשר   נמצא | ג C אין אתה (ג את) יכול. שלא יהא   לוקח | גפ כלוקח   קורדום | ג קרדום
3 ליה | ג להן   היה | גפ -   מחלפן | ג מחליפן פ מחליפו   מתנייה | פ מתניה   פתרין | גפ אמרין   לה דברי הכל כההיא | גפ כיי   4 דמר | פ דאמ'   והכא | ג והכה פ וכא   חבקר נדרו | ג הבקירו   5 והורון | ג והורו

לֵית הָדָא פְלִיגָא עַל רִבִּי יוֹחָנָן. דְּרִבִּי יוֹחָנָן אָמַר. מִכֵּיוָן שֶׁעָבַר עָלָיו וּשְׁכָחוֹ הֲרֵי הוּא שִׁכְחָה. שְׁנִיָּיה הִיא בְּעָרִיס שֶׁדַּרְכּוֹ לִבָּחֵן. אֲפִילּוּ עַל דְּרִבִּי אוֹשַׁעְיָה לֵית הִיא פְלִיגָא. דְּרִבִּי הוֹשַׁעְיָה אָמַר. רוֹמֶשׂ הָיִיתִי זֵיתִים עִם רִבִּי חִיָּיה הַגָּדוֹל. וְאָמַר לִי. כָּל־זַיִת שֶׁאַתְּ יָכוֹל לִפְשׁוֹט יָדְךָ וְלִיטְלוֹ אֵינוֹ שִׁכְחָה. שְׁנִיָּיא הִיא. שֶׁכָּל־רוֹגָלוֹת וְרוֹגָלוֹת אוּמָן בִּפְנֵי עַצְמוֹ.

1 הדא | ג הדה   פליגא | ג פליגה   מכיון | ג כיון   שעבר | ג שעברו   2 לבחן | ג לבחין   אפי' | פ ואפי'   אושעיה | ג הושעיה פ הושעיא   3 הושעיה | פ הושעיא ואמ' | פ אמ'   4 ידך | ג את ידך וליטלו | פ ליטלו   רוגלות ורוגלות | ג רוגלית ורוגלית פ רוגליות ורוגליות

Rebbi Ḥiyya bar Abba[179] asked before Rebbi Mana: It is impossible[180] to eat without redemption[181] since Temple property cannot leave without redemption. If one redeems and eats it, it would be as if one bought an axe with Sabbatical money[182]. He said to him, the treasurer[183] exchanges it through a third person. Rebbi Mattaniah said, why do we not explain it[184] according to everybody, as Rebbi Johanan said[185], the words of Rebbi Yose

HALAKHAH NINE

because his vow precedes his declaration of abandonment. But here[186] the vow of abandonment precedes his dedication[187]. Rebbi Johanan said, it happened that they gave instructions following Rebbi Yose[188].

[189]Does this not contradict Rebbi Johanan, since Rebbi Johanan said, if he passed over it and forgot it, it is forgotten. There is a difference, for a trellis is usually checked[190]. And it does not even contradict Rebbi Hoshaia, for Rebbi Hoshaia said, when I was mashing olives with the great Rebbi Hiyya, he told me that any olive you can reach when stretching out your hand is not forgotten[191]. There is a difference, since every single freestanding vine is a separate planting.

---

179 While this is the text here and in *Peah*, it is impossible since the third generation R. Hiyya bar Abba cannot be a student either of the first generation R. Mana I nor of the fifth generation R. Mana II. Therefore with ג one has to read "R. Hiyya bar Ada" (second generation).

180 Here the corrector, trained in Babylonian Aramaic, corrupted the text. Following the other two sources, both times "אי" has to be deleted since the Yerushalmi distinguishes between אֶפְשָׁר "possible" and אִיפְשַׁר "impossible".

181 This refers to the statement earlier that produce dedicated to the Temple is subject to the rules of the Sabbatical. Sabbatical produce must be eaten (*Lev.* 25:6) but Temple produce cannot be eaten without first being redeemed and the sanctity transferred to the redemption money.

182 The Temple has no need for money for food since the public sacrifices must be paid from the Temple tax of half a *šeqel* and private sacrifices are paid by the donors. Valuables donated to the Temple are used for building upkeep, vessels, and implements. Any monetary gain from Sabbatical produce for these purposes is forbidden; how can the Temple accept illegal money?

183 The Temple treasurer has the right and the obligation to sell all Temple property which is not directly used for sacrifices in order to raise money for the upkeep of the Temple. The Sabbatical produce is not sold but directly exchanged for vessels or implements needed by the Temple. This exchange is permitted; it removes the holiness of Temple property but has no influence on the Sabbatical status of the produce. The third party may use or sell the produce as Sabbatical food.

184 That the laws of the Sabbatical year apply to Temple property.

185 This refers to Mishnah *Nedarim* 6:10: Two people A and B are on the road. B had made a vow not to use anything belonging to A. A has food with him, B has nothing to eat. A gives food to a third person C as a gift; C gives the food to B who may use it. If no third person is present, A puts the food up on a fence or on a rock and says, this is abandoned to anybody who wants it. B may

take and eat it, but R. Yose forbids. R. Johanan notes that R. Yose only forbade because the food was forbidden to B before it was abandoned. But if anything was abandoned before a vow was made, R. Yose agrees that a vow cannot retroactively influence the status of abandoned property.

186 In the cases of the vineyards (Notes 174 and 178), the abandonment both of the gleanings and the Sabbatical year are written in the Torah and certainly precede any dedication.

187 Since the abandonment of the Sabbatical year is not invalidated by the dedication, the Sabbatical produce should not need any redemption.

188 Who requires in Mishnah *Peah* 4:8 that the Temple be reimbursed for the produce grown in its possession, deciding with R. Hiyya bar Ada against R. Mattaniah.

189 The following paragraph refers only to the last part of Mishnah *Peah* 7:8: "What are forgotten grapes? On a trellis, anything one cannot stretch out his hand and take; on a single growing vine once he is done with it." The paragraph is copied from there and has no relevance for *Pesahim*, nor is it related to the statement of R. Johanan just quoted.

190 On a trellis the branches are stretched out widely; one can go over the branches as many times as he wants as long as he does not move away.

191 But Mishnah *Peah* 7:8 makes it clear that one may go around a free-standing vine as many times as he wants, as long as he does not move away.

(31b line 56) רִבִּי אַבָּא בַּר כַּהֲנָא בְעָא קוֹמֵי רִבִּי אִימִּי. הַמַּשְׂכִּיר בַּיִת לַחֲבֵירוֹ וְנִצְרַךְ לְדָמָיו. אָמַר לֵיהּ. לֹא עָלָה עַל דַּעַת שֶׁיָּמוּת בָּרָעָב. רִבִּי זְעִירָא רִבִּי לָא תְּרֵיהוֹן אָמְרִין. מִיסְתְּיוֹסִיס כְּאוֹנֵי הִיא וְנִקְנֵית בְּמֶקַח. תַּנֵּי. הַמַּשְׂכִּיר בַּיִת לַחֲבֵירוֹ וְעָמַד וְהִקְדִּישׁוֹ. הֲרֵי זֶה דָר בְּתוֹכוֹ וּמַעֲלֶה שָׂכָר לְהֶקְדֵּשׁ. אֵימָתַי. בִּזְמַן שֶׁלֹּא הִקְדִּים לוֹ שְׂכָרוֹ. אֲבָל בִּזְמַן שֶׁהִקְדִּים לוֹ שְׂכָרוֹ. הֲרֵי זֶה דָר בְּתוֹכוֹ חִנָּם. בְּיוֹמוֹי דְּרִבִּי מָנָא הֲוָת נִימוֹרָה בְּצִיפּוֹרִין. וַהֲוֹון בְּנֵיהוֹן מִישְׁכּוֹנִין גַּבֵּין. מִיאָתָאֵי מֵיזַל לוֹן אַפִּיק רִבִּי מָנָא כָּהֵין דוּן דְּרִבִּי אִימִּי. אָמַר. לָא דַּאֲנָא סָבַר כְּדַעְתֵּיהּ. אֶלָּא בְּגִין צִיפְרַיָּיא דְלָא יַחְלְטוּן בְּהֵיהוֹן.

1 בעא | בעה אימי | ג אמי 2 עלה | ג עלת[192] זעורא | ג זעורה לא | ג הילןא] 3 ונקנית | ג וניקנית 4 להקדש | ג להקדיש אימתי | ג אמתי שכרו | ג שכר (2) 5 הימורה | ג נמירה והוון | ג והווה - | ג דציפוריי גבין | ג גבון 6 מיאתאי מיזל | ג מאתי מזל כדון | ג כרוז כהיא | ג כהדה אימי | ג אמי דאנא סבר כדעתיה | ג דאנה סבור דכוותה 7 ציפרייא | ג ציפוריי

Rebbi Abba bar Cahana asked before Rebbi Immi: If one leased his house to another and needs the money? He said to him, it is unthinkable that he should have to starve to death[193]. Rebbi Ze`ira, Rebbi [Il]la both say, μίστωσις like ὠνή is acquired by buying[194]. It was stated[195]: If one leased his house to another and went and dedicated it, [the renter] lives in it and pays the rent to the Sanctuary. When? If he did not pay the rent in advance, but if he paid the rent in advance he lives there for free. In the days of Rebbi Mana there was a company[196] in Sepphoris, and their children were taken as pledges.

When they were about to leave, Rebbi Mana published (so) [a proclamation]¹⁹⁷ following Rebbi Immi. He said, not that I am of his opinion, but because of the Sepphoreans that they should not permanently lose their children¹⁹⁸.

192 עלה is the corrector's text; עלת is reported as R. Immi's statement also in *Bava Meṣi'a* 8:11 (Note 52).
193 He accepts the rule of Roman law that sale breaks lease.
194 S. Liebermann's remark is convincing that they choose to formulate the statement in Greek terms, "lease is acquired like a buy by acquisition" to make the point of their rejection of the Roman law clear to all traders. They consider the right to use leased property as a valuable asset which once acquired in due form cannot be taken away.
195 Babli *Arakhin* 21a. Since property donated to the Temple is given only for its money's worth, not the house was given but the future income.
196 Latin *numerus;* a military unit of native auxiliaries in the late Roman Empire. For nonpayment, the government threatened to enslave the children.
197 The text of ג [in brackets] seems preferable.
198 This was an emergency measure (probably to permit sale of houses to Gentiles). He could not have agreed with the underlying principle since he was a student of his father R. Jonah, student of R. Jeremiah, student of R. Ze`ira.

(31b line 65) וְאוֹכְלִין מִתַּחַת הַנְּשָׁרִים. מַה נָן קַיָימִין. אִם בְּשֶׁנָּשְׁרוּ מֵעֶרֶב יוֹם טוֹב. דִּבְרֵי הַכֹּל מוּתָּר. אִם בְּשֶׁנָּשְׁרוּ בְיוֹם טוֹב. דִּבְרֵי הַכֹּל אָסוּר. אֶלָּא כִי נָן קַיָימִין. בִּסְתָּם.

1 הנשרים | ג הנשרין   קיימין | ג קימין

"They ate wind-fall." Where do we hold? If it fell off before the holiday, everybody agrees that it is permitted; if it fell off on the holiday, everybody agrees that it is forbidden. But we must hold if it is unknown¹⁹⁹.

199 Since fruit on the tree at nightfall of a Sabbath or holiday is *muqseh*, it cannot become permitted on the Sabbath or holiday. The only problem is whether *muqseh* is to be considered as rabbinic prohibition, which would require a case of doubt to be treated leniently as permitted, or as biblical, which requires a case of doubt to be treated restrictively as prohibited. Since the principle of *muqseh* is recognized by Sadducees (cf. Introduction to Tractates *Šabbat* and *Eruvin*), the Mishnah treats it as biblical prohibition. Quoted by Tosaphot 56b *s. v.* מחלוקת.

(31b line 67) וְנוֹתְנִין פֵּיאָה לַיָרָק. לֹא הָיוּ נוֹתְנִין אֶלָּא מִן הַלֶּפֶת וּמִן הַקְּפַלוֹטוֹת שֶׁלְּקִיטָתָן כְּאַחַת. רִבִּי יוֹסֵה אוֹמֵר. אַף לָאַכְרוּב. מַעֲשֶׂה בְּבֶן מֵבִיא יַיִן שֶׁנָּתַן בְּנוֹ פֵּיאָה לַיָרָק לַעֲנִיִּים. וּבָא אָבִיו וּמְצָאָן עוֹמְדִין עַל פֶּתַח הַגִּינָה. אָמַר לָהֶן. הַנִּיחוּ מַה שֶׁבְּיֶדְכֶם. וְהִנִּיחוּ מַה שֶׁבְּיָדָן. וְנָתַן לָהֶם בְּכִפְלֵיהֶן מְעוּשָּׂרִין. לֹא שֶׁהָיְתָה עֵינוֹ צָרָה. אֶלָּא שֶׁהָיָה חוֹשֵׁשׁ לְדִבְרֵי חֲכָמִים. חַד זְמַן צָרְכוּן רַבָּנָן נִדְבָּא. שְׁלָחוּן לְרִבִּי עֲקִיבָה וּלְחַד מִן רַבָּנִין עִמֵּיהּ. אָתוֹן בָּעֵיי מֵיעוֹל לְגַבֵּיהּ וְשָׁמְעוּן קָלֵיהּ דְּטַלְיָיא. אֲמַר לֵיהּ. מַה נִיזְבּוֹן לָךְ יוֹמָא דֵין. אֲמַר לֵיהּ. טְרוֹכְסִימוֹן. לָא מִן יוֹמָא דֵין אֶלָּא מִן דְּאֶתְמוֹל. דְּהוּא כָמִישׁ וּזְלִיל. שָׁבְקוּן לֵיהּ וְאָזְלוּן לוֹן. מִן דְּזָכוּן כָּל־עַמָּא אָתוֹן לְגַבֵּיהּ. אֲמַר לוֹן. לָמָּה לֹא אֲתִיתוֹן גַּבַּיי קַדְמָיי כְּמָה דַהֲוֵיתוֹן נְהִיגִין. אָמְרִין. כְּבָר אֲתֵינָן וּשְׁמָעִינָן קָלֵיהּ דְּטַלְיָיא אָמַר לָךְ. מַה נִיזְבּוֹן לָךְ יוֹמָא דֵין. וְאָמַרְתְּ לֵיהּ. טְרוֹכְסִימוֹן. לָא מִן דְּיוֹמָא דֵין אֶלָּא מִן דְּאֶיתְמוֹל. דְּהוּא כָמִישׁ וּזְלִיל. אָמַר. מַה דְּבֵינִי לְבֵין טַלְיָיא יְדַעְתּוּן. יְדַעְתּוֹן מַה בֵּינִי לְבֵין בָּרָיי. אַף עַל פִּי כֵן אַזְלוּן וְאָמְרוּן לָהּ וְהִיא יָהֲבָה לְכוֹן חַד מוֹדֵיי דְּדִינָרִין. אָזְלוּן וְאָמְרוּן לָהּ. אֲמָרָה לוֹן. מָה אֲמַר לְכוֹן. גְּדִיל אוֹ מְחִיק. אֲמָרוּ לָהּ. סָתָם אֲמַר לוֹן. אֲמָרָה לוֹן. אֲנָא יָהֲבָה לְכוֹן גְּדִיל. וְאֵין אֲמַר. גְּדִיל. הָא כְמִילוּי. וְאֵין לָא. אֲנָא מְחַשְּׁבְּנָא גוּדְלָנָא מִן פֵּרְנִי. כֵּיוָן שֶׁשָּׁמַע בַּעֲלָהּ כָּךְ. כָּפַל לָהּ אֶת כְּתוּבָּתָהּ.

¹ אלא מן הלפת והקפלוטות | ג ללפת ולקפלוטות - | ג מפני 2 לאכרוב | ג מן האכרוב לירק | ג ירק 4 רבנן | ג רבנין נידבא | ג נדבה 5 שלחון | ג שלחון ליה ולחד | ג חד 6 ניזבון | ג נזבון דין | ג דו טרוכסימון { ג טרוכסימון דין | ג דו מן דאתמול | ג מדאתמל 7 דהוא | ג דו - | ג שמעון קליה ואזלון | ג ואזלין דזכון | ג דגבון 8 נהיגין | ג ילפין - | ג ליה ושנעינן קליה דטלייא | ג ושמענן קלה דטליא - | א' 9 יזבון | ג נזבון ואמרת | ג ואמרית טרוכסימון | ג טרוכסימון מן דאיתמול | ג מדאתמל דהוא | ג דו 10 אמ' | ג אמ' לון דביני | ג ביני טלייא | ג טלי ידעתון | ג ידעתם ידעתון מה ביני לבין ברי | ג מה ביני לבין ברי ידעתון אעפ"כ | ג אפילו כן 11 והיא | ג והי מודיי | ג מודי לון | ג להון 12 אמרו | ג אמרון לון | ג לן אנא | ג אנה ואין | ג אין 13 ואין לא | ג ואילא מחשבנא גודלנה | ג מחשבה גדלוניה כך | ג -

"They gave *peah* from vegetables." ²⁰⁰"They only gave for beets and leeks²⁰¹ since these are harvested once. Rebbi Yose said, also cabbage."

²⁰²It happened that the son of Ben Meviyayin²⁰³ gave *peah* of vegetables to the poor. His father came and found them standing at the door of the garden plot. He told them, put down what is in your hands, they put down what was in their hands. He gave them double from what had been tithed. Not that he was a miser, but he was concerned about the words of the Sages. Once the rabbis needed contributions; they sent to him Rebbi Aqiba and another rabbi with him. When they came to enter at his place they heard the voice of a lad saying to him, what shall we buy for you today? He said, endives²⁰⁴, not from today but from yesterday which are wilted and cheap. They left him and went away. After all people had (acquired merit) [contributed]²⁰⁵, they came to him. He said to them, why did you not come to me first, as you were used to? They told him, we already came but heard the voice of a lad saying to you,

what shall we buy for you today? You said, endives, not from today but from yesterday which are wilted and cheap. He said, you know what was between me and the lad; do you know what is between me and my Creator? Nevertheless, go and tell her[206] to give you a *modius*[207] of denars. They went and told her. She said to them, what did he say to you, heaped or flat? They answered her, he said it vaguely. She told them, I am giving you heaped. If he said so, I filled it. If not, I shall account for the excess from my dowry[208]. When her husband heard this, he doubled her *ketubah*.

200 Tosephta 3:20.
201 Greek κεφαλωτόν "headed".
202 *Esther rabba* 2, on v. 1:4.
203 "Importer of wine".
204 Greek τρώξιμον vegetable "eaten raw".
205 The text from the Leiden ms. is in parentheses, from ו in brackets.
206 His wife.
207 A measure of volume; Roman 8.5 l, Syrian 17 l.
208 Greek φερνή, ἡ.

תמיד נשחט פרק חמישי

(fol.31c) **משנה א**: תָּמִיד נִשְׁחָט בִּשְׁמוֹנֶה וּמֶחֱצָה וְקָרֵב בְּתֵשַׁע וּמֶחֱצָה. עֶרֶב פְּסָחִים נִשְׁחָט בְּשֶׁבַע וּמֶחֱצָה וְקָרֵב בִּשְׁמוֹנֶה וּמֶחֱצָה בֵּין בַּחוֹל בֵּין בַּשַּׁבָּת. חָל עֶרֶב פְּסָחִים לִהְיוֹת עֶרֶב שַׁבָּת נִשְׁחָט בְּשֵׁשׁ וּמֶחֱצָה וְקָרֵב בְּשֶׁבַע וּמֶחֱצָה וְהַפֶּסַח אַחֲרָיו:

Mishnah 1: The daily sacrifice[1] is slaughtered at [hour] eight and a half and brought at nine and a half. On Passover Eve it is slaughtered at [hour] seven and a half and brought at eight and a half whether it be weekday or Sabbath[2]. If Passover Eve falls on a Friday, it is slaughtered at [hour] six and a half and brought at seven and a half[3]. The *Pesaḥ* is following[4].

1 The service of the daily afternoon sacrifice which concludes the Temple service for the day is concluded at 3:30 pm local time every day of the year except Passover Eve. In Roman style, an hour is defined as $1/12$ of the time of daylight. The night is divided into watches, not hours.

2 Since the *Pesaḥ* is slaughtered after the service of the daily sacrifice is completed, there must be time for several groups of people to prepare their *Pesaḥ*. Since it must be done on the 14th of Nisan, the rules of the *Pesaḥ* have precedence over those of the Sabbath.

3 In this case, roasting the *Pesaḥ* is an obligation of the 14th of Nisan, and it does not push aside the Sabbath prohibitions on the 15th if that day be a Sabbath. The slaughter has to be early enough to allow for roasting before nightfall.

4 In all cases, the *Pesaḥ* follows the completion of the ordinary Temple service.

(31c line 63) תָּמִיד נִשְׁחָט כול'. כָּתוּב וְזֶה אֲשֶׁר תַּעֲשֶׂה עַל־הַמִּזְבֵּחַ וגו'. הָיִיתִי אוֹמֵר. יְקָרְבוּ שְׁנֵיהֶן בְּשַׁחֲרִית וּשְׁנֵיהֶן בֵּין הָעַרְבַּיִם. אֶת־הַכֶּבֶשׂ הָאֶחָד תַּעֲשֶׂה בַבֹּקֶר. תַּלְמוּד לוֹמַר. הָיִיתִי אוֹמֵר. יִקְרַב שֶׁלְּשַׁחַר עִם הֶנֵץ הַחַמָּה. וְשֶׁלְּבֵין הָעַרְבַּיִם עִם דִּמְדּוּמֵי הַחַמָּה. תַּלְמוּד לוֹמַר. בֵּין הָעַרְבַּיִם. נֶאֱמַר כָּאן בֵּין הָעַרְבַּיִם. וְנֶאֱמַר לְהַלָּן בֵּין הָעַרְבַּיִם: מַה בֵּין הָעַרְבַּיִם שֶׁנֶּאֱמַר לְהַלָּן מִשֵּׁשׁ שָׁעוֹת וּלְמַעְלָן. אַף בֵּין הָעַרְבַּיִם שֶׁנֶּאֱמַר כָּאן מִשֵּׁשׁ שָׁעוֹת וּלְמַעְלָן. מַה חָמִית מֵימַר בֵּין הָעַרְבַּיִם מִשֵּׁשׁ שָׁעוֹת וּלְמַעְלָן. [אַף עַל פִּי שֶׁאֵין רְאָיָה לַדָּבָר זֵכֶר לַדָּבָר.] אוֹי לָנוּ כִּי־פָנָה הַיּוֹם כִּי יִנָּטוּ צִלְלֵי־עָרֶב: מַה עֶרֶב שֶׁנֶּאֱמַר לְהַלָּן מִשֵּׁשׁ שָׁעוֹת וּלְמַעְלָן. אַף עֶרֶב שֶׁנֶּאֱמַר כָּאן מִשֵּׁשׁ שָׁעוֹת וּלְמַעְלָן. וִיהֵא כָשֵׁר מִשֵּׁשׁ שָׁעוֹת וּלְמַעְלָן. רִבִּי יֹשׁוּעַ בֶּן לֵוִי אָמַר. בֵּין הָעַרְבַּיִם. כֵּיצַד. חָלוּק בֵּין הָעַרְבַּיִם. וְתֶן לוֹ שְׁתֵּי שָׁעוֹת וּמֶחֱצָה לְפָנָיו וּשְׁתֵּי שָׁעוֹת וּמֶחֱצָה לְאַחֲרָיו. וְשָׁעָה אַחַת לְאִסּוּקוֹ. נִמְצֵאתָ אוֹמֵר שֶׁהַתָּמִיד קָרֵב בְּתֵשַׁע שָׁעוֹת וּמֶחֱצָה.

2 שניהן | ג שניהם   ושניהן | ג ושניהם   3 יקרב שלשחר עם הנץ החמה ושלבין הערבים עם | ג יקריב C 6] [| ג יקריב

גS - 7 ערב | ג הערב כאן | ג כן   8 יישוע | ג יהושע   9 יהושע כיצד | ג הא כיצד   9 ושעה | ג שעה

"The daily sacrifice is slaughtered," etc. It is written: *The following you shall do on the altar*[5], etc. I would have said, both of them should be sacrificed in the morning, or both of them in the afternoon. The verse says[6], *one sheep you shall do in the morning*. I would have said, the morning one should be sacrificed at dawn and the evening one at dusk; the verse says[6], *between the evenings*. It is said here *between the evenings* and it is said there[7] *between the evenings*. Since *between the evenings* which is said there means after six hours[8], also *between the evenings* which is said here must mean after six hours. What did you see that makes you say, *between the evenings* means after six hours? [Even though it is no proof there is a hint:][9] *woe on us that the day has turned, that evening shadows are turned*[10]. Since *evening* which is said there means after six hours[11], also *evening* which is said here must mean after six hours. Then should it not be qualified after six hours[12]? Rebbi Joshua ben Levi said, what is *between the evenings*? Split the evening into two, give it two and a half hours before, two and a half hours afterwards, and one hour for its work[13]. It turns out that the daily sacrifice is brought at nine hours and a half.

5   *Ex.* 29:38. As usual the reference is to the second part of the verse, not quoted in the text: *sheep, yearlings, two per day, in perpetuity.*
6   *Ex.* 29:39.
7   *Ex.* 12:6, about the *Pesaḥ* sacrifice.
8   As noted immediately afterwards, this assertion is unproven.
9   This sentence was not written by the scribe, and also is missing in ג. It was added by the corrector from the parallels, *Sifra Emor Pereq* 11, *Mekhilta deR. Ismael Bo Parasha* 5 (ed. Horovitz-Rabin p. 17).
10 *Jer.* 6:4.
11 The verse shows that "evening" is the time when shadows point East. The Babli holds (58a) that this starts not at noontime but about half an hour later. But it seems that for Yerushalmi, Sifra and Mekhilta "six hours" means 12 noon.
   The argument is only a hint, not a proof, since the thesis that a word can have only one meaning is valid only for the Pentateuch, not for later biblical books.
12 S. Liebermann thinks that this refers to the *Pesaḥ* since the Mishnah states that on a 14th of Nisan which is a Friday the daily sacrifice is brought at 12:30 pm. This time must be qualified on all days. But this is a Babli argument, not valid for the Yerushalmi. The question is about the daily sacrifice; why on a 14th of Nisan which is a Friday is the service of the daily evening sacrifice not started at noon?
13 Since from noon to sunset there are 6 variable hours, the sacrifice should be

brought at 3 pm. Since one does not consider smaller units of time, "3 pm" really means "from 2:30 pm to 3:30 pm". Babli *Zevahim* 11b.

(31c line 76) אָמַר רִבִּי יוֹסֵה. שָׁבַק רִבִּי יְהוֹשֻׁעַ בֶּן לֵוִי רֵישָׁא וְאָמַר סוֹפָא. דְּל כֵּן [כְּהָדָא דְּתַנֵּי]. חֲנַנְיָה בֶּן יְהוּדָה אוֹמֵר. שׁוֹמֵעַ אֲנִי בֵּין הָעַרְבַּיִם. בֵּין עֲרָבִים. בֵּין עַרְבּוֹ שֶׁלְאַרְבָּעָה עָשָׂר וּבֵין עַרְבּוֹ שֶׁלַחֲמִשָּׁה עָשָׂר. יָכוֹל הַיּוֹם וְהַלַּיְלָה בִּכְלָל. תַּלְמוּד לוֹמַר יוֹם. [כְּשֶׁהוּא אוֹמֵר יוֹם יָצָא לַיְלָה.] אִי יוֹם. יָכוֹל בִּשְׁתֵּי שָׁעוֹת בַּיּוֹם. תַּלְמוּד לוֹמַר בָּעֶרֶב. אִי בָּעֶרֶב יָכוֹל מִשֶּׁתֶּחְשָׁךְ. תַּלְמוּד לוֹמַר בֵּין הָעַרְבַּיִם. הָא כֵּיצַד. חָלוֹק בֵּין הָעַרְבַּיִם וְתֵן שְׁתֵּי שָׁעוֹת וּמֶחֱצָה לְפָנָיו וּשְׁתֵּי שָׁעוֹת וּמֶחֱצָה לְאַחֲרָיו וְשָׁעָה אַחַת לְאִיסּוּקוֹ. נִמְצֵאתָ אוֹמֵר שֶׁהַתָּמִיד קָרֵב בְּתֵשַׁע שָׁעוֹת וּמֶחֱצָה.

1 יושע | ג יהושע רישא | ג ראשה דל | ג דלא כהדא | ג כהדה   2 שומע | ג שומיע בין | ג בין שני ערבו | ג עירבו

Rebbi Yose said, Rebbi Joshua ben Levi left out the beginning[14] and said the end; is that not what was stated: "Hanania ben Jehudah[15] says, I hear *between evenings*, between [two][16] evenings, between the evening of the 14th and the evening of the fifteenth[17]. I could think that day and night are included; the verse says, *day*[18]. Since He said *day*, this excludes the night. If it is day, I could think at two hours into the day; the verse says, *in the evening*. If *in the evening*, I could think after it became dark. The verse says, *between the evenings*. How is this? Split the evening into two, give it two and a half hours before, two and a half hours afterwards, and one hour for its work. It turns out that the daily sacrifice[19] is brought at nine hours and a half."

14 The statement of R. Joshua ben Levi actually is an older *baraita* which makes it explicit that the times of the evening daily sacrifice and the *Pesah* are identical.

15 In *Mekhilta deR. Simeon ben Yoḥai* (p. 12, *ad Ex.* 12:6), which according to J. N. Epstein is the *Tanna debe Ḥizqiah*: Ḥanania ben Hakinai).

16 Added from ג and *Mekhilta deR. Simeon ben Yohai*.

17 Reading עַרְבַּיִם as עֲרָבִים. For the rest of the Halakhah ג is not readable.

18 *Ex.* 12:6: *It should be guarded by you until the fourteenth day of this month*.

19 And the *Pesah*.

(31d line 9) אָמַר רִבִּי יוֹסֵה. הָדָא דְתֵימַר לְמִצְוָה. אֲבָל לַעֲכּוּב הָדָא הִיא דְתַנִּינָן. שְׁחָטוֹ קוֹדֶם לַחֲצוֹת פָּסוּל. לְאַחַר חֲצוֹת כָּשֵׁר מִיָּד. קוֹדֶם לַתָּמִיד כָּשֵׁר. וְיֵימַר אַף בְּשַׁחֲרִית כֵּן. הָכָא כְתוּב בֵּין הָעַרְבַּיִם: אִית לָךְ מֵימַר תַּמָּן בֵּין הַבְּקָרִים.

Rebbi Yose said, that is, for merit[20]. But for invalidation it is what we have stated[21]: "If one slaughtered it before noon it is disqualified; after noon it

HALAKHAH ONE   163

is immediately qualified. Before the daily evening sacrifice it is qualified." Could one say that it also is the same for the morning[22]? Here it is written *between the evenings*; do you have a verse *between the mornings*[23]?

20 If one follows all the rules, both *Pesah* and the daily evening sacrifice have to be brought at 3:30 pm. But as the Mishnah shows, a deviation does not invalidate the sacrifice.

21 Mishnah 5:3. The Mishnah supports the Yerushalmi position that "6 hours" means exactly this and not "half past twelve". Any *Pesah* or daily evening sacrifice slaughtered before noon is invalid.

22 Meaning that the daily morning sacrifice should preferably be slaughtered at 2½ hours (8:30 am), rather than at dawn?

24 Since it says "morning" but never "between the mornings", there is no reason why it should not be meritorious to start the morning service at soon as possible.

(31d line 13) רִבִּי יְושֻעַ בֶּן לֵוִי אָמַר. תְּפִילּוֹת מֵאָבוֹת לָמְדוּ. גֵּרַשׁ עַד אַף עַל פִּי כֵן לֹא הוֹרִידוּ אוֹתוֹ מִגְּדוּלָתוֹ אֶלָּא מִינּוּ אוֹתוֹ אַב בֵּית דִּין.

Rebbi Joshua ben Levi said, they learned prayers from the patriarchs. One repeats this[25] up to "but made him head of the court."

25 Here one should insert a copy of the text in *Berakhot* 4:1 (Notes 11-124). A number of Medieval authorities (e. g., Rav Nissim Gaon in his Commentary to *Berakhot* 27b, penultimate line) note that the text of *Berakhot* also appears in *Pesahim* (and partially in *Ta'aniot* 4:1). In the Venice *editio princeps* and the later printed editions the sentence has been shortened to become unintelligible.

(31d line 14) מָאן תַּנָּא בֵּין בַּחוֹל בֵּין בַּשַּׁבָּת. רִבִּי יִשְׁמָעֵאל. דְּתַנֵּי. כְּסִידּוּרוֹ בַּחוֹל כָּךְ סִידּוּרוֹ בַּשַּׁבָּת. דִּבְרֵי רִבִּי יִשְׁמָעֵאל. רִבִּי עֲקִיבָה אוֹמֵר. כְּסִדּוּרוֹ בְּעֶרֶב שַׁבָּת כָּךְ סִידּוּרוֹ בַּשַּׁבָּת. הָא רִבִּי יִשְׁמָעֵאל מְאַחֵר שָׁעָה לְפִלְפּוּלוֹ. וְרִבִּי עֲקִיבָה מַקְדִּים שָׁעָה אַחַת לְעִיסּוּקוֹ. כְּדֵי שֶׁלֹא יִכָּנְסוּ לְמִצְוָה מְשׁוּפָּרִין. וִיקָרֵב פֶּסַח תְּחִילָּה וְתָמִיד אַחֲרָיו. אִם אוֹמֵר אַתְּ כֵּן נִמְצֵאתָ מְבַטֵּל בֵּין הָעַרְבַּיִם שֶׁלְפֶּסַח. אִם מְקַיֵּים אַתְּ בֵּין הָעַרְבַּיִם שֶׁלְפֶּסַח לֹא נִמְצֵאתָ מְבַטֵּל בֵּין הָעַרְבַּיִם שֶׁלְתָּמִיד. תָּמִיד אִם מְבַטְּלוֹ אַתְּ עַכְשָׁיו אַתְּ מְקַיְּימוֹ לְאַחַר זְמַן. פֶּסַח אִם מְבַטְּלוֹ אַתְּ עַכְשָׁיו אֵימָתַי אַתְּ מְקַיְּימוֹ. וְיַקְרִיב פֶּסַח תְּחִילָּה וְתָמִיד אַחֲרָיו. יְאוּחַר דָּבָר שֶׁנֶּאֱמַר בּוֹ בָּעֶרֶב וּבֵין הָעַרְבַּיִם לְדָבָר שֶׁלֹּא נֶאֱמַר בּוֹ אֶלָּא בֵּין הָעַרְבַּיִם [בִּלְבָד].

Who is the Tanna of "whether it be weekday or Sabbath"? Rebbi Ismael, as it was stated[26]: "As its order is on a weekday so its order is on a Sabbath, the words of Rebbi Ismael. Rebbi Aqiba says, as its order is on a Friday so is its order on a Sabbath." This means that Rebbi Ismael makes it an hour later for its arguments[27], and Rebbi Aqiba makes it an hour earlier to occupy oneself with it, so they would not fulfill the commandment while inebriated[28]. Could not the *Pesaḥ* be brought first and the daily sacrifice afterwards[29]? If you are saying so, you are eliminating *between the evenings* of the *Pesaḥ*. If you are keeping *between the evenings* of the *Pesaḥ*, are you not eliminating *between the evenings* of the daily sacrifice? If you are neglecting *between the evenings* of the daily sacrifice now, you can observe it at other times. If you are neglecting it now for the *Pesaḥ*, when can you ever observe it? Could not *Pesaḥ* be brought first, followed by the daily sacrifice? The one about which is written *in the evening*[30] and *between the evenings* shall be delayed more than one about which is written [only] *between the evenings*.

רִבִּי יִרְמְיָה בָּעֵי. מַה חֲמִיתְ מֵימַר עֶרֶב מְאוּחָר אוֹ נֹאמַר עֶרֶב מוּקְדָּם. אֶלָּא כֵינִי. יְאוּחַר דָּבָר שֶׁנֶּאֱמַר בּוֹ בֵּין הָעַרְבַּיִם כְּבוֹא הַשֶּׁמֶשׁ לְדָבָר שֶׁלֹּא נֶאֱמַר בּוֹ אֶלָּא בֵּין הָעַרְבַּיִם לְבַד. לְשׁוֹן מַתְנִיתָהּ מְסַייְעָה לְרִבִּי יִרְמְיָה. שָׁם תִּזְבַּח אֶת־הַפֶּסַח בָּעָרֶב. בָּעֶרֶב אַתָּה זוֹבֵחַ. כְּבוֹא הַשֶּׁמֶשׁ אַתָּה אוֹכֵל. מוֹעֵד צֵאתְךָ מִמִּצְרָיִם: אַתָּה צוֹלֶה. אִית תַּנָּיֵי תַנֵּי. בָּעֶרֶב אַתָּה אוֹכֵל. כְּבוֹא הַשֶּׁמֶשׁ אַתָּה זוֹבֵחַ. מוֹעֵד צֵאתְךָ מִמִּצְרָיִם: אַתָּה צוֹלֶה.

Rebbi Jeremiah asked, what did you see to say that *evening* is later[31]; could we not say that *between the evenings is later*? But it must be: The one about which is written *between the evenings at sundown*[31] shall be delayed more than one about which is written only *between the evenings*. The formulation of a *baraita*[32] supports Rebbi Jeremiah: *"There you shall slaughter the Pesaḥ in the evening. In the evening you are slaughtering, at sundown you are eating, at the time of your exodus from Egypt you are roasting*[33]." There are Tannaim who state: "*In the evening you are eating, at sundown you are slaughtering, at the time of your exodus from Egypt you are roasting.*"

26 Babli 58a. In *Sifry zuṭa Beha`alotekha* 9(3) (Yalquṭ 720) the name tradition is the opposite of that of the Talmudim.

27 In *Ma`aser šeni* 1:1 (Note 19) פְּלְפּוּלוֹ refers to the discussion of the rules of tithe money. So it seems that here the interpretation of *Pene Moshe* is correct, that there is time to solve all questions that arise before the sacrifice is slaughtered on a tight schedule.

28 Since it is a Sabbath where usually three meals with bread and wine are prescribed, he makes sure that the entire

afternoon no alcohol is consumed and the people are awake for the celebration in the night.

29   Since if the 14th is a Friday neither the *Pesaḥ* nor the daily sacrifice are brought at the time which was determined to be the correct *between the evenings,* it should not make any difference which sacrifice was brought first.

30   *Deut. 16:6: There you shall slaughter the Pesaḥ in the evening, at sundown, at the time of your exodus from Egypt.* Babli 59a.

31   Since starting at 12:01 pm one greets with "good evening".

32   Babli *Berakhot* 9a, *Sifry Deut*. 113 in the name of R. Eliezer; different wording and authors *Mekhilta dR. Ismael Bo* 5, last sentence.

33   Since obviously roasting must precede eating and the day of the Exodus was the 15th of Nisan, the day after the night dedicated to the *Pesaḥ*, with the parallel sources one has to understand "roasting" as "burning" the remainders (*Ex* 12:10).

(31d line 32) וְיִקְרְבוּ שְׁנֵיהֶן כְּאַחַת. אָמַר רִבִּי יוֹסֵה. כֶּבֶשׁ שֵׁנִי. אֵין פֶּסַח שֵׁנִי. תַּנֵּי. רִבִּי נָתָן אוֹמֵר. בְּכָל־יוֹם תָּמִיד נִשְׁחָט בִּשְׁמוֹנֶה וּמֶחֱצָה וְקָרֵב בְּתֵשַׁע וּמֶחֱצָה. מָהוּ בְּכָל־יוֹם וָיוֹם. בְּכָל־עֶרֶב פֶּסַח וּפֶסַח. אָמַר רִבִּי יוֹסֵה בֵּירִבִּי בּוּן. טַעֲמֵיהּ (דָּהֵן) [דְּהָדֵין] תַּנָּיָה כְּדֵי לִיתֵּן חֲצִי שָׁעָה בֵּין כַּת לְכַת.

Could not both be brought simultaneously? Rebbi Yose said, the sheep is second, the *Pesaḥ* is not second[34]. It was stated: Rebbi Nathan says, every day the daily sacrifice was slaughtered at eight and a half, and brought at nine and a half. What means "every day"? Every Passover Eve. Rebbi Yose ben Rebbi Abun said, the reason of this Tanna is to allow half an hour between one group and the next[35].

תַּנֵּי. דַּם תָּמִיד וְאֵיבָרָיו קוֹדְמִין לַפֶּסַח וּפֶסַח לַקְּטוֹרֶת וְהַקְּטוֹרֶת לְהַטָּבַת נֵירוֹת. אִית תַּנָּיֵי תַּנֵּי. דַּם תָּמִיד וְאֵיבָרָיו קוֹדְמִין לַקְּטוֹרֶת וְהַקְּטוֹרֶת לַפֶּסַח וּפֶסַח לְהַטָּבַת הַנֵּירוֹת. כְּדֵי שֶׁיִּקְרְבוּ נִסְכֵּי תָמִיד עִמּוֹ. וְאֵין מוּקְדָּם לַתָּמִיד שֶׁלַּשַּׁחַר וְלֹא מְאוּחָר לַתָּמִיד שֶׁלְּבֵין הָעַרְבַּיִם אֶלָּא הַפֶּסַח וְהַקְּטוֹרֶת בְּעַרְבֵי פְסָחִים. מִנַּיִין שֶׁלֹּא יְהֵא דָּבָר קוֹדֵם לַתָּמִיד שֶׁלַּשַּׁחַר. תַּלְמוּד לוֹמַר עָלֶיהָ עוֹלָה. וּמִנַּיִן שֶׁלֹּא יְהֵא דָּבָר מְעַכֵּב לַתָּמִיד שֶׁלְּבֵין הָעַרְבַּיִם. תַּלְמוּד לוֹמַר עָלֶיהָ שְׁלָמִים. רִבִּי שִׁמְעוֹן בֶּן לָקִישׁ אָמַר. וְעָרַךְ עָלֶיהָ עוֹלָה אֵין כָּתוּב כָּאן. אֶלָּא וְעָרַךְ עָלֶיהָ הָעוֹלָה. שֶׁלֹּא תְהֵא הָעוֹלָה קוֹדֶמֶת לַתָּמִיד שֶׁל שַׁחַר. רִבִּי יִשְׁמָעֵאל בְּנוֹ שֶׁלְּרִבִּי יוֹחָנָן בֶּן בְּרוֹקָה אוֹמֵר. מְחוּסְרֵי כַפָּרָה מְבִיאִין כַּפָּרָתָן אַחַר הַתָּמִיד שֶׁלְּבֵין הָעַרְבַּיִם כְּדֵי שֶׁיִּטְבְּלוּ וְיֹאכְלוּ פִסְחֵיהֶן לָעֶרֶב. אָמַר רִבִּי יוּדָן. הָדָא דְתֵימַר בִּמְצוֹרָע עָשִׁיר. אֲבָל בִּמְצוֹרָע עָנִי לֹא עוֹף הוּא מֵבִיא. אָמַר רִבִּי שְׁמוּאֵל בַּר אֲבוּדִימָא. אֵינוֹ מֵבִיא אָשָׁם.

It was stated[36]: "The blood of the daily sacrifice and its limbs precede the *Pesaḥ*, and the *Pesaḥ* the incense, and the incense the trimming of the lights.[37]" There are Tannaim who state: "The blood of the daily sacrifice and its limbs precede the incense, and the incense the *Pesaḥ*, and the *Pesaḥ* the trimming of the lights, so that the libations of the daily sacrifice should be accompanying it[38]." There is nothing preceding the daily morning sacrifice and nothing later than the daily evening sacrifice except *Pesaḥ* and incense on Passover Eve. "[39]From where that nothing should precede the daily morning sacrifice? The verse says, *on it `olah*[40]. And from where that nothing should invalidate the daily evening sacrifice? The verse says, *on it šelamim*[41]. Rebbi Simeon ben Laqish says, it is not written here *he arranges on it `olah* but *he arranges on it the `olah*, that no elevation offering precede the daily morning sacrifice[42]. It was stated: Rebbi Ismael the son of Rebbi Johanan ben Beroqa says, people lacking expiation[43] bring their expiatory sacrifices after the daily evening sacrifice to enable them to immerse themselves and eat their *Pesaḥ* in the evening. Rebbi Yudan said, that is, for a rich sufferer from skin disease. But a poor sufferer from skin disease, does he not bring a bird[44]? Said Rebbi Samuel ben Eudaimon, does he not bring a reparation sacrifice[45]?

36 *Sifry Num.* 143, Babli 58b. The argument seems to be that the *Pesaḥ*, while a personal sacrifice from the offerers, has the status of a public sacrifice, since only public sacrifices can override Sabbath prohibitions and be offered if the people are impure (Mishnah 9:3). Then the verse states that the daily evening offering has to be the second public offering of the day, not the third. (This implies that the additional offerings of Sabbath and holidays are counted as appendices to the daily morning sacrifice.)
37 *Ex.* 27:2.
38 "It" here is the burning of the incense on the golden altar in the Temple. Since the burning of incense does not involve the altar of the sacrifices, it is not dependent on the daily sacrifices and in the morning may precede, in the evening follow, the daily offering (Babli 59a).
39 *Sifra Ṣaw Pereq* 2(10).
40 S. Liebermann conjectures that here one reads עולה as Aramaic אוּלָא "first".
41 Reading שְׁלוּמִים "finishing".
42 Babli 58b. The definite article describes an offering that certainly is brought on the altar immediately after it is readied for service; this must be the daily morning sacrifice.
43 People forbidden access to *sancta* unless a reparation sacrifice has been brought in the Temple on their behalf: The woman after childbirth (*Lev.* 12:6-8), the male sufferer from gonorrhea (*Lev.* 15:14-15), the female sufferer from flux (*Lev.* 15:29-30), and the person healed from skin disease (*Lev.* 14:19,31). Babli 59a.
44 It is clear from *Lev.* 14:19 that of the

two sacrifices offered, an elevation (עולה) and a reparation (חטאת) one, only the latter is expiatory. But in case this is a bird (in all cases except the wealthy sufferer from skin disease), nothing is burned on the altar, only its blood is squeezed out on wall and bottom of the altar (*Lev.* 5:9). Therefore these offerings by their nature are not subject to the limitations imposed on offerings of which parts are burned on the altar.

45   And *Lev.* 14:21 declares also the reparation offering as expiatory.

(fol. 31c) **משנה ב**: הַפֶּסַח שֶׁשְּׁחָטוֹ שֶׁלֹּא לִשְׁמוֹ קִבֵּל וְהִילֵּךְ וְזָרַק שֶׁלֹּא לִשְׁמוֹ אוֹ לִשְׁמוֹ וְשֶׁלֹּא לִשְׁמוֹ אוֹ שֶׁלֹּא לִשְׁמוֹ וְלִשְׁמוֹ פָּסוּל. כֵּיצַד לִשְׁמוֹ וְשֶׁלֹּא לִשְׁמוֹ. לְשֵׁם פֶּסַח וּלְשֵׁם שְׁלָמִים. שֶׁלֹּא לִשְׁמוֹ וְלִשְׁמוֹ. לְשֵׁם שְׁלָמִים וּלְשֵׁם פֶּסַח:

Mishnah 2: *Pesaḥ* which he[46] slaughtered not for its purpose, received [the blood], transported it, or poured it, not for its purpose, or for its purpose and not for its purpose, or not for its purpose and for its purpose, is disqualified. What is "for its purpose and not for its purpose"? As *Pesaḥ* and as well-being offering. "Not for its purpose and for its purpose"? As well-being offering and as *Pesaḥ*.

46   The sacrifice may be slaughtered by its owner, or by a Levitic slaughterer attached to the Temple. The blood must be received in a vessel, transported to the altar, and sprinkled on the walls of the altar by a Cohen. Everybody involved in the service must have the intent of performing his duty explicitly for the *Pesaḥ*. If he started with the correct idea but in the act changed his mind and thought, e. g., that he is performing for the festival offering (Mishnah 6:6), we do not say that his prior thought is a dedication which excludes additional dedications, but the association of *Pesaḥ* and any other kind of sacrifice in any order disqualifies the sacrifice; it must be disposed of by burning outside the Temple district.

(31d line 50) **הלכה ב**: מְנַיִין שֶׁהוּא צָרִיךְ לְשׁוֹחֲטוֹ לִשְׁמוֹ. רִבִּי בָּא בְשֵׁם רַב. וַאֲמַרְתֶּם זֶבַח־פֶּסַח הוּא. לוֹמַר. אִם שְׁחָטוֹ לְשֵׁם פֶּסַח הֲרֵי הוּא פֶּסַח. וְאִם לָאו אֵינוֹ פֶסַח. שְׁאָר כָּל־מַעֲשָׂיו מְנַיִין. וְעָשִׂיתָ [פֶּסַח]. שֶׁיְּהוּ כָל־מַעֲשָׂיו לְשֵׁם פֶּסַח. מֵעַתָּה אֲפִילוּ הֶקְטֵר אֵימוּרִין. תַּלְמוּד לוֹמַר זֶבַח. מַה זְּבִיחָה מְיוּחֶדֶת שֶׁהִיא הָעַכֶּבֶת אֶת הַכַּפָּרָה. יָצְאוּ הֶקְטֵר אֵימוּרִין שֶׁאֵינָן מְעַכְּבִין אֶת הַכַּפָּרָה.

חַטָּאת מְנַיִין. וְשָׁחַט אֹתָהּ לְחַטָּאת. וּשְׁאָר כָּל־מַעֲשָׂיו מְנַיִין. וְעָשָׂה אֶת־הָאֶחָד חַטָּאת.
מֵעַתָּה אֲפִילוּ הֶקְטֵר אֵימוּרִין. תַּלְמוּד לוֹמַר וְשָׁחַט. מַה שְּׁחִיטָה מְיוּחֶדֶת שֶׁהִיא הָעַכֶּבֶת אֶת
הַכַּפָּרָה. יָצְאוּ הֶקְטֵר אֵימוּרִין שֶׁאֵינָן מְעַכְּבִין אֶת הַכַּפָּרָה.

Halakhah 2: [47]From where that he must slaughter it for its purpose? Rebbi Abba in the name of Rav: *And you shall say, a Pesaḥ slaughter it is*[48]; to imply that if he slaughtered it for the purpose of *Pesaḥ* it is *Pesaḥ*, otherwise it is not *Pesaḥ*. From where the remainder of its actions? *You shall make [a Pesaḥ]*[49], that all its actions shall be for the purpose of *Pesaḥ*. But then also the burning of its parts[50]? The verse says, *slaughter* But then also the burning of its parts[50]? The verse says, *slaughter*[51]. Since slaughter is particular in that it invalidates expiation[52], this excludes the burning of its parts which does not invalidate expiation.

From where for purification offerings? *He shall slaughter it as purification offering*[53]. From where the remainder of its actions? *[He] shall make*[49] *one as purification offering*[54]. But then also the burning of its parts[50]? The verse says, *he shall slaughter*. Since slaughter is particular in that it invalidates expiation, this excludes the burning of its parts which does not invalidate expiation.

47 Babli *Zevahim* 7b. The topic here really is Mishnah *Zevahim* 1:1 : "All sacrifices which were not slaughtered specifically for the benefit of their owners are qualified except for *Pesaḥ* and purification offerings." In all matters of required intent, the rules for *Pesaḥ* and purification offerings are equal.

48 *Ex.* 20:27. Quoted in this sense in *Mekhilta dR. Simeon ben Yoḥai* (p. 26, line 20).

49 *Deut.* 16:1. The unspecific עשה always is interpreted to include all necessary actions.

50 Greek αἱ μοῖραι [τοῦ θεοῦ], the fat which is forbidden for human consumption.

51 זבח indicates slaughter in preparation of a meal; often "sacrifice of which at least a part is consumed as sanctum"; whereas שחט (سحط) specifically means "to cut the throat".

52 Since it is spelled out that *the blood is it which atones for the soul* (*Lev.* 17:11), if anything goes wrong in any action necessary up to the pouring of the blood on the altar's wall the sacrifice is invalid, but nothing that happens afterwards can invalidate the offering. If the parts to be burned become impure, they have to be burned outside the Temple district but the sacrifice remains valid.

53 *Lev.* 4:33.

54 There is no verse exactly as quoted in the text. The reference seems to be to *Lev.* 16:30, *the Cohen shall bring one as*

purification offering.

(31d line 59) חַטָּאת לְשֵׁם בְּעָלִים מְנַיִין. אָמַר רִבִּי יִרְמְיָה. וְעָשָׂה הַכֹּהֵן אֶת־הַחַטָּאת וְכִפֶּר עַל־הַמִּטַּהֵר מְטּוּמְאָתוֹ. אָמַר לֵיהּ רִבִּי יוֹסֵי. מֵעַתָּה אֲפִילוּ הֶקְטֵר אֵימוּרִין. תַּלְמוּד לוֹמַר וְכִפֶּר. מַה זְרִיקָה מְיוּחֶדֶת שֶׁהִיא הָעַכֶּבֶת אֶת הַכַּפָּרָה. יָצְאוּ הֶקְטֵר אֵימוּרִין שֶׁאֵינָן מְעַכְּבִין אֶת הַכַּפָּרָה.

2 הקטר | K הקטיר   אימורין | K אמו'   ת"ל וכפר. מה זריקה מיוחדת שהיא מעכבת את הכפרה. יצאו הקטר אימורין | K -

פֶּסַח לְשֵׁם בְּעָלִים מְנַיִין. וְדִין הוּא. מָה אִם הַחַטָּאת שֶׁאֵין מַחֲשֶׁבֶת עָרֵלִים וּטְמֵאִים פּוֹסְלִין בָּהּ צְרִיכָה שֶׁתְּהֵא לְשֵׁם בְּעָלִים. פֶּסַח שֶׁפַּחֲשֶׁבֶת עָרֵלִים וּטְמֵאִים פּוֹסְלִין בּוֹ אֵינוּ דִין שֶׁיְהֵא [צָרִיךְ] לְשֵׁם בְּעָלִים. לֹא. אִם אָמַרְתָּ בְּחַטָּאת שֶׁהִיא קָדְשֵׁי קָדָשִׁים. תֹּאמַר בַּפֶּסַח. שֶׁהוּא קָדָשִׁים קַלִּין. אָמַר רִבִּי יוֹסֵה. וְלֹא מִמַּחֲשָׁבָה לְמַדְנָּ. הַתּוֹרָה רִיבְּת מַחֲשָׁבָה בַּפֶּסַח יוֹתֵר מִן הַחַטָּאת. אָמַר רִבִּי חֲנַנְיָה קוֹמֵי רִבִּי מָנָא. וּמֵחַטָּאתוֹ שֶׁלַּמְצוֹרָע אָנוּ לְמֵידִין. וְכִי חַטָּאתוֹ שֶׁלַמְצוֹרָע לֹא לְחִידוּשָׁהּ יָצָאת. שֶׁתְּהֵא טְעוּנָה נְסָכִים לְשֵׁם בְּעָלִים. וְדָבָר שֶׁיָּצָא לְחִידוּשׁוֹ אֵין לְמֵידִין מִמֶּנּוּ. אָמַר לֵיהּ. וְכִי חַטָּאתוֹ שֶׁלַמְצוֹרָע מֵאֵיכָן לְמֵידָה שֶׁתְּהֵא פְסוּלָה שֶׁלֹּא לִשְׁמָהּ. לֹא מִן הָדֵין קַרְיָיא דִכְתִיב וְשָׁחַט אוֹתָהּ לְחַטָּאת. וּכְתִיב זֹאת תּוֹרַת הַחַטָּאת. תּוֹרָה אַחַת לְכָל־הַחַטָּאוֹת. אֶלָּא מִמָּקוֹם שֶׁהִיא לְמֵידָה מִשָּׁם הִיא מְלַמֶּדֶת.

1 בעלים | K בעלין   ערלים וטמאים | K ערלין וטמאין   2 בעלים | K בעלין   ערלים וטמאים | K ערלין וטמאין   3 בעלים | K בעלין   אמרת | K אמרתה   4 קלין | K קלים   למדת | K למדתה   5 שלמצורע | K -   למידין | K למידים   6 בעלים | K בעלין   ודבר | K ולדבר   7 ממנו | K -   מאיכן | K מאיכין   למידה | K למדה   8 קרייא | K קרייה   זאת | K -

From where that a purification sacrifice must be for the name of its owner[55]? Rebbi Jeremiah said, *the Cohen shall make the purification offering and expiate for the one who purifies himself from his impurity*[56]. Rebbi Yose said to him, but then also the burning of its parts[50]? The verse says, *and expiate*. Since pouring is particular in that it invalidates expiation[52], this excludes the burning of its parts which does not invalidate expiation.

From where that a *Pesaḥ* must be in the name of its owner? Is it not a logical argument[57]? Since a purification sacrifice, where intent for the uncircumcised or impure[58] does not invalidate it, needs to be in the name of the owner, *Pesaḥ*, where intent for the uncircumcised or impure does invalidate it, is it not logical that it needs to be in the name of its owner? No. If you are saying about purification sacrifice which is most holy[59], would you say that about *Pesaḥ* which is a simple *sanctum*[60]? Rebbi Yose said, did you not argue about intent? The Torah insisted about intent for *Pesaḥ* more than for purification sacrifice. Rebbi Hananiah said before Rebbi Mana: Do we infer this from the purification sacrifice of the sufferer from skin disease? But is not the purification sacrifice of the sufferer from skin disease separate for something new[61]? And one cannot infer from anything which is separate for something new[62]. He told him, from where do you infer that it be invalid if not for its purpose? Not from the following verse, *he shall slaughter it as purification sacrifice*[63], and it is written: *this is the doctrine of the purification sacrifice*[64]. There is one doctrine for all purification sacrifices. But from the place where it is being inferred, there it permits inferences[65].

55 All Temple personnel dealing with the sacrifice have to know the name of the owner, and the purpose of the sacrifice, and have to intend to help his expiation.

56 Lev. 14:19. Babli *Zevahim* 8a in the name of Rava, a contemporary of R. Jeremiah.

From here through Chapter 7 there exists a series of Genizah fragments from the Kaufmann collection in Budapest, published by S. Loewinger in the Hebrew part of the Alexander Marx Jubilee Volumes (New York 1950), indicated here by K.

57 דין usually introduces an informal argument *de minore ad majus*.

58 Sacrifices of the uncircumcised (e. g., a hemophiliac who may not be circumcised) or an impure person (e. g., a resident outside the Land) sent through third persons are accepted in the Temple. But any uncircumcised is excluded from the *Pesah* (*Ex.* 12:48) and the person who will not be pure by nightfall is excluded by the requirement that the *Pesah* be slaughtered for the group of subscribers (*Ex.* 12:3-4); adding the name of a person prohibited from eating sacred food will invalidate the slaughter. This argument is somewhat circular; since the argument is rejected for other reasons, this does not have to be pointed out.

59 It may be eaten only by male Cohanim in the Temple precinct.

60 It may be eaten by every pure person within the walls of the city of the Temple.

61 As stated in Mishnah *Menahot* 9:6, no purification offering other than that of the sufferer from skin disease needs accompanying offerings of flour and wine. The offering of flour is explicit in *Lev.* 14:10; that of wine is inferred in *Sifra Mesora` Pereq* 2(10).

62 This is R. Ismael's 12th hermeneutical principle: Anything which was in a group, but is taken from the group to be under a separate rule, cannot be returned to its original group unless the verse returns it explicitly. An example is the reparation sacrifice of the sufferer from skin disease, whose blood is not for the altar but for the right thumb and right great toe of the owner, but which *Lev.* 14:13 declares to follow the rules of reparation sacrifices in all respects. Such a note is missing for the purification sacrifice. The Babli, *Zevahim* 8a, accepts the argument as valid.

63 *Lev.* 4:33. *Sifra Wayyiqra II (Hovah)*

Pereq 11(3).
64 *Lev.* 6:18. Babli *Zevahim* 9a. Interpreted differently in *Sifra Saw Parašah* 3(1).
65 Since the flour offering does not accompany the purification offering of the sufferer from skin disease but his elevation offering (14:20), the attribution of the wine offering to the purification offering is an inference of the oral tradition which cannot override *Lev.* 6:18.

(31d line 76) שְׁחָטוֹ לִשְׁמוֹ לִזְרוֹק דָּמוֹ שֶׁלֹּא לִשְׁמוֹ. אָמַר רִבִּי יוֹחָנָן. יֵשׁ שֶׁלֹּא לִשְׁמוֹ מֵעֲבוֹדָה לַעֲבוֹדָה וְהוּא פוֹסֵל. רִבִּי שִׁמְעוֹן בֶּן לָקִישׁ אָמַר. יֵשׁ שֶׁלֹּא לִשְׁמוֹ מֵעֲבוֹדָה לַעֲבוֹדָה. וִיהֵא כָשֵׁר. אָמַר רִבִּי אִילָא. מִמַּחֲשֶׁבֶת פִּיגּוּל לִימֵּד רִבִּי יוֹחָנָן. אִילּוּ זָרַק שֶׁלֹּא לִשְׁמוֹ שֶׁמָּא אֵינוֹ פִיגּוּל. שְׁחָטוֹ לִשְׁמוֹ לִזְרוֹק דָּמוֹ שֶׁלֹּא לִשְׁמוֹ פָּסוּל. אָמַר רִבִּי יוֹסֵי. מִן תַּרְתֵּין מִילִין לֹא דָמְיָא מַחֲשֶׁבֶת פִּיגּוּל לְמַחֲשֶׁבֶת פְּסוּל. אִילּוּ שְׁחָטוֹ לִשְׁמוֹ לְקַבֵּל דָּמוֹ שֶׁלֹּא לִשְׁמוֹ שֶׁמָּא אֵינוֹ כָשֵׁר. שְׁחָטוֹ לִשְׁמוֹ לְקַבֵּל דָּמוֹ שֶׁלֹּא לִשְׁמוֹ פָּסוּל. אִילּוּ שְׁחָטוֹ לִשְׁמוֹ לְהַקְטִיר אֵימוֹרָיו שֶׁלֹּא לִשְׁמוֹ שֶׁמָּא אֵינוֹ פִיגּוּל. שְׁחָטוֹ לִשְׁמוֹ לְהַקְטִיר אֵימוֹרָיו שֶׁלֹּא לִשְׁמוֹ כָשֵׁר.

2 פוסל K | פסול יש K | אין K | ויהא K | והוא K | ואילא 3 אילא K | הילא K | פיגול K | פסול אילו K | אלו זרק K | זרק דמו 4 יוסי K | יוסה מן תרתין מילין K | מתרתין מלין דמיא K | דמייה 5 אילו K | אלו 6 SK לשמו C | שלא לשמו לשמו K - C | שלא לשמו פיגול K | פסול אימורין K | אמוריו 7 פיגול K | פסול כשר K | כשיר

If he slaughtered for its purpose with the intent to sprinkle its blood not for its purpose[66]. Rebbi Johanan said, there is transfer of "not for its purpose" from service to service and it is disqualified. Rebbi Simeon ben Laqish said, is there transfer of "not for its purpose" from service to service[66a]? It should be qualified. Rebbi Ila said, Rebbi Johanan learned this from thought of *piggul*[67]. If he poured not for its purpose would that not cause *piggul*[68]? If he slaughtered for its purpose with the intent to pour its blood not for its purpose, it is disqualified. Rebbi Yose said, in two aspects is the intent of *piggul* not equivalent to the intent of disqualification[69]. If he slaughtered for its purpose with the intent to receive its blood not for its purpose, would that not be qualified[70]? If he slaughtered for its purpose and received its blood not for its purpose, it is disqualified[71]. If he slaughtered for its purpose in order to burn its parts not for its purpose, would that not be *piggul*? If he slaughtered for its purpose and in order to burn its parts not for its purpose, it is qualified.

66 The slaughterer, who most probably is not priestly, is different from the person who will pour the blood. He has the correct intention for his own action, but intends a future action to be disqualifying. Does this have an influence on the status of *Pesah* or purification offering? Babli *Zevahim* 9b/10a, *Hulin* 39a.

66a In K: "Rebbi Simeon ben Laqish said, there is no transfer of 'not for its purpose' from service to service."

67 The source is *Lev.* 19:7. A well-being offering must be eaten on the day of its offering and the next. *But if it is intended to be eaten on the third day, it is piggul* ("mushy") *and will not be wanted.* Eating from sacrificial meat on the third day is sinful, but this has no influence on the validity of the sacrifice. But from the start intending to eat on the third day disqualifies the sacrifice and any consumption of its meat, even on the first day, is a deadly sin. This clearly is disqualification by intent for a future action by a different person. The argument is accepted in both Babli sources.

68 It would cause disqualification but not *piggul*.

69 He objects of comparing required actions in the presentation of sacrifices to *piggul*.

70 Since the Cohen who receives the blood must be present at the moment of slaughter, the Cohen's intent is what counts; a contrary intent by the slaughterer is irrelevant since it cannot precede the Cohen's.

71 In this sentence and the next, only the scribe's text is reproduced and translated; the corrector's additions and deletions are disregarded. The scribe's text is fully confirmed by K.

The argument goes as follows: For any action up to the pouring of the blood, the wrong intent before or during the action disqualifies. But for actions required after the pouring of the blood, such as burning of the parts or eating the meat, a wrong intent before the pouring of the blood disqualifies, but a wrong intent at the moment of the action is irrelevant. Therefore, the rules of *piggul* cannot be used to infer rules for actions preceding the pouring of the blood.

(32a line 10) אָמַר רִבִּי יוֹסֵה. אֲנָא חֲמִית לְרִבִּי יִרְמְיָה תְּפִיס לְרִבִּי בָּא. אֲמַר לֵיהּ. אֱמוֹר לִי טַעֲמָא דְּרִבִּי יוֹחָנָן. לָמָּה שְׁחָטוֹ לִשְׁמוֹ לִזְרוֹק דָּמוֹ שֶׁלֹּא לִשְׁמוֹ פָּסוּל. נַעֲשָׂה מִשָּׁעָה רִאשׁוֹנָה כְּשׁוֹחֲטוֹ לִשְׁמוֹ וּשֶׁלֹּא לִשְׁמוֹ וְהוּא פָּסוּל. אֲמַר לֵיהּ. וְאִין כֵּינִי אֲפִילוּ שְׁחָטוֹ שֶׁלֹּא לְאוֹכְלָיו לִזְרוֹק אֶת דָּמוֹ שֶׁלֹּא לְאוֹכְלָיו. וְיֵעָשֶׂה מִשָּׁעָה רִאשׁוֹנָה כְּשׁוֹחֲטוֹ לְאוֹכְלָיו וְשֶׁלֹּא לְאוֹכְלָיו וִיהֵא כָשֵׁר. לֵית יְכִיל. +דָּמַר רִבִּי אִילָא בְּשֵׁם רִבִּי יוֹחָנָן. שְׁחָטוֹ לְאוֹכְלָיו לִזְרוֹק דָּמוֹ שֶׁלֹּא לְאוֹכְלָיו כָּשֵׁר. אָתָא רִבִּי יַעֲקֹב בַּר אָחָא בְּשֵׁם רִבִּי יוֹחָנָן. שְׁחָטוֹ לְאוֹכְלָיו לִזְרוֹק דָּמוֹ שֶׁלֹּא לְאוֹכְלָיו כָּשֵׁר. רִבִּי יוֹסֵי נְסִי[נ]ב] חֲלֵיהּ מִן תְּרֵין טַעֲמוֹי דְּרִבִּי יוֹחָנָן. לָמָּה שְׁחָטוֹ לִשְׁמוֹ לִזְרוֹק דָּמוֹ שֶׁלֹּא לִשְׁמוֹ פָּסוּל. נַעֲשָׂה מִשָּׁעָה רִאשׁוֹנָה כְּשׁוֹחֲטוֹ לִשְׁמוֹ וּשֶׁלֹּא לִשְׁמוֹ וְהוּא פָּסוּל. לָמָּה שְׁחָטוֹ לְאוֹכְלָיו לִזְרוֹק דָּמוֹ שֶׁלֹּא לְאוֹכְלָיו כָּשֵׁר. נַעֲשָׂה כְּמִשָּׁעָה הָרִאשׁוֹנָה כְּשׁוֹחֲטוֹ לְאוֹכְלָיו וְשֶׁלֹּא לְאוֹכְלָיו וְהוּא כָשֵׁר.

1 אנא K | אנה אמור K | אימר 2 כשוחטו K | כשחט ואין K | ואן שלא K | - 4 את K | - 5 דמר K | דאמ' אילא K | הילא 6 אחא K | אחה K | שחטו K | אפילו שחטו 7 נסיב חיליה K | חייל 9 כמשעה K | משעה

רִבִּי חֲנַנְיָה אָמַר קוֹמֵי רִבִּי מָנָא בְּשֵׁם רִבִּי יוּדָן. טַעֲמָא דְּרִבִּי יוֹחָנָן. כָּל־שֶׁאִילּוּ יָבוֹא לְאוֹתָהּ הָעֲבוֹדָה וְאֵינוֹ מְחַשֵּׁב לָהּ. מְחַשֵּׁב הוּא מֵעֲבוֹדָה אַחֶרֶת לָהּ. אִילּוּ שְׁחָטוֹ לִשְׁמוֹ לִזְרוֹק דָּמוֹ שֶׁלֹּא

לִשְׁמוֹ שֶׁמָּא אֵינוֹ פִיגּוּל. שְׁחָטוֹ לִשְׁמוֹ לִזְרוֹק דָּמוֹ שֶׁלֹּא לִשְׁמוֹ פָּסוּל. אִילּוּ שְׁחָטוֹ לִשְׁמוֹ לְקַבֵּל דָּמוֹ שֶׁלֹּא לִשְׁמוֹ שֶׁמָּא אֵינוֹ כָשֵׁר. וּבִשְׁעַת קַבָּלָה מְחַשֵּׁב הוּא. הֲרֵי כָּל־שֶׁאִילּוּ יָבוֹא לְאוֹתָהּ הָעֲבוֹדָה וְאֵינוֹ מְחַשֵּׁב לָהּ. הוּא מְחַשֵּׁב מֵעֲבוֹדָה אַחֶרֶת לָהּ. אִילּוּ שְׁחָטוֹ לִשְׁמוֹ לְהַקְטִיר אֵימוּרָיו שֶׁלֹּא לִשְׁמוֹ שֶׁמָּא אֵינוֹ פִיגּוּל. וּבִשְׁעַת הַקְטָרָה אֵינוֹ מְחַשֵּׁב. הֲרֵי כָּל־שֶׁאִילּוּ יָבוֹא לְאוֹתָהּ הָעֲבוֹדָה וְהוּא מְחַשֵּׁב לָהּ אֵינוֹ מְחַשֵּׁב מֵעֲבוֹדָה אַחֶרֶת לָהּ. אָמַר לֵיהּ. לָא תְתִיבֵינִי מְפִיגּוּל עַל פָּסוּל. דָּמַר רִבִּי יוֹסֵה. מִן תְּרֵין מִילִּין לֹא דַּמְיָיא מַחֲשֶׁבֶת פִּיגּוּל לְמַחֲשֶׁבֶת פָּסוּל.

1 כל שאילו K | הרי כל שאלו 3 אילו K | אלו 5 היא מחשב K | מחשב הוא 6 אימוריו K | אמורי 7 תתיביני K | תתיבני 8 מן תרין מילין K | מתרתין מלין דמייא K | דמיה

Rebbi Yose said, I saw Rebbi Jeremiah grabbing Rebbi Abba and saying to him, tell me the reason of Rebbi Johanan, why it is disqualified if one slaughtered for its purpose with the intent to pour its blood not for its purpose? It is made from the start as if he slaughtered for its purpose and not for its purpose, and it is disqualified. He told him, if this is so, even if he slaughtered not[72] for its eaters and to sprinkle its blood not for its eaters, it should be as if from the start he slaughtered for its eaters and not for its eaters and be qualified[73]. This you cannot do, as Rebbi Ila said in the name of Rebbi Johanan, if he slaughtered for its eaters and to pour its blood not for its eaters, it is qualified[74]. There came Rebbi Jacob bar Aha in the name of Rebbi Johanan, if he slaughtered for its eaters and to pour its blood not for its eaters, it is qualified[75]. Rebbi Yose got his strength[76] from the two reasons of Rebbi Johanan. Why is it disqualified if one slaughtered for its purpose with the intent to pour its blood not for its purpose? It is made from start as if he slaughtered for its purpose and not for its purpose, and is disqualified. Why is it qualified if he slaughtered for its eaters and to pour its blood not for its eaters? It is made from the start as if he slaughtered for its eaters and not for its eaters, and is qualified.

Rebbi Hananiah said before Rebbi Mana in the name of Rebbi Yudan. The reason of Rebbi Johanan that if one would come to perform a certain action without thinking[77], one continues thinking from another action. If one slaughtered for its purpose with the intent to pour its blood not for its purpose, would that not be *piggul*[68]? If one slaughtered for its purpose with the intent to pour its blood not for its purpose, it is disqualified. If one slaughtered for its purpose and to receive its blood not for its purpose, would that not be qualified, since on the act of receiving he is thinking[70]. Therefore, if one would come to perform a certain action without thinking, one continues the thinking from another action. If one slaughtered for its purpose with the intent to burn its parts not for its purpose, would that not be *piggul*? If at the moment of burning he does not think, then if one would come to perform a certain action without thinking, one continues the thinking from another action[78]. He told him, do not object to me about disqualification because of *piggul*, since Rebbi Yose said, in two aspects is the intent of *piggul* not equivalent to the intent of disqualification.

72 For the text to make sense, this word has to be deleted with K.
73 Mishnah 3.
74 Obviously, here one has to read "disqualified," even though the text is confirmed by K.
75 The argument of R. Yose is correct; the tradition of R. Ila is incorrect, and R. Johanan is consistent in his opinions.
76 To reject a comparison with *piggul*.
77 Since sacrifices may become disqualified if a necessary action is made with the wrong intent, it is preferable that the Cohen not have any thought other than doing his duty for whom and for what it is needed.
78 As stated in Note 71, the intent at the moment of the action after the pouring of the blood cannot have retroactive influence on the validity of the sacrifice.

(32a line 33) מָה נָפִיק מִן בֵּינֵיהוֹן. אָמַר רִבִּי שְׁמוּאֵל בַּר אֲבַדּוּמָא. חִילוּפִין. בִּשְׁאָר יְמוֹת הַשָּׁנָה. שְׁחָטוֹ לִשְׁמוֹ לִזְרוֹק דָּמוֹ שֶׁלֹּא לִשְׁמוֹ בִּשְׁאָר יְמוֹת הַשָּׁנָה. עַל דַּעְתֵּיהּ דְּרִבִּי יוֹחָנָן כָּשֵׁר. עַל דַּעְתֵּיהּ דְּרִבִּי שִׁמְעוֹן בֶּן לָקִישׁ פָּסוּל.

1 נפיק | K נפק אבדומא | K אבודמא   2 לזרוק דמו שלא לשמו | K לזרוק דמו שלא לשמו לזרוק דמו שלא לשמו

What results from the difference between them? Rebbi Samuel ben Eudaimon said, switching on the other days of the year. If one slaughtered for its purpose with the intent to sprinkle its blood not for its purpose, on the other days of the year. In the opinion of Rebbi Johanan it is qualified; in the opinion of Rebbi Simeon ben Laqish it is disqualified[79].

79 For R. Johanan, *Pesah* at any other day is a well-being sacrifice which is not disqualified by an action not done for its purpose (Mishnah *Zevahim* 1:1). For R. Simeon ben Laqish, *Pesah* on any other day is out of order.

(32a line 36) אָמַר רִבִּי יוֹחָנָן. עַל דָּא עֲלֵי אַבָּא בַּר אַבָּא. דְּאִינּוּן אֲמְרִין. מְנַיִּין שֶׁהַפֶּסַח מִשְׁתַּנֶּה לְשֵׁם שְׁלָמִים. וְאִם־מִן־הַצֹּאן קָרְבָּנוֹ לְזֶבַח שְׁלָמִים. כָּל־שֶׁהוּא מִן הַצֹּאן בָּא שְׁלָמִים. הֲתִיבוּן. הֲרֵי עוֹלָה מִן הַצֹּאן. דָּבָר שֶׁאֵינוֹ בָא אֶלָּא מִן הַצֹּאן. יָצָאת עוֹלָה שֶׁהִיא בָאָה אֲפִילוּ מִן הַבָּקָר. הֲתִיבוּן. הֲרֵי אָשָׁם. אָמַר רִבִּי בּוּן בַּר כַּהֲנָא. מִן־הַצֹּאן. דָּבָר הַבָּא מִכָּל־הַצֹּאן. יָצָא אָשָׁם שֶׁאֵינוֹ בָא אֶלָּא מִן הָאֵילִים בִּלְבָד. בְּכָל־אָתָר אַתְּ אוֹמֵר. מִן לְרַבּוֹת. וְהָכָא אַתְּ אָמַר. מִן לְמַעֵט. אָמַר רִבִּי מָנָא. מִיעוּטוֹ. שֶׁאֵינוֹ בָא אֶלָּא מִן הָאֵילִים בִּלְבָד. הֲתִיבוּן. וְהִכְתִיב וְאִם־מִן־הַצֹּאן קָרְבָּנוֹ מִן־הַכְּשָׂבִים אוֹ מִן־הָעִזִּים לְעוֹלָה. מֵעַתָּה מוּתָּר הַפֶּסַח בָּא עוֹלָה. אָמַר רִבִּי אָבוּן. מְשַׁנִּין דָּבָר שֶׁהוּא לַאֲכִילָה בְדָבָר שֶׁהוּא לַאֲכִילָה. [וְאֵין מְשַׁנִּין דָּבָר שֶׁהוּא לַאֲכִילָה בְדָבָר שֶׁאֵינוֹ לַאֲכִילָה.] אָמַר רִבִּי יוֹסֵי בֵּירִבִּי בּוּן. מְשַׁנִּין קָדָשִׁים קַלִּין לְשֵׁם קָדָשִׁים קַלִּין וְאֵין מְשַׁנִּין קָדָשִׁים קַלִּים לְשֵׁם קָדְשֵׁי קָדָשִׁים. אָמַר רִבִּי יוֹחָנָן עַל דְּעָלֵי רִבִּי חֲנִינָה דְּאָתוֹן אֲמְרִין. אֵין הַפֶּסַח מִשְׁתַּנֶּה לְשֵׁם שְׁלָמִים אֶלָּא אִם כֵּן שְׁחָטוֹ לְשֵׁם שְׁלָמִים. וַאֲנִי אוֹמֵר. אֲפִילוּ לְשֵׁם עוֹלָה. אָמַר רִבִּי לָא. טַעֲמֵיהּ דְּרִבִּי יוֹחָנָן. וְאִם־מִן־הַצֹּאן קָרְבָּנוֹ לְזֶבַח שְׁלָמִים. כָּל שֶׁהוּא זֶבַח בָּא שְׁלָמִים. מִשְׁתַּנֶּה לְמַחֲשֶׁבֶת פָּסוּל. הֵיךְ עֲבִיד. שְׁחָטוֹ לְשֵׁם עוֹלָה עַל מְנַת לִזְרוֹק דָּמוֹ לְמָחָר. מִכָּל־מָקוֹם פָּסוּל הוּא. אֵין תֵּימַר. מִשְׁתַּנֶּה לְמַחֲשֶׁבֶת פָּסוּל. פִּיגּוּל. אֵין תֵּימַר. אֵינוֹ מִשְׁתַּנֶּה לְמַחֲשֶׁבֶת פָּסוּל. פָּסוּל.

1 אמ' ר' יוחנן | ש ר' יוחנן אמ' | דא עלי | Kש דעלי ש דא עליל בר אבא | ש בר בא 2 לשם שלמים | ש לשלמים ואם | ש אם לזבח שלמים | ש - בא | ש - 3 שלמים | ש לשלמים K שלמין יצאת | ש יצא שהיא באה | ש שבאה 4 בון | ש ביבי K אבון הבא | Kש שהוא בא 5 מכל | ש מן כל שאינו | ש שאין האילים | שש האלים - | ש התיב ר' בון מן לרבות { M מלרבות ש מן להוציא 6 והכא | K והכה מן למעט | שM מלמעט ש מן לרבות מנא | ש אבין - | ש ה"נ מלמעט מיעוט שאינו בא בן שני שנים ואינו בא נקיבה וגבי אשם נמי מן למעט הוא האילים | שש האלים התיבון והכת' | ש כתב 7 ואם | K אם או מן העזים לעולה | ש - בא עולה | ש לעולה 8 אבון | ש אבין בדבר | Kש לדבר 9 בדבר | ש לדבר יוסי | K יוסה קדשים | K קדשין קלין | ששש האלים קדשים | K קדשין קלים | Kששש קלין לשם | ש לשום אמ' ר' יוחנן | ש ר' יוחנן אמ' | דעלי | ש דא עליל חנינא | ש חנינה 10 דאתון | K דאינון לשם שלמים | ש לשלמים לשם | ש לשום לשם | ש שחטו לשום לשם | ש לשום 12 אפי' | Kש אפי' שחטו לא | K הילא שש אילא ואם | ש אם שהוא | ש - 13 בא | ש - משתנה | K ומשתנה ש נשתנה עביד | Kש עבידה ש היאך עבידה לשם | ש לשום 14 מכל | ש בכל אין תימר | ש ואם תאמר (2) משתנה | ש נשתנה פיגול | K פיגול הו[א] 15 אינו | ש אין משתנה | ש נשתנה פסול | ש פיגול

⁸⁰Rebbi Johanan said, about this Abba bar Abba⁸¹ enlightened me, for they are saying, from where that *Pesaḥ* is changed⁸² into the denomination of well-being sacrifices? The verse says⁸³, *and if his sacrifice be from small cattle as meal well-being offering*; anything from small cattle comes as well-being offering. They objected, is there not an elevation offering [from small cattle]⁸⁴? Anything which only comes from small cattle; this eliminates the elevation offering which even may come from large cattle. They objected, is there not reparation offering⁸⁵? Rebbi Abun bar Cahana said, *"from small cattle"*. this eliminates the reparation offering, which only comes from rams.

[Rebbi Abun objected,][84] everywhere you are saying that מִן is to include, but here you are saying that מִן is to exclude[86]? Rebbi Mana said, it excludes it, since it only comes from rams. They objected, is there not written,[87] *and if his sacrifice be from small cattle, from sheep or goats, as elevation offering*; then excess *Pesaḥ* should become elevation offering? Rebbi Abun said, one changes something to be eaten into something to be eaten, [but one does not change something to be eaten into something not to be eaten.][88] Rebbi Yose ben Rebbi Abun said, one changes simple *sancta* into simple *sancta*, but one does not change simple *sancta* into most holy sacrifices[89]. Rebbi Joḥanan said, about what Rebbi Ḥanina enlightened, that you are saying, *Pesaḥ* is changed[82] into a well-being offering only if he slaughtered it for the purpose of well-being offering; but I am saying, even for the purpose of an elevation offering. Rebbi [Il]la said, the reason of Rebbi Joḥanan: *And if his sacrifice be from small cattle as meal well-being offering*[83]; anything to be consumed as *sanctum* is a well-being offering. Does it change with respect to disqualifying thoughts[90]? How is this? If he slaughtered it for the purpose of an elevation offering in order to pour its blood the next day[91]. In any case, it is disqualified. If you are saying that it changes with respect to disqualifying thoughts, it is *piggul*[92]. If you are saying that it does not change with respect to disqualifying thoughts, it is disqualified.

80 This paragraph also appears in *Šeqalim* 2:4 (ש). The readings of the *editio princeps* of the Babli with Yerushalmi *Šeqalim* are noted (ש); those of interest of the very shortened Munich ms. of the Babli as (M). The version of *Šeqalim* in the Babli is characterized by much babylonized spelling; there is an addition in Babylonian Aramaic directly taken from the parallel in the Babli *Zevahim* 8b-9a.

81 He is the father of Samuel (Babli *Zevahim* 8b), head of the school of Nahardea in the generation of transition from Tannaim to Amoraim. He reports a Babylonian tradition.

82 An offering in the Temple declared as *Pesaḥ* on any day other than the 14th of Nisan automatically is for well-being. Therefore animals dedicated as *Pesaḥ* but not needed on the 14th, at nightfall of the 15th automatically become dedicated well-being offerings.

83 *Lev.* 3:6.

84 Scribe's text, incorrectly deleted by corrector and missing in printed editions but confiirmed by ש. K is lacunary at this point.

85 Which never comes from large cattle.

86 The text is difficult since it is standard rabbinic interpretation to consider prefix *mem* or מִן as privative, excluding certain

categories (cf. *Šabbat* 7 Note 26, *Ševuot* 1:2 Note 75, *Bava Mesia'* 4:8 Note 122, *Nazir* 5:4 Note 105). Also in the next sentence, R. Mana gives the interpretation that here מִן is privative. On the other hand, the testimony of K, M, and the scribe's text of ש do not permit emendation. It seems that here "every where" is derogatory, meaning Babylonian. The sequence of arguments leads to a contradiction. Abba bar Abba treats מִן as inclusive, R. Abun bar Cahana as exclusive. R. Mana explains that מִן always is partitive; automatic switch to well-being offerings is possible only for sacrifices that totally correspond to the declaration צאן, i. e., both sheep and goats, male and female.

87 *Lev.* 1:10.

88 Addition by the corrector from ש, confirmed by K.

89 The latter category includes both elevation and reparation sacrifices.

90 If the animal dedicated as *Pesaḥ* is used against the rules for something other than a well-being offering, do the rules of the other kind apply or is it disqualified and no rules of intent apply.

91 This being forbidden certainly disqualifies.

92 If the animal still is a sacrifice, now under the rules of elevation sacrifices, the intention to perform any required action out of its prescribed time-frame generates *piggul*, which is a deadly sin causing extirpation.

92 If the animal is disqualified and not under the rule of any kind of sacrifice, the illegitimate intent is inconsequential.

(32a line 55)   לִשְׁמוֹ וְשֶׁלֹּא לִשְׁמוֹ בִּשְׁאָר יְמוֹת הַשָּׁנָה. רְבִּי בּוּן בַּר חִיָּיה בְּשֵׁם שְׁמוּאֵל בַּר אַבָּא. מִכֵּיוָן שֶׁאֵין לוֹ שֵׁם נַעֲשָׂה כְּשׁוֹחֲטוֹ לִשְׁמוֹ וְשֶׁלֹּא לִשְׁמוֹ בִּשְׁתִיקָה וְהוּא כָשֵׁר. אָמְרוּ לֵיהּ. וְאִין כֵּינִי. אֲפִילוּ שְׁחָטוֹ לִשְׁמוֹ לִזְרוֹק דָּמוֹ שֶׁלֹּא לִשְׁמוֹ וְיֵיעָשֶׂה מִשָּׁעָה רִאשׁוֹנָה כְּשׁוֹחֲטוֹ לִשְׁמוֹ וְשֶׁלֹּא לִשְׁמוֹ בִּשְׁתִיקָה וִיהֵא כָשֵׁר. אָמַר רְבִּי אַבָּא מָרִי. מָאן אָמַר בִּשְׁתִיקָה כָּשֵׁר. אוֹ נֹאמַר. בִּשְׁתִיקָה פָּסוּל.

1 בשאר | ש לשאר   ר׳ בון בר חייה | ש ר׳ ביבין בשם ר׳ חייא M ר׳ ביבין ב״ר ר׳ חייא אבא K | אבה   2 שאין לו שם | ש שחלשו והוא | ש יהא אמ׳ ליה. ואין כיני | ש אם כן הוא ואין | K ואן   3 לזרוק | ש ונזרק וייעשה | K ש יעשה ש נעשה ש ראשונה | ש הראשונה   4 בשתיקה ויהא כשר | K ויהא פסיל | ש יהא מרי | ש מר אחוה דר׳ יוסי   מאן אמ׳ | ש מה נא׳ K מן אמר

[93]For its purpose and not for its purpose on the other days of the year[94]? Rebbi Abun bar Ḥiyya in the name of Samuel bar Abba: Since it is left without a name it is as if from the start he slaughtered for its purpose and not for its purpose in silence and is qualified[95]. They said to him. if it is so, even if he slaughtered for its purpose to pour the blood not for its purpose it should be treated as if from the start he slaughtered for its purpose and not for its purpose in silence and be qualified[96]. Rebbi Abba Mari said, who says that in silence it is qualified[97]? Or may we say, in silence it is disqualified?

93 This paragraph also has a parallel in *Šeqalim*.

94 The slaughterer has intent both for *Pesaḥ* and for well-being offering. Since the *Pesaḥ* then is a well-being offering, it should not make any difference.

95 Since now *Pesaḥ* and well-being offering mean the same, there is no contradiction. But since the names are different, it may be treated as if it was slaughtered for "what may apply". It is presumed that slaughtering a simple sacrifice without spelling out the category is qualified.

96 Since two different designations were used, the presumption should be that this is disqualified, as given in K.

97 The premise of Samuel bar Abba is unproven. The question remains unanswered.

משנה ג: שְׁחָטוֹ שֶׁלֹּא לְאוֹכְלָיו וְשֶׁלֹּא לִמְחוּיָו, לָעֲרֵלִים וְלַטְּמֵאִים פָּסוּל. לְאוֹכְלָיו וְשֶׁלֹּא (fol. 31c) לְאוֹכְלָיו לִמְנוּיָיו וְשֶׁלֹּא לִמְנוּיָיו לַמּוּלִים וְלָעֲרֵלִים לַטְּמֵאִים וְלַטְּהוֹרִים כָּשֵׁר. שְׁחָטוֹ קוֹדֶם לַחֲצוֹת פָּסוּל שֶׁנֶּאֱמַר בּוֹ בֵּין הָעַרְבָּיִם. קוֹדֶם לַתָּמִיד כָּשֵׁר. וּבִלְבַד שֶׁיְּהֵא אֶחָד מְמָרֵס בְּדָמוֹ עַד שֶׁיִּזָּרֵק דַּם הַתָּמִיד. וְאִם נִזְרַק כָּשֵׁר:

Mishnah 3: If he slaughtered it for those who cannot not eat it[98], for those who did not subscribe to it[99], for the uncircumcised,[100] or for the impure[101], it is disqualified[102]. For those who eat it and those who will not eat it, for those who subscribed to it and those who did not subscribe to it, for the circumcised and the uncircumcised, or for the pure and the impure, it is qualified[103]. If one slaughtered it before noon it is disqualified since it was said about it: *between the evenings*[104]. If one slaughtered it before the daily evening sacrifice it is qualified, on condition that somebody stir the blood until after the blood of the daily evening sacrifice was poured;[105] but if the blood was poured it is qualified[106].

98 For example a sick person who will not be able to eat a full olive-sized piece of meat.

99 The *Pesaḥ* may be eaten only by people who beforehand formed a group to this purpose, *Ex.* 12:4.

100 He is forbidden to participate even if he is a hemophiliac who may not be circumcised, *Ex.* 12:48.

101 If he will be impure in the evening, such as a person impure in the impurity of the dead who is impure for seven days. For an impure person eating *sancta* is a deadly sin, *Lev.* 7:21.

102 The meat of a simple sacrifice must be eaten; it may not be slaughtered in the

absence of people who would consume it.

103 Since people may decide to join the group until the blood is poured on the walls of the altar, which is after slaughtering, the slaughter is qualified as long as there is at least one person for whom it is validly slaughtered.

104 See Halakhah 1.

105 Since any sacrifice may be slaughtered by a lay person and the sacral activities only

start with the reception of the blood in a sacral vessel by a Cohen, the status of a *Pesaḥ* slaughtered before the daily sacrifice, whose blood was stirred to prevent jellying and which then was poured on the walls of the altar after the daily sacrifice, is identical with one which was slaughtered after the daily sacrifice.

106 Even if the pouring was done before the daily sacrifice. Cf. Note 20.

(32a line 60) **הלכה ג**: מְנַיִין שֶׁהוּא צָרִיךְ לְשׁוֹחֲטוֹ לְאוֹכְלָיו. רִבִּי יוֹחָנָן בְּשֵׁם רִבִּי יִשְׁמָעֵאל. אִישׁ לְפִי אָכְלוֹ תָכֹסּוּ. אָמַר רִבִּי יֹאשִׁיָּה. לְשׁוֹן סוּרְסִי הוּא זֶה. כְּאָדָם שֶׁהוּא אוֹמֵר לַחֲבֵירוֹ. כּוֹס לִי אֶת הַטָּלֶה הַזֶּה.

1 לאוכליו | K לאוכלו   2 תבסו | K לפי איכליו תכוסו

Halakhah 3: From where that he needs to slaughter for those who will eat it? Rebbi Johanan in the name of Rebbi Ismael: *For each man according to his eating you shall cut*[107]. Rebbi Josia said, it is a Syriac expresssion, as if a person say to his neighbor, slaughter for me this lamb.

107 Ex. 12:4. This translation reads the *hapax* תָכֹסּוּ with Ibn Ezra as derived from a root כסס "to cut into pieces", as in Accadic. R. Josia reads it as imperative of Syriac נכס "to slaughter". *Mekhilta dR. Ismael Bo*

Parašah 3, end. Differetly Babli, 61a, 78b.

K reads: *For each man according to his eating*, one has to slaughter according to its eaters.

(32a line 63) כֵּיצַד שֶׁלֹּא לְאוֹכְלָיו. שְׁחָטוֹ לְשֵׁם חוֹלֶה לְשֵׁם זָקֵן שֶׁאֵינָן יְכוֹלִין לוֹכַל כְּזַיִת. כֵּיצַד שֶׁלֹּא לִמְנוּיָיו. שְׁחָטוֹ לְשֵׁם חֲבוּרָה אַחֶרֶת. הָדָא אָמְרָה. שֶׁהַקָּטָן יֵשׁ לוֹ מִינְיָין לִפָסוּל. הָדָא אָמְרָה. הָיָה נָתוּן בְּדֶרֶךְ רְחוֹקָה וּשְׁחָטוֹ לִשְׁמוֹ פָּסוּל. הָדָא אָמְרָה. הָדָא מְסַייְעָא לִדְרוֹמַיי. דִּדְרוֹמַיי אָמְרִין. אֵימוֹרִין שֶׁאֲבָדוּ מְחַשֵּׁב לָהֶן כְּמִי שֶׁהֵן קַייָמִין. הָדָא אָמְרָה. שְׁחָטוֹ שֶׁתֵּאָכֵל מִמֶּנּוּ חֲצִי חֲבוּרָתוֹ פָּסוּל. אָמַר רִבִּי חַגַּיי קוֹמֵי רִבִּי יוֹסֵה. תִּיפְתָּר שֶׁהָיוּ כּוּלָּן חוֹלִין. אָמַר לֵיהּ. נִיתְנֵי לְשֵׁם בְּנֵי חֲבוּרָה פְּסוּלִין. אָמַר לֵיהּ. בְּשֶׁהָיוּ שָׁם כְּשֵׁירִין וּשְׁחָטוֹ לְשֵׁם פְּסוּלִין.

1 לשם זקן | K ולשם זקן כזהת | K ממנו כזהת   4 אימורין | K אמורין   5 כולן חולין | K כולם חולים   6 פסולין | K פסולה

אָמַר רִבִּי אֶלְעָזָר. מַתְנִיתָה בְּשֶׁשְּׁחָטוֹ לְאוֹכְלָיו וְנִתְכַּפֵּר בּוֹ לְאוֹכְלָיו וְשֶׁלֹּא לְאוֹכְלָיו. אֲבָל אִם שְׁחָטוֹ מִשָּׁעָה הָרִאשׁוֹנָה בּוֹ לְאוֹכְלָיו וְשֶׁלֹּא לְאוֹכְלָיו פָּסוּל.

1 אלעזר | K לעזר ונתכפר | K וניתכפר   2 ונתכפר | K וניתכפר

"How is 'those who cannot eat it'? If he slaughtered it in the name of a sick person, in the name of an old person, who cannot eat the volume of an olive. How about 'those who did not subscribe to it'? If he slaughtered it in the name of a different group.[108]" This implies that a baby can be counted to disqualify[109]. This implies that if one was on a distant trip[110] and he slaughtered it in this person's name, it is disqualified. This implies that it supports the Southerners. since the Southerners are saying, one thinks about parts which were lost as if they were in existence[111]. This implies that if one slaughtered so that half of the group should eat, it is disqualified[112]. Rebbi Haggai said before Rebbi Yose, explain it that all of them were sick[113]. He told him, then one should have stated, "in the name of disqualified members of the group." He said to him, if there were qualified people, but he slaughtered in the name of the disqualified[114].

Rebbi Eleazar said, the Mishnah if he slaughtered it for those who eat it, but it was covered by those who eat it and those who cannot eat it. But it is disqualified if from the start he slaughtered it so that it should be covered by those who eat it and those who cannot eat it[115].

108 Tosephta 4:2; Babli 61a.
109 Since the baby cannot eat solid food. In *Mekhilta dR. Ismael Ba, Parašah* 3, the baby is mentioned instead of the old person.
110 Who cannot possibly be near the central sanctuary to participate in the *Pesaḥ*; *Num.* 9:9.
111 *Me'ilah* 7a.

It has been stated before that the validity of a sacrifice depends on the intent of the slaughterer. There is a general rule, that intent regarding less than the volume of an olive is disregarded (Note 125; Babli *Zevaḥim* 29b,31a). But if the intent was for at least the volume of an olive, but in fact it was impossible that it be the volume of an olive, as in the case of the baby or the sick person, it is intent that counts and not the fact. Similarly, if the intent was that parts should be burned out of time, it makes the sacrifice *piggul* even if the parts are lost and it is physically impossible to burn them out of time.

112 Part of the group were sick and could not eat the volume of an olive. If the *Pesaḥ* was slaughtered for those who can eat and those who cannot, it is qualified as stated in the Mishnah. But if it was slaughtered for all of them as being able to eat the volume of an olive, the slaughter was not "for those who eat it and those who will not eat it" and therefore those who cannot eat it will make it disqualified.
113 Certainly as a group they are able to consume meat in the volume of an olive.
114 Then certainly the sacrifice is invalid.

115 It seems that R. Eleazar interprets the Mishnah that the sacrifice is qualified if the slaughterer intended it for the entire group, without inquiring whether all members of the group were entitled to eat or able to consume a minimum. If then it turned out that some members were barred or unable to participate, there was no false intent and the sacrifice is qualified. But if from the start there was explicit intent to include incapable or disqualified persons, the intent was disqualifying (S. Liebermann).

(32a line 73) רִבִּי שִׂמְלָאי אֲתָא גַּבֵּי רִבִּי יוֹנָתָן. אֲמַר לֵיהּ. אַלְפִין אֲגָדָה. אֲמַר לֵיהּ. מְסוֹרֶת בְּיָדִי מֵאֲבוֹתַיי שֶׁלֹּא לְלַמֵּד אֲגָדָה לֹא לְבַבְלִי וְלֹא לִדְרוֹמִי. שֶׁהֵן גַּסֵּי רוּחַ וּמְעוּטֵי תוֹרָה. וְאַתְּ נְהַרְדְּעָאי וְדָר בְּדָרוֹם. אֲמַר לֵיהּ. אֱמוֹר לִי הָדָא מִילְתָא. מַה בֵּין לִשְׁמוֹ וְשֶׁלֹּא לִשְׁמוֹ. מַה בֵּין לְאוֹכְלָיו וְשֶׁלֹּא לְאוֹכְלָיו. אֲמַר לֵיהּ. לִשְׁמוֹ וְשֶׁלֹּא לִשְׁמוֹ פְּסוּלוֹ מִגּוּפוֹ. לְאוֹכְלָיו וְשֶׁלֹּא לְאוֹכְלָיו פְּסוּלוֹ מֵאֲחֵרִים. לִשְׁמוֹ וְשֶׁלֹּא לִשְׁמוֹ אֵין אַתְּ יָכוֹל לָבוּר פְּסוּלוֹ מִתּוֹךְ הֲכָשֵׁירוֹ. לְאוֹכְלָיו וְשֶׁלֹּא לְאוֹכְלָיו אַתְּ יָכוֹל לָבוּר פְּסוּלוֹ מִתּוֹךְ הֲכָשֵׁירוֹ. לִשְׁמוֹ וְשֶׁלֹּא לִשְׁמוֹ נוֹהֵג בְּכָל־הַקֳּדָשִׁים. לְאוֹכְלָיו וְשֶׁלֹּא לְאוֹכְלָיו אֵינוֹ נוֹהֵג אֶלָּא בַפֶּסַח.

1 שמלאי K שמליי | אתא K אתה | גבי K לגבי | אלפין K אלפי | 2 לבבלי K לבבליים | לדרומי K [ולד]רומיים | 3 נהרדעאי K נהרדעי | בדרום K בדרום ועוד קטן | הדא K הדה | מילתא K מילתה | מה K ומה | 5 מאחרים K [מא]חרי | את K אין את הקדשים K הקדשין | 6 את C

Rebbi Simlai came to Rebbi Jonathan[116]. He said to him, teach me homiletics. He answered him, I have a tradition from my forefathers not to teach homiletics either to a Babylonian or to a Southerner, since they are gross in spirit and have little learning. And you are from Nahardea and live in the South. He said to him, tell me this one thing, what is the difference between "for its purpose and not for its purpose" and "for those who eat it and those who cannot eat it"[117]? He answered him, "for its purpose and not for its purpose", the disqualification is intrinsic. "For those who eat it and those who cannot eat it", the disqualification is of others. "For its purpose and not for its purpose", you cannot pick out the disqualified from the qualified. ["For those who eat it and those who cannot eat it", you can pick out the disqualified from the qualified.][118a] "For its purpose and not for its purpose", applies to all sacrifices[118]; "for those who eat it and those who cannot eat it" applies only to the *Pesah*.

116 Babli 62b. R. Simlai became famous as a preacher. K and the Medieval sources add that he was too young to be taught these matters.

117 Why is the former disqualified and the latter qualified.

118 Mishnah *Zevahlm* 1:1: "All sacrifices, except *Pesah* and purification offerings,

which were slaughtered not for their purpose are qualified but do not relieve their owners from their obligations."

118* The corrector's addition is justified by K, which reads "you can't" instead of "you can.

(32b line 6) אָמַר רִבִּי יוֹסֵה. מִן הָדָא דְרִבִּי לְעָזָר אַתְּ שְׁמַע אִתְּ תַּרְתֵּיי. דָּמַר רִבִּי לְעָזָר. מַתְנִיתָה בְּשֶׁשְּׁחָטוֹ לְאוֹכְלָיו וְנִתְכַּפֶּר בּוֹ לְאוֹכְלָיו וְשֶׁלֹּא לְאוֹכְלָיו. אֲבָל אִם שָׁחַט מִשָּׁעָה הָרִאשׁוֹנָה וְנִתְכַּפֶּר בּוֹ לְאוֹכְלָיו וְשֶׁלֹּא לְאוֹכְלָיו פָּסוּל. הֲרֵי פְסוּלוֹ מֵחֲמַת אֲחֵרִים וְאַתְּ יָכוֹל לָבוּר פְּסוּלוֹ מִתּוֹךְ הֶכְשֵׁירוֹ. וְאַתְּ אָמַר הָכֵין. אֶלָּא כֵינִי. לִשְׁמוֹ וְשֶׁלֹּא לִשְׁמוֹ נוֹהֵג בְּכָל־הַקֳּדָשִׁים. לְאוֹכְלָיו וְשֶׁלֹּא לְאוֹכְלָיו אֵינוֹ נוֹהֵג אֶלָּא בַפֶּסַח. אָמַר רִבִּי אָבִין. אִית לָךְ חוֹרֵי. לִשְׁמוֹ וְשֶׁלֹּא לִשְׁמוֹ נוֹהֵג בְּכָל־הָעֲבוֹדוֹת. לְאוֹכְלָיו וְשֶׁלֹּא לְאוֹכְלָיו אֵינוֹ נוֹהֵג אֶלָּא בִשְׁחִיטָה.

1 הדא K | הדה   4 ואת אמר K | ותמר   הקדשים K | הקדשין   5 אבין K | אבון

Rebbi Yose said, from that of Rebbi Eleazar one may deduce two [conclusions]. Since Rebbi Eleazar said, the Mishnah if he slaughtered it for those who eat it, but it was covered by those who eat it and those who cannot eat it. But it is disqualified if from the start he slaughtered for those who eat it and it was covered by those who eat it and those who cannot eat it[115]. Then its disqualification is of others and you can pick out the disqualified from the qualified, and you are saying so? But it must be the following, "for its purpose and not for its purpose", applies to all sacrifices[118]; "for those who eat it and those who cannot eat it" applies only to the *Pesah*[119]. Rebbi Abin said, there are others. "For its purpose and not for its purpose", applies to all services[120]; "for those who eat it and those who cannot eat it" applies only to slaughtering.

119 Of all the arguments of R. Jonathan, only the last is valid.

120 Mishnah *Zevahim* 1:4: The sacrifice becomes disqualified [by wrong intent] in four cases: For slaughter, for reception of the blood, for carrying the blood to the altar, for pouring the blood.

(32b line 14) לְאוֹכְלָיו כְּזַיִתִין וְשֶׁלֹּא לְאוֹכְלָיו כְּזַיִתִין כָּשֵׁר. לְאוֹכְלָיו כְּזֵיתִין וְשֶׁלֹּא לְאוֹכְלָיו כַּחֲצִי זֵיתִין כָּל־שֶׁכֵּן כָּשֵׁר. לְאוֹכְלָיו כַּחֲצִי זֵיתִין וְשֶׁלֹּא לְאוֹכְלָיו כַּחֲצִי זֵיתִים מָה אָנֻן קַיָּימִין. אִם כְּשֶׁהָיְתָה הַמַּחֲשָׁבָה לַכּוֹשֶׁר תְּהֵא הַמַּחֲשָׁבָה לִפְסוּל. אִם אֵינָהּ הַמַּחֲשָׁבָה לִפְסוּל תְּהֵא הַמַּחֲשָׁבָה לַכּוֹשֶׁר. אָמַר רִבִּי יוֹסֵה. מַתְנִיתָהּ אָמְרָה שֶׁהַמַּחֲשָׁבָה לַכּוֹשֶׁר. דְּתַנִּינָן תַּמָּן. לוֹכַל כַּחֲצִי זַיִת וּלְהַקְטִיר כַּחֲצִי זַיִת כָּשֵׁר. שֶׁאֵין אֲכִילָה וְהַקְטָרָה מִצְטָרְפִין. שְׁחָטוֹ שֶׁנִּתְכַּפֵּר בּוֹ חֲצִי חֲבוּרָתוֹ. רִבִּי יוֹנָה פּוֹסֵל. נַעֲשָׂה כְּמַתְפִּיס כַּפָּרַת אֵילוּ לָאֵילוּ. מֵאַחַר שֶׁלֹּא נִתְכַּפֵּר לָאֵילוּ לֹא נִתְכַּפֵּר

לְאֵילוּ. רִבִּי יוֹסֵה אָמַר. כָּשֵׁר. בַּמַּחֲזוֹרָה תִּינְיָינָא חֲזַר בֵּיהּ רִבִּי יוֹסֵי. אָמַר לֵיהּ רִבִּי פִּינְחָס. לֹא
כֵן אִילְפָן רִבִּי. כָּשֵׁר. אָמַר לֵיהּ. הָא קָבִיעָה גַבָּךְ כְּמַסְמְרָא.

1 כזיתין K | כזיתים (3)   2 זיתין K | זיתים (2)   כשר K | כשיר   מה אנן | מהנן K | המחשבה K | מחשבה
(first and last)   לפסול K | לפסול   לכושר K | לכושר   4 לכושר K | לפסול   לוכל K | לאכל   5 שנתכפר K | שתתכפר   6
פוסל K | אמ' פסול   לאילו K | לאלו (2)   7 אילו K | לאלו   תינייאנא K | תנינה   יוסי K | יוסה   8 אילפן | K
אלפן

For those who eat it in volumes of an olive and those who cannot eat it in volumes of an olive, it is qualified[121]. For those who eat it in volumes of an olive and those who cannot eat it in volumes of half an olive, it is qualified *a fortiori*. For those who eat it in volumes of half an olive and those who cannot eat it in volumes of half an olive? Where do we hold? If intent was qualifying, intent is disqualifying[122]. If intent is not disqualifying then the intent should be qualifying.[123] Rebbi Yose said, a Mishnah implies that the intent in qualifying, as we have stated there[124]: "To eat half the volume of an olive and to burn half the volume of an olive is qualified since slaughter and burning do not combine[125]." If he slaughtered it that half of its group should be covered, Rebbi Jonah disqualifies. It is as grabbing the cover for these and those. Since these are not covered, neither are those covered[126]. Rebbi Yose said, it is qualified. During the second cycle[127], Rebbi Yose retracted. Rebbi Phineas said to him, did the rabbi not teach us, it is qualified. He told him, is this fixed for you by nails?

121 This is the normal case mentioned in the Mishnah.
122 If intent regarding consumption of less than the volume of an olive is counted as qualifying, then it also must be counted as disqualifying. In this case, the rule formulated by R. Eleazar applies as if the intent was for volumes of an olive.
123 If intent regarding consumption of less than the volume of an olive is disregarded, then the slaughter was made without special condition, "for whom it may apply", and is qualified.
124 Mishnah *Zevahim* 2:5.
125 The sacrifice was slaughtered with the intent that half the volume of an olive should be eaten out of its allotted time and half the volume of an olive be burned on the altar out of its allotted time. Since it is stated that the sacrifice is qualified, it follows that any intent about half the volume of an olive is disregarded. Therefore in the preceding case the intent is disregarded and the sacrifice is qualified.
126 Since an entire group paid for the *Pesah*, they are its owners. If the intent was to eliminate part of the owners, the *Pesah* is slaughtered not for its owners and therefore disqualified.
127 When the entire material of the

Yerushalmi was reviewed a second time in the Academy of RR. Yose in Tiberias, he

(32b line 24) שְׁחָטוֹ קוֹדֶם לַחֲצוֹת פָּסוּל. [לְאַחַר חֲצוֹת] מִיָּד כָּשֵׁר. קוֹדֶם לַתָּמִיד כָּשֵׁר. וְתָנֵי כֵן. יָכוֹל אִם קָדַם פֶּסַח לְתָמִיד לֹא יֵאָחֵר הַתָּמִיד. תַּלְמוּד לוֹמַר תַּעֲשֶׂה. רִיבָה. אָמַר רִבִּי אָבוּן. מַתְנִיתָה אָמְרָה. פֶּסַח עַצְמוֹ כָשֵׁר. אִין תֵּימַר. פָּסוּל. כְּמִי שֶׁלֹּא קְדָמוֹ.

1 כשר K | כשיר   2 אבון K | בון

תַּמָּן אַתְּ אָמַר. דַּם תָּמִיד וְאֵיבָרָיו קוֹדְמִין לַפֶּסַח. וּפֶסַח לַקְּטוֹרֶת. וְהַקְּטוֹרֶת לְהַטָּבַת הַנֵּרוֹת. וָכָא אַתְּ אָמַר אָכֵן. אָמַר רִבִּי לָא. כָּאן בְּחַי וְכָאן בְּשָׁחוּט.

1 ואיבריו K | ואבריו והקטורת K | וקטורת   2 הנרות K | הנירות וכא K | והכה לא K | הילא כאן בחי | K כן בחיי וכאן | K וכן

"If one slaughtered it before noon it is disqualified," [after noontime] immediately it is qualified. "If one slaughtered it before the daily sacrifice it is qualified." It was stated thus[128]: One could think that if *Pesaḥ* preceded the daily sacrifice, the daily sacrifice could not be delayed. The verse says, *do*, adding. Rebbi Abun said, the Mishnah implies that the *Pesaḥ* itself is qualified. If you would say, it is disqualified, it would be as if it did not precede.

There[36], you are saying: "The blood of the daily sacrifice and its limbs precede the *Pesaḥ*, and the *Pesaḥ* the incense, and the incense the trimming of the lights.[37]" And here you are saying so? Rebbi La said, one if it is living, the other if it is slaughtered[129].

128 *Sifry zuta Pinḥas* 28(3). The question was whether slaughter of the *Pesaḥ* prohibits later slaughter of the daily sacrifice. The answer is that the wording of the verse *Num*. 28:4, וְאֵת הַכֶּבֶשׂ הַשֵּׁנִי תַּעֲשֶׂה בֵּין הָעַרְבָּיִם when it would have been possible to say simply וְאֵת הַכֶּבֶשׂ הַשֵּׁנִי בֵּין הָעַרְבָּיִם implies that it must be broughtr in any case.

129 The *baraita* requires that the *Pesaḥ* be brought after the limbs of the daily sacrifice are on the altar, but Mishnah 3 mentions only pouring of the blood, without mention of the limbs. If the *Pesaḥ* is still alive, one has to wait until the limbs have been disposed of; if it is slaughtered, one waits only for the pouring of the blood.

(fol. 31c) **משנה ד**: הַשּׁוֹחֵט אֶת הַפֶּסַח עַל הֶחָמֵץ עוֹבֵר בְּלֹא תַעֲשֶׂה. רִבִּי יְהוּדָה אוֹמֵר אַף הַתָּמִיד. רִבִּי שִׁמְעוֹן אוֹמֵר אַף הַפֶּסַח בְּאַרְבָּעָה עָשָׂר לִשְׁמוֹ חַיָּב וְשֶׁלֹּא לִשְׁמוֹ פָּטוּר. וּשְׁאָר

כָּל־הַזְּבָחִין בֵּין לִשְׁמָן וּבֵין שֶׁלֹּא לִשְׁמָן פָּטוּר. וּבַמּוֹעֵד לִשְׁמוֹ פָּטוּר וְשֶׁלֹּא לִשְׁמוֹ חַיָּב. וּשְׁאָר כָּל־הַזְּבָחִין בֵּין לִשְׁמָן וּבֵין שֶׁלֹּא לִשְׁמָן חַיָּב חוּץ מִן הַחַטָּאת שֶׁשְּׁחָטָהּ שֶׁלֹּא לִשְׁמָהּ׃

Mishnah 4: One who slaughters the *Pesaḥ* on leavened matter transgresses a prohibition[130]; Rebbi Jehudah says, also the daily sacrifice[131]. Rebbi Simeon says, the *Pesaḥ* on the Fourteenth, if for its purpose, he is liable, not for its purpose he is not liable[132]. All other sacrifices, whether for their purposes or not for their purposes, he is not liable[133]. On the holiday, for its purpose he is not liable, not for its purpose he is liable[134]; for all other sacrifices, whether for their purposes or not for their purposes, he is liable except for the purification offering which he slaughtered not for its purpose[135].

130 *Ex.* 23:18; 34:25: *Do not sacrifice on leavened matter the blood of My sacrifice; the sacrifice of the Pesaḥ pilgrimage.* "On leavened matter" means that he has leavened matter in his possession.

131 Since this is an elevation offering which is completely burned, it is *My sacrifice*.

132 A disqualified sacrifice is no sacrifice at all and therefore not a subject of the prohibition.

133 Since the verse refers only to the *Pesaḥ*.

134 R. Simeon reads the verse as referring not only to the 14th of Nisan but also to the entire Holiday of Unleavened Bread, Nisan 15-21. Since the *Pesaḥ* slaughtered for its purpose on any day other than the 14th is disqualified, it does not count. But not for its purpose it is a qualified well-being sacrifice.

135 Which is disqualified (Mishna *Zevahim* 1:1).

(32b line 30) **הלכה ד**: מְנַיִין לַשּׁוֹחֵט אֶת הַפֶּסַח עַל הֶחָמֵץ שֶׁהוּא עוֹבֵר בְּלֹא תַעֲשֶׂה. תַּלְמוּד לוֹמַר לֹא־תִשְׁחַט עַל־חָמֵץ דַּם־זִבְחִי. אֵין לִי אֶלָּא הַשּׁוֹחֵט. הַזּוֹרֵק מְנַיִין. תַּלְמוּד לוֹמַר לֹא עַל־חָמֵץ דַּם. אָמַר רִבִּי שְׁמוּאֵל בַּר רַב יִצְחָק. מִמַּה שֶׁהוּא מִתְחַיֵּיב עַל הַזְּרִיקָה הָדָא אֲמָרָה. פֶּסַח עַצְמוֹ כָּשֵׁר. אָמַר רִבִּי יוֹסֵה. תִּיפְתַּר שֶׁנִּתְמַנֶּה לוֹ חָמֵץ בֵּין שְׁחִיטָה לִזְרִיקָה. אוֹ שֶׁהָיָה זֶה שׁוֹחֵט וְזֶה זוֹרֵק׃

2 השוחט K ‖ שוחט K ‖ הזורק K ‖ זור]ק[K ‖ לא K ‖ ולא 3 רב K ‖ בב הדא K הדה

Halakhah 4: From where that one who slaughters the *Pesaḥ* on leavened matter transgresses a prohibition? The verse says[130], *do not slaughter on leavened matter the blood of My sacrifice.* I have not only the slaughterer, from where the one who pours the blood? The verse says, *not on leavened matter the blood.* Rebbi Samuel bar Rav Isaac said, since he becomes guilty for pouring, this implies that the *Pesaḥ* be qualified[132,136]. Rebbi Yose said, explain it that leavened matter came to him between slaughter and pouring or that one person was slaughtering and another pouring[137].

136 Tosephta 4:3.
137 In both cases the slaughter was correct and only the pouring incorrect. One still has to assume that the *Pesaḥ* slaughtered on leavened matter even in the afternoon of the 14th is disqualified.

(32b line 35) תַּנֵּי חִזְקִיָּה. לֹא־תִשְׁחַט עַל־חָמֵץ דַּם־זִבְחִי. הַתּוֹרָה קָרָאת אוֹתוֹ זֶבְחִי. אָמַר רַבִּי מָנָא. אִילוּלֵי דְתַנִּיתָהּ חִזְקִיָּה מָצִינוּ דָבָר פָּסוּל וְחַיָּבִין עָלָיו חַטָּאת. הַמְחַמֵּץ אֶת הַפְּסוּלָה. אִית תַּנָּיֵי תַנֵּי. חַיָּיב. אִית תַּנָּיֵי תַנֵּי. פָּטוּר. אָמַר רַב חִסְדָּא. מָאן דְּאָמַר. חַיָּיב. בְּשֶׁנִּפְסְלָה מַחְמַת חִימּוּצָהּ. מָאן דְּאָמַר. פָּטוּר. בְּשֶׁלֹּא נִפְסְלָה מַחְמַת חִימּוּצָהּ.

2 דתניתה J | דתנתה 5 מאן דאמ' | K מן דמר 4 מאן דאמ' | K ומן דמר

הַקְטֵיר אֵימוּרִין עַל חָמֵץ. אִית תַּנָּיֵי תַנֵּי. חַיָּיב. אִית תַּנָּיֵי תַנֵּי. פָּטוּר. מָאן דְּאָמַר. חַיָּיב. דָּם מִכָּל־מָקוֹם. מָאן דְּאָמַר. פָּטוּר. זֶבַח. מַה זְּבִיחָה מְיוּחֶדֶת שֶׁהִיא מְעַכֶּבֶת אֶת הַכַּפָּרָה. יָצְאוּ הָקְטֵיר אֵימוּרִין שֶׁאֵינָן מְעַכְּבִין אֶת הַכַּפָּרָה.

1 אימורין K | אמורין   מאן דאמ' | K מן דמר   2 מאן דאמ' | K מן דמר   3 אימורין K | אמורין

מָלַק עוֹף עַל חָמֵץ. אִית תַּנָּיֵי תַנֵּי. חַיָּיב. אִית תַּנָּיֵי תַנֵּי. פָּטוּר. מָאן דְּאָמַר. חַיָּיב. דָּם מִכָּל־מָקוֹם. מָאן דְּאָמַר. פָּטוּר. זֶבַח. יָצָא עוֹף שֶׁאֵינוֹ זֶבַח. רִבִּי יַעֲקֹב בַּר זַבְדִּי בְּעָא קוֹמֵי רִבִּי יוֹסֵה. מָאן דְּאָמַר. חַיָּיב. נִיחָא. כְּמָה דְתֵימַר לְעִנְיָין פָּטוּר. מָאן דְּאָמַר. פָּטוּר. מַה טַּעַם. אָמַר לֵיהּ. לְמֵידִין עוֹנֶשׁ מֵעוֹנֶשׁ וְאֵין לְמֵידִין עוֹנֶשׁ מִפָּטוּר.

1 מאן דאמ' | K מן דמר   2 מאן דאמ' | K מן דמר   עוף K דם בעא K בעה   3 מאן דאמ' | K מן דמר ניחא K ניחה   דתימר K דתמר   לעניין K לעיניין

Ḥizqiah stated: *Do not slaughter on leavened matter the blood of My sacrifice*[130], the Torah called it "My sacrifice"[138]. Rebbi Mana said, if Ḥizqiah had not stated this, do we find anything disqualified because of which one is liable for a purification sacrifice[139]? If somebody leavens the disqualified[140]. There are Tannaim who state, he is liable; there are Tannaim who state, he is not liable. Rav Ḥisda said, he who says liable, if it became disqualified because of its leavening[241]; he who says not liable, if it did not become disqualified because of its leavening.

The burning of the parts on leavening[142]. There are Tannaim who state, he is liable; there are Tannaim who state, he is not liable. He who says liable, *blood* anywhere. He who says not liable, *sacrifice*. Since slaughtering for sacrifice is particular in that it is indispensable for atonement, this excludes burning of the parts, which is not indispensable for atonement.

If one broke a bird's neck on leavening[143]. There are Tannaim who state, he is liable; there are Tannaim who state, he is not liable. He who says liable, *blood* anywhere. He who says not liable, *sacrifice*. This excludes the bird which is not slaughtered as sacrifice[144]. Rebbi Jacob bar Zavdi asked before Rebbi Yose. Him who said "liable" one understands as you are saying for freeing from liability[144a]. What is the reason of him who frees from liability? He said to him, one may infer punishment from punishment but one may not infer punishment from exemption.

138 This implies that it is a valid sacrifice. Cf. *Mekhilta dR. Simeon ben Yohai* p. 219, line 1.

139 Without Hizqiah"s statement we would have declared the sacrifice disqualified since in fact we find that a person who sacrifices outside the official sanctuary is liable (i. e., for extirpation or a purification sacrifice) both for the slaughter and for burning on an altar even though the slaughter disqualifies (Mishnah *Zevahim* 13:1).

140 This refers to flour offerings the entire year. They are required to be unleavened, *Lev.* 2:11.

141 According to the Babli, even if it already was disqualified because of leavening, *Šabbat* 111a, top line. *Menahot* 57a.

142 On the afternoon of the 14th of Nisan. Differently Babli 63b-64a.

143 This must refer to the middle days of the holiday following R. Simeon, since it was stated earlier that on the 14th one is liable only for the *Pesaḥ* and possibly the daily sacrifice.

144 זֶבַח is a *sanctum*, parts of which are consumed by lay people. A bird sacrifice, not killed by *šeḥitah*, if eaten at all is reserved for priests.

144a Scribe's text deleted by corrector, therefore iy is not found in the printed texts. But it is confirmed by K and necessary to understand R. Yose's response. R. Jacob bar Zavdi argues that since bird sacrifices are treated as equal to animal sacrifices on the 14th, there is no liability if the owner still has leavened matter while bringing his offering, they also should be treated like animal sacrifices on the holiday and there should be liability.

(32b line 48) רַבָּנָן דְּקַיְסָרִין בְּעַיָין. יָכוֹל הַמְקַבֵּל וְהַמְהַלֵּךְ עַל חָמֵץ יְהֵא חַיָּיב. תַּלְמוּד לוֹמַר זֶבַח. מַה זְּבִיחָה מְיוּחֶדֶת שֶׁחַיָּיבִין עָלֶיהָ בַחוּץ. יָצָא הַמְקַבֵּל וְהַמְהַלֵּךְ עַל חָמֵץ שֶׁאֵין חַיָּיבִין עֲלֵיהֶן בַּחוּץ. יָכוֹל הַמַּקְטִיר אֵימוֹרִין עַל חָמֵץ יְהֵא חַיָּיב. תַּלְמוּד לוֹמַר זְרִיקָה מְיוּחֶדֶת שֶׁהִיא מְעַכֶּבֶת אֶת הַכַּפָּרָה. יָצְאוּ הֶקְטֵר אֵימוֹרִין שֶׁאֵינָן מְעַכְּבִין אֶת הַכַּפָּרָה. רִבִּי יַעֲקֹב

בַּר זַבְדִּי בְּעָא קוֹמֵי רִבִּי יוֹסֵה. עַד דְּאַתְּ דַּיָּין לָהּ לִפְטוֹר. דּוּנָהּ לְחִיּוּב. דּוֹנָה לְחִיּוּב. יָכוֹל הַמְקַבֵּל וְהַמְהַלֵּךְ עַל חָמֵץ יְהֵא פָטוּר. תַּלְמוּד לוֹמַר זֶבַח. מַה זְּבִיחָה מְיוּחֶדֶת שֶׁחַיָּיבִין עָלֶיהָ בַחוּץ. אַף אֲנִי אַרְבֶּה הֶקְטֵר אֵימוּרִין שֶׁחַיָּיבִין עֲלֵיהֶן בַּחוּץ. יָכוֹל הַמַּקְטִיר אֵימוּרִין עַל חָמֵץ יְהֵא פָטוּר. תַּלְמוּד לוֹמַר וְכִפֶּר. מַה זְּרִיקָה מְיוּחֶדֶת שֶׁהִיא מְעַכֶּבֶת אֶת הַכַּפָּרָה. אַף אֲנִי אַרְבֶּה הַמְקַבֵּל וְהַמְהַלֵּךְ שֶׁהֵן מְעַכְּבִין אֶת הַכַּפָּרָה. אָמַר לֵיהּ. דָּבָר שָׁוֶה בִשְׁנֵיהֶן מְלַמֵּד. דָּבָר שֶׁאֵינוֹ שָׁוֶה בִשְׁנֵיהֶן אֵינוֹ מְלַמֵּד. זֶבַח. מַה זְּבִיחָה מְיוּחֶדֶת שֶׁהִיא מְעַכֶּבֶת אֶת הַכַּפָּרָה וְחַיָּיבִין עָלֶיהָ בַחוּץ. יָצָא הַמְקַבֵּל וְהַמְהַלֵּךְ עַל חָמֵץ שֶׁאֵין חַיָּיבִין עֲלֵיהֶן בַּחוּץ. יָצְאוּ הֶקְטֵר אֵימוּרִין שֶׁאֵינָן מְעַכְּבוֹת אֶת הַכַּפָּרָה.

1 חמץ K | החמץ יהא חייב K | יהא]ון] חייבין 2 יצא K | יצאו 3 אימורין K | אמורין חמץ K | החמץ 4 אימורין K | אמורין שאינן K | שאין 5 בעא K | בעה לפטור K | לעיניין פטור דונה K | דוניה 6 חמץ K | החמץ 7 הקטר K | הקטיר אימורין K | אמורין (2) שחייבין K | שיהוא חנ]ייבין] 8 אני - K | שהן K | שיהוא 9 בשניהן K | בשניהם (2) 10 וחייבין K | חייבין 11 על חמץ K | - הקטר K | הקטיר אימורין K | אמורין שאינן K | שאין מעכבות K | מעכבין

The rabbis of Caesarea asked: I could think that the one who receives or carries [the blood][145] on leavened matter be liable. The verse says, *sacrifice*. Since slaughtering for sacrifice is particular in that one is liable for it outside [the Sanctuary], this excludes the one who receives or carries on leavened matter for which one is not liable outside[146]. I could think that one who burns parts on leavened matter be liable. The verse says, *and he atones*[147]. Since pouring is particular in that it is indispensable for atonement, this excludes burning of the parts, which is not indispensable for atonement. Rebbi Jacob bar Zavdi asked before Rebbi Yose. Instead of arguing for absence of liability, argue for liability. I could think that the one who receives or carries [the blood][148] on leavened matter not be liable. The verse says, *sacrifice*. Since slaughtering for sacrifice is particular in that for it one is liable outside [the Sanctuary], I also am adding burning of the parts for which one is liable outside. I could think that one who burns parts on leavened matter[149] not be liable. The verse says, *and he atones*. Since pouring is particular in that it is indispensable for atonement, I also am adding the one who receives or carries who is indispensable for atonement[150]. He said to him, anything equal in both respects instructs; anything not equal in both respects does not instruct. *Sacrifice*. Since slaughtering for sacrifice is particular in that it is indispensable for atonement and for it one is liable outside [the Sanctuary], this excludes the one who receives or carries on leavened matter for which one is not liable outside; it excludes burning of the parts, which is not indispensable for atonement[151].

145 The Cohen who receives the blood of the sacrifice slaughtered by a layman or Levite, and the one who carries it to the altar. These two actions are biblically required. Reception of the blood in a sanctified vessel is mentioned explicitly; the action of carrying the blood is required implicitly since slaughter of the sacrifice must be performed away from the altar (North of the altar for most holy sacrifices, *Lev.* 1:11; before the Tent of Meeting for simple sacrifices, *Lev.* 3:2,8,13).

146 In the prohibition of sacrifices outside the Sanctuary (*Lev.* 17), only slaughter (v.4), pouring and burning of the parts (v. 6) are mentioned. There exists liability for extirpation or a purification sacrifice even if the slaughter was performed so that collection of the blood and carrying it was not necessary.

147 This expression is never used for the *Pesah*. The reference is to the verses referring to purification sacrifices, *Lev.* 4:26,31, from which it would appear that the burning of the fat on the altar is the atoning agent but which in *Sifra Wayyiqra II (Hovah) Pereq* 11(5-6) is explained to refer only to the pouring of the blood.

148 The argument shows that instead of "the one who receives or carries" one has to read "one who burns parts".

149 The argument shows that instead of "one who burns parts" one has to read "the one who receives or carries".

150 The argument of the rabbis of Caesarea is invalid since it can be turned upside down.

151 The statement of the rabbis of Caesarea is correct but their argument is incomplete.

(32b line 62) תַּמָּן תַּנֵּינָן. [בֵּית שַׁמַּאי אוֹמְרִים] שְׂאוֹר כַּזַּיִת וְחָמֵץ כַּכּוֹתָבֶת. וּבֵית הִלֵּל אוֹמְרִים זֶה וָזֶה בְּכַזַּיִת: רִבִּי זְרִיקָן בְּשֵׁם רִבִּי יֹסֵה בֶּן חֲנִינָא. לֹא שָׁנוּ אֶלָּא לְבִיעוּרוֹ. אֲבָל לַאֲכִילָה כַּזַּיִת. רִבִּי אַבָּהוּ בְשֵׁם רִבִּי יוֹחָנָן. בֵּין לִבְעוּרוֹ בֵּין לַאֲכִילָה כַּזַּיִת. קָם רִבִּי מָנָא עִם רִבִּי חִזְקִיָּה. אָמַר לֵיהּ. מְנָן שְׁמַע רִבִּי הָדָא מִילְתָא. אֲמַר לֵיהּ. מִן רִבִּי אַבָּהוּ. אֲמַר לֵיהּ. וַאֲנַן אֲמְרִין. רִבִּי אַבָּהוּ בְשֵׁם רִבִּי יוֹחָנָן. בֵּין לִבְעוּרוֹ בֵּין לַאֲכִילָה כַּזַּיִת.

1 שמאי K | שמיי   אומרים K | אומרין   ובית K | בית   2 בכזית K | כזית   חנינא K | חנינה   3 אבהו K | אבהיא   4 הדא K | הדה   מן ר' אבהו K | מר' אבהוא ואנן K | אנן   אבהו | אבהוא K   5 יוחנן K | -   לביעורו K | לבעורו

שְׁחָטוֹ עַל חָמֵץ. אַחַר מִי אַתְּ מְהַלֵּךְ. אַחַר אֲכִילָתוֹ אוֹ אַחַר בִּיעוּרוֹ. תַּמָּן אָמַר רִבִּי יִרְמְיָה בְּשֵׁם רִבִּי זְעוּרָה. שְׁנֵי חֲצָאֵי זֵיתִים בְּתוֹךְ הַבַּיִת אֵין הַבַּיִת מִצְטָרֵף. בְּתוֹךְ הַכֵּלִי הַכֵּלִי מִצְטָרֵף שְׁחָטוֹ עֲלֵיהֶן. מֵאַחַר שֶׁאֵילּוּ בְּתוֹךְ הַבַּיִת וְאֵין הַבַּיִת מִצְטָרֵף פָּטוּר. אוֹ מֵאַחַר שֶׁאֵילּוּ בְּתוֹךְ הַכֵּלִי הַכֵּלִי מִצְטָרֵף חַיָּיב. שְׁחָטוֹ עַל סִיעוּר. מֵאַחַר דְּאָמַר רַב הוּנָא בְשֵׁם רַב. מוּתָּר לְהַאֲכִילוֹ לְכַלְבּוֹ. פָּטוּר. אוֹ מֵאַחַר דְּרַב אָמַר. לוֹקִין עַל אֲכִילָתוֹ. חַיָּיב.

2 חצאי J | חצי זיתים K | זיתין   4 היכלי והכלע מצרף K | הבית   סיעור K | סיאור   דאמ' רב הונא K | דמר

חונא

[152]There, we have stated[153]: "The House of Shammai say, leavening in the volume of an olive, and leavened matter in the volume of a dried fig." Rebbi Zeriqan in the name of Rebbi Yose ben Ḥanina: They stated this only for its elimination, but for eating the volume of an olive[154]. Rebbi Abbahu in the name of Rebbi Joḥanan, whether for elimination or eating, the volume of an olive[155]. Rebbi Mana was standing with Rebbi Ḥizqiah; he said to him, from where did the rabbi hear this?. He told him, from Rebbi Abbahu. He answered, we also are saying, Rebbi Abbahu in the name of Rebbi Joḥanan, whether for elimination or eating, the volume of an olive[156].

If one slaughtered on leavened matter, after what are you going? After eating or after elimination? There[157] did Rebbi Jeremiah say in the name of Rebbi Ze'ira: Two volumes of half an olive in one house, the house does not combine them; in one vessel, the vessel does combine them. If one slaughtered on them, if they were in the house, and the house did not combine them, he is not liable; or if they were in one vessel and the vessel combines them, he is liable. If he slaughtered on leavening. Since Rav Huna said in the name of Rav, he is permitted to feed it to his dog[158], he is not liable; or since Rav said, one flogs for eating it, he is liable[159].

152 This paragraph has a parallel in *Yom Tov* 1:1 (end).
153 Mishnah *Yom Tov* (*Besah*) 1:1.
154 Even the House of Shammai agree that eating leavened matter in the volume of an olive on Passover creates liability.
155 This statement refers only to the opinion of the House of Hillel. While leavened matter is forbidden on Passover in the most minute amount, liability is created only by the volume of an olive, whether active leavening or passive leavened matter.

156 In this version, nothing can be learned from the discussion between RR. Mana and Ḥizqiah. In *Yom Tov* the statement of R. Abbahu continues with a proof, that if there were different standards for leavening and leavened matter, the Mishnah in *Keritut* which enumerates the transgressions causing extirpation should have enumerated them separately.
157 Halakhah 3:2, beginning.
158 Halakhah 2:1, Note 9.
159 The questions are not answered.

(32b line 75) רִבִּי שִׁמְעוֹן בֶּן לָקִישׁ אָמַר. עַד שֶׁיְּהֵא לַשּׁוֹחֵט לְאֶחָד מִבְּנֵי חֲבוּרָה. רִבִּי יוֹחָנָן אָמַר. לַשּׁוֹחֵט אַף עַל פִּי שֶׁאֵינוֹ מִבְּנֵי חֲבוּרָה. לְאֶחָד מִבְּנֵי חֲבוּרָה אַף עַל פִּי שֶׁאֵינוֹ שׁוֹחֵט. רִבִּי יוֹחָנָן אָמַר. אֲפִילוּ נָתוּן עִמּוֹ בִּירוּשָׁלֵם. רִבִּי שִׁמְעוֹן בֶּן לָקִישׁ אָמַר. עַד שֶׁיְּהֵא נָתוּן עִמּוֹ בַּעֲזָרָה.

דֵּין כְּדַעְתֵּיהּ וְדֵין כְּדַעְתֵּיהּ. דְּאִיתְפַּלְגוּן. שְׁנֵי יָמִים טוֹבִים שֶׁלְגָּלִיּוֹת. רִבִּי יוֹחָנָן אָמַר. מְקַבְּלִין הַתְרָיָיה עַל סָפֵק. רִבִּי שִׁמְעוֹן בֶּן לָקִישׁ אָמַר. אֵין מְקַבְּלִין הַתְרָיָיה עַל סָפֵק. הַכֹּל מוֹדִין שֶׁאִם הָיָה נָתוּן כְּנֶגְדּוֹ בַּחַלּוֹן בִּירוּשָׁלֵם. מָאן דְּאָמַר. סָפֵק. וַדַּאי. מָאן דְּאָמַר. בָּעֲזָרָה. בִּירוּשָׁלֵם הוּא.

1 לשוחט K | שוחט   2 לאחד K | ר' יעקב בר... ר'... לשוחט אף על פי שאינו מבני חבורה לאחד   שוחט K | לשוחט   5 ספק K | הספק (2)   6 מאן K | מן   K | וודאי   K | ודיי   מאן K | ומן

Rebbi Simeon ben Laqish said, only if it belongs to the slaughterer who is one of the group[160]. Rebbi Joḥanan said, to the slaughterer even if he is not of the group, to one of the group even if he is not the slaughterer. Rebbi Joḥanan said, even if it is with him in Jerusalem; Rebbi Simeon ben Laqish said, only if it is with him in the Temple courtyard[161]. [162]Each of them follows his own opinion, since they disagreed: about the two holidays of the diaspora[163]. Rebbi Joḥanan said, one accepts forewarning in case of a doubt; Rebbi Simeon ben Laqish said, one does not accept forewarning in case of a doubt. Everybody agrees if it was lying opposite him in a window in Jerusalem. He who said, a doubt[164], it is certain. He who said, in the Temple courtyard, it is in Jerusalem.

160 What does it mean, "one who slaughters the *Pesaḥ* on leavened matter"? Whose leavened matter?

161 He reads "on" as meaning "physically close" (Babli *Menaḥot* 98a).

In the text of K, the opinion of R. Joḥanan is repeated (supported) by R. Jacob bar [Aha].

162 *Yebamot* 11:7 Note 171, *Nazir* 8:1 Notes 48,49. Babli 64b, *Ševuot* 3b.

163 Before the publication of the computed calendar, communities which could not be informed by messengers about the determination of the first days of the months of Nisan and Tishri, kept two days of holidays to account for possible variations in the dates. Since each day was only one of a possible two, and in talmudic interpretation no infraction could be prosecuted unless the perpetrator was duly warned by two witnesses not to commit the crime, work on the holidays could not be prosecutable unless the warning was given for both days, the infraction occurred on both days, and this kind of long-term conditional warning was accepted in court. [After the publication of the calendar computations, the first day of a holiday is of biblical character; the second day is purely rabbinic and is kept only because the algorithm was published on condition that its users continue to keep the second day (*Eruvin* 3, Note 190; Babli *Beṣah* 4b).]

164 The disagreement of RR. Joḥanan and Simeon ben Laqish can be explained as one about warnings in cases of doubt only if the leavened matter is not visible by the slaughterer at the moment of slaughter, for it

might have been disposed of in the meantime. If it is visible to the slaughterer on the Temple Mount the doubt does not apply. But if the reason is that "on" means physical presence, R. Simeon ben Laqish still will declare the slaughterer not liable even though the leavened matter is visible in Jerusalem.

(32c line 8) מַה טַעֲמָא דְרִבִּי יוּדָה. דִם זבחי. דַם פֶּסַח וְדַם תָּמִיד.

אָמַר רִבִּי יוֹחָנָן. טַעֲמָא דְרִבִּי שִׁמְעוֹן. כָּתוּב אֶחָד אוֹמֵר. לֹא־תִשְׁחַט עַל־חָמֵץ דַּם־זִבְחִי. וְכָתוּב אַחֵר אוֹמֵר לֹא־תִזְבַּח עַל־חָמֵץ דַּם־זִבְחִי. אֶחָד הַפֶּסַח בְּאַרְבָּעָה עָשָׂר. אֶחָד שְׁאָר כָּל־הַזְּבָחִים בְּחוּלוֹ שֶׁלְּמוֹעֵד. מָה רָאִיתָ לְרַבּוֹתָן בְּחוּלוֹ שֶׁלְּמוֹעֵד וּלְהוֹצִיאָן מִן אַרְבָּעָה עָשָׂר. אַחַר שְׁרִיבָה הַכָּתוּב מִיעֵט. מְרַבֶּה אֲנִי אוֹתָן בְּחוּלוֹ שֶׁלְּמוֹעֵד שֶׁהוּא בַל יֵרָאֶה וּבַל יִמָּצֵא. וּמוֹצִיאָן מֵאַרְבָּעָה עָשָׂר שֶׁאֵינָן בַּל יֵרָאֶה וּבַל יִמָּצֵא. וְאַתְיָא כַּיֵי דְאָמַר רִבִּי מֵאִיר. דְרִבִּי מֵאִיר אָמַר. מִשֵּׁשׁ שָׁעוֹת וּלְמַעְלָן מִדִּבְרֵיהֶן. אָמַר רִבִּי מָנָא. כְּלָהֶן דִּכְתִיב זֶבַח חַג הַפֶּסַח אַרְבָּעָה עָשָׂר אָנוּ קַיָּימִין.

2 אחד K | ואחד   3 ראית K | ראיתה   K | ולהוציאן K | ולהוציאם מן ארבעה K | מארבעה   5 שאינן K | שאינו ואתיא K | ותייה כיי K | כההיא   דאמ' ר' K | דר'   7 אנן K | נן

What is Rebbi Jehudah's reason? *The blood of my sacrifices*, the blood of *Pesaḥ* and the blood of the daily sacrifice[165].

Rebbi Johanan said, the reason of Rebbi Simeon: One verse says[166], *do not slaughter on leavened matter the blood of my sacrifice*, and another verse[167] says, *do not sacrifice on leavened matter the blood of my sacrifice*. One refers to the *Pesaḥ* on the Fourteenth, one[168] to all other consumed sacrifices on the workdays of the holiday. How did you understand to add them on the workdays of the holiday and to exclude them from the Fourteenth? After that the verse added, it subtracted[169]. I am adding them on the workdays of the holiday since these are subject to "it should not be seen nor found"[170], and exclude them from the Fourteenth where they are not under "it should not be seen nor found". And this parallels what Rebbi Meïr said; as Rebbi Meïr said, after noontime it is of their words[171]. Rebbi Mana said, there where it says, *the consumed sacrifice of the Pesaḥ holiday of pilgrimage*, we hold that it refers to the Fourteenth[172].

166 R. Jehudah in the Mishnah includes the daily sacrifice in the prohibition of leavened matter. He reads זִבְחֵי instead of זְבָחַי. Babli 64a.

167 The second verse is *Ex.* 23:18, where it says לֹא־תִזְבַּח, the first is *Ex.*.34:25. Babli 64a.

168 This is formulated as if the second

verse referred to the intermediate days of the holiday.

169 *Ex.* 23:18 is general, referring to sacrifices eaten by its owners in general, while *Ex.*.34:25 explicitly mentions the *Pesaḥ* and therefore restricts its meaning.

170 Chapter 2:2 Note 90.
171 Chapter 1:4, Notes 109-110.
172 *Ex.*.34:25 must refer to the 14th of Nisan; the anonymous majority is justified in rejecting R. Simeon's position.

(32c line 17) אָמַר רִבִּי יוֹחָנָן. חֲבוּרָה הָיְתָה מַקְשָׁה. מָה אֲנָן קַיָּימִין. אִם בְּשֶׁאָבַד וְנִמְצָא קוֹדֶם לַכַּפָּרָה. בֵּין לִשְׁמוֹ בֵּין שֶׁלֹּא לִשְׁמוֹ כָּשֵׁר וְנִיתָּק לִרְעִיָה. אִם בְּשֶׁאָבַד וְנִמְצָא לְאַחַר כַּפָּרָה. בֵּין לִשְׁמוֹ בֵּין שֶׁלֹּא לִשְׁמוֹ פָּסוּל שְׁלָמִים הוּא. וְקַיָּימִנָה בְּשֶׁנִּיטְמְאוּ הַבְּעָלִים אוֹ שֶׁהֵזִידוּ וּכְבָר נִדְחָה לְפֶסַח שֵׁינִי. לִשְׁמוֹ פָּטוּר וְהוּא פָּסוּל. שֶׁלֹּא לִשְׁמוֹ חַיָּיב וְהוּא כָּשֵׁר. וְהַיי דֵּינוֹ לִשְׁמוֹ פָּטוּר. תַּמָּן אָמְרִין בְּשֵׁם רַב חִסְדָּא. בְּשֶׁעָבְרָה שְׁנָתוֹ בֵּין רִאשׁוֹן לַשֵּׁינִי. רִבִּי לָא בְשֵׁם רִבִּי יוֹחָנָן. בְּשֶׁעִיבֵּר זְמַן כַּפָּרָתוֹ. פֶּסַח שֶׁעִיבֵּר זְמַנּוֹ וּשְׁחָטוֹ לִשְׁמוֹ בִזְמַנּוֹ. אוֹ שֶׁשָּׁחַט אֲחֵרִים לִשְׁמוֹ בִזְמַנּוֹ. רִבִּי לִיעֶזֶר פּוֹסֵל וְרִבִּי יְהוֹשֻׁעַ מַכְשִׁיר. רִבִּי לִיעֶזֶר פּוֹסֵל שֶׁהוּא כְשׁוֹחֵט פֶּסַח לְשֵׁם שְׁלָמִים. וְרִבִּי יְהוֹשֻׁעַ מַכְשִׁיר שֶׁהוּא כְשׁוֹחֵט שְׁלָמִים לְשֵׁם פֶּסַח. מִכֵּיוָן שֶׁעִיבֵּר זְמַנּוֹ לֹא שַׁנְיָיא. הִיא הַשּׁוֹחֵט פֶּסַח לְשֵׁם שְׁלָמִים. הִיא הַשּׁוֹחֵט שְׁלָמִים לְשֵׁם פֶּסַח. עַל דַּעְתֵּיהּ דְּרַב חִסְדָּא. בְּשֶׁעִיבֵּר שְׁנָתוֹ בֵּין רִאשׁוֹן לַשֵּׁינִי. עַל דַּעְתֵּיהּ דְּרִבִּי לָא בְשֵׁם רִבִּי יוֹחָנָן. בְּשֶׁעִיבֵּר זְמַן כַּפָּרָתוֹ.

1 אנן | K נן   2 לכפרה | K לכפרה   C לרעיה | KS לראיה   3 שלמים | K ושלמים   4 שלא | K ושלא והיא | K שהיא   והיי | K דינו והיידנו | K   5 לא | K הילא   7 יושוע | K ישוע יהושע (2) | K   8 כשוחט | K שוחט   שוחט שנייא | K שנייה   השוחט | K שוחט   9 השוחט | K שוחט   10 לא | K הילא

[173]Rebbi Johanan said, the company was asking, where are we holding[174]? If it was lost and found before propitiation, whether it was for its purpose or not for its purpose it is qualified and sent to grazing[175]. If it was lost and found after propitiation, whether for its purpose or not for its purpose, it is disqualified as well-being offering[176]. But we confirmed it when the owner became impure or acted criminally and already pushed to the Second *Pesaḥ*[177]. For its purpose, he is not liable and it is disqualified. Not for its purpose, he is liable and it is qualified[134]. There they are saying in the name of Rav Ḥisda: If its year was completed between First and Second[178]. Rebbi La in the name of Rebbi Johanan: When the time for its propitiation was passed[179]. "If a *Pesaḥ* whose time had passed was slaughtered for its purpose at its time[180], or that he slaughtered another one for its purpose at its time[181], Rebbi Eliezer disqualifies and Rebbi Joshua qualifies. Rebbi Eliezer disqualifies since he is like one who slaughters a *Pesaḥ* for the purpose of a well-being sacrifice. Rebbi Joshua qualifies since he is like one who slaughters a well-being

sacrifice for the purpose of a *Pesaḥ*.[182]" Since its time is passed, there is no difference whether he slaughtered a *Pesaḥ* for the purpose of a well-being sacrifice or he slaughtered a well-being sacrifice for the purpose of a *Pesaḥ*. In the opinion of Rav Ḥisda, if its year was completed between First and Second. In the opinion of Rebbi La in the name of Rebbi Joḥanan, when the time for its propitiation was passed[183].

173 The different commentators offer different emendations of this paragraph. The following commentary is offered as a tentative explanation of the text as it stands.

174 Discussion of the statement of the Mishnah, "on the holiday, for its purpose he is not liable, not for its purpose he is liable."

175 Mishnah 9:5. If an animal had been designated as *Pesaḥ*, was lost, another animal was designated, and then the original was found before the other was slaughtered, it is qualified as sacrifice but cannot be used as *Pesaḥ*. A qualified sacrifice cannot be redeemed (*Lev.* 27:10); therefore it shall graze until it develops a defect, then be sold and the money used to buy well-being offerings.

176 While Mishnah 9:5 states clearly that a *Pesaḥ* animal, which was lost and only found after the replacement was slaughtered, is a qualified well-being offering, there is an opinion in Halakhah 9:6 that "the body of any which was acceptable as a *Pesaḥ* cannot be brought as well-being offering." While this is explained away in Halakhah 9:6, it seems to be the basis of the statement here.

177 The offering on the 14th of Iyar for those incapable of coming to the Sanctuary on the 14th of Nisan; *Num.* 9:9-14.

178 The *Pesaḥ* lamb must be a yearling., *Ex.* 12:5. If the animal was dedicated before Passover but then its owner was prevented from coming to the Sanctuary in time, it automatically is dedicated for the Second *Pesaḥ*. If then it will be too old, it is automatically dedicated as well-being offering and can be used as such during the holiday; this is "not for its purpose" as *Pesaḥ*.

179 If for some reason it was not used on the 14th and its owner is not eligible to celebrate the Second *Pesaḥ*, it may be used as well-being sacrifice during the holiday.

180 An old animal, which had been dedicated when young, slaughtered on the 14th as *Pesaḥ*.

181 An animal dedicated as well-being offering used as *Pesaḥ*.

182 The Babylonian version of the *baraita* is in Babli *Zevaḥim* 11a, Tosephta *Pesaḥim* 4:5.

183 Interpretations of : "*Pesaḥ* whose time had passed."

(fol. 31c) **משנה ה**: הַפֶּסַח נִשְׁחָט בְּשָׁלֹשׁ כִּתּוֹת שֶׁנֶּאֱמַר וְשָׁחֲטוּ אֹתוֹ כֹּל קְהַל עֲדַת יִשְׂרָאֵל קָהָל וְעֵדָה וְיִשְׂרָאֵל. נִכְנְסָה כַּת הָרִאשׁוֹנָה וְנִתְמַלֵּאת הָעֲזָרָה נָעֲלוּ דַּלְתוֹת הָעֲזָרָה תָּקְעוּ וְהֵרִיעוּ וְתָקְעוּ הַכֹּהֲנִים עוֹמְדִין שׁוּרוֹת שׁוּרוֹת וּבִידֵיהֶם בָּזִיכֵי כֶסֶף וּבָזִיכֵי זָהָב. שׁוּרָה שֶׁכּוּלָּהּ כֶּסֶף כֶּסֶף. שׁוּרָה שֶׁכּוּלָּהּ זָהָב זָהָב. לֹא הָיוּ מְעוֹרָבִין וְלֹא הָיוּ לַבָּזִיכִין שׁוּלַיִם שֶׁמָּא יַנִּיחוּם וְיִקְרַשׁ הַדָּם:

Mishnah 5: The *Pesaḥ* was being slaughtered in three groups, as it is said[184], *and they shall slaughter it, the entire assembly of the community of Israel*, assembly, community, and Israel. When the first group entered, the courtyard was filled, they locked the doors of the courtyard. They[185] blew the trumpets, straight, modulated, and straight. The priests were standing in rows[186] and in their hands were silver and golden cups; one row only silver, one row only gold, they were not mixed. The cups had no flat bottoms lest they would be put down and the blood jellying[187].

184 *Ex.* 12:6.
185 The priests whose duty it was to blow horns for the daily sacrifice. "Straight" means an extended single tone.
186 The people went in with their lambs and stood in front of the priests, one priest per lamb.
187 That it could no longer be sprinkled on the wall of the altar.

(32c line 31) **הלכה ה**: רִבִּי יַעֲקֹב בַּר אָחָא בְשֵׁם רִבִּי יָסָא. נִיתַּן כֹּחַ בְּקוֹלוֹ שֶׁלְּמֹשֶׁה וְהָיָה קוֹלוֹ מְהַלֵּךְ בְּכָל־אֶרֶץ מִצְרַיִם מַהֲלַךְ מ' יוֹם. וּמַה הָיָה אוֹמֵר. מִמָּקוֹם פְּלוֹנִי עַד מָקוֹם פְּלוֹנִי כַּת אַחַת. וּמִמָּקוֹם פְּלוֹנִי עַד מָקוֹם פְּלוֹנִי כַּת אַחַת. וְאַל תִּתָּמַהּ. וּמַה אִם אָבָק שֶׁאֵין דַּרְכּוֹ לְהַלֵּךְ אַתְּ מַר וְהָיָה לְאָבָק בְּכָל־אֶרֶץ מִצְרָיִם. קוֹל שֶׁדַּרְכּוֹ לְהַלֵּךְ לֹא כָל־שֶׁכֵּן. אָמַר רִבִּי לֵוִי. כְּשֶׁם שֶׁנִּיתַּן כֹּחַ בְּקוֹלוֹ שֶׁלְּמֹשֶׁה כָּךְ נִיתַּן כֹּחַ בְּקוֹלוֹ שֶׁלְּפַרְעֹה. [וְהָיָה קוֹלוֹ מְהַלֵּךְ בְּכָל־אֶרֶץ מְהַלַּךְ אַרְבָּעִים יוֹם.] וּמַה הָיָה אוֹמֵר. קוּמוּ צְּאוּ מִתּוֹךְ עַמִּי. לְשֶׁעָבַר הֱיִיתֶם עַבְדֵי פַרְעֹה. מִיכָּן וְהֵילַךְ אַתֶּם עַבְדֵי יי. בְּאוֹתָהּ שָׁעָה הָיוּ אוֹמְרִים הַלְלוּ יָהּ | הַלְלוּ עַבְדֵי יי. וְלֹא עַבְדֵי פַרְעֹה.

1 כח *K* כוח קולו *K* | - 2 מ' *K* | ארבעים מה *K* ומה 3 וממקום *K* ממקום מה *K* ומה 4 בכל *K* על כל כח *K* כוח 5 שלפרעה *K* שלפרעה הרשע קולו *K* | - 6 ומה *K* מה עמי *K* עמי גם אתם גם בני יש' ולכו עבדו את יי עבדי פרעה *K* עבדיי והילך *K* והלך 7 אתם *K* אתן

Halakhah 5: [188]Rebbi Jacob bar Aḥa in the name of Rebbi Yasa. Power was given to Moses's voice and his voice went through the entire land of Egypt, a distance of 40 days of travel[189]. What did he say? From place X to place Y one group, from place Z to place U one group. You should not be astonished. If about dust, which does not usually move, it is said[190], *it will be* *dust in the entire land of Egypt*, voice which usually is moving, not so much more? Rebbi Levi said, just as power was given to Moses's voice, so power was given to Pharao's voice, [and his voice went through the entire land of Egypt, a distance of forty days of travel.][191] What did he say? *Get up, leave from the midst of my people*[192]. In the past you were servants of Pharao, from now on you are servants of the Eternal. At that moment, they were saying[193], *Hallelujah, give praise, servants of the Eternal*, but not servants of Pharao.

188 A sermon, introducing the recitation of the "Egyptian Hallel", *Ps.* 113-118, in the Passover night celebration. Cf. the author's *The Scholar's Haggadah* p. 319; *Midrash Tehillim* 113(2), *Mekhilta dR. Ismael Bo Parashah* 14.
189 Or 400 Egyptian parasangs.
190 *Ex.* 9:9.

191 Addition by the corrector, confirmed by K and Medieval sources.
192 *Ex.* 12:31. The argument is based on the part of the verse not quoted here, but quoted in K: *both you and the Children of Israel and go to serve the Eternal.*
193 *Ps.* 113:1.

(32c line 40) תַּנֵּי. תָּמִיד שֶׁיֵּשׁ לוֹ נְסָכִים תּוֹקְעִין לִנְסָכִים. פֶּסַח שֶׁאֵין לוֹ נְסָכִים [תּוֹקְעִין] לִשְׁחִיטָתוֹ.

1 לו K | לו שני   לנסכים K | לנסכין (2)   2 לשחיטתו K | על שחיטתו

It was stated: For the daily sacrifice, which is accompanied by libations, one blows the trumpets for the libations[194]. For the *Pesaḥ*, which has no libations, one blows the trumpets for its slaughter.

194 Mishnah *Tamid* 7:2; *Num.* 10:10.

(32c line 41) דַּלְמָה. רִבִּי זְעוּרָה וְרִבִּי יַעֲקֹב בַּר אָחָא וְרִבִּי אַבִּינָא הֲווֹן יְתִיבִין. אָמַר רִבִּי אַבִּינָא מִפְּנֵי הָרַמָּאִין. אָמַר לֵיהּ רִבִּי יַעֲקֹב בַּר אָחָא. בְּכָל־פּוּמָךְ. אָמַר לֵיהּ רִבִּי זְעִירָא. אֱמוֹר לֵיהּ בְּפַלְגּוּת [פּוּמָ]. אָתָא רִבִּי יִרְמְיָה בְּשֵׁם רִבִּי יוֹחָנָן. מִפְּנֵי הָרַמָּאִין.

1 אבינא K | אבונא (2)   2 הרמאין K | הרמין   פומך K | פמך   זעירא K | זעורה   אמ' ליה K - | 3 C פומך | פומך K   פמך הרמאין K | הרמיין

Explanation[195]. Rebbi Ze`ira, and Rebbi Jacob bar Aha, and Rebbi Abinna were sitting. Rebbi Abinna said, because of the tricksters[196]. Rebbi Jacob bar Aha said to him, a mouthful[197]. Rebbi Ze`ira said to him, say it with half a mouthful. There came Rebbi Jeremiah in the name of Rebbi Joḥanan: because of the tricksters.

PESAHIM CHAPTER FIVE

195 Greek δήλωμα; cf. *Berakhot* 1:1 Note 72.

196 The vessels in one row of Cohanim are all of the same metal lest a Cohen bring a silver vessel from home and substitute it for a gold vessel of the Temple.

197 It is insolent to suspect that holy priests would steal from the Temple. Accepted by the Babli, 64b.

(fol. 31c) **משנה ו**: שָׁחַט יִשְׂרָאֵל וְקִבֵּל הַכֹּהֵן נוֹתְנוֹ לַחֲבֵירוֹ וַחֲבֵירוֹ לַחֲבֵירוֹ מְקַבֵּל אֶת הַמָּלֵא וּמַחֲזִיר אֶת הָרֵיקָן. כֹּהֵן הַקָּרוֹב אֵצֶל הַמִּזְבֵּחַ זוֹרְקוֹ זְרִיקָה אַחַת כְּנֶגֶד הַיְסוֹד:

Mishnah 6: The Israel slaughters[198] and the Cohen receives[199]; he hands it to his colleague and the colleague to his colleague; he accepts the full [cup] and returns the empty one[200]. The Cohen standing next to the altar pours it in one pouring in the direction of the foundations[201].

198 If he so wishes since slaughter is permitted to everybody.

199 The blood; an action for which only priests are qualified.

200 So that one Cohen may serve many slaughterers.

201 Foundation stones extending one cubit outside the altar proper; Mishnah *Middot* 3:1.

(32c line 45) **הלכה ו**: כָּתוּב אֶחָד אוֹמֵר אַךְ בְּכוֹר־שׁוֹר אוֹ־בְכוֹר כֶּשֶׂב אוֹ־בְכוֹר עֵז לֹא תִפְדֶּה קוֹדֶשׁ הֵם אֶת־דָּמָם תִּזְרֹק עַל־הַמִּזְבֵּחַ וְכָתוּב אַחֵר אוֹמֵר וְדַם־זְבָחֶיךָ יִשָּׁפֵךְ עַל־מִזְבַּח יְיָ אֱלֹהֶיךָ. אִם שְׁפִיכָה לָמָה זְרִיקָה. וְאִם זְרִיקָה לָמָה שְׁפִיכָה. תַּנֵּי. יִשָּׁפֵךְ. לֹא יַטִּיף. יִשָּׁפֵךְ. לֹא יָזֶה. יִשָּׁפֵךְ. לֹא יִזְרוֹק. וּפֵירֵשׁ בַּקַּבָּלָה. כֹּהֲנִים זוֹרְקִין אֶת הַדָּם מִיַּד הַלְוִיִּם. הַכֹּל מוֹדִין בִּשְׁפִיכָה דִּי הָכֵין. בְּהַזָּיָיה דִּי הָכֵין. [וּמַה] מַפְלִיגִין. בִּזְרִיקָה. רִבִּי מָנָא אָמַר. זְרִיקָה כְּעֵין שְׁפִיכָה. רִבִּי חֲנַנְיָה אָמַר. זְרִיקָה כְּעֵין הַזָּיָיה. אָמַר רִבִּי יוֹחָנָן בַּר מַדְיָיא. קִרְיָיא מְסַיֵּיעַ לְרִבִּי חֲנַנְיָה. כִּי מֵי נִדָּה לֹא־זוֹרַק עָלָיו טָמֵא יִהְיֶה וגו'. הָא דִּי לֹא קַיָּים גַּבָּה הַזָּיָיה וְאַתְּ צְוַוח לָהּ זְרִיקָה.

1-2 לא תפדה... על המזבח K | - K | 2 אחר K | אחד 3 ואם K | אם K | ישפיך K | ישפך 4 ישפך K | ופירש K | פירש כהנים K | הכהנים מודין K | מודים 5 הכין K | הכן C (2) ומה K | מה מפליגין K | פליגין ר' חנניני ור' מנא 6 מדייא K | מדיא קרייא K | קריה 7 וגו' K | - K | הא דיי K | והייד גבה K | גבי ואת K | והיא

Halakhah 6: One verse says[202], *but a firstling bull, or a firstling sheep, or a firstling goat, shall not be redeemed; holy they are; and their blood you shall pour on the altar*. Another verse says[203], *and the blood of your sacrifices shall be spilled on the altar of the Eternal, your God*. If spilling, why pouring, and if pouring, why spilling? It was stated, *shall be spilled*, he may not let it fall in drips. *Shall be spilled*, he shall not sprinkle. *Shall be spilled*, he shall not pour. And it is explained in tradition[204] that the priests pour the blood from the hands of the Levites. Everybody agrees on spilling how it is done; about sprinkling how it is done. Where do they disagree? About pouring. Rebbi Mana said, pouring is like spilling. Rebbi Hananiah said, pouring is like sprinkling. Rebbi Johanan bar Marius said, a verse supports Rebbi Hananiah: *For the throwing water was not poured on him, impure he shall be*[205], etc. Does he not talk about sprinkling and calls it pouring?

202 *Num.* 18:17.
203 *Deut.* 12:27.
204 *2 Chr.* 35:11.

205 *Num.* 19:20, about sprinkling with water containing ashes of the Red Cow. Cf. *Zevahim* 36b/37a.

(fol. 31c) **משנה ז**: יָצְאָת כַּת הָרִאשׁוֹנָה וְנִכְנְסָה שְׁנִיָּה יָצְאָת שְׁנִיָּה וְנִכְנְסָה שְׁלִישִׁית. כְּמַעֲשֵׂה הָרִאשׁוֹנָה כָּךְ מַעֲשֵׂה שְׁנִיָּה וּשְׁלִישִׁית. קָרְאוּ אֶת הַהַלֵּל אִם גָּמְרוּ שָׁנוּ וְאִם שָׁנוּ שִׁלֵּשׁוּ אַף עַל פִּי שֶׁלֹּא שִׁלֵּשׁוּ מִימֵיהֶם. רִבִּי יְהוּדָה אוֹמֵר מִימֵיהֶן שֶׁל כַּת שְׁלִישִׁית לֹא הִגִּיעַ לְאָהַבְתִּי כִּי יִשְׁמַע ה' אֶת־קוֹלִי מִפְּנֵי שֶׁעֲמָהּ מוּעָטִין:

Mishnah 7: When the first group left, the second entered; when the second left, the third entered. Like the arrangement for the first, so is the arrangement for second and third. They read the *Hallel*[206]; when they finished they repeated, after they repeated they tripled, even though they never tripled. Rebbi Jehudah says, during the existence of a third group they never reached *I am loving; truly the Eternal listened to my voice*[207], since its people were few.

206 *Ps.* 113-118, sung by the Levites (cf. Note 188).
207 *Ps.* 116:1

(32c line 55) **הלכה ז**: תַּמָּן תַּנִּינָן. יָצְאוּ וְאָכְלוּ וְשָׁתוּ. וּבָאוּ בֵּין הָעַרְבַּיִם וְקָרְאוּ הַלֵּל הַגְּדוֹלָה: אֵיזוֹ הִיא הַלֵּל הַגְּדוֹלָה. רִבִּי פַּרְנַךְ בְּשֵׁם רִבִּי חֲנִינָה. הוֹדוּ לֵאלֹהֵי הָאֱלֹהִים. אָמַר רִבִּי יוֹחָנָן. וּבִלְבַד מֵשֶׁעוֹמְדִים בְּבֵית יי. לָמָּה בְּאִילֵין תַּרְתֵּין פָּרְשָׁתָא. רִבִּי זְעוּרָא רִבִּי אַבָּהוּ בְּשֵׁם רִבִּי שְׁמוּאֵל בַּר נַחְמָן. מִפְּנֵי שֶׁיְּרִידַת גְּשָׁמִים כְּלוּלָה בָהֶן. עַל דַּעְתֵּיהּ דְּרִבִּי יוֹחָנָן נִיחָא. דִּכְתִיב מַעֲלֶה נְשִׂיאִים מִקְצֵה הָאָרֶץ. וּכְרִבִּי חֲנִינָה מָה. בְּגִין דִּכְתִיב נֹתֵן לֶחֶם לְכָל־בָּשָׂר כִּי לְעוֹלָם

חִסְדּוֹ: רִבִּי בָא וְרִבִּי סִימוֹן תְּרֵיהוֹן אֳמָרִין. הָדָא דִידָן. רִבִּי יֹושׁוּעַ בֶּן לֵוִי אָמַר. הָדָא דִידָן. בַּר
קַפָּרָא אָמַר. הָדָא דִידָן. בַּר קַפָּרָא כְדַעְתֵּיהּ. דְּתַנִּינָן. מִימֵיהֶן שֶׁל כַּת הַשְּׁלִישִׁית לֹא הִגִּיעָה
לְאָהַבְתִּי כִּי יִשְׁמַע ה' אֶת־קֹולִי תַחֲנוּנָי. מִפְּנֵי שֶׁעַמָּהּ מְמוּעָטִין. תַּנֵּי בַּר קַפָּרָא. זֹו הִיא הַלֵּל
הַגְּדֹולָה. חַד בַּר אַבַּיָּיה עֳבַר קֹומֵי תֵיבוּתָא. אָמַר לֹון. עַנּוּן בַּתְרָיי מַה דַּנָה אָמַר. הָדָא אָמְרָה.
לֵית הָדָא דִידָן. אָמַר רִבִּי מָנָא. הָדָא דִידָן. נִסָּא הֲוָה רַב. בְּגִין כֵּן אָמַר לֹון. עַנּוּן בַּתְרָיי מַה
דַּנָא אָמַר.

2 - | ו כי לעולם חסדו. הודו לאדוני האדונים כי לעולם חסדו. 3 למה | ו ולמה 6 יושוע | ו יהושע 7 דתנינן
| ו דתנינן תמן 8 את קולי תחנוניי | ו - 9 אבייה | ו אביי דנה | דאנא 10 נסא | ו ניסא 11 דנא | דאנא

Halakhah 7: [208]There, we have stated: "They went, ate, and drank. In the evening they returned and red the Great *Hallel*." What is the Great *Hallel*? Rebbi Parnakh in the name of Rebbi Ḥaninah; *Give thanks to Almighty God*[209]. Rebbi Joḥanan said, on condition of *who stand in the Eternal's house*[210]. Why these two chapters? Because rainfall is included in them. In the opinion of Rebbi Joḥanan it is understandable, for it is written[211], *He brings up vapors from the ends of the earth*. How is it for Rebbi Ḥaninah? Because it is written[212], *He gives nourishment to all flesh; Truly, His kindness is forever*. Rebbi Abba, Rebbi Simon, both are saying, ours[213]. Rebbi Joshua ben Levi said, ours. Bar Qappara said, ours. Bar Qappara follows his opinion, as it was stated: "during the existence of a third group they never reached *I am loving; truly the Eternal listened to my voice, my supplication*, since its people were few." Bar Qappara stated, this is the Great Hallel. A patrician stood before the Ark[214]; he said to them, repeat after me what I am saying. This implies that it is not ours[215]. Rebbi Mana said, it is ours. The miracle was great; therefore he said to them, repeat after me what I am saying[216].

---

208 Mishnah *Taʿaniot* 3:14, about a fast in a year of drought which was cut short by rainfall. The text is Halakhah 3:14 in *Taʿaniot* (1).
209 *Ps.* 136. Babli 118a.
210 *Ps.* 135 as introduction to *Ps.* 136.
211 *Ps.* 135:7.
212 *Ps.* 136:25.
213 *Ps.* 113-118.

214 To be the reader in a service of thanksgiving for rain relieving a drought.
215 If it were the regular *Hallel*, the congregation would not repeat the verses but answer every half-verse with "Hallelujah" (cf. *Šabbat* 16, Note 59).
216 Because of the extraordinary nature of the event, he changed the usual response to repetition of the entire *Hallel*.

(32c line 68) תָּנֵי. הִיא הָיְתָה נִקְרֵאת כַּת עֲצֵלִים. אָמַר רִבִּי אָבוּן. מַה אִם דָּבָר שֶׁמִּצְוָתוֹ לָכֵן הִיא הָיְתָה נִקְרֵאת כַּת עֲצֵלִים. מִי שֶׁהוּא מִתְעַצֵּל בְּמִצְוָה עַל אַחַת כַּמָּה וְכַמָּה.

It was stated: It was called the group of the lazy ones[217]. Rebbi Abun said, If in a case where the commandment is followed[218] it is called the group of the lazy ones, in a case one is lazy in fulfilling a commandment so much more.

217 Babli 65a.
218 Since "between the evenings" implies that late afternoon is preferred.

(fol. 31c) **משנה ח**: כְּמַעֲשֵׂהוּ בַחוֹל כָּךְ מַעֲשֵׂהוּ בַשַּׁבָּת אֶלָּא שֶׁהַכֹּהֲנִים מְדִיחִין אֶת הָעֲזָרָה שֶׁלֹּא בִרְצוֹן חֲכָמִים. רִבִּי יְהוּדָה אוֹמֵר כּוֹס הָיָה מְמַלֵּא מִדַּם הַתַּעֲרוֹבֶת וּזְרָקוֹ זְרִיקָה אַחַת עַל גַּבֵּי הַמִּזְבֵּחַ וְלֹא הוֹדוּ לוֹ חֲכָמִים:

Mishnah 8: As it is done on weekdays it is done on the Sabbath, only that the priests rinse the courtyard against the wish of the Sages[219]. Rebbi Jehudah says, one was filling a cup of the mixture of blood[220] and poured it in a single pouring on the altar, but the Sages did not agree with him.

219 Between two groups entering the courtyard they were stopping the flow of the water canal passing through the courtyard to flood the stone floor and thereby cleansing it (Tosephta 4:12). This is a rabbinic Sabbath infraction.
220 Covering the floor.

(32c line 71) **הלכה ח**: אָמַר רִבִּי יוֹנָתָן. לֹא כָל־שְׁבוּת הִתִּירוּ בַּמִּקְדָּשׁ. וְהָיוּ הַכֹּהֲנִים מְשֻׁתַּקְעִין בַּדָּם עַד אַרְכֻּבּוֹתֵיהֶן. כֵּיצַד הָיוּ עוֹשִׂין. מַסְטָוִיּוֹת הָיוּ עוֹשִׂין לָהֶן.

Halakhah 8: Rebbi Jonathan said[221], not every rabbinic Sabbath prohibition was permitted in the Temple. The priest would have sunk into the blood up to their knees[222]. How did they do it? They made them benches[223].

221 In *Eruvin* 10 (Note 133), the statement is in the name of the last generation R. Yose ben R. Abun instead of the first generation R. Jonathan. The statement explained why the inundating of the Temple courtyard was frowned upon by the pharisaic establishment.
222 This would have dirtied the priestly garments and made them unfit for service. The sweeping was necessary and therefore the displeasure of the Sages misplaced.
223 The priests stood on elevated benches above the accumulated blood. Since the priestly garments are enumerated in *Ex.* 28

and shoes are not mentioned there, the priests had to officiate barefoot, their feet touching the floor of the courtyard. Therefore one has to assume that the benches were rows of stones connected to the floor and counted as floor. Babli 65b.

(32c line 73) תַּמָּן תַּנֵּינָן. רִבִּי יְהוּדָה מְחַיֵּב בְּדַם הַתַּמְצִית: אָמַר רִבִּי יוֹחָנָן. לֹא רִיבָה אוֹתָהּ רִבִּי יוּדָה אֶלָּא לְהִכָּרֵת. אָתָא רִבִּי חִזְקִיָּה רִבִּי אַבָּהוּ בְּשֵׁם רִבִּי יוֹחָנָן. לֹא רִיבָה אוֹתָהּ רִבִּי יוּדָה אֶלָּא לְהִכָּרֵת. תַּמָּן אָמְרִין בְּשֵׁם רַב חִסְדָּא מַתְנִיתָא כו. אָמְרוּ לוֹ. וַהֲלֹא דַם הַתַּמְצִית הוּא. וְדַם תַּמְצִית פָּסוּל עַל גַּבֵּי הַמִּזְבֵּחַ. וְעוֹד מִן הָן 201 לֹא נִתְקַבֵּל בִּכְלִי. וְדָם שֶׁלֹּא נִתְקַבֵּל בִּכְלִי פָּסוּל מֵעַל גַּבֵּי הַמִּזְבֵּחַ. וְאִית לְרִבִּי יוּדָה דַּם מְבַטֵּל דָּם. כָּמָה דְלֵית לֵיהּ הָדָא וְהוּא מְקַבֵּל מִינְהוֹן. כֵּן לֵיהּ הָכָא וְהוּא מְקַבֵּל מִינְהוֹן. רִבִּי יוֹסֵי בֵּירִבִּי בּוּן בְּשֵׁם רַב חִסְדָּא. מַתְנִיתָהּ אָֽמְרָה כֵן. אֵין לִי אֶלָּא דַם הַנֶּפֶשׁ בְּמוּקְדָּשִׁין דָּבָר שֶׁהוּא רָאוּי לַכַּפָּרָה. מְנַיִין דַם הַנֶּפֶשׁ בְּחוּלִּין. וְדָם תַּמְצִית בֵּין בְּחוּלִּין בֵּין בְּמוּקְדָּשִׁין. תַּלְמוּד לוֹמַר דָּם. וְכָל־דָּם. כְּשֶׁהוּא אֵצֶל נֶפֶשׁ הוּא מַזְכִּיר כַּפָּרָה. אֵצֶל תַּמְצִית אֵינוֹ מַזְכִּיר כַּפָּרָה.

There, we have stated[224]: "Rebbi Jehudah declares liable for squeezed blood[225]." Rebbi Johanan said, Rebbi Jehudah added it only for extirpation[226]. There came Rebbi Hizqiah, Rebbi Abbahu in the name of Rebbi Johanan: Rebbi Jehudah added it only for extirpation. There[227], they are saying in the name of Rav Hisda: a *baraita*[227] says so: "They said to him, is that not squeezed blood? And squeezed blood is disqualified on the altar[228]. And also from the following, most of it was not received in a vessel, and blood not received in a vessel is disqualified on the altar[229]." Does Rebbi Jehudah hold that blood invalidates blood[230]? Since he did not reply, it follows that he accepted their position[231]. Since in the other case he does not hold so but did not respond, so here he does not hold so but did not respond[232]. Rebbi Yose ben Rebbi Abun in the name of Rav Hisda: a *baraita*[233] says so: "Not only life blood for *sancta*, matter appropriate for atonement, from where life blood for profane animals and squeezed blood for both *sancta* and profane animals? The verse says *blood* and *all blood*. When it is about life it mentions atonement, for squeezed blood it does not mention atonement[234].

224 Mishnah *Keritut* 5:1.
225 If an animal is slaughtered by having its throat cut, the blood pumped out from the carotid arteries by the heart is called "life blood"; all other blood is "squeezed out" blood unfit for sacrificial use. For the majority, all blood is prohibited (*Lev.* 7:23) but only life blood is forbidden on penalty of extirpation (*Lev.* 17:10). R. Jehudah disagrees since life blood is mentioned only

in v. 17:11.

226 He agrees that only life blood is qualified for the altar.

227 Tosephta 4:12; Babli 65a, *Zevahim* 34b, 60a.

228 As explained at the end of the paragraph.

229 Mishnah *Zevahim* 2:1.

230 In Mishnah *Zevahim* 8:6, R. Jehudah is quoted as saying that no blood invalidates blood. Therefore if only a small portion of the blood collected in the cup was qualified, the remainder is disregarded and the entire contents can be poured on the altar.

231 A possible interpretation of the Mishnah here.

232 Since we know that R. Jehudah holds that no blood invalidates blood and he is not reported to have answered the argument in the Tosephta, nothing can be inferred from his silence in the Mishnah.

233 Babli *Keritut* 22a.

234 This is R. Jehudah's argument. In *Lev.* 17:10 *all blood* is prohibited under penalty of extirpation. In *Lev.* 17:11 *blood* is the carrier of life, showing that life blood used for atonement is less than *all blood*. Babli 65a.

(fol. 31c) **משנה ט:** כֵּיצַד תּוֹלִין וּמַפְשִׁיטִין אוּנְקְלָיוֹת שֶׁל בַּרְזֶל הָיוּ קְבוּעִין בַּכְּתָלִים וּבָעַמּוּדִים שֶׁבָּהֶן תּוֹלִין וּמַפְשִׁיטִין. כָּל־מִי שֶׁאֵין לוֹ מָקוֹם לִתְלוֹת וּלְהַפְשִׁיט מַקְלוֹת דַּקִּין חֲלָקִים הָיוּ שָׁם וּמַנִּיחַ עַל כְּתֵיפוֹ וְעַל כֶּתֶף חֲבֵירוֹ וְתוֹלֶה וּמַפְשִׁיט. רִבִּי אֱלִיעֶזֶר אוֹמֵר אַרְבָּעָה עָשָׂר שֶׁחָל לִהְיוֹת בַּשַּׁבָּת מַנִּיחַ יָדוֹ עַל כֶּתֶף חֲבֵירוֹ וְיַד חֲבֵירוֹ עַל כְּתֵיפוֹ וְתוֹלֶה וּמַפְשִׁיט:

Mishnah 9: How does one hang and skins[235]? Iron hooks[236] were fixed in the walls and on the pillars where one hangs and skins. For anybody who does not find a place to hang and skin there were thin smooth rods; he puts one on his shoulder and another's shoulder, and hangs and skins. Rebbi Eliezer says, if the Fourteenth falls on a Sabbath, he puts his arm on another's shoulder who puts his arm on the first person's shoulder[237], and hangs and skins.

235 The *Pesah* has to be roasted whole; for this it has to be skinned. For this purpose the carcass it hung on its hind feet and stripped from there to the head. This has to be done in the Temple enclosure since the required innards have to be burned on the altar and sacrificial meat which leaves the Temple precinct becomes disqualified for the altar.

236 Greek ἀγκύλη, ἡ.

237 Since he holds that the rods are *muqseh* and may not be used on the Sabbath.

(32d line 9) **הלכה ט**: רִבִּי זְעִירָא בְשֵׁם רִבִּי אֶלְעָזָר. קָנִים וּמַקְלוֹת קוֹדֶם לְהַתָּרַת הַכֵּלִים נִשְׁנוּ.

Halakhah 9: Rebbi Ze'ira in the name of Rebbi Eleazar: Half-pipes and rods were stated before the permission of vessels[238].

238 This is quoted from *Šabbat* 17 (Notes 32,33), Babli *Šabbat* 123b. The half-pipes mentioned in Mishnah *Menahot* 11:6 which separate between the loaves of the shew-bread, where it is mentioned that they cannot be removed or put in on the Sabbath. This clearly contradicts Mishnah *Šabbat* 17:1 which declares that all implements may be moved on the Sabbath.

The rods are mentioned here. In view of Mishnah *Šabbat* 17:1 there is no reason not to use the rods on the Sabbath. It would be easy to say that practice does not follow R. Eliezer, but since he is a very reliable historical source there can be no doubt that he accurately reports Temple practice from his own experience. One has to conclude that the general permission to use all implements (with the exception of expensive tools of trade) has to be dated to the council of Jabneh after the destruction of the Second Temple.

(fol. 31c) **משנה י**: קְרָעוֹ וְהוֹצִיא אֶת אֵימוּרָיו נְתָנוֹ בַּמָּגֵס וְהִקְטִירָם עַל גַּבֵּי הַמִּזְבֵּחַ. יָצְאָת כַּת הָרִאשׁוֹנָה וְיָשְׁבָה לָהּ בְּהַר הַבַּיִת. שְׁנִיָּה בַּחֵיל. הַשְּׁלִישִׁית בִּמְקוֹמָהּ עוֹמֶדֶת. חֲשֵׁיכָה יָצְאוּ וְצָלוּ אֶת פִּסְחֵיהֶן:

Mishnah 10: He tears it open and removes the parts[50] which he[239] puts in a tureen and burns on the altar. The first group left and sat on the Temple Mount[240], the second within the inner wall of the Temple Mount, the third stood[241] at its place. When it got dark, they left and roasted their *Pesaḥ*.

239 The officiating priest.
240 According to Rashi and Maimonides, this refers only to a Sabbath, when they could not carry outside the enclosure of the Temple Mount.
241 Being inside the sacred district, they could not sit down.

(32d line 10) **הלכה י**: כָּתוּב וְהִזָּה מִמֶּנּוּ. מִכּוּלוֹ. אָמַר רִבִּי אֲבוּנָא. וּבִלְבַד מִזְבֵּחַ שָׁלֵם. כְּתוּב וְהִקְטִירוּ אוֹתוֹ. וְהִקְטִירָם. וְהִקְטִירוּ אוֹתוֹ. מַה תַּלְמוּד לוֹמַר וְהִקְטִירוּ אוֹתוֹ. הַכָּשֵׁר וְלֹא הַפָּסוּל. וְהִקְטִירוּ. שֶׁלֹּא יְעָרֵב חֲלָבִים בַּחֲלָבִים. וְהִקְטִירָם. כּוּלָּם כְּאַחַת. הָכָא אַתְּ מַר. וְהִקְטִירוּ. שֶׁלֹּא יְעָרֵב חֲלָבִים בַּחֲלָבִים. וְהָכָא אַתְּ מַר. הִקְטִירָן. כּוּלָּם כְּאַחַת. אָמַר רִבִּי לָא. כָּאן בְּמַגֵּס. וְכָאן עַל גַּבֵּי הַמִּזְבֵּחַ

Halakhah 10: It is written, *he sprinkled from it*[242], from its entirety. Rebbi Abuna said, only from a complete sacrifice. [243]"It is written, *they shall burn it, and he shall burn it, and he shall burn them*[244]. Why does the verse say *they shall burn it*, the qualified, not the disqualified[245]. *And he shall burn it*, that he may not mix fat with fat. *And he shall burn them*, all of them together." Here you are saying, *and he shall burn it*, that he may not mix fat with fat; and there you are saying, *and he shall burn them*, all of them together. Rebbi La said, here in the tureen, there on the top of the altar[246].

לֹא כֵן תַּנֵּי רִבִּי חִיָּיה. לֹא הָיְתָה יְשִׁיבָה בָעֲזָרָה אֶלָּא לְמַלְכֵי בֵית דָּוִד בִּלְבָד. וְאָמַר רִבִּי אִימִּי בְּשֵׁם רִבִּי שִׁמְעוֹן בֶּן לָקִישׁ. אֲפִילוּ לְמַלְכֵי בֵית דָּוִד לֹא הָיְתָה יְשִׁיבָה בָעֲזָרָה. תִּיפְתָּר שֶׁסַּמַּךְ עַצְמוֹ לַכּוֹתֶל וְיָשַׁב לוֹ. וְהָא כָתוּב וַיָּבֹא הַמֶּלֶךְ דָּוִיד וַיֵּשֶׁב לִפְנֵי יְי וגו׳. אָמַר רִבִּי אַייבוֹ בַּר נַגָּרִי. וַיְיַשֵּׁב עַצְמוֹ לִתְפִילָה.

Did not Rebbi Hiyya state, "nobody could sit in the Temple courtyard except kings of the Davidic dynasty"[247]? And Rebbi Immi said in the name of Rebbi Simeon ben Laqish, even the kings of the Davidic dynasty could not sit in the Temple courtyard. Explain it that he leaned on the wall as if sitting. But is it not written, *King David came and sat before the Eternal*[248], etc.? Rebbi Ayvo bar Naggari said, he concentrated[249] for prayer.

יָצְאַת כַּת רִאשׁוֹנָה וְיָשְׁבָה לָהּ בְּהַר הַבַּיִת. שְׁנִיָּה בַחֵיל. שְׁלִישִׁית בִּמְקוֹמָהּ. רִבִּי נַחְמָן בְּשֵׁם רִבִּי מָנָא. מָה אֲתֵינָן מִיתְנֵי. וְיָשְׁבָה בִּמְקוֹמָהּ. עָמְדָה לָהּ בִּמְקוֹמָהּ.

"The first group left and sat on the Temple Mount, the second within the inner wall of the Temple Mount, the third at its place." Rebbi Nahman in the name of Rebbi Mana: Did we state "sat at its place"? "Stood at its place[250]".

---

242 There is no verse like this; probably what is meant is *Lev.* 8:11: וַיַּז מִמֶּנּוּ. Cf. Babli *Bekhorot* 39b.

243 *Sifra Wayyiqra I Parsheta* 14(10).

244 The three expressions, from *Lev.* 3:5, 3:11, 3:16, all refer to well-being sacrifices, the first of cattle, the second of sheep, the third of goats. All three expressions are taken to refer to all three kinds, each one implying a different rule.

245 Since "it" is expressed by a separate word, it is for emphasis: This one but not one which does not follow the rules.

246 Once the priest has started, he may not stop before all parts lifted from one animal are burned.

247 Babli *Yoma* 25a,69b, *Sotah* 40a, *Tamid* 27a, *Sanhedrin* 101b; Yerushalmi *Yoma* 3:2, *Sotah* 7:7.

248 *1Chr.* 17:16.

249 Since in Mishnaic Hebrew יִשּׁוּב דַּעַת means "concentration".

250 The preceding paragraph explains why the third group is required to stand.

The text implies that the reading in the Mishnah was simply שְׁלִישִׁית בִּמְקוֹמָהּ "the third at its place."

אילו דברים פרק שישי

(fol.32d) **משנה א**: אֵילּוּ דְבָרִים בַּפֶּסַח דּוֹחִין אֶת הַשַּׁבָּת שְׁחִיטָתוֹ וּזְרִיקַת דָּמוֹ וּמִיחוּי קְרָבָיו וְהֶקְטֵר חֲלָבָיו. אֲבָל צְלִיָּיתוֹ וַהֲדָחַת קְרָבָיו אֵינָן דּוֹחִין. הַרְכָּבוֹ וַהֲבָאָתוֹ מִחוּץ לַתְּחוּם וַחֲתִיכַת יַבַּלְתּוֹ אֵינָן דּוֹחִין. רִבִּי אֱלִיעֶזֶר אוֹמֵר דּוֹחִין:

Mishnah 1: The following items about the *Pesah* push aside the Sabbath[1]: Its slaughter, and the pouring of its blood, and emptying its intestines[2], and the burning of its fat. But its roasting and washing of its intestines[3] do not push aside. Carrying it[4], or bringing it from outside the Sabbath domain, or cutting its wart[5], do not push aside; Rebbi Eliezer says, they push aside[6].

1 If the 14th of Nisan falls on a Sabbath.
2 Cleaning out the bowels so the carcass will not start to smell before nightfall when it can be roasted.
3 To clean them thoroughly to prepare them as food.
4 Carrying the lamb on one's shoulder.
5 Since a wart is a defect which disqualifies an animal as sacrifice (*Lev.* 22:22), the animal could not have been dedicated if it had developed one by the time of dedication. If it was dedicated without defect, a wart which developed later may be cut.
6 He holds that if an action supersedes the rules of the Sabbath, all preparatory actions also supersede the Sabbath (*Šabbat* 19:1).

(33a line 3) אֵילּוּ דְבָרִים בַּפֶּסַח כול'. זוֹ הֲלָכָה נֶעֶלְמָה מִזִּקְנֵי בָתֵירָה. פַּעַם אַחַת חָל אַרְבָּעָה עָשָׂר לִהְיוֹת בַּשַּׁבָּת. וְלֹא הָיוּ יוֹדְעִין אִם פֶּסַח דּוֹחֶה אֶת הַשַּׁבָּת אִם לָאו. אָמְרוּ. יֵשׁ כָּאן בָּבְלִי אֶחָד וְהִלֵּל שְׁמוֹ. שֶׁשִּׁימֵּשׁ אֶת שְׁמַעְיָה וְאַבְטַלְיוֹן. יוֹדֵעַ אִם פֶּסַח דּוֹחֶה אֶת הַשַּׁבָּת אִם לָאו. אֶיפְשָׁר שֶׁיֵּשׁ מִמֶּנּוּ תּוֹחֶלֶת. שָׁלְחוּ וְקָרְאוּ לוֹ. אָמְרוּ לוֹ. שָׁמַעְתָּ מִיָּמֶיךָ. כְּשֶׁחָל אַרְבָּעָה עֶשְׂרֵה לִהְיוֹת בַּשַּׁבָּת. אִם דּוֹחֶה אֶת הַשַּׁבָּת אִם לָאו. אָמַר לָהֶן. וְכִי אֵין לָנוּ אֶלָּא פֶּסַח אֶחָד בִּלְבָד דּוֹחֶה אֶת הַשַּׁבָּת בְּכָל־שָׁנָה. וַהֲלֹא כַּמָּה פְסָחִים יִדְחוּ אֶת הַשַּׁבָּת בְּכָל־שָׁנָה. אִית תַּנָּיֵי תַנֵּי. מֵאָה. אִית תַּנָּיֵי תַנֵּי. מָאתַיִם. אִית תַּנָּיֵי תַנֵּי. שְׁלֹשׁ מֵאוֹת. מָאן דְּאָמַר. מֵאָה. תְּמִידִין. מָאן דְּאָמַר. מָאתַיִם. תְּמִידִין וּמוּסְפֵי שַׁבָּתוֹת. מָאן דְּאָמַר. שְׁלֹשׁ מֵאוֹת. תְּמִידִין וּמוּסְפֵי שַׁבָּתוֹת שֶׁלְּיָמִים טוֹבִים וְשֶׁלְּרָאשֵׁי חֳדָשִׁים וּמְגִזֵּרָה שָׁנָה. מֵהֶקֵּשׁ. הוֹאִיל וְתָמִיד קָרְבַּן צִיבּוּר וּפֶסַח קָרְבַּן צִיבּוּר. מַה תָּמִיד קָרְבַּן צִיבּוּר וְדוֹחֶה [שַׁבָּת]. אַף פֶּסַח קָרְבַּן צִיבּוּר דּוֹחֶה אֶת הַשַּׁבָּת. מִקַּל וָחוֹמֶר. מַה אִם תָּמִיד שֶׁאֵין חַיָּיבִין עַל עֲשִׂיָּיתוֹ כָּרֵת דּוֹחֶה אֶת הַשַּׁבָּת. פֶּסַח שֶׁחַיָּיבִין עַל

עֲשִׂיָּתוֹ כָּרֵת אֵינוֹ דִין שֶׁיִּדְחֶה אֶת הַשַּׁבָּת. מִגְזֵירָה שָׁוָה. נֶאֱמַר בְּתָמִיד בְּמוֹעֲדוֹ וְנֶאֱמַר בְּפֶסַח בְּמוֹעֲדוֹ: מַה תָּמִיד שֶׁנֶּאֱמַר בּוֹ בְּמוֹעֲדוֹ דּוֹחֶה אֶת הַשַּׁבָּת. אַף פֶּסַח שֶׁנֶּאֱמַר בּוֹ בְּמוֹעֲדוֹ דּוֹחֶה אֶת הַשַּׁבָּת. אָמְרוּ לוֹ. כְּבָר אָמַרְנוּ אִם יֵשׁ תּוֹחֶלֶת מִבַּבְלִי. הֶקֵּישׁ שֶׁאָמַרְתָּ יֵשׁ לוֹ תְשׁוּבָה. לֹא. אִם אָמַרְתָּ בְּתָמִיד שֶׁכֵּן יֵשׁ לוֹ קִיצְבָה. תֹּאמַר בְּפֶסַח שֶׁאֵין לוֹ קִיצְבָה. קַל וָחוֹמֶר שֶׁאָמַרְתָּ יֵשׁ לוֹ תְשׁוּבָה. לֹא. אִם אָמַרְתָּ בְּתָמִיד שֶׁהוּא קָדְשֵׁי קָדָשִׁים. תֹּאמַר בְּפֶסַח שֶׁהוּא קָדָשִׁים קַלִּים. גְּזֵירָה שָׁוָה שֶׁאָמַרְתָּ. שֶׁאֵין אָדָם דָּן גְּזֵירָה שָׁוָה מֵעַצְמוֹ.

"The following items about the *Pesaḥ*," etc. [7]This question left the Elders of Bathyra at a loss. Once the Fourteenth fell on the Sabbath and they did not know whether *Pesaḥ* pushes aside the Sabbath or not. They said, we have here a Babylonian who served Shemaya and Avtalion[8] and knows whether *Pesaḥ* pushes aside the Sabbath or not. It is possible that there be hope from him. They sent and called him. The said to him, did you ever hear, if the Fourteenth falls on the Sabbath, whether *Pesaḥ* pushes aside the Sabbath or not? He told them, do we have only one *Pesaḥ* which pushes aside the Sabbath every year? Are there not many *Pesaḥim* which push aside the Sabbath every year? There are Tannaim who state: 100. There are Tannaim who state: 200. There are Tannaim who state: 300. He who says 100, the daily sacrifices of the Sabbath. He who says 200, the daily and additional sacrifices of the Sabbath. He who says 300, the daily and additional sacrifices of the Sabbath, and of holidays, and of New Moons, and of semi-holidays. They told him, already we said, there is hope from you. He started to explain to them by analogy, by an argument *de minore ad majus*, and by equal cut. By analogy: The daily sacrifice is a public offering and *Pesaḥ* is a public offering. Since the daily sacrifice as a public offering pushes aside the Sabbath, also *Pesaḥ* as a public offering pushes aside the Sabbath. By an argument *de minore ad majus*. Since the daily sacrifice, whose action is not subject to extirpation, pushes aside the Sabbath, it is only logical that *Pesaḥ*, whose action is subject to extirpation, push aside the Sabbath. By equal cut. It is said about the daily sacrifice, *at its fixed time*[9], and it is said about *Pesaḥ*, *at its fixed time*[10]. They said to him, we already said, is there hope from a Babylonian? The analogy which you proposed can be answered. No, if you said this about daily sacrifices which are fixed in number, what can you infer for *Pesaḥ* which is not fixed in number? The argument *de minore ad majus* which you proposed can be answered. No, if you said this about daily sacrifices which are most holy, what can you infer for *Pesah* which is a simple sacrifice[11]? Concerning the equal cut which you proposed, nobody can introduce an equal cut by himself[12].

7   Babli 66a; Tosephta 4:13-14.
8   The heads of the Pharisaic establishment in the preceding generation.
9   *Num.* 28:2.
10 *Num.* 9:2.
11 The relationship between daily sacrifice and *Pesah* is not that of minor and major; the argument is intrinsically invalid.
12 Equal expressions in the Pentateuch imply equal legal status only if there is a documented tradition that these words were written for this purpose. Babli 66a.

(33a line 26) רִבִּי יוֹסֵי בֵּירִבִּי בּוּן אָמַר בְּשֵׁם רִבִּי אַבָּא בַּר מָמָל. אִם בָּא אָדָם לָדִין אַחַר גְּזֵירָה שָׁוָה [מֵעַצְמוֹ] עוֹשֶׂה אֶת הַשֶּׁרֶץ מְטַמֵּא בָאֹהֶל. וְאֶת הַמֵּת מְטַמֵּא בְכָעֲדָשָׁה. דּוּ דָרַשׁ. בֶּגֶד עוֹר בֶּגֶד עוֹר לִגְזֵירָה שָׁוָה. כָּךְ אִם יִהְיֶה הַשֶּׁרֶץ בְּיָדוֹ שֶׁלְאָדָם אֲפִילוּ טוֹבֵל בְּמֵי שִׁילוֹחַ אוֹ בְמֵי בְרֵאשִׁית אֵין לוֹ טַהֲרָה עוֹלָמִית. הִשְׁלִיכוֹ מִיָּדוֹ מִיָּד הוּא טָהוֹר. רִבִּי יוֹסֵה בֵּירִבִּי בּוּן בְּשֵׁם רִבִּי בָּא בַּר מָמָל. אָדָם דָּן גְּזֵירָה שָׁוָה לְקַייֵם תַּלְמוּדוֹ. וְאֵין אָדָם דָּן גְּזֵירָה שָׁוָה לְבַטֵּל תַּלְמוּדוֹ. רִבִּי יוֹסֵי בֵּירִבִּי בּוּן בְּשֵׁם רִבִּי בָּא בַּר מָמָל. אָדָם דָּן קַל וָחוֹמֶר לְעַצְמוֹ וְאֵין אָדָם דָּן גְּזֵירָה שָׁוָה לְעַצְמוֹ. לְפִיכָךְ מְשִׁיבִין מִקַּל וָחוֹמֶר וְאֵין מְשִׁיבִין מִגְּזֵירָה שָׁוָה.

1 יוסי | ג יוסה אבא | ג בא אדם | ג [א]דן לדין | ג לדון אחר | ג -   2 באהל | ג באהיל בכעדשה | ג בכעדסה עור | ג ועור   3 עור | ג ועור כך אם יהיה... מיד הוא טהור | ג -   5 אדם | ג אדן (2)   6 יוסי | ג יוסה אדם | ג אדן לעצמו | ג מעצמו   7 לעצמו | ג מעצמו

[13]Rebbi Yose ben Rebbi Abun said in the name of Rebbi Abba bar Mamal: If a person could construct an equal cut by himself, he could make a creeping animal causing impurity in a tent and a corpse causing impurity in the volume of a lentil, by explaining *textile, leather; textile, leather*[14]. So if a creeping animal is in a person's hand, even if he immerses himself in the waters of the Siloam, or in waters of a primeval ocean, he never can achieve purity. If he throws it away, immediately he becomes pure[15]. Rebbi Yose ben Rebbi Abun in the name of Rebbi Abba bar Mamal: A person may use an equal cut to confirm what he has learned; nobody may use an equal cut to invalidate what he has learned[16]. Rebbi Yose ben Rebbi Abun in the name of Rebbi Abba bar Mamal: A person may argue *de minore ad majus* by himself; a person may not argue an equal cut by himself[16]. Therefore one can contradict an argument *de minore ad majus*; one cannot contradict an equal cut.

13 Here a Genizah fragment (*Ginze Schechter* pp. 446-447) becomes readable again (ג).

14 A dead creeping animal (of the list *Lev.* 11:29-30) imparts impurity in the volume of a lentil; a human corpse only in the volume of an olive. A human corpse imparts impurity to everything under the same roof with it, a dead creeping one imparts impurity only by contact. The argument is incomprehensible but the text is confirmed not only by ג but also by *Sefer Hapardes* from the school of Rashi (*Pardes Gadol* §175, ed. H. L. Ehrenreich p. 230), and *Meïri Pesahim* (ed. Y. Klein, col. 290a). While *textile and leather* are written about the creeping animal in *Lev.* 11:32, they are not mentioned in the Chapter about tent impurity (*Num.* 19). It is mentioned in the Chapter about *sāra'at* impurity of textiles (*Lev.* 13:47-59) although not in the exact wording of 11:32. The argument should be that the equal cut is illegitimate since minimal sizes for impurity of animals are determined by volume while those of textiles by surface area; the rules cannot be transferred.

15 This argument does not belong here, it is not in ג, nor in *Pardes*, nor in Meïri. It is part of a sermon in *Ta`anit* (Yerushalmi 2:1 69a line 69, Babli 16a.)

16 Since it is part of oral tradition.

(33a line 35) אַף עַל פִּי שֶׁהָיָה יוֹשֵׁב וְדוֹרֵשׁ לָהֶן כָּל־הַיּוֹם לֹא קִיבְּלוּ מִמֶּנּוּ עַד שֶׁאָמַר לָהֶן. יָבוֹא עָלַי כֵּן שָׁמַעְתִּי מִשְּׁמַעְיָה וְאַבְטַלְיוֹן. כֵּיוָן שֶׁשָּׁמְעוּ מִמֶּנּוּ כֵּן עָמְדוּ וּמִינּוּ אוֹתוֹ נָשִׂיא עֲלֵיהֶן. כֵּיוָן שֶׁמִּינּוּ אוֹתוֹ נָשִׂיא עֲלֵיהֶן הִתְחִיל מְקַנְתְּרָן בִּדְבָרִים וְאוֹמֵר. מִי גָרַם לָכֶם לְצֹרֶךְ לַבַּבְלִי הַזֶּה. לֹא עַל שֶׁלֹּא שִׁימַּשְׁתֶּם לִשְׁנֵי גְדוֹלֵי עוֹלָם לִשְׁמַעְיָה וְאַבְטַלְיוֹן שֶׁהָיוּ יוֹשְׁבִין אֶצְלְכֶם. כֵּיוָן שֶׁקִּינְתְּרָן בִּדְבָרִים נֶעֶלְמָה הֲלָכָה מִמֶּנּוּ.

1 קיבלו ממנו | ג קבלו עליהן יבוא | ג יבא   2 עלי | ג עליי כן | ג אם לא   ממנו | ג הימנו   3 ואו' | ג ואומר להן   4 לשני גדולי עולם לשמעיה ואבטליון | ג לשמעיה ואבטליון ש[ני גדולי עולם]

Even though he was sitting and explaining the entire day they did not accept it from him until he said, it should come over me, so I heard from Shemaya and Avtalion. When they heard this from him, they rose and appointed him Patriarch over them. After they had appointed him Patriarch over them, he started to goad[16*] them with words, and said: What caused you to need this Babylonian? Not that you did not serve the two greats of the world, Shemaya and Avtalion? When he started to goad them with words, practice disappeared from him.

אָמְרוּ לוֹ. מַה לַעֲשׂוֹת לָעָם וְלֹא הֵבִיאוּ סַכִּינֵיהֶן. אָמַר לָהֶן. הֲלָכָה זוֹ שָׁמַעְתִּי וְשָׁכַחְתִּי. אֶלָּא הַנִּיחוּ לְיִשְׂרָאֵל אִם אֵינָן נְבִיאִים בְּנֵי נְבִיאִים הֵן. מִיָּד כָּל־מִי שֶׁהָיָה טָלֶה פְּסָחוֹ פְּסָחוֹ הָיָה תּוֹחֲבָה בְגִיזָּתוֹ. גְּדִי הָיָה קוֹשְׁרוֹ בֵּין קַרְנָיו. נִמְצְאוּ פִּסְחֵיהֶן מְבִיאִין סַכִּינֵיהֶן עִמָּהֶן. כֵּיוָן שֶׁרָאָה אֶת הַמַּעֲשֶׂה נִזְכַּר אֶת הַהֲלָכָה. אָמַר. כָּךְ שָׁמַעְתִּי מִפִּי שְׁמַעְיָה וְאַבְטַלְיוֹן.

רִבִּי זְעִירָה בְשֵׁם רִבִּי אֶלְעָזָר. כָּל־תּוֹרָה שֶׁאֵין לָהּ בֵּית אָב אֵינָהּ תּוֹרָה. תַּמָּן תַּנִּינָן. רָכַב
עָלֶיהָ. נִשְׁעַן עָלֶיהָ. נִתְלָה בְזְנָבָהּ. עָבַר בָּהּ אֶת הַנָּהָר. קִיפֵּל עָלֶיהָ אֶת הַמּוֹסֵירָה. נָתַן טַלִּיתוֹ
עָלֶיהָ. פְּסוּלָה. [אֲבָל קוֹשְׁרָהּ בַּמּוֹסֵרָה. עָשָׂה לָהּ סַנְדָּל בִּשְׁבִיל שֶׁלֹּא תַחֲלִיק. פֵּרַס טַלִּיתוֹ עָלֶיהָ
מִפְּנֵי הַזְּבוּבִין. כְּשֵׁרָה. זֶה הַכְּלָל. כֹּל שֶׁהוּא לְצָרְכָהּ כְּשֵׁרָה. לְצוֹרֶךְ אַחֵר פְּסוּלָה:] הָדָא יַלְפָּה
מִן הַהִיא וְהַהִיא יַלְפָּה מִן הָדָא. הָדָא יַלְפָּה מִן הַהִיא. שֶׁאִם תָּלָה בָהּ סַכִּין לְשׁוֹחֲטָהּ כְּשֵׁירָה.
וְהַהִיא יַלְפָה מִן הָדָא. שֶׁכָּל־עֲבוֹדָה שֶׁהִיא לְשֵׁם קֳדָשִׁים אֵינָהּ עֲבוֹדָה. וְיַתִּירוּ לָהֶן עַל יְדֵי חוֹלָה.
אֶלָּא כְרִבִּי אִימִּי. וַאֲפִילוּ תֵימַר כְּרִבִּי סִימוֹן. כְּשֵׁם שֶׁנֶּעֶלְמָה זוֹ כָּךְ נֶעֶלְמָה זוֹ. אָמַר רִבִּי אָבוּן.
וַהֲלֹא [אִי] אֶיפְשָׁר לִשְׁנֵי שָׁבוּעוֹת שֶׁלֹּא חָל אַרְבָּעָה עָשָׂר לִהְיוֹת בְּשַׁבָּת. וְלָמָּה נֶעֶלְמָה הֲלָכָה
מֵהֶן. כְּדֵי לִיתֵּן גְּדוּלָה לְהִלֵּל.

[17]They said to him: What to do with people who did not bring their knives with them? He told them, I was informed of the practice, but I forgot. But let Israel act; if they are not prophets they are descendants of prophets. Then everybody whose Passover sacrifice was a lamb stuck them in its fleece, for a kid goat he bound them to its horns; it turned out that the Passover sacrifices brought their knives with them. When he saw the action he remembered the practice. He told them, this is what I heard from Shemaya and Avtalion.

Rebbi Ze`ira in the name of Rebbi Eleazar. Any teaching which has no pedigree is no teaching. There, we have stated[18]: "If he rode on it, leaned on it, hung on it, used it to cross a river, folded the bridle on it, put his toga on it, it is disqualified. [But if he tied it with the bridle, made it a shoe lest it slip, put his toga on it because of flies, it is qualified. This is the principle: Anything for its needs, it is qualified. For any other need, it is disqualified.]" This learns from that and that learns from this. This learns from that that if he hung on it a knife to slaughter it it remains qualified. That learns from this, that any action which is done for *sancta* is not work. Why did they not allow it to them by means of walls of people? It must follow Rebbi Immi. Even if you are saying following Rebbi Simon, just as they could not remember this so they did not remember that. Rebbi Abun said, but it is impossible that in two Sabbatical periods there should be no 14th which falls on the Sabbath! How could they not have remembered? To confer greatness on Hillel.

16* Greek κεντρόω "to spur, goad, hit with a sharp instrument".

17 This is copied from *Šabbat* 19, Notes 59-66, where readings are noted and the text is explained. While the text fits in here, its origin is in *Šabbat* since the disagreement

between R. Immi and R. Simon mentioned in the paragraph does not refer to anything discussed here.

18 Mishnah *Parah* 2:3. The text in parentheses was added by the corrector from the Mishnah.

(33a line 56) אָמַר רִבִּי מָנָא. אֲנָא שְׁמָעִית מֵרִבִּי יוּדָן וּמִן כָּל־רַבָּנִין. מִפְּנֵי מָה נוֹהֲגִין בְּבֵית דִּין שֶׁלְּמַטָּן בְּכָבוֹד. שֶׁלֹּא יִרְבּוּ מַחֲלוֹקוֹת בְּיִשְׂרָאֵל. שְׁלֹשָׁה הִנִּיחוּ כִתְרָן בָּעוֹלָם הַזֶּה וְיָרְשׁוּ חַיֵּי הָעוֹלָם הַבָּא. וְאֵילוּ הֵן. יוֹנָתָן בֶּן שָׁאוּל. וְאֶלְעָזָר בֶּן עֲזַרְיָה. וְזִקְנֵי בְתֵירָה. יוֹנָתָן בֶּן שָׁאוּל. אָמַר רִבִּי לָא. אֲפִילוּ נָשִׁים מֵאֲחוֹרֵי הַקּוּרְיָין יוֹדְעוֹת הָיוּ שֶׁדָּוִד עָתִיד לִמְלוֹךְ. אֶלְעָזָר בֶּן עֲזַרְיָה תִּנְיָין הֲוָה. לֵית לָךְ כְּהָדָא דְזִקְנֵי בְתֵירָה דְשָׁרוֹן גַּרְמוֹן מִן נְשִׂייוּתָא וּמְנוּנְיֵהּ נָשִׂיא. רַבָּנִין דְּקַיְסָרִין אָמְרִין. אַף רִבִּי חֲנִינָה דְצִיפּוֹרִין לְרִבִּי מָנָא. אָמַר רִבִּי יוֹשׁוּעַ בֶּן קַבְסַיי. כָּל־יוֹמַי הָיִיתִי בּוֹרֵחַ מִן הַשְּׂרָרָה. עַכְשָׁיו שֶׁנִּכְנַסְתִּי. כָּל־מִי שֶׁבָּא וּמוֹצִיאֵנִי. כְּקוּמְקוּם הַזֶּה אֲנִי יוֹרֵד לוֹ. מַה הַקּוּמְקוּם הַזֶּה כּוֹוֶה וּמַפְצִיעַ וּמְפַחֵם בּוֹ. כָּךְ אֲנִי יוֹרֵד לוֹ. אָמַר רִבִּי יוֹסֵי בֵירִבִּי בּוּן. חַס וְשָׁלוֹם דַּהֲוָה בָעֵי לָהּ. אֶלָּא דַהֲוָה אָמַר. מָאן יֵימַר לִי דְחוֹרָן מְקַדֵּשׁ שֵׁם שָׁמַיִם דִּכְוָותִי.

1 אנא | ג אנה מר' | ג מן ר' דין | ג - 3 יונתן | ג יוחנ 4 לא | ג אל[א] נשים | ג נשין שדוד | ג שדויד 5 הוה | ג היו כחדא | ג אלא [כחד]ה דשרון | ג דישרון נשייותא | ג נשייותה דקיסרין | ג [ד]קוסרין 6 יושוע בן קבסיי | ג יהושע בן קוסיי 7 עכשיו | ג וכיון שבא | ג שהוא בא לו | ג אליו מה | ג מן 8 ומפחם | ג ומפחס בד | ג - יוסי | ג יוסה דהוה | ג דהווה 10 מאן ההמר | ג מן יימר

Rebbi Mana said, I heard from Rebbi Yudan and from all the rabbis, why does one honor the lower house[19]? So that divisions should not grow in Israel. Three put down their crowns in this world and inherited the life of the Future World. And these are: Jonathan the son of Saul, and Eleazar ben Azariah, and the Elders of Bathyra. Jonathan the son of Saul. Rebbi La said, even the women behind the loom[20] did know that David would rule in the future. Eleazar ben Azaria was Second in rank[21]. There are among these only the Elders of Bathyra who freed themselves of the Patriarchate and appointed him Patriarch. The rabbis of Caesarea said, also Rebbi Ḥanina of Sepphoris for Rebbi Mana. Rebbi Joshua ben Qabusai[22] said, all my days I fled from authority. Now that I entered, anybody who would remove me I would treat like a water kettle. As the kettle burns, and injures, and chars, so I would treat him. Rebbi Yose ben Rebbi Bun said, heaven forbid that he wanted this. But he said, who could tell me that he would sanctify the Name of Heaven as I am doing.

19 Following ג, we read "the earthly House", meaning the Patriarchate (as recognized by L. Ginzberg), not "the earthly court". While Hillel became Patriarch because of his intellectual stature, in Talmudic times the descendants of Rebbi

were no longer the leading scholars. The question then is asked, why they should retain their status as Patriarchs. They are needed since their pronouncements can guarantee unity of practice in Judaism.
20 Greek καῖρος, ό.
21 While he volunteered to re-establish Rabban Gamliel as Patriarch (*Berakhot* 4:1

Notes 114-124). ג reads "there was a stipulation," that he would remain Chief Justice if Rabban Gamliel was re-instated as Patriarch.
22 Since the name tradition is not uniform, it cannot be determined who exactly was the person referred to.

(33a line 67) עַל שְׁלֹשָׁה דְבָרִים עָלָה הִלֵּל מִבָּבֶל. טָהוֹר הֲוּא. יָכוֹל יִפָּטֵר וְיֵלֵךְ לוֹ. תַּלְמוּד לוֹמַר וְטִהֲרוֹ הַכֹּהֵן. אִי וְטִהֲרוֹ הַכֹּהֵן יָכוֹל אִם אָמַר הַכֹּהֵן עַל טָמֵא טָהוֹר יְהֵא טָהוֹר. תַּלְמוּד לוֹמַר טָהוֹר הֲוּא וְטִהֲרוֹ הַכֹּהֵן: כָּל זֶה עָלָה הִלֵּל מִבָּבֶל.

כָּתוּב אֶחָד אוֹמֵר. וְזָבַחְתָּ פֶּסַח לַיָי אֱלֹהֶיךָ צֹאן וּבָקָר. וְכָתוּב אֶחָד אוֹמֵר. מִן־הַכְּבָשִׂים וּמִן־הָעִזִּים תִּקָּחוּ· הָא כֵיצַד. צֹאן לַפֶּסַח. וְצֹאן וּבָקָר לַחֲגִיגָה.

כָּתוּב אֶחָד אוֹמֵר. שֵׁשֶׁת יָמִים תֹּאכַל מַצּוֹת. וְכָתוּב אֶחָד אוֹמֵר. שִׁבְעַת יָמִים מַצּוֹת תֹּאכֵלוּ. הָא כֵיצַד. שִׁשָּׁה מִן הֶחָדָשׁ וְשִׁבְעָה מִן הַיָּשָׁן. וְדָרַשׁ וְהִסְכִּים וְעָלָה וְקִיבֵּל הֲלָכָה.

Because of three questions Hillel immigrated from Babylonia. *He is pure.* I could think that he was rid of it and may take leave, the verse says, *the Cohen shall declare him pure.* If *the Cohen shall declare him pure* then I could think that if the Cohen declared him pure while he was impure that he was pure, the verse says, *he is pure and the Cohen shall declare him pure*[23]. For this Hillel immigrated from Babylonia[24].

One verse says[25], *you shall sacrifice a Pesah to the Eternal, your God, small cattle and large cattle.* Another verse says[26], *from sheep and goats you shall take.* How is this? Small cattle for *Pesah*, small and large cattle for the festival sacrifice[27].

One verse says[28], *you shall eat mazzot for six days;* another verse says[29], *seven days you shall eat mazzot.* How is this? Six days from the new crop[30], seven days from the old. He interpreted, and agreed, and immigrated, and received practice[31].

23 *Lev.* 13:37.
24 *Sifra Tazria` Pereq* 9(15).
25 *Deut.* 16:2.
26 *Ex.* 12:5.
27 Babli 70b, *Sifry Deut.* 129, not in the name of Hillel.
28 *Deut.* 16:8.
29 *Ex.* 12:5.

30 After the *Omer* ceremony on the second day of the Holiday of Unleavened Bread, when grain from the new harvest becomes permitted (*Lev.* 23:14). *Sifry Deut.* 134 in the name of R. Simeon, 5 generations after Hillel; *Mekhilta dR. Ismael Bo, Parašah* 8, anonymous.

31 He had found the solutions himself; he immigrated into Palestine to have his explanations accepted by Shemaya and Avtalion and to have it harmonized with existing practice.

(33a line 74) מִיחוֹי קִרְבָיו. אָמַר רִבִּי יוֹחָנָן. כָּל פָּעַל יְיָ לַמַּעֲנֵהוּ. שֶׁלֹּא יְהֵא נִרְאֶה כְנוֹטֵל אֵימוֹרִין מִתּוֹךְ זֶבַח מְנוּוָל. הַפְשֵׁיטוֹ דּוֹחֶה אֶת הַשַּׁבָּת. תַּנֵּי רִבִּי יִשְׁמָעֵאל. תַּנֵּי רִבִּי יִשְׁמָעֵאל בְּנוֹ שֶׁל רִבִּי יוֹחָנָן בֶּן בְּרוֹקָה אוֹמֵר. בַּשַּׁבָּת הָיָה מַפְשִׁיט אֶת הֶחָזֶה. מַה טַעֲמֵיהּ דְּרִבִּי יִשְׁמָעֵאל. שֶׁלֹּא יְהֵא נִרְאֶה כְנוֹטֵל אֵימוֹרִין מִתּוֹךְ זֶבַח מְנוּוָל. מַה עָבַד לָהּ רִבִּי יִשְׁמָעֵאל בְּנוֹ שֶׁל רִבִּי יוֹחָנָן בֶּן בְּרוֹקָה. מִתּוֹךְ שֶׁהוּא הוֹפְכוֹ אֵינוֹ כְנוֹטֵל אֵימוֹרִין מִתּוֹךְ זֶבַח מְנוּוָל. אָמַר רִבִּי יוֹחָנָן. רִבִּי יִשְׁמָעֵאל וְרִבִּי יִשְׁמָעֵאל בְּנוֹ שֶׁל רִבִּי יוֹחָנָן בֶּן בְּרוֹקָה אָמְרוּ דָבָר אֶחָד. כְּמָה דְּרִבִּי יִשְׁמָעֵאל אָמַר. מוּבְחָר דּוֹחֶה. אֵין מוּבְחָר מִן הַמּוּבְחָר דּוֹחֶה. [כֵּן רִבִּי יִשְׁמָעֵאל בְּנוֹ שֶׁל רִבִּי יוֹחָנָן בֶּן בְּרוֹקָא אוֹמֵר. מוּבְחָר דּוֹחֶה. אֵין מוּבְחָר מִן הַמּוּבְחָר דּוֹחֶה. אִין תֵּימַר. מוּבְחָר הוּא. יִקְרָעֶנּוּ וְיוֹצִיא אֵימוֹרָיו. אָמַר רִבִּי יוֹסֵי בֵּירִבִּי בּוּן. לֹא אַתְיָא אֶלָּא כְּרִבִּי שִׁמְעוֹן.

דְּתַנֵּי. הַגּוֹרֵר הַקּוֹדֵחַ הַקּוֹצֵץ כָּל־שֶׁהוּא בַּשַּׁבָּת חַיָּיב. רִבִּי שִׁמְעוֹן בֶּן אֶלְעָזָר אוֹמֵר. הַגּוֹרֵר עַד שֶׁיִּגּוֹר כָּל־צוֹרְכּוֹ. הַקּוֹדֵחַ עַד שֶׁיִּקְדַּח כָּל־צוֹרְכּוֹ. הַקּוֹצֵץ עַד שֶׁיְּקַצֵּץ כָּל־צוֹרְכּוֹ. וְהַמְעַבֵּד אֶת הָעוֹר עַד שֶׁיְּעַבֵּד כָּל־צוֹרְכּוֹ. אָמַר רִבִּי יַעֲקֹב בַּר אָחָא. לֹא אַתְיָא אֶלָּא כְּרִבִּי שִׁמְעוֹן. דְּרִבִּי שִׁמְעוֹן לֹא עָבַד מִקְצָת מְלָאכָה כְּכוּלָּהּ. וְרַבָּנָן עָבְדִין מִקְצָת מְלָאכָה כְּכוּלָּהּ.

וְקַשְׁיָא עַל דְּרַבָּן שִׁמְעוֹן בֶּן גַּמְלִיאֵל. אִילּוּ נָטַל לִקְצוֹר וְלֹא קָצַר שֶׁמָּא כְלוּם הוּא. אָמַר רַב. אַתְיָא דְּרַבָּן שִׁמְעוֹן בֶּן גַּמְלִיאֵל כְּרִבִּי יְהוּדָה. דְּתַנֵּי. הַשּׁוֹבֵט וְהַמְקַטְקֵט עַל הָאָרִיג חַיָּיב מִפְּנֵי שֶׁהוּא כִמְיַישֵּׁב בְּיָדוֹ. וְהָכָא מִפְּנֵי שֶׁהוּא כִמְיַישֵּׁב בְּיָדוֹ.

"Emptying its intestines". Rebbi Joḥanan said, *all the Eternal's works are for Himself*[32]; that it should not look as if he took the parts from a disgusting sacrifice[33]. Rebbi Ismael stated, its skinning pushes the Sabbath aside[34]. It was stated: Rebbi Ismael the son of Rebbi Joḥanan ben Beroqa says, on the Sabbath one was skinning the breast[35]. What is Rebbi Ismael's reason? That it should not look as if he took the parts from a disgusting sacrifice. What does Rebbi Ismael the son of Rebbi Joḥanan ben Beroqa do with this? Because he turns it around, it is not as if he was taking the parts from a disgusting sacrifice[36]. Rebbi Joḥanan said, Rebbi Ismael and Rebbi Ismael the son of Rebbi Joḥanan ben Beroqa said the same. As Rebbi Ismael said, choice pushes aside but choicest does not push aside[37], so Rebbi Ismael the son of

Rebbi Johanan ben Beroqa said choice pushes aside but choicest does not push aside. If you are saying, this is choice, can he not tear it open and remove the parts[38]? Rebbi Yose ben Rebbi Abun said, it only follows Rebbi Simeon.

[39]As it was stated[7]: "One who scratches, who drills, who chops anything is liable; Rebbi Simeon ben Eleazar says, one who scratches only if he scratches completely, one who drills only if he drills completely, one who chops only if he chopped completely, one who tans hides only if he tanned completely." And Rebbi Jacob bar Ada said, this only follows Rebbi Simeon since Rebbi Simeon did not treat partial work as whole work, but the rabbis do treat partial work as whole work[40].

[41]And it is difficult about Rabban Simeon ben Gamliel. If one took [tools] to harvest but did not harvest, is that perhaps anything? Rebbi Ada said, Rabban Simeon ben Gamliel parallels Rebbi Jehudah, as it was stated: "One who hits or smooths a piece of weaving is liable. He is liable because he equalizes with his hand." And here because he equalizes with his hand.

32 Prov. 16:4. Quoted Babli *Šabbat* 116b.
33 Since for profane use the emptying of the intestines would be a Sabbath violation.
34 But for profane use it would be a Sabbath violation.
35 With Tosephta 4:10 one has to read: "One was skinning up to the breast (starting with the feet)."
36 Since it is obvious that one skins from the feet for sacrificial use, it is not necessary to push aside the Sabbath more than a minimum.
37 In Mishnah *Menahot* 6:1, R. Ismael states that while on a Sabbath the 'Omer ($^3/_{10}$ of a *seah*) of barley flour was sifted from three *seah* of grain while on weekdays it was from five. This implies that for the Temple service one uses choice material but only on weekdays it must be of the choicest kind if it is a matter of pushing aside Sabbath prohibitions.
38 If we interpret R. Ismael ben R. Johanan ben Beroqa in this way, then R. Ismael would be inconsistent by requiring total stripping of the *Pesah*. Also R. Ismael ben R. Johanan ben Beroqa could obtain the desired result with much less Sabbath desecration. Therefore R. Johanan's statement cannot be correct.
39 This is from *Šabbat* 12, Notes 47-49.
40 Therefore R. Ismael ben R. Johanan ben Beroqa disagrees with R. Ismael and holds that skinning the *Pesah* on the Sabbath is forbidden as action for profane use; he only permits partial skinning since for him it is not a Sabbath desecration. Cf. *Menahot* 63b-64a.

41 This paragraph, continuation of the preceding one, is copied from *Šabbat* 12, Notes 50-53; it refers to Mishnah *Šabbat* 12:1 and has no meaning here.

(33b line 18) וְהִקְטִיר חֲלָבָיו. וְלֹא־יָלִין חֵלֶב־חַגִּי עַד־בֹּקֶר: וְאֵימוֹרֵי חוֹל קְרֵיבִין בְּיוֹם טוֹב. אָמַר רִבִּי אַבָּהוּ. קִיַּימְתִּיהָ בְּשְׁחָל אַרְבָּעָה עָשָׂר לִהְיוֹת בַּשַׁבָּת. רִבִּי יוֹנָה בָעֵי. אִם בְּשְׁחָל אַרְבָּעָה עָשָׂר לִהְיוֹת בַּשַׁבָּת אֵין חֲגִיגָה בָאָה עִמּוֹ. אָמְרָה תוֹרָה. הַקְרִיבֵהוּ מִבְּעוֹד יוֹם. שֶׁלֹּא יָבוֹא לִידֵי בַל תָּלִין. וְהָכָא. הַקְרִיבֵהוּ מִבְּעוֹד יוֹם. שֶׁלֹּא יָבוֹא לִידֵי בַל תְּאַחֵר. אָמַר רִבִּי חִינְנָא. אִילוּ עָבַר וְהֵבִיא שֶׁמָּא אֵינוֹ כָשֵׁר. מֵאַחַר שֶׁאִילוּ עָבַר וְהֵבִיא כָּשֵׁר עוֹבֵר.

[42]"And the burning of its fat." *The fat of my holiday offering shall not stay until the morning*[43]. But could parts from weekday be brought on a holiday[44]? Rebbi Abbahu said, I confirmed it, if the Fourteenth fell on a Sabbath. Rebbi Jonah asked, if the Fourteenth fell on a Sabbath, no holiday offering comes with it, that the Torah has to say, bring it to the altar when it is still daylight lest it come to "not stay"[45]? (And here, bring it to the altar when it is still daylight lest it come to "not tarry"[46].) Rebbi Ḥinena said, if he transgressed and brought, is it not qualified[47]? Since it is qualified if he transgressed and brought, he would transgress[48].

42 This paragraph also appears word for word in *Roš Haššanah* 1:1 (56c l. 13), which seems to be the original source.

43 *Ex.* 23:18. The first part of the verse is about slaughtering the *Pesaḥ* (Chapter 5, Note 130). The second part quoted here explicitly mentions the holiday offering, the required family sacrifice on the occasion of the holiday pilgrimage, but is interpreted to include the fat of the *Pesaḥ*.

44 Since the 15th of Nisan is a holiday, it seems obvious that parts of a sacrifice brought on the 14th have to be burned before the start of the holiday; the verse seems to be meaningless.

45 Even if we restrict the meaning of the sentence to holiday offerings, since there is none if the 14th falls on a Sabbath, the explanation of R. Abbahu seems pointless.

46 This sentence, referring to *Deut.* 23:22, belongs to *Roš Haššanah* and has no meaning here.

47 This argument that a holiday offering, brought in error on the 14th which is a Sabbath, is qualified and the person who brought it is not liable for a Sabbath infraction, is not found in the Babli and the surviving Tosephta mss.; it is quoted as R. Meïr's opinion in the Tosephta of the Bomberg Babli, 5:4.

48 If one brings a holiday offering on a 14th which is a Sabbath, the explanation of R. Abbahu applies. The verse is not meaningless.

(33b line 24) אֲבָל צְלִיָּיתוֹ וַהֲדָחַת קְרָבָיו אֵינָן דּוֹחִין. תַּנִּינָן. יָצְאוּ וְצָלוּ אֶת פִּסְחֵיהֶן וְאִתְּ אָמַר הָכֵין. לְשִׁילְשׁוּלוֹ לַתַּנּוּר.

הַרְכָּבוֹ וַהֲבָאָתוֹ מִחוּץ לַתְּחוּם. לֹא אָמַר אֶלָּא חוּץ לִירוּשָׁלֵם. הָא חוּץ לָעֲזָרָה מוּתָּר מִשּׁוּם שְׁבוּת שֶׁהִתִּירוּ בַּמִּקְדָּשׁ.

"But its roasting, and washing of its intestines, do not push aside." We have stated, "When it got dark, they left and roasted their *Pesaḥ*," and you are saying so? For hanging into the oven[49].

"Carrying it, or bringing it from outside the Sabbath domain." He said only, from outside Jerusalem. Therefore from outside the Temple courtyard it is permitted because of rabbinic Sabbath restriction[50] which they permitted in the Temple.

49 In Mishnah *Šabbat* 1:15 roasting the *Pesaḥ* on the Sabbath is permitted if the 14th is a Friday. Why is it prohibited if the 14th is a Sabbath? The roasting essentially os automatic; it is starting the process which is forbidden on a Sabbath, whether the 14th is a Friday or a Sabbath.

50 Since Jerusalem is a walled city, inside the city there can be no public domain by biblical standards; restrictions of carrying within the city walls are rabbinic.

(32b line 28) חֲתִיכַת יַבֶּלְתּוֹ. תַּמָּן תַּנִּינָן. חוֹתְכִין יַבֶּלֶת בַּמִּקְדָּשׁ, אֲבָל לֹא בַּמְּדִינָה. וְאִם בִּכְלִי, כָּאן וְכָאן אָסוּר: הָכָא אַתְּ אָמַר. דּוֹחָה. וְהָכָא אַתְּ אָמַר. אֵינוֹ דוֹחָה.

רִבִּי סִימוֹן רִבִּי יְהוֹשֻׁעַ בֶּן לֵוִי בְּשֵׁם בַּר פְּדָיָיה. מִפְּנֵי קִילְקוּל פַּייסוֹת. אָמַר רִבִּי יוֹסֵה. וְהֵן שֶׁהִפִּיסוּ. רִבִּי שִׁמְעוֹן בֶּן לָקִישׁ בְּשֵׁם רִבִּי סוֹבַיָיה. כָּאן בְּנִפְרֶכֶת וְכָאן בְּשֶׁאֵינָהּ נִפְרֶכֶת. רִבִּי שִׁמְעוֹן בֶּן יָקִים אָמַר. כָּאן בְּלַחָה בְּון בִּיבֵישָׁה. רִבִּי יוֹסֵי בֵּירִבִּי חֲנִינָה אָמַר. כָּאן בְּיָד וְכָאן בִּכְלִי. אַתְיָא דְּרִבִּי שִׁמְעוֹן בֶּן לָקִישׁ כְּבַר קַפָּרָא. וּדְרִבִּי יוֹסֵי בַּר חֲנִינָה כְּרִבִּי יוֹחָנָן. דְּתַנֵּי. כָּל־הַמְקַלְקְלִין פְּטוּרִין חוּץ מִן הַמַּבְעִיר וְהָעוֹשֶׂה חַבּוּרָה. בַּר קַפָּרָא אָמַר. אֲפִילּוּ אֵינוֹ צָרִיךְ לְדָם. אֲפִילּוּ אֵינוֹ צָרִיךְ לְאֵפֶר. אָמַר רִבִּי יוֹחָנָן. וְהוּא שֶׁיְּהֵא צָרִיךְ לְדָם. וְהוּא שֶׁיְּהֵא צָרִיךְ לְאֵפֶר. רִבִּי אָחָא רִבִּי חֲנִינָה בְּשֵׁם רִבִּי יוֹחָנָן. כָּאן וְכָאן בְּלַחָה אֲנָן קַיָּימִין. וְהוּא שֶׁיְּהֵא צָרִיךְ לְדָם.

"Cutting its wart." There, we have stated[51]: "One cuts a wart at the Temple but not in the countryside; using an implement is forbidden here and there." Here[52], you are saying, it pushes aside; there, you are saying, it does not push aside.

[53]Rebbi Simon in the name of Rebbi Joshua ben Levi in the name of Bar Pedaya: Because of vitiation of the lotteries. Rebbi Yose said, but only if they drew lots. Rebbi Simeon ben Laqish said in the name of Rebbi Sobaya: Whether it can be scraped off or cannot be scraped off. Rebbi Simeon ben Yaqim said, one if it is moist, the other if it is dry. Rebbi Yose ben Ḥanina said, here by hand, there by implement. It turns out that Rebbi Simeon ben Laqish parallels Bar Qappara, and Rebbi Yose ben Ḥanina Rebbi Joḥanan, as it was stated: All who destroy are not liable, except the incendiary and one causing an injury. Bar Qappara said, even if he did not need the blood, even if he did not need the ashes. Rebbi Joḥanan said, only if he needed the blood or the ashes. Rebbi Aḥa, Rebbi Ḥanina in the name of Rebbi Joḥanan: In both cases if it is moist, and only if he needs the blood.

51 Mishnah *Eruvin* 10:11.
52 In *Eruvin,* showing that this is the origin of the Halakhah.
53 This paragraph is from *Eruvin* 10, Notes 141-148.

משנה ב: אָמַר רִבִּי אֱלִיעֶזֶר וּמַה אִם שְׁחִיטָה שֶׁהִיא מִשּׁוּם מְלָאכָה דּוֹחָה אֶת הַשַּׁבָּת. אֵילּוּ שֶׁהֵן מִשּׁוּם שְׁבוּת לֹא יִדְחוּ אֶת הַשַּׁבָּת. אָמַר לוֹ רִבִּי יְהוֹשֻׁעַ יוֹם טוֹב יוֹכִיחַ שֶׁהִתִּיר בּוֹ מִשּׁוּם מְלָאכָה וְאָסַר בּוֹ מִשּׁוּם שְׁבוּת. אָמַר לוֹ רִבִּי אֱלִיעֶזֶר מַה זֶּה יְהוֹשֻׁעַ מָה רְאָיָה רְשׁוּת לַמִּצְוָה. (fol. 32d)

Mishnah 2: Rebbi Eliezer said, if slaughter which is work[54] pushes the Sabbath aside, should not these[55], which are because of Sabbath rest, push the Sabbath aside? Rebbi Joshua said to him, holiday is a counter example, where He permitted the work but forbade because of Sabbath rest[56]. Rebbi Eliezer answered whim, what is this, Joshua? What proof is option for obligation[57]?

54 Slaughter is one of the 49 categories of work biblically forbidden on the Sabbath.
55 The Mishnah is a continuation of Mishnah 1, where R. Eliezer holds that all actions needed for the *Pesah* push aside the Sabbath. The discussion in particular is about the list of rabbinically prohibited actions at the end of Mishnah 1, which are permitted by R. Eliezer but prohibited by the Sages (represented by R. Joshua.)
56 Since preparation of food is permitted on a holiday, slaughter for meat is permitted.

But the rules of rabbinic Sabbath rest apply to holiday as to the Sabbath.

57 Rules of preparation of profane food cannot teach anything for sacrifices.

(33b line 39) **הלכה ב**: הֲבָאָתוֹ חוּץ לַתְּחוּם שְׁבוּת. הָדָא מְסַיְּיעָא לְהָא דָּמַר רִבִּי יוֹנָתָן קוֹמֵי רִבִּי חִיָּיה רִבָּה בְּשֵׁם רִבִּי שִׁמְעוֹן בַּר יוֹסֵי בַּר לַקוֹנְיָא. לוֹקִין עַל תְּחוּמֵי שַׁבָּת דְּבַר תּוֹרָה. אָמַר לֵיהּ רִבִּי חִיָּיה רַבָּה. וַהֲלֹא אֵין בַּשַּׁבָּת אֶלָּא סְקִילָה וְכָרֵת. אָמַר לֵיהּ. וְהָכְתִיב אַל־תֹּאכְלוּ מִמֶּנּוּ נָא . אָמַר לֵיהּ מִי כְתִיב לֹא. אַל כְּתִיב. אָמַר לֵיהּ. וְהָכְתִיב שְׁבוּ | אִישׁ תַּחְתָּיו אַל־יֵצֵא אִישׁ מִמְּקוֹמוֹ בַּיּוֹם הַשְּׁבִיעִי׃ אָמַר לֵיהּ. מַה כְתִיב לֹא. אַל כְּתִיב. אָמַר רִבִּי יוֹסֵי בֵּירִבִּי בּוּן. אַף עַל פִּי כֵן זֶה עוֹמֵד בִּשְׁמוּעָתוֹ וְזֶה עוֹמֵד בִּשְׁמוּעָתוֹ. חֲתִיכַת יַבַּלְתּוֹ בִּכְלִי שְׁבוּת. אָמַר רִבִּי אַבָּהוּ. לֹא תַנֵּי רִבִּי יוֹסֵי בֶּן חֲנִינָא אֶלָּא הֶרְכֵּבוֹ וַהֲבָאָתוֹ. הָא חֲתִיכַת יַבַּלְתּוֹ לֹא. מִן בְּגִין דּוּ סָבַר בָּכְלִי. הָא אִין לָא סָבַר בָּכְלִי. שְׁבוּת. לֹא כֵן אָמַר רִבִּי אַבָּהוּ בְּשֵׁם רִבִּי יוֹסֵי בֶּן חֲנִינָא. מַפְלִיגִין. בְּשֶׁנְּטָלוֹ הוּא. אֲבָל אִם נְטָלוֹ אַחֵר מָאוּסִין הֵן. וְהָדֵין זֶבַח כְּאַחֵר הוּא. אָמַר רִבִּי יוֹסֵה. שַׁנְיָיא הִיא הָכָא דִכְתִיב זֶבַח. אָמַר רִבִּי מָנָא. הָזַיָּיה שְׁבוּת וְאֵילוּ שְׁבוּת. הַזָּיָה דּוֹחִין וְאֵילוּ אֵינָן דּוֹחִין. אֶלָּא שֶׁזֶּה בְזֶבַח וְזֶה בְזוֹבֵחַ. מִילְּתֵיהּ דְּרִבִּי זְעוּרָא אָמְרָה. הִיא זֶבַח הִיא זוֹבֵחַ. תַּנֵּי רִבִּי יוּדָה בַּר פָּזִי דְּבַר קַפָּרָה קוֹמֵי רִבִּי זְעֵירָא. תִּמְהוֹנַי חֲדָא קִיבֵּל רִבִּי לִיעֶזֶר מֵרִבִּי יְהוֹשֻׁעַ אֶת הַתְּשׁוּבָה שֶׁזֶּה בְזֶבַח וְזֶה בְזוֹבֵחַ. בַּר קַפָּרָה תַּמָּה. אָמַר לֵיהּ. רִבִּי לִיעֶזֶר לֹא תַמָּהּ.

10 דוחין K | דוחה 11 זעורא K | זעורה 12 זעיורא K | זעורה יהושע K | יישע את התשובה K | תשובה 13 קפרה K קפרא

Halakhah 2: Is bringing it from outside the Sabbath domain a matter of Sabbath rest[58]? [59]This supports what Rebbi Jonathan said before the Elder Rebbi Ḥiyya in the name of Rebbi Simeon ben Rebbi Yose ben Laqonia: One whips because of Sabbath domains as word of the Torah. Rebbi Ḥiyya the Elder said to him, but for Sabbath there is only stoning or extirpation! He said to him, is there not written[60], *do not eat from it raw*? He said to him, is there written לא? No, it is written אל! He said to him, is there not written[61], *stay everybody where he is, no person shall leave his place on the Seventh day*? He said to him, is there written לא? No, it is written אל. Rebbi Yose ben Rebbi Abun said, nevertheless each one kept to his tradition[62]. Is cutting its wart with an implement a matter of Sabbath rest[63]? Rebbi Abbahu said, Rebbi Yose ben Ḥanina stated only carrying it and bringing it; therefore not cutting its wart[64]. That is because he thinks it[65] is with an implement. Therefore if he were not of the opinion that it was with an implement, would it be a matter of Sabbath rest? [66]Did not Rebbi Abbahu say in the name of Rebbi Yose ben Ḥanina, where do they disagree? If he removed it with an implement. But if another person removed it it is disgusting[67], and is not the sacrifice another? Rebbi Yose said, there is a difference because there is written "a sacrifice". Rebbi Mana said, sprinkling[68] is a matter of Sabbath rest, and these are because of Sabbath rest. Sprinkling is pushed aside[69] but these should not be pushed aside? Only that these are about the sacrifice and this is for the person who sacrifices. The word of Rebbi Ze`ira implies that there is no difference between sacrifice and sacrificer: Rebbi Jehudah bar Pazi stated Bar Qappara's before Rebbi Ze`ira: I wonder how Rebbi Eliezer received Rebbi Joshua's answer that these are about the sacrifice and this is for the person who sacrifices[70]? He told him, Bar Qappara was wondering, Rebbi Eliezer was not wondering[71].

58 Since the argument of R. Eliezer and R. Joshua is about rabbinic restrictions because of Sabbath rest, it is implied that the list of items in Mishnah 2 about which R. Eliezer dissents contains only rabbinic prohibitions. But bringing anything from outside the Sabbath domain is a biblical prohibition.

59 The next sentences are from *Eruvin* 3, Notes 127-131.

60 *Ex.* 12:9. This belongs to the discussion there whether all pentateuchal prohibitions are legally prosecutable, or only those formulated as לא whereas those introduced by the negation אל are simply moral obligations. Since the latter then cannot be enforced in court by biblical standards, they are equal in rank to rabbinic prohibitions.

61 *Ex.* 16:28.

62 This is the end of the parallel in *Eruvin* 3.

63 This is making a wound, biblically forbidden under the category of slaughtering.

64 In Mishnah 1, he does not read "cutting its wart".

65 Cutting the wart. Everybody agrees that biting off the wart is unprofessional, therefore does not create liability, and is only rabbinically forbidden.

66 Quoted from *Eruvin* 10(7), Note 64. It is stated there that cutting the wart creates liability only if done professionally with a surgeon's knife.

67 Therefore not causing biblical liability. Babli *Šabbat* 94b.

68 Purifying a person impure by the impurity of the dead by sprinkling with water containing of the ashes of the Red Cow. In Second Temple times this was a public act (Mishnah *Parah* 11:4) not performed on the Sabbath.

69 If the 14th of Nisan is a Sabbath and a person's seventh day of impurity falls on that day, he may not be purified by sprinkling, but this is not biblically forbidden, and he has to celebrate his *Pesah* on the 14th of Iyar. Cf. Mishnaiot 3,4.

70 Since R. Joshua's argument is about the slaughterer, not the animal being slaughtered.

71 Their discussion makes sense only if there is no difference whether one speaks about sacrifice or sacrificer. This confirms what R. Ze'ira said.

(33b line 55) מַה שְׁבוּת. לֹא כֵן תַּנִּינָן. הַמְחַלֵּל אֶת הַקֳּדָשִׁים. וְהַמְבַזֶּה אֶת הַמּוֹעֲדוֹת. וְהַמֵּפֵר בְּרִיתוֹ שֶׁלְּאַבְרָהָם אָבִינוּ. וְהַמְגַלֶּה פָנִים בַּתּוֹרָה. אַף עַל פִּי שֶׁיֵּשׁ בְּיָדוֹ תּוֹרָה וּמַעֲשִׂים טוֹבִים אֵין לוֹ חֵלֶק לָעוֹלָם הַבָּא· אָמַר רִבִּי יִרְמְיָה. מָהוּא רְשׁוּת. רָצָה בִּישֵּׁל רָצָה לֹא בִּישֵּׁל

1 והמפר K | והמפיר   2 שלאברהם אבינו K| אבינו אברהם   תורה ומעשים טובים K | מעשׂין טובין   3 לעולם הבא . . . לא בישל K | -

אָמַר רִבִּי יוֹסֵה. הָכֵין הֲוָה רִבִּי לִיעֶזֶר צָרִיךְ מִתְבַּזֶּה לְרִבִּי יְהוֹשֻׁעַ. הֲרֵי חֲגִיגַת יוֹם טוֹב לְשִׁיטָתָךְ תּוֹכִיחַ. שֶׁהִתִּירוּ בָהּ מִשֵּׁם מְלָאכָה וְאָסְרוּ בָהּ מִשֵּׁם שְׁבוּת. וַהֲוָה לֵיהּ מֵימַר בָּהּ. לֹא. אִם אָמַרְתְּ בַּחֲגִיגַת יוֹם טוֹב שֶׁאֵין חַיָּיבִין עָלֶיהָ כָרֵת. תֹּאמַר בַּפֶּסַח שֶׁחַיָּיבִין עָלָיו כָרֵת. וִיתִיבִינֵיהּ כְּמַתְנִיתִין. לֹא. אִם אָמַרְתְּ בְּיוֹם טוֹב שֶׁאֵין חַיָּיבִין עָלֶיהָ כָרֵת. תֹּאמַר בַּפֶּסַח שֶׁחַיָּיבִין עָלָיו כָרֵת. כַּיי דָּמַר רִבִּי אִימִּי. עֲשִׁירִין הָיוּ בִּתְשׁוּבוֹת. אוֹ יָבֹא כַּיי דָּמַר רִבִּי נָסָא. כְּאִינָשׁ דְּאִית לֵיהּ תְּרֵין טְעָמִין וְהוּא מָתִיב חַד מִינְּהוֹן.

1 אמ' ר' יוסה . . . מתבזה K | -   2 לשיטתך K | כשיטתך   מימר בה K | מימור ליה   4 ויתיביניה K | ויתבניניה עליה K | עליו   5 כיי K | אמ' ר' מנא שניה היא יום טוב שאין חייבין עליו כרת כההיא   אימי K | אמי   או ייבא כיי K | כההיא   6 מתיב K | מתיב

What does Sabbath rest mean? Did we not state[72] "One who desecrates *sancta*, or abases the holidays, or breaks the Covenant of our father Abraham, or is insolent against the Torah, even if in his hands are learning and good deeds, has no part in the Future World." Rebbi Jeremiah said, what is optional[73]? If he wants he cooks, if he does not want he does not cook.

Rebbi Yose said, so should Rebbi Eliezer have embarrassed Rebbi Joshua. Does not the festival offering disprove according to your system, where they permitted the category of work but prohibited the category of Sabbath rest[74]? He should have answered, no. If you are saying this about the festival offering about which one is not liable for extirpation, what can you say about *Pesaḥ* where one is liable for extirpation? He also could have objected as in the Mishnah: No, if you are saying this about the holiday about which one is not liable for extirpation, what can you say about *Pesaḥ where* one is liable for extirpation? It is as Rebbi Immi said, they were rich in answers[75]. Or it may be as Rebbi Nassa said, like a man who has two arguments but he moves one of them.

72 Mishnah *Avot* 3:11. Since there is an obligation to honor the holidays, is there not an obligation to slaughter animals for holiday meals. How can R. Eliezer call this optional?

73 There could have been meals prepared beforehand. There is no religious obligation to slaughter on a holiday, it truly is optional.

74 Since R. Eliezer is a follower of the House of Shammai, who permit the festival sacrifice to be brought on the holiday but prohibit the (biblically required but purely rabbinically prohibited) laying of hands on the sacrificial animal, he would have to agree that not all rabbinic restrictions are waived on Sabbath and holiday.

75 The same statements *Kilaim* 2:5 Note 89, *Nazir* 5:4 Note 109.

(fol. 32d) **משנה ג**: הֵשִׁיב רַבִּי עֲקִיבָה הַזָּיָה תּוֹכִיחַ שֶׁהִיא מִצְוָה וְהִיא מִשּׁוּם שְׁבוּת וְאֵינָהּ דּוֹחָה אֶת הַשַׁבָּת. אַף אַתָּה אַל תִּתְמַהּ עַל אֵילּוּ שֶׁאַף עַל פִּי שֶׁהֵן מִצְוָה וְהֵן מִשּׁוּם שְׁבוּת לֹא יְדֲחוּ אֶת הַשַׁבָּת.

Mishnah 3: Rebbi Aqiba answered, sprinkling[68] is a counter example, for it is a commandment and because of Sabbath rest does not push aside the Sabbath[69]. So you should not wonder about these[55], even though they are commandments and because of Sabbath rest but shall not push aside the Sabbath.

(33b line 66) **הלכה ג**: שְׁלֹשׁ עֶשְׂרֵה שָׁנָה עָשָׂה רִבִּי עֲקִיבָה נִכְנָס אֵצֶל רִבִּי לִיעֶזֶר וְלֹא הָיָה יוֹדֵעַ בּוֹ. וְזוֹ הִיא תְשׁוּבָתוֹ הָרִאשׁוֹנָה לִפְנֵי רִבִּי לִיעֶזֶר. אָמַר לוֹ רִבִּי יְהוֹשֻׁעַ, הֲלֹא זֶה הָעָם אֲשֶׁר מָאַסְתָּ בּוֹ צֵא־נָא עַתָּה וְהִלָּחֶם בּוֹ:

2 היא K | היא תחילת ליעזר K | אליעזר

Halakhah 3: Thirteen years did Rebbi Aqiba enter at Rebbi Eliezer's and he did not take notice of him. This is his first retort before Rebbi Eliezer. Rebbi Joshua said to him, *is this not the people which you despised; go now and fight against it*[76].

76 *Jud.* 9:38.

(33b line 69) תַּמָּן תַּנִּינָן. אֵי זוֹ הִיא דֶּרֶךְ רְחוֹקָה מִן הַמּוֹדִיעִית וְלַחוּץ. וּכְמִידָּתָהּ לְכָל רוּחַ. דִּבְרֵי רִבִּי [עֲקִיבָא. רִבִּי אֱלִיעֶזֶר אוֹמֵר. מֵאַסְקוּפַּת עֲזָרָה וְלַחוּץ.] אָמַר רִבִּי יוֹחָנָן. לֹא אָמַר רִבִּי לִיעֶזֶר אֶלָּא לְפוֹטְרוֹ מִן הַהַכָּרֵת. אָמַר רִבִּי לְעָזָר. מַתְנִיתָהּ אֲמָרָה כֵן. הֵשִׁיב רַבִּי עֲקִיבָה. הַזָּיָיה תּוֹכִיחַ. שֶׁהִיא מִצְוָה. וּמִצְוָה לְהַזֹּאת. תִּיפְתַּר שֶׁחָל יוֹם הַשְּׁבִיעִי שֶׁלּוֹ לִהְיוֹת בָּאַרְבָּעָה עָשָׂר שֶׁחָל לִהְיוֹת בַּשַׁבָּת. שֶׁאִילּוּ חוֹל הָיָה. הָיָה מַזֶּה עָלָיו וְאַחַר כָּךְ בָּא וְשׁוֹחֵט לוֹ אֶת פִּסְחוֹ וְהוּא נִכְנַס

וְאוֹכְלוֹ בָעֶרֶב. מִכֵּיוָן שֶׁהִיא שַׁבָּת וְאֵינוֹ מַזֶּה עָלָיו נִמְצָא מִתְעַכֵּב מִן הַמִּצְוֹת. אָמַר רַב הוֹשַׁעְיָה. תִּיפְתָּר שֶׁחָל יוֹם הַשְּׁבִיעִי שֶׁלּוֹ לִהְיוֹת בִּשְׁלֹשָׁה עָשָׂר שֶׁחָל לִהְיוֹת בַּשַּׁבָּת. שֶׁאִילּוּ חוֹל הָיָה. הָיָה מַזֶּה עָלָיו וּלְמָחָר הוּא בָא וְשׁוֹחֵט לוֹ אֶת פִּסְחוֹ וְהוּא נִכְנָס וְאוֹכְלוֹ לָעֶרֶב. מִכֵּיוָן שֶׁהִיא שַׁבָּת וְאֵינוֹ מַזֶּה עָלָיו נִמְצָא מִתְעַכֵּב מִן הַמִּצְוֹת. אַשְׁכַּח תַּנֵּי כְּהָדֵין קַדְמָיָא.

2 C עקיבא K | עקיבה C אלעזר K | ליעזר K קדמייא | 9 קדמייא K קדמיה

There[77], we have stated: "What is 'far away'[78]? From Modiin and farther away, and in the same distance in every direction, the words of Rebbi Aqiba. Rebbi Eliezer says, from the doorstep[79] of the Temple courtyard and farther away." Rebbi Johanan said, Rebbi Eliezer said this only not to make him liable for extirpation[80]. Rebbi Eleazar said, the Mishnah implies this: "Rebbi Aqiba answered him, sprinkling is a counter example, for it is a commandment." Is it a commandment to sprinkle[81]? Explain it that his seventh day happened to be the Fourteenth which fell on a Sabbath. If it had been a weekday, one would have sprinkled on him, then he would have come, slaughtered his *Pesah*[82], and entered and eaten it in the evening. Because it is a Sabbath and one does not sprinkle on him, it results that he he is prevented from fulfilling the commandment. Rav Hoshaia said, explain it that his seventh day happened to be the Thirteenth which fell on a Sabbath. If it had been a weekday, one would have sprinkled on him, then the next day he would have come, slaughtered his *Pesah*, and entered and eaten it in the evening. Because it is a Sabbath and one does not sprinkle on him, it results that he is prevented from fulfilling the commandment. It was found stated[83] following the first [explanation].

אָמַר רִבִּי יוּדָה בַּר פָּזִי. תִּיפְתָּר כְּמָאן דְּאָמַר. מֵאַסְקוּפַת יְרוּשָׁלֵם וְלַחוּץ. מְשִׁיבִין דָּבָר מִחוּץ לִירוּשָׁלֵם עַל דָּבָר שֶׁבִּירוּשָׁלֵם

1 כמאן דאמ' K | כמן דמר מאסכופת KC | מאסקופת משיבין K | ומשיבין

Rebbi Jehudah bar Pazi said, explain it following him who said, from the doorstep of Jerusalem and outside. Would one object from outside Jerusalem to something inside Jerusalem[84]?

וְאִית בַּר נַשׁ אֲמַר לְרַבֵּיהּ. אוֹ חִילּוּף. לְפִי שֶׁהָיָה רִבִּי לִיעֶזֶר מְלַמְּדוֹ הֲלָכָה וּבָא שְׁאֵין חֲגִיגָה דּוֹחָה שַׁבָּת וְכָפַר בּוֹ בִּשְׁעַת הַדִּין. לְפוּם כָּךְ הוּא אֲמַר לֵיהּ. אוֹ חִילּוּף.

2 שבת K | את השבת לפום K לפם

Is there anybody who says to his teacher, it is the other way around? Since Rebbi Eliezer was teaching him practice currently that the festival offering does not push aside the Sabbath and he objected to him at the time of argument, therefore he told him, it is the other way around[85].

77 Mishnah 9:2.
78 That a person at this place on the 14th of Nisan is not obligated to bring his *Pesaḥ* on the 14th of Nisan (*Num.* 9:13).
79 Accadic *askuppu*.
80 But he will agree that anybody within commuting distance to the Temple is obligated by a positive commandment (*Num.* 9:2) to offer the *Pesaḥ*.
81 The purification from the impurity of the dead is an obligation for anybody coming to the Sanctuary. If he is not going there, there is no obligation to be sprinkled on.
82 This is an inexact statement. The person who was sprinkled with the water containing the ashes of the Red Cow on the 3rd and 7th days of his impurity and then immerses himself in a *miqweh* is able to enter the sanctuary and eat *sancta* after sundown (*Num.* 19:19). This means that another person has to slaughter the *Pesaḥ* for him; but he can then come and eat from the sacrifice in the night. Rav Hoshaia holds that one may not slaughter for a person who could not slaughter by himself; therefore he has to transfer the situation to the 13th.
83 A *baraita* (not quoted) supports R. Eleazar against Rav Hoshaia.
84 S. Liebermann has noted that this statement refers to Tosephta 8:2 where R. Eliezer defines "far away" as "outside the place where [the *Pesaḥ*] is consumed" and argues by comparing *Pesaḥ* to Second Tithe. Both definitions point to Jerusalem, and not the Temple courtyard, as R. Eliezer's "not far away"; else one would compare "outside of Jerusalem" with "inside Jerusalem (but outside the Temple enclosure)." The version of the Tosephta is supported against the version of the Mishnah.
85 This refers to their discussion in Mishnah 4. S. Liebermann points out that the use of כָּפַר in the meaning of "contradict" is characteristic of *Sifry zuṭa*, and the remark refers to the formulation of the Mishnaic discussion in *Sifry zuṭa Beha'alotekha* 9(2).

(fol. 32d) **משנה ד**: אָמַר לוֹ רִבִּי אֱלִיעֶזֶר וְעָלֶיהָ אֲנִי דָן. מָה אִם שְׁחִיטָה שֶׁהִיא מִשּׁוּם מְלָאכָה דּוֹחָה אֶת הַשַּׁבָּת. הַזָּיָיה שֶׁהִיא מִשּׁוּם שְׁבוּת לֹא תִדְחֶה אֶת הַשַּׁבָּת. אָמַר לוֹ רִבִּי עֲקִיבָה אוֹ חִלּוּף מָה אִם הַזָּיָיה שֶׁהִיא מִשּׁוּם שְׁבוּת אֵינָהּ דּוֹחָה אֶת הַשַּׁבָּת אַף שְׁחִיטָה שֶׁהִיא מִשּׁוּם מְלָאכָה לֹא תִדְחֶה אֶת הַשַּׁבָּת.

Mishnah 4: Rebbi Eliezer said to him, about this I am arguing. Since slaughter, which is work, pushes the Sabbath aside, sprinkling, which is because of Sabbath rest, shall push aside the Sabbath. Rebbi Aqiba said to him, or the other way. Since sprinkling, which is because of Sabbath rest, does not push aside the Sabbath, slaughter, which is work, shall not push the Sabbath aside[86].

משנה ה: אָמַר לוֹ רִבִּי אֱלִיעֶזֶר. עֲקִיבָה עָקַרְתָּ מַה שֶּׁכָּתוּב בַּתּוֹרָה, בֵּין הָעַרְבַּיִם בְּמוֹעֲדוֹ בֵּין בַּחֹל בֵּין בַּשַּׁבָּת. אָמַר לוֹ רַבִּי הֲבֵא לִי מוֹעֵד לְאֵלּוּ כַּמּוֹעֵד בַּשְּׁחִיטָה. כְּלָל אָמַר רִבִּי עֲקִיבָה כָּל־מְלָאכָה שֶׁאֶיפְשָׁר לָהּ לֵיעָשׂוֹת מֵעֶרֶב שַׁבָּת אֵינָהּ דּוֹחָה אֶת הַשַּׁבָּת. שְׁחִיטָה שֶׁאֵי אֶיפְשָׁר לָהּ לֵיעָשׂוֹת מֵעֶרֶב שַׁבָּת דּוֹחָה אֶת הַשַּׁבָּת:

Mishnah 5: Rebbi Eliezer said to him, Aqiba! You uprooted what is written in the Torah, *between the evenings, at its fixed time*[87], whether on weekdays or on the Sabbath. He answered him, Rabbi, bring me a fixed time for these similar to the fixed time for slaughter[88]. Rebbi Aqiba formulated a principle: Anything which can be done on Friday does not push the Sabbath aside. Slaughter which cannot be done on Friday pushes the Sabbath aside.

---

86 Since it is agreed that the obligation to slaughter the *Pesaḥ* on the Sabbath if it is the 14th of Nisan is a biblical decree (Halakhah 6:1), what R. Aqiba proves is that biblical and rabbinic decrees cannot be compared in formal or informal arguments *de minore ad majus*.

87 *Num*. 9:2.

88 There is no biblical authorization for preparations of the *Pesaḥ* to be executed in violation of Sabbath rules.

(33c line 9) **הלכה ד:** תַּנֵּי. רִבִּי לִיעֶזֶר אוֹמֵר. כְּשֵׁם שֶׁהַשְּׁחִיטָה דּוֹחָה שַׁבָּת. כָּךְ מַכְשִׁירֵי שְׁחִיטָה דּוֹחִין אֶת הַשַּׁבָּת. אָמַר לוֹ רִבִּי עֲקִיבָה. לֹא. אִם אָמַרְתְּ בִּשְׁחִיטָה שֶׁאֵי אֶיפְשָׁר לָהּ לֵעָשׂוֹת מֵעֶרֶב שַׁבָּת דּוּחָה אֶת הַשַּׁבָּת. תֹּאמַר בְּמַכְשִׁירֵי שְׁחִיטָה שֶׁאֶיפְשָׁר לָהֶם לֵיעָשׂוֹת מֵעֶרֶב שַׁבָּת (אֵין)[89] דּוֹחִין אֶת הַשַּׁבָּת. אָמַר לוֹ רִבִּי אֱלִיעֶזֶר. אֵימוֹרֵי צִיבּוּר יוֹכִיחוּ. שֶׁהוּא יָכוֹל לַעֲשׂוֹתָן מוֹצָאֵי שַׁבָּת וַהֲרֵי הֵן דּוֹחִין אֶת הַשַּׁבָּת. מָה לִי מַכְשִׁירֵי שְׁחִיטָה לִפְנֵי שְׁחִיטָה. מָה לִי מַכְשִׁירֵי שְׁחִיטָה לְאַחַר שְׁחִיטָה. אָמַר לוֹ רִבִּי עֲקִיבָה. מָה לְמַכְשִׁירֵי שְׁחִיטָה לְאַחַר שְׁחִיטָה דּוֹחִין אֶת הַשַּׁבָּת שֶׁכְּבָר דָּחַת שְׁחִיטָה אֶת הַשַּׁבָּת. יִדָּחוּ מַכְשִׁירֵי שְׁחִיטָה לִפְנֵי שְׁחִיטָה וַאֲדַיִין לֹא דָחַת שְׁחִיטָה אֶת הַשַּׁבָּת. דָּבָר אַחֵר. שֶׁאִם יִמָּצֵא הַזֶּבַח פָּסוּל וְנִמְצָא דוֹחֶה אֶת הַשַּׁבָּת בְּלֹא שְׁחִיטָה.

1 שבת K | את השבת   2 אמרת K | אמרתה   שאי איפשר K | שאיפשר   3 לעשות K | ליעשות   תאמר K | תומר   שאיפשר K | שאפשר   ליעשות K | להעשות   4 אין דוחין K | שידחו   אליעזר K | ליעזר   אימורי K | אמורי   5 מה K | ומה   שחיטה K | לי מכשירי   שחיטה דוחין את השבת K | שחיטה דוחין את השבת למכשירי   8 הזבח K | זבח   - K

גַּבֵּי [תִינוֹק] מַה אִית לָךְ. שֶׁמָּא יֶחֱלֶה הַתִּינוֹק וְנִמְצָא דּוֹחֶה אֶת הַשַּׁבָּת בְּלֹא מִילָה. הֵתִיבוּן. הֲרֵי מִזְבֵּחַ שֶׁנָּפַל בַּשַּׁבָּת. הֲרֵי אֵינוֹ רָאוּי לִיבָּנוֹת מֵאֶתְמוֹל. הַגַּע עַצְמָךְ שֶׁנּוֹלְדָה לוֹ יַבּוֹלֶת. הֲרֵי אֵינוֹ רָאוּי לְחוֹתְכָהּ בַּשַּׁבָּת. מִין יַבּוֹלֶת רְאוּיָה לִיחָתֵךְ מֵאֶתְמוֹל. הַגַּע עַצְמָךְ שֶׁחָל יוֹם הַשְּׁבִיעִי שֶׁלּוֹ לִהְיוֹת בַּשַּׁבָּת. הֲרֵי אֵינוֹ רָאוּי לְהַזּוֹת בַּשַּׁבָּת. מִין הַזָּיָה רְאוּיָה לְהַזּוֹת מֵאֶתְמוֹל.

1 K תינוק | S - | 2 ראוי | K - | ליבנות | K להבנות מאתמול K בשבת מין מזבח ראוי להבנות מאיתמל לו | K לה

⁹⁰It was stated: "Rebbi Eliezer says, just as slaughter pushes the Sabbath aside so the preparations of slaughter push the Sabbath aside. Rebbi Aqiba said to him, no. If you speak about slaughter which is impossible to be done on Friday and pushes the Sabbath aside, what can you infer about preparations of slaughter than can be done on Friday, should they push the Sabbath aside? Rebbi Eliezer said to him, the public parts shall prove which he could do after the Sabbath and which nevertheless push aside the Sabbath. What is the difference between preparations of slaughter before the slaughter and preparations of slaughter after slaughter? Rebbi Aqiba said to him, about preparations of slaughter after slaughter which push aside the Sabbath when the slaughter already had pushed away the Sabbath, what does this imply for preparations of slaughter before slaughter when the slaughter had not yet pushed away the Sabbath? Another explanation: Maybe the sacrifice would be found disqualified, then it turned out that the Sabbath was pushed aside without a slaughter."

What can you say [about a baby]? Maybe the baby would become sick; then the Sabbath would be pushed aside without circumcision. They objected: If the altar collapsed on the Sabbath, it will not be possible to build on the Sabbath!⁹¹ Think of it, if it developed a wart? It cannot be cut on the Sabbath! Warts can be cut on the day before. Think of it, if his Seventh day falls on a Sabbath, there cannot be sprinkling on the Sabbath⁸¹! Sprinkling may be done on the day before.

89 Unwarranted addition by the corrector, not translated.

90 These paragraphs also are *Šabbat* 19 (17a line 16), Notes 66-76. The origin of the first paragraph is here, the second (of which part of the introduction and a sentence are missing here) is from there.

91 Added from K: Some kind of altar can be built the day before.

HALAKHAH FIVE   225

(fol. 32d) **משנה ו**: אֵימָתַי מְבִיאִין עִמּוֹ חֲגִיגָה בִּזְמַן שֶׁהוּא בָּא בַּחֹל בְּטָהֳרָה וּבְמוּעָט. בִּזְמַן שֶׁהוּא בָּא בַּשַּׁבָּת בִּמְרוּבֶּה וּבְטוּמְאָה אֵין מְבִיאִין עִמּוֹ חֲגִיגָה:

Mishnah 6: When does one bring a festival offering[92] with it? When it comes on a weekday, in purity, and in small portions[93]. When it comes on the Sabbath, in large portions, or in impurity[94], one does not bring a festival offering with it.

משנה ז: חֲגִיגָה הָיְתָה בָּאָה מִן הַצֹּאן מִן הַבָּקָר מִן הַכְּבָשִׂים וּמִן הָעִזִּים מִן הַזְּכָרִים וּמִן הַנְּקֵבוֹת וְנֶאֱכֶלֶת לִשְׁנֵי יָמִים וְלַיְלָה אֶחָד:

Mishnah 7: The festival offering came from small cattle or bovines, from sheep or goats, from males and females[95], and may be eaten during two days and one night[96].

92 Since every group had only one *Pesah*, if the number of participants was large so that only a small portion of the meat was available for each participant, the main dish as the meal was another sacrifice which was given under the rules of festival sacrifices even though it could not be counted as satisfying the biblical requirement of such an offering during the holiday itself.

93 If only small portions of *Pesah* meat were available for each participant, not enough to satisfy. Then the festival offering had to be consumed first.

94 If most of the public is impure, only public sacrifices may be offered in the Temple. The *Pesah* has the status of a public sacrifice in this respect, but the accompanying festival offering does not.

95 Whereas the *Pesah* must be a male goat or sheep.

96 In this case really 2 times 24 hrs.

(33c line 24) **הלכה ה**: תַּנֵּי. חֲגִינַת אַרְבָּעָה עָשָׂר הָיְתָה בָּאָה מִן הַמַּעֲשֵׂר. רִבִּי יַעֲקֹב בַּר אָחָא בְּשֵׁם שְׁמוּאֵל בַּר אַבָּא. זֹאת אוֹמֶרֶת שֶׁהִיא רְשׁוּת. אֵין תֵּימַר חוֹבָה. דָּבָר שֶׁהוּא בָּא חוֹבָה בָּא מִן הַמַּעֲשֵׂר.

תַּנֵּי. חֲגִיגָה הַבָּאָה עִם הַפֶּסַח נֶאֱכֶלֶת תְּחִילָּה כְּדֵי שֶׁיֵּיאָכֵל הַפֶּסַח לַשֹּׂבַע. וְלֹא יֵיאָכֵל הַפֶּסַח לַשֹּׂבַע. רִבִּי יוֹסֵי בֵּירִבִּי בּוּן בְּשֵׁם רִבִּי יַעֲקֹב בַּר דֹּסַאי. שֶׁלֹּא יָבֹא (לִפְנֵי) [לִידֵי] שְׁבִירַת עֶצֶם.
1 יֵיאָכֵל K | יאכל   2 יוֹסֵי K | יוסי   K | יוסה   יבא K | יצא

תַּנֵּי. חֲגִיגָה הַבָּאָה עִם הַפֶּסַח הָיְתָה מִתְבַּעֶרֶת עִמּוֹ. אִיתָא חֲמֵי. חֲגִיגָה נֶאֱכֶלֶת לִשְׁנֵי יָמִים וּפֶסַח נֶאֱכָל עַד חֲצוֹת. וְתֵימַר הָכֵין. בְּעוֹלִין עִמּוֹ עַל שׁוּלְחָנוֹ. הַתַּבְשִׁילִין הָעוֹלִין עִמּוֹ עַל שׁוּלְחָנוֹ צְרִיכִין לְהִתְבָּעֵר עִמּוֹ. אָמַר רִבִּי יוֹסֵה. הָדָא אָמְרָה. הָהֵין דַּאֲכַל חוֹבֵץ וּבְדַעְתֵּיהּ מֵיכוֹל קוּפָּד צָרִיךְ מְבַעֲרָה פִּיסְתָהּ.
1 איתא חמי חגיגה K | אתה או'   2 ותימר הכין K | ותמר הכן   שולחנו K | השלחן   (2) התבשילין K | תבןשילין]   3 הדא K | הדה   מיכול K | מיכל   4 מבערה K | למבערה

Halakhah 5: It was stated: The festival offering of the Fourteenth could come from tithe. Rebbi Jacob bar Aha in the name of Samuel bar Abba: This means that it is voluntary. If you would say that it is obligatory, can anything which is obligatory come from tithe[97]?

It was stated: The festival offering which comes with the *Pesaḥ* is eaten first so that the *Pesaḥ* be eaten when one is satiated[98]. Why should the *Pesaḥ* not be eaten so one be satiated? Rebbi Yose ben Rebbi Bun in the name of Rebbi Jacob bar Dosay: Lest one come to break a bone[99].

It was stated: The festival offering which comes with the *Pesaḥ* has to be eliminated with it. Come and see, a festival offering may be eaten for two days but the *Pesaḥ* only until midnight, and you are saying so? If it comes to the table with it[100]. Dishes who come to the table with it have to be eliminated with it[101]. Rebbi Yose said, this implies that he who ate soft cheese and wants to eat meat must eliminate the bread slices[102].

---

97 Animal tithe (*Lev.* 27:32) automatically is a *sanctum* which must be sacrificed and eaten by the family; therefore it is no longer at the disposal of the owner to use it to fulfill any obligation. If it is acceptable for use with the *Pesaḥ*, this cannot represent fulfilling an obligation. Babli *Hagigah* 7b-8a.

98 Tosephta 5:3.

99 Babli 70a. *Mekhilta dR. Ismael Bo* 6 (ed. Horovitz-Rabin p. 20).

99 Since remainders of the *Pesaḥ* have to be burned (*Ex.* 12:10), any dish which came into contact with the *Pesaḥ* has to be burned with it since it may be contaminated with particles of the *Pesaḥ*. The Babli 70a disagrees and holds that it must be eliminated (as a biblical requirement) only in the opinion of Ben Tema.

101 Tosephta 5:3, opinion of R. Simeon ben Elazar.

102 Accepted by *Šulhan Arukh Yoreh De`a* 89(4).

(fol. 32d) **משנה ח**: הַפֶּסַח שֶׁשְּׁחָטוֹ שֶׁלֹּא לִשְׁמוֹ בַּשַּׁבָּת חַיָּיב עָלָיו חַטָּאת. וּשְׁאָר כָּל־הַזְּבָחִים שֶׁשְּׁחָטָן לְשֵׁם פֶּסַח אִם אֵינָן רְאוּיִין חַיָּיב. וְאִם רְאוּיִין הֵן רִבִּי אֱלִיעֶזֶר מְחַיֵּיב חַטָּאת. וְרִבִּי יְהוֹשֻׁעַ פּוֹטֵר.

Mishnah 8: He who slaughters the *Pesaḥ* not for its purpose[103] on the Sabbath is for this liable for a purification sacrifice[104]. For any other sacrifice which he slaughtered for the purpose of *Pesaḥ*, if they are not suitable[105] he is liable, if suitable, Rebbi Eliezer declares him liable for a purification sacrifice but Rebbi Joshua declares not liable[106].

משנה ט: אָמַר רִבִּי אֱלִיעֶזֶר מָה אִם הַפֶּסַח שֶׁהוּא מוּתָּר לִשְׁמוֹ כְּשֶׁשִּׁינָּה שְׁמוֹ חַיָּב. זְבָחִים שֶׁהֵן אֲסוּרִין לִשְׁמָן כְּשֶׁשִּׁינָּה אֶת שְׁמָן אֵינוֹ דִין שֶׁיְּהֵא חַיָּב. אָמַר לוֹ רִבִּי יְהוֹשֻׁעַ. לֹא. אִם אָמַרְתָּ בַּפֶּסַח שֶׁשִּׁינָּהוּ אֶת שְׁמוֹ בְדָבָר אָסוּר. תֹּאמַר בַּזְּבָחִים שֶׁשִּׁנָּן בְּדָבָר מוּתָּר. אָמַר לוֹ רִבִּי אֱלִיעֶזֶר. אֵימוּרֵי צִיבּוּר יוֹכִיחַ. שֶׁהֵן מוּתָּרִין לִשְׁמָן הַשּׁוֹחֵט לִשְׁמָן חַיָּב. אָמַר לוֹ רִבִּי יְהוֹשֻׁעַ. לֹא. אִם אָמַרְתָּ בְּאֵימוּרֵי צִיבּוּר שֶׁכֵּן יֵשׁ לָהֶן קִיצְבָה. תֹּאמַר בַּפֶּסַח שֶׁאֵין לוֹ קִצְבָה. רִבִּי מֵאִיר אוֹמֵר. אַף הַשּׁוֹחֵט לְשֵׁם אֵימוֹרֵי צִיבּוּר פָּטוּר:

Mishnah 9: Rebbi Eliezer said to him, since for *Pesaḥ*, which is permitted for its purpose[107], he is liable if he changed its purpose, sacrifices which are forbidden for their purpose[108], it should be logical that he be liable if he changed their purpose. Rebbi Joshua answered him, no. If you argue about *Pesaḥ*, which he changed to something forbidden, what can you infer about sacrifices which he changed to something permitted[109]? Rebbi Eliezer said to him, public parts[110] should prove it, which are permitted for their purpose and he who slaughters for their purpose is liable[111]. Rebbi Joshua answered him, no. If you argue about public parts which are fixed in number, what can you infer about *Pesaḥ* which is not fixed in number? Rebbi Meïr says, also he who slaughters for the purpose of public parts is not liable[112].

103 As well-being sacrifice.
104 If he slaughtered in error, i. e., either if he did not know that slaughtering not for its purpose is forbidden or if he did not realize that it was a Sabbath.
105 If they are not male sheep or goat yearlings.
106 For him a valid sacrifice even if wrongly presented cannot trigger liability.
107 If the 14th is a Sabbath.
108 Festival offerings or general well-being offerings on a Sabbath.
109 Since anything called *Pesaḥ* may be slaughtered on a 14th of Nisan which is a Sabbath.
110 The altar's parts of those public sacrifices of which the rest is consumed by the priests, such as holiday purification sacrifices and the public well-being sacrifice of Pentecost.
111 If he erroneously slaughters any other sacrifice for the purpose of public sacrifice.
112 Since he slaughtered with the intent of fulfilling a commandment, there can be no liability, and R. Eliezer's premise is incorrect.

(33c line 36) **הלכה ו:** מַתְנִיתָה בְּיוֹדֵעַ בּוֹ שֶׁהוּא פֶסַח וּשְׁחָטוֹ לְשֵׁם שְׁלָמִים. הָיָה יוֹדֵעַ בּוֹ שֶׁהוּא שְׁלָמִים וּשְׁחָטוֹ לְשֵׁם עוֹלָה. רְבִּי מָנָא אָמַר. יֵשׁ בַּעֲשִׂיָּיתוֹ מִצְוָה. רְבִּי יוֹסֵה אָמַר. אֵין בַּעֲשִׂיָּיתוֹ מִצְוָה. אֵילֵי צִיבּוּר שֶׁהָיָה סָבוּר שֶׁהֵן כְּבָשִׂים וּשְׁחָטָן לְשֵׁם אֵלִים שֶׁמָּא לֹא עָלוּ לַצִּיבּוּר לְשֵׁם אֵלִים. וְתַנֵּי כֵן. אֵילֵי צִיבּוּר שֶׁהָיָה סָבוּר שֶׁהֵן כְּבָשִׂים וּשְׁחָטָן לְשֵׁם אֵלִים כְּבָר עָלוּ לַצִּיבּוּר לְשֵׁם חוֹבָה. מַתְנִיתָה בְסָבוּר בּוֹ שֶׁהוּא פֶסַח וּשְׁחָטוֹ לְשֵׁם פֶּסַח. הָיָה יוֹדֵעַ בּוֹ שֶׁהוּא שְׁלָמִים אֶלָּא שֶׁהָיָה סָבוּר לוֹמַר שֶׁמּוּתָּר לְשַׁנּוֹת שְׁלָמִים לְשֵׁם פֶּסַח. רְבִּי מָנָא אָמַר. אֵין בַּעֲשִׂיָּיתוֹ מִצְוָה. רְבִּי יוֹסֵה אָמַר. יֵשׁ בַּעֲשִׂיָּיתוֹ מִצְוָה. מִסְתַּבְּרָא דְרְבִּי מָנָא בְּקַדְמִייָתָא וּדְרְבִּי יוֹסֵי בָּאַחֲרִיתָה

1 מתנית' K | מתניתה אמרה בו K | - K | 3 אילי K | אילו אילי K | כבשין K אלים K אילין 4 אילי | K אילו אילי שהן | K בהן שהן כבשים K כבשין כבר K | - לשם חובה K משם אילים 7 בקדמייתא | K בקדמייתה

Halakhah 6: The Mishnah if he realized that it was *Pesaḥ* but he slaughtered it for the purpose of well-being offerings[113]. If he knew that it was a well-being offering but he slaughtered it for the purpose of an elevation offering. Rebbi Mana said, there is fulfilling of a commandment in his action. Rebbi Yose said, there is no fulfilling of a commandment in his action[114]. Rams of the public which he thought were sheep and he slaughtered them for the purpose of rams, are they perhaps not counted as rams for the public[115]? It was stated thus: Rams of the public which he thought were sheep and he slaughtered them for the purpose of rams, already are counted for the public as fulfillment of their obligation. The Mishnah applies if he thought it was *Pesaḥ* and he slaughtered it for the purpose of *Pesaḥ*[116]. If he knew that it was a well-being sacrifice but thought to say that it is permitted to change well-being sacrifice into *Pesaḥ*, Rebbi Mana said, there is no fulfilling of a commandment in his action; Rebbi Yose said, there is fulfilling of a commandment in his action[117]. It is reasonable following Rebbi Mana in the first case, following Rebbi Yose in the last.

113 If he knew that it was *Pesah* and intentionally changed the purpose, there is liability if he erred in thinking that this was permitted, since his intent was executed. But if it was *Pesah*, only the slaughterer thought that it was a well-being offering and he slaughtered it as well-being offering, it is valid *Pesah* since an intent based on a false premise has no legal consequence. Cf. Babli 72a.

114 This is a continuation of the preceding argument. The animal was dedicated as *Pesah*, the slaughterer thought that it was a well-being offering and he slaughtered it as elevation offering. R. Mana holds that the slaughterer's intent is ineffective since it is based on a wrong premise; the sacrifice is qualified as *Pesah*. R. Yose holds that in all

cases the slaughterer's intent determines qualification.

115 Rams are supplementary elevation sacrifices on holidays, as are the sheep mentioned here. Babli *Menahot* 49a.

116 The second case of Mishnah 8, "for any other sacrifice which he slaughtered for the purpose of *Pesaḥ*, . . .", if an animal was dedicated as well-being offering but is of the kind qualified for *Pesaḥ*, and was slaughtered as *Pesaḥ*, R. Joshua declares him not liable since the sacrifice is qualified

and he erred in the fulfillment of a commandment.

117 The difference here is the interpretation of R. Joshua's stance. R. Mana holds that since he knew that the animal was not a *Pesaḥ*, it cannot be called error in the fulfillment of a commandment and even R. Joshua will agree that he is liable. R. Yose holds that since the sacrifice is qualified it must be called error in the fulfillment of a commandment and R. Joshua will hold that he is not liable.

(33c line 50) **הלכה ז**: אָמְרִין. לֵית הָדָא דְרִבִּי לִיעֶזֶר תְּתוּבָה עַל דְּרִבִּי יְהוֹשֻׁעַ. דּוּ יָכִיל מֵימַר לֵיהּ. הֵיאַךְ אַתְּ מְשִׁיבֵינִי מִדָּבָר שֶׁדַּרְכּוֹ לַחֲלָף עַל דָּבָר שֶׁאֵין דַּרְכּוֹ לְיִתְחַלֵּף. וְלֹא הָדָא דְרִבִּי יְהוֹשֻׁעַ תְּתוּבָה עַל דְּרִבִּי אֱלִיעֶזֶר. דּוּ יָכִיל מֵימַר לֵיהּ. הֲרֵי פִּסְחוֹ שֶׁל רְאוּבֵן שֶׁשְּׁחָטוֹ לְשֵׁם שִׁמְעוֹן הֲרֵי שִׁינָּהוּ לְדָבָר כָּשֵׁר. וְתֵימַר. חַיָּיב.

2 לחלף K | להתחלף הדא K - | 3 יושע K יהושע אליעזר K ליעזר מימור K מימר 4 חדבר K לשם דבר

Halakhah 7[118]: They said, that argument of Rebbi Eliezer is no answer to Rebbi Joshua, since he could say to him, how can you answer me with an argument about something that is apt to change for something that is not apt to being changed[119]? Neither is the argument of Rebbi Joshua an answer to Rebbi Eliezer, since he could say to him, the *Pesaḥ* of Reuben which he slaughtered in the name of Simeon is changed into something qualified[120]; and you are saying, he is liable?

118 Discussion of Mishnah 9.

119 The *Pesaḥ* after the 14th is automatically a well-being offering; but animals dedicated as well-being offerings cannot validly be changed into anything else.

120 Mishnah 5:3.

(33c line 54) רִבִּי מֵאִיר אוֹמֵר. אַף הַשּׁוֹחֵט לְשֵׁם אֵימוּרֵי צִבּוּר פָּטוּר: אָמַר רִבִּי לְעָזָר. דִּבְרֵי רִבִּי מֵאִיר אֲפִילוּ עֵגֶל. אַתְּ שְׁמַע מִינָּהּ תַּרְתֵּיי. אַתְּ שְׁמַע מִינָּהּ. דָּבָר שֶׁאֵין לוֹ קִיצְבָה וְדָבָר שֶׁאֵין דַּרְכּוֹ לְהִתְחַלֵּף וְיֵשׁ בַּעֲשִׂיָּיתוֹ מִצְוָה. רִבִּי שִׁמְעוֹן בֶּן לָקִישׁ אָמַר. יֵשׁ בַּעֲשִׂיָּיתוֹ מִצְוָה כְּגוֹן יְבִמְתּוֹ נִדָּה וּבָא עָלֶיהָ. רִבִּי יוֹחָנָן אָמַר. (יֵשׁ) [אֵין] בַּעֲשִׂיָּיתוֹ מִצְוָה כְּגוֹן שְׁנֵי שְׁפוּדִין אֶחָד שֶׁלִּשְׁחוּטָה וְאֶחָד שֶׁלִּנְבֵילָה. וּבִיקֵּשׁ לוֹכַל מִזֶּה וְאָכַל מִזֶּה. מַתְנִיתָה פְלִיגָא עַל רִבִּי יוֹחָנָן. שָׁכַח וּמָל אֶת שֶׁל

אַחַר שַׁבָּת בַּשַׁבָּת. רִבִּי אֱלִיעֶזֶר מְחַיֵּיב חַטָּאת. וְרִבִּי יְהוֹשֻׁעַ פּוֹטֵר: הֲרֵי אֵין בָּעֲשִׂיָּיתוֹ מִצְוָה וְרִבִּי יְהוֹשֻׁעַ פּוֹטֵר. שְׁמוּאֵל קַפּוֹדְקָיָּא אָמַר. לְמָחָר יֵשׁ בָּעֲשִׂיָּיתוֹ מִצְוָה.

2 קיצבה K | קצבה   3 להשתנות K | לישתנות

"Rebbi Meïr says, also he who slaughters for the purpose of public parts is not liable." Rebbi Eleazar said, the words of Rebbi Meïr: even a calf[121]. You understand from here two things. You understand something which has no fixed number, or that is apt to being changed, only if the act is meritorious[122]. Rebbi Simeon ben Laqish said, if the act is meritorious, for example his sister-in-law which is menstruating and he slept with her[123]. Rebbi Johanan said, if the act is [not][124] meritorious, for example two spits, one with slaughtered meat, the other with carcass meat, and he intended to eat from one but ate from the other[125]. A Mishnah disagrees with Rebbi Johanan[126]: "If he forgot and circumcised the one for Sunday on the Sabbath, Rebbi Eliezer makes him liable for a purification sacrifice but Rebbi Joshua declares him not liable." In this case the act is not meritorious and Rebbi Joshua declares not liable. Samuel from Cappadocia said, the next day it is meritorious[127].

121 No public sacrifice is a calf. According to him, R. Meïr in interpreting R. Joshua's position that no action resulting in a qualified sacrifice can trigger liability.

122 Even if there are two detriments as enumerated in the Mishnah, as long as there is an angle of merit there is no liability.

123 If the sister-in-law is a childless widow the brother-in-law is biblically obligated to sleep with her (*Deut.* 25:5). Incidentally by this act she becomes his wife, but this is not the point here. Since his act is in obeying a biblical commandment it cannot be sanctioned; even though he was negligent in not asking her whether sex with her was permissible; in the interpretation of R. Joshua's position given here, the purification offering due for erroneously sleeping with a menstruating woman is neither due nor possible in this case.

124 An addition by the corrector which seems to be erroneous.

125 This sentence seems to be corrupt. Eating non-kosher meat is a simple violation, not a deadly sin whose commission in error would require a purification sacrifice. One might try to amend the text; which has been done in very many different ways, none of which is convincing. If one assumes that the uncorrected text is genuine, one has to assume, in the general spirit of the discussion, that the kosher meat is *sanctum*, whose consumption is meritorious. R. Johanan asserts that if the intended act was meritorious, the actual action, while a sin, cannot be sinful.

126 *Šabbat* 19:4, about two babies to circumcise, one on the Sabbath and one on Sunday.

127 Since on Sunday the baby is lawfully

circumcised, the Mishnah cannot be used to show that R. Joshua declares not liable even if no commandment was obeyed in the action.

(33c line 63) אָמַר רִבִּי יוֹחָנָן. דְּרִבִּי מֵאִיר הִיא. דְּרִבִּי מֵאִיר אָמַר. דָּבָר שֶׁיֵּשׁ בַּעֲשִׂיָּיתוֹ מִצְוָה [פָּטוּר. דָּבָר שֶׁאֵין בַּעֲשִׂיָּיתוֹ] מִצְוָה חַיָּיב כְּמַחֲלוֹקֶת. רִבִּי שִׁמְעוֹן אוֹמֵר. דָּבָר שֶׁיֵּשׁ בַּעֲשִׂיָּיתוֹ מִצְוָה חַיָּיב. וְשֶׁאֵין בַּעֲשִׂיָּיתוֹ מִצְוָה פָּטוּר כְּמַחֲלוֹקֶת. רִבִּי יָסֵי רִבִּי מֵאִיר וְהוּא דִּבְרֵי רִבִּי יוֹחָנָן. שֶׁיְּהֵא שֶׂה תָמִים וּבֶן שָׁנָה וּשְׁלָמִים וְרָאוּי לְהִשְׁתַּנּוֹת לְשֵׁם פֶּסַח. אַתְּ שָׁמַע מִינָהּ תְּלַת. אַתְּ שָׁמַע מִינָהּ. דָּבָר שֶׁאֵין לוֹ קִצְבָה. וְדָבָר שֶׁאֵין דַּרְכּוֹ לְהַחֲלִיף. וְדָבָר שֶׁיֵּשׁ בַּעֲשִׂיָּיתוֹ מִצְוָה. מָה אִית לָךְ דָּבָר שֶׁאֵין לוֹ קִיצְבָה. רִבִּי יִרְמְיָה סָבַר מֵימַר שֶׁלֹּא נָתְנָה הַתּוֹרָה קִצְבָה כַּמָּה פְּסָחִים יִדָּחוּ אֶת הַשַּׁבָּת בְּכָל־שָׁנָה. רִבִּי יוֹסֵי סָבַר מֵימַר. שֶׁאֵין אַתְּ יָכוֹל לַעֲמוֹד עַל מִינְיָינָן. רִבִּי יוֹסֵי כַּד הֲוֵי מַטֵּי לְאִילֵּין תִּינוֹקוֹת סְפֵיקוֹת הֲוָה אָמַר. יָפֶה לִימְּדָנוּ רִבִּי יִרְמְיָה. שֶׁאֵין אַתְּ יָכוֹל לַעֲמוֹד עַל מֵינְיָינָן. אֶלָּא שֶׁלֹּא נָתְנָה הַתּוֹרָה קִיצְבָה כַּמָּה פְּסָחִים יִדָּחוּ אֶת הַשַּׁבָּת בְּכָל־שָׁנָה. אָמַר רַב חִסְדָּא. דִּבְרֵי רִבִּי שִׁמְעוֹן תִּיפְתָּר שֶׁהָיָה שָׁם חֲבוּרָה אַחַת שֶׁלֹּא שָׁחֲטָה. אָמַר רִבִּי זְעוּרָא. מִילְּתֵיהּ דְּרִבִּי יַנַּאי אָמְרָה. וְהוּא שֶׁשָּׁכַח וּמָל אֶת שֶׁלְּשַׁבָּת בְּעֶרֶב שַׁבָּת. מָלוֹ בְּשַׁחֲרִית. רִבִּי זְעוּרָא אָמַר. סָבַר רִבִּי יַנַּאי. פָּטוּר. רִבִּי אַבָּא אָמַר. חַיָּיב. וְלֵיידָה מִילָּה אָמְרָהּ רִבִּי יַנַּאי. בָּא לְהוֹדִיעֲךָ הֵיאַךְ דַּרְכָּן שֶׁלְּתִּינוֹקוֹת לְהִתְחַלֵּף. עַל דַּעְתֵּיהּ דְּרִבִּי זְעוּרָא כְּרִבִּי יַנַּאי. עַל דַּעְתֵּיהּ דְּרַב כְּרִבִּי מֵאִיר. אָמַר רִבִּי מָנָא קוֹמֵי רִבִּי יוֹסֵה. מַה דְּאָמַר רַב חִסְדָּא כְּרִבִּי שִׁמְעוֹן. וּמָה דְּאָמַר רִבִּי יַנַּאי כְּרִבִּי מֵאִיר. מְשִׁיבִין דָּבָר בֵּין רִבִּי מֵאִיר לְרִבִּי שִׁמְעוֹן. אַשְׁכְּחָן פְּלוּגְנָא בֵּין רִבִּי מֵאִיר לְרִבִּי שִׁמְעוֹן בְּשִׁיּוּר. אִילֵּין תִּינוֹקוֹת סְפֵיקוֹת מַה אַתְּ עָבֵד לוֹן. כִּדְבָר שֶׁיֵּשׁ לוֹ קִיצְבָה אוֹ כִדְבָר שֶׁאֵין לוֹ קִיצְבָה. [אֵין תַּעֲבַדִינוּן כִּדְבָר שֶׁיֵּשׁ לוֹ קִיצְבָה.] אֲפִילוּ אֵין שָׁם תִּינוֹק אֶחָד לָמוּל. וְאִין תַּעֲבַדִינוּן כִּדְבָר שֶׁאֵין לוֹ קִצְבָה. וְהוּא שֶׁיְּהֵא שָׁם תִּינוֹק אֶחָד לָמוּל. אִיתָא חֲמֵי. הִקְדִּים זְמַנּוֹ פָּטוּר. אִיחַר זְמַנּוֹ חַיָּיב. רַב הוּנָא אָמַר. מַחְלְפָה הִיא מַתְנִיתָהּ. דְּתַנֵּי. אָמַר רִבִּי שִׁמְעוֹן. לֹא נֶחְלַק רִבִּי לִיעֶזֶר וְרִבִּי יְהוֹשֻׁעַ עַל מִי שֶׁהָיָה לוֹ לָמוּל לְאַחַר שַׁבָּת וּמָלוֹ בַּשַּׁבָּת שֶׁהוּא חַיָּיב. וְעַל מַה נֶּחְלָקוּ. עַל מִי שֶׁהָיָה לוֹ לָמוּל בְּעֶרֶב שַׁבָּת וּמָלוֹ בַּשַּׁבָּת. שֶׁרִבִּי אֱלִיעֶזֶר מְחַיֵּיב חַטָּאת וְרִבִּי יְהוֹשֻׁעַ פּוֹטֵר. אָמַר רִבִּי יוֹסֵי בֵּירִבִּי בּוּן. מִן קוּשְׁיֵי מַקְשִׁי לָהּ רִבִּי יַנַּאי. וְהוּא שֶׁשָּׁכַח וּמָל אֶת שֶׁלְּשַׁבָּת בְּעֶרֶב שַׁבָּת. רַב אַדָא בַּר אֲחַוָה אָמַר. זוֹ דִּבְרֵי רִבִּי מֵאִיר וְרִבִּי שִׁמְעוֹן. אֲבָל דִּבְרֵי רִבִּי יוֹסֵי. אֲפִילוּ דָּבָר שֶׁאֵין בַּעֲשִׂיָּיתוֹ מִצְוָה הוֹאִיל וְטוֹעִין בּוֹ לְשֵׁם מִצְוָה פָּטוּר.

3 שיהא K | שיהא שם 4 ושלמים K | - ושלמים 5 קצבה K | קיצבה להחליף K | להתחלף 6 קצבה K | קיצבה פסחים K | פסחין ידחו K | שידחו 7 יוסי K | יוסה מימר K | מינינן K | מניין 8 לאילין K | לאלין 9 מינייני K | מינינן 10 אמ' רב חסדא ... מלו בשחרית K | ר' יוסה סבר מימר מימר והוא ששכח ומל שלשבת בערב שבת ומלו בשחרית 12 זעורא K | זעורה סבר K | סבר מימר ינאי K | יניי (2) פטור K | שהוא פטור בא K | אבא חייב K | שהיא חייב 13 זעורא K | זעורה ינאי K | יניי 14 רב חסדא K | ר' חסדא 15 ינאי K | יניי פלוגא K | פלגה 16 אילין K | אלין 17 CS - | K] אפי' K | ואפלו אחד K | אחר 18 אין תעבדינון K | - אחד למול ... K | איתא K | אתא 21 אליעזר ליעזר 22 יוסי K | יוסה ומל K | המל 24 יוסי K | יוסה

פֵּירֵשׁ אֵינוֹ חוֹזֵר אֶלָּא עַל צִיצִין הַמְעַכְּבִין אֶת הַמִּילָה. אָמַר רִבִּי יוֹחָנָן. דִּבְרֵי רִבִּי יוֹסֵי. אֲפִילוּ פֵּירֵשׁ חוֹזֵר אַף עַל הַצִּיצִין שֶׁאֵין מְעַכְּבִין אֶת הַמִּילָה. הֵיידֵין רִבִּי יוֹסֵי. הֲהוּא דְתַנֵּינָן. רִבִּי יוֹסֵי אוֹמֵר. יוֹם טוֹב הָרִאשׁוֹן שֶׁלְחַג שֶׁחָל לִהְיוֹת בַּשַּׁבָּת שָׁכַח וְהוֹצִיא אֶת הַלּוּלָב בִּרְשׁוּת הָרַבִּים. פָּטוּר. מִפְּנֵי שֶׁהוֹצִיאוֹ בִרְשׁוּת׃ אַף בְּסַכִּין שֶׁלְמִילָה כֵּן. אַף בְּמַצָּה כֵּן. מִן מַה דְּאָמַר רִבִּי יוֹחָנָן. דִּבְרֵי רִבִּי יוֹסֵי. אֲפִילוּ פֵּירֵשׁ וְחָזַר אֲפִילוּ עַל הַצִּיצִין שֶׁאֵין מְעַכְּבִין אֶת הַמִּילָה. הָדָא אָמְרָה. אַף בְּסַכִּין שֶׁלְמִילָה כֵּן. אַף בְּמַצָּה כֵּן

1 המעכבין K | המעכבים יוסי K | יוסה   2 אף K | אפילו הציצין K | הציצים שאין K | שאינו היידין K | היידן יוסי K | יוסה דתנינן K | דתנינן תמן   3 יוסי K | יוסה שכח K | ושכח   4 מן מה K | ממה   5 יוסי K | יוסה פירש K | פרש שאין K | שאינו   6 הדא K | הדה

[128]Rebbi Johanan said, it is Rebbi Meïr's, since Rebbi Meïr said, for something where there is a commandment performed one is not liable, but if no commandment is performed whether he is liable is disputed. Rebbi Simeon says, where there is a commandment performed one is liable, but if no commandment is performed whether he is not liable is disputed. Rebbi Yose, Rebbi Johanan: The words of Rebbi Meïr are, on condition that it be a sheep without blemish, a yearling, and a well-being sacrifice fit to be changed into a Passover sacrifice. One understands from this three consequences. One understands something which is not a fixed number. And which is not usually exchanged. And doing something which fulfills a commandment. What means "something which is not a fixed number"? Rebbi Jeremiah wanted to say that the Torah did not specify how many *Pesaḥ* sacrifices should push the Sabbath aside in any given year. Rebbi Yose wanted to say, where you cannot determine the amount. When Rebbi Yose came to these "children in doubt" he used to say, Rebbi Jeremiah taught us correctly. Could you say that you cannot determine the amount? But the Torah did not specify how many *Pesaḥ* sacrifices should push the Sabbath aside in any given year. Rav Ḥisda said, one may explain the words of Rebbi Simeon if a group was there which did not slaughter. Rebbi Ze`ira said, the word of Rebbi Yannai implies that he forgot and circumcised the one for the Sabbath on Friday. It he circumcised him in the morning, Rebbi Ze`ira said that Rebbi Yannai was of the opinion that he is not liable. Rebbi Abba said, he is liable. In relation to what did Rebbi Yannai say it? He comes to tell you in which cases can there be a switching of children. In Rebbi Ze`ira's opinion following Rebbi Yannai Rav followed Rebbi Meïr. Rebbi Mana said before Rebbi Yose, what Rav Ḥisda

said follows Rebbi Simeon, and what Rebbi Yannai said follows Rebbi Meïr. Can one object anything between Rebbi Meïr and Rebbi Simeon? Do we find a difference between Rebbi Meïr and Rebbi Simeon about the remainder? How do you treat the babies in doubt? Like something which is a fixed amount or something which is not a fixed amount? If you are treating it like something which is a fixed amount, even if there is no (one) [other] baby to circumcise. If you are treating it like something which is not a fixed amount, only if there remains (one) [another] baby to circumcise. Come and see: If he anticipated his time he is not liable, if he delayed his time he is liable? Rav Huna said, the Mishnah is the other way around, as it was stated: Rebbi Simeon said, Rebbi Eliezer and Rebbi Joshua did not disagree about one which was to be circumcised after the Sabbath if he circumcised him on the Sabbath that he is liable, but one who was to be circumcised before the Sabbath if he circumcised him on the Sabbath where Rebbi Eliezer makes him liable for a purification sacrifice and Rebbi Joshua declares him not liable. Rebbi Yose ben Rebbi Abun said, because of this objection it was difficult for Rebbi Yannai, only if he forgot and circumcised the one of the Sabbath on Friday. Rebbi Ada bar Ahawah said, these are the words of Rebbi Meïr and Rebbi Simeon, but the words of Rebbi Yose [are]: Even if no commandment is performed he is not liable since he erred on behalf of a commandment.

If he finished he can return only for fibers which would invalidate the circumcision. Rebbi Johanan said, the words of Rebbi Yose, even if he finished he may even return for fibers which do not invalidate the circumcision. Which [statement of] Rebbi Yose? That which we stated, "Rebbi Yose says, if the first day of Tabernacles falls on a Sabbath, if he forgot and took the *lulav* out into the public domain he is not liable because he took it out with permission." Does the same hold for a knife for circumcision, the same for unleavened bread? Since Rebbi Johanan said, the words of Rebbi Yose, even if he finished he may even return for fibers which do not invalidate the circumcision; this implies the same even for a knife for circumcision, the same for unleavened bread.

128 The text from here to the end of the Halakhah is from *Šabbat* 19, Notes 110-141.

The connection with the topics here seems to be the mention of *mazzah* in the last two sentences.

(fol. 32d) **משנה י**: שְׁחָטוֹ שֶׁלֹּא לְאוֹכְלָיו וְשֶׁלֹּא לִמְנוּיָיו לַעֲרֵלִים וְלִטְמֵאִים חַיָּב. לְאוֹכְלָיו וְשֶׁלֹּא לְאוֹכְלָיו לִמְנוּיָיו וְשֶׁלֹּא לִמְנוּיָיו לַמּוּלִים וְלָעֲרֵלִים לַטְּהוֹרִים וְלִטְמֵאִים פָּטוּר. שְׁחָטוֹ וְנִמְצָא בַעַל מוּם חַיָּב. שְׁחָטוֹ וְנִמְצָא טְרֵפָה בַסֵּתֶר פָּטוּר. שְׁחָטוֹ וְנוֹדַע שֶׁמָּשְׁכוּ הַבְּעָלִים אֶת יָדָן אוֹ שֶׁמֵּתוּ אוֹ שֶׁנִּיטְמְאוּ פָּטוּר מִפְּנֵי שֶׁשָּׁחַט בִּרְשׁוּת:

Mishnah 10: He is liable if he slaughtered it[129] not for its eaters, or not for its subscribers, for the uncircumcised, or for the impure[130]. He is not liable if for its eaters and not for its eaters, for its subscribers and not for its subscribers, for the circumcised and the uncircumcised, for the pure and the impure[131]. If he slaughtered and it was found defective, he is liable[132]. If he slaughtered and it was found internally torn, he is not liable[133]. He is not liable if he slaughtered and it became known that the owners became disinterested in it, or they died, or they became impure, because he slaughtered with permission[134].

129 For a *Pesah* on the Sabbath he is liable for a purification sacrifice if acting in error.
130 Since a *Pesah* is disqualified if nobody is able to eat it.
131 Mishnah 5:3.
132 Since the *Pesah* may not be defective (*Ex.* 12:5), it is necessary to inspect the animal before slaughter.
133 Since this cannot be determined beforehand, no guilt can be incurred. The last two statements are equally valid for the Sabbath sacrifices during the year.
134 R. Joshua's opinion in the preceding Halakhah.

(33d line 25) **הלכה ח**: אָמַר רִבִּי לְעָזָר. לְמִי נִצְרְכָה. לְרִבִּי מֵאִיר. אַתְיָא דְרִבִּי לְעָזָר כְּרִבִּי שִׁמְעוֹן בֶּן לָקִישׁ. כַּמָּה דְרִבִּי שִׁמְעוֹן בֶּן לָקִישׁ אָמַר. יֵשׁ בַּעֲשִׂיָּיתוֹ מִצְוָה. כֵּן רִבִּי לְעָזָר אָמַר. יֵשׁ בַּעֲשִׂיָּיתוֹ מִצְוָה. אִין תֵּימָר. שַׁנְיָיא הִיא. שֶׁהוּא בַעַל מוּם. וּבַעַל מוּם אֵין דַּרְכּוֹ לְהִתְחַלֵּף. הֲרֵי עֵגֶל הֲרֵי אֵין דַּרְכּוֹ לְהִתְחַלֵּף וְאָמַר רִבִּי לְעָזָר. דִּבְרֵי רִבִּי מֵאִיר אֲפִילוּ עֵגֶל. אָמַר רִבִּי יוֹסִי. אֵין יִסְבּוֹר רִבִּי לְעָזָר כְּרִבִּי יוֹחָנָן אַתְיָא הִיא. דְּאָמַר רִבִּי יוֹחָנָן. בַּעַל מוּם אֵין דַּרְכּוֹ לְהִתְחַלֵּף. עֵגֶל דַּרְכּוֹ לְהִתְחַלֵּף. שֶׁכֵּן נִצְרְכָה (לְהִלֵּל) [לְחָלָל]. הָא בְנָלוּי חַיָּב.
1 אתיא K | אמ' ר' ירמיה אתייה 3 שנייא K שנייה 4 הרי K | - לעזר K | אלעזר יוסי K | יוסה 5 אתיא K | אתייה 6 KS להלל | C לחלל

אָמַר רִבִּי יוֹחָנָן. דְּרִבִּי שִׁמְעוֹן הִיא. רִבִּי יַעֲקֹב בַּר אָחָא רִבִּי אִימִּי בְּשֵׁם רִבִּי שִׁמְעוֹן בֶּן לָקִישׁ. דְּרִבִּי שִׁמְעוֹן הִיא. רִבִּי חָמָא בַּר עוּקְבָה בְּשֵׁם רִבִּי יוֹסִי בֵּירִבִּי חֲנִינָה. הַמּוֹשֵׁךְ יָדוֹ מִפִּסְחוֹ גוּפוֹ

קָרֵב שְׁלָמִים. רִבִּי יוֹנָה אָמַר. שְׁלָמִים כְּשֵׁירִים. רִבִּי יוֹסֵה אָמַר. שְׁלָמִים פְּסוּלִים. וְהָא תַנִּינָן. פָּטוּר. סָבְרִין מֵימַר. פָּטוּר וְ[כָ]שֵׁר. פְּתָרִין לֵיהּ. פָּטוּר פָּסוּל. רִבִּי יָסָא בְּשֵׁם רִבִּי יוֹחָנָן. אֵין לְךָ פֶּסַח גּוּפוֹ קָרֵב שְׁלָמִים אֶלָּא שֶׁאָבַד וְנִמְצָא מֵאַחַר שֶׁכִּיפְּרוּ הַבְּעָלִים. וְהָא תַנִּינָן. פָּטוּר. סָבְרִין מֵימַר. פָּטוּר כָּשֵׁר. פְּתָרִין לֵיהּ. פָּטוּר פָּסוּל. שְׁמוּאֵל אָמַר. כָּל־שֶׁאָמְרוּ בַחַטָּאת מֵתָה כְּיוֹצֵא בּוֹ בַפֶּסַח גּוּפוֹ קָרֵב שְׁלָמִים. וְהָא תַנִּינָן. פָּטוּר. סָבְרִין מֵימַר. פָּטוּר פָּסוּל. פְּתָרִין לֵיהּ. פָּטוּר כָּשֵׁר.

2 חמא K | חמה יוסי K | יוסה ביר' K | בן 3 כשרים K | כשרין פסולים K | פסולין 4 C וכשר KS | כשר יסא K | יסי

רִבִּי יָסָא בְּשֵׁם רִבִּי יוֹחָנָן. דְּרִבִּי יְהוּדָה הִיא. דְּתַנִּינָן תַּמָּן. אֵין שׁוֹחֲטִין אֶת הַפֶּסַח עַל הַיָּחִיד. דִּבְרֵי רִבִּי יְהוּדָה. וְרִבִּי יוֹסֵה מַתִּיר. רִבִּי זְעוּרָה בְּעָא קוֹמֵי רִבִּי מָנָא. הוֹ אֲשִׁכְּחָן פָּטוּר וְכָשֵׁר. אֲמַר לֵיהּ. תַּנִּינָן הָכָא. פָּטוּר. וְתַנִּינָן תַּמָּן. כָּשֵׁר. וְעַל כּוּלָם הָיָה רִבִּי יִשְׁמָעֵאל בְּנוֹ שֶׁלְּרִבִּי יוֹחָנָן בֶּן בְּרוֹקָה אוֹמֵר. תְּעוּבַּר צוּרָתוֹ וְיֵצֵא לְבֵית הַשְּׂרֵיפָה רִבִּי לְעָזָר בֵּירִבִּי יוֹסֵי בְּעָא קוֹמֵי רִבִּי יוֹסֵי. נִיחָא שֶׁמֵּתוּ וְשֶׁנִּיטְמְאוּ. שֶׁמָּשְׁכוּ הַבְּעָלִים אֶת יָדָם. מָה אֲנָן קַיָּימִין. אִם בַּחַיִּים. פָּסוּל מַכְשִׁיר. פָּסוּל הוּא. אִם לְאַחַר שְׁחִיטָה. יֵשׁ מְשִׁיכָה לְאַחַר שְׁחִיטָה. מִכֵּיוָן שֶׁיֵּשׁ לוֹ רְשׁוּת לִמְשׁוֹךְ. פָּסוּל מַכְשִׁיר הוּא. וְטָעוּן צוּרָה.

2 יהודה K | ידה ור' K | ר' 3 וכשר K | נו]כשיר הכא K | הכה 4 תעובר K | תעבר יוסי K | יוסה העא K | בעה 5 יוסי K | יוסה שמתו K | שמיתו ושניטמאו K | ושניטמו הבעלים K | הבעלין ידם K | ידן אנן K | נן בחיים K | בחיין 6 מכשיר K | למכשיר פסול - K | מכיון K | אלא כר' שמע' דר' שמעון אמ' יש משיכה לאחר שחיטה מכיון

Halakhah 8: Rebbi Eleazar said, for whom is this[135] needed? For Rebbi Meïr. Does Rebbi Eleazar parallel Rebbi Simeon ben Laqish? Just as Rebbi Simeon ben Laqish requires that his action be meritorious, does Rebbi Eleazar require that his action be meritorious[136]? If you are saying that there is a difference, since this one has a defect, and a defective animal is not apt to be changed[137], also a calf is not apt to be changed, and Rebbi Eleazar said, the words of Rebbi Meïr: even a calf[121]. Rebbi Yose said, if Rebbi Eleazar were of Rebbi Johanan's opinion, it would be understandable, since Rebbi Johanan said, a defective animals is not apt to be changed, but a calf is apt to be changed, because (it was a problem for Hillel) [it is needed for the slain][138]. Therefore {if it was torn} in the open, he is liable[139].

Rebbi Johanan said, it[140] is Rebbi Simeon's. Rebbi Jacob bar Aha, Rebbi Immi in the name of Rebbi Simeon ben Laqish, it is Rebbi Simeon's. Rebbi Hama bar Uqba in the name of Rebbi Yose ben Rebbi Hanina: If somebody became disinterested in his *Pesaḥ*, its body is brought as well-being offering[141]. Rebbi Jonah said, qualified well-being offering. Rebbi Yose said, disqualified well-being offering. But did we not state, "not liable"[142]? They wanted to say, not liable and qualified. They explain it, not liable and disqualified. Rebbi Yasa in the name of Rebbi Johanan, the only *Pesaḥ* which itself is brought as well-being offering is what was lost and found after the owner had fulfilled his obligation[143]. But did we not state, "not liable"? They wanted to say, not liable and qualified. They explain it, not liable and disqualified[144]. Samuel said, in any case where they said that a purification sacrifice is allowed to die[145], a *Pesaḥ* will be brought as well-being sacrifice. But did we not state, "not liable"? They wanted to say, not liable and disqualified. They explain it, not liable and qualified[143].

Rebbi Yasa in the name of Rebbi Johanan, it[146] is Rebbi Jehudah's, as we have stated there[147]: "One does not slaughter the *Pesaḥ* for a single individual, the words of Rebbi Jehudah, but Rebbi Yose permits." Rebbi Ze`ira asked before Rebbi Mana: Where do we find "not liable and qualified"? He told him, here we stated "not liable", and there we stated "qualified"[148]. But about all of them did Rebbi Ismael the son of Rebbi Johanan ben Beroqa say, it should lose its shape and be brought to be burned[149]. Rebbi Eleazar ben Rebbi Yose asked before Rebbi Yose, one understands if they died or became impure. If the owners became disinterested[150]? If they are alive, does disqualification qualify? It is disqualified. If after it was slaughtered, can one become disinterested after slaughter? Since he has the right to become disinterested, the disqualification qualifies[151], and it needs {losing its} shape.

135 This discusses the statement in the Mishnah that he who slaughters a defective *Pesaḥ* on a Sabbath is liable for a purification sacrifice.

136 Since a defective animal never is acceptable as a sacrifice, it cannot be dedicated as a *Pesaḥ*, nor can it ever be used for any purpose in the Temple.

137 The previous argument, while probably true, is not proven, since R. Meïr also requires that the sacrifice be apt to be changed into one of the correct type, Note 122.

138 The correct text is the sribe's one in parentheses, confirmed by K. Since Hillel raised the question why a *Pesaḥ* cannot be a calf when there is a verse seemingly endorsing its use (Note 25), is using a calf as *Pesaḥ* not an excusable error? The text in brackets is the corrector's, it makes little sense. (Maybe the corrector did not understand the scribe's text, reading הַלֵּל instead of הִלֵּל). A calf is used in the rite of atonement of an unsolved murder, *Deut.* 22:

1-9, but this is not a Temple ceremony.

139 This refers to the next clause in the Mishnah, if there was a defect in an internal organ, the sacrifice is disqualified but the slaughterer is not liable. (Not only is he not liable, but he did not commit any sin.) But if the defect was visible, it is a case of the previous clause; there is liability.

140 The statement in the Mishnah, when the *Pesah* was slaughtered even though the owners decided to belong to a different group. In the preceding text from *Šabbat* 19, R. Simeon is more restrictive than R. Meïr; therefore if the Mishnah is compatible with R. Simeon's position, it certainly is with R. Meïr's.

141 Since a *Pesah* whose time has passed automatically is dedicated as well-being offering, the case here must be that it was slaughtered on the 14th of Nisan. If it is not *Pesah*, it must be a well-being offering. The question is whether it is qualified and must be eaten, or is disqualified and may not be eaten. If it is disqualified the next question is whether it is disqualified *Pesah* and must be burned immediately outside the Temple district or is qualified but unused and as well-being sacrifice has to wait until the third day, when it biblically becomes forbidden and must be burned there (Mishnaiot 7:6-7).

142 "Not liable" implies that a sinful act was committed, only it is not criminally prosecutable.

143 Babli 97a.

144 In the case of the Mishnah, the *Pesah* which is left without eaters.

145 Mishnah *Temurah* 4:1-2: The offspring of an animal dedicated as purification offering, the (illegal) replacement of a purification offering, a purification offering whose owner had died, a purification offering which had been lost and was found after the owner had used a replacement, and one who became too old.

146 The last sentence in the Mishnah, that if the owner(s) lost interest, died, or became impure, the slaughterer on the Sabbath is not liable. A difficulty is created by idiomatic rabbinic Hebrew, where "owner" is בְּעָלִים with the verb in the plural whether there is one owner or there are many owners.

147 Mishnah 8:7. R. Jehudah may read the Mishnah here that if a *Pesah* was slaughtered for a number of subscribers, and all of them except one either lost interest, or died, or became impure, the sacrifice still is valid even though it would not have been permitted to be slaughtered if the facts had been known beforehand.

148 In Mishnah 8:7 R. Jehudah only says "one does not slaughter;" he does not state that if one slaughtered for a single eater the *Pesah* was disqualified. Therefore it is qualified even for R. Jehudah.

149 Babli 73b. Since the disqualification is extrinsic, the sacrifice cannot be burned immediately; one has to wait until it must be burned even if it is treated as well-being offering.

150 In the first two cases, it is an accident and one understands that the sacrifice cannot be burned immediately. But if the owner became disinterested, the animal may not be slaughtered. If it was slaughtered anyhow, the action is illegitimate and the carcass should be burned immediately.

151 K: "It must be R. Simeon's, since R. Simeon said, one may become disinterested after slaughtering" (up to the time of

pouring the blood, Mishnah 8:3) is suspect as *lectio facilior*. In keeping with the earlier statements, one may read the scribe's text as implying that, since before slaughter one may subscribe or cancel the subscription at will, cancelling after slaughter is an excusable error, not intrinsic, and has to follow the general rules of sacrifices becoming disqualified by extrinsic factors.

כיצד צולין פרק שביעי

(fol.33d) **משנה א**: כֵּיצַד צוֹלִין אֶת הַפֶּסַח שִׁפּוּד שֶׁל רִמּוֹן תּוֹחָבוֹ מִתּוֹךְ פִּיו עַד בֵּית נְקוּבָתוֹ וְנוֹתֵן אֶת כְּרָעָיו וְאֶת בְּנֵי מֵעָיו לְתוֹכוֹ דִּבְרֵי רִבִּי יוֹסֵי הַגְּלִילִי. רִבִּי עֲקִיבָה אוֹמֵר כְּמִין בִּישׁוּל הוּא זֶה אֶלָּא תוֹלִין חוּצָה לוֹ:

Mishnah 1: How does one roast the *Pesah*[1]? A spit of pomegranate wood[2] he sticks from its mouth to its buttocks and puts the hooves and its innards into it, the words of Rebbi Yose the Galilean. Rebbi Aqiba says, this is a kind of cooking[3]; but one hangs them outside.

1 Since the verse *Ex.* 12:9 requires: *Do not eat from it raw, or cooked in water, but roasted in fire, its head with its hooves and its innards.*
2 Hardwood which will not ooze sap into the meat. The sap would cook the meat near the spit; and the meat may not be eaten as Pesah.
3 Since the innards will be heated not by the fire but by hot moist meat.

(34a line 24) כֵּיצַד צוֹלִין אֶת הַפֶּסַח כול'. לָמָּה שֶׁלְּרִימּוֹן. אָמַר רִבִּי חִייָה בַּר בָּא. כָּל־הָעֵצִים בּוֹצְצִין מַשְׁקִין וְשֶׁלְּרִימּוֹן אֵינוֹ בוֹצֵץ מַשְׁקִין. מָה אֲנָן קַיָּימִין. אִם בְּלַחִין. אֲפִילוּ שֶׁלְּרִימּוֹן בּוֹצֵץ. אִם בִּיבֵישִׁין. אֲפִילוּ כָּל־הָעֵצִים אֵינָן בּוֹצְצִין. אֶלָּא כֵינִי. כָּל־הָעֵצִים יְבֵישִׁין מִבַּחוּץ וְלַחִין מִבִּפְנִים. רִימּוֹן יָבֵשׁ מִבַּחוּץ יָבֵשׁ מִבִּפְנִים.

1 למה K ולמה שלרימון K | בשל רמון 2 ושלרימון K ושלרמון K אנן K | נן שלרימון K שלרמון 3 העצים K העצין (2) 4 רימון K רמון | יבש K ויבש

"How does one roast the *Pesah*" etc. Why of pomegranates? Rebbi Hiyyas bar Abba said, all wood oozes fluid, but of pomegranates does not ooze fluid. Where do we hold? If fresh, even pomegranate {[wood} oozes. If dry, all other wood does not ooze. But it is so: All other wood if it is dry outside still is moist inside. Pomegranate {wood} if dry outside is dry inside.

תַּנֵּי בְשֵׁם רִבִּי יוּדָה. צוֹלֶה אוֹתוֹ בְשִׁפּוּד שֶׁלְּמַתֶּכֶת. אָמְרוּ לוֹ. וַהֲרֵי הוּא רוֹתֵחַ וּמַרְתִּיחַ. אָמַר לָהֶן. [כְּשֵׁם] שֶׁלְּעֵץ אֵינוֹ נִשְׂרָף כָּךְ שֶׁלְּמַתֶּכֶת אֵינוֹ מַרְתִּיחַ. אָמְרוּ לוֹ. לֹא דוֹמֶה הָעֵץ לַמַּתֶּכֶת. שֶׁהָעֵץ חַם מִקְצָתוֹ לֹא חַם כּוּלוֹ. שֶׁלְּמַתֶּכֶת חַם מִקְצָתוֹ חַם כּוּלוֹ.

2 להן K להם S 2 - | KC כשם 3 שלמתכת K מתכת כולו K -

It was stated[4] in the name of Rebbi Jehudah: He roasts it on a metal spit. They said to him, is it not hot and heats[5]? He said to them, just as the wooden one is not burned, so the metal one does not heat. They said to him, wood is not comparable to metal, for wood, if it is hot somewhere, is not hot everywhere, but metal if hot somewhere is hot everywhere.

4 Tosephta 5:8; Babli 74a.
5 Then the inner parts of the lamb are cooked by the heat of the spit, not roasted by the fire outside; cf. Halakhah 2.

(34a line 33) אִית תַּנָּיֵי תַנֵּי. תּוֹחְבוֹ מִבֵּית נְקוּבָתוֹ עַד שֶׁהוּא מַגִּיעַ לְתוֹךְ פִּיו. עַל דַּעְתֵּיהּ דְּהָדֵין תַּנְיָיה בָּרְיָיה חוֹזֵר וְהוֹפְכוֹ.

מַה. כְּיָרֵךְ [עָבָה] עָבַד לֵיהּ רִבִּי יוֹסֵי הַגָּלִילִי. אוֹ קָרֵיי דָרַשׁ רֹאשׁוֹ עַל־כְּרָעָיו וְעַל־קִרְבּוֹ: מַה נָפַק מִבֵּינֵיהוֹן. צָלָיו כִּגְדִי שְׁלָחוּלִין. אִין תֵּימַר כְּיָרֵךְ עָבָה עָבַד לֵיהּ רִבִּי יוֹסֵי הַגָּלִילִי. פָּסוּל. אִין תֵּימַר קָרֵיי דָרַשׁ רֹאשׁוֹ עַל־כְּרָעָיו וְעַל־קִרְבּוֹ. כָּשֵׁר. חָתַךְ מִמֶּנּוּ בָּשָׂר וּצְלָיוֹ בּוֹ. אִין תֵּימַר כְּיָרֵךְ עָבָה עָבַד לֵיהּ רִבִּי יוֹסֵי הַגָּלִילִי. כָּשֵׁר. אִין תֵּימַר קָרֵיי דָרַשׁ רֹאשׁוֹ עַל־כְּרָעָיו וְעַל־קִרְבּוֹ. פָּסוּל. צְלָיוֹ בַּחֲבַל שֶׁלְּקְדֵירָה. אִין תֵּימַר כְּיָרֵךְ עָבָה עָבַד לֵיהּ רִבִּי יוֹסֵי הַגָּלִילִי. פָּסוּל. אִין תֵּימַר קָרֵיי דָרַשׁ רֹאשׁוֹ עַל־כְּרָעָיו וְעַל־קִרְבּוֹ. כָּשֵׁר. לֹא כֵן תַּנֵּי. צְלִי־אֵשׁ. לֹא צְלִי קְדֵירָה. [שְׁנֵי לָהּ]. בְּנוֹגֵעַ בְּגוּפָהּ שֶׁלְּקְדֵירָה. הָדָא אָמְרָה. קָרֵיי דְרִישׁ.

1 S - | KC עבה ליה K | לה יוסי K | יוסה K מביניהון 2 מן ביניהון K עבה - | K | יוסי K יוסה 3
K | וצליו K וצליי 5 צלייו K | צלי יוסי K | יוסה K שני לה KS - | C 6 שלקדירה K שלקדרה חדא K הדה

There are Tannaim who stated, he sticks from its buttocks to its mouth. In the opinion of this *baraita* teacher he turns it around[6].

What? Does Rebbi Yose the Galilean consider it as thick hips[7], or does he explain the verse[8], *its head, on its hooves, and on its innards*. What is the difference between them? If he roasted it like a profane lamb[9]. If you are saying that Rebbi Yose the Galilean considers it as thick hips, it is disqualified[10]; if you are saying that he explains the verse, *its head, on its hooves, and on its innards*, it is qualified[11]. If he cut some meat from it and roasted it inside, if you are saying that Rebbi Yose the Galilean considers it as thick hips, it is qualified; if you are saying that he explains the verse, *its head, on its hooves, and on its innards*, it is disqualified[12]. If he roasted it in the steam of a pot, if you are saying that Rebbi Yose the Galilean considers it as thick hips, it is disqualified[13]; if you are saying that he explains the verse, *its head, on its hooves, and on its innards*, it is qualified[14]. But did one not state, *roasted in fire*, not roasted in a pot. [Explain it,] if it touched the body of the pot. This[15] implies that he explained the verse.

6   The argument implies that the lamb was roasted on a vertical spit, like shawarma. According to the Tanna of the Mishnah, the pointed end of the stick stands out at the top; the lamb, whose meat has not been koshered, hangs down and the blood can flow out through the cut in the neck; koshering is not needed. But in the scenario of the *baraita*, the spit has to be turned around, with the pointed end at the bottom.

7   Is his argument a practical one? Since it is assumed that the inner parts also will be roasted by the fire burning under the lamb, there is no reason that the innards, if put inside, will not be roasted.

8   *Deut.* 12:9. As explained in the next paragraph, he reads "on" to mean in direct bodily contact; and this is guaranteed at all times only if the hooves and innards are tucked inside the body.

9   Innards and hooves separate from the body.

10 One has to read "qualified". This is the reading of the quote in *Or Zarua*` II §229. This author is usually trustworthy in his readings.

11 Read: disqualified, confirmed by *Or zarua*`. Clearly, if the innards hang in the fire separate from the body, they will be roasted but the verse is violated.

12 In the first case the meat will be roasted, therefore being qualified as *Pesah*; but the verse does not permit to roast anything inside the body except innards and hooves.

13 Read: qualified (*Or zarua*`).

14 Read: disqualified (*Or zarua*`).

15 Not the preceding inconclusive discussion but the following discussion of the verse.

(34a line 44) הַכֹּל מוֹדִין בְּעָלָיו שֶׁהוּא סָמוּךְ. מַה פְּלִיגִין. בְּעַל. אַבָּא שָׁאוּל אוֹמֵר. עַל הַמַּעֲרָכָה סָמוּךְ לַמַּעֲרָכָה. וְרַבָּנִין אֲמְרִין. עַל הַמַּעֲרָכָה עַל גַּנָּה שֶׁלְמַעֲרָכָה. אַתְיָא דְאַבָּא שָׁאוּל כְּרִבִּי עֲקִיבָה. וּדְרַבָּנִין כְּרִבִּי יוֹסֵי הַגְּלִילִי. רִבִּי אוֹמֵר. אֲפִילוּ עֲשָׂאָן שְׁנֵי סְדָרִין שֶׁלְאַרְבַּע עֶשְׂרֵה רוֹאִין אֶת הָעֶלְיוֹנוֹת כְּאִילוּ אֵינָן וְהַתַּחְתּוֹנוֹת כְּשֵׁירוֹת. רִבִּי יוֹסֵי בֵּירִבִּי בּוּן בְּשֵׁם רִבִּי יוֹחָנָן. רִבִּי וְאַבָּא שָׁאוּל בְּשִׁיטַת רִבִּי מֵאִיר בְּשׁוּלְחָן.

1 סמוך K | סמוך לו אבא K | אבה   2 אתיא K | אתייה דאבא K | דאבה   3 ר' | K ר' יוסה הגלילי   4 יוסי | K יוסה   5 ואבא K | ואבה

תּוֹךְ בַּר דִּבְרֵי רִבִּי טַרְפוֹן. רִבִּי יִשְׁמָעֵאל אוֹמֵר. מְקוּלָּס. אַתְיָא דְרִבִּי טַרְפוֹן כְּרִבִּי עֲקִיבָה. וּדְרִבִּי יִשְׁמָעֵאל כְּרִבִּי יוֹסֵי הַגְּלִילִי. דְּתַנֵּי. רִבִּי יוֹסֵי [הַגְּלִילִי] אוֹמֵר. אֵי זֶהוּ גְדִי מְקוּלָּס. כּוּלוֹ צָלִי. רֹאשׁוֹ עַל־כְּרָעָיו וְעַל־קִרְבּוֹ. שָׁלַק מִקְצָת אוֹ בִישֵּׁל מִקְצָת אֵין זֶה גְדִי מְקוּלָּס. מַכְנִיסִין גְּדִי מְקוּלָּס בְּלֵילֵי יוֹם טוֹב הָרִאשׁוֹן שֶׁלְחַג וּבְיוֹם טוֹב הָאַחֲרוֹן שֶׁלְפֶּסַח. מַכְנִיסִין עֵגֶל מְקוּלָּס בְּלֵילֵי יוֹם טוֹב הָרִאשׁוֹן שֶׁלְפֶּסַח. אֲבָל לֹא גְדִי מְקוּלָּס.

1 אתיא K | אתייה   2 יוסי S יוסי C יוסי הגלילי K | יוסה (2) דתני K | תנה אי זהו K | אה הוא   3 או בישל K ובישל   4 האחרון K | הראשון

תַּנֵּי. אָמַר רִבִּי יִסָּה. תּוֹדוֹס אִישׁ רוֹמִי הִנְהִיג אֶת אֲנָשֵׁי רוֹמִי שֶׁיְּהוּ אוֹכְלִין גְּדָיִים מְקוּלָּסִין בְּלֵילֵי פְסָחִים. שָׁלְחוּ חֲכָמִים וְאָמְרוּ לוֹ. אִילוּלֵי שֶׁאַתְּ תּוֹדַס לֹא הָיִינוּ מְנַדִּין אוֹתָךְ. מַהוּ

תֵּוּדַס. אָמַר רִבִּי חֲנַנְיָה. דַּהֲוָה מְשַׁלֵּחַ פַּרְנָסָתְהוֹן דְּרַבָּנִין. לֹא נִמְצֵאתָ מֵבִיא אֶת הָרַבִּים לִידֵי אֲכִילַת קֳדָשִׁים בַּחוּץ. שֶׁכָּל־הַמֵּבִיא אֶת הָרַבִּים לִידֵי אֲכִילַת קֳדָשִׁים בַּחוּץ צָרִיךְ נִידּוּי.

1 יוסה | ק יוסי תודוס | צק תודוס את | K על שיהו | K שיהוא גדיים | K גדיין 2 פסחים | K פסחין חכמים | K חכמין שאת | K שאתה מהו | K מהיא 3 חנניה | K חניה דרבנין | צק דרבנן

Everybody agrees that "on it" means "in contact". Where do they disagree? About "on". [16]Abba Shaul says, *on the array*, near the array. But the rabbis say, *on the array*, on top of the array. It turns out that Abba Shaul parallels Rebbi Aqiba, and the rabbis Rebbi Yose the Galilean[17]. Rebbi says, even if he made them two arrangements of fourteen, one considers the upper one as nonexistent and the lower ones are qualified[18]. Rebbi Yose ben Rebbi Abun in the name of Rebbi Johanan: Rebbi and Abba Shaul use in the method of Rebbi Meïr for the table[19].

Inside-out, the words of Rebbi Tarphon. Rebbi Ismael says, helmeted[20]. It turns out that Rebbi Tarphon parallels Rebbi Aqiba, and Rebbi Ismael Rebbi Yose the Galilean; as we have stated: Rebbi Yose the Galilean said, [21]"what is a helmeted kid-goat? Entirely roasted, *its head, on its hooves, and on its innards*. If he parboiled part of it, or cooked part of it, this is not a helmeted kid-goat. One serves helmeted kid-goat in the evening of the first day of Tabernacles, and on the last day of Passover[22]. One serves helmeted calf on the first night of Passover but not helmeted kid-goat[23]."

[24]It was stated: Rebbi Yose said, Theudas of Rome led the people of Rome to eat helmeted kid-goat in the Passover nights. the Sages sent and said to him, if you were not Theudas, would we not put you in the ban? Who was Theudas? Rebbi Hananiah said, because he was providing for the rabbis. Are you not causing the public to eat *sancta* outside the Temple? And anybody causing the public to eat *sancta* outside the Temple has to be put in the ban.

16 This refers to Mishnah *Menahot* 11:5, Babli *Menahot* 97a, about the placement of incense on the table with the shew-bread. The verse says (*Lev.* 24:7): *Put pure incense on the array* (מַעֲרָכָה not מַעֲרֶכֶת). Abba Shaul says nearby, the rabbis say on top.

17 Since R. Aqiba requires the innards to bu hung outside, i. e. nearby.

18 There are twelve shew-breads. If one made two too many, 7 to a row instead of 6, the additional two can be disregarded and the incense put on top, since we do not read "on" to imply touching.

19 Mishnah *Menahot* 11:5 The table in the Tabernacle was 2 cubits long. According to R. Jehudah, the cubit was 5 hand-breadths, according to R. Meïr 6 hand-breadths. Six shew-breads in one row took up 10 hand-

breadths. This leaves 2 hand-breadths space where according to Abba Shaul the incense was placed, and according to Rebbi another bread could be placed.

The argument shows that the text of the Leiden ms. is correct, attributing the statement about the shew-bread to Rebbi, against the reading of K which attributes it to R. Yose the Galilean.

20 Rashi's explanation, Babli 74a.

21 Tosephta *Yom Tov* 2:15. The same text in *Besah* 2:7 (61c line 62); cf. Babli 74a.

22 This is the Tosephta's and the corrector's text in *Besah*; one Tosephta ms.

and K have "on the first day of Passover". Both texts are acceptable; the roasted kid-goat is forbidden only during the first night. It is remarkable that Pentecost is not mentioned in this context; this may indicate an early form of the usage of German Jews to eat dairy on the first day of Pentecost.

23 Roast meat is acceptable as long as it is not sheep or goat.

24 In addition to the *Besah* text (צ), this paragraph also is in *Mo`ed qatan* 3:1 (81d line 27,פ). Babli 53a, *Berakhot* 19a, *Besah* 23a.

(34a line 62) רִבִּי יוֹסֵה בֵּירִבִּי בּוּן בְּשֵׁם רַב. זֹאת אוֹמֶרֶת שֶׁאָסוּר לָאָדָם לוֹמַר לַחֲבֵירוֹ. הֵא לָךְ אֶת הַמָּעוֹת וּצֵא וְקַח לָךְ בָּהֶם בָּשָׂר לְפֶסַח. אֲבָל אוֹמֵר הוּא לוֹ. הֵא לָךְ אֶת הַמָּעוֹת הַלָּלוּ וּצֵא וְקַח לִי בָּהֶם בָּשָׂר לִצְלוֹת.

2 בהם K | - הוא K | - בהם K | 3 בהן לצלות K | לצלי

רִבִּי אִימִּי בָעֵי. גָּרַף אֶת הַתַּנּוּר וּצְלָיוֹ בוֹ. אָמַר רִבִּי יִרְמְיָה. מַה צְרִיכָה לֵיהּ כְּרִבִּי יוֹסֵי הַגְּלִילִי. בְּרַם כְּרִבִּי עֲקִיבָה פְּשִׁיטָה לֵיהּ. אָמַר רִבִּי יוֹסֵי. וַאֲפִילוּ כְרִבִּי עֲקִיבָה צְרִיכָה לֵיהּ. מִשֶּׁל גְחָלִים לָאֲוֵיר הַתַּנּוּר נִצְלָה לַחֲצִי שָׁעָה. גְחָלִים לָאֲוֵיר הָעוֹלָם נִצְלָה לְשָׁעָה. מַה בֵין נִצְלָה מִקְצָתוֹ מַחֲמַת הַתַּנּוּר מַה בֵין נִצְלָה כּוּלוֹ מַחֲמַת הַתַּנּוּר. אָמַר רִבִּי יוֹסֵה בֵּירִבִּי בּוּן. תַּנּוּר אֵינוֹ מוֹעִיל לַגֶּחָלִים כְּלוּם. אֵינוֹ אֶלָּא מַכְנִיס אֶת הַהֶבֶל. בְּשָׁעָה שֶׁהַגֶחָלִים בָּאֲוֵיר הַתַּנּוּר נִצְלָה לַחֲצִי שָׁעָה. בְּשָׁעָה שֶׁהַגֶחָלִים לָאֲוֵיר הָעוֹלָם נִצְלָה לְשָׁעָה.

1 אימי K | אמי וצלייו K | וצליו יוסי K | יוסה 2 יוסי K | יוסה ואפילו K | אפילו משל K | בשעה 3 גחלים K | שהגחלים לאויר K | לאביר נצלה K | ניצלה לחצי K | - גחלים K | גחלין לאויר K | לאביר נצלה K | ניצלה (2) 4 נצלה K | ניצלה יוסי K | יוסה 5 הבל K | ההבל באויר K | באביר נצלה K | ניצלה 6 לאויר K | לאביר נצלה K | ניצלה לשעה K | לחצי שעה

Rebbi Yose ben Rebbi Abun in the name of Rav: This[25] implies that a person is forbidden to say to another, here you have money and use it to buy meat for *Pesaḥ* for yourself[26]. But he may say to him, here you have money and buy me meat to roast.

Rebbi Immi asked, if one cleaned out the *tannur* and roasted it in it[27]? Rebbi Jeremiah said, his problem is following Rebbi Yose the Galilean, but it is obvious for him following Rebbi Aqiba[28]. Rebbi Yose said, even following Rebbi Aqiba it is problematic for him. From the coals into the air of the *tannur* it is roasted in half an hour. From the coals into free air it is roasted in one hour. What is the difference between being roasted half because of the *tannur* or being roasted entirely because of the *tannur*? Rebbi Yose ben Rebbi Abun said, the *tannur* does nothing for the coals, it only keeps the heat together[29]. If the coals are inside the *tannur* it is roasted in half an hour; if the coals are in free air it is roasted in one hour.

25 The story of Theudas.
26 Babli 53a.
27 The *tannur* is a truncated clay cone with an open top and some vents on the bottom, used to generate more heat by creating a draft and keeping the heat together in its walls. The question is whether by hanging the lamb into a *tannur* one roasts it in fire, as required by the verse, or one roasts it in the *tannur*, which would be forbidden just as using a metal spit is forbidden (see also Halakhah 2. Babli 95a.)

28 Since for R. Yose the Galilean the innards are roasted indirectly, inside the lamb, it is possible that he accept the use of a *tannur* while for R. Aqiba it should be clear that the roast must be in the open air.
29 One has to say that since in open air one may increase the heat by using bellows to increase the flames, the bottom vents of the *tannur* do not make the roasting a funxtion of the *tannur*. *Tosaphot* 95a s.v. וברפו.

(fol. 33d) **משנה ב**: אֵין צוֹלִין אֶת הַפֶּסַח לֹא בִּשְׁפּוּד וְלֹא בָּאַסְכָּלָה. אָמַר רִבִּי צָדוֹק מַעֲשֶׂה בְּרַבָּן גַּמְלִיאֵל שֶׁאָמַר לְטָבִי עַבְדּוֹ צֵא וּצְלֵה לָנוּ אֶת הַפֶּסַח עַל הָאַסְכָּלָה. נָגַע בְּחַרְסוֹ שֶׁל תַּנּוּר יִקְלוֹף אֶת מְקוֹמוֹ. נָטַף מֵרוֹטְבּוֹ עַל הַחֶרֶס וְחָזַר עָלָיו יִטּוֹל אֶת מְקוֹמוֹ. נָטַף מֵרוֹטְבּוֹ עַל הַסּוֹלֶת יִקְמוֹץ אֶת מְקוֹמוֹ:

Mishnah 2: One roasts the *Pesaḥ* neither on a spit[30] nor on a grill[31]. Rebbi Ṣadoq said, it happened that Rabban Gamliel said to his slave Tabi, go and roast us the *Pesaḥ* on a sacrificial hearth[32]. If it touched the pottery of the *tannur*, he has to shave off its place[33]. If some of its fluid fell on clay and returned, one has to remove this place[34]. If some of its fluid fell on flour, one has to remove its place[35].

30 A metal spit.
31 Greek ἐσχάρα, ἡ.
32 He holds that anything heated by fire is as good as fire itself. Since the metal gets all its heat from the fire, it is permitted. This Rabban Gamliel must be Gamliel I, preceding R. Jehudah (Note 4) by three generations, showing that Rebbi Jehudah is

a reliable historical source.
33 Since that place on the surface of the meat was cooked by the wall of the *tannur*, not roasted by the air heated by the fire.
34 The the fluid was heated by the clay walls; falling back onto the meat it penetrated into it and therefore surface shaving is insufficient.
35 Since the entire lamb has to be consumed *roasted in fire*, the fluid in the flour may not be consumed; it has to be removed and burned separately.

(34a line 72) **הלכה ב:** צְלִי־אֵשׁ. לֹא צְלִי שְׁפוּד. לֹא צְלִי קְדֵירָה. לֹא צְלִי אִסְכָּלָה. לֹא צְלִי [מַתֶּכֶת. וְלֹא] כָּל־דָּבָר.

1 קדירה K קדרה   2 C מתכת. ולא צלי KS -

מְכוַת־אֵשׁ. יָכוֹל מוּרֶרֶת. תַּלְמוּד לוֹמַר וְהָיְתָה מִחְיַת הַמִּכְוָה. [אִם מִחְיַת הַמִּכְוָה] יָכוֹל עַד שֶׁתֵּעָשֶׂה צַלֶּקֶת. תַּלְמוּד לוֹמַר מִכְוַת־אֵשׁ. הָא כֵּיצַד. חָיְתָה לֹא חָיְתָה. וְכֵן הוּא אוֹמֵר לְמַטָּן צָרֶבֶת הַמִּכְוָה הִיא. עַד שֶׁתִּקְרוֹם כִּקְלִיפַת הַשּׁוּם. וְכָא הוּא אוֹמֵר הָכֵין. אָמַר רִבִּי לָעְזָר. תַּמָּן צְלִי־אֵשׁ. כִּי אִם־צְלִי־אֵשׁ. שָׁנָה עָלָיו הַכָּתוּב לְעִיכּוּב. בְּרַם הָכָא וְהָיְתָה מִחְיַת הַמִּכְוָה. מִכָּל־מָקוֹם. אָמַר רִבִּי שְׁמוּאֵל בַּר אֲבוּדְּמָא. תַּמָּן חוּקַּת תּוֹרָה מְעַכֵּב. הָכָא מָה אִית לָךְ.

1 C אם מכות המכוה K אם מכות המגווה S - 2 מכות K מכוות חיתה K חייתה (2) למטן K מלמטן כי 3 שתקרום K שתיקרום וכא היא או' K והכה אתמר הכין K הכן   4 והייתה K והיתה 5 הכא K הכה

Halakhah 2: *Fire roasted*, not spit roasted, nor pot roasted, nor grill roasted, nor metal roasted, nor roasted in any other way[36].

"*A fire burn*[37], I could think if it stays moist[38], the verse says, *if the burn was healed*[39]. If the burn was healed, I could think until it becomes scar tissue, the verse says, *a fire burn*. How is that? It was partially healed; and so it says below, *it is a burn scar*;[40] until it forms a membrane in the thickness of a garlic peel."[41] And here he says so[42]? Rebbi Eleazar says, there *fire roasted, only fire roasted*[43], the verse repeated it to make it indispensable. But here, *if the burn was healed*, in any way. Rebbi Samuel bar Eudaimon said, there "law, teaching" makes it indispensable[44]. But here what do you have?

36 *Mekhilta dR. Ismael Bo* 6 (p. 19); cf. Babli 74a, 76a. The corrector's addition is only found in the Babli.
37 *Lev.* 13:24, in the rules of skin disease.
38 This is Maimonides's interpretation (*Nega`im* 7:8), based on the reading in *Sifra* מורדת. The reading here, מוררת could be interpreted, parallel to Arabic استمرّ "to stay unchanged", that the wound does not heal.
39 *Lev.* 13:27.
40 *Lev.* 13:28.
41 *Sifra Tazria Pereq* 7(3).
42 Why for skin disease does one include anything which minimally corresponds to the description in the verses, but for *Pesah* one excludes everything but strict adherence

to the prescribed manner.
43 *Ex.* 12:8,9. Babli 95a.
44 For the *Pesaḥ* "law" is written in *Ex.* 12:43, "teaching" in 12:49. Any commandment labelled "law" or "teaching" must be kept to the letter; Babli *Menaḥot* 19a. For skin disease, "teaching" is mentioned the first time for the purification rites (*Lev.* 14:43).

(34b line 3) לֵית לְרַבָּן גַּמְלִיאֵל צְלִי־אֵשׁ. [אִית לֵיהּ. פֶּסַח מִצְרַיִם צְלִי־אֵשׁ.] אֵין פֶּסַח הַדּוֹרוֹת צְלִי־אֵשׁ. אָמַר רִבִּי יוֹסֵי בֵּירִבִּי בּוּן. רַבָּן גַּמְלִיאֵל לֹא עָבַד תּוֹלְדוֹת אֵשׁ כְּאֵשׁ. וְרַבָּנִין עָבְדִין תּוֹלְדוֹת אֵשׁ כְּאֵשׁ. רַבָּן גַּמְלִיאֵל חָלוּק עַל חֲכָמִים וְעוֹשֶׂה הֲלָכָה כְּיוֹצֵא בוֹ.

C1 מצרים צלי K | מצרים וצלי הדורות K | דורות 2 יוסי K | יוסה 3 חלוק K | חולק

Does Rabban Gamliel not have *fire roasted*? He does. The *Pesaḥ* in Egypt was fire roasted; the *Pesaḥ* for generations is not fire roasted[45]. Rebbi Yose ben Rebbi Abun said, Rabban Gamliel did not consider consequences of fire as fire; the rabbis consider consequences of fire as fire[46]. Rabban Gamliel disagrees with the rabbis and in practice acts on his own opinion[47].

45 In the rules for the *Pesaḥ* to be observed in the future, at the end of *Ex.* 12 and the beginning of *Num.* 9, roasting in fire is not mentioned.
46 It is obvious that the places of "did not consider" and "consider" have to be switched. Since the problematic text also is in K, it is not a scribal error.
  The Babli, 95a top, explains the problem away.
47 Cf. *Berakhot* 1:2, Note 111; also *Avodah zarah* 3:12, Note 252.

(34b line 7) אִילּוּ אָמַר לֹא תֹאכְלוּ מִמֶּנּוּ כִּי אִם צְלִי אֵשׁ וְלֹא נֶאֱמַר נָא. הָיִיתִי אוֹמֵר. הִבְהֲבוֹ וּצְלָיוֹ מוּתָּר. הֲוֵי צוֹרֶךְ הוּא שֶׁיֹּאמַר נָא. אוֹ אִילּוּ אָמַר. (לֹא) [אַל תֹּאכְלוּ] מִמֶּנּוּ כִּי אִם צְלִי אֵשׁ וְלֹא אָמַר וּבָשֵׁל. שְׁלָקוֹ וּצְלָיוֹ יְהֵא מוּתָּר. הֲוֵי צוֹרֶךְ הוּא שֶׁיֹּאמַר וּבָשֵׁל. אוֹ אִילּוּ אָמַר. אַל תֹּאכְלוּ מִמֶּנּוּ כִּי אִם צְלִי אֵשׁ וְלֹא אָמַר מְבוּשָּׁל. בִּישְּׁלוֹ וּצְלָיוֹ יְהֵא מוּתָּר. הֲוֵי צָרִיךְ הוּא שֶׁיֹּאמַר נָא. וְצָרִיךְ הוּא שֶׁיֹּאמַר [בָּשֵׁל. וְצָרִיךְ הוּא שֶׁיֹּאמַר] מְבוּשָּׁל.

1 נאמ' K | אמ' 3 וצלייו K | וצליו הוי K | הווי 4 וצלייו K | וצליו הוי K | הווי 5 צריך K | צורך וצריך K | וצורך

If it had said "do not eat from it except fire roasted" and had not said "raw", I would have said that if he singed it and roasted it would be permitted; therefore he needed to say, "raw". Or if it had said "do not [eat from it] except fire roasted" and had not said "cooked", I would have said that if he parboiled it and roasted it, it would be permitted; therefore he needed to say, "cooked". Or if it had said "do not eat from it except fire roasted" and had not said "thoroughly cooked", I would have said that if he cooked it and roasted it would be permitted. Therefore it was needed to say "raw", and it was needed to say ["cooked", and it was needed to say] "thoroughly cooked."[48]

48 Cf. *Mekhilta dR. Ismael Bo* 6, ed. Horovitz-Rabin p. 21; Babli 41a. "Raw" is interpreted as "rare". C"s addition is confirmed by K.

(34b line 13) אָכַל כְּזַיִת נָא מִבְּעוֹד יוֹם. אִית תַּנָּיֵי תַנֵּי. חַיָּיב. וְאִית תַּנָּיֵי תַנֵּי. פָּטוּר. מָאן דְּאָמַר. חַיָּיב. אַל־תֹּאכְלוּ מִמֶּנּוּ נָא מִכָּל־מָקוֹם. וּמָאן דְּאָמַר. פָּטוּר. בְּשָׁעָה שֶׁהוּא בְקוּם אֲכוֹל צְלִי הוּא בְּבַל תֹּאכַל נָא. בְּשָׁעָה שֶׁאֵינוֹ בְקוּם אֲכוֹל צְלִי אֵינוּ בְּבַל תֹּאכַל נָא.

1 ואית K | אית   מאן דאמ' K | מן דמר   2 ומאן דאמ' K | מן דמר   3 בבל K | בל   שאינו K | שהיא

שָׁבַר בּוֹ עֶצֶם מִבְּעוֹד יוֹם. אִית תַּנָּיֵי תַנֵּי. חַיָּיב. אִית תַּנָּיֵי תַנֵּי. פָּטוּר. מָאן דְּאָמַר. חַיָּיב. וְעֶצֶם לֹא תִשְׁבְּרוּ־בוֹ כו' מִכָּל־מָקוֹם. וּמָאן דְּאָמַר. פָּטוּר. בְּשָׁעָה שֶׁאֵינוֹ בְקוּם אֲכוֹל צְלִי אֵינוּ מִשּׁוּם וְעֶצֶם לֹא תִשְׁבְּרוּ־בוֹ׃ בְּשָׁעָה שֶׁהוּא בְקוּם אֲכוֹל צְלִי הוּא מִשּׁוּם וְעֶצֶם לֹא תִשְׁבְּרוּ־בוֹ׃

1 מאן דאמ' K | מן דמר   2 ומאן דאמ' K | ומן דמר   שאינו K | שהיא   אינו K | היא   3 שהיא K | שאינו   היא K | אינו

If somebody ate the volume of an olive raw when it still was daylight[49]. There are Tannaim who state, he is liable, and there are Tannaim who state, he is not liable[50]. He who says that he is liable, *do not eat from it raw*[53], in any case. But he who says that he is not liable, at a time when he is obligated to eat fire-roasted he is under obligation not to eat raw; at a time when he is not obligated to eat fire-roasted he is not obligated not to eat raw.

If he broke a bone of it when it still was daylight. There are Tannaim who state, he is liable, and there are Tannaim who state, he is not liable[51]. He who says that he is liable, *do not break a bone in it*[53] etc., in any case. But he who says that he is not liable, at a time when he is not obligated to eat fire-roasted there is no *do not break a bone in it*; at a time when he is obligated to eat fire-roasted there is *do not break a bone in it*.

49 On the 14th of Nisan.
50 Babli 41b.
51 Babli 84b.
53 *Ex.* 12:46.

(34b line 21) נָגַע בְּחַרְסוֹ שֶׁלַּתַּנּוּר. פָּסוּל גּוּף [הוּא] וְנִשְׂרָף מִיָּד. נָטַף מֵרוּטְבּוֹ עַל הַחֶרֶס. פָּסוּל מַכְשִׁיר [הוּא] וְטָעוּן צוּרָה. נָטַף מֵרוּטְבּוֹ עַל הַסּוֹלֶת [יִקְמוֹץ אֶת מְקוֹמוֹ]. חִייָה בַּר אָדָא בְּשֵׁם רִבִּי שִׁמְעוֹן בֶּן לָקִישׁ. הָדָא דְתֵימַר בְּרוֹתַחַת. אֲבָל בְּצוֹנֶנֶת אָסוּר. אָמַר רִבִּי לְעָזָר. לֹא אָמְרָה הַתּוֹרָה. הוּא לֹא יִצָּלֶה אֶת אֲחֵרִים. אֶלָּא הוּא לֹא יִצָּלֶה מַחֲמַת אֲחֵרִים.

1 ונישרף K | ונישרף 2 C י 2 קמוץ את מקומו KS | - 2 הדא דתימר K | הדה דתמר   בתוננת K | בתונינית לעזר K | אליעזר   4 התורה K | - את אחרים K | אחרין   אחרים K | אחריו

"If it touched the pottery of the *tannur*," it is a disability of its body and it has to be burned immediately. "If of its fluid fell on clay," it is a disability on the instrument and needs [losing its] shape[53]. "If of its fluid fell on flour, one has to remove its place." Ḥiyya bar Ada in the name of Rebbi Simeon ben Laqish: that is, if it is hot[54]. But if it is cool, it is forbidden[55]. Rebbi Eleazar, the Torah did not say, it should not cook others, but it should not be cooked because of others[56].

53 It may not be eaten but because it is indirectly disqualified one has to wait until it would have to be burned even if qualified; cf. Chapter 6, after Note 151.
54 Babli 75b/76a.
55 In contrast to "liable", "forbidden" means rabbinically forbidden.
56 He disagrees and notes that since there is no biblical prohibition if the hot fluid falls into cold edibles; there is no reason for a rabbinic prohibition either.

(fol. 33d) **משנה ג**: סָכוּ בְשֶׁמֶן שֶׁל תְּרוּמָה אִם חֲבוּרַת כֹּהֲנִים יֹאכֵלוּ. אִם שֶׁל יִשְׂרָאֵל אִם חַי יְדִיחֶנּוּ. וְאִם צָלִי יְקַלוֹף אֶת הַחִיצוֹן. סָכוּ בְשֶׁמֶן שֶׁל מַעֲשֵׂר שֵׁנִי לֹא יַעֲשֶׂנּוּ דָמִים עַל בְּנֵיחֲבוּרָה שֶׁאֵין מוֹכְרִין מַעֲשֵׂר שֵׁנִי בִירוּשָׁלָֽיִם:

Mishnah 3: If he basted it with heave oil, if there is a group of priests, they shall eat it. If of Israel[57], if it is raw he shall soak it, if roasted he has to peel off the outside. If he basted it with oil of Second Tithe[58], he may not charge the members of the group for it since one may not sell Second Tithe in Jerusalem.

57 For whom consumption of heave is a deadly sin.
58 Which is property of the farmer, to be eaten in purity at the place of the Temple. Second Tithe may be redeemed outside of Jerusalem, with the sanctity of the produce transferred to the money which has to be spent on pure food in Jerusalem. There is neither redemption nor sale of Second Tithe in Jerusalem.

(34b line 26) **הלכה ג**: לֹא אָמַר אֶלָּא סָכוּ. הָא אִם טִיבְּלוֹ. אָסוּר. חַד בַּר נַשׁ בִּישֵׁל תַּרְנְגוֹלְתָּא בְשֶׁמֶן שְׂרֵיפָה. אֲתָא שְׁאִיל לְרִבִּי בִּיסְנָא. אֲמַר לֵיהּ. אֲזַל שׁוּלְקָהּ.

1 C לֹא SK | סכו לא   תרנגולתא K | תרנגולת   2 אתא K | -

כֵּינֵי מַתְנִיתָה. אֵין פּוֹדִין מַעֲשֵׂר שֵׁנִי בִירוּשָׁלֵם:

Halakhah 3: He only said "basted". Therefore, if he immersed it, it is forbidden[59]. A person cooked a chicken using oil to be burned[60]. He came and asked Rebbi Bisna, who told him, go and cook it in water for an extended period.

So is the Mishnah: "One does not redeem Second Tithe in Jerusalem.[61]"

59 Either this means that if the lamb absorbed too much of the oil, no Israel will be allowed to eat from it in any way. Or it may be that טִיבְּלוֹ stands for תִּיבְּלוֹ "spiced it", when it will be forbidden to everybody since the spices cover the taste of the lamb's meat.

60 "Oil to be burned" is impure heave oil. While it may not be consumed, it may be used by a Cohen as fuel. Use as fuel by an Israel is stealing from the Cohanim. R. Bisna's order has to be classified as imposing a fine.

61 The text of the Mishnah in the Babli.

(fol. 33d) **משנה ד:** חֲמִשָּׁה דְבָרִים בָּאִין בְּטוּמְאָה וְאֵינָן נֶאֱכָלִין בְּטוּמְאָה. הָעוֹמֶר וּשְׁתֵּי הַלֶּחֶם וְלֶחֶם הַפָּנִים וְזִבְחֵי שַׁלְמֵי צִבּוּר וּשְׂעִירֵי רָאשֵׁי חֳדָשִׁים. הַפֶּסַח שֶׁבָּא בְטוּמְאָה נֶאֱכָל בְּטוּמְאָה שֶׁלֹּא בָא מִתְּחִילָּתוֹ אֶלָּא לַאֲכִילָה:

Mishnah 4: Five kinds[62] are brought in impurity but are not eaten in impurity: The `Omer[63], and the Two Breads[64], and the shew-bread[65], and public well-being offerings[66], and the goats of New Moons[67]. *Pesaḥ* which is brought in impurity is eaten since from the start this is what it is for[68].

62 The only impurity permitted in the Temple is the impurity of the dead, which can be removed only by a lengthy procedure and depends on the availability of the ashes of a red cow. All other impurities prevent a person from entering the sacred precinct. If most or all of the people are impure, the public service is conducted by the Cohanim without interruption. Most of the public sacrifices are elevation sacrifices which are totally burned on the altar; for them the question of consumption does not arise. The only time impure non-Cohanim are admitted to the sacred precinct is the 14th of Nisan, for the *Pesaḥ*.

63 The offering of barley flour from the new harvest, *Lev.* 23:9-14, of which a fistful is burned on the altar and the remainder eaten be the Cohanim. If offered in impurity everything has to be burned.

64 The two leavened breads of new wheat harvest presented on Pentecost, *Lev.* 23:17, intended to be eaten entirely by the Cohanim.

65 *Lev.* 24:9.
66 The two sheep accompanying the two breads, to be eaten by the Cohanim with the breads; *Lev.* 23:19-20.
67 The obligatory purification offerings, not only for New Moons but also all holidays, of which only a small part is burned on the altar and most of it eaten by the Cohanim in the Temple precinct; *Num.* 28:15,22,30; 29:5.11,16, 19,22,25,28,31,34, 38.
68 Since it is written (*Ex.* 12:4), *Everybody according to his eating you should slaughter the lamb.*

(34b line 29) **הלכה ד**: וְכָל־קָרְבְּנוֹת צִיבּוּר אֵינָן בָּאִין בְּטוּמְאָה. לָא אֲתָא אֶלָּא מֵימוּר לָךְ. אַף עַל פִּי שֶׁהֵן בָּאִין בְּטוּמְאָה אֵינָן נֶאֱכָלִין בְּטוּמְאָה. בֵּין כְּמַאן דְּאָמַר. הַלֶּחֶם עִיקָּר. בֵּין כְּמַאן דְּאָמַר. כְּבָשִׂים עִיקָּר. אַרְבָּעָה אִינּוּן. תַּנָּיָיה חָשׁ לוֹן וּתְנָנְתּוֹן חֲמִשָּׁה.

1 ציבור K | הציבור   2 נאכלין K באין כמאן דאמ' K כמן דמר   3 כמאן דאמ' K כמן דמר כבשים K כבשין

אִית תַּנָּיֵי תַנֵּי. כּוּלְּהוֹם לְמֵידִין מִן הַפֶּסַח. אִית תַּנָּיֵי תַנֵּי. כָּל־אֶחָד וְאֶחָד לָמֵד מִמְּקוֹמוֹ. מָאן דְּאָמַר. כּוּלְּהוֹן לְמֵידִין מִן הַפֶּסַח. מַה מוֹעֲדוֹ שֶׁנֶּאֱמַר (כָּאן) [בַּפֶּסַח דּוֹחֶה אֶת הַטוּמְאָה. אַף מוֹעֲדוֹ שֶׁנֶּאֱמַר בְּכוּלָּן] דּוֹחֶה אֶת הַטוּמְאָה. מָאן דְּאָמַר. כָּל־אֶחָד וְאֶחָד לָמֵד מִמְּקוֹמוֹ מְנַיִין לֵיהּ. וְאַתְיָא כְהָדָא דְתַנֵּי. רִבִּי אוֹמֵר. מַה תַלְמוּד לוֹמַר וַיְדַבֵּר מֹשֶׁה אֶת־מֹעֲדֵי יְיָ. לְפִי שֶׁלֹּא לַמְדֵנוּ אֶלָּא עַל הַפֶּסַח וְהַתָּמִיד שֶׁיִּדְחוּ אֶת הַשַּׁבָּת. שֶׁנֶּאֱמַר בָּהֶם בְּמוֹעֲדוֹ. שְׁאָר כָּל־קָרְבְּנוֹת צִיבּוּר מְנַיִין. תַּלְמוּד לוֹמַר אֵלֶּה תַּעֲשׂוּ לַיְיָ בְּמוֹעֲדֵיכֶם. לָעוֹמֶר וּלְקָרֵב עִמּוֹ וְלִשְׁתֵּי הַלֶּחֶם וּלְקָרֵב עִמֵּהּ לֹא שְׁמַעֲנוּ. וּכְשֶׁהוּא אוֹמֵר וַיְדַבֵּר מֹשֶׁה אֶת־מֹעֲדֵי יְיָ אֶל־בְּנֵי יִשְׂרָאֵל קָבְעָן חוֹבָה. שֶׁכּוּלָּם יָבוֹאוּ בְּטוּמְאָה. וּכְשֵׁם שֶׁהֵן בָּאִין בְּטוּמְאָה כָּךְ יְהוּא נֶאֱכָלִין בְּטוּמְאָה. גְּזֵירַת הַכָּתוּב הוּא. וְהַבָּשָׂר אֲשֶׁר־יִגַּע בְּכָל־טָמֵא לֹא יֵאָכֵל. וְאָמַר אַף בַּפֶּסַח כֵּן. שְׁנִיָּיה הִיא. שֶׁלֹּא בָא מִתְּחִילָּתוֹ אֶלָּא לַאֲכִילָה:

1 כולהום K | כולהון למד K | למיד   2 מאן דאמ' K | מן דמר מועדו K | במועדו   3 בכולן C | בכולהון מאן דאמ' K | מן דמר מנין K | מנן   4 ואתיא K | ואתייה כחדא K | כחדה יי K | יי אל בני ישראל 5 פסח K | הפסח והתמיד K | יעל תמיד שנ' בהם בנגדו ציבור K | הציבור   6 ולקרב K | וליקריב ולקרב K | ולקריב עמו K | עמהן   7 שעולם K | שיהוא כולם יבואו K | באין   9 לא יאכל K | - ואמר K | ומר

Halakhah 4: Are not all public sacrifices brought in impurity? He only comes to tell you, even though they are brought in impurity they are not eaten in impurity. Both for him who says that the bread is the main item, as also for him who says that the sheep are the main item, there should be only four[69]. The Tanna takes note of them and stated them as five.

There are Tannaim who state that all of them are inferred from the *Pesaḥ*. There are Tannaim who state that each of them is inferred from its place. He who said that all of them are inferred from the *Pesaḥ*, since *at its fixed time* which is said (here) [about *Pesaḥ* pushes impurity aside, also *at its fixed time* which is written about all of them] pushes impurity aside[70]. He who said that each of them is inferred from its place, from where does he have it? It comes as it is stated[71]: "Rebbi says, why does the verse say, *Moses told the holidays of the Eternal*[72]. Since we learned only about *Pesaḥ* and the daily sacrifices that they push the Sabbath aside, since it is said about them *at its fixed time*[73], from where the rest of public offerings? The verse says, *these you shall offer to the Eternal at your fixed times*[74]. For the *Omer* and what is brought with it, and for the Two Breads and what is brought with them, we have no information. But since it is said, *Moses told the holidays of the Eternal to the Children of Israel*[71], this fixed it as obligation that all of them have to be offered in impurity." Just as they are brought in impurity, should they not be eaten in impurity? It is a decision of the verse: *Any meat that touched anything impure may not be eaten*[75]. One would say that the same is valid for the *Pesaḥ*. This is different since from the start this is what it is for[68].

69 A dispute between R. Aqiba and R. Simeon ben Nanas in Mishnah *Menaḥot* 4:3. The verse states that the lambs of the well-being sacrifice of Pentecost have to be brought *on the bread*, which R. Aqiba reads as meaning that the Two Breads are indispensable for bringing the lambs, but not the other way around, and R. Simeon ben Nanas holds the opposite opinion.

70 Since it says (*Lev.* 23:4): *These are the times of the Eternal, holy convocations, which you have to proclaim at their fixed times.* Cf. Chapter 6, Halakhah 1.

71 Babli 77a, *Menaḥot* 73a, *Sifra Emor Pereq* 17(13).

72 *Lev.* 23:44.

73 *Num.* 9:2, 28:2.

74 *Num.* 29:39.

75 *Lev.* 7:19/

משנה ה: נִטְמָא הַבָּשָׂר וְהַחֵלֶב קַיָּם אֵינוֹ זוֹרֵק אֶת הַדָּם. נִטְמָא הַחֵלֶב וְהַבָּשָׂר קַיָּם זוֹרֵק אֶת הַדָּם. וּבַמּוּקְדָּשִׁין אֵינוֹ כֵן אֶלָּא אַף עַל פִּי שֶׁנִּטְמָא הַבָּשָׂר וְהַחֵלֶב קַיָּם זוֹרֵק אֶת הַדָּם: נִטְמָא קָהָל אוֹ רוּבּוֹ אוֹ שֶׁהָיוּ הַכֹּהֲנִים טְמֵאִים וְהַקָּהָל טָהוֹר יֵעָשֶׂה בְטוּמְאָה. נִטְמָא מִיעוּט הַקָּהָל הַטְּהוֹרִין עוֹשִׂין אֶת הָרִאשׁוֹן וְהַטְּמֵאִין עוֹשִׂין אֶת הַשֵּׁנִי: הַפֶּסַח שֶׁנִּזְרַק דָּמוֹ וְאַחַר כָּךְ נוֹדַע שֶׁהוּא טָמֵא הַצִּיץ מְרַצֶּה. נִטְמָא טוּמְאַת הַגּוּף אֵין הַצִּיץ מְרַצֶּה מִפְּנֵי שֶׁאָמְרוּ נָזִיר וְעוֹשֶׂה פֶסַח הַצִּיץ מְרַצֶּה עַל טוּמְאַת הַדָּם וְאֵין הַצִּיץ מְרַצֶּה עַל טוּמְאַת הַגּוּף. נִטְמָא טוּמְאַת הַתְּהוֹם הַצִּיץ מְרַצֶּה:

Mishnah 5: If the meat became impure while the fat is unchanged, he does not pour the blood[76]. If the fat became impure while the meat is unchanged, he pours the blood. With sacrifices it is not so, but even if the meat became impure while the fat is unchanged, he pours the blood[77]. If the public or a majority of it were impure or the Cohanim were impure and the public pure, it should be brought in impurity[78]. If a minority of the public were impure, the pure people make the first and the impure the second[79]. If blood was poured of a *Pesaḥ* when later it became known that it was impure, the diadem makes acceptable[80]. An impurity of the body[81] the diadem does not make acceptable since they said that for the *nazir* and the offerer of the *Pesaḥ* the diadem makes impurity of the blood acceptable but not impurity of the body. If the impurity was caused by impurity of the abyss[82], the diadem makes acceptable.

76 Since the *Pesaḥ* is brought only to be eaten, if there is no meat to be eaten, there is no *Pesaḥ*. If the *Pesaḥ* was brought but the blood may not be poured, the owner has to bring a second *Pesaḥ* on the 14th of Iyar.

77 Since for *sancta* burned on the altar only pouring the blood permits the parts to be brought to the altar.

78 Since the *Pesaḥ* cannot be slaughtered without Cohanim ready to receive and pour the blood.

79 The Second *Pesaḥ* is made on the 14th of Iyar; *Num.* 9:10-12.

80 The golden diadem worn by the High Priest, whose object is *to carry away the iniquities of the sacrifices offered by the Children of Israel*; *Ex.* 28:37.

81 The body of the offerer.

82 Impurity buried in the ground which previously was totally unknown and is only recently uncovered. Since it is impossible to guard against this kind of impurity there can be no penalty for "tent impurity" of this kind.

(34b line 45) **הלכה ה**: וּדְלָא כְרַבִּי נָתָן. דְּרַבִּי נָתָן אָמַר. יוֹצְאִין בִּזְרִיקָה בְּלֹא אֲכִילָה. מַה טַעֲמָא. וְשָׁחֲטוּ אוֹתוֹ כָּל קְהַל עֲדַת־יִשְׂרָאֵל בֵּין הָעַרְבָּיִם: אוֹתוֹ אַף עַל פִּי שֶׁאֵין שָׁם אֶלָּא פֶּסַח אֶחָד כּוּלְּהוֹן יוֹצְאִין בִּזְרִיקָה אַחַת. וְאִיפְשַׁר כְּזַיִת לְכָל־אֶחָד וְאֶחָד.

1 ודלא K | דלא   3 כולהון K | כולחן

Halakhah 5: This does not follow Rebbi Nathan[83], for Rebbi Nathan says, one fulfills one's obligation by pouring without eating. What is the reason? *All of Israel shall slaughter it between the evenings*[84]. "It", even if there is only one *Pesaḥ*, all fulfill their obligation with one pouring. Ii is impossible that there be an olive-sized bit for everyone[85].

83 Babli 78b.
84 *Ex.* 12:6.
85 If the entire people bring only one lamb, there is not one olive-size bite for every one.

But eating less than an olive-size bite is not counted, it is equivalent to nobody eating anything.

(34b line 48) פְּשִׁיטָא דָא מִילְּתָא. נִטְמָא הַבָּשָׂר וְהָאֵימוֹרִין קַיָּימִין. זוֹרֵק אֶת הַדָּם עַל [הָאֵימוֹרִין. נִטְמָא הָאֵימוֹרִין וְהַבָּשָׂר קַיָּם. זוֹרֵק אֶת הַדָּם עַל] הַבָּשָׂר. נִיטְמָא הַבָּשָׂר וְאָבְדוּ הָאֵימוֹרִין. אָמַר רִבִּי שַׁמַּי. וְהֵן קַיָּימִין לֹא כְּמִי שֶׁנִּיטְמָא הַבָּשָׂר וְאָבְדוּ הָאֵימוֹרִין הוּא. אַתְּ אָמַר קוֹמֶץ. אוֹף הָכָא זוֹרֵק. אָמַר רִבִּי. תִּיפְתָּר כְּרִבִּי לִיעֶזֶר. דְּרִבִּי לִיעֶזֶר אָמַר. אַף עַל פִּי שֶׁאֵין שְׁיָרֵים יֵשׁ קוֹמֶץ.

1 פשיטא דא מילתא K | פשיטה הדה מילתה K | והאימורין C 2 האימורין K | והאמורין K | האמורין (2) 3 האמורין K | האמורין (2) שמי K | שמי קיימין K | קומץ 4 את אמר K | ותמר הכא K | הכה זורק K | קומץ ר' K | ר' מנא 5 שיריים K | שיריין

The following is obvious: If the meat became impure but the parts are unchanged, one pours the blood for [the parts. If the parts became impure and the meat is unchanged, one pours the blood for] the meat[86]. If the meat became impure and the parts were lost, Rebbi Shammai said, is the (existing) [fistful][87] not as if the meat became impure and the parts were lost[88]? You are saying that he takes the fistful; also here he pours. Rebbi [Mana][87] said, explain it following Rebbi Eliezer, since Rebbi Eliezer says, even if there is no remainder there is a fistful[89].

86 Since for all Temple sacrifices which are partially eaten, neither Heaven's parts can be brought to the altar nor the meat eaten before the blood was poured on the walls of the altar. If one of the two kinds still exists in pure shape, pouring the blood is a positive act and therefore permitted.
87 Reading of K.
88 A flour offering is eaten by the priests after a fistful has been burned on the altar. If after the fistful was in the hand of the Cohen but before it was brought to the altar the flour became impure, or was burned, or lost, R. Eliezer permits to burn the fistful on the altar but R. Joshua forbids (Mishnah *Menahot* 3:4). The situation can be compared to that of animal sacrifices when only the blood is left.
The text of K has to be followed here; the text of S is a scribal error.
89 In practice we follow R. Joshua. Babli 77b.

(34b line 53) בָּא בְטוּמְאַת עוֹבְדִין. הֵיךְ עֲבִידָה. שְׁחָטוּ אוֹתוֹ בַּעֲלֵי מוּמִין וְזָרְקוּ אוֹתוֹ טְהוֹרִין. אָמַר רִבִּי הִילָא. וְהַבָּשָׂר אֲשֶׁר־יִגַּע בְּכָל־טָמֵא לֹא יֵאָכֵל. הֲרֵי לֹא נָגַע בּוֹ טָמֵא. (וְהַטָּהוֹר)

{וְהַבָּשָׂר} כָּל־טָהוֹר יֹאכַל בָּשָׂר: הֲרֵי יֵשׁ כָּאן טְהוֹרִים שֶׁיֹּאכְלוּהוּ. רִבִּי זְעוּרָה. מֵאַחַר שֶׁאִילּוּ הַפֶּסַח הַבָּא בְטוּמְאָה וְנֶאֱכַל בְטוּמְאָה [וְהָכָא כְמִי שֶׁבָּא בְטוּמְאָה]. וַיְיִדָא אָמַר. רִבִּי שְׁמוּאֵל אָמַר. רִבִּי זְעוּרָה בָעֵי. בָּא בְטוּמְאַת הַדָּם הֵיךְ עֲבִידָא. מֵאַחַר שֶׁאֵין מַתִּירִין לוֹ לִזְרוֹק כְּמִי שֶׁבָּא בְטוּמְאָה. אוֹ מֵאַחַר שֶׁאִילּוּ עָבַר וְזָרַק הוּרְצָה כְּמִי שֶׁלֹּא בָא בְטוּמְאָה. נִשְׁמְעִינָהּ מִן הָדָא דְאָמַר רִבִּי הוֹשַׁעְיָה. וְנָשָׂא אַהֲרֹן אֶת־עֲוֺן הַקֳּדָשִׁים. עֲוֺן הַקְּרֵיבִים. לֹא עֲוֺן הַמַּקְרִיבִים. הִפְרִישׁ בֵּין קְרֵיבִין לְיָחִיד לִקְרֵיבִין לַצִּיבּוּר. הַקְּרֵיבִין לְיָחִיד אִם יֵשׁ לוֹ אוֹמְרִין לוֹ. הָבֵא. [וְאִם לָאו. אֵין מַתִּירִין לוֹ לִזְרוֹק אֶת דָּמוֹ.] עָבַר וְזָרַק הוּרְצָה. הַמַּקְרִיבִין לְיָחִיד בֵּין שֶׁיֵּשׁ לוֹ בֵּין שֶׁאֵין לוֹ [לֹא הוּרְצָה. הַקְּרֵיבִין לַצִּבּוּר אִם יֵשׁ אוֹמְרִין לוֹ. הָבֵא. וְאִם לָאו מַתִּירִין לוֹ לִזְרוֹק בַּתְּחִילָּה. הַמַּקְרִיבִין לַצִּיבּוּר בֵּין שֶׁיֵּשׁ לוֹ בֵּין שֶׁאֵין לוֹ עָבַר] וְזָרַק הוּרְצָה.

2 לא יאכל K | - K | 3 זעורה K | זעורא K | 4 הבא בטומאה K | כבא בטומאה K | והיא הא[כל] C | והכא K | והכה C בטומאה K | בטומאה ונאכל בטוצאה K | ויידא K | והיידה K | אמ' K | אמרה דא 5 עבידא K | עבידה 6 נישמעינה K | נשמעינא הדא K | הדה 7 ר' הושעיה K | ר' לעזר בשם ר' הישעיה K | עון הקריבים | K עוון הקריבין עון המקריבים K | כוון המקריבין C 8 אין K | 9- C 11 לא הורצה ... עבר | KS -

If it comes in impurity of the officiants[90]? How is that? If defective persons[91] slaughtered and pure[92] ones poured. Rebbi Hila said, *any meat that touched anything impure may not be eaten*[75], but here it was not touched by anybody impure. *The meat, anybody pure may eat meat*[75]; there are pure ones available to eat it[93]. Rebbi Ze'ira: Since *Pesaḥ* made in impurity is eaten, [this one is as if brought in impurity][94]. And where was this[95] said? Rebbi Samuel said, Rebbi Ze'ira asked: If it comes with impurity of the blood[96], what is done? Since one does not permit him to pour, is it as if brought in impurity? Or since if he transgressed and poured, it was made acceptable, is it as if not brought in impurity? Let us hear from the following which was said by [Rebbi Elazar in the name of][87] Rebbi Hoshaia: *Aaron shall carry the iniquities of the sacrifices*[97], the iniquities of the sacrifices, not the iniquities of the sacrificers[98]. He separated between what is offered on behalf of an individual and what is offered on behalf of the public. If offered for an individual, if he has another one[99], one tells him, bring! If not, [one does not permit him to pour the blood;] if he transgressed and poured, it was made acceptable. The sacrificers for an individual, whether he has or does not have, [it was not made acceptable. If offered for the public, if he has another one, one tells him, bring! If not, one permits him to pour the blood *a priori*. The sacrificers for the public, whether he has or does not have,] it was made acceptable.

HALAKHAH FIVE   255

90 The case mentioned in the Mishnah, that the people were pure but all officiating priests impure.

91 It could have stated, "a pure non-priest". The statement seems to imply that a priest with a bodily defect, who is barred from officiating (*Lev.* 21:16-24), still is permitted to act as slaughterer in the Temple. Here it is presumed that he is pure.

92 Obviously one has to read: impure. (K is not legible at this point.) The impure (by the impurity of the dead) priest does not come into direct contact with the sacrificial animal. While the blood collected in the vessel which he holds will be impure, it does not make the carcass impure through the stream of blood falling into his vessel.

93 The people, as stated in the Mishnah.

94 Since the people are pure, the argument of R. Hoshaia is superfluous.

95 The source of R. Ze`ira's argument.

96 The carcass is pure, the priests are pure, but the blood has become impure. Since only the blood pumped out at the moment of slaughter is acceptable on the altar (Chapter 5, Note 234), it cannot be replaced.

97 *Ex.* 28:38. Explained in more detail in the Babli 16b, *Yoma* 7a, *Zevahim* 23a.

98 The diadem will not cover deficiencies in either the owners or the officiants of a sacrifice. Babli *Zevahim* 23b.

99 Another animal to offer.

The following text in brackets is a corrector's addition which by the concurrent testimony of the original scribe and K should be deleted.

(34b line 67) אָמַר רִבִּי לְעָזָר. מַתְנִיתָה בְּבָא בְּטוּמְאָה מִשָּׁעָה רִאשׁוֹנָה. אֲבָל אִם בָּא בְּטַהֳרָה וְנִיטְמָא אֵינוֹ נֶאֱכָל בְּטוּמְאָה. שְׁחָטוֹ בְּטַהֳרָה וְנִיטְמָא הַצִּיבּוּר. יִיזָרֵק הַדָם בְּטַהֳרָה וְאַל יֵיאָכֵל הַבָּשָׂר בְּטוּמְאָה. (וְאָמַר אַף בִּזְרִיקָה כֵן.) [רִבִּי לָא בְּשֵׁם רִבִּי יוֹחָנָן. דְּרִבִּי נָתָן הִיא. רִבִּי נָתָן אָמַר. יוֹצְאִין בִּזְרִיקָה בְּלָא אֲכִילָה. שְׁחָטוֹ בְּטַהֳרָה וְנִיטְמָא הַדָּם הַצָּבוּר. יִיזָרֵק הַדָּם בְּטוּמְאָה וְאַל יֵיאָכֵל הַבָּשָׂר בְּטוּמְאָה. רִבִּי יִרְמְיָה בְּשֵׁם רִבִּי יוֹחָנָן. מִפְּנֵי מַרְאִית הָעַיִן. שֶׁלֹּא יֹאמְרוּ. רָאִינוּ פֶּסַח בָּא בְּטַהֳרָה וְנִזְרָק בְּטוּמְאָה. מֵעַתָּה לֹא יִיזָרֵק הַדָּם בְּטוּמְאָה.] שֶׁלֹּא יְהוּ אוֹמְרִין. רָאִינוּ פֶּסַח שֶׁבָּא בְּטַהֳרָה וְנִזְרָק בְּטוּמְאָה. הָא סוֹפָךְ מֵימַר דְּרִבִּי נָתָן הִיא. מוֹדֶה רִבִּי נָתָן בְּחוֹלֶה וּבִזְקֵן. מוֹדֶה רִבִּי נָתָן הִיא בַּחֲבוּרָה שֶׁנִּיטְמָא עוֹבֵד שֶׁלָּהּ. שֶׁהֵן נִידָּחִין לַפֶּסַח הַשֵּׁינִי. מוֹדֶה רִבִּי נָתָן בַּחֲבוּרָה שֶׁנִּמְצֵאת יַבֶּלֶת בְּעוֹרָהּ. שֶׁהֵן נִידָּחִין לַפֶּסַח הַשֵּׁינִי.

<small>1 בבא | K בשבא   בטהרה | K בטומאה   2 אינו נאכל בטומאה | K כבא בטומאה הוא ולוקים על אכילתו   ייזרק | K יזרק   ייאכל | K יאכל   3 ואמר אף בזריקה כן | - | K לא | K הילא ר' | K דר'   4 הצבור | K והציבור   5 יאמרו | K יהוא אומרין   6 ונזרק | K ונאכל   7 הא | K הוי מודה | K מודי   8 מודה | K מודי   (2) שניטמא | K שנטמא   השיני | K שיני   9 השיני | K שיני</small>

Rebbi Eleazar said, the Mishnah is about one "which comes in impurity from the start."[100] But if it came in purity and then became impure, it cannot be eaten in impurity. "If it was slaughtered in purity but then the public became impure, the blood shall be poured in purity[101] but the meat not eaten in impurity." (Should one not say the same for pouring?[102]) [Rebbi La in the name of Rebbi Johanan: It is Rebbi Nathan's, as Rebbi Nathan said, one has fulfilled his duty by pouring without eating[103]. "If it was slaughtered in purity but then the blood collected became impure[104], the blood may be poured in impurity but the meat may not be eaten in impurity." Rebbi Jeremiah in the name of Rebbi Johanan: Because of the bad impression, lest they say, we have seen a *Pesah* brought in purity which was [poured] {eaten}[105] in impurity. Then should not the blood be poured in impurity?] Lest they say, we have seen a *Pesah* brought in purity for which it was poured in impurity. You have to end up saying that it is Rebbi Nathan's. Rebbi Nathan agrees for a sick or an old person[106]. Rebbi Nathan agrees for a group whose officiant became impure[107], that they are pushed to the Second *Pesah*. Rebbi Nathan agrees for a group where a wart was found[108], that they are pushed to the Second *Pesah*.

100 Tosephta 6:1.

101 Obviously if everybody is impure, the blood in the vessel carried by the impure Cohen cannot remain pure. One has to read with the Tosephta: impure.

102 Text written by the scribe and deleted by the corrector; missing in K, which supports the corrector's text. There seems to be no reason why the blood could be poured in impurity if the blood is only needed to permit the meat to be consumed when the meat is forbidden for consumption.

103 Babli 78b. The pouring of the blood frees the group subscribing to this particular *Pesah* from having to bring another animal at the Second *Pesah*.

104 This sentence does not make any sense, although it is confirmed by the *editio princeps* of the Tosephta (6:1). One has to read with K and the Tosephta mss. either והציבור or וצבור: "If it was slaughtered in purity but then the public became impure, the blood may be poured in impurity but the meat may not be eaten in impurity."

105 As the following shows, one has to prefer {the text of K} over [the corrector's text].

106 R. Nathan only declares pouring the blood as sufficient if at the start there was a possibility that the meat would be eaten, "since from the start this is what it is for." If nobody in the group is able to eat a full olive-sized piece, there can be no *Pesah*.

107 If the slaughterer makes the sacrifice impure, there can be no pouring of the blood.

108 If the animal from the start was unfit to be a sacrifice, there can be no sacrifice.

(34c line 2) חָמֵשׁ חֲבוּרוֹת שֶׁנִּתְעָרְבוּ עוֹרוֹת פִּסְחֵיהֶן וְנִמְצֵאת יַבּוֹלֶת בְּעוֹרָהּ שֶׁלְאַחַת מֵהֶן. כּוּלְהוֹן יָצְאוּ לְבֵית הַשְּׂרֵיפָה וּפְטוּרִין מִלַּעֲשׂוֹת פֶּסַח שֵׁינִי. סָבְרִין מֵימַר דְּרִבִּי נָתָן הִיא. תִּיפְתָּר דִּבְרֵי הַכֹּל בִּמְיטָמֵא בִּסְפֵק קֶבֶר הַתְּהוֹם. וּכְרִבִּי נָתָן זוֹרֵק אֶת הַדָּם.

3 במיטמא | K ועשו אותו כמיטמא

"If the skins of the *Pesaḥ* sacrifices of five groups were intermingled and a wart was found on one of them, all of them[109] have to be brought to the place of burning, but they[110] are not liable to bring a Second *Pesaḥ*.[111]" They wanted to say that this is Rebbi Nathan's. Explain it following everybody, {they made it}[87] like one which has become impure by a doubt of a grave of the abyss[112]. Following Rebbi Nathan would he have poured the blood[113]?

109 The sacrifices have to be brought to the spot where disqualified sacrifices were burned outside the sacred precinct.

110 The members of the groups. Since the animal with the wart never was a potential sacrifice, the group bringing this particular animal must be considered as not having offered a *Pesaḥ* at all, and obligated to bring a Second *Pesaḥ*. But since for each person there only is a 20% probability that his *Pesaḥ* was the invalid one, and a Second *Pesaḥ* may not be brought by a person not obligated, nobody is provably obligated and therefore nobody is entitled to bring a Second *Pesaḥ*.

111 Babli 88b.

112 Since if the blood was poured for the *Pesaḥ* of a person who assumes that he was pure and between this act and the consumption of the sacrifice he was informed that possibly he was made impure by stepping over a previously unknown grave, he cannot eat, so also here all members of the group whose *Pesaḥ* possibly was a non-sacrifice cannot eat from it.

113 Even following R. Nathan, the situation is possible only if the wart was discovered after the blood was poured; even R. Nathan does not allow pouring the blood of a non-sacrifice. Babli 88b, opinion of Abbai.

(34c line 6) רִבִּי יוֹחָנָן רִבִּי יִשְׁמָעֵאל בְּשֵׁם רִבִּי יְהוֹשֻׁעַ. כָּתוּב אֶחָד אוֹמֵר אַךְ בְּכוֹר־שׁוֹר אוֹ־בְכוֹר כֶּשֶׂב אוֹ־בְכוֹר עֵז וגו'. וְכָתוּב אֶחָד אוֹמֵר וְזָרַק הַכֹּהֵן אֶת־הַדָּם עַל־מִזְבַּח יְי פֶּתַח אֹהֶל מוֹעֵד וְהִקְטִיר הַחֵלֶב לְרֵיחַ נִיחֹחַ לַיי. עַד שֶׁיְּהֵא שָׁם אוֹ בָשָׂר לַאֲכִילָה אן אֵימוּרִין לְהַקְטָרָה. תַּמָּן תַּנִּינָן. נִטְמְאוּ שְׁיָרֶיהָ נִשְׂרְפוּ שְׁיָרֶיהָ אָבְדוּ שְׁיָרֶיהָ. כְּמִידַּת רִבִּי אֱלִיעֶזֶר כְּשֵׁירָה וּכְמִידַּת רִבִּי יְהוֹשֻׁעַ פְּסוּלָה. [שֶׁלֹּא בִּכְלִי שָׁרֵת פְּסוּלָה. רִבִּי יִשְׁמָעֵאל מַכְשִׁיר. הִקְטִיר קַמְצוֹ פַּעֲמַיִם. כְּשֵׁרָה:] עַל דַּעְתֵּיהּ דְּרִבִּי אֱלִיעֶזֶר. אִם אֵין דָּם אֵין בָּשָׂר. אַף עַל פִּי שֶׁאֵין בָּשָׂר יֵשׁ דָּם. אִם אֵין קוֹמֶץ אֵין שְׁיָרַיִם. אַף עַל פִּי שֶׁאֵין שְׁיָרַיִים יֵשׁ קוֹמֶץ. עַל דַּעְתֵּיהּ דְּרִבִּי יְהוֹשֻׁעַ. אִם אֵין דָּם אֵין בָּשָׂר. אִם אֵין בָּשָׂר אֵין דָּם. אִם אֵין קוֹמֶץ אֵין שְׁיָרַיִים. אִם אֵין שְׁיָרַיִים אֵין קוֹמֶץ. אָמַר רִבִּי מָנָא. תִּיפְתָּר כְּרִבִּי אֱלִיעֶזֶר. דְּרִבִּי אֱלִיעֶזֶר אָמַר. אַף עַל פִּי שֶׁאֵין שְׁיָרִים יֵשׁ קוֹמֶץ. אָמַר רִבִּי

יוֹסֵי בֵּירִבִּי בּוּן. רַב וְרִבִּי יוֹחָנָן תְּרֵיהוֹן אֲמָרִין. מוֹדֶה רִבִּי יְהוֹשֻׁעַ שֶׁאִם עָבַר וְזָרַק אֶת הַדָּם שֶׁהוּרְצָה.

2 וגו' | K לא תפדה קדש הם את דמם תז' על ימז' ואת חל' תק'   פתח אהל מועד | K -   4 אליעזר | K ליעזר   וכמידת | K כמידת   5 C שלא בכלי שרת פסולה. ר' ישמעאל מכשיר. הקטיר קמתו פעמים כשרה KS | -   6 אליעזר | K ליעזר בשר | K -   7 שיריים K שירים (2)   8 שיריים (2)   9 אליעזר | K ליעזר (2)   שיריים | K שירים   10 יוסי K | יוסה

[114]Rebbi Johanan, Rebbi Ismael in the name of Rebbi Joshua: One verse says, *but a firstling of cattle, or a firstling of sheep, or a firstling of goats*[115], etc. And another verse says[116] *the Cohen shall pour the blood on the Eternal's altar at the door of the Tent of Meeting, and burn the fat for a pleasant smell before the Eternal.* Only if there be there either meat be be eaten or parts to be burned[117]. There we have stated[118]: "If the remainders became impure, the remainders were burned, the remainders were lost. In the rules of Rebbi Eliezer it is qualified, in the rules of Rebbi Joshua it is disqualified. [Not in a vessel of service it is disqualified; Rebbi Ismael[119] qualifies. If he burned the fistful in two parts it is qualified."] In Rebbi Eliezer's opinion, if there is no blood there is no meat; even though if there is no meat there is blood[120]. If there is no fistful there are no remainders, even though if there are no remainders there is a fistful. In Rebbi Joshua's opinion, if there is no blood there is no meat; if there is no meat there is no blood[121]. If there is no fistful there are no remainders, if there are no remainders there is no fistful. Rebbi Mana said, explain it[114] following Rebbi Eliezer, since Rebbi Eliezer said, even though there are no remainders there is a fistful. Rebbi Yose ben Rebbi Abun said, Rav and Rebbi Johanan both are saying, Rebbi Joshua agrees that if he transgressed and poured the blood that it was made acceptable[122].

114 Discussion of the statement of the Mishnah that both the *Omer* and the Two Breads are brought in impurity even though they cannot be consumed by the priest and it is questionable whether a fistful of the *Omer* can be burned or the breads presented before the altar if that action seems purposeless since it does not serve to permit anything to be eaten.

115 *Num.* 18:17. The verse continues: *pour their blood on the altar, and burn their fat, . . ., and their meat shall be yours.*

116 *Lev.* 17:6.

117 Since *Num.* 18:17 mentions fat and meat but *Lev.* 17:6 only fat, it follows that the sacrifice is acceptable if the blood is poured either to permit the fat to be burned or the meat to be eaten.

118 Mishnah *Menahot* 3:4. For flour offerings, the fistful to be burned on the altar

permits the remainder to be eaten by the Cohanim; the relationship of the fistful taken by the priest for the altar to the remainder to be consumed in the sacred domain is parallel to that of blood to be poured and the parts to be burned or the meat to be eaten.

119 The second part of the Mishnah was added by the corrector; by the testimony of K this should be deleted. "R. Ismael" is a scribal error for "R. Simeon" in the Mishnah and in a quote of the Mishnah in *Yoma* 2:1, 39c line 32.

120 For him, pouring the blood is a sacral act independent of the fact that pouring the blood is needed to enable the parts to be burned and the meat to be eaten.

121 If nothing is to be enabled, the act of pouring becomes meaningless and therefore has to be avoided. But then R. Joshua cannot permit the *Omer* to be brought in impurity, since this also would be a meaningless act.

122 Since the diadem justifies the act retroactively, the same can be said for the *Omer* and the entire Mishnah may be R. Joshua's.

(34c line 18) **הלכה ו**׳: מָאן תַּנָּא רוֹב. רִבִּי מֵאִיר. דְּתַנֵּי. רִבִּי מֵאִיר אוֹמֵר. הִיא מַחֲצִית כָּל־הַשְּׁבָטִים הִיא מַחֲצִית כָּל־שֵׁבֶט וָשֵׁבֶט. וּבִלְבַד רוֹב. רִבִּי יוּדָה אוֹמֵר. חֲצִי כָל־שֵׁבֶט וָשֵׁבֶט. וּבִלְבַד רוֹב שְׁבָטִים שְׁלֵימִים. שֵׁבֶט אֶחָד גּוֹרֵר כָּל־הַשְּׁבָטִים. רִבִּי מֵאִיר אוֹמֵר. כָּל־הַשְּׁבָטִים קְרוּיִים קָהָל. רִבִּי יוּדָה אוֹמֵר. כָּל־שֵׁבֶט וָשֵׁבֶט קָרוּי קָהָל. מַה נָּפַק מִבֵּינֵיהוֹן. גְּרִירָה. רִבִּי מֵאִיר אוֹמֵר. אֵין שֵׁבֶט אֶחָד גּוֹרֵר כָּל־הַשְּׁבָטִים. רִבִּי יוּדָה אוֹמֵר. שֵׁבֶט אֶחָד גּוֹרֵר כָּל־הַשְּׁבָטִים. אָתְיָא דְרִבִּי יוּדָה כְּרִבִּי שִׁמְעוֹן. כְּמָה דְרִבִּי שִׁמְעוֹן אָמַר. שֵׁבֶט אֶחָד גּוֹרֵר כָּל־הַשְּׁבָטִים. כֵּן רִבִּי יוּדָה אוֹמֵר. שֵׁבֶט אֶחָד גּוֹרֵר כָּל־הַשְּׁבָטִים. אַף עַל גַּב דְּרִבִּי יוּדָה אָמַר. שֵׁבֶט אֶחָד גּוֹרֵר כָּל־הַשְּׁבָטִים. מוֹדֶה וְהוּא שֶׁתְּהֵא הוֹרָיָה מִלִּשְׁכַּת הַגָּזִית. אָמַר רִבִּי יוֹסֵה. טַעֲמֵיהּ דָּהֵין תַּנָּיָיה מִן־הַמָּקוֹם הַהוּא אֲשֶׁר יִבְחַר יי. מַה טַעֲמֵיהּ דְּרִבִּי יוּדָה. וְנִסְלַח לְכָל־עֲדַת בְּנֵי יִשְׂרָאֵל. מַה טַעֲמָא דְּרִבִּי שִׁמְעוֹן. כִּי לְכָל־הָעָם בִּשְׁגָגָה. מַה מְּקַיֵּים רִבִּי שִׁמְעוֹן טַעֲמֵיהּ דְּרִבִּי יוּדָה וְנִסְלַח לְכָל־עֲדַת בְּנֵי יִשְׂרָאֵל. פְּרָט לְנָשִׁים וְלִקְטַנִּים. מַה מְּקַיֵּים רִבִּי יוּדָה טַעֲמֵיהּ דְּרִבִּי שִׁמְעוֹן כִּי לְכָל־הָעָם בִּשְׁגָגָה. פְּרָט לְשֶׁתְּחִילָּתָהּ בְּזָדוֹן וְסוֹפָהּ בִּשְׁגָגָה. רִבִּי אָבוּן בְּשֵׁם רִבִּי בִּנְיָמִין בַּר לֵוִי. קִרְיָיא מְסַיֵּיעַ לְמָאן דְּאָמַר. כָּל־שֵׁבֶט וָשֵׁבֶט קָרוּי קָהָל. גּוֹי וּקְהַל גּוֹיִם יִהְיֶה מִמֶּךָּ. וַאֲדַיִין לֹא נוֹלַד בִּנְיָמִין. אָמַר רִבִּי חִיָּיא בַּר בָּא. כְּשֵׁם שֶׁהֵן חוֹלְקִין כָּאן כָּךְ הֵן חֲלוּקִין בְּטוּמְאָה. דְּתַנֵּי. הָיָה הַצִּבּוּר חֶצְיָם טְהוֹרִין וְחֶצְיָן טְמֵאִין. הַטְּהוֹרִין עוֹשִׂין אֶת הָרִאשׁוֹן וְהַטְּמֵאִים עוֹשִׂין אֶת הַשֵּׁנִי. דִּבְרֵי רִבִּי מֵאִיר. רִבִּי יְהוּדָה אוֹמֵר. הַטְּהוֹרִין עוֹשִׂין לְעַצְמָן וְהַטְּמֵאִין עוֹשִׂין לְעַצְמָן. אָמְרוּ לוֹ. אֵין הַפֶּסַח בָּא חֲצָיִין. אֶלָּא אוֹ כוּלָּם יַעֲשׂוּ בְטָהֳרָה אוֹ כוּלָּם יַעֲשׂוּ בְטוּמְאָה. מָנוּ אָמְרוּ לוֹ. רִבִּי מֵאִיר. מַחְלְפָה שִׁטָּתֵיהּ דְּרִבִּי יוּדָה. דְּתַנִּינָן תַּמָּן. נִיטְמֵאת אַחַת מִן הַחֲלוֹת אוֹ אֶחָד מִן הַסְּדָרִים רִבִּי יוּדָה אוֹמֵר. שְׁנֵיהֶם יֵצְאוּ לְבֵית הַשְּׂרֵיפָה. שֶׁאֵין קָרְבָּן צִבּוּר חָלוּק. וַחֲכָמִים אוֹמְרִים. הַטָּמֵא בְטוּמְאָתוֹ וְהַטָּהוֹר יֵאָכֵל. רִבִּי יוֹסֵה בֶּרְבִּי בּוּן בְּשֵׁם רִבִּי יוֹחָנָן. מָנִי אָמְרוּ לוֹ. חֲכָמִים שֶׁהֵן כְּשִׁיטַת רִבִּי מֵאִיר.

1 מאן תנא K | מן תמה ר' מאיר או' | K - 2 ושבט | K - 3 שלימים K שלמים 4 מביניהון | K מן

5 או' K | אמ' K 6 אתייא K | אתייה K 8 יוסה K | יונסה] ביר' בון 11 ולקטמים K | ולקטנין 12 ביניהון
לשתחילתן וסופה K | וסופן 13 למאן K | למן קריי K | קרויין דכת' 14 חייא K | חייה לשתחילתה K | לשתחילתן
חולקין K | חלוקין 15 חציים K | חציין והטמאים עושין K | והטמאין 16 יהודה K | יודה 17 אלא K | -
19 הסדרים K | הסדרין שניהם K | או שניין 21 חכמים K | חכמין

Halakhah 6: Who is the Tanna of "majority"[123]? Rebbi Meïr[124], as it was stated: Either half of the tribes or half of each tribe, if only it be a majority[125]. Rebbi Jehudah says, half of each tribe, but only a majority of entire tribes[126]. One tribe drags all tribes[127].

Rebbi Meïr says, all tribes are called "the public"[128]. Rebbi Jehudah says, each single tribe is called "public". What is between them? Dragging. Rebbi Meïr says, a single tribe does not drag all tribes[129], but Rebbi Jehudah says, one tribe drags all tribes. And Rebbi Jehudah follows Rebbi Simeon. Just as Rebbi Simeon said, one tribe drags all tribes[130], so Rebbi Jehudah says, one tribe drags all tribes. Even though Rebbi Jehudah says, one tribe drags all tribes, he agrees that only if the ruling came from the ashlar hall[131]. Rebbi Yose said, the reason of that Tanna: *From this place which the Eternal will choose*[132]. What is the reason of Rebbi Jehudah? *The entire community of the Children of Israel will be forgiven*[133]. What is the reason of Rebbi Simeon? *Since the entire people acted in error*[133]. How does Rebbi Simeon uphold Rebbi Jehudah's reason, *the entire community of the Children of Israel will be forgiven*? Except women and children[134]. How does Rebbi Jehudah uphold Rebbi Simeon's reason, *since the entire people acted in error*? Except if the beginning was criminal and the conclusion in error. Rebbi Abun in the name of Rebbi Benjamin bar Levi: The verse supports him who said that each tribe is called "public", as it is written[137]: *A people and a public of peoples will come from you,* and Benjamin was not yet born.

Rebbi Hiyya bar Abba said, just as they differ here, so they differ about impurity, as it was stated: If the public was half pure and half impure; pure [people] celebrate the first [*Pesaḥ*] and impure the second, the words of Rebbi Meïr. Rebbi Jehudah says, the pure ones celebrate for themselves, and the impure ones celebrate for themselves[138]. They told him, there is no split Passover; either all celebrate in purity or all celebrate in impurity. Who is "they told him"? Rebbi Meïr. The argument of Rebbi Jehudah seems inverted, as we have stated there[139]: "If one of the loaves or one of the orders became impure, Rebbi Jehudah said, both have to be brought to be burned[140] for a public offering cannot be split[141]. But the Sages say, the impure in its impurity, and the pure shall be eaten[142]." Rebbi Yose ben Rebbi Abun in the name of Rebbi Johanan: who is "they told him"? The Sages who argue like Rebbi Meïr[143].

123 Discussion of the statement in the Mishnah, that *Pesah* is celebrated in impurity if most (50%+1) of the people are impure. The following is an extended version of Halakhah 1:6 in *Horaiot*, where the problem is what is called "community".

124 He holds that everywhere 50%+1 represent "all"; Babli *Horaiot* 5b.

125 In order to trigger the ceremony required if *all the community acts in error* (*Lev.* 4:14), by following an erroneous ruling either of the High Court at the central sanctuary or of a majority of tribal High Courts.

126 The language is somewhat self-contradictory. He also requires that a majority of Israel follow the erroneous ruling but in addition he demands that in a majority of tribes a majority follow the ruling. Babli *Horaiot* 5b.

127 If one tribe has more members than all the others together, the action of one tribe triggers the obligation of all of them. He does not hold that the law about erroneous rulings of the High Court became moot with the exile of the Ten Tribes. Even later, when the tribe of Jehudah represented the overwhelming majority of Israel, a majority of the people can be considered a majority of all twelve tribes and the majority of Judeans triggers the obligation for all tribes.

128 The purification sacrifice for an erroneous ruling by the Court has to be brought by "the public" (*Lev.* 4:14). The difference of opinions in the Mishnah is traced to different interpretations of this notion. R. Meïr holds that only the entire people of Israel qualify as "public"; RR. Jehudah and Simeon consider each tribe as a separate public. (Babli *Horaiot* 5b, *Pesahim* 80a, *Menahot* 15a).

129 Therefore he requires a separate sacrifice for the people of Israel in their entirety.

130 In *Horaiot*, the opposite is asserted, that in this particular R. Simeon sides with R. Meïr; this also is required by the later statements in this Halakhah. R. Simeon agrees that each single tribe is called "public".

131 Even though each tribe has to bring its own sacrifice, the ruling of a tribal High Court cannot trigger an obligation of any other tribe; only the Court sitting at the central sanctuary has this power.

132 *Deut.* 17:10.

133 *Num.* 15:26. R. Jehudah argues that the verse promises forgiveness for all of Israel even if only one tribe followed an erroneous ruling; this proves that "one tribe drags all the other tribes." R. Simeon disagrees since the last clause in the verse states that the *entire* people have to be in error; only a majority of the tribes

triggers the obligation.

134 Not that they will not be forgiven but they are not counted in determining what is a majority.

137 *Gen.* 35:11, said to Jacob after the birth of 11 sons. Babli *Horaiot* 5b.

138 Both offer their sacrifices in the Temple, in separate groups. For this to happen, the number of pure people in Jerusalem on the 14th of Nisan must be *exactly* equal to the number of impure ones. Tosephta 6:2 in the name of R. Simeon. This latter attribution seems to be correct since in the paragraph after the next the Amoraim explain that R. Jehudah never considers this case but requires that the number of pure people present be diminished.

139 Mishnah *Menahot* 2:2.

The Mishnah refers to the two public cereal offerings which have to be baked, *viz.*, the weekly show-bread and the two leavened loaves presented at Pentecost. The 12 show-breads were presented in two rows, here called "orders" (*Lev.* 24:6).

140 Outside the Temple precinct.

141 Cf. Babli 79a.

142 By the officiating priests.

143 In *Horaiot*: R. Jehudah. In any case, the question should not arise since the objecting Sages, while adopting the point of view of one of the protagonists, are not bound to follow him in all details.

(34c line 44) עַל דַּעְתֵּיהּ דְּרִבִּי מֵאִיר. הָהֵן מֶחֱצָה עַל מֶחֱצָה מָה אַתְּ עֲבַד לֵיהּ. כְּרוֹב כְּמִיעוּט. אֵין תֵּימַר כְּרוֹב. הַטְּהוֹרִין אֵינָן עוֹשִׂין אֶת הָרִאשׁוֹן. הַטְּמֵאִין אֵין עוֹשִׂין אֶת הַשֵּׁנִי. אָמַר רִבִּי יוֹסֵה. לֹא אָמַר. רוֹב טְהוֹרִים אֵינָן עוֹשִׂין אֶת הָרִאשׁוֹן. רוֹב טְמֵאִין אֵינָן עוֹשִׂין אֶת הַשֵּׁנִי. לֹא אָמַר אֶלָּא. רוֹב טְמֵאִין לֹא יִדָּחוּ לְפֶסַח שֵׁנִי.

1 כמיעוט K | כמעוט 2 אין K | אינן 3 טהורים K | הטהורין רוב K | ורוב 4 לא K | אמ' ר' יוסה לא אלא K | - ייֹדחו K | ידחו

עַל דַּעְתֵּיהּ דְּרִבִּי יוּדָה. הָהֵן מֶחֱצָה עַל מֶחֱצָה מָה אַתְּ עֲבַד לֵיהּ. רִבִּי בָּא מִשֵּׁם רַב. מְטַמְּאִין אֶחָד בְּשָׂרָץ. שְׁמוּאֵל אָמַר. מְשַׁלְּחִין אוֹתוֹ לְדֶרֶךְ רְחוֹקָה. אַתְיָא כְּמַאן דְּאָמַר. הַיָּחִיד מַכְרִיעַ עַל הַטּוּמְאָה. בְּרַם כְּמַאן דְּאָמַר. אֵין הַיָּחִיד מַכְרִיעַ עַל הַטּוּמָאה. מְשַׁלְּחִין שְׁנַיִם. דְּרַב כְּרִבִּי אֶלְעָזָר. כְּמָה דְּאָמַר רִבִּי לְעָזָר. הָיָה הַצִּיבּוּר מַגָּעֵי נְבֵילוֹת מַגָּעֵי שְׁרָצִים. עוֹשִׂין בְּטוּמְאָה. שֶׁאֵין שָׁם מַיִם לִטְבוֹל. [אֲבָל] אִם יֵשׁ שָׁם מַיִם לִטְבוֹל. אֵינָן עוֹשִׂין בְּטוּמְאָה. אָמַר רִבִּי לְעָזָר. הַבָּא בְּטוּמְאַת כְּלִי שֶׁרֶת הַבָּא בְּטוּמְאָה. הוּא בָא בְּטוּמְאַת כְּלִי שֶׁרֶת הַבָּא בְּטוּמְאַת יָדַיִם הַבָּא בְּטוּמְאַת סַכִּינִין.

1 ההן K | ההין ליה K | לה משם K | בש' 3 על הטומאה K | לטומאה (2) שנים K | שניים אתייה 5 שאין K | בשאין 6 בטומאה K | בטומאת הבא K | כבא בא K | הבא כלי K | הבא כלי ידים K | ידיין

הָיָה צִיבּוּר שְׁלִישׁ זָבִין שְׁלִישׁ טְמֵאִין שְׁלִישׁ טְהוֹרִין. רִבִּי מָנָא בְּשֵׁם חִזְקִיָּה. זָבִין וּטְמֵאִין רַבִּין עַל הַטְּהוֹרִין וְעוֹשִׂין בְּטוּמְאָה. זָבִין אֵינָן עוֹשִׂין לֹא אֶת הָרִאשׁוֹן וְלֹא אֶת הַשֵּׁנִי. אָמַר רִבִּי זְעוּרָה. הַזָּב עָשׂוּ אוֹתוֹ כִּמְשׁוּפָּד בְּהוֹרָיָיה. כְּמָה דְּתֵימַר תַּמָּן. הַמְשׁוּפָּד בְּהוֹרָיָיה אֵינוֹ לֹא מַעֲלֶה וְלֹא מוֹרִיד. אוֹף הָכָא אֵינוֹ לֹא מַעֲלֶה וְלֹא מוֹרִיד.

1 ציבור K | הציבור שליש K | ושליש (2) 3 דתימ' תמן K | דתמר המשומד K | משומד 4 אוף הכא K

וְהָכָא בְּנֵי חֲבוּרָה שֶׁנִּיטְמָא אֶחָד מֵהֶן. וְאֵין יָדוּעַ אֵי זֶהוּ. [צְרִיכִין לַעֲשׂוֹת פֶּסַח שֵׁנִי. צִבּוּר שֶׁנִּטְמָא אֶחָד מֵהֶן. וְאֵין יָדוּעַ אֵי זֶהוּ.] רִבִּי זְעוּרָא אָמַר. יַעֲשׂוּ בְטוּמְאָה. תַּנֵּי רִבִּי הוֹשַׁעְיָה. יַעֲשׂוּ כִסְפֵיקָן. לֹא מִסְתַּבְּרָא דְלֹא כְהָדָא דְתַנֵּי רִבִּי הוֹשַׁעְיָה. שֶׁלֹּא לַעֲנוֹשׁ לְיָחִיד כָּרֵת.

1 שניטמא K שנטמא זהו K זה היא 2 זהו K זה היא זעורא K זעורה 2-3 יעשו כספיקן. לש מסתברא דלא כהדא דתני ר' הושעיה K -

רִבִּי אִימִּי בְשֵׁם רִבִּי שִׁמְעוֹן בֶּן לָקִישׁ. לְהוֹרָיָיה הִילְכוּ אַחַר יְשִׁיבַת אֶרֶץ יִשְׂרָאֵל. לְטוּמְאָה הִילְכוּ אַחַר רוֹב נִכְנָסִין לָעֲזָרָה. מָה. בְּכָל־כַּת וָכַת מְשַׁעֲרִין. אוֹ אֵין מְשַׁעֲרִין אֶלָּא כַת הָרִאשׁוֹנָה בִלְבָד. אָמַר רִבִּי יוֹסֵה בֵּרִבִּי בּוּן. עַד שֶׁהֵן מִבַּחוּץ הֵן מְשַׁעֲרִין עַצְמָן. אָמַר רִבִּי יְהוֹשֻׁעַ בֶּן לֵוִי. לַרְאִייָה הִילְכוּ מִלְּבוֹא חֲמָת עַד נַחַל מִצְרָיִם. רִבִּי תַנְחוּמָא בְשֵׁם רִבִּי חוּנָה. טַעֲמֵיהּ דְּרִבִּי יְהוֹשֻׁעַ בֶּן לֵוִי וַיַּעַשׂ שְׁלֹמֹה בָעֵת־הַהִיא ׀ אֶת־הֶחָג וְכָל־יִשְׂרָאֵל עִמּוֹ וגו'.

1 אימי K אמי 2 נכנסין K הנכנסין 3 בר' K ביר' אמ' ר' יהושע בן לוי K ר' יהושע בן לוי אמ' 4 עד K ועד יהושע K ישוע 5 וגו' K ק' ג' מל' חמ' ר' נ' מצ'

In Rebbi Meïr's opinion[144], how does one act if they are half and half? As majority or as minority? If you are saying as a majority, the pure persons cannot make the First. If you are saying as a minority, the impure persons cannot make the Second[145]. Rebbi Yose said, he did not say that a majority of pure persons cannot make the First, a majority of impure persons cannot make the Second. He only said, a majority of impure persons is not pushed to the Second *Pesaḥ*[146].

In Rebbi Jehudah's opinion, how does one act if they are half and half? Rebbi Abba in the name of Rav: One defiles one person with a crawling animal[147]. Samuel said, one sends one person on a far-away trip[148]. This follows him who said, a single person clinches for impurity[149]. But for him who said, a single person does not clinch for impurity, one has to send two persons away. Rav's opinion parallels Rebbi Eleazar, as Rebbi Eleazar said, if the public was touching carcasses, touching crawling animals, one makes it in impurity if there is not water there to immerse in; but if there is water to immerse in, one does not make it in impurity[150]. Rebbi Eleazar said, if it comes while the Temple vessels are impure, comes in impurity; if it comes in impurity of Temple vessels, comes in impurity of hands, comes in impurity of knives[151].

If the public were one third sufferers from gonorrhea[152], one third impure[153], and one third pure. Rebbi Mana in the name of Ḥizqiah: The sufferers from gonorrhea and the impure form a majority against the pure and one brings in impurity. The sufferers from gonorrhea bring neither the First nor the Second[154]. Rebbi Ze'ira said, they made the sufferer from gonorrhea like the apostate for ruling[155]. As one says there, the apostate in matters of ruling neither adds nor subtracts, also here he neither adds nor subtracts.

If one of the members of a group became impure[153] but it is not known who it is, they must make the Second. If one of the public became impure but it is not known who it is, Rebbi Ze'ira said, they shall make the Second. Rebbi Hoshaia stated, they shall be treated as a case of doubt[156]. It is reasonable following Rebbi Hoshaia, not to subject the individual to punishment of extirpation.

[157]Rebbi Immi in the name of Rebbi Simeon ben Laqish: For ruling[158] they went after the population of the Land of Israel; for impurity they went after a majority of those entering the Temple courtyard. Does one estimate according to all groups or does one estimate only for the first group? Rebbi Yose ben Rebbi Abun said, they have to estimate by themselves as long as they are outside[159]. Rebbi Joshua ben Levi said, for appearance[160] they went from Lavo-Ḥamat to the Brook of Egypt. Rebbi Tanḥuma in the name of Rebbi Huna: The reason of Rebbi Joshua ben Levi, *At that time Solomon made the pilgrimage holiday, and all of Israel with him*[161], etc.

144 This name attribution seems to be in error since R. Meïr is quoted in the preceding paragraph that in this case the pure persons celebrate the First *Pesaḥ* and the impure the Second. One has to read "R. Simeon".

145 The formulation is not very clear. If one considers the impure (by the impurity of the dead) as a majority, then the service in the Temple is conducted in impurity, and the pure persons cannot make their sacrifice in purity. If the pure are considered a minority, there is no Second *Pesaḥ* for the impure.

146 The problem only is apparent, not real. For the *Pesaḥ* to be offered in impurity one needs a real majority; a 50-50 split in practice is equal to a majority of the pure.

147 He is impure, but can become free of impurity by immersion in a *miqweh*, which will make him pure for *sancta* at sundown. This kind of impurity does not prevent a person to be counted in a group eating the *Pesaḥ* in purity; accepting the person in the count of the impure is questionable; Babli 80a, 80b.

148 Babli 80a. He automatically must bring the Second *Pesaḥ*.

149 Babli 80a, Tosephta 6:2.

150 Since these are impurities which are eliminated by immersion in water.

151 This means that *Pesaḥ* is brought in

impurity if the necessary Temple implements are impure and cannot be purified in time; this could happen only in times of a siege of Jerusalem.

152 A person who suffers a single episode of gonorrhea is impure for the day and can be purified by immersion in a *miqweh*. If he has two episodes in at most two consecutive days, he is impure for seven days; after seven days in remission he can be purified by immersion in a *miqweh*. After three episodes he still needs seven days in remission but then is still prohibited *sancta* unless on the eighth day he brings a couple of birds as sacrifice to the Temple. A sufferer from gonorrhea who is impure for seven days, on the seventh day is a questionable candidate for *Pesaḥ* since if he suffers another episode he has to start all over again.

153 Impure in impurity of the dead.

154 The First he cannot bring being impure. If he should be healed between the 14th of Nisan and the 14th of Iyar, in this case he cannot bring the Second *Pesah* since the latter is instituted for people impure in the impurity of the dead or away on a trip (*Num.* 9:9). While healed sufferers from gonorrhea can bring the Second *Pesah* (Halakhah 9:1), there can be no Second *Pesah* if the First was celebrated in impurity.

155 If it is a question whether most of the people followed an erroneous ruling of the Supreme Court, apostates are not counted as part of the people. Applied to the case here, sufferers from gonorrhea are counted neither with the impure nor with the pure, in opposition to the rule stated earlier.

156 They cannot bring a *Pesah* since they cannot risk that one of the group eat *sanctum* while impure, a deadly sin punishable by extirpation.

157 This paragraph also is in *Horaiot* 1:2, Notes 92-97.

158 To determine whether a majority of the people followed an erroneous ruling of the Supreme Court, the entire adult male population of the Land is counted.

159 Since the impure are not permitted on the Temple Mount unless a majority of the people are impure, it is obvious that the count of a majority cannot be determined by the people entering the Temple precinct but must be made before people enter the Temple Mount. The Babli 94b has only the statement which is rejected here.

160 The duty for *all your men to be seen before the Eternal three times a year* (*Deut.* 15:16).

161 *IK.* 8:65. The verse continues: *a big crowd, from Levo-Hamat to the Brook of Egypt* (Central Syria to Wadi El-Arish).

(34c line 71) **הלכה ז:** מַתְנִיתָה בְּשֶׁנִּיטְמָא מִשֶּׁיָּרַד לַאֲוִירוֹ שֶׁלְּכֵלִי. אֲבָל אִם נִטְמָא עַד שֶׁהוּא מִלְמַעְלָן נַעֲשָׂה כִּמְקַבֵּל מַיִם.

1 בשניטמא K | בשנטמא לאוירו K לאבירו

Halakhah 7: [162]The Mishnah if it became impure after it fell into the vessel. But if it became impure when still higher it is as if he received water[163].

162 Discussion of the last part of Mishnah 5 (in the independent Mishnah mss. Mishnah 7), that the diadem covers up impurity of the blood for *Pesah* and the *nazir*.

163 If the Cohen received pure blood in a sacred vessel, the owner's act in the sacrifice is completed. If then something happens in the custody of the Cohen, the High Priest's diadem covers the fault; the blood may be poured on the walls of the altar and the meat consumed. But if the blood becomes impure before being received in the vessel, there is no qualified sacrifice; the carcass has to be burned outside the Temple district.

(34c line 72) מְנַיִין לִסְפֵק קֶבֶר הַתְּהוֹם. רִבִּי יַעֲקֹב בַּר אָחָא בְשֵׁם רַבָּנָן. אוֹ בְדֶרֶךְ רְחֹקָה לָכֶם. מַה לָכֶם בְּגָלוּי אַף כָּל־דָּבָר שֶׁהוּא בְגָלוּי. יָצָא קֶבֶר הַתְּהוֹם שֶׁאֵינוּ בְגָלוּי. עַד כְּדוֹן עוֹשֵׂי פֶסַח. נָזִיר מְנַיִין. רִבִּי יוֹחָנָן בְשֵׁם רִבִּי וְכִי־יָמוּת מֵת עָלָיו. מַה עָלָיו שֶׁהוּא בְגָלוּי אַף כָּל־דָּבָר שֶׁהוּא בְגָלוּי. יָצָא קֶבֶר הַתְּהוֹם שֶׁאֵינוּ בְגָלוּי.

1 אחא K | אחה רבנן K | רבנין 2 עושי K | עושה 3 ר' יוחנן בשם ר' | אמ' ר' יוחנן בשם ר' ינייֵ שהוא K | - K

[164]From where about a doubtful case of a grave in the abyss[165]? Rebbi Jacob bar Aḥa in the name of the rabbis: *Or on a far trip for you*. What is in the open for you, including everything in the open. This excludes the case of a grave in the abyss which is not open. So far for the people celebrating Passover. From where the *nazir*? Rebbi Joḥanan in the name of Rebbi [Yannai][87]: *If a person dies suddenly on him*[166]. Since on him it is in the open, so everything in the open. This eliminates the grave in the abyss which is not in the open[167].

164 From here on, the text is also found in *Nazir* 9:2, Notes 58-94.

165 Both for the person going to celebrate the *Pesah* and the *nazir* who finished his term, the impurity caused by a doubtful case of a grave in the abyss is disregarded. In view of the central role of purity in everything connected with the Sanctuary, it is obvious that some biblical justification has to be found for the rule. In the case of Passover, the argument notes that *Num.* 9:9 could have stated that a person *on a far trip* was required to celebrate the Second *Pesah*. The addition *for you* seems to be superfluous. It is interpreted to mean just as the road is open to the wanderer, so the impurity has to be in the open for the impure person. The same argument is in the Babli 81b.

166 *Num.* 6:9.

167 The same argument as before; Babli 81b, *Sifry Num.* 28.

1) (34d line 1) צִיבּוּר שֶׁנִּיטְמָא בִּסְפֵק הַתְּהוֹם מַהוּ שֶׁיְּרַצֶּה עָלָיו הַצִּיץ. קַל וָחוֹמֶר. מָה אִם הַיָּחִיד שֶׁהוֹרְעַתְּ כּוֹחוֹ בְטוּמְאָה יְדוּעָה יִפִּיתָה כּוֹחוֹ בִּסְפֵק קֶבֶר הַתְּהוֹם. צִיבּוּר שֶׁיִּפִּיתָה כּוֹחוֹ בְטוּמְאָה יְדוּעָה אֵינוֹ דִין שֶׁיִּפִּיתָה כּוֹחוֹ בִּסְפֵק קֶבֶר הַתְּהוֹם. קַל שֶׁאַתְּ מֵקִיל בְּיָחִיד אַתְּ מַחְמִיר בְּצִיבּוּר. קַל שֶׁאַתְּ מֵקִיל בְּיָחִיד. שֶׁאִם נִתְוַודַּע לוֹ לִפְנֵי זְרִיקָה יֵעָשָׂה כְּמִי שֶׁנִּיטְמָא לְאַחַר זְרִיקָה בִּשְׁבִיל שֶׁלֹּא יָדְחֶה לַפֶּסַח שֵׁינִי. אַתְּ מַחְמִיר עָלָיו בַּצִּיבּוּר. שֶׁאִם נִתְוַודַּע לוֹ לְאַחַר זְרִיקָה יֵעָשָׂה כְּמִי שֶׁנִּיטְמָא לִפְנֵי זְרִיקָה בִּשְׁבִיל שֶׁלֹּא יֹאכַל הַבָּשָׂר. קַל שֶׁאַתְּ מֵיקִיל בְּנָזִיר טָהוֹר. שֶׁאִם נִתְוַודַּע לוֹ לִפְנֵי זְרִיקָה יֵעָשָׂה כְּמִי שֶׁנִּיטְמָא לְאַחַר זְרִיקָה שֶׁלֹּא יָבִיא קׇרְבָּן טוּמְאָה. אַתְּ מַחְמִיר בְּנָזִיר טָמֵא. שֶׁאִם נִתְוַודַּע לוֹ לְאַחַר זְרִיקָה יֵעָשָׂה כְּמִי שֶׁנִּיטְמָא וְנִיטְמָא. מֵבִיא קׇרְבָּן טוּמְאָה לְכָל־אֶחָד וְאֶחָד. [כַּהֲדָא דְּתַנָּא. נִטְמָא וְחָזַר וְנִטְמָא. מֵבִיא קׇרְבָּן טוּמְאָה עַל כָּל־אֶחָד וְאֶחָד.] עוֹבֵד שֶׁלַּפֶּסַח מַהוּ שֶׁיְּרַצֶּה עָלָיו אֶת הַצִּיץ. קַל וָחוֹמֶר. וּמָה אִם הַבְּעָלִים. שֶׁהוֹרְעָתָה כּוֹחָן בְּזָקֵן וּבְחוֹלֶה. יִפִּיתָה כּוֹחָן בִּסְפֵק קֶבֶר הַתְּהוֹם. עוֹבֵד שֶׁיִּפִּיתָה כּוֹחוֹ בְּזָקֵן וּבְחוֹלֶה. אֵינוֹ דִין שֶׁתִּיַּיפֶּה כּוֹחוֹ בִּסְפֵק קֶבֶר הַתְּהוֹם. לֹא. אִם אָמַרְתְּ בַּבְּעָלִים. שֶׁיִּפִּיתָה כּוֹחָן בִּשְׁאָר כָּל־הַטּוּמְאוֹת שֶׁבַּשָּׁנָה. תֹּאמַר בָּעוֹבֵד. שֶׁהוֹרְעָתָה כּוֹחוֹ בִּשְׁאָר כָּל־הַטּוּמְאוֹת שֶׁבַּשָּׁנָה. הוֹאִיל וְהוֹרְעָתָה כּוֹחוֹ בִּשְׁאָר כָּל־הַטּוּמְאוֹת שֶׁלְּכָל־הַשָּׁנָה תּוֹרַע כּוֹחוֹ בְטָמֵא מֵת בַּפֶּסַח. מַאי כְּדוֹן. רִבִּי נַחְמָן בְּשֵׁם רִבִּי מָנָא. לָכֶם. בֵּין לוֹ בֵּין לְעוֹבֵד שֶׁלּוֹ. עַד כְּדוֹן עוֹשֵׂי פֶסַח. נָזִיר מְנַיִין. רִבִּי יוֹסֵף בְּשֵׁם רַב חִסְדָּא. הֲוֵינָן סָבְרִין מֵימַר. עָלָיו. לֹא עַל הָעוֹבֵד שֶׁלּוֹ. מִן מַה דְּתַנֵּי. הִיא נָזִיר הִיא עוֹשֶׂה פֶסַח. הָדָא אֲמָרָה. מַה דְּנָפַל לְדֵין נָפַל לְדֵין.

1 ציבור K | צבור קל K | קול 2 ייפיתה K | יפיתה שייפיתה K | שיפיתה 4 שניטמא K | שנטמא שיני K | שני 6 לאחר K | לפני ייעשה K | יעשה שניטמא שנטמא לפני K | לאחר 7 טהור K | טהור את מחמיר בנזיר טמא קל את מיקל בנזיר טהור ייעשה K | יעשה 8 טומאה K | טמאה לאחר K | לפני 9 מביא K | בשביל שיביא טומאה K | טמאה לכל K | על כל C כהדא דתנא K | כהדה דתני C שניטמא | K ניטמא ונטמא K | וניטמא 10 טומאה K | טמאה מהו K | מהיא את K | - ומה K | מה 11 הבעלים K | הבעלין ייפיתה K | יפיתה 12 שתייפה K | שתיפה בספק קבר K | בקבר בבעלים K | בבעלין 13 שייפיתה K | שיפיתה הטומאות K | טמאות שבשנה K | שבשנא שבכל שנה K | שבכל שנא תאמר K | תומר 14 הטומאות K | טמאות שבשנה K | שבכל שנה הטומאות K | טמאות שבכל השנה K | שבשנא 15 מהו K | מהיא ר' נחמן K | רב נחמן לעובד K | העובד 16 עושי K | עושה יוסי K | יוסה ביר' בון חסדא K | חיסדא 17 הדא K | הדה לדין K | להן (2)

If the public became impure in a doubtful case of a grave in the abyss, does the diadem make it acceptable? It is a conclusion *de minore ad maius*. Since in the case of a single person, whose position you clarified to his disadvantage in the case of known impurity[168], you clarified to his advantage in the case of a grave in the abyss[169], for the public, whose position you clarified to its advantage in the case of known impurity[170], it only is logical that you should clarify it to its advantage in a doubtful case of a grave in the abyss. A leniency which you apply to a single person you treat as a restriction for the public[171]. A leniency which you apply to a single person, so that if it became known to him[172] before pouring he should be treated as if he became impure after pouring, that he should not be pushed to the Second *Pesaḥ*, you restrict him in public, so that if it became known to him after pouring he should be treated as if he became impure before pouring, that he should not be able to eat the meat[173]. The leniency which you apply to the pure *nazir*, so that if it became known to him before pouring he is treated as impure after pouring, that he should not have to bring a sacrifice of impurity[174], you treat as a restriction for the impure *nazir*, that if it became known to him after pouring he is treated as somebody repeatedly becoming impure; he has to bring a sacrifice of impurity for each single case[175]. [As it was stated: If he repeatedly became impure, he has to bring a sacrifice for each single case[176].] If somebody is officiating for the *Pesaḥ*, does the diadem make it acceptable? It is a conclusion *de minore ad majus*. Since for the owner [of the *Pesaḥ*] whose position you clarified to his disadvantage in the case of the infirm and the aged[177], you clarified to their advantage in the case of a grave in the abyss, it should be only logical that for the officiating, whose position you clarified to his advantage in the case of the infirm and the aged, you should clarify it to his advantage in the case of a grave in the abyss. No. Since for the owner you clarify to his disadvantage in the case of impurity during the rest of the year; what can you say for the officiating where you clarify his position to his disadvantage in the case of impurity during the rest of the year[178]. Since you clarify his position to his disadvantage in the case of impurity during the rest of the year, you also clarify his position to his disadvantage in the case of the impurity of the dead on Passover. How is it really? *For you*[165], whether for him or for the one officiating for him. So far for the people celebrating Passover. From where the *nazir*? Rebbi Yose in the name of Rav Ḥisda: We thought to say, *on him*[166], not on the one officiating for him. Since we stated that the same rules apply to the *nazir* and to those celebrating Passover, it means that what holds for the one holds for the other[179].

168 Since a single person impure on the 14th of Nisan is required to celebrate the Second *Pesaḥ*, his standing is inferior to that of the public who celebrate the First *Pesaḥ* in impurity.

169 The case of a grave in the abyss can arise only in a private domain since in a public domain all doubts are automatically

resolved in favor of purity (*Sotah* 1:2, Note 88). For a private person, a case of doubt in matters of a grave in the abyss in a private domain is treated as if it were occurring in the public domain.

170 In that they may bring the *Pesaḥ* in impurity.

171 This is how one intends to disprove the argument *de minore ad majus*.

172 The impurity of a grave in the abyss never forces a person to the Second *Pesaḥ*; so if he was told before pouring it is as if he became otherwise impure after pouring, where the sacrificial act was completed and while he cannot eat his part of the *Pesaḥ* he has discharged all his obligations.

173 If the public are impure, the *Pesaḥ* is slaughtered and eaten in impurity. But if it was slaughtered as pure and then it became impure or became known to be impure, it cannot be eaten.

174 Mishnah *Nazir* 9:2. Corrector's addition supported by K.

175 But if the *nazir* became aware of the second impurity before he offered his sacrifice of impurity, he has to bring only one sacrifice.

176 *Nazir* Halakhah 6:8, Note 198.

177 While a person unable to eat the volume of an olive of the *Pesaḥ* may not subscribe to it, an old or sick priest is able to serve in the Temple as long as his infirmity is not of the kind listed in *Lev*, 21:18-20.

178 An impure person, including a *nazir* not impure by the impurity of the dead, can send his sacrifice other than the *Pesaḥ* to the Temple by a pure agent, but an impure priest cannot officiate, irrespective of the nature of his impurity.

179 Babli 80b.

(34d line 23) אֵי זֶהוּ קֶבֶר תְּהוֹם. הַמֵּת שֶׁנִּקְבַּר בְּקַשׁ וּבְתֶבֶן וּבְעָפָר וּבִצְרוֹרוֹת. אֲבָל אִם נִקְבַּר בַּמַּיִם וּבַאֲפֵילָה וּבְנִקְקִיקֵי סְלָעִים אֵינוֹ עוֹשֶׂה קֶבֶר תְּהוֹם. כְּלָלוֹ שֶׁל דָּבָר. כָּל־שֶׁאַתְּ יָכוֹל לְפַנּוֹתוֹ עוֹשֶׂה קֶבֶר תְּהוֹם. וְכָל־שֶׁאֵין אַתְּ יָכוֹל לְפַנּוֹתוֹ אֵינוֹ עוֹשֶׂה קֶבֶר תְּהוֹם. וְקַשׁ וְתֶבֶן אֵין אַתְּ יָכוֹל לְפַנּוֹתוֹ. מַתְנִיתָהּ דְּלָא כְרִבִּי יוֹסֵי. דְּרִבִּי יוֹסֵי אָמַר. תֶּבֶן וּבִיטְלוֹ. בָּטֵל. רִבִּי יוֹסֵי בֵּרִבִּי בּוּן בְּשֵׁם רַב חִסְדָּא. דִּבְרֵי הַכֹּל הִיא. מָה דְאָמַר רִבִּי יוֹסֵי. בְּשֶׁבִּלֵּל בֶּעָפָר. יֵשׁ תֶּבֶן שֶׁהוּא כְעָפָר. וְיֵשׁ עָפָר שֶׁהוּא כְתֶבֶן. תֶּבֶן שֶׁאֵין אַתְּ עָתִיד לְפַנּוֹתוֹ הֲרֵי הוּא כְעָפָר. וְעָפָר שֶׁאַתְּ עָתִיד לְפַנּוֹתוֹ הֲרֵי הוּא כְתֶבֶן. דְּבֵית רִבִּי יַנַּאי אָמְרִי. חִיפָּהוּ מַחֲצָלִיּוֹת בָּטֵל. אִיתָא חֲמֵי. מִילֵּהוּ מַחֲצָלוֹת לֹא בָטֵל. חִיפָּהוּ מַחֲצָלִיּוֹת בָּטֵל. מִילֵּהוּ חָרִיוֹת צְרִיכָה. רִבִּי זְרִיקָן רִבִּי אָמִי בְּשֵׁם רִבִּי שִׁמְעוֹן בֶּן לָקִישׁ. וַאֲפִילוּ רָק.

1 זהו K | זה היא אם נקבר K | הניקבר K | סלעים 2 | הסלעים K | יוסי 4 | יוסי K | יוסה וביטלו K | ביטלו יוסי |
K | יוסה 5 | חסדא K | חיסדה יוסי K | יוסה בשבלל K | בשבללו ויש עפר K | ועפר 7 | ינאי K | ינײ
K | אמרי | אמרין K | איתא K | אתא K | לט בטל K | - | 8 | חריות K | חיות אמי K | אימי 9 | רק K | ריק

"What is a grave of the abyss? A corpse buried in stubble, straw, dust, or pebbles[180]. But if it was buried in water, a dark spot, or rock crevices, it does not create a grave of the abyss[181]." The principle: Any place from where it can be removed creates a grave of the abyss; any place from where it cannot be removed does not create a grave of the abyss[182]. Can stubbles and straw not be removed? Does the Mishnah not follow Rebbi Yose, since Rebbi Yose said, straw said to be disregarded is disregarded[183]? Rebbi Yose ben Rebbi Abun in the name of Rav Hisda: It is everybody's opinion. What Rebbi Yose said, if he mixed it with dust[184]. "There is straw which is treated like dust and dust which is treated like straw. Straw not to be removed is like dust; dust to be removed is like straw.[185]" In the House of Rebbi Yannai they said: If he covered it with mats it is disregarded. Come and see: If he filled it with mats it is not disregarded[186], if he covered it with mats it is disregarded[187]. If he filled it with branches of date palms it is problematic[188]. Rebbi Zeriqan, Rebbi Immi, in the name of Rebbi Simeon ben Laqish: Even thin sheets[189].

180 Tosephta *Zavim* 2:9; quoted in the Babli, 81b, and *Nazir* 63b, without further discussion. As explained in the next paragraph, "grave of the abyss" is that of a person killed by an accident not witnessed by anybody. If one finds a corpse buried under a heap of straw, one has to assume that he suffocated when the straw fell on him. A corpse buried in dust or pebbles probably was the victim of an accident.

181 In this case, the person also probably was the victim of an accident. But since it could have been seen by a passer-by, the competent authorities should have been alerted; this is not an unknown body.

182 Obviously, the clauses in this sentence are switched (here and in *Nazir*). As explained in the preceding notes, one must read: "Any place from where it cannot be removed creates a grave of the abyss; any place from where it can be removed does not create a grave of the abyss." A corpse whose existence is unknown cannot be removed.

183 The remainder of this paragraph also is in *Eruvin* 7, Notes 58-62.

This refers to the rules of the tent-impurity caused by a corpse. A "tent" is any covered space in which there is at least one hand-breadth of space between the corpse and the roof. If the space is enclosed, the impurity is restricted to the "tent"; anything above the ceiling and below the floor of the "tent" is pure. But if the entire space between floor and ceiling is filled with matter, there is no tent and the impurity extends indefinitely above and below the tent space. This is known as "squeezed impurity" (Mishnah *Ahilut* 15:1,5,6). It is implied in Tosephta *Ahilut* 15:5 that R. Yose restricts "squeezed impurity" to material permanently deposited; but a storage of straw which is to be removed in the future is not counted as filler.

184 Not really "mixed with", but "treated like," as formulated in the Tosephta.

185 Statement of R. Yose in Tosephta *Ahilut* 15:5; quoted in *Eruvin* 79a. "Straw" stands here for "material to be removed," "dust" for "permanent filling."

186 Since the filling can easily be

removed, the ditch still separates.
187 If a ditch is filled with any material, even straw, but this is covered with mats to create a floor from one side to the other, the courtyards become one and require one *eruv*. *Šabbat* 100a.

188 No ruling is available in this case.
189 This translation is tentative; it follows the *Pesahim* text, reading רָק. Neither the text in *Eruvin* רוֹק "spittle" nor the one in K and *Nazir* רִיק "emptiness" are appropriate.

(34d line 34) אֵי זֶהוּ קֶבֶר הַתְּהוֹם. כָּל־שֶׁאֵין אָדָם זוֹכְרוֹ. וְחָשׁ לוֹמַר. שֶׁמָּא אֶחָד בְּסוֹף הָעוֹלָם יוֹדֵעַ. בְּחֶזְקַת הַחַי כַּחַי. תִּיפְתָּר שֶׁמְּצָאוֹ קַמְצִיץ.

1 זהו K | זה היא בסוף K | מסוף   2 החי כחי K | החיי כחיי תיפתר K | תפתר

תַּנֵּי. אֵין לְךָ עוֹשֶׂה קֶבֶר הַתְּהוֹם אֶלָּא הַמֵּת בִּלְבָד. הָא נְבֵילָה לֹא. קַל וָחוֹמֶר. מָה אִם הַמֵּת שֶׁאֵינוֹ עוֹשֶׂה מִשְׁכָּב וּמוֹשָׁב עוֹשֶׂה קֶבֶר תְּהוֹם. נְבֵילָה שֶׁהִיא עוֹשָׂה מִשְׁכָּב וּמוֹשָׁב אֵינוֹ דִין שֶׁתַּעֲשֶׂה קֶבֶר תְּהוֹם. לְאֵי זֶה דָבָר נֶאֱמַר. אֵין לְךָ עוֹשֶׂה קֶבֶר תְּהוֹם אֶלָּא הַמֵּת בִּלְבַד. לְהוֹצִיא מִשְׁכָּב וּמוֹשָׁב.

1 קל K | קול   2 תהום K | התהום   3 תהום K | התהום (2)

"What is a grave of the abyss? Any which nobody remembers." Should we not be cautious and say, maybe one at the end of the world knows[190]? And is the permanence of the living not like living[191]? Explain that he was found compressed[192].

It was stated: "Only a corpse creates a grave of the abyss."[193] Therefore, not a carcass[194]. An argument *de minore ad maius*. Since a corpse, which does not cause impurity of couch and seat, creates a grave of the abyss, should a carcasss which causes impurity of couch and seat not create a grave of the abyss? Why was it said that only a corpse creates a grave of the abyss? To exclude couch and seat[195].

190 Tosephta *Zavim* 2:9, Babli 81b.
191 He might know of the grave even if we do not.
192 Cf. *Gittin* 3:3, Notes 81,87. If any person left from here, when that person left he was alive and we have to apply the legal principle of permanence of the status quo and consider him permanently alive, disregarding the notion of "unknown grave".
193 Which clearly shows that he was not buried by humans but was the victim of an accident. Since the accident was not noticed when it occurred, there is nobody "at the end of the world" who would know of it.
193 Tosephta *Zavim* 2:9, Babli 80b.
194 Obviously, only a human corpse has a grave that presents problems of impurity. A buried animal carcass does not produce impurity. Carcasses cause impurity only when touched or carried. The meaning of this sentence can be clarified: Only for the impurity of the dead do we find a rule that

sometimes allows one to disregard biblical impurity.

195 This argument does not make any sense. There are several distinct ways to emend the passage to create sense; therefore, no textual emendation is proposed but the meaning can easily be clarified.

A person who is the source of his own impurity (a male or female sufferer from genital discharges) causes original impurity to any couch or personal seat he is using (Lev. 15:4-6,21-22,26). But any impurity induced on an inanimate object by a corpse is only derivative. The argument shows that the rules of the impurity of the dead and impurity produced by a living human body are not comparable: Each kind of impurity has its own severities and leniencies not found in the other.

Here ends the parallel to *Nazir*.

(34d line 41) תַּמָּן תַּנִּינָן. כָּל־הַזְּבָחִים שֶׁקִּיבֵּל דָּמָן זָר. אוֹנֵן. וּטְבוּל יוֹם. מְחוּסַּר בְּגָדִים. מְחוּסָּר כִּיפּוּרִים. וְשֶׁלֹּא רְחוּץ יָדַיִם וְרַגְלַיִם. עָרֵל. טָמֵא. יוֹשֵׁב. עוֹמֵד עַל גַּבֵּי כֵלִים. עַל גַּבֵּי [בְהֵמָה. עַל גַּבֵּי] חֲבֵירוֹ. פָּסַל. דְּרוֹמָאֵי אָמְרֵי. בְּטָמֵא טוּמְאַת זִיבָה וְטוּמְאַת צָרַעַת אֲנָן קַיָּימִין. אֲבָל בְּטָמֵא מֵת אֵינוֹ מְחַלֵּל. מֵאַחַר שֶׁהוּתַּר מִכְּלָל טוּמְאָה לָרַבִּים כַּפֶּסַח. מְתִיב רִבִּי שִׁמְעוֹן בֶּן לָקִישׁ לִדְרוֹמָאֵי. מָה אִם הַבְּעָלִים שֶׁיִּפִּיתָן כּוֹחָן בִּשְׁאָר כָּל־הַטֻּמְאוֹת שֶׁבַּשָּׁנָה. הוֹרְעָתָה כּוֹחָן בְּטָמֵא מֵת בַּפֶּסַח. עוֹבֵד. שֶׁהוּרְעָתָה כּוֹחוֹ בִּשְׁאָר טֻמְאוֹת שֶׁלְּכָל־הַשָּׁנָה. אֵינוֹ דִין שֶׁתּוֹרַע כּוֹחוֹ בְּטָמֵא מֵת בַּפֶּסַח. וְעוֹד שֶׁשָּׁנָה רִבִּי. הַצִּיץ מְרַצֶּה עַל טוּמְאַת הַדָּם. אֵין הַצִּיץ מְרַצֶּה עַל טוּמְאַת הַגּוּף. אֵין תֵּימַר בְּטָמֵא טוּמְאַת זִיבָה וְטוּמְאַת צָרַעַת אֲנָן קַיָּימִין. לֵית יְכִיל. דְּתַנִּינָן. מְטַמֵּא טוּמְאַת תְּהוֹם הַצִּיץ מְרַצֶּה: מָה עָבְדִין לָהּ דְּרוֹמָאֵי. פָּתְרִין לָהּ בַּבְּעָלִים. וְהָא תַּנִּינָן. נָזִיר. פָּתְרִין לָהּ בָּעוֹבְדִין. עַל דַּעְתֵּיהּ דְּרִבִּי שִׁמְעוֹן בֶּן לָקִישׁ. לֹא שַׁנְיָיא. הִיא בְעָלִים הִיא עוֹבְדִין. אָמַר רִבִּי יִרְמְיָה. הֲרֵי זֶה קַל וָחוֹמֶר שֶׁיֵּשׁ עָלָיו תְּשׁוּבָה. דְּאִינּוּן יָכְלִין מֵימַר לֵיהּ. לֹא. אִם אָמַרְתָּ בִּבְעָלִים. שֶׁהוּרְעָתָה כּוֹחָן בְּזָקֵן וּבְחוֹלֶה. תֹּאמַר בְּעוֹבֵד. שֶׁיִּפִּיתָה כּוֹחוֹ בְּזָקֵן וּבְחוֹלֶה. וְכָל־קַל וָחוֹמֶר שֶׁיֵּשׁ עָלָיו תְּשׁוּבָה בָּטֵל קַל וָחוֹמֶר. אָמַר רִבִּי חֲנַנְיָה. הֲרֵי זֶה קַל וָחוֹמֶר שֶׁיֵּשׁ עָלָיו תְּשׁוּבָה. דְּאִינּוּן יָכְלִין מֵימַר לֵיהּ. לֹא. אִם אָמַרְתָּ בִּבְעָלִים. שֶׁמִּילַת זְכָרָיו וַעֲבָדָיו מְעַכְּבִין אוֹתוֹ. תֹּאמַר בְּעוֹבֵד. שֶׁאֵין מִילַת זְכָרָיו וַעֲבָדָיו מְעַכְּבִין אוֹתוֹ. וְכָל־קַל וָחוֹמֶר שֶׁיֵּשׁ עָלָיו תְּשׁוּבָה בָּטֵל קַל וָחוֹמֶר.

1 הזבחים K | הזבחין K | אונן K | ואונן K | וטביל K | טביל K | בגדים K | בגדין   2 מחוסר כיפורים K | ומחבר כיפורין   2-3 על גבי כלים. על גבי [בהמה. על גבי] חבירו. פסל K | -   3 דרו מאיי K | דרומייה אמרי K | אמרין לרבים K | לרבין   4 מחלל K | מחולל   5 לדרומאיי K | לדרומייה   K הבעלים K | הבעלין שייפיתה K שיפיתה   6 כוחא K | כוחן   K כוחן טמאות של כל השנה K | כל טמאות שבכל שנה K | הטמאות שבשנה K | טמאות שבכל שנה   9 תהום K | התהום   10 שנייא K | שנייה K בעלים K | בעלין   12 בבעלים K | בבעלין שייפיתה K שיפיתה   13 וכל K | כל K תשובה | K - K חנניה | K חנייה   14 דאינון יכלין מימר ליה K | דו יכיל מימר לון K בבעלים K | בבעלין שמילת K שאין מילת K תומר K תאמר   15 שאין מילת K שמילת K וכל K כל

There, we have stated[196]: "All sacrifices whose blood was collected by a non-Cohen, a deep mourner[197], one immersed on this day[198], missing garments[199], missing atonement[200], with unwashed hands or feet[201], uncircumcised[202], impure[203], sitting[204], standing on utensils, on [an animal, on] another person[205], disqualified it." The Southerners say, we hold this for those impure by the impurity of gonorrhea or the impurity of skin disease[206], but impurity of the dead does not desecrate since it was permitted in case of the impurity of the many for the *Pesaḥ*. Rebbi Simeon ben Laqish objected to the Southerners: Since for the owner, where you clarified to his advantage in case of all other impurities during the course of the year[207], you clarified to his disadvantage in case of impurity of the dead for *Pesaḥ*[208], for the officiant, where you clarified to his disadvantage in case of all other impurities during the course of the year[209], it is only logical that you should clarify to his disadvantage in case of impurity of the dead for *Pesaḥ*. In addition to what Rebbi stated, "the diadem makes impurity of the blood acceptable but not impurity of the body." If you want to say that this refers to the impurity of gonorrhea or the impurity of skin disease, you cannot, since we have stated, "if the impurity was caused by impurity of the abyss[82], the diadem makes acceptable.[210]" What are the Southerners doing with this? They explain if for the owner[211]. But did we not state "a *nazir*"[212]? They explain it for the officiant. In Rebbi Simeon ben Laqish's opinion, there is no difference; it is equal for owner or officiant. Rebbi Jeremiah said, this is an argument *de minore ad maius* that can be contradicted, for they can say to him, no. If you argue about the owner whose position you clarified to his disadvantage in the case of the infirm and the aged[177], what can you say about the officiating, whose position you clarified to his advantage in the case of the infirm and the aged. And any argument *de minore ad majus* that can be contradicted, the argument *de minore ad majus* is invalid. Rebbi Ḥananiah said, this is an argument *de minore ad majus* that can be contradicted, for they can say to him, no. If you argue about the owner for whom the circumcision of his males and his slaves are indispensable for him[213], what can you say about the officiating, for whom the circumcision of his males and his slaves are not indispensable[214]. And any argument *de minore ad majus* that can be contradicted, the argument *de minore ad majus* is invalid.

196 Mishnah *Zevahim* 2:1.
197 A person obligated to bury a close relative, such as defined in *Lev.* 21:2-3, who from the moment of the death to the burial is barred from all sacral acts; inferred from *Deut.* 26:14.
198 Who is no longer impure but barred from sacral acts until sundown; *Lev.* 22:7.
199 A Cohen serving while not wearing all priestly garments commits a deadly sin; *Ex.* 28:43.
200 A person healed from skin disease or gonorrhea who needs not only immersion in water and waiting for sundown but is excluded from sacral rites until be bring a purifying sacrifice, *Lev.* 14:1-32 for skin disease, 15:14-15 for the sufferer from gonorrhea.
201 *Ex.* 30:19-20.
202 As the Babli points out, *Zevahim* 22b, there is no pentateuchal verse forbidding service to an uncircumcised priest, but there is one in Ezechiel, 44:9, which forbids entry to the Temple domain to any uncircumcised person, including a hemophiliac who may not be circumcised.
203 *Lev.* 22:2-3.
204 Since the verses never permit any action in sitting, and the priests are required to be barefoot, no service is possible unless the priest is standing with his feet in direct contact with the floor of the Temple court, the Temple interior, or the altar.
205 Meaning that another priest puts his hands under the feet of the officiating priest. Then he is not in contact with the floor.

206 They read the expression "impurity of the body" used in the Mishnah to describe what the diadem does not make acceptable as impurity caused by the person's body (i. e., in addition to skin disease and gonorrhea also sexual activity, *Lev.* 15:15,18.)
207 They may send their sacrifices through an agent if they are disabled by impurity.
208 He must celebrate the Second *Pesah*.
209 He may never serve being impure.
210 Since impurity of the abyss only is caused by a corpse, it is not caused by the person's body. If it is stated that the diadem makes acceptable in this case, it follows that the diadem is inactive in all cases of known impurity caused by external influences.
211 The diadem only covers abyss impurity of the owner, but not proven impurity of the dead; one may still read "impurity of the body" as referring to impurity produced by the body.
212 The only impurity forbidden for the *nazir* is the impurity of the dead, so in Mishnah 5 the reference must be to this kind of impurity.
213 Since *Ex.* 12:48 notes that *no one uncircumcised may eat it* [the *Pesah*], in v. 44, *a man's slave, bought with money, if you circumcise him he may eat it*, "he" is read to refer to the owner; the owner may not eat *Pesah* if there are uncircumcised males in his *familia*. *Mekhilta dR. Ismael Bo* 15, *dR. Simeon ben Yohai* p. 35
214 Cf. Note 202. An uncircumcised Cohen may not serve; nothing is said about his dependents.

(34d line 60) רִבִּי יִצְחָק בַּר גּוּפְתָּא בְּעָא קוֹמֵי רִבִּי מָנָא. אִילּוּ יָחִיד בַּפֶּסַח לָמֶד מִן הַצִּיבּוּר בַּפֶּסַח. עוֹבֵד בִּשְׁאָר יְמוֹת הַשָּׁנָה לָמֶד מִן הַצִּיבּוּר בַּפֶּסַח. רִבִּי אַמִּי בָּעֵי. הָכֵן טָמֵא מָה אַתְּ עָבַד

לֵיהּ. כְּטָמֵא טוּמְאַת זִיבָה וְטוּמְאַת צָרַעַת. מְחוּסְרֵי כַפָּרָה. וְהָתַנִּינָן. אִם מְשֻׁטָּבָל הוּא מְחַלֵּל. לֹא כָּל־שֶׁכֵּן עַד שֶׁלֹּא טָבַל. הָהֵן טְבוּל יוֹם מַה אַתְּ עָבַד לֵיהּ. בִּטְבוּל יוֹם מִן הַמֵּת. אִיתָא חֲמִי. טָמֵא מֵת אֵינוֹ מְחַלֵּל. לֹא כָּל־שֶׁכֵּן טְבוּל יוֹם מִן הַמֵּת. אֶלָּא טְבוּל יוֹם מִן הַשֶּׁרֶץ. אִיתָא חֲמִי. טְבוּל יוֹם מִן הַמֵּת אֵינוֹ מְחַלֵּל. לֹא כָּל־שֶׁכֵּן טְבוּל יוֹם מִן הַשֶּׁרֶץ. אָמַר רִבִּי שְׁמוּאֵל בַּר יוּדָן. מַגְּעֵי זָבִין. רַבָּנָן דְּקַיסָרִין פֶּתְרִין כּוֹלָּהּ בְּזָב. טְבוּל יוֹם שְׁרָאָה אַחַת. טָמֵא (מת) שֶׁרָאָה שְׁתַּיִם. מְחוּסָּר כִּיפּוּרִים שֶׁרָאָה שָׁלֹשׁ. עַל דַּעְתִּין דִּדְרוֹמָאֵי. מַגַּע זָב כְּזָב. נִשְׁמְעִינַהּ מִן הָדָא. דְּאָמַר רִבִּי אֶלְעָזָר בְּשֵׁם רִבִּי הוֹשַׁעְיָה. וְנָשָׂא אַהֲרֹן אֶת־עֲוֹן הַקֳּדָשִׁים. עֲוֹן הַקְּרֵיבִין. לֹא עֲוֹן הַמַּקְרִיבִין. מָהוּ עֲוֹן הַקְּרֵיבִין. דַּם זָב. לֹא מַגַּע זָב. וְדִכְוָותָהּ. עֲוֹן הַמַּקְרִיבִין. מַגְּעֵי הַזָּב. הֲדָא אָמְרָה. הָיָה הַצִּיבּוּר מַגְּעֵי זָבִין וּמַגְּעֵי זָבוֹת. אֵינָן עוֹשִׂין בְּטוּמְאָה.

1 גופתא K גופתה | בעא K בעה | למד K למיד 2 למד K למיד | טמא K טמא מת 3 ליה K לה | והתנינין K והא תנינן 4 בטבול K טבול | איתא K איתא 5 איתא K אתא לא - K | 7 מגעי K | במגעי רבנן K רבנין 8 כיפורים K כיפורין | דעתין K דעתיין | דדרומאי K דדרומייה | מן הדא K גו הזב דאצ׳ K דמר אלעזר K לעזר 9 הקריבין K הקריבים | הדא K הדה 10 הדא K הדה

Rebbi Isaac bar Gufta asked before Rebbi Mana: If an individual could learn from the public for the *Pesaḥ*, the officiant during the rest of the year might infer from the public for the *Pesaḥ*[215]. Rebbi Immi asked: how do you explain this "impure"? Impure by the impurity of gonorrhea or the impurity of skin disease? But did we not state, "missing atonement"? If he desecrates when he had been immersed, not so much more before he was immersed[216]! How do you explain "immersed on this day"? If he immersed himself on that day because of a corpse. Come and see: the one impure from a corpse does not desecrate, not so much more one immersed on that day because of a corpse? But he must be immersed on that day because of a crawling animal[147]. Come and see: the immersed on that day because of a corpse does not desecrate, not so much more one immersed on that day because of a crawling animal[217]? Rebbi Samuel bar Yudan said, people having touched sufferers from gonorrhea[218]. The rabbis of Caesarea explain everything from a sufferer from gonorrhea[152]. "One immersed on this day[198]," if he had one episode. "Impure" (in the impurity of the dead)[218*] if he had two episodes. "Missing atonement[200]," if he had three episodes. Are people having touched a sufferer from gonorrhea like a sufferer from gonorrhea in the opinion of the Southerners? Let us hear from the following, as Rebbi Eleazar said in the name of Rebbi Hoshaia: *Aaron shall carry the iniquities of the sacrifices*[97], the iniquities of the sacrifices, not the iniquities of the sacrificers[98]. What is iniquity of the sacrifices? The blood of a sufferer from gonorrhea? No, what was touched by a sufferer from gonorrhea[219]. Similarly, the iniquity of the sacrificers, who touched a sufferer from gonorrhea. This implies that if the public were impure because they had touched sufferers from gonorrhea or women suffering from flux, they cannot make it[220] in impurity.

215 But since the individual must make a Second *Pesaḥ* which the public never makes, the original argument of R. Simeon ben Laqish is incorrect.

216 The statement of Mishnah *Zevahim* 2:1 seems redundant.

217 And from impurity of a corpse one has to wait for seven days while of a dead crawling animal one may immerse himself immediately.

218 Who are impure until sundown after immediate immersion in water, *Lev.* 15:4,7.

218* The text in parentheses has to be deleted even though it is confirmed by K.

219 Since gonorrhea causes impurity only in humans, the impurity cannot be the victim's.

220 The only cause for *Pesaḥ* in impurity is the impurity of the dead.

(fol. 34a) **משנה ו:** נִטְמָא שָׁלֵם אוֹ רוּבּוֹ שׂוֹרְפִין אוֹתוֹ לִפְנֵי הַבִּירָה מֵעֲצֵי הַמַּעֲרָכָה. נִטְמָא מִיעוּטוֹ וְהַנּוֹתָר שׂוֹרְפִין אוֹתוֹ בְחַצְרוֹתֵיהֶן אוֹ עַל גַּגּוֹתֵיהֶן מֵעֲצֵי עַצְמָן. הַצַּיְקָנִין שׂוֹרְפִין אוֹתוֹ לִפְנֵי הַבִּירָה בִּשְׁבִיל לֵיהָנוֹת מֵעֲצֵי הַמַּעֲרָכָה:

Mishnah 6: If it became impure whole or most of it, one burns it before the citadel on altar wood. If a minor part became impure or leftovers[220] one burns in the courtyards or on their roofs on their own wood. The misers burn it before the citadel in order to profit from altar wood.

220 What was not eaten by midnight (Mishnah 10:)

(34d line 74) **הלכה ח:** רִבִּי חָמָא בַּר עוּקְבָה בְשֵׁם רִבִּי יוֹסֵי בֶּן חֲנִינָה. כְּדֵי לְפַרְסְמוֹ. לְהוֹדִיעַ שְׁקִילְקֵל בּוֹ. אָמַר. הֲרֵינִי שׂוֹרְפוֹ לִפְנֵי הַבִּירָה מֵעֲצֵי עַצְמוֹ. אֵין שׁוֹמְעִין לוֹ. לֹא צוֹרְכָה דְלֹא [אָמַר.] הֲרֵינִי שׂוֹרְפוֹ עַל גַּגֵּי מֵעֲצֵי עַצְמִי. כָּל־שֶׁכֵּן אֵין שׁוֹמְעִין לוֹ

רִבִּי יִרְמְיָה בְשֵׁם רִבִּי הִילָא. לְהוֹדִיעַ לָבוֹא אַחֲרָיו שֶׁהוּא צִוִּיקָן. תֵּדַע לָךְ. בְּכָל־אֲתָר לֹא צָוַוח לֵיהּ צְוִיקָן. וְכָא אַתְּ צְחִחַח לֵיהּ צְוִיקָן. קַל הֵקִילוּ בָּאכְסְנָיֵי.

1 הילא K | הלא תדע K תידע לא K | לית   2 הכא K והכה

אָמַר רִבִּי יוֹחָנָן. מִגְדָּל הָיָה עוֹמֵד בְּהַר הַבַּיִת וְהָיָה קָרוּי בִּירָה. רִבִּי שִׁמְעוֹן בֶּן לָקִישׁ אָמַר. כָּל־הַר הַבַּיִת קָרוּי בִּירָה. לַעֲשׂוֹת הַכֹּל וְלִבְנוֹת הַבִּירָה אֲשֶׁר־הֲכִינוֹתִי.

2 קרוי | K היה קרוי   לעשות הכל | K -

Halakhah 8: Rebbi Ḥama bar Uqba in the name of Rebbi Yose ben Ḥanina: To publicize him, to make it known that he spoiled it[221]. If he said, I am going to burn it before the citadel on my own wood, one does not listen to him; it is not necessary to note that if he says, I will burn it on my roof on my own wood that one does not listen to him[222].

Rebbi Jeremiah in the name of Rebbi Hila: To inform the next in line that he is a miser. You should know that nowhere else is he called miser, but here you are calling him miser[223]. They made it easy for the guest[224].

[225]Rebbi Joḥanan said, a tower was standing on the Temple Mount which was called "citadel". Rebbi Simeon ben Laqish said, the entire Temple Mount was called citadel, *to do everything and to build the citadel which I prepared*[226].

221 Babli 81b.
222 Here it refers to the Mishnah here; but the statement in Tosephta 3:13 that before the citadel one may not use private wood refers to Mishnah 3:8 (Note 150), and emphasizes that before the citadel one never uses any but altar wood.
223 This now refers to the end of the Mishnah. In Mishnah 3:8, where people burn disqualified private sacral meat before the citadel on altar wood, they are not called miser.
224 Babli 82a. Most people in Jerusalem at holiday time are guests, without their own supply of fire wood.
225 *Yoma* 2b, *Zevahim* 104b.
226 *1Chr.* 28:19.

(fol. 34a) **משנה ז**: הַפֶּסַח שֶׁיָּצָא אוֹ שֶׁנִּטְמָא יִשָּׂרֵף מִיָּד. נִטְמְאוּ הַבְּעָלִים אוֹ שֶׁמֵּתוּ תְּעוּבַּר צוּרָתוֹ וְיֵצֵא לְבֵית הַשְּׂרֵיפָה. רַבִּי יוֹחָנָן בֶּן בְּרוֹקָה אוֹמֵר אַף זֶה יִשָּׂרֵף מִיָּד שֶׁאֵין לוֹ אוֹכְלִין:

Mishnah 7: *Pesaḥ* which left[227] or which became impure has to be burned immediately[228]. If the owners became impure or died it shall lose its shape[229] and be brought to the place of burning[229a]. Rebbi Joḥanan ben Beroqa says, this one also has to be burned immediately since it has no eaters.

227 The walls of Jerusalem.
228 On the 14th of Nisan.
229 Be spoiled and become unusable as sacral meat.
229a The place where disqualified sacrifices and those to be burned outside the sacred domain have to be disposed of.

(35a line 6) תָּנֵי רִבִּי חִיָּיה. פְּסוּל גּוּף [פִּיגּוּל הוּא וְ]נִשְׂרָף מִיָּד. [נִטְמְאוּ בְעָלִים אוֹ שֶׁמֵּתוּ] פְּסוּל מַכְשִׁיר טָעוּן צוּרָה. אָמַר רִבִּי יוֹסֵה. מַתְנִיתָה אֲמָרָה כֵן. פֶּסַח שֶׁיָּצָא אוֹ שֶׁנִּיטְמָא. פְּסוּל גּוּף הוּא וְנִשְׂרָף מִיָּד. נִיטְמְאוּ הַבְּעָלִים אוֹ שֶׁמֵּתוּ. פְּסוּל מַכְשִׁיר הוּא וְטָעוּן צוּרָה.

C 1 פיגול הוא | KS - | KS ונשרף | C נשרף KS | C נטמאו בעלים או שמתו | KS - | 3 ניטמאו K | ניטמו הבעלים K | הבעלין

Rebbi Ḥiyya stated[230]: "A disqualification of the body [is *piggul* and] is immediately burned. [If the owners became impure or died it is] a disqualification of enabler and needs to lose its shape. Rebbi Yose said, the Mishnah says so: *"Pesaḥ* which left or which became impure is a disqualification of the body and has to be burned immediately. If the owner became impure or died it is a disqualification of the enabler and it shall lose its shape."

230 Babli 34b, 73b, 82b; Tosephta 6:6. As K shows, the corrector's additions are superfluous and should be deleted.

(35a line 10) רִבִּי חָמָא בַּר עוּקְבָה בְשֵׁם רִבִּי יוֹסֵה בַּר חֲנִינָה. רִבִּי נְחֶמְיָה וְרִבִּי יוֹחָנָן בֶּן בְּרוֹקָה שְׁנֵיהֶם אֲמְרוּ דָבָר אֶחָד. דְּתַנֵּי. אָמַר רִבִּי נְחֶמְיָה. וְכִי מִפְּנֵי אֲנִינָה נִשְׂרָף. וְהָא לֹא נִשְׂרַף אֶלָּא מִפְּנֵי הַטּוּמְאָה. שֶׁאִילּוּ מִפְּנֵי אֲנִינָה נִשְׂרָף הָיָה לוֹ לְשַׁלְּשְׁתָּן לִישָּׂרֵף. דָּבָר אַחֵר. וַהֲלֹא פִינְחָס הָיָה עִמָּהֶן. דָּבָר אַחֵר. וַהֲלֹא מוּתָּר לְאוֹכְלוֹ מִבְּעָרֶב. עַל דַּעְתֵּיהּ דְּרִבִּי נְחֶמְיָה יִשְׂרוֹף וְיִמָּנֶה. סָבַר רִבִּי נְחֶמְיָה. שֶׁלְּשָׁתָּן נִשְׂרְפוּ. הָיָה לוֹ לְפִינְחָס לוֹכַל. וַאֲדַיִין לֹא נִתְמַנֶּה כֹּהֵן גָּדוֹל. וְהָיָה לוֹ לְאַהֲרוֹן לוֹכַל מִבְּעָרֶב. סָבַר רִבִּי נְחֶמְיָה. אֲנִינָה [לַיְלָה] תּוֹרָה. אָמַר רִבִּי יִרְמְיָה. אוֹף רִבִּי יוֹסֵי הַגְּלִילִי דִּכְוָותְהוֹן. דְּתַנִינָן תַּמָּן. חַטָּאת שֶׁקִּיבֵּל דָּמָהּ בִּשְׁנֵי כוֹסוֹת. יָצָא אֶחָד מֵהֶן לַחוּץ. הַפְּנִימִי כָשֵׁר. נִכְנַס אֶחָד מֵהֶן לִפְנִים. רִבִּי יוֹסֵי הַגְּלִילִי מַכְשִׁיר בַּחִיצוֹן. וַחֲכָמִים פּוֹסְלִין. [אָמַר רִבִּי יוֹסֵי הַגְּלִילִי. וּמָה אִם בְּמָקוֹם שֶׁמַּחֲשָׁבָה פוֹסֶלֶת בַּחוּץ. לֹא עָשָׂה בָהּ הַמְשׁוּאָר כַּיּוֹצֵא. מָקוֹם שֶׁאֵין הַמַּחֲשָׁבָה פּוֹסֶלֶת בִּפְנִים אֵינוֹ דִין שֶׁלֹּא נַעֲשָׂה הַמְשׁוּאָר כַּנִּכְנָס. נִכְנַס לְכַפֵּר. אַף עַל פִּי שֶׁלֹּא כִפֵּר. פָּסוּל. דִּבְרֵי רִבִּי אֱלִיעֶזֶר. רִבִּי שִׁמְעוֹן אוֹמֵר. עַד שֶׁיְּכַפֵּר. רִבִּי יוּדָא אוֹמֵר. אִם הִכְנִיס שׁוֹגֵג. כָּשֵׁר. כָּל הַדָּמִים פְּסוּלִין שֶׁנִּתְּנוּ עַל גַּבֵּי הַמִּזְבֵּחַ לֹא הוּרְצָה הַצִּיץ אֶלָּא עַל טָמֵא. שֶׁהַצִּיץ מְרַצֶּה עַל הַטָּמֵא וְאֵינוֹ מְרַצֶּה עַל הַיּוֹצֵא] אָמַר רִבִּי לְעָזָר. תֵּדַע לָךְ שֶׁהוּא פָסוּל מַכְשִׁיר כְּרִבִּי יוֹסֵי הַגְּלִילִי. שֶׁהֲרֵי חֲבֵירוֹ מִבַּחוּץ וְהוּא כָשֵׁר. תֵּדַע לָךְ שֶׁהוּא פָסוּל גּוּף כְּרַבָּנָן. שֶׁהֲרֵי הוּא בִמְחִיצָתוֹ וְהוּא פָסוּל. רַבָּנָן דָּרְשִׁין. מִפְּנֵי שֶׁלֹּא נִכְנַס מִקְצָת דָּמָהּ לִפְנִים אָכֹל תֹּאכְלוּ אֹתָהּ. הָא אִם נִכְנַס מִקְצָת דָּמָהּ לִפְנִים [יָפָה עֲשִׂיתֶם] שֶׁשְּׂרַפְתֶּם. רִבִּי יוֹסֵי הַגְּלִילִי דָּרֵשׁ. מִפְּנֵי שֶׁלֹּא נִכְנַס כָּל דָּמָהּ לִפְנִים [אָכֹל תֹּאכְלוּ אֹתָהּ.   הָא אִם נִכְנַס כָּל דָּמָהּ לִפְנִים] יָפָה עֲשִׂיתֶם שֶׁשְּׂרַפְתֶּם. מַה טַּעֲמוֹן דְּרַבָּנָן. וְכָל־חַטָּאת אֲשֶׁר יוּבָא מִדָּמָהּ. אֲפִילוּ מִקְצָת דָּמָהּ. מַה טַעֲמֵיהּ דְּרִבִּי יוֹסֵי הַגְּלִילִי. הֵן לֹא־הוּבָא אֶת־דָּמָהּ אֶל־הַקֹּדֶשׁ פְּנִימָה. [כִּהֲדָא דְ]תַנֵּי. רִבִּי יוֹסֵי הַגְּלִילִי

אוֹמֵר. אֵין כָּל־הָעִנְיָין הַזֶּה מְדַבֵּר אֶלָּא בַּפָּרִים וּבַשְּׂעִירִין הַנִּשְׂרָפִין וּבַשְּׂעִירִין הַנִּשְׂרָפִין לִיתֵּן עֲלֵיהֶן לֹא תַעֲשֶׂה עַל אֲכִילָתָן וּלְלַמֵּד שֶׁפְּסוּלֵיהֶן נִשְׂרָפִין בְּבֵית הַבִּירָה. אָמְרוּ לוֹ. מִנַּיִין לַחַטָּאת שֶׁאִם נִכְנַס מִדָּמָהּ לִפְנִים שֶׁהִיא פְּסוּלָה. לֹא מִן הָדֵין קִרְיָיא הֵן לֹא־הוּבָא אֶת־דָּמָהּ אֶל־הַקּוֹדֶשׁ פְּנִימָה. הָא אֵינוֹ אוֹמֵר מִדָּמָהּ אֶלָּא כָל־דָּמָהּ. תְּשׁוּבָה לְרִבִּי עֲקִיבָה שֶׁהָיָה אוֹמֵר. מִדָּמָהּ. לֹא כָל־דָּמָהּ.

2 והא K | והלא   3 נשרף K | נישרף שלשתן לישרף K | לשריף   5 שלשתן K | שלושתן   היה K | והיה לוכל K | לאכול לאהרן K | -   6 לוכל K | לאכול   אנינה K | אנינות יוסי K | יוסה   7 שקיבל K | שקבל 8 מה K | -   יוסי K | יוסה   KS | [text in brackets] C 13-8   15 במחיצתו K | עומד במחיצתו]   17 הא אם K | האם   18 דרבנן K | דרבניו   יוסי K | יוסה   19 פנימה K | -   כהדא K | כהדה יוסי K | יוסה 20 מדבר K | המדבר   לא K | בלא   21 וללמד K | ללמד   בבית K | לפני   22 שהיא K | תהא   - K | אמ' להן   קרייה K | קרייה דכת'   24 לא כל דמה K | אפילו מקצת דמה

Rebbi Ḥama bar Uqba in the name of Rebbi Yose bar Ḥanina: Rebbi Nehemiah and Rebbi Joḥanan ben Beroqa both said the same[231], as it was stated[232]: "it was burned because of deep mourning[233]? Was it not burned only because of impurity? But it was not burned because of impurity, since if it had been burned because of mourning, all three of them[234] should have been burned. Another opinion, was not Phineas with them[235]? Another opinion, would it not have been permitted to be eaten in the evening[236]?" In the opinion of Rebbi Nehemiah it should be burned but be counted[237]. Rebbi Nehemiah is of the opinion that all three of them were burned. Should not Phineas have eaten? He was not yet appointed {High) Priest[238]. Should not Aaron have eaten in the evening? Rebbi Nehemiah is of the opinion that deeo mourning in the night is from the Torah. Rebbi Jeremiah said, also Rebbi Yose the Galilean is with them[239].

[240]And we have stated there:[241] "A purification sacrifice whose blood was received in two cups, of which one was brought outside[242]; the one inside is qualified. If one of them was brought to the interior[243], Rebbi Yose the Galilean declares qualified but the Sages declare disqualified. [Rebbi Yose the Galilean said, since in a case where intent disqualifies outside[244] the remainder was not made equal to what was brought outside, in a case where intent does not disqualify in the interior[245] is it not logical that we not make the remainder to what was brought inside? If it was brought into the interior to atone, even if it did not atone it is disqualified, the words of Rebbi Eliezer[246]. Rebbi Simeon says, only if it atones[247]. Rebbi Jehudah says, if it was brought into the interior in error, it remains qualified. Of all disqualified

blood which one gave on the altar, the diadem only makes the impure acceptable; for the diadem makes the impure acceptable but not what was brought outside."] Rebbi Eleazar said, you have to know that for Rebbi Yose the Galilean it is disqualification of the enabler since the other part is outside[248] and it is qualified. You have to know that for the rabbis it is disqualification of the body since it is within its enclosure[249] and it is disqualified. The rabbis explain, since nothing of the blood was brought to the interior, *you shall certainly eat it*[250]. Therefore if some of the blood had been brought to the interior, you[251] [would have done well] in burning it. Rebbi Yose the Galilean explains, since not all of the blood was brought to the interior, [*you shall certainly eat it*. Therefore if all of the blood had been brought inside,] you would have done well in burning it. What is the rabbis' reason? *Any purification offering of whose blood was brought*; even part of the blood[252]. What is Rebbi Yose the Galilean's reason? *Behold, its blood was not brought inside the Sanctuary*[250,253]. [This fits with] what was stated: Rebbi Yose the Galilean says, the entire matter only speaks of bulls to be burned and goats to be burned[254], to prohibit eating them and to teach that if they are disqualified they are burned inside the citadel[255]. They asked him, from where that a purification sacrifice becomes disqualified if some of its blood is brought inside? Not from this verse, *behold, its blood was not brought inside the Sanctuary*? There it does not say *of whose blood* but all of its blood[256]. An answer to Rebbi Aqiba who was saying, *of whose blood*, not all of its blood[257].

231 That under certain circumstances a disqualified sacrifice must be burned immediately, without waiting that it lose its shape, even if the disqualification is not in the victim's body.

232 *Sifra Šeminy Pereq* 2(8-10).

233 This is R. Nehemiah's statement. The discussion refers to *Lev.* 10:16-17. Since tradition fixes the inauguration of Tabernacle and Priesthood on a First of Nisan (*Seder Olam* Chapter 7, in the author's edition p. 82; cf. Rashi *ad* 9:1), there were three goats as purification offering: the one required for every New Moon (*Num.* 28:15), the people's initiation sacrifice (*Lev.* 10:3), and the one offered by the chief of the tribe of Judah (*Num.* 7:16). Only the first of these was presented pursuant a permanent law; the other two were one time affairs from which no conclusions could be drawn for generally valid principles. R. Nehemiah holds that since a

deep rnourner on the day of burial is biblically excluded from all sacral rites, the order given in 18:12-15 to Aaron and his sons to eat *sancta* even though Aaron's sons Nadav and Avihu had been buried on that day necessarily was restricted to the one time offerings of that day, to the exclusion of offerings presented following a permanent prescription. But the mourning of the priests is a condition of the enablers, not of the victim, and nevertheless Moses agreed that the purification offering correctly had been burned and not eaten.

234 Since in Moses's order to eat the *sancta* purification offerings are not mentioned.

235 Phineas was born in Egypt (*Ex.* 6:25). As a nephew of Nadav and Avihu he had no biblical obligation to mourn and could legally have eaten all sacrifices. Since there was one eater, R. Johanan ben Beroqa would agree that the sacrifice cannot be burned.

236 Since the talmudic rule is that only the day of burial is biblically forbidden. While his sons would have to observe seven days of mourning, the High Priest is forbidden mourning where it is not prescribed; in the following night he could have joined Phineas. Purification offerings are eaten by the priests during the day of offering and the following night.

237 There is no doubt that the obligation for which the sacrifice was brought had been fulfilled.

238 In the initiation rites (*Lev.* Chapter 8), only Aaron and his sons are mentioned, not his grandson Phineas. This is the basis of the opinion that Phineas was not originally included in the priesthood; priesthood was conferred on him only after the incident with Zimry (*Num.* 25:13); Babli *Zevahim* 101b.

239 In the same Chapter of *Sifra* (Halakhah 5), he deduces from *Lev.* 10:18 that any purification sacrifice whose blood was brought into the sanctuary is disqualified and must be burned immediately. This proves that he agrees with R. Nehemiah that the verses have to be interpreted referring to the ordinary Temple service, and that disqualification of the enabler may trigger an obligation of immediate burning.

240 This paragraph has no direct connection with the preceding; the connection being that R. Yose the Galilean interprets *Lev.* 10:18..

241 Mishnah *Zevahim* 8:12.

242 Since purification sacrifice has to be eaten by the priests in the Temple courtyard (*Lev.* 6:19), if any part leaves the sacred domain it becomes disqualified. Since pouring the blood on the walls of the altar enables the meat to be eaten, if blood is brought outside before it was poured the sacrifice is disqualified.

243 As noted later, this is required/permitted only in extraordinary cases. The Mishnah here refers to ordinary sacrifices. Since then the blood is not in the courtyard, it is outside its prescribed domain and disqualified.

244 Slaughtering a victim with the intent of pouring the blood outside the sacred precinct disqualifies the sacrifice; Mishnah *Zevahim* 2:2.

The text in brackets was added by a corrector from a different source; it is neither in the scribe's text nor in K.

245 The intent to pour the blood in the Temple itself does not disqualify; Mishnah *Zevahim* 3:6.

246 The fact that the blood was inside when it should not have been makes it "outside its

place" and disqualifies.

247 Only if something was done against the rules with the blood; the interior of the Temple still is sacred domain.

248 In the case that one cup was brought to the interior.

249 Since one cup remained outside, it could be poured on the walls of the altar even if the cup inside became unusable.

250 *Lev.* 10:18.

251 Aaron's sons, addressed by Moses.

252 *Lev.* 6:33. As usual, a prefixed *mem* is interpreted to mean "some, not all".

253 If *Lev.* 10:18 is read to refer to rules of the purification sacrifices applicable at all times then it seems to contradict *Lev.* 6:33 since the prefixed *mem* is missing.

254 The purification offering of the High Priest (*Lev.* 4:1-12), of the people (*Lev.* 4:13-21), and of the day of Atonement (*Lev.* 1627). Babli 83a top, *Zevahim* 82a.

255 Whereas all the other disqualified sacrifices have to be burned outside like the impure *Pesah*.

256 Since this is the formulation in the actual case decided by Moses, it is the operative version.

257 Whose opinion is that of the "Sages" opposing R. Yose the Galilean.

(fol. 34a) **משנה ז**: הָעֲצָמוֹת וְהַגִּידִין וְהַנּוֹתָר יִשָּׂרְפוּ בְשִׁשָּׁה עָשָׂר. וְאִם חָל שִׁשָּׁה עָשָׂר לִהְיוֹת בַּשַּׁבָּת יִשָּׂרְפוּ בְשִׁבְעָה עָשָׂר דּוֹחִין לֹא אֶת הַשַּׁבָּת וְלֹא אֶת יוֹם טוֹב:

Mishnah 7: The bones, the sinews, and leftovers are to be burned on the Sixteenth. But if the Sixteenth falls on a Sabbath they are to be burned on the Seventeenth since this pushes aside neither Sabbath nor holiday.

(35a line 62) **הלכה**: עֶצֶם שֶׁאֵין עָלָיו בָּשָׂר. רִבִּי יוֹחָנָן אָמַר. אָסוּר לְשׁוֹבְרוֹ. רִבִּי שִׁמְעוֹן בֶּן לָקִישׁ אָמַר. מוּתָּר לְשׁוֹבְרוֹ. מָתִיב רִבִּי יוֹחָנָן לְרִבִּי שִׁמְעוֹן בֶּן לָקִישׁ. וְהָא תַּנִּינָן. הָעֲצָמוֹת וְהַגִּידִין וְהַנּוֹתָר יִשָּׂרְפוּ בְשִׁשָּׁה עָשָׂר. וְיִקּוֹץ. מִפְּנֵי הַמּוֹחַ שֶׁבַּקּוּלִית. וְיַחֲלוֹץ אֶת הַבָּשָׂר מִן הָעֶצֶם וִיהֲנֶה מִן הָעֶצֶם. סָבְרִין מֵימַר. אֵין חוֹלְצִין אֶת הַפָּסוּל. אָמַר רִבִּי לְעָזָר. וַאֲפִילוּ תֵּימַר. חוֹלְצִין. פָּתַר לָהּ כְּרִבִּי יַעֲקֹב. דְּרִבִּי יַעֲקֹב אָמַר. הָכָא בְכוֹשֵׁר מִשָּׁעָה רִאשׁוֹנָה וְנִיטְמָא אָסוּר בִּשְׁבִירַת הָעֶצֶם. רִבִּי אִימִּי בְּשֵׁם רִבִּי לְעָזָר. מַה טַּעַם אָמְרוּ. הָעֲצָמוֹת וְהַגִּידִין וְהַנּוֹתָר יִשָּׂרְפוּ בְשִׁשָּׁה עָשָׂר. שֶׁהַשּׂוֹרֵף יֵשׁ בּוֹ מִשּׁוּם שׁוֹבֵר. שְׁמוּאֵל אָמַר. נִימְנִין עַל מוֹחַ שֶׁבָּרֹאשׁ וְאֵין נִימְנִין עַל מוֹחַ שֶׁבַּקּוּלִית. נִימְנִין עַל מוֹחַ שֶׁבָּרֹאשׁ. שֶׁהוּא יָכוֹל לְהוֹצִיאוֹ דֶּרֶךְ הָאֹזֶן. וְאֵין נִימְנִין עַל מוֹחַ שֶׁבַּקּוּלִית. שֶׁאֵינוֹ יָכוֹל לְהוֹצִיאוֹ אֶלָּא דֶּרֶךְ שְׁבִירָה. רִבִּי יוֹחָנָן אָמַר. נִימְנִין עַל מוֹחַ שֶׁבַּקּוּלִית. רִבִּי יַעֲקֹב בַּר אָחָא בְשֵׁם רִבִּי יוֹחָנָן. אֵין נִימְנִין עַל מוֹחַ שֶׁבַּקּוּלִית. וְאִם נִמְנָה נִמְנָה. עַל דַּעְתֵּיהּ דְּרִבִּי יוֹחָנָן. יִשְׂרוֹף וְיִמְנֶה. מִפְּנֵי אָבְדָן קֳדָשִׁים. עַל דַּעְתֵּיהּ דִּשְׁמוּאֵל. יִשְׂרוֹף וְיִמְנֶה. סָבַר שְׁמוּאֵל כְּרִבִּי יַעֲקֹב. [דְּרִבִּי יַעֲקֹב] אָמַר. הָכָא בְכוֹשֵׁר מִשָּׁעָה רִאשׁוֹנָה וְנִיטְמָא אָסוּר בִּשְׁבִירַת הָעֶצֶם.

1 לשוברו K לשברו   2 ר' יוחנן K | -   4 אין K שאין ואפי' K אפילו חולצין K חולצין את הפסול   5
וניטמא K ונטמא בשבירת K בשביעית   6 אימי K אמי   7 שמואל K ר' שמואל שבראש K שבקולית
ואין K | -   8 שבקולית K שבראש   נימנין על מוח שבראש. שהיא יכול להוציאו דרך האוזן K ואין מנימנין
דרך האוזן   10 על מוח שבקולית K | -   11 אבדן K אובדן

מַה חֲמִית מֵימַר. וְלֹא־תוֹתִירוּ מִמֶּנּוּ עַד־בּוֹקֶר וְהַנוֹתָר מִמֶּנּוּ עַד־בּוֹקֶר בָּאֵשׁ תִּשְׂרוֹפוּ: אַחַר שְׁנֵי בְקָרִים אַחַר בּוֹקְרוֹ שֶׁלָּאַרְבָּעָה עָשָׂר וְאַחַר בּוֹקְרוֹ שֶׁלָּחֲמִשָּׁה עָשָׂר. וְכָתוּב וְהַנוֹתָר מִבְּשַׂר הַזֶּבַח בַּיּוֹם הַשְּׁלִישִׁי בָּאֵשׁ יִשָּׂרֵף:

1 מימר K | מימר כן   2 בקרים K בקרין   שלארבעה K| שלחמשה   שלחמשה K| שלששה   3 ביום השלישי באש ישרף K | -

מָהוּ לְהַצִּית אֶת הָאוּר בִּמְדוּרַת חָמֵץ. מָאן דְּיָלִיף מִן הַנּוֹתָר. אָסוּר. מָאן דְּלָא יָלִיף מִן הַנּוֹתָר. מוּתָר. אָמַר רִבִּי בּוּן בַּר חִיָּיה. יָרְדוּ לָהּ בְּשִׁטַּת רִבִּי יִשְׁמָעֵאל (וכו'). [כָּמָה דְרִבִּי יִשְׁמָעֵאל אָמַר תַּמָּן. תִּינוֹק שֶׁעָבַר זְמַנּוֹ נִימוֹל בֵּין בַּיּוֹם בֵּין בַּלַּיְלָה. וְהָכָא עִבֵּר זְמַנּוֹ נִשְׂרָף בֵּין בַּיּוֹם בֵּין בַּלַּיְלָה.]

1 מהו K מהוא   מאן K | מן   דיליף K | דיליף   (2) דיליף לה K | -   2 כמה דר' ישמעאל K | -

Halakhah: A bone with no meat on it, Rebbi Johanan said, one is forbidden to break it; Rebbi Simeon ben Laqish said, one is permitted to break it[258]. Rebbi Johanan objected to Rebbi Simeon ben Laqish: Did we not state, "the bones, the sinews, and leftovers are to be burned on the Sixteenth[258a]"? Could he not chop? Because of the marrow in a marrow-bone[259]. Could one not strip off all meat from the bone and profit from the bone? They wanted to say that one may not strip off from the disqualified. Rebbi Eleazar said, and even if you say that one may strip, he explains it following Rebbi Jacob, since Rebbi Jacob said, the prohibition of breaking a bone applies if at the start it was qualified and then became impure[260]. Rebbi Immi in the name of Rebbi Eleazar: why did they say, "the bones, the sinews, and leftovers are to be burned on the Sixteenth"? Because he who burns causes breaking[261]. Samuel said, one may subscribe to the brain in the head but one may not subscribe to the marrow in a marrow bone[262]. One may subscribe to the brain in the head because one can take it out through the ear. But one may not subscribe to the marrow in a marrow bone since one could only extricate it by breaking. Rebbi Johanan said, one may subscribe to the marrow in a marrow bone. Rebbi Jacob bar Aha in the name of Rebbi Johanan, one may not subscribe to the marrow in a marrow bone, but if he subscribed, he subscribed[263]. In Rebbi Johanan's opinion, could he not burn and subscribe? Because of the loss of *sancta*[264]. In Samuel's opinion, could he not burn and subscribe? Samuel thinks like Rebbi Jacob, as Rebbi Jacob said, the prohibition of breaking a bone applies if at the start it was qualified and then became impure.

[265]What did you see that you said so? *You shall not leave any leftovers until the morning; what is left over from it until morning you shall burn in fire*[266]. After two mornings, one the morning of the (14th) and the other the morning of the (15th)[267]. And it is written[268], *what is left of the well-being sacrifice should be burned on the third day.*

May one start fire on a pyre of leavened matter[269]? For him who infers from leftovers it is prohibited; for him who does not infer from leftovers it is permitted[270]. Rebbi Abun bar Ḥiyya said, they came to it [271] following the argument of Rebbi Ismael. (etc.) [Just as Rebbi Ismael said, a baby whose time has passed can be circumcised either during the day or during the night, so when its time has passed the *sanctum* may be burned either during the day or during the night.]

258 While it is a biblical commandment not to break a bone of the *Pesaḥ* (*Ex.* 12:46), it is generally accepted that bone material is inert like wood; cf. *Orlah* 1:4, Note 163. Therefore the prohibition can only refer to a bone with some meat on it or to the marrow inside the bone. The question may be asked only for a bone whose marrow does not add up to the volume of an olive, since otherwise the marrow, being edible, becomes leftover and has to be burned with the leftover meat.

258a Text of the Mishnah in the independent Mishnah mss. and the Babli.

259 One treats all bones as marrow bones to avoid problems in borderline cases. A different approach in Babli 84b referring to Mishnah 8.

260 Babli 84b. The prohibition of breaking a bone applies even to the leftovers with or without marrow; cf. *Mekhilta dR. Ismael Bo* 15 (pp. 53-54).

261 It is forbidden when roasting the lamb on the 14th to cut the meat from the bones and expose the bones to direct fire to cause them to break and give access to the bone marrow.

262 Babli 84b.

263 He disagrees with the previous statement that burning is like breaking. Since the *Pesaḥ* may be eaten only by the subscribers to it, if somebody subscribed to the marrow he may open the bone by holding it into the fire; even though this is frowned upon it is not forbidden.

264 Since some of the edible marrow also will be burned and become inedible.

265 This paragraph is copied from *Šabbat* 2, Notes 50-51; it starts with a question the reason of which is found only there. Here it is used to explain why the Mishnah requires the leftovers to be burned on the Sixteenth when from the verse one would have expected that it would be the 15th.

266 *Ex.* 12:9.

267 The correct version is in K and *Šabbat*, 15th and 16th.
268 *Lev.* 7:17.
269 May one dispose of one's leavened matter by making a pyre on the 14th and have it burn into the 15th which is a holiday.

270 This is the disagreement between R. Jehudah and the rabbis explained in Halakhah 2:1, Notes 66 ff. As stated in the Mishnah, leftover *sacra* may not be burned on a holiday.
271 This is from *Šabbat* 2, Notes 58-59.

(fol. 34a) משנה ח: כָּל הַנֶּאֱכָל בְּשׁוֹר הַגָּדוֹל יֵאָכֵל בִּגְדִי הָרַךְ וְרָאשֵׁי כְנָפַיִם וְהַסְחוּסִין. הַשּׁוֹבֵר אֶת הָעֶצֶם בְּפֶסַח טָהוֹר הֲרֵי זֶה לוֹקֶה אַרְבָּעִים אֲבָל הַמּוֹתִיר בַּטָּהוֹר וְהַשּׁוֹבֵר בַּטָּמֵא אֵינוֹ לוֹקֶה אֶת הָאַרְבָּעִים:

Mishnah 8: Anything eaten of a large bull shall be eaten of the soft lamb[272], including the ends of the shoulder bone and cartilage. He who breaks a bone of a pure *Pesaḥ* is whipped forty [lashes]; but he who leaves over of a pure[273] or who breaks of an impure is not whipped forty [lashes].

272 Since it is forbidden to break a bone of the *Pesaḥ* (*Ex.* 12:46), any part of the animal which cannot be eaten of an adult bull even after extended cooking is considered bone also of a lamb whose sinews are still soft. Since these may not be broken they cannot be eaten. The borderline cases are cartilage and shoulder tendons which become edible in adult cattle by extended cooking. These are considered meat and the number of subscribers to one *Pesaḥ* may be increased accordingly.
273 Even though it is prohibited to have edible leftovers of the *Pesaḥ* (*Ex.* 12:10), leaving leftovers is a transgression by inaction which cannot be prosecuted.

(35a line 62) הלכה: גִּידִים הָרַכִּים. רִבִּי יוֹחָנָן אָמַר. נִימְנִין עֲלֵיהֶן. רִבִּי שִׁמְעוֹן בֶּן לָקִישׁ אָמַר. אֵין נִימְנִין עֲלֵיהֶן. רִבִּי יַעֲקֹב בַּר אָחָא בְשֵׁם רִבִּי זְעוּרָה. מַחְלָפָה שִׁיטָתֵיהּ דְּרִבִּי יוֹחָנָן. מַחְלָפָה שִׁיטָתֵיהּ דְּרִבִּי שִׁמְעוֹן בֶּן לָקִישׁ. דְּאִיתְפַּלְגוֹן. [דְּתַנִּינַן תַּמָּן.] אֵילוּ שֶׁעוֹרוֹתֵיהֶן כִּבְשָׂרָן. עוֹר הָאָדָם וְעוֹר חֲזִיר שֶׁל יִישׁוּב. רִבִּי יוֹסֵה אוֹמֵר. אַף עוֹר שֶׁלְּחֲזִיר חַבָּר. [עוֹר חֲטָרוֹת גָּמַל הָרַכָּה. עוֹר הָרֹאשׁ שֶׁל עֵגֶל הָרַךְ. עוֹר בֵּית הַפְּרָסוֹת. עוֹר בֵּית הַבּוֹשֶׁת. וְעוֹר הַשָּׁלִיל. וְעוֹר שֶׁתַּחַת הָאַלְיָה. וְעוֹר הָאֲנָקָה וְהַכֹּחַ וְהַלְטָאָה וְהַחוֹמֶט. רִבִּי יְהוּדָה אוֹמֵר. הַלְּטָאָה כַּחוּלְדָּה. וְכוּלָן שְׁעִיבְּדָן. אוֹ שֶׁהִילֵּךְ בָּהֶן כְּדֵי עֲבוֹדָה. טְהוֹרִין. חוּץ מֵעוֹר הָאָדָם. רִבִּי יוֹחָנָן בֶּן נוּרִי אוֹמֵר. שְׁמֹנָה שְׁרָצִים יֵשׁ לָהֶן עוֹרוֹת:] אָמַר רִבִּי יוֹחָנָן. לֹא שָׁנוּ אֶלָּא לְאִיסּוּר וּלְטוּמְאָה. אֲבָל לִלְקוֹת. עוֹר הוּא. וְאֵין לוֹקִין עָלָיו מִשּׁוּם נְבֵילָה. רִבִּי שִׁמְעוֹן בֶּן לָקִישׁ אָמַר. מִשְׁנָה שְׁלֵימָה שָׁנָה רִבִּי. בֵּין לְאִיסּוּר בֵּין לִלְקוֹת בֵּין לְטוּמְאָה. מַחְלָפָה שִׁיטָתֵיהּ דְּרִבִּי שִׁמְעוֹן בֶּן לָקִישׁ. תַּמָּן הוּא עָבֵד

לֵיהּ בָּשָׂר. וְכָא לָא עָבַד לֵיהּ בָּשָׂר. אָמַר רִבִּי יוּדָה בַּר פָּזִי. שַׁנְיָיא הִיא תַמָּן שֶׁהוּא עוֹר. וְעוֹר סוֹפוֹ לְהַקְשׁוֹת. כָּל־שֶׁכֵּן מַחְלְפָה שִׁיטָתֵיהּ דְּרִבִּי שִׁמְעוֹן בֶּן לָקִישׁ. מַה אִין תַּמָּן שֶׁסּוֹפוֹ לְהַקְשׁוֹת הוּא עָבַד לֵיהּ בָּשָׂר. כָּאן שֶׁאֵין סוֹפוֹ לְהַקְשׁוֹת לֹא כָל־שֶׁכֵּן. אָמַר רִבִּי אָבוּן. טַעֲמָא דְּרִבִּי שִׁמְעוֹן בֶּן לָקִישׁ וְאָכְלוּ אֶת־הַבָּשָׂר. לֹא גִידִים

1 גידים K | 2 מחלפה K | ומחלפה K | 3 דאיתפלגון K | דאתפלגון 4 חזיר של יישוב K | החזיר שליושב C | [text in brackets] KS | - 8 אמר K | ואמ' לאיסור K | לאסור 9 משום K | משם שלימה K | תמימה K | לאיסור K | לאסור 10 הוא K | - ליה K | ליה K | לה וכא K | והכא 11 ליה K | - שנייא K | שניה 12 אין K | אן ליה K | לה 14 גידים K | גידין

Halakhah: [274]What is the rule about soft sinews? Rebbi Johanan said, one subscribes to them; Rebbi Simeon ben Laqish said, one does not subscribe to them. Rebbi Jacob bar Aha in the name of Rebbi Ze`ira: The argument of Rebbi Johanan is inverted; the argument of Rebbi Simeon ben Laqish is inverted. As they disagreed about what is stated there[275]: "The following have their hides treated like their flesh: Human skin, and the hides of domesticated pigs, Rebbi Yose says also of wild pigs. [276][The soft skin of camel's hump, the soft skin of a calf's head, the skin near the hooves, the skin of genitals, the skin of an embryo, the skin under the fat tail, and the skin of *anaqa, koah, leta'ah,* and *homet* lizards.[277] Rebbi Jehudah says, a lizard is like a mole. In all cases, if one tanned them, or started to use them as working material, they are pure, except for human skin. Rebbi Johanan ben Nuri says, the "eight crawling animals" have hides[278]."] Rebbi Johanan said, this was only said as prohibition and regarding impurity, but for flogging it is hide. Rebbi Simeon ben Laqish said, Rebbi stated a complete Mishnah, for prohibition, for flogging, for impurity. The reasoning of Rebbi Simeon ben Laqish seems inverted. There, he treats it as flesh, but here, he does not treat it as meat. Rebbi Judah bar Pazi said, there is a difference, since there one refers to skin which in the end will become hard. This emphasizes that the reasoning of Rebbi Simeon ben Laqish seems inverted! Since there, where in the end it will harden, he treats it as flesh, here where in the end it will not harden[279], not so much more? Rebbi Abun said, the reason of Rebbi Simeon ben Laqish is: *they shall eat the meat in that night*[280], not sinews.

274 This paragraph also is in *Sanhedrin* 8:2, Note 23-29.
275 Mishnah *Hulin* 9:2. Mishnah 9:1 states that in general the hide of an animal is subject to the rules of impurity of food, but not to those of impurity of carcasses. Then

Mishnah 2 lists some animals whose hides follow the rules of flesh in all respects; general consensus exists only for humans and domesticated pigs. R. Johanan holds that for eating pigskin one never can be prosecuted, while R. Simeon ben Laqish holds that eating pigskin, not yet transformed into leather, is as punishable as eating pork.

276 The text in brackets, the remainder of the Mishnah, was added by the corrector; it is neither in K nor in *Sanhedrin* and is not relevant for the discussion here.

277 The lizards in the list of "crawling animals", *Lev.* 11:29-30, whose carcasses are severely impure.

278 None of the animals mentioned in *Lev.* 11:29-30 fall under the exceptions of Mishnah 9:2.

279 Animal hide will become inedible; soft sinews and cartilage will remain edible after cooking.

280 *Ex.* 12:8.

(35b line 4) רַבָּנָן דְּקַיְסָרִין אָמְרִין. רִבִּי חִיָּיה רִבִּי אִיסִי חַד מִיחֲלַף וְחַד כְּהָדֵין תַּנְיָיא. מָאן דְּמִחֲלַף לֵית לֵיהּ כְּאִילֵּין קִישְׁוַיָּא. וְכַמָּה יְשַׁבּוֹר. רִבִּי יוֹסֵי וְרִבִּי זְעוּרָא בְּשֵׁם רִבִּי יוֹחָנָן. עַד כְּדֵי שֶׁתְּהֵא הַיָּד מְחַגֶּרֶת. רִבִּי יוֹנָה אָמַר. רִבִּי זְעוּרָא וְרִבִּי בָּא תְּרֵיהוֹן בְּשֵׁם רִבִּי יוֹחָנָן. חַד אָמַר. עַד כְּדֵי שֶׁתְּהֵא הַיָּד מְחַגֶּרֶת. וְחוֹרָנָה אָמַר. אֲפִילוּ צִפּוֹרֶן. מָאן דְּאָמַר. יָד. כָּל־שֶׁכֵּן צִפּוֹרֶן. מָאן דְּאָמַר. צִפּוֹרֶן. אֲבָל יָד לֹא. רִבִּי יוֹחָנָן וְרִבִּי שִׁמְעוֹן בֶּן לָקִישׁ תְּרֵיהוֹן אָמְרִי. לְעוֹלָם אֵינוּ חַיָּיב עַד שֶׁיִּשְׁבּוֹר עֶצֶם שֶׁיֵּשׁ עָלָיו בָּשָׂר וּמִמָּקוֹם בָּשָׂר. רִבִּי יַעֲקֹב בַּר אָחָא אָמַר. שְׁמוּאֵל בַּר אַבָּא בָּעֵי. מֵיתָה. לְעוֹלָם אֵינוּ חַיָּיב עַד שְׁיִּטּוֹל אֶבֶן וִירַסֵּס. עֶצֶם. לְחַיֵּיב עַל כָּל־עֶצֶם וָעֶצֶם. הֲדָא דְתֵימַר. בְּהַתְרָיָיה אַחַת. אֲבָל בִּשְׁתֵּי הַתְרָיוֹת. שֶׁכֵּן אֲפִילוּ עֶצֶם אֶחָד וְשִׁבְרוֹ וְחָזַר וְשִׁבְרוֹ חַיָּיב שְׁתַּיִם. רִבִּי יִרְמְיָה בָּעֵי. לֵית הָדָא פְלִיגָא עַל רִבִּי שִׁמְעוֹן בֶּן לָקִישׁ. דְּרִבִּי שִׁמְעוֹן בֶּן לָקִישׁ אָמַר. עֶצֶם שֶׁאֵין עָלָיו בָּשָׂר מוּתָּר לְשׁוֹבְרוֹ. לֹא אָמַר אֶלָּא שֶׁלֹּא יְלָקֶה. הָא לֶאֱסוֹר אָסוּר.

1 איסי K | יבי מיחלף K | מחלף תנייא K | תנייה מאן K | מן K. End of K.

The rabbis of Caesarea are saying, Rebbi Ḥiyya and Rebbi Issy[281], one switches and one follows as it was stated[282]. The one who switches does not have these problems[283].

And how much does he have to break[284]? Rebbi Yose and Rebbi Ze'ira in the name of Rebbi Joḥanan: until the hand be grated[285]. Rebbi Jonah said, Rebbi Ze'ira and Rebbi Abba both in the name of Rebbi Joḥanan. One said, until the hand be grated; but the other said, even a finger nail[286]. He who said the hand, so much more the finger nail. He who said the finger nail, but not the hand.

Rebbi Joḥanan and Rebbi Simeon ben Laqish both are saying, one never is liable unless one break a bone on which there is meat in the size of an olive, at one place of meat[287]. Rebbi Jacob bar Aḥa said, Samuel bar Abba asked, then he never should be liable unless he take a stone and smash it into little pieces[288]. *A bone*, to make him liable for each single bone[289]. This is, with one warning[290]. But with two warnings, then he will be twice liable even for a single bone which he broke repeatedly. Rebbi Jeremiah asked, does this not disagree with Rebbi Simeon ben Laqish? Since Rebbi Simeon ben Laqish said, one is permitted to break a bone without meat. He said this only that he cannot be whipped, but as a prohibition, it is prohibited[291].

281 Since Issy also is a nickname for Josef, probably one should read "Yasa". K reads "Yasi" R. Hiyya here is R. Hiyya bar Abba.

282 The disagreement of R. Johanan and R. Simeon ben Laqish.

283 If the names are switched in the statement, the arguments of each one of the parties are consistent.

284 How much of the bone has to be broken to constitute a prosecutable offense. In the following, "liable" means liable to possible criminal prosecution and punishment by whipping.

285 If passing with the back of the hand over the bone, the skin is grated.

286 One notices a dent in the surface of the bone if moving a finger nail along its surface.

287 Babli 84b.

288 Since if one starts to break a bone with meat on it, the meat will be loosened in the process and then there no longer will be an olive sized piece firmly attached to the bone unless the breaking is done with one stroke or by smashing with a stone.

289 The singular used in *Ex.* 12:46 implies that breaking multiple bones is counted as multiple offenses.

290 Since there can be no criminal prosecution unless the perpetrator was duly warned that his intended behavior was criminal, no prosecution can exceed the scope of the warning (cf. *Introduction to Tractate Sanhedrin*, on Chapter Five). Unless the warning was extended to cover both breaking multiple bones and multiple breaking of one bone, only one prosecution is possible.

291 Breaking any bone of the *Pesah* always is sinful, even if not prosecutable.

(35b line 17)   אֲבָל הַמוֹתִיר[בַּטָהוֹר] וְהַשׁוֹבֵר בַּטָמֵא אֵינוֹ לוֹקֶה אַרְבָּעִים: רִבִּי אָבוּן בְּשֵׁם רִבִּי אֶלְעָזָר. מַתְנִיתָא כְּשֶׁבָּא בְטוּמְאָה מִשָּׁעָה רִאשׁוֹנָה. אֲבָל אִם בָּא בְטַהֲרָה וְנִטְמָא כְּבָא בְטַהֲרָה וְלוֹקִין עַל שְׁבִירָתוֹ.

"But he who leaves over of a pure {*Pesah*} or who breaks of an impure is not whipped forty {ashes}." Rebbi Abun in the name of Rebbi Eleazar: The Mishnah if it came in impurity from the start. But if it came in purity[292] and became impure it is as if coming in purity and one is whipped for its breaking[293].

292 If the blood was poured in purity.
293 This is in line with his earlier statement,

Note 260. In the Babli 84a-b this is a matter of disagreement of Tannaim.

(fol. 34a) **משנה ט**: אֵבֶר שֶׁיָּצָא מִקְצָתוֹ חוֹתֵךְ עַד שֶׁמַּגִּיעַ לָעֶצֶם וְקוֹלֵף עַד שֶׁמַּגִּיעַ לַפֶּרֶק וְחוֹתֵךְ וּבַמּוּקְדָּשִׁין קוֹצֵץ בַּקּוֹפִיץ שֶׁאֵין בּוֹ מִשּׁוּם שְׁבִירַת הָעֶצֶם.

Mishnah 9: A limb which partially was taken out[294] one cuts until he reaches the bone, and pares until he reaches the joint, where he cuts[295]; but for sacrifices[296] he cuts with a dagger since there breaking bones is not forbidden..

משנה י: מִן הָאֲגַף וְלִפְנִים כְּלִפְנִים מִן הָאֲגַף וְלַחוּץ כְּלַחוּץ. הַחַלּוֹנוֹת וְעוֹבִי הַחוֹמָה כְּלִפְנִים:

Mishnah 10: From the wing and inside it is like inside; from the wing and outside it is like outside[297]. Windows and the thickness of the wall are like inside[298].

294 If part of a limb was taken out of Jerusalem and therefore became impure, or in the night of the 15th of Nisan was taken out of the house where it was eaten and therefore became forbidden as food (*Ex.* 12:46).
295 At the joint he cuts the sinews, not the bone, to remove the bone. The meat pared from the bone remains edible.
296 All other sacrifices.
297 The wing is the place of the hinges and the door bay.
298 Windows are slits in the wall without glass. Since there was nothing to close off parts of the wall from the interior, the entire thickness of the wall is counted as interior.

(35b line 20) **הלכה**: מָתִיב רִבִּי יוֹחָנָן לְרִבִּי שִׁמְעוֹן בֶּן לָקִישׁ. וְהָא תַנִּינָן. הָעֲצָמוֹת וְהַגִּידִים וְהַנּוֹתָר יִשָּׂרְפוּ בְשִׁשָּׁה עָשָׂר. וְיִקּוֹץ. מִפְּנֵי מוֹחַ. וְיַחֲלוֹץ בָּשָׂר מִן הָעֶצֶם. וְיִקּוֹץ. שֶׁלֹּא לְפַקֵּעַ תַּחַת הַבָּשָׂר.

Halakhah: Rebbi Johanan objected to Rebbi Simeon ben Laqish: Did we not state, "the bones, the sinews, and leftovers are to be burned on the Sixteenth"? Could he not chop? Because of the marrow[259]. Could one not strip off all meat from the bone and cut? Not to break under the flesh[299].

299 Except for the last sentence this is copied from earlier, Halakhah 9. Here it is R. Johanan's objection to R. Simeon ben Laqish who declares breaking a bone without flesh not prosecutable. Then why does the Mishnah require that one take out the entire bone after stripping off the meat; could one not strip off the meat and then

290 PESAHIM CHAPTER SEVEN

break the bone, without cutting the sinews at the next joint? The answer is that in theory one could do this but in practice one could never be sure whether all meat was safely stripped off; for R. Simeon ben Laqish Mishnah 9 is rabbinical prescription. (Babli 85a, opinion of Abbai.)

(35b line 23) רִבִּי סִימוֹן רִבִּי יְהוֹשֻׁעַ בֶּן לֵוִי בְשֵׁם בֶּן פְּדָיָיה. הַפִּיגּוּל וְהַנּוֹתָר מִצְטָרְפִין לְטַמֵּא אֶת הַיָּדַיִם עַד כְּדֵי עוֹנְשָׁן בַּכְּזַיִת. מַהוּ שֶׁיִּפְסְלוּ בִתְרוּמָה. קַל וָחוֹמֶר. אִם מְטַמְּאִין אֶת הַיָּדַיִם לִפְסוֹל בַּתְרוּמָה. הֵן עַצְמָן לֹא כָל־שֶׁכֵּן. הָהֵן יוֹצֵא מָה אַתְּ עָבַד לֵיהּ. מְטַמֵּא אֶת הַיָּדַיִם אוֹ אֵינוֹ מְטַמֵּא אֶת הַיָּדַיִם. אִין תֵּימַר. הָהֵן יוֹצֵא מְטַמֵּא אֶת הַיָּדַיִם. פִּיגּוּל וְנוֹתָר אֵינָן פּוֹסְלִין בַּתְרוּמָה. אִין תֵּימַר. פִּיגּוּל וְנוֹתָר אֵינָן פּוֹסְלִין בַּתְרוּמָה. הָהֵן יוֹצֵא לֹא גָזְרוּ עָלָיו כְּלוּם. דְּלֹא כֵן יְטַמֵּא צַד הַחִיצוֹן וְצַד הַפְּנִימִי. אֲמַר רִבִּי אַבִּין. מָאן אִית לֵיהּ דָּבָר טָמֵא מַחֲמַת עַצְמוֹ. לֹא רִבִּי מֵאִיר. לֹא כֵן אֲמַר רִבִּי יוֹחָנָן. כָּל־הַדְּבָרִים טְהוֹרִין בְּרוּבָּן. כֵּיוָן שֶׁחֲתָכוֹ רוּבָּן לָאו כְּפָרוּשׁ הוּא. וִיהֵא כְמַגִּיעֵי בוֹ וִיהֵא פָסוּל. אֲמַר רִבִּי חֲנַנְיָה. בִּמְחַתֵּךְ כָּל־שֶׁהוּא וּמַשְׁלִיךְ.

1 בשם בר פדייה | 10 - 2 עד - 10 | שיפסלו | 10 שיפסול 3 בתרומה | 10 את התרומה 4 פיגול ונותר | 10 הפיגול והנותר 5 אין תימר פיגול ונותר אינו פוסלין בתרטומה | 10 - ההן | 10 וההן דלא | 10 דל 6 מחמת | 10 מחמת מגע 7 טהורין | 10 טהורים ויהא | 10 ויעשה 7 כמגיעי | 10 במגיע כל שהוא | 10 כל שהוא כל שהוא

[300]Rebbi Simon, Rebbi Joshua ben Levi in the name of Bar Pedaya: *Piggul*[301] and leftovers add together to make hands impure[302] in the amount that exposes to punishment, the volume of an olive. Do they disqualify heave? It is a argument *de minore ad majus*. If they make hands impure to disqualify heave, they themselves not so much more? This which left[294] what are you doing with it? Does it make hands impure or does it not make hands impure? If you are saying that this which left makes hands impure, would *piggul* and leftovers not disqualify heave[303]? If you are saying that *piggul* and leftovers do not disqualify heave, about that which left they did not decide anything[304]. For if it were not so, the outer part would make the inner part impure[305]. Rebbi Abbin said, who holds that something can become impure by [touching][306] itself? Rebbi Meïr[307]. Did not Rebbi Johanan say, everything becomes pure by its greater part? When he cut off the greater part, is it not separated[308]? Then it would be touching and be disqualified. Rebbi Hananiah said, if he cuts off minimal pieces and throws away[309].

300 This paragraph is copied in the last Halakhah of Chapter 10 (10).
301 Cf. Chapter 5, Note 67.

302 The impurity of hands as separate from impurity of the body is not pentateuchal. By tradition, it is an institution of First Temple

times.

303 Since they make hands impure and the touch of impure hands disqualifies heave, it is obvious that the touch of *piggul* and leftovers must disqualify heave. Cf. *Me`ilah* 17b.

304 In contrast to *piggul* and leftovers, use of *sancta* which were taken out of their required places are not infractions punishable by extirpation.

305 The outer part of the bone, which became impure, touching the inner part would make the inner part and with it the entire *Pesah* impure and disqualified.

306 Added from 10, needed for clarity.

307 The previous argument has to be qualified. Everybody agrees that touching at interior parts (מַגַּע בֵּית הַסְּתָרִים "touch of secret places") does not transmit impurity (*Sifra Mesora` Pereq* 6(10), quoted Babli *Niddah* 44b). Rebbi Meïr excludes from this rule the case that an object be partially impure and partially pure; then the inner contact of both parts makes everything impure. Therefore the preceding argument is valid only for R. Meïr, who is not followed in practice.

308 If the pure part is larger than the impure, the object is pure. There is no problem for the *Pesah* since the bone cannot be cut, the impurity is not transmitted since the touch is interior, and the entire bone is removed. But for other *sancta*, the moment the bone is cut, the touch is external and transmits impurity, which disqualifies the entire sacrifice. How can the Mishnah permit cutting the bone in this case?

309 The bone cannot be cut but must be shaved off in pieces smaller than the size of an olive which then are discarded immediately. Quoted in *Tosaphot* 85a, *s.v.* ולרבינא.

(35b line 33) רִבִּי בָּא בְשֵׁם רַב יְהוּדָה. לֹא קִידְּשׁוּ תַּחַת הָאֵגוּף שֶׁבִּירוּשָׁלֵם. רִבִּי יִרְמְיָה בְשֵׁם רַב שְׁמוּאֵל בַּר רַב יִצְחָק. כְּדֵי שֶׁיִּהוּ מְצוֹרָעִין מָגִינִין תַּחְתֵּיהֶן בַּחַמָּה מִפְּנֵי הַחַמָּה וּבַגְּשָׁמִים מִפְּנֵי הַגְּשָׁמִים. וְדִכְוָותָהּ. לֹא קִידְּשׁוּ תַּחַת הָאֵגוּף שֶׁלְּהַר הַבַּיִת. כְּדֵי שֶׁיִּהוּ זָבִין מָגִינִין תַּחְתֵּיהֶן בַּחַמָּה מִפְּנֵי הַחַמָּה וּבַגְּשָׁמִים מִפְּנֵי הַגְּשָׁמִים. מְצוֹרָע אֵין לוֹ אֵיכָן לְהָגֵן. זָב יֵשׁ לוֹ אֵיכָן לְהָגֵן בְּכָל־יְרוּשָׁלֵם. רִבִּי יוֹחָנָן בַּר מַרְיָיא בְשֵׁם רִבִּי פִינְחָס. מִן מַה דַאֲנַן חֲמֵי רַבָּנָן שְׁלְחִין סַנְדְּלֵיהוֹן תַּחַת הָאֵגוּף שֶׁלְּהַר הַבַּיִת הָדָא אָמְרָה שֶׁלֹּא קִידְּשׁוּ תַּחַת הָאֵגוּף שֶׁלְּהַר הַבַּיִת. רַב שָׁאַל לְרִבִּי חִייָה רְבָּה. גַּגּוֹת יְרוּשָׁלֵם מָה הֵן. אָמַר לֵיהּ. מִן מַה דְּמַתְלִין מַתְלָא. פִּיסְחָא בְזֵיתָא וְהַלֵּילָה מִתְבַּר אַגְרִיָּיא. הָדָא אָמְרָה. גַּגּוֹת יְרוּשָׁלֵם קוֹדֶשׁ. רִבִּי יִרְמְיָה רִבִּי מַייָשָׁא רִבִּי שְׁמוּאֵל בַּר רַב יִצְחָק בְּשֵׁם רַב. גַּגּוֹת יְרוּשָׁלֵם חוֹל. וְהָא תַנִּינָן. מִן הָאֵגוּף וְלִפְנִים כְּלִפְנִים. מִן הָאֵגוּף וְלַחוּץ כְּלַחוּץ. פָּתַר לָהּ בְּגַג מְבוּצָר לַאֲוִיר חָצֵר הִיא מַתְנִיתָהּ. הַחַלוֹנוֹת וְעוֹבֵי הַחוֹמָה כְּלִפְנִים: עוֹד הִיא בְגַג מְבוּצָר לַאֲוִיר חָצֵר הִיא מַתְנִיתָהּ. וְאַתְיָיא כְהָהִיא דְּאָמַר רִבִּי אָחָא בְשֵׁם רִבִּי חִינָּנָא. וַיַּאֲבָל־חֵיל וְחוֹמָה. שׁוּרָא וּבַר שׁוּרָה. אִם עוֹבֵי הַחוֹמָה קִידְּשׁוּ כָּל־שֶׁכֵּן חָלוֹן. אָמַר רִבִּי אָחָא. בְּחַלּוֹן שֶׁעַל גַּבֵּי הָאֵגוּף נִצְרְכָה. אַף עַל גַּב דְּתֵימַר. לֹא קִידְּשׁוּ תַּחַת הָאֵגוּף שֶׁלִּירוּשָׁלֵם. חָלוֹן שֶׁעַל גַּבֵּי הָאֵגוּף קִידְּשׁוּ.

תַּנֵּי בְשֵׁם רִבִּי יְהוּדָה. מְחִילוֹת שֶׁתַּחַת הַהֵיכָל חוֹל וְנִגּוֹת הַהֵיכָל קוֹדֶשׁ. רִבִּי אִמִּי בְשֵׁם רִבִּי שִׁמְעוֹן בֶּן לָקִישׁ. מַתְנִיתָהּ אֲמָרָהּ כֵּן. מְדוּרָה הָיְתָה שָׁם וּבֵית כִּסֵּא שֶׁלְּכָבוֹד. וְזֶה הָיָה כְבוֹדוֹ [מְצָאוֹ נָעוּל. יוֹדֵעַ שֶׁיֵּשׁ שָׁם אָדָם. פָּתוּחַ. יוֹדֵעַ שֶׁאֵין שָׁם אָדָם.] אָמַר רִבִּי יוֹסֵה. וְכִי צוֹאָה טוּמְאָה. וַהֲלֹא אֵינָהּ אֶלָּא נְקִיּוּת. וַיי דָא אֲמָרָה דָא. יוֹצֵא וְהוֹלֵךְ לוֹ בִּמְסִבָּה הַהוֹלֶכֶת תַּחַת הַבִּירָה. וְנֵירוֹת דּוֹלְקִין מִיכָּן וּמִיכָּן. עַד שֶׁהוּא מַגִּיעַ לְבֵית הַטְּבִילָה. אִם קָדוֹשׁ הוּא יֵלֵךְ לוֹ בְקִצְרָה.

Rebbi Abba in the name of Rav Jehudah: They did not sanctify under the wing in Jerusalem[310]. Rebbi Jeremiah in the name of Rav Samuel bar Rav Isaac: That the sufferers from skin disease[311] might find shelter in summer from the sun and in the rainy season from rain. Did they similarly not sanctify under the wing of the Temple Mount, that sufferers from gonorrhea and flux[311] might find shelter in summer from the sun and in the rainy season from rain? The sufferer from skin disease has no place to find shelter; the sufferer from gonorrhea finds shelter in all of Jerusalem. Rebbi Johanan bar Marius in the name of Rebbi Phineas: Since we see that the rabbis take off their sandals under the wing of the Temple Mount[312], this implies that they did not sanctify under the wing of the Temple Mount. Rav asked the Elder Rebbi Hiyya: What is the status of roofs in Jerusalem? He told him, since one uses as proverb: the *Pesah* in an olive-sized bit and *Hallel* breaks the roof,[313] this implies that the roofs of Jerusalem are sanctified. Rebbi Jeremiah, Rebbi Miasha, Rebbi Samuel bar Rav Isaac in the name of Rav: The roofs of Jerusalem are profane. But did we not state, "From the wing and inside it is like inside; from the wing and outside it is like outside[314]"? Explain it that the Mishnah speaks about a roof surrounded by buildings forming a courtyard[315]. But did we not state, "windows and the thickness of the wall are like inside[316]"? Explain it again that the Mishnah speaks about a roof surrounded by buildings forming a courtyard. This parallels what Rebbi Aha said in the name of Rebbi Hinena: *glacis and wall mourned*[317], the wall and the ante-wall. If they sanctified the thickness of the wall, not so much more the window? Rebbi Aha said, it is necessary for the window on top of the wing. Even though you are saying that they did not sanctify under the wing of Jerusalem, they sanctified the window over the wing.

It was stated in the name of Rebbi Jehudah: the tunnels under the Temple were profane, the Temple roofs were sanctified[318]. Rebbi Immi in the name of Rebbi Simeon ben Laqish: A Mishnah[319] says so, "there was a fireplace there, and an honorable bathroom. [What was its honor? If one found it locked, one knew that it was occupied, unlocked one knew that it was unoccupied."] Rebbi Yose said, is excrement impure? Is it not simply cleanliness? But the following is it, "he[320] leaves and goes in the walkway under the Temple, and lights were burning on both sides, until he comes to the place of immersion." If it were sanctified he would have to go by the shortest way[321].

310 The gates of the walls of Jerusalem were sanctified, to be used as place for the consumption of *sancta*, only within the closed doors.

311 While the verse *Num.* 5:2 says, *they shall exile from the camp any sufferer from skin disease, any sufferer from gonorrhea, and any one defiled by a corpse*, the rabbinic interpretation is that the sufferers from skin disease have to be exiled from any walled city, the sufferer from gonorrhea only from the Temple Mount, and the person impure by the impurity of corpses only from the Temple district proper. Babli 67a, *Sifry Num.* 1.

312 Since it is forbidden to walk with shoes on the Temple Mount proper; Mishnah *Berakhot* 9:8.

313 So many people have subscribed to one *Pesaḥ* that each only got one olive-sized piece, and the noise of the *Hallel* which they were singing while eating on the roof damaged the roof. This proves that the *Pesaḥ* was eaten on the roof, and therefore the roofs of the houses of Jerusalem were sanctified.

314 Since the roofs are of houses inside the walls, the blanket statement that all inside is sanctified also includes the roofs.

315 Roofs on street level of houses dug out from the earth, not built on it.

316 The "thickness of the wall" cannot refer to the material since this is inaccessible; it cannot refer to the windows which are mentioned separately. Therefore it must refer to the roofs.

317 *Thr.* 2:8. Babli 86a.

318 Babli 86a.

319 Mishnah *Tamid* 1:1.

320 A priest watching in the Temple who becomes impure has to leave immediately by the shortest way.

(fol. 34a) **משנה יא:** שְׁתֵּי חֲבוּרוֹת שֶׁהָיוּ אוֹכְלוֹת בְּבַיִת אֶחָד אֵילוּ הוֹפְכִין אֶת פְּנֵיהֶם הֵילָךְ וְאוֹכְלִין וְאֵילוּ הוֹפְכִין אֶת פְּנֵיהֶם הֵילָךְ וְאוֹכְלִין וְהַמֵּחַם בָּאֶמְצַע. וּכְשֶׁהַשַּׁמָּשׁ עוֹמֵד לִמְזוֹג

קוֹפֵץ אֶת פִּיו וּמַחֲזִיר אֶת פָּנָיו עַד שֶׁמַּגִּיעַ אֵצֶל חֲבוּרָתוֹ וְאוֹכֵל. וְהַכַּלָּה הוֹפֶכֶת אֶת פָּנֶיהָ וְאוֹכֶלֶת׃

Mishnah 11: Two groups which were eating in the same room, these are turning their faces in one direction while eating, and those are turning their faces in one direction while eating[321], and the samovar[322] is in the middle. When the waiter stands to mix, he closes his mouth and turns his head[323] unless he is near his own group and eats. But the newly-wed[324] may turn aside her face and eat.

321 Either (Babli) two different groups have subscribed to different parts of one and the same *Pesah* or (*Mekhilta dR. Ismael*) eating different *Pesahim*. Both cases are possible for the Yerushalmi. They may use the same room only if they are sitting back to back.

322 Producing hot water to mix the wine for the required Four Cups in the standard ratio of one part wine to two parts water.

323 So people will not suspect him to eat with a group to whose part of the *Pesah* he did not subscribe.

324 Who is not yet used to be in company; she may turn her face away from the company and will not be suspected of not eating with her own group.

(35b line 58) **הלכה**: כָּתוּב וְלֹא תוֹצִיא מִן־הַבַּיִת מִן־הַבָּשָׂר חוּצָה. אֵין לִי אֶלָּא חוּץ לַבָּיִת. חוּץ לַחֲבוּרָה מְנַיִין. תַּלְמוּד לוֹמַר לֹא תוֹצִיא חוּצָה. אָמַר רִבִּי יוּדָן. מִיכָּן שֶׁאִם (אָמַר הֲרֵינִי) [הוֹצִיא] חוּץ לַחֲבוּרָה. שֶׁהוּא מִתְחַיֵּיב. אָמַר רִבִּי מָנָא. יֹאמַר קִרְיָיא. לֹא תוֹצִיא חוּצָה. וְנָן אָמְרִין. אִם חוּץ לַחֲבוּרָה שֶׁהוּא מִתְחַיֵּיב. לֹא כָל־שֶׁכֵּן חוּץ לַבָּיִת.

רִבִּי אִימִי בָּעֵי. הוֹצִיא מֵחֲבוּרָה לַחֲבוּרָה כְּשָׁנֵי זֵיתִים חַיָּיב שְׁתַּיִם. מִשּׁוּם לֹא־תוֹצִיא מִן־הַבַּיִת וּמִשּׁוּם לֹא תוֹצִיא חוּצָה. הוֹצִיא אֶחָד כְּזַיִת חַיָּיב. שְׁנַיִם שְׁלֹשָׁה פְּטוּרִין. מִפְּנֵי שֶׁבְּנֵי חֲבוּרָתָן רְאוּיִין לְהִימָּשֵׁךְ אֶצְלָן. אֶלָּא שֶׁהֵן עוֹבְרִין בַּעֲשֵׂה. וּכְרִבִּי שִׁמְעוֹן אֲפִילוּ בַעֲשֵׂה אֵינָן עוֹבְרִין. דְּתַנֵּי. עַל הַבָּתִּים אֲשֶׁר־יֹאכְלוּ אוֹתוֹ בָּהֶם. מְלַמֵּד שֶׁהַפֶּסַח נֶאֱכָל בִּשְׁנֵי מְקוֹמוֹת. יָכוֹל אַף אוֹכְלָיו יְהוּ אוֹכְלִין אוֹתוֹ בִּשְׁנֵי מְקוֹמוֹת. תַּלְמוּד לוֹמַר בְּבַיִת אֶחָד יֵאָכֵל. הָא כֵּיצַד. פֶּסַח נֶאֱכָל בִּשְׁנֵי מְקוֹמוֹת. וְאֵין אוֹכְלָיו אוֹכְלִין אוֹתוֹ בִּשְׁנֵי מְקוֹמוֹת. [וְרִבִּי שִׁמְעוֹן אוֹמֵר. אַף אוֹכְלָיו אוֹכְלִין אוֹתוֹ בִּשְׁנֵי מְקוֹמוֹת.] מַה מְקַיֵּים רִבִּי שִׁמְעוֹן בְּבַיִת אֶחָד יֵאָכֵל. שֶׁלֹּא תְהֵא חֲבוּרָה מִקְצָתָהּ אוֹכֶלֶת בִּפְנִים וּמִקְצָתָהּ אוֹכֶלֶת בַּחוּץ. יָחִיד שֶׁהוֹצִיא כְזַיִת חוּץ לַחֲבוּרָה. מִפְּנֵי שֶׁבְּנֵי חֲבוּרָתוֹ רְאוּיִים לִימָּשֵׁךְ אֶצְלוֹ. נִפְטַר מִלֹּא תַעֲשֶׂה. רִבִּי חִייָה בַּר בָּא בָּעֵי. לָמָּה לִי כְּרִבִּי שִׁמְעוֹן. אֲפִילוּ כְרַנָּנְן. מִפְּנֵי שֶׁבְּנֵי חֲבוּרָתָן רְאוּיִין לִימָּשֵׁךְ אֶצְלָן נִפְטְרוּ מִלֹּא תַעֲשֶׂה. אֲפִילוּ בַעֲשֵׂה לֹא יְהוּ.

שַׁמָּשׁ שֶׁאָכַל כְּזַיִת וְהוּא בְּצַד הַתַּנּוּר. אִם הָיָה פִּיקֵחַ מְמַלֵּא אֶת כְּרֵיסוֹ מִמֶּנּוּ. אִם רָצוּ לַחֲלוֹק לוֹ כָּבוֹד. בָּאִין וְאוֹכְלִין עִמּוֹ בְּצַד הַתַּנּוּר. וְאִם לָאו. נוֹתְנִין לוֹ חֶלְקוֹ וְאוֹכֵל בִּמְקוֹמוֹ.

תַּמָּן אָמְרִין. דְּרִבִּי שִׁמְעוֹן הִיא. וְלָא שָׁמְעִין דַּאֲמַר רִבִּי הִילָא רִבִּי אִיסֵי רִבִּי אֶלְעָזָר בְּשֵׁם רִבִּי הוֹשַׁעְיָה. הַכֹּל מוֹדִין בַּתְּחִילָה שֶׁיֵּין חוֹלְקִין. בַּסּוֹף שֶׁאֵינָן חוֹלְקִין. מַה פְלִיגִין. בְּשֶׁהָיוּ יוֹשְׁבִין וּפְקָעָה עֲלֵיהֶן הַקּוֹרָה. רִבִּי שִׁמְעוֹן אוֹמֵר. עוֹקְרִין הֵן חֶלְקָן וְאוֹכְלִין בְּמָקוֹם אַחֵר. וְרַבָּנִין אָמְרִין. אֵיהָן עוֹקְרִין אֶת חֶלְקָן וְאוֹכְלִין בְּמָקוֹם אַחֵר.

Halakhah: "It is written, *do not remove any meat from the house to the outside*[325]. I have not only outside the house, from where outside the group? The verse says, *do not remove to the outside.*"[326] Rebbi Yudan said, from here that he makes himself liable if he (said I am) [removed] away from the group[327]. Rebbi Mana said, the verse should have said, *do not remove to the outside*, and we would have said, if he makes himself liable outside the group, not so much more outside the house[328]?

Rebbi Immi asked, if he removed from group to group (the volume of two olives)[329] he is twice liable, because of *do not remove from the house* and *do not remove to the outside*. If they subscribed to a *Pesaḥ*, and an individual removed the volume of an olive, he is liable. Two or three persons are not liable since the members of the group may be drawn after them; but they infringe on a positive commandment[330]; and following Rebbi Simeon they do not infringe. As it was stated, *over the houses in which they are eating it there*[331], this teaches that the *Pesaḥ* may be eaten in two places[332]. I could think that its eaters also could eat it in two places, the verse says, *in one house it shall be eaten*. How is that? A *Pesaḥ* may be eaten in two places, but its eaters may not eat it in two places. [Rebbi Simeon says, also its eaters could eat it in two places.] How does Rebbi Simeon uphold *in one house it shall be eaten*? Lest part of one group eat inside and another part outside. An individual who removed the volume of an olive, since the members of the group may be drawn after him, becomes absolved from the positive commandment. Rebbi Ḥiyya bar Abba asked, why following Rebbi Simeon? Even following the rabbis, since the members of the group may be drawn after him, they are absolved from the prohibition; neither should they be under the positive commandment[333].

The waiter who ate the volume of an olive when he was near the oven,[334] if he is intelligent he fills his belly from it. If they want to honor him, they come and eat with him near the oven; otherwise they give him his part and he eats at his place. There[335], they are saying, this is Rebbi Simeon's, since they did not hear what Rebbi Hila, Rebbi Issy[281], Rebbi Eleazar said in the name of Rebbi Hoshaia: Everybody agrees that at the start they may split, at the end they may not split[336]. Where do they disagree? When they were sitting and a beam cracked over them. Rebbi Simeon says, part of them remove themselves and eat at another place, but the rabbis say, no part of them may remove themselves and eat at another place[338].

325 *Ex.* 12:46.
326 Babli 86a, Tosephta 6:11, *Mekhilta dR. Ismael Bo* 15 (p. 55), *dR. Simeon bar Yohai* p. 36, *Tanhuma Bo* 10, also cf. the *Targumim*.
327 The text in parentheses is the scribe's, the one in brackets the corrector's. Since in the corrector's text R. Yudan adds nothing to the *baraita*, the scribe's text must be the correct one. If a person (after the pouring of the blood) declares himself not to be part of his group, he commits a sin.
328 The mention of the house seems to be superfluous. *Mekhilta dR. Ismael* disagrees; the meat becomes disqualified and impure only by being removed to the outside.
329 It seems that instead of כִּשְׁנֵי זֵיתִים one should read בִּשְׁנֵי בָתִּים "in two houses".

Since "house" usually means a one-room dwelling, "house" also may mean "room" in a big house.
330 Beginning of v. 12:46: *In one house it shall be eaten.*
331 *Ex.* 12:7.
332 In the same room, as described in the Mishnah. Babli 86a/b.
333 Since the question is not answered it seems to be accepted. The positive commandment referred to is not in Maimonides's list of commandments.
334 In which the one *Pesah* is roasted.
335 In the same house.
336 Once they start eating.
337 They have to move; the question is whether they have to move as a group or as individuals. Babli 86a.

(35c line 8) רִבִּי חִיָּיא בַּר בָּא אָמַר רִבִּי יוֹסֵי בֶּן חֲנִינָה בָעֵי. מֵעַתָּה הַמּוֹצִיא אֵינוֹ חַיָּיב עַד שָׁעָה שֶׁיֹּאכַל. אֲתָא רִבִּי שְׁמוּאֵל רִבִּי אַבָּהוּ בְשֵׁם רִבִּי יוֹחָנָן. הַמּוֹצִיא אֵינוֹ חַיָּיב עַד שָׁעָה שֶׁיֹּאכַל. אָמַר רִבִּי זְעוּרָא. וְתַנֵּי תַמָּן. יָחִיד שֶׁהוֹצִיא כְזַיִת חוּץ לַחֲבוּרָה חַיָּיב. וְלֹא פָסַל עַצְמוֹ מִפְּנֵי חֲבוּרָתוֹ. הָדָא אָמְרָה. אֲפִילוּ לֹא אָכַל. אֲבָל. אִין תֵּימַר. לָמָּה לִי לֹא פָסַל עַצְמוֹ מִבְּנֵי חֲבוּרָתוֹ. אָמַר רִבִּי יוֹסֵה. כֵּיוָן שֶׁהוֹצִיאוֹ פְּסָלוֹ. אֲפִילוּ אָכַל. דָּבָר פָּסוּל אָכַל. וַיֵּי דָא אָמַר דָא. יֵשׁ שׁוֹבֵר אַחַר שׁוֹבֵר. אֵין מוֹצִיא אַחַר מוֹצִיא. אוֹ הָדָא אָמְרָה כֵּיוָן שֶׁהוֹצִיאוֹ פְּסָלוֹ. אוֹ הָדָא אָמְרָה. הַמּוֹצִיא אֵינוֹ חַיָּיב עַד שָׁעָה שֶׁיֹּאכַל.

פְּשִׁיטָא דָא מִילְתָא. הִתְחִילוּ אִילוּ וְנִטְמְאוּ אִילוּ. זָכוּ טְהוֹרִין בְּחֶלְקָן שֶׁלַּטְּמֵאִין. וְלֹא עוֹד אֶלָּא אֲפִילוּ הִתְחִילוּ אִילוּ וְנִיטְמוּ הֵן. זָכוּ טְהוֹרִין בְּחֶלְקָן שֶׁלַּטְּמֵאִין. אֲבָל הִתְחִילוּ אִילוּ וְאִילוּ וְנִיטְמָא אֶחָד מֵהֶן. לֹא זָכוּ טְהוֹרִין בְּחֶלְקָן שֶׁלַּטְּמֵאִין.

יָחִיד מַפְשִׁיט יָדוֹ בְּכָל־הַבַּיִת. וְאֵין חֲבוּרָה מֵפְשֶׁטֶת יָדָהּ בְּכָל־הַבַּיִת. וְהָא תַנִּינָן. שְׁתֵּי חֲבוּרוֹת. לֹא אָמַר אֶלָּא שְׁתַּיִם. הָא אַחַת לֹא. וְהָא תַנִּינָן. הַמֵּחַם בָּאֶמְצַע. מְקוֹם שֶׁהַשַּׁמָּשׁ מוֹכִיחַ עָלָיו שָׁם הִיא חֲבוּרָתוֹ. וְהָא תַנִּינָן. הַכַּלָּה הוֹפֶכֶת פָּנֶיהָ וְאוֹכֶלֶת: אָמַר רִבִּי חִייָה בַּר בָּא מִפְּנֵי הַבּוּשָׁה.

Rebbi Hiyya bar Abba said, Rebbi Yose ben Ḥanina asked: Then[338] one who removes should not be liable up to the moment when he eats. Rebbi Samuel, Rebbi Abbahu in the name of Rebbi Joḥanan: One who removes is not liable up to the moment when he eats. Rebbi Zeʼira said, but it was stated there, an individual who removed the volume of an olive from a group is liable but he did not disqualify himself as a member[339] of the group. This implies, even if he did not eat. If you would say, he ate, why did he not disqualify himself as a member of the group? Rebbi Yose said, when he removed it he disqualified it. Even if he ate, he ate something disqualified. Where was this said? There is breaking after breaking but not removing after removing[340]. Either this means that when he removes it, he disqualifies it, or it means that he is not liable up to the moment when he eats[341].

The following is obvious: If one group started eating when the other became impure, the pure group acquired the part of the impure[342]. Not only this but even if one group started eating and they became impure, the pure group acquired the part of the impure. But if both had started eating when one of them became impure, the pure group did not acquire the part of the impure[343].

An individual can move his part in the entire room, but a group cannot move their part in the entire room[344]. But did we not state "two groups"[345]? He only said two; therefore not one. But did we not state, "the samovar in the middle"[346]? The place of the waiter proves where his group is. But did we not state, "the newly-wed may turn aside her face and eat"[347]? Rebbi Hiyya bar Abba said, because of shyness.

338 Since the rabbis agree that a group may split into two before they start eating, there is no fixed place of the *Pesah* before they start eating and there can be no removal.

339 Reading מִבְּנֵי with the next sentence for מִפְּנֵי in the text.

340 (Cf. Note 290). It is sinful to break a broken bone of a *Pesah*, but it is not sinful to further remove a removed part.

341 Either there can be no removal after

removal because the first removal disqualifies the meat, and moving disqualified *Pesah* is not sanctioned, or "removing" means "removing and eating" and the first removal did not count.

342 Since both groups subscribe to the same animal and one group becomes unable to use it.

343 Since each group already took possession of its part.

344 A single person eating a *Pesah* may change his place while eating while members of a group have to remain sitting where they started eating.

345 They are eating from the same *Pesah* at two distinct tables. But one single group cannot be separated.

346 It serves both groups at the same time; the hot water has to be transported through the entire room. But the waiter shows by his behavior as described in the Mishnah to which group he belongs.

347 Does she not show by turning away from the group that she does not want to belong?

האשה פרק שמיני

(fol.35c) **משנה א**: הָאִשָּׁה בִּזְמַן שֶׁהִיא בְּבֵית בַּעֲלָהּ שָׁחַט עָלֶיהָ בַּעֲלָהּ וְשָׁחַט עָלֶיהָ אָבִיהָ תֹּאכַל מִשֶּׁל בַּעֲלָהּ. הָלְכָה רֶגֶל הָרִאשׁוֹן לַעֲשׂוֹת בְּבֵית אָבִיהָ שָׁחַט עָלֶיהָ אָבִיהָ וְשָׁחַט עָלֶיהָ בַּעֲלָהּ תֹּאכַל מִמָּקוֹם שֶׁהִיא רוֹצָה. יָתוֹם שֶׁשְּׁחָטוּ עָלָיו אֲפִיטְרוֹפִּין יֹאכַל מִמָּקוֹם שֶׁהוּא רוֹצָה. עֶבֶד שֶׁל שְׁנֵי שׁוּתָּפִין לֹא יֹאכַל מִשֶּׁל שְׁנֵיהֶם. חֲצִי עֶבֶד וַחֲצִיוֹ בֶן חוֹרִין לֹא יֹאכַל מִשֶּׁל רַבּוֹ:

Mishnah 1: A woman living in her husband's house[1], and both her husband and her father slaughtered for her[2], should eat of her husband's. If she went to her father's house for the first holiday[3] and both her father and her husband slaughtered for her, she may eat where she desires. An orphan for whom guardians[4] slaughtered may eat where he desires. A slave of two owners may not eat from either of them[5]. A person who is half slave and half freedman may not eat of his master's[6].

1 If she only is preliminarily married, she still lives in her father's house and eats *Pesah* as her father's child.

2 Both are in Jerusalem and both counted her on the list of subscribers to their *Pesah*.

3 There was a general custom of the bride returning to her father's house for the first holiday after the definitive marriage.

4 If there are multiple guardians (Greek ἐπίτροπος, ὁ).

5 Since neither of the joint owners has the right to take from the other, the part of the slave belonging to one cannot profit from the other's food. He has to participate in a separate *Pesah*.

6 He has to behave like a free person.

(35c line 66) הָאִשָּׁה בִּזְמַן שֶׁהִיא בְּבֵית בַּעֲלָהּ כול'. אָמַר רִבִּי יוֹחָנָן. אַרְבָּעָה מְחוּסְּרֵי כַפָּרָה מַפְרִישִׁין עֲלֵיהֶן חוּץ מִדַּעְתָּן. וְאֵילוּ הֵן. זָב וְזָבָה וְיוֹלֶדֶת וּמְצוֹרָע. שֶׁכֵּן אָדָם מַפְרִישׁ עַל בְּנוֹ הַקָּטָן וְהוּא נָתוּן בַּעֲרִיסָה. נִיחָא זָב וְזָבָה וּמְצוֹרָע. יוֹלֶדֶת. וְיֵשׁ קְטַנָּה יוֹלֶדֶת. לֹא כֵן אָמַר רִבִּי רְדִיפָה רִבִּי יוֹנָה בְשֵׁם רַב חוּנָה. עִיבְּרָה וְיָלְדָה עַד שֶׁלֹּא הֵבִיאָה שְׁתֵּי שְׂעָרוֹת. הִיא וּבְנָהּ מֵתִים. מִשֶּׁהֵבִיאָה שְׁתֵּי שְׂעָרוֹת. הִיא וּבְנָהּ חַיִּים. עִיבְּרָה עַד שֶׁלֹּא הֵבִיאָה שְׁתֵּי שְׂעָרוֹת וְיָלְדָה מִשֶּׁהֵבִיאָה שְׁתֵּי שְׂעָרוֹת. הִיא חָיָה וּבְנָהּ מֵת. מַאי כְדוֹן. שֶׁכֵּן אָדָם מַפְרִישׁ עַל בִּתּוֹ קְטַנָּה. מִכֵּיוָן שֶׁהִשִּׂיאָהּ לֹא כְבַר יָצְאָה מֵרְשׁוּת אָבִיהָ. אֶלָּא שֶׁכֵּן אָדָם מַפְרִישׁ עַל אִשְׁתּוֹ חֵרֶשֶׁת. וְכָאן סוֹטָה קְטַנָּה אֵין אַתְּ יָכִיל. דְּאָמַר רִבִּי זְעוּרָה רִבִּי יוֹסֵא בְשֵׁם רִבִּי יוֹחָנָן. קְטַנָּה שֶׁאֵינְךָ אֵין לָהּ רָצוֹן לֵיאָסֵר עַל בַּעֲלָהּ. וְחֵרֶשֶׁת אֵין אַתְּ יָכִיל. דִּכְתִיב וְאָמְרָה הָאִשָּׁה אָמֵן | אָמֵן. אָמַר רִבִּי אָבוּן. שַׁנְייָא הִיא. דִּכְתִיב וְשָׂמַחְתָּ אַתָּה וּבֵיתֶךָ:

"A woman living in her husband's house," etc. [7]Rebbi Joḥanan said, for the four who are missing atonement[8] others may dedicate without their knowledge; these are the following: Man or woman [healed from] genital discharges, the woman after childbirth and one [healed from] skin disease, since a father may dedicate for his small son who is lying in a crib[9]. One understands man or woman [healed from] genital discharges or [healed from] skin disease, but a woman after childbirth? May a minor give birth? [10]Did not Rebbi Redifa, Rebbi Jonah, say in the name of Rav Huna: If a woman became pregnant and gave birth before she grew two hairs, she and her son will die. After she grew two hairs, she and her son will live. If she became pregnant before she grew two hairs and gave birth after she grew two hairs, she will live but her son will die. How is the situation? Since a man may dedicate for his underage daughter[11]. Since he married her off[12], she already left his power. But it must be since a man may dedicate for his deaf-mute wife. Here, in the case of the suspected wife, the case of the minor does not apply since [13]Rebbi Ze'ira, Rebbi Yosa[14] said in the name of Rebbi Joḥanan: An underage girl who whored has no will to be forbidden to her husband. The case of the deaf-mute does not apply since it is written[15]: *The woman shall say: Amen, amen.* Rebbi Abun said, since it is written[16]: *You shall enjoy together with your house.*

7 This paragraph is from *Sotah* 2:1, Notes 15-23 which is the original since the last sentence, which makes the argument intelligible, is missing here.

8 Anyone whose own body was the source of impurity, when he is pure again cannot enter the Temple precinct unless he first brought a sacrifice of cleansing: The woman after childbirth (*Lev.* 12:6-8), the person healed from skin disease (*Lev.* 14:1-32) and the persons healed from genital discharges (*Lev.* 15:14-15,29-30).

9 Who could have been afflicted with skin disease and, if female, with a discharge at her birth mimicking menstruation.

10 This text also is in *Yebamot* 1:2, Note 153. It implies that a woman giving birth is an adult and no longer in her father's power.

11 Therefore, he should be able to dedicate for his wife who also is dependent upon him.

12 Even without growing pubic hair, if he married her off she is emancipated from him.

13 This statement also is in *Sotah* 1:2, Note 91. In the language of the Babli, *Yebamot* 33b, "the seduction of an under-age girl is rape."

14 With the text in *Sotah* read: Yasa.

15 *Num.* 5:22. The answer of the wife is a

requirement that cannot be waved. Therefore, a mute woman cannot undergo the *sotah* ordeal. The Babli concurs, *Sotah* 27b, quoted in *Num. rabba* 9(18).

16 *Deut.* 14:26. *A man's house* usually means his wife. The missing final sentence explains that since he cannot enjoy himself if his wife is forbidden to him, she cannot hinder him in the preparations for her rehabilitation. This answers the original question for the husband. At the same time, R. Abun disagrees with R. Johanan and holds that only the husband may dedicate the purgation offering of the woman after childbirth without her knowledge since he has a direct interest in it. While the woman after childbirth is permitted to her husband once she is recovered and pure, she cannot enjoy the holiday sacrifices with him as long as her sacrifice has not been handed over to the Temple personnel.

(35d line 3) רִבִּי יִרְמְיָה בְשֵׁם רִבִּי יוֹחָנָן. אָדָם קוֹבֵעַ עַל חֲבֵירוֹ קָרְבַּן נָזִיר שֶׁלֹּא מִדַּעְתּוֹ. אֲבָל אֵינוֹ מַפְרִישׁוֹ שֶׁלֹּא מִדַּעְתּוֹ. רִבִּי זְעוּרָא בְשֵׁם רִבִּי יוֹחָנָן. אָדָם קוֹבֵעַ עַל חֲבֵירוֹ חַטָּאת חֵלֶב שֶׁלֹּא מִדַּעְתּוֹ. אֲבָל אֵינוֹ מַפְרִישׁוֹ שֶׁלֹּא מִדַּעְתּוֹ.

Rebbi Jeremiah in the name of Rebbi Johanan: A person chooses another's *nezirut* sacrifice without the other's knowledge. But he cannot dedicate it without the other's knowledge[17]. Rebbi Ze`ira in the name of Rebbi Johanan: A person chooses another's purification sacrifice for fat[18] without the other's knowledge. But he cannot dedicate it without the other's knowledge.

17 Cf. *Nazir* 2:5 Note 84. Since an animal cannot be brought to the Temple without having been dedicated, and the dedication has to be for a specific obligation, the *nazir* whose sacrifices are paid for must be informed of the dedication for it to be valid. Denied by the Babli, *Nedarim* 36a.

18 A general name for inadvertent sins punishable by extirpation, cf. *Lev.* 7:25. Denied by the Babli, *Nedarim* 36a.

(35d line 6) רִבִּי זְעוּרָא בְשֵׁם רִבִּי אֶלְעָזָר. אָדָם שׁוֹחֵט פִּסְחוֹ שֶׁלַּחֲבֵירוֹ שֶׁלֹּא מִדַּעְתּוֹ. אֲבָל אֵינוֹ מַפְרִישׁוֹ אֶלָּא מִדַּעְתּוֹ. אָמַר רִבִּי אֶלְעָזָר. מַתְנִיתָה אָמְרָה כֵן. הָאִשָּׁה בִּזְמַן שֶׁהִיא בְּבֵית בַּעֲלָהּ. שָׁחַט עָלֶיהָ אָבִיהָ שָׁחַט עָלֶיהָ בַּעְלָהּ. תֹּאכַל מִשֶׁלְּבַעֲלָהּ. מַה נָן קַייָמִין. אִם בְּמַמְחִין. סְתָם אִשָּׁה מַמְחָה לוֹמַר. אֵצֶל בָּנַי אֲנִי רוֹצָה. אִם בְּשֶׁאֵינָן מַמְחִין. מַתְנִיתָה בְּמַמְחִין. אָתָא רִבִּי יִרְמְיָה בְשֵׁם רִבִּי יוֹחָנָן. מַתְנִיתָה בְּמַמְחִין. לֵית הָדָא פְלִינָא עַל דְּרִבִּי אֶלְעָזָר. דְּרִבִּי אֶלְעָזָר אָמַר. אָדָם שׁוֹחֵט פִּסְחוֹ שֶׁלַּחֲבֵירוֹ שֶׁלֹּא מִדַּעְתּוֹ. אֲבָל אֵינוֹ מַפְרִישׁוֹ שֶׁלֹּא מִדַּעְתּוֹ. שַׁנְיָיא הִיא פֶּסַח. שַׁנְיָיא הִיא חַטָּאת. פֶּסַח לִכְשֶׁתַּגְדִּיל רָאוּי הוּא לְהִתְכַּפֵּר בּוֹ. חַטָּאת לִכְשֶׁתַּגְדִּיל אֵינוֹ רָאוּי הוּא לְהִתְכַּפֵּר בּוֹ.

אָמַר רִבִּי יוֹחָנָן. בְּרֶגֶל רְדוּפִין שָׁנוּ. אֵי זֶהוּ רֶגֶל רְדוּפִין. אָמַר רִבִּי יוֹסֵה בֵּירִבִּי בּוּן. זֶה רֶגֶל רִאשׁוֹן שֶׁאָבִיהָ רוֹדְפָהּ לְבֵית בַּעְלָהּ. לֹא הָלְכָה רֶגֶל הָרִאשׁוֹן. רֶגֶל הַשֵּׁינִי מָהוּ שֶׁיֵּיעָשֶׂה רֶגֶל רְדוּפִין. לְעוֹלָם יֵשׁ לָהּ רֶגֶל רְדוּפִין. אַלְמָנָה מָהוּ שֶׁיְּהֵא לָהּ רֶגֶל רְדוּפִין. נִשְׁמְעִינָהּ מִן הָדָא. הָלְכָה רֶגֶל הָרִאשׁוֹן לַעֲשׂוֹת בְּבֵית אָבִיהָ. אוֹ הָדָא אֲמָרָה. לְעוֹלָם יֵשׁ לָהּ רֶגֶל רְדוּפִין. אוֹ הָדָא אֲמָרָה. אַלְמָנָה מָהוּ יֵשׁ לָהּ רֶגֶל רְדוּפִין. אָמַר רִבִּי יוֹסֵה בֵּירִבִּי בּוּן. תִּיפְתָּר שֶׁיֵּשׁ לָהּ בָּנִים וְאֵין לָהּ בַּעַל. וּסְתָם הָאִשָּׁה מַמְחָה לוֹמַר. אֵצֶל בָּנַיי אֲנִי רוֹצָה.

Rebbi Ze`ira in the name of Rebbi Eleazar: A person may slaughter another's *Pesaḥ* without his knowledge, but he cannot dedicate it without his knowledge. Rebbi Eleazar said, the Mishnah says so: "A woman living in her husband's house, and both her father and her husband slaughtered for her, should eat of her husband's.[19]" Where do we hold? If giving instructions[20], normally a woman gives instructions saying, I want to be with my children[21]. So not giving instructions[22]. The Mishnah may be about giving instructions[23]. There came Rebbi Jeremiah in the name of Rebbi Johanan, the Mishnah is about giving instructions. Does this not disagree with Rebbi Eleazar, since Rebbi Eleazar said, a person may slaughter another's *Pesaḥ* without his knowledge, but he may not choose it without his knowledge[24]? There is a difference between *Pesaḥ* and a purification sacrifice. If a *Pesaḥ* grows it may be used to satisfy an obligation[25]; a purification sacrifice if it grows may not be used to satisfy an obligation[26].

Rebbi Johanan said, they taught this about the follow-holiday[27]. What is the follow-holiday? Rebbi Yose ben Rebbi Abun said, that is the first holiday when her father follows her to her husband's house. If she did not go for the first holiday, does the second holiday become the follow-holiday[28]? She always has a follow-holiday. Does a widow have a follow-holiday? Let us hear from the following: "If she went to her father's house for the first holiday." Either this means that she always has a follow-holiday or it means that a widow has a follow-holiday[29]. Rebbi Yose ben Rebbi Abun said, explain it that she has children but no husband. Normally a woman gives instructions saying, I want to be with my children[30].

19 The fist sentence of the Mishnah, which prescribes the wife's place, seems to contradict the second, which gives her	freedom of choice. It is to be assumed that neither her father nor her husband are permanent dwellers in Jerusalem so that for

the *Pesah* she actually is neither in her husband's nor in her father's permanent home.

20 Reading מִמְחָה as מַמְחָה; not derived from any of the roots מחה "protest; erase, rub out".

21 So one may assume that the Mishnah does not refer tot a wife who already has children.

22 Neither father nor husband had her agreement to eat with him. This would follow R. Eleazar who allows slaughtering the *Pesah* without the knowledge of the other person.

23 The Mishnah cannot be used to prove that practice agrees with R. Eleazar.

24 Then she at least has to be informed beforehand. Babli, *Nedarim* 36a.

25 An animal dedicated for *Pesah* but not used automatically is dedicated as well-being sacrifice to be used later for satisfying a vow by the owner.

26 An animal dedicated as purification sacrifice but not used may not be used for anything else.

27 Using the root רדף not in the biblical sense "to pursue" but the related meaning "to follow closely", Arabic ردف. The definition of follow-holiday is from *Ketubot* 7:5 (Notes 43-45), Babli *Ketubot* 71b.

28 So if that should be Passover she has a choice whether to join her father or her husband for the *Pesah*.

29 To make sense of the duplication in the Mishnah since following R. Johanan also the first sentence of the Mishnah refers to a newly-wed who still has no child.

30 Once she has children, the question of where she celebrates the *Pesah* is resolved; she no longer has to be asked where she wants to be.

(35d line 23) אָמַר רִבִּי לְעָזָר. פִּיסְחָן שֶׁלְּנָשִׁים רְשׁוּת. וְדוֹחִין עָלָיו אֶת הַשַּׁבָּת. רִבִּי יַעֲקֹב בַּר אָחָא בְּשֵׁם רִבִּי אֶלְעָזָר. פִּיסְחָן שֶׁלְּנָשִׁים וְשֶׁלַעֲבָדִים רְשׁוּת. כָּל־שֶׁכֵּן דּוֹחִין עָלָיו אֶת הַשַּׁבָּת. מַצָּתָן מָה הִיא. רִבִּי לְעָזָר אָמַר. חוֹבָה. רִבִּי זְעוּרָא אָמַר. רְשׁוּת. רִבִּי הִילָא אָמַר. דִּבְרֵי הַכֹּל. מַתְנִיתָהּ מְסַייְעָא לְדֵין וּמַתְנִיתָהּ מְסַייְעָא לְדֵין. מַתְנִיתָהּ מְסַייְעָא לְרִבִּי זְעִירָא. חֲזֶרֶת מַצָּה וּפֶסַח לַיְלָה הָרִאשׁוֹן חוֹבָה. וּשְׁאַר כָּל־הַיָּמִים רְשׁוּת. מַתְנִיתָהּ מְסַייְעָא לְרִבִּי הִילָא. לֹא־תֹאכַל עָלָיו חָמֵץ שִׁבְעַת יָמִים תֹּאכַל־עָלָיו מַצּוֹת לֶחֶם עוֹנִי. אֶת שֶׁהוּא בְּבַל תֹּאכַל חָמֵץ הֲרֵי הוּא בְּקוּם אֲכוֹל מַצָּה. וְנָשִׁים הוֹאִיל וְהֵן בְּבַל תֹּאכַל חָמֵץ הֲרֵי הֵן בְּקוּם אֲכוֹל מַצָּה. וְהָא תַנִּינָן. כָּל־מִצְוַת עֲשֵׂה שֶׁהַזְּמָן גְּרָמָא הָאֲנָשִׁים חַייָבִין וְהַנָּשִׁים פְּטוּרוֹת. אָמַר רִבִּי מָנָא. חוֹמֶר הִיא מִצְוַת עֲשֵׂה שֶׁהִיא בָאָה מִכֹּחַ בְּלֹא מַעֲשֶׂה.

[31]Rebbi Eleazar said: The *Pesah* of women is voluntary[32], but one pushes the Sabbath away for it[33]. Rebbi Jacob bar Aha in the name of Rebbi Eleazar: The Passover sacrifice from women and slaves is voluntary; certainly one does push the Sabbath away for it. What is their *mazzah*? Rebbi Eleazar said, it is obligatory. Rebbi Ze`ira said, it is voluntary[34]. Rebbi Hila said, it is everybody's {opinion}. A *baraita* supports the one and a *baraita* supports the

other. A *baraita* supports Rebbi Ze'ira: Lettuce, *mazzah* and *Pesaḥ* are obligatory the first night; on all other days they are voluntary. A *baraita* supports Rebbi Hila: It was said: *Do not eat leavened matter with it, for seven days you shall eat with it mazzot, the bread of deprivation*[35]. Anybody under the prohibition of leavened matter is under the obligation to eat *mazzah*, and women, being under the prohibition of leavened matter, are under the obligation to eat *mazzah*[36]. But did we not state: "For any positive commandment triggered by time, men are obligated but women are free"[37]? Rebby Mana said, it is a powerful positive commandment since it is implied by a prohibition[38].

וְאִתְיָא כְמאן דְּאָמַר. פִּסְחָן שֶׁלְּנָשִׁים רְשׁוּת. תַּנֵּי. הָאִשָּׁה עוֹשָׂה פֶּסַח הָרִאשׁוֹן לְעַצְמָהּ וְהַשֵּׁינִי טְפֵילָה לַאֲחֵרִים. דִּבְרֵי רִבִּי מֵאִיר. רִבִּי יוֹסֵה אוֹמֵר. הָאִשָּׁה עוֹשָׂה פֶּסַח שֵׁינִי לְעַצְמָהּ אֲפִילוּ בַשַּׁבָּת. וְאֵין צָרִיךְ לוֹמַר הָרִאשׁוֹן. רִבִּי שִׁמְעוֹן בֶּן אֶלְעָזָר אוֹמֵר. הָאִשָּׁה עוֹשָׂה פֶּסַח הָרִאשׁוֹן טְפֵילָה לַאֲחֵרִים וְאֵינָהּ עוֹשָׂה פֶּסַח שֵׁינִי. מַה טַּעֲמֵיהּ דְּרִבִּי מֵאִיר. אִישׁ שֶׂה לְבֵית אָבוֹת. אִם רָצוּ לַבָּיִת. מַה טַּעֲמֵיב דְּרִבִּי יוֹסֵי. אִישׁ שֶׂה לְבֵית אָבוֹת. כָּל־שֶׁכֵּן לַבָּיִת. מַה טַּעֲמֵיהּ דְּרִבִּי לְעָזָר בֵּירִבִּי שִׁמְעוֹן. אִישׁ. לֹא אִשָּׁה. מַה מְקַיְימִין רַבָּנָן אִישׁ. פְּרָט לְקָטָן. אָמַר רִבִּי יוֹנָה. וַאֲפִילוּ כְמאן דְּאָמַר. פְּסָחִים שֶׁלְּנָשִׁים רְשׁוּת. שַׁנְיָיא הִיא שֶׁהַדָּבָר מְסוּיָּים. שֶׁלֹּא יִקָּבַע הַדָּבָר חוֹבָה.

[39]Does it follow him who says the *Pesaḥ* of women is voluntary? It was stated[40]: "A woman may make the First *Pesaḥ* by herself and the Second joining \others, the words of Rebbi Meïr. Rebbi Yose says, a woman may make the Second *Pesaḥ* by herself, and certainly the First. Rebbi Simeon ben Eleazar[41] says, a woman may make the First *Pesaḥ* joining others but does not make the Second." What is the reason of Rebbi Meïr? *Every man a sheep for the family*, if they want *for the house*[42]. What is the reason of Rebbi Yose, *every man a sheep for the family*, a fortiori *for the house*. What is the reason of Rebbi Eleazar ben Rebbi Simeon? "Every man", not a woman. How do the rabbis uphold "man"? A man, not a minor. Rebbi Jonah said, even according to him who says it is an obligation, it is different here since the occasion was news, lest it become an obligation[43].

31 This paragraph also appears in *Qiddušin* 1:7, Notes 612-623. The origin probably is here.

32 S. Liebermann has emphasized repeatedly that in the Yerushalmi רשות

means "meritorious act which is not obligatory." The Babli disagrees in the name of R. Eliezer, 91a.

In the Babli and related texts, it is taken for granted that women present in Jerusalem on Passover eve are obligated to take part in the Passover meal, based on *Ex.* 12:4 which designates the participants as "persons", not "men" (*Mekhilta dR. Ismael, Pisha* 3, *Mekhilta dR. Simeon b*en *Yohai* p. 10; cf. Mishnah 8:1,7 Tosephta 8:10; Babli 91a/b.) But it should be noted that missing the sacrificial meal is a deadly sin only for men (*Num.* 9:13); only men are required (and permitted) to make up the missed sacrifice on the 14th of Iyar (*Num.* 9:13; Tosephta 8:10).

The statement means that an unaffiliated female, living neither in her father's nor a husband's house, is not obligated to seek a group with which to celebrate Passover. It would be considered most inappropriate if a single woman would join a group of men unrelated to her. But since she is included in the circle of celebrants of Passover by biblical law, if she alone or a group of similarly situated women want to organize their own *Pesah* and meal, they are authorized to do so.

Circumcised slaves are included in the group of Passover celebrants in *Ex.* 12:44. The owner of uncircumcised slaves is prohibited from bringing a *Pesah*.

33 Since women are biblically empowered to celebrate Passover, the rule also applies to groups of women.

34 In *Qiddušin:* This is in dispute.

35 *Deut* 17:3. Rules stated in the same verse must be of one and the same category.

36 In the Babli, 91b, this is a statement by R. Eleazar, probably the Tanna. In *Sifry Deut*. 130, its contrapositive is a statement of R. Simeon.

37 Mishnah *Qiddušin* 1:7.

38 And therefore follow the rules of prohibitions, obligatory for women.

39 This paragraph is from *Hallah* 4:12 and originates there. It refers to Mishnah *Hallah* 4:12 which reports that a certain Joseph Hakohen brought his entire family, women and children, to celebrate Second *Pesah* but the Temple authorities admitted only the adult males.

40 Tosephta 8:10.

41 This should read with the other sources: R. Eleazar ben R. Simeon.

42 *Ex.* 12:3. Everywhere "house" is read as synonym of "wife".

43 If a renowned authority does something, everybody will rush to emulate him and in the next generation it will already be a common standard and acquire the status of "practice of the forefathers from time immemorial". Even R. Yose will agree that in such a situation one should not allow a public display of special devotion.

(35d line 43) יָתוֹם שֶׁשָּׁחֲטוּ עָלָיו אֶפִּיטְרוֹפִּין יאכַל בְּמָקוֹם שֶׁהוּא רוֹצֶה. מַתְנִיתָא בְיָתוֹם קָטָן. אֲבָל בְּיָתוֹם גָּדוֹל נַעֲשָׂה כִּמְמַנֶּה עַצְמוֹ עַל שְׁנֵי פְסָחִים כְּאַחַת. דְּתַנֵּי רְבִּי חִייָה. הַנִּמְנֶה עַל שְׁנֵי פְסָחִים כְּאַחַת אוֹכֵל מֵאֵי זֶה מֵהֶן שֶׁנִּשְׁחַט רִאשׁוֹן. אָמַר רְבִּי יוֹסֵה. מַתְנִיתָא אָמְרָה כֵן. שָׁחַט גְּדִי וְטָלֶה יאכַל מִן הָרִאשׁוֹן.

"An orphan for whom guardians[4] slaughtered may eat where he desires." The Mishnah refers to an underage orphan. But an adult orphan is like one who subscribed to two *Pesaḥim*; as Rebbi Ḥiyya stated[44], one who subscribed to two *Pesaḥim* eats from the one which was slaughtered first[45]. Rebbi Yose says, the Mishnah says so, "if he slaughtered a kid goat and a lamb, one eats from the first.[46]"

44 Tosephta 7:3; cf. Babli 89b.
45 Therefore the adult orphan has no choice but the order of slaughter determines where he is obligated to eat.

46 Mishnah 8:2, referring to a case where the person who slaughtered was fully empowered to do so.

(35d line 47) עֶבֶד שֶׁלִּשְׁנֵי שׁוּתָּפִין לֹא יֹאכַל מִשֶּׁלִּשְׁנֵיהֶם. רִבִּי יוֹסֵה אוֹמַר. אֵין רְשׁוּת לְרַבּוֹ לוֹמַר לוֹ. אֵיפְשַׁר שֶׁתִּמָּנֶה עַל הַפֶּסַח. אֲבָל אוֹמְרִים הוּא לוֹ. אֵיפְשִׁי שֶׁתִּמָּנֶה עַל זֶה וְלֹא אֶלָּא עַל זֶה. פְּעָמִים שֶׁהוּא נִמְנֶה עַל שְׁלֹשָׁה פְסָחִים כְּאַחַת. הֵיךְ עֲבִידָא. עֶבֶד שֶׁלִּשְׁנֵי שׁוּתָּפִין צָרִיךְ לְהִימָּנוֹת עַל הַפֶּסַח. שִׁיחְרֵר אֶחָד מֵהֶן חֶלְקוֹ. צָרִיךְ לְהִימָּנוֹת עַל פֶּסַח אַחֵר. שִׁיחְרְרוּ שְׁנֵיהֶן. צָרִיךְ לְהִימָּנוֹת עַל פֶּסַח אַחֵר. שְׁמוּאֵל בַּר אַבָּא בָעֵי. עֶבֶד מָהוּ שֶׁיֹּאכַל מִשְּׁלָשְׁתָּן. אָמַר רִבִּי יוֹסֵי. אִם אוֹמֵר אַתְּ. עֶבֶד לֹא יֹאכַל מִשְּׁלָשְׁתָּן. מֵעַתָּה לֹא יִימָּנֶה עַל הַפֶּסַח. שֶׁמָּא יִימָלֵךְ רַבּוֹ וִישַׁחְרְרוֹ וְנִמְצָא הַקְּדֵּשׁ פָּסוּל מְעוּרָב בַּעֲבוֹדָה. רִבִּי יַעֲקֹב בַּר אָחָא אָמַר רִבִּי זְעוּרָא בָעֵי. הָרַב מַהוּ שֶׁיֵּצֵא בְהֶקְדֵּשׁ הָעָבֶד. וְלָאו מַתְנִיתָא הִיא. הָאוֹמֵר לְעַבְדּוֹ. צֵא וּשְׁחוֹט עָלַי אֶת הַפֶּסַח. מַתְנִיתָא מִדַּעַת רַבּוֹ. מַה צְּרִיעָה לֵיהּ שֶׁלֹּא מִדַּעַת רַבּוֹ.

"A slave of two owners may not eat from either of them." Rebbi Yose said, his master has no right to say, it is impossible that you should be counted for a *Pesaḥ*, but he may say to him, you may not be counted for this one, only for that one[47]. Sometimes he is counted for three *Pesaḥim* simultaneously. How is this? A slave of two owners must subscribe to a *Pesaḥ*. If one of them freed his part, he has to subscribe to another *Pesaḥ*[48]. If both of them freed, he has to subscribe to yet another *Pesaḥ*. Samuel bar Abba asked, may the slave eat from all three of them? If you are saying that the slave may not eat from all three of them, then he should not be able to subscribe to a *Pesaḥ*, since perhaps his master might want to free him and it turns out that an invalid dedication is mixed up in the offering[49]. Rebbi Jacob bar Aḥa said that Rebbi Ze`ira asked, may the owner fulfill his obligation by the slave's dedication? Is that not a Mishnah: "One says to his slave, go and slaughter the *Pesaḥ* for me.⁵⁰" The Mishnah on the instruction of his master, what is problematic for him not on the instruction of his master.

47 To resolve the problem spelled out in the Mishnah, one of the masters may bar him from his own *Pesaḥ* and thereby force him to eat from the other owner's *Pesaḥ*. But he cannot forbid him a *Pesaḥ* since it is a biblical obligation.

48 The part of his which is free cannot fulfill his absolute obligation with the dedication for the limited obligation of a slave.

49 It is a biblical obligation that circumcised slaves eat from their master's *Pesaḥ* (and the master is barred from *Pesaḥ* if he owns uncircumcised slaves). If manumission would invalidate the dedication, neither slaveholder nor his slaves would be able to eat any *Pesaḥ* since there always would be the possibility that the master manumit a slave which would retroactively invalidate the dedication and an undedicated animal may not be sacrificed. Therefore it is clear that manumission does not invalidate dedication.

50 Mishnah 2. It is clear from the remainder of the text of this Mishnah that the slave is authorized to buy the animal for *Pesaḥ* and to dedicate it on behalf of his master.

(35d line 59) חֶצְיוֹ עֶבֶד וְחֶצְיוֹ בֶן חוֹרִין לֹא יֹאכַל מִשֶּׁל רַבּוֹ: רִבִּי חִייָה בְשֵׁם רִבִּי יוֹחָנָן. מִי שֶׁחֶצְיוֹ עֶבֶד וְחֶצְיוֹ בֶן חוֹרִין. קִידֵּשׁ אִשָּׁה. אֵין חוֹשְׁשִׁין לְקִידּוּשָׁיו. וְדִכְוָותָהּ. גֵּירֵשׁ. אֵין חוֹשְׁשִׁין לְגֵירוּשָׁיו. שְׁמוּאֵל אָמַר. חוֹשְׁשִׁין לְגֵירוּשָׁיו. אַתְיָא דִשְׁמוּאֵל כְּרִבִּי יוּדָה. דְּתַנִּינָן תַּמָּן. גָּנַב מִי שֶׁחֶצְיוֹ עֶבֶד וְחֶצְיוֹ בֶן חוֹרִין. רִבִּי יוּדָה מְחַיֵּיב. וַחֲכָמִים פּוֹטְרִין:

"A person who is half slave and half freedman may not eat of his master's." Rebbi Ḥiyya in the name of Rebbi Joḥanan: If a man who is half slave and half freedman preliminarily married a woman, one disregards his preliminary marriage. It is the same for divorce⁵². Samuel says, one takes notice of his divorce. Samuel's statement parallels Rebbi Jehudah's, as we have stated, "One who kidnapped a person half slave and half free Rebbi Jehudah declares punishable but the Sages make him not prosecutable.⁵³"

52 Obviously if there can be no marriage there can be no divorce. Therefore the text, which also is copied in *Gittin* 4:5 (Notes 135-141), has to be interpreted in the light of the explanation given there, following the House of Hillel who say that he works for his owner one day and for himself the other day. On his owner's day he is a slave unable either to marry or divorce; on his own day he can marry preliminarily (but is unable to consummate the marriage, as explained there.) In *Gittin* and in *Qiddušin* 1:1 (Note 139), the statement about divorce is a straight declarative sentence which is unchallenged. Here it is possible to read it as a question: is it the same for divorce?

Samuel holds that since on his own day he may contract a preliminary marriage, just as a half-freed woman can contract a preliminary marriage to be consummated after her complete emancipation, so he can dissolve the preliminary marriage on his own day

52 Mishnah *Sanhedrin* 11:2.

(fol. 35a) **משנה ב**: הָאוֹמֵר לְעַבְדּוֹ צֵא וּשְׁחוֹט עָלַי אֶת הַפֶּסַח. שָׁחַט גְּדִי יֵאָכֵל שָׁחַט טָלֶה יֵאָכֵל. שָׁחַט גְּדִי וְטָלֶה יאָכַל מִן הָרִאשׁוֹן. שָׁכַח מָה אָמַר לוֹ רַבּוֹ כֵּיצַד יַעֲשֶׂה. יִשְׁחוֹט גְּדִי וְטָלֶה וְיֹאמַר אִם גְּדִי אָמַר לִי רַבִּי גְּדִי שֶׁלּוֹ וְטָלֶה שֶׁלִּי. וְאִם טָלֶה אָמַר לִי רַבִּי טָלֶה שֶׁלּוֹ וּגְדִי שֶׁלִּי. שָׁכַח רַבּוֹ מָה אָמַר לוֹ שְׁנֵיהֶן יֵצְאוּ לְבֵית הַשְּׂרֵפָה וּפְטוּרִין מִלַּעֲשׂוֹת פֶּסַח שֵׁנִי:

Mishnah 2: One says to his slave, go and slaughter the *Pesah* for me[53]. If he slaughtered a kid goat, it should be eaten; if he slaughtered a lamb, it should be eaten. If he slaughtered kid goat and lamb, one eats from the first. If he forgot what his master had told him[54], what can he do? He shall slaughter a kid goat and a lamb and say, if my master said to me a kid goat, the kid goat is his and the lamb mine, but if my master said to me a lamb, the lamb is his and the kid goat mine. If his master had forgotten what he told him, both shall be brought to the place of burning[55] but they are free from bringing the Second *Pesah*.

53 He delegates him to dedicate and slaughter the *Pesah* without detailed instructions about what to do.

54 But he remembers that he was instructed to buy a particular kind of animal. Then he is not empowered to dedicate an animal not conforming to his master's instructions; also a *Pesah* may not be dedicated if it is known beforehand that it will not be eaten. Since only two kinds of animal are allowed fur *Pesah*, the slave can resolve the problem by buying two animals and making sure that there are people able to eat either one of them.

55 Since it cannot be determined which animal has to be slaughtered for him and since "*Pesah* comes only for its eaters," the slaughter cannot permit the meat to be eaten. But since an attempt was made to bring the First *Pesah*, the conditions for a Second are not satisfied.

(35b line 63) **הלכה ב**: תַּנֵּי רִבִּי חִייָה. הַנִּמְנֶה עַל שְׁנֵי פְסָחִין כְּאַחַת אוֹכֵל מֵאֵי זֶה מֵהֶן שֶׁנִּשְׁחַט רִאשׁוֹן. אָמַר רִבִּי יוֹסֵה. מַתְנִיתָה אֲמָרָהּ כֵּן. שָׁחַט גְּדִי וְטָלֶה יֹאכַל מִן הָרִאשׁוֹן. רִבִּי לָעְזָר וְרִבִּי יוֹחָנָן תְּרֵיהוֹן אָמְרִין. דְּרִבִּי נָתָן הִיא. דְּרִבִּי נָתָן אָמַר. יוֹצְאִין בִּזְרִיקָה בְּלֹא אֲכִילָה. רִבִּי חִזְקִיָּה

בְּשֵׁם רִבִּי בָּא בַּר מָמָל. תִּיפְתָּר שֶׁשָּׁכַח רַבּוֹ בֵּין שְׁחִיטָה לַזְרִיקָה. אָמַר רִבִּי חִזְקִיָּה. מָתִיב חַד מִן רַבָּנָן. וְאָמְרִין. הוּא הֲוָה. וְהָא תַּנִּינָן. שָׁכַח רַבּוֹ מָה אָמַר לוֹ. יִשְׁחוֹט גְּדִי וְטָלֶה. אָמַר רִבִּי יוֹחָנָן. הִפְרִישׁ פִּסְחוֹ עַד שֶׁלֹּא נִתְגַּיֵּיר וְנִתְגַּיֵּיר. עַד שֶׁלֹּא נִשְׁתַּחְרֵר וְנִשְׁתַּחְרֵר. עַד שֶׁלֹּא הֵבִיא שְׁתֵּי שְׂעָרוֹת וְהֵבִיא שְׁתֵּי שְׂעָרוֹת. צָרִיךְ לְהִמָּנוֹת עַל פֶּסַח אַחֵר. אָמַר רִבִּי יוּדָן. כָּל־הַסְּפֵיקוֹת דְּרִבִּי נָתָן אִינּוּן. חוּץ מִן הַזּוֹרֵק דַּם חַטָּאתוֹ וְדַם אֲשָׁמוֹ. סָפֵק בַּלַּיְלָה זָרַק סָפֵק בַּיּוֹם זָרַק. נַעֲשָׂה כִּסְפֵק כַּפָּרָה. וּסְפֵק כַּפָּרָה כִּיפֵּר.

Halakhah 2: Rebbi Hiyya stated[44]: One who simultaneously subscribed to two *Pesaḥim* eats from the one which was slaughtered first. Rebbi Yose said, the Mishnah implies this; "if he slaughtered kid goat and lamb, one eats from the first." Rebbi Eleazar and Rebbi Joḥanan both are saying, this is Rebbi Nathan's since Rebbi Nathan said, one fulfills his obligation by pouring without eating. Rebbi Ḥizqiah in the name of Rebbi Abba bar Mamal: Explain it that the master forgot between slaughter and pouring[56]. Renni Ḥizqiah said, one of the rabbis objected; some say that it was himself: Did we not state, "If he forgot what his master had told him, he shall slaughter a kid goat and a lamb[57]"?

Rebbi Joḥanan said, if he dedicated a *Pesaḥ* before he converted and then converted[58], before he was manumitted and then was manumitted, before he grew two pubic hairs[59] and then grew two pubic hairs, has to subscribe to another *Pesaḥ*[60]. Rebbi Yudan said, all doubts[61] follow Rebbi Nathan, except for him who pours the blood of his purification offering or the blood of his reparation offering when there is a doubt whether he poured during nighttime or poured during daytime[62], where there is a doubt of atonement, and every doubt of atonement atones[63].

56 Babli 88b. Then the blood was poured when it was known that the *Pesaḥ* would be eaten and it is qualified according to everybody.

57 Since this presupposes that the master knows what he told him, the next sentence must deal with the case that the master did nor remember at the time of slaughter and the Mishnah necessarily follows R. Nathan.

58 Since a Gentile may bring a well-being offering, and an unused *Pesaḥ* automatically reverts to a well-being offering, since the Gentile is barred from offering a *Pesaḥ*, he dedicated a well-being offering, and after conversion is without a dedicated *Pesaḥ*.

59 An adult is a person growing two pubic hairs. As a minor he has no obligation to bring a *Pesaḥ*; therefore he cannot dedicate one.

60 However Maimonides (*Qorban Pesaḥ*

4:9) and Meïri (*Pesahim*, ed. Y. Klein, Jerusalem 1964, p. 366b) read: "he brings [the animal when he is ineligible] as *Pesah*."

61 Whether a sacrifice required to be eaten (either by the Cohanim or by lay people) is acceptable in case that its blood was poured but it could not be eaten.

62 No sacrificial act is possible (except burning excess sacrifices) during nighttime.

63 Even following the majority no other sacrifice is required.

(fol. 35c) **משנה ג:** הָאוֹמֵר לְבָנָיו הֲרֵינִי שׁוֹחֵט אֶת הַפֶּסַח עַל מְנָת מִי שֶׁיַּעֲלֶה מִכֶּם רִאשׁוֹן לִירוּשָׁלַיִם כֵּיוָן שֶׁהִכְנִיס הָרִאשׁוֹן רֹאשׁוֹ וְרוּבּוֹ זָכָה בְחֶלְקוֹ וּמְזַכֶּה אֶת אֶחָיו עִמּוֹ. לְעוֹלָם אֵין נִמְנִין עָלָיו עַד שֶׁיְּהֵא בוֹ כַּזַּיִת לְכָל אֶחָד וְאֶחָד. נִמְנִין וּמוֹשְׁכִין אֶת יְדֵיהֶן מִמֶּנּוּ עַד שֶׁיִּשָּׁחֵט. רִבִּי שִׁמְעוֹן אוֹמֵר עַד שֶׁיִּזָּרֵק עָלָיו אֶת הַדָּם:

Mishnah 3: If one says to his children, I am going to slaughter the *Pesah* in the name of whoever of you will come first to Jerusalem. When the first of them entered with his head and most of his body, he acquired his part and acquires for his siblings with him. Forever one subscribes to it as long as there is the volume of an olive for each participant. One subscribes to it or cancels until it has been slaughtered; Rebbi Simeon says until the blood is poured.

(35b line 76) **הלכה ג:** אָמַר רִבִּי יוֹחָנָן. לֵית כָּאן הֲרֵינִי שׁוֹחֵט. אֶלָּא הֲרֵינִי מַקְדִּישׁ. וְלָמָּה תְנִינָתָהּ. הֲרֵינִי שׁוֹחֵט. כְּדֵי לְזָרְזוֹ.

Halakhah 3: Rebbi Johanan said, there is no "I am going to slaughter" here, only "I am going to dedicate.[64]" And why was it stated "I am going to slaughter"? To urge him on.

64 Since after slaughter the animal is Heaven's property, nobody can acquire a part of the animal. If the Mishnah mentions that the first to come acquires his own part and those of his siblings, by necessity this must be for the dedication as sacrifice.

(36a line 1) רִבִּי לְעֶזָר בְּשֵׁם רִבִּי הוֹשַׁעְיָה. תְּנַיֵּי בֵית דִּין הוּא שֶׁיְּהֵא זֶה מַפְרִישׁ אֶת פִּסְחוֹ וְזֶה מַפְרִישׁ אֶת מְעוֹתָיו. מִמֶּנּוּ אוֹתוֹ עַל שֶׁלּוֹ וְהַמָּעוֹת יוֹצְאִין לַחוּלִין מֵאֵילֵיהֶן. מַה. יוֹצֵא לַחוּלִין וְחָזַר וְקָדַשׁ. אוֹ לְכָךְ הִקְדִּישׁוֹ מִשָּׁעָה רִאשׁוֹנָה. מַה נָפַק מִבֵּינֵיהוֹן. מַפְרִישׁ מֵאָה מָנֶה לְפִסְחוֹ וְהִימְנָה אוֹתוֹ עַל חֲמִשִּׁים. אִין תֵּימַר. יוֹצֵא לַחוּלִין וְחוֹזֵר וְקָדַשׁ. שְׁאָר הַמָּעוֹת חוּלִין הֵן. אִין תֵּימַר. לְכָךְ הִקְדִּישׁוֹ מִשָּׁעָה רִאשׁוֹנָה. שְׁאָר הַמָּעוֹת (חוּלִין) [הֶקְדֵּשׁ] הֵן. רִבִּי יַעֲקֹב בַּר אָחָא

אָמַר. שְׁמוּאֵל בַּר אַבָּא בָעֵי. הַגַּע עַצְמָךְ שֶׁהִמְנֶה אוֹתוֹ עַל חִנָּם. מַה אִית לָךְ יוֹצֵא לַחוּלִין וְחוֹזֵר וְקָדֵשׁ. מִילֵּיהוֹן דְּרַבָּנָן אָמְרֵי שֶׁאֵינוֹ יוֹצֵא לַחוּלִין וְחוֹזֵר וְקָדֵשׁ. תַּמָּן תַּנִּינָן. נָתַן לָהּ כְּסָפִים הֲרֵי אֵלּוּ מוּתָּרִין. יֵינוֹת שְׁמָנִים וּסְלָתוֹת וְכָל־דָּבָר שֶׁכַּיּוֹצֵא בוֹ קָרֵב עַל גַּבֵּי מִזְבֵּחַ. אָסוּר. רִבִּי שִׁמְעוֹן בֶּן לָקִישׁ אָמַר. בִּמְמַנֶּה אוֹתוֹ עַל פִּסְחוֹ וְעַל חֲגִיגָתוֹ. הָדָא אָמְרָה שֶׁאֵינוֹ יוֹצֵא לַחוּלִין וְחוֹזֵר וְקָדֵשׁ. אִין תֵּימַר שֶׁהוּא יוֹצֵא לַחוּלִין וְחוֹזֵר וְקָדֵשׁ. יְהֵא אָסוּר מִשּׁוּם אֶתְנָן. פָּתַר לָהּ בְּשֶׁלֹּא נִכְנַס לְתוֹךְ יָדוֹ כְּלוּם. תֵּדַע לָךְ. דְּתַנִּינָן תַּמָּן. מַקְרִיב עָלָיו קִינֵּי זָבִים זָבוֹת קִינֵּי יוֹלְדוֹת. לֹא בְּשֶׁלֹּא נִכְנַס לְתוֹךְ יָדוֹ כְּלוּם. אוֹף הָכָא בְּשֶׁלֹּא נִכְנַס לְתוֹךְ יָדוֹ כְּלוּם.

Rebbi Eleazar in the name of Rebbi Hoshaia: It is a stipulation of the Court that one dedicate his *Pesaḥ* and the other his money[65]. He lets him subscribe to his [part] and the money automatically becomes profane. How? It becomes profane and then dedicated again? Or for this purpose it was dedicated from the start[66]? What is the difference between them? If he dedicated 100 *mina* for his *Pesaḥ* and used 50 to subscribe[67]. If you are saying that it becomes profane and is dedicated again, the remainder of the monies are profane. If you are saying that for this purpose he dedicated it from the start, the rest of the monies are (profane) [dedicated][68]. Rebbi Jacob bar Aḥa said, Samuel bar Abba asked: Think of it if he lets him subscribe gratis. Where do you have "becomes profane and is dedicated again"[69]? The words of the rabbis imply that it does not become profane and then dedicated again. We have stated there[70]: "If he gave her monies, they are permitted; wines, oils, and fine flour, or anything of whose kind one offers on the altar, are forbidden." Rebbi Simeon ben Laqish said, if he lets him[71] subscribe to his *Pesaḥ* and to his festival offering. This implies that it does not become profane and then dedicated again. If you would say that it becomes profane and then dedicated again, it would be forbidden as harlot's wages[72]. Explain it if nothing was given into his hand; you should know as it was stated there[73], "he can bring for him nests for male or female sufferers from genital discharges, nests for childbirth;" not if nothing came into his hands? Here also if nothing came into his[71] hands.

65 The problem is, how can one have people subscribe to a *Pesaḥ* that already is dedicated as a sacrifice? It is Heaven's property and no longer can be considered the owner's; how can he take money for participation? Subscription is only possible because of a stipulation, probably part of Ezra's reorganization of Jewish worship,

that a *Pesaḥ* be open to subscription and that money dedicated for this purpose become profane in the hand of the person who dedicated the animal.

66 Since no Mishnah in *Pesaḥim* mentions the monetary aspect, it is up to Amoraim to determine how to harmonize this exception with the generally known rules of dedication of *sancta*. Either the *Pesaḥ* after dedication is not considered a *sanctum* but becomes one piecewise when olive-sized parts of it are sold to a subscriber and the sanctity of the dedicated money is transferred to the piece of the *Pesaḥ* while the money becomes profane in the hand of the seller, as is the general rule for money dedicated for sacrifices which become profane in the hand of the seller of the animal which is dedicated in being bought as sacrifice, or the money dedicated for *Pesaḥ* has a status different from money dedicated for any other sacrifice in that it is intrinsically profane with the restriction to be used only for the *Pesaḥ*. Cf. Babli 89b.

67 This is a typically 3rd Century example from the time of the inflation of the Military Anarchy in the Roman Empire. 100 *mina* are 10'000 *drachma* (*denar*), while in the old (Augustean) Mishnah *Ḥagigah* 1:2 the value of a sacrifice is between an *obolus* ($^1/_6$ *denar*) and 2 *denar*.

68 The text in parentheses is the original text of the scribe, the one in brackets his own correction. It seems that the scribe felt compelled to correct the text since in the preceding sentence he wrote "profane". But it seems more logical to assume that the first "profane" is in error and should be replaced by "dedicated" while in the second sentence "profane" is the correct expression.

In the preceding sentence "it" refers to the *Pesaḥ* animal, to which the sanctity of the subscription money is transferred while the unused part in the hand of the buyer is not touched by the transaction; it remains dedicated. But if the dedication of the money was conditional for the stated purpose of acquiring part of a *Pesaḥ*, the remaining money never was dedicated and is profane.

69 Since no money changes hands, there is dedicated money whose sanctity can be transferred to parts of the *Pesaḥ*. In order to have a fully dedicated sacrifice it should be forbidden to invite non-paying guests for the *Pesaḥ*. This is a restriction which nowhere is mentioned and has to be rejected.

70 Mishnah *Temurah* 6:4, dealing with wages of prostitution which may not be used for Temple dedications (*Deut.* 23:19). The reference is to the sentence following the quote, "if he (the customer) gave her (the prostitute) *sancta*, they are permitted (as sacrifice)" since as Heaven's property they never became the prostitute's.

71 This must be "her". R. Simeon ben Laqish holds that a sacrifice in the hands of a prostitute is barred from the Temple, but if the prostitute is paid by a subscription to his *Pesaḥ* or his festival offering it is an acceptable arrangement. *Temurah* 30b.

72 Mishnah *Nedarim* 4:3, detailing what A can legally do for B if A made a vow that B may not have any usufruct from him. A can pay for B's sacrifices as long as no money comes into B's hand, since sacrifices dedicated for B are Heaven's, not B's property.

HALAKHAH THREE

(36a line 16) רִבִּי יַעֲקֹב בַּר אָחָא בְּשֵׁם רִבִּי אִמִּי. אִיתְפַּלְּגוּן רִבִּי יוֹחָנָן וְרִבִּי שִׁמְעוֹן בֶּן לָקִיש. חַד אָמַר. מַקְדִּישִׁין. וְחַד אָמַר. אֵין מַקְדִּישִׁין. רַבָּנִן דְּקֵיסָרִין מְפָרְשִׁין לְהוֹן. רִבִּי יוֹחָנָן אָמַר. מַקְדִּישִׁין. כַּתְּחִילָּה בְּיוֹם טוֹב. רִבִּי שִׁמְעוֹן בֶּן לָקִיש אָמַר. אֵין מַקְדִּישִׁין. כַּתְּחִילָּה בְּיוֹם טוֹב. אִית תַּנָּיֵי תַנֵּי. הוֹלֵךְ לוֹ אֵצֶל מוֹכְרֵי טְלָאִים. אִית תַּנָּיֵי תַנֵּי. הוֹלֵךְ לוֹ אֵצֶל מוֹכְרֵי פְסָחִים. מָאן דְּאָמַר. הוֹלֵךְ אֵצֶל מוֹכְרֵי טְלָאִים. כְּמָאן דְּאָמַר. מַקְדִּישִׁין. מָאן דְּאָמַר. הוֹלֵךְ אֵצֶל מוֹכְרֵי פְסָחִים. כְּמָאן דְּאָמַר. אֵין מַקְדִּישִׁין. הָדָא אָמְרָה. אֵינוֹ יוֹצֵא לַחוּלִּין וְחוֹזֵר וְקָדֵש. אִין תֵּימַר שֶׁהוּא יוֹצֵא לַחוּלִּין וְחוֹזֵר וְקָדֵש. יְהֵא אָסוּר מִשּׁוּם מַקְדִּיש. וְתַנִּינָן. אֵין מַקְדִּישִׁין. רִבִּי חֲנַנְיָה וְרִבִּי מָנָא. חַד אָמַר. בְּמַקְדִּישׁ לְמָחָר. וְחוֹרָנָה אָמַר. בְּמַקְדִּישׁ לְבֶדֶק הַבַּיִת. אָמַר רִבִּי שַׁמַּי. וַאֲפִילוּ כְּמָאן דְּאָמַר. בְּמַקְדִּישׁ בָּעֲזָרָה. מִשֵּׁם שְׁבוּת שֶׁהִתִּירוּ בַּמִּקְדָּש.

2 וחד | צ וחורנה   6 אינו | צ שאינו   7 שהיא | צ -   9 במקדיש | צ מקדישין

[73]Rebbi Jacob bar Aha in the name of Rebbi Immi: Rebbi Joḥanan and Rebbi Simeon ben Laqish disagreed. One said, one dedicates; the other said, one does not dedicate. The rabbis of Caesarea make it explicit: Rebbi Joḥanan said, one dedicates without problems on a holiday; Rebbi Simeon ben Laqish said, one does not dedicate. without problems on a holiday[74]. There are Tannaim who state, he goes to sellers of lambs; there are Tannaim who state, he goes to sellers of *Pesaḥim*[75]. He who says, he goes to sellers of lambs, follows him who says, one dedicates. He who says, he goes to sellers of *Pesaḥim*, follows him who says, one does not dedicate. This implies that it does not become profane and then dedicated again. If you would say that it becomes profane and then dedicated again, it should be forbidden because of dedicating, and we have stated, "one does not dedicate.[76]" Rebbi Ḥananiah and Rebbi Mana, one said, if he dedicates for the next day; but the other said, if he dedicated for the upkeep of the Temple[77]. Rebbi Shammai said, even for him who said that one dedicates[78], in the Temple Court because rabbinic Sabbath prohibitions were permitted in the Temple.

73 This paragraph also is in *Besah* 5:2 (צ).
74 There is no doubt that biblically one is permitted to dedicate animals as sacrifices on a holiday; the question is whether there is a rabbinic prohibition.
75 If the 14th of Nisan is a Sabbath. In the first formulation, the lambs are profane and have to be dedicated on the Sabbath to be permitted into the Temple court; in the second version they already are dedicated (cf. Babli *Šabbat* 148b).
76 Mishnah *Besah* 5:2.
77 Dedication of a sacrifice to be eaten on the holiday has to be considered part of the preparation of food and is permitted; what the Mishnah forbids are dedications either not for use on the holiday or not for food at

all.
78 It seems that one has to read "that one does not dedicate". Since Mishnah *Beṣah* 5:2 explicitly declares that the prohibition of dedication of sacrifices is rabbinical, it implies that inside the Temple precinct proper the prohibition does not apply. In this situation there is no disagreement between R. Johanan and R. Simeon ben Laqish and no inference may be drawn about the status of monies dedicated for *Pesah*.

(36a line 27) מְנַיִין שֶׁהֵן נִמְנִין. תַּלְמוּד לוֹמַר בְּמִכְסַת נְפָשׁוֹת. מְנַיִין שֶׁהֵן מְמַנִּין. נֶאֱמַר כָּאן שֶׂה וְנֶאֱמַר בְּמִצְרַיִם שֶׂה. מַה שֶׂה שֶׁנֶּאֱמַר בְּמִצְרַיִם חַי לֹא שָׁחוּט. אַף שֶׂה שֶׁנֶּאֱמַר כָּאן חַי לֹא שָׁחוּט. מַה טַעֲמָא דְּרִבִּי שִׁמְעוֹן. אִילּוּ מֵתוּ בֵּין שְׁחִיטָה לִזְרִיקָה שֶׁמָּא אֵין הַבְּעָלִים מִתְכַּפְּרִין. מַה בֵּין מֵתוּ מַה בֵּין מָשְׁכוּ הַבְּעָלִים אֶת יְדֵהֶם מִמֶּנּוּ.

From where that one subscribes? The verse says, *by the number of souls*[79]. From where that one appoints[80]? It is said here *a lamb*, and it is said in Egypt *a lamb*. Since the lamb quoted in Egypt is live, not slaughtered, so the lamb quoted here is live, not slaughtered[81]. What is Rebbi Simeon's reason? If he dies between slaughtering and pouring, would it not count for the owner as merit? What is the difference between the owner dying or the owner withdrawing from it[83].

79 Ex. 12:4. By biblical decree a person not counted as participant is barred from eating the *Pesah*. Babli 89a.
80 Appoints people as eaters.
81 "Lamb" is mentioned in v. 12:4 which, since its topic is not otherwise dealt with in the Pentateuch, refers to *Pesah* at all times. "Lamb" also is mentioned in v. 12:3 which uniquely refers to the *Pesah* in Egypt since only there was the lamb selected on the 10th of Nisan. Since the lamb was slaughtered only in the evening of the 14th; on both occasions the reference is to a living lamb. This implies that the count must be made while the lamb is alive, the position of the anonymous majority.
82 From this argument it seems that R. Simeon also agrees that one may subscribe only to a living lamb; he only permits later withdrawal.

(fol. 35c) **משנה ד**׃ הַמְמַנֶּה אֲחֵרִים עִמּוֹ עַל חֶלְקוֹ רַשָּׁאִין לִיתֵּן לוֹ אֶת שֶׁלּוֹ וְהוּא אוֹכֵל מִשֶּׁלּוֹ וְהֵן אוֹכְלִין מִשֶּׁלָּהֶן׃

Mishnah 4: If somebody lets others subscribe to his part, they are empowered to give him his part, so that he eats of his and they eat of theirs[83].

83 A person subscribed to a *Pesaḥ* as an individual but now appears with several people which he has invited without paying for them. They may give him the portion of an individual and tell him to divide it among his guests while everybody else get the full volume for which he has paid.

(36a line 31) **הלכה ד**: בְּנֵי חֲבוּרָה שֶׁהָיוּ יָדוֹת שֶׁלְאֶחָד מֵהֶן יָפוֹת. רַשָּׁאִין לוֹמַר לוֹ. טוֹל חֶלְקָךְ וֶאֱכוֹל לְעַצְמָךְ. לֹא סוֹף דָּבָר פֶּסַח. אֶלָּא אֲפִילוּ עָשׂוּ סִינְבּוֹל רַשָּׁאִין לוֹמַר לוֹ. טוֹל חֶלְקָךְ וֶאֱכוֹל לְעַצְמָךְ. אִם הָיוּ מַכִּירִין אוֹתוֹ. לְכָךְ הִתְנוּ מִשָּׁעָה רִאשׁוֹנָה.

Halakhah 4: The members of a group of which one had beautiful hands[84] were entitled to tell him, take your part and eat alone Not only *Pesaḥ*, but even if they made a meal by contributions[85] they are entitled to tell him, take your part and eat alone, if they did know him[86], since this was a stipulation from the start.

84 The traditional explanation is: He grabs a lot and eats an inordinate amount of food. Babli 89b, Tosephta 7:9.

85 Greek συμβόλαια, τά, "contributions to partake in a common meal/"

86 They did know from the start that letting him participate might be unfair to the remainder of the group.

(36a line 35) רַב חוּנָא אָמַר. הִפְרִישׁ פִּסְחוֹ וְאָמַר. עַל מְנָת שֶׁלֹּא יִימָּנֶה אַחֵר עִמִּי. אֵין אַחֵר נִמְנֶה עִמּוֹ. הִפְרִישׁוֹ סְתָם. כָּל־מַה שֶׁיָּבוֹאוּ מִינּוּיָיו הֵן. רִבִּי יַעֲקֹב בַּר אָחָא בְשֵׁם רִבִּי זְעִירָא. מַתְנִיתָהּ אֲמָרָה כֵן. וְאִם־יִמְעַט הַבַּיִת. מְלַמֵּד שֶׁהֵן מִתְמַעֲטִין וְהוֹלְכִין. בִּלְבַד שֶׁיְּהֵא שָׁם אֶחָד מִבְּנֵי חֲבוּרָה הָרִאשׁוֹנָה וְאֶחָד מִבְּנֵי חֲבוּרָה הַשְּׁנִייָה. דִּבְרֵי רִבִּי יוּדָה. רִבִּי יוֹסֵה אוֹמֵר. בֵּין מִן הָרִאשׁוֹנָה בֵּין מִן הַשְּׁנִייָה. בִּלְבַד שֶׁלֹּא יַנִּיחוּ אֶת הַפֶּסַח כְּמוֹת שֶׁהוּא. אֵין תֵּימַר. כָּל־מַה שֶׁיָּבוֹאוּ מִינּוּיָיו הֵן. הֵן בְּנֵי חֲבוּרָה הָרִאשׁוֹנָה הֵן בְּנֵי חֲבוּרָה הַשְּׁנִייָה. מַה נְפַק מִבֵּינֵיהוֹן. הִפְרִישׁ פִּסְחוֹ וּמָשַׁךְ יָדוֹ וְנִמְנָה אַחֵר עִמּוֹ. עַל דַּעְתֵּיהּ דְּרַב חוּנָה. כָּשֵׁר. עַל דַּעְתֵּיהּ דְּרִבִּי זְעִירָא. פָּסוּל. עַל דַּעְתֵּיהּ דְּרַב חוּנָה. הֶקְדֵּשׁ יָחִיד הוּא. וְהֶקְדֵּשׁ יָחִיד עוֹשֶׂה תְמוּרָה. עַל דַּעְתֵּיהּ דְּרִבִּי זְעִירָה. הֶקְדֵּשׁ שׁוּתָּפִין הוּא. וְאֵין הֶקְדֵּשׁ שׁוּתָּפִין עוֹשֶׂה תְמוּרָה. נִמְנוּ עָלָיו מֵאָה בְּנֵי אָדָם כְּאַחַת. רַב חוּנָה אָמַר. אִם יֵשׁ כְּזַיִת לְכָל־אֶחָד וְאֶחָד. כָּשֵׁר. וְאִם לָאו פָּסוּל. אָמַר רִבִּי זְעִירָא. מָקוֹם שֶׁיֵּשׁ [כְּזַיִת לְכָל־אֶחָד וְאֶחָד] מֵהֶם. כָּשֵׁר. וְאִם לָאו. פָּסֵל. וְתִנֵּי כֵן. נִמְנוּ עָלַי וְחָזְרוּ וְנִמְנוּ עָלָי. עַד מָקוֹם שֶׁיֵּשׁ כְּזַיִת לְכָל־אֶחָד וְאֶחָד מֵהֶם. כָּשֵׁר. וְאִם לָאו. פָּסוּל.

Rav Huna said, if somebody dedicated his *Pesaḥ* and said, on condition that nobody else subscribe with me, nobody else can subscribe with him. If he dedicated it without specification, any who join are its subscribers[87]. Rebbi Jacob bar Aḥa in the name of Rebbi Ze`ira: Does the Mishnah say so? "*If the house be less*[88], this teaches that they may continuously diminish, on condition that there always be one of the first group and one of the second group, the words of Rebbi Jehudah. Rebbi Yose says, either from the first or from the second, if only the *Pesaḥ* not be left alone.[89]" If you are saying that any who join are its subscribers, then the members of the first group are the members of the second group[90]. What is the difference between them? If he dedicated his *Pesaḥ*, withdrew from it but another person subscribed to it. In the opinion of Rav Huna it is qualified, in the opinion of Rebbi Ze`ira disqualified[91]. In the opinion of Rav Huna it is dedication by an individual and subject to the laws of substitution; in the opinion of Rebbi Ze`ira it is dedication by partners and dedication of partners is not subject to the laws of substitution[92]. If a hundred people subscribed to it simultaneously, Rav Huna said, if there is the volume [of an olive for each of them], it is qualified, otherwise disqualified. Rebbi Ze`ira said, as long as there is the volume of an olive for each of them, it is qualified, otherwise disqualified[93]. And it was stated thus: "If they subscribed and added subscribers, as long as there is the volume of an olive for each of them, it is qualified, otherwise disqualified.[94]"

87 From the start the *Pesaḥ* is dedicated for anybody who will come to join.

88 *Ex.* 12:4.

89 Babli 99a, Tosephta 7:7, *Mekhilta dR. Ismael Bo* 3, *dR. Simeon ben Yoḥai* p. 9. It is presumed that practice follows R. Yose (the Tanna, ben Halafta.)

90 According to Rav Huna, every subscriber is counted as original subscriber; there can be no first and second group.

91 For Rav Huna, the second person is an original subscriber. For R. Ze`ira the *Pesaḥ* was left without subscriber for a moment; this disqualifies.

92 If the first subscriber left; his replacement now is the original dedicator and all the rules of Tractate *Temurah* (*Lev.* 27:10) do apply. But for R. Ze`ira, supposing that the second subscriber came before the first one left and the *Pesaḥ* still is qualified, it now is dedication by partners and any attempt at substitution is invalid and therefore inconsequential.

93 Since for Rav Huna all subscribers are original dedicators, simultaneous subscription is possible. The subscriptions either are all valid or all invalid. For R. Ze`ira only sequential subscriptions are possible; as long as there is the volume of an olive available for a new subscriber he is accepted, otherwise he is rejected, but the rejection has no influence on the status of subscribers accepted earlier.

94 Babli 78b.

(fol. 35c) **משנה ה**: זָב שֶׁרָאָה שְׁתֵּי רְאִיּוֹת שׁוֹחֲטִין עָלָיו בַּשְּׁבִיעִי. רָאָה שָׁלֹשׁ שׁוֹחֲטִין עָלָיו בַּשְּׁמִינִי. וְכֵן שׁוֹמֶרֶת יוֹם כְּנֶגֶד יוֹם שׁוֹחֲטִין עָלֶיהָ בַּשֵּׁנִי. רָאֲת שְׁנֵי יָמִים שׁוֹחֲטִין עָלֶיהָ בַּשְּׁלִישִׁי. וְהַזָּבָה שׁוֹחֲטִין עָלֶיהָ בַּשְּׁמִינִי:

Mishnah 5: For a sufferer from gonorrhea after two episodes one slaughters on the seventh {day}, if he had three episodes one slaughters for him on the eighth. Similarly for a woman watching day for day one slaughters on the second, if she had episodes on two consecutive days one slaughters on the third; but for the sufferer from flux one slaughters on the eighth[95].

95 A person who suffers a single episode of gonorrhea is impure for the day and can be purified by immersion in a *miqweh*. If he has two episodes in at most two consecutive days, he is impure for seven days; after seven days in remission he can be purified by immersion in a *miqweh*. After three episodes he still needs seven days in remission but then is still prohibited *sancta* unless on the eighth day he brings a couple of birds as sacrifice to the Temple. He can subscribe to a *Pesah* if there is a reasonable chance that he will be permitted *sancta* after nightfall.

A menstruating woman is impure for seven days, *Lev.* 15:19. A woman having non-menstrual discharges for *many days* (*Lev.* 15:25), interpreted as three days, is in the same situation as a male sufferer from gonorrhea after three episodes (15:28-29). For isolated episodes on one or two days, she may immerse herself in a *miqweh* on the next day and become pure for *sancta* at nightfall.

(36a line 50) **הלכה ה**: תַּנֵּי רִבִּי חִיָּיה. נִדָּה שׁוֹחֲטִין עָלֶיהָ בַּשְּׁמִינִי. בּוֹעֵל נִדָּה שׁוֹחֲטִין עָלָיו בַּשְּׁבִיעִי. אָמַר רִבִּי יוֹסֵה. הָדָא אָמְרָה שֶׁבּוֹעֵל נִדָּה טָהוֹר בַּיּוֹם הַשְּׁבִיעִי שֶׁלּוֹ.

Halakhah 5: Rebbi Hiyya stated: "For the menstruating woman one slaughters on her eighth day. For a man having had intercourse with a menstruating woman one slaughters on his seventh day." Rebbi Yose said, this implies that a man having had intercourse with a menstruating woman is pure on his seventh day[96].

96 For a woman it is written *seven days she shall stay in her separation* (*Lev..* 15:19) which is read to mean that she can go to a *miqweh* only after nightfall at the end of the seventh day. The next sundown which permits her to partake of *sancta* therefore is the sundown of the eighth day (Babli 90b). But for a male who lies with her it says (*Lev..* 15:24) *he is impure for seven days*, and since part of a day is counted as a full day, he can purify himself on the seventh day before nightfall (Babli *Yoma* 6a).

(fol. 35c) **משנה ו**: הָאוֹנֵן וְהַמְפַקֵּחַ בַּגַּל וְכֵן מִי שֶׁהִבְטִיחוּהוּ לְהוֹצִיאוֹ מִבֵּית הָאֲסוּרִין הַחוֹלֶה וְהַזָּקֵן שֶׁהֵן יְכוֹלִין לוֹכַל כַּזַּיִת שׁוֹחֲטִין עֲלֵיהֶן. וְעַל כּוּלָּן אֵין שׁוֹחֲטִין עֲלֵיהֶן בִּפְנֵי עַצְמָן שֶׁלֹּא יָבִיאוּהוּ אֶת הַפֶּסַח לִידֵי פָּסוּל. לְפִיכָךְ אִם אֵירַע בָּהֶן פְּסוּל פְּטוּרִין מִלַּעֲשׂוֹת פֶּסַח שֵׁנִי חוּץ מִן הַמְפַקֵּחַ בַּגַּל שֶׁהָיָה טָמֵא מִתְּחִלָּתוֹ׃

Mishnah 6: One slaughters for the deep mourner[97], and one who digs out a collapsed building[98], and one who was promised that he would be freed from jail, the sick person or the old who are able to eat the volume of an olive. But for all of these one does not slaughter for themselves lest the *Pesaḥ* become disqualified[99]. Therefore if a disqualification should occur they are not liable for the Second *Pesaḥ* except for one who digs out a collapsed building who from the start could expect to be impure.

97 The status of a person a close relative of whom has died, between the time of death and burial. As a deep mourner he is barred from all religious rites, but if he does not become impure by the impurity of the dead by nightfall he is able to participate in religious ceremonies.

98 He searches for survivors or for the corpses of the slain. If he finds no corpses he remains pure and can eat the *Pesaḥ*, but this is very uncertain.

99 If something happened, the *Pesaḥ* would be without eaters and would have to be burned.

(36a line 52) **הלכה ו**: רִבִּי יוֹסֵה בֵּירִבִּי בּוּן אַבָּא בַּר בַּר חָנָה בְּשֵׁם רִבִּי יוֹחָנָן. מַתְנִיתָה בְּשֶׁחֲבָשׁוּהוּ יִשְׂרָאֵל. אֲבָל אִם חַבָּשׁוּהוּ גוֹיִם. אֲשֶׁר פִּיהֶם דִּבֶּר־שָׁוְא וִימִינָם יְמִין שָׁקֶר. בְּנָתוּן חוּץ לִירוּשָׁלֵם. אֲבָל בְּנָתוּן בְּתוֹךְ לִירוּשָׁלַם. אֲפִילוּ לֹא הִבְטִיחוּ. כְּמִי שֶׁהִבְטִיחוּ.

רִבִּי יוֹנָה וְרִבִּי יוֹסֵה תְּרֵיהוֹן אָמְרִין. בְּקַדְמִיתָא הֲוֵינָן אָמְרִין. יִשְׂרָאֵל עָרֵל מַוִּין עָלָיו. וְלָא הֲוֵינָן אָמְרִין כְּלוּם. תַּנָּא רִבִּי סִימוֹן בַּר זַבְדִּי קוֹמֵי רִבִּי הִילָא. נֶאֱמַר כָּאן וְאָז יִקְרַב לַעֲשׂוֹתוֹ. וְנֶאֱמַר לְהַלָּן אָז יֹאכַל בּוֹ. מַה אָז שֶׁנֶּאֱמַר לְהַלָּן עַד שֶׁיְּהֵא כָשֵׁר בִּשְׁעַת אֲכִילָה. אַף אָז שֶׁנֶּאֱמַר כָּאן עַד שֶׁיְּהֵא כָשֵׁר בִּשְׁעַת (אֲכִילָה) [שְׁחִיטָה].

פְּעָמִים שֶׁהוּא נַעֲשָׂה כְיוֹצֵא בָהֶם. פְּעָמִים שֶׁהֵן נַעֲשִׂים כְּיוֹצֵא בוֹ. פְּעָמִים שֶׁהוּא נַעֲשָׂה כְיוֹצֵא בָהֶם. בְּגַל אָרוֹךְ. אֲנִי אוֹמֵר. נִזְרַק עָלָיו הַדָּם עַד שֶׁלֹּא הִגִּיעַ לַטּוּמְאָה. פְּעָמִים שֶׁהֵן נַעֲשִׂין כְּיוֹצֵא בוֹ. בְּגַל עָגוּל. אֵירַע בָּהֶן פְּסוּל בֵּין שְׁחִיטָה לִזְרִיקָה הֵן נַעֲשִׂין כְּיוֹצֵא בוֹ בְּגַל עָגוּל.

Halakhah 6: Rebbi Yose ben Rebbi Abun, Abba bar bar Ḥana in the name of Rebbi Joḥanan: The Mishnah[100] if he was jailed by Jews. But if he was jailed by gentiles. *whose mouth speaks vanity and whose oath is false oath*[101]. If he was held outside of Jerusalem, but if he was held in Jerusalem even if they did not promise it is as if they had promised[102].

HALAKHAH SIX

Rebbi Jonah and Rebbi Yose both are saying, in the beginning we used to say that one may sprinkle on an uncircumcised Jew; but we were saying nothing[103]. Rebbi Simon bar Zavdi stated before Rebbi Hila: It is said here *then he shall come near to make it*, and it is said there, *then he may eat of it*[104]. Since *then* mentioned there presumes that he is qualified at the time of eating, so also *there* mentioned here presumes that he is qualified at the time of (eating) [slaughter][105].

Sometimes he[106] has the status of them and sometimes they have the status of him. Sometimes he has the status of them, a long collapsed building. I am saying that the blood was poured for him before he reached the impurity[107]. Sometimes they have the status of him, at a circular collapsed building[108]; if a disqualification occurred for them between slaughter and pouring, they have the status of him at a circular collapsed building.

100 About the person who had been promised that he would be freed.

101 *Ps.* 144:8.

102 Since they can bring the *Pesah* to the jail and eat there with him.

103 Sprinkling with water mixed with ashes of the Red Cow belongs to the ritual of cleansing the impurity of the dead; it is applicable to all Jews including those uncircumcised (cf. Note 160). But for people intending to eat *Pesah*, this applies only to those already circumcised, as explained in the following sentence.

104 In the rules of the *Pesah*, *Ex.* 12:43-50, it is said of the slave (v.44) that he must be circumcised, *then he may eat of it*, and of the proselyte (v.48) that all his males have to be circumcised, *then he may come near to make it*. Since the verse about the slave states that circumcision is what is needed before he can eat, the same is true for the proselyte, and he must be circumcised and receive sprinkling before he can eat. Babli *Yebamot* 71a.

105 The text in parentheses was first written by the scribe who then corrected it to the text in brackets. It is obvious that the original text is the correct one.

106 The person digging for victims in a collapsed building who is obligated for Second *Pesah*.

107 Then he may not bring a Second *Pesah*. Babli 91a.

108 Where in all likelihood he stood over the corpse if any was found at all, then he is impure by "tent impurity".

(fol. 35c) **משנה ז**: אֵין שׁוֹחֲטִין אֶת הַפֶּסַח עַל הַיָּחִיד דִּבְרֵי רִבִּי יְהוּדָה. וְרִבִּי יוֹסֵי מַתִּיר. אֲפִילוּ חֲבוּרָה שֶׁל מֵאָה שֶׁאֵינָן יְכוֹלִין לוֹכַל כַּזַּיִת אֵין שׁוֹחֲטִין עֲלֵיהֶן. וְאֵין עוֹשִׂין חֲבוּרָה נָשִׁים וַעֲבָדִים וּקְטַנִּים:

Mishnah 7: One does not slaughter the *Pesaḥ* for a single person, the words of Rebbi Jehudah; but Rebbi Yose permits. One does not slaughter for a group, even of a hundred, if none of them can eat the volume of an olive[109], and one does not form a group of women, slaves, and minors.

109 Even though together they eat more than the volume of an olive.

(36a line 66) **הלכה ז**: אָמַר רִבִּי יוֹחָנָן. טַעֲמֵיהּ דְּרִבִּי יוּדָה. לֹא תוּכַל לִזְבּוֹחַ אֶת־הַפֶּסַח בְּאַחַד שְׁעָרֶיךָ. מַה מְקַייֵם רִבִּי יוֹסֵי טַעֲמֵיהּ דְּרִבִּי יוּדָא. פָּתַר לָהּ כְּרִבִּי אֶלְעָזָר בֶּן מַתְיָה. דְּתַנֵּי. רִבִּי אֶלְעָזָר אוֹמֵר. יָכוֹל יְהֵא הַיָּחִיד מַכְרִיעַ עַל הַטּוּמְאָה. תַּלְמוּד לוֹמַר לֹא תוּכַל לִזְבּוֹחַ אֶת־הַפֶּסַח בְּאַחַד. אָמַר רִבִּי יוֹחָנָן. מוֹדֶה רִבִּי יוּדָה שֶׁאִם עָבַר וְזָרַק אֶת הַדָּם שֶׁהוּרְצָה. עָבַר וְשָׁחַט מַתִּירִין לוֹ לִזְרוֹק.

תַּנֵּי. אֵין עוֹשִׂין חֲבוּרָה נָשִׁים וַעֲבָדִים וּקְטַנִּים מִפְּנֵי שֶׁהֵן מַרְבִּין בְּתִיפְלָה. תַּנֵּי בַּר קַפָּרָא. שֶׁלֹּא יָבִיאוּ אֶת הַקֳּדָשִׁים לִידֵי בִיזָּיוֹן. רִבִּי יַעֲקֹב בַּר אָחָא בְשֵׁם רִבִּי אִיסִי. אֵין עוֹשִׂין חֲבוּרָה שֶׁלְּגֵרִים. מִתּוֹךְ שֶׁהֵן [מְקוּלְקָלִין אֵין] מְדַקְדְּקִין בּוֹ. וְהֵם מְבִיאִין אוֹתוֹ לִידֵי פָסוּל.

Halakhah 7: Rebbi Joḥanan said, the season of Rebbi Jehudah: *You may not sacrifice the Pesaḥ in one of your gates*[110] How does Rebbi Yose interpret Rebbi Jehudah's reason? He explains it following Rebbi Eleazar ben Matthew, as it was stated: Rebbi Eleazar says, I could think that a single person clinches for impurity, the verse says, *you may not sacrifice the Pesaḥ in one*[111]. Rebbi Joḥanan said, Rebbi Jehudah concedes that if he transgressed and poured, it was made acceptable; if he transgressed and slaughtered one permits him to pour.

It was stated: one does not form a group of women, slaves, and minors, since they increase lewd behavior[112]. Bar Qappara stated, because they bring *sancta* to disqualification[113]. Rebbi Jacob bar Aha in the name of Rebbi Issy: One does not form a group from proselytes. Since they are [faulty they are not][114] diligent about it and bring it to disqualification.

110 *Deut.* 16:5. Halakhah 9:9, Babli 91a,99a; *Sifry Deut.* #132.
111 Cf. Chapter 7, Note 149.
112 Without the presence of adult free males.
113 Cf. *Šabbat* 11, Note 58.

114 The text in brackets is an addition at the margin of the ms. The text without the addition is that of the Babli 91b, the text with the addition is quoted there by Tosaphot *s.v.* שמא.

(fol. 35c) **משנה ח**: אוֹנֵן טוֹבֵל וְאוֹכֵל פִּסְחוֹ לָעֶרֶב אֲבָל לֹא בַקֳּדָשִׁים. הַשּׁוֹמֵעַ עַל מֵתוֹ וּמִי שֶׁנִּתְלַקְּטוּ לוֹ עֲצָמוֹת טוֹבֵל וְאוֹכֵל בַּקֳּדָשִׁים. גֵּר שֶׁנִּתְגַּיֵּיר עֶרֶב פֶּסַח. בֵּית שַׁמַּאי אוֹמְרִים טוֹבֵל וְאוֹכֵל אֶת פִּסְחוֹ לָעֶרֶב. וּבֵית הִלֵּל אוֹמְרִים הַפּוֹרֵשׁ מִן הָעָרְלָה כְּפוֹרֵשׁ מִן הַקֶּבֶר:

Mishnah 8: The deep mourner immerses himself and eats his *Pesaḥ* in the evening but not [other] *sancta*[97,115]. He who hears about a death or for whom bones were collected immerses himself and eats *sancta*[116]. A proselyte who converted on Passover eve, the House of Shammai say that he immerses himself[117] and eats his *Pesaḥ* in the evening, but the House of Hillel say that he who separates from the prepuce is like one who separates from a grave[118].

115 In line with Mishnah 6 it is held that the biblical rules for deep mourning only apply during daytime; the extension to the following night is rabbinical and is waved for the *Pesaḥ*, whose omission is a deadly sin, but not for other *sancta*.

116 If he did not become impure by the impurity of the dead, the immersion required for *sancta* is purely rabbinical; this rabbinic extension of the rules of deep mourning in no case extends to the night (Mishnah *Hagigah* 3:3).

117 An immersion for *sancta*, additional to that required for conversion.

118 After conversion he has to be sprinkled with water containing ashes of the Red Cow on the 3rd and 7th days after conversion.

(36a line 74) **הלכה ח**: אָמַר רִבִּי יוֹסֵי בֵּירִבִּי בּוּן. מַתְנִיתָהּ בְּשֶׁנַּעֲשָׂה אוֹנֵן מִשָּׁעָה רִאשׁוֹנָה בֵּין שְׁחִיטָה לִזְרִיקָה. אֲבָל אִם נַעֲשָׂה אוֹנֵן לְאַחַר כַּפָּרָה כְּבָר הוּרְצָה.

וְתַנֵּי כֵן. אֵי זוֹ הִיא אֲנִינָה. מִשְּׁעַת מִיתָה וְעַד שְׁעַת קְבוּרָה. דִּבְרֵי רִבִּי. וַחֲכָמִים אוֹמְרִים. כָּל־הַיּוֹם כּוּלּוֹ. אַשְׁכָּחַת חֲמָר. קַלּוֹת וַחֲמוּרוֹת עַל דְּרִבִּי. קַלּוֹת וַחֲמוּרוֹת עַל דְּרַבָּנָן. קַלּוֹת עַל דְּרִבִּי. מֵת וְנִקְבַּר בְּשַׁעְתּוֹ. עַל דַּעְתֵּיהּ דְּרִבִּי. אֵינוֹ אָסוּר אֶלָּא אוֹתָהּ שָׁעָה בִּלְבָד. עַל דַּעְתְּהוֹן דְּרַבָּנָן אָסוּר כָּל הַיּוֹם כּוּלּוֹ. קַלּוֹת עַל דְּרַבָּנָן. מֵת וְנִקְבַּר לְאַחַר שְׁלֹשָׁה יָמִים. עַל דַּעְתְּהוֹן דְּרַבָּנָן אָסוּר כָּל־אוֹתוֹ הַיּוֹם. עַל דַּעְתֵּיהּ דְּרִבִּי. אָסוּר עַד שְׁלֹשָׁה יָמִים. אֲתָא רִבִּי אַבָּהוּ בְּשֵׁם רִבִּי יוֹחָנָן וְרַב חוּנָה תְּרֵיהוֹן אָמְרִין. מוֹדֶה רִבִּי לַחֲכָמִים שֶׁאֵינוֹ אָסוּר אֶלָּא אוֹתוֹ הַיּוֹם בִּלְבָד. וְתַנֵּי כֵן. רִבִּי אוֹמֵר. תֵּדַע לָךְ שֶׁאֵין אֲנִינוּת [הַלַּיְלָה] תּוֹרָה. שֶׁהֲרֵי אָמְרוּ. אוֹנֵן טוֹבֵל וְאוֹכֵל פִּסְחוֹ

לָעֶרֶב. וַהֲרֵי אֲנִינוּת יוֹם עָשׂוּ אוֹתָהּ תּוֹרָה. רִבִּי יוֹסֵה בֵּירִבִּי בּוּן בְּשֵׁם רִבִּי חִסְדָּא. תִּיפְתָּר בְּשֶׁנִּקְבַּר עִם דִּמְדּוּמֵי הַחַמָּה. וְלֵית שְׁמַע מִינָהּ כְּלוּם.

Halakhah 8: Rebbi Yose ben Rebbi Abun said, the Mishnah is about one who newly became a deep mourner between slaughter and pouring[119]. But if he became a deep mourner after atonement it already was accepted[120].

[121]And it was stated[122]: "What is deep mourning? From the moment of death until the moment of burial, the word of Rebbi. Bur the Sages say, the entire day." It turns out that one describes leniencies and stringencies following Rebbi, leniencies and stringencies following the rabbis. What leniencies following Rebbi? If he died and was buried within the hour. Following Rebbi he is forbidden only that hour, following the rabbis he is forbiddden the entire day. Leniencies following the rabbis? If he died and was buried after three days. Following the rabbis, he is forbidden the entire day; following Rebbi he is forbidden up to three days. There came Rebbi Abbahu in the name of Rebbi Johanan, and Rav Huna, both of whom said that Rebbi agrees with the Sages that he is forbidden only during the first day, as it was stated[123]: Rebbi said, you know that deep mourning [in the night] is not biblical, since they said, "the deep mourner immerses himself and eats his *Pesaḥ* in the evening." But they declared deep mourning during daytime as biblical. Rebbi Yose ben Rebbi Abun in the name of Rav Hisda: Explain it that he was buried close to sundown and one cannot infer anything.[124]

119 It may have occurred earlier. The reason for this formulation is explained at the end of the paragraph.
120 Since the sacrifice is accepted, there is no reason to wave any rules and the deep mourner may not eat from the *Pesaḥ* but he has fulfilled his religious duty.
121 This also is in *Sanhedrin* 2:1 (Notes 52-55), *Horaiot* 3:2.

122 *Babli Zevahim* 100b; a suspect text in *Semahot* 4:4.
123 *Babli Zevahim* 100b.
124 The Mishnah only refers to the unlikely case that the deep mourner was not defiled with the impurity of the dead in a case in which both Rebbi and the Sages will agree on the duration of the deep mourning.

(36b line 12) רִבִּי אַבָּהוּ בְּשֵׁם רִבִּי לָעְזָר. אֵין אֲנִינָה אֶלָּא לְמֵת בִּלְבָד. דִּכְתִיב וְאֲנִי וְאֲבֵלוּ פְתָחֶיהָ. הָתִיב רִבִּי חִייָה בַּר אָדָא. וְהָכְתִיב וְאָנוּ הַדַּייָגִים וְאָבְלוּ כָּל־מַשְׁלִיכֵי בַיְאוֹר חַכָּה. אָמַר רִבִּי חֲנָנָה. כֵּינִי מַתְנִיתָא. אֵין אֲנִינָה טְמֵאָה אֶלָּא לְמֵת בִּלְבַד.

[121]Rebbi Abbahu in the name of Rebbi Eleazar: "Deep sorrow"[125] is only for the dead, for it is written[126]: *Its gates are in deep sorrow and mourning.* Hiyya bar Ada objected: Is it not written[127]: *the fishermen are in deep sorrow, and mourning all who throw a fishing hook into the Nile*? Rebbi Ḥanina said, so is the *baraita*: there is no deep sorrow in impurity except for the dead.

125 In its legal implications, that the person not only be forbidden to eat sanctified food but also cannot be counted in a quorum for religious services; cf. *Berakhot* 3:1, Note 42.
126 *Is.* 3:26. The gates of Jerusalem are in sorrow because all its men are dead.

127 *Is.* 19:8. The fishermen are in *deep sorrow* (and they *mourn* as quoted in the two parallel texts) because the Nile dried up. This proves that both terms used for the religious obligations of a person whose close relative died are used in the Bible also to describe other situations.

(36b line 15) תַּנֵּי. יוֹם שְׁמִיעָה כְיוֹם קְבוּרָה. לִקְרַע וּלְאִיבּוּל וְלִסְפִירַת שִׁבְעָה וְלִסְפִירַת שְׁלשִׁים. וְלֶאֱכוֹל בַּקֳּדָשִׁים הֲרֵי הֵן כְּלִיקוּטֵי עֲצָמוֹת (טוֹבֵל וְאוֹכֵל בַּקֳּדָשִׁים). וְלִיקוּטֵי עֲצָמוֹת טוֹבֵל וְאוֹכֵל בַּקֳּדָשִׁים. רִבִּי יוֹסֵי בֵּירִבִּי בּוּן בְּשֵׁם רַב חִסְדָּא. תִּיפְתָּר שֶׁנִּקְבַּר מִשֶּׁחֲשֵׁיכָה. וְזֶה וָזֶה טוֹבְלִין וְאוֹכְלִין אֶת פִּסְחֵיהֶן לָעָרֶב. וּקְבוּרָה אוֹכֶלֶת בַּקֳּדָשִׁים. אָמַר רִבִּי יוֹסֵי בֵּירִבִּי בּוּן. תַּרְתֵּיהוֹן בִּשְׁמִיעָה. שָׁמַע שֶׁמֵּת לוֹ מֵת מֵאֶתְמוֹל. טוֹבֵל וְאוֹכֵל בַּקֳּדָשִׁים. שָׁמַע שֶׁנִּתְלַקְטוּ לוֹ עֲצָמוֹת מֵאֶתְמוֹל. טוֹבֵל וְאוֹכֵל בַּקֳּדָשִׁים.

It was stated[128]: "The day of information is like the day of burial as regards tearing[129], and mourning[130], and counting Seven and Thirty; but to eat *sancta* it is like gathering bones, (he immerses himself and eats *sancta*)[131]." About gathering bones, may he immerse himself and eat *sancta*[132]? Rebbi Yose ben Rebbi Abun in the name of Rav Ḥisda, explain it if he was buried after nightfall[133]. "In both cases they immerse themselves and eat their *Pesaḥ* in the evening.[134]" After burial may one eat *sancta*? Rebbi Yose ben Rebbi Abun said, both are about information. If he was informed that a relative died the day before, he immerses himself and eats *sancta*; if he was informed that bones were collected the day before, he immerses himself and eats *sancta*[135].

128 Babli *Zevahim* 100b; *Semahot* 12:1. In both sources, "and eats *sancta* in the evening." From the following it is clear that this also was the reading of the Yerushalmi.
129 The obligation to tear his clothes.

130 To observe the rules of the seven days of intensive followed by the thirty days of lesser mourning.
131 The text in parentheses was written by the scribe but then was deleted. The

deletion is in error as shown by the question following the statement.

132 Why is the qualification "in the evening" missing in the Mishnah?

133 Then he can eat *sancta* only a day later.

134 Since the Mishnah states that the rules of deep mourning are waved for *Pesaḥ* but not for other *sancta*, it seems that here one should read *sancta* for *Pesaḥ*.

135 But in the evening of the day itself only *Pesaḥ* may be eaten, not *sancta* in general.

(36b line 22) תַּנֵּי. הַמַּעֲבִיר אָרוֹן מִמָּקוֹם לְמָקוֹם. אֵין בּוֹ מִשּׁוּם לִיקּוּטֵי עֲצָמוֹת. אָמַר רִבִּי אֲחָא. הָדָא דְאַתְּ אָמַר בְּאָרוֹן שֶׁלְּאֶבֶן. אֲבָל בְּאָרוֹן שֶׁלְעֵץ יֵשׁ בּוֹ מִשּׁוּם לִיקּוּטֵי עֲצָמוֹת. אָמַר רִבִּי יוֹסֵה. וַאֲפִילוּ בְאָרוֹן שֶׁלְעֵץ אֵין בּוֹ מִשּׁוּם לִיקּוּטֵי עֲצָמוֹת. אֵי זֶהוּ לִיקּוּט עֲצָמוֹת. הַמַּעֲבִידָן בָּאֶפִּיקְרֵיסִין מִמָּקוֹם לְמָקוֹם. רִבִּי חַגַּי בְּשֵׁם רִבִּי זְעוּרָה. לִיקּוּט עֲצָמוֹת כִּשְׁמוּעָן. וְתַנֵּי כֵן. לִיקּוּט עֲצָמוֹת מְלַקֵּט עֶצֶם עֶצֶם מִשֶּׁיִּתְאַכֵּל הַבָּשָׂר. תַּנֵּי. אֵין שְׁמוּעָה לְלִיקּוּט עֲצָמוֹת. אָמַר רִבִּי חַגַּי. וְהוּא שֶׁשָּׁמַע לְמָחָר. אֲבָל אִם שָׁמַע בּוֹ בַיּוֹם יֵשׁ שְׁמוּעָה לְלִיקּוּטֵי עֲצָמוֹת. וְיֵשׁ שִׁיעוּר לְלִיקּוּטֵי עֲצָמוֹת. תַּנָּא נִיקוֹמָכִי קוֹמֵי רִבִּי זְעוּרָה. אֵין שִׁיעוּר לְלִיקּוּטֵי עֲצָמוֹת. כְּהָדָא רִבִּי מָנָא הוֹרֵי לְרִבִּי הִלֵּל דִּכְיפְרָא לִקְרוֹעַ וּלְהִתְאַבֵּל כְּרִבִּי אֲחָא. וְשֶׁלֹּא לְהִיטַמּוֹת כְּרִבִּי יוֹסֵי. תַּנֵּי. לִיקּוּטֵי עֲצָמוֹת אֵין אוֹמְרִין עֲלֵיהֶן קִינִים וְנֶהִי. וְאֵין אוֹמְרִין עֲלֵיהֶן לֹא בִרְכַּת אֲבֵלִים וְלֹא תַנְחוּמֵי אֲבֵלִים. אֵילּוּ הֵן בִּרְכֹת אֲבֵלִים. מַה שֶׁהֵן אוֹמְרִים בְּבֵית הַכְּנֶסֶת. אֵילּוּ הֵן תַּנְחוּמֵי אֲבֵלִים. מַה שֶׁהֵן אוֹמְרִים בַּשּׁוּרָה. תַּנֵּי. אֲבָל אוֹמְרִין עֲלֵיהֶן דְּבָרִים. מָהוּ דְבָרִים. רַבָּנָן דְּקַיְסָרִין אָמְרִין. קִילּוּסִין.

1 ליקוטי | מ ליקוט 2 דאת | מ דת ליקוטי | מ ליקוטי אמ' | מ אמ' ליה 3 יוסה | מ יוסי ואפי' | מ ואפי' תימא 4 באפיקריסין | מ באפיקרסין 5 ליקוט | מ ליקוטי ליקוטי | מ ליקוטי 6 חגי | מ חגיי לליקוטי | מ לליקוטי 7 לליקוטי | מ לליקוט (2) 8 ושלא להיטמות | מ שלא להיטמאות 9 ואין | מ אין

[136]It was stated: If a person transports a casket from place to place the rules[137] of collecting bones do not apply. Rebbi Aḥa said, that only is about a stone sarcophagus. But to a wooden casket the rules of collecting bones do apply. Rebbi Yose said, even to a wooden casket the rules of collecting bones do not apply. When is there collecting bones? If one transports them in a striped garment[138] from place to place. Rebbi Haggai in the name of Rebbi Ze`ira: Collecting bones [is] what it means[139]. And it was stated thus: In collecting bones one collects them bone by bone after the flesh has decomposed. It was stated: There is no information[140] about collecting bones. Rebbi Haggai said, that is if he was informed the next day. But on the day itself there is information about collecting bones. Is there a minimum for collecting bones? Nikomachos stated before Rebbi Ze`ira: There is no minimum about collecting bones. About this, Rebbi Mana instructed Rebbi

Hillel from Kifra to tear and mourn following Rebbi Aha but not to defile himself following Rebbi Yose[141]. It was stated: When collecting bones one does not recite lamentations and dirges; one recites neither the blessings for mourners nor the consolations for mourners. These are blessings for mourners: what is recited in the synagogue. These are consolations of mourners, what is said in the row[142]. It was stated: But one says words. What are words? The rabbis of Caesarea are saying, eulogies[143].

136 This text is from *Mo`ed qatan* 1:5 (ס). There also exists a Genizah text for most of the Halakhah there.
137 Prescribing mourning rites.
138 Greek ἐπικάρσιον, τό.
139 The rules apply only to the act of collecting bones, not of transporting.
140 No prescribed mourning rites when one is informed of the act.
141 R. Hillel was a Cohen; he was instructed to follow R. Aha to observe mourning rites when his parents' bone were brought in ossuaries but not to violate the biblical rules which prohibit a Cohen from becoming impure in the impurity of the dead except for the burial of close relatives. The rules spelled out by R. Aha are purely rabbinic.
142 After the burial the people attending form two rows between which the mourners walk and are greeted with a wish that "the Omnipresent may console you with all the mourners of Zion and Jerusalem."
143 קילוס "praise" is derived from Greek καλῶς! "beautiful, excellent". For the use as "eulogy" compare καλολογέω, same as ἐυλογέω (E. G.).

(36b line 37) מַה טַּעֲמוֹן דְּבֵית שַׁמַּי. אַתֶּם וּשְׁבִיכֶם. מַה אַתֶּם לֹא נִטְמֵאתֶם עַד שֶׁנִּכְנַסְתֶּם לַבְּרִית. אַף שְׁבִיכֶם לֹא נִטְמְאוּ עַד שֶׁנִּכְנַס לַבְּרִית. מַה טַּעֲמוֹן דְּבֵית הִלֵּל. אַתֶּם וּשְׁבִיכֶם. מַה אַתֶּם טְעוּנִין הַזָּיָה בַּשְּׁלִישִׁי וּבַשְּׁבִיעִי. אַף שְׁבִיכֶם טְעוּנִין הַזָּיָה בַּשְּׁלִישִׁי וּבַשְּׁבִיעִי. וְאֵינוֹ מְחוּוָּר. דְּאָמַר רַב חִיָּיה בַּר יוֹסֵף גִּידּוּל בַּר בִּנְיָמִן בְּשֵׁם רַב. מוֹדַיי בֵּית הִלֵּל שֶׁאִם עָבַר וְזָרַק אֶת הַדָּם שֶׁיּוּרְצָה.

What is the reason of the House of Shammai? *You and your captives*[144]. Since you could not be impure before you entered the covenant, also your captives cannot be impure before they enter the covenant[145]. What is the reason of the House of Hillel? *You and your captives*. Since you need sprinkling on the third and seventh {days}, so your captives need sprinkling on the third and seventh {days}. But it is not logically consistent[146], since Rav Hiyya bar Joseph, Giddul bar Benjamin said in the name of Rav: The House of Hillel agree that if he transgressed and poured the blood, that it is accepted.

144 *Num.* 31:19, speaking of the captive Midianite women.

145 While it seems from the text there that a Gentile corpse imparts impurity of the dead by touch, it is clear that a living Gentile cannot biblically be impure; the impurities attributed to Gentiles are of purely rabbinic character and must be disregarded in matters of conversions. *Sifry Num.* # 157 notes that mention of the captives in relation to impurity implies that these had to be converted.

146 There is no claim that the restrictive practice of the House of Hillel is biblical.

(36b line 43) נָזִיר שֶׁנִּיטְמָא בִסְפֵק רְשׁוּת הַיָּחִיד[(וְאֵינוּ] בַּפֶּסַח. רִבִּי הוֹשַׁעְיָה רַבָּה אָמַר. הַנָּזִיר מְגַלֵּחַ. רִבִּי יוֹחָנָן אָמַר. אֵין הַנָּזִיר מְגַלֵּחַ. דְּתַנִּינָן תַּמָּן. כָּל־טוּמְאָה מִן הַמֵּת שֶׁהַנָּזִיר מְגַלֵּחַ עָלֶיהָ [חַיָּיבִין עָלֶיהָ] (וְ)עַל בִּיאַת הַמִּקְדָּשׁ. וְכָל־טוּמְאָה מִן הַמֵּת שֶׁאֵין הַנָּזִיר מְגַלֵּחַ עָלֶיהָ [אֵין חַיָּיבִין עָלֶיהָ] (וְ)עַל בִּיאַת הַמִּקְדָּשׁ. הַיי דֵּינוֹ סָפֵק. רִבִּי יוֹחָנָן אָמַר. רֹאשָׁא דְפִירְקָא. רִבִּי הוֹשַׁעְיָה רַבָּה אָמַר. הָהֵן דְּהָכָא. יָחִיד שֶׁנִּיטְמָא בִסְפֵק רְשׁוּת הַיָּחִיד בַּפֶּסַח. רִבִּי הוֹשַׁעְיָה רַבָּה אָמַר. יִדָּחֶה לְפֶסַח שֵׁינִי. רִבִּי יוֹחָנָן אָמַר. מְשַׁלְּחִין אוֹתוֹ לְדֶרֶךְ רְחוֹקָה. וְאַתְיָא כָּיי דָּמַר רִבִּי יוֹחָנָן. נִיטְמָא בְטוּמְאַת בֵּית פָּרָס. מְשַׁלְּחִין אוֹתוֹ דֶּרֶךְ רְחוֹקָה. צִיבּוּר שֶׁנִּיטְמָא בִסְפֵק רְשׁוּת הַיָּחִיד בַּפֶּסַח. רִבִּי יוֹחָנָן אָמַר. יַעֲשׂוּ בִסְפֵיקָן. רִבִּי הוֹשַׁעְיָה רַבָּה אָמַר. יַיעֲשׂוּ בְטוּמְאָה. (אוֹמֵר) [אוֹף] רִבִּי הוֹשַׁעְיָה [מוֹדֶה] שֶׁיַּעֲשׂוּ בִסְפֵיקָן. לֹא אָמַר רִבִּי הוֹשַׁעְיָה אֶלָּא לְחוּמַרִין.

[147]A *nazir* who became impure by a doubt relating to a private domain[148] (on Qassover) [not related to the *Pesaḥ*.[149]] The great Rebbi Hoshaia said, the *nazir* shaves. Rebbi Joḥanan said, the *nazir* does not shave[150], since we have stated there[151]: "For any impurity caused by a corpse for which the *nazir* shaves, [one is liable] if entering the Sanctuary, but any impurity caused by a corpse for which the *nazir* does not shave, [one is not liable] if entering the Sanctuary." What kind of doubt? Rebbi Joḥanan said, the start of the Chapter[152]. The great Rebbi Hoshaia said, the one here[153]. A person who became impure by a doubt relating to a private domain for the *Pesaḥ*. Rebbi Hoshaia said, he should be pushed to the Second *Pesaḥ*. Rebbi Joḥanan said, one sends him on a far journey[154]. This follows what Rebbi Joḥanan said, if he became impure by the impurity of the broken field[155], one sends him on a far journey. The community who became impure by a doubt relating to a private domain on Passover. Rebbi Joḥanan said, they should present it in their doubt[156]. Does the great Rebbi Hoshaia say, it should be made in impurity? Rebbi Hoshaia (said) [also agrees] that it should be presented in their doubt; what Rebbi Hoshaia said referred only to restrictions.

147 This paragraph is a reformulation of one in *Nazir* 8:1 (Notes 56-63) but, as the quotes in the paragraph show clearly, the source is *Nazir*, in contrast to the next paragraph which in *Nazir* is a copy from *Pesahim*.

148 The general principle is that a doubt about impurity arising in a private domain is treated as certain impurity, in the public domain as certain purity. The rule becomes void if the character of the place itself is doubtful.

149 The scribe wrote "on *Pesah*" and the corrector inserted "not". Both words should be deleted.

150 The essence of a vow of *nazir* is that the person must let his hair grow, abstain from all products of the vine, and avoid any impurity of the dead. If he should become impure in this impurity, he has to shave, bring required sacrifices, and start his *nezirut* all over again.

151 Mishnah *Nazir* 7:4. In Mishnah 7:2 it is explained that the *Nazir* shaves only if the cause of the impurity is a verified part of a corpse; the cases of doubt enumerated in Mishnah 7:3 are excluded. The liability for entering the Sanctuary in impurity is for a sacrifice if inadvertent or for extirpation if intentional.

152 Mishnah *Nazir* 8:1: A person saw that one of two *nezirim* became impure but he cannot identify whom he saw. Then there certainly is impurity but it is not known to whom it refers.

153 One of the cases of Mishnah *Nazir* 7:3, where t is not known whether actually impurity was created.

154 For him also the person has to bring the *Second Pesah*, but he holds that like any other sacrifice it may be brought for a certain, rather than a possible, obligation.

155 A field which contained a grave ploughed under. Not only is the suspected place of the grave impure by biblical standards but the entire field is rabbinically impure since the plough might have caught a bone and transported it to another part of the field.

156 If the majority of the public is certainly impure, all *Pesahim* are made in impurity. If the majority is in doubt whether they are impure, the pure minority brings their offerings in purity and the possibly impure majority theirs in possible impurity.

(36b line 55) רִבִּי יוֹחָנָן בְּשֵׁם רִבִּי בְּנָיָיה. יִשְׂרָאֵל עָרֵל מַזִּין עָלָיו. שֶׁכֵּן מָצָאנוּ שֶׁקִּיבְּלוּ אֲבוֹתֵינוּ בַּמִּדְבָּר הַזָּיָיה עֲרֵלִים. אָמַר רַב חִסְדָּא. אַתְיָא כְמָאן דְּאָמַר. בְּאַחַד עָשָׂר מָלוּ. בְּרַם כְּמָאן דְּאָמַר. בָּעֲשִׂירִי מָלוּ. לֹא קִיבְּלוּ הַזָּיָיה עֲרֵלִים. אָמַר רִבִּי אָבוּן. מִכָּל־מָקוֹם לֹא מָנוּ לַהַזָּיָיה עֲרֵלִים. רִבִּי לְעָזָר בְּשֵׁם רִבִּי חֲנִינָה. מַעֲשֶׂה בְכֹהֵן עָרֵל שֶׁהִזָּה וְיוּכְשְׁרוּ הַזָּיוֹתָיו. וְתַנֵּי כֵן. רִבִּי אֱלִיעֶזֶר בֶּן יַעֲקֹב אוֹמֵר. אִיסְרַטְיוֹטוֹת הָיוּ שׁוֹמְרִין צִירִין בִּירוּשָׁלֵם וְטָבְלוּ וְאָכְלוּ פִּסְחֵיהֶן לָעֶרֶב.

Rebbi Joḥanan in the name of Rebbi Benaiah: One sprinkles on an uncircumcised Jew[157], for we find that our forefathers in the desert[158] received sprinkling when uncircumcised. Rav Ḥisda said, following him who said that they circumcised on the eleventh[159]. But for him who said that they circumcised on the tenth, they did not count sprinkling when uncircumcised.

Rebbi Abun said, did they not have to count for sprinkling when uncircumcised in any case[160]? Rebbi Eleazar in the name of Rebbi Hanina: It happened that an uncircumcised Cohen sprinkled[161] and the sprinklings were declared valid. It was stated so: Rebbi Eliezer ben Jacob says, there were soldiers[162] and gate keepers in Jerusalem who immersed themselves and ate their *Pesaḥ* in the evening[163].

156 *Nazir* 8:1, Notes 64-71. A parallel discussion is in the Babli, *Yebamot* 17b.

157 The position of the House of Hillel in the Mishnah is rejected. It is asserted that the uncircumcised can purify himself from the impurity and, being circumcised later, participate in the *Pesaḥ* celebration as asserted by the House of Shammai.

158 Not in the desert, but after crossing the Jordan on the 10th of Nisan (*Jos.* 4:19). They were then circumcised (*Jos.* 5:2-8) and celebrated the *Pesaḥ* on the 14th (*Jos.* 5:10).

159 If they were circumcised on the 11th they had to be sprinkled on the 10th, when they still were uncircumcised, in order to become pure on the 14th.

160 Rav Hisda's argument has to be rejected since if sprinkling on an uncircumcised person is ineffective, the underlying counting (of the third, seventh days) also must be ineffective. But for the *Pesaḥ* on the 14th, the counting had to start on the 7th, when according to the biblical text everybody (except Joshua, Caleb, and possibly Levites and/or Priests) were uncircumcised. He will hold that the first Passover in Canaan was held in impurity. This argument, represented in the Babli, *loc. cit.*, by Mar Zutra, there is rejected by Rav Ashi.

161 In *Nazir*: "he was sprinkled" (passive voice).

162 Greek στρατιώτης, ὁ.

163 They were Gentiles who converted to Judaism, were circumcised, immersed themselves in a *miqweh* on the 14th of Nisan, and participated in Passover, not needing cleansing by sprinkling following the House of Shammai

מי שהיה טמא פרק תשיעי

(fol.36b) **משנה א**: מִי שֶׁהָיָה טָמֵא אוֹ בְדֶרֶךְ רְחוֹקָה וְלֹא עָשָׂה אֶת הָרִאשׁוֹן יַעֲשֶׂה אֶת הַשֵּׁנִי. שָׁגַג אוֹ נֶאֱנַס וְלֹא עָשָׂה אֶת הָרִאשׁוֹן יַעֲשֶׂה אֶת הַשֵּׁנִי. אִם כֵּן לָמָּה נֶאֱמַר טָמֵא אוֹ שֶׁהָיָה בְדֶרֶךְ רְחוֹקָה שֶׁאֵלּוּ פְטוּרִין מִן הַהִכָּרֵת וְאֵלּוּ חַיָּיבִין בַּהִכָּרֵת:

Mishnah 1: He who was impure or on a far trip and did not make the First shall make the Second[1]. If in error or by force[2] he did not make the First shall make the Second. If this is so, why was it said[3] *impure or on a far trip*? Because these are not liable for extirpation[4] but those are liable for extirpation.

1 A person impure and/or at a distance from Jerusalem on the afternoon of the 14th of Nisan is obligated to bring a *Pesah* on the 14th of Iyar.
2 He was pure and in Jerusalem on the 14th of Nisan but forcibly prevented from participating in a *Pesah*.
3 *Num.* 9:9.
4 The Second *Pesah* is a positive commandment for which no penalties are indicated in case of omission, in contrast to the First whose intentional omission is a deadly sin implying extirpation. In contrast to the Babli (93b), the Yerushalmi does not expect that those who missed the First in error or by force are subject to extirpation if they intentionally miss the Second.

(36c line 45) מִי שֶׁהָיָה טָמֵא כול׳. טָמֵא | לָנֶפֶשׁ. אֵין לִי אֶלָּא טָמֵא לַנֶּפֶשׁ. אֲנוּסִים אוֹ שׁוֹגְגִין מְנַיִין. תַּלְמוּד לוֹמַר אִישׁ אִישׁ. [רִיבָּה] עַד כְּדוֹן כְּרִבִּי עֲקִיבָה. כְּרִבִּי יִשְׁמָעֵאל. תַּנֵּי רִבִּי יִשְׁמָעֵאל. לֹא טָמֵא נֶפֶשׁ כַּהֲרֵי דֶרֶךְ רְחוֹקָה וְלֹא דֶרֶךְ רְחוֹקָה כַּהֲרֵי טָמֵא נֶפֶשׁ. הַצַּד הַשָּׁוֶה שֶׁבָּהֶן שֶׁלֹּא עָשָׂה אֶת הָרִאשׁוֹן יַעֲשֶׂה אֶת הַשֵּׁנִי. אַף אֲנִי אַרְבֶּה אֲנוּסִין אוֹ שׁוֹגְגִין שֶׁלֹּא עָשׂוּ אֶת הָרִאשׁוֹן יַעֲשׂוּ אֶת הַשֵּׁנִי. מֵזִיד מְנַיִין. אָמַר רִבִּי זְעוּרָה. וְהָאִישׁ לְרַבּוֹת אֶת הַמֵּזִיד. אָנָן תַּנִּינָן. שָׁגַג אוֹ נֶאֱנָס. תַּנֵּי רִבִּי חִיָּיה. שָׁגַג אוֹ נֶאֱנַס אוֹ הֵזִיד. אָמַר רִבִּי יוֹסֵה. מַתְנִיתָא אָמְרָה כֵן. שֶׁאֵילּוּ פְטוּרִין מִן הַהַכָּרֵת וְאֵילּוּ חַיָּיבִין בַּהִכָּרֵת: מַה אִית לָךְ חַיָּיב בְּהִכָּרֵת. לֹא מֵזִיד.

"He who was impure," etc. *Impure by a corpse*[5], I not only have impure by a corpse, from where forced or in error? The verse says, *every man*, [it added][6]. So far following Rebbi Aqiba; following Rebbi Ismael? Rebbi Ismael stated, *impure by a corpse* is not equal to *a far-away trip*, nor is *a far-away trip* equal to *impure by a corpse*, what is common to them[7] is that he did not make the First and shall make the Second; also I am adding those forced or in error who did not make the First that they shall make the Second. Intentional from where? Rebbi Ze'ira said, *but the man*, to add the one acting intentionally[8]. We have stated; "if in error or by force;" Rebbi Ḥiyya stated, "if in error, or by force, or intentional.[9]" Rebbi Yose said, the Mishnah implies this, "because these are not liable for extirpation but those are liable for extirpation;" who is subject to extirpation if not intentional?

5 *Num.* 9:10.	Aqiba in the Tosephta, that both those impure by a corpse and those on a far trip are prevented from making the First *Pesaḥ* and therefore the third hermeneutical principle excludes the one who intentionally omitted the First even though he was pure and not far away. Cf. Babli 93a/b.
6 Babli 93a.	
7 This is the third hermeneutical principle of R. Ismael. *Sifry Num.* 69, Tosephta 8:2 (in the name of R. Aqiba); Targum Pseudo-Jonathan 9:10.	
8 *Num.* 9:13: *But the man who was pure.* This contradicts the position of R.	9 Tosephta 8:1.

(36c line 54) טָמֵא | לְנֶפֶשׁ. אֵין לִי אֶלָּא טָמֵא | לְנֶפֶשׁ. טָמֵא זִיבָה וְטָמֵא צָרַעַת מְנַיִין. תַּלְמוּד לוֹמַר טָמֵא מֵת[10] רִיבָּה. מַה תַּלְמוּד לוֹמַר טָמֵא נֶפֶשׁ. אֶלָּא אִישׁ טָמֵא נֶפֶשׁ נִדְחִין לְפֶסַח שֵׁינִי. וְאֵין צִיבּוּר טָמֵא נֶפֶשׁ נִדְחָה לְפֶסַח שֵׁינִי. טָמֵא זִיבָה וְטָמֵא צָרַעַת נִדְחִין לְפֶסַח שֵׁינִי. טוּמְאַת עֲבוֹדָה זָרָה עָשׂוּ אוֹתָהּ כְּטָמֵא זִיבָה וְטָמֵא צָרַעַת. נִיתַּן לְיִשְׂרָאֵל לִבְנוֹת בֵּית הַבְּחִירָה. יָחִיד עוֹשֶׂה פֶּסַח שֵׁינִי וְאֵין צִיבּוּר עוֹשִׁין פֶּסַח שֵׁינִי. רִבִּי יוּדָה אוֹמֵר. צִיבּוּר עוֹשֶׂה פֶּסַח שֵׁינִי שֶׁכֵּן מָצִינוּ בְחִזְקִיָּה שֶׁעָשָׂה פֶּסַח שֵׁנִי. הָדָא הוּא דִכְתִיב כִּי מַרְבִּית הָעָם רַבַּת מֵאֶפְרַיִם וּמְנַשֶּׁה וגו׳.

Impure by a corpse. I have not only *impure by a corpse*; impure by genital discharge, impure by skin disease, from where? The verse says impure (by the dead)[10], it added. Why does the verse say, *impure by a corpse*[11]? A man impure by a corpse is pushed to the Second *Pesaḥ*, but a public impure by the impurity of a corpse are not pushed to the Second *Pesaḥ*. Those impure by genital discharge or impure by skin disease are pushed to the Second *Pesaḥ*. They made the impurity of idolatry equal to the impure by genital discharge or impure by skin disease[12]. If Israel had the possibility to build the Temple[13], individuals celebrate the Second *Pesaḥ* but the public does not celebrate the Second *Pesaḥ*. [14]Rebbi Jehudah says, the public celebrates the Second *Pesaḥ* since we find that Hezekia celebrated the Second *Pesaḥ*.

This is what is written, *for most of the people from Ephraim and Manasse*[15], etc.

10 This word should be deleted since there is no verse containing this expression. The argument is that while one would expect the accents to be טָמֵא לָנֶפֶשׁ "impure by a corpse," the first word carries *legarmeh*, a dividing accent, טָמֵא | לָנֶפֶשׁ, correctly translated "impure, [e. g.,] by a corpse." Babli 93a, *Sifry Num.* 69.
11 The argument is not really from this quote but from the entire first part of the verse: *every single man who would be impure, by a corpse.*
12 As explained in the paragraph after the next.
13 If the Temple could be rebuilt after the 14th of Nisan but before the 14th of Iyar.
14 From here on, the text is from *Nazir* 6:13 (Notes 83-109), *Sanhedrin* 1:2 (Notes 209-219).
15 *2Chr.* 30:18.

(36c line 63) אִית תַּנָּיֵי תַנֵי. מְעַבְּרִין אֶת הַשָּׁנָה מִפְּנֵי הַטּוּמְאָה. אִית תַּנָּיֵי תַנֵי. אֵין מְעַבְּרִין אֶת הַשָּׁנָה מִפְּנֵי הַטּוּמְאָה. מָאן דְּאָמַר אֵין מְעַבְּרִין אֶת הַשָּׁנָה מִפְּנֵי הַטּוּמְאָה. מַה מְקַיֵּים כִּי־אָכְלוּ אֶת־הַפֶּסַח בְּלֹא כַכָּתוּב. שֶׁעִיבְּרוּ אֶת נִיסָן וְאֵינוֹ מְעוּבָּר אֶלָּא אָדָר. וְאָתְיָא כַּיי דָּמַר רִבִּי סִימוֹן בַּר זַבְדִּי. גּוּלְגּוֹלְתּוֹ שֶׁלְּאָרְנָן הַיְבוּסִי מָצְאוּ תַחַת הַמִּזְבֵּחַ.

Some Tannaïm state: One intercalates the year because of impurity[16]. Some Tannaïm state: One does not intercalate the year because of impurity. He who says, one does not intercalate, how does he uphold: *for they ate the Passover contrary to what is written*[17]? They intercalated in Nisan but only Adar can be intercalated. This follows what Rebbi Simon bar Zavdi said: they found the skull of Ornan the Yebusite under the altar[18].

16 One does not intercalate a 13th month to give people time to purify themselves in time for the *Pesaḥ* on the 14th of Nisan.
17 *2Chr.* 30:18. Hezeqiah celebrated *Pesah* a month late; that is exactly what Scripture prescribes for impure individuals.
18 This statement is from *Sotah* 5:2, Note 90; it must refer to the construction of the altar by Solomon. Hezekiah moved the month because the Temple was not usable in Nisan since similarly the Temple was found to be a "tent" over human bones and thus impure. Ornan was the original owner of the Temple Mount (*1Chr.* 21:18-26); the text does not imply that Gentiles create tent impurity. Babli *Sanhedrin* 12a.

(36c line 67) כְּתִיב וַיָּחֵילוּ בְּאֶחָד לַחוֹדֶשׁ הָרִאשׁוֹן לְקַדֵּשׁ וּבְיוֹם שְׁמוֹנָה לַחוֹדֶשׁ. וַהֲלֹא בְיוֹם אֶחָד הָיוּ יְכוֹלִין לְבַעֵר כָּל־עֲבוֹדָה זָרָה שֶׁהָיָה שָׁם. אָמַר רִבִּי אִידִי. מִפְּנֵי צַלְמֵי כַשְׂדִּים שֶׁהָיוּ חֲקוּקִים בַּשֵּׁשָׁר. כְּתִיב כָּל־לְבָבוֹ הֵכִין לִדְרוֹשׁ הָאֱלֹהִים | יְי אֱלֹהֵי אֲבוֹתָיו. רִבִּי סִימוֹן בַּר זַבְדִּי

וְרִבִּי שְׁמוּאֵל בַּר נַחְמָנִי. חַד אָמַר. אֲפִילוּ עָשָׂה כַּמָּה בְטָהֳרַת הַקּוֹדֶשׁ לֹא יָצָא יְדֵי טָהֳרַת הַקּוֹדֶשׁ. וְחוֹרָנָה אָמַר. אֲפִילוּ כָּל־מַעֲשִׂים טוֹבִים שֶׁעָשָׂה לְטָהֳרַת הַקּוֹדֶשׁ לֹא יָצָא יְדֵי טָהֳרַת הַקּוֹדֶשׁ.

It is written[19]: *They started on the first of the first month, and on the eighth day . . ..* Could they not have eliminated all idolatry from there in one day? Rebbi Idi said, because of Chaldean idols which were engraved in vermilion. It is written[20]: *With all his heart he prepared himself to seek the Eternal, the God of his forefathers.* Rebbi Simon bar Zavdi and Rebbi Samuel bar Nahman: One said, with all he did for the purity of the Temple, he did not fully establish the purity of the Temple. One said, with all the good works he did, he did not fully do his duty for the purity of the Temple.

שִׁשָּׁה דְּבָרִים עָשָׂה חִזְקִיָּהוּ מֶלֶךְ יְהוּדָה. עַל שְׁלשָׁה הוֹדוּ לוֹ וְעַל שְׁלשָׁה לֹא הוֹדוּ לוֹ. וְאֵילוּ שְׁלשָׁה שֶׁהוֹדוּ לוֹ. כִּיתֵּת נְחַשׁ הַנְּחוֹשֶׁת וְהוֹדוּ לוֹ. גִּירֵר עַצְמוֹת אָבִיו עַל מִיטָּה שֶׁלַחֲבָלִים וְהוֹדוּ לוֹ. גָּנַז טַבְלָה שֶׁלִרְפוּאוֹת וְהוֹדוּ לוֹ. וְאֵילוּ שֶׁלֹא הוֹדוּ לוֹ. קִיצֵּץ דַּלְתוֹת הַהֵיכָל וְלֹא הוֹדוּ לוֹ. סָתַם אֶת מוֹצָא מֵימֵי גִיחוֹן וְלֹא הוֹדוּ לוֹ. עִיבַּר נִיסָן בְּנִיסָן. וְלֹא הוֹדוּ לוֹ.

Six things did Hezekiah, the King of Judea, do; with three they agreed, with three they did not agree[21]. For the following they agreed with him. He smashed the bronze snake[22] and they agreed with him. He dragged his father's bones on a bier of ropes[23], and they agreed with him. He hid the table of medicines[24], and they agreed with him. For the following they disagreed with him. He cut down the Temple doors[25] and they disagreed with him. He enclosed the upper Gihon spring[26], and they disagreed with him. He intercalated Nisan in Nisan[27]; and they disagreed with him.

19 *2Chr.* 29:17. They finished cleansing the Temple of idolatry on the 16th.
20 *2Chr.*30:19. The verse ends: *except for the Temple's purity.*
21 This is the last Mishnah in Chapter 4 of the Babli; Maimonides in his Mishnah commentary declares it to be a Tosephta (cf. 8:5). Babli 56a, *Berakhot* 10b, *Sanhedrin* 47a.
22 The bronze snake made by Moses, *2K.* 18:4. "They" are the Heavenly Court.
23 He buried him in an undignified way to atone for his sins. The basis is a note in *2Chr.* 28:27 that Ahaz was not buried in the kings' graves, contradicting *2K.* 16:20.
24 According to Maimonides a book of magical remedies.
25 *2K.* 18:16; to pay tribute to Assyria.
26 It seems that they did not connect *2Chr.* 32:30 with *2K.* 20:20. The statement is denied in *Avot dR. Nathan A,* Chapter 2.
27 As explained in the preceding paragraph, the celebration of Passover was wrong from beginning to end; the

intercalation would have to precede Nisan, and if it was Iyar it should not be a mass celebration.

(36d line 3) הָיָה הַצִּיבּוּר חֶצְיָים זָבִים וְחֶצְיָין טְמֵאִין. רַב אָדָא בַּר אֲהָבָה אָמַר. זָבִין נַעֲשִׂין אֵצֶל טְמֵאִין כִּטְמֵאִין אֵצֶל טְהוֹרִין. אֵינָן עוֹשִׂין זָבִין נִידָחִין לְפֶסַח שֵׁינִי. רַב חוּנָה אָמַר. אֵין תַּשְׁלוּמִין לַפֶּסַח הַבָּא בְטוּמְאָה.

הָיָה הַצִּיבּוּר רוּבָּן טְהוּרִין וּמִיעוּטָן טְמֵאִין. וּמֵתוּ מִן הַטְּהוֹרִים בֵּין שְׁחִיטָה לִזְרִיקָה. אַחַר מִי אַתְּ מְהַלֵּךְ. אַחַר שְׁחִיטָה [אוֹ] אַחַר זְרִיקָה. אִין תֵּימַר. אַחַר שְׁחִיטָה. אֵינָן עוֹשִׂין בְּטוּמְאָה. אִין תֵּימַר. אַחַר זְרִיקָה. עוֹשִׂים בְּטוּמְאָה. הָיָה הַצִּיבּוּר רוּבָּן טְמֵאִין וּמִיעוּטָן טְהוּרִין. וּמֵתוּ מִן הַטְּמֵאִים בֵּין שְׁחִיטָה לִזְרִיקָה. אַחַר מִי אַתְּ מְהַלֵּךְ. אַחַר שְׁחִיטָה אוֹ אַחַר זְרִיקָה. אִין תֵּימַר. אַחַר שְׁחִיטָה. עוֹשִׁין בְּטוּמְאָה. אִין תֵּימַר. אַחַר זְרִיקָה. אֵינָן עוֹשִׂין בְּטוּמְאָה.

If the public was half suffering from gonorrhea and half impure. Rav Ada bar Ahava said, the sufferers from gonorrhea relate to the impure as the impure relate to the pure. They do not make it; the sufferers from gonorrhea are pushed to the Second *Pesaḥ*. Rav Huna said, there is no make-up for *Pesaḥ* celebrated in impurity[28].

If most of the public were pure but a minority impure[29], and some of the pure died between slaughter and pouring. After what are you going? Slaughter [or] pouring? If you are saying after slaughter, one does not celebrate in impurity; if you are saying after pouring, one celebrates in impurity. If most of the public were impure but a minority pure, and of the impure died between slaughter and pouring. After what are you going? Slaughter or pouring? If you are saying after slaughter, one celebrates in impurity; if you are saying after pouring, one does not celebrate in impurity[30].

28 While sufferers from gonorrhea (and in general, all people whose impurity is generated by their own body) are impure and excluded from the sanctuary, only people impure in the impurity of the dead are counted in determining whether *Pesaḥ* is celebrated in impurity. The only difference is that in this case, where everybody is impure, the impure celebrate *Pesaḥ* in impurity if they make up 50% of the population, not 50%+2, and the healed sufferers from gonorrhea and similar impurity then may celebrate the Second. Cf. Halakhah 7:6, Note 154/

29 Impure in the impurity of the dead.

30 Since the case cannot happen, no answer is required.

(fol. 36b) **משנה ב**: וְאֵיזוֹ הִיא דֶרֶךְ רְחוֹקָה מִן הַמּוֹדִיעִית וְלַחוּץ וּכְמִידָּתָהּ לְכָל רוּחַ דִּבְרֵי רִבִּי עֲקִיבָה. רִבִּי אֱלִיעֶזֶר אוֹמֵר מֵאִסְקוּפַת עֲזָרָה וְלַחוּץ. אָמַר רִבִּי יוֹסֵי לְפִיכָךְ נָקוּד עַל הֵ"א לוֹמַר לֹא מִפְּנֵי שֶׁרְחוֹקָה וַדַּאי אֶלָּא מֵאִסְקוּפַת הָעֲזָרָה וְלַחוּץ:

Mishnah 2: What is a far-away trip[31]? From Modi`in[32] and farther away, and the same distance in every direction, the words of Rebbi Aqiba. Rebbi Eliezer says, outside the doorstep of the Temple Courtyard. Rebbi Yose said, therefore there is a dot on the ה[33] to indicate not that it be really far but outside the doorstep of the Temple Courtyard.

31 That a person being there on the 14th of Nisan be obligated for Second *Pesah*.
32 In the foothills West of Jerusalem.
33 The masoretic text is רחקה, using the technique that instead of deleting letters one makes dots over them.

(36d line 12) **הלכה ב**: רִבִּי סִימוֹן אָמַר. אִתְפַּלְגוּן רִבִּי חִייָה רַבָּה וּבַר קַפָּרָה. חַד אָמַר. כְּדֵי שֶׁיָּבוֹא וְיֹאכַל. וְחוֹרָנָה אָמַר. כְּדֵי שֶׁיָּבוֹא וְיִזְרוֹק. וַאֲפִילוּ כְּמָאן דְּאָמַר. כְּדֵי שֶׁיָּבוֹא וְיֹאכַל. וְהוּא שֶׁיְּהֵא בְּתוֹךְ אַלְפַּיִם לַתְּחוּם עַד שֶׁלֹא חֲשִׁיכָה. אָמַר רִבִּי זְעוּרָה. וְתַנֵּי תַמָּן. הָיָה נָתוּן מִן הַמּוֹדִיעִית וְלִפְנִים וְרַגְלָיו רָעוֹת. יָכוֹל יְהֵא חַייָב. תַּלְמוּד לוֹמַר וְחָדָל. יָצָא זֶה שֶׁלֹּא חָדָל. הָיָה נָתוּן מִן הַמּוֹדִיעִית וְלַחוּץ וְהַסּוּס בְּיָדוֹ. יָכוֹל יְהֵא חַייָב. תַּלְמוּד לוֹמַר וּבְדֶרֶךְ לֹא־הָיָה. יָצָא זֶה שֶׁהָיָה בַדֶּרֶךְ. הָיָה נָתוּן מִן הַמּוֹדִיעִית וְלִפְנִים קוֹדֶם לְשֵׁשׁ שָׁעוֹת. יָצָא לוֹ קוֹדֶם שֵׁשׁ שָׁעוֹת. יָכוֹל יְהֵא חַייָב. תַּלְמוּד לוֹמַר וְחָדַל לַעֲשׂוֹת. הֶחְדֵּל בְּשִׁבְעַת עֲשִׂייָה חַייָב. שֶׁלֹּא בְּשִׁבְעַת עֲשִׂייָה פָּטוּר. רִבִּי אַבָּהוּ בְשֵׁם רִבִּי יוֹחָנָן. שְׁנֵיהֶן מִקְרָא אֶחָד הֵן דּוֹרְשִׁין. שָׁם שָׁם. חַד אָמַר חוּץ לַעֲשִׂייָתוֹ. וְחוֹרָנָה אָמַר. חוּץ לִמְחִיצָתוֹ. חֲבֵרַייָא בְשֵׁם רִבִּי יוֹחָנָן. וְהָאִישׁ אֲשֶׁר־הוּא טָהוֹר וּבְדֶרֶךְ לֹא־הָיָה. יָצָא זֶה שֶׁהָיָה בַדֶּרֶךְ. רִבִּי זְעוּרָה בְשֵׁם רִבִּי יוֹחָנָן. כְּשֶׁהוּא מַזְהִיר הוּא מַזְכִּיר רְחוֹקָה. כְּשֶׁהוּא עוֹנֵשׁ אֵינוֹ מַזְכִּיר רְחוֹקָה. וְרַבָּנָן אָמְרֵי. בְּשָׁעָה שֶׁהַכְּתָב רָבָה עַל הַנְּקוּדָה. אַתְּ דּוֹרֵשׁ אֶת הַכְּתָב וּמְסַלֵּק אֶת הַנְּקוּדָה. וּבְשָׁעָה שֶׁהַנְּקוּדָה רָבָה עַל הַכְּתָב. אַתְּ דּוֹרֵשׁ אֶת הַנְּקוּדָה וּמְסַלֵּק אֶת הַכְּתָב. אָמַר רִבִּי. אַף עַל פִּי שֶׁאֵין שָׁם אֶלָּא נְקוּדָה אַחַת מִלְּמַעְלָן אַתְּ דּוֹרֵשׁ אֶת הַנְּקוּדָה וּמְסַלֵּק אֶת הַכְּתָב. הֵ"א שֶׁבִּרְחוֹקָה נָקוּד. אִישׁ רָחוֹק. וְאֵין דֶּרֶךְ רְחוֹקָה.

Halakhah 2: Rebbi Simeon said, the Great Rebbi Hiyya and bar Qappara disagreed. One said, that he could come and eat[34]; the other one said that he could come and pour[35]. And even following him who said, that he could come and eat; on condition that he be within the two thousand cubits of the [Sabbath] domain before nightfall[36]. Rebbi Ze`ira said, there[37] they stated, if he happened to be closer than Modi`in but his feet were bad, I could think that he be liable, the verse said, *he refrained*[38], this excludes one who did not refrain. If he happened to be farther than Modi'in but had a horse at his disposal, I could think that he be liable, the verse said, *and he was not on a trip*, this excludes this one who was on a trip. If he happened to be closer than Modi'in before noontime but left before noontime, I could think that he be liable, the verse said, *he refrained from doing*, he who refrains at the time of doing is liable, not at the time of doing is not liable.

Rebbi Abbahu in the name of Rebbi Johanan: Both of them[39] explained the same verse, *there, there*[40]. One said, away from doing it, but the other one said, away from its enclosure.

The colleagues in the name of Rebbi Johanan: *But the man who is pure and was not on the road*[38], this excludes the one on the road. Rebbi Ze'ira in the name of Rebbi Johanan: when He warned, He mentioned *far away*, when He punishes He does not mention "far away"[41]. But the rabbis are saying, in case that the letters are more than what is dotted, one explains the letters and disregards what is dotted; in case that the dotted is more than the letters, one explains the dotted and disregards the letter[42]. Rebbi[42] said, even though that in this case there is only one letter dotted on top, one explains the dotted and disregards the letters. The *he* in רחוקה is dotted: the man is far away, not the road far away.

34 A person is not "far away" to be absolved from participating in the First *Pesaḥ* if he can reach the walled city of Jerusalem in time for the eating of the *Pesaḥ*, i. e., between nightfall and midnight.
35 He must be there at the time of pouring the blood at the altar walls, in the late afternoon.
36 Since on the holiday he is not permitted to walk more than 2'000 cubits from the place at which he started the holiday, it is clear that nobody farther than 2'000 cubits from Jerusalem at sundown can participate.
37 In Babylonia. In the text of the extracts from the Yerushalmi in *Yalqut Šimony* published by L. Ginzberg in his *Genizah Fragments* (p. 321): "Tannaim state."
38 *Num.* 9:13.
39 R. Aqiba and R. Eliezer, quoted in the Mishnah.
40 It is said about the *Pesaḥ* (*Deut.* 16:6) *there you shall slaughter the Pesaḥ in the evening*, and it is said about Second Tithe (*Deut.* 14:22): *you shall eat before the Eternal, your God, at the place which He will select to have His Name dwell there*. Both *Pesaḥ* and Second Tithe have to be eaten at the place of the Sanctuary, and Tithe has to be accompanied by a sacrifice of appearance. Therefore "there" may be

interpreted either as place of the sacrifice, in this case the Temple, or the place of consumption, Jerusalem, with the corresponding meaning of "far away".

41 "Far away" is mentioned in *Num.* 9:9, where the Second *Pesah* is defined, but missing in 9:13 where omission of both *Pesahim* is declared to be a deadly sin.

42 As in *Gen.* 18:9 where אַיּוֹ is read as איו "where?"

43 In *Yalqut Šimony* it reads: ר' יוסי אומ' אפילו אין אלא נקודה אחת. "R. Yose says, even if there is only one point. " This seems to be the correct text.

(fol. 36b) **משנה ג**: מַה בֵּין פֶּסַח הָרִאשׁוֹן לַשֵּׁנִי. הָרִאשׁוֹן אָסוּר בְּבַל יֵרָאֶה וּבַל יִמָּצֵא. וְהַשֵּׁנִי מַצָּה וְחָמֵץ עִמּוֹ בַּבָּיִת. הָרִאשׁוֹן טָעוּן הַלֵּל בַּאֲכִילָתוֹ וְהַשֵּׁנִי אֵינוֹ טָעוּן הַלֵּל בַּאֲכִילָתוֹ. זֶה וָזֶה טְעוּנִין הַלֵּל בַּעֲשִׂיָּיתָן. וְנֶאֱכָלִין צָלִי עַל מַצָּה וּמְרוֹרִים וְדוֹחִין אֶת הַשַּׁבָּת:

Mishnah 3: What is the difference between the First and the Second *Pesah*? The First is forbidden [leavened matter] to be seen or found. For the Second, leavened matter and *mazzah* are with him in the house. The First needs *Hallel* when it is eaten, but the Second does not need *Hallel* when it is eaten[44]. Both need *Hallel* when it is offered[45], and they are eaten roasted, with unleavened bread and bitter herbs, and push the Sabbath aside.

44 The First is a family celebration, the Second a ritual restricted to adult males.

45 *Pss.* 113-117 sung by the Levitic choir in the Temple, not the family at the table.

(36d line 31) **הלכה ג**: כָּתוּב לֹא־יַשְׁאִירוּ מִמֶּנּוּ עַד בּוֹקֶר. אִם לֶאֱכוֹל. זֶה מִצְוַת עֲשֵׂה שֶׁבּוֹ. וְעֵצָם לֹא יִשְׁבְּרוּ־בוֹ זֶה מִצְוַת לֹא תַעֲשֶׂה שֶׁבּוֹ. וּכְשֶׁהוּא אוֹמֵר. כְּכָל־חוּקַּת הַפֶּסַח יַעֲשׂוּ אוֹתוֹ: יָכוֹל שֶׁאֲנִי מַרְבֶּה לְבִיעוּר חָמֵץ וְלַאֲכִילַת מַצָּה כָּל־שִׁבְעָה. תַּלְמוּד לוֹמַר עַל־מַצּוֹת וּמְרוֹרִים יֹאכְלוּהוּ: אֵין לָךְ דָּבָר חוּץ מִגּוּפוֹ מְעַכְּבוֹ אֶלָּא מַצּוֹת וּמְרוֹרִים בִּלְבַד. דְּרִבִּי יִשְׁמָעֵאל אָמַר. כְּלָל וּפְרָט הַכֹּל בִּכְלָל. יָכוֹל יְהוּ כָּל־הַדְּבָרִים מְעַכְּבִין אוֹתוֹ. תַּלְמוּד לוֹמַר עַל־מַצּוֹת וּמְרוֹרִים יֹאכְלוּהוּ: אֵין לָךְ דָּבָר חוּץ מִגּוּפוֹ מְעַכְּבוֹ אֶלָּא מַצּוֹת וּמְרוֹרִים בִּלְבַד. אִית תַּנָּיֵי תַנֵּי. עַל הַשֵּׁינִי הוּא עָנוּשׁ כָּרֵת. עַל הָרִאשׁוֹן אֵינוֹ עָנוּשׁ כָּרֵת. אִית תַּנָּיֵי תַנֵּי. עַל הָרִאשׁוֹן הוּא עָנוּשׁ כָּרֵת. עַל הַשֵּׁינִי אֵינוֹ עָנוּשׁ כָּרֵת. בֵּין עַל הָרִאשׁוֹן בֵּין עַל הַשֵּׁינִי עָנוּשׁ כָּרֵת. מָאן דְּאָמַר. עַל הָרִאשׁוֹן הוּא עָנוּשׁ כָּרֵת. חֶטְאוֹ יִשָּׂא בָּרִאשׁוֹן. מָאן דְּאָמַר. עַל הַשֵּׁינִי הוּא עָנוּשׁ כָּרֵת. חֶטְאוֹ יִשָּׂא בַשֵּׁינִי. מָאן דְּאָמַר. בֵּין עַל הָרִאשׁוֹן בֵּין עַל הַשֵּׁינִי עָנוּשׁ כָּרֵת. חֶטְאוֹ יִשָּׂא בֵּין עַל הָרִאשׁוֹן בֵּין עַל הַשֵּׁינִי. מָאן דְּאָמַר. עַל הַשֵּׁינִי. אֵינוֹ עָנוּשׁ כָּרֵת אֶלָּא

אִם כֵּן לֹא עָשָׂה אֶת הָרִאשׁוֹן. כִּי | אֶת קָרְבַּן יי לֹא הִקְרִיב בְּמוֹעֲדוֹ. בָּרִאשׁוֹן חֶטְאוֹ יִשָּׂא. בַּשֵּׁנִי.

אָמַר רִבִּי יוֹחָנָן בְּשֵׁם רִבִּי שִׁמְעוֹן בֶּן יוֹצָדָק. כָּתוּב הַשִּׁיר יִהְיֶה לָכֶם כְּלֵיל הִתְקַדֶּשׁ־חָג. בָּא לֵילֵי פֶסַח לְלַמֵּד עַל מַפַּלְתּוֹ שֶׁלְסַנְחֵרִיב וְנִמְצָא לָמֵד מִמֶּנּוּ. מַה זֶה טָעוּן הַלֵּל אַף זֶה טָעוּן הַלֵּל. אִי מַה זֶה טָעוּן חֲגִיגָה אַף זֶה טָעוּן חֲגִיגָה. אָמַר רִבִּי זְעִירָה. כְּלֵיל הִתְקַדֶּשׁ־חָג. אֶת טָעוּן הַלֵּל טָעוּן חֲגִיגָה. אֶת שֶׁאֵינוֹ טָעוּן הַלֵּל אֵינוֹ טָעוּן חֲגִיגָה.

וְדוֹחֶה אֶת הַטּוּמְאָה. אָמַרְתְּ. כָּל־עַצְמוֹ אֵינוֹ בָא אֶלָּא מִפְּנֵי הַטּוּמְאָה. וְאַתְּ אָמַר. דּוֹחֶה אֶת הַטּוּמְאָה

Halakhah 3: It is written: *they shall not leave anything until morning*[46]. If it relates to eating, this is the relevant positive commandment. *No bone of it may be broken*, that is the relevant prohibition. So when He says, *according to all rules of the Pesaḥ they shall make it*, I could think that I have to add the elimination of leavened matter and *mazzah* for seven days. The verse says, *on mazzot and bitter herbs they shall eat it*[47]. Nothing external to its body impedes it except *mazzot* and bitter herbs. And following Rebbi Ismael? Since Rebbi Ismael says, a principle followed by a detail, everything is in the principle, I could think that everything impedes it; the verse says, *on mazzot and bitter herbs they shall eat it*. Nothing external to its body impedes it except *mazzot* and bitter herbs[48].

Some Tannain stated, he is punished by extirpation for the Second, he is not punished by extirpation for the First. Some Tannain stated, he is punished by extirpation for the First, he is not punished by extirpation for the Second. And there are Tannaim who state, both for the First as for the Second he is punished by extirpation. He who says, he is punished by extirpation for the First; *he shall bear his sin* about the First. He who says, he is punished by extirpation for the Second; *he shall bear his sin* about the Second. He who says, both for the First as for the Second he is punished by extirpation, *he shall bear his sin* about the First and the Second. He who said, for the Second, he is not punished by extirpation except if he missed the First: *For the sacrifice of the Eternal he did did not bring at its appointed time*, the First, *his sin he shall bear*, about the Second[49].

Rebbi Joḥanan said in the name of Rebbi Simon ben Joṣadaq: It is written, *the song shall be for you like the night at the start of the holiday of pilgrimage*[50]. The Passover night comes to instruct about the downfall of Sanherib and taken instruction from it. Since the one needs *Hallel*. so the other needs *Hallel*. But then since the one needs a sacrifice of pilgrimage, does the other need a sacrifice of pilgrimage? Rebbi Ze`ira said, *like the night at the start of the holiday of pilgrimage*, anything needing *Hallel* needs a sacrifice of pilgrimage; anything not needing *Hallel* does not need a sacrifice of pilgrimage.

It pushes aside impurity. You say, in itself it only comes because of impurity, and you are saying, it pushes aside impurity[51]?

---

46 *Num.* 9:12, stating the rules of the Second *Pesah*.
47 *Num.* 9:11. Cf. Babli 95a.
48 In *Sifry Num.* 69, the argument is based on another hermeneutical principle of R. Ismael: "Anything mentioned in one setting and repeated in a different setting cannot be considered part of the original setting unless referred to explicitly by the verse." Since the details, to be eaten with *mazzah* and bitter herbs, not to be left until morning, and no bone being broken, are repeated from the laws of the First *Pesah*, they and only they are transferred to the Second.
49 While *Num.* 9:13 is written with the laws of the Second *Pesah*, it is formulated in terms of the First. Therefore it is not clear whether it refers to the First (as understood by *Sifry Num.*70 and Pseudo-Jonathan), the Second, or both.
50 *Is.* 30:29; Babli 95b.
51 Babli 95b, *Sifry Num.*70. It is clear that the Second *Pesah* only can be offered in purity.

(fol. 36b) **משנה ג:** הַפֶּסַח שֶׁבָּא בְטוּמְאָה לֹא יאכְלוּ מִמֶּנּוּ זָבִין וְזָבוֹת נִדּוֹת וְיוֹלְדוֹת. וְאִם אָכְלוּ פְּטוּרִים מִכָּרֵת וְרִבִּי אֱלִיעֶזֶר פּוֹטֵר אַף עַל בִּיאַת מִקְדָּשׁ:

Mishnah 3 (continued): Male and female sufferers from genital discharges, menstruating women, and those after childbirth, may not eat from *Pesah* which is brought in impurity[52]; but if they ate they are not subject to extirpation, and Rebbi Eliezer also frees from {punishment for} entering the Sanctuary[53].

---

52 Since only the impurity of the dead is lifted for the *Pesah*, but no other impurity. On the other hand, extirpation for eating *sancta* in impurity is written for all impurities; if this is lifted for one kind it cannot be enforced for any other.
53 Since in *Num.* 5:2, sufferers from skin disease and genital discharges are excluded

from sacred domains together with those impure by the impurity of the dead. If one kind of impure person is admitted, the others cannot be punished for entering.

(36d line 54) **הלכה ד**: תַּנֵּי. רִבִּי מֵאִיר מְחַיֵּיב וְרִבִּי שִׁמְעוֹן פּוֹטֵר. מַה טַעֲמָא דְּרִבִּי שִׁמְעוֹן. וְהַבָּשָׂר כָּל־טָהוֹר יֹאכַל בָּשָׂר: וְהַנֶּפֶשׁ אֲשֶׁר־תֹּאכַל בָּשָׂר מִזֶּבַח הַשְּׁלָמִים. אֶת שֶׁהוּא מוּתָּר לַטְהוֹרִין חַייָבִין עָלָיו מִשּׁוּם טוּמְאָה. יָצָא פֶסַח שֶׁבָּא בְטוּמְאָה וַאֲכָלוּ מִמֶּנּוּ זָבִים וְזָבוֹת נִדוֹת וְיוֹלְדוֹת. אֶת שֶׁאֵינוֹ מוּתָּר לַטְהוֹרִין אֵין חַייָבִין עָלָיו מִשּׁוּם טוּמְאָה. אָכַל עוֹלָה אָכַל אֵימוּרִין. מֵאַחַר שֶׁאֵין מוּתָּר לַטְהוֹרִין אֵין חַייָבִין עָלָיו.

נִכְנַס בַּלַּיְלָה. נִכְנַס קוֹדֶם לְשֵׁשׁ שָׁעוֹת. אָמַר רִבִּי יוֹסֵי. אִין יִסְבּוֹר רִבִּי אֱלֶעָזֶר כְּרִבִּי שִׁמְעוֹן. מַה טַעֲמָא בְּכָל־קוֹדֶשׁ לֹא־תִגָּע וְאֶל־הַמִּקְדָּשׁ לֹא תָבוֹא. אֶת שֶׁהוּא חַייָב עַל אֲכִילַת קוֹדֶשׁ חַייָב עַל בִּיאַת הַמִּקְדָּשׁ. וְאֶת שֶׁאֵינוֹ חַייָב עַל אֲכִילַת קוֹדֶשׁ אֵינוֹ חַייָב עַל בִּיאַת הַמִּקְדָּשׁ. אִין יִסְבּוֹר רִבִּי שִׁמְעוֹן כְּרִבִּי לְעֶזֶר מַה טַעֲמָא בְּכָל־קוֹדֶשׁ לֹא־תִגָּע וְאֶל־הַמִּקְדָּשׁ לֹא תָבוֹא. אֶת שֶׁהוּא חַייָב עַל בִּיאַת הַמִּקְדָּשׁ חַייָב עַל אֲכִילַת קוֹדֶשׁ. וְאֶת שֶׁאֵינוֹ חַייָב עַל בִּיאַת מִקְדָּשׁ אֵינוֹ חַייָב עַל אֲכִילַת קוֹדֶשׁ.

Halakhah 4: It was stated: Rebbi Meïr declares liable but Rebbi Simeon declares not liable[54]. What is Rebbi Simeon's reason? *The meat, every pure person shall eat meat. But the person who would eat meat from the well-being sacrifice*[55], for any which is permitted to pure persons one is liable for impurity, but for any which is not permitted to pure persons one is not liable for impurity[56]. If he ate elevation offerings, if he ate parts[57], since they are not permitted to pure persons one is not liable for it.

If he[58] entered in the night, if he entered before noontime? Rebbi Yose said, if Rebbi Eliezer would hold with Rebbi Simeon, what is the reason on *she may not touch any sancta and into the Sanctuary she may not come*[59]? In case one be liable for eating *sancta* one is liable for entering the Sanctuary, and in case one be not liable for eating *sancta* one is not liable for entering the Sanctuary. If Rebbi Simeon would hold with Rebbi Eliezer, what is the reason on *she may not touch any sancta and in the Sanctuary she may not come*? In case one is liable for entering the Sanctuary one is liable for eating *sancta* and in case one is not liable for entering the Sanctuary one is not liable for eating *sancta*[60].

54 The people whose impurity is caused by their own body who eat from *Pesah* slaughtered for people impure by the impurity of the dead. The Mishnah is R. Simeon's. In *Sifra Saw Pereq* 14, the argument is attributed to R. Josua, in

Tosephta 8:9 R. Simeon in the name of R. Joshua; in the Babli 95b it is anonymous.
55 *Lev.* 7:19-20.
56 But naturally he still is liable for a sacrifice to atone for the unauthorized use of *sancta* (מְעִילָה).
57 The fat to be burned on the altar and forbidden for human consumption (Chapter 5, Note 50).
58 The persons whose impurity is caused by their own body, who are excluded from the sacred domain, entering at a time when the *Pesaḥ* (which is to be brought in impurity) cannot be slaughtered. The question presupposes that practice follows R. Eliezer.
59 *Lev.* 12:4, of the woman after birth and before she brought the sacrifice which permits her to enter the sacred domain.
60 The Mishnah is consistent; the anonymous part and that attributed to R. Eliezer express the same principles.

(fol. 36b) **משנה ד**: מַה בֵּין פֶּסַח מִצְרַיִם לְפֶסַח דּוֹרוֹת. פֶּסַח מִצְרַיִם מִקְחוֹ מִבְּעָשׂוֹר וְטָעוּן הַזָּיָה וַאֲגֻדַּת אֵזוֹב עַל הַמַּשְׁקוֹף וְעַל שְׁתֵּי מְזוּזוֹת וְנֶאֱכָל בְּחִפָּזוֹן לַיְלָה אֶחָד וּפֶסַח דּוֹרוֹת נוֹהֵג כָּל־שִׁבְעָה:

Mishnah 4: What is the difference between Passover in Egypt and the Passover of generations[61]? The *Pesaḥ* in Egypt was bought on the Tenth[62], and needed sprinkling with a bunch of hyssop on the lintel and two door-posts[63], and was eaten in a hurry[64], during one night[65]. But Passover of generations is all of seven [days].

61 Passover for future generations.
62 *Ex.* 12:3.
63 *Ex.* 12:22.
64 *Ex.* 12:11.
65 The following day was a common workday on which they left Egypt.

(36d line 67) אִית תַּנָּיֵי תַנֵּי. דּוּקִים וְתַבְלוּלִים פּוֹסְלִין בּוֹ. אִית תַּנָּיֵי תַנֵּי. אֵין דּוּקִים וְתַבְלוּלִים פּוֹסְלִין בּוֹ. מָאן דְּאָמַר. דָּקִים וְתַבְלוּלִין פּוֹסְלִין בּוֹ. נִיחָא. דִּכְתִיב שֶׂה תָמִים. מָאן דְּאָמַר. אֵין דּוּקִים וְתַבְלוּלִים פּוֹסְלִין בּוֹ. מַה מְקַיֵים שֶׂה תָמִים. אֲפִילוּ בְּקָרְבָּנוֹת בְּנֵי נֹחַ אֵינוֹ. לֹא כֵן אָמַר רִבִּי יָסָא. פָּשַׁט רִבִּי לְעָזָר לַחֲבֵרַיָּיא. מִכָּל־הַחַי מִכָּל־בָּשָׂר. שֶׁיְּהוּ שְׁלֵימִין בְּאֵיבָרֵיהֶן. תַּפֶּן יֵשׁ מֵהֶן לַמִּזְבֵּחַ. בְּרַם הָכָא אֵין מֵהֶם לַמִּזְבֵּחַ. רִבִּי חוּנָה בְּשֵׁם רִבִּי יִרְמְיָה. מִכֵּיוָן שֶׁכָּתוּב בָּהּ כַּפָּרָה כְּקֳדָשִׁים כְּמִי שֶׁיֵּשׁ מֵהֶם לַמִּזְבֵּחַ. וְתַנֵּי כֵן. שָׁלֹשׁ מִזְבְּחוֹת הָיוּ לַאֲבוֹתֵינוּ בְמִצְרַיִם. מַשְׁקוֹף וּשְׁתֵּי מְזוּזוֹת. אִית תַּנָּיֵי תַנֵּי. אַרְבָּעָה. סַף וּמַשְׁקוֹף וּשְׁתֵּי מְזוּזוֹת. אִית תַּנָּיֵי תַנֵּי. סַף כֶּלִי. אִית תַּנָּיֵי תַנֵּי. סַף אַסְקוּפָה. מָאן דְּאָמַר. סַף כֶּלִי. וְאֶת הַסִּיפִים וְאֶת הַמְזַמְּרוֹת וְאֶת הַמִּזְרָקוֹת. מָאן דְּאָמַר. סַף אַסְקוּפָה. בְּתִתָּם סִפָּם אֶת־סִיפַּי. מָאן דְּאָמַר. כֶּלִי. נִיחָא. דִּכְתִיב מִן־הַדָּם

אֲשֶׁר בַּסֵּף. מָאן דְּאָמַר. סַף אַסְקוּפָה. מַה מְקַיֵּים סַף כְּלִי. מֵבִיא סַף כְּלִי וְנוֹתֵן עַל הָאַסְקוּפָה וְטוֹבֵל וּמַזֶּה.

תַּנֵּי. בֶּן בַּגְבַּג אוֹמֵר. שֶׂה תָמִים. אֵין גִּיזָה תְמִימָה. וְהָתַנֵּי. מִן הַצֹּאן. לְהוֹצִיא אֶת הַחֲלָקִים שֶׁבָּהֶן. אָמַר רִבִּי אָבוּן. לְהוֹצִיא אֶת שֶׁחִלְּקָה [לָךְ הַתּוֹרָה]. רוֹבֵעַ וְנִרְבַּע וּמוּקְצָה וְנֶעֱבָד.

אָמַר רִבִּי יוֹסֵה. אַף רִבִּי יוֹסֵה הַגְּלִילִי דִכְוָותְהוֹן. דְּתַנֵּי. רִבִּי יוֹסֵי הַגְּלִילִי אוֹמֵר. אוֹמֵר אֲנִי שֶׁלֹּא הָיָה פֶסַח מִצְרַיִם אֶלָּא יוֹם אֶחָד בִּלְבָד. שֶׁנֶּאֱמַר וְלֹא יֵאָכֵל חָמֵץ הַיּוֹם.

Some Tannaim state, membranes over the eyes and cataracts were disqualifying for it[66]. Some Tannaim state, membranes over the eyes and cataracts were not disqualifying for it[67]. He who said, membranes over the eyes and cataracts were disqualifying for it, is understandable, since it is written, *a perfect lamb*[68]. He who said, membranes over the eyes and cataracts were not disqualifying for it, how does he confirm *a perfect lamb*? [69]Even for offerings of the descendants of Noah it is impossible! Did not Rebbi Yasa say that Rebbi Eleazar made it clear to the colleagues, *from all living, from all flesh*[70], that they were complete in their limbs. There, some of them were for the altar, here nothing is for the altar. [71](Rebbi Huna in the name of Rebbi Joḥanan, since you say, purgation is written there as for sacrifices, but here the altar has no part) But is was stated thus: Our forefathers in Egypt had three altars, the lintel and two door-posts. Some Tannaim state, four: the door-step, and the lintel, and two door-posts. Some Tannaim state, סַף is a vessel. Some Tannaim state, סַף is the door-step. He who said, סַף is a vessel, *the cups, and the pruning knives, and the vessels for pouring*[72]. He who said, סַף is the door-step, *when they used My door-step and their door-step*[73]. He who said, סַף is a vessel, is understandable[74]; *from the blood in the* סַף. He who said, סַף is the door-step, how does he confirm that סַף may mean a vessel? He brings a cup as סַף, puts it down on the door-step, dunks and sprinkles.

It was stated: Ben Bag-bag says, *a perfect lamb,* shorn is not perfect. But was it not stated, *of small cattle*[75], to exclude the smooth of them. Rebbi Abun said, to exclude those which the Torah separated[76], the male or female used for bestiality, one dedicated for idolatrous worship, and one worshipped.

Rebbi Yose said, also Rebbi Yose the Galilean is with them[77], as it was stated: Rebbi Yose the Galilean said, I am saying that Passover in Egypt was only one day, as it is said, *no leavened matter shall be eaten; today*[78].

66 As they are disqualifying for sacrifices; Lev. 22:22-24. *Mekhilta dR. Isamel Bo* 4.

67 Tosephta 8:11.

68 *Ex.* 12:5.

69 The next sentences are from *Sotah* 9:5, Notes 109-112.

70 *Gen.* 6:19. *From all living creatures, each one with its entire flesh*, i. e., a whole body. Babli *Avodah zarah* 5b.

Since Noah sacrificed some of the pure animals after the Flood, they must have conformed to the rules of sacrificial animals. But the *Pesah* in Egypt was not an altar sacrifice.

71 This sentence belongs to *Sotah*, it has no place here.

72 *1K.* 6:50. The words are badly misspelled. The word is סף I.

73 *Ez.* 43:8, סף II.

74 *Ex.* 12:22.

75 *Lev.* 1:2. As always, prefix *mem* is read as: from some, not all.

76 *Sifra Wayyiqra I (Nedavah) Pereq* 2.

77 With the author of the last statement in the Mishnah, that Passover in Egypt was only one day. Tosephta 8:21, as minority opinion.

78 *Ex.* 13:3-4.

(fol. 36c) **משנה ה**: אָמַר רִבִּי יְהוֹשֻׁעַ שָׁמַעְתִּי שֶׁתְּמוּרַת הַפֶּסַח קְרֵיבָה וּתְמוּרַת הַפֶּסַח אֵינָהּ קְרֵיבָה וְאֵין לִי לְפָרֵשׁ. אָמַר רִבִּי עֲקִיבָה אֲנִי אֲפָרֵשׁ. הַפֶּסַח שֶׁנִּמְצָא קוֹדֶם שְׁחִיטַת הַפֶּסַח יִרְעֶה עַד שֶׁיִּסְתָּאֵב. וְיִמָּכֵר וְיָבִיא בְדָמָיו שְׁלָמִים וְכֵן תְּמוּרָתוֹ. לְאַחַר שְׁחִיטַת הַפֶּסַח קָרֵב שְׁלָמִים. וְכֵן תְּמוּרָתוֹ:

Mishnah 5: Rebbi Joshua said, I have heard that the substitute of a *Pesah* is sacrificed and that the substitute of a *Pesah* is not sacrificed, and I cannot explain it. Rebbi Aqiba said, I shall explain it. The *Pesah* which is found[79] before the time of slaughtering the *Pesah* shall graze until it becomes unusable[80], then be sold, and for the money one shall bring well-being offerings; the same holds for its substitute[81]. After the time of slaughtering the *Pesah*, it shall be brought as well-being offering[82]; the same holds for its substitute.

79 An animal had been designated as *Pesah* when it was lost and another animal was designated in its stead. If then it is found before the afternoon of the 14th of Nisan, it remains dedicated but cannot be sacrificed since only one *Pesah* is possible for one group. A sacrifice which could not be used for the intended purpose cannot be

used anymore.

80 Either is develops a defect which disqualifies it for the altar or it becomes too old. Then it may be sold and the dedication is removed from the animal and transferred to the money, which only may be used to buy sacrificial animals.

81 This refers to unauthorized substitutes, where the act of substitution is sinful but the substituted animal nevertheless acquires the status of the animal for which it is substituted (*Lev.* 27:10).

82 Since the dedication as *Pesah* after the 14th of Nisan automatically becomes dedication as well-being offering.

(37a line 10) **הלכה ה**׃ רִבִּי יוּדָן בָּעֵי. אַף בִּתְמוּרַת אָשָׁם כֵּן. תְּמוּרַת אָשָׁם קְרֵיבָה וּתְמוּרַת אָשָׁם אֵינָהּ קְרֵיבָה. אָמַר רִבִּי יוֹסֵה. פֶּסַח שֶׁהִקְרִיבָה [בְּשַׁחֲרִית] אֵינָהּ פֶּסַח. עוֹלָה הִקְרִיבָהּ בְּשַׁחֲרִית עוֹלָה הִיא.

הֵמִיר בָּהּ בִּשְׁלֹשָׁה עָשָׂר. רִבִּי זְעוּרָה אָמַר. תְּמוּרָתָהּ קְרֵיבָה שְׁלָמִים. רִבִּי שְׁמוּאֵל בַּר רַב יִצְחָק אָמַר. אֵין תְּמוּרָתוֹ קְרֵיבָה שְׁלָמִים. חֵיילֵיהּ דְּרִבִּי שְׁמוּאֵל בַּר רַב יִצְחָק מִן הָדָא. לְאַחַר הַפֶּסַח יָבִיא שְׁלָמִים. וְכֵן תְּמוּרָתוֹ׃ אִין תֵּימַר. הֵמִיר בּוֹ בִּשְׁלֹשָׁה עָשָׂר וּתְמוּרָתוֹ קְרֵיבָה שְׁלָמִים. וְיְתִיבִינֵיהּ. לֹא מוּטָב לִלְמֵד תְּמוּרַת פֶּסַח מִפֶּסַח וְלֹא לִלְמֵד תְּמוּרַת שְׁלָמִים מִפֶּסַח.

רִבִּי הִילָא בְשֵׁם שְׁמוּאֵל. מֵתוּ בְעָלִים בִּשְׁלֹשָׁה עָשָׂר. גּוּפוֹ קָרֵב שְׁלָמִים. וְלָמָּה לֹא אָמַר. בְּאַרְבָּעָה עָשָׂר. כָּל־שֶׁגִּנְרָאָה לִיקָּרֵב בְּפֶסַח אֵין גּוּפוֹ קָרֵב שְׁלָמִים.

Halakhah 5: Rebbi Yudan asked, is it the same for the substitute of a reparation offering, that the substitute of a reparation offering is sacrificed and the substitute of a reparation offering is not sacrificed[83]? [84]Rebbi Yose said, a *Pesah* which one sacrificed [in the morning] is no *Pesah*; an elevation offering which one sacrificed in the morning is an elevation offering.

If he substituted for it on the Thirteenth, Rebbi Ze`ira said, the substitute is brought as a well-being offering[85]; Rebbi Samuel ben Rav Isaac said, the substitute is not brought as a well-being offering[86]. The strength of Rebbi Samuel ben Rav Isaac is from the following: "after the time of slaughtering the *Pesah*, it shall be brought as well-being offering." If you are saying, if he substituted for it on the Thirteenth and the substitute is brought as a well-being offering, is it not better to infer the {rules of the} substitute of a *Pesah* from the {rules of the} *Pesah* than to infer the [rules of the] substitute of a well-being sacrifice from the {rules of the} *Pesah*[87]?

Rebbi Hila in the name of Samuel: If the owner died[88] on the Thirteenth, its body is offered as a well-being sacrifice. Why did he not say, on the

Fourteenth? Any {animal} which is due to be sacrificed as *Pesah*, its body is not offered as a well-being sacrifice[89].

83 *Lev.* 27:10 prescribes that the status of an (illegal) substitute of a sacrifice is that of the sacrifice for which it is substituted. But this condition cannot be fulfilled for a reparation sacrifice since for one obligation only one sacrifice is possible. Therefore it is decreed (Mishnsh *Temurah* 3:3) that in all cases the substitute of a reparation sacrifice (in contrast to substitutes of purification sacrifices) should be sent to graze until it becomes unusable, then be sold, and for the money one shall buy elevation sacrifices. The question is why, if the animal was lost and only found after the original had been sacrificed, it cannot be used directly as elevation sacrifice. No answer is given. As S. Liebermann points out, in the opinion of Tosaphot (73a, *s.v.* אשם), by biblical standards any substitute of a reparation sacrifice could be brought as elevation offering and the circuitous route via grazing is purely rabbinic; since the original rule does not mention exceptions, the question should not have been asked.

84 This sentence is copied from Chapter 4:1, Note 27. However, only the first part is relevant here. It defines "the time of slaughtering the *Pesah*" mentioned in the Mishnah: this is the afternoon of the Fourteenth of Nisan. Therefore, in the following, "Thirteenth" really means "Thirteenth and morning of Fourteenth", and "Fourteenth" means "Afternoon of the Fourteenth".

85 Since the dedication of a *Pesah* animal which is not used automatically is that of well-being sacrifice.

86 But it must be sent to graze, as spelled out in the Mishnah.

87 The Mishnah, which treats the substitute together with the lost and found animal is more logically consistent than R. Ze`ira's correction; the Mishnah should be followed to the letter.

88 And no family member is subscribing. Babli 98a, Tosephta 9:16.

89 The rule that an animal which had been designated for a certain sacrifice, but at the moment of actual sacrifice was not used, never could be used for another sacrifice, has precedence over the rule which states that a designation of *Pesah* automatically reverts to that of well-being sacrifice after the 14th of Nisan.

(27a line 20) תַּמָּן תַּנִּינָן. וְלַד חַטָּאת וּתְמוּרַת חַטָּאת וְחַטָּאת שֶׁמֵּתוּ בְעָלֶיהָ וְשֶׁעִיבְּרָה שְׁנָתָהּ וְשֶׁאָבְדָה וְנִמְצֵאת בַּעֲלַת מוּם.

וְלַד חַטָּאת דְּאִיתְפַּלְגוֹן. צִיבּוּר שֶׁהִפְרִישׁ נְקֵיבָה. וְכֵן נָשִׂיא שֶׁהִפְרִישׁ שְׂעִירָה. רִבִּי יִרְמְיָה אָמַר. לֹא קָדְשָׁה וּוְלָדָהּ קָרֵב. רִבִּי יוֹסֵה אוֹמֵר. קָדְשָׁה וּוְלָדָהּ מֵת. חִילֵיהּ דְּרִבִּי יוֹסֵי מִן הָדָא. אֵין אַתְּ יָכוֹל לוֹמַר. וְלַד חַטָּאת בְּצִיבּוּר. שֶׁאֵין הַצִיבּוּר מְבִיאִין נְקֵיבָה. לֹא אָמַר אֶלָּא. אֵין אַתְּ יָכוֹל. הָא אִם הִקְדִּישָׁהּ קָדְשָׁה. אָמַר רִבִּי יוֹסֵי בֵּירִבִּי בּוּן. יָאוּת אָמַר רִבִּי יִרְמְיָה. וְלֹא רִבִּי שִׁמְעוֹן הִיא. דְּרִבִּי שִׁמְעוֹן אָמַר. נְקֵיבָה לְעוֹלָה לֹא קָדְשָׁה אֶלָּא הֶקְדֵּשׁ דָּמִים.

וּתְמוּרַת חַטָּאת דְּאִיתְפַּלְגוּן. הֵמִיר בָּהּ בִּשְׁלֹשָׁה עָשָׂר. רִבִּי זְעוּרָה אָמַר. תְּמוּרָתוֹ קְרֵיבָה שְׁלָמִים. רִבִּי שְׁמוּאֵל בַּר רַב יִצְחָק אָמַר. אֵין תְּמוּרָתוֹ קְרֵיבָה שְׁלָמִים.
וְחַטָּאת שֶׁמֵּתוּ בְעָלֶיהָ [נָמוּתוּ.] כַּיִי דָמַר] (אָמַר) רִבִּי הִילָא בְּשֵׁם שְׁמוּאֵל. מֵתוּ בְעָלָיו בִּשְׁלֹשָׁה עָשָׂר. גּוּפוֹ קָרֵב שְׁלָמִים. וְלָמָּה { } אָמַר בְּאַרְבָּעָה עָשָׂר. כָּל־עַמָּא מוֹדֵיי. כָּל־שֶׁנִּרְאָה לִקָּרֵב בְּפֶסַח אֵין גּוּפוֹ קָרֵב שְׁלָמִים.
וְשֶׁעִיבְרָה שְׁנָתָהּ. כַּיִי דָמַר רַב חִסְדָּא. בְּשֶׁעִיבְרָה שְׁנָתָהּ בֵּין רִאשׁוֹן לַשֵּׁינִי. רִבִּי הִילָא בְּשֵׁם רִבִּי יוֹחָנָן. בְּשֶׁעִיבֵּר זְמַן כַּפָּרָתוֹ.
וְשֶׁאָבְדָה וְנִמְצֵאת. (בַּעַל מוּם) [בְּרִי מוּתָּר.] רִבִּי יָסָא בְּשֵׁם רִבִּי יוֹחָנָן. אֵין לָךְ פֶּסַח גּוּפוֹ קָרֵב שְׁלָמִים אֶלָּא שֶׁאָבַד וְנִמְצָא מֵאַחַר שֶׁכִּיפְּרוּ הַבְּעָלִים.
וּבַעֲלַת מוּם. רִבִּי זְעוּרָא בְּעָא קוֹמֵי רִבִּי יָסָא. לֹא מִסְתַּבְּרָא בָהֶן בַּעַל מוּם דְּתַנֵּינָן הָכָא בָּאֲבִיד הוּא. אָמַר לֵיהּ. אוֹף אֲנָא סְבַר כֵּן.

There[90], we have stated: "The offspring of a purification offering[91], and the substitute of a purification offering, and a purification offering whose owner died[92], . . . [93], and whose year has passed[94], and which was lost and found, defective[95]."

[96]"The offspring of a purification offering," as they disagreed: If the community dedicated a female, and so the prince who dedicated a she-goat, Rebbi Jeremiah said, it is not dedicated[97] and its offspring may be offered; Rebbi Yose said, it is dedicated and its offspring must die[98]. The strength of Rebbi Yose is from the following[99]: "You cannot speak about the offspring of a purification offering of the community, since the community does not bring a female." He only said, "you cannot speak about"; therefore if he dedicated it[100] it is dedicated. Rebbi Yose ben Rebbi Abun said, Rebbi Jeremiah said it correctly. Is it not Rebbi Simeon's? As Rebbi Simeon said, a female as elevation offering is dedicated only for its money's worth[101].

"And the substitute of a purification offering," as they disagreed: if he substituted for it on the Thirteenth, Rebbi Ze`ira said, the substitute is brought as a well-being offering[85]; Rebbi Samuel ben Rav Isaac said, the substitute is not brought as a well-being offering[86].

"And a purification offering whose owner died," [has to die. Parallel to what] Rebbi Hila said in the name of Samuel, If the owner died[88] on the Thirteenth, its body is offered as a well-being sacrifice. Why did he {not} say, on the Fourteenth? Everybody agrees that the body of any {animal} due to be sacrificed as *Pesah*, is not offered as a well-being sacrifice[89].

"And whose year has passed." Parallel to what Rav Hisda said[102], If its year was completed between First and Second. Rebbi Hila in the name of Rebbi Johanan: When the time for its propitiation was passed.

"And which was lost and found." (Defective.) [Is it not certainly permitted?] Rebbi Yasa in the name of Rebbi Johanan: No body of a *Pesah* is brought as well- being sacrifice except the one which was lost but found only after the owners propitiated[103].

"And the defective." Rebbi Ze'ira asked before Rebbi Yasa: Is it not reasonable that the defective quoted here is the one which was lost[104]? He said to him, I also am of this opinion.

---

90 Mishnah *Temurah* 4:1.

91 The purification offering from a private person is a female sheep or goat. If it produces a lamb, the lamb is a *sanctum* but since only its mother can be sacrificed, it may neither be redeemed nor used for any other sacrifice.

92 Since it is dedicated, it may not be redeemed. As a purification offering, the dedication may not be transferred to the benefit of any other person (Mishna *Zevahim* 1:1).

93 The portion missing here states that all the previously enumerated animals must be allowed to die since they cannot be used; even if they develop a defect they cannot be sold.

94 Sheep are acceptable as sacrifice only if one year old.

95 The question whether one has to read "which was lost and found defective" or "which was lost and found, and the defective" is resolved in the discussion in favor of the first alternative. For this second group the Mishnah prescribes that they have to die if found after the owners had offered a substitute but if found before that time they are to be put out to graze, to be sold once no longer qualified as sacrifices.

96 The Mishnah is discussed item by item, the hypothesis being that any animal which if dedicated as purification offering is left to die, as *Pesah* is brought as well-being offering, but those put out to graze follow the same rules in both cases.

97 Since the purification offering of the community has to be a bull (*Lev.* 4:14) and that of a prince (*Lev.* 4:23) a ram. He holds that a dedication against the rules is void.

98 The dedication is valid but obviously the animal cannot be used. Not only the calf but also its mother must die.

99 A *baraita* also quoted in the Babli, *Temurah* 16a.

100 The *baraita* does not state that there is no dedication.

101 An elevation offering has to be male (*Lev.* 1:3,10). The dedication of a female is valid as gift to the Temple but invalid as sacrifice; therefore the animal has to be

given to the Temple to be sold for its benefit. (A matter of dispute in the Babli, *Temurah* 20a/b.) R. Jeremiah may also hold that the value of the animals is dedicated to the Temple, but this does not imply any sacrificial status.

102 Chapter 5, Notes 178-179.

103 In all other cases, while he agrees that the value of the animal is dedicated for well-being offerings, he demands that the animal be put out to grazing, to be sold once disqualified as sacrifice. Babli 97b.

The scribe's text "defective" is certainly a scribal error from the following paragraph. 104 Since a defective animal cannot be dedicated as sacrifice; its dedication automatically would only be for its money's worth. It is to be sold without delay for the benefit of the Temple.

(37a line 40) הִפְרִישׁ פִּסְחוֹ וְאָבַד וְהִפְרִישׁ אַחֵר תַּחְתָּיו. לֹא הִסְפִּיק לְהַקְרִיב אֶת הַשֵּׁינִי עַד שֶׁנִּמְצָא הָרִאשׁוֹן. וַהֲרֵי שְׁנֵיהֶן עוֹמְדִין. אִית תַּנָּיֵי תַנֵּי. מִצְוָה לְהַקְרִיב אֶת הָרִאשׁוֹן. אִית תַּנָּיֵי תַנֵּי. מִצְוָה לְהַקְרִיב אֶת הַשֵּׁינִי. וְתַנֵּי שְׁמוּאֵל כֵּן. בּוֹרֵר אֶת הַיָּפֶה שֶׁבָּהֶן וְהַשֵּׁינִי יִרְעֶה עַד שֶׁיִּסְתָּאֵב. וְיִמָּכֵר וְיָבִיא בְדָמָיו שְׁלָמִים בְּשִׁשָּׁה עָשָׂר. רִבִּי לְעֶזֶר אוֹמֵר. הוּא עַצְמוֹ קָרֵב שְׁלָמִים בְּשִׁשָּׁה עָשָׂר. אַתְיָא דְרִבִּי כְּרִבִּי לְעֶזֶר. וּשְׁמוּאֵל תַּנִּיתָהּ כִּשְׁיטָתֵיהּ. דְּתַנֵּי. רִבִּי אוֹמֵר. אֵין חַטָּאת {מֵתָה} אֶלָּא שֶׁנִּמְצֵאת מֵאַחַר שֶׁכִּיפְּרוּ בָהּ הַבְּעָלִים. אֵין הַמָּעוֹת הוֹלְכוֹת לְיָם הַמֶּלַח אֶלָּא שֶׁנִּמְצָאוּ מֵאַחַר שֶׁכִּיפְּרוּ הַבְּעָלִים.

If he dedicated his *Pesah*, but it became lost, and he dedicated another in its stead. Before he could sacrifice the second, the first was found, and now both are at his disposal. There are Tannaim who state, it is meritorious to sacrifice the first; there are Tannaim who state, it is meritorious to sacrifice the second. Samuel stated as follows: He selects the better of the two, and the other one shall graze until it becomes unusable, then be sold, and he shall bring for its value well-being offerings on the Sixteenth[105]. Rebbi Eleazar says, itself shall be brought as well-being offering on the Sixteenth. Rebbi comes with Rebbi Eleazar, and Samuel stated according to his system[89], as it was stated[106]: "Rebbi says, no purification offering {dies}[107] but one which was found after that the owner had been atoned[95], no money is thrown into the Dead Sea except which was found after the owner had been atoned[108]."

105 In Tosephta 9:12 the text is: "If he dedicated his *Pesah*, but it became lost, and he dedicated another in its stead. Before he could sacrifice the second, the first was found, and now both are at his disposal. He should bring the one he chooses following the words of the Sages. Rebbi Yose says, it is meritorious to sacrifice the first one, but if the second is better he should sacrifice that one and the first one shall graze until it

becomes unusable, then be sold, and he shall bring for its value well-being offerings on the Sixteenth."

The excess sacrifice cannot be brought before the Sixteenth since the Fifteenth is a holiday and only obligatory sacrifices are permitted on that day. No commentary known to me addresses the problem that first it is required that the animal graze for an indeterminate period but then be sacrificed on short notice on the second day after the first sacrifice. Probably one should read the text as "not before the Sixteenth".

106 The Babli 97a, *Temurah* 22b, has a completely different tradition. One may not emend the Yerushalmi according to the Babli, in particular in this case where R. Salomon Adani in his commentary מלאכת שלמה to the Mishnah quotes the Yerushalmi from a Yemenite ms. in the form given here.

107 The word is missing in the text here but is quoted by R. Salomon Adani and is needed for understanding. The quote is based on the rule explained in Note 96, that any animal left to die as purification sacrifice is brought as well-being sacrifice in the case of *Pesaḥ*.

108 No animal had been bought yet but money was dedicated to be used for a purification sacrifice. Since gifts to Heaven are irrevocable (Mishnah *Qiddušin* 1:6), if the money was lost and only found after a substitute animal had been offered, it has to be destroyed in a way in which nobody could have future usufruct of any kind, such as throwing the coins into the Dead Sea where the metal will quickly be dissolved.

(fol. 36c) **משנה ו**: הַמַּפְרִישׁ נְקֵיבָה לְפִסְחוֹ אוֹ זָכָר בֶּן שְׁתֵּי שָׁנִים יִרְעֶה עַד שֶׁיִּסְתָּאֵב וְיִמָּכֵר וְיִפְּלוּ דָמָיו לִנְדָבָה. הַמַּפְרִישׁ פִּסְחוֹ וָמֵת לֹא יְבִיאֶנּוּ בְנוֹ אַחֲרָיו לְשֵׁם פֶּסַח אֶלָּא לְשֵׁם שְׁלָמִים:

Mishnah 6: If he dedicates a female as his *Pesaḥ* or a two year old male[109], it shall graze until it becomes unusable, then be sold, and the monies given for voluntary sacrifices[110]. If he dedicates his *Pesaḥ* and dies, his son may not bring it after him as *Pesaḥ* but as well-being offering[111].

109 Since *Ex.* 12:5 requires *a male yearling*, the dedications as *Pesaḥ* are invalid. Since the animal never was a *Pesaḥ*, the rule that a dedication of *Pesaḥ* implies a dedication as well-being offering cannot be applied.

110 The Temple account from which elevation offerings are paid to cover periods where otherwise the altar would be empty.

111 Only if the *Pesaḥ* was left without subscribers; i. e., the son was not a subscriber to his father's *Pesaḥ* (Tosephta 9:17).

(37a line 44) **הלכה**: מַתְנִיתָא לְאַחַר כַּפָּרָה. וּכְרִבִּי שִׁמְעוֹן. דְּתַנֵּי. קוֹדֶם לַפֶּסַח תְּהֵא רוֹעָה עַד שֶׁתִּסְתָּאֵב וְתִימָּכֵר וְיָבִיא בְדָמֶיהָ פָּסַח. לְאַחַר הַפֶּסַח תָּבוֹא שְׁלָמִים. רִבִּי שִׁמְעוֹן אוֹמֵר. קוֹדֶם

לַפֶּסַח תִּימָּכֵר שֶׁלֹּא בְמוּם. לְאַחַר הַפֶּסַח תָּבוֹא שְׁלָמִים. לָא כֵן סָבְרָנָן מֵימַר. כָּל־שֶׁנִּרְאָה לִקְרַב בַּפֶּסַח אֵין גּוּפוֹ קָרֵב שְׁלָמִים. פָּתַר לָהּ כְּשֶׁהִפְרִישׁ מָעוֹת.

Halakhah: The Mishnah after propitiation[112], following {neither Rebbi nor[113] Rebbi Simeon, as it was stated[114]: "Before Passover it shall graze until it becomes unusable, then be sold, and he shall bring for its value a *Pesaḥ*[115]. After Passover it shall be brought as well-being sacrifice. Rebbi Simeon[116] says, before Passover it shall be sold without a defect, after Passover it shall be brought as well-being sacrifice." Did we not understand that "the body of any {animal} due to be sacrificed as *Pesaḥ* is not offered as a well-being sacrifice[89]"? Explain it if he dedicated coins.

112 The question is why in the first sentence of the Mishnah one does not distinguish as always between the situations before and after the 14th of Nisan. The sentence cannot deal with the situation before Passover when everything stilll can be put in order.

113 These words are missing in the ms., they are quoted by R. Salomon Adani from a Yemenite ms. of the Yerushalmi and are necessary for the understanding of the text. The agreement of Rebbi and R. Simeon is in Tosephta 9:19.

114 Tosephta 9:20, about a female sheep dedicated as *Pesaḥ*.

115 Since the money always was intended for *Pesaḥ*.

116 In the Tosephta: "R. Simeon ben Jehudah".

(fol. 36c) **משנה ז**: הַפֶּסַח שֶׁנִּתְעָרְבָה בַּזְּבָחִים כּוּלָּן יִרְעוּ עַד שֶׁיִּסְתָּאֲבוּ וְיִמָּכְרוּ וְיָבִיא בִּדְמֵי הַיָּפֶה שֶׁבָּהֶן מִמִּין זֶה וּבִדְמֵי הַיָּפֶה שֶׁבָּהֶן מִמִּין זֶה וְיַפְסִיד הַמּוֹתָר מִבֵּיתוֹ. נִתְעָרַב בַּבְּכוֹרוֹת רְבִּי שִׁמְעוֹן אוֹמֵר אִם חֲבוּרַת כֹּהֲנִים יֹאכֵלוּ:

Mishnah 7: If a *Pesaḥ* was mingled with sacrifices[117], all of them shall graze until they become unusable, then be sold, and for the value of the best among them he shall bring one of each kind and lose the difference on his account[118]. If it was mingled with firstlings, Rebbi Simeon says, if it is a company of priests, they shall eat[119].

117 Other than well-being sacrifices, since a *Pesaḥ* mixed with well-being sacrifices is brought as well-being sacrifice on the 16th of Nisan.

118 He redeems all animals and but spends money in a multiple of the proceeds obtained for the best in the flock.

119 Since the Temple service for *Pesaḥ* and

firstlings is identical. The majority disagrees since firstlings may be eaten during two days and the night in between but a *Pesaḥ* only half a night.

(37a line 49) **הלכה**: תַּנֵּי. אֵין לוֹקְחִין שְׁבִיעִית בְּכֶסֶף מַעֲשֵׂר. רִבִּי יוֹסֵה אָמַר. כְּמַחֲלוֹקֶת. אָמַר רִבִּי יוֹנָה. דִּבְרֵי הַכֹּל הִיא. אוֹכְלֵי תְרוּמָה זְרִיזִין הֵן. הָתִיב רִבִּי חֲנַנְיָה קוֹמֵי רִבִּי מָנָא. וְהָתַנִּינָן. נִתְעָרְב בַּבְּכוֹרוֹת רִבִּי שִׁמְעוֹן אוֹמֵר אִם חֲבוּרַת כֹּהֲנִים יֹאכֵלוּ: וְתַנֵּי עֲלָהּ. יֹאכְלוּ כֶּחָמוּר שֶׁבָּהֶן. אָמַר לֵיהּ. אוֹכְלֵי פְסָחִים בִּשְׁעָתָן זְרִיזִין הֵן כְּאוֹכְלֵי תְרוּמָה. תֵּדַע לָךְ. דְּתַנִּינָן. אֵין צוֹלִין בָּשָׂר בָּצָל וּבֵיצָה אֶלָּא כְּדֵי שֶׁיִּצוֹלוּ. וְתַנִּינָן. מְשַׁלְשְׁלִין אֶת הַפֶּסַח בַּתַּנּוּר עִם חֲשֵׁכָה.
1 ר' יוסח אמ' | ס אמ' ר' יוסי   3 והתנינין | ס והא תנינן   נתערב | ס נתערבו   לך | ס לך שהיא כן

Halakhah: [120]It was stated: "One does not buy Sabbatical [produce] with tithe money." Rebbi Yose said, that is a disagreement. Rebbi Jonah said, that is the opinion of everybody. The eaters of heave are careful. Rebbi Ḥananiah objected before Rebbi Mana: Did we not state: "If they were mingled with firstlings, Rebbi Simeon says, if it is a company of Cohanim they should eat." And we have stated on that, they should be eaten following the more stringent rules. He said to him, eaters of the *Pesaḥ* in its time are as careful as the eaters of heave. You should know this since we have stated[121]: "One roasts meat, onion, or egg only that they should be roasted", but we have stated:[122] "One lowers the *Pesaḥ* into the oven at nightfall."

120 This Halakhah also is a paragraph in *Ma`aser Šeni* 3:2 (ס) Notes 28-36. Sabbatical produce must be consumed by humans, Second Tithe money must be used to buy produce to be eaten in purity at the place of the Temple. The situation is similar to that of a *Pesaḥ* mingled with a firstling; the question is whether the disagreement of R. Simeon and the rabbis carries over to tithes and Sabbatical produce.

121 Mishnah *Šabbat* 1:14. "They should be roasted before nightfall".

122 Mishnah *Šabbat* 1:15, contradicting the preceding Mishnah unless one accepts R. Mana's argument (which is that of his father R. Jonah).

(fol. 36c) **משנה ח** חֲבוּרָה שֶׁאָבַד פִּסְחָהּ אָמְרוּ לְאֶחָד צֵא וּבַקֵּשׁ וּשְׁחוֹט עָלֵינוּ וְהָלַךְ וּמָצָא וְשָׁחַט וְהֵם לָקְחוּ וְשָׁחָטוּ. אִם שֶׁלּוֹ נִשְׁחַט רִאשׁוֹן הוּא אוֹכֵל מִשֶּׁלּוֹ וְהֵן אוֹכְלִין עִמּוֹ. אִם שֶׁלָּהֶן נִשְׁחַט רִאשׁוֹן הוּא אוֹכֵל מִשֶּׁלּוֹ וְהֵן אוֹכְלִין מִשֶּׁלָּהֶן. אֵין יָדוּעַ אֵי זֶה מֵהֶן נִשְׁחַט רִאשׁוֹן אוֹ שֶׁשָּׁחֲטוּ שְׁנֵיהֶן כְּאַחַת הֵן אוֹכְלִין מִשֶּׁלָּהֶן וְהוּא אֵינוֹ אוֹכֵל עִמָּהֶן וְשֶׁלּוֹ יֵצֵא לְבֵית הַשְּׂרֵפָה וּפָטוּר מִלַּעֲשׂוֹת פֶּסַח שֵׁנִי.

Mishnah 8: A group whose *Pesaḥ* was lost and they said to one of them go, and search for it, and slaughter for us. He went, found[123], and slaughtered, and they bought and slaughtered. If his was slaughtered first, he eats of his, and they eat with him[124]; but if theirs was slaughtered first, they eat of theirs, and he eats of his[125]. If it is not known which one was slaughtered first, or they slaughtered simultaneously, they eat of theirs, but he does not eat with them[126]. His is brought to be burned[127], and he is not liable for a Second *Pesaḥ*.

123 The original sheep.
124 Since all of them are subscribers to the one.
125 By their action they cancelled their subscription to the first sheep, but he never was involved with the second.

126 Since it is not known whether they still are subscribers to their sheep or whether the subscription was cancelled by their action.
127 This disposal of any disabled *sanctum* is by burning outside the sacred domain.

(37a line 60) **הלכה:** אָמַר רִבִּי יוֹחָנָן. דְּרִבִּי נָתָן הִיא. דְּרִבִּי נָתָן אָמַר. יוֹצְאִין בִּזְרִיקָה בְּדֹא אֲכִילָה.

Halakhah: Rebbi Joḥanan said, this[128] is Rebbi Nathan's, since Rebbi Nathan said, one fulfills one's obligation by pouring without eating.

128 The statement in this and the following Mishnah that one is not liable for a Second *Pesaḥ* since the blood of their sheep was correctly poured on the altar, even though it turned out that they could not eat from it.

(fol. 36c) **משנה ט:** אָמַר לָהֶן אִם אֵיחַרְתִּי שַׁחֲטוּ עָלַי. הָלַךְ וּמָצָא וְשָׁחַט וְהֵם לָקְחוּ וְשָׁחֲטוּ. אִם שֶׁלָּהֶן נִשְׁחַט רִאשׁוֹן הֵן אוֹכְלִין מִשֶּׁלָּהֶן וְהוּא אוֹכֵל עִמָּהֶן. וְאִם שֶׁלּוֹ נִשְׁחַט רִאשׁוֹן הוּא אוֹכֵל מִשֶּׁלּוֹ וְהֵן אוֹכְלִין מִשֶּׁלָּהֶן. אֵין יָדוּעַ אֵיזֶה מֵהֶן נִשְׁחַט רִאשׁוֹן אוֹ שֶׁשָּׁחֲטוּ שְׁנֵיהֶן כְּאַחַת הוּא אוֹכֵל מִשֶּׁלּוֹ וְהֵן אֵינָם אוֹכְלִין עִמּוֹ וְשֶׁלָּהֶן יֵצֵא לְבֵית הַשְּׂרֵפָה וּפְטוּרִין מִלַּעֲשׂוֹת פֶּסַח שֵׁנִי.

אָמַר לָהֶן אִם אֵיחַרְתִּי צְאוּ וְשַׁחֲטוּ עָלַי. הָלַךְ וּמָצָא וְשָׁחַט וְהֵם לָקְחוּ וְשָׁחֲטוּ. אִם שֶׁלָּהֶן נִשְׁחַט רִאשׁוֹן הֵן אוֹכְלִין מִשֶּׁלָּהֶן וְהוּא אוֹכֵל עִמָּהֶן. וְאִם שֶׁלּוֹ נִשְׁחַט רִאשׁוֹן הוּא אוֹכֵל מִשֶּׁלּוֹ וְהֵן אוֹכְלִין מִשֶּׁלָּהֶן. וְאִם אֵינוֹ יָדוּעַ אֵיזֶה נִשְׁחַט רִאשׁוֹן אוֹ שֶׁשָּׁחֲטוּ שְׁנֵיהֶן כְּאַחַת הֵן אוֹכְלִין מִשֶּׁלָּהֶן וְהוּא אֵינוֹ אוֹכֵל עִמָּהֶן וְשֶׁלּוֹ יֵצֵא לְבֵית הַשְּׂרֵפָה וּפָטוּר מִלַּעֲשׂוֹת פֶּסַח שֵׁנִי.

Mishnah 9: If he told them, if I would tarry, slaughter for me; he went, found, and slaughtered, and they bought and slaughtered. If theirs was slaughtered first, they eat of theirs, and he eats with them; but if his was slaughtered first, he eats of his and they eat of theirs. If it is not known which one was slaughtered first, or they slaughtered simultaneously, he eats of his, but they he may not eat with him; and theirs is brought to be burned, but they are not liable for a Second *Pesah*[129].

If he told them, if I would tarry, go and slaughter for me; he went, found, and slaughtered, and they bought and slaughtered. If theirs was slaughtered first, they eat of theirs, and he eats with them[130]; but if his was slaughtered first, he eats of his and they eat of theirs. If it is not known which one was slaughtered first, or they slaughtered simultaneously, they eat of theirs, and he may not eat with them; and his is brought to be burned[131], but he is not liable for a Second *Pesah*.

משנה י אָמַר לָהֶן וְאָמְרוּ לוֹ. אוֹכְלִין כּוּלָּם מִן הָרִאשׁוֹן. לֹא אָמַר לָהֶן וְלֹא אָמְרוּ לוֹ אֵינָן אַחֲרָאִין זֶה לָזֶה:

Mishnah 10: If he said to them and they said to him, all of them eat of the first. If he did not talk to them nor did they talk to him, they are not responsible for one another.

משנה יא שְׁתֵּי חֲבוּרוֹת שֶׁנִּתְעָרְבוּ פִּסְחֵיהֶן אֵילוּ מוֹשְׁכִין לָהֶן אֶחָד וְאֵילוּ מוֹשְׁכִין לָהֶן אֶחָד. אֶחָד מֵאֵילוּ בָּא לוֹ אֵצֶל אֵילוּ וְאֶחָד מֵאֵילוּ בָּא לוֹ אֵצֶל אֵילוּ. וְכֵן הֵן אוֹמְרִים אִם שֶׁלָּנוּ הוּא הַפֶּסַח הַזֶּה יָדֶיךָ מְשׁוּכוֹת מִשֶּׁלְּךָ וְנִמְנֵית עַל שֶׁלָּנוּ. וְאִם שֶׁלְּךָ הוּא הַפֶּסַח הַזֶּה יָדֵינוּ מְשׁוּכוֹת מִשֶּׁלָּנוּ וְנִמְנִינוּ עַל שֶׁלְּךָ.

Mishnah 11: Two groups whose *Pesahim* were commingled[132], each of them draws one for them. One of each group joins the other and they[133] declare: If this *Pesah* is ours, your hand is removed from yours and you are subscribing to ours, and if this *Pesah* is yours, our hand is removed from ours and we are subscribing to yours.

משנה יב וְכֵן חָמֵשׁ חֲבוּרוֹת שֶׁל חֲמִשָּׁה חֲמִשָּׁה וְשֶׁל עֲשָׂרָה עֲשָׂרָה מוֹשְׁכִין לָהֶן אֶחָד מִכָּל חֲבוּרָה וַחֲבוּרָה וְכָךְ הָיוּ אוֹמְרִים:

Mishnah 12: The same holds for five groups of five members each, or ten of ten, one exchanges members of each group and so they declare[134].

129 The text of the Mishnah in the Yerushalmi is that of the *editio princeps*, it is not part of the manuscript text. It is obvious that this Mishnah was copied twice; the text of the second version is that of the Babli and Maimonides. Since the Mishnah is not discussed, it is impossible to decide between the versions. Maimonides declares the Mishnah to be obvious and not in need of explanation.

130 Since he does not renounce his membership in the group and their *Pesah* was slaughtered first, which makes his redundant.

131 Since he had made them his agents to slaughter a *Pesah*, the slaughter of the first makes his redundant.

132 When the animals are alive and it is possible to change affiliations.

133 Each group has to make a separate declaration.

134 If *n Pesahim* were commingled, each group must have at last *n* members so that one member of each group joins another. They all have to make the declaration formulated in the previous Mishnah.

(37a line 56) תַּנֵּי בַּר קַפָּרָא. יָפָה שְׁתִיקָה לַחֲכָמִים. קַל הָחוֹמֶר לַטִּיפְּשִׁים. וְכֵן שְׁלֹמֹה אוֹמֵר. גַּם אֱוִיל מַחֲרִישׁ חָכָם יֵחָשֵׁב. וְאֵין צָרִיךְ לוֹמַר. חָכָם מַחֲרִישׁ.

Bar Qappara stated: Silence behoves the Sages, and so much more the fools. And also Solomon says[135], *also a silent dolt is considered to be wise*, and it is not necessary to say, a silent sage[136].

135 *Prov.* 17:28.
136 Since the only uncomplicated case in the Mishnaiot is when nobody says anything. Babli 99a.

(fol. 36c) **משנה יג**: שְׁנַיִם שֶׁנִּתְעָרְבוּ פִּסְחֵיהֶן זֶה מוֹשֵׁךְ לוֹ אֶחָד וְזֶה מוֹשֵׁךְ לוֹ אֶחָד. זֶה מְמַנֶּה עִמּוֹ אֶחָד מִן הַשּׁוּק וְזֶה מְמַנֶּה עִמּוֹ אֶחָד מִן הַשּׁוּק זֶה בָּא אֵצֶל זֶה וְזֶה בָּא אֵצֶל זֶה וְכָךְ הוּא אוֹמֵר אִם שֶׁלִּי הוּא הַפֶּסַח זֶה יָדֶיךָ מְשׁוּכוֹת מִשֶּׁלְּךָ וְנִמְנֵית עַל שֶׁלִּי. וְאִם שֶׁלְּךָ הוּא הַפֶּסַח זֶה יָדַי מְשׁוּכוֹת מִשֶּׁלִּי וְנִמְנֵיתִי עַל שֶׁלְּךָ:

Mishnah 13: If the *Pesahim* of two people were intermingled[137], each of them takes one, and each one invites another from the street to subscribe with him[138]. One of each group joins the other, and each one declares[139] as follows: If this *Pesah* be mine, your hand is removed from yours and you are subscribing to mine, and if this *Pesah* be yours, my hand is removed from mine and I am subscribing to yours.

137 And no other people subscribed to these *Pesahim*. They cannot simply re-subscribe each to one of the animals since then the dedicated *Pesahim* would for a moment be left without subscribers and therefore disqualified.

138 Then there are two groups of two people whose *Pesahim* were intermingled and one may apply the rule spelled out in Mishnah 11.

139 To the one who comes to join the other group.

(37a line 59) **הלכה:** אָמַר רִבִּי יוֹחָנָן. דְּרִבִּי יוּדָה הִיא. דְּתַנִּינָן תַּמָּן. אֵין שׁוֹחֲטִין אֶת הַפֶּסַח עַל הַיָּחִיד דִּבְרֵי רִבִּי יְהוּדָה. וְרִבִּי יוֹסֵי מַתִּיר. הָא שֶׁלְאַרְבָּעָה עָשָׂר לֹא. לֹא כֵן אָמַר רִבִּי יוֹחָנָן. דְּרִבִּי יוּדָה הִיא. אָמַר רִבִּי יוֹסֵה. כָּל־גַּרְמָהּ אֶמְרָה דְּהִיא דְּרִבִּי יוּדָה. דְּתַנִּינָן תַּמָּן. אֵין שׁוֹחֲטִין אֶת הַפֶּסַח עַל הַיָּחִיד דִּבְרֵי רִבִּי יְהוּדָה. וְרִבִּי יוֹסֵי מַתִּיר.

Halakhah. [140]Rebbi Johanan said, this is Rebbi Jehudah's as we have stated there[141], "One does not slaughter the *Pesah* for a single person, the words of Rebbi Jehudah; but Rebbi Yose permits." Therefore not of the Fourteenth. Did not Rebbi Johanan say, this is Rebbi Jehudah's? Rebbi Yose said, does it proclaim that it is Rebbi Jehudah's? As we have stated there, "One does not slaughter the *Pesah* for a single person, the words of Rebbi Jehudah; but Rebbi Yose permits."

140 S. Liebermann writes: "I cannot explain this paragraph without major emendations." In fact, as R. Yose the Amora notes in the second part of the paragraph, Mishnah 13 must follow R. Yose the Tanna, since according to R. Jehudah every *Pesah* belongs to a group of at least 2 subscribers and therefore should be treated following Mishnah 11. A minimally invasive emendation would be to read in R. Johanan's statement: "This is not R. Jehudah's."

141 Mishnah 8:7.

ערב פסחים פרק עשירי

(fol.37a) **משנה א**: עֲרָב פְּסָחִים סָמוּךְ לַמִּנְחָה לֹא יֹאכַל אָדָם עַד שֶׁתֶּחְשַׁךְ. וַאֲפִילוּ עָנִי שֶׁבְּיִשְׂרָאֵל לֹא יֹאכַל עַד שֶׁיָּסֵב. וְלֹא יִפְחֲתוּ לוֹ מֵאַרְבָּעָה כוֹסוֹת שֶׁל יַיִן וַאֲפִילוּ מִן הַתַּמְחוּי:

Mishnah 1: In the afternoon of Passover Eve close to the time of afternoon prayers one should not eat until it gets dark[1]. And even the poorest person in Israel should not eat until he lies on a couch[2]. One shall not give him less than four cups of wine, even from the communal tray[3].

1   The time of the usual afternoon prayers starts at about 3:30 pm. Close to the time would be about 3 pm. One should not eat in the afternoon so as to eat with appetite the formal meal in the night.

2   Since in those times every formal dinner was eaten on couches. סבב really means "to form a circle", since the couches were arranged in almost circular fashion in the *triclinium*.

3   The תַּמְחוּי is the communal chest where contributions to charity are collected in kind. Four cups of wine have to be drunk by every participant of the *Seder* ceremony in the evening of the first day of Passover. For the entire Chapter, see the author's commentary in *The Scholar's Haggadah*, Northvale NJ 1995, pp. 183-377.

(37b line 42) עֲרָב פְּסָחִים סָמוּךְ לַמִּנְחָה כול'. מַתְנִיתָא דְּרִבִּי יוּדָה. דְּתַנֵּי. עֲרָב שַׁבָּת מִן הַמִּנְחָה וּלְמַעְלָן לֹא יִטְעוֹם אָדָם כְּלוּם עַד שֶׁתֶּחְשַׁךְ כְּדֵי שֶׁיִּכָּנֵס לַשַּׁבָּת בְּתַאֲבָה. דִּבְרֵי רִבִּי יוּדָה. רִבִּי יוֹסֵה אוֹמֵר. אוֹכֵל וְהוֹלֵךְ עַד שָׁעָה שֶׁהוּא מַשְׁלִים. מַפְסִיקִין לַשַּׁבָּת. דִּבְרֵי רִבִּי יוּדָה. רִבִּי יוֹסֵה אוֹמֵר. אֵין מַפְסִיקִין. מַעֲשָׂה בְרַבָּן שִׁמְעוֹן בֶּן גַּמְלִיאֵל וְרִבִּי יוֹסֵי בֶּן חֲלַפְתָּא שֶׁהָיוּ מְסוּבִּין בְּעֶרֶב שַׁבָּת בְּעַכּוֹ וְקָדְשָׁה עֲלֵיהֶן הַשַּׁבָּת. אָמַר לוֹ רַבָּן שִׁמְעוֹן בֶּן גַּמְלִיאֵל לְרִבִּי יוֹסֵי בֶּן חֲלַפְתָּא. רְצוֹנָךְ שֶׁנִּפְסוֹק לַשַּׁבָּת. אָמַר לוֹ. כָּל־הַיּוֹם הָיִיתָ מְחַבֵּב דְּבָרַי לִפְנֵי רִבִּי יְהוּדָה. וְעַכְשָׁיו אַתְּ מְחַבֵּב דִּבְרֵי רִבִּי יְהוּדָה בְּפָנַי. הֲגַם לִכְבּוֹשׁ אֶת־הַמַּלְכָּה עִמִּי בַּבָּיִת. אָמַר לוֹ. אִם כֵּן לֹא נַפְסִיק. שֶׁלֹּא תִיקָּבַע הֲלָכָה בְּיִשְׂרָאֵל כְּרִבִּי יְהוּדָה. לֹא זָזוּ מִשָּׁם עַד שֶׁקָּבְעוּ הֲלָכָה כְּרִבִּי יוֹסֵי. רַב יְהוּדָה בְשֵׁם שְׁמוּאֵל. זוֹ דִּבְרֵי רִבִּי יְהוּדָה וְרִבִּי יוֹסֵה. אֲבָל דִּבְרֵי חֲכָמִים פּוֹרֵשׂ מַפָּה וּמְקַדֵּשׁ. מַהוּ לוֹכַל מִינֵי כִיסָנִין. מַהוּ לוֹכַל מִינֵי תַרְגִּימָא. רִבִּי יוּדָן נְשִׂיָּיא סָחָה וּצְחָה. שָׁאַל לְרִבִּי מָנָא. בְּגִין דַּאֲנָא צְחִי מָהוּ נִשְׁתֵּי. אָמַר לֵיהּ. תַּנֵּי רִבִּי חִיָּיא. אָסוּר לָאָדָם לִטְעוֹם כְּלוּם עַד שֶׁתֶּחְשַׁךְ.

"In the afternoon of Passover Eve close to the time of afternoon prayers," etc. The Mishnah is Rebbi Jehudah's, as it was stated:[4] "On Sabbath Eve starting at the time of afternoon prayers one should not taste anything until nightfall in order to enter the Sabbath with an appetite, the words of Rebbi Jehudah. Rebbi Yose says, he continues eating until he finishes." [5]"One interrupts[6] for the Sabbath, the words of Rebbi Jehudah. Rebbi Yose says, one does not interrupt." [7]"It happened that Rabban Simeon ben Gamliel and Rebbi Yose ben Ḥalaphta were lying on couches in Acco on Sabbath Eve, and in the meantime the Sabbath became holy. Rabban Simeon ben Gamliel said to Rebbi Yose ben Ḥalaphta, do you want to interrupt for the Sabbath? He answered him, the entire day you preferred my words over those of Rebbi Jehudah, and now you are preferring the words of Rebbi Jehudah over mine, *also to rape the queen in my palace*[8]? He said to him, therefore we shall not interrupt, that practice in Israel should not be fixed following R. Jehudah. They did not leave there before they fixed practice following Rebbi Yose." Rav Jehudah in the name of Samuel: These are the words of Rebbi Jehudah and Rebbi Yose. But the words of the Sages, one spreads a cloth and makes *qiddush*[9]. May one eat kinds of cookies[10]? May one eat kinds of dried fruit[11]? Rebbi Yudan the Prince bathed and became thirsty. He asked Rebbi Mana, since I am thirsty, may I drink? He told him, Rebbi Ḥiyya stated: A person may not taste anything before nightfall[12].

4 Bali 99b, Tosephta *Berakhot* 5:1. The Babli denies that in the special case of Passover Eve R. Yose disagrees.
5 Babli 100a.
6 R. Jehudah requires that one formally end the meal by reciting Grace and, probably after Evening prayers, restarts the meals by reciting *qidduš*.
7 Babli 100a, Tosephta *Berakhot* 5:2.
8 *Esth.* 7:8.
9 This disagrees with R. Yose since one acknowledges the Sabbath by a short interruption of the meal, it also disagrees with R. Jehudah since one is not required to formally close the meal or to recite Grace.
10 Since these are eaten without bread, they cannot be considered a meal.
11 Greek τράγημα, τό.
12 Therefore the previous questions have to be answered in the negative. The Babli disagrees, 107b.

(37b line 57) אָמַר רִבִּי לֵוִי. הָאוֹכֵל מַצָּה בָּעֶרֶב הַפֶּסַח כְּבָא עַל אֲרוּסָתוֹ בְּבֵית חָמִיו. וְהַבָּא עַל אֲרוּסָתוֹ בְּבֵית חָמִיו לוֹקֶה. תַּנֵּי. רִבִּי יוּדָה בֶּן בָּתִירָה אוֹמֵר. בֵּין חָמֵץ בֵּין מַצָּה אָסוּר. רִבִּי סִימוֹן בְּשֵׁם רִבִּי יְהוֹשֻׁעַ בֶּן לֵוִי. רִבִּי לֹא הָיָה אוֹכֵל לֹא חָמֵץ וְלֹא מַצָּה. לֹא מַצָּה מִן הָדָא דְרִבִּי לֵוִי. לֹא חָמֵץ מִן הָדָא דְרִבִּי יוּדָה בֶּן בָּתִירָה. וְרִבִּי תַלְמִידֵיהּ דְּרִבִּי יוּדָה בֶּן בָּתִירָה הֲוָה. לֹא.

תַּלְמִידֵיהּ דְּרִבִּי יַעֲקֹב בַּר קוֹרְשַׁיי הֲוָה. אֶלָּא בְגִין דַּהֲוָה בְכוֹר. אָמַר רִבִּי מָנָא. רִבִּי יוֹנָה אַבָּא הֲוָה בְכוֹר וַהֲוָה אֲכִיל. אָמַר רִבִּי תַּנְחוּמָא. לֹא מִן הָדָא אֶלָּא מִן הָדָא. רִבִּי אִיסְתְּנֵיס הֲוָה. כַּד הֲוָה אֲכִיל בִּימָמָא לָא הֲוָה אֲכִיל בְּרַמְשָׁא. וְלָמָּה לָא הֲוָה אֲכִיל הָכָא בִימָמָא. כְּדֵי שֶׁיִּכָּנֵס לַשַּׁבָּת בְּתַאֲוָה.

Rebbi Levi said, he who eats *mazzah* on Passover Eve is like one who sleeps with his betrothed in his father-in-law's house[13], and he who sleeps with his betrothed in his father-in-law's house is flogged. It was stated: Rebbi Jehudah ben Bathyra says, both bread and *mazzah* are forbidden[14]. Rebbi Simon in the name of Rebbi Joshua ben Levi: Rebbi ate neither bread nor *mazzah*. No *mazzah* because of that of Rebbi Levi, and no bread because of that of Rebbi Jehudah ben Bathyra. Was Rebbi a student of Rebbi Jehudah ben Bathyra? No, he was a student of Rebbi Jacob ben Qorshai. But it was because he was a firstborn[15]. Rebbi Mana said, my father Rebbi Jonah was a firstborn and he ate. Rebbi Tanḥuma said, it is neither for this nor for that reason; Rebbi was asthenic[16] and when he ate during the day, he could not eat in the night. Why did he not eat during this day? To enter the Sabbath with appetite[17].

13 After the preliminary but before the definitive marriage, when she is forbidden to him.
14 On the entire 14th of Nisan, even in the morning when leavened matter still is permitted.
15 Even though this reason is refuted in the following and it is not mentioned in the Babli, under the influence of Good Friday the fast of the firstborn has become a holy rite (*Tur Šulhan Arukh Orah Hayyim* §470).
16 Greek ἀσθενής. Cf. Babli 108a, about Rav Sheshet.
17 Therefore it seems that Rebbi fasted every Friday.

(37b line 66) אָמַר רִבִּי לֵוִי. לְפִי שֶׁדֶּרֶךְ עֲבָדִים לִהְיוֹת אוֹכְלִין מְעוּמָד. וְכָאן לִהְיוֹת אוֹכְלִין מְסוּבִּין. לְהוֹדִיעַ שֶׁיָּצְאוּ מֵעַבְדּוּת לַחֵירוּת. רִבִּי סִימוֹן בְּשֵׁם רִבִּי יְהוֹשֻׁעַ בֶּן לֵוִי. אוֹתוֹ כְזַיִת שֶׁאָדָם יוֹצֵא בוֹ בַּפֶּסַח צָרִיךְ לְאוֹכְלוֹ מֵיסַב. רִבִּי יוֹסֵי בָּעָא קוֹמֵי רִבִּי סִימוֹן. אֲפִילוּ עֶבֶד לִפְנֵי רַבּוֹ. אֲפִילוּ אִשָּׁה לִפְנֵי בַעֲלָהּ. אָמַר לֵיהּ. בְּרִבִּי. עַד כָּאן שָׁמַעְתִּי.

אָמַר רִבִּי חִייָה בַּר אָדָא. לְפִי שֶׁאֵין עָרֵב לְאָדָם לוֹכַל מִן הַקּוּפָּה. וְכָאן אֲפִילוּ מִן הַתַּמְחוּי.

[18]Rebbi Levi said, because usually slaves eat while standing, and here one is forced to eat lying on couches, to proclaim that they went from slavery to freedom. Rebbi Simon in the name of Rebbi Joshua ben Levi: This

olive-sized bit with which a person fulfills his obligation on Passover he must eat lying down. Rebbi Yose asked before Rebbi Simon, even a slave before his master, even a woman before her husband[19]? He said to him, great personality, that is all I heard.

Rebbi Ḥiyya bar Ada said, because it is not agreeable for a person to eat from public assistance, and here even from the tray[20].

18 Here starts the detailed discussion of the Mishnah.
19 For the entire paragraph, see Babli 108a. According to the Babli, only aristocratic women have to lie down.
20 In general, people are encouraged not to use public assistance even if they are entitled to it. But for the Passover *Seder* it is an obligation of the poor to apply even to the distribution of food in kind, which is more demeaning than distribution of money, if otherwise he could not fulfill the requirements of the meal.

(37b line 72) תַּנֵּי. צָרִיךְ הוּא אָדָם לְשַׂמֵּחַ אֶת אִשְׁתּוֹ וְאֶת בָּנָיו בָּרֶגֶל. בַּמֶּה מְשַׂמְּחָן. בְּיַיִן. רִבִּי יוּדָה אוֹמֵר נָשִׁים בָּרָאוּי לָהֶן וּקְטַנִּים בָּרָאוּי לָהֶן. נָשִׁים בָּרָאוּי לָהֶן. כְּגוֹן מְסָאנִין וְצוּצְלָיו. וּקְטַנִּים בָּרָאוּי לָהֶן. כְּגוֹן אֱגוֹזִין וְלוּזִין. אָמְרִין. הֲוָה רִבִּי טַרְפוֹן עָבִיד כֵּן.

It was stated[21]: "A man has to make his family happy on a feast of pilgrimage. How does he make them happy? With wine. Rebbi Jehudah used to say, women with what is appropriate for them, and minors with what is appropriate for them. Women with what is appropriate for them, for example shoes[22] and belts, and minors with what is appropriate for them, for example nuts and pistachios." They said, Rebbi Tarphon acted in this way.

21 Babli 109a.
22 Reading מסאנין. N. J. Epstein reads ביסניו, Greek βύσσινα, "(garments) made of byssos, fine linen". It probably is better to read "shoes", which are accessories like belts, rather than "luxury linen garments" which are not quite what the Babli recommends for women in the Land of Israel.

(37b line 76) מִנַּיִין לְאַרְבָּעָה כוֹסוֹת. רִבִּי יוֹחָנָן בְּשֵׁם רִבִּי בִּנְיָיה. כְּנֶגֶד אַרְבַּע גְּאוּלוֹת. לָכֵן אֱמֹר לִבְנֵי־יִשְׂרָאֵל אֲנִי יי וְהוֹצֵאתִי אֶתְכֶם וגו'. וְלָקַחְתִּי אֶתְכֶם לִי לְעָם וגו'. וְהוֹצֵאתִי. וְהִצַּלְתִּי. וְגָאַלְתִּי. וְלָקַחְתִּי. רִבִּי יְהוֹשֻׁעַ בֶּן לֵוִי אָמַר. כְּנֶגֶד אַרְבַּע כּוֹסוֹת שֶׁלְפַּרְעֹה. וְכוֹס פַּרְעֹה בְּיָדִי. וָאֶשְׁחַט אֹתָם אֶל־כּוֹס פַּרְעֹה. וָאֶתֵּן אֶת־הַכּוֹס עַל־כַּף פַּרְעֹה: וְנָתַתָּ כוֹס־פַּרְעֹה בְּיָדוֹ. רִבִּי לֵוִי אָמַר. כְּנֶגֶד אַרְבַּע מַלְכוּיוֹת. וְרַבָּנָן אָמְרֵי. כְּנֶגֶד אַרְבָּעָה כוֹסוֹת שֶׁלְפּוּרְעָנוּת שֶׁהַקָּדוֹשׁ בָּרוּךְ הוּא

עָתִיד לְהַשְׁקוֹת אֶת אוּמוֹת הָעוֹלָם. כִּי כֹה אָמַר יְיָ אֱלֹהֵי יִשְׂרָאֵל אֵלַי קַח אֶת־כּוֹס הַיַּיִן הַחֵימָה וגו'. כּוֹס־זָהָב בָּבֶל בְּיַד־יְיָ. כִּי כוֹס בְּיַד־יְיָ. יַמְטֵר עַל־רְשָׁעִים פַּחִים אֵשׁ וְגָפְרִית וְרוּחַ זִלְעָפוֹת מְנָת כּוֹסָם: מָהוּ מְנָת כּוֹסָם. רִבִּי אָבוּן אָמַר. דִּיפְלֵי פוֹטִירִין. כְּדִיפְלֵי פוֹטִירִין אַחַר הַמֶּרְחַץ. וּכְנֶגְדָּן עָתִיד הַקָּדוֹשׁ בָּרוּךְ הוּא לְהַשְׁקוֹת אֶת יִשְׂרָאֵל אַרְבַּע כּוֹסוֹת שֶׁלְּנֶחָמָה. יְיָ מְנָת־חֶלְקִי וְכוֹסִי. דִּשַּׁנְתָּ בַשֶּׁמֶן רֹאשִׁי כּוֹסִי רְוָיָה: וְהָדֵין כּוֹס־יְשׁוּעוֹת אֶשָּׂא תְּרֵיִין.

[23]From where the Four Cups? Rebbi Johanan in the name of Rebbi Benaiah: Corresponding to the four deliveries[24]: *Therefore, say to the Children of Israel, I am the Eternal, and I shall take you out*, etc. *And I shall take you as My people*, etc. *I shall take you, I shall save you, I shall free you, I shall take you.* Rebbi Joshua ben Levi said, corresponding to the four cups of Pharao: *The cup of Pharao was in my hand; I took the grapes and squeezed them into Pharao's cup, and gave the cup in Pharao's hand. You will give the cup in the hand of Pharao*[25]. Rebbi Levi said, corresponding to the four kingdoms. But our teachers say, corresponding to the four cups of doom that the Holy One, praise to Him, will make the Gentiles drink at the end of days. *Truly, so said the Eternal, the God of Israel, to me: take this cup of the wine of wrath*[26]. *The golden cup of Babylon is in the hand of the Eternal*[27]. *Truly a cup is in the hand of the Eternal, intoxicating wine, fully to be mixed; He shall sprinkle from it but its dregs shall be drunk, squeezed to the last, by all the wicked of the earth*[28]. *He shall let coals rain on the wicked; fire, sulphur, and burning wind is the portion of their cup*[29]. What does *the portion of their cup* mean? R. Abun said: a double cup[30] like the double cup taken after a thermal bath. And in accordance with this correspondingly the Holy One, praised be He, will let Israel drink four cups of consolation at the End of Days: *The Eternal is the portion of my part and my cup*[31]. *You anointed my head with oil; my cup is overflowing*[32]. *I shall lift up the cup of salvations*[33] counts for two.

23 For an explanation of this paragraph, see the author's *The Scholar's Haggadah*, pp. 186-187.
24 *Ex.* 6:7-8.
25 *Gen.* 40:11,13. The relation to Passover is explained in Targum Pseudo-Jonathan *ad loc.*
26 *Jer.* 23:15.
27 *Jer.* 51:7.
28 *Ps.* 75:9.
29 *Ps.* 11:6.
30 Greek διπλόν ποτήριον, τό.
31 *Ps.* 16:5.
32 *Ps.* 23:5/

33 *Ps.* 116:13.

(37c line 13) תַּמָּן תַּנִּינָן. הַמּוֹצִיא יַיִן כְּדֵי מְזִיגַת הַכּוֹס. רִבִּי זְעוּרָה שָׁאַל לְרִבִּי יוֹשִׁיָּה. כַּמָּה הוּא שִׁיעוּרָן שֶׁלְכּוֹסוֹת. אָמַר לֵיהּ. נִלְמוֹד סָתוּם מִן הַמְפוֹרָשׁ. דְּתָנֵי רִבִּי חִייָה. אַרְבָּעָה [כוסות] שֶׁאָמְרוּ יֵשׁ בָּן רְבִיעִית יַיִן בָּאִיטַלְקִי.

[34]"One who brings out wine to mix a cup," etc. Rebbi Ze`ira asked Rebbi Joshiah, what is the measure of cups? He told him, let us infer the hidden from the explicit since Rebbi Ḥiyya stated, the Four Cups which they said add up to an Italic *quartarius* of wine.

תַּמָּן תַּנִּינָן. מְפַנִּין אֲפִילוּ אַרְבַּע וְחָמֵשׁ קוּפּוֹת. רִבִּי זְעוּרָה שָׁאַל לְרִבִּי יוֹשִׁיָּה. כַּמָּה הִיא שִׁיעוּרָהּ שֶׁלְּקוּפָּה. אָמַר לֵיהּ. נִלְמוֹד סָתוּם מִן הַמְפוֹרָשׁ. דְּתַנִּינָן תַּמָּן. בְּשָׁלֹשׁ קוּפּוֹת שֶׁל שָׁלֹשׁ שָׁלֹשׁ סְאִין תּוֹרְמִין אֶת הַלִּשְׁכָּה.

There, we have stated[35]: "One removes four or five baskets." Rebbi Ze`ira asked Rebbi Joshiah, what is the measure of baskets? He told him, let us infer the hidden from the explicit since we have stated there[36]: "The contributions for the Temple were removed in three baskets of three *seah* each."

רִבִּי יוֹסֵה בֶּרִבִּי בּוּן בְּשֵׁם רִבִּי יוֹחָנָן. דְּרִבִּי [יוּדָא] הִיא. דְּתָנֵי. מַיִם כְּדֵי גְמִייָה. רִבִּי יוּדָה אוֹמֵר. כְּדֵי מְזִיגַת (הַכּוֹס) [הַמּוֹזֵג] מָזוּג בְּכַמָּה. נִשְׁמְעִינָהּ מִן הָדָא. מַיִם כְּדֵי גְמִייָה. רִבִּי יוּדָה אוֹמֵר. כְּדֵי מְזִיגַת הַכּוֹס. יַיִן כְּדֵי גְמִייָה. רִבִּי יוּדָה אוֹמֵר. כְּדֵי מְזִיגַת הַכּוֹס. כַּמָּה הוּא שִׁיעוּרָן שֶׁלְכּוֹסוֹת. רִבִּי מָנָא אָמַר. טִיטַרְטוֹן וּרְבִיעַ.

Rebbi Yose ben Rebbi Abun said, it is Rebbi Jehudah's. As it was stated[37] "Water, a gulp; Rebbi Jehudah says, for the mixer's mixing. Mixed by how much? Let us hear from the following: "Water. a gulp; Rebbi Jehudah says, for mixing a cup. Wine. a gulp; Rebbi Jehudah says, for mixing a cup." What is the measure of cups? Rebbi Abun said, τέταρτον[37a] is a quarter.

מַהוּ לִשְׁתּוֹתָן בְּכֶרֶךְ אֶחָד. מִן מַה דְּאָמַר רִבִּי יוֹחָנָן. הִלֵּל אִם שְׁמָעָן בְּבַיִת הַכְּנֶסֶת יָצָא. הָדָא אֲמָרָה. אֲפִילוּ שְׁתַּיִן בְּכֶרֶךְ אֶחָד יָצָא. מַהוּ לִשְׁתּוֹתָן מְפוּסָּקִין. כְּלוּם אָמְרוּ שֶׁיִּשְׁתֶּה לֹא שֶׁלֹּשְׁתַּכֵּר. אִם שׁוֹתָהּ הוּא מְפוּסָּקִין אֵינוֹ מִשְׁתַּכֵּר. מַהוּ לָצֵאת בְּיַיִן שֶׁלִּשְׁבִיעִית. תַּנֵּי רִבִּי הוֹשַׁעְיָה. יוֹצְאִין בְּיַיִן שֶׁלִּשְׁבִיעִית. מַהוּ לָצֵאת בְּקוּנְדִּיטוֹן. מִן מַה דְּתָנֵי בַּר קַפָּרָא. קוֹנְדִּיטוֹן כְּיַיִן. הָדָא אֲמָרָה יוֹצְאִין בְּקוּנְדִּיטוֹן. מַהוּ לָצֵאת בָּהֶן מְזוּגִין. מִן מַה דְּתָנֵי רִבִּי חִייָה. אַרְבָּעָה [כוסות] שֶׁאָמְרוּ יוֹצְאִין בָּהֶן בֵּין חַיִּין בֵּין מְזוּגִין. וְהוּא שֶׁיְּהֵא בָּהֶן טַעַם וּמַרְאֵה יַיִן. אָמַר רִבִּי יִרְמְיָה. מִצְוָתָהּ לָצֵאת בְּיַיִן אָדוֹם. [שֶׁנֶּאֱמַר.] אַל־תֵּרֶא יַיִן כִּי יִתְאַדָּם. תַּנֵּי. מְבוּשָּׁל כְּדֵי תַּבֶל.

מָהוּ לָצֵאת בְּיַיִן מְבוּשָׁל. רִבִּי יוֹנָה אָמַר. יוֹצְאִין בְּיַיִן מְבוּשָׁל. רִבִּי יוֹנָה כְדַעְתֵּיהּ. דְּרִבִּי יוֹנָה שָׁתֵי אַרְבַּעְתֵּי כָסוֹי דְּלֵילֵי פִסְחָא וְחָזִיק רֵישֵׁיהּ עַד עֲצַרְתָּא.

May one drink them together? Since Rebbi Joḥanan said about *Hallel*, if he heard it in the synagogue he has fulfilled his obligation, this implies that if he drank them together he fulfilled his obligation. May one drink them with interruptions? They said that he should drink, not that he should get drunk. If he drinks them with interruptions, would he not become drunk? May one fulfill his obligation with Sabbatical wine? Rebbi Hoshaia stated, one may fulfill his obligation with Sabbatical wine. May one fulfill his obligation with spiced wine? Since Bar Qappara stated, spiced wine is like wine, which implies that one may fulfill his obligation with spiced wine. May one fulfill his obligation with mixed wine? Since Rebbi Ḥiyya stated: the Four Cups which they prescribed, one may fulfill his obligation either with unmixed or mixed, on condition that it have the taste and looks of wine. Rebbi Jeremiah said, it is meritorious to fulfill one's obligation with red wine. What is the reason? *Do not see wine when it shows its red color*[38]. It was stated, cooked for spice. May one fulfill his obligation with cooked wine? Rebbi Jonah said, one may fulfill his obligation with cooked wine. Rebbi Jonah follows his own opinion, since Rebbi Jonah drank his four cups in the Passover night and had a headache until Pentecost.

רִבִּי יוּדָה בֵּירִבִּי אִילְעַאי שָׁתֵי אַרְבַּעְתֵּי כָסוֹי דְּלֵילֵי פִסְחָא וְחָזִיק רֵישֵׁיהּ עַד חַגָּא. חַמְתֵּיהּ חָדָא מַטְרוֹנָא אַפּוֹי נְהִירִין. אָמְרָה לֵיהּ. סַבָּא סַבָּא. חָדָא מִן תְּלַת מִילִין אִית בָּךְ. אוֹ שָׁתֵי חֲמַר אַתְּ. אוֹ מַלְוֵה בְּרִיבִּית אַתְּ. אוֹ מְגַדֵּל חֲזִירִים אַתְּ. אֲמַר לָהּ. תִּיפַּח רוּחָהּ דַּהִיא אִיתְּתָא. חָדָא מִן אִילֵּין תַּלְתֵּי מִילַּיָּא לֵית בִּי. אֶלָּא אוּלְפָּנִי שְׁכִיחַ לִי. דִּכְתִיב חָכְמַת אָדָם תָּאִיר פָּנָיו.

רִבִּי אַבָּהוּ נְחַת לִטִיבֶּרְיָא. חֲמוֹנֵיהּ תַּלְמִידוֹי דְּרִבִּי יוֹחָנָן אַפּוֹי נְהִירִין. אָמְרוּן קוֹמֵי רִבִּי יוֹחָנָן. אַשְׁכַּח רִבִּי אַבָּהוּ סִימָא. אֲמַר לוֹן. לָמָה. אָמְרִין לֵיהּ. אַפּוֹי נְהִירִין. אֲמַר לוֹן. דִּילְמָא אוֹרַיְתָא חַדְתָא שְׁמַע. סְלִיק לְגַבֵּיהּ. אֲמַר לֵיהּ. מַאי אוֹרַיְתָא חַדְתָא שְׁמַעְתְּ. אֲמַר לֵיהּ. תּוֹסֶפְתָּא עַתִּיקְתָּא. וְקָרָא עֲלוֹי. חָכְמַת אָדָם תָּאִיר פָּנָיו.

Rebbi Jehudah bar Ilai drank his four cups in the Passover night and had a headache until Tabernacles. A lady saw that his face was shiny. She said to him, old man, old man, one of three things applies to you. Either you are drunk from wine, or you are lending on interest, or you are raising pigs. He answered her, this woman's spirit shall be blown away, not one of these three things applies to me, but my learning is ever present with me, as it is written, *a man's wisdom illuminates his face.*

Rebbi Abbahu descended to Tiberias. The students of Rebbi Johanan saw that his face was shining. They said before Rebbi Johanan, Rebbi Abbahu found a treasure. He asked them, why? They told him, his face is shining. He said to them, maybe he understood a new teaching. He came to visit him. He asked him, what new teaching did you hear? He said, an old Tosephta. He recited about him, *a man's wisdom illuminates his face*

אָמַר רִבִּי חֲנִינָה. לוֹגָא דְאוֹרָיְיתָא תוֹמַנְתָּא עַתִּיקְתָּא דְּמוּרְיָיסָא דְצִיפּוֹרִין. אָמַר רִבִּי יוֹנָה. חֲכִים אֲנָא לָהּ. דְּבֵית רִבִּי יַנַּאי מְכִילִין בָּהּ דְּבַשׁ. תַּנֵּי. חֲצִי שְׁמִינִית טִיבֶּרְנִית יְשָׁנָה. אָמַר רִבִּי יוֹחָנָן. הָדָא דִידָן הֲוַת. וְלָמָּה לֹא אָמַר. עַתִּיקְתָּא. בְּגִין דַּהֲוַת בְּיוֹמוֹי. אִית דְּאָמְרִין. דַּהֲוַת זְעִירָא. וְרָבַת וּזְעִירַת. וְלֹא זְעֵרַת כַּמָּה דַהֲוַת. כַּמָּה הוּא שִׁיעוּרוֹ שֶׁלְּכוֹס. רִבִּי יוֹסֵה בְשֵׁם רִבִּי יוּדָה בַּר פָּזִי רִבִּי יוֹסֵי בֵּירִבִּי בּוּן בְּשֵׁם שְׁמוּאֵל. אֶצְבָּעַיִם עַל אֶצְבָּעַיִם עַל רוּם אֶצְבַּע וּמֶחֱצָה וּשְׁלִישׁ אֶצְבַּע. תַּנֵּי. יָבֵשׁ כְּזַיִת. דִּבְרֵי רִבִּי נָתָן. רַבָּנָן דְּקַיְסָרִין רִבִּי יוֹסֵה בֵּירִבִּי בּוּן בְּשֵׁם רִבִּי יוֹחָנָן. אַתְיָא דְּרִבִּי [נָתָן] כְּרִבִּי שִׁמְעוֹן. כְּמָה דְרִבִּי שִׁמְעוֹן אָמַר. בָּרְבִיעִית. כֵּן רִבִּי נָתָן אָמַר. לִכְשֶׁיִּקְרַשׁ יְהֵא בוֹ כְזַיִת.

Rebbi Hanina said, the *log* of the Torah is the old Sepphorean eighth of fish sauce. Rebbi Jonah said, I know it. In the House of Rebbi Yannai they were measuring honey with it. It was stated, half of the old Tiberian eighth. Rebbi Johanan said, this one we used. Why did he not say, the old one? Because it was in his days. Some are saying, it was small, then was enlarged, and diminished, but it was not made small as before. What is the measure of a cup? Rebbi Yose in the name of Rebbi Jehudah bar Pazi, Rebbi Yose ben Rebbi Abun in the name of Samuel: Two fingers by two fingers high a finger and a half and a third of a finger[40]. It was stated, dried like the volume of an olive, the words of Rebbi Nathan. The rabbis of Caesarea in the name of Rebbi Yose ben Rebbi Abun in the name of Rebbi Johanan: Rebbi Nathan follows Rebbi Simeon. Just as Rebbi Simeon says, a *quartarius*, so Rebbi Nathan says, a *quartarius*, when it jells it will have the volume of an olive.

34 This text is from *Šabbat* 8, Notes 23-50.
35 Mishnah *Šabbat* 18:1.
36 Mishnah *Šeqalim* 3:2.
37 Tosephta *Šabbat* 8:10.
37a Τεταρτεύς, -έως, ὁ, or τεταρτηρόν, τό, a measure of capacity.

38 *Prov.* 23:31.

39 *Eccl.* 8:1.

40 This value of $2 \times 2 \times 1^5/_6 = 7^1/_3$ cubic digits compares to a Babylonian value of 10.8 cubic digits (Babli 109a). A cubit is 24 digits. Various cubits were in use; therefore it is difficult to define this volume in modern terms. The variability of the cubit is mirrored in the Greek world by the many values given for the *stadion*, which varies from 148 m for the (Egyptian) *itinerant stadion* to the Greek sacramental 184 m. Based on the itinerant *stadion* and 1 mile = 7.5 stadia = 2000 cubits, one would obtain 91 cm³ for the cup.

In *Terumot* 10:7 (Note 80), a *log* is defined as (volume corresponding to a weight of) 200 denar. If volume of water is intended, this would make a cup of 155 cm³. In *Terumot* 5:3, the *log* is defined as the volume of 4 eggs, the *modius* (16 *log*) as 96 eggs (in the Babli, *Eruvin* 83a, 217 eggs, which, however, refers not to the Roman but the Syrian *modius*, twice the volume of the Roman). For the standard *modius* of 8.536 l, this gives the volume of a cup as the standard *quartarius* of 133 cm³ (Note 1).

(fol. 37a) **משנה ב**: מָזְגוּ לוֹ כוֹס רִאשׁוֹן בֵּית שַׁמַּאי אוֹמְרִים מְבָרֵךְ עַל הַיּוֹם וְאַחַר כָּךְ מְבָרֵךְ עַל הַיַּיִן. וּבֵית הִלֵּל אוֹמְרִים מְבָרֵךְ עַל הַיַּיִן וְאַחַר כָּךְ מְבָרֵךְ עַל הַיּוֹם:

Mishnah 2: One mixes him[41] the first cup. The House of Shammai say, he pronounces the benediction of the day and after that he pronounces the benediction over the wine. But the House of Hillel say, he pronounces the benediction over the wine and after that he pronounces the benediction of the day.

41 The celebrant of the *Seder*. Everybody else's cup also is filled but only the celebrant recites the benediction of *Qiddush*. The Mishnah is paralleled by Mishnah *Berakhot* 8:1 (referring to the Sabbath). Halakhah 2 in its entirety is paralleled in *Berakhot* 8:1(ב), Notes 2-18.

(37c line 54) **הלכה ב**: מַה טַעֲמְהוֹן דְּבֵית שַׁמַּי. שֶׁקְּדוּשַׁת הַיּוֹם גָּרְמָה לַיַּיִן שֶׁיָּבוֹא. וּכְבָר נִתְחַיֵּיב בִּקְדוּשַׁת הַיּוֹם עַד שֶׁלֹּא בָא הַיַּיִן. מַה טַעֲמְהוֹן דְּבֵית הִלֵּל. שֶׁהַיַּיִן גּוֹרֵם לִקְדוּשַׁת הַיּוֹם שֶׁתֵּיאָמֵר. דָּבָר אַחֵר. הַיַּיִן תָּדִיר וּקְדוּשָׁה אֵינָהּ תְּדִירָה.

Halakhah 2: What is the reason of the House of Shammai? The Sanctification of the Day causes the wine to be served; he was obligated for the Sanctification of the Day before the wine was served. What is the reason of the House of Hillel? The wine causes the Sanctification of the Day to be recited. Another explanation: The wine is frequent, Sanctification is less frequent.

אָמַר רִבִּי יוֹסֵי. מִדִּבְרֵי שְׁנֵיהֶן. יַיִן וְאַבְדָּלָה הַיַּיִן קוֹדֵם. כְּלוּם טַעֲמְהוֹן דְּבֵית שַׁמַּי לֹא שֶׁקְּדוּשַׁת הַיּוֹם גֵּרְמָה לַיַּיִן. וְכָאן הוֹאִיל וְאַבְדָּלָה גֵּרְמָה לַיַּיִן שֶׁיָּבוֹא. הַיַּיִן קוֹדֵם. כְּלוּם טַעֲמְהוֹן דְּבֵית הִלֵּל אֶלָּא שֶׁהַיַּיִן תָּדִיר וּקְדוּשָׁה אֵינָהּ תְּדִירָה. וְכָאן הוֹאִיל וְהַיַּיִן תְּדִירָה וְאַבְדָּלָה אֵינָהּ תְּדִירָה. הַיַּיִן קוֹדֵם. אָמַר רִבִּי מָנָא. מִדִּבְרֵי שְׁנֵיהֶן. יַיִן וְאַבְדָּלָה אַבְדָּלָה קוֹדֵם. כְּלוּם טַעֲמְהוֹן דְּבֵית שַׁמַּי אֶלָּא שֶׁכְּבָר נִתְחַיֵּיב בִּקְדוּשַׁת הַיּוֹם עַד שֶׁלֹּא בָא הַיַּיִן. וְכָאן הוֹאִיל וְנִתְחַיֵּיב בָּאַבְדָּלָה עַד שֶׁלֹּא בָא הַיַּיִן. אַבְדָּלָה קוֹדֶמֶת. כְּלוּם טַעֲמְהוֹן דְּבֵית הִלֵּל אֶלָּא שֶׁהַיַּיִן גּוֹרֵם לִקְדוּשַׁת הַיּוֹם שֶׁתֵּיאָמֵר. וְכָאן הוֹאִיל וְהַיַּיִן גּוֹרֵם לָאַבְדָּלָה שֶׁתֵּיאָמֵר. אַבְדָּלָה קוֹדֶמֶת.

1 יוסי | ב יוסה ואבדלה | ב והבדלה לא | ב אלא 2 ליין | ב ליין שיבוא ואבדלה | ב ולא אבדלה 3 וכאן | ב הכן תדירה | ב תדיר נ 4 קודם | ב קודמת 5 באבדלה | ב בהבדלה 7 וחיין | ב ואין היין

Rebbi Yose said: From the words of both of them it follows that for wine and *Havdalah*, the wine comes first. Is not the reason of the House of Shammai that the Sanctification of the Day causes the wine to be served? But here, *Havdalah* does {not}[42] cause the wine to be served; wine therefore has precedence. Is not the reason of the House of Hillel that the wine is frequent, Sanctification of the Day is less frequent? Also here, wine is frequent and *Havdalah* is less frequent: the wine has precedence. Rebbi Mana said: From the words of both of them it follows that for wine and *Havdalah*, *Havdalah* comes first. Is not the reason of the House of Shammai that he was obligated for the Sanctification of the Day before the wine came? Also here, since he is obligated for *Havdalah* before the wine came, *Havdalah* has precedence. Is not the reason of the House of Hillel that the wine causes the Sanctification of the Day to be recited? But here, the wine does {not}[42] cause *Havdalah* to be recited: *Havdalah* has precedence.

אָמַר רִבִּי זְעוּרָה. מִדִּבְרֵי שְׁנֵיהֶן. מַבְדִּילִין בְּלֹא יַיִן וְאֵין מְקַדְּשִׁין אֶלָּא בְיַיִן. הִיא דַעְתֵּיהּ דְּרִבִּי זְעוּרָה. דְּרִבִּי זְעוּרָה אָמַר. מַבְדִּילִין עַל שֵׁכָר. וְאָזְלִין מִן אָתָר לְאָתָר לְמִישְׁמַע קִידּוּשָׁא.

1 זעורה | ב זעירא 2 זעורה | ב זעירא (2) | ב שכר | ב שכר למשמע קידושא | ב משום קדושה

Rebbi Ze'ira said: One infers from the words of both of them that one may make *Havdalah* without wine but one may not make *Qiddush* without wine. That is the opinion of Rebbi Ze'ira since Rebbi Ze'ira said: One makes

Havdalah on alcoholic beverages but one goes from one place to another to hear *Qiddush*.

אָמַר רִבִּי יוֹסֵי בֵּירִבִּי בּוּן. נְהִגִין תַּמָּן. בְּמָקוֹם שֶׁאֵין יַיִן שְׁלִיחַ צִיבּוּר יוֹרֵד לִפְנֵי הַתֵּיבָה וְאוֹמֵר בְּרָכָה אַחַת מֵעֵין שֶׁבַע. וְחוֹתֵם. מְקַדֵּשׁ יִשְׂרָאֵל וְיוֹם הַשַּׁבָּת.

1 נהיגין | ב נהיגין יורד | ב עובר   2 מקדש | ב במקדש

Rebbi Yose ben Rebbi Abun said: There, they have the custom that at a place without wine, the reader descends before the Ark, recites one benediction that contains seven, and closes by "He Who sanctifies Israel and the Sabbath Day".

42 Added from *Berakhot*, missing here, but logically necessary.

(fol. 37b) **משנה ג:** הֵבִיאוּ לְפָנָיו יְרָקוֹת וַחֲזֶרֶת מְטַבֵּל בַּחֲזֶרֶת עַד שֶׁהוּא מַגִּיעַ לְפַרְפֶּרֶת הַפַּת. הֵבִיאוּ לְפָנָיו מַצָּה וַחֲזֶרֶת וַחֲרוֹסֶת וּשְׁנֵי תַבְשִׁילִין אַף עַל פִּי שֶׁאֵין חֲרוֹסֶת מִצְוָה. רִבִּי לְעָזֶר בִּי רִבִּי צָדוֹק אוֹמֵר מִצְוָה. וּבַמִּקְדָּשׁ מְבִיאִין לְפָנָיו גּוּפוֹ שֶׁל פֶּסַח:

Mishnah 3: They bring before him vegetables and Romaine lettuce[43]. One dips Romaine lettuce[44], until he comes to filling the bread[45], when one brings before him[46] *mazzah*, and Romaine lettuce, and *haroset*[47], and two dishes[48], even though *haroset* is not an obligation; Rebbi Eliezer ben Rebbi Sadoq says, it is an obligation. In the Temple[49] one brings before him the body of the *Pesah*.

43 "Romaine lettuce" is used as stand-in for all bitter herbs admissible for the *Seder*, Mishnah 2:5. General vegetables are mentioned only in the Mishnah of the Yerushalmi; from the Halakhah which mentions that one is permitted non-bitter vegetables for the first dip it seems that they were not mentioned in the Mishnah underlying the Halakhah.

44 As an appetizer, since on Passover the cookies usually served as appetizers may not be used; cf. *The Scholar's Haggadah*, pp. 228-233.

45 After the discussion of the Exodus, described in Mishnaiot 4,5,6. "Filling the bread" refers to the meal where in the absence of forks and knives one ate everything as fillers of pitta-bread; in this case, freshly baked soft *mazzah*.

46 Unless the entire plate was brought on a table at the start.

47 A moist mixture of fruits and spices in

which the bitter herbs have to be dipped.

48 As the Halakhah explains, a remembrance of the *Pesaḥ* and the festival offerings of Temple times.

49 In Jerusalem in Temple times.

(37c line 71) **הלכה ג**: חֲבֵרַיָּיא בְשֵׁם רִבִּי יוֹחָנָן. צָרִיךְ לִטְבֹּל בַּחֲזֶרֶת שְׁנֵי פְעָמִים. רִבִּי זְעוּרָה בְשֵׁם רִבִּי יוֹחָנָן. אֵינוֹ צָרִיךְ לִטְבֹּל בַּחֲזֶרֶת שְׁנֵי פְעָמִים. רִבִּי שִׁמְעוֹן בֶּן לָקִישׁ אָמַר. אִם לֹא טָבַל פַּעַם רִאשׁוֹנָה צָרִיךְ לִטְבֹּל פַּעַם שְׁנִיָּיה. מַתְנִיתָא פְלִינָא עַל רִבִּי שִׁמְעוֹן בֶּן לָקִישׁ. שֶׁבְּכָל־הַלֵּילוֹת אָנוּ מַטְבִּילִין פַּעַם אַחַת. הַלַּיְלָה הַזֶּה שְׁתֵּי פְעָמִים. סָבַר רִבִּי שִׁמְעוֹן בֶּן לָקִישׁ עַל הָדָא דְבַר קַפָּרָה. מַתְנִיתָא פְלִינָא עַל בַּר קַפָּרָא.. שֶׁבְּכָל־הַלֵּילוֹת אָנוּ מַטְבִּילִין אוֹתוֹ אִם הַפָּת. וְכַאן אָנוּ מַטְבִּילִין אוֹתוֹ בִּפְנֵי עַצְמוֹ. מַתְנִיתָא פְלִינָא עַל רִבִּי יוֹחָנָן. יוֹצְאִין בַּמַּצָּה בֵּין שֶׁכִּיוַּון. בֵּין שֶׁלֹּא כִיוַּון. וְהָכָא מִכֵּיוָן שֶׁהֵיסַב. חֲזָקָה כִּיוֵּין. מְתִיב רִבִּי יִרְמְיָה קוֹמֵי רִבִּי זְעוּרָה. מַתְנִיתָא פְלִינָא עַל רִבִּי שִׁמְעוֹן בֶּן לָקִישׁ. הֵבִיאוּ לְפָנָיו מַצָּה וַחֲזֶרֶת וַחֲרוֹסֶת. אַף עַל פִּי שֶׁאֵין חֲרוֹסֶת מִצְוָה. חֲזֶרֶת מִצְוָה. אָמַר לֵיהּ. שֶׁכֵּן רַב מְטַבֵּל בַּתְּרָדִין.

Halakhah 3: The colleagues in the name of Rebbi Joḥanan: One has to dip Romaine lettuce twice. Rebbi Ze`ira in the name of Rebbi Joḥanan: One need not dip Romaine lettuce twice[50]. Rebbi Simeon ben Laqish said, if he did not dip the first time, he has to dip the second time[51]. The Mishnah disagrees with Rebbi Simeon ben Laqish; "On all other nights we dip once, this night twice." Rebbi Simeon ben Laqish is of one opinion with Bar Qappara; the Mishnah disagrees with Bar Qappara: On all other nights we dip with bread[52], but here we dip it by itself. The Mishnah disagrees with Rebbi Joḥanan, one fulfills his obligation with *mazzah,* whether he intended it or did not intend[53]. But here since he was lying on a couch, the presumption is that he intended[54]. Rebbi Jeremiah objected before Rebbi Ze`ira, does not the Mishnah disagree with Rebbi Simeon ben Laqish? "one brings before him *mazzah*, and Romaine lettuce, and *ḥaroset*, . . . even though *ḥaroset* is not an obligation." Romaine lettuce is an obligation[55]. He said to him, since Rav dips with beets[56].

50 He holds that after the *Qiddush* one has to eat vegetable, with the appropriate benediction of "Him Who created the produce of the earth," and at the start of the meal one has to eat bitter herbs, in fulfillment of the biblical obligation, without a benediction on the bitter herbs as food. The only problem is whether the benediction for the food must be for bitter herbs, or whether any vegetable is fine, and the benediction can be intended to include the bitter herbs consumed later. There are two

conflicting traditions in the name of R. Johanan.

51 He holds that the first dipping is optional, an opinion rejected by the Babli 114b.

52 One fills the pitta with food and dips the bread in sauce; without knives and forks this is the usual way to eat dinner. To dip vegetable without bread is uncommon.

53 Since in his opinion a biblical obligation is discharged when the required action is completed, with or without particular intention, then it should be impossible to eat bitter herbs the second time in fulfillment of the biblical obligation since the obligation already was discharged unintentionally with the first dipping.

54 But for vegetables this cannot be presupposed.

55 This question implies that in his version of the Mishnah, "vegetables" were not mentioned. Since *haroset* is singled out as optional, it follows that bitter herbs are not optional even for the first dipping, and that a benediction for non-bitter vegetables as food would not be valid for bitter herbs.

56 Therefore it is preferable to use some other vegetable for the benediction over food and reserve bitter herbs for the biblically ordained ceremony. Babli 115a.

(37d line 10) תַּגָּרֵי יְרוּשָׁלֵם הָיוּ אוֹמְרִים. בּוֹאוּ וּטְלוּ לָכֶם תַּבְלֵי מִצְוָה. בְּנֵי בֵיתֵיהּ דְּאִיסִי בְשֵׁם אִיסִי. וְלָמָּה נִקְרָא שְׁמָהּ (דּוּכָה) [רוֹבָה]. דּוּ דוּכָה עִימּוֹ. רִבִּי יְהוֹשֻׁעַ בֶּן לֵוִי אָמַר. צְרִיכָה שֶׁתְּהֵא עָבָה. מִילְתֵיהּ אֲמָרָה. זֵיכֶר לַטִּיט. אִית תַּנָּיֵי תַנֵּי. צְרִיכָה שֶׁתְּהֵא רַכָּה. מִילְתֵיהּ אָמַר. זֵיכֶר לַדָּם.

תַּנֵּי. וּבִגְבוּלִין צְרִיכִין שְׁנֵי תַבְשִׁילִין אֶחָד זֵיכֶר לַפֶּסַח וְאֶחָד זֵיכֶר לַחֲגִיגָה.

The traders of Jerusalem used to say, "come and buy spices for the meritorious deed.[57]" The family of Issy in the same of Issy: Why is it[57] called "pounded"? Because one pounds[58] for it. Rebbi Joshua ben Levi said, it has to be thick. His word implies that it is a remembrance of the mortar[59]. There are Tannaim who state, it has to be soft[60]. This word implies that it is a remembrance of the blood.

It was stated: Outside Jerusalem one needs two dishes[61], one as remembrance of the *Pesaḥ*, and one as remembrance of the holiday offering.

57 The *haroset*. Babli 116a.
58 The spices and fruits are pounded to produce *haroset*.
59 The mortar used by the Israelite slaves in Egypt.
60 It needs added wine. (In Medieval sources, such as *Or Zarua`* 2, §256, the text is very different.)
61 The common usage is a roasted bone and an egg. Babli 114b.

(fol. 37b) **משנה ד**: מָזְגוּ לוֹ כּוֹס שֵׁנִי וְכָאן הַבֵּן שׁוֹאֵל. אִם אֵין דַּעַת בַּבֵּן לִשְׁאוֹל אָבִיו מְלַמְּדוֹ מַה נִּשְׁתַּנָּה הַלַּיְלָה הַזֶּה מִכָּל־הַלֵּילוֹת. שֶׁבְּכָל־הַלֵּילוֹת אָנוּ מַטְבִּילִין פַּעַם אַחַת וְהַלַּיְלָה הַזֶּה שְׁתֵּי פְעָמִים. שֶׁבְּכָל־הַלֵּילוֹת אָנוּ אוֹכְלִין חָמֵץ וּמַצָּה וְהַלַּיְלָה הַזֶּה כּוּלוֹ מַצָּה. שֶׁבְּכָל־הַלֵּילוֹת אוֹכְלִין בָּשָׂר צָלִי שָׁלוּק וּמְבוּשָּׁל וְהַלַּיְלָה הַזֶּה כּוּלוֹ צָלִי. וּלְפִי דַעְתּוֹ שֶׁל בֵּן אָבִיו מְלַמְּדוֹ. מַתְחִיל בִּגְנוּת וּמְסַייֵם בְּשֶׁבַח וְדוֹרֵשׁ מֵאֲרַמִּי אוֹבֵד אָבִי עַד שֶׁהוּא גוֹמֵר כָּל־הַפָּרָשָׁה.

Mishnah 4: One mixes him the second cup, and here the son asks[62]. If the son does not know how to ask, his father instructs him[63]: What is the difference between this night and all other nights? For every night we dip once[64], but this night we dip twice. For every night we eat leavened and unleavened bread, but this night only unleavened. For in all other nights we eat meat roasted, preserved[65], or cooked, but in this night only roasted. According to the son's understanding the father teaches him[66]. He starts with ignominy[67] and ends with praise and explains from "a lost Aramean was my father" until he finishes the paragraph[68].

62 He is supposed spontaneously to ask why this dinner is different from the usual set-up.

63 The following catalogue is an example of the questions with which the instruction may start. The order of the questions is the same in Maimonides's text, different in the Babli.

64 As explained in Note 52.

65 By extended cooking. This always is mentioned as a separate category of preparation of food.

66 Along the lines explained in Mishnah 5. If children or women do not understand Hebrew, this implies the duty to translate the Haggadah text.

67 As explained in Halakhah 5.

68 *Deut*. 26:5-8. The Babli text, "until he finishes the paragraph completely", would instruct to include also v. 9, not included in the Haggadah text identical with *Sifry Deut.* on *Deut*. 26:5-8.

(37d line 15) **הלכה ד**: תַּנֵּי רִבִּי חִייָה. כְּנֶגֶד אַרְבָּעָה בָנִים דִּיבְּרָה תוֹרָה. בֵּן חָכָם בֵּן רָשָׁע בֵּן טִיפֵּשׁ בֵּן שֶׁאֵינוֹ יוֹדֵעַ לִשְׁאָל. בֵּן חָכָם מָהוּ אוֹמֵר. מָה הָעֵדֹת וְהַחֻקִּים וְהַמִּשְׁפָּטִים אֲשֶׁר צִוָּה יְי אֱלֹהֵינוּ אוֹתָנוּ. אַף אַתָּה אֱמוֹר לוֹ. בְּחוֹזֶק יָד הוֹצִיאָנוּ יְיָ מִמִּצְרַיִם מִבֵּית עֲבָדִים: בֵּן רָשָׁע מָהוּ אוֹמֵר. מָה הָעֲבוֹדָה הַזֹּאת לָכֶם. מַה הַטּוֹרַח הַזֶּה שֶׁאַתֶּם מַטְרִיחִין עָלֵינוּ בְּכָל־(שָׁעָה וְשָׁעָה) [שָׁנָה וְשָׁנָה]. מִכֵּיוָן שֶׁהוֹצִיא אֶת עַצְמוֹ מִן הַכְּלָל אַף אַתָּה אֱמוֹר לוֹ. בַּעֲבוּר זֶה עָשָׂה יְי לִי· לִי עָשָׂה. לְאוֹתוֹ הָאִישׁ לֹא עָשָׂה. אִילּוּ הָיָה אוֹתוֹ הָאִישׁ בְּמִצְרַיִם לֹא הָיָה רָאוּי לְהִיגָּאֵל מִשָּׁם לְעוֹלָם. טִיפֵּשׁ מָהוּ אוֹמֵר. מַה־זֹּאת. אַף אַתְּ לַמְּדוֹ הִילְכוֹת הַפֶּסַח. שֶׁאֵין מַפְטִירִין אַחַר הַפֶּסַח אֲפִיקוֹמָן. מָהוּ

אֱפִיקוֹמָן. שֶׁלֹּא יְהֵא עוֹמֵד מֵחֲבוּרָה זוֹ וְנִכְנָס לַחֲבוּרָה אַחֶרֶת. בֶּן שֶׁאֵינוֹ יוֹדֵעַ לִשְׁאָל אַתְּ פְּתַח לוֹ תְּחִילָּה. אָמַר רִבִּי יוֹסֵה. מַתְנִיתָא אָמְרָה כֵן. אִם אֵין דַּעַת בַּבֵּן אָבִיו מְלַמְּדוֹ.

Halakhah 4: Rebbi Ḥiyya stated[69] "The Torah spoke about Four Children, a wise child, a wicked child, a stupid child, and a child who does not know how to ask. What does the wise child say? *What are the testimonials, the ordinances, and the laws, that the Eternal, our God, commanded us*[70]? Also you shall tell him, *with a strong hand did the Eternal lead us out of Egypt, the house of slaves*[71]. What does the wicked son say? *What does this service mean to you*[72]? What is this exertion which you impose on us every (moment) [year]? Since he excluded himself from the community, also you shall tell him, *because of this did the Eternal do for me when I left Egypt*[73]. For me, He did it, for that man He did not do it. If that man had been in Egypt, he would not have been worthy ever to be redeemed. What does the stupid child say? *What is this*[74]? Tell him the rules of Passover, that one may not follow the Pesaḥ ἐπὶ κῶμον[75]. What means ἐπὶ κῶμον? That one not leave one company and join another company. With the child who does not know how to ask[76], you have to begin and initiate with him." Rebbi Yose said, that is what the Mishnah says, "if the son does not know how to ask, his father instructs him."

---

69 The Babylonian parallel, used in the common Haggadah, is in *Mekhilta dR. Ismael, Bo, Pisqa* 18. There the answers to the wise and stupid children are switched.

70 *Deut.* 6:20. The text of R. Ḥiyya and the Mekhilta is that underlying the LXX; the masoretic text has the child asking, *what are the testimonials, . . . commanded you*. This is a natural formulation for a child born later, asking a member of the generation which first received the Torah. The formulation of the Yerushalmi/Mekhilta was common in all Haggadot until corrected by pedantic editors who copied the masoretic text, disregarding talmudic tradition in Biblical quotes.

Following Naḥmanides, the "testimonials" are obligations in remembrance of His miracles, the "ordinances" are those commandments for which no reason is hinted at in the Torah, and the "laws" are the legal instructions to the court.

71 *Ex.* 13:14, the biblical answer to the question of the stupid child. The answer addresses the reason why one is obligated to follow the rules of Jewish worship, which is much more expensive than gentile rites.

72 *Ex.* 12:26.

73 *Ex.* 13:8.

74 *Ex.* 13:14. The question is not about Passover but about the obligation of

sacrificing the firstlings of the flock. In order that the child should understand the answer given to the wise child, he first has to learn by rote all the rules, up to the last Mishnah dealing with the rules of the Passover celebration.

75 A (frequently drunken) revelry, characteristic of Greek celebrations and most objectionable to Jews.

76 The child who does not know how to ask is alluded to in *Ex.* 13:8, *you must tell your child on that day as follows: . . .*, without a question preceding.

(37d line 27) **הלכה ה:** רַב אָמַר. מִתְּחִילָה. צָרִיךְ לְהַתְחִיל בְּעֵבֶר הַנָּהָר יָשְׁבוּ אֲבוֹתֵיכֶם וגו'. וָאֶקַּח אֶת־אֲבִיכֶם אֶת־אַבְרָהָם מֵעֵבֶר הַנָּהָר וגו'. וָאַרְבֶּה. אָמַר רִבִּי אָחָא. וָאַרְבְּ כְּתִיב. כַּמָּה רִיבִים עָשִׂיתִי עִמּוֹ עַד שֶׁלֹּא נָתַתִּי לוֹ אֶת יִצְחָק. דָּבָר אַחֵר. נַעֲשִׂיתִי לוֹ אוֹרֵב. אִין חָטָא מִיתָּן לֵיהּ. וְאִין זָכָה מִיתָּן לֵיהּ.

Halakhah 5: [77]Rav said, a priori he has to start with[78] *your forefathers always lived on the far side of the River*, etc. *But I took your father Abraham from the far side of the River, etc And I increased.* Rebbi Aḥa said, the *ketib* is וארב. How may quarrels I made for him before I gave him Isaac[79]. Another explanation, I prepared an ambush for him[80]. If he would sin, to repay him, if he would acquire merit, to reward him.

77 This explains the expression in the Mishnah, "he starts with ignominy." The Babli 116a reports that this is the Galilean version; the autochthonous Babylonian version was different. (The name tradition in modern prints of the Babli is unreliable; it is discussed in detail in *The Scholar's Haggadah* pp. 252-255.)

78 *Jos.* 24:2-4.

79 The word is explained not from the root רבה "to increase" but ריב "to quarrel".

80 Root ארב "to ambush".

(fol. 37b) **משנה ה:** רַבָּן גַּמְלִיאֵל הָיָה אוֹמֵר כָּל־שֶׁלֹּא אָמַר שְׁלֹשָׁה דְבָרִים אֵילּוּ בַּפֶּסַח לֹא יָצָא יְדֵי חוֹבָתוֹ. פֶּסַח מַצָּה וּמְרוֹרִים. פֶּסַח עַל שֵׁם שֶׁפָּסַח הַמָּקוֹם עַל בָּתֵּי אֲבוֹתֵינוּ בְמִצְרָיִם. מַצָּה עַל שֵׁם שֶׁנִּגְאֲלוּ אֲבוֹתֵינוּ מִמִּצְרַיִם. מָרוֹר עַל שׁוּם שֶׁמֵּרְרוּ הַמִּצְרִיִּים אֶת חַיֵּי אֲבוֹתֵינוּ בְמִצְרָיִם. בְּכָל דּוֹר וָדוֹר חַיָּיב אָדָם לִרְאוֹת אֶת עַצְמוֹ כְּאִילּוּ הוּא יָצָא מִמִּצְרַיִם שֶׁנֶּאֱמַר וְהִגַּדְתָּ לְבִנְךָ בַּיּוֹם הַהוּא לֵאמֹר בַּעֲבוּר זֶה עָשָׂה יי לִי בְּצֵאתִי מִמִּצְרָיִם. לְפִיכָךְ אָנוּ חַיָּיבִין לְהוֹדוֹת

לְהַלֵּל לְשַׁבֵּחַ לְפָאֵר לְרוֹמֵם לְנַצֵּחַ לְגַדֵּל לְמִי שֶׁעָשָׂה לָנוּ אֶת כָּל הַנִּסִּים הָאֵילוּ וְהוֹצִיאָנוּ מֵעַבְדוּת לְחֵרוּת וְנֹאמַר לְפָנָיו, הַלְלוּיָהּ׃

Mishnah 5: Rabban Gamliel used to say, anybody who did not teach these three words on Passover did not fulfill his duty, *Pesaḥ, mazzah*, and bitter herbs. *Pesaḥ* because the Omnipresent passed over the houses of our forefathers in Egypt. *mazzah* because our forefathers were freed from Egypt[81]. Bitter herbs because the Egyptians embittered the lives of our forefathers in Egypt. In every generation a person is required to see himself as if he himself had gone out of Egypt, as it was said, *you shall tell your son on that day, this is on account of what the Eternal did for me when I left Egypt.* Therefore we are required to thank, sing His praise, laud, glorify, exalt, praise in perpetuity, to glorify, Him who did all these miracles for us[82] and led us from slavery to freedom; let us say before Him *Hallelujah*[83].

משנה ו: עַד אֵיכָן הוּא אוֹמֵר בֵּית שַׁמַּאי אוֹמְרִים עַד אֵם הַבָּנִים שְׂמֵחָה. וּבֵית הִלֵּל אוֹמְרִים, עַד הַחַלָּמִישׁ לְמַעְיְנוֹ מָיִם. וְחוֹתֵם בִּגְאוּלָה.

Mishnah 6: How far does he say? The House of Shammai say, up to *a happy mother of children*[84]. But the House of Hillel are saying, up to *the pebble into a source of water*[85], and he finishes with "redemption.[96]"

81 A reference to *Ex.* 12:39 is understood, but is not included in any reliable Mishnah ms.
82 Since everybody has to consider himself as if he left Egypt, it is appropriate that here "our forefathers" are not mentioned, in contrast to the Mishnah in the Babli.
83 The *Hallel, Pss.* 113-118.
84 *Ps.* 113 only.
85 *Ps.* 114, starting with *Ps.* 113.

(37d line 31) **הלכה ו**: אָמְרוּ לָהֶן בֵּית שַׁמַּי. וְכִי יָצְאוּ יִשְׂרָאֵל מִמִּצְרַיִם שֶׁהוּא מַזְכִּיר יְצִיאַת מִצְרַיִם. אָמְרוּ לָהֶן בֵּית הִלֵּל. אִילוּ מַמְתִּין עַד קְרוֹת הַגֶּבֶר אַדַּיִין לֹא הִגִּיעוּ לַחֲצִי גְאוּלָה. הֵיאַךְ מַזְכִּירִין גְּאוּלָה וַאֲדַיִין לֹא נִגְאֲלוּ. וַהֲלֹא לֹא יָצְאוּ אֶלָּא בַחֲצִי הַיּוֹם. שֶׁנֶּאֱמַר וַיְהִי בְּעֶצֶם הַיּוֹם הַזֶּה הוֹצִיא יי אֶת בְּנֵי יִשְׂרָאֵל וגו'. אֶלָּא מִכֵּיוָן שֶׁהִתְחִיל בַּמִּצְוָה אוֹמְרִים לוֹ. מָרֵק. הֵתִיב רִבִּי אַבּוּנָה בַּר סְחוֹרָא. לֹא כְבָר הִזְכִּיר עַל הַכּוֹס.

Halakhah 6: [86]"The House of Shammai said to them, did Israel leave Egypt that he should mention the Exodus from Egypt[87]? The House of Hillel answered them, even if he would wait until the cock crows[88], they did not reach half the redemption," since they left only at noontime, as it is said[89], *in the middle of this day* did the Eternal lead out the Children of Israel, etc. But since one started fulfilling the obligation, on tells him to clean it up. Rebbi Abunah bar Sehora objected, did he not already mention it for the cup[90]?

86 Tosephta 10:9.
87 The first verse of *Ps.* 114 mentions the Exodus; the entire Psalm is more about the crossing of the Red Sea.
88 Since the House of Shammai also agree that after the meal one finishes the *Hallel* (Mishnah 8), even if this is said close to dawn it would be much too early.
89 *Ex.* 12:41; the remainder of the verse is misquoted.
90 Since the House of Shammai agree that in the *Qiddush* spoken over the first cup one mentions the Exodus, the objection of the House of Shammai seems without base.

(37d line 37) תַּנֵּי. אֵין אוֹמְרִים זְמַן אֶלָּא בִשְׁלֹשָׁה רְגָלִים בִּלְבָד. אָמַר רִבִּי מָנָא. מַתְנִיתָא אֲמְרָה כֵן. בְּחַג הַמַּצּוֹת וּבְחַג הַשָּׁבֻעוֹת וּבְחַג הַסּוּכּוֹת. תַּנֵּי. כָּל־שֶׁכָּתוּב בּוֹ מִקְרָא קוֹדֶשׁ צָרִיךְ לְהַזְכִּיר בּוֹ זְמַן. אָמַר רִבִּי תַנְחוּמָא. וְיֵאוּת. מִי שֶׁרָאָה תְאֵינָה בִּכּוֹרֶת שֶׁמָּא אֵין צָרִיךְ לְהַזְכִּיר זְמַן. הֲרֵי רֹאשׁ הַשָּׁנָה וְיוֹם הַכִּיפּוּרִים.

בִּיהוּדָה נָהֲגוּ כְרִבִּי עֲקִיבָה. וּבַגָּלִיל נָהֲגוּ כְרִבִּי יוֹחָנָן בֶּן נוּרִי. עָבַר וְעָשָׂה בִיהוּדָה כְגָלִיל וּבְגָלִיל כִּיהוּדָה. יָצָא. הֲרֵי פוּרִים. אֵילוּ קוֹרְאִים בְּאַרְבָּעָה עָשָׂר וְאֵילוּ קוֹרְאִין בַּחֲמִשָּׁה עָשָׂר. שַׁנְיָיא הִיא. דִּכְתִיב מִשְׁפָּחָה וּמִשְׁפָּחָה מְדִינָה וּמְדִינָה וְעִיר וָעִיר.

It was stated: One says "time"[91] only at the three festivals of pilgrimage. Rebbi Mana said, a *baraita* says so, *on the festival of mazzot, the festival of weeks, and the festival of booths*[92]. It was stated: For any {day} where it is stated "declaration as holy" one has to say "time"[93]. Rebbi Tanhuma said, this is correct. If somebody saw a fig as first fruit, does he not have to recite "time"[94]? This applies to New Year's Day and the Day of Atonement

[95](where in Judea one used to follow Rebbi Aqiba and in Galilee Rebbi Johanan ben Nuri. If he changed and in Judea acted as in Galilee or in Galilee as in Judea he discharged his obligation. But is there not Purim, where these read on the fourteenth and those on the fifteenth? There is a difference since it is written, *family and family, country and country, and town and town*.)

91 This refers to the benediction "Praise to You, Eternal, our God, King of the universe, Who has kept us alive, maintained us, and enabled us to reach this festive time." Babli *Eruvin* 40b. Since the benediction is said with *Qiddush*, this paragraph belongs with Halakhah 1.
92 *Deut.* 16:16. It seems that the *baraita*

notes that the verse singles out these three festivals at times one is obligated to enjoy.
93 This includes the day following the festival of booths, New Year's Day, and the Day of Atonement.
94 The benediction is for all festive occasions which happen not more than once a year.
95 The text in parenthesis is copied from Chapter 4:1, Notes 57-60, it is the continuation of the preceding half sentence, which also is the start of this text, but has no meaning in this context.

(fol. 37b) **משנה ז׃** רִבִּי טַרְפוֹן אוֹמֵר אֲשֶׁר גְּאָלָנוּ וְגָאַל אֶת אֲבוֹתֵינוּ מִמִּצְרַיִם וְהִגִּיעָנוּ הַלַּיְלָה הַזֶּה וְאֵינוּ חוֹתֵם. רִבִּי עֲקִיבָה אוֹמֵר כֵּן ה׳ אֱלֹהֵינוּ יַגִּיעֵנוּ לִרְגָלִים הַבָּאִים לִקְרָאתֵנוּ לְשָׁלוֹם שְׂמֵחִים בְּבִנְיַן עִירָךְ שָׂשִׂים בַּעֲבוֹדָתָךְ וּבְחִידּוּשׁ בֵּית מִקְדָּשָׁךְ. וְשָׁם נֹאכַל מִן הַפְּסָחִים וּמִן הַזְּבָחִים אֲשֶׁר הִגִּיעַ דָּמָם עַל קִיר מִזְבָּחָךְ לְרָצוֹן וְנוֹדֶה לְךָ עַל גְּאוּלָתֵינוּ. בָּרוּךְ אַתָּה יי גָּאַל יִשְׂרָאֵל:

Mishnah 7: Rebbi Tarphon says, [96]"Who freed us and freed our forefathers from Egypt and let us reach this night", and does not seal[97]. Rebbi Aqiba says, [98]"so Eternal, our God, let us reach other festivals coming towards us in peace, happy in the rebuilding of Your city, enjoying Your service, and the renewal of Your Temple. There may we eat from the *Pesah* and well-being offerings whose blood will reach to the wall of Your altar for pleasure and we shall thank You for our redemption. Praise to You, Eternal, Who redeems Israel."

96 Text of the benediction for redemption prescribed at the end of Mishnah 6.
97 For him the required benediction is "short", starting with the formula "Praise to You, Eternal, our God, King of the Universe," followed by a single sentence.
98 This text is in addition to R. Tarphon's. It is "long", closing with a separate sentence starting with "Praise to You, Eternal".

(37d line 46) **הלכה ז׃** כְּתִיב בִּפְרוֹעַ פְּרָעוֹת בְּיִשְׂרָאֵל בְּהִתְנַדֵּב עָם בָּרְכוּ יְי. הִתְנַדְּבוּ רָאשֵׁי עָם. כְּשֶׁהַקָּדוֹשׁ בָּרוּךְ הוּא עוֹשֶׂה לָכֶם נִיסִים יְהוּא אוֹמְרִין שִׁירָה. הַתִּיבוּן. הֲרֵי גְּאוּלַת מִצְרַיִם. שְׁנִיָּיא הִיא. שֶׁהִיא תְּחִילַת גְּאוּלָתָן. הֲרֵי מָרְדְּכַי וְאֶסְתֵּר. שְׁנִיָּיא הִיא. שֶׁהִיא בְּחוּץ לָאָרֶץ. וְאִית דְּבָעֵי מֵימַר. מָרְדְּכַי וְאֶסְתֵּר מִשּׁוּנְאֵיהֶם נִגְאֲלוּ. לֹא נִגְאֲלוּ מִן הַמַּלְכוּת.

Halakhah 7: [99]It is written[100]: *When retribution is retributed for Israel, when the people volunteered, praise the Eternal*; the heads of the people volunteered. When the Holy One, praise to Him, does wonders for Israel, they should sing a song. They objected: There is the redemption from Egypt[101]! That is something else since it was the beginning of their redemption. They objected. There is redemption of Mardocai and Esther! That is something else since they were outside the Land; some want to say that Mardocai and Esther were freed of their enemies, they were not freed from {Gentile] government.

99 This paragraph is copied from *Sotah* 5:6, Notes 138-141.
100 *Jud.* 5:2.
101 Meaning that the Song of the Sea also covers the Exodus, since the latter was confirmed only at the Sea. In the Babli and midrashic literature, *Ps.* 113 is the song of the Israelites during Passover night [*Pesahim* 117a, *Midrash Tehillim* 113; cf. *Cant. rabba* 1(37), *Mekhilta deR. Ismael, Shirah* 1; *deR. Simeon ben Yohai* p. 71]. Cf. *The Scholar's Haggadah,* pp. 314-319.

(fol. 37b) **משנה ח:** מָזְגוּ לוֹ כוֹס שְׁלִישִׁי מְבָרֵךְ עַל מְזוֹנוֹ. רְבִיעַ גּוֹמֵר עָלָיו אֶת הַהַלֵּל וְאוֹמֵר עָלָיו בִּרְכַּת הַשִּׁיר. בֵּין הַכּוֹסוֹת הַלָּלוּ אִם רוֹצֶה לִשְׁתּוֹת יִשְׁתֶּה. בֵּין שְׁלִישִׁי לִרְבִיעִי לֹא יִשְׁתֶּה:

אֵין מַפְטִירִין אַחַר הַפֶּסַח אָפִיקוֹמָן. יָשְׁנוּ מִקְצָתָן יֹאכֵלוּ. כּוּלָּם לֹא יֹאכֵלוּ. רִבִּי יוֹסֵי אוֹמֵר אִם נִתְנַמְנְמוּ יֹאכֵלוּ. נִרְדְּמוּ לֹא יֹאכֵלוּ:

Mishnah 8: One mixes him the third cup, he says Grace[102]. The fourth, over which he finishes the Hallel and recites the benediction of the song[103]. Between these cups[104], he may drink if he wants to drink; between the third and the fourth he may not drink.

After the *Pesaḥ* one may not serve *afiqoman*[105]. If part of them slept, they may eat; if all of them, they may not eat[106]. Rebbi Yose says, if they[107] were sleepy, they may eat, if they slept they may not eat.

102 Which requires a cup of wine anyhow.
103 The benediction after the recitation of the Hallel in the synagogue.
104 After the first cup up to the conclusion of the meal.
105 While in Halakhah 4 this was

interpreted as ἐπὶ κῶμον, the Halakhah here gives other interpretations.

106 Sacrifices become disqualified if they are not permanently guarded. If the entire company sleeps before the *Pesah* is consumed, the meat automatically is disqualified and impure.

107 The entire company subscribing to one *Pesah*.

(37d line 51) **הלכה ח**: לָמָּה. בִּשְׁבִיל שֶׁלֹּא יִשְׁתַּכֵּר. כְּבָר מְשׁוּכָּר הוּא. מַה בֵּין יַיִן שֶׁבְּתוֹךְ הַמָּזוֹן מַה בֵּין יַיִן שֶׁלְּאַחַר הַמָּזוֹן. יַיִן שֶׁלְּאַחַר הַמָּזוֹן מְשַׁכֵּר. שֶׁבְּתוֹךְ הַמָּזוֹן אֵינוֹ מְשַׁכֵּר. רִבִּי סִימוֹן בְּשֵׁם רִבִּי אִינְיָינֵי בַּר סִיסַיי. מִינֵי זֶמֶר. רִבִּי יוֹחָנָן אָמַר. מִינֵי מְתִיקָה. שְׁמוּאֵל אָמַר. עַרְדִּילֵי וְגוֹזְלַיָּא דַחֲנַנְיָה בַּר שִׁילַת.

Halakhah 8: Why? That he should not get drunk. Is he not already drunk? What is the difference between wine with the meal and wine after the meal? Wine after the meal intoxicates, wine with the meal does not intoxicate[108].

Rebbi Simeon in the name of Rebbi Inainy bar Sisay: kinds of songs[109]. Rebbi Johanan says, sweets. Samuel says, truffles and chick pigeons prepared by Hanania bar Shilat.

108 Tosaphot (in Babli 117b s.v. רביעי deduce from here that drinking water is permitted between the third and the fourth cups.

109 He reads the word as ἐπικῶμιον "drinking song", one of the more objectionable aspects of the κῶμος. The other explanations do not seem to be based on any Greek word. Babli 119b.

(fol. 37b) **משנה ט**: הַפֶּסַח אַחַר חֲצוֹת מְטַמֵּא אֶת הַיָּדַיִם. הַפִּיגּוּל וְהַנּוֹתָר מְטַמְּאִין אֶת הַיָּדַיִם. בֵּירַךְ בִּרְכַּת הַפֶּסַח פָּטַר אֶת שֶׁל זֶבַח. בֵּרַךְ אֶת שֶׁל זֶבַח לֹא פָטַר אֶת שֶׁל פֶּסַח דִּבְרֵי רִבִּי יִשְׁמָעֵאל. רִבִּי עֲקִיבָה אוֹמֵר לֹא זוֹ פוֹטֶרֶת זוֹ וְלֹא זוֹ פוֹטֶרֶת זוֹ:

Mishnah 9: The *Pesah* after midnight[110] makes hands impure. *Piggul*[111] and leftover[112] make the hands impure. If he recited the benediction for the *Pesah*[113] it exempted that of the family sacrifice[114]; the one for the family sacrifice does not exempt the one for the *Pesah*, the words of Rebbi Ismael. Rebbi Aqiba said, neither one exempts the other.

110 When rabbinically it may no longer be eaten (Mishnah *Zevahim* 5:8), it is treated as

leftover.

111 A sacrifice slaughtered with the intention of consuming it after its allotted time or at an unauthorized place. While it is a deadly sin to consume *piggul*, the impurity imposed on it is purely rabbinical and weaker than biblical impurity.

112 A qualified sacrifice left after the time allotted to its consumption.

113 "Praise to You, Eternal, our God, King of the universe, Who sanctified us by His commandments and commanded us to eat *Pesah*." (Tosephta 10:13).

114 "Praise to You, Eternal, our God, King of the universe, Who sanctified us by His commandments and commanded us to eat sacrifice." For R. Ismael, the *Pesah* is the main dish, the family sacrifice is a filler and does not need a separate benediction (Mishnah *Berakhot* 6:7). For R. Aqiba the two are coordinate, neither is subordinate to the other.

(37d line 56) **הלכה ט**: לָמָּה. מִפְּנֵי הִסִּיעַ דַּעַת אוֹ מִשּׁוּם שֶׁעָבַר עָלָיו חֲצוֹת. הַגַּע עַצְמָךְ שֶׁיֵּשׁ שָׁם חֲבוּרָה אַחֶרֶת. הֲרֵי לֹא עָבַר חֲצוֹת. הֱוֵי. לֵית טַעֲמָא דָא אֶלָּא מִפְּנֵי הִסִּיעַ דַּעַת.

Halakhah 9: Why? Because they did not think of it or because midnight had passed? Think of it, if there was another group and midnight had not passed? Therefore the reason only is because they did not think of it[115].

115 It seems that this paragraph does not refer to Mishnah 9 but to Mishnah 8. Why is the *Pesah* disqualified if the participants were sleeping? Is it rabbinically, for they may miss the deadline of midnight, or biblically because nobody guards the sacrifice? Since the Mishnah implies that the *Pesah* is disqualified even if there is another group in the house which would see to it that the first group would not miss the deadline, it follows that the reason must be the lack of attention given to the *Pesah*.

(37d line 58) רִבִּי סִימוֹן בְּשֵׁם רִבִּי יְהוֹשֻׁעַ בֶּן לֵוִי. הַפִּיגּוּל וְהַנּוֹתָר מִצְטָרְפִין לְטַמֵּא אֶת הַיָּדַיִם כְּדֵי עוֹנְשָׁן בְּכַזַּיִת. מַהוּ שֶׁיִּפְסוֹל אֶת הַתְּרוּמָה. קַל וָחוֹמֶר. אִם מְטַמְּאִין אֶת הַיָּדַיִם לִפְסוֹל אֶת הַתְּרוּמָה. הֵן עַצְמָן לֹא כָל־שֶׁכֵּן. הָהֵן יוֹצֵא מַה אַתְּ עָבַד לֵיהּ. מְטַמֵּא אֶת הַיָּדַיִם אוֹ אֵינוֹ מְטַמֵּא אֶת הַיָּדַיִם. אִין תֵּימַר הָהֵן יוֹצֵא מְטַמֵּא אֶת הַיָּדַיִם. הַפִּיגּוּל וְהַנּוֹתָר אֵינָן פּוֹסְלִין אֶת הַתְּרוּמָה. וְהָהֵן יוֹצֵא לֹא גָזְרוּ עָלָיו כְּלוּם. דְּלֹא כֵן יְטַמֵּא צַד הַחִיצוֹן וְצַד הַפְּנִימִי. [אָמַר רִבִּי אַבִּין. מָאן אִית לֵיהּ דָּבָר טָמֵא מַחְמַת מַגַּע עַצְמוֹ. לֹא רִבִּי מֵאִיר. וְלֹא כֵן אָמַר רִבִּי יוֹחָנָן. כָּל־הַדְּבָרִים טְהוֹרִים בְּרוּבָּן. כֵּיוָן שְׁחִיתֵּךְ רוּבָּן לָאו כְּפָרוּשׁ הוּא. וְיַעֲשֶׂה כְמַגִּיעַ בּוֹ וִיהֵא פָסוּל.] אָמַר רִבִּי חֲנַנְיָה. בִּמְחַתֵּךְ כָּל־שֶׁהוּא כָּל־שֶׁהוּא וּמַשְׁלִיךְ.

[116]Rebbi Simon in the name of Rebbi Joshua ben Levi: *Piggul* and leftovers add together to make hands impure in the amount that exposes to punishment, the volume of an olive. Do they disqualify heave? It is a argument *de minore ad maius*. If they make hands impure to disqualify

heave, they themselves not so much more? This which was left, what are you doing with it? Does it make hands impure or does it not make hands impure? If you are saying that this which was left makes hands impure, would *piggul* and leftovers not disqualify heave? About that which was left they did not decide anything⁴. For if it were not so, the outer part would make the inner part impure⁵. Rebbi Abbin said, who holds that something can become impure by touching itself? Rebbi Meïr. Did not Rebbi Johanan say, everything becomes pure by its greater part? When he cut off the greater part, is it not separated? Then it would be touching and be disqualified. Rebbi Hananiah said, if he cuts off minimal pieces and throws away.

אִית לָךְ מֵימַר. שֶׁעָבַר חֲצוֹת. לָא מִפְּנֵי הִסִּיעַ דַּעַת. הֲוֵיי. לֵית טַעֲמָא (דְלָא) [אֶלָּא] מִפְּנֵי הִסִּיעַ דַּעַת.

Can you say, because midnight has passed? No, because they did not think of it. Therefore the reason only is because they did not think of it¹¹⁷.

116 This paragraph is copied from Halakhah 7:11, Notes 300-309.

117 Since the preceding paragraph is about the *Pesaḥ* taken out from its place, long before midnight, it follows that also in that case it is disqualified and makes hands impure because one no longer guards it.

(37d line 70) אָמַר רִבִּי זְעוּרָה. דְּלֹא בֵירַךְ בִּרְכַּת הַפֶּסַח לֹא פָטַר שֶׁלְזֶבַח. וְשֶׁלְזֶבַח פָּטַר שֶׁלְפֶּסַח. שֶׁהַפֶּסַח בִּכְלָל הַזֶּבַח. אָמַר רִבִּי מָנָא. הַפֶּסַח עִיקָּר וְהַזֶּבַח טְפֵילָה.

Rebbi Ze'ira said, should not making the benediction for *Pesaḥ* not exempt the sacrifice, but for the sacrifice exempt the *Pesaḥ*, since the *Pesaḥ* is included in the notion of sacrifice¹¹⁸? Rebbi Mana said, the *Pesaḥ* is the main item, the {family} sacrifice a minor part¹¹⁹.

118 Since the formulation of the benediction for the festival sacrifice is general, and making a general benediction in general makes it impossible to recite the more appropriate specific benediction (Mishnah *Berakhot* 6:2), one can understand the position neither of R. Ismael nor that of R. Aqiba.

119 The principle of Mishnah *Berakhot* 6:2 is not applicable here for either R. Ismael or R. Aqiba.

Introduction to Tractate Yoma

"The Day" discussed in this Tractate is the Day of Atonement; the relevant biblical texts are *Lev.* Chapter 16 in its entirety, 23:26-32, and *Num.* 27:7-11. The text relevant for modern observation of the day is Chapter Eight. The first seven Chapters are dedicated to the rules of the Temple service.

Chapter One contains a general introduction and the rules from the preparation of the High Priest, who on the Day of Atonement must perform the entire ritual by himself, essentially unaided. The last Mishnaiot of the Chapter introduce the topic of Chapters Two and Three, the rules of the daily sacrifices which precede the service particular to the Day. These, like the concluding rites in the afternoon, are performed by the High Priest in his regular garments, worn all year round. Chapters Four to Six describe the rites of purification of the sanctuary as outlined in *Lev.* Chapter 16, to be performed in unadorned white linen garments. Chapter Seven is dedicated to the remaining duties of the High Priest at the conclusion of the Day.

Chapter 1-6 in this Tractate and 5-7 in *Pesahim*, which concentrate on the details of Temple service, can be considered the Yerushalmi's introduction to the Tractates of the fifth order, *Qodashim*, for which no Yerushalmi exists.

שבעת ימים פרק ראשון

(fol.38a) **משנה א**: שִׁבְעַת יָמִים קוֹדֶם לְיוֹם הַכִּפּוּרִים מַפְרִישִׁין כֹּהֵן גָּדוֹל מִבֵּיתוֹ לְלִשְׁכַּת פַּרְהֶדְרִין וּמַתְקִינִין לוֹ כֹהֵן אַחֵר תַּחְתָּיו שֶׁמָּא יֶאֱרַע בּוֹ פְסוּל. רִבִּי יְהוּדָה אוֹמֵר אַף אִשָּׁה אַחֶרֶת מַתְקִינִין לוֹ שֶׁמָּא תָמוּת אִשְׁתּוֹ שֶׁנֶּאֱמַר וְכִפֶּר בַּעֲדוֹ וּבְעַד בֵּית. בֵּיתוֹ הִיא אִשְׁתּוֹ. אָמְרוּ לוֹ חֲכָמִים אִם כֵּן אֵין לַדָּבָר סוֹף:

Mishnah 1: Seven days before the Day of Atonement one isolates the High Priest from his house[1] to the Parhedrin[2] lodge and one prepares another Cohen because he might become disqualified[3]. Rebbi Jehudah says, one also prepares for him another wife, since maybe his wife would die, for it is said, *he shall atone for himself and his house*[4], his house means his wife. The Sages said to him, in this case the procedure never ends[5].

1 Meaning his wife, as explained later in the Mishnah. To prevent him from becoming impure should the wife become impure by menstruation.

2 In the Halakhah the name also appears as פלהדרין with change of liquids. Possibly derived from πάρεδρος, ὁ, "adjunct"; cf. Note 113.

3 Since the entire Temple service of the Day of Atonement has to be performed by the High Priest himself, there must be somebody trained to act as High Priest in case the officiating one becomes somehow impure and unable to continue.

4 *Lev.* 16:6.

5 Since the substitute wife also could die, one would need an unlimited supply of wives, but the High Priest is biblically restricted to one wife. Disqualification can be foreseen, death cannot be foreseen.

(38a line 44) שִׁבְעַת יָמִים קוֹדֶם לְיוֹם הַכִּפּוּרִים כול'. רִבִּי בָּא בְשֵׁם רִבִּי יוֹחָנָן שָׁמַע לָהּ מִן הָדָא. כַּאֲשֶׁר עָשָׂה בַּיּוֹם הַזֶּה. אֵילּוּ שִׁבְעַת יְמֵי הַמִּילּוּאִים. צִוָּה יְיָ. לַדּוֹרוֹת. לַעֲשׂוֹת. זֶה שְׂעִיר שֶׁלְּיוֹם הַכִּיפּוּרִים. אוֹ אֵינוֹ אֶלָּא שָׂעִיר שֶׁלְּרֹאשׁ חוֹדֶשׁ. אָמַר רִבִּי בָא. לְכַפֵּר עֲלֵיכֶם. כַּפָּרָה שֶׁהִיא כָזוֹ. מַה זוֹ כַּפָּרַת אַהֲרֹן עַצְמוֹ כַּפָּרַת בָּנִים עַצְמָן. אַף זוֹ כַּפָּרַת אַהֲרֹן עַצְמוֹ כַּפָּרַת בָּנִים עַצְמָן.

רִבִּי יוֹנָה בְשֵׁם בַּר קַפָּרָא שָׁמַע לָהּ מִן הָדָא. כַּאֲשֶׁר עָשָׂה בַּיּוֹם הַזֶּה. אֵילּוּ שִׁבְעַת יְמֵי הַמִּילּוּאִים. צִוָּה יְיָ. זוֹ שְׂרֵיפַת הַפָּרָה. נֶאֱמַר כָּאן צִוָּה יְיָ. וְנֶאֱמַר לְהַלָּן זֹאת חוּקַת הַתּוֹרָה

אֲשֶׁר־צִוָּה יְיָ לֵאמֹר. לַעֲשׂוֹת. זֶה שָׂעִיר שֶׁלְיוֹם הַכִּיפּוּרִים. אוֹ אֵינוֹ אֶלָּא שָׂעִיר שֶׁלְרֹאשׁ חוֹדֶשׁ. כַּהִיא דְּאָמַר רִבִּי בָּא. לְכַפֵּר עֲלֵיכֶם: כַּפָּרָה שֶׁהִיא כָזוֹ. מַה זוֹ כַּפָּרָה שֶׁאֵינָהּ כְּשֵׁירָה אֶלָּא בְכֹהֵן גָּדוֹל. אַף זוֹ כַּפָּרָה שֶׁאֵינָהּ אֶלָּא בְכֹהֵן גָּדוֹל.

"Seven days before the Day of Atonement," etc. Rebbi Abba in the name of Rebbi Joḥanan understood it[6] from the following: *As he did on that day*[7], these are the seven days of initiation. *Did the Eternal command* for future generations[8]. *To make*, this is the goat of the Day of Atonement[9]. Or maybe it is the goat of a New Moon? Rebbi Abba said, *to atone for you*, an atonement which is like the other. Since the one[10] is atonement of Aaron himself and his sons themselves, the other also must be atonement of Aaron himself and his sons themselves

Rebbi Jonah in the name of Bar Qappara understood it from the following. *As he did on that day*, these are the seven days of initiation. *Did the Eternal command*, this is burning of the Cow[11]. It is said here, *did the Eternal command*, and it is said there[12], *this is the law of the Torah which the Eternal commanded, saying."* *To make*, this is the goat of the Day of Atonement[10]. Or maybe it is the goat of a New Moon? As Rebbi Abba said, *to atone for you*, an atonement which is like the other. Since the one is atonement valid only through the High Priest, the other also[13] is atonement through the High Priest.

6 That the separation of the High Priest from his wife for seven days has some biblical justification. A much shorter version covering both interpretations given here is in *Sifra Saw, Mekhilta deMilluim* 37; differently Babli 2a.

7 *Lev.* 8:34, referring to the dedication of the Tabernacle, where Aaron and his sons spent seven full days, day and night, at the Tabernacle, far from their families.

8 Since the Chapter starts with God's commandment to inaugurate the Tabernacle, the mention here of God's commandment is redundant and may be interpreted as a new commandment for future generations.

9 The verb עשה is used in *Lev.* 16:15 for the blood of the goat sacrificed on the Day of Atonement. The same verb also is used in 9:7 with reference to the goat sacrificed on the eighth day of dedication which happened to be the first of the first month.

10 The dedication ceremony, where Aaron had to bring an atoning sacrifice separate from that for his sons and the people, the other is the Day of Atonement where the same is true.

11 The priest in charge of burning the Red Cow to produce the ashes which cleanse from the impurity of the dead also had to be separated for seven days (Mishnah

Parah 3:1).
12 *Num.* 19:2.
13 The ceremonies of the Day of Atonement detailed in *Lev.* 16 refer exclusively to actions by the High Priest. Babli 3b.

(38a line 55) מַה בֵּין כֹּהֵן הַשּׂוֹרֵף אֶת הַפָּרָה לַכֹּהֵן הַגָּדוֹל בְּיוֹם הַכִּיפּוּרִים. שָׁזֶה אַפְרָשׁוּתוֹ בְּטַהֲרָה וְאֵין אֶחָיו הַכֹּהֲנִים נוֹגְעִין בּוֹ. וְזֶה אַפְרָשׁוּתוֹ בִּקְדוּשָׁה וְאֶחָיו הַכֹּהֲנִים נוֹגְעִין בּוֹ. עַל דַּעְתֵּיהּ דְּרִבִּי יוֹחָנָן דּוּ יָלִיף לָהּ מִן הָדֵין קְרָיָיא [שֶׁמַּעֲלָה הִיא בְּפָרָה. סִילְסוּל הִיא בְּפָרָה. נִיחָא. עַל דַּעְתֵּיהּ דְּבַר קַפָּרָא דְלָא יָלִיף לָהּ מִן קְרָיָיא] לָמָּה כָאן נוֹגְעִין וְכָאן אֵין נוֹגְעִין. אָמַר רִבִּי חִייָה בַּר אָדָא. שֶׁלֹּא יְטַמְּאוּ אוֹתוֹ אֶחָיו הַכֹּהֲנִים. [וְלֹא כָךְ אֵינוֹ טָמֵא מֵחֲמַת הַזָּיָיתוֹ.] אָמַר רִבִּי בּוּן. אַף בַּר קַפָּרָא אִית לֵיהּ מִשּׁוּם מַעֲלָה הִיא בְּפָרָה. סִילְסוּל הִיא בְּפָרָה.

What is the difference between the Cohen who burns the Cow and the High Priest on the Day of Atonement? The separation of the first is for purity and his brothers the priests refrain from touching him. The separation of the other is for holiness and his brothers the priests touch him. In the opinion of Rebbi Johanan, who infers[14] from that verse, [it is exceptional for the Cow, it is an embellishment for the Cow[15], one understands it. In the opinion of Bar Qappara who does not infer[16] it from this verse], why does one touch here but not touch there? Rebbi Hiyya bar Ada said, that his brothers the priests should not make him impure. [But will he not be impure because of his sprinkling[17]?] Rebbi Abun said, even Bar Qappara holds that it is exceptional for the Cow, it is an embellishment for the Cow[18].

14 Based on the preceding text, one has to read "does not infer" since in the explanation attributed to R. Johanan, burning of the Cow is not mentioned. (In the Babli 2a, an argument close to that of Bar Qappara here is attributed to R. Johanan, but this should be irrelevant for the study of the Yerushalmi.)
15 The separation of the priest who will burn the Cow is purely rabbinical; Tosephta *Parah* 3:1.
16 Here one has to read: "who infers."
17 Since it is to be presumed that the Cohen selected to burn the Cow was pure, water with ashes from prior Cows will make him impure (*Sifry Num.* 129). But this impurity is minor, it can be removed by immersion in a *miqweh* and the following sundown. It is obvious that no sprinkling can be done on the day of the burning.

In fact, a Pharisee Cohen burning the Cow is made impure and has to cleanse himself in a *miqweh* on the day of the ceremony because of a quarrel with Sadducees, Mishnah *Parah* 3:7.
18 Everybody agrees that the rules for the Cohen burning the Cow are purely rabbinical, not accepted by Sadducees, and

bar Qappara's mention of the burning of the Cow is a far-fetched simile, not an authoritative interpretation of the verse.

(38a line) רִבִּי שִׁמְעוֹן בֶּן לָקִישׁ בָּעָא קוֹמֵי רִבִּי יוֹחָנָן. אִי מַה אֵיל הַמִּילוּאִים מְעַכֵּב אַף שְׂעִיר שְׁלְיוֹם הַכִּיפּוּרִים מְעַכֵּב. וְהוּא מְקַבֵּל מִינֵּיהּ. [מִן מַה דָּמַר רִבִּי מָנָא. וּתְמִיהַּ אֲנִי הֵיךְ רִבִּי שִׁמְעוֹן בֶּן לָקִישׁ מָתִיב קוֹמֵי רִבִּי יוֹחָנָן וְהוּא מְקַבֵּל מִינֵּיהּ]. וְיָתִיבִינֵיהּ. לֹא מָצָאנוּ דָּבָר מְעַכֵּב לָמֵד מִדָּבָר שֶׁאֵינוֹ מְעַכֵּב. וְדָבָר שֶׁאֵינוֹ מְעַכֵּב לָמֵד מִדָּבָר שֶׁהוּא מְעַכֵּב. מָלָק וְהִקְטִיר. מָה מְלִיקָה בְּרֹאשׁ הַמִּזְבֵּחַ אַף (מְלִיקָה) [הַקְטָרָה] בְּרֹאשׁ הַמִּזְבֵּחַ. מְלִיקָה מְאַכֶּבֶת. אֵין הַקְטָרָה מְאַכֶּבֶת. תָּמִיד [תָּמִיד]. נֶאֱמַר תָּמִיד בַּחֲבִיתִּין וְנֶאֱמַר תָּמִיד בְּלֶחֶם הַפָּנִים. מַה [תָּמִיד הָאָמוּר בַּחֲבִיתִּין שְׁנֵים עֲשָׂרָה אַף תָּמִיד הָאָמוּר בְּלֶחֶם הַפָּנִים שְׁנֵים עָשָׂר.] לֶחֶם הַפָּנִים מְעַכֵּב. (אַף) [אֵין] חֲבִיתִּין מְעַכֶּבֶת. לְקִיחָה לְקִיחָה. נֶאֱמַר לְקִיחָה בְּמִצְרַיִם וְנֶאֱמַר לְקִיחָה בְּלוּלָב. [מַה לְקִיחָה הָאָמוּר בְּמִצְרַיִם אֲגוּדָה. אַף לְקִיחָה הָאָמוּר בְּלוּלָב אֲגוּדָה.] לוּלָב מְעַבֵּב. מִצְרַיִם אֵינָהּ מְעַכֶּבֶת. הֲרֵי מָצָאנוּ דָּבָר מְעַכֵּב לָמֵד מִדָּבָר שֶׁאֵינוֹ מְעַכֵּב. וְדָבָר שֶׁאֵינוֹ מְעַכֵּב לָמֵד מִדָּבָר מְעַכֵּב.

Rebbi Simeon ben Laqish asked before Rebbi Johanan[19]: But since the he-goat of initiation obstructs, does the he-goat of the Day of Atonement also obstruct[20]? And he accepted it from him[21]. [On that Rebbi Mana said, I am wondering how could Rebbi Simeon ben Laqish ask before Rebbi Johanan and he accepted it from him?] Should he not have objected to him that we do not find that anything obstructing can be inferred from anything not obstructing, nor can anything not obstructing be inferred from anything obstructing? "He breaks the neck", "to burn in smoke"[22]. Since (breaking the neck)[23] is done on top of the altar, so (breaking the neck) [burning in smoke][24] is done on the top of the altar. Breaking the neck obstructs, burning in smoke does not obstruct[25]. "Permanently," ["permanently]." "Permanently" is mentioned for the pan-baked breads[26] and "permanently" is mentioned for the shew-bread[27].] The shew-breads are obstructive, the pan-baked breads are not obstructive. Since ["permanently" mentioned for the pan-baked breads refers to twelve,] so "permanently" mentioned [for the shew-bread refers to twelve[28]. "Taking", "taking". "Taking" mentioned in Egypt[29], "taking" is mentioned for *lulav*[30]. [Since "taking" mentioned in Egypt implies a bundle[31], so also "taking" mentioned for *lulav* implies a bundle[32].] For the *lulav* it obstructs, in Egypt it did not obstruct. Therefore we found things obstructing can be inferred from anything not obstructing, and things not obstructing can be inferred from anything obstructing[34].

19 Babli 3b.

20 In the ceremonies for the eighth day of initiation, the commandment to Aaron to take a bull and a he-goat (*Lev.* 9:2) is one unit; there could be no bull without a he-goat. But in Mishnah *Menahot* 4:2 it is stated that for all holiday sacrifices bulls and he-goats are independent of one another. If the rules of the Day of Atonement are derived from the rules of the initiation rites, the Mishnah would have to state an exception for the Day of Atonement.

21 The rules of the Day of Atonement cannot be derived from the rules of the initiation rites.

22 In the rules of the elevation offering of a bird (*Lev.* 1:15), in the same verse it is required that the Cohen break the neck of the bird and burn it in smoke on the altar.

23 This must read: "burning in smoke".

24 The text in parentheses was first written by the scribe, the text in brackets is the correction. The original text in parentheses is the correct one. *Sifra Wayyiqra* I *Parshata* 7(4).

25 If the sacrifice would become impure and disqualified after the breaking of the neck but before the burning, the offerer has fulfilled his vow and it is not necessary to bring a second sacrifice.

26 Therefore one part of R. Mana's objection has been shown to be invalid.

26 The daily offering of the High Priest (*Lev.* 6:12-16), a tenth of an *epha* of fine flour baked into "breads" (v. 14) without a specified number. "Permanent" is stated in v. 13.

27 The shew-bread is specified as 12 loaves, *Lev.* 24:5. The arrangement is called "permanent" in v. 24:8.

28 It is obvious that here also one has to switch the places of "shew-bread" and "pan-baked breads". The number of breads of the High Priest is fixed as 12 in Mishnah *Menahot* 6:5, but a deviation from this number invalidates only shew-bread, not the High Priest's offering.

29 *Ex.* 12:22, the commandment to take "a bundle of hyssop".

30 *Lev.* 23;40, the commandment to take 4 kinds of plants; it is not mentioned that they must be tied as a bundle.

31 In the Babli *Sukkah* 11b, and *Sifra Emor Pereq* 16(1), this is rejected as R. Jehudah's minority opinion.

32 Both of R. Mana's objections were disregarded by Tannaim; R. Simeon ben Laqish is justified.

(38a line 76) הָא רִבִּי שִׁמְעוֹן בֶּן לָקִישׁ מַקְשֵׁי לָהּ. מִן הֵן מַיְיתֵי לָהּ רִבִּי שִׁמְעוֹן בֶּן לָקִישׁ. כְּהָדָא דְּתַנֵּי רִבִּי יִשְׁמָעֵאל. בְּזֹאת יָבֹא אַהֲרֹן אֶל־הַקּוֹדֶשׁ. בָּאֱמוּר בָּעִנְיָן. מָה אָמוּר בָּעִנְיָן מַפְרִישִׁין אוֹתוֹ כָּל־שִׁבְעָה וְעוֹבֵד כָּל־שִׁבְעָה וּמְחַנְּחִין אוֹתוֹ כָּל־שִׁבְעָה. אַף זֶה מַפְרִישִׁין אוֹתוֹ כָּל־שִׁבְעָה וְעוֹבֵד כָּל־שִׁבְעָה וּמְחַנְּחִין אוֹתוֹ כָּל־שִׁבְעָה. וְכִי אָמוּר הוּא בָּעִנְיָן. אֶלָּא מִכֵּיוָן שֶׁמִּיתַת בְּנֵי אַהֲרֹן אֲמוּרָה בָּעִנְיָן וְלֹא מֵתוּ אֶלָּא בְמִילוּאִין כְּמִי שֶׁהוּא אָמוּר בָּעִנְיָן. וְלֵית סוֹפֵיהּ דְּרִבִּי

שִׁמְעוֹן בֶּן לָקִישׁ מִישְׁמְעִינֵיהּ מִן הָדֵין קְרָיָא. אֶלָּא כְּאִינָשׁ דְּשָׁמַע מִילָּה וּמַקְשֵׁי עֲלָהּ. אָמַר רִבִּי יוֹסֵה בֵּירִבִּי בּוּן. טַעֲמֵיהּ דְּרִבִּי שִׁמְעוֹן בֶּן לָקִישׁ וַיִּשְׁכּוֹן כְּבוֹד־יְיָ עַל־הַר סִינַי. מַה מֹשֶׁה לֹא נִכְנַס לִפְנַיי לִפְנִים עַד שֶׁנִּתְקַדֵּשׁ בֶּעָנָן כָּל־שִׁבְעָה. אַף אַהֲרֹן לֹא נִכְנַס לִפְנַיי לִפְנִים עַד שֶׁנִּתְרַבֶּה בְשֶׁמֶן הַמִּשְׁחָה כָּל־שִׁבְעָה.

Since Rebbi Simeon ben Laqish has this objection, from where does Rebbi Simeon derive it[33]? Following that of Rebbi Ismael:[34] *With this Aaron shall come into the Sanctuary*[35], what was said in the matter[36]. One separates him all of seven days, he serves all of seven days, and one initiates him all of seven days. Also in this case one separates him all of seven days, he serves all of seven days, and one initiates him all of seven days. Is that spelled out in the matter? But since the death of Aaron's sons is mentioned in the matter[37] and they died during the initiation, it is as if the matter was mentioned. Does not in the end Rebbi Simeon ben Laqish understand it from the same verse[38]? But he is like a person who hears a statement and questions it. Rebbi Yose ben Rebbi Abun said, the reason of Rebbi Simeon ben Laqish is: *the glory of the Eternal was dwelling on Mount Sinai*[39]. Just as Moses did not enter the Holiest of Holies before he was sanctified in the cloud all of seven days, so Aaron did not enter the Holiest of Holies before he was inducted by the anointing oil all of seven days[40].

33 The rule that the High Priest is separated from his family for seven days before the Day of Atonement.
34 Babli 4a.
35 *Lev.* 16:3.
36 Of Aaron's induction into the High Priesthood.
37 *Lev.* 16:1.
38 He still has to explain the same verse used by R. Johanan and Bar Qappara, which he himself proved to be inadequate.
39 *Ex.* 24:16.
40 It is not a biblical requirement but popular usage supported by an aggadic argument.

(line 12 38b) עַל דַּעְתֵּיהּ דְּרִבִּי יוֹחָנָן. לָמָּה מִיתַת בְּנֵי אַהֲרֹן אֲמוּרָה בָּעִנְיָין וְלֹא מֵתוּ אֶלָּא בְמִילּוּאִים. אָמַר רִבִּי חִייָה בַּר בָּא. בְּנֵי אַהֲרֹן בְּאֶחָד בְּנִיסָן מֵתוּ. וְלָמָּה הוּא מַזְכִּיר מִיתָתָן בְּיוֹם הַכִּיפּוּרִים. לְלַמְּדָךְ שֶׁכְּשֵׁם שֶׁיּוֹם הַכִּיפּוּרִים מְכַפֵּר עַל יִשְׂרָאֵל כַּךְ מִיתָתָן שֶׁלְּצַדִּיקִים מְכַפֶּרֶת עַל יִשְׂרָאֵל. אָמַר רִבִּי בָּא בַּר בִּינָה. לָמָּה סָמַךְ הַכָּתוּב מִיתַת מִרְיָם לְפָרָשַׁת פָּרָה. לְלַמְּדָךְ שֶׁכְּשֵׁם שֶׁאֵפֶר הַפָּרָה מְכַפֶּרֶת עַל יִשְׂרָאֵל כֵּן מִיתָתָן שֶׁלְּצַדִּיקִים מְכַפֶּרֶת עַל יִשְׂרָאֵל. אָמַר רִבִּי יוּדָן

בֵּירַבִּי שָׁלוֹם. לָמָּה סָמַךְ הַכָּתוּב מִיתַת אַהֲרֹן לְשִׁיבּוּר הַלּוּחוֹת. לְלַמֶּדְךָ שֶׁמִּיתָתָן שֶׁלְצַדִּיקִים קָשָׁה לִפְנֵי הַקָּדוֹשׁ בָּרוּךְ הוּא כְּשִׁיבּוּר לוּחוֹת.

In Rebbi Johanan's opinion, why is the death of Aaron's sons mentioned in the matter when they died during initiation? Rebbi Hiyya bar Abba said, Aaron's sons died on the First of Nisan; why does He mention their death at the Day of Atonement[41]? To teach you that just as the Day of Atonement atones for Israel, so the death of the Just atones for Israel. Rebbi Ba bar Binah said, why did the verse append the death of Miriam to the Chapter of the Cow[42]? To teach you that just as the ashes of the Cow atone for Israel, so the death of the Just atones for Israel. Rebbi Yudan bar Shalom said, why did the verse append the death of Aaron to the breaking of the Tablets[43]? To teach you that the death of the Just is as hard for the Holy One, praise to Him, as the breaking of the Tablets.

41 *Lev.* 16:1.
42 The rules of the Red Cow and purification from the impurity of the dead are given in *Num.* 19; the death of Miriam is noted in v. 20:1.
43 The breaking of the Tablets and the story of the Golden Calf are quoted in *Deut.* 9:7-29; Aaron's death is mentioned in 10:6 in a verse which requires further explanation, given in the next paragraph without reference to the Day of Atonement. *Lev. rabba* 20, end.

(38b line 20) כָּתוּב וּבְנֵי יִשְׂרָאֵל נָסְעוּ מִבְּאֵרוֹת בְּנֵי־יַעֲקָן מוֹסֵרָה שָׁם מֵת אַהֲרֹן. וְכִי בְמוֹסֵירָה מֵת אַהֲרֹן. וַהֲלֹא בְהֹר הָהָר מֵת. הָדָא הוּא דִכְתִיב וַיַּעַל אַהֲרֹן הַכֹּהֵן [הֹר הָהָר] עַל־פִּי יְי וַיָּמָת שָׁם. אֶלָּא מִכֵּיוָן שֶׁמֵּת אַהֲרֹן נִסְתַּלְּקוּ עֲנָנֵי הַכָּבוֹד וּבִקְּשׁוּ הַכְּנַעֲנִים לְהִתְגָּרוֹת בָּם. הָדָא הוּא דִכְתִיב וַיִּשְׁמַע הַכְּנַעֲנִי מֶלֶךְ־עֲרָד יֹשֵׁב הַנֶּגֶב כִּי בָא יִשְׂרָאֵל דֶּרֶךְ הָאֲתָרִים וַיִּלָּחֶם בְּיִשְׂרָאֵל. מַהוּ דֶּרֶךְ הָאֲתָרִים. כִּי מֵת הַתַּיָּיר הַגָּדוֹל שֶׁהָיָה תָר לָהֶם אֶת הַדֶּרֶךְ. וּבָאוּ וְנִתְגָּרוּ בָם. וּבִקְשׁוּ יִשְׂרָאֵל לַחֲזוֹר לְמִצְרַיִם וְנָסְעוּ לַאֲחוֹרֵיהֶן שְׁמוֹנָה מַסָּעוֹת. וְרָץ אַחֲרָיו שִׁבְטוֹ שֶׁלְלֵוִי וְהָרַג מֵמֶּנּוּ שְׁמוֹנָה מִשְׁפָּחוֹת. אַף הֵם הָרְגוּ מִמֶּנּוּ אַרְבַּע. לַעֲמַרְמִי לַיִּצְהָרִי לַחֶבְרוֹנִי לַעֻזִּיאֵלִי. אֵימָתַי חָזְרוּ. בִּימֵי דָוִד. הָדָא הוּא דִכְתִיב יָפְרַח־בְּיָמָיו צַדִּיק וְרֹב שָׁלוֹם עַד־בְּלִי יָרֵחַ. אָמְרוּ. מִי גָרַם לָנוּ לַדָּמִים הַלָּלוּ. אָמְרוּ. עַל שֶׁלֹּא עָשִׂינוּ חֶסֶד עִם אוֹתוֹ הַצַּדִּיק. וְיָשְׁבוּ וְקָשְׁרוּ הֶסְפֵּידוֹ וְגָמְלוּ לַצַּדִּיק חֶסֶד. וְהֶעֱלָה עֲלֵיהֶן הַמָּקוֹם כְּאִילוּ מֵת שָׁם וְנִקְבַּר שָׁם וְגָמְלוּ לַצַּדִּיק חֶסֶד.

[44]It is written[45]: *and the Children of Israel travelled from the wells of Bene Yaaqon to Mosera; there Aaron died.* Did Aaron die at Mosera? Did he not die on Mount Hor? This is what is written[46], *Aaron the Priest ascended*

Mount Hor by the order of the Eternal and died there. But when Aaron died, the clouds of glory[47] disappeared and the Canaanites wanted to attack them. This is what is written[48], *the Canaanite, the king of Arad, who was dwelling in the Negev, heard that Israel came in the way of Atarim, and made war against Israel.* What means *"in the way of Atarim"*? That the great scout had died who had scouted the way for them. They came and attacked them. Then Israel wanted to return to Egypt and returned eight travel stations[49]. The tribe of Levi ran after them and killed from them eight families[50]. Also they killed from them four families, [51]*for the Amramite, the Yisharite, the Ḥevronite, the Uzzielite.* When did they recover? In the days of David. This is what is written[52], *in his days the just may bloom, immense peace, without moon-periods.* They said, what caused us all this bloodshed? They said, because we did not show compassion for this perfect person[53]. They sat down, organized his eulogies, and showed compassion for this Just; then the Omnipresent credited them as if he had died there, was buried there, and they showed compassion for the perfect person.

44 For this Aggada and more aggadic parts in this Tractate there exists a Medieval copy in the *Qonteros Aharon* of *Yalqut Shim'ony* reproduced by L. Ginsberg in his *Yerushalmi Fragments from the Genizah*, pp. 311-313, referred to by Q. A short parallel is in the Babli, *Roš Haššanah* 3a; parallels are in *Mekhilta dR. Ismael Bešallah, Masekhta deWayassa* 1; *Tanhuma Ḥuqqat* 18. The entire paragraph is discussed by Rashi in his Commentary to *Num.* 26:13.

45 *Deut.* 10:6. According to *Num.*, he did not die at Mosera and never was buried. In the text, the word [אל] has been added from the masoretic text and Q.

46 *Num.* 33:38.

47 Who had covered the Israelites' camp from the moment of the Exodus.

48 *Num.* 21:1.

49 As enumerated in *Num.* 33.

50 In Q: "16 families".

51 A redundant verse in *1Chr.* 26:23. (See Rashi, quoted in Note 44).

52 *Ps.* 72:6.

53 To organize due eulogies. In this context, גְּמִילוּת חֶסֶד means services to the living or the dead by a person himself, which cannot be bought by money.

(38b line 34) רִבִּי יוֹסֵי בֶּן חֲנִינָה אָמַר. עֲשִׂירִית הָאֵיפָה וּמְכַנָסַיִּים מְעַכְּבִין. מַה טַעֲמָא. זֶה וְזֶה עֲשִׂיָּיה. אָמַר רִבִּי חֲנִינָה. וְעָשִׂיתָ לְאַהֲרֹן וּלְבָנָיו כָּכָה. כָּל־הָאָמוּר בַּפָּרָשָׁה מְעַכֵּב. וְאַתְיָיא כַּיי דָּמַר רִבִּי שְׁמוּאֵל בַּר נַחְמָן בְּשֵׁם רִבִּי יוֹנָתָן. זֶה הַדָּבָר וְזֶה הַדָּבָר. אֲפִילוּ קְרִיַּת הַפָּרָשָׁה

מְעַכֶּבֶת. אָמַר רִבִּי יוֹחָנָן. כָּל־הַמְעַכֵּב לַדּוֹרוֹת מְעַכֵּב כָּאן. [וְכָל־שֶׁאֵין מְעַכֵּב לַדּוֹרוֹת אֵינוֹ מְעַכֵּב כָּאן]. מָה אִית לָךְ. סְמִיכָה וּשְׁיָרֵי דָמִים שֶׁאֵינָן מְעַכְּבִין לַדּוֹרוֹת מְעַכְּבִין כָּאן. אָמַר רִבִּי חֲנִינָה. צִיץ וּמִצְנַפְתּוֹ שֶׁלְאַהֲרֹן קוֹדֵם לָאַבְנֵטִים שֶׁלְבָּנִים. יְהוּדָה בְּרִיבִּי אוֹמֵר. וְחָגַרְתָּ אֹתָם אַבְנֵט אַהֲרֹן וּבָנָיו. אָמַר רִבִּי אִידִי. הָדָא דְאַתְּ אָמַר לְמִצְוָה. אֲבָל לְצִיווּי וַיַּקְרֵב מֹשֶׁה אֶת־אַהֲרֹן וְאֶת־בָּנָיו וַיִּרְחַץ אוֹתָם בַּמָּיִם. וְאַחַר כָּךְ וַיִּתֵּן עָלָיו אֶת־הַכֻּתֹּנֶת. וְאַחַר כָּךְ וַיַּקְרֵב מֹשֶׁה אֶת אַהֲרֹן וְאֶת בָּנָיו וַיַּלְבִּשֵׁם כֻּתֳּנֹת.

Rebbi Yose ben Ḥanina said, the tenth of an *ephah* and breeches obstruct[54]. What is the reason? Both are "making"[55]. Rebbi Ḥanina said, *and do with Aaron and his sons so*[56], all which is written in the Chapter obstructs. This comes following what Rebbi Samuel bar Naḥman said in the name of Rebbi Jonathan: *this is the word*[57], *and this is the word*[58], even reading the Chapter obstructs. Rebbi Joḥanan said, anything obstructing for future generations obstructs here, [and anything not obstructing for future generations does not obstruct here.] What do you have? The leaning of hands[59] and the remainders of the blood[60] which are not obstructing in future generations are obstructing here. Rebbi Ḥanina said, the diadem and Aaron's mitre precede the sons' belts[61]. Jehudah the great says, *you shall gird them with belts, Aaron and his sons*[62]. Rebbi Idi said, what you are saying is as a meritorious deed. But as a commandment, *Moses brought near Aaron and his sons and washed them in water,* and after that, *he put the vest on him*, and after that, *Moses brought Aaron and his sons near and clothed them with shirts*[63].

54 The presentation of twelve breads which is the daily offering of the High Priest (Note 26) and the initiation of offering of a common priest (*Lev.* 6:13) as well as the breeches which are part of the priests' holy garments (*Ex.* 28:42-43), even though they are mentioned neither in the instructions for the initiation rites given to Moses (*Ex.* 28) nor in the record of the execution of these instructions (*Lev.* 8), are necessary and the omission of the offering or failure to wear the breeches would have invalidated the entire proceedings. Babli 5b.

55 It is held that every commandment using the verb עשה requires strict adherence to the rules given by this verb. The verb is used for the initiation of a priest in *Lev.* 6:14, for the high priest in *Lev.* 6:15, and Moses is ordered to "make breeches" for the priests in *Ex.* 28:42.

56 *Ex.* 29:35. The verse continues, <u>all that I commanded you.</u>

57 *Lev.* 8:5, the declaration of Moses to the people explaining the initiation rites.

58 *Ex.* 29:1, the instruction for future initiation rites.

59 The leaning of hands of Aaron and his sons on the heads of the sacrificial animals (*Ex.* 29:10,15,19) which for the initiation rites is an essential act but in the rules of sacrifices (*Lev.* 1-5) is prescribed only for private offerings, and in no case would the failure to follow the requirement disqualify the sacrifice.

60 The remainder of the blood collected by the Cohen after the required sprinkling of blood on the altar walls has to be poured into the base of the altar. But this act is not required for validity of the sacrifice; if the blood becomes impure after the sprinkling, the blood has to be otherwise disposed of but the sacrifice is unquestionably valid. These cases represent the points of difference between R. Hanina and R. Johanan. Babli 4b (bottom), switching attributions.

61 In dressing of the priests in initiation.

62 *Ex.* 29:9, the commandment to Moses.

63 *Lev.* 8:6,7,13, description of the execution.

(38b line 46) אָמַר רִבִּי לָעֲזָר בֵּירִבִּי יוֹסֵי. פָּשֵׁט הוּא לָן שֶׁבַּחֲלוּק לָבָן שִׁימֵּשׁ מֹשֶׁה בִּכְהוּנָה גְדוֹלָה. אָמַר רִבִּי תַנְחוּם בַּר יוּדָן וְתַנֵּי לָהּ. כָּל־שִׁבְעַת יְמֵי הַמִּילוּאִים הָיָה מֹשֶׁה מְשַׁמֵּשׁ בִּכְהוּנָה גְדוֹלָה וְלֹא שָׁרַת שְׁכִינָה עַל יָדָיו. וְכֵיוָן שֶׁלָּבַשׁ אַהֲרֹן בִּגְדֵי כְהוּנָה גְדוֹלָה וְשִׁימֵּשׁ שָׁרַת שְׁכִינָה עַל יָדָיו. מָה טַעַם. כִּי הַיּוֹם יְי נִרְאָה אֲלֵיכֶם:

רִבִּי יוֹסֵה בַּר חֲנָנָה בָּעֵי. עֲשִׂירִית הָאֵיפָה הֵיאַךְ קְרֵבָה. (חֲצִיִּים) [חֲצָיָיהּ] קְרֵיבָה אוֹ שְׁלֵימָה קְרֵבָה. מִן מַה דִכְתִיב וַיָּבֹא מֹשֶׁה וְאַהֲרֹן אֶל־אֹהֶל מוֹעֵד. [מְלַמֵּד] שֶׁלֹּא בָא עִמּוֹ אֶלָּא לְלַמְּדוֹ עַל מַעֲשֶׂה הַקְּטֹרֶת. הֲדָא אֲמָרָה. חֲצָיִים קְרֵבָה. אִין תֵּימַר. שְׁלֵימָה קְרֵבָה. נִיתְנֵי. עַל מַעֲשֶׂה הַקְּטֹרֶת וְעַל עֲשִׂירִית הָאֵיפָה. אָמַר רִבִּי תַנְחוּם בַּר יוּדָן. וְלֹא בָעֲבוֹדוֹת שֶׁבִּפְנִים אֲנַן קַיָּימִין. כְּבָר לִימְּדוֹ עֲבוֹדוֹת שֶׁבַּחוּץ.

Rebbi Eleazar ben Rebbi Yose[64] said, it is clear to us that Moses officiated in the High Priesthood in a white robe. Rebbi Tanhum bar Yudan said, it was stated: [65]"All seven days of initiation did Moses officiate in the High Priesthood but the Divine Presence was not drawn through him. When Aaron dressed in the priestly garments and officiated, the Divine Presence was drawn through him." What is the reason? *For today the Eternal will appear to you*[66].

Rebbi Yose ben Hanina asked, how was the tenth of an *epha* brought? Was it brought half or [brought] whole[67]? Since it is written[68], *Moses and Aaron came to the Tent of Meeting*, this teaches that he only came with him to teach him the work of incense. [This implies that] half it was brought. If you are saying that it was brought whole, one should have stated, about he work of incense and the tenth of an epha. Rebbi Tanhum bar Yudan said, are we not concerned with service inside? He already had taught him about service outside⁶⁹.

64 The only talmudic Sage known of this name is the Tanna, son of R. Yose ben Halaphta. But since he *said*, not *stated*, and R. Tanhum objected that his assertion already was a tannaitic statement, he must be an otherwise unknown Amora.

Since Aaron entered the High Priesthood only on the eighth day, Moses must have acted as High Priest during the first seven. Babli *Avodah zarah* 34a as tannaitic statement.

65 *Sifra Šemini Milluim* 14.
66 *Lev.* 9:4.

67 Since the offering of the High Priest had to be brought half in the morning and half in the evening, but in the morning of the eighth day Aaron was not yet High Priest, the question is whether only the afternoon offering was made or the morning offering later in the morning.

68 *Lev.* 9:23.
69 The breads of the High Priest are burned on the outside altar; no service in the Tent is involved and the prior argument does not prove anything.

(38b line 56) מִילּוּאִים מָה הָיוּ. קָרְבַּן יָחִיד [אוֹ] קָרְבַּן צִיבּוּר. מִן מַה דִּכְתִיב וַיִּסְמְכוּ אַהֲרֹן וּבָנָיו אֶת־יְדֵיהֶם עַל־רֹאשׁ הָאָיִל: הָדָא אָמְרָה. קָרְבַּן יָחִיד. וְהָא תַנֵּי. קָרְבַּן צִיבּוּר. אָמַר רִבִּי אִידִי. נְתַנְדְּבוּ צִיבּוּר וּמְסָרוּם לָהֶם. מִילּוּאִים מֵאֵיכָן לָמְדוּ. מִן הַקָּרְבָּנוֹת אוֹ מִמַּעֲשֵׂה בְרֵאשִׁית. אִין תֵּימַר. מִן הַקָּרְבָּנוֹת. הַלַּיְלָה הוֹלֵךְ אַחַר הַיּוֹם. אִין תֵּימַר. מִמַּעֲשֵׂה בְרֵאשִׁית. הַיּוֹם הוֹלֵךְ אַחַר הַלַּיְלָה. אִין תֵּימַר. מִן הַקָּרְבָּנוֹת. לַיְלָה אַחֲרוֹן אֵין לוֹ יוֹם. אִין תֵּימַר. מִמַּעֲשֵׂה בְרֵאשִׁית. יוֹם רִאשׁוֹן אֵין לוֹ לַיְלָה.

What were the initiation sacrifices? Private sacrifice or public sacrifice? Since it is written⁷⁰, *Aaron and his sons leaned with their hands on the he-goat's head*, it follows that it was private sacrifice⁷¹. But it was stated, public sacrifice⁷². Rebbi Idi said, the community volunteered and handed them over to them. From where was initiation deduced⁷³? From sacrifices or from Creation? If you are saying from sacrifices, the night follows the day. If you are saying from Creation, the day follows the night. If you are saying from sacrifices, the last night has no day⁷⁴. If you are saying from Creation, the first day has no night.

70 *Lev.* 8:18.
71 Since public sacrifices never need leaning on the sacrificial animal.
72 *Sifra Ṣaw Mekhilta deMilluim* 13.

73 Since it is written (*Lev.* 8:35) that Aaron and his sons have to sit at the gate of the Tabernacle "seven days, day and night" All sacrifices which are eaten "one day and

one night" may be eaten during the day of the sacrifice and the following night.

74 Since on the eighth day they were permitted to leave the Sanctuary after the completion of services.

(38b line 63) תַּמָּן תַּנִּינָן. אֵילּוּ מוֹשְׁכִין וְאֵילּוּ מַנִּיחִין. וְטִפְחוֹ שֶׁלָּזֶה כְּנֶגֶד טִפְחוֹ שֶׁלָּזֶה שֶׁנֶּאֱמַר לְפָנַי תָּמִיד. מַתְנִיתָה דְרַבִּי מֵאִיר. מִדְּרִבִּי יוֹחָנָן מוֹדֶה רִבִּי מֵאִיר שֶׁאִם פֵּירְקוּ אֶת הַיְשָׁנָה בַשַּׁחֲרִית וְסִידְּרוּ אֶת הַחֲדָשָׁה בֵּין הָעַרְבַּיִם אַף זוֹ הָיְתָה תָּמִיד. רִבִּי יוֹסֵי אוֹמֵר. אַף אֵילּוּ נוֹטְלִין וְאֵילּוּ מַנִּיחִין אַף זוֹ הָיְתָה תָּמִיד. אָמַר רִבִּי יוֹחָנָן. מִישִׁיבַת אַהֲרֹן וּבָנָיו לָמַד רִבִּי יוֹסֵי. כַּמָה דְתֵימַר. בִּישִׁיבַת אַהֲרֹן וּבָנָיו צָרִיךְ שֶׁיִּמְסוֹר יוֹם לַלַּיְלָה וְלַיְלָה לַיּוֹם. וְהָכָא צָרִיךְ שֶׁיִּמְסוֹר יוֹם לַלַּיְלָה וְלַיְלָה לַיּוֹם. רִבִּי חִיָּיה בַּר יוֹסֵה אָמַר. מִכֵּיוָן שֶׁמָּסַר יוֹם לַלַּיְלָה דַּיּוֹ. מָה אָמַר רִבִּי חִיָּיה בַּר יוֹסֵף בִּישִׁיבַת אַהֲרֹן וּבָנָיו. מָה אִין תַּמָּן שֶׁכָּתוּב בּוֹ תָּמִיד אַתְּ אָמַר. מִכֵּיוָן שֶׁמָּסַר יוֹם לַלַּיְלָה דַּיּוֹ. כָּאן שֶׁאֵין כָּתוּב תָּמִיד לֹא כָל־שֶׁכֵּן. אַשְׁכַּחַת אֲמַר. עַל דַּעְתֵּיהּ דְּרִבִּי יוֹחָנָן הָיָה שָׁם שֶׁבַע עֲמִידוֹת וְשִׁשָּׁה פֵירוּקִין. עַל דַּעְתֵּיהּ דְּרִבִּי חִיָּיה בַּר יוֹסֵף הָיָה שָׁם אַרְבַּע עֲשָׂרָה עֲמִידוֹת וּשְׁלֹשׁ עֶשְׂרֵה פֵירוּקִין. תַּנֵּי. כָּל־שִׁבְעַת יְמֵי הַמִּילּוּאִים הָיָה מֹשֶׁה מוֹשֵׁחַ אֶת הַמִּשְׁכָּן וּמַעֲמִידוֹ וּמְפָרְקוֹ וְסוֹדֵר עָלָיו אֶת הָעֲבוֹדוֹת. וּבַיּוֹם הַשְּׁמִינִי הֶעֱמִידוֹ וְלֹא פֵירְקוֹ. רִבִּי יוֹסֵה בֵּירִבִּי יוּדָה אָמַר. אַף בַּיּוֹם הַשְּׁמִינִי הֶעֱמִידוֹ וּמְשָׁחוֹ וּפֵירְקוֹ. אָמַר רִבִּי זְעוּרָה. זֹאת אוֹמֶרֶת שֶׁהֲקָמַת הַלַּיְלָה פְסוּלָה לַעֲבוֹדַת הַיּוֹם. אַשְׁכַּחַת אֲמַר. עַל דַּעְתֵּיהּ דְּרִבִּי יוֹחָנָן כְּרִבִּי יוֹסֵה בֵּרִבִּי יוּדָה הָיָה שָׁם אַרְבַּע עֲשָׂרֵה עֲמִידוֹת וּשְׁלֹשׁ עֶשְׂרֵה פֵּירוּקִין. עַל דַּעְתֵּיהּ דְּרִבִּי חִיָּיה בַּר יוֹסֵף כְּרִבִּי יוֹסֵה בֵּרִבִּי יוּדָה הָיָה שָׁם עֶשְׂרִים וְאַחַת עֲמִידוֹת וְעֶשְׂרִים פֵּירוּקִין.

[75]There, we have stated[76]: "These take away and those put down. And the hand of one is close to the hand of the other, for it is said[77], *before Me always*." The Mishnah is Rebbi Meïr's[78]. But according to Rebbi Johanan does Rebbi Meïr agree that if they removed the old set in the morning and arranged the new set in the evening this is also "always"[79]. "Rebbi Yose says, also these may remove and those put down; for this also is 'always'.[76]" Rebbi Johanan said, Rebbi Yose inferred this from the sitting of Aaron and his sons[80]. As you are saying, at the sitting of Aaron and his sons it was necessary that the day deliver to the night and the night deliver to the day[81], so here it was necessary that the day deliver to the night and the night deliver to the day. Rebbi Hiyya bar Yose said, it was sufficient that the day deliver to the night[82]. What does Rebbi Hiyya bar Joseph say about the sitting of Aaron and his sons?, Since if there, where it is written "always", you are saying that it was sufficient that the day deliver to the night, here[83] where it is not written "always" not so much more? You have to say that in Rebbi Johanan's opinion

there were seven erections and six dismantlings[84]. In Rebbi Ḥiyya bar Joseph's opinion here were fourteen erections and thirteen dismantlings[85]. It was stated[86]: "All seven days of initiation did Moses anoint the Tabernacle, erected and dismantled it, and performed in it the services[87]. On the eighth day, he erected it and did not dismantle. Rebbi Yose ben Rebbi Jehudah said, on the eighth day also he erected, anointed, and dismantled." Rebbi Ze'ira said, this implies that erection in the night is invalid for service during the day[88]. You have to say that in Rebbi Joḥanan's opinion following Rebbi Yose ben Rebbi Jehudah there were fourteen erections and thirteen dismantlings. In Rebbi Ḥiyya bar Joseph's opinion following Rebbi Yose ben Rebbi Jehudah there were 21 erections and 20 dismantlings[89].

75 One discusses what it means that Aaron and his sons had to sit at the gate of the Tent of Meeting "seven days, day and night".

76 Mishnah *Menahot* 11:7, describing the order in which the shew-bread was removed from the table in the Tent of Meeting on the Sabbath and new bread deposited when the verse prescribes that the shew-bread always be on the table.

77 *Ex.* 25:30.

78 Since it is anonymous.

79 So even according to R. Meïr the arrangement that the twelve shew-breads were exchanged in a ceremony involving 24 priests so that the table should not be empty for one moment is recommended but not absolutely necessary.

80 Since it is understood that if there is no Tent of Meeting, Aaron and his sons could not sit at its gate and, as explained in the following paragraph, the Tent was every day (or also every night) disassembled and re-erected, the requirement that they sit there "seven days, day and night" could only mean that every day and every night they were sitting there for some time.

81 They actually had to be present there only at dusk and dawn.

82 His statement refers to the shewbreads. He reads "always" to mean that there shall be no day on which the table be empty. Since the breads were kept there from Sabbath to Sabbath, he only requires that the new breads be delivered before dusk at the end of the Sabbath.

83 At the initiation of the priests.

84 Since it is shown in the next paragraph that every morning the Tent had to be re-erected, and Aaron and his sons were to be present in the sacred precinct day and night, the Tent was erected on day 1, and on days 2 - 7 was disassembled and re-erected every morning after dawn.

85 Since *Lev.* 8:34 requires that Aaron and his sons not leave the sacred domain during 7 days, but v. 35 states that they have to sit there "day and night", it follows that they could not leave, and therefore the Tent could not be disassembled, during the days, but it could be disassembled in the night after nightfall, then re-erected for the night,

and disassembled after dawn.

86 *Sifra Saw Mekhilta deMilluim* 36; *Num. rabba* 12(18); *Seder Olam* Chapter 7.

87 Since Aaron and his sons entered service only on day 8, for the first 7 days Moses acted as High Priest (Note 64).

88 Since it was necessary to disassemble the Tent after the seventh night, it follows that services could be held only in presence of a Tent erected during daytime. *Num. rabba* 12(18).

89 Since for R. Johanan the Tent has to be standing every dawn and dusk (except for the first dawn) and R. Yose ben R. Jehudah requires (in the interpretation of R. Ze`ira) that the Tent be re-erected in the night but not for service, in 7 days and 7 nights there must be 14 erections and one less dismantling.

According to R. Hiyya ben Joseph the tent was erected every morning for services, disassembled and re-erected for dusk, and disassembled and re-erected for the night. In this opinion it makes no difference whether the Tent was disassembled before or after dawn. There are different name attributions in *Num. rabba* 12(18).

(38c line 8) מְנַיִן לַפֵּירוּקִין. אָמַר רִבִּי זְעוּרָה. וַיְהִי בְּיוֹם כַּלּוֹת מֹשֶׁה לְהָקִים אֶת־הַמִּשְׁכָּן. בַּיּוֹם שֶׁכָּלוּ הֲקָמוֹתָיו. רִבִּי שִׁמְעוֹן בֶּן לָקִישׁ אָמַר. כַּאֲשֶׁר עָשָׂה בַּיּוֹם הַזֶּה צִוָּה יי וגו'. וְלֹא כְבָר תַּנִּיתָהּ חָדָא בְּשֵׁם רִבִּי יוֹחָנָן וְחָדָא בְּשֵׁם רִבִּי שִׁמְעוֹן בֶּן לָקִישׁ.

בַּשְּׁמִינִי. אִית תַּנָּיֵי תַנֵּי. נִמְשַׁח. וְאִית תַּנָּיֵי תַנֵּי. לֹא נִמְשַׁח. אִית תַּנָּיֵי תַנֵּי. נִתְפָּרֵק. אִית תַּנָּיֵי תַנֵּי. לֹא נִתְפָּרֵק. אָמַר רִבִּי חָנִין. פְּשַׁט הוּא לָן. מָאן דְּאָמַר. נִמְשַׁח. נִתְפָּרֵק. וּמָאן דְּאָמַר. לֹא נִמְשַׁח. לֹא נִתְפָּרֵק. מָאן דְּאָמַר. נִמְשַׁח. נִיחָא. דִּכְתִיב וַיִּמְשָׁחֵם. וּמָאן דְּאָמַר. לֹא נִמְשַׁח. מַה מְּקַיֵּים וַיִּמְשָׁחֵם. מַעֲלֶה אֲנִי עֲלֵיכֶם כְּאִילּוּ שֶׁהוּא מְחוּסָּר מְשִׁיחָה וּמְשַׁחְתֶּם אוֹתוֹ. מָאן דְּאָמַר. נִתְפָּרֵק. נִיחָא. דִּכְתִיב שִׁבְעַת יָמִים יְכַפְּרוּ אֶת הַמִּזְבֵּחַ. מָאן דְּאָמַר. לֹא נִתְפָּרֵק. מַה מְּקַיֵּים שִׁבְעַת יָמִים יְכַפְּרוּ עַל־הַמִּזְבֵּחַ. כַּפָּרָה שֶׁהִיא בַדָּם. כְּהָדָא דְתַנֵּי. עַל זֶה וְעַל זֶה הָיוּ מַזִּין עָלָיו מִכָּל־הַחַטָּאוֹת שֶׁהָיוּ שָׁם כְּדֵי שֶׁיִּכָּנְסוּ הַמַּיִם תַּחַת הַדָּם. דִּבְרֵי רִבִּי יְהוּדָה. רִבִּי יוֹסֵה אוֹמֵר. תַּחַת הַדָּם וְתַחַת שֶׁמֶן הַמִּשְׁחָה.

From where the dismantlings? Rebbi Ze`ira said,[90] *it was on the day that Moses stopped erecting the Dwelling,* on the day the erections stopped. Rebbi Simeon ben Laqish said, *as he did on that day, did the Eternal command*[91]. Was this not already stated? One in the name of Rebbi Johanan[92], and one in the name of Rebbi Simeon ben Laqish.

On the Eighth {Day}. There are Tannaim who state, it[93] was anointed; and there are Tannaim who state, it was not anointed. There are Tannaim who state, it was dismantled; and there are Tannaim who state, it was not dismantled. Rebbi Ḥanin said, it is obvious for us that for him who said, it was anointed it was dismantled; and for him who said, it was not anointed it was not dismantled. Him who said, it was anointed, one understands since it is written *he anointed them*[90]. But he who said, it was not anointed, how does he uphold *he anointed them*? I consider it as if it were missing anointment and you anointed it. Him who said, it was anointed, one understands since it is written[94], *seven days they shall atone the altar*. But he who said, it was not dismantled, how does he uphold *seven days they shall atone the altar*? Atonement by blood, as it was stated[95]: On both of them they were sprinkling from all purifications[96] that were there, so that the water should penetrate under the blood, the words of Rebbi Jehudah; Rebbi Yose says, under the blood and under the anointing oil.

90 *Num.* 7:1. Since on this day the princes of the tribes started presenting their sacrifices, it must be the day when Aaron and his sons already officiated, the eighth day of initiation. Since the Tent of Meeting already was erected on the first day, finishing the erections on the eighth implies some dismantling in between.

91 *Lev.* 8:34. Since the verse implies that all of seven days the ritual commanded in *Ex.* 29 had to be repeated, including the erection of the Tent of Meeting.

92 He interprets the verse differently, Note 7.

93 The Tent of Meeting.

94 *Ex.* 29:37. If the altar was not put out of commission in the meantime because the Tent was dismantled, only one atonement would have been necessary. Therefore every day must have seen a new commissioning of the altar.

95 Babli 4a. The persons referred to are the High Priest for the service of the Day of Atonement and the priest chosen to burn the corpse of the Red Cow. The sprinkling water has to penetrate the prietly garments below the blood and oil by which they were dedicated.

98 Ashes from all Red Cows conserved in the Temple.

(38c line 21) פֵּירֵשׁ בֶּן בְּתִירָה. שֶׁמָּא יָבוֹא עַל אִשְׁתּוֹ נִדָּה וִידָחֶה כָּל־שִׁבְעָה. וְיִשְׂרָאֵל חֲשׁוּדִ׳ין עַל הַנִּידּוֹת. כַּיֵּי דְתַנִּינָן תַּמָּן. הָיָה מְשַׁמֵּשׁ עִם הַטְּהוֹרָה. אָמְרָה לוֹ. נִטְמֵאתִי פֵּירַשׁ מִיָּד חַיָּיב. שֶׁיְּצִיאָתוֹ הֲנָיָיה לוֹ כְּבִיאָתוֹ׃ אַשְׁכָּחַת אָמַר. מַאן דְּאָמַר. רִבִּי יוֹחָנָן. צְרִיכָה לְבֶן בְּתִירָה. מָאן דְּאָמַר. בֶּן בְּתִירָה. צְרִיכָה לְרִבִּי יוֹחָנָן. אִילּוּ אָמַר רִבִּי יוֹחָנָן וְלֹא אָמְרָהּ בֶּן בְּתִירָה הֲוִינָן אָמְרִין. יְשַׁמֵּשׁ מִיטָּתוֹ וְיָשֵׁן לוֹ בְּלִשְׁכַּת פַּלְהֶדְרִין. הֲוֵי צוֹרְכָה לְהִיא דְּאָמַר בֶּן בְּתִירָה. אִילּוּ אָמְרָהּ בֶּן בְּתִירָה וְלֹא אָמַר רִבִּי יוֹחָנָן. הֲוִינָן אָמְרִין. יִפְרוֹשׁ מִמִּיטָּתוֹ וְיָשֵׁן לוֹ בְּתוֹךְ בֵּיתוֹ. הֲוֵי צוֹרְכָה לְהִיא דְּאָמַר רִבִּי יוֹחָנָן. וְצוֹרְכָה לְהִיא דְּאָמַר בֶּן בְּתִירָה.

Ben Bathyra explained[99]: Perhaps he would sleep with his menstruating wife and be pushed away all of seven days[100]. But are Israel suspected about menstruating women[101]? Following what was stated there[102]: "If he was having sex with a pure one and she said to him, I became impure, if he separates immediately he is liable, for his separation is as pleasurable to him as his entry[103]." You have to say that he who transmits the statement of Rebbi Johanan needs that of Ben Bathyra, and he who transmits the statement of Rebbi Johanan needs that of Ben Bathyra. If Rebbi Johanan had said but not Ben Bathyra, we would have said that he may have sex but sleep in the Palhedrin lodge; therefore one needs that of Ben Bathyra. If Ben Bathyra had said but not Rebbi Johanan, we would have said, let him not have sex but he may sleep in his house; therefore one needs that of Rebbi Johanan, and one needs that of Ben Bathyra.

99 One returns to the discussion of Mishnah 1, explaining why the High Priest has to live in the Temple precinct for seven days prior to the Day of Atonement. Babli 6a, Tosephta 1:1.

100 *Lev.* 15:24.

101 Is not Ben Bathyra's explanation an insult to the High Priest? If this Ben Bathyra is the early Tanna (and not the later R. Jehudah ben Bathyra to whom the statement is attributed in the Babli), his argument might be an anti-Sadducee statement, since Sadducees and Pharisees accused one another of sleeping with menstruating women by following their sectarian interpretation of the biblical law; cf. *Niddah* 4:1 Note 3 (SJ 34).

102 Mishnah *Ševu'ot* 2:5, Notes 80,81.

103 If the wife becomes impure during intercourse, if then he stops moving immediately and separates after the erection has disappeared, he touched an impure woman, has to immerse himself in a *miqweh*, and becomes totally pure at the next sundown. But if he separates while still with erection, he had intercourse with a menstruating woman and is severely impure for seven days. Ben Bathyra's argument presupposes that the High Priest is an ignoramus.

(38c line 29) תַּנֵי. כָּל־הַלְּשָׁכוֹת שֶׁהָיוּ בַּמִּקְדָּשׁ הָיוּ פְטוּרוֹת מִן הַמְּזוּזָה חוּץ מִלִּשְׁכַּת פַּלְהֶדְרִין שֶׁהִיא דִירָה לַכֹּהֵן גָּדוֹל שִׁבְעַת יָמִים בַּשָּׁנָה. אָמַר רִבִּי יְהוּדָה. אַף הִיא גְזֵירָה גֶזְרוּ עָלֶיהָ. בִּשְׁעָרֶיךָ. אִית תַּנָּיֵי תַּנֵי. פְּרָט לְשַׁעֲרֵי הַר הַבַּיִת וְהָעֲזָרוֹת. אִית תַּנָּיֵי תַּנֵי. לָרַבּוֹת. מָאן דְּאָמַר. פְּרָט. רִבִּי יְהוּדָה. מָאן דְּאָמַר. לְרַבּוֹת. רַבָּנָן. יָאוּת אָמַר רִבִּי יְהוּדָה. מַה טַעֲמוֹן דְּרַבָּנָן. בִּשְׁעָרֶיךָ. וְכִי בֵית דִּירָה הֵן. הָתִיב רִבִּי יוֹסֵי בֵּירִבִּי בּוּן. וְהָתַנֵּי. בִּשְׁעָרֶיךָ. לְרַבּוֹת שַׁעֲרֵי הַמְּדִינָה. וְכִי בֵית דִּירָה הֵן. אֶלָּא שֶׁבָּהֶן נִכְנָסִין לְבֵית דִּירָה. וְהָכָא שֶׁבָּהֶן הָיוּ נִכְנָסִין לְבֵית דִּירָה.

חוּלְדַּת הַמּוּלִים חַיֶּבֶת בִּמְזוּזָה. חָלוֹן שֶׁהוּא אַרְבַּע עַל אַרְבַּע שֶׁעֲבָדִים יוֹשְׁבִין שָׁם וּמְנִיפִין לְרַבּוֹנֵיהֶם חַיָּיבִין בִּמְזוּזָה. לוּלִים אֵילוּ עַל גַּב אִילוּ חַיָּיבִין בִּמְזוּזָה. הֵן דּוּ דָרַס אַסְקוּפְתָּא אַרְעֵייָתָא. רִבִּי יוֹסֵי הֲוָה מִצְטָעֵר דְּלָא חָמָא לוּלָא דְרִבִּי אִילַי דַּהֲוָוה עָבִיד מִן דַּעְתּוֹן דְּכָל־רַבָּנָן.

3 אסקופתא | ל אסכופתא   4 אילי | ל אילעא   דעתון | ל דעתהון

"All lodges which were in the Temple were not liable for *mezuzah* except for the Palhedrin lodge which was the abode of the High Priest for seven days every year. Rebbi Jehudah said, also this is a decree which was decreed about it."[104] *In your gates*[105]. There are Tannaim who state, to exclude the gates of the Temple Mount and the Courtyards[106]. There are Tannaim who state, to include. He who said to exclude, Rebbi Jehudah. He who said to include, the rabbis. Rebbi Jehudah says it correctly; what is the rabbis' reason? *In your gates*, are these lodgings? Rebbi Yose ben Rebbi Abun asked, but did we not state, *in your gates*, to include city gates[107]? Are these lodgings? But through them one enters lodgings, so also here through them one enters lodgings.

[108]*Huldat hammulim*[109] is liable for *mezuzah*. A window, four by four {cubits} wide, in which slaves sit and make wind for their masters are liable for *mezuzah*. Coops one on top of the other are liable for *mezuzah*; one steps on the doorstep below[110]. Rebbi Yose was sorry not to have seen the coop of Rebbi Ilai which he had made according to all rabbis[111].

104 Babli 10a; Tosephta 1:2. R. Jehudah requires a *mezuzah* only for an apartment used for at least 30 days. Therefore the *mezuzah* on the High Priest's lodging is purely rabbinical.
105 *Deut.* 6:9.
106 Babli 11b, *Sifry Deut.* 36.
107 Babli 11a.
108 These lines are copied from the discussion of the laws of *mezuzah* in *Megillah* 4:12 (ל). They have no direct connection with the topic treated here.
109 A direct translation would be "mole of circumcised", which makes no sense. The explanation of *Qorban haEda*, "entrances of cave dwellings" has no linguistic basis and would be superfluous. A possibility is Jastrow's explanation, 'loading and unloading dock for mules", from מולא, Latin *mulus, mula*, the mule.
110 If the chicken coops are part of the house and are directly accessible from the doorstep, and the areas of the openings add up to four-by-four cubits.
111 That it was required to have a *mezuzah* according to everybody.

(38c line 42) לְלִשְׁכַּת פַּלְהֶדְרִין. אַבָּא שָׁאוּל הָיָה קוֹרֵא אוֹתָהּ לִשְׁכַּת בּוּלְווֹטִין. בָּרִאשׁוֹנָה הָיוּ קוֹרִין אוֹתָהּ לִשְׁכַּת בּוּלְווֹטִין. וְעַכְשָׁיו קוֹרִין אוֹתָהּ לִשְׁכַּת פַּלְהֶדְרִין. פְּרֵאייֵתֵי מִילָא עֲבִידָא.

בְּרִאשׁוֹן שֶׁהָיוּ מְשַׁמְּשִׁין הוּא וּבְנוֹ וּבֶן בְּנוֹ. שִׁימְּשׁוּ בוֹ שְׁמוֹנָה עָשָׂר כֹּהֲנִים. אֲבָל בַּשֵּׁנִי עַל יְדֵי שֶׁהָיוּ נוֹטְלִין בְּדָמִים. שֶׁהָיוּ הוֹרְגִין זֶה אֶת זֶה בִּכְשָׁפִים. שִׁימְּשׁוּ בוֹ שְׁמוֹנִים כֹּהֲנִים. וְיֵשׁ אוֹמְרִים. שְׁמוֹנִים וְאֶחָד. וְיֵשׁ אוֹמְרִים. שְׁמוֹנִים וּשְׁנַיִם. וְיֵשׁ אוֹמְרִים. שְׁמוֹנִים וְשָׁלֹשׁ. וְיֵשׁ אוֹמְרִים. שְׁמוֹנִים וְאַרְבַּע. וְיֵשׁ אוֹמְרִים. שְׁמוֹנִים וְחָמֵשׁ. וּמֵהֶן שִׁימְּשׁוּ שִׁמְעוֹן הַצַּדִּיק אַרְבָּעִים שָׁנָה. אָמַר רִבִּי אֲחָא. כְּתוּב יִרְאַת יי תּוֹסִיף יָמִים. אֵילוּ כֹהֲנִים שֶׁשִּׁימְּשׁוּ בַּבַּיִת הָרִאשׁוֹן. וּשְׁנוֹת רְשָׁעִים תִּקְצוֹרְנָה׃ אֵילוּ שֶׁשִּׁימְּשׁוּ בַּבִּנְיָין הַשֵּׁנִי. מַעֲשֶׂה בְאֶחָד שֶׁשִּׁילַּח בְּיַד בְּנוֹ שְׁתֵּי מִידוֹת שֶׁלְכֶּסֶף מְלֵיאוֹת כֶּסֶף וּמְחוּקֵיהֶן כֶּסֶף. וּבָא אַחֵר וְשִׁילַּח בְּיַד בְּנוֹ שְׁתֵּי מִידוֹת שֶׁלְזָהָב מְלֵיאוֹת זָהָב וּמְחוּקֵיהֶן זָהָב. אָמְרוּ. כָּפָה הַסַּיָּח אֶת הַמְּנוֹרָה.

"To the Palhedrin[2] lodge." Abba Shaul was calling it the council member's lodge[112]. Earlier it was called the council member's lodge. But now one calls it the Palhedrin lodge. The ex-priests[113], a passing[114] matter. In the first {Temple}, where he, his son, and his grandson served, there were eighteen priests serving. But in the second, where they bought it for money, but some say that they killed one another by sorcery[115], there served 80 priests, but some say 81, and some say 82, and some say 84, and some say 85. And from these Simeon the Just served for 40 years. Rebbi Aha said, it is written[116], *the fear of the Eternal adds days*, these are the priests who served in the first Temple, *but the years of the wicked ones will be shortened*; these are those who served in the second building. It happened that one sent through his son two measures of silver, full of silver, and their covers silver. Another came and sent through his son two measures of gold, full of gold, and their covers gold. They said, the foal overturned the candelabrum[117].

112 Greek βουλευταί, οἱ. Since under Persian rule the High Priest also was the political head of the commonwealth, it is reasonable to assume that during his stay at the lodge also the council meetings were held there. Babli 8b.
113 Allon's explanation in *Tarbiz* 13, p. 16, as προϊεραθέντες ex-priests, is the correct one.
114 Reading עבירה for עבידה. The meaning of Palhedrin should be seen as pejorative.
115 Since in theory the appointment as High Priest is for life, later generations had difficulty to understand how the appointment to the High Priesthood could be on a yearly basis. They had to assume that the acting High Priest died within his year.
116 *Pr.* 10:27. Babli 9a.
117 This popular saying refers to another story, told in *Pesiqta dR. Cahana, Ekha*: R. Levy said, it happened that a woman honored a judge with a silver candelabrum. Her opponent in the suit went and honored him with a golden foal. The next day the woman went and found the judgment against her. She said to him, My lord, may the

judgment be radiant before you like the silver candelabrum. He said to her, what can I do? The foal overturned the candelabrum.

The Yerushalmi text is quoted in *Sifry Num.* 131; *Pesiqta dR. Cahana Ahare Mot* towards end, *Lev. rabba* 21(8).

(38c line 55) מָצָאנוּ שֶׁלֹּא חָרַב הַבַּיִת בָּרִאשׁוֹנָה אֶלָּא שֶׁהָיוּ עוֹבְדִים עֲבוֹדָה זָרָה וּמְגַלִּים עֲרָיוֹת וְשׁוֹפְכֵי דָמִים. וְכֵן בַּשֵּׁנִי. רִבִּי יוֹחָנָן בַּר תּוֹרְתָא אָמַר. מָצָאנוּ שֶׁלֹּא חָרְבָה שִׁילֹה אֶלָּא שֶׁהָיוּ מְבַזִּים אֶת הַמּוֹעֲדוֹת וּמְחַלְּלִין אֶת הַקֳּדָשִׁים. מָצָאנוּ שֶׁלֹּא חָרַב הַבַּיִת בָּרִאשׁוֹנָה אֶלָּא שֶׁהָיוּ עוֹבְדִים עֲבוֹדָה זָרָה וּמְגַלֵּי עֲרָיוֹת וְשׁוֹפְכִין דָמִים. אֲבָל בַּשֵּׁנִי מַכִּירִין אָנוּ אוֹתָם שֶׁהָיוּ יְגִיעִין בַּתּוֹרָה וּזְהִירִין בַּמִּצְוֹת וּבְמַעְשְׂרוֹת וְכָל־וְסֶת טוֹבָה הָיְתָה בָהֶן. אֶלָּא שֶׁהָיוּ אוֹהֲבִין אֶת הַמָּמוֹן וְשׂוֹנְאִין אִילוּ לְאִילוּ שִׂנְאַת חִנָּם. וְקָשָׁה הִיא שִׂנְאַת חִנָּם שֶׁהִיא שְׁקוּלָה כְּנֶגֶד עֲבוֹדָה זָרָה וְגִילּוּי עֲרָיוֹת וּשְׁפִיכוּת דָמִים. דְלָמָה. רִבִּי זְעוּרָה וְרִבִּי יַעֲקֹב בַּר אָחָא וְרִבִּי אֲבוּנָה הֲווֹן יָתְבִין אֲמִרִין. בְּיוֹתֵר שֶׁבָּרִאשׁוֹן נִבְנָה וּבַשֵּׁנִי לֹא נִבְנָה. אָמַר רִבִּי זְעוּרָה. הָרִאשׁוֹנִים עָשׂוּ תְשׁוּבָה. וְהַשְּׁנִיִּים לֹא עָשׂוּ תְשׁוּבָה. אָמַר רִבִּי אֶלְעָזָר. הָרִאשׁוֹנִים נִתְגַּלָּה עֲוֹנָם וְנִתְגַּלָּה קִיצָּם. הַשְּׁנִיִּים נִתְגַּלָּה עֲוֹנָם וְלֹא נִתְגַּלָּה קִיצָּם. שְׁאָלוּ אֶת רִבִּי אֶלְעָזָר. דּוֹרוֹת הָאַחֲרוֹנִים כְּשֵׁרִים מִן הָרִאשׁוֹנִים. אָמַר לָהֶן. עֵידִיכֶם בֵּית הַבְּחִירָה יוֹכִיחַ. אֲבוֹתֵינוּ הֶעֱבִירוּ אֶת הַתִּקְרָה. וַיִּגֶל אֵת מָסַךְ יְהוּדָה. אֲבָל אָנוּ פְעַפְעָנוּ אֶת הַכְּתָלִים. הָאֹמְרִים עָרוּ | עָרוּ עַד הַיְסוֹד בָּהּ׃ אָמְרוּ. כָּל־דּוֹר שֶׁאֵינוֹ נִבְנֶה בְיָמָיו מַעֲלִין עָלָיו כְּאִילּוּ הוּא הֶחֱרִיבוֹ.

[118]We find that the Temple was destroyed the first time only because they were active idolators, and uncoverers of nakedness[119], and spillers of blood. And so the second time. Rebbi Joḥanan ben Torta said, we find that Shiloh was destroyed only because they slighted the holidays and desecrated the *sancta*. We find that the Temple was destroyed the first time only because they were active idolators, and uncoverers of nakedness, and spillers of blood. But of the second we know that they toiled in the Torah, were careful about the commandments and tithes, and every good custom[120] was in them; only they loved money and hated one another without reason. Hate without reason is hard for it is the equivalent if idolatry, and uncovering nakedness, and spilling of blood. An example. Rebbi Ze`ira, and Rebbi Jacob bar Aḥa, and Rebbi Abuna, were sitting and saying, it is worse since the first time it was rebuilt but the second time it was not rebuilt. Rebbi Ze`ira said, the first ones repented, the second ones did not repent. Rebbi Eleazar said, the first time their sin was brought into the open and so was their end; the second time their sin was brought into the open but their end was not brought into the open.

They asked Rebbi Eliezer, are the later generations more qualified than the first? He told them, your witness, the Temple, shall prove it. Our forefathers removed the ceiling, *the curtain of Jehudah was lifted*[121], but we blew out the walls, *who are saying, make bare, make bare, up to its foundations*[122]. They said, any generation in which it is not rebuilt is debited as if it had destroyed it.

118 Babli 9a/9b.
119 The technical term for incest and adultery (all crimes prohibited in *Lev.* 18.)
120 Latin *suetum* (E. G.).
121 *Is.* 22:8.
122 *Ps.* 137:7.

(38c line 72) מַתְקִינִין לוֹ כֹהֵן אַחֵר תַּחְתָּיו שֶׁמָּא יֶאֱרַע בּוֹ פְסוּל. מַה. מְיַיחֲדִין לֵיהּ עִמֵּיהּ. אָמַר רְבִּי חַגַּיי. מֹשֶׁה. דְּאִין מְיַיחֲדִין לֵיהּ עִמֵּיהּ דּוּ קָטַל לֵיהּ. אוֹתוֹ. אוֹתוֹ מוֹשְׁחִין וְאֵין מוֹשְׁחִין שְׁנַיִם. אָמַר רְבִּי יוֹחָנָן. מִפְּנֵי אֵיבָה.

[123]"One arranges for another Cohen as his replacement, maybe a disqualification of his will happen." How? Does one leave them alone together? Rebbi Haggai said, by Moses[8]! If one would leave them alone together, he would kill him! *Him*[124]. One anoints one, one does not anoint two. Rebbi Johanan said, because of rivalry[125].

123 From here on there is a parallel in *Horaiot* 3:3, Notes 146-188 and *Megillah* 1:12.
124 *Lev.* 6:12; the offering of the High Priest starting with the day he is anointed for his office. *Sifra Saw Parašah* 3(3). The singular indicates that only one High Priest can be appointed at one time. This implies that the reserve appointee for the day of Atonement cannot have the status of High Priest unless he actually is needed.
125 He disagrees and holds that while the two could not have been anointed on the same day, they could have been anointed on different days. The rule that the back-up Cohen has lower status is practical, not biblical, as is the entire institution of the back-up.

(38c line 75) עָבַר זֶה וְשִׁימֵּשׁ זֶה. הָרִאשׁוֹן כָּל־קְדוּשַׁת כְּהוּנָּה עָלָיו. הַשֵּׁינִי אֵינוֹ כָשֵׁר לֹא לְכֹהֵן גָּדוֹל וְלֹא לְכֹהֵן הֶדְיוֹט. אָמַר רְבִּי יוֹחָנָן. עָבַר וְעָבַד עֲבוֹדָתוֹ כְּשֵׁירָה. עֲבוֹדָתוֹ מִשֶּׁל מִי. נִשְׁמְעִינָהּ מִן הָדָא. מַעֲשֶׂה בְּבֶן אִילֵם מִצִּיפּוֹרִין שֶׁאִיַּרַע קֶרִי לְכֹהֵן גָּדוֹל בְּיוֹם הַכִּיפּוּרִים. וְנִכְנַס בֶּן אִילֵם וְשִׁימֵּשׁ תַּחְתָּיו בִּכְהוּנָּה גְדוֹלָה. וּכְשֶׁיָּצָא אָמַר לַמֶּלֶךְ. אֲדוֹנִי הַמֶּלֶךְ. פַּר וְשָׂעִיר שָׁלִיוֹם הַכִּיפּוּרִים

מָשְׁלִי הֵן קְרֵיבִין אוֹ מִשֶּׁלְּכֹהֵן גָּדוֹל. וְיָדַע הַמֶּלֶךְ מָה הוּא שׁוֹאֲלוֹ. אָמַר לוֹ. בֶּן אִילֵּם. אִילּוּ לֹא דַיֶּיךָ שֶׁשִּׁימַּשְׁתָּ שָׁעָה אַחַת לִפְנֵי מִי שֶׁאָמַר וְהָיָה הָעוֹלָם. וְיָדַע בֶּן אִלֵּם שֶׁהוּסַּע מִכְּהוּנָה גְדוֹלָה.

If one was incapacitated and the other officiated. The first has all the sanctity of the High Priesthood on him; the second one is qualified neither as High Priest nor as common priest[126]. Rebbi Johanan said, if he transgressed and officiated, his officiating is valid. Whose officiating? Let us hear from the following: It happened to Ben Illem from Sepphoris that the High Priest experienced an emission of semen on the Day of Atonement; Ben Illem entered and officiated in his stead. He went out and asked the king: "The bull and the he-goat which are brought today, are they offered from his or from the High Priest's property?[6]" The king understood what he was asking and answered him, "is it not enough for you that you served once before Him Who spoke and the world was created?" Ben Illem understood that he was removed from the High Priesthood.

126 As the Babli explains (*Yoma* 12b), "one increases in sanctity but never decreases" (cf. *Bikkurim* 3:3, Note 57; *Megillah* 1:12 72a l. 47, *Ševuot* 1:8, 33b l.13). Since the service of the Day of Atonement is valid only if performed by the High Priest, the substitute becomes a temporary High Priest. He cannot act as a High Priest if the actual High Priest's temporary disability is removed, and he is permanently barred from acting as a common priest. As the Babli points out, if the High Priest dies, the substitute automatically becomes his successor. Tosephta 1:4.

(38d line 8) מַעֲשֶׂה בְשִׁמְעוֹן בֶּן קַמְחִית שֶׁיָּצָא לְדַבֵּר עִם הַמֶּלֶךְ (עַרְבִי) [עֶרֶב יוֹם הַכִּיפּוּרִים]. וְנִתְּזָה צִינּוֹרָה שֶׁלּרוֹק מִפִּיו עַל בְּגָדָיו וְטִימַּתּוּ. וְנִכְנַס יְהוּדָה אָחִיו וְשִׁימֵּשׁ תַּחְתָּיו בִּכְהוּנָה גְדוֹלָה. וְרָאָת אִימָּן שְׁנֵי בָנֶיהָ כֹּהֲנִים גְּדוֹלִים בְּיוֹם אֶחָד. שִׁבְעָה בָנִים הָיוּ לָהּ לְקַמְחִית וְכוּלָּן שִׁימְּשׁוּ בִּכְהוּנָּה גְדוֹלָה. שָׁלְחוּ חֲכָמִים וְאָמְרוּ לָהּ. מַה מַּעֲשִׂים טוֹבִים יֶשׁ בְּיָדָךְ. אָמְרָה לָהֶן. יָבוֹא עָלַי אִם רָאוּ קוֹרוֹת בֵּיתִי שְׂעָרוֹת רֹאשִׁי [וְאִימְרַת חָלוּקִי] מִיָּמָיי. אָמְרוּן. כָּל־קַמְחַיָּיא קֶמַח. וְקִמְחָא דְקִימְחִית סוֹלֶת. נֶקֶרוּן עָלָה כָּל־כְּבוּדָּה בַת־מֶלֶךְ פְּנִימָה מִמִּשְׁבְּצוֹת זָהָב לְבוּשָׁהּ:

C 1 ערב יום הכיפורים | S ערבי

[127]It happened that Simeon ben Qimḥit went out to talk to (an Arab king) [the king on the eve of the Day of Atonement][128] and a drop of spittle squirted on his garment and defiled him. His brother Jehudah entered and officiated in his stead. On that day their mother saw two of her sons as High Priests.

Qimḥit had seven sons; all of them served as High Priests. They sent and asked Qimḥit, what good deeds are in your hand? She told them, there should come over me if the beams of the roof of my house ever saw the hair on my head or the seam of my undershirt. They said, all flours are flour but Qimḥit's flour is fine flour. They recited about her[129]: *All the honor of the king's daughter is inside; gold settings her garments*

127 In addition to the two parallels there are short versions in the Babli 47a, Tosephta 3:20, *Lev. rabba* 20 (end), *Tanhuma Ahare* 7, *Tanhuma Buber Ahare* 9 (Note 127), *Num. rabba 2 (end), Pesiqta dR. Cahana Ahare* (ed. Buber Note 126), *Avot deR. Natan* A, Chap. 35 (ed. Schechter fol. 35a.)

128 There can be little doubt that the scribe's text is the correct one; the corrector's text is an unjustified emendation. The question is discussed in detail by S. Liebermann, *Tosefta kiFshutah* iv, pp. 805-806. Speculations about the background of this tradition are in H. Grätz, *Geschichte der Juden* 3/2, Note 19ii (4th. ed., pp. 738-739).

129 *Ps.* 45:14.

(38d line 16) יָכוֹל יְהֵא מְשׁוּחַ מִלְחָמָה מֵבִיא עֲשִׂירִית הָאֵיפָה. תַּלְמוּד לוֹמַר תַּחְתָּיו מִבָּנָיו. אֶת שֶׁבְּנוֹ עוֹבֵד תַּחְתָּיו [מֵבִיא עֲשִׂירִית הָאֵיפָה.] יָצָא מְשׁוּחַ מִלְחָמָה שֶׁאֵין בְּנוֹ עוֹבֵד תַּחְתָּיו. וּמִנַּיִן לִמְשׁוּחַ מִלְחָמָה שֶׁאֵין בְּנוֹ עוֹבֵד תַּחְתָּיו. תַּלְמוּד לוֹמַר שִׁבְעַת יָמִים יִלְבָּשָׁם הַכֹּהֵן תַּחְתָּיו מִבָּנָיו. אֶת שֶׁהוּא בָא אֶל אֹהֶל מוֹעֵד לְשָׁרֵת בַּקּוֹדֶשׁ בְּנוֹ עוֹמֵד תַּחְתָּיו. יָצָא מְשׁוּחַ מִלְחָמָה שֶׁאֵינוֹ בָא אֶל אֹהֶל מוֹעֵד לְשָׁרֵת בַּקּוֹדֶשׁ. וּמִנַּיִן שֶׁהוּא מִתְמַנֶּה לִהְיוֹת כֹּהֵן גָּדוֹל. [שֶׁנֶּאֱמַר] וּפִינְחָס בֶּן־אֶלְעָזָר נָגִיד הָיָה עֲלֵיהֶם לְפָנִים יְיָ עִמּוֹ. רִבִּי יוֹסֵי כַד הֲוָה בָעֵי מְקַנְתְּרָה לְרִבִּי לְעָזָר בֵּירִבִּי יוֹסֵי הֲוָה אֲמַר לֵיהּ. לְפָנִים עִמּוֹ. בִּימֵי זִמְרִי מִיחָה. וּבִימֵי פִילֶגֶשׁ בְּגִבְעָה לֹא מִיחָה.

3 מבניו Q | מבניו אשר יבא לאהל מועד   4 את שהיא בא Q | הבא   5 להיות - Q

I could think that the Anointed for War[130] should bring his tenth of an *ephah*[131]. The verse says[132], *in his stead, of his sons*. One whose son will serve in his stead [brings a tenth of an *ephah*.] This excludes the Anointed for War whose son will not serve in his stead. From where that the Anointed's for War son will not serve in his stead? The verse says[133], *seven days shall the priest wear them in his stead, one of his sons*. If one officiates in the Tent of Meeting, his son will stand in his stead. This excludes the Anointed for War who does not officiate in the Tent of Meeting, From where that he can be appointed as High Priest? [134][As it is said,] *Phineas the son of Eleazar was leader over them; in earlier times the Eternal was with him.* When Rebbi

Yose wanted to needle Rebbi Eleazar ben Rebbi Yose, he said to him, "before, he was with him." In the days of Zimri[135], he protested. In the days of the concubine at Gibea[136], he did not protest.

130 The one appointed to deliver the exhortations prescribed in *Deut.* 20:1-15.
131 Prescribed for the High Priest in *Lev.* 6:15.
132 *Ex.* 29:30. The only hereditary office in Divine Service is that of the High Priest. Babli 72b/73a.
134 *1Chr.* 9:20. The leader of the priests is the High Priest. Phineas was appointed Anointed for War by Moses, *Num.* 31:6.

135 *Num.* 27:1-15.
136 *Jud.* 19-21. In the opinion of *Seder Olam,* based on the teachings of R. Yose the Tanna (who is the R. Yose quoted here), the affair at Gibea happened at the start of the period of the Judges, when Phineas was High Priest. Cf. the author's edition of *Seder Olam* (Northvale NJ 1998), pp. 122-123.

(28d line 26) מְנַיִין שֶׁהוּא נִשְׁאַל בִּשְׁמוֹנָה. רִבִּי חִיָּיה בְשֵׁם רִבִּי יוֹחָנָן. וּבִגְדֵי הַקּוֹדֶשׁ אֲשֶׁר לְאַהֲרֹן יִהְיוּ לְבָנָיו [אַחֲרָיו]. מַה תַּלְמוּד לוֹמַר אַחֲרָיו. אֶלָּא לִגְדוּלָּה שֶׁלְאַחֲרָיו. [וּמְנַיִין שֶׁהוּא עוֹבֵד בִּשְׁמוֹנָה. רִבִּי יִרְמִיָה בְשֵׁם רִבִּי יוֹחָנָן. וּבִגְדֵי הַקּוֹדֶשׁ אֲשֶׁר לְאַהֲרֹן יִהְיוּ לְבָנָיו. מַה תַּלְמוּד לוֹמַר אַחֲרָיו. לִקְדוּשָּׁה שֶׁלְאַחֲרָיו.] אָמַר לֵיהּ רִבִּי יוֹנָה. עִמָּךְ הָיִיתִי. לֹא אָמַר עוֹבֵד אֶלָּא נִשְׁאַל. [וּבַמֶּה נִשְׁאַל.] אַייְתִי רַב הוֹשַׁעֲיָה מַתְנִיתָא דְּבַר קַפָּרָא מִן דְּרוֹמָא וְתַנָּא. וַחֲכָמִים אוֹמְרִים. אֵינוּ עוֹבֵד לֹא בִּשְׁמוֹנָה שֶׁל כֹּהֵן גָּדוֹל וְלֹא בְאַרְבָּעָה שֶׁלְכֹּהֵן הֶדְיוֹט. אָמַר רִבִּי בָּא. בְּדִין הָיָה שֶׁיְּהֵא עוֹבֵד בְּאַרְבָּעָה. וְלָמָּה אֵינוֹ עוֹבֵד. שֶׁלֹּא יְהוּ אוֹמְרִין. רָאִינוּ כֹהֵן גָּדוֹל פְּעָמִים עוֹבֵד בְּאַרְבָּעָה [פְּעָמִים בִּשְׁמוֹנָה.] אָמַר רִבִּי יוֹנָה. וְלֹא מִבִּפְנִים הוּא עוֹבֵד. וְלֹא מִבַּחוּץ נִשְׁאַל. וְטוֹעִין מִבִּפְנִים לַבַּחוּץ. וְכִי רִבִּי טַרְפוֹן אֲבִיהֶן שֶׁלְכָּל־יִשְׂרָאֵל לֹא טָעָה בֵּין תְּקִיעַת הַקָּהֵל לִתְקִיעַת קָרְבָּן. דִּכְתִיב וּבְנֵי אַהֲרֹן הַכֹּהֲנִים יִתְקְעוּ בַּחֲצוֹצְרוֹת. תְּמִימִים לֹא בַעֲלֵי מוּמִין. דִּבְרֵי רִבִּי עֲקִיבָה. אָמַר לוֹ רִבִּי טַרְפוֹן. אֲקַפַּח אֶת בָּנַיי אִם לֹא רָאִיתִי אָחִי אִימִּי חִיגֵּר בְּאַחַת מֵרַגְלָיו עוֹמֵד בָּעֲזָרָה חֲצוֹצְרָתוֹ בְיָדוֹ וְתוֹקֵעַ. אָמַר לוֹ רִבִּי עֲקִיבָה. רִבִּי. שֶׁמָּא לֹא רָאִיתָה אֶלָּא בִשְׁעַת הַקָּהֵל. וַאֲנִי אוֹמֵר. בִּשְׁעַת קָרְבָּן. אָמַר לוֹ רִבִּי טַרְפוֹן. אֲקַפַּח אֶת בָּנַיי שֶׁלֹּא הִיטִיתָה יָמִין וּשְׂמֹאל. אֲנִי הוּא שֶׁשָּׁמַעְתִּי וְלֹא הָיָה לִי לְפָרֵשׁ. וְאַתָּה דוֹרֵשׁ וּמַסְכִּים לַשְּׁמוּעָה. הָא כָל־הַפּוֹרֵשׁ מִמָּךְ כְּפוֹרֵשׁ מֵחַיָּיו.

12 שמא G | שמה G 14 GS ששצעתי ולא היה הלי לפרש C | שראיתי את המעשה השכחתי גפורש G | כפוריש

And from where that he was asked in eight[137]? Rebbi Hiyya in the name of Rebbi Johanan: *And Aaron's holy garments shall be for his descendants [in his stead]*[138]. Why does the verse say, *in his stead*? For greatness after him[139]. And from where that he officiated in eight? Rebbi Jeremiah in the name of Rebbi Johanan: *And Aaron's holy garments shall be for his descendants.* Why does the verse say, *in his stead*? For sanctity after him. Rebbi Jonah said to him, I was with you;[140] he did not say "officiated" but "was asked". [In how many was he asked?] Rav Hoshaia brought a Mishnah of Bar Qappara from the South which stated: He officiates neither in the eight of a High Priest nor in the four of a common priest. Rebbi Abba said, it would be logical that he officiate in four. Why did they say that he did not officiate? Lest people say, we saw a High Priest who sometimes officiated in four like a simple priest. Rebbi Jonah said, would he not officiate inside and would he not be asked outside? Does one err between inside and outside? But did Rebbi Tarphon, the father of all of Israel, not err between blowing for assembly and the blowing for a sacrifice? As it is written: *The descendants of Aaron, the priests, shall blow the trumpets*[141], blameless ones, not with bodily defects, the words of Rebbi Aqiba. Rebbi Tarphon said to him, I would hit my sons if I did not see my mother's brother, lame in one of his legs, standing in the Temple court with his trumpet in his hand and blowing! Rebbi Aqiba answered him, Rebbi, maybe you saw him only at the time of assembly[141]; but I was saying, at the time of sacrifices. Rebbi Tarphon said to him, I would hit my sons but you did not deviate right or left. I am the one who heard but I could not explain[142]. You derive it and agree with tradition. Therefore, anybody who separates from you is as if he separated himself from his life.

137 The paragraph discusses the rules for the priest Anointed for War. It starts with an assertion that the Anointed for War officiates in the Temple in the High Priest's garb while later it is asserted without dissent that he be barred from any service in the Sanctuary. The entire topic is a reconstruction of the environment in which one has to place David's inquiries to God as recorded in the books of Samuel.

The Anointed for War has two jobs. One is to address the army as described in *Deut.* 20:1-9, the other to ask the Urim and Tummim oracle on behalf of the army commander. Since this oracle is mentioned only in connection with the High Priest's garments (*Ex.* 28:30) it is obvious that the Anointed for War must wear one of these garments for the oracle. But since all eight garments of the High Priest form an indivisible unit, he must wear all of them.

138 *Ex.* 29:30 continues: *To be anointed in them and inducted into office.* Since the one Anointed for War is anointed, he seems to qualify.

139 Since the Anointed for War was

anointed, he seems to qualify.

140 The name of R. Jonah's interlocutor is not given. It must be another student of R. Jeremiah (R. Yose?) since he points out that the words of his teacher were incorrectly transmitted and that R. Jeremiah's statement was identical with that of R. Abba bar Hiyya, the companion of R. Jeremiah's teacher R. Ze`ira. In the Babli, 73a, the students of R. Johanan point out that R. Johanan only gave his opinion on interrogation of the oracle, not of officiating.

141 *Num.* 10:8.

142 The command to call all the community in the desert by the sound of trumpets (*Num.* 10:3) is extended to use trumpets to introduce the public Torah reading in the Temple at Tabernacles in the Sabbatical Year (*Deut.* 31:10-13).

143 The text of the scribe is confirmed by all other sources but makes little sense here; it is a formula copied from other places where R. Tarphon comes to agree with R. Aqiba. The corrector's text, "I saw the happening but I forgot," is appropriate but conjectural.

(47d line 49) וְכִפֶּר הַכֹּהֵן אֲשֶׁר־יִמְשַׁח אוֹתוֹ. מַה תַּלְמוּד לוֹמַר. לְפִי שֶׁכָּל־הַפָּרָשָׁה אֲמוּרָה בְּאַהֲרֹן. אֵין לִי אֶלָּא אַהֲרֹן עַצְמוֹ. וּמִנַּיִין לְרַבּוֹת כֹּהֵן אַחֵר. תַּלְמוּד לוֹמַר אֲשֶׁר־יִמְשַׁח אוֹתוֹ. מְשׁוּחַ בְּשֶׁמֶן הַמִּשְׁחָה. הַמְרוּבָּה בִּבְגָדִים מְנַיִין. תַּלְמוּד לוֹמַר וַאֲשֶׁר יְמַלֵּא אֶת־יָדוֹ. וּמִנַּיִין לְרַבּוֹת כֹּהֵן אַחֵר הַמִּתְמַנֶּה. תַּלְמוּד לוֹמַר וְכִפֶּר הַכֹּהֵן. בַּמֶּה הוּא מִתְכַּפֵּר. רַבָּנָן דְּקֵיסָרִין בְּשֵׁם רִבִּי חִייָה בַּר יוֹסֵף. בְּפֶה. אָמַר רִבִּי זְעוּרָה. הָדָא אֲמָרָה שְׁמַמַּנִּין זְקֵנִים בַּפֶּה. אָמַר רִבִּי חִייָה בַּר אָדָא. מַתְנִיתָא אָמְרָה כֵן. חֲזוֹר בָּךְ בְּאַרְבָּעָה דְּבָרִים שֶׁהָיִיתָ אוֹמֵר. וְנַעֲשְׂךָ אַב בֵּית דִּין עַל יִשְׂרָאֵל.

The priest shall atone who was anointed[144]. Since the entire chapter is said about Aaron, from where to include another priest? The verse says, *who was anointed*; with the anointing oil. From where the one clothed in multiple garb[145]? The verse says, *who was inducted into office*. And from where another who was appointed[146]? The verse says, *the priest shall atone*[147]. How is he being appointed? The rabbis of Caesarea in the name of Rebbi Hiyya bar Joseph, by mouth[148]. Rebbi Ze`ira said, this implies that one may ordain Elders by word of mouth. Rebbi Hiyya bar Ada said, a Mishnah says so: "Recant the four things that you are used to say and we shall make you president of the Court for Israel.[149]"

144 *Lev.* 16:32. The problem is the legitimacy of a priest appointed *ad hoc* as High Priest to conduct the service of the Day of Atonement for which common priests are disqualified. *Sifra Ahara Mot Pereq* 8((4-5).

145 The High Priest in Second Temple times who was not anointed since the anointing oil prepared by Moses was lost.
146 In an emergency of the Day of Atonement where no formal session of a court can be held. Even when anointing oil was available, simple investiture was enough.
147 Since it does not stress "the High Priest", it follows that any priest can be appointed to fill the office.
148 It does not need the laying on of hands nor a document of appointment. (Tosaphot 12b s, v. כהן).
149 Mishnah *Idiut* 5:6. The oral promise was irrevocable.

Here end the parallels in *Horaiot* and *Megillah*.

(38d line 53) מְנַיִין כְּשֵׁם שֶׁמַּתְקִינִין לוֹ כֹּהֵן אַחֵר תַּחְתָּיו שֶׁמָּא יְאָרַע בּוֹ פְסוּל. כָּךְ מְקַדְּשִׁין לוֹ אִשָּׁה אֲחֶרֶת עַל תְּנַאי שֶׁמָּא יְאָרַע דָּבָר בְּאִשְׁתּוֹ. שֶׁנֶּאֱמַר וְכִפֶּר בַּעֲדוֹ וּבְעַד בֵּיתוֹ. בֵּיתוֹ זוֹ אִשְׁתּוֹ. דִּבְרֵי רִבִּי יְהוּדָה. אָמַר לוֹ רִבִּי יוֹסֵה. אִם כֵּן אֵין לַדָּבָר סוֹף. מָהוּ אֵין לַדָּבָר סוֹף. שֶׁמָּא תָמוּת אִשְׁתּוֹ וְתָמוּת אִשָּׁה אֲחֶרֶת. אָמַר רִבִּי מָנָא. עַד דְּאַתְּ מַקְשִׁי לָהּ עַח דְּרִבִּי יְהוּדָה קַשְׁיֵיתָהּ עַל דְּרַבָּנָן. שֶׁמָּא יְאָרַע קֶרִי לְכֹהֵן זֶה וְיֵאָרַע קֶרִי לְכֹהֵן אַחֵר. קֶרִי מָצוּי. מִיתָה אֵינָהּ מְצוּיָה. גָּזְרוּ עַל דָּבָר שֶׁהוּא מָצוּי. וְלֹא גָזְרוּ עַל דָּבָר שֶׁאֵינוֹ מָצוּי. הֵן אַשְׁכְּחַן דְּרִבִּי יְהוּדָה אָמַר. מִיתָה מְצוּיָה. [הֲדָא] הִיא דְתַנִּינָן תַּמָּן. רִבִּי יְהוּדָה אוֹמֵר אַף אִשָּׁה אַחֶרֶת מַתְקִינִין לוֹ שֶׁמָּא תָמוּת אִשְׁתּוֹ. תַּמָּן תַּנִּינָן. הַמֵּבִיא גֵט וְהִנִּיחוֹ זָקֵן אוֹ חוֹלֶה. נוֹתְנוֹ לָהּ בְּחֶזְקַת שֶׁהוּא קַיָּם. תַּמָּן אַתְּ אָמַר. אֵין מִיתָה מְצוּיָה. וְכָא אַתְּ אָמַר. מִיתָה מְצוּיָה. כָּאן בְּיָחִיד. וְכָאן בְּצִיבּוּר. חוֹמֶר הוּא בַצִּיבּוּר. וְהֵן אַשְׁכְּחָן דְּרִבִּי יְהוּדָה מַחֲמִיר בְּיָחִיד. דְּתַנֵּי. אָמַר רִבִּי יְהוּדָה. לֹא הָיָה שׁוֹפַר שֶׁלְּקִינִּים בִּירוּשָׁלֶם מִפְּנֵי הַתַּעֲרוֹבֶת. שֶׁמָּא תָמוּת אַחַת מֵהֶן וְנִמְצָא דְמֵי חַטָּאוֹת מֵיתוֹת מְעוֹרָבוֹת בַּקָּרְבָּן. וִיקַדֵּשׁ מֵאִתְמוֹל. וְכִפֶּר בַּעֲדוֹ וּבְעַד בֵּיתוֹ וְלֹא בְעַד שְׁנֵי בָתִּים. רִבִּי גַּמְלִיאֵל בַּר אִינְיָינֵי בְּעָא קוֹמֵי רִבִּי מָבָא. לֹא נִמְצָא כְקוֹנֶה קִינְיָין בַּשַּׁבָּת. אָמַר לֵיהּ. מִשּׁוּם שְׁבוּת שֶׁהִתִּירוּ בַמִּקְדָּשׁ. אָמַר רִבִּי מָבָא. הֲדָא אָמְרָה. אִילֵּין דִּכְנָסִין אַרְמְלָן צָרִיךְ לְכוֹנְסָן מִבְּעוֹד יוֹם. שֶׁלֹּא יְהֵא כְקוֹנֶה קִינְיָין בַּשַּׁבָּת.

"From where that just as one prepares another Cohen in his stead for maybe a disability will happen to him, so one preliminarily marries to him another wife in case something happen to his wife, as it is said[150], *and he atone for himself and for his house*; his house is his wife, the words of Rebbi Jehudah. Rebbi Yose said to him, in that case there is no end to it, maybe not only this wife but also the other wife would die[151]." Rebbi Mana said, before you question Rebbi Jehudah, question the rabbis! Maybe an emission[152] would happen both to this Cohen and to the other Cohen. Emissions are frequent, death is not frequent[153]. They decided about what is frequent, but did not decide about what is infrequent. We find that Rebbi Jehudah said, death is frequent; that is what we have stated there: "Rebbi Jehudah says, one also prepares for him another wife, maybe his wife would die." There we have stated[154]: "One who brings a bill of divorce and left him old or sick, delivers to her under the presumption that the man be alive." There you are saying, death is infrequent, and here you are saying, death is frequent. There it is a private matter, here a public act. Is one more restrictive in public acts, as we have stated[155]: "Rebbi Jehudah says, there was no horn for nests in Jerusalem because of mixing, maybe one of them[156] would die and it would turn out that money of purification sacrifices that must be left to die is mixed up in the offering." Could he not preliminarily marry her yesterday? *And he atone for himself and for his house*; but not for two houses. Rebbi Gamliel bar Inyani asked before Rebbi Mana: Is he not like one who acquires something on the Sabbath[156]? He answered him, it is because they permitted Sabbath restriction in the Sanctuary. Rebbi Mana said, this implies that those who marry a widow must take her in when it is still daytime, lest he be like someone who acquires on the Sabbath[157].

150 *Lev.* 16:11.
151 *Sifra Ahara Mot Pereq* 8(6). He cannot marry her outright since a High Priest (and any priest aspiring to that position) is restricted to a single wife, as explained later in the paragraph.
152 Emission of semen, an example of impurity which even if removed immediately disables a person from performing sacral acts before the next sundown.
153 Babli 13a.
154 Mishnah *Gittin* 3:3 (Note 79). While the Mishnah is anonymous, the fact that R. Jehudah does not oppose the ruling indicates that he approves of it.
155 Babli 55a, Tosephta *Šeqalim* 3:3, *Gittin* 7:4 (Notes 195-107). The horns were openings of boxes where people could deposit money for specified sacrifices and assume that the boxes would be emptied every day and the necessary sacrifices offered. In particular a woman after childbirth who may not eat *sancta* unless she brought her purification sacrifice may deposit the money and eat *sancta* after sundown without inquiring whether the offering had actually been brought. A "nest" is a couple of pigeons or turtle-doves.
156 If a woman designates a couple of birds as her sacrifice, one of them is a purification sacrifice. If she dies between designation and offering, the purification sacrifice can neither be offered nor redeemed. Therefore the money which she deposited in the horn cannot be used, but it

cannot be determined which coins are those coming from her.

157 Since the Day of Atonement follows the Sabbath rules and the High Priest would have to get a new wife immediately if his wife die after nightfall of the day, should not his wife's death disqualify him from the service since preliminary marriage is an act of acquisition forbidden on the Sabbath? (Since the High Priest is forbidden to defile himself for any corpse, in contrast to a common priest he is not disabled by the death of a close relative.)

158 This is a not quite suitable quote from *Ketubot* 1:1 (Note 14). In contrast to preliminary marriage which is a fictive buy, consummation of definitive marriage is actual transfer of rights of disposition of property from bride to groom. If the definitive marriage is on a Friday (a date disapproved of for the marriage of a virgin), the marriage has to be consummated before sundown.

(fol. 38a) **משנה ב**: כָּל־שִׁבְעַת הַיָּמִים הוּא זוֹרֵק אֶת הַדָּם וּמַקְטִיר אֶת הַקְּטוֹרֶת וּמֵטִיב אֶת הַנֵּרוֹת וּמַקְרִיב אֶת הָרֹאשׁ וְאֶת הָרַגְלַיִם. וּשְׁאָר כָּל־הַיָּמִים אִם רָצָה לְהַקְרִיב מַקְרִיב שֶׁכֹּהֵן גָּדוֹל מַקְרִיב חֵלֶק בָּרֹאשׁ וְנוֹטֵל חֵלֶק בָּרֹאשׁ:

Mishnah 2: All seven days he pours the blood[159], and burns the incense, and cleans the lights[160], and brings head and feet to the altar[161]. On any other day, if he wants to sacrifice he sacrifices since the High Priest is first in line to sacrifice his part[162] and to take his part[163].

159 Of the daily sacrifice, so that he should be used to it since on the Day of Atonement he has to perform all sacrificial acts unaided.

160 Of the candelabrum in the Temple, including lighting it anew; this also is his duty on the Day of Atonement.

161 The parts which are taken first to the altar (Mishnah 2:7).

162 While in general jobs in the Temple service are distributed by a lottery, the High Priest may perform any duty he chooses before the other jobs are distributed.

163 Even if he did not participate in the sacrificial acts.

(38d line 72) **הלכה ב**: וְאֵינוֹ טָמֵא מִשּׁוּם הַזָּיָיתוֹ. אָמַר רִבִּי יוֹסֵה בֵּירִבִּי בּוּן. מִשֶּׁהָיָה מַקְרִיב קָרְבְּנוֹתָיו הָעוּ מַזִּין עָלָיו.

Halakhah 2: Does he not become impure because of his sprinklings[164]? Rebbi Yose ben Rebbi Abun said, they were sprinkling on him after he had brought his offerings.

164 How can the High Priest officiate if he is sprinkled with the water containing ashes of the Red Cow (Note 95) since the ashes, while cleansing the person impure in the impurity of the dead, are defiling a pure person (*Sifry Num.* 129, based on *Num.* 19:21)? Cf. Note 17.

(38d line 74) שֶׁכֹּהֵן גָּדוֹל מַקְרִיב בָּרֹאשׁ וְנוֹטֵל חֵלֶק בָּרֹאשׁ: הֵיךְ עֲבִידָה. עוֹר זֶה שֶׁלִּי. חַלָּה אַחַת מִשְּׁתֵּי הַלֶּחֶם. שֵׁשׁ חַלּוֹת מִלֶּחֶם הַפָּנִים. הָכָא הוּא נָסֵב כּוּלָּהּ וְכָא הוּא נָסִיב פַּלְגָּא. אָמַר רִבִּי זְעוּרָה. כָּאן לְקָרְבָּן יָחִיד וְכָאן לְקָרְבָּן צִיבּוּר. תַּנֵּי. רִבִּי אוֹמֵר. אוֹמֵר אֲנִי שֶׁלֹּא יִטּוֹל אֶלָּא מֶחֱצָה. אִית תַּנָּיֵי תַנֵּי. רִבִּי אוֹמֵר. אוֹמֵר אֲנִי שֶׁיִּטּוֹל מֶחֱצָה. הֵיךְ עֲבִידָה. הָיָה שָׁם עוֹר אֶחָד. רַבָּנָן אֲמְרֵי. נוֹטֵל אֶת כּוּלּוֹ. רִבִּי אוֹמֵר. אוֹמֵר אֲנִי שֶׁלֹּא יִטּוֹל אֶלָּא מֶחֱצָה. הָיוּ שָׁם אַרְבָּעָה חֲמִשָּׁה עוֹרוֹת. רַבָּנָן אֲמְרֵי. נוֹטֵל אֶחָד. רִבִּי אוֹמֵר. אוֹמֵר אֲנִי. נוֹטֵל מֶחֱצָה. מַה טַעֲמָא דְּרִבִּי. וְהַנּוֹתֶרֶת מִן־הַמִּנְחָה לְאַהֲרֹן וּלְבָנָיו. וְכִי אֵין אָנוּ יוֹדְעִין שֶׁאַהֲרֹן בִּכְלַל בָּנָיו. וּמַה תַּלְמוּד לוֹמַר. לְאַהֲרֹן וּלְבָנָיו. אֶלָּא אָמַר. אַהֲרֹן יָסַב פַּלְגָּא וּבָנָיו יִסְבּוּן פַּלְגָּא.

כְּהָדָא בּוּלֵי וְאִסְטְרַטְגֵי הֲוָה לוֹן קְרִיבוּ. אֲתָא עוֹבְדָא קוֹמֵי רִבִּי וְאָמַר. אֵין בּוּלֵי בִּכְלַל אִסְטְרַטְגֵי. וְלַיי דָּא מִילָה אָמַר. בּוּלֵי וְאִסְטְרַטְגֵי. אֶלָּא אָמַר. אִילֵּין יִתְּנוּן פַּלְגָּא וְאִילֵּין יִתְּנוּן פַּלְגָּא. אָמַר רִבִּי יוֹסֵה בֵּירִבִּי בּוּן. רִבִּי כְּדַעְתֵּיהּ. דְּרִבִּי אָמַר. וְהָיְתָה לְאַהֲרֹן וּלְבָנָיו. לְאַהֲרֹן מֶחֱצָה וּלְבָנָיו מֶחֱצָה.

"Since the High Priest is first in line to sacrifice and to take his part first." How is this? "[165]This skin is mine; one loaf of the Two Breads[166], five loaves of the shew-bread.[167]" In one case he takes everything, in the other case he takes half? Rebbi Ze`ira said, in the first case, a private sacrifice, in the other case, a public sacrifice. It was stated:[165] "Rebbi said, I am saying that he takes only one half." There are Tannaim who state, "Rebbi said, I am saying that he takes one half." How is that? If there was one skin. The rabbis say, he takes it whole. Rebbi said, I am saying that he takes only one half. If there were four, five skins. The rabbis say, he takes one[168]. Rebbi said, I am saying that he takes half. What is Rebbi's reason? *The remainder of the offering is for Aaron and his sons*[169]. Do we not know that Aaron is together with his sons? Why does the verse say[170], *. for Aaron and his sons*? But it means, Aaron shall take half of it and his sons shall take half.

As in the following: The city council[171] and the military district[172] had to bring a gift[173]. The case came before Rebbi who said, the city council is not included in the military district. For which purpose did he say "city council and military district"? But that each party give one half. Rebbi Yose ben

Rebbi Abun said, Rebbi follows his opinion, as Rebbi said, *for Aaron and his sons*, half for Aaron and half for his sons.

165 Tosephta 1:5, Babli 17b.
166 The two leavened breads as public offering on Pentecost.
167 Of the 12 shew breads becoming available every Sabbath.
168 Since the Mishnah states that he takes "a part".
169 *Lev.* 2:3. *Sifra Wayyiqra I Pereq* 11(1).
170 *Lev.* 24:9 (on the shew-bread); *Sifra Emor Pereq* 18(10).

171 Greek βουλή, ἡ.
172 Greek στρατήγιον, τό, "the general's tent", the rural district under the direct command of the local military commander, not under the authority of the city council.
173 The entire district was under the obligation to contribute to a "voluntary" gift, such as crown money at the accession of a new emperor, requested (imposed) by the government.

(39a line 13) מְתִיב רִבִּי בָּא בַּר מָמָל. וְהָא מַתְנִיתָהּ פְּלִיגָא. הָאוֹמֵר. הֲרֵי עָלַי מֵאָה עֶשְׂרוֹנוֹת לְהָבִיאָן בִּשְׁנֵי כֵלִים. מֵבִיא חֲמִשִּׁים בִּכְלִי אֶחָד וַחֲמִשִּׁים בִּכְלִי אֶחָד. וְאִם הֵבִיא שִׁשִּׁים בִּכְלִי אֶחָד וְאַרְבָּעִים בִּכְלִי אֶחָד יָצָא. אִילוּ מִי שֶׁאָמַר. הֲרֵי עָלַי מֵאָה עֶשְׂרוֹנוֹת. סְתָם. וְלֹא אָמַר בְּכַמָּה כֵלִים הוּא מְבִיאָן. וְלֵיידָא מִילָּא אָמַר. לַהֲבִיאָן בִּשְׁנֵי כֵלִים. חֲמִשִּׁים בִּכְלִי אֶחָד וַחֲמִשִּׁים בִּכְלִי אֶחָד. וְתַנֵּי עֲלָהּ. אִם הֵבִיא שִׁשִּׁים בִּכְלִי אֶחָד וְאַרְבָּעִים בִּכְלִי אֶחָד יָצָא. אָמַר רִבִּי יוֹסֵה בֵּירִבִּי בּוּן. מִכֵּיוָן שֶׁעַד שִׁשִּׁים יְכוֹלִין לִיבָּלֵל כְּמִי שֶׁקָּבַע לוֹ שִׁשִּׁים מִשָּׁעָה רִאשׁוֹנָה. לֹא צוּרְכָא דְלֹא אֲמַר. הֲרֵי עָלַי שִׁשִּׁים עֶשְׂרוֹנוֹת לַהֲבִיאָן בִּשְׁנֵי כֵלִים. מֵבִיא שְׁלֹשִׁים בִּכְלִי אֶחָד וּשְׁלֹשִׁים בִּכְלִי אֶחָד. וְאִם הֵבִיא אַרְבָּעִים בִּכְלִי אֶחָד וְעֶשְׂרִים בִּכְלִי אֶחָד יָצָא. אַשְׁכַּח תַּנֵּי כֵן.

רִבִּי חֲנַנְיָה חַבְרוֹן דְּרַבָּנִין בָּעֵי. לְמִידִין מִידַּת הַדִּין מֵעִישְׂרוֹן. [אַשְׁכַּח תַּנֵּי. וְהוּא לָמַד מִידַּת הַדִּין מֵעִישְׂרוֹן.] אָמַר רִבִּי אָבוּן. בִּלְבַד שֶׁלֹּא יְבִיאֵם בִּשְׁלֹשָׁה כֵלִים. [וְרִבִּי בָּא בַּר מָמָל אָמַר. אֲפִילוּ בְּכַמָּה כֵלִים.]

Rebbi Abba bar Mamal objected: Does not a *baraita* disagree? "[174]If somebody says, I am taking on me the obligation to bring 100 *esronim*[175] in two vessels, he shall bring 50 in one vessel each. But if he brought 60[176] in one vessel and 40 in the other, he has fulfilled his obligation." Somebody could say, I am taking on me the obligation to bring 100 *esronim*, simply, without specifying the number of vessels in which be brings them; why does he specify "to bring them in two vessels"? To bring them 50 in one vessel each/ And we have stated on this, if he brought 60 in one vessel and 40 in the other, he has fulfilled his obligation[177]! .Rebbi Yose ben Rebbi Abun said, since up to 60 they can be mixed[178], it is as if from the start he fixed it at 60. It would be necessary to say, "if somebody says, I am taking on me the obligation to bring 60 *esronim* in two vessels, he shall bring 30 in one vessel each. But if he brought 40 in one vessel and 20 in the other, he has fulfilled his obligation.[179]" It was found stated thus[180].

Rebbi Ḥananiah the colleague of the rabbis asked: May one infer law of obligations from *issaron*[181]? It was found stated[182], "he inferred law of obligations from *issaron*." Rebbi Abun said, only he should not bring them[183] in three vessels. Rebbi Abba bar Mamal said, even in many vessels.

174 Tosephta *Menahot* 12:7.

175 The flour offerings in the Temple were all multiples of the *issaron*, one tenth of an *ephah*, or 3/10 of a *se`ah*, approximately 3.6 liter.

176 As quoted later in this paragraph, since flour offerings have to be brought *mixed with oil,* it is a rule (Mishnah *Menahot* 12:4) that the maximum flour offering which can be brought in one vessel is 60 *esronim*.

177 This is the essence of R. Abba bar Mamal's objection to Rebbi's interpretation of the verse. Since even if it should be clear that the intent was to split evenly, it is not a strict condition, therefore Rebbi's inference that the verse prescribes an even split between Aaron and his sons is not justified.

178 Mishnah *Menahot* 12:4; Tosephta 12:8-9/

179 R. Abba bar Mamal's objection could only be substantiated by a *baraita* which does not involve 60 *esronim*.

180 Therefore Rebbi's argument has to be rejected.

181 Since the Temple rules belong to ritual law, but the right of the High Priest is a matter of monetary claim, do they necessarily follow identical rules?

182 There was found a *baraita* which supports R. Abba bar Mamal. It is not clear which subject and which person the *baraita* refers to.

183 The person offering 60 *esronim*.

(39a line 26) רִבִּי יוֹסֵי בֵּירִבִּי בּוּן בְּשֵׁם רִבִּי יְבוֹשֻׁעַ בֶּן לֵוִי. בְּכָל־יוֹם כֹּהֵן גָּדוֹל מִתְלַבֵּשׁ בְּכֵלָיו וּבָא וּמַקְרִיב תָּמִיד שֶׁלְשַׁחַר. אִם יֵשׁ שָׁם נְדָרִים וּנְדָבוֹת הוּא מַקְרִיבָן וְהוֹלֵךְ בְּתוֹךְ בֵּיתוֹ וּבָא וּמַקְרִיב תָּמִיד שֶׁלְבֵּין הָעַרְבַּיִם וּבָא וְלָן בְּלִשְׁכַּת פַּלְהֶדְרִין. רִבִּי עוּקְבָה בְּשֵׁם רִבִּי יְהוֹשֻׁעַ בֶּן לֵוִי. לֹא הָיָה עוֹשֶׂה כֵן אֶלָּא בַשַּׁבָּתוֹת וּבְיָמִים טוֹבִים.

אֶת תַּנֵּי תַנֵּי. הַצִּיץ מְרֻצֶּה עַל מִצְחוֹ. אֶת תַּנֵּי תַנֵּי. אֲפִילוּ בְזָוִית. מָאן דְּאָמַר. הַצִּיץ מְרֻצֶּה עַל מִצְחוֹ. וְהָיָה עַל־מִצְחוֹ תָּמִיד. וּמָאן דְּאָמַר. אֲפִילוּ בְזָוִית. מִן הָדָא דְיוֹם הַכִּיפּוּרִים. מָאן דְּאָמַר. הַצִּיץ מְרֻצֶּה עַל מִצְחוֹ. מְסַיֵּיעַ לְרִבִּי יוֹסֵי בֵּירִבִּי בּוּן. מָאן דְּאָמַר. אֲפִילוּ בְזָוִית. מְסַיֵּיעַ לְרִבִּי עוּקְבָה.

Rebbi Yose ben Rebbi Abun in the name of Rebbi Joshua ben Levi: Every day[184] the High Priest dresses in his robes[185], comes, and sacrifices the daily morning sacrifice. If there are vows or voluntary sacrifices[186], he offers them. Then he goes to his house, and returns to bring the daily evening sacrifice, and comes to stay overnight in the Palhedrin lodge. Rebbi Uqba in the name of Rebbi Joshua ben Levi: He did this only on Sabbath and holidays[187].

There are Tannaim who state: the diadem[188] propitiates on his forehead. There are Tannaim who state: even in a corner. He who says, the diadem propitiates on his forehead, *it always shall be on his forehead*[189]. But he who says, even in a corner, from the Day of Atonement[190]. He who says, the diadem propitiates on his forehead, supports Rebbi Yose ben Rebbi Abun; he who says, even in a corner, supports Rebbi Uqba.

184 Of the seven days of preparation.
185 The eight garments prescribed for the High Priest.
186 The legal difference between a vow and a voluntary offering, which also needs dedication, is that a vow is formulated as a personal obligation, "I am taking upon me the obligation to offer such and such a sacrifice." In that case, if the animal selected for the sacrifice becomes disqualified for any reason, the maker of the vow has to bring a replacement. A voluntary offering is a dedication, "this animal shall be such-and-such a sacrifice."

If the animal becomes disqualified, no replacement is due.
187 He seems to imply every Sabbath and holiday during the year, including New Year's Day and the Sabbath preceding the day of Atonement.
188 The diadem (*Ex.* 28:36-38) which is worn *to eliminate iniquities of sancta*, to legitimate sacrifices even if they do not completely satisfy the prescribed rules.
189 *Ex.* 29:38.
190 When the High Priest officiates in white robes without the diadem.

(fol. 38a) **משנה ג**: מְסָרוּ לוֹ זְקֵנִים מִזִּקְנֵי בֵית דִּין קוֹרִין לְפָנָיו בְּסֵדֶר הַיּוֹם וְאוֹמְרִים לוֹ אִישִׁי כֹּהֵן גָּדוֹל קְרָא אַתָּה בְּפִיךָ שֶׁמָּא שָׁכַחְתָּ אוֹ שֶׁמָּא לֹא לָמַדְתָּ. עֶרֶב יוֹם הַכִּפּוּרִים שַׁחֲרִית מַעֲמִידִין אוֹתוֹ בְּשַׁעַר הַמִּזְרָח וּמַעֲבִירִין לְפָנָיו פָּרִים וְאֵילִים וּכְבָשִׂים כְּדֵי שֶׁיְּהֵא מַכִּיר וְרָגִיל בַּעֲבוֹדָה:

Mishnah 3: One sends him Elders from the Elders of the Court[191]; they read before him the Order of the Day[192] and say to him, Sir High Priest, read yourself with your mouth, maybe you forgot, or maybe you never learned. In the morning of the eve of the Day of Atonement one makes him stand at the Eastern Gate and brings before him oxen, and he-goats, and sheep, so he should recognize and be used to the service.

191 The Pharisaic High Court. The Mishnah has to be dated to Herodian times since the Hasmonean kings all acted as High Priests.

192 *Lev.* 16.

(39a line 36) **הלכה ג**׃ שֶׁמָּא שָׁכַחְתָּ אוֹ שֶׁמָּא לֹא לָמַדְתָּ. לֹא כֵן תַּנֵּי. וְהַכֹּהֵן הַגָּדוֹל מֵאֶחָיו. שֶׁתְּהֵא גְדוּלָּתוֹ מֵאֶחָיו. אֲשֶׁר־יוּצַק עַל־רֹאשׁוֹ ׀ שֶׁמֶן הַמִּשְׁחָה. רִבִּי אוֹמֵר. בְּנוֹי בְּעוֹשֶׁר בְּחָכְמָה וּבְמַרְאֶה. אָמַר רִבִּי יוֹסֵי בֵּירִבִּי בּוּן. כָּאן בָּרִאשׁוֹן וְכָאן בַּשֵּׁינִי.

Halakhah 3: "Maybe you forgot, or maybe you never learned." Did we not state[193], *"the priest, greater than his brethren*[194]*, that his greatness be from his brethren*[195]*, on whose head the anointing oil was poured.* Rebbi says, in beauty, in riches, in wisdom[196], and in looks." Rebbi Yose ben Rebbi Abun said, there in the first [Temple], here in the second[197].

193 Tosephta 1:6.
194 *Lev.* 21:10.
195 If he was not rich, the other Cohanim should donate money to make him rich.
196 Therefore an ignorant High Priest should be an impossibility.
197 Since these High Priests were not anointed (cf. *Horaiot* 3:4), the verse does not necessarily apply to Second Temple High Priests.

(39a line 39) מַעֲמִידִין אוֹתוֹ בְּשַׁעֲרֵי מִזְרָח. אֵיכָן הָיוּ מַעֲמִידִין אוֹתוֹ. מִבִּפְנִים אוֹ מִבַּחוּץ. אִין תֵּימַר. מִבִּפְנִים. כַּיי דְתַנִּינָן תַּמָּן. חָמֵשׁ טְבִילוֹת הָיָה שָׁם בְּאוֹתוֹ הַיּוֹם. אַחַת שֶׁלֹּא הָיָה אָדָם נִכְנָס לָעֲזָרָה לַעֲבוֹדָה אֲפִלּוּ טָהוֹר עַד שֶׁיְּהֵא טוֹבֵל. וְאַרְבַּע מַחֲמַת יוֹם הַכִּיפּוּרִים. אִין תֵּימַר. מִבַּחוּץ. כּוּלְּהוֹן מַחְמַת יוֹם הַכִּיפּוּרִים.

מַעֲבִירִין לְפָנָיו פָּרִים וְאֵילִים וּכְבָשִׂים. וְלָמָּה לֹא אָמַר. שָׂעִיר. אָמַר רִבִּי בָּא קַרְטִיגְנָא. בְּלֹא כָךְ אֵינוֹ זָקוּק לְהַעֲרוֹת. אַשְׁכַּח תַּנֵּי. וְשָׂעִיר.

"One makes him stand at the Eastern Gates." Where does one let him stand, inside or outside? If you are saying inside, what we stated there[198], "five immersions were there on that day, one because nobody entered the

Temple courtyard for service, even if he was pure, unless he immersed himself, and four because of the Day of Atonement." If you are saying outside, all of them were because of the Day of Atonement.

"One brings before him oxen, and he-goats, and sheep." Why did he not say, a goat[199]? Rebbi Abba from Carthage said, is he not anyhow obliged to pour?[200] It was found stated, "and a goat"[201].

198 A reformulation of Mishnah 3:3. Since the Mishnah here states that one lets him stand at the gate but not that he has first to immerse himself in a *miqweh*, it follows that a pure person may enter the Temple courtyard without an additional immersion if he does not intend to serve there. Therefore if the High Priest was standing inside the gate, the Mishnah here agrees with the Mishnah there that the first immersion of the High Priest on the Day of Atonement is not connected with the special rules of that day.

But if he was standing outside, no immersion is required, and nothing can be inferred from the Mishnah here.
199 Which also is part of the service of the Day of Atonement.
200 Even though this sentence seems to be part of this Halakhah in a badly preserved Genizah fragment (Ginzberg p. 117), it does not belong here but is a statement (quoted there in the name of R. Mana) in Halakhah 5:6 (Note 187).
201 Babli 18a.

(fol. 38a) **משנה ד**: כָּל־שִׁבְעַת הַיָּמִים לֹא הָיוּ מוֹנְעִין מִמֶּנּוּ מַאֲכָל וּמִשְׁתֶּה. עֶרֶב יוֹם הַכִּפּוּרִים עִם חֲשֵׁיכָה לֹא הָיוּ מַנִּיחִין אוֹתוֹ לוֹכַל הַרְבֵּה שֶׁהַמַּאֲכָל מֵבִיא אֶת הַשֵּׁינָה:

Mishnah 4: All of the seven days one does not prevent him from food and drink. On the Eve of the Day of Atonement one does not allow him to eat much because food induces sleep[202].

202 And in the following night he was not permitted to sleep.

(39a line 46) **הלכה ד**: תַּנֵּי. לֹא הָיוּ מַנִּיחִין אוֹתוֹ לוֹכַל לֹא חָלָב וְלֹא בֵצִים וְלֹא גְבִינָה וְלֹא בָשָׂר שָׁמֵן וְלֹא יַיִן וְלֹא יָשָׁן וְלֹא קוֹנְדִּיטוֹן וְלֹא גְרִיסִין שֶׁל פּוֹל וְלֹא עֲדָשִׁים. שְׁמוּאֵל אָמַר. וְלֹא אֶתְרוֹג. וְלֹא כָל־דָּבָר שֶׁהוּא מַרְגִּיל לְזִיבָה. אַף עַל פִּי כֵן הָיוּ קוֹרִין עָלָיו אֶת הַפָּסוּק הַזֶּה. אִם־יְיָ לֹא־יִבְנֶה בַיִת וגו׳. וְלֹא מִן הַנִּיסִּים שֶׁהָיוּ נַעֲשִׂין בְּבֵית בַּמִּקְדָּשׁ הֵן. אָמַר רִבִּי אָבוּן. עַל שֵׁם לֹא תְנַסּוּ. אָמַר רִבִּי יוֹסֵי בֵּירִבִּי בּוּן. כָּאן בָּרִאשׁוֹן וְכָאן בַּשֵּׁינִי.

Halakhah 4: It was stated[201]: One allows him neither milk, nor eggs, nor cheese, nor fat meat, nor old wine, nor spiced wine, nor bean groats, nor lentils, Samuel said, nor *citrus medica*, nor anything which causes emission of semen. Nevertheless one was quoting for him the verse[203], *if the Eternal does not build the house*, etc. But was this not of the miracles which happened in the Temple[204]? Rebbi Abun said, because of *you shall not try*[205]. Rebbi Yose ben Rebbi Abun said, there in the first {Temple}, here in the second[206].

203 Ps. 127:1. *If the Eternal does not build the house, in vain toil its builders.*
204 Enumerated in Mishnah *Avot* 5:5. One of the ten miracles was that never was the High Priest incapacitated by an emission of semen on the Day of Atonement.
205 *Deut.* 6:16.
206 Mishnah *Avot* 5:5 applies only to the First Temple.

(fol. 28a) **משנה ה**: מְסָרוּהוּ זִקְנֵי בֵית דִּין לְזִקְנֵי כְהוּנָּה הוֹלִיכוּהוּ לַעֲלִיַּית בֵּית אַבְטִינָס הִשְׁבִּיעוּהוּ וְנִפְטְרוּ וְהָלְכוּ לָהֶם. אָמְרוּ לוֹ אִישִׁי כֹּהֵן גָּדוֹל אָנוּ שְׁלוּחֵי בֵית דִּין וְאַתָּה שְׁלוּחֵנוּ וּשְׁלִיחַ בֵּית דִּין מַשְׁבִּיעִין אָנוּ עָלֶיךָ בְּמִי שֶׁשִּׁכֵּן שְׁמוֹ בַּבַּיִת הַזֶּה שֶׁלֹּא תְשַׁנֶּה דָבָר מִכָּל־מַה שֶּׁאָמַרְנוּ לְךָ. הוּא פוֹרֵשׁ וּבוֹכֶה וְהֵן פּוֹרְשִׁין וּבוֹכִין:

Mishnah 5: The Elders of the Court hand him over to the Elders of the priesthood; they lead him to the upper floor of the house of Eutinoos[207] They adjure him; this finishes their task and they leave. They say to him, Sir High Priest, we are the agents of the Court, and you are our agent and the Court's agent. We adjure you by Him Who let His Name dwell in this House that you will not change anything of all we told you. He turns aside and cries, and they turn aside and cry[208].

207 The place where the incense was prepared for use in the Temple.(Mishnah 3:11, *Tamid* 1:1.) They had first to instruct him in the Pharisee interpretation of the verses since the matter of presentation of the incense in the Temple was the only matter of controversy between Sadducees and Pharisees in the service of the day of Atonement. Then they had to make him swear to follow the Pharisaic rules.
208 As explained in the Halakhah.

HALAKHAH FIVE

(39a line 52) **הלכה ה׃** עַל גַּבֵּי שַׁעַר הַמַּיִם הָיִיתָהּ וְסָמוּךְ לְלִשְׁכָּתוֹ הָיִיתָהּ. הוּא פּוֹרֵשׁ וּבוֹכֶה. שֶׁנֶּחְשַׁד. וְהֵן פּוֹרְשִׁין וּבוֹכִין׃ שֶׁצָּרְכוּ לְכָךְ. וְלָמָּה מַשְׁבִּיעִין אוֹתוֹ. מִפְּנֵי הַבַּיְיתוֹסִין. שֶׁהָיוּ אוֹמְרִין. יַקְטִיר מִבַּחוּץ וְיַכְנִיס מִבִּפְנִים.

Halakhah 5: It[209] was located on top the the Water Gate[210] and close to his lodge.

"He turns aside and cries," that he was suspected. "And they turn aside and cry," that they needed to do this[211]. And why does one adjure him? Because of the Boethusians, who were saying that he starts the incense outside and brings it inside[212].

---

209 The place where incense was prepared.
210 The fourth gate on the South side of the Temple precinct proper. Babli 19a.
211 Babli 19b, Tosephta 1:8.
212 The problem is *Lev. 16:13: He shall put the incense on the fire before the Eternal, and the incense cloud shall cover the cover which is on the testimonials so that he should not die.* The Pharisaic interpretation is that the first part of the verse implies that the incense should be put into the fire inside the Holiest of Holies, which is *before the Eternal*. The Boethusian interpretation is based on the second part of the verse, that the cloud should cover him already at the entry into the Holiest of Holies.

(39a line 55) מַעֲשֶׂה בְּאֶחָד שֶׁהִקְטִיר מִבַּחוּץ וְהִכְנִיס מִבִּפְנִים. וּכְשֶׁיָּצָא אָמַר לְאָבִיו. אַף עַל פִּי שֶׁהָיִיתֶם דּוֹרְשִׁין כָּל־יְמֵיכֶם לֹא עֲשִׂיתֶם עַד שֶׁעָמַד אוֹתוֹ הָאִישׁ וְעָשָׂה. אָמַר לוֹ. אַף עַל פִּי שֶׁהָיִינוּ דּוֹרְשִׁין כָּל־יְמֵינוּ אֲבָל כִּרְצוֹן חֲכָמִים הָיִינוּ עוֹשִׂין. תְּמִיהַּ אֲנִי אִם יַאֲרִיךְ אוֹתוֹ הָאִישׁ יָמִים בָּעוֹלָם. אָמְרוּ. לֹא בָאוּ יָמִים קַלִּין עַד שֶׁמֵּת. וְיֵשׁ אוֹמְרִין. יָצָא חוֹטְמוֹ מְזַנֵּק תּוֹלָעִים וּכְמִין פַּרְסַת עֵגֶל עָלַת בְּתוֹךְ מִצְחוֹ.

[211]It happened that one person started the incense outside and brought it inside. When he left, he said to his father, even though you were interpreting all your days, you did not act until this man came and acted. He answered him, even though you were interpreting all our days, we acted only following the will of the Sages. I am wondering whether this man will have many days in the world. After a short time he died. But some are saying, his nose gushed out worms and something like a calf's hoof grew in his brain.

(39a line 61) אִית דְּבָעֵי מֵימַר. הִיא דְפָרָה הִיא דְסוּפָה הִיא דְיוֹם הַכִּיפּוּרִים. רִבִּי סִימוֹן לֹא אָמַר כֵּן. אֶלָּא אוֹ דְפָרָה וּדְסוּפָה חַד וּדְכִיפּוּרִים חַד. אוֹ דְפָרָה וּדְכִיפּוּרִים חַד וּדְסוּפָה חַד.

מָאן דְּאָמַר. לֹא בָאוּ יָמִים קַלִּים עַד שֶׁמֵּת. תַּלְתֵּיהוֹן עֲבַד. מָאן דְּאָמַר. יָצָא חוּטְמוֹ מְזַנֵּק תּוֹלָעִים וּכְמִין פַּרְסַת יָצָאת בְּתוֹךְ מִצְחוֹ. כְּמָאן דְּאָמַר. אוֹ דְּפָרָה וּדְסוּכָּה חַד וּדְכִיפּוּרִים חַד. אוֹ דְפָרָה וּדְכִיפּוּרִים חַד וּדְסוּכָּה חַד. צָוְוחָה עֲלֵיהֶן הָעֲזָרָה. צְאוּ מִיכָּן בְּנֵי עֵלִי. טִימַּאתֶּם בֵּית אֱלֹהֵינוּ. בּוֹ בַיּוֹם נִפְגְּמָה קֶרֶן הַמִּזְבֵּחַ וְנָתְנוּ עָלָיו גּוּשׁ שֶׁלְּמֶלַח שֶׁלֹּא יְהֵא נִרְאֶה כְפָגוּם. שֶׁכָּל־מִזְבֵּחַ שֶׁאֵין לוֹ קֶרֶן וְסוֹבֵב וִיסוֹד פָּסוּל הוּא.

1 דיום הכיפורים | כ דכיפורים   4 יצאת | כ -   ודכיפורים | כ ודסוכה   ודסוכה | כ ודכיפורים

בָּעוּן קוֹמֵי רִבִּי אַבָּהוּ. וְהָא כְתִיב. וְכָל־אָדָ֞ם לֹא־יִהְיֶ֣ה | בְּאֹ֣הֶל מוֹעֵ֗ד בְּבֹא֛וֹ לְכַפֵּ֥ר בַּקֹּ֖דֶשׁ עַד־צֵאת֑וֹ. אֲפִילוּ אוֹתָן שֶׁכָּתוּב בָּהֶן וּדְמוּת פְּנֵיהֶם פְּנֵי אָדָם לֹא יִהְיֶה בְּאֹהֶל מוֹעֵד. אָמַר לוֹן. בְּשָׁעָה שֶׁהוּא נִכְנָס כְּדַרְכּוֹ.

2 מועד | כ מועד בבואו לכפר בקודש

[213]Some want to say, he was the same for the Cow[214], on Tabernacles[215], and on the Day of Atonement. Rebbi Simon does not say so, but either the Cow and Tabernacles was one and Atonement one, or Cow and Atonement was one and Tabernacles one. He who said, after a short time he died, he did all three. He who said, his nose gushed out worms and something like a calf's hoof grew in his brain, follows him who said, either Cow and Tabernacles was one and Atonement one, or Cow and Atonement was one and Tabernacles one. The Courtyard cried about them, get out of here, sons of Eli, you defiled our God's Temple[216]. "On that day[217], the corner of the altar was damaged and they put a block of salt there lest it should look deficient since any altar without corner, or walkway[218], or base[219] is disqualified."

They asked before Rebbi Abbahu: Is it not written[220], *nobody shall be in the Tent of Meeting during his coming to atone in the sanctuary until he leaves*, not even those about whom it is written[221], *the shapes of their faces are human shapes* shall not be in the Tent of Meeting[222]? He answered them, if he enters following normal rules

213 This text also appears in *Sukkah* 4:8 (ב). It is an intellectual construct, rather than a historical report.

214 Where the Sadducees insisted that the Cohen who burns the Red Cow must be pure from the preceding sundown. However, it is difficult to square what is reported in Tosephta *Parah* 3:8 with what is presumed here: "It happened that a Sadducee was pure from the preceding sundown when he came to burn the Cow, but Rabban Johanan ben Zakkai realized it; he came and leaned both of his hands on him and told him, Sir High Priest, how wonderful you are as High Priest, go and immerse yourself . He went down and immersed himself. After he came

back he grated his earlobe and said to him, Ben Zakkai, when I shall be free to deal with you; he answered him, if you will be free. It was not three days before they put him in the grave."

Biblical impurity is only original impurity and derivative impurity in the first degree. Rabbinic impurity has derivative impurity in the second degree for unwashed hands, third degree impurity for heave, and fourth degree for sacrifices. Therefore, the intrinsically pure Ben Zakkai (who before the destruction of the Temple was not Rabban), by putting his second degree impure hands on the priest defiled the latter for *sacra* and forced him to immerse himself in a *miqweh*. Our sources seem to describe the Sadducee position correctly; cf. Dead Sea Scrolls fragment 4Q394, lines 16-18.

215 Mishnah *Sukkah* 4:8, Tosephta *Sukkah* 3:16. The popular ceremony of water offering on the altar has no explicit foundation in the biblical text and was opposed by Sadducees (possibly only by the Boethusian sect.) A priest who poured out the water in contempt of the rite was killed by the *etrogim* (*citrus medica*) which the people threw at him.

216 Babli *Pesahim* 57a, *Keritut* 28a.

217 At Tabernacles, when the people threw their *etrogim* at the priest standing on the altar. Tosephta *Sukkah* 3:16; Babli *Sukkah* 48b.

218 The extension at half-height of the altar, allowing a priest to walk around the altar and pour blood at its four corners.

219 A hollow at the base of the altar into which remnants of sacrificial blood were poured.

220 *Lev.* 16:17.

221 *Ez.* 1:10.

222 If the offending priest was hit on his head by a calf's foot it must have been by one of the four-headed angels seen by Ezechiel whose feet are calves' feet (*Ez.* 1:7).

(39a line 74) כָּתוּב וְהֵבִיא מִבֵּית לַפָּרֹכֶת: וְנָתַן אֶת־הַקְּטֹרֶת עַל־הָאֵשׁ לִפְנֵי יְיָ. שֶׁלֹּא יְתַקֵּן מִבַּחוּץ וְיַכְנִיס מִבִּפְנִים. שֶׁהֲרֵי הַצַּדּוּקִין אוֹמְרִין. יְתַקֵּן מִבַּחוּץ וְיַכְנִיס. אִם לִפְנֵי בָשָׂר וָדָם עוֹשִׂין כֵּן קַל וָחוֹמֶר לִפְנֵי הַמָּקוֹם. וְאוֹמֵר כִּי בֶּעָנָן אֵרָאֶה עַל־הַכַּפֹּרֶת: אָמְרוּ לָהֶן חֲכָמִים. וַהֲלֹא כְּבָר נֶאֱמַר וְנָתַן אֶת־הַקְּטֹרֶת עַל־הָאֵשׁ לִפְנֵי יְיָ. אֵינוֹ נוֹתֵן אֶלָּא מִבִּפְנִים. [אִם כֵּן לָמָּה נֶאֱמַר כִּי בֶעָנָן אֵרָאֶה עַל־הַכַּפֹּרֶת.] מְלַמֵּד שֶׁהוּא נוֹתֵן בָּהּ מַעֲלֵה עָשָׁן. וּמִנַּיִן שֶׁהוּא נוֹתֵן בָּהּ מַעֲלֵה עָשָׁן. תַּלְמוּד לוֹמַר וְכִסָּה | עֲנַן הַקְּטֹרֶת [אֶת־הַכַּפֹּרֶת אֲשֶׁר עַל־הָעֵדוּת וְלֹא יָמוּת:] הָא אִם לֹא נָתַן מַעֲלֵה עָשָׁן אוֹ שֶׁחִיסֵּר אַחַת מִסַּמְמָנֶיהָ חַיָּיב מִיתָה. וְלֹא יָמוּת הֲרֵי זֶה עוֹנֶשׁ. כִּי בֶעָנָן אֵרָאֶה עַל־הַכַּפֹּרֶת: הֲרֵי זֶה אַזְהָרָה.

אָמַר רִבִּי אֶלְעָזָר בֵּירִבִּי שִׁמְעוֹן. יָכוֹל עוֹנֶשׁ וְאַזְהָרָה נֶאֶמְרוּ קוֹדֶם לְמִיתַת בְּנֵי אַהֲרֹן. תַּלְמוּד לוֹמַר אַחֲרֵי מוֹת שְׁנֵי בְּנֵי אַהֲרֹן. אִי אַחֲרֵי מוֹת שְׁנֵי בְּנֵי אַהֲרֹן יָכוֹל שְׁנֵיהֶן נֶאֶמְרוּ אַחֲרֵי מִיתַת שְׁנֵי בְּנֵי אַהֲרֹן. תַּלְמוּד לוֹמַר כִּי בֶעָנָן אֵרָאֶה עַל־הַכַּפֹּרֶת: הָא כֵיצַד. אַזְהָרָה נֶאֶמְרָה קוֹדֶם לְמִיתַת שְׁנֵי בְּנֵי אַהֲרֹן. וְעוֹנֶשׁ נֶאֱמַר לְאַחַר מִיתַת שְׁנֵי בְּנֵי אַהֲרֹן. אָמַר רִבִּי זְעוּרָה. כִּי בֶעָנָן נִרְאֵיתִי אֵין כָּתוּב כָּאן אֶלָּא אֵרָאֶה. מִיכָּן שֶׁאֵין הַקָּדוֹשׁ בָּרוּךְ הוּא עוֹנֵשׁ אֶלָּא אִם כֵּן הִזְהִיר.

[223]It is written[224] *and he shall bring it inside the curtain, and put the incense in the fire before the Eternal,* that he should not prepare outside and bring inside, since the Sadducees are saying, he shall prepare outside and then bring inside. If one does this before flesh and blood, *a fortiori* before the Omnipresent. Also it says[225], *for in a cloud I shall appear over the cover.* The Sages said to them, has it not already been said, *he shall put the incense in the fire before the Eternal;* only inside he puts it on. If it is so, why was it said, *for in a cloud I shall appear over the cover*? This teaches that he has to put in smoke-creating herb. From where that he has to add smoke-creating herb? The verse says[226], *the incense shall cover the cover over the chest*[227], *lest he die.* If he failed to add smoke-creating herb or left out any of its ingredients he has committed a deadly sin[228]. *Lest he die,* that is the punishment. *For in a cloud I* shall appear over the cover. this is the warning.

[229]Rebbi Eleazar ben Rebbi Simeon said, I could think that punishment and warning had been said before the death of the two sons of Aaron, the verse says[230], *after the death of the two sons of Aaron.* If *after the death of the two sons of Aaron.* I could think that both had been said after the death of the two sons of Aaron, the verse says, *for in a cloud I shall appear over the cover.* How is that? The warning was said before the death of the two sons of Aaron, but the punishment was said after the death of the two sons of Aaron, Rebbi Ze'ura said, it does not say "because in a cloud I was seen over the cover," but *I shall be seen.* From here that the Holy One, praise to Him, does not punish unless he had warned[231].

223 Babli 53a, *Sifra Ahare Pereq* 3(11).
224 *Lev.* 16:12-13.
225 *Lev.* 16:2.
226 *Lev.* 16:13.
227 Corrector's misquote.
228 Babli *Keritut* 6a.
229 *Sifra Ahare Introduction* (13).
230 *Lev.* 16:1.
231 The tannaitic position is rejected. While the death of the two sons of Aaron made an atonement ceremony necessary, their deaths cannot be punishment for infractions of laws not yet promulgated.

(fol. 38a)) **משנה ו**: אִם הָיָה חָכָם דּוֹרֵשׁ. וְאִם לָאו תַּלְמִידֵי חֲכָמִים דּוֹרְשִׁין לְפָנָיו. אִם רָגִיל לִקְרוֹת קוֹרֵא. וְאִם לָאו קוֹרִין לְפָנָיו. וּבַמֶּה קוֹרִין לְפָנָיו. בְּאִיּוֹב וּבְעֶזְרָא וּבְדִבְרֵי הַיָּמִים. זְכַרְיָה בֶן קְבוּטָל אוֹמֵר פְּעָמִים הַרְבֵּה קָרִיתִי לְפָנָיו בְּדָנִיֵּאל:

Mishnah 6: If he was a scholar, he preaches[232]; otherwise scholars preach before him. If he was used to reciting[233] he recites; otherwise one recites before him. What does one recite before him? Job, Ezra, and Chronicles. Zacariah ben Qebutal says, many times I recited before him from Daniel.

232 Explains biblical verses either legalistically or as homilies.

233 As technical term, קורא always means reading biblical texts with the masoretic accents. (which in those times were not written but had to be memorized.)

(39b line 14) **הלכה ו**: תַּנֵּי. בְּמִשְׁלֵי וּבִתְהִילִים מִפְּנֵי שֶׁטַּעֲמָן מֵפִיג אֶת הַשֵּׁינָה. כַּהֲנָא שְׁאַל לְרַב. מַה נִיתְנֵי. קְבוּטָר קְבוּטָל. וַהֲוָה קָאִים מַצְלֵי וַחֲוֵי לֵיהּ בְּאֶצְבַּעְתֵּיהּ. צְפַר קְבּוֹטָר

Halakhah 6: It was stated, in Proverbs and Psalms, since their interest makes sleep disappear.

Cahana asked Rav, how shall we state, Qebutar or Qebutal[234]? He was standing in prayer and indicated to him by his finger, a bird, *kabōtar*[235].

234 Babli 19b; there the question is not between *r* and *l* but between *b* and *p* with opposite readings in the printed edition and the Munich ms.

235 "Dove". *kabōtar* in Pahlevi, کبوتر *kabūtar* in Farsi.

(fol. 38a) **משנה ז**: בִּיקֵּשׁ לְהִתְנַמְנֵם פִּרְחֵי כְהוּנָּה מַכִּין לְפָנָיו בְּאֶצְבַּע צְרָדָה וְאוֹמְרִים לוֹ אִישִׁי כֹהֵן גָּדוֹל עֲמוֹד וְהָפֵג אַחַת עַל הָרִצְפָּה. וּמַעֲסִיקִין אוֹתוֹ עַד שֶׁיַּגִּיעַ זְמַן הַשְּׁחִיטָה:

Mishnah 7: If he became sleepy, the young priests drum before him with a dry finger and say to him, Sir High Priest, stand up and take it easy once on the floor. One occupies him until the time of slaughter.

(39b line 17) **הלכה ז**: רַב חוּנָה אָמַר. בְּאֶצְבַּע צְרָדָה בַּפֶּה. וְרִבִּי יוֹחָנָן אָמַר. בְּאֶצְבַּע צְרָדָה בְּיָד. מַתְנִיתָה פְלִיגָה עַל וְרִבִּי יוֹחָנָן. בַּפֶּה. לֹא בְנֶבֶל וְלֹא בְכִינּוֹר. פָּתַר לָהּ. נְעִימָה הַנֶּאֱמֶרֶת בְּאֶצְבַּע צְרָדָה אוֹמְרָהּ בַּפֶּה. לֹא בְנֶבֶל וְלֹא בְכִינּוֹר.

Halakhah 7: Rav Huna said, "with a dry finger" orally. But Rebbi Johanan said, "with a dry finger", with the hand. A *baraita* disagrees with Rebbi Johanan "orally, not with harp nor with lute.[236]" He explains it, the melody indicated by the dry finger one says orally, not with harp nor with lute.

236 Tosephta 1:9, Babli 19b.

(fol. 38a) **משנה ח**: בְּכָל־יוֹם תּוֹרְמִין אֶת הַמִּזְבֵּחַ מִקְרוֹת הַגֶּבֶר אוֹ בְסָמוּךְ לוֹ מִלְּפָנָיו אוֹ מִלְּאַחֲרָיו. וּבְיוֹם הַכִּפּוּרִים מֵחֲצוֹת. וּבָרְגָלִים מֵאַשְׁמוּרָה הָרִאשׁוֹנָה. לֹא הָיְתָה קְרוֹת הַגֶּבֶר מַגַּעַת עַד שֶׁהָיְתָה עֲזָרָה מְלֵיאָה מִיִּשְׂרָאֵל:

Mishnah 8: Every day one removes ashes from the altar[237] about at the call of the cock, before it or after it. But on the Day of Atonement at midnight[238], and on holidays after the first watch[239]. The cock did not crow[240] before the Courtyard was full of Israel.

237 The removal of the ashes from the previous day is the required action before the service of the new day may start; *Lev.* 6:1-6.

238 To let the High Priest start the office of the day at the earliest possible moment.

2398 The end of the first third of the night.

On holidays not only were there many additional public offerings but also a very great number of private holiday offerings, taking up the entire day.

240 On holidays and the Day of Atonement.

(39b line 20) **הלכה ח**: אָמַר רִבִּי מָנָא. לֹא מִסְתַּבְּרָא. דְּלֹא יוֹם הַכִּפּוּרִים מֵאַשְׁמוּרָה הָרִאשׁוֹנָה. וּבָרְגָלִים מֵחֲצוֹת. שֶׁלֹּא יָבוֹאוּ לִידֵי צָמָאוֹן. אָמַר רִבִּי יוֹחָנָן. תְּרוּמַת הַדֶּשֶׁן תְּחִילַת עֲבוֹדָה שֶׁלְּמָחָר הִיא. וְצָרִיךְ לְקַדֵּשׁ יָדָיו וְרַגְלָיו מִן הַכִּיּוֹר הַמְשׁוּקָּע בַּמָּיִם.

Halakhah 8: Rebbi Mana said, would it not be understandable if on the day of Atonement it were after the first watch and on holidays from midnight, that they[241] should not become thirsty? Rebbi Johanan said, the removal of ashes is the start of the service of the next say and one had to sanctify his hands and feet from the basin which was immersed in water[242].

241 Everybody involved in the service of the fast day. R. Mana's opinion is not mentioned in the Babli.

242 Washing hands and feet before any sacral act is an absolute requirement, *Ex.* 30:17-21. But the water used on one day would become unusable the next day unless it is at least 40 *se`ah*, the minimum volume of a *miqweh* whose water always is pure. Therefore the wash basin of the priests has to be immersed in a large *miqweh* during the night and can be lifted for easy use only at dawn. For the removal of ashes on the special days, hands and feet have to be washed in the *miqweh*. In the interpretation of the Babli *Zevahim* 21b, R. Johanan holds that since the removal of the ashes is the start of the service of the next day, the Cohen washing for the removal does not have to wash again for the morning service.

בראשונה פרק שני

(fol.39b) **משנה א**: בָּרִאשׁוֹנָה כָּל־מִי שֶׁהוּא רוֹצֶה לִתְרוֹם אֶת הַמִּזְבֵּחַ תּוֹרֵם. בִּזְמַן שֶׁהֵן מְרוּבִּין רָצִין וְעוֹלִין בַּכֶּבֶשׁ וְכָל־הַקּוֹדֵם אֶת חֲבֵירוֹ לְתוֹךְ אַרְבַּע אַמּוֹת זָכָה. וְאִם הָיוּ שְׁנַיִם שָׁוִים הַמְמוּנֶּה אוֹמֵר לָהֶם הַצְבִּיעוּ. וּמָה הֵן מוֹצִיאִין אַחַת אוֹ שְׁתַּיִם וְאֵין מוֹצִיאִין אֲגוּדָּל בַּמִּקְדָּשׁ׃

Mishnah 1: Originally, anybody who wanted to remove the ashes[1] from the altar could remove them. If they were many of them, they ran up the ramp[2]; he who was first within four cubits[3] got the right to do it. If two were at equal times, the overseer used to say to them, show fingers[4]. What do they hold up? One or two[5]; but one does not show a thumb in the Temple[6].

1 The ritual removal of some ashes from the altar by a priest in special attire (*Lev.* 6:3), followed by the less formal removal of the remainder of the ashes, *Lev.* 6:4.

2 The ramp on the South side of the altar, leading to the top without stairs (*Ex.* 20:23).

3 4 cubits from the top of the altar.

4 Since people may not be counted, one counts fingers instead. The overseer calls out a large number and then counts down finger by finger repeatedly and the person whose finger is then number 1 is selected.

(In modern Hebrew, מצביע no longer means to show a finger, or to point with a finger, but "to vote"; a misinterpretation of this Mishnah..)

5 If a Cohen has arthritic fingers and cannot lift a single finger, he may show two which, being close to one another, will be counted as one.

6 Since the thumb is far from the other fingers, the thumb and one other finger might erroneously be counted as two persons.

(39b line 61) בָּרִאשׁוֹנָה כָּל־מִי שֶׁהוּא רוֹצֶה לִתְרוֹם אֶת הַמִּזְבֵּחַ כול'. רִבִּי מָנָא בָּעֵי. וְלָמָּה לֹא קָבְעוּ פַּיִיס לִתְרוּמַת הַדֶּשֶׁן. אִיתָא חֲמֵי. שְׁחִיטָה כְּשֵׁירָה בְזָר. וְאַתְּ אָמַר. יֶשׁ לָהּ פַּיִיס. תְּרוּמַת הַדֶּשֶׁן אֲסוּרָה בְזָר. וְאַתְּ אָמַר. אֵין לָהּ פַּיִיס. חָזַר רִבִּי מָנָא וְאָמַר. שְׁחִיטָה אֵינָהּ כְּשֵׁירָה אֶלָּא בַיּוֹם. אֲבָל תְּרוּמַת הַדֶּשֶׁן כְּשֵׁירָה כָּל־הַלַּיְלָה. אִם אוֹמֵר אַתְּ. יְפַיֵּס. אַף הוּא אֵינוֹ מַשְׁכִּים עַל הַסָּפֵק. מַאי חֲמִית מֵימַר כֵּן. כָּל־הַלַּיְלָה וְהֲרֵי. מִיכָּן לִתְרוּמַת הַדֶּשֶׁן שֶׁהִיא כְּשֵׁירָה כָּל־הַלַּיְלָה.

"Originally, anybody who wanted to remove the ashes from the altar," etc. Rebbi Mana asked, why did they not establish a lottery for the removal of ashes? Come and see, slaughter is valid by a non-Cohen, but you are saying that there is a lottery⁷. Removal of ashes is forbidden to a non-Cohen, and you are saying, there is no lottery? Rebbi Mana turned around and said, slaughter is valid only during daytime, but the removal of ashes is valid during the entire night. If you are saying that there is a lottery, he will not get up early for the doubt⁸. What did you see to say this? *All the night*⁹, *he shall remove*¹⁰. From here that the removal of ashes is valid during the entire night.

7 Mishnah 2:2.	night duty. Babli 22a.
8 If the chances are slim that he will be able to serve, no Cohen will show up for the	9 Lev. 6:2.
	10 Lev. 6:3.

(68 line 39b) זָר שֶׁתָּרַם. רִבִּי יוֹחָנָן אָמַר. חַיָּיב. רִבִּי שִׁמְעוֹן בֶּן לָקִישׁ אָמַר. פָּטוּר. מַה טַעֲמֵיהּ דְּרִבִּי שִׁמְעוֹן בֶּן לָקִישׁ. עֲבוֹדַת מַתָּנָה. יָצָא זֶה שֶׁהוּא בַהֲרָמָה. מַה טַעֲמֵיהּ דְּרִבִּי יוֹחָנָן. לְכָל־דְּבַר הַמִּזְבֵּחַ. רִבִּי יוֹסֵי בֵּירִבִּי בּוּן בְּשֵׁם רַב. אַרְבַּע עֲבוֹדוֹת שֶׁהַכֹּהֵן מִתְחַיֵּיב עֲלֵיהֶן מִבַּחוּץ זָר מִתְחַיֵּיב עֲלֵיהֶן מִבִּפְנִים. וְאֵי זוֹ הִיא. זוֹ הַקְטָרָה וּזְרִיקָה וְנִיסּוּךְ הַמַּיִם וְהַיַּיִן. וְאַתְיָא כְרִבִּי שִׁמְעוֹן בֶּן לָקִישׁ. לֵוִי אָמַר. אֲפִילוּ לִתְרוּמַת הַדֶּשֶׁן. וְאַתְיָא כְרִבִּי יוֹחָנָן. תַּפְלוּגְתָּא דְּרִבִּי יוֹחָנָן וּדְרִבִּי שִׁמְעוֹן בֶּן לָקִישׁ. הוֹצִיא שְׁאָר הַדֶּשֶׁן. תַּפְלוּגְתָּא דְּרִבִּי יוֹחָנָן וּדְרִבִּי שִׁמְעוֹן בֶּן לָקִישׁ. אַתְיָא כְמָאן דְּאָמַר. אַחֵרִים. פְּחוּתִים מֵהֶן. בְּרַם כְּמָאן דְּאָמַר. אַחֵרִים. לָרַבּוֹת בַּעֲלֵי מוּמִין. הִיא זָר הִיא בַעַל מוּם. הַכֹּל מוֹדִין בְּזָר שֶׁסִּידֵּר מַעֲרָכָה שֶׁלְּעֵצִים שֶׁהוּא חַיָּיב. אָמַר רִבִּי זְעִירָא. וּבִלְבַד שְׁנֵי גִיזִירֵי עֵצִים שֶׁהַכָּתוּב מַזְהִיר עֲלֵיהֶן לַעֲבוֹדַת כְּהוּנָה. וְנָתְנוּ בְּנֵי אַהֲרֹן הַכֹּהֵן אֵשׁ עַל־הַמִּזְבֵּחַ וְעָרְכוּ עֵצִים.

A non-Cohen who removed¹¹. Rebbi Johanan said, he is liable. Rebbi Simeon ben Laqish said, he is not liable. What is Rebbi Simeon ben Laqish's reason? *Service of bringing*¹². This excludes what is a removal. What is Rebbi Johanan's reason? *Anything concerning the altar*¹². Rebbi Yose ben Rebbi Abun in the name of Rav: The four kinds of service for which a Cohen would be liable if done outside¹³, the non-Cohen is liable for inside. What are these? Burning incense, and pouring blood, and making libations of water and wine. This follows Rebbi Simeon ben Laqish. Levi said, even removal of the ashes;¹⁴ this follows Rebbi Johanan. If he¹⁵ stirred the coals, the disagreement of Rebbi Johanan and Rebbi Simeon ben Laqish. If he¹⁵ removed the remainder of the ashes, the disagreement of Rebbi Johanan and Rebbi Simeon ben Laqish, following him who said, *others*¹⁶, of lesser value than these. But for him[17] who said *others*, to include people with bodily defects, there is no difference between a Cohen with a bodily defect and a non-Cohen. Everybody agreed that the non-Cohen who arranged the woods[18] is liable. Rebbi Ze`ira said, but only for the two logs on which the verse insists that they are Cohen's service: *Aaron's the priest's sons shall put fire on the altar and arrange woods*[19].

11   The formal removal of ashes from the altar.
12   *Num.* 18:7.
13   Outside a divinely approved place of worship; after the building of the Temple, outside of the Temple district. Worship outside the Temple is sinful only if it imitates Temple ceremonies. Babli 24a.
14   Babli 24a.
15   The non-Cohen.
16   *Lev.* 6:4. *Sifra Saw Pereq* 2(6).
17   According to *Sifra*, R. Eleazar (the Tanna.)
18   The logs of firewood on the altar.
19   *Lev.* 1:7. Since a simple plural always means 2 (Note 138); this establishes a formal requirement that two new logs be brought to the altar at the start of the morning service; *Lev.* 6:5. Babli 24b.

(39c line 5) תַּנֵּי. אָמַר רִבִּי יְהוּדָה. מְנַיִין לְהַצָּתַת הָאֲלִיתָא שֶׁלֹּא תְהֵא אֶלָּא בְכֹהֵן כָּשֵׁר וּבִכְלִי שָׁרֵת. תַּלְמוּד לוֹמַר וְנָתְנוּ בְּנֵי אַהֲרֹן הַכֹּהֵן אֵשׁ עַל־הַמִּזְבֵּחַ. אָמַר רִבִּי שִׁמְעוֹן. וְכִי עָלַת עַל לֵב שֶׁהַזָּר קָרֵב עַל גַּבֵּי הַמִּזְבֵּחַ. אִם כֵּן לָמָּה נֶאֱמַר וְנָתְנוּ בְּנֵי אַהֲרֹן הַכֹּהֵן אֵשׁ עַל־הַמִּזְבֵּחַ. לִימֵד עַל הַצָּתַת הָאֵשׁ שֶׁלֹּא תְהֵא אֶלָּא בְרֹאשׁוֹ שֶׁלְּמִזְבֵּחַ. הֲתִיבוּן. וְהָא כְתִיב וְהָאֵשׁ עַל־הַמִּזְבֵּחַ תּוּקַד־בּוֹ לֹא תִכְבֶּה. מִיכָּן לְהַצָּתַת הָאֵשׁ שֶׁלֹּא תְהֵא אֶלָּא בְרֹאשׁוֹ שֶׁלְּמִזְבֵּחַ. דִּבְרֵי רִבִּי יְהוּדָה. מְחִלְפָה שִׁיטָתֵיהּ דְּרִבִּי יְהוּדָה. תַּמָּן הִיא צְרִיכָה כֹהֵן כָּשֵׁר. וְכָא הוּא אֵינָהּ צְרִיכָה כֹּהֵן כָּשֵׁר. אָמַר רִבִּי תַּנְחוּם בַּר יוּדָן. מָה אַתְּ שְׁמַע מִינָהּ. נֶאֱמַר בְּרֹאשׁ הַמִּזְבֵּחַ וְזָר.

It was stated[20] "Rebbi Jehudah said, from where that kindling fire wood[21] may only be done by a qualified Cohen and with a vessel of service[22]? The verse says, *Aaron's the priest's sons shall put fire on the altar*. Rebbi Simeon said, could anybody think that a non-Cohen might approach the top of the altar? Then why is it said, *Aaron's the priest's sons shall put fire on the altar*? This teaches that kindling the fire may only be done on top of the altar" They objected, is it not written *"and the fire on the altar shall burn there, it shall not go out*[23], from here that kindling the fire may only be done on top of the altar, the words of Rebbi Jehudah[24]"? The argument of Rebbi Jehudah is inverted. There it needs a qualified Cohen, but here it does not need a qualified Cohen. Rebbi Tanhum bar Yudan said, what do you understand from here? Could we say on top of the altar and a non-Cohen[25]?

20 *Sifra Saw Pereq* 2(7).=; Babli 24b,45a.
21 Rashi's explanation.
22 The firewood had to be transported in a dedicated vessel.
23 Lev. 6:5.
24 Babli 45a.
25 Since it already was stated that no non-Cohen could be present at the altar, a mention of "Cohen" was superfluous in the second case.

(39c line 14) תָּרַם וְהִפְרִיחָתוֹ הָרוּחַ. תַּפְלוּגְתָּא דְרִבִּי יוֹחָנָן וּדְרִבִּי חֲנִינָה. דְּאָמַר רִבִּי חֲנִינָה. קוֹמֶץ שֶׁנְּתָנוֹ עַל גַּבֵּי הָאִישִׁים וְהִפְרִיחָתוֹ הָרוּחַ. בִּפְרִיחָה הָאַחֲרוֹנָה נִתְכַּפְּרוּ הַבְּעָלִים וְיָצְאוּ הַשִּׁיָּרִים יְדֵי מְעִילָה. רִבִּי יוֹחָנָן אָמַר. מִשֶּׁיּוֹחַז הָאוֹר בְּרוּבּוֹ. מַהוּ בְּרוּבּוֹ. בְּרוּבּוֹ שֶׁלְקוֹמֶץ אוֹ בְּרוֹב כָּל־פְּרִידָה וּפְרִידָה אִתְאֲמָרַת. אָתָא רִבִּי חִזְקִיָּה רִבִּי יוֹנָה רִבִּי בָּא רִבִּי חִיָּיה בְּשֵׁם רִבִּי יוֹחָנָן. בְּרוֹב כָּל־פְּרִידָה וּפְרִידָה אִתְאֲמָרַת.

If he removed and the wind blew it away[26], the disagreement between Rebbi Johanan and Rebbi Hanina, since Rebbi Hanina said, if a fistful[27] was put in the fire when the wind blew it away, by the last blowing the owner was atoned for and the remainders freed from larceny. Rebbi Johanan said, if[28] the fire engulfed most of it. What means "most of it"? Most of the fistful, or had it been said about most of each separate lump? There came Rebbi Hizqiah, Rebbi Jonah, Rebbi Abba, Rebbi Hiyya, in the name of Rebbi Johanan: It had been said about most of each separate lump.

26 Does one have to lift a second time?
27 A flour offering after dedication is most holy, all use is forbidden as larceny of *sancta*. The priest has to take a fistful of the flour mixed with oil, bring it to the top of the altar in a dedicated vessel, and empty the vessel into the fire. At that moment, the owners have fulfilled their vow, and the remainders of the offering are released to the priests as their property, to be eaten in the sacred precinct.
28 Meaning; *only if*. Babli *Menahot* 26b.

(39c line) תָּרַם (לְתַיִּים) [חֲצָיָיהּ]. תַּפְלוּגְתָּא דְרִבִּי יוֹחָנָן וּדְרִבִּי יְהוֹשֻׁעַ בֶּן לֵוִי. דְּאָמַר רִבִּי יוֹחָנָן. קוֹמֶץ שֶׁקִּדַּשׁ בְּכֵלִי וְהִקְטִירוֹ אֲפִילוּ שׁוּמְשְׁמִין יָצָא. רִבִּי יְהוֹשֻׁעַ בֶּן לֵוִי אָמַר. מַתְנִיתָא לֹא אָמְרָה כֵן אֶלָּא הִקְטִיר בְּקוּמְצוֹ פַּעֲמַיִם כְּשֵׁירָה. רִבִּי חָמָא בַּר עוּקְבָה בְּשֵׁם רִבִּי יְהוֹשֻׁעַ בֶּן לֵוִי. אֵין קְמִיצָה פָּחוּת מִשְּׁנֵי זֵיתִים. וְאֵין הַקְטָרָה פָּחוּתָה (מְקוֹמֶץ) [מִכַּזַּיִת]. רִבִּי יִצְחָק בֵּירִבִּי אֶלְעָזָר שָׁאַל. מֵאַתָּה כֹהֵן שֶׁאֵין יָדוֹ מַחֲזֶקֶת כִּשְׁנֵי זֵיתִים פָּסוּל מִן הָעֲבוֹדָה.

If he lifted half of it, the disagreement between Rebbi Johanan and Rebbi Joshua ben Levi, since Rebbi Johanan said, if the fistful had been sanctified in a vessel, he did his duty if he burned even a sesame grain's size of it. Rebbi Joshua ben Levi said, the Mishnah[29] does not say so, only if he burned his fistful in two parts it is qualified. Rebbi Ḥama bar Uqba in the name of Rebbi Joshua ben Levi: A fistful is not less than the volume of two olives, no burning is less than the volume of (a fistful) [an olive][30]. Rebbi Isaac ben Rebbi Eleazar asked, then a Cohen whose hand could not hold the volume of two olives would be disqualified from the service[31]?

29   *Menahot* 3:4, Babli *Menahot* 26a.
30   *Menahot* 26b. The corrector's change is suspect as adaptation to the Babli.

31   Since this disability does not appear in a list of defects which disqualify a Cohen, practice cannot follow R. Joshua ben Levi.

(29c line 25) תְּרַם בִּשְׂמֹאל. תַּפְלוּגְתָּא דְּרִבִּי יוֹחָנָן וּדְרִבִּי יְהוּדָה בֵּירִבִּי. דְּאָמַר רִבִּי יוֹחָנָן. קוֹמֶץ שֶׁקָּדַשׁ בְּכֵלִי וְהִקְטִירוֹ בֵּין בְּיָד בֵּין בִּכְלִי בֵּין בְּיָמִין בֵּין בִּשְׂמֹאל. יְהוּדָה בֵּירִבִּי אוֹמֵר. אוֹ כְחַטָּאת בְּיָד אוֹ כְאָשָׁם בִּכְלִי. וּבִלְבַד בְּיָמִין. הֲתִיבוּן. וְהָא תַנֵּי. קִיבֵּל בִּימִינוֹ וְנָתַן בִּשְׂמֹאלוֹ יַחֲזִיר לִימִינוֹ. אִם בִּשְׂמֹאל הוּא מַחֲזִיר לַמִּזְבֵּחַ לֹא כָל־שֶׁכֵּן לַבֶּזֶךְ. אָמַר רִבִּי לָא. אִם שָׁנְיָא אָדָם רִבִּי לְעָזָר בְּרִבִּי שִׁמְעוֹן שָׁנְיָיהּ. דְּתַנֵּי. רִבִּי אֶלְעָזָר בְּרִבִּי שִׁמְעוֹן אוֹמֵר. אֵינָהּ צְרִיכָה קִידּוּשׁ בֶּזֶךְ. אַתְיָא דְּרִבִּי לְעָזָר בְּרִבִּי שִׁמְעוֹן בְּשִׁיטַת רִבִּי שִׁמְעוֹן אָבִיו. דְּתַנִּינָן תַּמָּן. שֶׁלֹּא בִכְלִי שָׁרֵת פְּסוּלָה. וְרִבִּי שִׁמְעוֹן מַכְשִׁיר. מַאי כְדוֹן. רַבָּנִן דְּאִית לוֹן כְּלִי שָׁרֵת צְרִיכָה לוֹן יָמִין. רִבִּי שִׁמְעוֹן [דְּ]לֵית לֵיהּ כְּלִי שָׁרֵת לֹא צְרִיכָה לֵיהּ לְיָמִין. אָמַר רִבִּי מָנָא. וּתְמִיהּ אֲנָא הֵיךְ רַבָּנָן מְדַמֵּי תְּרוּמַת הַדֶּשֶׁן לְהַקְטָרָה. וְלֹא דָמְיָא אֶלָּא לִקְמִיצָה. שָׁאוּ בַּהֲרָמָה וְזוּ בַּהֲרָמָה.

If he removed with his left hand, the disagreement between Rebbi Johanan and Jehudah ben Rebbi, since Rebbi Johanan said, if a fistful[32] had been sanctified in a dedicated vessel and he burned it whether out of his hand or out of a vessel, whether by his right hand or by the left. Jehudah ben Rebbi said, either like a purification offering from the hand, or like a reparation offering from a vessel, but only with the right hand[33]. They objected: Was it not stated, if he received with his right hand and then put it into his left hand, he must return it to the right hand[34]? If from the left hand he returns it for the altar, not so much more to the cup? Rebbi La said, if somebody stated this, Rebbi Eleazar ben Rebbi Simeon stated it. As it was stated, it[35] does not need sanctification in a cup. Rebbi Eleazar ben Rebbi Simeon follows the argument of his father Rebbi Simeon, as we have stated there[36], "not in a dedicated vessel it is disqualified, but Rebbi Simeon qualifies it." How is it? The rabbis who require a dedicated vessel need the right hand[37]; Rebbi Simeon [who] does not require a dedicated vessel does not need the right hand. Rebbi Mana said, I am wondering how the rabbis could compare the removal of ashes to burning, but it can be compared only to the lifting of the fistful, since both are by lifting[38].

32 Of the flour offering.
33 In *Lev.* 6:10 it is stated that the flour offering is "most holy, like purification offering and like reparation offering." For purification offerings it is stated (*Lev.* 4:25,30,34) that the Cohen has to apply the blood of the sacrifice *with his finger* to the corners of the altar. This requirement is missing for the reparation sacrifice (*Lev.* 7:1-7.)
34 Mishnah *Zevahim* 3:1, *Zevahim* 32a,

speaking of the blood received in a vessel and brought to the altar to be poured at the wall.
35 The fistful taken from a flour offering.
36 Mishnah *Menahot* 3:4.
37 *Menahot* 26b.
38 Since everybody agrees that at all places where the verse requires that the action be done by a Cohen he must use his right hand; therefor the lifting of the fistful must be with the Cohen's right hand.

(39c line 36) וְהֵרִים. וְאֵין וְהֵרִים אֶלָּא בְשִׁשִׁיֵּיר. אֲשֶׁר תֹּאכַל. אֵין אֲכִילָה אֶלָּא בְכַזַּיִת. הָיָה בְכוּלּוֹ כַזַּיִת. לִיטּוֹל מִקְצָתוֹ אֵין אַתְּ יָכוֹל שֶׁאֵין בּוֹ כַזַּיִת. לִיטּוֹל אֶת כּוּלּוֹ אֵין אַתְּ יָכוֹל שֶׁאֵין כָּאן שִׁיּוּר. וְהֵרִים אֲשֶׁר תֹּאכַל הָאֵשׁ. יָכוֹל עֵצִים. תַּלְמוּד לוֹמַר עוֹלָה. אִי עוֹלָה יָכוֹל אֵיבָרֵי עוֹלָה. תַּלְמוּד לוֹמַר אֲשֶׁר תֹּאכַל הָאֵשׁ. הָא כֵיצַד. חוֹתָה מִן הַמְאוּכָּלוֹת הַפְּנִימִיּוֹת וְיוֹרֵד. מִצְוָה לְהַקְדִּים אֵשׁ לָעֵצִים. שֶׁנֶּאֱמַר וְעָרְכוּ עֵצִים עַל־הָאֵשׁ: קִידֵּם עֵצִים לָאֵשׁ. סִידֵּר עַד שֶׁלֹּא תָרַם מַשְׁחִיל וְתוֹרֵם מְפָרֵק וְתוֹרֵם.

And he shall lift[39]. There is no lifting unless he left a remainder[40]. *Which ate*, there is no eating less than the volume of an olive. If all of it[41] was the volume of an olive? You may not take part of it since there would not be the volume of an olive; you may not take all of it since there would not be a remainder. *And he lifts . . . what the fire ate.* I could think wood, the verse says, the elevation sacrifice[42]. If elevation sacrifice, I could think limbs of an elevation sacrifice[43]; the verse says, *what the fire ate.* How is this? He scoops up from what has been consumed in the middle[44] and descends. It is an obligation to bring wood before fire, as it is said[45], *they shall arrange on the fire*, He mentioned wood before fire. If one arranged before he removed, he throws down and removes, disassembles and removes[46].

39 Lev. 6:3.
40 Otherwise the verse would have said, "he takes away".
41 The ashes on the altar.
42 The verse reads: *He shall lift the ashes from where the fire ate the elevation sacrifice on the altar.*
43 Parts of the daily sacrifice which still are recognizable as such.
44 Where it is most likely from the sacrifice, not the fire wood. *Sifra Saw Pereq* 2(4).
45 Lev. 1:7.
46 Since it has been stated that the removal of ashes is first in the service of a new day, and arranging new logs precedes the morning daily sacrifice, any arrangement preceding the removal of ashes is simply addition to the preceding day's service and may be undone for the new day. *Sifra Wayyiqra* I *Pereq* 5(11).

(39c line 43) רִבִּי יַעֲקֹב בַּר אָחָא אָמַר. חִילְפַּיי שָׁאַל. קוֹמֶץ שֶׁנְּתָנוֹ עַל גַּבֵּי מַעֲרֶכֶת לַיְלָה מָה הֵן. [רִבִּי יִרְמְיָה אָמַר. חִילְפַּיי שָׁאַל. אֵימָרִין שֶׁנְּתָנָן עַל גַּבֵּי מַעֲרֶכֶת לַיְלָה מָה הֵן. וְלָאו מַתְנִיתָה הִיא. אֵין לָךְ קוֹדֶם לַתָּמִיד שֶׁלְּשַׁחַר אֶלָּא קְטוֹרֶת בִּלְבַד. מַתְנִיתָה לְמִצְוָה. מַה צְּרִיכָה לֵיהּ לְעִיכּוּב. צִיץ מָהוּ שֶׁיְרַצֶּה עַל טוּמְאַת יָדַיִם. יָדַיִם מָהוּ שֶׁיִּפָּסְלוּ מִשָּׁם יוֹצֵא. וְלָאו מַתְנִיתָה הִיא. קִידֵּשׁ יָדָיו וְרַגְלָיו וְנִיטְמוּ מַטְבִּילָן וְהֵן טְהוֹרוֹת. יָצָא לֹא נִפְסְלוּ מִשָּׁם יוֹצֵא. וְאַתְיָא כְמָאן דְּאָמַר. אֵין הַלִּינָה פּוֹסֶלֶת בַּיָּדַיִם. מַה צְּרִיכָה לֵיהּ. [בְּרַם הָכָא] כְּמָאן דְּאָמַר. לִינָה פּוֹסֶלֶת בַּיָּדַיִם. יָדַיִם מָהוּ שֶׁיִּפָּסְלוּ מִשָּׁם מְחוּסַּר זְמָן. וְלָאו מַתְנִיתָה הִיא. קִידֵּשׁ יָדָיו וְרַגְלָיו הַיּוֹם לַעֲבוֹדַת שֶׁלְּמָחָר.

אָמַר רִבִּי יוֹחָנָן. תְּרוּמַת הַדֶּשֶׁן תְּחִילַּת עֲבוֹדָה שֶׁלְּמָחָר הִיא. וְצָרִיךְ לְקַדֵּשׁ יָדָיו וְרַגְלָיו מִן הַכִּיּוֹר הַמְשׁוּקָּע בַּמַּיִם. רִבִּי חִייָא בַּר יוֹסֵף אָמַר. מִכֵּיוָן שֶׁמָּסַר יוֹם לַלַּיְלָה דַּיּוֹ. חֲבֵרַייָא בְּשֵׁם רִבִּי יוֹחָנָן. מַשֶּׁהוּ מַגְבִּיהוּ הוּא מַשְׁקִיעוֹ. מַתְנִיתָה פְּלִיגָא עַל רִבִּי חִייָא בַּר יוֹסֵף. קִידֵּשׁ יָדָיו וְרַגְלָיו בַּיּוֹם אֵינוֹ צָרִיךְ לְקַדְּשָׁן בַּלַּיְלָה. בַּלַּיְלָה צָרִיךְ לְקַדְּשָׁן בַּיּוֹם. דִּבְרֵי רִבִּי. רִבִּי לְעָזָר בֵּירִבִּי שִׁמְעוֹן אוֹמֵר. אֲפִילוּ עָסוּק בַּעֲבוֹדָה כָּל־שְׁלֹשָׁה אֵינוֹ צָרִיךְ לְקַדֵּשׁ יָדָיו וְרַגְלָיו. שֶׁאֵין הַלִּינָה פּוֹסֶלֶת בַּיָּדַיִם בִּשְׁיָירֵי עֲבוֹדוֹת. אֲבָל בִּתְחִילַּת עֲבוֹדוֹת צָרִיךְ.

[רִבִּי חִייָא בַּר יוֹסֵף פָּתַר מַתְנִיתָה. קִדֵּשׁ יָדָיו וְרַגְלָיו בַּיּוֹם אֵינוֹ צָרִיךְ לְקַדְּשָׁן בַּלַּיְלָה בִּשְׁיָירֵי עֲבוֹדוֹת. אֲבָל בִּתְחִילַּת עֲבוֹדוֹת צָרִיךְ לְקַדְּשָׁן בַּיּוֹם. דִּבְרֵי רִבִּי. רִבִּי אֶלְעָזָר בֵּירִבִּי שִׁמְעוֹן אוֹמֵר. אֲפִילוּ עָסוּק בַּעֲבוֹדָה כָּל־שְׁלֹשָׁה אֵינוֹ צָרִיךְ לְקַדֵּשׁ יָדָיו וְרַגְלָיו. שֶׁאֵין הַלִּינָה פּוֹסֶלֶת בַּיָּדַיִם בִּשְׁיָירֵי עֲבוֹדוֹת. אֲבָל בִּתְחִילַּת עֲבוֹדוֹת צָרִיךְ.]

רִבִּי יוֹחָנָן פָּתַר מַתְנִיתָה. קִדֵּשׁ יָדָיו וְרַגְלָיו בַּיּוֹם (אֵינוֹ) אֲינוֹ) צָרִיךְ לְקַדְּשָׁן בַּלַּיְלָה בֵּין בִּתְחִילַּת עֲבוֹדוֹת בֵּין בִּשְׁיָירֵי עֲבוֹדוֹת. אֲבָל בַּלַּיְלָה צָרִיךְ לְקַדְּשָׁן בַּיּוֹם. דִּבְרֵי רִבִּי. רִבִּי לְעָזָר בֵּירִבִּי שִׁמְעוֹן אוֹמֵר. אֲפִילוּ עָסוּק בַּעֲבוֹדָה [כָּל־שְׁלֹשָׁה] אֵינוֹ צָרִיךְ לְקַדֵּשׁ יָדָיו וְרַגְלָיו. שֶׁאֵין הַלִּינָה פּוֹסֶלֶת בַּיָּדַיִם בֵּין בִּתְחִילַּת עֲבוֹדוֹת בֵּין בִּשְׁיָירֵי עֲבוֹדוֹת.

חִילְפַיי אָמַר. כְּשֵׁם שֶׁאֵין הַלִּינָה פוֹסֶלֶת בַּיָדַיִם כָּךְ אֵין הַלִּינָה פוֹסֶלֶת בַּכִּיּוֹר. מַתְנִיתָה פְלִינָא עַל רְבִּי חִילְפַיי. קִידֵּשׁ יָדָיו וְרַגְלָיו בַּיּוֹם אֵינוֹ צָרִיךְ לְקַדֵּשׁ בַּלַּיְלָה. בַּלַּיְלָה צָרִיךְ לְקַדֵּשׁ בַּיּוֹם. דִּבְרֵי רְבִּי. רְבִּי לְעָזָר בֵּירְבִּי שִׁמְעוֹן אוֹמֵר. אֲפִילוּ עָסוּק בַּעֲבוֹדָה כָּל־שְׁלֹשָׁה אֵינוֹ צָרִיךְ לְקַדֵּשׁ יָדָיו וְרַגְלָיו. שֶׁאֵין הַלִּינָה פוֹסֶלֶת בַּיָדַיִם. הָא בַכִּיּוֹר פּוֹסֶלֶת. תַּלְמִידוֹי דְרְבִּי יוֹחָנָן בְּשֵׁם חִילְפַיי. הָכֵינִי. קִידֵּשׁ יָדָיו וְרַגְלָיו כול'. שֶׁאֵין הַלִּינָה פוֹסֶלֶת בַּיָדַיִם. הָא בַכִּיּוֹר פּוֹסֶלֶת. וּבִלְבַד מִיּוֹם לַלַּיְלָה.

Rebbi Jacob bar Aḥa said, Hilfai asked: What is the status of a fistful given on the setting of the night[47]? Rebbi Jeremiah said, Hilfai asked: What is the status of the public parts on the setting of the night[48]? Is that not a *baraita*? Nothing precedes the daily sacrifice but incense[49]. The *baraita* as commandment, what he is asking is as impediment[50]. Does the diadem cover up for impurity of the hands[51]? Do hands become disqualified by leaving[52]? Is that not a *baraita*? If he sanctified[51] his hands and feet and they became impure, he immerses them and they are pure; if he left they did not become disqualified because of leaving. This comes following the one who said, an overnight stay does not disqualify hands. What is his problem? [But here] it is following him who said, an overnight stay disqualifies hands. Do hands become impure for missing time? Is that not a *baraita*? If he sanctified his hands and feet today for tomorrow's service[53].

Rebbi Joḥanan said, the removal of ashes is the start of the service of the next day and one had to sanctify his hands and feet from the basin which was immersed in water[54]. Rebbi Ḥiyya ben Joseph said, it was sufficient that the day deliver to the night[55]. The colleagues in the name of Rebbi Joḥanan, after he lifted it he put it[56] back down. A *baraita* disagrees with Rebbi Ḥiyya bar Joseph. [57]"If he sanctified his hands and feet during the day, he does not have to sanctify them for the night; during the night, he has to sanctify them for the day[58], the words of Rebbi. Rebbi Eleazar ben Rebbi Simeon says, even if he is occupied with service for all of three days, he does not have to sanctify his hands and feet, since staying overnight does not disqualify hands during ancillary services. But to start services it is necessary."

[Rebbi Ḥiyya bar Joseph explains the *baraita*: If he sanctified his hands and feet during the day, he does not have to sanctify them for the night; for ancillary services. But to start service he has to sanctify them for the day, the words of Rebbi. Rebbi Eleazar ben Rebbi Simeon says, even if he is occupied with service for all of three days, he does not have to sanctify his hands and feet, since staying overnight does not disqualify hands during ancillary services[59]. But to start services it is necessary.]

Rebbi Joḥanan explains the *baraita*: If he sanctified his hands and feet during the day, he does (not)[60] have to sanctify them for the night; whether to start service or for ancillary services; during the night, he has to sanctify them for the day, the words of Rebbi. Rebbi Eleazar ben Rebbi Simeon says, even if he is occupied with service for all of three days, he does not have to sanctify his hands and feet, since staying overnight does not disqualify hands whether to start service or for ancillary services.

Hilfai said, just as staying overnight does not disqualify hands, so it does not disqualify the basin[61]. A *baraita* disagrees with Rebbi Hilfai. "If he sanctified his hands and feet during the day, he does not have to sanctify them for the night; during the night, he has to sanctify them for the day, the words of Rebbi. Rebbi Eleazar ben Rebbi Simeon says, even if he is occupied with service for all of three days, he does not have to sanctify his hands and feet, since staying overnight does not disqualify hands." Therefore it disqualifies the basin[62]. The students of Rebbi Joḥanan in the name of Hilfai. So it is: If he sanctified his hands and feet, etc., since staying overnight does not disqualify hands. Therefore it disqualifies the basin, only from day to night[63].

47 It is a biblical commandment that all leftovers from the service of a certain day have to be burned on the altar during the following night. Therefore the question has to be, what is the status of the next morning's flour offering which was brought to the altar at dawn before the required new wood was formally brought to the altar after the removal of the previous day's ashes.

48 The same question as before, only referring to the parts of the sacrificial animals brought before the ritual setting of new logs in the morning. The questions remain unanswered also in the Babli. *Menaḥot* 26b.

49 Since the daily sacrifice is scheduled בבוקר "in the morning (*Ex.* 29:39) but the incense בבוקר בבוקר "in the early morning (*Ex.* 30:7); cf. Halakhah 3:5. Babli *Pesaḥim* 59a.

50 Is the service invalid if the precedences indicated by the verses are not followed?

51 Since except for the biblically ordained washing ("sanctification") of hands and feet at the start of a priest's period of

service (*Ex.* 30:20,40:31-32) the rules of impurity of hands are purely rabbinical, and hands are purified by immersion in a *miqweh*, not by sanctification from the basin. The (unanswered) question is whether the diadem covers also non-biblical infractions of the rules.

52 It is obvious that if a Cohen leaves the sacred precinct because he has finished his tour of duty, for the next tour he has to sanctify his hands and feet again. The question is whether his hands become rabbinically impure if he leaves the sacred precinct for a prescribed ritual act, such as depositing excess ashes outside the sacred domain.

53 It seems that one has to complete the sentence: the sanctification is valid.

54 Chapter 1, Note 241, Babli *Zevahim* 20a.

55 Chapter 1, Note 82.

56 The basin has to stay in the cistern any time it is not used during the night. According to R. Hiyya ben Joseph this should be necessary only at dusk and dawn. According to R. Johanan, the new day starts in the preceding night, with the preparation for lifting ashes.

57 Tosephta 1:9, differently Tosephta *Menahot* 1:13. In that text, Rebbi agrees with R. Eleazar ben R. Simeon. Babli *Zevahim* 20b.

58 The night is used to burn the remainder of the previous day's service; it is an appendix to the day and, since no service is initiated during the night, does not need new preparation.

59 But if he were unoccupied during the entire night, the next day's service is a new beginning and needs sanctification of hands.

60 A word correctly written by the scribe and incorrectly deleted.

61 He disagrees with R. Johanan and holds that the water remaining i n the basin does not become disqualified at the next dawn.

62 Since the basin was not mentioned in the statement. Babli *Zevahim* 20a.

63 Not from night to day since the next day's service starts with the removal of ashes following R. Johanan, and not if the basin was in continuous use during dusk, following R. Hiyya bar Joseph.

(fol. 39b) **משנה ב**: מַעֲשֶׂה שֶׁהָיוּ שְׁנַיִם שָׁוִין וְרָצִין וְעוֹלִין בַּכֶּבֶשׁ וְדָחַף אֶחָד מֵהֶן אֶת חֲבֵירוֹ וְנִשְׁבְּרָה רַגְלוֹ. וּכְשֶׁרָאוּ בֵית דִּין שֶׁהֵן בָּאִין לִידֵי סַכָּנָה הִתְקִינוּ שֶׁלֹּא יְהוּ תוֹרְמִין אֶת הַמִּזְבֵּחַ אֶלָּא בְפַּיִיס. אַרְבַּע פְּיָסוֹת הָיוּ שָׁם וְזֶה הַפַּיִיס הָרִאשׁוֹן:

Mishnah 2: It happened that two were equally running up the ramp when one pushed the other who broke his leg. When the court saw that they might come into danger they enacted that they should remove the ashes from the altar only by lottery[4]. There were four lotteries, and this was the first of them.

(39c line 75) **הלכה ב**: מַה בֵּין בְּתוֹךְ אַרְבַּע אַמּוֹת לַכֶּבֶשׁ בְּתוֹךְ אַרְבַּע אַמּוֹת לַמִּזְבֵּחַ. מִן מַה דְתַנִּינָן. מַעֲשֶׂה שֶׁהָיוּ שְׁנַיִם שָׁוִין רָצִין וְעוֹלִין בַּכֶּבֶשׁ. הָדָא אֲמָרָה. בְּתוֹךְ אַרְבַּע אַמּוֹת לַמִּזְבֵּחַ. אָמַר רִבִּי יוֹסֵי בֵּירִבִּי בּוּן. בְּפֵירוּשׁ תַּנִּי לָהּ רִבִּי חִייָה. כָּל־הַקּוֹדֵם אֶת חֲבֵירוֹ לְתוֹךְ אַרְבַּע אַמּוֹת [לַמִּזְבֵּחַ] זָכָה.

Halakhah 2: [64]How, either within four cubits of the ramp or four cubits of the altar? Since we have stated, "It happened that two were equally running up the ramp," this implies within four cubits of the altar. Rebbi Yose ben Rebbi Abun said, explicitly did Rebbi Hiyya state, "he who is first within four cubits of the altar got the right to do it."

מַהוּ הִצְבִּיעוּ. הוֹצִיאוּ אֶצְבַּע. הוֹצִיאוּ אַחַת מוֹנִין לוֹ. שְׁתַּיִם מוֹנִין לוֹ. שָׁלֹשׁ אֵין מוֹנִין לוֹ. מָהוּ אֵין מוֹנִין. כָּל־עִיקָר. אֵין מוֹנִין לוֹ אֶת הַיְּתֵירָה. אַרְבַּע הַמְמוּנֶּה מַכֶּה אוֹתוֹ בַּפְּקִיעַ וּבָטֵל הַפַּיִיס.

What means הצביעו? Show a finger[65]. If one put up one, he is counted; two, he is counted[5]; three he is not counted. What means., "is not counted"? Not at all? One does not count the additional. Four, the overseer hits him with a whip and cancels the lottery.

אֵין מוֹצִיאִין אֲגוּדָּל בַּמִּקְדָּשׁ. מִפְּנֵי הָרַמָּאִין. אֵין אוֹמְרִין (מִמֶּנּוּ) [מִמִּי] בַּמִּקְדָּשׁ. אֶלָּא הַמְמוּנֶּה הָיָה מַגְבִּיהַּ מִצְנַפְתּוֹ שֶׁלְּאֶחָד מֵהֶן וְהֵן יוֹדְעִין שֶׁמִּמֶּנּוּ הָיָה הַפַּיִיס (מְהַלֵךְ) [מַתְחִיל]. וְחָשׁ לוֹמַר. שֶׁמָּא לְאוֹהֲבוֹ אוֹ לִקְרוֹבוֹ. כָּמִין קוּכְלַיִיס הָיוּ עוֹשִׂין. כֵּיצַד הָיָה הַפַּיִיס מְהַלֵךְ. לִימִין לִשְׂמֹאל. אָמַר רִבִּי בּוּן בַּר חִייָה. מִן מַה דְתַנֵּי. מִי שֶׁזָּכָה בַּקְטוֹרֶת אוֹמֵר לְזֶה שֶׁעַל יְמִינוֹ. אוּף אַתְּ לְמַחְתָּה. הָדָא אֲמָרָה. לִימִין הַפַּיִיס מְהַלֵךְ. תַּלְמִידוֹי דְרִבִּי יוֹנָה בְּשֵׁם רִבִּי חִילְפַי. הֲכֵינֵי. לִשְׂמֹאל הַפַּיִיס מְהַלֵךְ. הָאוּכָה זָכָה לִימִין. מוּטָב שֶׁיִּזְכָּה לְמִי שֶׁעָבַר עָלָיו הַפַּיִיס שְׁנֵי פְעָמִים מִזֶּה שֶׁלֹּא עָבַר עָלָיו הַפַּיִיס אֶלָּא פַּעַם אַחַת בִּלְבָד.

"One does not show a thumb in the Temple," because of the tricksters[6]. One does not say from whom[66] in the Temple, but the overseer lifts the cap of one of them and they know that the lottery (proceeds) [starts] from there. Should we not worry, maybe for a friend or a relative[67]? They formed a snail[68]. How was the lottery proceeding, to the right or to the left? Rebbi Yose ben Rebbi Abun said, since we did state, the one winning the incense says to the one on his right side, you are with me with the pan[69], this implies that it proceeded to the right. The students of Rebbi Jonah in the name of Rebbi Hilfai: It is as follows. The lottery proceeds to the left, the winner adds to the right. It is preferable that one should win over whom the lottery passed twice, rather than one over whom the lottery passed only once⁷⁰.

64 One starts with discussing the remainder of Mishnah 1, starting with the meaning of "within 4 cubits".
65 Since verbs from the root צבע usually meant "to color, to dye". Cf. Babli 23a.
66 The people were not identified by name.
67 That the overseer could predetermine the outcome and therefore the lottery was unfair.
68 Greek κοχλίας "snail with a spiral shell". Since the row of Cohanim was "snailing", the overseer could not determine the exact number of those present. Babli 25a.
69 On all days other than the Day of Atonement, presenting the incense on the interior altar needed two Cohanim, one carrying the incense and the other carrying hot coals on a pan.
70 The previous argument did not prove anything/

(39d line 15) מַעֲשֶׂה בְּאֶחָד שֶׁקָּדַם אֶת חֲבֵירוֹ בְּתוֹךְ אַרְבַּע אַמּוֹת שֶׁלְמִזְבֵּחַ. נָטַל חֲבֵירוֹ אֶת הַסַּכִּין וּתְקָעָהּ בְּלִיבּוֹ. עָמַד לוֹ רִבִּי צָדוֹק עַח מַעֲלוֹת הָאוּלָם. אָמַר לָהֶן. שְׁמָעוּנִי אֲחַיי בֵית יִשְׂרָאֵל. כָּתוּב כִּי־יִמָּצֵא חָלָל וגו'. וְיָצְאוּ זְקֵנֶיךָ וְשׁוֹפְטֶיךָ. אָנוּ מֵאַיכָן לָנוּ לָמוּד. מִן הַהֵיכָל מִן הָעֲזָרוֹת. שָׁרוֹן כָּל־עַמָּא בָכְיָין. עַד דְּאִינּוּן עֲסִיקִין בִּבְכִיָּה נִכְנַס אָבִיו שֶׁלְּאוֹתוֹ הַתִּינוֹק. אָמַר לָהֶן. אֲנִי כַּפָּרַתְכֶם. אַדַיְיין הַתִּינוֹק מְפַרְפֵּר וְלֹא נִטְמְאָת הַסַּכִּין. מְלַמֵּד שֶׁהָיְתָה טוּמְאָה קָשָׁה לָהֶן מִשְּׁפִיכוּת דָּמִים. לִגְנַיי.

⁷¹It happened that one preceded another to within four cubits of the altar. The other took the knife and stuck it into his heart. Rebbi Ṣadoq⁷² stood on the steps of the Hall and said to them, listen to me, my brethren, the House of Israel. It is written, *if a corpse be found*⁷³, etc. *Your elders and your judges shall go out*⁷⁴. From where do we have to measure, from the Temple or from the courtyards? All the people started to cry. While they still were crying, the father of the child⁷⁵ came and told them, I am atoning for you. The child is still fluttering, so the knife did not become impure⁷⁶. This teaches that impurity was worse for them than spilling blood, a shame.

71 Babli 23a, Tosephta 1:12, Tosephta *Ševuot* 1:4, *Sifry Num.* 161.
72 Since Rabban Johanan ben Zakkai asked Vespasian for medical treatment for R. Sadoq, the introduction of the lottery must be dated to the times of direct Roman rule in Judea.
73 *Deut.* 21:1.
74 *Deut.* 21:2.
75 In the impurity of the dead.

(fol. 39b) **משנה ג**: הַפַּיִס הַשֵּׁנִי מִי שׁוֹחֵט מִי זוֹרֵק מִי מְדַשֵּׁן אֶת הַמִּזְבֵּחַ הַפְּנִימִי מִי מְדַשֵּׁן אֶת הַמְּנוֹרָה. מִי מַעֲלֶה אֵיבָרִים לַכֶּבֶשׁ הָרֹאשׁ וְהָרֶגֶל וּשְׁתֵּי הַיָּדַיִם הָעוֹקֶץ וְהָרֶגֶל הֶחָזֶה וְהַגֵּרָה וּשְׁתֵּי הַדְּפָנוֹת וְהַקְּרָבַיִים וְהַסּוֹלֶת וְהַחֲבִיתִּים וְהַיָּיִן. וּשְׁלֹשָׁה עָשָׂר כֹּהֲנִים זָכִין בּוֹ. אָמַר בֶּן עַזַּאי לִפְנֵי רִבִּי עֲקִיבָה מִשֵּׁם רִבִּי יְהוֹשֻׁעַ כְּדֶרֶךְ הִילּוּכוֹ הָיָה קָרֵב:

Mishnah 3: The second lottery: Who slaughters[76], who pours[77], who removes the ashes from the interior altar, who cleans the candelabrum, and who brings the parts to the ramp[78]: head and leg[79], the two front legs, spine and leg[80], breast and fat[81], two side pieces[82], and the intestines,[83] and the fine flour[84], and the pan-baked breads[85], and the wine[86]. Thirteen Cohanim won here. Ben Azzai said before Rebbi Aqiba in the name of Rebbi Joshua, it was brought in the way of its walking[87].

76 The sheep of the daily morning sacrifice. He is the Cohen with whom the counting of the lottery stops; the following 12 are those lined up to his right.

77 The blood of the daily morning sacrifice.

78 The parts were first transported to the Western side of lower part of the ramp (Mishnah *Šeqalim* 8:8); then the Cohanim took a prayer break to recite the *Šema`* (Mishnah *Tamid* 4:3, end) and only afterwards were the parts brought to the fire on top of the altar. The way the sheep was cut up is detailed in *Tamid* 4:2-3.

79 The head and the right hind leg are carried by the fifth Cohen in line.

80 The left hind leg with tail and kidneys, by the 7th Cohen.

81 The breast with the neck and two ribs on each side connected to lung and heart.

82 With spine, liver, and spleen, by the 9th Cohen.

83 Brought in a vessel, with the feet lying on top.

83 The daily flour offering of a tenth of an *epha*.

82 The first part of the daily offering of the High Priest (paid for by the High Priest but not carried by him). Cf. Chapter 1, Note 26.

83 The wine offering, a quarter *hin*.

84 The order of carrying, and of distribution to the Cohanim, was not that indicated by the Mishnah but head, breast, front legs, two side pieces, spine and back leg (Note 130). The order of the first and the last four is not in dispute.

(39d line 22) **הלכה ג**: אָמַר רִבִּי יוֹחָנָן. כְּדֵי לַעֲשׂוֹת פּוּמְפֵּי לַדָּבָר. אָמַר רִבִּי. וַהֲלֹא כֹהֵן הַמְדַשֵּׁן אֶת הַמִּזְבֵּחַ הַפְּנִימִי יָכוֹל הוּא לְדַשֵּׁן אֶת הַמְּנוֹרָה. אֶלָּא לַעֲשׂוֹת פּוּמְפֵּי לַדָּבָר. תַּמָּן תַּנִּינָן. וְהִנִּיחַ אֶת הַכּוּז עַל מַעֲלָה שְׁנִייָה וְיָצָא. וְנָטַל אֶת הַכּוּז מִמַּעֲלָה שְׁנִייָה וְיָצָא: אָמַר רִבִּי יוֹחָנָן. וְלָמָּה הָיָה נִכְנַס לִקְטוֹרֶת שְׁנֵי פְעָמִים. אֶלָּא לַעֲשׂוֹת פּוּמְפֵּי לַדָּבָר. רִבִּי שִׁמְעוֹן בֶּן לָקִישׁ

אָמַר. דְּבַר תּוֹרָה הוּא. בַּבּוֹקֶר בַּבּוֹקֶר בְּהֵיטִיבוֹ אֶת־הַנֵּירוֹת יַקְטִירֶינָּה: מָה עֲבַד לָהּ רִבִּי יוֹחָנָן. עוֹבֵר לְהֵיטֵב וּמַקְטִיר.

Halakhah 3: Rebbi Joḥanan said, to make a procession[85] on the occasion. Rebbi said, could not the Cohen who was removing the ashes from the interior altar himself clean the candelabra? But to make a procession on the occasion. There, we have stated: "He deposits the flask on the second step and leaves;[86]" "he takes the flask from the second step and leaves.[87]" Rebbi Joḥanan said, why does he enter twice for incense? Only to make a procession on the occasion. Rebbi Simeon ben Laqish said, it is a biblical command: *in the morning, in the morning, when he cleans the lights he shall burn the incense*[88]. What does Rebbi Joḥanan do with this? He could enter to clean and to burn incense[89].

85 Latin *pompa*, Greek πομπή "solemn procession". One tries to have as many Cohanim as possible involved in order to increase the solemnity.
Babli 24b, bottom.
86 *Mishnah Tamid* 3:9, speaking of the Cohen who cleans 5 lights of the candelabrum and refills them with oil.
87 *Mishnah Tamid* 6:1; the same Cohen returns, cleans the remaining two lights on the candelabrum, refills, and lights them, when he enters the Sanctuary a second time.
88 *Ex.* 30:7.
89 The verse does not require different persons for the different jobs (also we already had interpreted *in the morning, in the morning* as meaning "early in the morning, cf. Note 49.)

(39d line 29) מְנַיִין לְדִישׁוּן הַמִּזְבֵּחַ הַפְּנִימִי. רִבִּי פְּדָת בְּשֵׁם רִבִּי לְעָזָר. וְהִשְׁלִיךְ אוֹתָהּ אֵצֶל הַמִּזְבֵּחַ קֵדְמָה אֶל־מְקוֹם הַדָּשֶׁן אֵינוֹ צָרִיךְ. אִם [לקבוע] לוֹ מָקוֹם. כְּבָר כָּתוּב אֵצֶל הַמִּזְבֵּחַ. אִם לְלַמֵּד שֶׁיִּינָתֵן בְּמִזְרָחוֹ שֶׁלַּכֶּבֶשׁ. כְּבָר כָּתוּב קֵדְמָה. אַף הוּא דָרַשׁ אֵצֶל הַמִּזְבֵּחַ אֵצֶל הַמִּזְבֵּחַ. מַה כָּאן מִזְרָחוֹ שֶׁלַּכֶּבֶשׁ אַף כָּאן מִזְרָחוֹ שֶׁלַּכֶּבֶשׁ. מְנַיִין שֶׁהוּא אָסוּר בַּהֲנָייָה. רִבִּי לָא בְשֵׁם רִבִּי לְעָזָר. אֶל־מָקוֹם טָהוֹר. שֶׁיְּהֵא מְקוֹמוֹ טָהוֹר. רִבִּי זְעוּרָה בְשֵׁם רִבִּי לְעָזָר לֹא אָמַר כֵּן אֶלָּא. מְנַיִין לְדִישׁוּן הַמִּזְבֵּחַ הַחִיצוֹן שֶׁהוּא אָסוּר בַּהֲנָייָה. תַּלְמוּד לוֹמַר אֶל־מְקוֹם הַדָּשֶׁן. שֶׁיְּהֵא מְקוֹמוֹ לְעוֹלָם. מְנַיִין לְדִישׁוּן מִזְבֵּחַ הַפְּנִימִי. וְהִזָּה עָלָיו וְהִקְטִיר. מַה הַזָּיָיה בְגוּפוֹ אַף הַקְטָרָה בְגוּפוֹ. מְנַיִין לְמִזְבֵּחַ הַפְּנִימִי שֶׁהוּא אָסוּר בַּהֲנָייָה. קוֹל הַחוֹמֶר. אִם מִזְבֵּחַ הַחִיצוֹן אָסוּר בַּהֲנָייָה הַפְּנִימִי לֹא כָל־שֶׁכֵּן.

From where the cleaning of the interior altar[90]? Rebbi Pedat in the name of Rebbi Eleazar: *He shall throw it next to the altar, to the East, on the place of ashes*[91]. It is unnecessary[92]. If to designate [the place], it already is written, *next to the altar*. If to teach you that it should be put to the East of the ramp, it already is written, *to the East*. Also he explained, *next to the altar, next to the altar*[93]. Since in one case it is to the East of the ramp, so in the other case it is to the East of the ramp. From where that it is forbidden for usufruct[94]? Rebbi La in the name of Rebbi Eleazar: *to a pure place*[95], that its place shall be pure[96]. Rebbi Ze`ira in the name of Rebbi Eleazar did not say so but, from where that the cleaning of the exterior altar is forbidden for usufruct? The verse says, *to the place of ashes*, that it be its place forever. From where the cleaning of the interior altar? *He shall sprinkle on it*[97], *he shall burn incense*[98]. Since sprinkling is on its body[99], also burning incense on its body. From where that the interior altar is forbidden for usufruct? An argument *de minore ad majus*. If from the exterior altar it is forbidden, so much more from the interior[100].

90 Since in contrast to the exterior altar, removing ashes from the interior incense altar is never mentioned in the Torah.

91 *Lev.* 1:16, referring to the crop of a pigeon brought as elevation offering. Cf. *Sifra Wayyiqra I Pereq* 9(3).

92 The mention *on the place of ashes* is not needed to fix the place; it instructs the Cohen where to put the ashes. Babli *Me`ilah* 12a.

93 The first quote is from *Lev.* 1:16, the second *Lev.* 6:3, about the ashes from the exterior altar formally deposited next to the altar. Since this case is explicit the exterior altar, the other is taken implicitly to refer to the interior altar.

94 Mishnah *Me`ilah* 3:4 states that from the ashes from the interior altar and the candelabrum one may not have usufruct but taking them is not larceny.

95 *Lev.* 6:4. The quote is inappropriate since the verse speaks of the remainder of the ashes on the exterior altar which are transported to a pure place outside the sacred precinct.

96 It seems that here "pure" is taken in the sense of "untouched".

97 *Lev.* 16:19.

98 *Ex.* 30:7. The quote is incomplete since the argument is a comparison of *he shall sprinkle on it*, and *he shall burn incense on it*.

99 As explained in Halakhah 5:7, the High Priest on the Day of Atonement is commanded to sprinkle blood on the interior altar *on it*, on the cleaned metal surface directly, not on ashes or unburned incense. The rule is then transferred to everyday's burning of incense since the same expression is used.

100 Since the external altar is accessible to all Cohanim at all times, the internal only to a selected Cohen twice a day.

(39d line 40) רִבִּי זְעוּרָה בְשֵׁם רִבִּי חֲנִינָה. קְטוֹרֶת שֶׁכָּבָת הוּמַמוּ אֲפִילוּ בְקַרְטִין. שֶׁאֵין כָּתוּב אִיכּוּל אֶלָא עַל מִזְבֵּחַ הַחִיצוֹן. פְּתִילָה שֶׁכָּבָת צְרִיכָה דִישׁוּן. מַה מִיָּד. תַּלְמִידוֹי דְּרִבִּי חִייָה בַּר לוּלְייָנֵי אֲמְרִין. מֵעַתָּה צָרִיךְ שֶׁיְּהֵא מֵיצָן. שֶׁמֶן מָהוּ שֶׁיְּהֵא צָרִיךְ דִישׁוּן. מִילְתֵיהּ דְרַבִּי שְׁמוּאֵל בַּר רַב יִצְחָק אֲמָרָה. שֶׁמֶן צָרִיךְ דִישׁוּן. רִבִּי שְׁמוּאֵל בַּר רַב יִצְחָק בָּעֵי. מֵעַתָּה בְּאֶחָד בִּתְקוּפַת טֵבֵת מֶחֱצֵי לוֹג לְכָל־נֵר. בְּאֶחָד בִּתְקוּפַת תַּמּוּז מֶחֱצִי לוֹג לְכָל־נֵר. אָמַר רִבִּי יוֹסֵה. אֵין מִן הָדָא לֵית שְׁמַע מִינָהּ כְּלוּם. דְּתַנִּינָן תַּמָּן. בֶּן בֵּבַי עַל הַפָּקִיעַ. שֶׁהָיָה מְזַוֵיג אֶת הַפְּתִילוֹת.

Rebbi Ze'ira in the name of Rebbi Ḥanina: Incense which was extinguished becomes defective even in carats[101]; for consumption is written only for the external altar[102]. A wick which was extinguished needs replacement[103]. Immediately? The students of Rebbi Ḥiyya bar Julianus say, first it needs to be cooled. Does the oil have to be replaced? The word of Rebbi Samuel bar Rav Isaac implies that oil has to be replaced. Rebbi Samuel bar Rav Isaac asked, now on the winter solstice half a *log* for each light, on the summer solstice half a log for each light[104]? Rebbi Yose said, from this you cannot conclude anything, as we have stated there[105], "Ben Bevay for the skeins", he was threading the wicks[106].

101 Even if entire grains of incense are not touched by the fire, they become disqualified. Babli *Menaḥot* 24b.

102 Lev. 6:3.

103 Babli *Menaḥot* 88b.

104 Since the candelabrum has to be lit "from evening to morning' (*Ex.* 27:21), one would assume that filling the same volume of oil in winter and summer means that in the summer the remnants of the previous night's oil have to be discarded. Cf. Babli 15a.

105 Mishnah *Šeqalim* 5:1.

106 If larger wicks are used in summer than in winter, the same amount of oil can be burned in all seasons. The Babli presumes without discussion that the oil has to be replaced, *Menaḥot* 88b.

(39d line 48) הָכָא אַתְּ אָמַר. מֵיטַב וְאַחַר כָּךְ מַקְטִיר. וְהָכָא אַתְּ אָמַר. מַקְטִיר וְאַחַר כָּךְ מֵיטַב. אָמַר רִבִּי יוֹחָנָן. תָּמִיד דְּרִבִּי שִׁמְעוֹן אִישׁ הַמִּצְפָּה הִיא. אָמַר רִבִּי יַעֲקֹב בַּר אָחָא. וְלֹא כוּלָּהּ אֶלָּא מִילִּין צְרִיכִין לְרַבָּנָן. רִבִּי חִזְקִיָּה רִבִּי אָחָא בְּשֵׁם רִבִּי אַבָּהוּ. מִדּוֹת דְּרִבִּי אֱלִיעֶזֶר בֶּן יַעֲקֹב הִיא. אָמַר רִבִּי יוֹסֵי בֵּירִבִּי בּוּן. וְלֹא כוּלָּהּ אֶלָּא מִילִּין צְרִיכִין לְרַבָּנָן. מַה טַעֲמָא דְּרִבִּי שִׁמְעוֹן אִישׁ הַמִּצְפָּה. בַּבּוֹקֶר בַּבּוֹקֶר בְּהֵיטִיבוֹ אֶת־הַנֵּירֹת יַקְטִירֶנָּה׃ רִבִּי אָחָא רִבִּי חִנָּנָא בְּשֵׁם רִבִּי שִׁמְעוֹן בְּרִבִּי. טַעֲמוֹן דְּרַבָּנָן. מִחוּץ לַפָּרֹכֶת הָעֵדוּת בְּאֹהֶל מוֹעֵד יַעֲרֹךְ אֹתוֹ אַהֲרֹן וּבָנָיו מֵעֶרֶב וְעַד בֹּקֶר. שֶׁלֹּא יְהֵא שָׁם אֶלָּא הֲטָבַת נֵרוֹת בִּלְבָד.

Here, you are saying, he cleans and then he burns the incense; but there, you are saying, he burns the incense and then he cleans[107]. Rebbi Johanan said, this is *Tamid* of Rebbi Simeon from Mitzpeh[108]. Rebbi Aha bar Jacob said, but not all of it; there are sayings questioned by the rabbis[109]. Rebbi Hizqiah, Rebbi Aha, in the name of Rebbi Abbahu: It is *Middot* of Rebbi Eliezer ben Jacob[110]. Rebbi Yose ben Rebbi Abun said, but not all of it; there are sayings questioned by the rabbis. What is the reason of Rebbi Simeon from Mitzpeh? *In the morning, in the morning, when he cleans the lights he shall burn the incense on it*[111]. Rebbi Aha, Rebbi Hinena in the name of Rebbi Simeon ben Rebbi: The reason of the rabbis, *outside the curtain of the testimonial in the Tent of Meeting, Aaron and his sons shall arrange it from evening to morning*[112]*;* that there shall be only the cleaning of the lights[113].

107 In Mishnah 1:2 it is stated that the High Priest first burns the incense and then cleans the lights; it is presumed that this was the order during the entire year when ordinary priests were serving. But in Mishnah 2:3 the cleaning of the candelabrum is part of the first lottery, while burning the incense is mentioned only in Mishnah 2:4 (confirmed by Mishnah *Tamid* 5:2). The Mishnaiot are inconsistent with one another.

108 Chapter 2 follows the Mishnah in *Tamid*, which follows the teachings of Rebbi Simeon from Mitzpeh. Tosephta 1:13.

109 Tractate *Tamid* is mostly, but not totally, based on the teachings of Rebbi Simeon from Mitzpeh.

110 The parts in *Tamid* inconsistent with the teachings of Rebbi Simeon from Mitzpeh are attributed to R. Eliezer ben Jacob I who is the source of most of Mishnah *Middot* (Babli 16a).

111 *Ex.* 30:7 clearly mentions cleaning the lights before burning the incense.

112 *Ex.* 27:21 (badly misquoted). If the burning of incense in the evening were after lighting the candelabrum, the lighting would not be the last action in the Sanctuary before the next morning.

(39d line 56) אָמַר רִבִּי יוֹחָנָן. לֹא קָבְעוּ פַּייס לַתָּמִיד שֶׁלְּבֵין הָעַרְבַּיִם אֶלָּא אָמְרוּ. מִי שֶׁזָּכָה בַּשַּׁחֲרִית יִזְכֶּה בֵין הָעַרְבַּיִם. וְהָא תַנֵּי. כְּפַייס שֶׁלְשַׁחֲרִית כֵּן פַּייס שֶׁל בֵּין הָעַרְבַּיִם. הַזָּכָה זָכָה לְעַצְמוֹ. רִבִּי חִזְקִיָּה בְשֵׁם רִבִּי בּוּן בַּר כַּהֲנָא. תִּיפִתָּר שֶׁהָיְתָה הַשַּׁבָּת אֶחָד מִשְׁמָר הַבָּא וְאֶחָד מִשְׁמָר הַיּוֹצֵא.

אָמַר רִבִּי יוֹחָנָן. לֹא גָזְרוּ עַל שְׁנֵי גִיזִירִין בַּשַּׁחֲרִית. אָמַר רִבִּי יוֹסֵה. מַתְנִיתָהּ אָמְרָה כֵן. בְּכָל־יוֹם אַיִל קָרֵב בֵּין הָעַרְבַּיִם בְּאַחַד עָשָׂר. וְלֹא אָמַר בְּשַׁחֲרִית כְּלוּם. רִבִּי שַׁמַּי בָּעֵי. וְלָמָּה לֹא גָזְרוּ עַל שְׁנֵי גִיזִירִין בַּשַּׁחֲרִית. [אָמַר רִבִּי מָנָא. וְלֹא שְׁמִיעַ רִבִּי שַׁמַּי דְּאָמַר רִבִּי יוֹחָנָן. לֹא גָזְרוּ עַל

שְׁנֵי גְזִירִין בַּשַּׁחֲרִית. וְאָמַר רִבִּי יוֹסֵי. מַתְנִיתָא אֲמָרָה כֵן. וְחָזַר וְאָמַר. אִין. דּוּ שְׁמִיעַ. אֶלָּא כְאִינַּשׁ דְּשָׁמַע מִילָּא וּמַקְשֵׁי עֲלָהּ. רִבִּי שַׁמַּי בָּעֵי. לָמָּה גָזְרוּ עַל שְׁנֵי גְזִירִין בֵּין הָעַרְבָּיִים וְלֹא גָזְרוּ עַל שְׁנֵי גְזִירִין בַּשַּׁחֲרִית.]

Rebbi Joḥanan said, they did not institute a lottery for the evening but said, he who won in the morning shall have won in the evening[113]. But was it not stated: Just as the lottery is in the morning, so it is in the evening? The winner won for himself. Rebbi Ḥizqiah in the name of Rebbi Abun bar Cahana: Explain it that it was on the Sabbath; one for the entering watch, the other for the leaving watch[114].

Rebbi Joḥanan said, they did not decide about the two logs in the morning[115]. Rebbi Yose said, a *baraita* says so, every day (a he-goat)[116] is brought by eleven, and it does not mention anything in the morning. Rebbi Shammai asked, why did they not decide about the two logs in the morning? Rebbi Mana said, did Rebbi Shammai not hear that Rebbi Joḥanan said, they did not decide about the two logs in the morning; and Rebbi Yose said, a *baraita* says so? He turned around and said, yes, he had heard. But he is a person who heard a statement and questions it: Why did they decide about two logs in the evening and did not decide about two logs in the morning[117]?

113 Babli 26a.
114 Since a new watch, another family of Cohanim, took over the service after the morning sacrifices, it is obvious that the Cohen who won in the morning is no longer present at the Temple in the afternoon.
115 There was no lottery to determine who brought the obligatory two logs to the altar in the morning, but the Cohen chosen to remove the ashes had to bring the new logs and set up an orderly fireplace on the altar.
116 This word is a misquote from Mishnah 6 which is not quoted here since one refers to Mishnah 5 about the daily sacrifice, which was a sheep.
117 Tosaphot *Menahot* 89b-90a, s. v. תמיד point out that the bringing of logs to the altar in the morning belongs to the preparation, covered by the first lottery. Only in the afternoon was the bringing of two logs part of the service of the daily sacrifice. Since the early morning preparation was in the night, there was no need to increase the number of participants for *pompa*.

(39d line 67) שְׁלֹשָׁה עָשָׂר זָכִין בּוֹ. וְתָנֵי עֲלָהּ. פְּעָמִים בְּאַרְבָּעָה עָשָׂר. פְּעָמִים בַּחֲמִשָּׁה עָשָׂר. פְּעָמִים בְּשִׁשָּׁה עָשָׂר. לֹא פָחוֹת וְלֹא יוֹתֵר. כְּדַרְכּוֹ בַּתְּשָׁעָה. וּבֶחָג בְּיַד אֶחָד צְלוֹחִית שֶׁל מַיִם. הֲרֵי עֲשָׂרָה. בֵּין הָעַרְבַּיִים בְּאַחַד עָשָׂר. שְׁנַיִם בְּיָדָם שְׁנֵי גִיזְרֵי עֵצִים. [וּ]בַשַּׁבָּת בְּאַחַד עָשָׂר

עָצְמוּ בְּתִשְׁעָה. שְׁנַיִם בְּיָדָם שְׁנֵי בְזִיכֵי לְבוֹנָה שֶׁלְלֶחֶם הַפָּנִים. הֲרֵי (חֲמִשָּׁה עָשָׂר) [אַרְבַּע עָשָׂר]. וּבַשַּׁבָּת שֶׁבְּתוֹךְ הֶחָג בְּיַד אֶחָד צְלוֹחִית שֶׁל מָיִם. הֲרֵי שִׁשָּׁה עָשָׂר.

תְּבִיאֶנָּה לִפְנֵי הַמּוּסָפִין. וּכְשֶׁהוּא אוֹמֵר תַּקְרִיב. אַף לְאַחַר הַנְּסָכִים. אִית תַּנָּיֵי תַנֵּי. קוֹדֶם לִנְסָכִים. מָאן דְּאָמַר. קוֹדֶם לִנְסָכִים. קוֹדֶם לְנִיסְכֵי יַיִן. מָאן דְּאָמַר. לְאַחַר נְסָכִים. לְאַחַר נִיסְכֵי סוֹלֶת. סֹלֶת קוֹדֶמֶת לַחֲבִיתִין. אַף עַל פִּי שֶׁזֶּה לָאִישִׁים. וְזֶה לָאִישִׁים. זֶה קָרְבַּן יָחִיד וְזֶה קָרְבַּן צִיבּוּר. חֲבִיתִּין קוֹדְמִין לַבְּזִיכִין. אַף עַל פִּי שֶׁזֶּה קָרְבַּן יָחִיד וְזֶה קָרְבַּן צִבּוּר. זֶה תָדִיר וְזֶה אֵינוֹ תָדִיר. חֲבִיתִּין קוֹדְמִין לַיַּיִן. שֶׁזֶּה לָאִישִׁים וְזֶה לַסְּפָלִים. בְּזִיכִין וְיַיִן מִי קוֹדֵם. וְלֹא מַתְנִיתָה הִיא. לְבוֹנָה לַיַּיִן. כָּאן לְקָרְבַּן יָחִיד. כָּאן לְקָרְבַּן צִיבּוּר.

"Thirteen won here." And it was stated on this[118]: "Sometimes fourteen, sometimes fifteen, sometimes sixteen, no less and no more." Normally by nine[119], and on Tabernacles in the hand of one a vial of water, these are ten[120]. In the evening by eleven; in the hands of two, two wooden logs. On the Sabbath by eleven, itself by nine, two, in their hands two cups of incense of the shew-bread; this makes (fifteen) [fourteen][121]. On the Sabbath of Tabernacles, in the hand of one a vial of water, this makes sixteen.

He shall bring it[122], before the additional sacrifices, but when he repeats *you shall sacrifice* even after the libations[123]. There are Tannaim who state, before the libations. He who says before the libations, before the wine libations. He who says after the libations, after the libations of fine flour. [124]The fine flour precedes the pan-baked breads; even though this is for the fire and that is for the fire, this is a private sacrifice[125] and the other a public sacrifice. The pan-baked bread precede the cups[126]; even though this is a private sacrifice and the other a public sacrifice, this is frequent but the other is not frequent[127]. The pan-baked breads precede the wine since this is for the fire but that is for the bowls[127]. Cups and wine, which one has precedence? Is that not the Mishnah, incense before the wine[128]? Here for a private offering[129], there for public offering.

118 Tosephta 1:13.
119 Plus the four who precede the presentation of the daily sacrifice makes 13.
120 Together 14.
121 Both in the evening of every day and in the morning of the Sabbath. The corrector's text clearly is in error.

122 *Lev.* 6:7, on the presentation of the High-Priest's pan-baked breads. Cf.i 34a
123 The libations of wine belonging to the daily sacrifice, preceding the additional sacrifices of special days.
124 Babli 34a.
125 The High Priest's private offering,

although part of the public ceremony.
126 On the Sabbath, containing the incense which accompanied the shew-bread on the table in the Sanctuary.
127 The wine libations accompanying the sacrifices were poured into bowls with small holes on the bottom through which the wine flowed onto the altar in sufficiently small amounts so that the wine evaporated and did not extinguish the flame.
128 Since in Mishnah 3 wine is mentioned last, and on the Sabbath one mentions the two cups containing incense with the daily sacrifice, it should be clear that incense precedes the wine.
129 The only open question is how to handle incense and wine brought with a private offering.

(40a line 4) כֵּינֵי מַתְנִיתָה. הָרֹאשׁ וְהָרֶגֶל הֶחָזֶה וְהַגֵּרה וּשְׁתֵּי יָדַיִם וּשְׁתֵּי דְפָנוֹת הָעוֹקֶץ וְהָרֶגֶל. אָמַר רִבִּי יוֹחָנָן. טַעֲמָא דְּבֶן עַזַּאי. וְהִקְטַרְתָּ אֶת־כָּל־הָאַיִל הַמִּזְבֵּחָה. כְּדֵי שֶׁיְּהֵא נִרְאֶה כְּמְהַלֵּךְ עַל גַּבֵּי הַמִּזְבֵּח. הָרֹאשׁ וְהָרֶגֶל. וְאַתְּ אָמַר הָכֵין. אָמַר רִבִּי מָנָא. פָּשַׁט רֹאשָׁהּ. עָקַר רַגְלָהּ.

So is the Mishnah[130]: head and leg[79], breast and fat[81], the two front legs, two side pieces[82], spine and leg[80]. Rebbi Johanan said, the reason of Ben Azzai: *You shall burn the entire he-goat on the altar*[131], it should look as if it went walking onto the altar. Head and leg, and you are saying so? Rebbi Mana said, if it stretches out its head[132] it lifts the foot.

130 The missing part of the Mishnah, the list according to Ben Azzai. Babli 25b.
131 *Ex.* 29:18.
132 In order to start walking.

(fol. 39b) **משנה ד**: הַפַּיִס הַשְּׁלִישִׁי חֲדָשִׁים לַקְּטוֹרֶת בּוֹאוּ וְהָפִיסוּ. רְבִיעִי חֲדָשִׁים עִם יְשָׁנִים מִי מַעֲלֶה אֵיבָרִים מִן הַכֶּבֶשׁ לַמִּזְבֵּחַ:

Mishnah 4: The third lottery, newcomers for incense come and participate in the lottery. The fourth, newcomers and old-timers, who brings the limbs from the ramp to the altar?

(40a line 8) **הלכה ד**. אָמַר רִבִּי חֲנִינָה. מִיָּמָיו לֹא הֵפִיס אָדָם בִּקְטוֹרֶת וְשָׁנָה. אָמַר רִבִּי יוֹסֵה. מַתְנִיתָה אָמְרָה כֵן. חֲדָשִׁים לַקְּטוֹרֶת בּוֹאוּ וְהָפִיסוּ. אָמַר רִבִּי חֲנִינָה. וְכֵן לַמַּחְתָּה. אָמַר רִבִּי יוֹסֵה. מַתְנִיתָה אָמְרָה כֵן. מִי שֶׁזָּכָה בִּקְטוֹרֶת אוֹמֵר לָזֶה שֶׁעַל יְמִינוֹ. אוּף אַתְּ לַמַּחְתָּה. נִמְצֵאתָהּ אוֹמֵר. שְׁנֵי כֹהֲנִים הָיוּ מִתְבָּרְכִים בְּכָל־פַּעַם. רַב אָמַר. בָּרֶךְ יי חֵילוֹ וּפוֹעַל יָדָיו תִּרְצֶה. מַעֲשֶׂה בְּאֶחָד שֶׁיָּבְשָׁה זְרוֹעוֹ וְלֹא הֵנִיחָהּ. לְקַיֵּים מַה שֶׁנֶּאֱמַר בָּרֶךְ יי חֵילוֹ וּפוֹעַל יָדָיו תִּרְצֶה.

Halakhah 4: Rebbi Hanina said, nobody ever participated in the lottery and repeated[133]. Rebbi Yose said, the Mishnah says so, "newcomers for incense come and participate in the lottery." Rebbi Hanina said, the same is true for the pan[69]. Rebbi Yose said, a *baraita* says so, "the one winning the incense says to the one on his right side, you are with me with the pan," You have to say that two Cohanim are blessed every time[134]. Rav said, *May the Eternal bless his might and may You desire the action of his hands*[135]. It happened that a man whose arm atrophied[136] but he did not refrain from it, to uphold what had been said, *may the Eternal bless his might and may You desire the action of his hands.*

133 It means that nobody ever won in that lottery and repeated. Babli 26a, where R. Hanina says that bringing the incense makes people rich.
134 Since obviously the man standing next to the winner also never won before.
135 *Deut.* 33:11, the blessing of Moses.

The Babli interprets חַיִל as "riches", whereas the Yerushalmi reads it as "physical power".
136 The arm could not really have atrophied since that would have disqualified the Cohen from serving; it must have been a case of weakness in the arm which was healed by his serving with the incense.

(fol. 39b) **משנה ה**: תָּמִיד קָרֵב בְּתִשְׁעָה בַּעֲשָׂרָה בְּאַחַד עָשָׂר בִּשְׁנַיִם עָשָׂר לֹא פָחוֹת וְלֹא יוֹתֵר. כֵּיצַד עַצְמוֹ בְתִשְׁעָה. בֶּחָג בְּיַד אֶחָד צְלוֹחִית שֶׁל מַיִם הֲרֵי עֲשָׂרָה. בֵּין הָעַרְבַּיִם בְּאַחַד עָשָׂר עַצְמוֹ בְתִשְׁעָה וּשְׁנַיִם בְּיָדָם שְׁנֵי גִיזִירֵי עֵצִים. בַּשַּׁבָּת בְּאַחַד עָשָׂר עַצְמוֹ בְתִשְׁעָה וּשְׁנַיִם בְּיָדָם שְׁנֵי בְזִיכֵי לְבוֹנָה שֶׁל לֶחֶם הַפָּנִים. וּבַשַּׁבָּת שֶׁבְּתוֹךְ הֶחָג בְּיַד אֶחָד צְלוֹחִית שֶׁל מַיִם:

Mishnah 5: The daily sacrifice is brought by nine persons, by ten, by eleven, by twelve, neither less nor more. How is this? Itself by nine[119], and on Tabernacles in the hand of one a vial of water, these are ten[120]. In the evening by eleven; itself by nine and in the hands of two, two wooden logs. On the Sabbath by eleven, itself by nine, two, in their hands two cups of incense of the shew-bread;.. On the Sabbath of Tabernacles, in the hand of one a vial of water.

(40a line 15) **הלכה ה:** וְעָרְכוּ. יָכוֹל מֵאָה. יָכוֹל מָאתַיִם. אָמַר רִבִּי עֲקִיבָה. כָּל־שֶׁשְּׁמוּעוֹ מְרוּבָּה וּשְׁמוּעוֹ מְמוּעָט. תָּפַשְׂתָּה מְרוּבָּה לֹא תָפַשְׂתָּה. תָּפַשְׂתָּה אֶת הַמְמוּעָט תָּפַשְׂתָּה. תַּנֵּי רִבִּי יְהוּדָה בֶּן בָּתֵירָה אוֹמֵר. שְׁתֵּי מִידוֹת. אַחַת כָּלָה וְאַחַת שֶׁאֵינָהּ כָּלָה. הַכֹּל מוֹדִין בְּמִידָה כָלָה וְאֵין מוֹדִין בְּמִידָה שֶׁאֵינָהּ כָּלָה. אָמַר רִבִּי נְחֶמְיָה. וְכִי מַה בָא הַכָּתוּב. לִפְתּוֹחַ אוֹ לִנְעוֹל. לֹא בָא לִנְעוֹל אֶלָּא לִפְתּוֹחַ. אִם אוֹמֵר. יָמִים. עֲשָׂרָה. אֵינָן אֶלָּא מֵאָה אֶלָּא מָאתַיִם. אֶלָּא אֶלֶף אֶלָּא רִיבּוֹא. וּכְשֶׁאַתָּה אוֹמֵר. יָמַיִם שְׁנָיִם. פָּתַחְתָּ. רִבִּי מָנָא אָמַר מִשּׁוּם רִבִּי יְהוּדָה. יָמִים שְׁנָיִם. יָכוֹל יָמִים הַרְבֵּה. אִם מְרוּבִּין הֵן. וַהֲלֹא כְבָר נֶאֱמַר רַבִּים. הָא לֹא דִיבֵּר אֶלָּא בְיָמִים מְעוּטִים. וְכַמָּה הֵן. הֱוֵי אוֹמֵר. שְׁנָיִם. רַבִּים שְׁלֹשָׁה. יָכוֹל (יָמִים) רַבִּים עֲשָׂרָה. אָמַר יָמִים וְאָמַר רַבִּים. מַה יָּמִים מִיעוּט יָמִים שְׁנָיִם. אַף רַבִּים מִיעוּט רַבִּים שְׁלֹשָׁה. יָכוֹל שְׁנָיִם וּשְׁלֹשָׁה הֲרֵי חֲמִשָּׁה. וְכִי נֶאֱמַר יָמִים [וְרַבִּים]. וַהֲלֹא לֹא נֶאֱמַר אֶלָּא יָמִים רַבִּים. הָא כֵיצַד. הָרַבִּים הַלָּלוּ יְהוּ מְרוּבִּין עַל שְׁנָיִם. וְכַמָּה הֵן. הֱוֵי אוֹמֵר. שְׁלֹשָׁה.

וְעָרְכוּ בְּנֵי אַהֲרֹן֒. יָכוֹל מֵאָה. תַּלְמוּד לוֹמַר וְעָרַךְ הַכֹּהֵן֒ אוֹתָם. [אִי וְעָרַךְ הַכֹּהֵן֒ אוֹתָם.] יָכוֹל יְהֵא כֹהֵן אֶחָד עוֹרֵךְ אֶת כָּל־הָאֵיבָרִים. תַּלְמוּד לוֹמַר וְעָרְכוּ. הָא כֵיצַד. כֹּהֵן אֶחָד עוֹרֵךְ שְׁנֵי אֵיבָרִים. וְכַמָּה הֵן אֵיבָרִים. עֲשָׂרָה. וְאֶחָד בִּקְרָבַיִם. נִמְצָא הַטָּלֶה עוֹלֶה בְשִׁשָּׁה. דִּבְרֵי רִבִּי יִשְׁמָעֵאל. רִבִּי עֲקִיבָה אוֹמֵר. וְעָרְכוּ שְׁנָיִם. בְּנֵי אַהֲרֹן֒ שְׁנָיִם. הַכֹּהֲנִים שְׁנָיִם. מְלַמֵּד שֶׁהַטָּלֶה עוֹלֶה בְשִׁשָּׁה. [הַכֹּהֲנִים. לְרַבּוֹת הַקְּרָחִים. דִּבְרֵי רִבִּי יוּדָא]

וַהֲלֹא בְּבֶן בָּקָר הַכָּתוּב מְדַבֵּר. מַה תַּלְמוּד לוֹמַר. בְּתָמִיד שֶׁלַּשַּׁחַר הַכָּתוּב מְדַבֵּר. שִׁמְעוֹן בַּר בָּא רִבִּי יוֹחָנָן בְּשֵׁם רִבִּי יַנַּאי. נֶאֱמַר כָּאן עֲרִיכָה. וְנֶאֱמַר לְהַלָּן וְעָרַךְ הַכֹּהֵן֒ אוֹתָם. מַה עֲרִיכָה שֶׁנֶּאֱמְרָה לְהַלָּן בְּתָמִיד שֶׁלַּשַּׁחַר הַכָּתוּב מְדַבֵּר. אַף עֲרִיכָה שֶׁנֶּאֱמְרָה כָּאן בְּתָמִיד שֶׁלַּשַּׁחַר הַכָּתוּב מְדַבֵּר. עוּלָא בַּר יִשְׁמָעֵאל בְּשֵׁם רִבִּי לַעֲזָר. אֵינוֹ צָרִיךְ. מִמַּשְׁמַע שֶׁנֶּאֱמַר וְעָרְכוּ אֵין אָנוּ יוֹדְעִין שֶׁהֵן שָׁמַיִם. וְאַתְּ דָּרֵשׁ. וְעָרְכוּ שְׁנָיִם. בְּנֵי אַהֲרֹן֒ שְׁנָיִם. הַכֹּהֲנִים שְׁנָיִם. וְתַנֵּי כֵּן. אֵין לְךָ קוֹדֶם לְתָמִיד שֶׁלַּשַּׁחַר אֶלָּא קְטוֹרֶת בִּחְבָד.

Halakhah 5: *They shall arrange*[137]. I could think, a hundred; I could think, a thousand. [138]Rebbi Aqiba said, anywhere you could understand many or you could understand few, if you took the many you took nothing, if you took few you took[139]. It was stated: Rebbi Jehudah ben Bathyra said, two measures; one finite, the other infinite. Everybody measures with the finite measure, but nobody measures with the infinite measure. Rebbi Nehemiah said, does the verse come to open or to lock in? It does not come to lock in but to open[140]. If you are saying *days*[141] are ten, they could be 100 or 200 or 1'000 or 10'000. But if you say *days* are two, you did unlock. Rebbi Muna[142] said in the name of Rebbi Jehudah. *Days* are two. I could think that *days* are many. If they are many, why is it said, *many*? Therefore the verse only spoke of few days. How much are they? It means two; *many* are three. I could think that *many (days)* means ten. It says *days* and it says *many*. Since the minimum of *days* are two, so for *many*, the minimum of many are three. I could think that two and three make five. But is it said, *days [and many]*? It only is said, *many days*. How is this? These *many* should be more than two. How many are they? It implies three.

[143]*The sons of Aaron shall arrange*[137]. I could think, a hundred; the verse says, *the Cohen shall arrange*[144]. [If *the Cohen shall arrange*,] I could think that a single Cohen should arrange all the limbs; the verse says, *they shall arrange*. How is this? One Cohen arranges two limbs. How many limbs are there? Ten, and one for the intestines. It turns out that the lamb comes up by six (priests}, the words of Rebbi Ismael. Rebbi Aqiba says, *they shall arrange*, two; *the sons of Aaron*, two; *the priests*, two[145]. This teaches that the lamb comes up by six {priests}. [*The priest*, to include the bald-headed, the words of Rebbi Jehudah.][146]

But does the verse not speak of cattle[146]? Where does the verse imply that it is written about the daily morning sacrifice? Simeon bar Abba, Rebbi Johanan in the name of Rebbi Yannai: It is written here[147] arranging, and it is written there, *the Cohen shall arrange them*. Since concerning the arrangement mentioned there, the verse speaks about the daily morning sacrifice, so also concerning the arrangement mentioned here, the verse speaks about the daily morning sacrifice. Ulla bar Ismael in the name of Rebbi Eleazar, this is unnecessary. From the meaning of *they shall arrange*, do we not understand that they are two? And you explain, *they shall arrange*, two; *the sons of Aaron*, two; *the priests*, two; and it was stated so: Nothing precedes the daily sacrifice but incense[49,148].

---

137 *Lev.* 1:7. The theme of the Halakhah is to find a biblical source for the number of Cohanim used to bring the parts of the daily sacrifices to the altar.

138 The remainder of the Paragraph also is *Sifra Mesora`Parashah* 5(5-9). Its topic is the interpretation of prescriptive biblical verses in the absence of numerical data. The theory expounded here is what the author has called the axiom of definiteness: Biblical language in legal contexts is definite (H. Guggenheimer, *Logical Problems in Jewish Tradition*, in: Confrontations with Judaism, Ph. Longworth ed.,

London 1966., pp. 171-196, in particular pp. 174-175.) In the situation considered here it is noted that the set of numbers >1 has a smallest element, 2, but no largest one. Therefore an indefinite plural used in a biblical law must mean 2, otherwise the meaning would not be definite. This is applied to the laws of *zava*, a woman impure by non-menstrual blood flow for *many days*. By the principle of definiteness this means that days are 2, the number of *many days* is the smallest number >2, or 3.

139 Babli *Megillah* 17a, *Sanhedrin* 5a.
140 In Babylonian sources, this statement is credited to R. Yose; *Seder Olam* Chapter 1 (in the author's edition, Northvale 1998, p. 3, Note 5, pp. 5-8.)
141 *Lev.* 15:25.
142 The Tanna.
143 This paragraph is *Sifra Wayyiqra I Pereq* 6(1).

144 *Lev.* 1:12.
145 Babli 27a.
146 The sentence in brackets was added by the corrector, probably from *Sifra*. It has no connection with the topic under discussion. Babli *Bekhorot* 43b.
147 *Lev.* 1:7 is written in the paragraph about elevation offerings of cattle; only *Lev.* 1:12 is about elevation offerings of sheep, including the daily sacrifice. The argument of the preceding paragraph seems pointless.
148 Ulla's argument goes as follows. Since arranging the wood on the altar belongs to the preparations of the morning service, and no cattle can be offered as elevation offering (or any other) before the daily morning sacrifice, necessarily *Lev.* 1:7 is written for the preparation of all offerings for the new day, including the daily sacrifice.

(fol. 39b) **משנה ו:** אַיִל קָרֵב בְּאַחַד עָשָׂר הַבָּשָׂר בַּחֲמִשָּׁה הַקְּרָבַיִם וְהַסֹּלֶת וְהַיַּיִן שְׁנַיִם שְׁנַיִם:

Mishnah 6: A he-goat is brought by eleven, the meat by five, the intestines, and the fine flour, and the wine, each by two.

(40a line 41) יְכוֹלִין הֵם שְׁלֹשָׁה לְהַעֲלוֹתוֹ. וְלָמָּה אַיִל קָרֵב בְּאַחַד עָשָׂר. אֶלָּא כְּדֵי לַעֲשׂוֹת פּוֹמְפֵּי.

Three could bring it up; why is a he-goat brought by eleven? Only to make a procession.

(fol. 39b) **משנה ז:** פַּר קָרֵב בְּעֶשְׂרִים וְאַרְבָּעָה. הָרֹאשׁ וְהָרַגְלַיִם הָרֹאשׁ בְּאֶחָד וְהָרֶגֶל בִּשְׁנַיִם. הָעֹקֶץ וְהָרַגְלַיִם הָעֹקֶץ בִּשְׁנַיִם וְהָרַגְלַיִם בִּשְׁנַיִם. הֶחָזֶה וְהַגֵּרָה הֶחָזֶה בְּאֶחָד וְהַגֵּרָה בִּשְׁלֹשָׁה. שְׁתֵּי יָדוֹת בִּשְׁנַיִם. וּשְׁתֵּי דְפָנוֹת בִּשְׁנַיִם. הַקְּרָבַיִם וְהַסֹּלֶת וְהַיַּיִן בִּשְׁלֹשָׁה שְׁלֹשָׁה. בַּמֶּה דְבָרִים אֲמוּרִים. בְּקָרְבְּנוֹת צִיבּוּר. אֲבָל בְּקָרְבְּנוֹת הַיָּחִיד אִם רָצָה לְהַקְרִיב מַקְרִיב. הַפְשֵׁיטָן וְנִיתּוּחָן שֶׁל אֵילוּ וָאֵילוּ שָׁוֶה:

Mishnah 7: A bull is brought by twenty-four. head and leg[79], the head by one and the leg by two; spine and leg[80], the spine by two and the leg by two; breast and fat[81], the breast by one and the fat by three; the two front legs by two; the two side pieces[82] by two; the intestines, and the fine flour[149], and the wine[150] by three each. When has this been said? For a public offering. But for a private offering, if one wants to sacrifice, he sacrifices[151]. Skinning and cutting into pieces is the same for these and for those[152].

149 Which is $3/10$ of an *epha* or about 3.6 liter of flour mixed with $1/2$ *hin* of oil, about 3.5 liter.
150 Also half a *hin*.

151 If a single Cohen wants to do all the carrying, he may do it.
152 It need not be done by Cohanim.

(40a line 43) רַבָּנָן דְּקַיְסָרִין אָמְרֵי. מִפְּנֵי מַה קָרֵב פָּר בְּעֶשְׂרִים וְאַרְבָּעָה. כְּדֵי לַעֲשׂוֹת פּוֹמְפֵּי לַדָּבָר. עַל שֵׁם בְּבֵית אֱלֹהִים נְהַלֵּךְ בְּרָגֶשׁ: וְאֵת דָּרַשׁ. וְעָרְכוּ שְׁנַיִם. בְּנֵי אַהֲרֹן שְׁנַיִם. הַכֹּהֲנִים שְׁנַיִם. מִיכָּן לְפָרוֹ שֶׁל יָחִיד שֶׁיְּהֵא קָרֵב בְּשִׁשָּׁה.

The rabbis of Caesarea say, why is a bull brought by 24? To make a procession on the occasion, under the heading, *in God's House we shall walk in excitement*[153]. Since one explains, *they shall arrange*, two; *the sons of Aaron*, two; *the priests*, two; from here that a private person's bull should be brought by six[154].

153 *Ps.* 55:15.
154 Since *Lev.* 1:7, to which this explanation refers, is written in the paragraph about private elevation offerings of cattle.

אמר להם הממונה פרק שלישי

(fol.40a) **משנה א**: אָמַר לָהֶן הַמְמוּנֶּה צְאוּ וּרְאוּ אִם הִגִּיעַ זְמַן הַשְּׁחִיטָה. אִם הִגִּיעַ הָרוֹאֶה אוֹמֵר בּוֹרְקַי. מַתְיָה בֶּן שְׁמוּאֵל אוֹמֵר הֵאִיר פְּנֵי כָל הַמִּזְרָח עַד שֶׁבְּחֶבְרוֹן. וְהוּא אוֹמֵר הֵין:

Mishnah 1: The overseer said to them[1], "go and see whether the time of slaughter has arrived." When it arrived, the lookout says "it is radiant." Mathatias ben Samuel[2] says, "was the entire East illuminated up to what is in Hebron[3]?" And he[4] answers "yes".

1 Every day of the year, when the daily morning sacrifice was brought at dawn.
2 He is mentioned in Mishnah *Šeqalim* 5:1 as overseer of the lotteries. The sources are not unanimous about the meaning of these names, whether they came with the job or are a remembrance of outstanding personalities who once filled these positions. Some moderns presume that the list is of the last officials serving in the Second Temple.
3 Even though Hebron is South of Jerusalem, as explained at the end of the Halakhah.
4 The lookout.

(40b line 22) אָמַר לָהֶן הַמְמוּנֶּה כול'. מָהוּ בּוֹרְקַי. בָּרֶקֶת. תַּמָּן אָמְרִין. בָּרוֹק בּוֹרְקָה. אַנְהַר מַנְהֲרָא.

1 אמרין | **א** אמרי   ברוק בורקה | **א** ברק ברקא

[5]"The overseer said to them," etc. What means *borqi*? *Bareqet*[6]. There[7], they are saying, בָּרוֹק בּוֹרְקָה, getting light, radiant.

5 The Halakhah is copied in *Roš Haššanah* 2:1 (**א**).
6 The word denotes one of the precious stones in the breast plate of the High Priest, usually identified as agate or emerald. The word means radiant, from בָּרָק "lightning".
7 In Babylonia; in the formulation of the Babli 28b בָּרָק בַּרְקַאי.

(40b line 23) וְעֵד אֶחָד נֶאֱמָן. שְׁנִיָּיא הִיא הָכָא שֶׁאֵין אַתְּ יָכוֹל לַעֲמוֹד עָלָיו. וְחָשׁ לוֹמַר. עַד דּוּ עָלִיל וּנְפַק הִיא מַנְתָרָה. חֲכִימָא הִיא מִילְּתָא. אָמַר עַד אֶחָד. נוֹלַד אִישׁ פְּלוֹנִי בַּשַׁבָּת. מַלִּין אוֹתוֹ עַל פִּיו. חֲשִׁיכָה מוֹצָאֵי שַׁבָּת. מְטַלְטְלִין אוֹתוֹ עַל פִּיו. רְבִּי אִימִּי מְטַלְטֵל עַל פּוּם מְלוּיִתָא. רִבִּי מַתַּנְיָה מְטַלְטֵל עַל פּוּם אִיבִירִיתָא דִּזְהֲרָה. רִבִּי אִמִּי מְטַלְטֵל עַל פּוּם נָשַׁיָּיא דְּאָמְרָן. שִׁמְשָׁא הֲוַת עַל סוּסִיתָה.

1 דו | **א** דחיא   2 מנהרה | **א** מנהרא   3 אימי | **א** אמי   4 מלויתה | **א** דמלויתה | **א** מתניה | **א** מתנייה   אמי | **א** אימי   מטלטל | **א** מל   על פום נשייא | **א** על פי נשים

May one witness be believed[8]? It is different here since one cannot control him; should we not worry and say, by the time somebody climbs up and goes out it will shine[9]? The matter can be verified. If one witness says, this male was born on the Sabbath, one circumcises him on his word[10]. Rebbi Immi was carrying on the result of elapsed time[11]. Rebbi Mattaniah was carrying on the saying of the moon shining[12]. Rebbi Immi was (carrying) {circumcising][13] on the saying of women, the sun was over Hippos[14].

8 The Babli holds in general that a single witness can be believed in matters of prohibitions; the biblical requirement of two witnesses is binding only in criminal cases and matters that may have implications in criminal law. From the present paragraph it seems that the Yerushalmi does not accept this in general but that in cases where one witness is sufficient there is no difference between male or female witnesses.

9 While the time indicated must be approximately correct, since one asks only at the end of the night, and by the time somebody climbs up to check it clearly will be dawn, this does not prove that at the time of the assertion dawn was really visible. The text cannot be amended and the "not" deleted since it is confirmed by both sources.

10 Even though circumcising on the Sabbath a child not born on the Sabbath is a deadly sin.

11 Arabic ملوة "interval of time". He computed the end of the Sabbath astronomically, for a smooth terrestrial globe; a severe restriction for Tiberias situated on a steep Eastern slope.

12 The translation of איבירייתא is conjectural. The direction of the shining part of the moon indicates the position of the sun, from which its position below the horizon (of a smooth terrestrial globe) can be inferred without complicated computations.

13 The text in parenthesis is from *Yoma*, the one in braces from *Roš Haššanah*. Since Hippos was on the Eastern shore of the Lake of Galilee, so that for people in Tiberias on the Western shore the sun shone over Hippos in the morning, the statement cannot refer to the Sabbath. The reading of *Roš Haššanah* has to be accepted. Since circumcision has to be performed during daytime, R. Immi is consistently restrictive; in this case he does not rely on astronomical computations of sunrise but on the much later observation of the sun appearing over the mountains to the East.

(40b line 29) וְלָמָּה   עַד שֶׁהוּא בְחֶבְרוֹן [וְהוּא] אוֹמֵר הֵיוּ׃ בָּא לְהַזְכִּיר זְכוּת אָבוֹת.

And why "up to who is in Hebron? And he answers yes"? He comes to commemorate the merit of the Patriarchs.

(fol. 40a) **משנה ב**: וְלָמָה הוּצְרְכוּ לְכָךְ שֶׁפַּעַם אַחַת עָלָה מְאוֹר הַלְּבָנָה וְדִימּוּ שֶׁהֵאִיר הַמִּזְרָח וְשָׁחֲטוּ אֶת הַתָּמִיד וְהוֹצִיאוּהוּ לְבֵית הַשְּׂרֵיפָה וְהוֹרִידוּ הַכֹּהֵן לְבֵית הַטְּבִילָה. זֶה הַכְּלָל הָיָה בַמִּקְדָּשׁ כָּל־הַמֵּסִיךְ אֶת רַגְלָיו טָעוּן טְבִילָה. וְכָל־הַמַּטִּיל מַיִם טָעוּן קִדּוּשׁ יָדַיִם וְרַגְלָיִם:

Why did they need this? Because once the moon shone[14] and they thought that it dawned to the East; they slaughtered the daily sacrifice and had to bring it outside to the place of burning[15]. Then they brought the Cohen[16] to the place of immersion. This was the rule in the Temple: Everybody who spread his legs[17] needed immersion[18]; and everybody who urinated needed sanctification of hands and feet[19].

14 As the Halakhah points out, this can happen only in the second half of a month and therefore could not refer to a Day of Atonement.
15 The outside place reserved for the burning of disqualified sacrifices or those whose blood was brought into the Sanctuary and which could not be burned on the altar.
16 All Babli and independent Mishnah texts read: The High Priest.
17 Defecated. A biblical expression *Jud.* 3:26.
18 Of his entire body in a *miqweh*.
19 From the basin in the courtyard.

(40b line 30) **הלכה ב**: מְאוֹר הַלְּבָנָה מְתַמֵּר וְעוֹלֶה. מְאוֹר הַחַמָּה פּוֹסָה עַל פְּנֵי כָל־הַמִּזְרָח. עַד כְּדוֹן דַּהֲוָה סוֹפֵיהּ דְּיַרְחָא. הֲוָה רֵישִׁיהּ.

Halakhah 2: Moonlight comes up as a beam; sunlight spreads over the entire East[20]. So far if it was the end of the month; if it was the start[21]?

20 The reason given in the Mishnah is difficult to accept. In the Babli 28b it is explained that it was a cloudy day where the moonlight also was diffuse.
21 Even if one accepts the explanation of the Mishnah, the inquiry would only be necessary towards the end of the month when the moon rises towards morning.

(40b line 32) אָמַר רִבִּי חֲנִינָה. מֵאֵילֶת הַשַּׁחַר עַד שֶׁיָּאִיר הַמִּזְרָח אָדָם מְהַלֵּךְ אַרְבַּעַת מִיל. וּמִשֶּׁיָּאִיר הַמִּזְרָח עַד שֶׁתְּנֵץ הַחַמָּה אָדָם מְהַלֵּךְ אַרְבַּעַת מִיל. וּמִנַּיִין שֶׁמֵּאֵילֶת הַשַּׁחַר עַד שֶׁיָּאִיר

הַמִּזְרָח אָדָם מְהַלֵּךְ אַרְבַּעַת מִילִין. [שֶׁנֶּאֱמַר] וּכְמוֹ הַשַּׁחַר עָלָה וַיָּאִיצוּ הַמַּלְאָכִים בְּלוֹט לֵאמֹר. מִן סְדוֹם לְצוֹעַר אַרְבָּעָה מִילִין. יָתֵיר הֲוָון. אָמַר רִבִּי זְעוּרָא. הַמַּלְאָךְ הָיָה מְקַדֵּד לִפְנֵיהֶן אֶת הַדֶּרֶךְ. וּמְנַיִין מְשֶׁיָּאִיר הַמִּזְרָח עַד הָנֵץ הַחַמָּה אָדָם מְהַלֵּךְ אַרְבַּעַת מִיל. כְּמוֹ וּכְמוֹ. מִילָה דַּמְיָא לַחֲבֶירְתַּהּ.

[22]Rebbi Ḥanina said: From the appearance of the "morning hind"[23] until the first rays of light in the East a man can walk four mil[24]. From the first rays of light in the East until sunrise a man can walk four mil[25]. From where do we know that from the appearance of "the morning hind" until the first rays of light on the East there are four mil? [ince it is written][26]: *and when the morning came, the angels urged Lot, saying*[27]. From Sodom to Zoar there are four mil. It is farther than that[28]. Rebbi Ze`ira said: the angel was flattening the road before them. And from where that from the first rays of light in the East until sunrise there are four mil? When, *and when*, one thing compares to another[29].

22 A somewhat garbled version of a text in *Berakhot* 1:1 (Notes 63-70) and *Gen. rabba* 50(15).

23 The zodiacal light.

24 Since a person is presumed to be able to walk 40 *mil* on a full day at the equinoxes, this comes to 72 min.

25 Babli *Pesahim* 94a,

26 *Gen.* 19:15.

27 It is clear that the argument is not relevant to the question asked here, but to the time elapsing between first dawn and sunrise. To complete the proof, one has tro add a reference to v. 23, found in *Berakhot* and *Gen. rabba*, which states that Lot arrived in Zoar at the time of sunrise.

28 In the Babli, *Pesahim* 93b, R. Hanina is quoted that he checked out the distance and it was 5 *mil*.

29 The additional *and* permits to compare the one time specified in Scripture to the other, the time between visibility of the zodiacal light and first dawn.

(40b line 39) אָמַר רִבִּי יוֹסֵי בֵּירִבִּי בּוּן. הָדָא אַיֶּלֶת דְּשַׁחֲרָא. מָאן דְּאָמַר. כּוֹכַבְתָּא הִיא. טָעֵי. זִמְנִין דְּהִיא מְקַדָּמָה וְזִמְנִין דְּהִיא מְאַחֲרָה. מַאי כְדוֹן. כְּמִין תְּרֵין דְּקַרְנִין דִּנְהוֹר דְּסַלְקִין מִן מַדִּינְחָא וּמְנַהֲרִין.

[וְ]דִלְמָא. רִבִּי חִייָא רוֹבָא וְרִבִּי שִׁמְעוֹן בֶּן חֲלַפְתָּא הֲווֹ מְהַלְּכִין בְּהָדָא בִּקְעַת אַרְבֵּל בַּקְרִיצְתָהּ רָאוּ אַיֶּלֶת הַשַּׁחַר שֶׁבָּקַע אוֹרָהּ. אָמַר רִבִּי חִייָא רוֹבָא לְרִבִּי שִׁמְעוֹן בֶּן חֲלַפְתָּא. בְּרִבִּי. כָּךְ הִיא גְאוּלָתָן שֶׁל יִשְׂרָאֵל. בַּתְּחִילָּה קִימְעָא קִימְעָא. כָּל־ שֶׁהִיא הוֹלֶכֶת הִיא הוֹלֶכֶת וּמֵאִיר. מַאי טַעֲמָא. כִּי יוֹשֵׁב בַּחֹשֶׁךְ יי אוֹר לִי׃ כָּךְ בַּתְּחִילָּה וּמָרְדֳּכַי יוֹשֵׁב בְּשַׁעַר־הַמֶּלֶךְ. וְאַחַר כָּךְ וַיָּשָׁב

מָרְדֳּכַי אֶל־שַׁעַר הַמֶּלֶךְ. וְאַחַר כָּךְ וַיִּקַּח הָמָן אֶת־הַלְּבוּשׁ וְאֶת־הַסּוּס. וְאַחַר כָּךְ וּמָרְדֳּכַי יָצָא | מִלִּפְנֵי הַמֶּלֶךְ בִּלְבוּשׁ מַלְכוּת. וְאַחַר כָּךְ לַיְּהוּדִים הָיְתָה אוֹרָה וְשִׂמְחָה.

[30]Rebbi Yose bar Abun said: Anybody who identifies the "morning hind" with the planet Venus is in error; that planet sometimes is too early and sometimes too late[31]. What is it? It is like two double horns of light that arise from the East and illuminate..

[32][Explanation[33]: The great Rebbi Ḥiyya and Rebbi Simeon ben Ḥalaphta were walking in the valley of Arbela before morning and saw "the morning hind" that started radiating. The great Rebbi Ḥiyya said to Rebbi Simeon ben Ḥalaphta: Great man, so will be the deliverance of Israel; it starts out very small and grows and radiates as it goes on. What is the reason [34]When he[35] shall dwell in darkness, the Eternal is my light. So also at the start [36]Mordocai was sitting at the king's gate." After that [37]Mordocai returned to the king's gate. After that [38]Haman took the garment and the horse. After that: [39]Mordocai left the king's presence in royal garb. After that: [40]The Jews had light and joy.]

30 This and the following paragraph also are from *Berakhot*.
31 Sometimes Venus sets still during the night and sometimes it still is seen after sunrise.
32 This paragraph was added to the ms. by a corrector. While there is no logical necessity for the addition of this text, it is copied from a *Yoma* text, not from *Berakhot*. In *Berakhot* the quotes from *Esther* make sense, v. 6:11 preceding 6:12. The paragraph also is copied in *Qonteros Aharon* (Q, Chapter 1, Note 44; p. 311) which also quotes 6:12 before v 6:11. The text of Q is identical with that given here except that the Aramaic endings are ה not א; babylonized spelling is to be expected from all correctors.
33 Greek δήλωμα.
34 *Micha* 7:8.
35 In the biblical text: I.
36 *Esth.* 2:21.
37 *Esth.* 6:12.
38 *Esth.* 6:11.
39 *Esth.* 8:15.
40 *Esth.* 8:16.

(40b line 49) תַּנֵּי. כֹּהֵן שֶׁיָּצָא לְדַבֵּר עִם חֲבֵירוֹ. אִם לְהַפְלִיג טָעוּן טְבִילָה. אִם לְשָׁעָה טָעוּן קִידּוּשׁ יָדַיִם וְרַגְלָיִם. וּסְנֻמַ[וִיכָה[41] לֹא שָׁעָה קַלָּה הִיא. שַׁנְיָיא הִיא סְנָמַ[וִיכָה[. שֶׁעָשׂוּ אוֹתָהּ כְּהֶפְלֵג.

תַּנֵּי. יָשֵׁן טָעוּן טְבִילָה. נִתְנַמְנֵם טָעוּן קִידּוּשׁ יָדַיִם וְרַגְלַיִם. וְיָשֵׁן טָעוּן טְבִילָה. לֹא כֵן תַּנֵּי רִבִּי חִייָא. לֹא הָיְתָה יְשִׁיבָה בַּעֲזָרָה אֶלָּא לַמְּלָכֵי בֵית דָּוִד בִּלְבָד. וְאָמַר רִבִּי אִמִּי בְּשֵׁם רִבִּי

שִׁמְעוֹן בֶּן לָקִישׁ. אַף לְמַלְכֵי בֵית דָּוִד לֹא הָיְתָה יְשִׁיבָה בָעֲזָרָה. תִּיפְתָּר שֶׁסָּמַךְ עַצְמוֹ לַכּוֹתֶל וְיָשַׁן לוֹ. וְהָא כְתִיב וַיָּבֹא הַמֶּלֶךְ דָּוִד וַיֵּשֶׁב לִפְנֵי יְי׳. אָמַר רִבִּי אַיְיבוֹ בַּר נַגְרִי. יִישֵׁב עַצְמוֹ בִּתְפִילָה.

It was stated[42]: "A Cohen who left to speak with another person, if to go a distance, he needs immersion[43]; if for a short time he needs sanctification of hands and legs[44]. But is defecation not for a short time? There is a difference for defecation since they treat it as if going a distance.

It was stated: A person sleeping needs immersion, being drowsy needs sanctification of hands and legs. Does a person sleeping need immersion? Did not Rebbi Hiyya state[45], "there was no sitting in the Temple courtyard except for the kings of the Davidic dynasty;" and Rebbi Immi said in the name of Rebbi Simeon ben Laqish, even for the kings of the Davidic dynasty there was no sitting in the Temple courtyard. Explain it that somebody was supporting himself on a wall and sleeping. But is it not written[46], *King David came and sat before the Eternal?* Rebbi Ayvo bar Naggari said, he concentrated in prayer[43].

41 The scribe wrote סיכה "anointing", the corrector changed to סמיכה "laying on hands"; both mistaken for מסיכה "defecation."
42 Tosephta 1:16, Babli *Zevahim* 20b, Yerushalmi *Kilaim* 9:2 Notes 47-48.
43 As requited by Mishnah 3.
44 Since when he returns he starts his service anew; cf. Chapter 2 Note 51.
45 Babli 25a,69b; *Sotah* 40b,41b; *Qiddušin* 78b; *Sanhedrin* 101b; *Tamid* 27b. Yerushalmi *Pesahim* 5:12 (Note 247), *Sotah* 7:7 (Note 219).
46 2S. 7:18.
47 Cf. *Pesahim* 5:12 Note 248.

(fol. 40a) **משנה ג**: אֵין אָדָם נִכְנָס לָעֲזָרָה לָעֲבוֹדָה אֲפִילּוּ טָהוֹר עַד שֶׁיִּטְבּוֹל. חָמֵשׁ טְבִילוֹת וַעֲשָׂרָה קִדּוּשִׁין טוֹבֵל כֹּהֵן גָּדוֹל וּמְקַדֵּשׁ בּוֹ בַיּוֹם וְכֻלָּם בַּקּוֹדֶשׁ בֵּית הַפַּרְוָה חוּץ מִזּוֹ בִלְבָד:

Mishnah 3: Nobody enters the courtyard to serve, even if he was pure, unless he immerses himself. Five immersions and ten sanctifications did the High Priest immerse himself and sanctify on that day, and all of them in the Sanctuary in the Parwa house[48], except this one alone[49].

48 A subterranean cave inside the walls enclosing the sacred domain. The Babli declares "Parwa" to be the name of a magus or sorcerer.

49 Since the Mishnah states that nobody can enter the sacred domain for service unless he immersed himself in water outside the sacred domain, it is obvious that before serving the High Priest also must immerse himself in a *miqweh* on the Temple Mount but outside the sacred domain

(40b line 57) **הלכה ג:** כִּינֵי מַתְנִיתָה. לֹא הָיָה אָדָם נִכְנָס לַעֲזָרָה וְלַעֲבוֹדָה[וַאֲפִילוּ טָהוֹ] עַד שֶׁהוּא טוֹבֵל. לֹא סוֹף דָּבָר לַעֲבוֹדָה אֶלָּא אֲפִילוּ שֶׁלֹּא לַעֲבוֹדָה.

Halakhah 3: So is the Mishnah: No person did enter the courtyard or for service[50], [even if he was pure,] unless he immerses himself. Not only for service but also not for service.

50 Nobody, Cohen or lay person, could enter the sacred domain without ablution. But the Cohen who entered not for service could not start to serve until he underwent a second immersion.

(40b line 59) שָׁאֲלוּ אֶת בֶּן זוֹמָא. מַה מָּקוֹם לִטְבִילָה זוֹ. אָמַר לָהֶם. מַה אִם בְּשָׁעָה שֶׁהוּא נִכְנָס מִקּוֹדֶשׁ לַקּוֹדֶשׁ טָעוּן טְבִילָה. מְחוֹל לַקּוֹדֶשׁ כָּל־שֶׁכֵּן. [לֹא צוֹרְכָה דְּלָא מִקּוֹדֶשׁ לַקּוֹדֶשׁ] לֹא יְהֵא טָעוּן טְבִילָה. מְחוֹל לַקּוֹדֶשׁ יְהֵא טָעוּן טְבִילָה. אָמַר רִבִּי שַׁמַּאי. וְכֵינִי. מַה אִם מִקּוֹדֶשׁ לַקּוֹדֶשׁ שֶׁאֵינוּ עָנוּשׁ כָּרֵת טָעוּן טְבִילָה. מְחוֹל לַקּוֹדֶשׁ שֶׁהוּא עָנוּשׁ כָּרֵת לֹא כָל־שֶׁכֵּן יְהֵא טָעוּן טְבִילָה. וַאֲפִילוּ מִקּוֹדֶשׁ לַקּוֹדֶשׁ יְהֵא עָנוּשׁ כָּרֵת. כַּיֵּי דִּתְנִינָן תַּמָּן. הִשְׁתַּחֲוָה אוֹ שֶׁשָּׁהָה בִּכְדֵי הִשְׁתַּחֲוָיָה. עַד כַּמָּה הִיא שִׁיעוּר הִשְׁתַּחֲוָיָה. רִבִּי סִימוֹן בְּשֵׁם רִבִּי יְהוֹשֻׁעַ בֶּן לֵוִי. [עַד כְּדֵי] וַיִּכְרְעוּ אַפַּיִם אַרְצָה עַל־הָרִצְפָה וַיִּשְׁתַּחֲווּ. רִבִּי אַבָּהוּ מוֹסִיף עַד וְהוֹדוֹת לַיָי כִּי טוֹב. רִבִּי מָנָא מוֹסִיף. כִּי לְעוֹלָם חַסְדּוֹ:

They asked Ben Zoma, where does this immersion come from[51]? He said to them, since when he enters the holy from the holy he needs immersion[52], from profane to holy so much more? It is not necessary, but from holy to holy he should not need immersion[53], from profane to holy he should need immersion[54]. Rebbi Shammai said, it is the following. Since from holy to holy where he is not subject to extirpation[55] he needs immersion, from profane to holy where he is subject to extirpation[56] not so much more that he should need immersion? And even from holy to holy he should be subject to extirpation, following what we have stated there[57]: "If he prostrated himself, or tarried that he could have prostrated himself.⁵⁸" What is the duration of prostration? Rebbi Simon in the name of Rebbi Joshua ben Levi⁵⁹, [as long as] ⁶⁰*they bowed down with their faces on the floor and prostrated themselves.* Rebbi Abbahu adds, *thanking the Eternal for He is good*, Rebbi Mana adds, *His grace is forever.*

51 Which does not seem to be biblical.
52 As stated later in the Mishnah, if the High Priest changes from his 8 garments used for service outside to white garments used inside the Sanctuary he both immerses himself and sanctifies hands and legs.
53 Since he already immersed himself at the start of the service.
54 This would be an answer to the question asked at the start of the paragraph, but it is contradicted by the later Mishnaiot.
55 If he is pure when entering the Sanctuary but becomes impure inside, if he leaves immediately he is not subject to extirpation (Mishnah *Ševuot* 2:4.)
56 If he enters the sacred domain while impure, he is subject to extirpation.
57 Mishnah *Ševuot* 2:4.
58 While impure, he is subject to extirpation.
59 In *Ševuot* 2:4, he gives a much shorter time frame. The criterion given here, the time necessary to recite half or all of the verse, is the one given by the Babli *Ševuot* 16b in the name of other Galilean authorities.
60 2Chr. 7:3.

(fol. 40a) **משנה ד**: פֵּרְשׂוּ סָדִין שֶׁל בּוּץ בֵּינוֹ לְבֵין הָעָם פָּשַׁט יָרַד וְטָבַל עָלָה וְנִסְתַּפָּג. הֵבִיאוּ לוֹ בִגְדֵי זָהָב וְלָבַשׁ וְקִידֵּשׁ יָדָיו וְרַגְלָיו.

Mishnah 4: They spread a byssus sheet⁶¹ between him and the people; he undressed, stepped down, and immersed himself, came up and dried himself with a towel. They brought him the golden garments⁶², and he dressed, and sanctified hands and legs.

61 The same material from which the white garments are made which the High Priest wears for the special functions on the Day of Atonement.
62 The eight garments which the High Priest wears all year long, of which the diadem was pure gold and the coat, belt, and breast-shield contained gold.

(40b line 70) **הלכה ד**: תַּנֵּי. אָמַר רִבִּי יְהוּדָה. כָּל־עַצְמָן לֹא הִתְקִינוּ טְבִילָה זוֹ אֶלָּא מִפְּנֵי טְבִילַת סֶרֶךְ. שֶׁפְּעָמִים שֶׁאָדָם הוֹלֵךְ לְרָחוֹץ וְהוּא נִזְכָּר קֶרִי יָשָׁן שֶׁיֵּשׁ בְּיָדוֹ וְחוֹזֵר וּבָא לוֹ. תַּמָּן

תַּנֵּינָן. הַמְשַׁמֶּשֶׁת שֶׁרָאָת נִדָּה צְרִיכִין טְבִילָה וְרִבִּי יוּדָה פּוֹטֵר: מַה חָלַק רִבִּי יוּדָה. עַל טְבִילַת סֶרֶךְ. אוֹ מִשׁוּם אֲפִילוּ טוֹבֵל מַה מוֹעִיל. מַה נָּפַק מִינָהּ. רָאָה קֶרִי. אִין תֵּימַר. חָלוּק רִבִּי יוּדָה עַל טְבִילַת סֶרֶךְ. דְּבַר תּוֹרָה הוּא. אִין תֵּימַר. אֲפִילוּ טוֹבֵל מַה מוֹעִיל. מוֹעִיל הוּא שֶׁהוּא טוֹבֵל. כְּהָדָא דְתַנֵּי. אָמַר רִבִּי יְהוּדָה. כָּל־עַצְמָן לֹא הִתְקִינוּ טְבִילָה זוֹ אֶלָּא מִפְּנֵי טְבִילַת סֶרֶךְ. שֶׁפְּעָמִים שֶׁאָדָם הוֹלֵךְ לִרְחוֹץ וְהוּא נִזְכָּר קֶרִי יָשָׁן שֶׁבְּיָדוֹ וְחוֹזֵר וּבָא לוֹ. [הָדָא אָמְרָה] לֹא חָלַק רִבִּי יוּדָה עַל טְבִילַת סֶרֶךְ אֶלָּא מִשֵּׁם אֲפִילוּ טוֹבֵל מַה הוּא מוֹעִיל.

Halakhah 4: It was stated: [63]Rebbi Jehudah says, they instituted this immersion only as immersion of discipline, for sometimes when a person goes to wash he remembers an old emission of semen which he had and turns back[64]. There, we have stated[65]: "the woman who started menstruating while having intercourse, needs immersion, but Rebbi Jehudah declares them not liable." Why does Rebbi Jehudah disagree? Is it about immersion of discipline or because even if he immerses himself what would be its use? What is the difference? If he[66] had an emission. If you say that Rebbi Jehudah disagrees about immersion of discipline, it is a word of the Torah[67]. If you say, even if he immerses himself, what would be its use? It is useful that he immerse himself, as it was stated, Rebbi Jehudah says, they instituted this immersion only as immersion of discipline, for sometimes when a person goes to wash he remembers an old emission of semen which he had and turns back. This implies that Rebbi Jehudah did not disagree about immersion of discipline but because even if he immerses himself, what would be its use?

63 Babli 30a.

64 In itself this immersion is useless. If a person actually is impure, he is forbidden to partake of *sancta* and to enter the sacred domain. Immersion in a *miqweh* will remove the impurity but the disability regarding *sancta* and the sacred domain is removed only by the following sundown (*Lev.* 22:7). Therefore immersion in the morning is only for pure persons; for R. Jehudah it is instituted so people should not inadvertently enter the sacred domain while still not qualified for it.

65 Mishnah *Berakhot* 3:6. The Mishnah is truncated; the full text explains the plural form of the verb: "The person with gonorrhea who had an emission of semen, as well as a menstruating woman who lost semen, and the woman who started menstruating while having intercourse, need immersion, but Rebbi Jehudah declares them not liable."

An emission of semen pollutes, but it is a minor impurity which is removed by immersion in water and, for *sancta*, the following sundown. But gonorrhea and menstruation cause severe impurity for which immersion is possible only after seven days (*Lev.* 15:13,19). An immersion because of emission, before the time where immersion for the severe impurity is possible, is totally ineffective.

A different version of the following discussion is in *Berakhot* 3:6, Notes 260-264.

66   The male sufferer from gonorrhea, mentioned in the Mishnah. He had an emission before he started suffering from gonorrhea. He was obligated for an immersion before he became severely impure.

67   *Lev.* 15:16.

(fol. 40a) **משנה ה**: הֵבִיאוּ לוֹ אֶת הַתָּמִיד. קְרָצוּ וּמֵירֵק אַחֵר שְׁחִיטָה עַל יָדוֹ. קִבֵּל אֶת דָּמוֹ וּזְרָקוֹ. נִכְנַס לְהַקְטִיר אֶת הַקְּטוֹרֶת לְהֵטִיב אֶת הַנֵּרוֹת לְהַקְרִיב אֶת הָרֹאשׁ וְאֶת הָאֵיבָרִים וְאֶת הַחֲבִיתִּין וְאֶת הַיַּיִן:

Mishnah 5: They brought him the daily sacrifice; he cut it,[68] and another completed the slaughter for him. He received the blood and poured it. He entered to burn the incense, to clean the lights, to sacrifice[69] the head, the limbs, the pan-baked breads, and the wine.

68   Since the entire service of the Day of Atonement has to be performed by the High Priest himself, he has a problem in that he has to slaughter the sheep (and later the other sacrifices) while at the same time receiving the blood, which has to be that pumped out by the heart, not what is flowing out later. Therefore he has to cut the legal minimum, throat and esophagus, and let another Cohen cut the carotid arteries, which action, while necessary for the slaughter, does not formally fall under the definition of שחט "to cut the throat".

69   On the large altar in the inner courtyard, outside the sanctuary/

(40c line 3) רִבִּי לְעָזָר בְּשֵׁם רִבִּי הוֹשַׁעְיָה. עַד שֶׁיִּשְׁחוֹט בּוֹ שְׁנַיִם אוֹ רוֹב שְׁנָיִם. אָמַר רִבִּי יוֹסֵה. מַתְנִיתָא אָמְרָה בֵן. [הֵבִיאוּ לוֹ אֶת הַתָּמִיד.] קְרָצוּ.
כָּתוּב קֶרֶץ מִצָּפוֹן בָּא בֵהּ: רִבִּי חֲנִינָה וְרִבִּי יְהוֹשֻׁעַ בֶּן לֵוִי. חַד אָמַר נְכוֹסָה. וְחוֹרָנָה אָמַר. נְסוֹחָה. מָאן דְּאָמַר. נְכוֹסָה. מִן הָדָא. הֵבִיאוּ לוֹ אֶת הַתָּמִיד. קְרָצוּ. מָאן דְּאָמַר. נְסוֹחָה. מַגְלְיָּינָא. מֵחוֹמֶר קוֹרְצְתִּי גַם־אָנִי.

Rebbi Eleazar in the name of Rebbi Hoshaiah: Until he cut two or most of two[70]. Rebbi Yose said, the Mishnah says so, "[they brought him the daily sacrifice;] he cut it."

It is written[71], *qeres from the North comes into it.* Rebbi Ḥanina and Rebbi Joshua ben Levi. One said, a butcher; but the other said, a remover. He who said, a butcher, from this, "they brought him the daily sacrifice; he cut it." He who said, a remover, an exiler, *from loam I also was cut off*[72].

70 "Two" is the technical term for windpipe and esophagus, see Note 68. Babli 32b.
71 *Jer.* 46:20 (Babli 32b).
72 *Job* 33:6. Hebrew קרץ may represent both قرص "to pinch, tweak, sting" and قرض "sever, cut off, clip".

(fol. 40a) **משנה ו:** קְטוֹרֶת שֶׁל שַׁחַר הָיְתָה קְרֵיבָה בֵּין דָּם לָאֵיבָרִים שֶׁל בֵּין הָעַרְבַּיִם הָיְתָה קְרֵיבָה בֵּין אֵיבָרִים לַנְּסָכִים. אִם הָיָה כֹהֵן גָּדוֹל זָקֵן אוֹ אִיסְטְנִיס מְחַמִּין לוֹ חַמִּין וּמַטִּילִין לְתוֹךְ הַצּוֹנֵן כְּדֵי שֶׁתָּפוּג צִנָּתָן:

Mishnah 6: The incense in the morning[73] was brought between blood and limbs; in the evening it was brought between limbs and libations[74]. If the High Priest was old or asthenic[75], one heats water for him[76] and pours into the cold water to mitigate its coldness.

73 Not only on the day of Atonement but every day of the year.
74 Not only libation but also the flour offering.
75 Greek ἀσθενής.
76 On the preceding day since cooking or heating is forbidden on the day of Atonement.

(40c line 9) **הלכה ה:** כָּתוּב בְּתָמִיד בַּבּוֹקֶר וְכָתוּב בָּעֵצִים בַּבּוֹקֶר. יְקַדּוֹם דָּבָר שֶׁנֶּאֱמַר בּוֹ בַּבּוֹקֶר לְדָבָר שֶׁלֹּא נֶאֱמַר בּוֹ אֶלָּא בַּבּוֹקֶר [אֶחָד]. מֵעַתָּה אֲפִילוּ לְדָמוֹ. אָמַר רִבִּי הִילָא. תַּעֲשֶׂה. הִקְדִּים בּוֹ מַעֲשֶׂה. כָּתוּב בַּבּוֹקֶר בְּתָמִיד. וְכָתוּב בַּקְטוֹרֶת בַּבּוֹקֶר. יְקַדּוֹם דָּבָר שֶׁנֶּאֱמַר בּוֹ בַּבּוֹקֶר לְדָבָר שֶׁלֹּא נֶאֱמַר בּוֹ אֶלָּא בַּבּוֹקֶר. מַה נָן קַיָּימִין. אִם לָאֵיבָרִין. וַהֲלֹא כְצֵצִים הֵן. אֶלָּא כִי נָן קַיָּימִין. אֲפִילוּ לְדָמוֹ. כָּתוּב בָּעֵצִים בַּבּוֹקֶר וְכָתוּב בַּקְטוֹרֶת בַּבּוֹקֶר. וְאֵינִי יוֹדֵעַ אֵי זֶה מֵהֶן יְקַדּוֹם. מִי מַכְשִׁיר אֶת מִי. עֵצִים מַכְשִׁירִין אֶת הַקְּטוֹרֶת. אַף הֵם יְקַדְּמוּ אֶת הַקְּטוֹרֶת. אִיתָא חֲמֵי. עֵצִים קוֹדְמִין אֶת הַדָּם וְהַדָּם קוֹדֶם לַקְּטוֹרֶת. וְתֵימַר הָכֵין. אָמַר רִבִּי הִילָא. לֹא. עַל שֶׁלֹּא זָכִיתִי בּוֹ מִן הַדִּין. שֶׁהָעֵצִים מַכְשִׁירִין אֶת הַקְּטוֹרֶת. וְאַצְרְכַתְּ הָדָא מַתְנִיתָא. הֲוֹון בָּעֵי מֵימַר. מִי מַכְשִׁיר אֶת הַקְּטוֹרֶת. גֶּחָלִים. אָמַר רִבִּי אֶלְעָזָר. מַעֲלֵה עָשָׁן.

Halakhah 5: It is written about the daily sacrifice *in the morning*[77], and it is written about wood *in the morning*[78]. Something about which is written *in the morning, in the morning,* shall precede something about which *in the morning* is written only once. Then even before its blood? Rebbi Hila said, *you shall do*[77], preceded action for it[79]. It is written about the daily sacrifice *in the morning*, and it is written about incense *in the morning, in the morning*[80]. Something about which is written *in the morning, in the morning,* shall precede something about which only [one] *in the morning* is written. Where do we hold? If about limbs, are they not like wood[81]? But we are holding, even for its blood. It is written about wood *in the morning, in the morning*, and it is written about incense *in the morning, in the morning,*, and I do not know which of the two is preceding. Which one is enabling what? Wood enables the incense; the wood shall precede the incense[82]. Come and see, wood precedes the blood and blood precedes incense, and you are saying so? Rebbi Hila said, no. Since I could not prove by a logical argument that wood enables the incense, you needed that *baraita*. They wanted to say, what enables the incense? Charcoal. Rebbi Eleazar said, smoke-creating herb[83].

77   *Ex.* 29:39; *Num.* 28:4.
78   This has to read: *in the morning, in the morning*; *Lev.* 6:5, referring to the two wooden logs which have to be ceremoniously put into the fire every morning. While this is not mentioned in the Mishnah, the presentation and arrangement of the two logs also is an obligation of the High Priest on the Day of Atonement.
79   The slaughter and the dissection of the daily sacrifice are not done on the altar; they are not covered by any argument about the number of "mornings" quoted. They have to be done as early as possible in the morning (and as late as possible in the evening.)
80   *Ex.* 30:7.
81   They are to be burned on the altar; they can be considered fuel of the altar.
82   *Sifra Saw Pereq* 2(8).
83   Cf. Chapter 2, Note 227.

(40c line 21) נֶאֱמַר בְּתָמִיד בֵּין הָעַרְבַּיִם וְנֶאֱמַר בִּקְטוֹרֶת בֵּין הָעַרְבַּיִם. סְמַךְ לַנֵּרוֹת. (וְלֹא) [תֹאמַר] בַּנֵּרוֹת מֵעֶרֶב וְעַד בּוֹקֶר. יְאוּחַר דָּבָר שֶׁנֶּאֱמַר בּוֹ בֵּין הָעַרְבַּיִם סָמַךְ לַנֵּירוֹת לְדָבָר שֶׁלֹּא נֶאֱמַר בּוֹ אֶלָּא בֵּין הָעַרְבַּיִם. מֵעַתָּה אֲפִילוּ לִנְסָכִין. אָמַר רִבִּי הִילָא. תֵּעָשֶׂה. אִיחַר בּוֹ מַעֲשֶׂה. רִבִּי בּוּן בַּר חִייָה בְּעָא קוֹמֵי רִבִּי הִילָא. הָכָא אַתְּ אָמַר. תֵּעָשֶׂה. הִקְדִּים בּוֹ מַעֲשֶׂה. וָכָא אַתְּ אָמַר. תֵּעָשֶׂה. אִיחַר בּוֹ מַעֲשֶׂה. אָמַר רִבִּי הִילָא. כָּל־אֶחָד וְאֶחָד כְּעִנְייָנוּ. תָּמִיד שֶׁלַּשַּׁחַר בִּכְלַל מְאוּחָר הָיָה. מַה תַּלְמוּד לוֹמַר תֵּעָשֶׂה. הִקְדִּים בּוֹ מַעֲשֶׂה. תָּמִיד שֶׁלְּבֵין הָעַרְבַּיִם בִּכְלַל מוּקְדָּם

הָיָה. מַה תַּלְמוּד לוֹמַר תַּעֲשֶׂה. אִיחַר בּוֹ מַעֲשֶׂה. וַהֲיָה רִבִּי זְעוּרָה מְקַלֵּס לֵיהּ וְצָוַוח לֵיהּ בְּנֵיהּ דְּאוֹרְיָיתָא.

It says for the afternoon daily sacrifice, *in the evening*[77], and it says about incense, *in the evening*, close to the lights[84]. (Not) [You say] about the lights, *from evening to morning*[85](?)[.] A matter where it is said *in the evening* close to the lights shall be delayed after a matter where only *in the evening* is said. Then even after the libations? Rebbi Hila said, *you shall do*[77], delayed action for it[86]. Rebbi Abun bar Ḥiyya asked before Rebbi Hila: Here you are saying, "*you shall do*, preceded action for it", and there you are saying, "*you shall do*, delayed action for it"? Rebbi Hila said, each one according to its subject. The daily morning sacrifice was shown to be later; *you shall do*, preceded action for it. The daily evening sacrifice was shown to be earlier, the verse says *you shall do*, delayed action for it. Rebbi Zeʿira acclaimed[87] him and called him "son of the Torah."

84 Ex. 30:8: *When Aaron kindles the light in the evening he shall burn incense on it* i. e., on the interior altar.
85 Ex. 27:21.
86 By an argument parallel to that of Note 79.
87 A Semitic adaptation of Greek καλόω.

(40c line 30) תַּנֵי. אָמַר רִבִּי יְהוּדָה. עֲשָׁתוֹת שֶׁלְּבַרְזֶל הָיוּ מַרְתִּיחִין אוֹתָן מֵעֶרֶב יוֹם הַכִּיפּוּרִים וּמַטִּילִין לְתוֹךְ הַצּוֹנִין כְּדֵי שֶׁתָּפוּג צִינָתָן. וְלֹא נִמְצָא כִּמְכַבֶּה בְּיוֹם הַכִּיפּוּרִים. אֶלָּא מִיסְּבוֹר סָבַר רִבִּי יוּדָה שֶׁאֵין אָבוֹת מְלָאכוֹת בְּיוֹם הַכִּיפּוּרִים. אֶלָּא רִבִּי יוּדָה וְרִבִּי שִׁמְעוֹן אָמְרוּ דָבָר אֶחָד. לֹא כֵן סָבַר מֵימוֹר. רִבִּי יוֹסֵי וְרִבִּי שִׁמְעוֹן שְׁנֵיהֶן אָמְרוּ דָבָר אֶחָד. נֵימַר. רִבִּי יוֹסֵי וְרִבִּי יוּדָה וְרִבִּי שִׁמְעוֹן שְׁלַשְׁתָּן אָמְרוּ דָבָר אֶחָד. אֶלָּא מִיסְּבוֹר סָבַר רִבִּי יוּדָה שֶׁאֵין תּוֹלֶדֶת אֵשׁ כְּאֵשׁ. אֶלָּא כֵינֵי. רִבִּי יוּדָה סָבַר מֵימוֹר שֶׁאֵין תּוֹלֶדֶת אֵשׁ כְּאֵשׁ. וְרַבָּנָן סָבְרִין מֵימַר. תּוֹלֶדֶת אֵשׁ כְּאֵשׁ. וְיֵחַם לוֹ חַמִּין. רִבִּי יְהוֹשֻׁעַ בַּר אָבִיּוֹן רִבִּי סִימוֹן בְּשֵׁם רִבִּי אִינְיָינֵי בַּר סוֹסַיּ. טַעְמָא דְהָדֵין תַּנָּיָא. שֶׁלֹּא יְהוּ אוֹמְרִים. רְאִינוּ כֹּהֵן גָּדוֹל טוֹבֵל בְּמַיִם שְׁאוּבִין בְּיוֹם הַכִּיפּוּרִים.

It was stated[88]: Rebbi Jehudah says, iron bars they were heating on the eve of the Day of Atonement which they dropped into the water to mitigate its cold. Would he be not like a person who extinguished {fire} on the Day of Atonement[89]? But would Rebbi Jehudah hold that there are no principal categories of work on the Sabbath[90]? But Rebbi Jehudah and Rebbi Simeon must have said the same[91]. Were we not of the opinion that Rebbi Yose and

Rebbi Simeon said the same⁹²? Let us say that Rebbi Yose, Rebbi Jehudah, and Rebbi Simeon, said the same⁹³! But Rebbi Jehudah must think that derivatives of fire are not like fire, and the rabbis think that derivatives of fire are like fire. Could one not heat water⁹⁴? Rebbi Joshua bar Abin, Rebbi Simon in the name of Rebbi Anyani bar Sosai: The reason of this Tanna, that they should not say, we saw the High Priest immersing himself in drawn water⁹⁵ on the Day of Atonement.

88   Babli 34b.
89   Presuming that the iron still was really hot by next morning. The Babli holds that the problem is that sudden cooling of iron bars is a step in the production of steel and as such forbidden on the Sabbath and the Day of Atonement, but in this case where the bars have been stored for an entire night the prohibition would only be rabbinic, which is not applied in the Temple.
90   But on the Day of Atonement all work is forbidden (*Lev.* 16:29) as on the Sabbath.
91   R. Simeon holds that an action whose forbidden aspect was not intended is not forbidden on the Sabbath; cf. *Šabbat* Chapter 2, Note 19.
92   *Šabbat* Chapter 2, Note 148. Babli *Šabbat* 31b.
93   But we know from Mishnah *Šabbat* that R. Jehudah disagrees.
94   Which may be poured into cold water on the Sabbath according to everybody.
95   A *miqweh* cannot be filled with drawn water; 3 *log* of drawn water invalidate a *miqweh* of 40 *seah* (960 *log*), Mishnah *Miqwaot* 2:4.

(fol. 40a) **משנה ז:** הֱבִיאוּהוּ לְבֵית הַפַּרְוָה וּבַקּוֹדֶשׁ הָיְתָה. פֵּרְסוּ סָדִין שֶׁל בּוּץ בֵּינוֹ לְבֵין הָעָם. קִדֵּשׁ יָדָיו וְרַגְלָיו וּפָשַׁט. רַבִּי מֵאִיר אוֹמֵר פָּשַׁט קִדֵּשׁ יָדָיו וְרַגְלָיו. יָרַד וְטָבַל עָלָה וְנִסְתַּפָּג. הֱבִיאוּ לוֹ בִגְדֵי לָבָן וְלָבַשׁ וְקִדֵּשׁ יָדָיו וְרַגְלָיו:

Mishnah 7: They brought him to the Parwa house⁴⁸, which was in the sacred domain. They spread a byssus sheet⁶¹ between him and the people; he sanctified hands and legs and undressed; Rebbi Meïr says, he undressed and sanctified hands and legs. He stepped down, and immersed himself, came up and dried himself with a towel. They brought him the white garments⁹⁶, he dressed and sanctified hands and legs.

96   The four garments (coat, slacks, belt, and turban) made of byssus required for all expiatory acts on the Day of Atonement, *Lev.* 16:4.

(40c line 41) **הלכה ו:** מַה טַעֲמָא דְּרִבִּי מֵאִיר. פָּשַׁט וְקִידֵּשׁ וְרָחַץ וְקִידֵּשׁ. מַה טַעֲמָא דְּרַבָּנָן. וּפָשַׁט וְלָבַשׁ. הִקִּישׁ פְּשִׁיטָה לִלְבִישָׁה. מַה לִבְישָׁה מְקַדֵּשׁ אַף פְּשִׁיטָה מְקַדֵּשׁ. אָמַר רִבִּי מָנָא קוֹמֵי רִבִּי יוּדָן. עַל דַּעְתֵּיהּ דְּרִבִּי מֵאִיר רְחִיצָה חוֹצֶצֶת. אָמַר לֵיהּ. מִיסְבּוֹר אַתְּ סְבוֹר. עַל דְּרִבִּי מֵאִיר. וּפָשַׁט וְקִידֵּשׁ וְרָחַץ וְקִידֵּשׁ. אֵינָהּ כֵּן אֶלָּא וּפָשַׁט וְקִידֵּשׁ וְרָחַץ וְלָבַשׁ וְקִידֵּשׁ.

שְׁמוּאֵל אָמַר. אַחַת פְּשׁוּט וְאַחַת לִבוּשׁ שְׁתֵּיהֶן לָבֹא. בַּר קַפָּרָא אָמַר. אַחַת לָבֹא וְאַחַת לְשֶׁעָבַר שְׁתֵּיהֶן לְבוּשׁ. אָמַר רִבִּי יוֹחָנָן. הַכֹּל מוֹדִין בְּקִידּוּשׁ הָרִאשׁוֹן שֶׁהוּא לָבֹא. אָמַר רִבִּי יוֹחָנָן. הַכֹּל מוֹדִין בְּקִידּוּשׁ הָרִאשׁוֹן שֶׁהוּא מְעַכֵּב. מַה טַעֲמָא. חוּקַּת עוֹלָם לְדוֹרוֹתֵיכֶם. אָמַר רִבִּי יוֹחָנָן. הַכֹּל מוֹדִין בְּקִידּוּשׁ הָאַחֲרוֹן שֶׁהוּא לְשֶׁעָבַר. אָמַר רִבִּי יוֹסֵה. מַתְנִיתָא אָמְרָה כֵן. הֱבִיאוּ לוֹ בִגְדֵי עַצְמוֹ וְלָבַשׁ. וְיֵשׁ אָדָם מְקַדֵּשׁ יָדָיו וְרַגְלָיו לִלְבּוֹשׁ בִּגְדֵי חוֹל. רִבִּי יוֹחָנָן אָמַר. וּלְבֵשָׁם. לְבִישָׁה מְעַכֶּבֶת. וְאֵין קִידּוּשׁ יָדַיִם וְרַגְלַיִם מְעַכֵּב. וְדִכְוָתָהּ. לְבִישָׁה מְעַכֶּבֶת. וְאֵין קִידּוּשׁ יָדַיִם וְרַגְלַיִם מְעַכֵּב.

Halakhah 6: What is Rebbi Meïr's reason? *He undressed* and sanctified, *and he washed* and sanctified.[97]. What is the rabbi's reason? *And he undressed, and he dressed*. It tied undressing to dressing[98]. Since for dressing he sanctifies, so for undressing he sanctifies. Rebbi Mana said before Rebbi Yudan, does washing separate in Rebbi Meïr's opinion[99]? He said to him, you think that Rebbi Meïr's reason is, *and he undressed* and sanctified, *and he washed* and sanctified.. It is not so, but *and he undressed* and sanctified, *and he washed and dressed* and sanctified.

Samuel said, both for undressing and for dressing are for the future[100]. Bar Qappara said, one for the future and one for the past, both for dressing[101]. Rebbi Johanan said, everybody agrees that the first sanctification is for the future[102]. Rebbi Johanan said, everybody agrees that the first sanctification is obstructive[103]. What is the reason? *An eternal law for your generations*[104]. Rebbi Johanan said, everybody agrees that the last sanctification is for the past. Rebbi Yose said, the Mishnah[105] says so. "They bring him his own clothing and he dresses." Does anybody sanctify his hands and legs to wear profane clothing? Rebbi Johanan said, *and he shall wear them*[106]. The dressing is obstructive[107], but sanctification of hands and legs is not obstructive. And similarly, the dressing is obstructive, but sanctification of hands and legs is not obstructive[108].

97 The argument is about *Lev.* 16:23-24, where at the end of the expiatory service Aaron is commanded first to take off his byssus garments, then to wash (immerse himself), and then to dress in the High Priest's garb for the ordinary afternoon service.

98 The argument is more explicit in *Sifra Aḥare Pereq* 6(6) and here in Halakhah 7:3, Babli 71a. It says in *Lev.* 16:23, *he shall take off the linen garments which he wore.* Since nobody can take off clothing which he does not wear, the reference is taken to v. 4 where Aaron is commanded *to wash his flesh in water and wear them.* Therefore all procedures connected with dressing are required for undressing, in the same order.

99 As formulated at the beginning, the second sanctification is tied to washing, not to dressing. This is unreasonable.

100 The sanctifications at a change of dress are not biblical. According to the reason given for the rabbis' position, both are intended for the next step in the service.

101 For him, each step in the service needs sanctification before and after. The second sanctification is not for taking off the garments but for the garments he is wearing at the moment of sanctification.

102 The first sanctification at the start of the morning service is a biblical requirement, *Ex.* 30:21. Therefore there is no requirement of sanctification when the High Priest takes off his profane clothing.

103 Without this sanctification, the High Priest would be disqualified from serving.

104 A misquote from *Ex.* 30:21.

105 Mishnah 7:4.

106 *Lev.* 16:4.

107 Obviously he cannot serve naked, but the emphasis is on *wear them*: all four garments enumerated in the verse form an inseparable unit.

108 All changes of dress during the day are biblical prescriptions but the accompanying sanctifications (except the first, as stated) are required but their omission does not disqualify. Babli *Zevahim* 19b.

(40c line 54) כדי. שֶׁיְּהוּ כְפוּלִים. וְקַיָּמִינָהּ דְּלָא כְּרַבִּי יוֹסֵה. רַבִּי שְׁמוּאֵל בַּר רַב יִצְחָק לָא נְחַת לְבֵית וַעֲדָא. קָם עִם רַבִּי זְעוּרָא. אָמַר לֵיהּ. מַה חַדְתּוֹן [הֲוָה לְכוֹן בְּבֵי מִדְרָשָׁא] יוֹמָא דֵין. [אָמַר לֵיהּ.] בַּד. שֶׁיְּהוּ כְפוּלִים. וְקַיָּמִינָהּ דְּלָא כְּרַבִּי יוֹסֵי. דְּתַנֵּי. וְלִבְנֵי אַהֲרֹן תַּעֲשֶׂה כֻתֳּנוֹת. רַבָּנָן אָמְרֵי. שְׁתֵּי כֻתֳּנוֹת לְכָל־אֶחָד וְאֶחָד. רַבִּי יוֹסֵי אוֹמֵר. אֲפִילוּ כֻתּוֹנֶת אַחַת לְכָל־אֶחָד וְאֶחָד. מַה טַעֲמָא דְרַבָּנָן. וְלִבְנֵי אַהֲרֹן תַּעֲשֶׂה כֻתֳּנוֹת. מַה טַעֲמָא דְּרַבִּי יוֹסֵי. לְמָאֵי בְנֵי אַהֲרֹן תַּעֲשֶׂה כֻתֹּנֶת. בַּד. שֶׁיְּהוּ חֲדָשִׁים. אִם אוֹמֵר אַתְּ שֶׁלֹּא יִלְבַּשׁ שְׁחָקִים. וְהָא תַּנֵּי. וּלְבֵשָׁם׃ אֲפִילוּ שְׁחָקִים. רַבִּי חֲנַנְיָה בְשֵׁם רַבִּי יָסָא. כְּמַחֲלוֹקֶת.

עוֹר שֶׁעֲיבְּדוֹ לְשֵׁם קָמֵיעַ מוּתָּר לִכְתּוֹב עָלָיו מְזוּזָה. רַבָּן שִׁמְעוֹן בֶּן גַּמְלִיאֵל אוֹסֵר. אוֹמַר רַבִּי יוֹסֵה. הֲוֵינָן סָבְרִין מֵימַר. מַה פְּלִיגִין. לְהֶדְיוֹט. הָא לַגָּבוֹהַּ לֹא. מִן מַה דְּתַנֵּי. אַבְנֵי קוֹדֶשׁ צָרִיךְ שֶׁתְּהֵא חֲצִיבָתָן בַּקּוֹדֶשׁ וּבַקּוֹדֶשׁ יֵחָצְבוּ. בִּגְדֵי קוֹדֶשׁ צָרִיךְ קוֹדֶשׁ שֶׁתְּהֵא אֲרִיגָתָן בַּקּוֹדֶשׁ וּבַקּוֹדֶשׁ יֵאָרְגוּ. וְאָמַר רַבִּי חֲנִינָה בְשֵׁם רַבִּי יָסָא. בְּמַחֲלוֹקֶת הִיא. הָדָא אָמְרָה. אַף לַגָּבוֹהַּ פְּלִיגִין. דְּתַנֵּי. הָעוֹשֶׂה כְלִי לַגָּבוֹהַּ. עַד שֶׁלֹּא נִשְׁתַּמֵּשׁ בּוֹ גָבוֹהַּ מוּתָּר לְהִשְׁתַּמֵּשׁ בּוֹ הֶדְיוֹט. מִשֶּׁנִּשְׁתַּמֵּשׁ בּוֹ גָבוֹהַּ

אָסוּר לְהִשְׁתַּמֵּשׁ בּוֹ הֶדְיוֹט. וְהָא תַנֵּי. הָעוֹשֶׂה כְלִי לַגָּבוֹהַּ אַל יִשְׁתַּמֵּשׁ בּוֹ הֶדְיוֹט. רִבִּי חֲנַנְיָה בְשֵׁם רִבִּי יָסָא. כְּמַחֲלוֹקֶת. דְּתַנֵּי. הָעוֹשֶׂה כְלִי לְהֶדְיוֹט. עַד שֶׁלֹּא נִשְׁתַּמֵּשׁ בּוֹ הֶדְיוֹט מוּתָּר לְהִשְׁתַּמֵּשׁ בּוֹ גָּבוֹהַּ. וּמִשֶּׁנִּשְׁתַּמֵּשׁ בּוֹ הֶדְיוֹט אָסוּר לְהִשְׁתַּמֵּשׁ בּוֹ גָּבוֹהַּ. וְהָא תַנֵּי. הָעוֹשֶׂה כְלִי לְהֶדְיוֹט. אַל יִשְׁתַּמֵּשׁ בּוֹ גָּבוֹהַּ. רִבִּי חוּנָה בְשֵׁם רַבָּנָן דְּתַמָּן. תִּיפְתָּר שֶׁבָּא מִתְּרוּמַת הַלִּשְׁכָּה. וְלֵית שְׁמַע מִינָהּ כְּלוּם.

כדי[109] that they should be double[110]. We determined that this does not follow Rebbi Yose. Rebbi Samuel bar Rav Isaac did not come to the assembly hall. He met Rebbi Ze'ira and asked him, what did you newly find [was for you in the house of study][111] on that day? He told him, *linen cloth, that they should be double*. We determined that this does not follow Rebbi Yose[112]. As it was stated, *and for Aaron's sons you shall make coats*[113]. The rabbis say, two coats for each one; Rebbi Yose says, even one coat for each one. What is the rabbis' reason? *And for Aaron's sons you shall make coats*. What is Rebbi Yose's reason? Make coats for 100 sons of Aaron. *Linen cloth*, that they should be new[110]. If you are saying that they should not be worn out, was it not stated, *and he shall wear them*[106], even if they are worn out? Rebbi Ḥananiah in the name of Rebbi Yasa, as the disagreement[114].

Leather which was tanned for an amulet. It is permitted to write a *mezuza* on it; Rabban Simeon ben Gamliel forbids[115]. Rebbi Yose said, we were of the opinion that where they disagree is about a private person; therefore not for Heaven. Since it was stated, holy stones have to be quarried in holiness, in holiness they have to be quarried[116]. Holy garments have to be woven in holiness, in holiness they have to be woven. And Rebbi Ḥaninah said in the name of Rebbi Yasa, this is as the disagreement. This implies that they disagree even for Heaven[117], as it was stated: If somebody makes a vessel for Heaven, as long as it was not used for Heaven, a lay person may use it; after it was used for Heaven, a lay person may not use it. But was it not stated, If somebody makes a vessel for Heaven, a lay person may not use it? Rebbi Ḥananiah in the name of Rebbi Yasa, as the disagreement. [As it was stated:][118] If somebody makes a vessel for a lay person, as long as it was not used for a lay person, Heaven may use it; after it was used for a lay person Heaven may not use it. But was it not stated, If somebody makes a vessel for a lay person, Heaven may not use it? Rebbi Huna in the name of the rabbis there: Explain it that it was paid for by the Temple tax[119] and you cannot infer anything.

109 This is misspelled for בד "linen cloth".

110 This is a discussion of a *baraita* reported in *Sifra Ahare Pereq* 1(5), Babli *Zevahim* 18b. The word "linen cloth" is repeated four times in *Lev.* 16:4. One of these is necessary to establish that the High Priest has to wear four linen garments; the other three are read to imply that the garments should be of byssus (expensive), new, and double (not transparent, in the Babli's version, woven from entwined thread.)

111 The text in parentheses was added by a corrector who did not understand the text. The addition is in the usual Babli style in this situation.

112 Since the discussion centers on a *baraita*, the discovery of the Amoraim was that the *baraita* cannot be R. Yose's.

113 *Ex.* 27:40.

114 R. Yose (the Tanna) does not accept that the garments have to be new every year. The Babli 12b attributes the disagreement to other Tannaim.

115 Rabban Simeon requires that the parchment on which the *mezuza* is written be especially prepared for sacramental use.

116 The duplication means that the stones (of the High Priest's breastplate) have to be quarried (and later, the priestly garment to be woven) with the intention to produce sacred utensils.

117 For use in the Temple. Tosephta *Menahot* 9:21.

118 The text in parentheses was added by a corrector who did not understand the text. The following text is not quoted as support of the prior statement but is discussed in its own right; the question is whether it is a parallel to the earlier statement or not.

119 Therefore it is Temple property and any non-sacramental use is larceny committed on Heaven's property.

(40c line 75) כְּלֵי שָׁרֵת מֵאֵימָתַי הֵן קְדֵישִׁין. מִיָּד אוֹ בִשְׁעַת הַתַּשְׁמִישׁ. אֵין תֵּימַר. מִיָּד. נִיחָא. אֵין תֵּימַר. בִּשְׁעַת הַתַּשְׁמִישׁ. כְּאַחַת הֵן קְדוֹשִׁין. נִיחָא שֶׁלְּמֹשֶׁה שֶׁנִּתְקַדְּשׁוּ בְּשֶׁמֶן הַמִּשְׁחָה. בְּרַם שֶׁלִּשְׁלֹמֹה כְּאַחַת הֵן קְדֵישִׁין וּמִתְקַדְּשִׁין. בִּכְנִיסָתָן לָאָרֶץ הָיוּ מְפַנִּין מִתּוֹךְ שֶׁל מֹשֶׁה לְתוֹךְ שֶׁלִּשְׁלֹמֹה. לֹא הָיָה שָׁם שֶׁלְּשְׁלֹמֹה כְּאַחַת הֵן קְדֵישִׁין וּמִתְקַדְּשִׁין. וּבַעֲלִיָּיתָן מִן הַגּוֹלָה הָיוּ מְפַנִּין מִתּוֹךְ שֶׁלִּשְׁלֹמֹה לְתוֹךְ שֶׁלָּהֶם. לֹא הָיָה שָׁם שֶׁלִּשְׁלֹמֹה כְּאַחַת הֵן קְדֵישִׁין וּמִתְקַדְּשִׁין.

2 הן קדושין | ל הם קדישין ומתקדישין   המשחה | ל המשחה ובדם   ברם | ל -   3 שלשלמה | ל ושל שלמה קדשין | ל קדשין   4 רדשים | ל רדשים   קדישין ומתקדישין | ל קדישים ומתקדשים   ובעלייתן | ל בעלייתן   5 שלהם | ל שלהן קדישין ומתקדישין | ל קדישים ומתקדשים

אֲבָנִים שֶׁחָצְבָן לְשֵׁם מֵת אֲסוּרִין בַּהֲנָיָיה. לְשֵׁם חַי וּלְשֵׁם מֵת מוּתָּרִין בַּהֲנָיָיה. הָאוֹרֵךְ כְּלִי לִפְנֵי מִיטָתוֹ שֶׁל מֵת לְתוֹךְ אַרְבַּע אַמּוֹת אָסוּר בַּהֲנָיָיה. כָּל־חוּץ לְאַרְבַּע אַמּוֹת מוּתָּר בַּהֲנָיָיה.

1 אסורין | ל אסורות   מותרין | ל מותרות   2 אמות | ל אמות [שלו]   כל | ל -

[120]From which moment on are vessels of Temple service holy? Immediately[121] or at the moment of use? If you are saying immediately, it is understandable. If you are saying at the moment of use, simultaneously they become holy {and make holy}[122]. One can understand for those of Moses which became holy by the anointing oil[123]. But those of Solomon simultaneously became holy and made holy. When they entered the Land they transferred from Moses's to Solomon's[124]. If none of Moses was available, they simultaneously became holy and made holy. When they returned from the Diaspora, they transferred from Solomon's[125] to theirs. If none of Solomon was available, they simultaneously became holy and made holy.

Stones quarried for a corpse are forbidden for usufruct[126]. For a corpse or a living person[127] they are permitted for usufruct. If somebody throws an implement near the bier of a corpse, within four cubits it is forbidden for usufruct; anything outside four cubits is permitted for usufruct.

120 The same text is in *Megillah* 3:1 (ל).
121 Is a declaration of intent to use the vessel in the Temple the equivalent of a formal dedication and donation to the Temple, or not? Since the contents of a sacred vessel automatically become holy, in the second case the holiness of the vessel and its power to convert profane to sacral start at the same moment.
122 Added from *Megillah*, necessary for understanding the sentence.
123 Before they were actually used. This is an action, not a declaration of intent.
124 But first to the Tabernacle at Shiloh.
125 The vessels given by Cyrus from the treasury of Babylon.
126 Since a grave and its appurtenances are forbidden for usufruct.
127 Babli *Sanhedrin* 48a: A mausoleum built for a person still living is permitted for usufruct.

(40d line 8) נִמְצֵאתָ אוֹמֵר. חָמֵשׁ טְבִילוֹת וַעֲשָׂרָה קִידּוּשִׁין טוֹבֵל וּמְקַדֵּשׁ בּוֹ בַיּוֹם. מִנְיָין שֶׁשְּׁנֵי קִידּוּשֵׁי יָדַיִם וְרַגְלַיִם עַל כָּל־טְבִילָה וּטְבִילָה. תַּלְמוּד לוֹמַר וְרָחַץ וּפָשַׁט וְרָחַץ (פָּשַׁט) [וְלָבַשׁ.] אָמַר רִבִּי אֶלְעָזָר בְּרִבִּי שִׁמְעוֹן. וְדִין הוּא. מַה אִם בְּמָקוֹם שֶׁאֵינוֹ טָעוּן טְבִילָה טָעוּן קִידּוּשׁ יָדַיִם וְרַגְלַיִם. כָּאן שֶׁהוּא טָעוּן טְבִילָה לֹא כָל־שֶׁכֵּן יְהֵא טָעוּן קִידּוּשׁ יָדַיִם וְרַגְלַיִם. טוֹל לָךְ מַה שֶׁהֵבֵאתָה. אִי מַה לְהַלָּן אַחַת כָּל־הַיּוֹם אַף כָּאן אַחַת כָּל־הַיּוֹם. תַּלְמוּד לוֹמַר וּפָשַׁט אֶת־בִּגְדֵי הַבָּד. שֶׁאֵין תַּלְמוּד לוֹמַר אֲשֶׁר לָבַשׁ. וְכִי עָלַת עַל דַּעְתֵּינוּ כְּלוּם הוּא פּוֹשֵׁט אֶלָּא מַה שֶׁהוּא לוֹבֵשׁ. אִם כֵּן לָמָּה נֶאֱמַר אֲשֶׁר לָבַשׁ. הִקִּישׁ פְּשִׁיטָה לִלְבִישָׁה. מַה לְבִישָׁה בְּקִידּוּשׁ יָדַיִם

וְרַגְלַיִם אַף פְּשִׁיטָה בְּקִידּוּשׁ יָדַיִם וְרַגְלַיִם. אָמַר רִבִּי מָנָא. לֹא מִסְתַּבְּרָה [דְלָא] {אֶלָּא} חִילּוּפִין. הָקִישׁ לְבִישָׁה לִפְשִׁיטָה. מַה פְּשִׁיטָה בְּקִידּוּשׁ יָדַיִם וְרַגְלַיִם אַף לְבִישָׁה בְּקִידּוּשׁ יָדַיִם וְרַגְלַיִם.

[128]"You find that by five immersions and ten sanctifications he immerses and sanctifies himself on that day. From where that there are two sanctifications for every immersion? The verse says[97], *and he undressed, and he washed, and he washed, (and he undressed) [and he dressed]*. Rebbi Eleazar ben Rebbi Simeon said, it is an argument *de minore ad majus*. Since at a place where he does not need immersion he needs sanctification of hands and legs[129], here where he needs immersion not so much more that he should need sanctification of hands and legs? Take away your argument. Since there it is once for the entire day, also here it would be once for the entire day[130]. The verse says, *and he shall take off the linen garments*, why does the verse say, *which he wore*? Could we ever think that he took off what he was not wearing? Then why does it say, *which he wore*? It bracketed undressing and dressing. Since dressing needs sanctification of hands and legs, also undressing needs sanctification of hands and legs[98]." Rebbi Mana said, it is reasonable the opposite way. It bracketed undressing and dressing. Since undressing needs sanctification of hands and legs, also dressing needs sanctification of hands and legs[131]."

128 One returns to the discussion of the Mishnah. Most of this paragraph is a *baraita* in *Sifra Ahare Pereq* 6(6).

129 During all other days of the year, there is only one sanctification at the start of the day's service.

130 Since the consequence of a logical argument cannot be stronger than the premise.

131 Since "washing" is mentioned after undressing and before dressing. Only the corrector's text is correct.

(fol. 40a) **משנה ח**: בַּשַּׁחַר הָיָה לוֹבֵשׁ פִּילוּסִין שֶׁל שְׁנֵים עָשָׂר מָנֶה וּבֵין הָעַרְבַּיִם הִינְדְּוָן שֶׁל שְׁמוֹנֶה מֵאוֹת זוּז דִּבְרֵי רִבִּי מֵאִיר. וַחֲכָמִים אוֹמְרִים בַּשַּׁחַר הָיָה לָבוּשׁ פִּילוּסִים שֶׁל שְׁמוֹנָה עָשָׂר מָנֶה. וּבֵין הָעַרְבַּיִם שֶׁל שְׁנֵים עָשָׂר מָנֶה הַכֹּל שְׁלֹשִׁים מָנֶה. אֵילוּ נוֹטֵל מִן הַהֶקְדֵּשׁ וְאִם רָצָה לְהוֹסִיף מוֹסִיף מִשֶּׁלּוֹ:

Mishnah 8: In the morning he was wearing Pelusian[132] worth twelve *mina*, and in the evening Indian[133] of 800 *denar*, the words of Rebbi Meïr. But the Sages say, in the morning he was wearing Pelusian worth eighteen *mina* and in the evening of twelve *mina*, all together thirty *mina*[134]. This he takes from Temple property; if he wants to add, he adds from his own.

132 Linen manufactured in Pelusium, the most expensive kind on the market.
132 Indian linen.
133 A *mina* was 100 *denar* (*drachma*); 30 *mina* = 3'000 silver *denar*. For first Century prices, this seems excessive, but the examples given later exclude the possibility that the data might be second Century re-interpretations. In Mishnah *Peah* 8:8 it is stated that a fortune of 200 *denar* disqualifies its owner from receiving welfare.

(40d line 10) וְאֵין שֵׁינִי שֶׁל פִּילוּסִין יָפֶה מִן הָרִאשׁוֹן שֶׁלְהִנְדְּוָין. מִשֵּׁם מִילָה דְשִׁמְעָה פְּרוּטֵי. תַּמָּן תַּנִּינָן. הָרִאשׁוֹן שֶׁבָּרִאשׁוֹן אֵין לְמַעֲלָה מִמֶּנּוּ.[הַשֵּׁנִי שֶׁבָּרִאשׁוֹן וְהָרִאשׁוֹן שֶׁבַּשֵּׁנִי שָׁוִין.] וְאֵין שֵׁינִי שֶׁבָּרִאשׁוֹן יָפֶה מִן הָרִאשׁוֹן שֶׁבַּשֵּׁנִי. מִשֵּׁם מִילָה דְשִׁמְעָה פְּרוּטֵי. מַאי כְדוֹן. רִבִּי נַחְמָן בְּשֵׁם רִבִּי מָנָא. בְּשַׁחַר כְּתוּב בַּד בַּד אַרְבָּעָה פְּעָמִים. וּבְמִנְחָה כָּתוּב בַּד.

מַעֲשֶׂה בְּיִרבִּי יִשְׁמָעֵאל בֶּן פִּיאָבִי שֶׁלָּבַשׁ כֻּתֳּנוֹת בְּמֵאָה מָנֶה וְעָלָה וְהִקְרִיב עַל גַּבֵּי הַמִּזְבֵּחַ. מַעֲשֶׂה בְּרִבִּי אֶלְעָזָר בֶּן חַרְסוֹם שֶׁלָּבַשׁ כֻּתֳּנוֹת בִּשְׁתֵּי רִיבּוֹא וְעָלָה וְהִקְרִיב עַל גַּבֵּי הַמִּזְבֵּחַ. וְהוֹרִידוּ אוֹתוֹ אֶחָיו הַכֹּהֲנִים שֶׁהָיָה נִרְאֶה מִתּוֹכָהּ עָרוֹם. מֶה עָשָׂה. מִילֵּא אוֹתָהּ מַיִם וְסָבַב אֶת הַמִּזְבֵּחַ שֶׁבַע פְּעָמִים.

But is not second quality of Pelusian better than first Indian[134]? A formulation which is an exaggeration[135]. There, we have stated[136]: "Nothing is better than the best of first quality. [Second tier of the first and first tier of the second are equal.]" But is not the second tier of first quality better than the first of second quality? A formulation which is an exaggeration. What about it? Rebbi Naḥman in the name of Rebbi Mana: In the morning, *linen* is written four times. In the afternoon, *linen* is written[137].

It happened that Rebbi Ismael ben Phiabi wore coats worth 100 *mina*, he went up and sacrificed on the altar[138]. It happened that Rebbi Eleazar ben Ḥartom wore coats worth 20'000[139], he went up and sacrificed on the altar, but his brothers the Cohanim took him down since he was seen naked under it. What did he do? He drenched it with water and circled the altar seven times[140].

134 Then why does the Mishnah not require second quality Pelusian linen for the afternoon service?

135 Arabic فرط "excess, exaggeration". The Mishnah is formulated to give leeway in the choice of materials.

136 Mishnah *Menahot* 8:5, about the oil qualified for the lamp and the flour sacrifices in the Temple. Since the Mishnah is known, the corrector's addition is not absolutely necessary.

137 In *Lev.* 16:23 linen is mentioned only once, in contrast to 4 times in v. 4.

138 First he cannot serve without first donating his garments to the Temple and second they will become unusable by the bloodstains that are unavoidable.

139 20'000 *denar* = 200 *mina*.

140 He made his garment opaque by soaking it with water and then drying it by circling the flames on the altar.

(fol. 40a) **משנה ט**: בָּא לוֹ אֵצֶל פָּרוֹ וּפָרוֹ הָיָה עוֹמֵד בֵּין הָאוּלָם וְלַמִּזְבֵּחַ רֹאשׁוֹ לַדָּרוֹם וּפָנָיו לַמַּעֲרָב הַכֹּהֵן עוֹמֵד בַּמִּזְרָח וּפָנָיו לַמַּעֲרָב. סָמַךְ שְׁתֵּי יָדָיו עָלָיו וְנִתְוַדֶּה וְכָךְ הָיָה אוֹמֵר אָנָּא הַשֵּׁם עָוִיתִי פָּשַׁעְתִּי חָטָאתִי לְפָנֶיךָ אֲנִי וּבֵיתִי. אָנָּא הַשֵּׁם כַּפֶּר נָא לָעֲוֹנוֹת וְלַפְּשָׁעִים וְלַחֲטָאִים שֶׁעָוִיתִי וְשֶׁפָּשַׁעְתִּי וְשֶׁחָטָאתִי לְפָנֶיךָ אֲנִי וּבֵיתִי כַּכָּתוּב בְּתוֹרַת מֹשֶׁה עַבְדְּךָ כִּי־בַיּוֹם הַזֶּה יְכַפֵּר עֲלֵיכֶם וגו': וְהֵן עוֹנִין אַחֲרָיו בָּרוּךְ שֵׁם כְּבוֹד מַלְכוּתוֹ לְעוֹלָם וָעֶד: בָּא לוֹ לְמִזְרַח הָעֲזָרָה לִצְפוֹן הַמִּזְבֵּחַ הַסָּגָן בִּימִינוֹ וְרֹאשׁ בֵּית אָב מִשְּׂמֹאלוֹ. וְשָׁם שְׁנֵי שְׂעִירִים וְקַלְפֵּי הָיְתָה שָׁם וּבָהּ שְׁנֵי גוֹרָלוֹת. שֶׁל אֶשְׁכְּרוֹעַ הָיוּ וַעֲשָׂאָן בֶּן גַּמְלָא שֶׁל זָהָב וְהָיוּ מַזְכִּירִין אוֹתוֹ לְשָׁבַח:

Mishnah 9: He comes to his bull[141]; his bull was standing between the Temple Hall and the altar, its head to the South and its face to the West[142], and the Cohen standing in the East with his face to the West. He leans his hands on it[143] and confesses, and thus he was saying: "Please Hashem[144], I acted criminally, I offended, I sinned[145] before You, I and my house. Please Hashem, please atone the criminal acts, and the offenses, and the sins, by which I offended, acted criminally, and sinned before You, I and my house, as is written in the Torah of Your servant Moses[146], *because on that day He will atone for you,* etc." They[147] answer him: "Praised be the glory of His Kingdom forever and ever" He comes to the Eastern part of the courtyard, North of the altar[148]; the executive officer[149] to his right and the head of the serving family[150] to his left. There were two he-goats,[151] and an urn[152] was there with two lots in it. They were of boxwood but Ben Gamla[153] made them from gold; he was remembered for praise.

141 The bull to be sacrificed which he is required to provide from his own money; Lev. 16:3,6.
142 The bull's body was standing North to South but its head was bent to the West, facing the Temple Hall.
143 Between its horns.
144 "The Name", the generally accepted sobriquet for the Divine Name, whose correct pronunciation was taught only to the High Priest and which he only used on the Day of Atonement in his confessions.
145 As explained in the Halakhah, עָוֹן is a criminal act, פֶּשַׁע is an intentional sin, and חֵטְא is an unintentional sin.
146 Lev. 16:30.
147 The priests and the people standing in the outer courtyards.
148 The prescribed place of slaughter of all most holy sacrifices.
149 The person overseeing the daily routine in the Temple.
150 The Cohanim were divided into 24 watches; each watch came to the Temple for one week to serve there (except for a few permanent offices, enumerated in Tractate Šeqalim.) Each watch was divided into 6 families; each family serving for one day, except for the Sabbath when the entire watch were serving together. The head of the family serving on the day of Atonement accompanies the High Priest.
151 Lev. 16:8.
152 Greek κάλπη.
153 The High Priest Joshua ben Gamla, contemporary of king Agrippa I, who instituted universal Jewish compulsory elementary education.

(40d line 29) **הלכה ז:** אֵי זֶהוּ צְפוֹנוֹ שֶׁלְמִזְבֵּחַ שֶׁהוּא כָשֵׁר בִּשְׁחִיטַת קָדְשֵׁי קָדָשִׁים. מְקִירוּ שֶׁלְמִזְבֵּחַ צְפוֹנִי וְעַד כּוֹתֶל הָעֲזָרָה צְפוֹנִי עַד כְּנֶגֶד כָּל־הַמִּזְבֵּחַ. יֶשְׁנוֹ כִּשְׁלֹשִׁים וּשְׁתַּיִם אַמָּה. דִּבְרֵי רִבִּי. רִבִּי אֶלְעָזָר בֵּירִבִּי שִׁמְעוֹן אוֹמֵר. מִכְּנֶגֶד בֵּית הַחִילָפוֹת עַד כְּנֶגֶד בֵּין הָאוּלָם וְלַמִּזְבֵּחַ וְעַד כּוֹתֶל הָעֲזָרָה הַמִּזְרָחִי. רִבִּי מוֹסִיף. מְקוֹם דְּרִיסַת רַגְלֵי יִשְׂרָאֵל אַחַת עֶשְׂרֵה אַמָּה. מְקוֹם דְּרִיסַת רַגְלֵי הַכֹּהֲנִים אַחַת עֶשְׂרֵה אַמָּה. מִקִּירוֹ שֶׁלְמִזְבֵּחַ הַצְּפוֹנִי וְעַד כּוֹתֶל הָעֲזָרָה הַמִּזְרָחִי.

Halakhah 7: What is "North of the altar" which is qualified for the slaughter of most holy sacrifices[154]? From the Northern wall of the altar to the Northern wall of the courtyard the entire width of the altar, i. e., 32 cubits[155], the words of Rebbi[156]. Rebbi Eleazar ben Rebbi Simeon says, from before the House of Knives[157] up to[158] between the Hall and the altar, to the Eastern[159] wall of the courtyard. Rebbi adds: the place where Cohanim can enter, eleven cubits, and the place where Israel can enter, eleven cubits[160], from the Northern rim of the altar to the Eastern wall of the courtyard.

154 For the elevation sacrifice this is required in *Lev.* 1:11; for all other most holy sacrifices it is prescribed that they be slaughtered "at the place of the elevation sacrifice.".

155 The length of each side of the square altar, Mishnah *Middot* 3:1.

156 In the Babli 36a (*Zevahim* 20a), "R. Yose ben R. Jehudah". This reading is required here also since Rebbi is quoted later to extend the permitted area another 22 cubits Eastward.

157 On the Northern wall between the Temple Hall and the altar there were 24 niches, one for each watch of priests, where they kept their slaughtering knives.

158 The word עד "up to" has to be deleted, since the place of the niches was there.

Many verses in *Lev.* instruct that all kinds of most holy sacrifices must be slaughtered "before the Eternal", i. e., to the East of the Temple Hall.

159 "Eastern" must be deleted and replaced by "Northern". The Eastern wall is at the entrance of the courtyard.

160 The area of the altar and westward could only be entered by Cohanim at the time of service; East of it was the courtyard of the Cohanim, 11 cubits wide, where Cohanim could enter at all times, even if not currently occupied. East of this was a space, also 11 wide, accessible to Israel males. Still further East was the women's courtyard, 135 cubits wide (*Middot* 2:6). Rebbi adds that part of the area of all courtyards which is North of the altar.

(40d line 35) אָמַר רִבִּי יוֹחָנָן. לֹא מַצָאנוּ שְׁחִיטָה כְשֵׁירָה בְזָר. רַב מְפַקֵּד לְתַלְמִידוֹי. בְּכָל־אֲתַר הֲוֹון תַּנֵּיי. שׁוֹחֵט. חוּץ מִפָּרָה הֲוֹון תַּנֵּיי. זוֹרֵק. וְאָמַר רִבִּי יוֹחָנָן. לֹא מַצָאנוּ שְׁחִיטָה (כְשֵׁירָה) [פְּסוּלָה] בְזָר. הָתִיב רִבִּי חִייָה בַּר בָּא. וְהָא כְּתִיב וְשָׁחַט וְהִזָּה. מָה הַזָּיָה לֹא הוּכְשְׁרָה בְאִשָּׁה כָּאִישׁ אַף שְׁחִיטָה לֹא הוּכְשְׁרָה בְאִשָּׁה כָּאִישׁ. אָמַר לֵיהּ. הֲרֵי הַזָּיָה מִיָּמָיהּ הֲרֵי הִיא כְשֵׁירָה בְזָר וּפְסוּלָה בְאִשָּׁה. אָמַר לֵיהּ. תַּמָּן לֵית כְּתִיב כֹּהֵן. וְלֵייְדָא מִילְּתָא כְּתִיב אִישׁ. לְהַכְשִׁיר אֶת הַזָּר. הִיא אִישׁ הִיא אִשָּׁה. בְּרַם הָכָא כְּתֵיב כֹּהֵן. הִיא זָר הִיא אִשָּׁה. אִין תֵּימַר שֶׁהִיא כְשֵׁירָה בְזָר תּוּכְשַׁר בְאִשָּׁה.

רִבִּי שְׁמוּאֵל בַּר רַב יִצְחָק רִבִּי יוֹחָנָן בְּשֵׁם רִבִּי שִׁמְעוֹן בֶּן יוֹחַי. פַּר שֶׁלְּיוֹם הַכִּיפּוּרִים צָרִיךְ כֹּהֵן. וְלָמָּה לֹא אָמַר וְשָׂעִיר. דּוּ קָרְייָא וְשָׁחַט וְהֵבִיא. מַה הֲבָאָה בְכֹהֵן אַף שְׁחִיטָה בְכֹהֵן. רִבִּי יַעֲקֹב בַּר אָחָא רִבִּי יָסָא רִבִּי יוֹחָנָן בְּשֵׁם רִבִּי שִׁמְעוֹן בֶּן יוֹחַי. פַּר וְשָׂעִיר שֶׁלְּיוֹם הַכִּיפּוּרִים צְרִיכִין כֹּהֵן.

Rebbi Johanan said, we do not find that slaughter be qualified[161] by a non-Cohen. Rav commanded his students, everywhere state "he slaughters", but for the Cow[162] state "sprinkles"; and Rebbi Johanan said, we do not find that slaughter be (qualified) [disqualified][163] by a non-Cohen. Rebbi Hiyya bar Abba objected. Is it not written, *he slaughters, he sprinkles*[164]? Since sprinkling is not qualified by a woman as by a man[165], also slaughter is not qualified by a woman as by a man. He said to him, but sprinkling always was qualified by a Non-Cohen and disqualified by a woman[166]. He answered him, there "Cohen" is not written[167]. For which purpose is written *a man*? To qualify a non-Cohen. There is no difference between man and woman. If you are saying that it is qualified by a non-Cohen, it has to be qualified by a woman.

Rebbi Samuel bar Rav Isaac, Rebbi Joḥanan in the name of Rebbi Simeon ben Iohai. The bull of the Day of Atonement requires a Cohen.[166] But why does he not say, "and the he-goat"? That is the verse, *and he slaughters, and he brings*[167]. Since bringing is by a Cohen, also the slaughter is by a Cohen. Rebbi Jacob bar Aḥa, Rebbi Yasa, Rebbi Joḥanan in the name of Rebbi Simeon ben Iohai. The bull and the he-goat of the Day of Atonement require a Cohen.

161 This must read "disqualified" since Mishnah *Zevahim* 3:1 states without dissent that slaughter of sacrifices by a Non-Cohen, a woman, or a slave, is qualified.

162 The Red Cow (*Num.* 19). Here one has to switch the places of "slaughters" and sprinkles." Rav instructed that in *baraitot* specifying where a Cohen is indispensable, it always should mention sprinkling (mostly pouring the blood on the altar) but not slaughtering. But he requires that the Cow be slaughtered by a Cohen even though *Num.* 19:3 states only that somebody has to slaughter the Cow in the Cohen's presence.

163 The text in parentheses is the scribe's, consistent with his earlier text, but materially wrong. The text in brackets is the corrector's; its correctness is shown by the following argument of R. Ḥiyya bar Abba.

164 *Num.* 19:3,4. This sprinkling is not that of water with the ashes of the Red Cow, but of its blood, and the verse specifies that it has to be done by the Cohen.

164 For sprinkling water with the ashes of the Red Cow *Num.* 19:18 specifies that it has to be performed by *a pure man*, excluding women. Babli 42b.

165 The main thrust of *Num.* 19:18 is that it describes a rite which does not require a Cohen.

166 If slaughter of sacrifices is permitted to laymen, why is the High Priest burdened with slaughter in addition to all his other duties on that day?

167 *Lev.* 16:15. While in the case of the bull, Aaron is only commanded *to sacrifice* (v. 6), in the case of the he-goat it is spelled out that he has to slaughter. There is more reason to require the High Priest to personally slaughter the he-goat than the bull.

(40d line 47) אָמַר רִבִּי חַגַּיי. בָּראשׁוֹנָה הוּא אוֹמֵר. אָנָּא הָשֵׁם. וּבַשְּׁנִייָה הוּא אוֹמֵר. אָנָּא בַשֵּׁם.

Rebbi Ḥaggai said, the first time he says "please Hashem", the second time he says, "please Bashem"[168].

168 The correct version of the Mishnah is that in the confession the reading is Hashem, but in the prayer for forgiveness it is Bashem. Obviously this does not refer to what the High Priest actually said, since he used the correct vocalization for YHWH on all three occasions in the ritual (in the confession, in the prayer for forgiveness, and in the quote from *Lev.* 16:30), but fixes the text for the re-enactment of the ritual in the *musaph* prayer of the Day of Atonement.

(40d line 48) [תַּנֵּי. כֵּיצַד מִתְוַדֶּה. עָוִיתִי פָּשַׁעְתִּי חָטָאתִי. וְאוֹמֵר נוֹשֵׂא עָוֹן וָפֶשַׁע וְחַטָּאָה.] וְאוֹמֵר וְהִתְוַדָּה עָלָיו אֶת־כָּל־עֲוֹנוֹת בְּנֵי יִשְׂרָאֵל. דִּבְרֵי רִבִּי מֵאִיר. וַחֲכָמִים אוֹמְרִים. עֲוֹנוֹת אֵילּוּ הַזְּדוֹנוֹת. פְּשָׁעֵיהֶם אֵילּוּ הַמּוֹרְדִים. חַטֹּאתָם אֵילּוּ הַשְּׁגָגוֹת. מֵאַחַר שֶׁהוּא מִתְוַדֶּה עַל הַזְּדוֹנוֹת וְעַל הַמּוֹרְדִים הוּא חוֹזֵר וּמִתְוַדֶּה עַל הַשְּׁגָגוֹת. אֶלָּא כָךְ הָיָה מִתְוַדֶּה. אָנָּא הָשֵׁם. חָטָאתִי עָוִיתִי פָּשַׁעְתִּי לְפָנֶיךָ אֲנִי וּבֵיתִי (כול׳) [וּבְנֵי אַהֲרֹן]. כַּכָּתוּב בְּתוֹרַת מֹשֶׁה עַבְדֶּךָ לֵאמֹר כִּי בַיּוֹם הַזֶּה וגו׳. וְהֵן עוֹנִין אַחֲרָיו. בָּרוּךְ שֵׁם כְּבוֹד מַלְכוּתוֹ לְעוֹלָם וָעֶד:] וְכֵן מָצִינוּ דֶרֶךְ כָּל־הַמִּתְוַדִּים מִתְוַדִּים. דָּוִד אָמַר חָטָאנוּ עִם־אֲבוֹתֵינוּ הֶעֱוִינוּ וְהִרְשָׁעְנוּ. שְׁלֹמֹה בְנוֹ אָמַר [חָטָאנוּ] הֶעֱוִינוּ רָשָׁעְנוּ. דָּנִיֵּאל אָמַר חָטָאנוּ עָוִינוּ הִרְשַׁעְנוּ וּמָרָדְנוּ. אַף הוּא כָךְ הָיָה מִתְוַדֶּה. חָטָאתִי עָוִיתִי פָּשַׁעְתִּי לְפָנֶיךָ. מָהוּ שֶׁמֹשֶׁה אָמַר. נוֹשֵׂא עָוֹן וָפֶשַׁע וְחַטָּאָה. וְאוֹמֵר וְהִתְוַדָּה עָלָיו אֶת־כָּל־עֲוֹנוֹת בְּנֵי יִשְׂרָאֵל וגו׳. אֶלָּא מִכֵּיוָן שֶׁהוּא מִתְוַדֶּה עַל הַזְּדוֹנוֹת וְעַל הַמּוֹרְדִים כְּאִילּוּ הֵן שְׁגָגוֹת לְפָנָיו.

[169][It was stated: "How does he confess? "I acted criminally, I rebelled, I sinned;' and it says[170], *He forgives crime, rebellion, and sin*; and it says[171], *and he shall confess over it all crimes of the Children of Israel*, etc., the words of Rebbi Meïr. But the Sages say, criminal acts are intentional crimes, offenses are rebellions[172], sins are inadvertent actions[173]. After he confesses about criminal acts he turns around and confesses about inadvertent acts? But he confesses as follows: Please Hashem, I sinned, I acted criminally, I rebelled before You, I and my house (etc..) [and the sons of Aaron. As is written in the Torah of Moses as follows, *for on that day he shall*, etc. They. answer him: "Praised be the glory of His Kingdom forever and ever".][174] And so we find that confessors do confess. David said[175], *we and our fathers sinned, we acted criminally and we led to bad behavior*. His son Solomon said[176], [*we sinned,*] *we acted criminally, behaved badly*. Daniel said[177], *we sinned, we acted*

criminally, we led to bad behavior, and we rebelled. Also he was confessing thus: I sinned, I acted criminally, I rebelled before You. What means this which Moses said, *He forgives crime, rebellion, and sin*; and it says, *and he shall confess over it all crimes of the Children of Israel*, etc.[178]? But since he confesses to criminal rebellious acts, it is as if they were inadvertent sins before Him."

169 Babli 36b, *Sifra Ahare Parashah* 2(4-6), the entire paragraph. The starting sentence was added by the corrector, probably from one of the parallel sources.
170 *Ex.* 34:7.
171 *Lev.* 16:21.
172 Sins intentionally committed as rebellion against God.
173 *Ševuot* 1:3 (Note 114), Babli *Ševuot* 12b, *Keritut* 25b.

174 The text in parentheses is the scribe's, the one in brackets the corrector's, probably added from one of the parallel sources.
175 *Ps.* 106:6. The *vaw* added to the last word is from the synagogue service of the Day.
176 *1K.* 8:47.
177 *Dan.* 9:5.
178 How can one explain the illogical order?

(40d line 62) עֲשָׂרָה פְּעָמִים הָיָה כֹּהֵן גָּדוֹל מַזְכִּיר אֶת הַשֵּׁם בְּיוֹם הַכִּיפּוּרִים. שִׁשָּׁה בְּפַר וּשְׁלֹשָׁה בְּשָׂעִיר וְאֶחָד בְּגוֹרָלוֹת. הַקְּרוֹבִים הָיוּ נוֹפְלִין עַל פְּנֵיהֶן. הָרְחוֹקִים הָיוּ אוֹמְרִין. בָּרוּךְ שֵׁם כְּבוֹד מַלְכוּתוֹ לְעוֹלָם וָעֶד: אֵילוּ וְאֵילוּ לֹא הָיוּ זָזִים מִשָּׁם עַד שֶׁהוּא מִתְעַלֵּם מֵהֶן. זֶה־שְׁמַי לְעוֹלָם. זֶה־שְׁמִי לְעַלַּם. בָּרִאשׁוֹנָה הָיָה אוֹמְרוֹ בְּקוֹל גָּבוֹהַּ. מִשֶּׁרַבּוּ הַפְּרוּצִין הָיָה אוֹמְרוֹ בְּקוֹל נָמוּךְ. אָמַר רִבִּי טַרְפוֹן. עוֹמֵד הָיִיתִי בֵּין אַחֵיי [הַכֹּהֲנִים] בַּשּׁוּרָה הִהְטִיתִי אָזְנִי כְּלַפֵּי כֹּהֵן גָּדוֹל וּשְׁמַעְתִּיו מַבְלִיעוֹ בִּנְעִימַת הַכֹּהֲנִים. בָּרִאשׁוֹנָה הָיָה נִמְסַר לְכָל־אָדָם. מִשֶּׁרַבּוּ הַפְּרוּצִים לֹא הָיָה נִמְסַר אֶלָּא לַכְּשֵׁירִים.

שְׁמוּאֵל הֲוָה עֲבַר. שְׁמַע פַּרְסָיָיא מְקַלֵּל לִבְרִייָה בֵּיהּ וָמִית. אָמַר. אֲזַל גַּבְרָא וּמָאן דְּשָׁמַע שָׁמַע. רִבִּי אִינְיָינֵי בֶּן סוֹסַיי סָלַק גַּבֵּי רִבִּי חֲנִינָה לְצִיפּוֹרִין. אָמַר. אִיתָא וַאֲנָא מְסַר יָתֵיהּ לָךְ. עָאַל לֵיהּ בְּרֵיהּ תְּחוֹתֵי עַרְסָא. עָטַשׁ וּשְׁמַע קָלֵיהּ. אָמַר. מָה אַתּוֹן נְהִיגִין גַּבֵּיכוֹן בִּדְמֵיהּ. אֲזַל. לָא לָךְ וְלָא לֵיהּ. חַד אֲסִי בְּצִיפּוֹרִין אָמַר לְרִבִּי פִּינְחָס בַּר חָמָא. אִיתָא וַאֲנָא מְסַר לִי לָךְ. אָמַר לֵיהּ. לֵית אֲנָא יָכִיל. אָמַר לֵיהּ. לָמָה. אָמַר לֵיהּ. דַּאֲנָא אָכַל מַעֲשַׂר. וּמָאן דְּרָגִיל לֵיהּ לָא יָכַל מֵיכוֹל מִבַּר נַשׁ כְּלוּם.

1 שמע Q שמע איתא מקלל Q מקלה אזל Q קא אזיל 2 איניני Q אבינא סוסיי Q סוסי לציפורין Q בציפורי אמ' Q אמ' ליה יתיה Q ליה 3 עאל ליה בריה Q ליה עלה ר' חייה בריה תחותי Q תחות עאש Q עטשא בדמיו Q ברמיו אזל Q זיל 4 חד אסי Q ר' יוסי בציפורין Q בציפורי אמ' Q אמר ליה פינחס Q פנחס לי Q ליה 5 ליה Q ביה

Ten times did the High Priest pronounce the Name on the Day of Atonement[179]: Six times with the bull[180], and three with the he-goat, and once with the lots[181]. Those near were falling on their faces, those farther away were saying "Praised be the glory of His Kingdom forever and ever". These and those did not move away from there before they forgot it. *This is My Name forever*[182], "this is My Name to conceal.[183]" In earlier times he was saying it aloud. Since the lawless increased, he said it softly. Rebbi Tarphon said, I was standing in a row with my brothers the Cohanim and turned my ear towards the High Priest, when I heard him mixing it with the song of the Cohanim[184]. In earlier times it was given to everybody. Since the lawless increased, it was given only to qualified ones.

[185]Samuel was passing by when he heard a Persian cursing his son by it[186]; he died. He said, a man is gone and [he] who heard, heard. Rebbi Iniany bar Sosay went up to Rebbi Ḥanina in Sepphoris. He said, come and I shall transmit it to you. His son went under the couch. He[187] sneezed and he[188] heard the sound. He said, why are you acting together in trickery[189], go! Neither for you nor for him. A physician[190] in Sepphoris said to Rebbi Phineas bar Ḥama, come and I shall transmit it to you. He told him, I am unable. He asked him, why? He said to him, because I am eating tithe, and anybody conversant with it[186] cannot eat anything from any person.

179 Babli 39b.
180 3 times with the bull confessing his sins the first time; 3 times with the bull confessing the sins of the Cohanim.
181 Mishnah 4:1.
182 *Ex.* 3:14.
183 Babli *Pesahim* 50a.
184 They sang "Praised be the glory of His Kingdom forever and ever" not after he had pronounced the name but immediately when he started pronouncing it.

185 A copy of this paragraph is in *Qonteros Aharon* (Q). The strict Aramaic used in the paragraph attests to its aggadic character, explaining why the knowledge of the correct pronunciation of the Name is lost.
186 The Name.
187 The son.
188 R. Ḥanina.
189 Translation of the text of Q.
190 In Q: R. Yose of Sepphoris.

(fol. 40b) **משנה י**: בֶּן קָטִין עָשָׂה שְׁנֵים עָשָׂר דַּד לַכִּיּוֹר שֶׁלֹּא הָיוּ לוֹ אֶלָּא שְׁנָיִם. וְאַף הוּא עָשָׂה מוּכְנִי לַכִּיּוֹר שֶׁלֹּא יִהְיוּ מֵימָיו נִפְסָלִין בְּלִינָה. מוֹנְבַּז הַמֶּלֶךְ הָיָה עוֹשֶׂה כָּל־יְדוֹת הַכֵּלִים שֶׁל יוֹם הַכִּפּוּרִים שֶׁל זָהָב. הִילְנִי אִמּוֹ עָשְׂתָה נִבְרֶשֶׁת שֶׁל זָהָב עַל פִּתְחוֹ שֶׁל הֵיכָל. וְאַף הִיא עָשְׂתָה טַבְלָא שֶׁל זָהָב שֶׁפָּרָשַׁת סוֹטָה כְּתוּבָה עָלֶיהָ. נִיקָנוֹר נַעֲשׂוּ נִסִּים לְדַלְתוֹתָיו וְהָיוּ מַזְכִּירִין אוֹתוֹ לְשֶׁבַח:

Mishnah 10: Ben Qaṭin made twelve spouts to the basin[191], which had only two. He also made a mechanical device for the basin that its water should not become disqualified overnight[192]. King Monobaz[193] made all handles of the vessels for the Day of Atonement of gold. His mother Helene made a golden chandelier at the door of the Temple. She also made a golden table with the Chapter about the deviant wife written on it. Miracles happened to Nicanor's doors; one remembers him for praise.

191 From which the Cohanim sanctify hands and legs.
192 That the basin is lowered into a cistern containing 40 *se'ah* of water which is enough to purify and therefore never becomes disqualified. Otherwise the sunrise of a new day disqualifies all remainders of the service of the previous day.
193 King of Adiabene in NE Mesopotamia, who converted to Judaism together with his mother.

(41a line 1) **הלכה ח**: אֵי זֶהוּ צְפוֹנוֹ שֶׁלְּמִזְבֵּחַ שֶׁהוּא כָּשֵׁר בִּשְׁחִיטַת קָדְשֵׁי קָדָשִׁים. מִקִּירוֹ שֶׁלְּמִזְבֵּחַ צְפוֹנִי. גְּרַס בְּהִלְכָתָא עִילֵיתָא עַד מִקִּירוּ שֶׁלְּמִזְבֵּחַ הַצְּפוֹנִי וְעַד כּוֹתֶל הָעֲזָרָה הַמִּזְרָחִי.

Halakhah 8: [194]What is "North of the altar" which is qualified for the slaughter of most holy sacrifices[154]? From the Northern wall of the altar; one repeats this from the preceding Halakhah up to "from the Northern rim of the altar to the Eastern wall of the courtyard."

חֲמִשָּׁה דְבָרִים הָיָה הַסְּגָן מְשַׁמֵּשׁ. הַסְּגָן אוֹמֵר לוֹ. אִישִׁי כֹהֵן גָּדוֹל הַגְבַּהּ יְמִינְךָ. הַסְּגָן בִּימִינוֹ וְרֹאשׁ בֵּית אָב מִשְּׂמֹאלוֹ. הֵנִיף הַסְּגָן בַּסּוּדָרִין. אָחַז הַסְּגָן בִּימִינוֹ וְהֶעֱלוּהוּ. לֹא הָיָה כֹהֵן גָּדוֹל מִתְמַנֶּה לִהְיוֹת כֹּהֵן גָּדוֹל עַד שֶׁהוּא נַעֲשָׂה סְגָן.

For five things did the executive officer serve. The executive officer says to him, Sir High Priest, lift your right hand[195]. The executive officer[149] to his right and the head of the serving family[150] to his left[196]. The executive officer swings scarves[197]. The executive officer grabs his hand and brings him up[198].

Nobody was appointed High Priest if he had not first been appointed executive officer.

194 Discussion of the second part of Mishnah 7 (Mishnah 9 in most Mishnah mss.)
195 Mishnah 4:1.
196 Anywhere the High Priest goes on the Day of Atonement.

197 Every day to signal to the Levites to start singing. Mishnah *Tamid* 7:3.
198 Everyday, if the High Priest wants to sacrifice, the executive officer has to help him after he climbed half of the ramp. *Tamid* 7:3.

(41a line 5) וְקַלְפֵּי הָיְתָה שָׁם וּבָהּ שְׁנֵי גוֹרָלוֹת. וְשֶׁלְאֶשְׁכְּרוֹעַ הָיוּ. מָהוּ אֶשְׁכְּרוֹעַ. פֻּסְקִינָן. רִבִּי שְׁמוּאֵל אֲחוּי דְּרַב בָּעֵי. אָבְדוּ. מָהוּ לַעֲשׂוֹת תַּחְתֵּיהֶן שֶׁלְזָהָב. יָבֹא כְהָדָא. שֶׁמַּעֲלִין בַּקֹּדֶשׁ וְלֹא מוֹרִידִין.

"And an urn[152] was there with two lots in it. They were of boxwood. What is "of boxwood"? Πύξινον[199]. Rebbi Samuel, Rav's brother, asked: If they were lost, must the replacement be made from gold[200]? It shall come following "one increases in holiness but does not decrease[201]."

199 Cf. *Ketubot* 7:11 (Note 177), *Gen. r.* 15(2).
200 After ben Gamla made the lots of gold, may the replacement be made of boxwood as it was originally or must any future replacement be made of gold?

No R. Samuel, Rav's brother, is otherwise known in talmudic literature. One may conjecture that the name is a scribal error for R. Samuel, R. Berekhiah's brother.
201 Mishnah *Šeqalim* 6:6.

(41a line 11) וְיַעֲשׂוּ דָדִין זֶה עַל גַּבֵּי זֶה. אָמַר רִבִּי יוֹנָה. כְּיוֹם מְרוּבֶּה שֶׁלְתָּמִיד. הָעֶלְיוֹן מְשַׁמֵּשׁ כְּלִי פָחוּת בְּרוּבּוֹ. וְהַתַּחְתּוֹן אֵין בּוֹ מִשּׁוּם אֲוִירוֹ שֶׁלְכְּלִי. אָמַר רִבִּי יְהוֹשֻׁעַ בֶּן לֵוִי. אַמַּת הַמַּיִם הָיְתָה מוֹשֶׁכֶת לוֹ מֵעֵיטָם. וְהָיוּ רַגְלֵי שֶׁבַּדָּרוֹם פְּחוּתִין כְּרִימּוֹנִים. רִבִּי שִׁמְעוֹן בַּר כַּרְסָנָא בְשֵׁם רִבִּי אָחָא. הַיָּם בֵּית טְבִילָה לַכֹּהֲנִים הוּא. וְהֶם לִרְחִיצַת לַכֹּהֲנִים בּוֹ¹ וְלֹא כְלִי הוּא. אַמַּת הַמַּיִם מוֹשֶׁכֶת לוֹ מֵעֵיטָם וְהָיוּ רַגְלֵי שֶׁבַּדָּרוֹם פְּחוּתִים כְּרִימּוֹנִים.

כְּתִיב וְאֵלֶּה מִסְפָּרָם אֲגַרְטְלֵי זָהָב שְׁלֹשִׁים. רִבִּי שְׁמוּאֵל בַּר נַחְמָן אָמַר. מָקוֹם שֶׁאוּגְרִין בּוֹ דָּמוֹ שֶׁלְטָלֶה. אֲגַרְטְלֵי־כֶסֶף אָלֶף. רִבִּי שִׁמְעוֹן בֶּן לָקִישׁ אָמַר. מָקוֹם שֶׁאוּגְרִין דָּמוֹ שֶׁלְפָּר. מַחֲלָפִים תִּשְׁעָה וְעֶשְׂרִים: אָמַר רִבִּי סִימוֹן. אֵילּוּ הַסַּכִּינִין. כַּיי דְּתַנִּינָן תַּמָּן. הוּא הָיָה נִקְרָא בֵּית הַחֲלִיפוֹת. שֶׁשָּׁם גּוֹנְזִין אֶת הַסַּכִּינִין.

1 ואלא Q | אלא שאוגרין Q | שאגרים Q | 3 אילו Q | - כיי Q | כהדא Q | תמן -

Could they make spouts one on top of the other[202]? Rebbi Jonah said, for the maximum day of the daily sacrifice[203]. The top because of a vessel reduced in its majority. But is the lower not in the category of volume inside a vessel[204]? Rebbi Joshua ben Levi said, a water canal was drawing from Etam[205], and the feet to the South were reduced in the size of pomegranates[206]. Rebbi Simeon ben Carsana in the name of Rebbi Aḥa: The Sea was a place of immersion of the Cohanim, *and the Sea for the Cohanim to wash in it*[207]. But was it not a vessel? A water canal was drawing from Etam, and the feet to the South were reduced in the size of pomegranates.

[207]It is written[208]: *And these are their numbers: gold basins 30*, Rebbi Samuel bar Naḥman said, places where the blood of the lamb was collected. *Silver basins 1'000*, Rebbi Simeon ben Laqish said, places where the blood of the bull was collected. *Knives 29*, Rebbi Simon said, these are the knives, as we have stated there[209], "it was called the place of knives since there they hid the knives."

202 Here starts the discussion of Mishnah 10. It is understood that Ben Qaṭina made 12 spouts level around the basin. Why was he restricted to 12?

203 By Mishnah 2:5, this is the maximum number of Cohanim needed for any morning daily sacrifice. Babli 37a.

204 How could there be a biblical requirement that the Cohanim sanctify themselves with water drawn from a basin? It is one of the general principles of the rules of purity that water only purifies if either it is flowing (in any amount) or is collected in a cistern (of at least 40 *seah*); water drawn in a container and poured into a cistern renders the latter disqualified. One has to prove that the basin does not qualify as a container. According to the Babli, the original two spouts were one on top of the other (37a).

As was noted in *Eruvin* (Chapter 1,

Notes 199-206) the Solomon's basin was a cylinder put on top of a rectangular solid. The upper part, being totally open to the bottom, is not a container. But the bottom seems to be a container.

205 *En Etam*, "the pools of Salomon", source of the water for the Temple.

206 The basin was not a container since the water in it was not at rest. It was filled from the water canal and the water flowed out of holes in the hooves of the three Southern bronze cattle on which the basin was resting (*1K*. 7:25). A hole in the size of a pomegranate makes any vessel pure since it cannot be a container even for solid food (Mishnah *Kelim* 17:1). (In Q, there is no mention of "Southern".)

207 This entire paragraph is copied in Q.

208 *2Chr*. 4:6. The topic is to find roots for the uncommon words אֲגַרְטְלֵי, מַחֲלָפִים.

209 Mishnah *Middot* 4:7.

(41a line 22) הִילְנִי אִמּוֹ עָשְׂתָה נִבְרֶשֶׁת שֶׁל זָהָב עַל פִּתְחוֹ שֶׁל הֵיכָל. תְּרֵין אֲמוֹרִין. חַד אָמַר. מְנַרְתָּא. וְחָרָנָה אָמַר. קוֹנְכִיתָא. תִּרְגֵּם אֲקִילַס. לְקַבֵּל נִבְרַשְׁתָּא לַמְפַּדֹס.

"His mother Helene made a golden chandelier at the door of the Temple.." Two Amoraim. One said, a chandelier. But the other said, a basin[210]. Aquila translated *before the chandelier*, λαμπάδος[211].

210 This translation is traditional; it is pure speculation. More likely is "a lamp (?) in shell form," Aramaic diminutive of Greek κόγχη, ἡ "mussel".

211 Genitive of λαμπάς, -άδος, ἡ, "torch". This is the translation of the Theodotion version of the LXX of *Dan.* 5:5.

(41a line 25) אַף הִיא עָשְׂתָה טַבְלָא שֶׁל זָהָב שֶׁפָּרָשַׁת סוֹטָה כְּתוּבָה עָלֶיהָ. שֶׁבְּשָׁעָה שֶׁהָיְתָה הַחַמָּה זוֹרַחַת הָיוּ הַנִּיצוֹצוֹת מְנַתְּזִין מִמֶּנָּה וְהָיוּ יוֹדְעִין שֶׁזָּרְחָה הַחַמָּה. וּמָה הָיָה כָתוּב עָלֶיהָ. רִבִּי שִׁמְעוֹן בֶּן לָקִישׁ בְּשֵׁם רִבִּי יַנַּאי. אָלֶ"ף בֵּי"ת הָיָה כָתוּב עָלֶיהָ. וְהָא תַנֵּי. כִּכְתָב שֶׁכָּאן כֵּן כְּתַב שֶׁכָּאן. לֹא מְעוּבֶּה וְלֹא מֵידַק אֶלָּא בֵינוֹנִי. פָּתַר לָהּ. כְּאָלֶ"ף שֶׁכָּאן [כֵּן] אָלֶ"ף שֶׁכָּאן. כְּבֵי"ת שֶׁכָּאן כֵּן בֵּי"ת שֶׁכָּאן. תַּנֵּי רִבִּי הוֹשַׁעְיָה. כָּל־פָּרָשַׁת סוֹטָה הָיָה כָתוּב עָלֶיהָ. שֶׁמִּמֶּנָּה הָיָה קוֹרֵא וּמְתַרְגֵּם כָּל־דִּקְדּוּקֵי הַפָּרָשָׁה.

1-2 שהיתה החמה | ס שהחמה   2 הניצוצות | ס הניצוצים   ומה | ס מה   3 ר' שמעון בן לקיש | ס ריש לקיש כתוב | ס כותב תני | ס תאני שכאן | ס שכן   4 כתב | ס כתיב כאן | ס כן שכאן | ס שכן כן | ס - שכאן | ס שכן   5 שכאן | ס שכן (2)   דקדוקי | ס דיקדוקי

[212]"Also she made a golden plate with the paragraph of the suspected wife written on it." When the sun rose, sparks were reflected on it and one knew that the sun had risen. What was written on it? Rebbi Simeon ben Laqish said in the name of Rebbi Yannai: Alef-Bet was written on it[213]. But did we not state: In the script there it was written here, not heavy, not thin, but average[214]. Explain "the Alef there" by "from the Alef there", "the Bet there" by "from the Bet there"[215]. Rebbi Hoshaia stated: The entire paragraph of the suspected wife was written there, and from it he was reading and explaining all details of the paragraph[216].

212 This paragraph is from *Sotah* 2:2 (Notes 91-97).

213 Single letters were written on the tablet, each letter being the first of its word. (Cf. P. Kahle, *Masoreten des Westens*, II, pp. 88-95).

214 The suspected wife's scroll had to be written in the way the letters were on the queen's tablet, not ornamental nor in italics. The questioner thought that the entire tablet had to be copied as it was written; then an abbreviated version would be impossible.

215 For each letter one copies the entire word. The first sentence of the scroll would

read on the tablet as
אם לשאאול שטתאהמההה
which would be copied as
אם לא שכב איש אתך ואם לא שטית טומאה תחת אישך הנקי ממי המרים המאררים האלה
where every first letter was copied exactly from the tablet and the rest of the word added in the same style of script. Babli 37b.

216 While writing, the Cohen explained the text homiletically to the suspected wife, so that she would understand the meaning of the ceremony.

(41a line 32b) נִיקָנוֹר נַעֲשׂוּ נִיסִּים לְדַלְתוֹתָיו. וּמַזְכִּירִין אוֹתוֹ לְשֶׁבַח: תַּנֵּי. מַעֲשֶׂה שֶׁהָיוּ בָאִין בִּסְפִינָה וְעָמַד עֲלֵיהֶן סַעַר גָּדוֹל בַּיָּם. וְנָטְלוּ אֶחָד מֵהֶם וְהִטִּילוּהוּ בַיָּם. וּבִקְשׁוּ לְהַטִּיל עוֹד שֵׁינִי וְעָמַד וְגִיפְפוֹ. אָמַר לָהֶן. אִם מַטִּילִין אַתֶּם אוֹתוֹ לַיָּם הַטִּילוּנִי עִמּוֹ. וְהָיָה בוֹכֶה וּמִתְאַבֵּל וּבָא עַד שֶׁהִגִּיעַ לִלְמֵינָהּ שֶׁל יָפוֹ. כֵּיוָן שֶׁהִגִּיעַ לִלְמֵינָהּ שֶׁל יָפוֹ הִתְחִיל מְבַעְבֵּעַ מִתַּחַת הַסְּפִינָה. כַּיי דְתַנִּינָן תַּמָּן. כָּל־הַשְּׁעָרִים שֶׁהָיוּ שָׁם נִשְׁתַּנּוּ לִהְיוֹת שֶׁלְּזָהָב חוּץ מְשַׁעֲרֵי נִיקָנוֹר מִפְּנֵי שֶׁנַּעֲשָׂה בָהֶן נֵס. וְיֵשׁ אוֹמְרִים מִפְּנֵי שֶׁנְּחוּשְׁתָּן מַצְהִיב: תַּנֵּי בְשֵׁם רְבִּי לִיעֶזֶר. נְחוּשְׁתָּן הָיָה (קָרוֹנְתִּיּוֹן) [מַצְהִיב וְיוֹתֵר] יָפֶה מִשֶּׁל זָהָב.

"Miracles happened to Nicanor's doors; one remembers him for praise." It was stated[217]: "It happened that they were traveling in a ship[218] when they ran into a big storm. They took one of the doors and threw it into the sea. When they wanted to throw also the second one he stood up and embraced it. He told them, it you are throwing it into the sea, throw me with it. He was crying and mourning continuously until he arrived at the port[219] of Jaffa. When he arrived at the port of Jaffa it started bubbling under the ship. As we have stated there[220], 'All doors there were changed into golden ones except Nicanor's doors since a miracle happened to them, but some say because their bronze had a golden shine.'" It was stated in the name of Rebbi Eliezer[221], "their bronze was (Corinthian)[222] [gold colored and more] beautiful than gold."

217 Babli 38a, Tosephta 2:4.
218 The parallel sources add: "From Alexandria".
219 Greek λιμήν, -ένες, ὁ.
220 Mishnah *Middot* 2:3.
221 In the parallel sources: R. Eliezer ben Jacob.

222 This is the correct scribe's text. The corrector who did not understand the word changed it to the text in brackets. Corinthian brass was the most expensive kind, used for luxury goods; a copper alloy probably containing some precious metal. Greek Κορίνθιον "Corinthian", *adj., n.*.

(fol. 40b) **משנה יא**: וְאֵילּוּ לִגְנַאי שֶׁל בֵּית גַּרְמוּ לֹא רָצוּ לְלַמֵּד עַל מַעֲשֵׂה לֶחֶם הַפָּנִים. שֶׁל בֵּית אַבְטִינָס לֹא רָצוּ לְלַמֵּד עַל מַעֲשֵׂה הַקְּטוֹרֶת. הוּגְדָּס בֶּן לֵוִי הָיָה יוֹדֵעַ פֶּרֶק בַּשִּׁיר וְלֹא רָצָה לְלַמֵּד. בֶּן קַמְצָר לֹא רָצָה לְלַמֵּד עַל מַעֲשֵׂה הַכְּתָב. עַל הָרִאשׁוֹנִים נֶאֱמַר זֵכֶר צַדִּיק לִבְרָכָה. וְעַל אֵילּוּ נֶאֱמַר וְשֵׁם רְשָׁעִים יִרְקַב:

Mishnah 11: But the following are for shame: The family Garmu did not want to teach the preparation of the shew-bread. The family Eutinos did not want to teach about preparation of the incense. [223]Hugdas ben Levi knew a chapter about song and did not want to teach. Ben Qamṣar did not want to teach writing technique. About the earlier ones it is said[224], *the remembrance of the just is for blessing*, and about those it is said, *but the name of evildoers shall rot*.

223 Only the first two cases are discussed in the Halakhah. According to the Babli, Hugdas knew how to amplify his voice and Ben Qamṣar knew how to write multiple letters simultaneously.

224 *Prov.* 10:3.

(41a line 40) **הלכה ט**: וְאֵילּוּ לִגְנַיי. בֵּית גַּרְמוּ. בֵּית גַּרְמוּ הָיוּ בְקִיאִין בְּמַעֲשֵׂה לֶחֶם הַפָּנִים וּבְרִדִּייָתוֹ וְלֹא רָצוּ לְלַמֵּד. שָׁלְחוּ וְהֵבִיאוּ אוּמָּנִים מֵאַלֶכְּסַנְדְּרִיָּה. וְהָיוּ בְקִיאִין בְּמַעֲשֵׂה לֶחֶם הַפָּנִים. וּבְרִדִּייָתוֹ לֹא הָיוּ בְקִיאִין. בֵּית גַּרְמוּ הָיוּ מַסִּיקִין מִבִּפְנִים וְרוֹדִין מִבַּחוּץ. וְלֹא הָיְתָה מְעַפֶּשֶׁת. וְאֵילּוּ מַסִּיקִין מִבַּחוּץ וְרוֹדִין מִבִּפְנִים. וְהָיְתָה מְעַפֶּשֶׁת. וְכֵיוָן שֶׁיָּדְעוּ חֲכָמִים בַּדָּבָר אָמְרוּ. כָּל־מַה שֶׁבָּרָא הַקָּדוֹשׁ בָּרוּךְ הוּא לִכְבוֹדוֹ בָּרָא. כָּל פָּעַל יְיָ לַמַּעֲנֵהוּ. שָׁלְחוּ אַחֲרֵיהֶם וְלֹא רָצוּ לָבוֹא עַד שֶׁכָּפְלוּ לָהֶן שְׂכָרָן. שְׁנֵים עָשָׂר מָנֶה הָיוּ נוֹטְלִין וְנָתְנוּ לָהֶן עֶשְׂרִים וְאַרְבַּע. רִבִּי יְהוּדָה אוֹמֵר. עֶשְׂרִים וְאַרְבַּע הָיוּ נוֹטְלִין וְנָתְנוּ לָהֶן אַרְבָּעִים וּשְׁמוֹנָה. אָמְרוּ לָהֶן. מִפְּנֵי מַה אֵין אַתֶּם רוֹצִין לְלַמֵּד. אָמְרוּ לָהֶן. מְסוֹרֶת הִיא בְיָדֵינוּ מֵאֲבוֹתֵינוּ שֶׁהַבַּיִת הַזֶּה עָתִיד לִיחָרֵב. שֶׁלֹּא יְלַמְדוּ אֲחֵרִים וְיִהְיוּ עוֹשִׂין כֵּן לִפְנֵי עֲבוֹדָה זָרָה שֶׁלָּהֶן. בִּדְבָרִים הַלָּלוּ מַזְכִּירִין אוֹתָן לְשֶׁבַח. שֶׁלֹּא יָצָא מִיַּד בְּנֵיהֶם פַּת נְקִייָה מֵעוֹלָם. שֶׁלֹּא יְהוּ אוֹמְרִים. מִמַּעֲשֵׂה לֶחֶם הַפָּנִים הֵן אוֹכְלִין.

4 מעפשת | **ש** מתעפשת C מעפשת | S מנפשת **ש** מתעפשת וכיון | **ש** כיון בדבר | **ש** בדבר הזה 5 - | שנא' 7 וארבע | **ש** וארבעה

Halakhah 9: "The following are for shame: The family Garmu." [225]"The family Garmu were experts in preparing the shew-bread and its removal from the oven, but they did not want to teach. They sent and brought craftsmen from Alexandria who were experts in preparing the shew-bread but were not experts in its removal from the oven. The family Garmu were heating from within and removing from the outside, and it did not become moldy[226]. But those were heating from the outside and removing from the inside, and it became moldy. When the Sages realized the situation, they said, everything which the Holy One, praise to Him, created, he created to His glory; *all work of the Eternal is for Himself*[227]. They sent after them, but they refused to come until they doubled their wages. They used to take twelve *mina*[228], so they gave them twenty-four. Rebbi Jehudah says, they used to take 24, so they gave them 48. They asked them, why do you not want to teach? They answered them, there is a tradition among us from our forefathers that this Temple will be destroyed in the future. Others should not learn and prepare the same before their foreign worship[229]. In the following matter one mentions them for praise, that in the hands of their children white bread was never found, so people should not say, from the preparation of shew-bread they are eating."

225 Tosephta 2:5, *Šeqalim* 5:2 (ש), Babli 38a, *Cant. rabba* 3:8. The *Šeqalim* text of the Babli *editio princeps* belongs to the spelling tradition of the Tosephta.
226 It had to stay fresh for a full week. The shew-bread was baked on clay forms in the shape of a ship.
227 Prov. 16:4.
228 As yearly wages. The Babli and *Cant. rabba* declare this weekly wages, an exaggeration.
229 Idolatry.

(41a line 54) שֶׁלְּבֵית אַבְטִינָס הָיוּ בְקִייִן בְּמַעֲשֵׂה הַקְּטוֹרֶת וּבְמַעֲלָה עָשָׁן וְלֹא רָצוּ לְלַמֵּד. שָׁלְחוּ וְהֵבִיאוּ אוּמָנִים מֵאַלֶכְּסַנְדְּרִיָּה. וְהָיוּ בְקִייִן בְּמַעֲשֵׂה הַקְּטוֹרֶת. וּבְמַעֲלָה עָשָׁן לֹא הָיוּ בְקִיאִין. שֶׁלְּבֵית אַבְטִינָס הָיְתָה מִתַּמֶּרֶת וְעוֹלָה וּפוֹסֶה וְיוֹרֶדֶת. וְשֶׁלָּאֵילוּ הָיְתָה פּוֹסָה מִיַּד. וְכֵיוָן שֶׁיָּדְעוּ חֲכָמִים בַּדָּבָר אָמְרוּ. כָּל־מַה שֶּׁבָּרָא הַקָּדוֹשׁ בָּרוּךְ הוּא לִכְבוֹדוֹ בָּרָא. שֶׁנֶּאֱמַר כֹּל הַנִּקְרָא בִשְׁמִי וגו'. שָׁלְחוּ אַחֲרֵיהֶן וְלֹא רָצוּ לָבוֹא כול' עַד לִפְנֵי עֲבוֹדָה זָרָה שֶׁלָּהֶן. בַּדְּבָרִים הַלָּלוּ מַזְכִּירִין אוֹתָן לְשֶׁבַח. שֶׁלֹּא יָצָאת אִשָּׁה שֶׁלְּאֶחָד מֵהֶן מְבוּשֶּׂמֶת מֵעוֹלָם. וְלֹא עוֹד אֶלָּא כְשֶׁהָיָה אֶחָד מֵהֶן נוֹשֵׂא אִשָּׁה מִמָּקוֹם אַחֵר הָיָה פּוֹסֵק עִמָּהּ שֶׁלֹּא תִתְבַּשֵּׂם.

אָמַר רִבִּי יוֹסֵי. מָצָאתִי תִּינוֹק אֶחָד מִבֵּית אַבְטִינָס. אָמַרְתִּי לוֹ. בְּנִי. מֵאֵי זוֹ מִשְׁפָּחָה אָתְּ. אָמַר לִי. מִמִּשְׁפַּחַת פְּלוֹנִית. אָמַרְתִּי לוֹ. בְּנִי. אֲבוֹתֶיךָ שֶׁנִּתְכַּוְּונוּ לְרַבּוֹת כְּבוֹדָם וּלְמַעֵט כְּבוֹד שָׁמַיִם לְפִיכָךְ נִתְמַעֵט כְּבוֹדָם וּכְבוֹד שָׁמַיִם נִתְרַבָּה. אָמַר רִבִּי עֲקִיבָה. סָח לִי שִׁמְעוֹן בֶּן (לגס) [לגסה]. מְלַקֵּט הָיִיתִי עֲשָׂבִים אֲנִי וְתִינוֹק אֶחָד מִבֵּית אַבְטִינָס. וְרָאִיתִי אוֹתוֹ שֶׁבָּכָה וְרָאִיתִי אוֹתוֹ שֶׁשָּׂחַק. אָמַרְתִּי לוֹ. בְּנִי. לָמָּה בָכִיתָה. אָמַר לִי. עַל כְּבוֹד בֵּית אַבָּא שֶׁנִּתְמַעֵט. וְלָמָּה שָׂחַקְתָּה. אָמַר לִי. עַל הַכָּבוֹד הַמָּתוּקָן לַצַּדִּיקִים לֶעָתִיד לָבוֹא. הֲרֵי מַעֲלֶה עָשָׁן לְנֶגְדִּי. נוֹמֵיתִי לוֹ. בְּנִי. הַרְאֵהוּ לִי. אָמַר לִי. מָסוֹרֶת בְּיָדִי מֵאֲבוֹתַיי שֶׁלֹּא לְהַרְאוֹתוֹ לִבְרִיָּיה. אָמַר רִבִּי יוֹחָנָן בֶּן נוּרִי. פָּגַע בִּי זָקֵן אֶחָד מִשֶּׁלְּבֵית אַבְטִינָס. אָמַר לִי. רִבִּי. לְשֶׁעָבַר הָיוּ בֵית אַבָּא צְנוּעִין וְהָיוּ מוֹסְרִין

אֶת הַמְגִילָה הַזֹּאת אֵילוּ לְאֵילוּ. וְעַכְשָׁיו שֶׁאֵינָן נֶאֱמָנִין הֵילָךְ אֶת הַמְגִילָה וְהִיזָּהֵר בָּהּ. וּכְשֶׁבָּאתִי וְהִרְצֵאתִי אֶת הַדְּבָרִים לִפְנֵי רִבִּי עֲקִיבָה זָלְגוּ דְמָעָיו וְאָמַר. מֵעַתָּה אֵין אָנוּ צְרִיכִין לְהַזְכִּירָן לִגְנַאי.

[230]"The family Eutinos were experts in preparing the incense and the smoke-creating herb, but they did not want to teach. They sent and brought craftsmen from Alexandria who were experts in preparing the incense but were not experts in the smoke-creating herb. The family Eutinos's was going straight up, and spread[231], and descended. But theirs was immediately spreading. When the Sages realized the situation, they said, everything which the Holy One, praise to Him, created, he created to His glory; as it is said[232], *all which is called by My Name,* etc. They sent after them, but they refused to come, etc.[233], up to "before their foreign worship[229]." In the following matter one mentions them for praise, that no woman of any of them ever went out perfumed. Not only that, but if one of them married a woman from outside, he contracted with her that she should not use perfume.

Rebbi Yose said, I found a child of the family Eutinos. I said to him, my son, from which family are you? he told me, from family X. I said to him, my son, because your forefathers intended to increase their prestige and to decrease Heaven's prestige, therefore their prestige was diminished and Heaven's prestige increased. Rebbi Aqiba said, Simeon ben Lagos[234] told me, 'I was collecting herbs, I and a youth from the family Eutinos, when I saw him crying and laughing. I said to him, my son, why did you cry? He said to me, about the prestige of my family which is diminished. And why did you laugh? About the glory prepared for the Just in the future world; there is smoke-creating herb before me! I said to him, my son, show it to me. He answered me, I have a tradition from my ancestors not to show it to any creature.' Rebbi Johanan ben Nuri said, I met an old man from the family Eutinos. He said to me, 'Rabbi. In the past my family were humble, and transmitting this scroll[235] one to the other. But now they are not trustworthy; here the scroll is yours and take care of it.' When I came and repeated these words before Rebbi Aqiba, his tears flowed and he said, from now on we do not have to mention them for shame."

230 Tosephta 2:6-7, *Šeqalim* 5:2, Babli 38a, *Cant. rabba* 3:8. The text here is slightly shortened.

231 فشى "to expand, spread".

232 *Is.* 43:7.

233 Here the corresponding text from the preceding paragraph has to be inserted.

234 This is the spelling of the scribe. The corrector changed this to *Logah* following the text in the other sources.

235 Containing the identification of the smoke-creating herb.

(41b line 1) וְכוּלְּהֹן מֶצְאוּ מַתְלָא לְדִבְרֵיהֶן חוּץ מִבֶּן קַמְצָר. כַּיֵי דְתַנִּינָן תַּמָּן. אֵילוּ הֵן הַמְמוּנִּין שֶׁהָיוּ בַּמִּקְדָּשׁ. רִבִּי חִזְקִיָּה אָמַר. רִבִּי סִימוֹן וְרַבָּנָן. חַד אָמַר. כְּשֵׁירֵי כָל־דּוֹר וָדוֹר בָּא לִמְנוֹת. וְחָרָנָה אָמַר. מִי שֶׁהָיָה בְאוֹתוֹ הַדּוֹר מָנָה מַה שֶׁבְּדוֹרוֹ. מָאן דְּאָמַר. כְּשֵׁירֵי כָּל־דּוֹר וָדוֹר בָּא לִמְנוֹת. עַל כּוּלָּם הוּא אוֹמֵר. זֵכֶר צַדִּיק לִבְרָכָה. מָאן דְּאָמַר. מִי שֶׁהָיָה בְאוֹתוֹ הַדּוֹר מָנָה מַה שֶׁבְּדוֹרוֹ. עַל כּוּלָּם הוּא אוֹמֵר. וְשֵׁם רְשָׁעִים יִרְקָב׃ עַל מִי נֶאֱמַר זֵכֶר צַדִּיק לִבְרָכָה. עַל בֶּן קָטִין וַחֲבֵירָיו.

1 כשירי | M מכשירי   2 למנות | ש למנות עליהן | ש וחרנה | ש ואחרינא   שהיה | ש שהיא   מנה | ש מונה   3 למנות | ש למנות עליהן²³⁶   על | ש -   כולם | ש כולן ש -   4 מנה | ש מונה עליהן   על | ש -   כולם | ש כולן ש -   על | ש ועל

וְעַל כּוּלָּן הָיָה בֶּן זוֹמָא אוֹמֵר. מִשֶּׁלְּךָ יִתְּנוּ לָךְ. וּבִשְׁמָךְ קוֹרִין אוֹתָךְ. וּבְשִׁבְחָךְ מוֹשִׁיבִין אוֹתָךְ. וְאֵין שִׁכְחָה לִפְנֵי הַמָּקוֹם. וְאֵין אָדָם נוֹגֵעַ בְּמוּכָן לָךְ.

All found an excuse for their behavior except Ben Qamsar. Also following what we have stated there[237].

"These are the appointees who were in the Sanctuary." Rebbi Hizqiah said, Rebbi Simon and the rabbis. One said, he comes to enumerate the qualified ones of every generation[238]. But the other said, he who was in a generation enumerated what was in his generation[239]. He who said, he comes to enumerate the qualified ones of every generation, about all of them he says[224], *the remembrance of the just is for blessing.* He who said, he who was in a generation enumerated what was in his generation, about all of them he says[224], *but the name of evildoers shall rot.* About whom was it said, *the remembrance of the just is for blessing*? About Ben Qatin and his kind.

About all of them, Ben Zoma says, from yours they will give you, and by your name they are calling you, and according to your praise they place you, and there is no forgetting before the Omnipresent, and nobody touches what is prepared for you[240].

236 Error of a learned copyist who understood מונה in the sense of "appointed" when it means "counted".

237 Mishnah *Šeqalim* 5:1. The following Paragraph also is there (Leiden ms. ש, Babli editio princeps ש, Munich ms. of the Babli M.)

238 The list is no historical document.

239 The list is a historical document from early Mishnaic times; time not otherwise determined.

240 He teaches an extreme doctrine of predestination, that the result of every action a person takes is predetermined in Heaven. Then even the exaggerated claims of the artisans working for the Temple would be predestined.

טרף בקלפי פרק רביעי

(fol.41b) **משנה א**: טָרַף בַּקַּלְפִּי וְהֶעֱלָה שְׁנֵי גוֹרָלוֹת. אֶחָד כָּתוּב עָלָיו לַשֵּׁם וְאֶחָד כָּתוּב עָלָיו לַעֲזָאזֵל הַסְּגָן בִּימִינוֹ וְרֹאשׁ בֵּית אָב מִשְּׂמֹאלוֹ. אִם שֶׁל שֵׁם עָלָה בִּימִינוֹ הַסְּגָן אוֹמֵר לוֹ אִישִׁי כֹּהֵן גָּדוֹל הַגְבֵּהַּ אֶת יְמִינֶךָ. וְאִם בִּשְׂמֹאלוֹ עָלָה רֹאשׁ בֵּית אָב אוֹמֵר לוֹ אִישִׁי כֹּהֵן גָּדוֹל הַגְבֵּהַּ אֶת שְׂמֹאלֶךָ. נְתָנָם עַל שְׁנֵי שְׂעִירִים וְאוֹמֵר לַיי חַטָּאת. רִבִּי יִשְׁמָעֵאל אוֹמֵר לֹא הָיָה צָרִיךְ לוֹמַר חַטָּאת אֶלָּא לַיי. וְהֵן עוֹנִין אַחֲרָיו בָּרוּךְ שֵׁם כְּבוֹד מַלְכוּתוֹ לְעוֹלָם וָעֶד:

Mishnah 1: He scrambled the urn[1] and brought up the two lots; one had written on it "for Hashem[2]", and the other had written on it "for Azazel[3]", with the executive officer to his right and the head of the serving family to his left. If the Eternal's came up in his right hand, the executive officer said to him, "Sir High Priest, lift you right hand." But if it came up in his left hand, the head of the serving family said to him. "Sir High Priest, lift your left hand." He puts them on the two he-goats[4] and says, "for Hashem a purification offering"[5]. Rebbi Ismael says, it was not necessary to say "a purification offering," only "for Hashem"[6], and they answer, "praised be the glory of His Kingdom forever and ever."

1 To make sure that he had no control about which lot he grabbed in each hand.
2 Cf. Chapter 3, Mishnah 9, Notre 144.
3 Since הָאֶבֶן הָאָזֵל (*IS.* 20:19) is a monolith, עז-אזז is a strong monolith, either a rocky mountain top or a sheer cliff, in the words of the verse (*Lev.* 16:22) "in a cut (or cut-off) land."
4 Standing between the two he-goats, the lot in his right hand is put on the he-goat to his right, and the one in his left on the he-goat to his left side.
5 In *Lev.* 16:9 the expression וְעָשָׂהוּ חַטָּאת cannot mean "sacrificed it as purification offering" since its slaughter is prescribed only in v. 15; it must mean "declare it as purification sacrifice."
6 Since both he-goats already were taken as purification sacrifices, v. 5.

(41b line 54) **הלכה א**: טָרַף בַּקַּלְפֵּי כול׳. לֹא סוֹף דָּבָר קַלְפֵּי אֶלָּא אֲפִילוּ קַלָּתוֹת. וְלָמָּה אָמְרוּ קַלְפֵּי. כְּדֵי לַעֲשׂוֹת פּוּמְפֵּי לַדָּבָר. וְיָבִיא שְׁנֵי חוּטִין. אֶחָד שָׁחוֹר וְאֶחָד לָבָן. וְיִקְשׁוֹר עֲלֵיהֶם וְיֹאמַר. זֶה לַשֵּׁם וְזֶה לַעֲזָאזֵל. תַּלְמוּד לוֹמַר גּוֹרָל אֶחָד לַיי. שֶׁיְּהֵא נִיכָּר שֶׁהוּא לַיי. וְגוֹרָל אֶחָד לַעֲזָאזֵל. שֶׁיְּהֵא נִיכָּר שֶׁהוּא לַעֲזָאזֵל. וְיָבִיא שְׁנֵי צְרוֹרוֹת. אֶחָד שָׁחוֹר וְאֶחָד לָבָן. [וְיִתֵּן עֲלֵיהֶם]

וְיֹאמַר. זֶה לַשֵּׁם וְזֶה לַעֲזָאזֵל. תַּלְמוּד לוֹמַר גּוֹרָל אֶחָד לַיי. [שֶׁיְּהֵא נִיכָּר שֶׁהוּא לַיי. וְגוֹרָל אֶחָד לַעֲזָאזֵל: שֶׁיְּהֵא נִיכָּר שֶׁהוּא לַעֲזָאזֵל. וְיִכְתּוֹב עֲלֵיהֶם וְיֹאמַר. זֶה לַשֵּׁם וְזֶה לַעֲזָאזֵל. תַּלְמוּד לוֹמַר גּוֹרָל אֶחָד לַיי.] שֶׁיְּהֵא מוֹכִיחַ עַל עַצְמוֹ שֶׁהוּא לַיי לְעוֹלָם. וְגוֹרָל אֶחָד לַעֲזָאזֵל: שֶׁיְּהֵא מוֹכִיחַ עַל עַצְמוֹ שֶׁהוּא לַעֲזָאזֵל לְעוֹלָם. הֲדָא אָמְרָה. חֲקוּקִים הָיוּ.

Halakhah 1: "He scrambled the urn," etc. Not only an urn but even baskets. And why did they say, an urn? To give solemnity to the act. Could one not bring two threads, one white and one black, tie them to them[7] and say, this is for Hashem and this is for Azazel? The verse says[8], *one lot for the Eternal*, that it shall be recognizable that it was for the Eternal, *and one lot for Azazel*, that it shall be recognizable that it was for Azazel. Could he not bring two pebbles, [put on them][9] and say, this is for Hashem and this is for Azazel? The verse says, *one lot for the Eternal*, [so it shall be recognizable that it was for the Eternal, *and one lot for Azazel*, that it shall be recognizable that it was for Azazel. Could one not write on them][9] saying this is for Hashem and this is for Azazel? The verse says, *one lot for the Eternal*, that it itself be proof that it was for the Eternal, *and one lot for Azazel*, that it itself be proof that it was for Azazel. This implies that they[10] were engraved.

7   Tie the threads to the horn of the he-goats.
8   *Lev.* 16:8.
9   Addition (probably unnecessary) by the corrector.
10   The lots, boxwood or gold, were used every year and were permanently engraved.

(41b line 64) וְתַנֵּי כֵן. בִּשְׁתֵּי קַלְפִּיּוֹת נִתְחַלְּקָה אֶרֶץ יִשְׂרָאֵל. אַחַת שֶׁהַגּוֹרָלוֹת נְתוּנִין בְּתוֹכָהּ וְאַחַת שֶׁשְּׁמוֹת הַשְּׁבָטִים בְּתוֹכָהּ. וּשְׁנֵי פִירְחֵי כְהוּנָה עוֹמְדִים. מַה שֶּׁזֶּה מַעֲלֶה וָזֶה מַעֲלֶה זָכָה. בִּשְׁלֹשָׁה דְבָרִים נִתְחַלְּקָה אֶרֶץ יִשְׂרָאֵל. בְּגוֹרָלוֹת בָּאוּרִים וְתוּמִּים וּבִכְסָפִים. הָדָא הוּא דִכְתִיב וַיַּשְׁלֵךְ לָהֶם יְהוֹשֻׁעַ גּוֹרָל לִפְנֵי יי בַּמִּצְפָּה. גּוֹרָל אִילּוּ הַגּוֹרָלוֹת. לִפְנֵי יי אִילּוּ אוּרִים וְתוּמִּים. רַב לְמֵעַט: אִילּוּ הַכְּסָפִים. אָמַר רִבִּי אַבִּין. אִילְמָלֵא שֶׁנָּתַן הַקָּדוֹשׁ בָּרוּךְ הוּא חֵן כָּל־מָקוֹם בְּעֵינֵי יוֹשְׁבָיו לֹא הָיְתָה אֶרֶץ יִשְׂרָאֵל מִתְחַלֶּקֶת לְעוֹלָם. וְתַנֵּי כֵן. שְׁלֹשָׁה חֵינִים הֵן. חֵן אִשָּׁה בְּעֵינֵי בַעֲלָהּ. חֵן מָקוֹם בְּעֵינֵי יוֹשְׁבָיו. חֵן מִקָּח בְּעֵינֵי לוֹקְחָיו. רִבִּי אַבָּא בְּרֵיהּ דְּרִבִּי פַּפִּי רִבִּי יְהוֹשֻׁעַ דְּסִיכְנִין בְּשֵׁם לֵוִי. אַף לֶעָתִיד לָבוֹא הַקָּדוֹשׁ בָּרוּךְ הוּא עוֹשֶׂה כֵן. הָדָא הִיא דִכְתִיב וְנָתַתִּי לָכֶם לֵב חָדָשׁ וגו'. וְנָתַתִּי לָכֶם לֵב בָּשָׂר וגו': שֶׁהוּא בּוֹשֵׁר בְּחֶלְקוֹ שֶׁלַּחֲבֵירוֹ.

It was stated similarly[11]: The Land of Israel was distributed by two urns, one containing the lots, the other containing the names of the tribes. Two young priests[12] were standing, what each of them brought up he won[13]. By three ways the Land of Israel was divided up, by lots, and Urim and Tummim, and by payments. That is what is written[14], *Joshua threw them lots before the Eternal at Mispeh*. *Lots*, these are the lots. *Before the Eternal*, these are the Urim and Tummim. *Between large and small*[15], these are payments[16]. Rebbi Abin said, unless the Holy One, praise to Him, made every place nice in the eyes of its inhabitants, the Land of Israel would never have been distributed. It was stated thus[17]: There are three graces. The grace of a woman in her husband's eyes. The grace of a place in the eyes of its inhabitants. The grace of a buy in the eyes of its buyer. Rebbi Abba the son of Rebbi Pappaeus, Rebbi Joshua of Sikhnin in the name of Levi: Even in the future the Holy one, praise to Him, will do the same. That is what is written[18], *I shall give you a new heart, etc., and shall give you a heart of flesh*, etc. He makes sour the part of others[19].

11 Babli *Bava batra* 122a.
12 Literally: Flowers of the priesthood.
13 They simultaneously drew lots before Eleazar the High Priest with Urim and Tummim, which paired territories with tribes.
14 Misquote of *Jos.* 18:10.
15 *Num.* 26:56.
16 The nature of these payments is nowhere spelled out. It seems that they were equalization payments so that the value of distributed land per head of the population would be approximately the same for all tribes; *Sifry Num.* 132; expanded quote in *Yalqut Šimony Pinehas.*#773.
17 Babli *Sotah* 47a.
18 *Ez.* 36:26.
19 Everybody will be satisfied with his part. *Gen. rabba* 34, end.

(41b line 75) נָגַע בָּהֶן כְּשֶׁהֵן לְמַטָּה וְנִתְעָרְבוּ. אֵין הַשְּׂעִירִים כְּמִצְוָתָן. וּמִשֶּׁהֶעֱלָה אוֹתָן נָגַע בָּהֶן וְנִתְעָרְבוּ. הַשְּׂעִירִים כְּמִצְוָתָן. וּבַעֲלִיָּתוֹ נָגַע בָּהֶן וְנִתְעָרְבוּ. אָמַר. אִם שְׁלֹשָׁם יַעֲלֶה בִימִינִי יְקֻדַּשׁ זֶה שֶׁעַל יְמִינִי. קָדַשׁ. אִם שְׁלֹשָׁם יַעֲלֶה בִשְׂמֹאלִי יְקֻדַּשׁ זֶה שֶׁעַל שְׂמֹאלִי. קָדַשׁ. וַאֲפִילוּ אִם אָמַר. אִם שְׁלֹשָׁם יַעֲלֶה בִימִינִי יְקֻדַּשׁ זֶה שֶׁעַל שְׂמֹאלִי. קָדַשׁ. אִם שְׁלֹשָׁם יַעֲלֶה בִשְׂמֹאלִי יְקֻדַּשׁ זֶה שֶׁעַל יְמִינִי. קָדַשׁ. אֲבָל אִם אָמַר. בֵּין שְׁלֹשָׁם יַעֲלֶה בִימִינִי בֵּין שְׁלֹשָׁם יַעֲלֶה בִשְׂמֹאלִי. לֹא יְקֻדַּשׁ אֶלָּא זֶה שֶׁעַל יְמִינִי. לֹא יְקֻדַּשׁ אֶלָּא זֶה שֶׁעַל שְׂמֹאלִי. לֹא קָדַשׁ. מִפְּנֵי שֶׁהוּא קוֹבְעָן בַּפֶּה.

אָמְרָה הַתּוֹרָה גּוֹרָלוֹת. גּוֹרָלוֹת שֶׁלְּכָל־דָּבָר. יָכוֹל יִתֵּן שְׁנֵי שְׁנֵי גוֹרָלוֹת עַל זֶה וּשְׁנֵי גוֹרָלוֹת עַל זֶה. תַּלְמוּד לוֹמַר גּוֹרָלוֹת גּוֹרָל אֶחָד לַיי וְגוֹרָל אֶחָד לַעֲזָאזֵל: יָכוֹל יִתֵּן שְׁלֹשָׁם וְשֶׁלַּעֲזָאזֵל עַל זֶה וְשֶׁלֹּשָׁם וְשֶׁלַּעֲזָאזֵל עַל זֶה. תַּלְמוּד לוֹמַר גּוֹרָל. וְלֹא דָא קַדְמִיָּיתָא. כֵּינִי. יָכוֹל מַשֶּׁהוּא נוֹתֵן

שְׁלָשָׁם עַל שְׁלָשָׁם וְשֶׁלַעֲזָאזֵל עַל שֶׁלַעֲזָאזֵל יַחֲזוֹר וְיַחֲלִיף. תַּלְמוּד לוֹמַר גּוֹרָל אֶחָד לַיְיָ. אֵין כָּאן לַשֵׁם אֶלָּא אֶחָד. וְגוֹרָל אֶחָד לַעֲזָאזֵל. אֵין כָּאן לַעֲזָאזֵל אֶלָּא אֶחָד.

If he touched them when they were down and they became mixed up. The he-goats are not as commanded[20]. If after they were lifted he touched them and they became mixed up, the he-goats are as commanded[21]. If he touched them while lifting and they became mixed up[22], if he said, if the Eternal's comes up in my right hand, the one on my right hand side shall be sanctified, it is sanctified. If the Eternal's comes up in my left hand, the one on my left hand side shall be sanctified, it is sanctified. And even if he said, if the Eternal's comes up in my right hand, the one on my left hand side shall be sanctified, it is sanctified; if the Eternal's comes up in my left hand, the one on my right hand side shall be sanctified, it is sanctified[23]. But if he said, whether the Eternal's comes up in my right hand or the Eternal's comes up in my left hand, only that to my right hand side shall be sanctified, only that to my left hand side shall be sanctified, it is not sanctified, since he established it by mouth[24].

[25]The Torah said, *lots*. Lots made of anything[26]. I could think that he should put two lots on one and two lots on the other, the verse says, *lots, one lot for the Eternal and one lot for Azazel*. I could think that he should give the Eternal's and Azazel's on one and the Eternal's and Azazel's on the other, the verse says, *lot*. Is that not the previous argument? It should be so: I could think that after he gave the Eternal's on the Eternal's and Azazel's on Azazel's, he could go back and switch, the verse says, *one lot for the Eternal*, there is only one for the Eternal, *and one lot for Azazel*, there is only one for Azazel.

20 Since lifting the lots is a requirement which cannot be waived, the ceremony is invalid and therefore the he-goats are disqualified; a new pair has to be presented and the ceremony repeated.

21 They remain qualified.

22 This situation is identical with the previous one, the remedy indicated in the sequel applies to every situation in which the High Priest held one lot in each hand and started lifting them.

23 Since all these cases are possibly correct.

24 The verse requires that the lot determine the fate of the he-goats, but the language in the last case excludes this.

25 *Sifra Ahare Pereq* 2(2); Babli 37a.

26 They may be made of any material.

(41c line 14) צִיץ הָיָה כָּתוּב עָלָיו קוֹדֶשׁ לַיי. קוֹדֶשׁ מִלְּמַטָּן וְשֵׁם מִלְּמַעְלָן כְּמֶלֶךְ שֶׁהוּא יוֹשֵׁב עַל קָתֶדְרִין שֶׁלּוֹ. וְדִכְוָותָהּ. אֶחָד מִלְּמַטָּן וְשֵׁם מִלְּמַעְלָן. אָמַר רִבִּי אֶלְעָזָר בֵּירִבִּי יוֹסֵי. אֲנִי רָאִיתִיו בְּרוֹמִי וְלֹא הָיָה כָּתוּב עָלָיו אֶלָּא שִׁיטָה אַחַת קוֹדֶשׁ לַיי.

The diadem was inscribed "Holy for the Eternal", "holy" below and "Eternal" above[27], like a king who sits on his throne[28]. And similarly, "one" below and the Name above[29]. Rebbi Eleazar ben Rebbi Yose said, I saw it in Rome[30] and it was written on it in one line, "Holy for the Eternal".

27 The diadem worn by the High Priest when officiating; *Ex.* 28:36. As explained in the parallels in the Babli (*Šabbat* 63b, *Sukkah* 5a) and in Yerushalmi *Megillah* 1:11(71d l. 57) only the four letters of the Name were in the upper line and קדוש ל on the bottom.
28 Greek καθέδριον, τὸ, "small chair".
29 On the lot was inscribed not only "for the Eternal" but "one for the Eternal".
30 He reports to have seen the High Priest's vestment in Rome, *Me`ilah* 17b.

(41c line 18) וְנָתַן אַהֲרֹן. אִם נָתַן זָר כָּשֵׁר. וְדִכְוָותָהּ. אִם הֶעֱלָה זָר פָּסוּל. קוֹל וָחוֹמֶר. מַה אִם נְתִינָה שֶׁכָּתוּב בָּהּ בְּנֵי אַהֲרֹן אִם נָתַן זָר כָּשֵׁר. הָעֲלִייָה שֶׁאֵין כָּתוּב בָּהּ בְּנֵי אַהֲרֹן לֹא כָל־שֶׁכֵּן. לֹא צוֹרְכָה דְלֹא. נְתִינָה שֶׁהִיא מְעַכֶּבֶת אִם נָתַן זָר כָּשֵׁר. הָעֲלִייָה שֶׁאֵינָהּ מְעַכֶּבֶת אִם הֶעֱלָה זָר פָּסוּל. וְאָמַר רִבִּי יִצְחָק בַּר חֲקוּלָה בְּשֵׁם רִבִּי יַנַּאי. הָעֲלִייָה מִתּוֹךְ קַילְפֵּי מְעַכֶּבֶת. אֵין נְתִינָה מְעַכֶּבֶת. אָמַר רִבִּי יוֹחָנָן. קוּבְעָן אֲפִילוּ בַּפֶּה. סָבְרִין מֵימַר. אֲפִילוּ אֶחָד הַיּוֹם וְאֶחָד לְמָחָר. עַל דַּעְתֵּיהּ דְּרִבִּי יוֹחָנָן דּוּ אָמַר. אֲפִילוּ אֶחָד הַיּוֹם וְאֶחָד לְמָחָר. נִיחָא. עַל דַּעְתֵּיהּ דְּרִבִּי יַנַּאי. לְאֵי זֶה דָבָר נֶאֱמַר גּוֹרָלוֹת. לְמִצְוָה. מַתְנִיתָה פְּלִיגָא עַל רִבִּי יוֹחָנָן. הַגּוֹרָל עוֹשֵׂהוּ חַטָּאת וְאֵין הַשֵּׁם עוֹשֵׂהוּ חַטָּאת. פָּתַר לָהּ בְּמַצְלִיחַ בַּגּוֹרָל. מַתְנִיתָה פְּלִיגָא עַל רִבִּי יַנַּאי. לֹא הִגְרִיל וְלֹא נִתְוַודֶּה כָּשֵׁר. אֶלָּא שֶׁחִיסֵּר מִצְוָה אַחַת.

לַיי. לְרַבּוֹת שָׂעִיר הַמִּשְׁתַּלֵּחַ שֶׁיְּהֵא פָסוּל מִשּׁוּם מְחוּסַּר זְמַן. וְאַתְיָא כַּיי דָּמַר רִבִּי יוֹחָנָן. קוּבְעָן אֲפִילוּ בַּפֶּה. סָבְרִין מֵימַר. אֲפִילוּ אֶחָד הַיּוֹם וְאֶחָד לְמָחָר. עַל דַּעְתֵּיהּ דְּרִבִּי יוֹחָנָן דּוּ אָמַר אֲפִילוּ אֶחָד הַיּוֹם וְאֶחָד לְמָחָר. נִיחָא. עַל דַּעְתֵּיהּ דְּרִבִּי יַנַּאי לְאֵי זֶה דָבָר נֶאֱמַר גּוֹרָלוֹת. וְחָשׁ לוֹמַר. שֶׁמָּא יַעֲלֶה לַשֵּׁם. פָּתַר לָהּ בְּרוֹצֶה לְהַגְרִיל.

Aaron shall put[8], if a non-Cohen puts it is qualified[31]. Similarly, if a non-Cohen draws it is disqualified[32]. An argument *de minore ad majus*. If putting, where Aaron's sons[33] are mentioned, is qualified if a non-Cohen puts it, drawing, where Aaron's sons[31] are not mentioned, not so much more[34]? No, it is not necessarily so. Putting on, which is obstructive[35], if a non-Cohen puts it is qualified. Drawing, which is not[35] obstructive, if a non-Cohen draws it is disqualified. And Rebbi Isaac ben Ḥaqula said in the name of Rebbi Yannai, drawing from the urn is obstructive, putting on is not obstructive[36]. Rebbi Johanan said, he establishes even by word of mouth[37]. They thought to say, even one today and one tomorrow[38]. In the opinion of Rebbi Johanan who said, even one today and one tomorrow, it is understandable. In the opinion of Rebbi Yannai, why does it say, *lots*[39]? As meritorious deed. A *baraita* disagrees with Rebbi Johanan: The lot makes it a purification sacrifice, giving it the name does not make it a purification sacrifice. He explains it, if the drawing succeeds[40]. A *baraita* disagrees with Rebbi Yannai: If he did not draw lots and did not confess it is qualified, only he missed a meritorious deed[41].

For the Eternal[42], to include the he-goat which is sent away that it can be disqualified for lacking time[43]. This comes following what Rebbi Johanan said, he establishes even by word of mouth[44]. They thought to say, even one today and one tomorrow. In the opinion of Rebbi Johanan who said, even one today and one tomorrow, it is understandable. In the opinion of Rebbi Yannai, why is there said, *lots*? Should we not be concerned that maybe it is drawn for the Eternal? He explains it if he wants to draw lots[45].

31 If a non-Cohen puts the lots on the he-goats, they remain qualified. This can happen only following Rebbi, who extends the space where the ceremony can be held in the courtyard of Israel. For everybody else the statement means that if the lots are not put on the he-goats the ceremony still is valid.

32 The drawing of lots from the urn by a non-Cohen is invalid and disqualifies the he-goats from being used in any sacrificial way.

33 Aaron's sons are not mentioned in the entire Chapter, only Aaron himself.

34 *Lev.* 16:8 mentions that Aaron has to put the lots on the he-goats; that the lots have to be drawn first is an inference, not a separate statement. If the drawing is not written in the verse, Aaron cannot be mentioned in connection with it.

35 From the preceding it follows that in the text the places of "obstructive" and "not obstructive" must be switched. "Obstructive" means that the ceremony (and all which follows) become invalid by its omission.

36 Babli 39b.

37 For him the drawing of lots is not indispensable; Babli 39b.

38 Since the entire service is restricted to one day, this can only mean that for R. Johanan it is possible to predetermine the he-goat which is to be the purification sacrifice.

39 These sentences have to be switched. For R. Yannai, for whom drawing of lots is

indispensable, the lots have to be mentioned. But for R. Johanan, for whom the fate of the he-goats can be predetermined, why are lots mentioned at all?

40 The position of R. Johanan is modified. He will agree that using an urn in the service is required. In the case that the High Priest loses the lots which he is lifting, the ceremony does not have to be repeated, the he-goats do not become disqualified, and he can proceed to select the he-goat to be sacrificed following the rules spelled out earlier.

41 Since the objection cannot be answered, practice has to follow R. Johanan. Babli 40a.

42 *Lev.* 22:26.

43 A he-goat which is not at least eight days old may not be used on the Day of Atonement. Even though the he-goat sent into the wilderness is not a sacrifice, by the process of drawing lots it is a potential sacrifice and has to be qualified as such. Babli 63b, *Sifra Emor Parasha* 8(6).

44 Since for him it might be the choice of the High Priest to select the he-goat as sacrifice, one understands that a separate verse is needed to require both he-goats to be eligible at the same time. But for R. Yannai, for whom only the drawing determines which animal is chosen, it should be obvious that both have to be eligible. Then why is a separate verse needed?

45 To prohibit that one could take the risk that an ineligible animal be drawn as sacrifice and in this case start again with another pair and a new drawing.

(41c line 34) שְׁנֵי שְׂעִירֵי יוֹם הַכִּיפּוּרִים שֶׁשְּׁחָטָן בַּחוּץ. אִית תַּנָּיֵי תַנִי. חַיָּיב. אִית תַּנָּיֵי תַנִי. פָּטוּר. אָמַר רַב חִסְדָּא. מָאן דְּאָמַר. חַיָּיב. בְּשֶׁקָּרַב הַשָּׂעִיר הַנַּעֲשָׂה בִּפְנִים. מָאן דְּאָמַר. פָּטוּר. בְּשֶׁלֹּא קָרַב הַשָּׂעִיר הַנַּעֲשָׂה בַחוּץ. אָמַר רִבִּי יוֹסֵה. רַב חִסְדָּא בָעֵי מְדַמָּתָהּ לַפֶּסַח וְלָא דָמְיָא. אָמַר רִבִּי מָנָא בַּר תַּנְחוּם. רִבִּי לְעָזָר וְרִבִּי יוֹחָנָן תְּרֵיהוֹן אָמְרִין. פֶּסַח שְׁעִיבֵּר זְמַנּוֹ מֵאֵילָיו הָיָה מִשְׁתַּנֶּה. בְּרַם הָכָא בִּשְׁחִיטָה הוּא מִשְׁתַּנֶּה. מַאי כְדוֹן. מָאן דְּאָמַר חַיָּיב. סָבְרִין מֵימַר. הַגְרָלָה מְעַכֶּבֶת. מָאן דְּאָמַר פָּטוּר. סָבְרִין מֵימַר. אֵין הַגְרָלָה מְעַכֶּבֶת כְּלוּם יֵשׁ כָּאן לַשֵּׁם אֶלָא אֶחָד. אָמַר רִבִּי שְׁמוּאֵל אֲחוֹי דְרִבִּי בֶּרֶכְיָה. אוֹ זֶה אוֹ זֶה מִשֶּׁהִגְרִיל חַיָּיב עַל שְׁלָשָׁם וּפָטוּר עַל שֶׁלְעַזָאזֵל. אָמַר רִבִּי בָּא. וְהוּא שֶׁנָּתַן מַתְּנַת הַפָּר. אֲבָל אִם לֹא נָתַן מַתְּנַת הַפָּר פָּטוּר. שֶׁשְּׁחִיטָתוֹ שֶׁלְשָׂעִיר מְעַכֶּבֶת מַתַּן דָּמוֹ שֶׁלְפָּר.

If one slaughtered outside[46] the two he-goats[47] of the Day of Atonement, there are Tannaim who state, he is liable; there are Tannaim who state, he is not liable. Rav Ḥisda said, he who said that he is liable, if the he-goat who is chosen for inside was sacrificed; he who said that he is not liable, if the he-goat who is chosen for outside was not sacrificed[48]. Rebbi Yose said, Rav Ḥisda wants to compare it to *Pesaḥ* but it is not comparable. Rebbi Mana bar Tanḥum said, Rebbi Eleazar and Rebbi Joḥanan both are saying, a *Pesaḥ* whose time passed is changed automatically[49], but here it changes by slaughter[50]. How is it? He who said liable wanted to say that drawing lots is obstructive; he who said not liable wanted to say that drawing lots is not obstructive[51]. There is only one here for Hashem[52]. Rebbi Samuel the brother of Rebbi Berekhiah said, either one of them, after he drew lots is liable for the Eternal's and is not liable for Azazel's[53]. Rebbi Abba said, only if he gave the bull's gift[54]. But if he did not give the bull's gift he is not liable since the slaughter of the he-goat obstructs giving the bull's blood[55].

46 Outside the Temple domain, which is a deadly sin for sacrifices.

47 There really are three he-goats on that day, the two mentioned in *Lev.* 16 and the holiday purification offering mentioned in *Num.* 29:11. The latter is referred to as "he-goat made outside" since its blood is poured onto the altar in the courtyard, where its inner parts are burned. The he-goat chosen as sacrifice by drawing lots is referred to as "he-goat made for inside" since its blood is sprinkled inside the sanctuary (and its body burned outside the sacred domain.) Since there is no reason to treat the holiday purification offering differently from all other holiday offerings, the question asked here must refer to the he-goats subject to drawing lots of which only one is going to be a sacrifice.

48 It is clear that for "inside" one has to read "outside" since the question is asked about the he-goat whose blood is to be brought inside, and if it was slaughtered in the Temple it cannot be slaughtered a second time outside. If the he-goat for outside was slaughtered, the main ceremony is concluded *Lev.* 16:24; the remaining he-goats cannot be sacrifices and their slaughter outside the sacred domain is no offense.

49 A *Pesaḥ* sacrifice after the 14th of Nisan is a well-being sacrifice. Babli 63a.

50 The he-goat chosen by the lot cannot be changed into the he-goat for outside.

51 Since the opinion of Rav Hisda is refuted, that the Tannaim refer to two different situations and do not disagree, one has to find the root of the disagreement. The text as it stands seems unintelligible; there seems to be unanimity that here also the mentions of "obstructive" and "not obstructive" have to be switched. If drawing is obstructive, neither of the two he-goats is a sacrifice before the drawing, and slaughter outside cannot be sinful. But if it is not obstructive, each one of the he-goats is a potential dedicated sacrifice and outside slaughter is sinful.

52 Since only one of the he-goats can become a sacrifice, the argument last given is invalid (unless both he-goats are simultaneously slaughtered outside.)

53 Since the latter he-goat is not a sacrifice.

54 As described in Mishnah 3, the blood of the bull has to be brought inside. This is called "the gift of the bull's blood."

55 The he-goat chosen to be the Eternal's

is slaughtered after the bull, but the bull cannot be slaughtered before the he-goat is chosen and ready to be slaughtered.

(41c line 46) רִבִּי בּוּן בַּר חִייָה בְּעָא קוֹמֵי רִבִּי זְעוּרָה. שָׁחַט אֶת הַפָּר עַד שֶׁלֹּא הִגְרִיל מָהוּ שֶׁיְּהֵא חַייָב. אָמַר לֵיהּ. נִישְׁמְעִינָהּ מִן הָדָא. פָּר מְעַכֵּב אֶת הַשָּׂעִיר. הַשָּׂעִיר מְעַכֵּב אֶת הַפָּר. הָדָא אָמְרָה. שָׁחַט אֶת הַפָּר עַד שֶׁלֹּא הִגְרִיל חַייָב. אִין תֵּימַר. פָּטוּר. נִיתְנֵי. אֵין הַשָּׂעִיר מְעַכֵּב אֶת הַפָּר. אָמַר רִבִּי שְׁמוּאֵל בַּר אֲבְדַּיְמִי. הָדָא דְתֵימַר. אֵין הַשָּׂעִיר מְעַכֵּב אֶת הַפָּר בְּמַתְּנוֹת הַבַּדִּים. אֲבָל בְּמַתְּנוֹת הַפָּרוֹכֶת שָׂעִיר מְעַכֵּב אֶת הַפָּר. הֵיךְ עֲבִידָא. שֶׁאֵינוֹ יָכוֹל לִיתֵּן מִדָּם הַפָּר עַל הַפָּרוֹכֶת עַד שֶׁיִּתֵּן מִדָּם הַשָּׂעִיר עַל בֵּין הַבַּדִּים.

Rebbi Abun bar Hiyya asked before Rebbi Ze`ira: If he slaughtered the bull before he drew lots, is he liable[56]? He said to him, let us hear from the following: The bull is obstructive of the he-goat, the he-goat is obstructive of the bull[57]. This implies that if he slaughtered the bull before he drew lots, he is liable. If you would say that he is not liable, one should state, the he-goat is not obstructive of the bull. Rebbi Samuel ben Eudaimon said, that is to say, the he-goat does not obstruct the bull in giving between the beams, but for giving on the curtain the he-goat is obstructive of the bull. How is this? He may not give of the bull's blood on the curtain before he gave of the he-goat's blood between the beams[58].

56 In the biblical narrative (Lev. 16), first the he-goat has to be selected by drawing lots (v. 8), then the bull has to be slaughtered (v. 11), then first incense (v. 12) and afterwards the bull's blood (v. 14) have to be brought into the Sanctuary, then the he-goat has to be slaughtered and its blood brought into the sanctuary (v. 15). If the order was reversed and the he-goat selected close to the time of its slaughter, is the ceremony invalid and therefore the slaughter a violation of the prohibition of work on the day of Atonement, and a deadly sin?

57 Slaughter of the bull is invalid unless the he-goat was selected; slaughter of the he-goat is invalid unless the bull was slaughtered first (and its blood brought inside, Babli 61a).

58 The blood has to be sprinkled first inside the Holiest of Holies at the place of the Ark in the First Temple, between the beams used to carry the Ark. In the Second Temple, the place was indicated by a stone, but the terminology was not changed. Then it had to be sprinkled in the Sanctuary onto the gobelin separating it from the Holiest of Holies. Babli 40a.

(fol. 41b) **משנה ב**: קָשַׁר לָשׁוֹן שֶׁל זְהוֹרִית בְּרֹאשׁ שָׂעִיר הַמִּשְׁתַּלֵּחַ הֶעֱמִידוֹ כְּנֶגֶד בֵּית שִׁלּוּחוֹ. וְלַנִּשְׁחָט כְּנֶגֶד בֵּית שְׁחִיטָתוֹ. בָּא לוֹ אֵצֶל פָּרוֹ שְׁנִיָּה וְסָמַךְ שְׁתֵּי יָדָיו עָלָיו וְנִתְוַדָה. וְכָךְ הָיָה אוֹמֵר אָנָּא הַשֵּׁם עָוִיתִי פָּשַׁעְתִּי חָטָאתִי לְפָנֶיךָ אֲנִי וּבֵיתִי וּבְנֵי אַהֲרֹן עַם קְדוֹשֶׁךָ. אָנָּא הַשֵּׁם כַּפֶּר נָא לַעֲוֹנוֹת וגו׳.

Mishnah 2: He tied a shiny strip on the head of the he-goat to be sent away[59] and put it next to its departure gate, and on the one to be slaughtered around the place of its slaughter[60]. He came to his bull a second time, leaned both his hands on it and confessed, and thus he was saying: "Please Hashem, I acted criminally, I offended, I sinned before You, I and my house, and the Sons of Aaron, your holy people. Please Hashem, please atone the criminal acts," etc[61].

59   Between its horns.
60   Around its neck, so it clearly would be distinguished from the he-goat chosen for the *musaph* sacrifice at the end of the service.
61   The text should be completed by the duly amended text of Mishnah 3:9.

(41c line 53) **הלכה ב**: רִבִּי שְׁמוּאֵל בַּר נַחְמָן בְּשֵׁם רִבִּי יוֹנָתָן. שְׁלֹשָׁה לְשׁוֹנוֹת הֵן. שֶׁלְּשָׂעִיר בְּסֶלַע. וְשֶׁלִּמְצוֹרָע בְּשֶׁקֶל. וְשֶׁלְּפָרָה בִּשְׁתֵּי סְלָעִים. אָמַר רִבִּי בָּא בַּר זַבְדָּא בְּשֵׁם רִבִּי שִׁמְעוֹן בֶּן חֲלַפְתָּא. שֶׁלְּפָרָה בִּשְׁתֵּי סְלָעִים וּמֶחֱצָה. אִית דְּמַפְקִין לִישָׁנָא. בַּעֲשָׂרָה זִין.

Halakhah 2: Rebbi Samuel bar Nahman in the name of Rebbi Jonathan: There are three strips[62]. The one for the he-goat for a tetradrachma, for the sufferer from skin disease for a sheqel[63], for the Cow for two tetradrachmas. Rebbi Abba bar Zavda in the name of Rebbi Simeon ben Halaphta, for the Cow for two tetradrachmas and a half; some express it in the formulation ten *zin*[64].

62   Strips of purple wool were used in the Temple not only rabbinically for the he-goats on the day of Atonement but also biblically for the purification ceremony of the person healed from skin disease (*Lev.* 14:4,6) and the preparation of the ashes of the Red Cow (*Num.* 19:6).
63   Rabbinically half a tetradrachma, two denarii. The old Canaanite (biblical) sheqel was about twice as much, cf *Qiddušin* 1:1, Note 122.
64   Defined in *Terumot* 10:7 (Note 80) as $1/100$ of a (probably Roman) pound. 2.5 *tetradrachma* are 10 *denarii*. Since an Augustean *denar* was $1/96$ of a Roman pound (silver), 10 *zin* are 9.6 *denarii*.

(fol. 41b) **משנה ג:** שְׁחָטוֹ וְקִיבֵּל בַּמִּזְרָק אֶת דָּמוֹ וּנְתָנוֹ לְמִי שֶׁהוּא מְמָרֵס בּוֹ עַל הָרוֹבֶד הָרְבִיעִי שֶׁבַּהֵיכָל כְּדֵי שֶׁלֹּא יִקָּרֵשׁ. נָטַל אֶת הַמַּחְתָּה וְעָלָה לְרֹאשׁ הַמִּזְבֵּחַ וּפָנָה גֶחָלִים אֵילָךְ וְאֵילָךְ וְחוֹתֶה מִן הַמְעוּכָּלוֹת הַפְּנִימִיוֹת וְיָרַד וְהִנִּיחָהּ עַל הָרוֹבֶד הָרְבִיעִי שֶׁבָּעֲזָרָה:

משנה ד: בְּכָל־יוֹם הָיָה חוֹתֶה בְּשֶׁל כֶּסֶף וּמְעָרֶה לְתוֹךְ שֶׁל זָהָב וְהַיּוֹם חוֹתֶה בְּשֶׁל זָהָב וּבָהּ הָיָה מַכְנִיס.

משנה ה: בְּכָל־יוֹם חוֹתֶה בְּשֶׁל אַרְבַּעַת קַבִּין וּמְעָרֶה בְּתוֹךְ שֶׁל שְׁלֹשֶׁת קַבִּין וְהַיּוֹם חוֹתֶה בְּשֶׁל שְׁלֹשֶׁת קַבִּין וּבָהּ הָיָה מַכְנִיס. רִבִּי יוֹסֵי אוֹמֵר בְּכָל־יוֹם חוֹתֶה בְּשֶׁל סְאָה וּמְעָרֶה בְּתוֹךְ שְׁלֹשֶׁת קַבִּין וְהַיּוֹם חוֹתֶה בִּשְׁלֹשֶׁת קַבִּין וּבָהּ הָיָה מַכְנִיס.

Mishnah 3: He slaughters it[65] and receives its blood in a pitcher which he hands to one[66] who stirs it on the fourth level[67] of the Temple Hall so it should not congeal[68]. He took a fire-pan and ascended to the top of the altar where he cleared away coals to both sides and collects coals on the fire pan from the interior well-burned ones, descends, and puts it on the fourth level in the courtyard.

Mishnah 4: Every day he collects coals in a silver fire-pan and empties them into one of gold; on this day he collects in a golden one and takes it inside[69].

Mishnah 5: Every day he collects in one of four *qab*[70] and empties into one of three *qab* but on this day he collects in one of three *qab* which he takes inside. Rebbi Yose says, every day he collects in one of a *seah*[71] and empties into one of three *qab* but on this day he collects in one of three *qab* which he takes inside.

65 The bull, which is large enough and has enough blood so that the High Priest does not need help in the slaughter..

66 An assisting Cohen.

67 There were twelve steps leading from the level of the altar to the entrance of the Temple Hall. Every third step was widened and denoted a level. The fourth, top level was level with the entrance door, so that the High Priest, when he returned from offering the incense, immediately could pick up the blood and re-enter the Temple.

68 After he picks up the incense which is to be given onto the coals inside the Temple. All coals mentioned here are charcoal; mineral coal being unknown at that time.

69 To make the officiating easier on the High Priest. It is obvious that these silver and gold vessels must have been made of alloys of baser metals to stand the heat.

70 A *qab* is 2.13 liter, 4 *quartarii*.

71 6 *qab*.

(41c line 57) **הלכה ג**: כֵּינֵי מַתְנִיתָא. עַל הָרוֹבֶד הָרְבִיעִי שֶׁבָּעֲזָרָה.

Halakhah 3: So is the Mishnah: on the fourth level in the courtyard[72].

73 In the Mishnah, "on the fourth level of the Temple Hall" is identical with "on the fourth level in the courtyard". It cannot mean "on the fourth level in the Temple Hall" since during the ceremonies of the day of Atonement nobody but the High Priest is permitted to enter the Sanctuary (*Lev.* 16:17). Babli 43b last line.

(41c line 58) תַּנֵּי. שָׁחַט בַּחוּץ חַיָּיב. חָפַן בִּפְנִים פָּטוּר. חָתָה וְהִקְטִיר וְנִשְׁפַּךְ הַדָּם יָבִיא פָר אַחֵר וְנִכְנַס בְּדָמוֹ. עַד שֶׁלֹּא הִקְטִיר נִשְׁפַּךְ הַדָּם חֲתִיָּיה פְסוּלָה הִיא וְהוּא צָרִיךְ לַחְתּוֹת כַּתְּחִילָּה. סָפֵק עַד שֶׁלֹּא הִקְטִיר נִשְׁפַּךְ הַדָּם וְסָפֵק מִשֶּׁהִקְטִיר נִשְׁפַּךְ הַדָּם. לְהָבִיא פַר אַחֵר וּלְהִיכָּנֵס בְּדָמוֹ אֵין אַתְּ יָכוֹל. שֶׁאֲנִי אוֹמֵר. עַד שֶׁלֹּא הִקְטִיר נִשְׁפַּךְ הַדָּם וְהִיא חֲתִיָּיה פְסוּלָה. וְהוּא צָרִיךְ לַחְתּוֹת כַּתְּחִילָּה. אֵין אַתְּ יָכוֹל. שֶׁאֲנִי אוֹמֵר. מִשֶּׁהִקְטִיר נִשְׁפַּךְ הַדָּם וְהִיא חֲתִיָּיה כְשֵׁירָה וְהוּא עוֹבֵר מִשּׁוּם הַכְנָסָה יְתֵירָה. וּבָטְלוּ הָעֲבוֹדוֹת. אַשְׁכָּחַת אֲמַר. בָּטְלוּ עֲבוֹדוֹת שֶׁלְּאוֹתוֹ הַיּוֹם. שָׁחַט וָמֵת. אַחֵר מָהוּ שֶׁיִּיכָּנֵס בְּדָמוֹ. רִבִּי שִׁמְעוֹן בֶּן לָקִישׁ אָמַר. בְּפָר. אֲבָל לֹא בְדָם. רִבִּי חֲנִינָה וְרִבִּי יוֹנָתָן תִּרֵיהוֹן אֱמָרִין. אֲפִילוּ בְדָם. מִילְּתֵיהּ דְּרִבִּי יְהוֹשֻׁעַ בֶּן לֵוִי אֱמָרָה. אֲפִילוּ בְדָם. דְּאָמַר רִבִּי חֲנִינָה רִבִּי בָּא בְשֵׁם רִבִּי יוֹחָנָן. אֲפִילוּ בְדָם. רִבִּי יְהוֹשֻׁעַ בֶּן לֵוִי שָׁאַל. חָפַן וָמֵת. מָהוּ שֶׁיִּיכָּנֵס בְּחָפְנָיו. מַה צְּרִיכָה לֵיהּ בְּחָפְנָיו. דִּכְתִיב וּמָלֵא חָפְנָיו. בְּרַם הָכָא לֵית כְּתִיב בְּדָמוֹ. פְּשִׁיטָא לֵיהּ. אֲפִילוּ בְדָם.

It was stated: If he slaughtered outside he is liable[74], if he took the fistful inside he is not liable[75]. If he collected coals and burned the incense when the blood was spilled, he has to bring another bull and enter with its blood[76]. If the blood was spilled before he burned the incense, it is an invalid collection of coals and he has to start again collecting coals. If there was a doubt whether the blood was spilled before he burned the incense or after he burned the incense, you cannot bring another bull and enter with its blood since I am saying that the blood was spilled before he burned the incense and the collection of coals was invalid, and he has to start again collecting coals. You cannot do this since I am saying that the blood was spilled after he burned the incense and the collection of coals was valid, and he is liable because of unnecessary entry. The service has to stop. You find to say, the services of that day are annulled.

If he slaughtered and died[79]. May the other[80] enter with his blood. Rebbi Simeon ben Laqish said, *with a bull*, but not with its blood[81]. Rebbi Ḥanina and Rebbi Jonathan both are saying, even with the blood. The word of Rebbi Joshua ben Levi implies even with the blood. For Rebbi Hanina[82], Rebbi Abba in the name of Rebbi Johanan, even with the blood. Rebbi Joshua ben Levi asked, if he took a fistful and then died, may one enter with his fistful[83]? Why does he question his fistful? For it is written, *his fistful*[8], but here it is not written "his blood"[4]. It is obvious for him, even with the blood.

74 If he slaughtered the bull outside the sacred domain, he is twice liable for extirpation, for violating the holiday and for sacrificing outside. This is obvious and only was stated as contrast to the next statement.

75 As explained in Mishnah 5:1, after he collected the coals other Cohanim bring to him the vessel containing the incense, of which he has to take a fistful and then enter the Sanctuary with the fire pan and the incense. It is difficult to see how he could take the fistful inside since no other Cohen is permitted there on this day, but if he did it the action is valid since there is no verse prescribing that the fistful has to be taken in the courtyard.

76 Since the verse is clear that incense may be burned only after the bull was slaughtered and that the bull's blood must be brought inside the Sanctuary after it was filled with incense smoke.

77 The High Priest after slaughtering the bull. Babli 49b.

78 The replacement as High Priest.

79 *Lev.* 16:3 requires that Aaron come to the sanctuary *with a bull*. R. Simeon ben Laqish reads the verse as implying that any other Cohen cannot use his bull's blood. All other authorities read the same verse as permitting the blood to another Cohen, as explained at the end of the paragraph.

80 This is the late Amora usually called R. Hinena. Babli 49a.

81 Presuming that somehow the incense did not become impure by the impurity of the dead, may the replacing Cohen use the first's fistful even though his own fist probably is of different size?

82 *Lev.* 16:12. For the blood it is not written "the blood which he collected"; therefore the blood is transferable.

(41c line 72) כַּיי דְתַנִּינָן תַּמָּן. נִתְפַּזֵּר מִמֶּנָּה כְּקַב גֶּחָלִים הָיָה מְכַבְּדָן לָאַמָּה. וּבַשַּׁבָּת כּוֹפִין עָלָיו (פְּסֶקוֹתֵּר) [פְּסֶכְתֵּר].

[83]As we have stated there[84]: "If about a *qab* of it was scattered, he swept them into the water canal; but on the Sabbath one covers it with a wine cooler[85]."

83 Discussion of Mishnah 5.

84 Mishnah *Tamid* 5:5, about the daily taking of coals from the altar for the incense burning.

85 Greek ψυκτήρ. The scribe's spelling is in parentheses, the corrector's in brackets.

(fol. 41b) **משנה ו**: בְּכָל־יוֹם הָיְתָה כְבֵידָה וְהַיּוֹם קַלָּה. בְּכָל־יוֹם הָיְתָה יָדָהּ קְצָרָה וְהַיּוֹם אֲרוּכָּה. בְּכָל־יוֹם הָיָה זְהָבָהּ יָרוֹק וְהַיּוֹם אָדוֹם דִּבְרֵי רַבִּי מְנַחֵם. בְּכָל יוֹם מַקְרִיב פְּרָס בְּשַׁחֲרִית וּפְרָס בֵּין הָעַרְבַּיִם וְהַיּוֹם מוֹסִיף מְלֹא חָפְנָיו. בְּכָל־יוֹם הָיְתָה דַקָּה וְהַיּוֹם דַּקָּה מִן הַדַּקָּה:

משנה ז: בְּכָל־יוֹם הַכֹּהֲנִים עוֹלִין בְּמִזְרָחוֹ וְיוֹרְדִין בְּמַעֲרָבוֹ וְהַיּוֹם עוֹלִן בָּאֶמְצַע וְיוֹרְדִין בָּאֶמְצַע. רַבִּי יְהוּדָה אוֹמֵר לְעוֹלָם כֹּהֵן גָּדוֹל עוֹלֶה בָּאֶמְצַע וְיוֹרֵד בָּאֶמְצַע.

משנה ח: בְּכָל יוֹם כֹּהֵן גָּדוֹל מְקַדֵּשׁ יָדָיו וְרַגְלָיו מִן הַכִּיוֹר וְהַיּוֹם מִן הַקִּיתוֹן שֶׁל זָהָב. רַבִּי יְהוּדָה אוֹמֵר לְעוֹלָם כֹּהֵן גָּדוֹל מְקַדֵּשׁ יָדָיו וְרַגְלָיו מִן הַקִּיתוֹן שֶׁל זָהָב:

Mishnah 6: Every day it[86] was heavy, but this day light. Every day its handle was short, but this day long. Everyday its gold was greenish[87], but this day reddish, the words of Rebbi Menahem. Every day he sacrifices one half[88] in the morning and one half in the evening, but on this day he adds a fistful[89]. Every day it was fine but this day finest[90].

Mishnah 7: Every day the Cohanim ascend on the East side {of the ramp} and descend on the West side, but this day they[91] ascend and descend in the middle. Rebbi Jehudah says, the High Priest always ascends in the middle and descendes in the middle.

Mishnah 8: Every day the High Priest sanctifies his hands and legs from the basin put this day from a gold pitcher[92]. Rebbi Jehudah says, always the High Priest sanctifies his hands and legs from a gold pitcher.

86 The fire-pan for the incense, which was adapted to make the High Priest's work easier.

87 As an alloy with coarse metal; reddish gold probably was a copper alloy.

88 Latin *pars, -rtis, f.* The full portion was the weight of one *mina*, or $^{25}/_{24}$ of a Roman pound (cf. Note 64).

89 The incense to be burned in the Holiest of Holies, in contrast to the larger amount burned on the incense altar in the sanctuary.

90 Incense to be burned on the altar is just called "incense" but the one destined for the Holiest of Holies has to be "fine incense" (*Lev.* 16:8); it is inferred that it has to be finer than regular incense.

91 "They" are only the High Priest, who this day does the sacral acts unaided. There is no danger of a traffic jam.

92 Identified by Buxtorf as Latin *cothon*, Greek κώθων, but this denotes a drinking vessel, not a pitcher.

(41c line 73) **הלכה ד**: בְּכָל־יוֹם הָיְתָה כְבֵידָה וְהַיּוֹם קַלָּה. שֶׁלֹּא לִיגַּע.

HALAKHAH FOUR

Halakhah 4: "Every day it was heavy, but this day light." Not to tire him.

בְּכָל־יוֹם הָיְתָה יָדָהּ קְצָרָה וְהַיּוֹם אֲרוּכָה. שֶׁלֹּא לְיַגְּעוֹ. בְּכָל־יוֹם לֹא הָיָה בָהּ אַמָּה גְמוּדָה. וְהַיּוֹם הָיָה בָהּ אַמָּה וּמֶחֱצָה. כְּדֵי שֶׁתְּהֵא הַזְּרוֹעַ מְסַייַעַת. בְּכָל־יוֹם לֹא הָיָה בָהּ נַרְתִּיק. וְהַיּוֹם הָיָה בָהּ נַרְתִּיק. כְּדֵי שֶׁלֹּא תִכָּבֶה. וְאֵינוּ חוֹצֵץ. אָמַר רִבִּי יוֹסֵי בֵּירִבִּי בּוּן. קוֹבְעוֹ בְּמַסְמֵר.

"Everyday its handle was short, but this day long." Not to tire him. Every day it was less that a short cubit[93], but this day it was a cubit, and a half, so that his arm could lend support. Everyday it did not have a sheath[94], this day it had a sheath, lest he should be burned[95]. But does this not separate[96]? Rebbi Yose ben Rebbi Abun said, it was held by a nail[97].

---

93 It is not clear whether this means a cubit of 5 hand-breadths or one of 6 hand-breadths of a small person.

94 Greek ναρθήκιον. The fire-pan was of metal.

95 With Tosaphot 44b *s. v.* בכל reading תכבה for יכוה.

96 Since the verse requires that the High Priest carry the fire-pan in his hand (*Lev.* 16:12), nothing may be between his hand and the fire-pan.

97 The sheath is an integral part of the pan; this is not separation. According to Tosaphot (44b *s.v.* בכל יום) this is possible even if the sheath was of leather.

(41d line) שִׁבְעָה זְהָבִים הֵן. זָהָב טוֹב. זָהָב טָהוֹר. זָהָב סָגוּר. זָהָב מוּפָז. זָהָב מְזוּקָק. זָהָב שָׁחוּט. זָהָב פַּרְוַויִם.

זָהָב טוֹב. כְּמַשְׁמָעוֹ. [וּזֲהַב הָאָרֶץ הַהוּא טוֹב.] אָמַר רִבִּי יִצְחָק. טוֹבוֹי דִי בְּבַיְיתֵיהּ. טוֹבוֹי דוּ בְּלוֹיָיתֵיהּ.

זָהָב טָהוֹר. שֶׁמַּכְנִיסִין אוֹתוֹ לָאוּר וְאֵינוֹ חָסֵר כְּלוּם. (וְהָא תַנֵּי) [וְאַתְיָיא כְּדִתְנֵי]. מַעֲשֶׂה בִמְנוֹרַת זָהָב שֶׁעָשָׂה מֹשֶׁה בַּמִּדְבָּר וְהָיְתָה יְתֵירָה דִּינָר זָהָב. וְהִכְנִיסוּהָ לַכּוּר שְׁמוֹנִים פַּעַם וְלֹא חָסְרָה כְּלוּם. וְיָאוּת. עַד שֶׁלֹּא יָקוּם עַל בְּרֵרֵיהּ הוּא חָסֵר סַגִּין. מִן דּוּ קַיָּים בְּרֵרֵיהּ לֹא חָסֵר כְּלוּם.

זָהָב סָגוּר. שֶׁהָיָה מַכְסִיף כְּעַד כָּל־הַזְּהָבִים שֶׁהָיוּ שָׁם. אָמַר רִבִּי שְׁמוּאֵל בַּר רַב יִצְחָק. כְּתוּב וְשִׁבְעַת אֲלָפִים כִּכַּר־כֶּסֶף מְזוּקָק לָטוּחַ קִירוֹת הַבָּיִת. וְאֶת־כָּל־הַבַּיִת צִפָּה זָהָב. וְאַתְּ אָמַר אָכֵן. אֶלָּא שֶׁהָיָה מַכְסִיף בְּעַד כָּל־הַזְּהָבִים שֶׁהָיוּ שָׁם.

זָהָב מוּפָז. רִבִּי פְּטְרוּקִי אֲחוּהָ דְרִבִּי דְרוֹסָא בְּשֵׁם רִבִּי בָּא בַּר בִּינָה. דּוֹמֶה לָאֵשׁ מַצֶּתֶת בְּגָפְרִית. אָמַר רִבִּי אַבִּין. לְשֵׁם מְקוֹמוֹ הוּא נִקְרָא. וְזָהָב מֵאוּפָז.

זָהָב מְזוּקָּק. שֶׁהָיוּ מְחַתְּכִין אוֹתוֹ כְּזֵיתִים וְטָחִים אוֹתוֹ בָּצֵק וּמַאֲכִילִין אוֹתוֹ לַנַּעֲמִיּוֹת. וְהֵן מְסַנְּנוֹת אוֹתוֹ. וְיֵשׁ אוֹמְרִים. שֶׁהָיוּ טוֹמְנִין אוֹתוֹ בַּזֶּבֶל שֶׁבַע שָׁנִים.

זָהָב שָׁחוּט. שֶׁהָיָה נִמְשָׁךְ כְּשַׁעֲוָה. אַדְרִיָינוּס הָיָה לוֹ מִשְׁקַל בֵּיצָה. דּוּקְלֵטִיָנוּס הָיָה לוֹ מִשְׁקַל דֵּינָר גּוֹרְדִּינוֹן.

זָהָב פַּרְוַיִים. רִבִּי שִׁמְעוֹן בֶּן לָקִישׁ אָמַר. אָדוֹם. דּוֹמֶה לְדָמוֹ שֶׁלְפָּר. וְיֵשׁ אוֹמְרִים. זָהָב שֶׁהוּא עוֹשֶׂה פֵירוֹת. כַּיֵי דְתַנִּינָן תַּמָּן. וְגֶפֶן שֶׁל זָהָב הָיְתָה עוֹמֶדֶת עַל פִּתְחוֹ שֶׁלְהֵיכָל. אָמַר רִבִּי אָחָא בַּר יִצְחָק. בַּשָּׁנָה שֶׁבָּנָה שְׁלֹמֹה אֶת בֵּית הַמִּקְדָּשׁ צָר כָּל־מִינֵי אִילָנוֹת לְתוֹכוֹ. וּבַשָּׁעָה שֶׁהָיוּ אִילוּ שֶׁבַּחוּץ [עוֹשִׂין פֵּירוֹת] הָיוּ אִילוּ שֶׁבִּפְנִים עוֹשִׂין פֵּירוֹת. הָדָא הוּא דִכְתִיב פָּרֹחַ תִּפְרַח וְתָגֵל אַף גִּילַת וְרַנֵּן וגו׳. אֵימָתַי יָבֵשׁוּ. אָמַר רִבִּי יִצְחָק חִינָּנָא בַּר יִצְחָק. בְּשָׁעָה שֶׁהֶעֱמִיד מְנַשֶּׁה צֶלֶם בַּהֵיכָל יָבֵשׁוּ. דִּכְתִיב וּפֶרַח לְבָנוֹן אוּמְלָל:

[98]There are seven kinds of gold: good gold[99], pure gold[100], closed gold[101], Mufaz gold[102], refined gold[103], drawn gold[104], Parwayim gold[105].

Good gold, as its name says. [*And the gold of this land is good.*[99,106]] Rebbi Isaac says, it is good to have in one's house, it is good to accompany one.

Pure gold, which one brings into the fire and nothing is missing. (As) [It comes as][107] it was stated: It happened that the golden candelabrum which Moses made in the desert was in excess of one denar, and they returned it to the fire eighty times and it did not lose anything[108]. This is correct. Before it is refined it loses a lot, once it is refined it will not miss anything.

Closed gold, which makes all other kinds of gold look like silver. Rebbi Samuel bar Rav Isaac said, it is written, *And seven thousand talents of refined silver to cover the walls of the House*[109]. *The entire House he covered with gold*[110], and you are saying so[111]? But it was making all other kinds of gold look like silver.

Mufaz gold. Rebbi Patroki the brother of Rebbi Drosa in the name of Rebbi Abba bar Bina: It looks like fire which was kindled with sulphur. Rebbi Abbin, it is called after its place, *and gold from Ufaz*[112].

Refined gold, one was cutting it up like olives, form it into dough, and feed it to ostriches; they filter it. But some are saying, that they were burying it in manure for seven years.

Drawn gold. It could be drawn like wax. Hadrian had the weight of an egg of it. Diocletian had the weight of a Gordian denar[113] of it.

Parwayim gold. Rebbi Simeon ben Laqish said, red, it is like ox blood, but some are saying, gold which produces fruits. As we have stated there[114], "a golden vine was standing at the door of the inner hall." Rebbi Aḥa bar Isaac said, at the time when Solomon built the Temple, he formed all kinds of trees in it and at the time when those outside where bearing fruit, those inside were bearing fruit. That is what is written[115], *blooming the blossom and jubilate, also enjoying and singing*, etc. When did they dry up? Rebbi Isaac Hinena bar Isaac said, when Manasse put up at statue in the Temple they dried up, as it is written, *and the flower of the Lebanon is wilted*[116].

98 Babli 44b, *Midrash Hazita (Shir rabba)* 3(17) on 3:9, *Num. rabba* 12.
99 *Gen.* 2:12.
100 *Ex.* 24:11,24; 25:17,32,36,37; 37:2,6
101 *1K.* 7:50.
102 *Dan.* 10:5.
103 "Refined" is found in the Bible only applied to silver, see the Halakhah.
104 *1K.* 10:10,17, *2Chr.* 9:15,16.
105 *2Chr.* 3:6.
106 Corrector's addition, probably from the parallels.
107 The text in parentheses is the scribe's (supported by the reliable parallel in *Midrash Hazita*); the one in brackets is the corrector's.
108 The text in *Midrash Hazita* seems original: The candelabrum the of Temple turned out to be in excess of that made in the desert by the weight of a Gordian *denar*; they refined it in fire 80 times until it lost that extra weight. The weight of the candelabrum itself is not defined in the Bible, only that the candelabrum and all its appurtenances have to be made from one talent (3'000 *sheqel*) of pure gold.
109 *1Chr.* 29:4, in the list of preparations David made for the Temple to be built by Solomon.
110 *1K.* 6:22, in the report on the actual building of the Temple.
111 Why is silver suddenly called gold?
112 *Jer.* 10:9.
113 One of the few coins minted during the inflationary period of the military anarchy in the Roman Empire with a reputation of being honest. Cf. D. Sperber, *Roman Palestine 200-400 Money and Prices*, Ramat Gan 1974.
114 Mishnah *Middot* 3:5. Babli 21b.
115 *Is.* 35:2.
116 *Nah.* 1:4. For "Lebanon" as sobriquet for the Temple cf, *1K.* 7:2.

(41d line) **הלכה ה:** פִּיטוּם הַקְּטוֹרֶת. הַצֳרֵי וְהַצִּפּוֹרֶן הַחֶלְבְּנָה וְהַלְּבוֹנָה מִשְׁקַל שִׁבְעִים שִׁבְעִים מָנֶה. מוֹר וּקְצִיעָה שִׁיבֹּלֶת נֵרְדְּ וְכַרְכֹּם מִשְׁקַל שִׁשָּׁה עָשָׂר שִׁשָּׁה עָשָׂר מָנֶה. קוֹשְׁטְ שְׁנֵים עָשָׂר. קִילוּפָה שְׁלֹשָׁה. קִינָּמוֹן תִּשְׁעָה. נִמְצֵאתָ אוֹמֵר. שְׁלֹשׁ מֵאוֹת וְשִׁשִּׁים וַחֲמֵשׁ מָנִים הָיוּ כְּנֶגֶד יְמוֹת הַשָּׁנָה. וּשְׁלֹשָׁה שֶׁלְּאוֹתוֹ הַיּוֹם. הָדָא הִיא דְּתַנִּינָן. וְהַיּוֹם מוֹסִיף מְלֹא חָפְנָיו. כָּרְשִׁינָה תִּשְׁעָה

קַבִּין. יֵין (קפניסין) [קַפְּרִיסִין] [קַפְּרִיסִין] שָׁלשׁ סְאִין וְשָׁלשׁ קַבִּין. אִם אֵין לוֹ יֵין קפניסין] [קַפְּרִיסִין] מֵבִיא חֲמַר חִיוּוְרָן עַתִּיק. מֶלַח סְדוֹמִית רוֹבַע. מַעֲלֶה עָשָׁן כָּל־שֶׁהוּא. רִבִּי נָתָן אוֹמֵר. אַף (קפרת) [כִּיפַּת] הַיַּרְדֵּן כָּל־שֶׁהוּא. נָתַן בָּהּ דְּבַשׁ פְּסָלָהּ. חִסַּר בָּהּ אַחַת מִכָּל סַמְמָנֶיהָ חַיָּיב מִיתָה.

Halakhah 5: [117]The compounding of the incense: balsamum, and cloves, galbanum and frankincense, each in the weight of 70 *maneh*[118]. Myrrh and cassia, spicenard and saffron, each in the weight of sixteen *maneh*. Costus twelve, bark three, cinnamon nine. You find that there were 365 *maneh* according to the days of the year and three for this day[119]. That is what we have stated: "but on this day he adds a fistful." Carshina[120] nine *qab*, (Qanrisin) [caper][121] wine three *seah* and three *qab*. If he has no (Qanrisin) [caper] wine he brings aged whitish wine. Sodom salt[122] a quarter. Some smoke producing herb. Rebbi Nathan says, also some (Qafra) [Kifa][123] of the Jordan. If he added honey he invalidated it. If he left out one of its ingredients he is liable for death[124].

תַּנֵּי. רַבָּן שִׁמְעוֹן בֶּן גַּמְלִיאֵל אוֹמֵר. הַצֲרִי אֵינוֹ אֶלָּא (סְרָף) [שְׂרָף] שֶׁלְּעֲצֵי (הַקְטָב) [הַקְטָף]. בְּרִית כַּרְשִׁינָה לָמָה הָיְתָה בָאָה. שֶׁבָּהּ שָׁפִין אֶת הַצִּפּוֹרֶן מִפְּנֵי שֶׁהִיא נָאָה. יֵין (קפניסין) [קַפְּרִיסִין] לָמָה הִיא בָאָה. שֶׁבָּהּ (שָׁפִין) [שׁוֹרִין] אֶת הַצִּפּוֹרֶן מִפְּנֵי שֶׁהִיא עַזָּה. וַהֲלֹא מֵי רַגְלַיִם יָפִין לָהּ. אֶלָּא שֶׁאֵין מַכְנִיסִין רֵיחַ רַע בָּעֲזָרָה מִפְּנֵי הַכָּבוֹד. וּכְשֶׁהָיָה מֵידַק הָיָה אוֹמֵר. הָדֵק הֵיטֵב. הָדֵק הֵיטֵב. שֶׁהַקּוֹל יָפֶה לַבְּשָׂמִים. חִסַּר בָּהּ אַחַת מִסַּמְמָנֶיהָ אוֹ שֶׁנָּתַן בָּהּ מְעַט דְּבַשׁ הָיְתָה פְּסוּלָה. לֹא נָתַן לְתוֹכָהּ מֶלַח אוֹ שֶׁנָּתַן לְתוֹכָהּ מַעֲלֵה עָשָׁן מִתְחַיֵּיב מִיתָה. אָמַר רִבִּי זְעוּרָה. וְעוֹבֵר מִשּׁוּם הַכְּנָסָה יְתֵירָה.

It was stated: Rabban Simeon ben Gamliel says, balsamum is only the sap of the (qtab) [qtaf][124] tree. For what comes Carshina lye? In it one polished the cloves. For what does (Qanrisin) [caper] wine come? In it one (polishes) [soaks][125] cloves that it should be strong. Would not be urine good for this? Only one does not introduce bad smell into the Temple courtyard because of decorum[126]. And when he was pulverizing he was saying: be well pulverized, be well pulverized, for voice is good for compounding. If he left out one of its ingredients or added honey he invalidated it. If he failed to add salt[127] or added[128] smoke producing herb he became liable for death. Rebbi Ze`ura said, and he sins because of unnecessary entry[129].

תַּנֵּי בַּר קַפָּרָא. הַפַּטָּמִים שֶׁבִּירוּשָׁלֵם הָיוּ אוֹמְרִים. אִילּוּ הָיָה נוֹתֵן לְתוֹכָהּ מְעַט דְּבַשׁ לֹא הָיָה כָל־הָעוֹלָם כּוּלּוֹ יָכוֹל לַעֲמוֹד בְּרֵיחָהּ.

It was stated: Bar Qappara said, the perfumers in Jerusalem were saying, if one would add some honey, the entire world could not withstand its smell.

תַּנֵּי. פִּיטְמָהּ חֲצָיִים כְּשֵׁירָה. שִׁילְשִׁים וְרְבָעִים לֹא שָׁמַעְנוּ. רִבִּי אוֹמֵר. כְּמִידָּתָהּ הָיְתָה כְּשֵׁירָה. וְדָא דְאַתְּ אָמַר. פִּיטְמָהּ חֲצָיִים כְּשֵׁירָה. חֲצִי כָל־סַמְמָן וְסַמְמָן. אַחַת לְשִׁשִּׁים לְשִׁבְעִים שָׁנָה הִיא הָיְתָה בָּאָה חֲצָיִים מִן הַשִּׁירַיִים. הָדָא הִיא מוֹתַר הַקְּטוֹרֶת מֶה הָיוּ עוֹשִׂין בָּהּ

It was stated: If one compounded half of it it is qualified. Thirds and quarters we did not hear. Rebbi said, in its proportion it is qualified. Therefore, what one said, if one compounded half of it it is qualified, half of every ingredient. Once in sixty or seventy years half of it was coming from leftovers. That is, "what was one doing with excess incense"[130]?

117 Babli *Keritut* 6a/b.
118 It is not obvious whether the reference is to the Semitic *maneh*, 60 *šeqel*, or the Greek *mnā*, 100 *denar* (*drachmē*). In the rabbinic system 1 *šeqel* = 2 *denar*. Since in all other circumstances we find that מנה denotes 100 *denar* (weight or money) there is no reason to assume that here the situation is different, even though the traditional vocalization in this context is מָנֶה.
119 The total amount adds up to 368 *maneh*.
120 Name of a plant, usually leeks (in Arabic, peas or a related vegetable.) In the Babli, "Carshina lye"; as shown by the next paragraph, this must be the reading here also. *Qab* as a volume is a fluid measure.
121 The text in parentheses is the scribe's, the one in brackets the corrector's. Since the scribe was very consistent in his spelling of the name, his is not a scribal error and the corrector's has to be classified as copied from the Babli. The word used by the scribe is a hapax, its meaning is unknown. If it is from قَنّٰر "small onions", the meaning of the Yerushalmi term is close to the of the Babli, wine with added vegetable aroma.
122 Dead Sea salt.
123 Here also the corrector's version in brackets is the Babli text, against the scribe's in parentheses. An aromatic plant also mentioned in Tosephta *Demai* 1:29 (cf. S.Liebermann, *Tosefta ki-fshutah, Zeraim* vol, 1, New York 1955, p. 208).
124 Babli 53a.
Again spelling of corrector following the Babli. Probably the Babylonian pronunciation of *qtaf* was close to the Galilean of *qtav*. עֵץ can mean both "tree" and "bush".
125 Here the correction of the corrector following the Babli seems to be correct.
126 Babli *Roš Haššanah* 32a.
127 Babli *Menahot* 20a.
128 Obviously this must read "did not add". Babli 53a.
129 If the incense is disqualified, entering the Sanctuary with it is sinful.

131 Mishnah *Šeqalim* 4:5. The Mishnah implies that leftover incense powder at the end of the year was a common occurrence.

(41d line 50) תַּנֵּי. הִקְטִיר כְּזַיִת בַּחוּץ חַיָּיב. פָּחוּת מִכְּזַיִת בִּפְנִים פָּטוּר. רִבִּי זְעוּרָה בְשֵׁם רַב יִרְמְיָה. נִפְטְרוּ הַצִּיבּוּר יְדֵי חוֹבָתָן. רִבִּי יוֹסֵי בֵּירִבִּי בּוּן בְּשֵׁם רִבִּי יִרְמְיָה. מִן מַה דְתַנֵּי. הִקְטִיר כְּזַיִת בַּחוּץ חַיָּיב. מִינָהּ אַתְּ שְׁמַע. פָּחוּת מִכְּזַיִת בִּפְנִים פָּטוּר.

It was stated[131]:: If he burned[132] the size of an olive outside he is liable; less than the volume of an olive inside he is not liable[133]. Rebbi Ze'ira in the name of Rav Jeremiah[134]: The public has fulfilled its obligation[135]. Rebbi Yose ben Rebbi Abun in the name of Rebbi Jeremiah[136], since it was stated that if he burned the size of an olive outside he is liable, from this you infer that less than the volume of an olive inside he is not liable[137].

131 Babli *Zevahim* 109a.
132 Of incense correctly compounded.
133 "Not liable" usually means "forbidden but not punishable." The Babli, probably more correctly, has :less than a *pars* (Note 90).
134 The first generation. Babylonian Amora.
135 Since no weights or measures are given in the biblical text.
136 The student of R. Ze'ira.
137 If he only is liable for a full olive-sized amount outside, he cannot be liable for less than an olive-sized piece inside. If this is formulated as separate statement, it must mean that he is not liable and the action is irrelevant. The statement of Rav Jeremiah must be in the Babylonian tradition referring to a *pars*.

(41d line 54) דַּקָּה. מַה תַּלְמוּד לוֹמַר. לְפִי שֶׁנֶּאֱמַר וְשָׁחַקְתָּ מִמֶּנָּה הָדֵק. אִם כֵּן לָמָּה נֶאֱמַר דַּקָּה. שֶׁתְּהֵא דַקָּה מִן הַדַּקָּה. כֵּיצַד הוּא עוֹשֶׂה. מַפְרִישׁ שְׁלֹשֶׁת מָנִים מֵעֶרֶב יוֹם הַכִּיפּוּרִים וּמַחֲזִירָן לַמַּכְתֶּשֶׁת כְּדֵי לְמַלְּאוֹת מִמֶּנָּה חָפְנָיו כְּדֵי לְקַיֵּים בָּהּ דַּקָּה מִן הַדַּקָּה.

Fine[138]. What does the verse say? Because it was said, *you shall pulverize it finely*[139]. Then why is it said, *fine*? That it be most fine. What does he do? He separates the *mina* on the Eve of the Day of Atonement and returns it to the mortar to fill from it his fistful to observe "most fine.[140]"

138 *Lev.* 16:12.
139 *Ex.* 31:36. If the entire year the incense must be a fine powder, what does the remark mean that on the Day of Atonement it be fine?
140 Babli 45a, *Keritut* 6b.

(41d line 57) אָמַר רִבִּי יוֹנָה. חוּץ מִקִידוּשׁ הָרִאשׁוֹן. אָמַר רִבִּי יוֹסֵה. וַאֲפִילוּ מִקִידוּשׁ הָרִאשׁוֹן. מַתְנִיתָהּ פְּלִיגָא עַל רִבִּי יוֹנָה. כָּל־הַכֵּלִים שֶׁהָיוּ בַמִּקְדָּשׁ הָיוּ רְאוּיִין לְקִידוּשׁ יָדַיִם וְרַגְלָיִם. פָּתַר לָהּ. חוּץ מִקִידוּשׁ הָרִאשׁוֹן. מַתְנִיתָהּ פְּלִיגָא עַל רִבִּי יוֹסֵה. הַכִּיּוֹר וְהַכֵּן מְעַכְּבִין. פָּתַר לָהּ. מְקוֹמָן מְעַכֵּב.

Rebbi Jonah said, except for the first sanctification[141]. Rebbi Yose said, even for the first sanctification. A *baraita* disagrees with Rebbi Jonah: All vessels[142] in the Temple were qualified for sanctifying hands and legs. He explains it, except for the first sanctification. A *baraita* disagrees with Rebbi Yose: the basin and its base are obstructive. He explains it, their place is obstructive[143].

141 This now refers to Mishnah 8, that the High Priest does not use the basin but a golden pitcher. Since the first sanctification from the basis is a biblical requirement (*Ex.* 30:20-21, 40:30) it cannot be waved.

142 All containers. *Zevahim* 21b/22a.
143 The place between the Tent of Meeting and the altar (*Ex.* 30:18). If the basin is not in its place, no service can be held.

(fol. 41b) **משנה ט**: בְּכָל־יוֹם הָיוּ שָׁם אַרְבַּע מַעֲרָכוֹת וְהַיּוֹם חָמֵשׁ דִּבְרֵי רִבִּי מֵאִיר. רִבִּי יוֹסֵי אוֹמֵר. בְּכָל־יוֹם שָׁלֹשׁ וְהַיּוֹם אַרְבַּע. רִבִּי יְהוּדָה אוֹמֵר בְּכָל־יוֹם שְׁתַּיִם וְהַיּוֹם שָׁלֹשׁ:

Mishnah 9: Every day there were four arrangements[144] and this day five[145], the words of Rebbi Meïr. Rebbi Yose says, everyday three and this day four. Rebbi Jehudah says, every day two and this day three.

144 The formal arrangement of wood on the altar. For R. Meïr the first one is in the morning for the daily sacrifice, the second for taking charcoal for the daily burning of incense on the interior altar, the third to make sure the fire is not extinguished for the remainder of the day, the fourth to burn through the night.

145 Additional logs from which the High Priest takes charcoal to bring into the Holiest of Holies.

(41d line 62) **הלכה ו**: מַה טַעֲמָא דְרִבִּי מֵאִיר. וְהָאֵשׁ עַל־הַמִּזְבֵּחַ תּוּקַד־בּוֹ לֹא תִכְבֶּה זוֹ מַעֲרֶכֶת קִיּוּמֵי הָאֵשׁ. וּבִעֵר עָלֶיהָ הַכֹּהֵן זוֹ מַעֲרֶכֶת אִיכּוּל אֵיבָרִין וּפְדָרִים. וְעָרַךְ עָלֶיהָ הָעֹלָה זוֹ מַעֲרָכָה גְדוֹלָה. וְהִקְטִיר עָלֶיהָ חֶלְבֵי הַשְּׁלָמִים זוֹ קְטוֹרֶת. וְלֵית לְרִבִּי יוֹסֵה מַעֲרֶכֶת אִיכּוּל

אֵיבָרִין. וְלֵית לְרִבִּי יְהוּדָה מַעֲרֶכֶת קִיּוּמֵי אֵשׁ. מַה מְקַיֵּים רִבִּי יְהוּדָה אֵשׁ תָּמִיד. אֵשׁ שֶׁאָמַרְתִּי לָךְ תְּהֵא תָּמִיד לֹא תְהֵא אֶלָּא עַל מִזְבֵּחַ הַחִיצוֹן.

Halakhah 6: What is Rebbi Meïr's reason? [148]*And the fire on the altar shall be lit there, you shall not extinguish*, that is the arrangement which keeps the fire. *And the Cohen shall burn on it*, that is the arrangement for disposal of limbs and fat. *And arrange on it the elevation sacrifice*, this is the main arrangement. *And burn as incense on it the fats of the well-being sacrifices*, this is the incense. Rebbi Yose does not have the arrangement for disposal of limbs. Rebbi Jehudah does not have the arrangement which keeps the fire. How does Rebbi Jehudah explain *a permanent fire*[147]? The fire which I told you that it be permanent only shall be on the outer altar[148].

146 *Lev.* 6:5; cf. *Sifra Ṣaw Pereq* 2(11); Babli 45a.
147 *Lev.* 6:6.
148 He holds that any Sanctuary fire can be made only on top of the outer altar, including the one used to light the candelabrum. Babli 45b.

(41d line 63) אָמַר רִבִּי אֶלְעָזָר. הָאֵיבָרִין וְהַפְּדָרִין שֶׁלֹּא נִתְאַכְּלוּ מִבְּעֶרֶב עוֹשֶׂה אוֹתָן מְדוּרָה וְשׂוֹרְפָן בִּפְנֵי עַצְמָן. וְדוֹחִין עֲלֵיהֶן אֶת הַשַּׁבָּת. רִבִּי יַעֲקֹב בַּר אָחָא בְּשֵׁם רִבִּי שְׁמוּאֵל בַּר אַבָּא. מַתְנִיתָא אָמְרָה כֵן. בְּכָל־יוֹם הָיוּ שָׁם אַרְבַּע מַעֲרָכוֹת. מָה אַתְּ שְׁמַע מִינָהּ. אָמַר רִבִּי מָנָא. וְהַיּוֹם חָמֵשׁ. רִבִּי בּוּן בַּר חִיָּיה בְּעָא קוֹמֵי רִבִּי זְעוּרָה. דָּבָר שֶׁאֵינוֹ מְעַכֵּב דּוֹחֶה. אָמַר לֵיהּ. הֲרֵי עֵידֵי הַחוֹדֶשׁ הֲרֵי אֵינָן מְעַכְּבִין וְדוֹחִין. דְּתַנִּינָן תַּמָּן. שֶׁעַל מַהֲלַךְ לַיְלָה וָיוֹם מְחַלְּלִין אֶת הַשַּׁבָּת וְיוֹצְאִין לְעֵידוּת הַחֹדֶשׁ.

Rebbi Eleazar said, limbs and fat which were not consumed before the evening one builds into a pyre[149] and burns them separately; for them one pushes aside the Sabbath[150]. Rebbi Jacob bar Aha in the name of Rebbi Samuel bar Abba: The Mishnah implies this: "Every day there were four arrangements." What does one understand from here[151]? Rebbi Mana said, "and this day five[152]". Rebbi Abun bar Ḥiyya asked before Rebbi Ze'ira: May something which is not obstructive push aside[153]? He answered him, there are the witnesses for the New Moon who are not obstructive[154] and push aside, as we have stated there[155]: "for a distance of a night and day one desecrates the Sabbath and comes for testimony of the New Moon."

149 On the altar.
150 The remainders of Friday sacrifices have to be burned in the following night which is Sabbath.
151 Maybe "every day" excludes Friday evening.
152 Since everything forbidden on the Sabbath is forbidden on the Day of Atonement (Mishnah *Megillah* 1:5), if the special arrangement for the night is prescribed for the day of Atonement it also must be prescribed for the Sabbath.
153 Since the sacrifice is valid if the blood was poured on the walls of the altar, the later disposal cannot invalidate. If one would leave the remainders unburned and after the Sabbath burn them outside the sacred domain, everything would remain valid. Why should the Sabbath be pushed aside for this, even though it has biblical justification?
154 Even in times when the New Moon was proclaimed on the basis of testimony, the Supreme Court had the possibility of declaring the New Moon based on their computations (Mishnah *Roš Haššanah* 2:11.
155 Mishnah *Roš Haššanah* 1:11.

(41d line 75) מְנַיָּין לְמַעֲרֶכֶת יוֹם הַכִּפּוּרִים. רִבִּי יִרְמְיָה בְשֵׁם רִבִּי פְדָת. גֶּחָלֵי. מַה תַלְמוּד לוֹמַר אֵשׁ. שֶׁהִיא בְטֵילָה עַל גַּבֵּי נַחֲלֶיהָ. גֶּחָלֵי. יָכוֹל עוֹמְמוֹת. תַלְמוּד לוֹמַר אֵשׁ. אִי אֵשׁ יָכוֹל שַׁלְהֶבֶת. תַלְמוּד לוֹמַר גַּחֲלֵי־אֵשׁ. הָא כֵיצַד. מִן הַלוֹחֲשׁוֹת הַלָּלוּ. וּמְנַיָּין שֶׁתְּהֵא הָאֵשׁ בְּטֵילָה עַל גַּבֵּי גְחָלִים. תַלְמוּד לוֹמַר גַּחֲלֵי־אֵשׁ.

From where the arrangement of the Day of Atonement[156]? Rebbi Jeremiah in the name of Rebbi Pedat: *Coals*[157]. Why does the verse say, *of fire*? That it should be insignificant on its coals. [158]"*Coals*, I could think smouldering; the verse says *of fire*. If *of fire*, I could think flames; the verse says *coals of fire*, from those crackling ones. And from where that the fire should be insignificant on the coals? The verse says, *coals of fire*."

156 That the wood on the altar has to be prepared specially for the requirements of the day and therefore needs an extra arrangement, in addition to the daily ones.
157 Lev. 16:12.
158 *Sifra Ahare Pereq* 3(5); Babli *Pesahim*
75b.. The following text is Tannaitic, not of the sayings of R. Jeremiah. It is missing in a Genizah fragment (Ginzberg, p. 118) and therefore may be a later addition. This explains the reduplication of the argument.

(42a line 4) רִבִּי יְהוֹשֻׁעַ בֶּן לֵוִי אָמַר. אֵין לֶחֶם הַפָּנִים נִפְסָל בְּשִׁעַת מַסָּעוֹת. [רִבִּי יוֹחָנָן אָמַר. לֶחֶם הַפָּנִים נִפְסָל בְּשִׁעַת מַסָּעוֹת.] רִבִּי חִיָּיה בְשֵׁם רִבִּי יְהוֹשֻׁעַ בֶּן לֵוִי. כַּאֲשֶׁר יַחֲנוּ כֵּן יִסָּעוּ. מַה בַחֲנִייָתָם אֵינוֹ נִפְסָל אַף בִּנְסִיעָתָם אֵינוֹ נִפְסָל. רִבִּי אִמִּי בְשֵׁם רִבִּי יְהוֹשֻׁעַ בֶּן לֵוִי. וְנָסַע אוֹהֶל מוֹעֵד מַחֲנֵה הַלְוִיִּם בְּתוֹךְ הַמַּחֲנוֹת. כִּבְתוֹךְ הַמַּחֲנוֹת.

רִבִּי יַעֲקֹב בַּר אָחָא רִבִּי אִמִּי בְשֵׁם רִבִּי אֶלְעָזָר. הַשּׂוֹרֵף קֳדָשִׁים בַּחוּץ בִּשְׁעַת מַסָּעוֹת לוֹקֶה. אָמַר רִבִּי יוֹחָנָן. קֳדָשִׁים נִדָּחִין בִּשְׁעַת מַסָּעוֹת. טְמֵאִים פְּרוּשִׁים כָּל־אֶחָד וְאֶחָד בִּמְחִיצָתוֹ. אָמַר רִבִּי יוֹסֵה. תְּדִירָה הָא מִילְתָא בְּפוּמְהוֹן דְּרַבָּנָן. נִסְתַּלְּקוּ הַפָּרְכוֹת הוּתְּרוּ הַמְּחִיצוֹת לְזָבִין וְלִמְצוֹרָעִין. מַתְנִיתָה מְסַיְּיעָה לְדֵין וּמַתְנִיתָה מְסַיְּיעָה לְדֵין. מַתְנִיתָה מְסַיְּיעָה לְרִבִּי יְהוֹשֻׁעַ בֶּן לֵוִי. תָּמִיד. תָּמִיד אֲפִילוּ בַשַּׁבָּת. תָּמִיד אַף בְּטוּמְאָה. מַתְנִיתָה מְסַיְּיעָה לְרִבִּי יוֹחָנָן. לֹא תִכְבֶּה. אַף בַּמַּסָּעוֹת. [בִּשְׁעַת מַסָּעוֹת] מֶה הָיוּ עוֹשִׂין לָהּ. הָיוּ כוֹפִין עָלֶיהָ (פְּסַקְתֵּיר) [פְּסַכְתֵּיר]. דִּבְרֵי רִבִּי יְהוּדָה. רִבִּי שִׁמְעוֹן אוֹמֵר. אַף בִּשְׁעַת מַסָּעוֹת הָיוּ מְדַשְּׁנִין אוֹתָהּ. שֶׁנֶּאֱמַר וְדִשְּׁנוּ אֶת־הַמִּזְבֵּחַ וּפָרְשׂוּ עָלָיו בֶּגֶד אַרְגָּמָן. הָא אִילּוּ הָיָה הַמִּזְבֵּחַ דָּלֵיק לֹא הָיָה בֶּגֶד אַרְגָּמָן נִשְׂרָף. מַה עָבַד לָהּ רִבִּי יוּדָה. (פְּסַקְתֵּיר) [פְּסַכְתֵּיר]. הָיוּ כוֹפִין עָלֶיהָ מִלְּמַעֲלָה. מַה מְקַיֵּים רִבִּי יוּדָה. וְדִשְּׁנוּ אֶת־הַמִּזְבֵּחַ. וְיֵרווֹן. כַּיי דָמַר רִבִּי יוּדָה בֶּן פָּזִי. וְאָכַל וְשָׂבַע וְדָשֵׁן.

Rebbi Joshua ben Levi said, the shew-bread did not become disqualified during travel time[159]. [Rebbi Johanan said, the shew-bread became disqualified during travel time.][160] Rebbi Ḥiyya in the name of Rebbi Joshua ben Levi: *just as they camped so they travelled*[161], since it did not become disqualified when they were camping so it did not become disqualified when they were travelling. Rebbi Immi in the name of Rebbi Joshua ben Levi: *The Tent of Meeting, the encampment of the Levites, shall travel in the midst of*[161] *camps*, as if in the center of camps.

Rebbi Jacob bar Aḥa, Rebbi Immi in the name of Rebbi Eleazar: One who burns *sancta* outside during travel time is flogged[162]. Rebbi Joḥanan said, *sancta* became rejects during travel time[163]; the impure remain separated each one according to his partition[164]. Rebbi Yose said, the following is frequent in the mouth of the rabbis: When the gobelins were removed, the partitions were permitted to sufferers from gonorrhea and skin disease[165]. A *baraita* supports the one and a *baraita* supports the other.[166] A *baraita*[167] supports Rebbi Joshua ben Levi: "*Permanent*, even on the Sabbath; *permanent* even in impurity." A *baraita* supports Rebbi Joḥanan, "*you shall not extinguish it, even during travel*[168]. What did they do [at travel time][169]? They put a wine-cooler[87] over it, the words of Rebbi Jehudah. Rebbi Simeon says, even at travel time they were removing ashes from it, as it is said[170], *they shall remove the ashes from the altar and spread a purple cloth over it.*" If the altar were burning, would the purple cloth not be burned? What does Rebbi Jehudah do with this? They put a wine-cooler over it. How does Rebbi

Jehudah validate *they shall remove the ashes from the altar*? They shall saturate it; as Rebbi Jehudah ben Pazi said, *he ate, and was sated, and saturated*[171].

159 Since the shew-bread has to be on the table in the Sanctuary (*Lev.* 24:5-9) it is obvious that bread taken out of a stationary Sanctuary becomes disqualified. The question is whether it also became disqualified when the Sanctuary around it was removed by divine command during the wanderings of he Israelites in the desert.

160 Addition by the corrector; sentence missing in the Genizah fragment published by Ginzberg (Note 159). The Babli, *Menahot* 95a, reports a disagreement of R. Joshua ben Levi and R. Johanan about this subject.

161 *Num.* 2:17.

162 Private altars and sacrifices outside the central sanctuary are forbidden, *Lev.* 17. In the absence of a central sanctuary, private altars are permitted, Mishnah *Zevahim* 14:4-8. If a central Sanctuary exists but is temporarily unavailable, the prohibition remains in place; *Menahot* 95a.

163 Sacrifices must either be burned on the altar in the courtyard of the Sanctuary or eaten within sanctified enclosures. If all enclosures are removed, all leftovers of sacrifices are automatically disqualified. Babli *Zevahim* 60b as tannaitic statement.

164 *Num.* 5:1-4. A person suffering from gonorrhea is excluded from the dwelling of the Levites, a sufferer from skin disease also from the camp of the Israelites. Since they were marching in military order, the impure were excluded from the marching order. Babli *Zevahim* 60b as tannaitic statement.

165 During travel times there is no inside and the impure cannot be sent outside.

166 Since R. Joshua ben Levi is not mentioned in the present paragraph, the reference to him has to be to the preceding one. The reference to R. Johanan is incomprehensible; the quoted *baraita* does not refer to any previous statement but to the following of R. Jehudah.

167 *Sifra Saw Pereq* 2(10), a *baraita* of R. Jehudah. Anywhere "permanent" is mentioned, it overrides restrictions. Since "permanent" is mentioned for the fire of that altar, *Lev.* 6:6, the priests have to tend the fire on the Sabbath even if all of them are impure. But "permanent" also is mentioned for the shew-bread (*Lev.* 24:8); this overrides the absence of the walls of the Sanctuary. By the same token, R. Joshua ben Levi has to hold that the altar fire has to be tended on the march; following R. Jehudah in the sequel.

168 Continuation of *Sifra Saw Pereq* 2(10) on *Lev.* 6:6.

169 Addition by the corrector; it should be deleted since by removing it the sentence and the next are again continuation of *Sifra Saw Pereq* 2(10).

170 *Num.* 4:13.

171 In all cognate languages דשן, دسم means "to be fat". The use of דשן as "ashes" must mean "ashes from fatty material". R. Jehudah will not extend the extended meaning of the noun to the corresponding verb.

הוציאו לו את הכף פרק חמישי

(fol.42a) **משנה א**: הוֹצִיאוּ לוֹ אֶת הַכַּף וְאֶת הַמַּחְתָּה וְחָפַן מְלֹא חָפְנָיו וְנָתַן לְתוֹךְ הַכַּף הַגָּדוֹל לְפִי גָדְלוֹ וְהַקָּטָן לְפִי קָטְנוֹ וְכָךְ הָיְתָה מִדָּתָן. נָטַל אֶת הַמַּחְתָּה בִּימִינוֹ וְאֶת הַכַּף בִּשְׂמֹאלוֹ. מְהַלֵּךְ בַּהֵיכָל עַד שֶׁמַּגִּיעַ לְבֵין שְׁנֵי הַפָּרוֹכֹת הַמַּבְדִּילוֹת בֵּין הַקּוֹדֶשׁ וּבֵין קוֹדֶשׁ הַקֳּדָשִׁים וּבֵינֵיהֶן אַמָּה. רִבִּי יוֹסֵי אוֹמֵר לֹא הָיְתָה שָׁם אֶלָּא פָּרוֹכֶת אַחַת בִּלְבַד שֶׁנֶּאֱמַר וְהִבְדִּילָה הַפָּרוֹכֶת לָכֶם בֵּין הַקּוֹדֶשׁ וּבֵין קֹדֶשׁ הַקֳּדָשִׁים.

Mishnah 1: They brought him the cup and the pan[1]; he took his full fistfuls and put it into the cup, a big person according to his bigness, and a small person according to his smallness, this was their measure. He took the fire-pan[2] into his right hand and the cup in his left, went into the Temple until he reached the space between the two gobelins which separate between the Holy and the Holiest of Holies with one cubit between them. Rebbi Yose says, there was only one gobelin as it was said[3], *and the gobelin shall separate for you between the Holy and the Holiest of Holies.*

משנה ב: הַחִיצוֹנָה פְרוּפָה מִן הַדָּרוֹם וְהַפְּנִימִית מִן הַצָּפוֹן וּמְהַלֵּךְ בֵּינֵיהֶן עַד שֶׁמַּגִּיעַ לַצָּפוֹן. הִגִּיעַ לַצָּפוֹן הָפַךְ פָּנָיו לַדָּרוֹם הָלַךְ לִשְׂמֹאלוֹ עִם הַפָּרוֹכֶת עַד שֶׁמַּגִּיעַ לָאָרוֹן הִגִּיעַ לָאָרוֹן נוֹתֵן אֶת הַמַּחְתָּה בֵּין שְׁנֵי הַבַּדִּים צָבַר אֶת הַקְּטוֹרֶת עַל גַּבֵּי גֶחָלִים וְנִתְמַלֵּא הַבַּיִת עָשָׁן. יָצָא וּבָא לוֹ דֶּרֶךְ כְּנִיסָתוֹ. מִתְפַּלֵּל תְּפִלָּה קְצָרָה וְלֹא הָיָה מַאֲרִיךְ בִּתְפִלָּתוֹ שֶׁלֹּא לְהַבְעִית אֶת יִשְׂרָאֵל:

Mishnah 3: The outer one was tied open from South and the inner one from North. He walks between them until he arrives at the North end. When he arrived at the North end he turns his face to the South; he walks with his left along the gobelin[4] until he arrives at the Ark. When he came to the Ark he puts the fire-pan between the two beams[5], he piles the incense on the coals and the entire House is filled with smoke. He leaves and returns in the way he entered[6]. He prays a short prayer[7] but not prolonging his prayer so as not to frighten Israel[8].

1 Other Cohanim bring him an empty cup and the censer full of the incense specially prepared for this day.

2 With the hot coals, which he had deposited on the uppermost step at the entrance to the Temple.

3   Ex. 26:33.
4   The Holiest of Holies being very dark, he guides his way along the inner gobelin with his left hand in which he holds the cold incense powder.
5   With which the Ark was carried (Ex. 25:13-15). For the Second Temple, where there was no Ark, see Mishnah 3.
6   He walks backwards with his face towards the Ark inside the Holiest of Holies and towards the North between the two gobelins.
7   In the main Temple Hall.
8   Who might be afraid that something had happened to him.

(42b line 3) הוֹצִיאוּ לוֹ אֶת הַכַּף כול'. וְלֹא כְבָר תַּנִּיתָהּ. נָטַל אֶת הַמַּחְתָּה וְעָלָה לְרֹאשׁ הַמִּזְבֵּחַ. כֵּינִי מַתְנִיתָא. אֶת הַכַּף וְאֶת הַבַּזָּךְ. מָהוּ כַף. מָגִיס. אָמַר רִבִּי יוֹסֵה. הָדָא אֲמָרָה. כְּלִי חוֹל הוּא. אֵין תֵּימַר. כְּלִי קוֹדֶשׁ. דָּבָר שֶׁקָּדַשׁ בִּכְלִי נִפְדֶּה.

דְּאִתְפַּלְגוּן. פִּיטְמָהּ בַּחוּלִּין. רִבִּי יוֹסֵה בֶּן חֲנִינָה אָמַר. פְּסוּלָה. רִבִּי יְהוֹשֻׁעַ בֶּן לֵוִי אָמַר. כְּשֵׁירָה. מַה טַּעֲמָא דְּרִבִּי יוֹסֵה בַּר חֲנִינָה. קוֹדֶשׁ הִיא. שֶׁתְּהֵא הֲבָאָתָהּ בַּקּוֹדֶשׁ. מַה טַּעֲמָא דְּרִבִּי יְהוֹשֻׁעַ בֶּן לֵוִי. קוֹדֶשׁ הִיא. שֶׁתְּהֵא בָאָה מִתְּרוּמַת הַלִּשְׁכָּה. אָמַר רִבִּי יוֹסֵה בֵּירִבִּי בּוּן. אַתְיָא דְּרִבִּי יוֹסֵה בֶּן חֲנִינָה כִּשְׁמוּאֵל וּדְרִבִּי יְהוֹשֻׁעַ בֶּן לֵוִי כְּרִבִּי יוֹחָנָן. דְּתַנִּינָן. הַמַּקְדִּישׁ נְכָסָיו וְהָיוּ בָהֶן דְּבָרִים רְאוּיִין לְקָרְבְּנוֹת צִיבּוּר. רִבִּי יוֹחָנָן אָמַר. קְטוֹרֶת. אָמַר רִבִּי הוֹשַׁעְיָה. תִּיפְתָּר בְּאוֹמָן שֶׁל בֵּית אַבְטִינָס [שֶׁהָיָה נוֹטֵל בִּשְׂכָרוֹ קְטוֹרֶת.] וּדְרִבִּי יוֹסֵה בֶּן חֲנִינָה כִּשְׁמוּאֵל. דְּאָמַר רִבִּי חוּנָה בְּשֵׁם שְׁמוּאֵל. מַכְתֶּשֶׁת עָשׂוּ אוֹתָהּ כְּלֵי שָׁרֵת לַקּוֹדֶשׁ. אָמַר רִבִּי יוֹסֵה בֵּירִבִּי בּוּן. אֲמָרָהּ רִבִּי חוּנָה קוֹמֵי רִבִּי יוֹסֵה. דָּבָר שֶׁקָּדַשׁ בִּכְלִי נִפְדֶּה. אָמַר לֵיהּ. וְלָאו שְׁמוּאֵל הִיא. וּשְׁמוּאֵל אָמַר. קַל הוּא בְּמוֹתָר. דְּאִתְפַּלְגוּן. הוֹתִירוּ תְמִידִין. שְׁמוּאֵל אָמַר. נִפְדִּין כִּתְמִימִין. רִבִּי יוֹחָנָן אָמַר. נִפְדִּין כִּפְסוּלֵי הַמּוּקְדָּשִׁין. הוֹתִירוּ שְׂעִירִים. עַל דַּעְתֵּיהּ דִּשְׁמוּאֵל. אִם עוֹלָה נִפְדֵּית לֹא כָּל־שֶׁכֵּן חַטָּאת. עַל דַּעְתֵּיהּ דְּרִבִּי יוֹחָנָן רִבִּי זְעֵירָא אָמַר. יֵרְעוּ. אָמַר רִבִּי שְׁמוּאֵל בַּר רַב יִצְחָק. מְקַיְּיצִים בָּהּ אֶת הַמִּזְבֵּחַ. וְקַשְׁיָא. יֵשׁ חַטָּאת קְרֵיבָה עוֹלָה. אָמַר רִבִּי יוֹסֵה. שָׁנְיָא הִיא. שֶׁאֵין קָרְבְּנוֹת צִיבּוּר נִקְבָּעִין אֶלָּא בִשְׁחִיטָה. אָמַר רִבִּי חֲנַנְיָה בֶּן תְּרַדְיוֹן. תָּנֵי בֵית דִּין הוּא עַל הַמּוֹתָרוֹת שֶׁיִּקְרְבוּ עוֹלוֹת.

שֶׁקְרוֹבָה עוֹלָה. אָמַר רִבִּי יוֹסֵי שַׁנְיָיה הִיא. שֶׁאֵין קָרְבְּנוֹת צִיבּוּר נִקְבָּעִין אֶלָּא בִשְׁחִיטָה. אָמַר רִבִּי חֲנִינָא. תְּנַאי בֵּית דִּין הוּא עַל הַמּוֹתָרוֹת שֶׁיִּקְרְבוּ עוֹלוֹת.

"They brought him the cup," etc. But was it not already stated[9], "he took a fire-pan and ascended to the top of the altar"? So is the Mishnah: The cup and the bowl. What is a כַּף? A tureen[10]. Rebbi Yose said, this implies that it is a profane vessel. If you would say, a sanctified vessel, may something sanctified in a vessel be redeemed[11]?

[12]As they disagreed: If it was compounded as profane, Rebbi Yose ben Hanina said, it is disqualified; Rebbi Joshua ben Levi said, it is qualified. What is Rebbi Yose ben Hanina's reason? *It is holy*[14], that it shall be brought into the Sanctuary[15]. What is Rebbi Joshua ben Levi's reason? *It is holy*, that it shall be brought from the contributions to the treasury[16]. Rebbi Yose ben Rebbi Bun said, Rebbi Yose ben Hanina's parallels Samuel and Rebbi Joshua ben Levi's Rebbi Johanan, as we have stated, "if one dedicated his property to the Temple and there were objects appropriate as public offerings[17]." Rebbi Johanan said, incense. Rebbi Hoshaia said, explain it about an artisan of the family Eutinos [who took incense as his wages.[18]] And Rebbi Joshua ben Levi's is like Samuel, as Rebbi Huna[19] said in the name of Samuel, they made the mortar a vessel of sacred service[20]. Rebbi Yose ben Rebbi Abun said, Rebbi Huna said this before Rebbi Yose: something sanctified in a vessel may be redeemed[11]. He said to him, is that not Samuel's? Since Samuel said, it is slight in the case of leftovers[22]. As they disagreed: If daily sacrifices were left over, Samuel says, they are redeemed unblemished[23]. Rebbi Johanan said, they are redeemed as disqualified *sancta*[24]. Leftover he-goats[25], in Samuel's opinion if elevation sacrifices are redeemed, a purification sacrifice so much more. In Rebbi Johanan's opinion? Rebbi Ze'ira said, they shall graze[26]. Rebbi Samuel bar Rav Isaac said, one uses them to adorn the altar[27]. This is difficult. May a purification sacrifice be brought as elevation sacrifice? Rebbi Yose said, there is a difference, for public sacrifices are determined only by slaughter[28]. Rebbi Hananiah ben Tradion[29] said, it is a stipulation of the Court that all leftovers should be brought as elevation sacrifices[30].

9 Mishnah 4:3. The same expression מַחְתָּה is used in Mishnah 4:3 and in 5:1. But if the High Priest already used the מַחְתָּה before, it cannot be brought to him now

from a storage facility.

10 From a rabbinic Hebrew root מגיס "to stir, to mix dough" which may have been induced by Greek μαγίς "dough".

11 This would contradict *Lev.* 27:10 stating that anything dedicated and fit for Divine service may not be redeemed.

12 The incense used in the Temple.

13 The text also is in *Šeqalim* 4:5 (48b l. 1) ש. The Babli text of *Šeqalim*, given separately under the heading ש, is from a different tradition, possibly a corruption. The question is whether the incense may be compounded outside the sacred domain and not in a dedicated vessel.

14 There is no such verse; similar verses about incense would be *Ex.* 30:36, *most holy it shall be for you,* Ex. 30:37, *holy it shall be for you.* Babli *Keritut* 6a.

15 It seems that the correct text is in *Šeqalim*: That its existence shall be in the holy space. The Babli text there adds: "and it shall be brought from the contributions to the treasury," i. e., from the Temple tax.

16 In the Babli text: "that it shall be brought into the Sanctuary" which in our text is the *Yoma* version of R. Yose ben Ḥanina. In the Babli *Šeqalim* text it makes sense; the preparation may be in profane terrain, only the use must be in the Sanctuary.

17 Mishnah *Šeqalim* 4:6.

18 Addition of the corrector from *Šeqalim*. As explained in *Šeqalim*, incense of each year has to bought by the proceeds of the Temple tax of that year. In order to avoid that any leftovers at the end of the year became disqualified, the leftovers are given to the workers and artisans working for the Temple as their wages. The Temple can then buy back the incense from the workers with money of the next year and the incense remains qualified. (Private use of incense compounded by the Temple's formula is a deadly sin, *Ex.* 30:38.) R. Johanan's argument that the Mishnah can only be interpreted as referring to incense is given in the Babli, *Keritut* 6a.

19 Read with *Šeqalim*: Rav Huna.

20 Here one has to read with the Babli *Šeqalim*: did *not* make. The incense always is prepared in a profane vessel; it becomes dedicated by being used on the dedicated fire-pan or the interior altar.

21 Answering his question in the negative. R. Yose holds that practice does not follow Samuel.

22 Animals and supplies bought with Temple tax monies but not used by the end of a fiscal year, which cannot be used for the next year.

23 It is impossible to redeem animals qualified to be sacrifices, *Lev.* 27:10. Samuel proposes to treat the surplus animals similar to how surplus incense was treated: The animals are redeemed with the past year's excess money, which then is used for repair or improvement of the Temple building as explained in *Šeqalim* Chapter 4. Then the animals are bought again with money of the new fiscal year and become newly qualified.

24 He requires that the excess sheep be let grazing until either they develop a defect or become disqualified by age; then they may be redeemed like any other disqualified animal. A different tradition Babli *Ševuot* 11b.

25 Bought for public purification

sacrifices on holidays and days of the New Moon.
26 Same procedure as for sheep, Note 24.
27 To be used as elevation offerings in periods where the altar otherwise would be empty. These sacrifices not being obligatory cannot be bought with money from the Temple tax; one uses dedicated animals which are not being used for their original purpose. The statement is erroneously missing in the Babli *Šeqalim*.

28 If they never had been dedicated as purification sacrifices, the rules of the latter do not apply. Accepted as opinion both by Samuel and R. Johanan in Babli *Ševuot* 12b.
29 With the *Šeqalim* texts delete the last two words; the tradent is a late Amora not the early Tanna..
30 Since the stipulation preceded the acquisition of the animals by the Temple, R. Yose's answer is unnecessary.

(42b line 24) **הלכה ב:** מְלֹא קוּמְצוֹ. יָכוֹל מָלֵא קוּמְצוֹ מְבוֹרָץ. תַּלְמוּד לוֹמַר בְּקֻמְצוֹ. אִי בְּקֻמְצוֹ יָכוֹל יִקְמוֹץ בְּרָאשֵׁי אֶצְבְּעוֹתָיו. תַּלְמוּד לוֹמַר מְלֹא קוּמְצוֹ. הָא כֵיצַד. חוֹפֶה אֶת פַּס יָדוֹ בַּמַּחֲבַת וּבְמַרְחֶשֶׁת וּמוֹחֵק בְּאֶצְבָּעוֹ מִלְמַעְלָן לְמַטָן.

תַּמָּן אַתְּ אָמַר. מְלֹא קֻמְצוֹ בְּקֻמְצוֹ. וְהָכָא אַתְּ אָמַר מְלֹא קוּמְצוֹ. רִבִּי יַעֲקֹב בַּר אָחָא רִבִּי סִימוֹן בְּשֵׁם רִבִּי יְהוֹשֻׁעַ בֶּן לֵוִי. מַה לְהַלָן קוֹמֶץ הֶחָסֵר פָּסוּל וְהָכָא קוֹמֶץ הֶחָסֵר פָּסוּל. חָפְנַיִם מָהוּ שֶׁיֵּעָשׂוּ כִּכְלִי שָׁרֵת לְקַדֵּשׁ. אַחֵר מַהוּ שֶׁיַּחְפּוֹן וְיִתֵּן לְתוֹךְ חָפְנָיו. מָהוּ שֶׁיַּעֲשֶׂה מִידָה לְחָפְנָיו. בְּכָל־חָפְנַיִם מְשַׁעֲרִין אוֹ אֵין מְשַׁעֲרִין אֶלָּא בְחָפְנָיו. רִבִּי יְהוֹשֻׁעַ בֶּן לֵוִי שָׁאַל. חָפַן וָמֵת. אַחֵר מַהוּ שֶׁיִּיכָּנֵס בְּחָפְנָיו. אֵין תֵּימַר. חָפְנַיִם עָשׂוּ אוֹתָן כִּכְלִי שָׁרֵת לַקּוֹדֶשׁ. הָדָא אָמְרָה. חָפַן וָמֵת אֵין אַחֵר נִכְנָס בְּחָפְנָיו. אֵין אַחֵר חוֹפֵן וְנוֹתֵן לְתוֹךְ חָפְנָיו. וְעוֹשִׂין מִידָה לְחָפְנָיו. וְאֵין מְשַׁעֲרִין בְּכָל־חָפְנַיִם. אֵין תֵּימַר. חָפְנַיִם לֹא עָשׂוּ אוֹתָן כִּכְלִי שָׁרֵת לַקּוֹדֶשׁ. הָדָא אָמְרָה. חָפַן וָמֵת. אַחֵר נִכְנָס בְּחָפְנָיו. אַחֵר חוֹפֵן וְנוֹתֵן לְתוֹךְ לְפָנָיו. וְאֵין עוֹשִׂין מִידָה לְחָפְנָיו. וּמְשַׁעֲרִין בְּכָל־חָפְנַיִם.

Halakhah 2: [31]"*His full handful*[32]. I could assume an overstuffed handful, the verse says, *with his handful*[33]. If *with his handful*, I could assume that he picks it up with his finger tips, the verse says, *his full handful*. How is this? He sinks his hand into the baking pan[34] or frying pan[35] and wipes clean with his finger from top to bottom."

There, you are saying, *his full handful, with his handful*, and here you are saying, *his full handful*[36]. Rebbi Jacob bar Aḥa, Rebbi Simon in the name of Rebbi Joshua ben Levi, since there a deficient handful is disqualified, here also a deficient handful is disqualified. Are his fists considered vessels of service to sanctify[37]? May another person take the fistful and puts it in his fist[38]? Should it be made to measure for his fists[39]? Do you estimate for all possible fists or you estimate for his fist only? Rebbi Joshua ben Levi asked: If he took a fistful and died, may another person enter with his fistful[40]? If you are saying that they did not consider his fists a vessel of service of the Sanctuary, this implies that another person may enter with his fistful; another person may take the fistful and put it in his fist; one makes to measure for his fists; one does not estimate for all possible fists[41]. If you are saying that they considered his fists a vessel of service of the Sanctuary, this implies that another person may not enter with his fistful; another person may not take the fistful and put in his fist; one does not make to measure for his fists; one estimates for all possible fists.

31 Babli 47a, *Menahot* 11a, *Sifra Wayyiqra I Parshata* 9(6).
32 Lev. 2:2.
33 Lev. 6:8.
34 Lev. 2:5.
35 Lev. 2:7.
36 The following text implies that here one has to read וּמִלֹא חָפְנָיו (*Lev.* 16:12), the expression used for the service of the Day of Atonement. It is asserted that the meaning of חָפְנַיִם used in Chapter 16 is identical with קוֹמֶץ used in Chapters 2 and 6, except naturally that the קוֹמֶץ, used in the singular, refers to his right hand only whereas the חָפְנַיִם need both hands.
37 The paragraph is R. Joshua ben Levi's teaching, who asserted before that the incense is compounded in a profane vessel. The question then arises at which moment the incense becomes sanctified to be used in the Temple service, in the hand of the High Priest when he takes it out of the profane cup or in the bowl in which he deposits it.

The bowl certainly is a Temple vessel only used for sanctified contents.
38 Babli 49a.
39 "It" is the empty bowl into which the High Priest deposits his fistful of incense. The next sentence really is a repetition of the question here, whether the same vessel is used for all High Priests or not.
40 May his successor use his incense, presuming it did not become impure by the death. Babli 49a.
41 If only the bowl turns the incense into dedicated material, taking the fistful is a necessary action but must not necessarily be done by him personally; therefore also the successor may continue to use the incense taken by the first High Priest. But it is necessary to switch the last two statements, "one makes to measure for his fists; one does not estimate for all possible fists" to the case that his fists are consecrating, and read here "one does not make to measure for his fists; one estimates for all possible fists."

(42b line 40) הַגָּדוֹל לְפִי גוֹדְלוֹ. אֲפִילוּ כְּבֶן קְמְחִית כְּבֶן קְמְחִית שֶׁהָיְיתָה יָדוֹ מַחְזֶקֶת כְּאַרְבַּעַת קַבִּין. וְהַקָּטָן לְפִי קוֹטְנוֹ. אֲפִילוּ כְּבֶן גַּמְלָא שֶׁלֹּא הָיְתָה יָדוֹ מַחְזֶקֶת אֶלָּא כִשְׁנֵי זֵיתִים.

"A big person according to his bigness," even like Ben Qimḥit whose hand contained about four *qab*[42], "and a small person according to his smallness," even like Ben Gamla, whose hand contained only about two olives.

הִילּוּךְ בְּזָר מָהוּ. חִזְקִיָּה אָמַר. הִילּוּךְ בְּזָר כָּשֵׁר. רִבִּי יַנַּאי אָמַר. הִילּוּךְ בְּזָר פָּסוּל. מַתְנִיתָה פְלִיגָא עַל רִבִּי יַנַּאי. קִבֵּל בִּימִינוֹ וְנָתַן לִשְׂמֹאלוֹ יַחֲזִיר לִימִינוֹ. וּשְׂמֹאלוֹ לֹא כְזָר הִיא. תִּיפְתָּר שֶׁהָיְתָה שְׂמֹאלוֹ כְּלַפֵּי לִפְנִים. אָמַר רִבִּי בָא. וַאֲפִילוּ תֵימַר. כְּלַפֵּי לַחוּץ. שַׁנְיָיא הִיא הִילּוּךְ בְּזָר שַׁנְיָיא הִיא מֵאֵילָיו. אָמַר רִבִּי זְעוּרָה. פְּשִׁיטָא יָד לֹא עָשׂוּ אוֹתָהּ כְּהִילּוּךְ. מַתְנִיתָה פְלִיגָא עַל רִבִּי יַנַּאי. נִשְׁפַּךְ מִן הַכְּלִי עַל הָרִצְפָּה וַאֲסָפוֹ כָּשֵׁר. אָמַר רִבִּי בֵּיבַי. תִּיפְתָּר שֶׁהָיָה מִתְגַּלְגֵּל כְּלַפֵּי לִפְנִים. אָמַר רִבִּי בָא. וַאֲפִילוּ תֵימַר. כְּלַפֵּי לַחוּץ. שַׁנְיָיא הִיא הִילּוּךְ בְּזָר שַׁנְיָיא הִיא הִילּוּךְ מֵאֵילָיו. אָמַר רִבִּי זְעוּרָה. פְּשִׁיטַת יָד עָשׂוּ אוֹתָהּ כְּהִילּוּךְ. מַתְנִיתָה פְלִיגָא עַל רִבִּי יַנַּאי. נָטַל אֶת הַמַּחְתָּה בִּימִינוֹ וְאֶת הַכַּף בִּשְׂמֹאלוֹ. שַׁנְיָיא הִיא שֶׁאֵינוֹ יָכוֹל לַעֲשׂוֹתוֹ. יִתְּלֶה אוֹתוֹ בִזְרוֹעוֹ. אֵינוֹ דֶרֶךְ כָּבוֹד. וְיַחֲלִיף. סָבְרִין מֵימַר. אִם הֶחֱלִיף פָּסוּל. וְיַחְתִּי. אִם הֶחֱתִי מִימִינוֹ לִשְׂמֹאלוֹ כָּשֵׁר. וְאָמַר אוֹף תַּמָּן. תַּמָּן אִם הֶחֱתִי פָּסוּל. [אִם הֶחֱלִיף פָּסוּל.] בְּרַם הָכָא אִם הֶחֱתִי כָּשֵׁר. אִם הֶחֱלִיף פָּסוּל.

הַכֹּל מוֹדִין שֶׁאִם הִכְנִיסָן אַחַת אַחַת כִּיפֵּר. אֶלָּא שֶׁהוּא עוֹבֵר מִשֵּׁם הַכְנָסָה [יְתֵירָה]. עַל אֵיזֶה מֵהֶן הוּא עוֹבֵר. חֲבֶרַיָּא אָמְרִי. עַל הָאַחֲרוֹנָה. אָמַר לוֹ רִבִּי יוֹסֵי. אוֹמֵר לוֹ. הִיכָּנֵס. וְאַתְּ אָמַר הָכֵין. אֶלָּא עַל הָרִאשׁוֹנָה. תַּמָּן תַּנֵּינָן. הִשְׁתַּחֲוָה אוֹ שֶׁשָּׁהָה בִּכְדֵי הִשְׁתַּחֲוָיָה. עַל אֵיזֶה מֵהֶן הוּא עוֹבֵר. חֲבֶרַיָּא אָמְרִי. עַל הָרִאשׁוֹנָה. אָמַר לוֹ רִבִּי יוֹסֵי. אוֹמֵר לוֹ. צֵא. וְאַתְּ אָמַר הָכֵין. אֶלָּא עַל הָאַחֲרוֹנָה.

What is the status of motion by an Non-Cohen[43]? Hizqiah said, motion by a Non-Cohen is qualified. Rebbi Yannai said, motion by a Non-Cohen is disqualified. A Mishnah disagrees with Rebbi Yannai[44]: "If he received with his right hand and put it in his left hand, he shall return it to his right hand." Is his left hand not like a Non-Cohen? Explain it if his left hand was towards the inside[45]. Rebbi Abba said, even if you are saying, towards the outside, there is a difference between motion by a Non-Cohen and one which is automatic. Rebbi Ze`ira said, they did not consider a movement of his hand as motion. A Mishnah disagrees with Rebbi Yannai:[46] "If from the vessel something was spilled on the floor and he collected it, it is qualified." Rebbi Bevai said, explain it if it was rolling towards the inside. Rebbi Abba said, even if you are saying towards the outside, there is a difference between motion by a Non-Cohen and one which is automatic. Rebbi Ze`ira said, they did consider a movement of his hand as motion. The Mishnah disagrees with Rebbi Yannai: "He took the fire-pan[2] into his right hand and the cup in his left." There is a difference because he cannot do it otherwise. Should he hang it on his arm? It is not respectful. May he switch? They wanted to say[47], if he switched it was disqualified. Should he lower it[48]? If he lowered it from his right hand to his left hand it is qualified. Could we say that also there[49], let him lower it? There if he lowered it it is disqualified. [If he switched it is disqualified.][50] But here if he lowered it it is qualified; if he switched it is disqualified[51].

Everybody agrees that if he brought them inside one by one, he atoned, but he transgresses because of unnecessary entry[52]. About which one does he transgress? The colleagues say, about the last one. Rebbi Yose said to him, one tells him to enter and you are saying so? But it is about the first one. There, we have stated[53]: "If he prostrated himself, or tarried that he could have prostrated himself, or left on a lengthy path, he is liable[60]." About which one is he liable? The colleagues say, about the first one. Rebbi Yose said to him, one tells him to leave and you are saying so? But it is about the last one.

42 About 8 liter.

43 This question cannot be about the Day of Atonement, where not even an ordinary Cohen may perform one of the duties of the High Priest, but of the regular service in the Temple, except those where the verse explicitly prescribes that a Cohen has to move the object; cf. *Lev.* 1:15.

44 Mishnah *Zevahim* 3:2. As a rule, sacral acts by the priests have to be performed with their right hands. Therefore the blood of a sacrifice has to be collected by the Cohen in a sacred vessel held in his right hand; if later he temporarily switches the vessel to his left hand he may return it to his right hand and it remains qualified.

45 If he returns the vessel to the right hand he increases its distance from the altar; this is not part of the transport of the blood to the altar.

46 Mishnah *Zevahim* 3:2.

47 The unanimous opinion of the members of the Academy although there is no tannaitic statement to guide the decision.

48 Put the vessel in his left hand under the right hand to support the right hand.

49 Can one say in the case from *Zevah*im that the vessel could remain in his left hand if it is held on his right hand side below his right hand?

50 Addition by the corrector; correct but not absolutely necessary.

51 If the fire pan is in his left hand and the cup with the dry incense powder in his right hand.

52 An unnecessary entry into the Holiest

of Holies is a deadly sin, *Lev.* 16:2.

53 Mishnah *Ševuot* 2:4 (Note 60). The text there, reported in slightly different formulation, seems to be the correct one: "How is that? About which of them does he become liable? About the first or the last? The colleagues say, about the first. Rebbi Yose told them, one says to him, leave, and you say about the first? But we must hold about the last." The improper behavior was that he tarried, not that he entered when pure. This parallels the first case, where the first entry was necessary and therefore legitimate, only the second one is unnecessary and sinful.

(42b line 62) וּבֵינֵיהֶן אַמָּה. אָמַר רִבִּי הִילָא. זֵיכֶר לַדָּבָר. כַּהִיא דְתַנִּינָן תַּמָּן. אַמָּה טַרְקְסִין. עֶשְׂרִים אַמָּה לְבֵית קוֹדֶשׁ הַקֳּדָשִׁים. מַהוּ אַמָּה טַרְקְסִין. רִבִּי יוֹנָה בּוֹצְרָיָא אָמַר. טִירְקְסוֹן. מַה מִבִּפְנִים מִבַּחוּץ. אָמַר רִבִּי יוֹסֵי. מִן מַה דִכְתִיב וְאַרְבָּעִים בָּאַמָּה הָיָה הַבַּיִת הוּא הַהֵיכָל לִפְנָיִי. הָדָא אָמְרָה. מִבִּפְנִים. אָמַר לֵיהּ רִבִּי מָנָא. וְהֶכְתִיב וַיַּעַשׂ אֶת־בֵּית קוֹדֶשׁ הַקֳּדָשִׁים עֶשְׂרִים אַמָּה. הֲוֵי מִבַּחוּץ. מַה טַעֲמוֹן דְּרַבָּנָן. וְהִבְדִּילָה הַפָּרֹכֶת לָכֶם וגו׳. מַה עָבַד לָהּ רִבִּי יֹסֵי. בֵּין קוֹדֶשׁ קָדָשִׁים שֶׁלְמַעְלָן לְקוֹדֶשׁ קָדָשִׁים שֶׁלְמַטָּן. וְלֵית לְרַבָּנָן כֵּן. אִית לוֹן כַּהִיא דְתַנִּינָן. וְרוֹשֶׁם פְּסִיפָּסִין מַבְדִּיל בָּעֲלִיָּה בֵּין קוֹדֶשׁ לְבֵין קוֹדֶשׁ הַקֳּדָשִׁים.

"With one cubit between them." Rebbi Hila said, this[54] is hinted at as we have stated there[55], "One cubit *taraqsin*, twenty cubits for the building of the Holiest of Holies." What is "one cubit *taraqsin*"? Rebbi Jonah from Bostra said, "confusion", what is inside-outside[56]. Rebbi Yose said, since it is written[57], *forty cubits was the House, that is the inner Temple*, it means that it is counted inside. Rebbi Mana said to him, but it is written[58], *he made the building of the Holiest of Holies, . . . , twenty cubits*, it means that it is counted outside. What is the rabbis' reason? *The gobelin shall separate for you*[59], etc.? What does Rebbi Yose do with this[60] Between the Holiest of Holies above and the Holiest of Holies below[61]. Do the rabbis not have this? They have it as we have stated[62], "the impression of pebbles[63] distinguish above between holy and the Holiest of Holies."

54 That in contrast to the First temple, the Second had two gobelins, the interior one belonging to the Holiest of Holies and the exterior one belonging to the Temple Hall, with a cubit in between. The problem whether the cubit between interior and exterior gobelins belongs to the Temple Hall or the Holies of Holies is quoted as undecidable in *Kilaim* 8:5 where part of the text is found (Notes 93-95) and Babli 52a.

55 Mishnah *Middot* 4:7.

56 Jastrow's conjecture that טרקסין is Greek τάραξιν, accusative of τάραξις, "confusion"; cf. *Kilaim* 8:5 Note 93.

57 *1K.* 6:17.
58 *2Chr.* 3:8. Since the reports about the first Temple do not mention the cubit in between, all they prove is that the interior gobelin belongs to the Holiest of Holies and the exterior one to the Temple Hall.
59 *Ex.* 26:33. This is R. Yose's (the Tanna) reason that only one gobelin is possible between the Temple Hall and the Holiest of Holies. How can the rabbis explain the verse?
60 In this and the next sentence, the places of "R. Yose" and "the rabbis" have to be switched since the simple meaning of the verse supports R. Yose. Tosephta 2:12.
61 The rabbis will dispute that even in the first Temple there was only one gobelin. Since there must be an opening for the High Priest to enter the Holiest of Holies, a complete separation so that the Holiest of Holies cannot be seen from the Temple Hall requires a minimum of two gobelins, one being closed at the place where the other is open. But on the roof of the building there was only one separating line.
62 Mishnah *Middot* 4:5.
63 Greek ψῆφος.

(42b line 70) **הלכה ג׃** תַּנֵּי. מִן הַמְּנוֹרָה וּלְדָרוֹם הָיָה נִכְנָס. דִּבְרֵי רִבִּי מֵאִיר. רִבִּי יוֹסֵי אוֹמֵר. מִן הַשּׁוּלְחָן וּלְצָפוֹן הָיָה נִכְנָס. אִית תַּנָּיֵי תַנֵּי. מִמִּזְבֵּחַ הַזָּהָב וְלַמְּנוֹרָה הָיָה נִכְנָס. מְהַלֵּךְ בֵּינֵיהֶן עַד שֶׁהוּא מַגִּיעַ לַצָּפוֹן. דּוֹחֵק הָיָה בָּאַצִּילֵי יָדָיו שֶׁלֹּא יִשָּׂרְפוּ הַפָּרֹכוֹת. הִגִּיעַ לַצָּפוֹן וְהָפַךְ פָּנָיו לַדָּרוֹם. חוֹזֵר הָיָה לַאֲחוֹרָיו כְּדֵי שֶׁלֹּא יְהֵא נִרְאֶה כְּמַפְסִיעַ בֵּין הַבַּדִּים. כֵּיצַד הוּא עוֹשֶׂה. אָמַר רִבִּי חֲנִינָה. מַנִּיחַ אֶת הַכַּף בָּאָרֶץ וְזוֹרְקָהּ בָּאַוֵּיר וְקוֹלְטָהּ בַּמַּחְתָּה. שְׁמוּאֵל אָמַר. בּוֹדְדָהּ בְּרַגְלוֹ. אָמַר רִבִּי יוֹחָנָן. מְעָרֶה מִתּוֹךְ הַכַּף וְהִיא מְתַמֶּרֶת וְעוֹלָה. וְאַחַר כָּךְ הִיא פוֹסָה וְיוֹרֶדֶת.

Halakhah 3: [64]It was stated: He enters South of the candelabrum,[65] the words of Rebbi Meïr; Rebbi Yose says, he enters North of the Table[66]. Some Tannaim state, he was entering between the golden altar and the candelabrum[67]. He walks between them until he reaches the North. He pushes with his elbows so that the gobelins should not be burned. When he arrives at the North he turns his face to the South. He retraces his steps lest he be seen as striding between the beams. How does he do it? Rebbi Hanina said, he puts the bowl on the ground, throws it in the air and catches it with the fire-pan[68]. Samuel said, he pushes it with his hands. Rebbi Johanan said, he empties the cup[69] and it rises straight up, then it expands and descends.

64 Starting discussion of Mishnah 2.
65 Which is standing at the South wall of the Sanctuary, *Ex.* 40:24, 2.5 cubits from the wall, Tosephta 2:12.
66 R. Yose admits only one gobelin. The table was at the North wall, *Ex.* 40:22.
67 Somewhat North of the candelabrum Tosephta 2:12, Babli 51b.
68 He and Samuel read the requirement that the High Priest put "his full fistfuls" of

incense into the fire that in the Holiest of Holies he also has to use both his hands to put the incense in the fire, which leaves no hand free to hold the cup, forcing an acrobatic feat. Differently Babli 49b.

69 He holds that the biblical requirement is satisfied by using his fists in putting the incense into the cup. Having deposited the fire pan, the High Priest may take the cup into his right hand and empty it into the firepan. Opinion not mentioned in the Babli.

(42c line 2) יָצָא וּבָא לוֹ דֶּרֶךְ כְּנִיסָתוֹ. כְּרִבִּי יוֹסֵה. בְּרַם כְּרִבִּי מֵאִיר אֲפִילוּ בָעֵי לָא יָכִיל. לָמָּה. שֶׁלֹּא יִתֵּן אֲחוֹרָיו לַקּוֹדֶשׁ.

כְּתִיב וַיָּבֹא שְׁלֹמֹה לַבָּמָה אֲשֶׁר־בְּגִבְעוֹן יְרוּשָׁלִָם. מָה נָן קַייָמִין. אִם מִירוּשָׁלֵם הָיָה בָא. נֵימַר מִירוּשָׁלַיִם לַבָּמָה. אִם מִבָּמָה הָיָה בָא. נֵימַר מִבָּמָה לִירוּשָׁלַיִם הָיָה בָא. אָמַר רִבִּי שְׁמוּאֵל בַּר אֶבוּדָמָא. לַבָּמָה הָיָה בָא שֶׁלֹּא לִיתֵּן אֲחוֹרָיו לַקּוֹדֶשׁ.

"He leaves and returns in the way he entered." Following Rebbi Yose, but following Rebbi Meïr, even if he wants he cannot do it. Why? Not to have his back turned to the Holiness[70].

It is written[71], *Solomon came to the high place in Gibeon to Jerusalem*. Where do we hold? If he came from Jerusalem, we should say "from Jerusalem to the high place." If he came from the high place, we should say, "he came from the high place to Jerusalem." Rebbi Samuel bar Eudaimon said, he came to the high place not to turn his back to the Holiness[72].

70 There is no problem walking backwards according to R. Yose since he simply backs out. But for R. Meïr when he passes back between the gobelins from the North end to the middle he would turn his back towards the Ark, which is a sign of disrespect. Therefore R. Meïr should require that he back out until he is between the gobelins, then go forward until he is close to half way to the South, turn right (West) to face the Ark, and a little later make another 90° turn and walk backwards until he exits into the Temple hall.

71 2 *Chr.* 1:13. In the description of the Chronicler, the Ark was in Jerusalem in a tent erected by David but the Tent of Meeting and Bezalel's altar were in Gibeon. Since the verse is written at the end of the description of Solomon's visit to Gibeon, one would have expected "from the high place" מִבָּמָה (as read by LXX, most modern translators, and the Babli 53a), not "to the high place", לַבָּמָה.

72 Going to Gibeon from Jerusalem he had his face always turned to face the Ark.

(42c line) וּמִתְפַּלֵּל תְּפִלָּה קְצָרָה בַּבַּיִת הַחִיצוֹן. וְכָךְ הָיְתָה תְפִילָּתוֹ שֶׁלְכֹּהֵן גָּדוֹל בְּיוֹם הַכִּיפּוּרִים בְּצֵאתוֹ בְשָׁלוֹם מִן הַקּוֹדֶשׁ. יְהִי רָצוֹן מִלְּפָנֶיךָ י"י אֱלֹהֵינוּ וֵאלֹהֵי אֲבוֹתֵינוּ שֶׁלֹּא תֵצֵא

עָלֵינוּ גָלוּת לֹא בַיוֹם הַזֶּה וְלֹא בַשָּׁנָה הַזֹּאת. וְאִם יָצְאָה עָלֵינוּ גָלוּת בַּיוֹם הַזֶּה אוֹ בַשָּׁנָה הַזֹּאת תְּהָא גָלוּתֵינוּ לִמָקוֹם שֶׁלַּתּוֹרָה. יְהִי רָצוֹן מִלְפָנֶיךָ י"י אֱלֹהֵינוּ וֵאלֹהֵי אֲבוֹתֵינוּ שֶׁלֹא יֵצֵא עָלֵינוּ חִסָרוֹן לֹא בַיוֹם הַזֶּה וְלֹא בַשָּׁנָה הַזֹּאת. וְאִם יָצָא עָלֵינוּ חִסָרוֹן בַּיוֹם הַזֶּה אוֹ בַשָּׁנָה הַזֹּאת יְהֵא חֶסְרוֹנֵינוּ בְחֶסְרוֹן שֶׁלְמִצְווֹת. [וִיהִי רָצוֹן מִלְפָנֶיךָ ה' אֱלֹקֵינוּ וֵאלֹקֵי אֲבוֹתֵינוּ שֶׁתְּהֵא הַשָּׁנָה הַזֹּאת שְׁנַת זוֹל. שְׁנַת שׂוֹבַע. שְׁנַת מַשָׂא וּמַתָּן. שְׁנַת גְשׁוּמָה וּשְׁחוּנָה וּטְלוּלָה. וְשֶׁלֹא יִצְטָרְכוּ עַמְּךָ יִשְׂרָאֵל אֵלוּ לָאֵלוּ. וְאַל תִּפְנֶה לִתְפִילַת יוֹצְאֵי דְרָכִים. רַבָּנָן דְקַסָרִין אָמְרִין. יַעַל עַמְּךָ יִשְׂרָאֵל שֶׁלֹא יִגְבְּהוּ שְׂרָרָה זוּ עַל גַב זוּ]. וְעַל אַנְשֵׁי הַשָּׁרוֹן הָיָה אוֹמֵר. יְהִי רָצוֹן מִלְפָנֶיךָ י"י אֱלֹהֵינוּ וֵאלֹהֵי אֲבוֹתֵינוּ שֶׁלֹא יֵעָשׂוּ בָתֵּיהֶן קִבְרֵיהֶ

"He prays a short prayer." And this was the High Priest's prayer on the Day of Atonement when he left the Holiness in peace: "May it be the will before You, Eternal our God and God of our fathers, that there shall be no exile decreed over us, not today and not this year. But if exile was decreed over us today or this year that our exile be at a place of Torah. May it be the will before You, Eternal our God and God of our fathers, that there shall be no loss decreed over us, not today and not this year. But if loss was decreed over us today or this year that it be loss for good deeds. [May it be the will before You, Eternal our God and God of our fathers, that this year be a year of cheapness, a year of satiety, a year of trade, a year of rains, sunshine, and dew, and that your people Israel should not need one another, and do not turn to the prayer of travellers. The rabbis of Caesarea are saying, and on your people Israel that they not erect dominion one over the other.]⁷³ And for the people of Sharon he was saying, may it be the will before You, Eternal our God and God of our fathers, that their houses not turn into their graves⁷⁴".

73 The text in brackets is a corrector's addition; it is from a source close to *Lev. rabba* 20(4). Since there, instead of "The rabbis of Caesarea are saying, and on your people Israel that they not erect dominion one over the other" one reads, "the rabbis of Caesarea were saying about our brothers in Caesarea, that they should not be oppressed by officials," it seems that both the original Yerushalmi text as quite certainly the corrector's addition (and similarly the Babli's text in *Ta`anit* 24b) are not meant to prescribe a prayer text to the High Priest but indicate the text of the High Priest's prayer in the re-enactment of his service in the *Musaf*-prayer of the Day of Atonement and describe the political situation in the 4ᵗʰ Cent. C. E..

The undesirable prayer of travellers is one for absence of rains in the rainy season.

74 Their adobe houses are in danger of collapse during the rainy season. In *Lev. rabba* 20(4) the text reads: "The rabbis of the South (meaning of Lydda) said about our

brethren in the Sharon, that their houses should not turn into their graves." This also is from the Yerushalmi *Musaf* service.

(42c line 22) וְלֹא הָיָה מַאֲרִיךְ שֶׁלֹּא לְהַבְעִית אֶת יִשְׂרָאֵל: מַעֲשֶׂה בְּאֶחָד שֶׁהֶאֱרִיךְ וְגָמְרוּ לְהִיכָּנֵס אַחֲרָיו. אָמְרוּ. שִׁמְעוֹן הַצַּדִּיק הָיָה. אָמְרוּ לוֹ. לָמָּה הֶאֱרַכְתָּה. אָמַר לָהֶן. מִתְפַּלֵּל הָיִיתִי עַל מִקְדַּשׁ אֱלֹהֵיכֶם שֶׁלֹּא יֵחָרֵב. אָמְרוּ לוֹ. אַף עַל פִּי כֵן לֹא הָיִיתָ צָרִיךְ לְהַאֲרִיךְ.

אַרְבָּעִים שָׁנָה שִׁימֵּשׁ שִׁמְעוֹן הַצַּדִּיק אֶת יִשְׂרָאֵל בִּכְהוּנָּה גְדוֹלָה. וּבַשָּׁנָה הָאַחֲרוֹנָה אָמַר לָהֶן. בַּשָּׁנָה הַזֹּאת אֲנִי מֵת. אָמְרוּ לוֹ. מֵאַיְכָן אַתָּה יוֹדֵעַ. אָמַר לָהֶן. כָּל־שָׁנָה וְשָׁנָה שֶׁהָיִיתִי נִכְנָס לְבֵית קוֹדֶשׁ הַקֳּדָשִׁים הָיָה זָקֵן אֶחָד לְבוּשׁ לְבָנִים וְעָטוּף לְבָנִים נִכְנָס עִמִּי וְיוֹצֵא עַמִּי. וּבַשָּׁנָה הַזּוֹ נִכְנָס עִמִּי וְלֹא יָצָא עִמִּי. בְּעוֹן קוֹמֵי רִבִּי אַבָּהוּ. וְהָכְתִיב כָּל־אָדָ֞ם לֹא־יִהְיֶ֣ה ׀ בְּאֹ֤הֶל מוֹעֵד֙ בְּבֹא֣וֹ לְכַפֵּ֣ר בַּקֹּ֔דֶשׁ עַד־צֵאת֑וֹ. אֲפִילוּ אוֹתָן שֶׁכָּתוּב בָּהֶן וּדְמוּת פְּנֵיהֶם פְּנֵי אָדָם לֹא יִהְיֶה בְּאֹהֶל מוֹעֵד. אָמַר לוֹן. מַה אֲמַר לִי דַּהֲוָה בַּר נָשׁ. אֲנִי אוֹמֵר. הַקָּדוֹשׁ צָּבָרוּךְ הוּא הָיָה.

"He was not prolonging his prayer not to frighten Israel." [75]It happened that one prolonged and they decided to enter after him[76]. One said, it was Simeon the Just. They said to him, why did you prolong? He answered them, I was praying for the Sanctuary of your God that it should not be destroyed. They said to him, nevertheless, you should not have prolonged.

[77]Simeon the Just served Israel as High Priest for forty years, and in the last year he told them, in this year I am going to die. They asked him, from where do you know? He said to them, every year when I entered the Holiest of Holies, an old man dressed in white and his head wrapped in white entered with me and left with me. But this year he entered with me but did not leave with me. [78]They asked before Rebbi Abbahu: Is it not written[79], *nobody shall be in the Tent of Meeting during his coming to atone in the sanctuary until he leaves*, not even those about whom it is written[80], *the shapes of their faces are human shapes* shall not be in the Tent of Meeting? He answered them, who tells me that it was a person? I am saying that it was the Holy One, praise to Him[81].

75 Babli 53b
76 To search for his corpse.
77 Babli 39b, *Menahot* 109b; Tosephta *Sotah* 13:8.. The first sentence is quoted in the next Chapter, 6:3.
78 Cf Chapter 1, Notes 220 ff.
79 *Lev.* 16:17.
80 *Ez.* 1:10.
81 In the apparition known as *Shekhina*.

(fol. 42a) **משנה ג:** מִשֶּׁנִּטַּל הָאָרוֹן אֶבֶן הָיְתָה שָׁם מִימוֹת הַנְּבִיאִים הָרִאשׁוֹנִים וּשְׁתִיָּה הָיְתָה נִקְרֵאת גְּבוֹהָה מִן הָאָרֶץ שְׁלֹשָׁה אֶצְבָּעוֹת וְעָלֶיהָ הָיָה נוֹתֵן:

Mishnah 3: From when the Ark was removed there was a stone there from the time of the earlier prophets; it was called Foundation, higher than the ground by three finger widths. On it he deposed it[82].

משנה ד: נָטַל אֶת הַדָּם מִמִּי שֶׁהָיָה מְמָרֵס בּוֹ נִכְנַס לַמָּקוֹם שֶׁנִּכְנַס וְעָמַד בַּמָּקוֹם שֶׁעָמַד וְהִזָּה מִמֶּנּוּ אַחַת לְמַעְלָן וְשֶׁבַע לְמַטָּן וְלֹא הָיָה מִתְכַּוֵּין לְהַזּוֹת לֹא לְמַעְלָן וְלֹא לְמַטָּן אֶלָּא כְּמַצְלִיף. וְכָךְ הָיָה מוֹנֶה. אַחַת. אַחַת וְאַחַת. אַחַת וּשְׁתַּיִם. אַחַת וְשָׁלֹשׁ. אַחַת וְאַרְבַּע. אַחַת וְחָמֵשׁ. אַחַת וָשֵׁשׁ. אַחַת וָשֶׁבַע. יָצָא וְהִנִּיחוֹ עַל כַּן הַזָּהָב שֶׁהָיָה בַּהֵיכָל:

Mishnah 4: He took the blood from the one who was stirring it, entered to the place where he had entered[83], and stood at the place where he had stood, and sprinkled from it once upwards and seven times downwards[84]. He did not intend upwards nor downwards but like one who was spanking[85]. And so was he counting: One, one and one, one and two, one and three, one and four, one and five, one and six, one and seven. He left and put it down on the golden pedestal which was in the Temple.

משנה ה: הֵבִיאוּ לוֹ אֶת הַשָּׂעִיר שְׁחָטוֹ קִבֵּל בַּמִּזְרָק אֶת דָּמוֹ. נִכְנַס לַמָּקוֹם שֶׁנִּכְנַס וְעָמַד בַּמָּקוֹם שֶׁעָמַד וְהִזָּה מִמֶּנּוּ אַחַת לְמַעְלָן וְשֶׁבַע לְמַטָּן וְלֹא הָיָה מִתְכַּוֵּין לְהַזּוֹת לֹא לְמַטָּן וְלֹא לְמַעְלָן אֶלָּא כְּמַצְלִיף. וְכָךְ הָיָה מוֹנֶה וכו'. יָצָא וְהִנִּיחוֹ עַל כַּן הַשֵּׁנִי שֶׁהָיָה בַּהֵיכָל. רִבִּי יְהוּדָה אוֹמֵר לֹא הָיָה שָׁם אֶלָּא כֵן אֶחָד בִּלְבָד.

Mishnah 5: They brought him the he-goat, he slaughtered it and received its blood in a bowl. He entered to the place where he had entered[83], and stood at the place where he had stood, and sprinkled from it once upwards and seven times downwards. He did not intend downwards nor upwards but like one who was spanking. And so was he counting, etc.[86] He left and put it down on the second pedestal which was in the Temple. Rebbi Jehudah says, only one pedestal was there.

משנה ו: נָטַל דַּם הַפָּר וְהִנִּיחַ דַּם הַשָּׂעִיר וְהִזָּה מִמֶּנּוּ עַל הַפָּרוֹכֶת שֶׁכְּנֶגֶד הָאָרוֹן מִבַּחוּץ אַחַת לְמַעְלָן וְשֶׁבַע לְמַטָּן וְלֹא הָיָה מִתְכַּוֵּין לְהַזּוֹת לֹא לְמַעְלָן וְלֹא לְמַטָּן אֶלָּא כְּמַצְלִיף. וְכָךְ הָיָה מוֹנֶה. נָטַל דַּם הַשָּׂעִיר וְהִנִּיחַ דַּם הַפָּר וְהִזָּה מִמֶּנּוּ עַל הַפָּרוֹכֶת שֶׁכְּנֶגֶד הָאָרוֹן מִבַּחוּץ אַחַת לְמַעְלָן וְשֶׁבַע לְמַטָּן וְלֹא הָיָה מִתְכַּוֵּין לְהַזּוֹת לֹא לְמַעְלָן וְלֹא לְמַטָּן אֶלָּא כְּמַצְלִיף. וְכָךְ

הָיָה מוֹנֶה. עֵירָה דַם הַפָּר לְתוֹךְ דַּם הַשָּׂעִיר וְנָתַן אֶת הַמָּלֵא לְתוֹךְ הָרֵיקָן: וְיָצָא אֶל הַמִּזְבֵּחַ אֲשֶׁר לִפְנֵי ה' וְכִפֶּר עָלָיו זֶה מִזְבַּח הַזָּהָב.

Mishnah 6: He took the blood of the bull, and put down the blood of the he-goat[87], and sprinkled from it on the gobelin at the place of the Ark from the outside[88] and sprinkled from it once upwards and seven times downwards. He did not intend upwards nor downwards but like one who was spanking. And so was he counting[86]. He took the blood of the he-goat, and put down the blood of the bull, and sprinkled from it on the gobelin at the place of the Ark from the outside and sprinkled from it once upwards and seven times downwards. He did not intend upwards nor downwards but like one who was spanking. And so was he counting[86]. He poured the blood of the bull into the blood of the he-goat and emptied the full vessel into the empty one[89]. *He shall go out to the altar which is before the Eternal*[90], that is the golden altar[91].

82   The fire pan which in Mishnah 2 was described as being put down between the beams of the Ark.

83   The Holiest of Holies.

84   As the verse prescribes (*Lev.* 16:14), once on the cover of the Ark and seven times in front of it.

85   Lifting his finger to let a drop fly off, and then dropping the finger for another drop.

86   As detailed in Mishnah 4.

87   This Mishnah follows R. Jehudah who insists that there was only one pedestal; therefore the bowl with the bull's blood had to be lifted before the one with the he-goat's blood could be deposited.

88   On the gobelin in the Temple Hall, just opposite the place of the Ark in the Holiest of Holies.

89   In order to improve the mixing of the two kinds of blood.

90   *Lev.* 16:18/

91   The incense altar in the Temple Hall.

(42c line 34) **הלכה ד**: תַּנֵּי. עַד שֶׁלֹּא הִגְנַז הָאָרוֹן הָיָה נִכְנָס וְיוֹצֵא לְאוֹרוֹ שֶׁלָּאָרוֹן. מִשֶּׁנִּיטַל הָאָרוֹן הָיָה מְנַשֵּׁשׁ וְנִכְנָס מְנַשֵּׁשׁ וְיוֹצֵא.

אָמַר רִבִּי יוֹחָנָן. לָמָּה נִקְרָא שְׁמָהּ אֶבֶן שְׁתִיָּיה. שֶׁמִּמֶּנָּה הוּשְׁתָה הָעוֹלָם. תַּנֵּי רִבִּי חִיָּיה. וְלָמָּה נִקְרָא אֶבֶן שְׁתִיָּיה. שֶׁמִּמֶּנָּה הוּשְׁתָה הָעוֹלָם. כָּתוּב מִזְמוֹר לְאָסָף אֵל | אֱלֹהִים י"י דִּבֶּר וַיִּקְרָא־אָרֶץ וגו'. מִצִּיּוֹן מִכְלַל יֹפִי אֱלֹהִים הוֹפִיעַ· וְאוֹמֵר הִנְנִי יִסַּד בְּצִיּוֹן אָבֶן וגו'.

Halakhah 4: It was stated: Before the Ark was hidden[92] he entered and exited by the light of the Ark. After the Ark was removed he was groping and entering, groping and leaving.

[93]Rebbi Johanan said, why is it called Foundation Stone? Because on it the world is based. Rebbi Hiyya stated:[94] "Why is it called Foundation Stone? Because on it the world is based.. It is written[95], *a psalm of Asaph; the power, God, the Eternal, spoke and called the earth*, etc., *from Zion, the perfection of beauty, God appears*. And it says[96], *behold I founded in Zion a stone*, etc."

92	Babli 53b/54a; cf. *Šeqalim* 6:1-2.	95	*Ps.* 50:1-2.
93	Babli 54b.	96	*Is.* 28:16.
94	Tosephta 2:14.		

(42c line 39) מַהוּ כְּמַצְלִיף. רִבִּי שְׁמוּאֵל בַּר חֲנַנְיָה בְשֵׁם רִבִּי לְעָזָר. כִּמְטַוְורֵד. אָמַר רִבִּי יוֹחָנָן. כְּדֵי שֶׁלֹּא יִטְעֶה. אָמַר רִבִּי זְעִירָא. כְּדֵי שֶׁיִּגְמוֹר הַזִּיּוֹתָיו מִתּוֹךְ שֶׁבַע. וְהָא קָתַנֵּי. שֶׁבַע וָאַחַת. אָמַר רִבִּי בּוּן. כָּתוּב אֶל פְּנֵי הַכַּפֹּרֶת שֶׁבַע. מַה תַּלְמוּד לוֹמַר יַזֶּה. כְּדֵי שֶׁתְּהֵא הַזָּייָה רִאשׁוֹנָה נִמְנֵית עִמָּהֶן.

What means כְּמַצְלִיף? Rebbi Samuel bar Hananiah in the name of Rebbi Eleazar: Like one who whips[97].

Rebbi Johanan said, so he should not err[98]. Rebbi Ze'ira said, that he should finish his sprinkling with "seven"[99]. But was it not stated[100], "seven and one"? Rebbi Abun said, it is written[101], *before the cover .. seven*. Why does the verse say, *he shall sprinkle*? That the first sprinkling should be counted with them[102].

97 Explanation of the Babli. *Arukh* reads כמטברר and explains "moves his hand towards the navel."
98 This refers to the way of counting as explained in Mishnah 4. Why does he have to count 1+n? Babli 55a.
99 Since in all he has to sprinkle 8 times, it is preferable to end with "7" which is an odd number and means "luck".
100 The prefix ק is Babylonian Aramaic.

The version in which the second number precedes the first is R. Jehudah's in Tosephta 2:14, R. Meïr's in the Babli 55a.
101 *Lev.* `16:14; cf. Note 84.
102 Sprinkling is mentioned separately for the blood on the cover of the Ark and the seven times in front of the Ark. Therefore they have to be mentioned separately in counting. Babli 55a.

(42c line 43) **הלכה ה**: כָּתוּב וְהִזָּה אוֹתוֹ עַל־הַכַּפֹּרֶת. יָכוֹל עַל גַּגָּהּ. תַּלְמוּד לוֹמַר לִפְנֵי הַכַּפֹּרֶת. יָכוֹל עַל מִצְחָהּ. תַּלְמוּד לוֹמַר עַל וְלִפְנֵי. רִבִּי זְעוֹרָה אָמַר. צָרִיךְ שֶׁיְּהֵא נוֹגֵעַ. רִבִּי

שְׁמוּאֵל בַּר רַב יִצְחָק אָמַר. אֵינוֹ צָרִיךְ שֶׁיְּהֵא נוֹגֵעַ. אָמַר רִבִּי בּוּן בַּר חִיָּיה. טַעֲמָא דְרִבִּי שְׁמוּאֵל בַּר רַב יִצְחָק. וְהִזָּה אוֹתוֹ עַל־הַכַּפּוֹרֶת וְלִפְנֵי הַכַּפּוֹרֶת. מַה כַּפּוֹרֶת שֶׁנֶּאֱמַר לְהַלָּן. עַל מִצְחָהּ לֹא עַל גַּנָּהּ וְאֵינוֹ צָרִיךְ שֶׁיְּהֵא נוֹגֵעַ. אַף כַּפּוֹרֶת שֶׁנֶּאֱמַר כָּאן עַל מִצְחָהּ לֹא עַל גַּנָּהּ וְאֵינוֹ צָרִיךְ שֶׁיְּהֵא נוֹגֵעַ. אָמַר רִבִּי יוֹסֵה. מִיסָּבוֹר סָבַר רִבִּי בּוּן בַּר חִיָּיה. הַזָּיוֹת שָׂעִיר שֶׁלְּמַעֲלָה לְמֵידוֹת מֵהַזָּיוֹת פָּר שֶׁלְּמַעֲלָן. וְאֵינוֹ כֵּן. אֶלָּא הַזָּיוֹת [שָׂעִיר] שֶׁלְּמַעֲלָן לְמֵידוֹת מֵהַזָּיוֹת פָּר שֶׁלְּמַטָּן.

Halakhah 5: It is written[103], *he shall sprinkle it on the cover*. I could think on its top, the verse says, *in front of the cover*. I could think on its front, the verse says, *on, in front of*[104]. Rebbi Ze`ira said, it needs to touch; Rebbi Samuel bar Rav Isaac said, it does not need to touch. Rebbi Abun bar Ḥiyya said, the reason of Rebbi Samuel bar Rav Isaac: *he shall sprinkle it on the cover and in front of the cover*. Since "the cover" mentioned there[105] means in front of but not on its top and it does not need to touch, also "the cover" mentioned here[106] means in front of but not on its top and it does not need to touch. Rebbi Yose said, Rebbi Abun bar Ḥiyya thinks that the upwards sprinkling of the he-goat is inferred from the upwards sprinkling of the bull, but it is not so, but the upwards sprinkling of the he-goat is inferred from the downwards sprinkling of the bull[107]:

103 *Lev.* 16:15, about the blood of the he-goat.

104 Therefore the blood of the he-goat must be sprinkled both on and in front of the cover. No numbers are indicated.

105 About the bull, where it is spelled out (v. 14) that the High Priest with his finger sprinkles *to the East towards the front of the cover* and *seven times in front of the cover*.

106 About the he-goat's blood (v. 15).

107 Therefore the disagreement between R. Ze`ira and R. Samuel bar Rav Isaac remains open.

וְהִזָּה אוֹתוֹ [לִפְנֵי הַכַּפּוֹרֶת]. מְלַמֵּד שֶׁהוּא נוֹתֵן אַלַּת לְמַעֲלָן. וְלִפְנֵי הַכַּפּוֹרֶת. אֵינִי יוֹדֵעַ כַּמָּה. הֲרֵי אֲמִי דָן. נֶאֱמַר מַתַּן דָּמִים בְּפָר לְמַטָּן. וְנֶאֱמַר מַתַּן דָּמִים בְּשָׂעִיר לְמַטָּן. מַה מַתַּן דָּמִים אֲמוּרִין בְּפָר לְמַטָּן שֶׁבַע אַף מַתַּן דָּמִים אֲמוּרִין בְּשָׂעִיר לְמַטָּן שֶׁבַע. (הָא) [אוֹ לְכָה] לְךָ לְדֶרֶךְ הַזּוֹ. נֶאֶמְרוּ דָמִים לְמַעֲלָן וְנֶאֱמְרוּ דָמִים לְמַטָּן. מַה דָּמִים אֲמוּרִין בּוֹ לְמַעֲלָן אַחַת אַף דָּמִים אֲמוּרִין בּוֹ לְמַטָּן אַחַת. נִרְאָה לְמִי דוֹמֶה. דָּנִין שֶׁלְּמַטָּן מִשֶּׁלְּמַטָּן. וְאֵין דָּנִין שֶׁלְּמַטָּן מִשֶּׁלְּמַעֲלָן. אוֹ לְכָה לְךָ לְדֶרֶךְ הַזּוֹ. דָּנִין דַּם הַשָּׂעִיר מִדַּם הַשָּׂעִיר. וְאֵין דָּנִין דַּם הַשָּׂעִיר מִדַּם הַפָּר. תַּלְמוּד לוֹמַר וְעָשָׂה אֶת־דָּמוֹ כַּאֲשֶׁר עָשָׂה לְדַם הַפָּר. מַה דַּם הַפָּר לְמַטָּן שֶׁבַע אַף דַּם הַשָּׂעִיר לְמַטָּה שֶׁבַע. וְאֵינִי יוֹדֵעַ כַּמָּה לִיתֵּן מִדַּם הַפָּר לְמַעֲלָן. נֶאֱמַר מַתַּן דָּמִים בְּשָׂעִיר לְמַעֲלָן וְנֶאֱמַר מַתַּן דָּמִים בַּפָּר לְמַעֲלָן. מַה דָּמִים הָאֲמוּרִין בְּשָׂעִיר לְמַעֲלָן אַחַת אַף מַתַּן דָּמִים

הָאֲמוּרִין בַּפָּר לְמַעְלָן אָחַת. אוֹ לְכָה לָךְ לְדֶרֶךְ הַזּ. נֶאֶמְרוּ דָמִים לְמַטָּן. נֶאֶמְרוּ דָמִים לְמַעְלָן. מַה דָּמִים אֲמוּרִין בּוֹ לְמַטָּה שֶׁבַע אַף דָּמִים אֲמוּרִין בּוֹ לְמַעְלָן שֶׁבַע. נִרְאֶה לְמִי דוֹמֶה. דָּנִין שֶׁלְּמַעְלָן מִשֶּׁלְּמַעְלָן. וְאֵין דָּנִין שֶׁלְּמַעְלָן מִשֶּׁלְּמַטָּן. אוֹ לְכָה לָךְ לְדֶרֶךְ הַזּ. דָּנִין דַּם הַפָּר מִדַּם הַפָּר. וְאֵין דָּנִין דַּם הַפָּר מִדַּם הַשָּׂעִיר. תַּלְמוּד לוֹמַר וְעָשָׂה אֶת־דָּמוֹ כַּאֲשֶׁר עָשָׂה לְדַם הַפָּר. שֶׁיִּהְיוּ כָּל־מַעֲשָׂיו שָׁוִין. מַה מַה דַּם הַפָּר לְמַטָּן שֶׁבַע אַף דַּם הַשָּׂעִיר לְמַטָּן שֶׁבַע. מַה דַּם הַשָּׂעִיר לְמַעְלָן אַחַת אַף דַּם הַפָּר לְמַעְלָן אַחַת.

[108]"*He shall sprinkle it*[103], [*in front of the cover*][109], this teaches that he gives a single one upwards[110]. *In front of the cover*, I do not know how many[111]. So I am arguing: It mentions giving the bull's blood downwards, and it mentions giving the he-goat's blood downwards. Since giving the bull's blood downwards as mentioned is seven times[112], so giving the he-goat's blood downwards as mentioned must be seven times. Or go in the following way: Blood is mentioned upwards and blood is mentioned downwards. Since the blood mentioned upwards is once, so the blood mentioned downwards must be once. Let us see to what it is comparable. One argues downwards from downwards; one does not argue downwards from upwards. Or go in the following way: One argues he-goat's blood from he-goat's blood; but one does not argue he-goat's blood from bull's blood. The verse says, *he shall treat its blood as he treated the bull's blood.* Since the bull's blood is downwards seven times, also the he-goat's blood is downwards seven times. But I do not know how many times to give the bull's blood upwards. Giving the blood upwards is mentioned for the he-goat and giving the blood upwards is mentioned for the bull. Since giving the blood upwards as mentioned for the he-goat is once, so giving the blood upwards as mentioned for the bull is once. Or go in the following way: Blood is mentioned downwards; blood is mentioned upwards. Since the blood mentioned downwards is seven, so the blood mentioned upwards must be seven. . Let us see to what it is similar. One argues upwards from upwards; one does not argue upwards from downwards. Or go in the following way: One argues bull's blood from bull's blood; but one does not argue bull's blood from he-goat's blood. The verse says, *he shall treat its blood as he treated the bull's blood,* that all its works be the same. Since the bull's blood is seven

times downwards, also the he-goat's blood is seven times downwards. Since the he-goat's blood is once upwards, also the bull's blood is once upwards[113]."

108 *Sifra Ahare Parashah* 3(3-7), Babli 55a.
109 Unjustified addition by the corrector.
110 The singular "it" implies a single sprinkling.
111 No numbers are mentioned in *Lev.* 16:15.
112 Explicit in *Lev.* 16:14.
113 The number of sprinklings are uniquely determined, upwards by inference from v. 15, downwards explicitly in v.14.

(42c line 73) הַקּוֹדֶשׁ. צָרִיךְ לְכַוֵּין כְּנֶגֶד הַקּוֹדֶשׁ. אָמַר רִבִּי נְחֶמְיָה. לְפִי שֶׁמָּצָאנוּ בַּפָּר הַבָּא עַל כָּל־הַמִּצְוֹת שֶׁהוּא עוֹמֵד חוּץ לַמִּזְבֵּחַ וּמַזֶּה עַל הַפָּרוֹכֶת בְּשָׁעָה שֶׁהוּא מַזֶּה. יָכוֹל אַף זֶה כֵן. תַּלְמוּד לוֹמַר אֲשֶׁר לִפְנֵי י"י. וְאֵיכָן הָיָה. לִפְנִים מִן הַמִּזְבֵּחַ. אוֹ אֵינוֹ מְדַבֵּר אֶלָּא עַל מִזְבֵּחַ הַחִיצוֹן. תַּלְמוּד לוֹמַר אֲשֶׁר לִפְנֵי י"י. הָא אֵינוֹ מְדַבֵּר אֶלָּא עַל מִזְבֵּחַ הַפְּנִימִי.
הַכֹּל מוֹדִין בַּפַּר מָשִׁיחַ וְעֵדָה שֶׁאֵינוֹ צָרִיךְ שֶׁיְּהֵא נוֹגֵעַ. מַה פְלִיגִין. בְּפַר וְשָׂעִיר שֶׁלְיוֹם הַכִּיפּוּרִים. אִית תַּנָּיֵי תַנֵּי. צָרִיךְ שֶׁיְּהֵא נוֹגֵעַ. אִית תַּנָּיֵי אֵינוֹ צָרִיךְ שֶׁיְּהֵא נוֹגֵעַ. אָמַר רִבִּי לְעָזָר בֵּירִבִּי יוֹסֵי. אֲנִי רְאִיתִיהָ בְּרוֹמִי מְלִיאָה טִיפִּין שֶׁלְדָּם. אָמַרְתִּי. אִילּוּ מִן הַדָּמִים שֶׁהָיוּ מַזִּין עָלֶיהָ בְּיוֹם הַכִּיפּוּרִים. הָדָא אָמְרָה. צָרִיךְ שֶׁיְּהֵא נוֹגֵעַ. [וַאֲפִילוּ תֵּימָא. אֵין צָרִיךְ שֶׁיְּהֵא נוֹגֵעַ.] (וְ)אִם נָגַע נָגַע.

The holiness[114]. He has to aim vis-a-vis the holiness[115]. [116]"Rebbi Nehemiah said, since we find about the bull which comes for all commandments[117] that he stands before the altar and sprinkles on the gobelin at the moment of his sprinkling[118], I could think that here it is the same; the verse says[119], *which is before the Eternal*. Where was he[120]? Inside of the altar. Or does he speak only of the outer altar? The verse says, *which is before the Eternal*. Therefore he only speaks of the inner altar[121]."

Everybody agrees about the bull of the anointed and the community that it need not touch[122]. Where do they disagree? About the bull and the he-goat of the day of Atonement. There are Tannaim who state, it needs to touch. There are Tannaim: it does not need to touch[123]. Rebbi Eleazar ben Rebbi Yose said, I saw it in Rome[124] full of drops of blood. I said, these are of the blood sprinkled on it on the Day of Atonement. This implies that it needs to touch. [Even if you say that it does not need to touch][125], (but)[126] if it touched, it touched.

114 *Lev.* 16:16.
115 This explains the statement of Mishnah 6 that blood sprinkled on the gobelin in the Temple Hall must be applied at the spot in front of the Ark.
116 *Sifra Ahare Pereq* 3(7-8). Babli 59b.
117 This is the expression of the verse (*Lev.* 4:2) to describe the purification offerings required for an anointed High Priest and the High Court; cf. Introduction to Tractate *Horaiot*.
118 Since the High Priest is commanded to bring the blood into the Sanctuary (*Lev.* 4:5), to sprinkle from it seven times on the gobelin (v.6), and without moving give blood on the four corners of the incense altar (v.7), it is clear that he has to stand in front of the altar and sprinkle the blood long distance in the direction of the gobelin.
119 *Lev.* 16:18: *He shall exit to the altar which is before the Eternal.*

120 Coming from the Holiest of Holies the High Priest stands between the gobelin and the altar.
121 Which is standing in the Temple hall directly opposite the ark in the Holiest of Holies.
122 Since the High Priest is standing too far away from the gobelin.
123 The disagreement between R. Ze`ira and R. Samuel bar Rav Isaac is a much older controversy.
124 Babli 37a; cf. 4:1 Note 40. Tosephta 2:14.
125 Addition by the corrector; the argument could be implied by the scribe's text. The form תימא, derived from the Accadic/Babylonian Aramaic root אמא "to speak", is impossible in a Yerushalmi text.
126 Scribe's text.

(42d line 7) נָתַן מִכְּלִי קוֹדֶשׁ לְתוֹךְ כְּלִי חוֹל פָּסַל. הָא מִכְּלִי קוֹדֶשׁ לְתוֹךְ כְּלִי קוֹדֶשׁ לֹא פָסַל. אָמַר רִבִּי חַגַּיי קוֹמֵי רִבִּי יוֹסֵה. מַתְנִיתָה אָמְרָה כֵן. עֵירָה דַם הַפָּר לְתוֹךְ דַּם הַשָּׂעִיר. מַה אַתְּ שָׁמַע מִינָהּ. אָמַר רִבִּי מָנָא. נֵימַר. מִדַּם הַפָּר שֶׁהוּא מָלֵא לְתוֹךְ דַּם הַשָּׂעִיר שֶׁהוּא רֵיקָם. אָמַר רִבִּי יוֹסֵה בֵּירִבִּי בּוּן. עֵירָה דַם הַפָּר לְתוֹךְ דַּם הַשָּׂעִיר מָלֵא. מִיכָּן וְהֵילַךְ חוֹזֵר וּבוֹלְלָן לְתוֹךְ כְּלִי אַחֵר כְּדֵי שֶׁיִּבָּלְלוּ כָּל־צוֹרְכָן.

If one gave from a sanctified vessel[127] to a profane vessel he disqualified[128]. Does this imply that from a sanctified vessel to a sanctified vessel it remains qualified[129]? Rebbi Ḥaggai said before Rebbi Yose, the Mishnah implies this: "He poured the blood of the bull into the blood of the he-goat. Rebbi Mana said, could we say, the blood of the bull from a full vessel into the blood of the he-goat in an empty vessel[130]? Rebbi Yose ben Rebbi Abun said, he poured the blood of the bull from a full vessel into the blood of the he-goat in a full vessel; after that he again mixes them into another vessel[131] to make a perfect mixture.

127 A vessel dedicated to the Temple service.
128 The disqualification is not absolute since Mishnah *Zevahim* 3:2 states that the blood will be qualified if returned to a sanctified vessel . The Babli has another reading of the question, 58a.
129 This question is asked not for the day of Atonement but for all year round. Does blood received in a sanctified vessel have to be brought to the altar in this vessel or not?

130 The Mishnah does not prove anything since the second vessel is not empty; the second vessel is not a replacement of the first.
131 Which in the Mishnah is the original vessel of the bull's blood, but for the mixture it is a new vessel. Therefore in this case one is required to pour blood from the original sanctified vessel into another sanctified vessel. This proves R. Haggai's point.

(42d line 13) מְנַיִין שֶׁהוּא זָקוּק לְהָעֲרוֹת. תַּלְמוּד לוֹמַר וְנָתַן מִדַּם הַפָּר וּמִדַּם הַשָּׂעִיר. בִּזְמַן שֶׁהֵן מְעוּרָבִין. יָכוֹל מִזֶּה בִּפְנֵי עַצְמוֹ וּמִזֶּה בִּפְנֵי עַצְמוֹ. תַּלְמוּד לוֹמַר וְכִפֶּר אַהֲרֹן עַל־קַרְנֹתָיו אַחַת בַּשָּׁנָה. אַחַת בַּשָּׁנָה הוּא מְכַפֵּר. וְאֵינוֹ מְכַפֵּר שְׁתַּיִם בַּשָּׁנָה. אוֹ נֵימַר. דַּם הַפָּר אַחַת בַּשָּׁנָה. לֹא שְׁתַּיִם בַּשָּׁנָה. תַּנֵּי רִבִּי יִשְׁמָעֵאל. מִדַּם חַטַּאת הַכִּפֻּרִים אַחַת בַּשָּׁנָה יְכַפֵּר עָלָיו לְדֹרֹתֵיכֶם. אַחַת בַּשָּׁנָה הוּא מְכַפֵּר. וְאֵינוֹ מְכַפֵּר שְׁתַּיִם בַּשָּׁנָה. הַכֹּל מוֹדִין בְּשֶׁבַע הַזָּאוֹת שֶׁלְּמַטָּן שֶׁהוּא צָרִךְ לְהָעֲרוֹת. דִּכְתִיב [שֶׁבַע] וְלֹא אַרְבַּע עֶשְׂרֵה.

From where that he is required to pour out[132]? The verse says[133], *he shall give of the blood of the bull and the blood of the he-goat*, when they are mixed. I could think each one by itself, the verse says[134], *Aaron shall atone on its corners once yearly*, he atones once yearly, he does not atone twice yearly[135]. Or should we say, the bull's blood once yearly, not twice yearly? Rebbi Ismael stated, *from the blood of the atoning purification offering*[134], he atones once yearly, he does not atone twice yearly. Everybody agrees that for the seven sprinklings downward[136] he has to pour[137], for it is written *seven*, not fourteen.

132 Why must the blood of the bull and the blood of the he-goat be mixed before given on the corners of the golden altar; Mishnah 6. The Babli does not necessarily accept the Mishnah, 57b-58a.
133 *Lev.* 16:18, misquoted.
134 *Ex.* 30:10.
135 Not even one directly after the other.

136 Regarding the incense altar, it is required by *Lev.* 16:19 that the High Priest sprinkle on its top "seven times of the blood." Since no mention is made of bull or he-goat, the verse must refer to the mixed blood. *Sifra Ahare Pereq* 4(8).
137 I. e., to mix..

HALAKHAH FIVE

(42d line 20) קִיבֵּל מִדַּם הַפָּר בִּשְׁלשָׁה כוֹסוֹת וּמִדַּם הַשָּׂעִיר בִּשְׁלשָׁה כוֹסוֹת לִיתֵּן מֵאֶחָד עַל הַבַּדִּין. מֵאֶחָד עַל הַפָּרֹכוֹת. מֵאֶחָד עַל מִזְבַּח הַזָּהָב. אֵי זֶה מֵהֶן זָקוּק לְהֵעָרוֹת. וְיֵשׁ אָדָם מְחַשֵּׁב חֲצִי כַפָּרָה. אֶלָּא כֵינִי. קִיבֵּל מִדַּם הַפָּר בִּשְׁלשָׁה כוֹסוֹת [וּמִדַּם הַשָּׂעִיר בִּשְׁלשָׁה כוֹסוֹת] לִיתֵּן מֵאֶחָד עַל הַבַּדִּים. וּמֵאֶחָד עַל הַפָּרֹכוֹת. וּמֵאֶחָד עַל מִזְבַּח הַזָּהָב. אֵי זֶה מֵהֶן הוּא זָקוּק לְהֵעָרוֹת. תַּפְלוּגְתָּא דְרִבִּי זְעוּרָה וּדְרִבִּי הִילָא. דְּאִיתְפַּלְגוֹן.

הִגְרִיל שְׁלשָׁה זוּגוֹת לִיתֵּן מֵאֶחָד עַל הַבַּדִּים. מֵאֶחָד עַל הַפָּרֹכוֹת. מֵאֶחָד עַל מִזְבַּח הַזָּהָב. אֵי זֶה מֵהֶן מִשְׁתַּלֵּחַ. רִבִּי זְעוּרָה אָמַר. לְכַפֵּר עָלָיו. אֶת שֶׁהוּא מְכַפֵּר בּוֹ חֲבֵירוֹ מִשְׁתַּלֵּחַ. אֶת שֶׁאֵינוֹ מְכַפֵּר אֵין חֲבֵירוֹ מִשְׁתַּלֵּחַ. רִבִּי הִילָא אָמַר. לְכַפֵּר עָלָיו. אֶת שֶׁהוּא גוֹמֵר בּוֹ כָּל־הַכַּפָּרָה חֲבֵירוֹ מִשְׁתַּלֵּחַ. אֶת שֶׁאֵינוֹ גוֹמֵר בּוֹ כָּל־הַכַּפָּרָה אֵין חֲבֵירוֹ מִשְׁתַּלֵּחַ. עַל דַּעְתֵּיהּ דְּרִבִּי זְעוּרָה. שְׁלָשְׁתָּן מִשְׁתַּלְּחִין. עַל דַּעְתֵּיהּ דְּרִבִּי הִילָא. אֵינוֹ מִשְׁתַּלֵּחַ אֶלָּא אַחֲרוֹן בִּלְבָד.

1 זוגות | 6 - הבדים | 6 הבדין 3 אין | 6 בו אין

וְהָכָא עַל דַּעְתֵּיהּ דְּרִבִּי זְעוּרָה. שְׁלָשְׁתָּן הוּא זָקוּק לְהֵעָרוֹת. עַל דַּעְתֵּיהּ דְּרִבִּי הִילָא. אֵינוֹ זָקוּק לְהֵעָרוֹת אֶלָּא אוֹתוֹ שֶׁהִזָּה מִמֶּנּוּ.

If he received of the bull's blood in three cups and of the he-goat's blood in three cups, to give from one between the beams, from one on the gobelins, from one on the golden altar. Which of them is he obligated to pour[138]? May a person think of half an atonement[139]? But it is so: If he received of the bull's blood in three cups [and of the he-goat's blood in three cups,][140] to give from one between the beams, and from one on the gobelins, and from one on the golden altar. Which of them is he obligated to pour? It is a disagreement between Rebbi Ze`ira and Rebbi Hila, since they disagreed:

[141]If he drew lots for three pairs[142], to give from one between the beams, from one on the gobelins, from one on the golden altar. Which of them is sent away? Rebbi Ze`ira said, *to atone on him*[143], one with whom one atones, the companion is sent away; one with whom one does not atone, the companion is not sent away.. Rebbi Hila said, *to atone on him*, one with whom one completes atonement, the companion is sent away. one with whom one does not complete atonement, the companion is not sent away. In Rebbi Ze`ira's opinion, all three are sent away. In Rebbi Hila's opinion, only the last one is sent away.

And here, in Rebbi Ze`ira's opinion, he must pour all three; in Rebbi Hila's opinion, he must pour only the one from which he sprinkled[144].

138 To mix for sprinkling on the top of the golden altar. It is obvious that the discussion here presupposes that there be no mixing for giving the blood on the corners of the golden altar; otherwise there would be only two cups possible.

139 Since the he-goat was made a purification sacrifice (Chapter 4 Note 5) and is disqualified if the blood was not received with the appropriate intention (Mishnah *Zevahim* 1:1), the blood must be received with the intent to be used for full atonement. The objection contradicts the anonymous Tanna in Mishnah 9, for whom all actions of the day separate atonements. As seen from the next section, the objection and the reformulation can be disregarded.

140 Addition of the corrector which must be deleted following the argument of the preceding Note.

141 This paragraph is repeated in Halakhah 6:1 (6).

142 Instead of one pair of he-goats there were three; for each group of sprinkling one was slaughtered while the other was alive.

143 *Lev.* 16:10.

144 On the corners of the altar.

(42d line 36) קִיבֵּל דַּם הַפָּר בִּשְׁלשָׁה כוֹסוֹת וּמִדַּם הַשָּׂעִיר בִּשְׁלשָׁה כוֹסוֹת לִיתֵּן מֵאֶחָד עַל הַבַּדִּין. מֵאֶחָד עַל הַפָּרֹכוֹת. מֵאֶחָד עַל מִזְבַּח הַזָּהָב. אֵי זֶה מֵהֶן נִשְׁפָּךְ עַל הַיְסוֹד. תַּפְלוּגְתָּא דְּרִבִּי וּדְרִבִּי אֶלְעָזָר בֵּירִבִּי שִׁמְעוֹן. דְּאִיתְפַּלְגוּן. חַטָּאת שֶׁקִּיבֵּל דָּמָהּ בְּאַרְבָּעָה כוֹסוֹת. נָתַן מִזֶּה אֶחָד וּמִזֶּה אֶחָד וּמִזֶּה אֶחָד. מְנַיִין שֶׁכּוּלָּם נִשְׁפָּכִין עַל הַיְסוֹד. תַּלְמוּד לוֹמַר. אֶת דָּמָהּ יִשְׁפֹּךְ. יָכוֹל אֲפִילוּ לֹא נָתַן מֵאֶחָד מֵהֶן מַתָּן אַרְבַּע יְהוּ כּוּלָּם נִשְׁפָּכִין. תַּלְמוּד לוֹמַר. וְאֶת־כָּל־דָּמָהּ יִשְׁפֹּךְ. הָא כֵיצַד. הוּא נִשְׁפָּךְ עַל הַיְסוֹד וְהֵן נִשְׁפָּכִין לָאַמָּה. דִּבְרֵי רִבִּי. רִבִּי אֶלְעָזָר בֵּירִבִּי שִׁמְעוֹן. מְנַיִין אֲפִילוּ לֹא נָתַן מֵאֶחָד מֵהֶן אֶלָּא אַרְבַּע מַתָּן אַרְבַּע יְהוּ כוּלָּן נִשְׁפָּכִין עַל הַיְסוֹד. תַּלְמוּד לוֹמַר. וְאֶת דָּמָהּ יִשְׁפֹּךְ. עַל דַּעְתֵּיהּ דְּרִבִּי אֶלְעָזָר בֵּירִבִּי שִׁמְעוֹן. כּוּלְּהוֹן נִשְׁפָּכִין עַל הַיְסוֹד. עַל דַּעְתֵּיהּ דְּרִבִּי. אֵין לְךָ נִשְׁפָּךְ עַל הַיְסוֹד אֶלָּא אוֹתוֹ שֶׁהִיָּה מִמֶּנּוּ.

If he received of the bull's blood in three cups and of the he-goat's blood in three cups, to give from one between the beams, from one on the gobelins, from one on the golden altar. Which of them is poured into the base[145]? The disagreement between Rebbi and Rebbi Eleazar ben Rebbi Simeon, as they disagreed: [146]"A purification offering whose blood was received in four cups and from each one he gave one giving[147], from where that all of them are poured on the base? The verse says[148], *and its blood he shall pour.* I could think that if he {only}[149] gave all four givings from one of them, all of them should be poured, the verse says,[150] *and all its blood he shall pour.* How is this? It is poured on the base, and they are emptied into the canal[151], the words of Rebbi. Rebbi Eleazar ben Rebbi Simeon: From where that even if he gave all four givings from one of them, all of them shall be poured on the base? The verse says, *and its blood he shall pour*. In Rebbi Eleazar ben Rebbi Simeon's opinion, all are poured into the base. In Rebbi's opinion, only the one from which he sprinkled is poured[152].

145 While it is not mentioned in *Lev.* 16, it is understood from *Lev.* 4 that the blood remaining after some of it was sprinkled on the four corners of the large altar is poured onto the base of the altar (*Lev.*4:25,30,34). The same is done with the blood of the bull of the anointed and the community (*Lev.*4:7,18) and therefore also applies to the purification offerings of the Day of Atonement.

146 *Sifra Wayyiqra II (Hovah) Pereq* 10(4-6), Babli 57b, *Zevahim* 34b.

147 The "giving" is sprinkling of blood on one corner of the large altar.

148 A misquote from *Lev.*4:25 (it should be דָּמוֹ not דָּמָהּ. All quotes from v. 25 should be replaced by v. 30,34 and vice-versa.

149 Word missing in the text, added from the parallels and needed for logical consistency.

150 *Lev.*4:30,34. See Note 148.

151 The water supply to the Temple which emptied into the Siloam pool.

152 In Rebbi's opinion, only the actual use of blood in a vessel qualifies the remainder to be poured on the base of the altar; in R. Eleazar ben R. Simeon's opinion, all eligible blood in a Temple vessel which is not disqualified is qualified to be poured on the base.

(42d line 47) חֲבֵרַיָּא אָמְרֵי. נִתְפַּגֵּל זֶה נִתְפַּגֵּל זֶה. אָבְדוּ אֵימוּרָיו שֶׁלָּזֶה מַזִּין עַל אֵימוּרָיו שֶׁלָּזֶה. הַכֹּל מוֹדִין בְּפַר מָשִׁיחַ וְעֵדָה עַד שֶׁיְּהֵא שָׁם מַתָּנָה אַחַת מִשֶּׁל שְׁנֵיהֶן. חֲבֵרַיָּא אָמְרֵי. אֵימוּרִין כְּשֵׁירִין שֶׁנִּתְעָרְבוּ בִּפְסוּלִין עַד שֶׁיְּהֵא שָׁם מַתָּנָה אַחַת מִשֶּׁל כְּשֵׁירִין. מָה פְלִיגִין. בְּדַם שְׁנֵי חַטָּאוֹת שֶׁנִּתְעָרְבוּ. רִבִּי אוֹמֵר. אוֹמֵר אֲנִי. רוֹאִין אֶת הַדָּם. אִם יֶשׁ בּוֹ כְדֵי מַתָּנָה אַחַת מִזֶּה וּכְדֵי מַתָּנָה אַחַת מִזֶּה כָּשֵׁר. וְאִם לָאו פָּסוּל. וַחֲכָמִים אוֹמְרִים. אֲפִילוּ אֵין בּוֹ אֶלָּא מַתָּנָה אַחַת [מִשֶּׁל שְׁנֵיהֶן] כָּשֵׁר. עַל דַּעְתֵּיהּ דְּרִבִּי. יֵשׁ שִׁיעוּר לַמַּתָּנוֹת. עַל דַּעְתֵּין דְּרַבָּנָן. אֵין שִׁיעוּר לַמַּתָּנוֹת. הָדָא אָמְרָה. נִתְפַּגֵּל זֶה נִתְפַּגֵּל זֶה. אָבְדוּ אֵימוּרָיו שֶׁלָּזֶה מַזִּין עַל אֵימוּרָיו שֶׁלָּזֶה.

The colleagues say[153], if one becomes *piggul*[154], so does the other; if the parts[155] of one were lost, one sprinkles for the parts of the other. Everybody agrees about the bull of the Anointed or the community[122], unless there be one giving of each of them. The colleagues say, qualified parts which were mixed up with disqualified parts, only if there was a giving[147] of the qualified. Where do they disagree? About the blood of two purification sacrifices which were mixed up. [156]Rebbi says, I am saying one investigates the blood; if there is enough for one giving for each one it is qualified, otherwise it is disqualified. But the Sages say, even if there is only one giving [for both of them]¹⁵⁷ it is qualified. In Rebbi's opinion, there is a measure for givings, in the Sages' opinion there is no measure for givings¹⁵⁸. This implies¹⁵⁹, if one becomes *piggul*, so does the other; if the parts of one were lost, one sprinkles for the parts of the other.

153 They have a tradition that Rebbi disagrees also if the blood of two purification offerings were mixed together in one vessel.

154 *Piggul* is consumption of sacrifices out of their allotted time (*Lev.* 19::7) our out of the proper place. Since a sacrifice cannot become disqualified retroactively, the technical term *piggul* is used to describe the disqualification caused by the intent of future *piggul* in any of the required actions in processing the sacrifice (slaughter, reception of the blood, bringing to the altar, sprinkling on the corners). Processing *piggul* sacrifice is sinful; therefore blood containing *piggul* blood cannot be used; it is disqualified.

155 The fat which is forbidden for human consumption, cf. Chapter 5:2, Note 50.

156 Babli *Zevahim* 95a.

157 Corrector's addition.

158 If Rebbi requires visibly enough blood for two givings, he must require more than a tiny drop for each giving. This amount is not spelled out anywhere. For the Sages a tiny drop is enough and this is available in any mixture, even if not recognizable separately.

159 For the Sages, whom practice has to follow, two separate purification offerings whose blood has been mixed are treated as one body.

(fol. 42a) **משנה ז:** הִתְחִיל מְחַטֵּא וְיֹרֵד. מֵהֵיכָן הוּא מַתְחִיל. מִקֶּרֶן מִזְרָחִית צְפוֹנִית. צְפוֹנִית מַעֲרָבִית. מַעֲרָבִית דְּרוֹמִית. דְּרוֹמִית מִזְרָחִית. מָקוֹם שֶׁהוּא מַתְחִיל בַּחַטָּאת עַל מִזְבֵּחַ הַחִיצוֹן מִשָּׁם הָיָה גוֹמֵר עַל מִזְבֵּחַ הַפְּנִימִי. רִבִּי אֱלִיעֶזֶר אוֹמֵר בִּמְקוֹמוֹ הָיָה עוֹמֵד וּמְחַטֵּא.

Mishnah 7: He¹⁶⁰ started purifying¹⁶¹ and moves. Where does he start? At the Northeast corner¹⁶², Northwest, Southwest, Southeast. At the place where he starts purifyng on the outer altar¹⁶³, there he finishes on the inner altar. Rebbi Eliezer says, he was standing on his place and purifying¹⁶⁴.

160 The High Priest, exiting from the Holiest of Holies, standing at the Southwest corner of the Temple Hall with his face to the West. As the Halakhah explains, he has to continue walking backwards with his face to the West until he stays East of the golden altar; then he turns right to the Northeast corner of the golden altar.

161 This meaning of the root חטא is derived from *Lev.* 14:49. Here it means sprinkling blood on the four corners of the golden altar.

162 If the High Priest stands in front of the altar, the NE corner is the first corner to his right, and there he starts since there is a rule that all voluntary turns in the Temple have to be to the right, the lucky side.

163 There is a walkway around the large outer altar at half height. Since this altar is accessed by the ramp on its South side, if the Cohen turns to his right entering the walkway, the first corner he arrives at is the SE corner. (On the walkway he naturally has to make 4 left turns, but these are forced by his original right turn.)

(42d line 52) **הלכה ו׃** וְיַתְחִיל בְּקֶרֶן מִזְרָחִית דְּרוֹמִית. אָמַר רִבִּי הִילָא. יְמָנִית אֵין זוֹ יְמָנִית. וְיַתְחִיל מִקֶּרֶן צְפוֹנִית מַעֲרָבִית. אָמַר רִבִּי אֶלְעָזָר. וְיָצָא אֶל־הַמִּזְבֵּחַ. וְיַתְחִיל מִקֶּרֶן מַעֲרָבִית דְּרוֹמִית. שֶׁלֹּא יִתֵּן אֲחוֹרָיו לַקּוֹדֶשׁ. וְאֵין סוֹפוֹ לִיתֵּן אֲחוֹרָיו לַקּוֹדֶשׁ. חוֹזֵר הָיָה לַאֲחוֹרָיו. וְיַעֲמוֹד בַּדָּרוֹם וְיַתְחִיל מִקֶּרֶן מִזְרָחִית צְפוֹנִית. כַּיי דְּאָמַר רִבִּי הִילָא. יְמָנִית אֵין זוֹ יְמָנִית.

Halakhah 6: Should he not start at the Southeast corner? Rebbi Hila said, right turn. This is no right turn[164]. Should he not start at the Northwest corner? Rebbi Eleazar said, *he shall leave to the altar*[165]. Should he not start at the Southwest corner? Not to turn his back on the Holiness[166]. Does he not end to turn his back on the Holiness? He was returning backwards[167]. He shall stand in the South and start at the Northeast corner, as Rebbi Hila said, right turn. This is no right turn.

164 If he stands in front of the altar to the South, he might go straight ahead to the SE corner, but if it is required that he start with a right turn by necessity he comes to the NE corner.

165 *Lev.* 16:18. This is read to require that he stand in front of the altar before starting the sprinkling. Therefore he has to start to the East.

166 Leaving the gobelins he stands in the SW between gobelin and altar. To start at the SW corner, he has to turn around.

167 If he starts at the NE corner, in the end he has to go from the SW to the SE corners turning his back to the Ark. Therefore he has to walk this stretch backwards, facing W. The rule of the Mishnah is the only one compatible with all constraints.

(42d line 62) תַּנֵּי. רִבִּי לִיעֶזֶר אוֹמֵר. מִמְּקוֹמוֹ הָיָה עוֹמֵד וּמְחַטֵּא. וְעַל כּוּלָּן הוּא נוֹתֵן מִלְּמַעְלָן לְמַטָּן חוּץ מִזּוּ שֶׁהָיָה לְפָנָיו [לוֹכְסָן] שֶׁהָיָה נוֹתְנָן מִלְּמַטָּן לְמַעְלָן. רִבִּי אַבָּהוּ בְּשֵׁם רִבִּי יוֹחָנָן.

שְׁנֵיהֶן מִקְרָא אֶחָד דָּרְשִׁין. סָבִיב. [וְרַבָּנָן אָמְרִין. סָבִיב לַהֲלוֹךְ. רִבִּי לִיעֶזֶר אוֹמֵר. סָבִיב] לַקְּרָנוֹת.

שְׁנֵי כֹהֲנִים בָּרְחוּ בַּפּוֹלֶמוֹסִיּוֹת. אֶחָד אוֹמֵר. עוֹמֵד הָיִיתִי וּמְחַטֵּא. וְאֶחָד אוֹמֵר. מְהַלֵּךְ הָיִיתִי וּמְחַטֵּא. אָמַר רִבִּי יוּדָן. הָדָא אָמְרָה. מָאן דַּעֲבַד הָכֵין לָא חֲשַׁשׁ. וּמַאן דַּעֲבַד הָכֵין לָא חֲשַׁשׁ.

It was stated:[168] Rebbi Eliezer says, he was standing at his place and purifying. On all of them he was giving from top to bottom except for the one he was standing in front of [in the diagonal][169], where he was giving from bottom to top[170]. Rebbi Abbahu in the name of Rebbi Joḥanan: Both of them were explaining the same verse[171], *around*. [The rabbis are saying, around walking. Rebbi Eliezer is saying, around][171] the corners.

Two Cohanim escaped the wars[172]. One said, I was standing and purifying; the other one said, I was walking and purifying. Rebbi Yudan said, this implies, he who does it one way does not worry, and he who does it the other way does not worry[173].

168 Tosephta 3:1, *Sifra Ahare Pereq* 4(10), Babli 59a. The text here seems to be the correct one, against the three witnesses to the Babylonian text.

169 Addition of the corrector from the Tosephta. Greek λοξόν, "oblique".

170 Since the top of the golden altar was only 1 cubit square, it was easily possible to sprinkle on all horns when standing in front of one corner.

171 Lev. 16:18. The blood must be sprinkled around; the way of delivery is not indicated.

172 Greek πόλεμος, ὁ "war"; in this case the first war against the Romans. Babli 59a.

173 Disregarding both Talmudim, Maimonides rules against R. Eliezer both in his Mishnah commentary and in his Code.

(fol. 42a) **משנה ח**: עַל כּוּלָּן הוּא נוֹתֵן מִלְּמַטָּה לְמַעְלָן חוּץ מִזּוֹ שֶׁהָיְתָה לְפָנָיו שֶׁהָיָה נוֹתֵן מִלְמַעְלָן לְמַטָּן: הִזָּה עַל טִיהֳרוֹ שֶׁל מִזְבֵּחַ שֶׁבַע פְּעָמִים. שְׁיָרֵי הַדָּם הָיָה שׁוֹפֵךְ עַל יְסוֹד מַעֲרָבִי שֶׁל מִזְבֵּחַ הַחִיצוֹן וְשֶׁל מִזְבֵּחַ הַחִיצוֹן הָיָה שׁוֹפֵךְ עַל יְסוֹד דְּרוֹמִי. אֵלּוּ וָאֵלּוּ מִתְעָרְבִין בָּאַמָּה וְיוֹצְאִין לְנַחַל קִדְרוֹן וְנִמְכָּרִין לַגַּנָּנִין לְזֶבֶל וּמוֹעֲלִין בּוֹ:

Mishnah 8: On all of them he gives from bottom to top except the one he is standing in front of, where he gives from top to bottom[174]. He sprinkles on the surface of the altar seven times[175]. The rest of the blood he poured on the

Western base of the outer altar[176]; those of the outer altar one pours on the southern base. This and that combine in the water canal[151] and leave towards the Kidron valley where it is sold to gardeners as fertilizer; one commits larceny with it[177].

174 This follows R. Eliezer. If he would give the blood with his finger on the horn directly in front of him from bottom to top, some blood would flow back onto his arm and dirty his white robe.
175 *Lev.* 16:19.
176 While this is not prescribed in *Lev.* 16, as explained in the Halakhah it is inferred from the treatment of the blood of the bull of the Anointed Priest, whose remainders have to be poured on the "base of the altar which is in front of the Tent of Meeting." "In front of" is taken to refer to "base", this is the Western side of the base of the altar.
177 The water coming out of the Temple is made to drip into the earth, where the blood is absorbed, and at the bottom clear water is reappearing. The earth enriched with the blood is sold to vegetable growers as fertilizer. Since this was part of the construction of the Temple, the Temple does not renounce proprietorship of the blood suspended in the water; therefore use of the enriched earth without paying redemption money to the Temple is stealing from Heaven's property.

(42d line 69) **חלכה ז:** וְהִזָּה עָלָיו. לֹא עַל אֲפָרָ[יו. עָלָיו. לֹא עַל גֶּחָלָיו. אִית תַּנָּיֵי תַנֵּי. צַד צָפוֹנִי. אִית תַּנָּיֵי תַנֵּי. צַד דְּרוֹמִי. מָאן דְּאָמַר. צַד צְפוֹנִי. רִבִּי לִיעֶזֶר. וּמָאן דְּאָמַר. צַד דְּרוֹמִי. רַבָּנָן.

אָמַר רִבִּי יוֹסֵה. זֶה סִימָן. כָּל־הַנִּיטָּל (מִבִּפְנִים) [מִבַּחוּץ] לְהִינָּתֵן (בַּחוּץ נִיתָּן) [בִּפְנִים נִיטַּל] מִן הַסָּמוּךְ לִפְנִים. וְעַל־הַיּוֹצֵא מִבִּפְנִים לְהִינָּתֵן בַּחוּץ נִיתָּן מִן הַסָּמוּךְ לִפְנִים.

רִבִּי יִרְמְיָה בְשֵׁם רִבִּי פְדָת. גֶּחָלִים שֶׁבְּכָל־יוֹם וְנֵר הַמַּעֲרָבִי לְמֵידִיו מִגֶּחָלִים שֶׁלְּיוֹם הַכִּיפּוּרִים. וּשְׁנֵי בְזִיכֵי לְבוֹנָה לְמֵידִין מִשְּׁיָרֵי דָמִים.

Halakhah 7: *He shall sprinkle on it*[178], not on its ashes. *On it,* not on its coals[179]. There are Tannaim who state, the North side. There are Tannaim who state, the South side. He who says, the North side, Rebbi Eliezer; he who says the South side, the rabbis[180].

[181]"Rebbi Yose said, this is a memorandum: Anything taken from inside to be given outside is given to what is close to the inside. [Anything taken from the outside to be given inside is taken from what is close to the inside.] And all that comes out from the inside to be given outside is given from what is close to the inside[182]."

Rebbi Jeremiah in the name of Rebbi Pedat. The coals of every day and the Western light[183] are inferred from the Day of Atonement. And the two censers are inferred from the remainder blood[184].

178 Lev. 16:19.
179 Babli 59a, Tosephta 3:2.
180 Since for R. Eliezer the High Priest always stands at the NE corner of the golden altar. For the rabbis, he finishes giving the blood on the corners at the SE corner, when he starts to sprinkle the top seven times.
181 Tosephta 3:7, *Sifra Ahare Pereq* 3(7); *Zevahim* 58b. The text of the second sentence is the scribe's, the one in brackets the corrector's. Since the two sentences of the scribe are essentially identical, the corrector's text should be accepted (even though the parallel sources show that it would have been better to correct the second sentence.)

182 Anything taken from inside, the remainder of blood used on the Day of Atonement or of the bull of the Anointed or of the commonwealth, outside has to be given close to the inside, i. e., on the Western base of the altar. Similarly, the incense taken from the table with the shew-bread to be burned on the outside altar has to be burned on the Western side of the altar. And anything taken from the outside to be taken inside, coals for the incense altar and fire to light the candelabrum, have to be taken from the Western side of the outside altar close to the Temple entrance.
183 On the candelabrum.
184 As explained in Note 182.

(42d line 76) וְאֶת | כָּל־דַּם הַפָּר יִשְׁפֹּךְ. לְרַבּוֹת פָּר דַּם יוֹם הַכִּיפּוּרִים לִשְׁפִיכָה. וְלָמָּה לֹא אָמַר. וְשָׂעִיר. אָמַר רִבִּי מָנָא. בְּלֹא כָךְ אֵינוֹ זָקוּק לְהֵעָרוֹת. אַשְׁכַּחַת אָמַר. וְאֶת | כָּל־דַּם הַפָּר יִשְׁפֹּךְ. לְרַבּוֹת דַּם פָּר יוֹם הַכִּיפּוּרִים וְשָׂעִיר לִשְׁפִיכָה.

[185]"*And all blood of the bull he shall pour*[186], to include the blood of the bull of the Day of Atonement in pouring." And why did he not say, "and the he-goat"? Rebbi Mana said, is it not required to be mixed[187]? You conclude in saying, *and all blood of the bull he shall pour*, to include the blood of the bull and the he-goat of the Day of Atonement in pouring.

185 *Sifra Wayyiqra II (Hovah) Parashah* 3(12); Babli 52a.
186 Lev. 4:7.
187 If the bull's blood has to be poured on the base of the large altar, the pouring of the he-goat's blood is an automatic consequence and does not have to be spelled out as a separate commandment. Cf. Chapter 1, Note 200.

(43a line 4) וְכִלָּה מִכַּפֵּר אֶת־הַקּוֹדֶשׁ. אִית תַּנָּיֵי תַנֵי. אִם כִּילָּה כִּיפֵּר. אִית תַּנָּיֵי תַנֵי. אִם כִּיפֵּר כִּלָּה. רִבִּי אַבָּהוּ בְשֵׁם רִבִּי יוֹחָנָן. מַחֲלוֹקֶת בֵּינֵיהוֹן. מָאן דְּאָמַר. אִם כִּיפֵּר כִּלָּה. הַשִּׁיּיֵרִים מְעַכְּבִין. מָאן דְּאָמַר. אִם כִּילָּה כִּפֵּר. אֵין הַשִּׁיּיֵרִים מְעַכְּבִין. רִבִּי יְהוֹשֻׁעַ בֶּן לֵוִי אָמַר. מַשְׁמָעוּת בֵּינֵיהוֹן. מַה הַשִּׁיּיֵרִים מְעַכְּבִין{) אֵין הַשִּׁיּיֵרִים מְעַכְּבִין. רִבִּי סִימוֹן בְּשֵׁם רִבִּי יְהוֹשֻׁעַ בֶּן לֵוִי. אֵין הַשִּׁיּיֵרִים מְעַכְּבִין. מַאי כְדוֹן. מָאן דְּאָמַר. אִם כִּלָּה כִּיפֵּר. עוֹשֶׂה אוֹתָן אַרְבַּע מַתָּנוֹת. מָאן דְּאָמַר. אִם כִּיפֵּר כִּלָּה. אֵינוֹ עוֹשֶׂה אוֹתָן אֶלָּא מַתָּנָה אַחַת.

When he finished atoning the sanctuary[188]. There are Tannaim who state, when he finished, he atoned[189] There are Tannaim who state, when he atoned, he finished[190]. Rebbi Abbahu in the name of Rebbi Johanan: They differ by disagreement. He who said, when he atoned, he finished, the remainder is obstructive[191]. He who said, when he finished, he atoned, the remainder is not obstructive. Rebbi Joshua ben Levi said, they differ in understanding. About the remainder (is it obstructive?), the remainder is not obstructive. Rebbi Simon in the name of Rebbi Joshua ben Levi, the remainder is not obstructive. How is this? He who said, when he finished, he atoned, makes it four givings[192]. He who said, when he finished, he atoned, makes it only one giving[193].

188 Lev. 16:20.
189 If he correctly finished the ceremonies, automatically he atoned. Cf. Babli 60b.
190 Only if he did everything required for atoning he is finished.
191 If the remaining blood is not poured on the Western base of the exterior altar, the interior ceremonies are invalid. Babli,

Zevahim 111a.
192 There are four ceremonies: Blood in the Holiest of Holies, on the gobelins, on the corners of the interior altar, and on its top. If one of them is invalid, it has to be repeated.
193 If part is invalid, the entire ceremony has to be repeated from the start.

(43a line 11) תַּנֵּי. אָמַר רִבִּי יִשְׁמָעֵאל. מָה אִם שְׁיָרֵי חַטָּאת שֶׁאֵינָן מְכַפְּרִין נִיתָּנִין עַל הַיְסוֹד. תְּחִילַּת עוֹלָה שֶׁהִיא מְכַפֶּרֶת אֵינוֹ דִין שֶׁתִּינָתֵן עַל הַיְסוֹד. אָמַר לוֹ רִבִּי עֲקִיבָה. לֹא. אִם אָמַרְתָּ בִּשְׁיָרֵי חַטָּאת שֶׁאֵינָן מְכַפְּרִין וְאֵינָן רְאוּיִין לְכַפֵּר נִיתָּנִין עַל הַיְסוֹד. תְּחִילַּת עוֹלָה שֶׁהִיא מְכַפֶּרֶת וּרְאוּיָה לְכַפֵּר אֵינוֹ דִין שֶׁתִּינָתֵן עַל הַיְסוֹד. מָאן דְּאָמַר. אֵין מְכַפְּרִין. אֵין מְכַפְּרִין בִּשְׁאָר יְמוֹת הַשָּׁנָה. הָא בְיוֹם הַכִּיפּוּרִים מְכַפְּרִין. מָאן דְּאָמַר. אֵינָן מְכַפְּרִין וְאֵינָם רְאוּיִים לְכַפֵּר אֵין מְכַפְּרִין לֹא בְרֹאשׁ הַשָּׁנָה וְלֹא בְיוֹם הַכִּיפּוּרִים. מַה נָן קַייָמִין. אִם לְמִצְוָה. מִצְוָה לִיתֵּן עַל הַיְסוֹד. אֶלָּא אִם אֵינוֹ עִנְיָין לְמִצְוָה תְּנֵיהוּ עִנְיָין לְעִיכּוּב.

אָמַר רְבִּי שַׁמַּי. מַתְנִיתָה אָמְרָה שֶׁהַשְּׁיָרַיִים מְעַכְּבִין. דְּתַנִּינָן. מָה לַתַּחְתּוֹנִים. אִם נְתָנָן לְמַעְלָן לֹא הוּרְצוּ. שֶׁאֵין מֵהֶן קָרֵב לְמַעְלָן. תֹּאמַר בָּעֶלְיוֹנִים. אִם נְתָנָן לְמַטָּן הוּרְצוּ. שֶׁיֵּשׁ מֵהֶן קָרֵב לְמַטָּן. הַפְּנִימַיִים יוֹכִיחוּ. שֶׁיֵּשׁ מֵהֶן קָרֵב בַּחוּץ. וְאִם נְתָנָן בַּחוּץ לֹא הוּרְצוּ. מָה לִפְנִימַיִים. אִם נְתָנָן בַּחוּץ לֹא הוּרְצוּ. שֶׁאֵין מִזְבֵּחַ מְמָרְקָן. אִם נְתָנָן לְמַטָּן הוּרְצוּ. שֶׁהֲרֵי הַקְּרָנוֹת מְמָרְקוֹת אוֹתָן. הוֹאִיל וְהַקְּרָנוֹת מְמָרְקוֹת אוֹתָן. אִם נְתָנָן לְמַטָּן תְּהֵא כְשֵׁירָה. תַּלְמוּד לוֹמַר אוֹתָהּ. שֶׁיִּתֵּן דָּמֶיהָ לְמַעְלָן. לֹא שֶׁיִּתֵּן דָּמֶיהָ לְמַטָּן. מָהוּ אֵין (הַמִּזְבֵּחַ הַפְּנִימִי) מְמָרְקָן. אָמַר רְבִּי יוֹסֵי בֵּירְבִּי בּוּן. שֶׁאֵינוֹ מְמָרְקָן לַעֲשׂוֹתָן שְׁיָרַיִים. שֶׁעַל יְדֵי הַבַּדִּין וְעַל יְדֵי הַפָּרֹכוֹת הֵן נַעֲשׂוֹת שְׁיָרַיִים.

אָמַר רְבִּי יוֹסָה. מַתְנִיתָה אָמְרָה שֶׁאֵין הַשְּׁיָרַיִים מְעַכְּבִין. דְּתַנִּינָן. אִם לֹא נָתַן לֹא עִכֵּב: רְבִּי בּוּרְקַיי בְּשֵׁם רְבִּי יוֹחָנָן. מַתְנִיתָה אָמְרָה שֶׁהַשְּׁיָרַיִים מְעַכְּבִין. דְּתַנִּינָן. וְכִפֶּר אֶת־מִקְדַּשׁ הַקֹּדֶשׁ זֶה לִפְנַי לִפְנִים. וְאֶת אוֹהֶל מוֹעֵד זֶה הַהֵיכָל. וְאֶת־הַמִּזְבֵּחַ זֶה מִזְבַּח [הַזָּהָב]. יְכַפֵּר אַף עַל הָעֲזָרוֹת. מָה אִית לָךְ כַּפָּרָה בָעֲזָרוֹת. לֹא הַשְּׁיָרַיִים. [רְבִּי בּוּן בַּר חִיָּא בָעֵי. כְּמַאן דָּמַר. הַשְּׁיָרִים] מְעַכְּבִין. מְקוֹמָן מְעַכֵּב. נוֹתְנָן בַּפַּיְלָה שׁוֹחֵט עָלֶיהָן בַּתְּחִילָה. חַבְרַיָּיא בָעֵי. מְחַשֵּׁב לָהֶן. רְבִּי יוּדָן בָּעֵי. אָבְדוּ. מָה הֵן צְרִיכָה לֵיהּ כְּשֶׁהִתְחִיל לִיתֵּן וְחָסְרוּ. אֲבָל אִם לֹא הִתְחִיל לִיתֵּן כָּל־עַמָּא מוֹדֵיי מַשֶּׁהוּא מְשַׁיֵּיר שֶׁהֵן שְׁיָרִים.

It was stated: [194]"Rebbi Ismael said, if the remainder blood of purification sacrifices which does not atone[195] is given on the base, the start of an elevation sacrifice which is atoning[196] it is only logical that it be given on the base[197]. Rebbi Aqiba said to him, No. If you said that the remainder blood of purification sacrifices which does not atone and is not able to atone are given on the base, the start of an elevation sacrifice which is atoning and is able to atone is only logical that it be given on the base." He who said "does not atone", they do not atone during all other days of the year; therefore on the Day of Atonement they atone[198]. He who says "does not atone and is not able to atone", they do not atone either on New Year's Day[198a] and not on the Day of Atonement. Where do we hold? If for a commandment, it is a commandment to give on the base. But if it cannot refer to the commandment, let it refer to obstruction[199].

Rebbi Shammai said, a *baraita* implies that the remainders are obstructive, as we have stated: [200]"The lower ones, if given on the upper did not placate since nothing of them is brought on the upper, should you not say about the upper ones, if given on the lower they placate since something of them is brought below[201]? The inner ones[202] shall prove, since some of them is given outside, but if he gave them outside[203] it did not placate, since the altar did not cleanse them[204], what should you say about the upper ones, if given on the lower they should placate since the horns cleanse them[205]. Since the horns cleanse them, if he gave them below it should be qualified. The verse says *it*[206], that he give the blood on the upper, but not that he give in the lower." What does it mean, "the altar did not cleanse them"? Rebbi Yose ben Rebbi Abun said, it does not cleanse them to turn them into remainders; only through the beams and the gobelins[207] they become remainders.

Rebbi Yose said, a Mishnah implies that the remainders are not obstructive, as we have stated:[208] "If he did not give, it does not obstruct." Rebbi Borqai in the name of Rebbi Johanan: a *baraita* implies that remainders are obstructive, as we have stated: [209]"*He shall atone for the holy Sanctuary*, that is the innermost room, *and the tent of Meeting*, this is the Temple Hall, *and the altar*, this is the [golden][210] altar, *he shall atone*, also for the courtyards." What atonement do you have for the courtyards? Not the remainders[211]? [Rebbi Abun bar Hiyya asked, according to him who said that][212] remainders are obstructive, is their place obstructive[213]? If he gave them in the night, does he have to slaughter a new sacrifice for them[214]? The colleagues asked: Does one think about them[215]? Rebbi Yudan asked: if they are lost? What is problematic for him, if he started and they became deficient. But if he did not start to give everybody agrees that what he leaves over are leftovers[216].

194 *Sifra Wayyiqra II (Hovah) Pereq* 9(2); cf. Basbli 52a.
195 The blood on the corners of the altar atones. In general if the blood becomes disqualified after this the purification sacrifice remains qualified. The only problem is the status of blood which was brought into the Sanctuary.
196 The blood of the elevation sacrifice which, in contrast to the purification sacrifice, is not given on the four horns of the altar at the corners but only on the lower walls of two diagonally opposed corners so that blood is splattered on all four walls of the altar.. The question is, which pair of corners, SW and NE, or NW and SE? While the elevation offering is voluntary, it is stated in *Lev*. 1:4 that it is atoning. While the verse does not detail for what it is atoning, it is concluded in *Sifra Wayyiqra I Pereq* 4(8) that it is for the transgressions which do not qualify for a purification offering, infraction of positive commandments and of minor prohibitions. The

"start" is giving the blood on the walls of the altar.

197 The SE corner of the altar had no base stones standing out from the walls of the altar. The argument shows that the blood of the elevation sacrifice has to be applied to the SW and NE corners. (Mishnah *Tamid* 4:1).

198 Since the ritual of the Day of Atonement in *Lev.* 16:29 is called *an eternal law*, any particular action required is essential for Atonement. But an action is certainly obstructive only if it is mentioned in Chapter 16.

198a "On New Year's Day" may be a scribal error for כָּל־יְמוֹת הַשָּׁנָה "all days of the year."

199 Since it was established earlier (Note 185) that it is a commandment to pour the remaining blood on the base, the difference between R. Ismael and R. Aqiba can only be whether pouring the blood on the base is obstructive or not.

200 Babli *Zevahim* 52b, *Sifra Saw Pereq* 3(4).

201 Blood of elevation and well-being sacrifices which has to be given on the walls of the altar below the walkway at half-height certainly cannot validly be given on the upper part of the walls, but blood of purification sacrifices which must be given on the horns of the altar (by a Cohen standing on the walkway) should be valid if given on the lower walls since at the end the remainder of the blood is poured on the base which is below the lower walls.

202 Blood used inside the Sanctuary, of the day of Atonement, and of the bulls of the Anointed and the community.

203 If none of the blood was brought inside, the ceremony certainly is invalid.

204 Since the altar is the place of only the third and fourths stops in the use of the blood inside the Sanctuary.

205 After blood of purification sacrifices was given on the horns, what is left becomes remainder.

206 *Lev.* 6:19. The purification sacrifice except for the parts destined for the altar is eaten by the Cohanim, but only if the priest *purified it*, i. e., followed all the prescribed rules.

207 Blood on the altar is invalid if from it was not previously given between the beams and on the gobelins.

208 Mishnah *Zevahim* 5:1, speaking of the remainders of the blood brought inside.

209 *Sifra Ahare Pereq* 8(8) on *Lev.* 16:29; Babli 61a.

210 Addition by the corrector; a correct statement but unnecessary as shown by the parallels.

211 And anything needed for atonement is obstructive.

212 Corrector's addition.

213 It seems that here are two different texts. The scribe's text is "Are not the remainders obstructive? Their place is obstructive." After having proved that the *baraita* presupposes that remainders are obstructive it is stated that if the remainders of blood brought into the sanctuary are not given on the base to the West of the exterior altar, the procedure is invalid. In the corrector's text this is a question, not an assertion.

214 No necessary action in the Temple can be performed in the night; only leftovers from the preceding day are burned on the altar. Pouring remainders of blood on the

base in the night clearly is invalid; the question is whether this requires a new sacrifice. The question cannot be asked about the service of the Day of Atonement, it must be about the bull of the Anointed or the community.

215 Since it is agreed that pouring the remainder blood on the base in a commandment, if a sacrifice is slaughtered with the intent not to pour, or the blood is brought to the alter with the intent not to pour the remainder on the base, is the sacrifice disqualified from the moment of the illegitimate thought? Answered in the affirmative in the Babli, *Zevahim* 29a.

216 The commandment to pour the remainders on the base is conditional; if there are no remainders, there is no obligation to pour.

(43a line 38) תַּנֵּי. מוֹעֲלִין הָיוּ בַדָּמִים. דִּבְרֵי רִבִּי מֵאִיר וְרִבִּי שִׁמְעוֹן. וַחֲכָמִים אוֹמְרִים. אֵין מְעִילָה בַדָּמִים. רִבִּי אַבָּהוּ בְשֵׁם רִבִּי יוֹחָנָן. כִּי־הַדָּם הוּא בַּנֶּפֶשׁ יְכַפֵּר: אֵין לְךָ בּוֹ אֶלָּא כַּפָּרַת נֶפֶשׁ בִּלְבַד. רִבִּי חִייָה בְשֵׁם רִבִּי יוֹחָנָן. כָּל־אֹכְלָיו יִכָּרֵת: אֵין לְךָ בּוֹ אֶלָּא כָרֵת נֶפֶשׁ בִּלְבַד. אָמַר רִבִּי זְעוּרָה. הִקְדִּישׁ דָּם בֵּינֵיהוֹן. מָאן דְּאָמַר. אֵין לְךָ בּוֹ אֶלָּא כַפָּרַת נֶפֶשׁ בִּלְבַד. וְזֶה הוֹאִיל וְאֵין בּוֹ כַפָּרָה אֵין בּוֹ מְעִילָה. מָאן דְּאָמַר. אֵין לְךָ בּוֹ אֶלָּא כָרֵת נֶפֶשׁ בִּלְבַד. וְזֶה הוֹאִיל יֵשׁ בּוֹ כָרֵת יֵשׁ בּוֹ מְעִילָה. אֲתָא רִבִּי בָּא רִבִּי חִייָה בְשֵׁם רִבִּי יוֹחָנָן. הִקְדִּישׁ דָּם וּבָדֵק הַבַּיִת בֵּינֵיהוֹן. וַהֲוָה רִבִּי זְעוּרָה חֲדֵי בָהּ. סָבַר עַל דְּרַבָּנָן אִיתְאָמָרַת. אֲמַר לֵיהּ. וּמַה בְיָדָךְ. וְעַל דְּרִבִּי שִׁמְעוֹן אִיתְאָמָרַת.

רִבִּי בָּא בְּרֵיהּ דְּרִבִּי חִייָה בַּר בָּא. כָּךְ מְשִׁיבִין חֲכָמִים לְרִבִּי שִׁמְעוֹן. אִילוּ מְכָרָן שֶׁמָּא אֵינוֹ תוֹפֵס דְּמֵיהֶן. מָה בֵּינֵיהֶן וּמָה בֵין דְּמֵיהֶן. וּפְלִיג עַל הֲהִיא דְּאָמַר רִבִּי לָעְזָר. יֵשׁ מֵהֶן שֶׁאָמְרוּ. לֹא נֶהֱנִין וְלֹא מוֹעֲלִין. לְפִיכָךְ אִם מְכָרָן אֵינוֹ תוֹפֵשׂ אֶת דְּמֵיהֶן. וְיֵשׁ מֵהֶן שֶׁאָמְרוּ. לֹא נֶהֱנִין וְלֹא מוֹעֲלִין. לְפִיכָךְ אִם מְכָרָן תּוֹפֵשׂ אֶת דְּמֵיהֶן. דִּישׁוּן הַמִּזְבֵּחַ הַפְּנִימִי וְהַמְּנוֹרָה לֹא נֶהֱנִין וְלֹא מוֹעֲלִין. לְפִיכָךְ אִם מְכָרָן אֵינוֹ תוֹפֵשׂ אֶת דְּמֵיהֶן. הַדָּמִים לֹא נֶהֱנִין וְלֹא מוֹעֲלִין בָּהֶן. לְפִיכָךְ אִם מְכָרָן תּוֹפֵשׂ אֶת דְּמֵיהֶן.

It was stated[217]: "One commits larceny with blood[218], the words of Rebbi Meïr and Rebbi Simeon, but the Sages are saying, there is no larceny with blood." Rebbi Abbahu in the name of Rebbi Johanan, *for the blood is it, it atones for the person*[219]. You only have atonement of persons from it. Rebbi Hiyya in the name of Rebbi Johanan, *any who eats it will be extirpated*[220]. You only have extirpation of persons from it[221]. Rebbi Ze'ira said, they differ if he dedicated blood[222]. He who said, you only have atonement of persons from it, and this since there is no atonement from it there is no larceny with it. He who says, you only have extirpation of persons from it, and since there is extirpation from it there is larceny with it[223]. There came Rebbi Abba, Rebbi

Hiyya in the name of Rebbi Johanan, they differ if he dedicated blood or for the upkeep of the Temple. Rebbi Ze'ira enjoyed it; he thought that it had been said about the rabbis. He said to him, what do you have in your hand? It was said about Rebbi Simeon[224].

Rebbi Abba the son of Rebbi Hiyya bar Abba: So the Sages are answering Rebbi Simeon. If he sold them, would it not transfer sanctity to the money? What is the difference between them and their money's worth[225]? This disagrees with what Rebbi Eleazar said: There are those of them of which they said, one has no usufruct but one does not commit larceny, therefore it one sold them it does not transfer sanctity to the money, and there are those of them of which they said, one has no usufruct but one does not commit larceny, therefore if one sold them it transfers sanctity to the money. Of the ashes of the interior altar and the candelabrum one has no usufruct but one does not commit larceny, therefore if one sold them it does not transfer sanctity to the money[226]. Of blood one has no usufruct but one does not commit larceny, therefore if one sold it, it transfers sanctity to the money.

---

217 Tosephta *Zevahim* 6:9; Babli *Yoma* 59a, Me'ilah 11a.

218 Illegitimate use of *sancta* is larceny which requires restitution, payment of a fine, and a sacrifice (*Lev.* 5:14-16). The question is whether this applies also to the blood when it flows out of the Temple domain after all ceremonies have successfully been completed.

219 *Lev.* 17:11.

220 *Lev.* 17:14.

221 In both cases, the argument is that after the blood has left the Temple precinct it is profane. It still may be Temple property, but no sacrilege is involved in unauthorized use and no sacrifice for me'ilah can be due.

222 It is not clear what this means. It could be that one refers to blood of sacrifices which somehow became disqualified for the altar, or of the blood of animals unfit for the altar which from the start were donated only for the upkeep of the Temple, and whose illicit use is me'ilah.

223 Both possibilities apply to both interpretations given in the preceding Note.

224 R. Simeon holds that the remainders of blood used on the altar, as the blood mentioned in Mishnah 8, as well as the blood of animals dedicated to the upkeep of the Temple, are subject to me'ilah (and the Mishnah follows R. Simeon), but about blood unfit for atonement he agrees that there can be no me'ilah. Therefore the expression "they differ" does not refer to the Amoraim reporting in the name of R. Johanan, but to R. Sineon and the Sages in the Tosephta.

225 Since anything given to the Temple for its upkeep is there to be sold and the money used for sacred purposes, the holiness of the

dedicated object is transferred to the money while the object reverts to profane status. But *me'ilah*, larceny committed on *sacra*, only applies to profane use of sacred objects, not to redemptions (or to use that can be legitimized by redemption.) Therefore the distinction made by R. Simeon is not consistent with our rules.

226 Mishnah *Me'ilah* 3:4.

(fol. 42a) **משנה ט**: כָּל מַעֲשֵׂה יוֹם הַכִּפּוּרִים הָאָמוּר עַל הַסֵּדֶר אִם הִקְדִּים מַעֲשֶׂה לַחֲבֵירוֹ לֹא עָשָׂה כְלוּם. הִקְדִּים דַּם הַשָּׂעִיר לְדַם הַפָּר יַחֲזוֹר וְיַזֶּה מִדַּם הַשָּׂעִיר לְאַחַר דַּם הַפָּר. אִם עַד שֶׁלֹּא גָמַר אֶת הַמַּתָּנוֹת שֶׁבִּפְנִים נִשְׁפַּךְ הַדָּם יָבִיא דָם אַחֵר וְיַחֲזוֹר וְיַזֶּה בַּתְּחִלָּה מִבִּפְנִים. וְכֵן בַּהֵיכָל וְכֵן בְּמִזְבַּח הַזָּהָב שֶׁכּוּלָּן כַּפָּרָה וְכַפָּרָה בִּפְנֵי עַצְמָן. רִבִּי אֶלְעָזָר וְרִבִּי שִׁמְעוֹן אוֹמְרִים מִמָּקוֹם שֶׁפָּסַק מִשָּׁם הוּא מַתְחִיל:

Mishnah 9: All actions of the Day of Atonement which have been prescribed in their sequence[227], if he advanced one action to another he did not do anything. If he advanced he-goat's blood to the bull's blood he has to sprinkle he-goat's blood after the bull's blood. If the blood was spilled before he finishes all givings required in the interior[228], he has to bring other blood and starts sprinkling anew in the interior. So it is in the Temple Hall and so it is with the golden altar, since all of these are separate atonements[229]. Rebbi Eleazar and Rebbi Simeon are saying, he starts at the place where he interrupted[230].

227 The order of actions prescribed to the High Priest in *Lev.* 16 must be followed exactly.

228 In the Holiest of Holies.

229 If the blood was spilled after an action was completed, new animals and new blood only are required for the subsequent actions; one does not have to start from the beginning.

230 While the anonymous Tanna requires the repetition of any partially complete action, R. Eleazar and R. Simeon accept completion with other blood of actions partially executed.

(43a line 55) **הלכה ח**: תַּנֵּי. אָמַר רִבִּי יְהוּדָה. בַּמֶּה דְּבָרִים אֲמוּרִים. בָּעֲבוֹדוֹת הַנַּעֲשׂוֹת בִּפְנִים בְּבִגְדֵי לָבָן. אֲבָל בָּעֲבוֹדוֹת הַנַּעֲשׂוֹת בַּחוּץ בְּבִגְדֵי זָהָב. אִם הִקְדִּים מַעֲשֶׂה לַחֲבֵירוֹ מַה שֶּׁעָשָׂה עָשׂוּי. וַחֲכָמִים אוֹמְרִים. אַף הַנַּעֲשׂוֹת בַּחוּץ בְּבִגְדֵי זָהָב. אִם הִקְדִּים מַעֲשֶׂה לַחֲבֵירוֹ לֹא עָשָׂה כְלוּם. רִבִּי אַבָּהוּ בְּשֵׁם רִבִּי יוֹחָנָן. שְׁנֵיהֶן מִקְרָא אֶחָד הֵן דּוֹרְשִׁין. מִדַּם חַטָּאת הַכִּפֻּרִים אֶחָת.

רַבָּנָן אֱמְרֵי. עֲבוֹדוֹת שֶׁהוּא נִכְנָס [פַּעַם] אַחַת בַּשָּׁנָה. רִבִּי יְהוּדָה אוֹמֵר. מָקוֹם שֶׁהוּא נִכְנָס בּוֹ [פַּעַם] אַחַת בַּשָּׁנָה.

Halakhah 8: It was stated:[231] "Rebbi Jehudah said, when has this[232] been said? About service performed inside in white garments. But service performed outside in golden garments if he advanced one action to another, what he did is done. And the Sages are saying, even for service performed outside in golden garments if he advanced one action to another, he did not do anything." Rebbi Abbahu in the name of Rebbi Joḥanan[233]: Both of them are explaining the same verse[234]: *of the blood of the atoning sacrifice once.* The rabbis are saying, service which is performed one [time][235] in the year. Rebbi Jehudah is saying, a place in which he enters one [time][235] per year.

231 Tosephta 3:4, Babli 60a.
232 That a change in the sequence of actions invalidates the service.
233 Babli 60a/b.

234 *Ex.* 30:10.
235 Corrector's addition, probably from the parallel in the Babli.

(43a line) רִבִּי הוֹשַׁעְיָה בְשֵׁם רִבִּי פֵס. בְּמַתְּנוֹת הַבַּדִּים. אֲבָל בְּמַתְּנוֹת הַפָּרוֹכֶת שָׂעִיר מְעַכֵּב אֶת הַפָּר. אָמַר רִבִּי לְעָזָר. וְנָתַן מִדַּם הַפָּר עַל בֵּין הַבַּדִּים וְעַל בֵּין הַפָּרְכוֹת וְאַחַר כָּךְ שָׁחַט אֶת הַשָּׂעִיר הַנַּעֲשָׂה בַתְּחִילָה כָּשֵׁר. אָמַר רִבִּי יוֹסֵה. אִילּוּ נִשְׁפַּךְ מִדַּם הַפָּר וּמִדַּם הַשָּׂעִיר הַמוּנָח בַּכּוֹס שֶׁמָּא אֵינוֹ מֵבִיא פָר אַחֵר וְכָשֵׁר. מַה בֵּין שָׁחַט עַד שֶׁלֹּא נָתַן מַה בֵּין שָׁחַט מִשֶּׁנָּתָן. אִילּוּ אָמַר וְנָתַן יָאוּת.

Rebbi Hoshaia in the name of Rebbi Ephes: About givings between the beams; but givings between the gobelins the he-goat is obstructive for the bull[236]. Rebbi Eleazar said, if he gave of the bull's blood between the beams and between the gobelins and afterwards freshly slaughtered the he-goat it is qualified[237]. Rebbi Yose said, if the bull's and the he-goat's blood in the cup was spilled, would he not bring another bull and it would be qualified[238]? What is the difference whether he slaughtered before he gave or slaughtered after he gave? If it had said "he gives" that would have been correct[239].

236 Chapter 4:1, Note 55.
237 Babli 40a, disputing the assertion of R. Ephes.
238 This cannot mean that the bull's and the he-goat's blood were mixed in one cup since this is scheduled only after both kinds of blood were sprinkled on the gobelins. R. Yose argues in support of R. Eleazar, since

the blood in the cup could be spilled at any moment, then the slaughter can happen at any moment.

238 R. Yose's argument is invalid. Since the biblical text never uses the expression "he gives" from which it would follow that the deposit of the blood on Ark, gobelin, or altar, is determining, but it always says, "he sprinkles" and "he slaughters", which means that the actions of the High Priest are what counts and the order of prescribed actions cannot be changed, supporting R. Hoshaia here (and R. Abba in Chapter 4).

(43a line 68) רַבָּנָן אָמְרֵי. שָׁלֹשׁ לָכּוֹשֶׁר וְשָׁלֹשׁ לִפְסוּל. רִבִּי לְעָזָר וְרִבִּי שִׁמְעוֹן אוֹמְרִין. אַרְבָּעִים וְשָׁלֹשׁ לָכּוֹשֶׁר וְאַרְבָּעִים וְשָׁלֹשׁ לִפְסוּל. וְרַבָּנָן אָמְרֵי. כָּל־שֶׁבַע וְשֶׁבַע כַּפָּרָה בִּפְנֵי עַצְמָהּ. [וְרִבִּי אֶחְעָזָר וְרִבִּי שִׁמְעוֹן אָמְרֵי. כָּל־אֶחָד וְאֶחָד כַּפָּרָה בִּפְנֵי עַצְמוֹ.] רִבִּי זְעוּרָה בְשֵׁם רִבִּי לְעָזָר. טַעֲמָא דְרִבִּי לְעָזָר בֵּירִבִּי שִׁמְעוֹן. וְכִלָּה מִכַּפֵּר אֶת־הַקּוֹדֶשׁ. אֲפִילוּ אֵין שָׁם אֶלָּא מַתָּנָה אַחַת אָמְרָה הַתּוֹרָה כִּלָּה.

The rabbis say, three for qualification and three for disqualification. Rebbi Eleazar and Rebbi Simeon are saying, 43 for qualification and 43 for disqualification[239]. Therefore the rabbis say, any seven[240] are atonement by themselves. [Rebbi Eleazar and Rebbi Simeon are saying, each single one is atonement by itself.][241] Rebbi Ze'ira in the name of Rebbi Eleazar[242], the reason of Rebbi Eleazar and[243] Rebbi Simeon: *he finished atoning for the holy*[244], even if there is only one giving, the Torah says "he finished"[245].

239 For the rabbis each group of sprinkling, in the Holiest of Holies, on the gobelins, and on the altar, forms a unit. If anything was incomplete or disqualifying in one of the actions, the entire action must be repeated. For R. Eleazar and R. Simeon every single sprinkling is a commandment by itself. In all there are 7+1 sprinklings of bull's blood and the same number of he-goat's blood in the Holiest of Holies, the same number of both kinds of blood on the gobelins, 4 of the combined blood on the horns of the golden altar and 7 on its top, for a total of 4x8+11 = 43.

240 This really should read "eight".
241 Corrector's addition.
242 The Amora ben Pedat, not the Tanna, ben Arakh, quoted in the Tosephta.
243 Reading וְ instead of the similar sounding בֵּ.
244 *Lev.* 16:20.
245 Since emphasis is on finishing, even if only a single sprinkling is needed to complete the ceremony it is counted and valid.

(43a line 73) אָמַר רִבִּי לְעָזָר. נָתַן מִקְצָת מַתָּנוֹת וְנִשְׁפַּךְ הַדָּם מֵבִיא אֲחֵרִים תַּחְתֵּיהֶן. אִילוּ [וְאֵילוּ] נִשְׁפָּכִין כְּמִצְוָתָן. לָכֵן צְרִיכָה כְּשֶׁנִּקְרָא עֲלֵיהֶן לְשֵׁם פָּסוּל. אָמַר רִבִּי יוֹסֵה. וְיָאוּת. אִילוּ

נָתַן מִקְצָת מַתָּנוֹת וְנִשְׁפַּךְ הַדָּם שֶׁמָּא אֵינוֹ מֵבִיא אֲחֵרִים תַּחְתֵּיהֶן וּמוֹעֲלִין בָּרִאשׁוֹנִים. רִבִּי חַגַּיי בְּעָא קוֹמֵי רִבִּי יוֹסֵה. עַד כְּדוֹן בְּשֶׁשָּׁחַט אֶת הָרִאשׁוֹנִים לְשֵׁם כּוֹשֶׁר וְהַשְּׁנִיִּים לְשֵׁם פָּסוּל. שָׁחַט אֶת הָרִאשׁוֹנִים לְשֵׁם פָּסוּל וְאֶת הַשְּׁנִיִּים לְשֵׁם כּוֹשֶׁר. אָמַר רִבִּי יוֹסֵה. מָצִינוּ פָּסוּל [מוֹצִיא] מִיַּד פִּיגוּל. מָצִינוּ פָּסוּל מוֹצִיא מִיַּד כּוֹשֶׁר.

[246]"Rebbi Eleazar[247] said, if he gave part of the givings when the blood was spilled, he brings others in their place; these [and those][248] are (emptied)[249] following their commandments." We need this only if an designation of disqualification was applicable to them[250]. Rebbi Yose said, this is correct. if he gave part of the givings when the blood was spilled, he brings others in their place; and the first ones are subject to *me`ilah*[251]. Rebbi Ḥaggai asked before Rebbi Yose, so far if he slaughtered the first ones for qualification and the second one for disqualification[252]. If he slaughtered the first ones for disqualification and the second one for qualification? Rebbi Yose said, we find that disqualification [eliminates][253] *piggul*[254]; do we find that disqualification eliminates qualification[255]?

246 *Sifra Ahare Parashah* 4(3); a minority opinion in the Babli, 61b.
247 The Tanna.
248 Addition by the corrector. While the statement is correct, the addition is questionable. As is clear from the text of *Sifra* and the remark following the quote, everybody agrees and it is obvious from the biblical text (*Lev.* 20:27) that the bull and the he-goat on whose blood the ceremony is completed have to be burned outside the city of Jerusalem and the people occupied with this burning become severely impure. The question is whether the animals whose blood was first brought into the sanctuary but was not used to finish the ceremonies, either because it was spilled or because of some disqualification, have to be disposed in the same way. This is asserted by R. Eleazar but negated by RR. Meïr and Simeon.
249 For "emptied" read נשרפין "burned". If the blood was spilled, it cannot be emptied a second time.
250 Or if it was spilled, cf. Note 248.
251 This is equivalent to saying that they did not completely lose their status as *sancta* and therefore have to be burned following the biblical rules.
252 Disqualification not of the second but the first couple of animals. Slaughter of animals with the intent that they be disqualified makes them disqualified and removes sacral status.
253 Necessary corrector's addition.
254 *Piggul (Lev.* 19:7) is slaughter with the intent that the sacrificial meat be eaten outside its allotted time frame. Only *sancta*, parts of which may be eaten, can become *piggul*, a disqualification which prevents the meat from being eaten, automatically removes *piggul*. Mishnah *Zevahim* 2:3.

255 R. Haggai's question is baseless; the disqualification of the first sacrifice cannot have influence on the status of the second..

שני שעירי פרק ששי

(fol.43b) **משנה א**: שְׁנֵי שְׂעִירֵי יוֹם הַכִּפּוּרִים מִצְוָתָן שֶׁיִּהְיוּ שָׁוִין בְּמַרְאֶה וּבְקוֹמָה וּבְדָמִים וּבִלְקִיחָתָן כְּאַחַת. וְאַף עַל פִּי שֶׁאֵינָן שָׁוִין כְּשֵׁרִים. לָקַח אֶחָד הַיּוֹם וְאֶחָד לְמָחָר כְּשֵׁרִים. מֵת אֶחָד מֵהֶן אִם עַד שֶׁלֹּא הִגְרִיל מֵת אֶחָד מֵהֶן יִקַּח זוּג לַשֵּׁנִי. וְאִם מִשֶּׁהִגְרִיל מֵת יָבִיא שְׁנַיִם וְיַגְרִיל עֲלֵיהֶם בַּתְּחִילָּה.

Mishnah 1: The commandment for the two he-goats of the Day of Atonement is that they be equal in looks, in height, and in value, and be bought simultaneously. Even if they are not equal they are qualified; if one was bought one day and the other the next day[1] they are qualified. If one of them dies, if it died before he[2] drew lots he should take a match for the second one; if it dies after he drew lots one brings two and he draws new lots for them.

משנה ב: וְיֹאמַר אִם שֶׁל שֵׁם מֵת זֶה שֶׁעָלָה עָלָיו הַגּוֹרָל לַשֵּׁם יִתְקַיֵּים תַּחְתָּיו. וְאִם שֶׁל עֲזָאזֵל מֵת זֶה שֶׁעָלָה עָלָיו הַגּוֹרָל לַעֲזָאזֵל יִתְקַיֵּים תַּחְתָּיו. וְהַשֵּׁנִי יִרְעֶה עַד שֶׁיִּסְתָּאֵב וְיִמָּכֵר וְיִפְּלוּ דָמָיו לִנְדָבָה שֶׁאֵין חַטַּאת צִיבּוּר מֵתָה. רִבִּי יְהוּדָה אוֹמֵר תָּמוּת. וְעוֹד אָמַר רִבִּי יְהוּדָה נִשְׁפַּךְ הַדָּם יָמוּת הַמִּשְׁתַּלֵּחַ. מֵת הַמִּשְׁתַּלֵּחַ יִשָּׁפֵךְ הַדָּם:

Mishnah 2: Then he shall say if the one for Hashem[3] dies, "the one for which the lot for Hashem is drawn shall be taken in its stead.[4]" And if the one for Azazel died, "the one for which the lot for Azazel is drawn shall be taken in its stead." The second one shall graze until it becomes unfit, then be sold, and its proceeds used for voluntary sacrifices[5] since no public purification sacrifice is allowed to die[6]. Rebbi Jehudah says, it shall die. In addition, Rebbi Jehudah says, if the blood is spilled the one to be sent away shall die, if the one to be sent away dies the blood shall be spilled[7].

1 Or any other day.
2 The High Priest.
3 Cf. Chapter 4, Note 2.
4 Since only one new he-goat is needed; the second one was taken only to satisfy the requirement that lots be drawn for any he-goat used in the service.
5 The monies to be used to buy elevation sacrifices for times when otherwise the altar would be idle.
6 In contrast to private purification sacrifices which are not used because the

owner used another animal in its stead. It cannot be used for another person, cannot be redeemed, and cannot be used in any other way.

7 Since R. Jehudah holds that if for any reason one of the he-goats or its blood cannot be used, the other cannot be used either and has to be let to die.

(43b line 49) שְׁנֵי שְׂעִירֵי יוֹם הַכִּפּוּרִים כול׳. שְׂעִירִים. מִיעוּט שְׂעִירִים שְׁנַיִם. אִם כֵּן לָמָּה נֶאֱמַר שְׁנֵי. שֶׁיְּהוּ שָׁוִין.

[כְּבָשִׂים. מִיעוּט כְּבָשִׂים שְׁנַיִם. אִם כֵּן לָמָּה נֶאֱמַר שְׁנֵי. שֶׁיְּהוּ שָׁוִין.]

צִפֳּרִים. מִיעוּט צִפֳּרִים שְׁתַּיִם. אִם כֵּן לָמָּה נֶאֱמַר שְׁתֵּי. שֶׁיְּהוּ שָׁווֹת.

חֲצוֹצְרוֹת. מִיעוּט חֲצוֹצְרוֹת שְׁתַּיִם. אִם כֵּן לָמָּה נֶאֱמַר שְׁתֵּי. שֶׁיְּהוּ שָׁווֹת.

הֵתִיב רִבִּי חַגַּי קוֹמֵי רִבִּי יוֹסֵה. וְהָא כְתִיב וְעָמְדוּ שְׁנֵי־הָאֲנָשִׁים אֲשֶׁר־לָהֶם הָרִיב לִפְנֵי יְי׳. מֵעַתָּה אֲנָשִׁים. מִיעוּט אֲנָשִׁים שְׁנַיִם. אִם כֵּן לָמָּה נֶאֱמַר שְׁנֵי. שֶׁיְּהוּ שָׁוִין. וְהָא כְתִיב לֹא תַטֶּה מִשְׁפַּט גֵּר יָתוֹם. הֲרֵי מָצִינוּ גֵר דָּן עִם מִי שֶׁאֵינוּ גֵר. יָתוֹם דָּן עִם מִי שֶׁאֵינוּ יָתוֹם. אַלְמָנָה עִם מִי שֶׁאֵינָהּ אַלְמָנָה. מַה תַּלְמוּד לוֹמַר שְׁנֵי. אֶלָּא מִפְּנִייָא לְהַקִּישׁ לִגְזִירָה שָׁוָה. נֶאֱמַר כָּאן שְׁנֵי וְנֶאֱמַר לְהַלָּן שְׁנֵי. מַה שְׁנֵי שֶׁנֶּאֱמַר לְהַלָּן אֲנָשִׁים וְלֹא נָשִׁים וְלֹא קְטַנִּים. אַף שְׁנֵי שֶׁנֶּאֱמַר כָּאן אֲנָשִׁים וְלֹא נָשִׁים וְלֹא קְטַנִּים. הֲרֵי לָמַדְנוּ שֶׁאֵין הָאִשָּׁה (דָּנָה) מְעִידָה. מֵעַתָּה אֵין הָאִשָּׁה (מְעִידָה) [דָּנָה].

רִבִּי יוֹסֵה בֵּי רִבִּי בּוּן רִבִּי חוּנָא בְּשֵׁם רַב יוֹסֵף. נֶאֱמַר כָּאן שְׁנֵי [עַל־פִּי | שְׁנַיִם עֵדִים]. וְנֶאֱמַר לְהַלָּן שְׁנֵי. וַיִּשָּׁאֲרוּ שְׁנֵי־אֲנָשִׁים | בַּמַּחֲנֶה. מַה שְׁנֵי שֶׁנֶּאֱמַר לְהַלָּן אֲנָשִׁים וְלֹא נָשִׁים וְלֹא קְטַנִּים. אַף שְׁנֵי שֶׁנֶּאֱמַר כָּאן אֲנָשִׁים וְלֹא נָשִׁים וְלֹא קְטַנִּים. אִם כֵּן לָמָּה נֶאֱמַר (שְׁנֵי) [וְעָמְדוּ שְׁנֵי־הָאֲנָשִׁים]. שֶׁלֹּא יְהֵא אֶחָד עוֹמֵד וְאֶחָד יוֹשֵׁב. [אֶחָד שׁוֹתֵק וְאֶחָד מְדַבֵּר.] אֶחָד מְדַבֵּר כָּל־צוֹרְכּוֹ. וְאֶחָד אַתְּ אוֹמֵר [לוֹ]. קַצֵּר בִּדְבָרֶיךָ. שֶׁלֹּא יְהֵא הַדַּיָּין מַסְבִּיר פָּנִים כְּנֶגֶד אֶחָד וּמֵעִיז פָּנִים כְּנֶגֶד אֶחָד. מַעֲמִיד לָזֶה וּמוֹשִׁיב לָזֶה. [מִשּׁוּם רִבִּי יִשְׁמָעֵאל אָמְרוּ. אוֹמְרִין לוֹ. לְבוֹשׁ כְּשֵׁם שֶׁהוּא לוֹבֵשׁ. אוֹ הַלְבִּישׁוֹ כְּשֵׁם שֶׁאַתָּה לָבוּשׁ.]

אָמַר רִבִּי יְהוּדָה. שָׁמַעְתִּי שֶׁאִם רָצָה הַדַּיָּין לְהוֹשִׁיב אֶת שְׁנֵיהֶן מוֹשִׁיב. וְאֵי זֶה אָסוּר. שֶׁלֹּא יְהֵא אֶחָד עוֹמֵד וְאֶחָד יוֹשֵׁב. אֶלָא מְדַבֵּר כָּל־צוֹרְכּוֹ וְכוּל׳.

רִבִּי בָּא בְשֵׁם רַב הוּנָא. צְרִיכִין הָעֵדִים לִהְיוֹת עוֹמְדִין כְּשֶׁהֵן מְעִידִין עֵדוּתָן. רִבִּי יִרְמְיָה בְשֵׁם רִבִּי אַבָּהוּ. אַף הַנִּידּוֹנִין צְרִיכִין לִהְיוֹת עוֹמְדִין בְּשָׁעָה שֶׁהֵן מְקַבְּלִין עֵדוּתָן.

"The two he-goats of the Day of Atonement," etc. [8]*He-goats*[9], the minimum of he-goats are two. If so, why does it say *two*? That they be equal.

[*Sheep*[10], the minimum of sheep are two. If so, why does it say *two*? That both be equal.][11]

Birds[12], the minimum of *birds* are two. If so, why does it say *two*? That both be equal.

Trumpets[13], the minimum of *trumpets* are two. If so, why does it say *two*? that both be equal.

Rebbi Haggai objected before Rebbi Yose. Is there not written[14]: *The two men who have the lawsuit shall stand before the Eternal*? Now *men*, is not two the minimum of "men"? If so, why does it say *two*? That both be equal? But it is written[15]: *Do not bend the lawsuit of the proselyte, the orphan*, . . . So we find that a proselyte can have a lawsuit against one who is not a proselyte, an orphan may have a lawsuit against one who is not an orphan, a widow against somebody who is not a widow. Then why does the verse say *two*? It is free to be combined and one may infer from it an *equal cut*. It is said here *two* and it is said there *two*. Since there *two* means men but not women nor underaged, also here *two* means men but not women nor underaged. From this we learn that a woman may not be a (judge) [witness]; consequently a woman may not be a (witness) [judge][16].

Rebbi Yose ben Rebbi Abun, Rebbi Huna in the name of Rebbi Yose. It is said here *two*, [*by the mouth of two witnesses*[17]], and it is said there *two*, *two men remained in the camp*[18]. Since there *two* means men but not women nor underaged, also here *two* means men but not women nor underaged. Then why is it said (*two*) [*and the two men shall stand*][19]? Lest one of them be standing while the other be sitting; [one is silent while the other talks][11], one says everything he has to say, but to the other one says, make your statement short. With one the judge is friendly, to the other he is unfriendly, lets one sit and the other stand. [They said in the name of Rebbi Ismael, one says to him, either you dress as he is dressed or pay him to be dressed as you are.][11]

Rebbi Jehudah said, I heard that if the judge wants to let both of them sit, he may tell them to sit down. What is forbidden is that one be standing and the other sitting; or that one says everything he has to say, but to the other one says, make your statement short, etc.

Rebbi Abba said in the name of Rav Huna: The witnesses have to stand while testifying. Rebbi Jeremiah in the name of Rebbi Abbahu: Also the parties have to stand at the moment the testimony is delivered..

8   The following is a slightly changed verson of a text appearing in *Sanhedrin* 3:10 (Notes 150-162) and *Ševuot* 4:1 (Notes 7-17).

9 Lev. 16:5,7,8. Babli 62b, *Sifra Ahare Parashah* 2(1).	14 *Deut.* 19:17.
10 *Ex.* 27:38, *Num.* 28:3.	15 *Deut.* 24:17.
11 Corrector's addition from the parallel sources.	16 The scribe's text in parentheses conforms to the parallels; the corrector's in brackets is more logical.
12 *Lev* 14:4.	17 *Deut.* 17:6.
13 *Num.* 10:2.	18 *Num.* 11:27.

(43b line 76) שָׁוִין בְּדָמִים וְאֵין שָׁוִין בְּשָׁבַח הַדָּמִים. אֵין הַשְּׂעִירִין כְּמִצְוָתָן. שָׁוִין בְּשָׁבַח הַדָּמִים וְאֵין שָׁוִין בְּדָמִים. הַשְּׂעִירִים כְּמִצְוָתָן. מְשׁוּבָּח בְּגוּפוֹ מְשׁוּבָּח בְּמַרְאָיו מִי קוֹדֵם. רִבִּי יִרְמְיָה סָבַר מֵימַר. מִישְׁמְעִינָהּ מִן הָדָא. אָבִיב קָצוּר יָבֵשׁ לִקְצוֹר. אָבִיב קָצוּר קוֹדֵם. הָדָא אָמְרָה מְשׁוּבָּח בְּגוּפוֹ [מְשׁוּבָּח בְּמַרְאָיו]. מְשׁוּבָּח בְּגוּפוֹ קוֹדֵם.

If they are equal in price but unequal in value, the he-goats are not as commanded[19]; equal in value but not equal in price, the he-goats are as commanded. Better in its body[20] or better in its looks, what is preferable? Rebbi Jeremiah thought to say[21] that we may understand it from the following: Of cut greenish and dry uncut, cut greenish is preferable[22]. This implies, better in its body [or better in its looks][23], better in its body is preferable.

19 If actually the same price was paid for the two he-goats used on the Day of Atonement, but if they were regularly sold in the market one of them clearly would fetch a higher price, they are not disqualified but do not fulfill the biblical requirement of equality.

20 Having more meat.

21 This is the only opinion we have on the problem but it is not necessarily to be followed in practice if the Temple will be rebuilt.

22 This refers to the `omer, the sacrifice of first barley (*Lev.* 2:14) which has to be greenish grain parched with fire, peeled barley of the fresh ear. While the `omer should be freshly cut, if the choice is only between cut moist or uncut completely dry barley, cut moist grain is preferable since this is explicitly required by the verse. אָבִיב is barley which is edible but still has a moist greenish tint; in Southern Germany known as *Grünkern*. Cf. Tosephta *Menahot* 10:33.

23 Corrector's addition. It might be that the scribe's second "better in its body" is dittography, which would make the correction unnecessary.

(43c line 5) כֵּינֵי מַתְנִיתָה. יָבִיא שְׁנַיִם וְיַגְרִיל עֲלֵיהֶם כַּתְּחִילָּה. וְיֹאמַר. זֶה שֶׁעָלָה עָלָיו הַגּוֹרָל לַשֵּׁם יִתְקַיֵּים תַּחְתָּיו. אֵי זֶה מֵהֶן קָרֵב תְּחִילָּה. רַב אָמַר. שֵׁינִי שֶׁבְּזוּג שֵׁינִי. רִבִּי יוֹחָנָן אָמַר. שֵׁינִי שֶׁבֵּין זוּג רִאשׁוֹן. אָמַר רִבִּי זְעוּרָה. טַעֲמָא דְּרִבִּי יוֹחָנָן. וְעָשָׂהוּ חַטָּאת. בָּרִאשׁוֹן. אָמַר רִבִּי

לָא. טַעֲמָא דְרִבִּי יוֹחָנָן. וְעָשָׂהוּ חַטָּאת.   קְבָעוֹ בַּתְּלִיָּה שֶׁלֹּא יִדָּחֶה. וְאַתְיָא כָּהִיא דְּאָמַר רִבִּי יוֹנָה בְּשֵׁם רִבִּי זְעוּרָה. וְעָשָׂהוּ חַטָּאת.   קְבָעוֹ בַּתְּלִיָּה שֶׁיִּזְדַּוֵוג לוֹ חֲבֵירוֹ. עַל דַּעְתֵּיהּ דְּרִבִּי יוֹחָנָן. מֵת שֵׁינִי שֶׁבַּזּוּג זוּג שֵׁינִי. שֵׁינִי שֶׁבַּזּוּג זוּג רִאשׁוֹן מָהוּ שֶׁיִּידָּחֶה. אֲתָא רִבִּי בָּא רִבִּי חִייָה בְּשֵׁם רִבִּי יוֹחָנָן. שֵׁינִי שֶׁבַּזּוּג זוּג רִאשׁוֹן כְּבָר נִדְחָה. [כָּל־שֶׁכֵּן מַחְלְפָיהּ שִׁיטָתֵיהּ דְּרַב. מֵת שֵׁינִי שֶׁבַּזּוּג רִאשׁוֹן. שֵׁינִי שֶׁבַּזּוּג שֵׁינִי כְּבָר נִדְחָה.]

So is the Mishnah: "One brings two and he draws new lots for them. He shall say, 'the one for which the lot for Hashem is drawn shall be taken in its stead.'[24]" Which of them is sacrificed first[25]? Rav said, the second in the second pair; Rebbi Joḥanan said, the second in the first pair[26]. Rebbi Ze'ira said, the reason of Rebbi Joḥanan: *he shall make it a purification sacrifice*[27], of the first {pair.[28]} Rebbi La said, the reason of Rebbi Joḥanan: *he shall make it a purification sacrifice,* he established it for dependency lest it be pushed aside[29]. This is parallel to what Rebbi Jonah said in the name of Rebbi Ze'ira, *he shall make it a purification sacrifice,* he established it for dependency that its companion be paired with it. In Rebbi Joḥanan's opinion, if the second in the second pair died, would the second in the first pair be pushed aside⁰? There came Rebbi Abba, Rebbi Ḥiyya in the name of Rebbi Joḥanan: then the second in the first pair already is pushed aside[30]. [So much more would Rav's reasoning be inverted? If the second in the second pair died, the second in the second pair already is pushed aside.[31]]

24 As it was translated in Mishnah 2, the clause אִם שֶׁל שֵׁם מֵת "if the one for Hashem dies," describes the background of the required action; it is not part of the declaration by the High Priest.

25 This now refers to the case that the he-goat to be sent to the Azazel dies and one is left with two he-goats as prospective sacrifices.

26 Rav holds that since the sacrifice of the first he-goat becomes invalidated if the he-goat for Azazel died, since it was stated that if the he-goat for the Azazel died after the first he-goat had been slaughtered, the blood has to be poured out and the entire ceremony started anew with a new pair of he-goats, a sacrifice which became invalidated never can be reinstated. While it is a general principle that a sacrifice which became invalidated never can be reinstated, R. Joḥanan holds that the living he-goat is not disqualified if its companion he-goat died, but it only is suspended. If a second he-goat is newly chosen, the suspension of the first is removed.

27 Lev. 16:19.

28 Since the verse refers to the first pair, the first he-goat is irrevocably made a sacrifice.

29 A different formulation of the same

idea.

30 If the replacement he-goat for the Azazel also died, R. Johanan might agree that a double suspension is equivalent to invalidation.

31 Addition of the corrector. The question here is different. One brings a second pair and draws lots. According to the Mishnah, the new he-goat for the Azazel is selected. If then the first he-goat dies, following Rav's original position the second drawing of lots was made under erroneous hypotheses, and a third pair of he-goats would be needed.

The corrector's source is unknown.

(43c line 15) הִגְרִיל שְׁלֹשָׁה לִיתֵּן מֵאֶחָד עַל הַבַּדִּין. מֵאֶחָד עַל הַפָּרֹכוֹת. מֵאֶחָד עַל מִזְבַּח הַזָּהָב. אֵי זֶה מֵהֶן מִשְׁתַּלֵּחַ. רִבִּי זְעוּרָה אָמַר. לְכַפֵּר עָלָיו. אֶת שֶׁהוּא מְכַפֵּר בּוֹ חֲבֵירוֹ מִשְׁתַּלֵּחַ. אֶת שֶׁאֵינוֹ מְכַפֵּר בּוֹ אֵין חֲבֵירוֹ מִשְׁתַּלֵּחַ. רִבִּי הִילָא אָמַר. לְכַפֵּר עָלָיו. אֶת שֶׁהוּא גוֹמֵר בּוֹ אֶת כָּל־הַכַּפָּרָה חֲבֵירוֹ מִשְׁתַּלֵּחַ. אֶת שֶׁאֵינוֹ גוֹמֵר בּוֹ אֶת כָּל־הַכַּפָּרָה אֵין חֲבֵירוֹ מִשְׁתַּלֵּחַ. עַל דַּעְתֵּיהּ דְּרִבִּי זְעוּרָה. שְׁלָשְׁתָּן מִשְׁתַּלְּחִין. עַל דַּעְתֵּיהּ דְּרִבִּי הִילָא. אֵינוֹ מִשְׁתַּלֵּחַ אֶלָּא אַחֲרוֹן בִּלְבָד.

[32]If he drew lots for three pairs[2], to give from one between the beams, from one on the gobelins, from one on the golden altar. Which of them is sent away? Rebbi Ze`ira said, *to atone on him*, one with whom one atones, the companion is sent away; one with whom one does not atone, the companion is not sent away. Rebbi Hila said, *to atone on him*, one with whom one completes atonement, the companion is sent away. one with whom one does not complete atonement, the companion is not sent away. In Rebbi Ze`ira's opinion, all three are sent away. In Rebbi Hila's opinion, only the last one is sent away.

32   Text from Chapter 5, Notes 141-143.

(43c line 21) שֶׁאֵין חַטָּאת צִיבּוּר מֵתָה. רִבִּי יְהוּדָה אוֹמֵר תָּמוּת. וְקַשְׁיָא עַל דְּרִבִּי יְהוּדָה. וְיֵשׁ אָדָם מַגְרִיל לְמִיתָה מִשָּׁעָה רִאשׁוֹנָה. אָמַר רִבִּי אָבוּן. וְלֹא אַשְׁכְּחָן כֵּן עַל דְּרִבִּי אֱלִיעֶזֶר. דְּרִבִּי אֱלִיעֶזֶר אָמַר. יָמוּתוּ. אָמַר רִבִּי מָנָא. הֵן דְּאַתְּ מַקְשֵׁי לָהּ עַל דְּרִבִּי יְהוּדָה קַשְׁיתָהּ עַל דְּמַתְנִיתָהּ. דְּתַנִּינָן תַּמָּן. וְלַד חַטָּאת וּתְמוּרַת חַטָּאת וְחַטָּאת שֶׁמֵּתוּ בְעָלֶיהָ יָמוּתוּ. וְיֵשׁ אָדָם מֵימַר לְמִיתָה מִשָּׁעָה הָרִאשׁוֹנָה.

"Since no public purification sacrifice is let to die[6]. Rebbi Jehudah says, it shall die." It is difficult for Rebbi Jehudah: does one draw lots originally to die? Rebbi Abun said, do we not find this following Rebbi Eliezer[33], as Rebbi Eliezer said, they shall die? Rebbi Mana said, what you ask about Rebbi

Jehudah you should ask about the Mishnah, as we have stated there[34], "the calf of a purification offering, and the replacement of a purification offering, and a purification offering whose owners died, shall die." Would a person replace originally to die?

33 It is sinful to try to replace a validly dedicated animal by an other (*Lev.* 27:10). In the case of (voluntary) well-being offerings, both animals are dedicated as well-being offerings. For obligatory offerings, two animals cannot be brought instead of one. In Mishnah *Temurah* 3:3, the majority rules that the replacement of a valid reparation offering and any of its offspring shall be put out to graze until they develop a defect which makes them unfit as sacrifices, then be sold, and the proceeds given to the Temple to be used for additional sacrifices, But R. Eliezer rules that they have to be allowed to die immediately without any benefit to the Temple. R. Jehudah as student of his father R. Illay, a student of R. Eliezer, can be presumed to follow the latter's teachings.

34 Mishnah *Temurah* 4:1. In case of a purification offering everybody agrees with R. Eliezer, and one of the he-goats for which lots are drawn is a purification offering.

(fol. 43b) מִשְׁנָה ג: בָּא לוֹ אֵצֶל שָׂעִיר הַמִשְׁתַּלֵּחַ וְסָמַךְ שְׁתֵּי יָדָיו עָלָיו וְנִתְוַדָּה. וְכָךְ הָיָה אוֹמֵר אָנָּא הַשֵּׁם עָווּ פָּשְׁעוּ חָטְאוּ לְפָנֶיךָ עַמְּךָ בֵּית יִשְׂרָאֵל. אָנָּא הַשֵּׁם כַּפֶּר נָא וְגוֹ׳. מְסָרוֹ לְמִי שֶׁהוּא מוֹלִיכוֹ. הַכֹּל כְּשֵׁרִין לְהוֹלִיכוֹ אֶלָּא שֶׁעָשׂוּ כֹהֲנִים גְדוֹלִים קֶבַע וְלֹא הָיוּ מַנִּיחִין יִשְׂרָאֵל לְהוֹלִיכוֹ. אָמַר רִבִּי יוֹסֵי מַעֲשֶׂה וְהוֹלִיכוֹ עַרְשְׁלָא מִצִּיפּוֹרִין וְיִשְׂרָאֵל הָיָה:

Mishnah 3: He came to the he-goat to be sent away and leaned on it with both his hands and confessed. And thus he was saying: "Please Hashem, they acted criminally, offended, sinned before You, Your people, the House of Israel. Please Hashem, please atone the criminal acts," etc[35]. He handed him over to the one who led him. Everybody is qualified to lead him, but the High Priests made it an institution that they did not let an Israel lead him. Rebbi Yose said, it happened that Arsela[36] from Sepphoris led it, and he was an Israel.

35 Cf. Chapter 4, Note 61.

36 "Hammock", a nickname.

(43c line 21) **הלכה ב**: תַּנֵּי בַּר קַפָּרָא. עָווּ פָּשְׁעוּ חָטְאוּ. שֶׁלֹּא לְהַזְכִּיר גְנוּיָין שֶׁלְיִשְׂרָאֵל.

יַעֲמַד־חָי. מְלַמֵּד שֶׁהוּא עָתִיד לָמוּת. עַד מָתַי הוּא חָיָיה. עַד וְכִלָּה מִכַּפֵּר אֶת־הַקֹּדֶשׁ. דִּבְרֵי רִבִּי יְהוּדָה. רִבִּי שִׁמְעוֹן אוֹמֵר. עַד שְׁעַת הַוִידּוּי. עַל דַּעְתֵּיהּ דְּרִבִּי יְהוּדָה הַוִידּוּי מְעַכֵּב. עַל דַּעְתֵּיהּ דְּרִבִּי שִׁמְעוֹן אֵין הַוִידּוּי מְעַכֵּב. מַה נָפַק מִן בֵּינֵיהוֹן. שְׁלָחוֹ בְלֹא וִידּוּי. עַל דַּעְתֵּיהּ דְּרִבִּי יְהוּדָה צָרִיךְ לְהָבִיא שָׂעִיר אַחֵר. עַל דַּעְתֵּיהּ דְּרִבִּי שִׁמְעוֹן אֵינוֹ צָרִיךְ לְהָבִיא שָׂעִיר אַחֵר. אַף בַּפָּר כֵּן. שְׁחָטוֹ בְלֹא וִידּוּי. עַל דַּעְתֵּיהּ דְּרִבִּי יְהוּדָה צָרִיךְ לְהָבִיא פָר אַחֵר. עַל דַּעְתֵּיהּ דְּרִבִּי שִׁמְעוֹן אֵינוֹ צָרִיךְ לְהָבִיא פָר אַחֵר. נִתְוַדָּה וּשְׁחָטוֹ וְנִשְׁפַּךְ הַדָּם. וְאַתְּ אָמַר. צָרִיךְ לְהָבִיא פָר אַחֵר. צָרִיךְ לְהִתְוַדּוֹת עָלָיו פַּעַם שְׁנִיָּיה אוֹ כְבָר יָצָא בְוִידּוּיוֹ שֶׁלָּרִאשׁוֹן. אַף בְּשָׂעִיר הַמִּשְׁתַּלֵּחַ כֵּן. צָרִיךְ לְהַגְרִיל עָלָיו פַּעַם שְׁנִיָּיה אוֹ כְבַר יָצָא בְהַגְרִילוֹ שֶׁלָּרִאשׁוֹן.

Halakhah 2: Bar Qappara stated, "they acted criminally, offended, sinned," in order not to mention the shame of Israel[37].

[38]*It shall be made standing alive*, This teaches that in the end it will die[39]. [40]How long must it live? Up to *he will finish atoning the Sanctuary*[41], the words of Rebbi Jehudah. Rebbi Simeon says, up to the moment of confession. In Rebbi Jehudah's opinion, the confession is indispensable. In Rebbi Simeon's opinion, the confession is not indispensable[42]. What is the difference between them? If he sent it without a confession. In Rebbi Jehudah's opinion, he must bring another he-goat. In Rebbi Simeon's opinion, he does not have to bring another he-goat. The same holds for the bull. If he slaughtered without confession. In Rebbi Jehudah's opinion, he must bring another bull. In Rebbi Simeon's opinion, he does not have to bring another bull. If he confessed, slaughtered, then the blood was spilled. Do you say, does he have to bring another bull and confess a second time or did he do his duty with the first confession? The same holds for the scapegoat; must he cast lots a second time or did he do his duty with the first confession[43]?

37 In his text, the High Priest does not mention "Your people, the House of Israel."

38 *Sifra Ahare Pereq* 2(5),

39 *Lev.* 16:9. Since the he-goat could not stand if he were not alive, the emphasis on "alive" in this verse implies that later it will not be alive, that it should not be let free in the desert but be thrown from a cliff.

40 This paragraph is a slight rewrite of a paragraph in *Ševuot* 1:10 (Notes 127-241).

41 *Lev.* 16:20. Since there can be no atonement without confession, this will include the last confession of the High Priest even though it is mentioned only in v. 21.

42 It remains unresolved whether for R. Simeon no confession is obstructive or only the last one which is mentioned after the atonement of the Sanctuary was declared complete.

43 It already had been stated that there

has to be another drawing of lots with new animals,, the question is only about the confessions.

(43c linr 38) **הלכה ג**׳ וְשִׁלַּח בְּיַד־אִישׁ. לְהַכְשִׁיר אֶת הַזָּר. עִתִּי. שֶׁיְּהֵא עָתִיד. עִתִּי. שֶׁיְּהֵא מְזוּמָּן. עִתִּי. אַף בַּשַּׁבָּת. עִתִּי. אַף בְּטוּמְאָה. לֹא הָיָה עָתִיד וְהוּא מְזוּמָּן. אֶלָּא שֶׁלֹּא יְשַׁלְּחֻנּוּ בְּיַד שְׁנַיִם. שִׁילְּחוֹ בְּיַד שְׁנַיִם מָהוּ שֶׁיְּטַמֵּא בְגָדִים. נִשְׁמְעִינָהּ מִן הָדָא. וְהַמְשַׁלֵּחַ. לֹא הַמְשַׁלֵּחַ אֶת הַמְשַׁלֵּחַ. הָדָא אָמְרָה. שִׁילְּחוֹ בְּיַד שְׁנַיִם אֵינוֹ מְטַמֵּא בְגָדִים.

בָּרַח דֶּרֶךְ הֲלִיכָה מְטַמֵּא בְגָדִים. דֶּרֶךְ חֲזִירָה אֵינוֹ מְטַמֵּא בְגָדִים.

Halakhah 3: *He shall send him by a man*[44], to qualify the non-Cohen[45]. *Timely*[44]. that he be ready; *timely*, that he be prepared. *Timely*, even on the Sabbath; *timely*, even in impurity. Can he be not ready but prepared[46]? But that he should not send him by two people. If he sent him by two people, does he make clothing impure[47]? Let us hear from the following: *And the one who sends*[48]; not who was sending the one who sends. This implies that if he sent him by two people, it does not make clothing impure[49].

If it escapes in the direction in which it is going, it makes clothing impure, in the opposite direction it does not make clothing impure[51].

44   Lev. 16:21.
45   Since "man" is unspecific. Babli 66a/b.
46   Ready and prepared are practically the same, the duplication is unwarranted.
47   Lev. 16:26 states that the person bringing the scapegoat to the desert becomes impure together with his clothing.
48   Lev. 16:26.
49   Only the person first appointed to the task becomes impure.
50   If the scapegoat escapes and disappears in the desert, the biblical requirement is satisfied. But if it escapes in the direction of a cultivated area and is not recaptured, it was not sent to the desert and the mission of the person leading it is not fulfilled.

(43c line 44) שָׁאֲלוּ אֶת רִבִּי אֱלִיעֶזֶר. חָלָה הַשָּׁלִיחַ. אָמַר לָהֶן. כָּךְ תְּהוּ בְשָׁלוֹם. וְאִם חָלָה הַמִּשְׁתַּלֵּחַ. אָמַר לָהֶן. יָכוֹל הוּא לִטְעוֹן אֶתְכֶם וְלִי. דְּחָיָיו וְלֹא מֵת. אָמַר לָהֶן. כֵּן יְהוּ כָּל־אוֹיְבֵי הַשָּׁמַיִם. לֹא שֶׁהָיָה רִבִּי אֱלִיעֶזֶר מַפְלִיגָן אֶלָּא שֶׁלֹּא הָיָה אוֹמֵר לָהֶן דְּבָרִים שֶׁלֹּא שָׁמַע מִפִּיו. וַחֲכָמִים אוֹמְרִים. חָלָה הַשָּׁלִיחַ מְשַׁלְּחוֹ בְּיַד אַחֵר. חָלָה הַמִּשְׁתַּלֵּחַ מַרְכִּיבוֹ עַל הַחֲמוֹר. דְּחָיָיו וְלֹא מֵת. יוֹרֵד אַחֲרָיו וּמְמִיתוֹ.

[51]"They asked Rebbi Eliezer, if the agent got sick? He said to them, so you shall be in peace. If the scapegoat fell ill? He said to them, it can carry

you and me. If he pushed it but it did not die? He said to them, so it shall happen to all enemies of Heaven. Not that Rebbi Eliezer wanted to distract them, only that he did not tell them statements which he never had heard[52]. But the Sages are saying, if the agent got sick, he[53] sends it[54] by somebody else/ If the scapegoat fell ill, he[55] lets it[54] be carried on a donkey. If he[55] pushed it[54] but it did not die, he[55] has to descend after it and kill it."

51 Babli 66b, Tosephta 3:14.	service.
52 Which probably means that the cases never had happened before during the ascendancy of the Pharisees in the Temple	53 The High Priest.
	54 The scapegoat.
	55 The designated agent.

(43c line 49) כָּל־יָמִים שֶׁהָיָה שִׁמְעוֹן הַצַּדִּיק קַיָּים לֹא הָיָה מַגִּיעַ לְמַחֲצִית הָהָר עַד שֶׁנַּעֲשָׂה אֵיבָרִין אֵיבָרִין. מִשֶּׁמֵּת שִׁמְעוֹן הַצַּדִּיק הָיָה בּוֹרֵחַ לַמִּדְבָּר וְהַסַּרְקִיִּין אוֹכְלִין אוֹתוֹ. כָּל־יָמִים שֶׁהָיָה שִׁמְעוֹן הַצַּדִּיק קַיָּים הָיָה גּוֹרָל שֶׁלְּשֵׁם עוֹלֶה מִיָּמִין. מִשֶּׁמֵּת שִׁמְעוֹן הַצַּדִּיק פְּעָמִים בַּיָּמִין פְּעָמִים בַּשְׂמֹאל. כָּל־יָמִים שֶׁהָיָה שִׁמְעוֹן הַצַּדִּיק קַיָּים הָיָה נֵר מַעֲרָבִי דוֹלֵק. מִשֶּׁמֵּת שִׁמְעוֹן הַצַּדִּיק פְּעָמִים כָּבָה פְּעָמִים דּוֹלֵק. כָּל־יָמִים שֶׁהָיָה שִׁמְעוֹן הַצַּדִּיק קַיָּים הָיָה לְשׁוֹן שֶׁלִּזְהוֹרִית מַלְבִּין. מִשֶּׁמֵּת שִׁמְעוֹן הַצַּדִּיק פְּעָמִים מַלְבִּין פְּעָמִים מַאֲדִים. כָּל־יָמִים שֶׁהָיָה שִׁמְעוֹן הַצַּדִּיק קַיָּים הָיָה אוֹר הַמַּעֲרָכָה מִתְגַּבֵּר וְעוֹלֶה. מִשֶּׁהָיוּ נוֹתְנִין שְׁנֵי גִיזְרֵי עֵצִים בַּשַּׁחֲרִית לֹא הָיוּ נוֹתְנִין כָּל־הַיּוֹם. מִשֶּׁמֵּת שִׁמְעוֹן הַצַּדִּיק תָּשַׁשׁ כּוֹחָהּ שֶׁלַּמַּעֲרָכָה וְלֹא הָיוּ נִמְנָעִין לִהְיוֹת נוֹתְנִין עֵצִים כָּל־הַיּוֹם. כָּל־יָמִים שֶׁהָיָה שִׁמְעוֹן הַצַּדִּיק קַיָּים הָיְתָה בְרָכָה מְשׁוּלַּחַת בִּשְׁתֵּי הַלֶּחֶם וּבְלֶחֶם הַפָּנִים. וְהָיָה נוֹפֵל לְכָל־אֶחָד וְאֶחָד עַד כְּזַיִת. וְיֵשׁ מֵהֶן שֶׁהָיוּ א(ו)כְלִין וּשְׂבֵיעִין. וְיֵשׁ מֵהֶן שֶׁהָיוּ א(ו)כְלִין וּמוֹתִירִין. מִשֶּׁמֵּת שִׁמְעוֹן הַצַּדִּיק נִיטְלָה בְרָכָה מִשְּׁתֵּי הַלֶּחֶם וּמִלֶּחֶם הַפָּנִים. וְהָיָה נוֹפֵל לְכָל־אֶחָד וְאֶחָד עַד כְּאַפּוּן. הַצְּנוּעִים הָיוּ מוֹשְׁכִין אֶת יְדֵיהֶן. וְהַגַּרְגְּרָנִים הָיוּ פּוֹשְׁטִין אֶת יְדֵיהֶן. מַעֲשֶׂה בְכֹהֵן אֶלָּד בְּצִיפּוֹרִין שֶׁנָּטַל חֶלְקוֹ וְחֵלֶק חֲבֵירוֹ. וְהוּא הָיָה נִקְרָא בֶּן הָאַפּוּן עַד הַיּוֹם. הוּא שֶׁדָּוִד אָמַר אֱלֹהַי פַּלְּטֵנִי מִיַּד רָשָׁע מִכַּף מְעַוֵּל וְחוֹמֵץ.

[תַּנֵּי.] אַרְבָּעִים שָׁנָה עַד שֶׁלֹּא חָרַב בֵּית הַמִּקְדָּשׁ הָיָה נֵר מַעֲרָבִי כָּבָה וְלָשׁוֹן שֶׁלִּזְהוֹרִית מַאֲדִים וְגוֹרָל שֶׁלְּשֵׁם עוֹלֶה בַשְׂמֹאל. וְהָיוּ נוֹעֲלִין דַּלְתוֹת הַהֵיכָל מִבָּעֶרֶב וּמַשְׁכִּימִין וּמוֹצְאִין אוֹתָן פְּתוּחִין. אָמַר לוֹ רַבָּן יוֹחָנָן בֶּן זַכַּאי. הֵיכָל. לָמָּה אַתָּה מְבַהֲלֵינוּ. יוֹדְעִין אָנוּ שֶׁסּוֹפָךְ לִיחָרֵב. שֶׁנֶּאֱמַר פְּתַח לְבָנוֹן דְּלָתֶיךָ וְתֹאכַל אֵשׁ בַּאֲרָזֶיךָ:

[56]"All during Simeon the Just's lifetime he[54] did not fall down half the mountain before he dissolved into limbs; after Simeon the Just's death he fled to the desert and was eaten by the Saracens. All during Simeon the Just's lifetime the lot for Hashem[57] came up in his right hand; after Simeon the Just's

death sometimes it came up to the right, sometimes to the left. All during Simeon the Just's lifetime the Easternmost light[58] was burning; after Simeon the Just's death sometimes it was extinguished, sometimes burning. All during Simeon the Just's lifetime the shiny strip[59] turned white; after Simeon the Just's death sometimes it turned white, sometimes it turned red. All during Simeon the Just's lifetime the fire on the altar steadily increased; after they had put on two logs in the morning[60] they did not add anything during the day. After Simeon the Just's death the fire weakened; the had to add wood all day long. All during Simeon the Just's lifetime a blessing was in the Two Breads[61] and the shew-bread; the part of each one came to an olive sized bite; some of them ate and were full, some of them ate and left over. After Simeon the Just's death the blessing was taken from the Two Breads and the shew-bread; the part of each one came only to a pea-sized bit. The decent ones refrained from taking; the gluttons stretched out their hands. It happened that a Cohen from Sepphoris took his and another's part; he was called "pea-sized one" to this day. This is what David said[62], *My God, let me escape from the hand of the evildoer, from the palm of the criminal and oppressor.*"

[63]It was stated: "Forty years before the Temple was destroyed was the Eastern light extinguished, and the shiny strip became red, and the lot of the Name came up in the left hand. They were locking the doors of the Temple hall in the evening and in the morning they found them open. Rabban Joanan ben Zakkai addressed it: 'Temple hall, why do you frighten us? We know that in the end you will be destroyed, as it was said[64], *Lebanon*[65], *open your doors so fire may consume your cedars.*'"

---

56 Babli 39a, Tosephta *Sotah* 13:6-8.
57 Mishnah 4:1.
58 In the evening, the easternmost light of the candelabrum was lit first but in the morning it was serviced last. It was one of the miracles of the Temple that it outlasted all other lights of the candelabrum.
59 Mishnah 6.
60 Chapter 2, Note 19.
61 The two leavened breads required for the service of Pentecost; *Lev.* 23:17.
62 *Ps.* 71:4.
63 Babli 39b.
64 *Zach.* 11:1.
65 The Temple is identified with "Lebanon", cf. *Targum Onqelos* to *Deut.* 3:25; *Sifry Num.* 134, *Deut.* 28. The last source identifies the Temple Mount as "Lebanon".

(43c line 73) אַרְבָּעִים שָׁנָה שִׁימֵּשׁ שִׁמְעוֹן הַצַּדִּיק אֶת יִשְׂרָאֵל בִּכְהוּנָה גְדוֹלָה. וּבַשָּׁנָה הָאַחֲרוֹנָה אָמַר לָהֶן. בַּשָּׁנָה הַזֹּאת אֲנִי מֵת. אָמְרוּ לוֹ. לְמִי נִמְנֶה אַחֲרֶיךָ. אָמַר לָהֶן. הֲרֵי נְחוֹנְיוֹן בְּנִי לִפְנֵיכֶם. הָלְכוּ וּמִינּוּ אֶת נְחוֹנְיוֹן. וְקִינְּא בּוֹ [שִׁמְעוֹן] אָחִיו וְהָלַךְ וְהִלְבִּישׁוֹ [אוּנְקְ]לָה וַחֲגָרוֹ (צוּצָל) [צִלְצָל]. אָמַר לָהֶן. רְאוּ מַה נָדַר לַאֲהוּבָתוֹ. אָמַר לָהּ. לִכְשֶׁאֲשַׁמֵּשׁ בִּכְהוּנָה גְדוֹלָה אַלְבִּישׁ נַקְלָה שֶׁלָּךְ וְאֶחְגּוֹר (בְּצוּצָל) [בְּצִלְצָל] שֶׁלָּךְ. בָּדְקוּ אֶת הַדְּבָרִים וְלֹא מָצְאוּ [אוֹתוֹ]. אָמְרוּ. מִשָּׁם בָּרַח לְהַר הַמֶּלֶךְ. מִשָּׁם בָּרַח לְאַלֶכְּסַנְדְּרִיָּיאָה וְעָמַד וּבָנָה שָׁם מִזְבֵּחַ. וְקָרָא עָלָיו אֶת הַפָּסוּק הַזֶּה בַּיּוֹם הַהוּא יִהְיֶה מִזְבֵּחַ לַי' בְּתוֹךְ אֶרֶץ מִצְרָיִם. וַהֲרֵי הַדְּבָרִים קַל הַחוֹמֶר. וּמָה אִם זֶה שֶׁבָּרַח מִן הַשְּׂרָרָה רָאוּ הֵיאַךְ נֶחֱזַר עָלֶיהָ בַסּוֹף. מִי שֶׁהוּא נִכְנָס וְיוֹצֵא עַל אַחַת כַּמָּה וְכַמָּה. תַּנֵּי. זוֹ דִּבְרֵי רִבִּי מֵאִיר. רִבִּי יְהוּדָה אוֹמֵר. לֹא כִי אֶלָּא מִינּוּ אֶת שִׁמְעוֹן. וְקִינְּא בּוֹ נְחוֹנְיוֹן אָחִיו וְהָלַךְ וְהִלְבִּישׁוֹ נַקְלָה וַחֲגָרוֹ (צוּצָל) [צִלְצָל]. אָמַר לָהֶן. רְאוּ מַה נָדַר לַאֲהוּבָתוֹ כּוּל' הֵיךְ קַדְמִייָא. וַהֲרֵי הַדְּבָרִים קַל הַחוֹמֶר. וּמָה אִם מִי שֶׁלֹּא נִכְנַס לַשְּׂרָרָה רָאוּ הֵיאַךְ הֶעֱשִׂיא אֶת יִשְׂרָאֵל לַעֲבוֹדָה זָרָה. מִי שֶׁהוּא נִכְנָס וְיוֹצֵא עַל אַחַת כַּמָּה וְכַמָּה.

[66] Simeon the Just served Israel as High Priest for forty years, and in the last year he told them, in this year I am going to die. [67] They asked him, whom shall we appoint in your stead? He told them, there is my son Onias before you. They went and appointed Onias. His brother [Simon][68] was jealous of him, he went and dressed him in an undershirt[69] and girded him with a belt[70]. He told them, look what this one vowed to his sweetheart: when I shall serve as High Priest I shall wear your undershirt and gird myself with your belt[71]. They investigated and did not find [him][72]. It is said, he fled to King's Mountain, from there he fled to Alexandria, based himself there and built there an altar, over which he recited this verse[73], *on that day there will be an altar for the Eternal inside the Land of Egypt.* Is that not an argument *de minore ad majus*? See how this one who fled from prominence went to seek it at the end[74], if one attained it and lost it not so much more? It was stated, these are the words of Rebbi Meïr. Rebbi Jehudah said, it was not so but they appointed Simeon; his brother Onias was jealous of him, he went and dressed him in an undershirt and girded him with a belt. He told them, look what this one vowed to his sweetheart etc., as before[75] Is that not an argument *de minore ad majus*? See how this one who never attained prominence forced Israel to foreign worship[76], if one attained it and lost it not so much more?

66 Chapter 5, Note 77.
67 A different version in the Babli, *Menahot* 109b. Josephus dates the building of the Onias Temple three generations later.

68 Name added by the corrector, consistent with quote later of R. Jehudah's statement. In the Babli, the name is Simei, a more likely name for a son of Simeon.

69 Cf. *Šabbat* 16, Note 111. The spelling in the Hebrew text here is the corrector's following the Babli, erasing the Yerushalmi spelling retained later in the parallel statement of R. Jehudah.

70 The word in parentheses is the scribe's Yerushalmi spelling, the words in brackets the corrector's from the Babli. The form צוצל should be recognized by the dictionaries as Yerushalmi spelling.

71 Since the garments to be worn in Temple service are prescribed in *Ex.* 25, this plot presupposes an extremely ignorant High Priest.

72 Corrector's addition, probably incorrect. The investigation showed that the charges were unfounded, not that Onias was not to be found.

73 *Is.* 16:16.

74 Onias preferred not to become High Priest rather than become an object of an investigation. Nevertheless he became a kind of High Priest in Egypt.

75 Aramaic note of the scribe; the text of the previous *baraita* has to be inserted here.

79 In the Babli *Menahot* 109b there is a discussion whether the illegitimate Onias Temple is classified as idolatry or not.

(fol. 43b) **משנה ד:** וְכֶבֶשׁ עָשׂוּ לוֹ מִפְּנֵי הַבַּבְלִיִּים שֶׁהָיוּ מְתַלְּשִׁים בִּשְׂעָרוֹ וְאוֹמְרִים לוֹ טוֹל וָצֵא טוֹל וָצֵא. יְקִירֵי יְרוּשָׁלַיִם הָיוּ מְלַוִּין אוֹתוֹ עַד סוּכָּה הָרִאשׁוֹנָה. עֶשֶׂר סוּכּוֹת מִירוּשָׁלַיִם וְעַד צוּק תִּשְׁעִים רִיס שִׁבְעָה וּמֶחֱצָה לְכָל מִיל:

Mishnah 4: They built him a ramp because of the Babylonians[80] who were plucking his hair and saying to him, go quickly, go quickly. The venerables of Jerusalem were accompanying him to the first hut[81]. There were ten huts between Jerusalem and the cliff, 90 stadia, 7½ per *mil*[82].

משנה ה: עַל כָּל סוּכָּה וְסוּכָּה אוֹמְרִים לוֹ הֲרֵי מָזוֹן וַהֲרֵי מַיִם וּמְלַוִּין אוֹתוֹ מִסּוּכָּה לְסוּכָּה חוּץ מִן הָאַחֲרוֹן שֶׁבָּהֶן שֶׁאֵינוֹ מַגִּיעַ עִמּוֹ לַצּוּק אֶלָּא עוֹמֵד מֵרָחוֹק וְרוֹאֶה אֶת מַעֲשָׂיו:

Mishnah 5: At each hut one tells him, here is food, here is water, and one accompanies him from hut to hut except for the last leg where one does not come with him to the crag but stands afar and observes his actions[82].

80 In the Babylonian tradition (Babli 66b) the misbehaving people were Alexandrians. This is rejected in the Yerushalmi.

81 The person leading the scapegoat has the obligation to go to the desert; the people accompanying him cannot leave their Sabbath domain, 2'000 cubits or 7½ stadia.

82 30 *stadia* are 1 *parasang* or 4 *mil*.. The Greek *stadion* is a very badly defined measure; the reference here probably is to Egyptian measures; cf. *Introduction to Tractates Šabbat and Eruvin.*

The huts were equally spaced, one *mil* apart. 90 *stadia* are 12 *mil*; as indicated in Mishnah 5 the people whose Sabbath domain was centered at the tenth hut could accompany him only for one *mil*; the last *mil* to the cliff he had to go by himself.

(43d line 14) **הלכה ד**: אִית תַּנָּיֵי תַנֵּי. כָּבַשׁ גוּפוֹ. אִית תַּנָּיֵי תַנֵּי. כֶּבֶשׁ מַמָּשׁ.

אָמַר רִבִּי חִיָּיה בַּר יוֹסֵף. אֲלֶכְּסַנְדְּרִיִּין הָיוּ אוֹמְרִין. עַד מָתַי אַתֶּם תּוֹלִין אֶת הַקַּלְקָלָה בָּנוּ.

Halakhah 4: There are Tannaim who state, he compressed his body[83]. There are Tannaim who state, a genuine ramp.

Rebbi Hiyya bar Joseph said, the Alexandrians were saying, until when do you attribute the misconduct to us[80]?

83 The verb כבש means "to compress" (also to preserve edibles by vinegar or extended cooking, processes which shrink the volume); the noun כבש means "a ramp" ("preserve" is כבוש). It is left undecided whether the Mishnaic expression is to be read as a verb, that the man accompanying the scapegoat has to make himself inconspicuous, or as a noun, as translated in Mishnah 4.

(43d line 16) יַקִּירֵי יְרוּשָׁלַיִם הָיוּ מְלַוִּין אוֹתוֹ עַד סוּכָּה הָרִאשׁוֹנָה. תַּנֵּי. עֶשֶׂר סוּכּוֹת בְּתוֹךְ שְׁנֵים עָשָׂר מִיל. דִּבְרֵי רִבִּי מֵאִיר. רִבִּי יְהוּדָה אוֹמֵר. עֶשֶׂר סוּכּוֹת בְּתוֹךְ עֲשָׂרָה מִיל. רִבִּי יוֹסֵי אוֹמֵר. חָמֵשׁ. [וְכוּלָּן עַל יְדֵי עֵירוּב.] וְכֵן אָמַר לִי אֱלִיעֶזֶר בְּנִי. יָכוֹל אֲנִי לַעֲשׂוֹתָן שְׁתַּיִם עַל יְדֵי עֵירוּב.

"The venerables of Jerusalem were accompanying him to the first hut[81]." It was stated[84]. "Ten huts within twelve *mil*, the words of Rebbi Meïr. Rebbi Jehudah says, ten[85] huts within ten *mil*. Rebbi Yose said, five [and all of them by *eruv*;][86] and so my son Eliezer said to me, I can make them five by *eruv*[87].

84 Tosephta 3:13, Babli 67a.
85 In the parallel sources: Nine. There is no reason to adapt the Yerushalmi to the Babli sources. If each hut is at distance 1 *mil* from the preceding, the last hut is at *mil* 10, from which it is another two *mil* to the crag. In the reading of the Babli, the distance of the crag from the wall of Jerusalem would only be 11 *mil* for R. Jehudah.
86 Corrector's addition from the Babli, probably incorrect, since in the Yerushalmi version R. Yose accepts that his son's R. Eliezer's (should be R. Eleazar) argument parallels his own.
87 If one does not accept the corrector's

addition, the huts postulated by R. Yose are at distances 2,4,6,8,10. The venerables of Jerusalem go halfway to the first hut, where they are met by people from the first hut who will accompany the scapegoat halfway to the second hut, etc., and the people of the fifth hut will stop one *mil* from the crag, as described in the Mishnah. In the version of R. Eliezer (Eleazar) ben R. Yose (in the Tosephta, R. Yose ben R. Jehudah), the venerables of Jerusalem make an *eruv* outside the city walls which allows them to accompany the scapegoat for two *mil*. At the end of these two *mil* they are met by people from the first hut who made an *eruv* halfway to the meeting point; they accompany to the first hut which is at distance 4 from the city wall. Another group of people who made an *eruv* in the opposite direction accompany the scapegoat halfway to the next hut which is at distance 8. In this version, the person leading the scapegoat has to walk the last two *mil* alone since the second group of people from the second hut have to stop at *mil* 10.

(43d line 20) עַל כָּל סוּכָּה וְסוּכָּה אוֹמְרִים לוֹ. הֲרֵי מָזוֹן וַהֲרֵי מַיִם. לְיַיפּוֹת אֶת כּוֹחוֹ. לָמָה. שֶׁאֵין יֵצֶר הָרָע תָּאֵב אֶלָּא דָבָר שֶׁהוּא אָסוּר לוֹ. כְּהָדָא רִבִּי מָנָא סָלַק מְבַקְּרָה לְרִבִּי חַגַּי דַהֲוָה תָּשִׁישׁ. אָמַר לֵיהּ. צְהִינָא. אֲמַר לֵיהּ. שְׁתֵה. שָׁבְקֵיהּ וּנְחַת לֵיהּ. בָּתָר שָׁעָה סָלַק לְגַבֵּיהּ. אֲמַר לֵיהּ. מָה עָבְדַת הַהִיא צְהִיוּתָךְ. אֲמַר לֵיהּ. כַּד שָׁרִית לִי אָזְלַת לָהּ. רִבִּי חִייָא בַּר בָּא הֲוָה מְשַׁתְּעֵי הָדֵין עוֹבְדָא. חַד בַּר נַשׁ הֲוָה מְהַלֵּךְ בַּשׁוּקָא וּבְרַתֵּיהּ עִימֵּיהּ. אָמְרָה לֵיהּ בְּרַתֵּיהּ. אַבָּא. צְהִיָא אֲנָא. אֲמַר לָהּ. אוֹרְכִין צִיבְחַר. אָמְרָה לֵיהּ. אַבָּא. צְהִיָא אֲנָא. אֲמַר לָהּ. אוֹרְכִין צִיבְחַר. וּמִיתַת. רִבִּי אָחָא כַּד מְפַנֵּי מוּסָפָא הֲוָה אֲמַר קוֹמֵיהוֹן. אָחֵינָן. מָאן דְּאִית לֵיהּ מֵיינוּק יֵזִיל בְּגִינֵיהּ.

"At each hut one tells him, here is food, here is water." In order to strengthen him. Why? For the evil inclination desires only what is forbidden to him. As the following: Rebbi Mana went to visit Rebbi Ḥaggai who was weak[88]. He told him, I am thirsty; he answered him, drink[89]! He left him and went away. After an hour he visited him and asked him, how is your thirst? He told him, the moment you permitted me it went away. Rebbi Hiyya bar Abba told the following case: A man was walking in public[88] with his daughter. His daughter said to him, my father, I am thirsty. He said to her, wait a little bit. She said to him, my father, I am thirsty. He said to her, wait a little bit, and she died. When Rebbi Aha finished the *musaf* prayer[88] he said before them[90], our brothers, he who has small children should leave because of them[91].

88 On the Day of Atonement.
89 R. Haggai was very old at this moment, having been a student of R. Ze`ira, the teacher of R. Jeremiah, the teacher of R. Jonah, father and teacher of R. Mana.
90 His congregants.
91 To feed them and give them to drink. Since little children are not required to fast, permitting them to drink would not quell their thirst; they actually have to be given to drink.

(fol. 43b) **משנה ו:** וּמֶה הָיָה עוֹשֶׂה. חָלָק לָשׁוֹן שֶׁל זְהוֹרִית חֶצְיוֹ קָשַׁר בַּסֶּלַע וְחֶצְיוֹ קָשַׁר בֵּין שְׁתֵּי קַרְנָיו וְדוֹחֲפוֹ לַאֲחוֹרָיו מִתְגַּלְגֵּל וְיוֹרֵד לֹא הָיָה מַגִּיעַ לַחֲצִי הָהָר עַד שֶׁהוּא נַעֲשֶׂה אֲבָרִים אֲבָרִים. בָּא וְיָשַׁב לוֹ תַּחַת הַסֻּכָּה הָאַחֲרוֹנָה עַד שֶׁתֶּחְשַׁךְ. מֵאֵימָתַי מְטַמֵּא בְגָדִים מִשֶּׁיָּצֵא חוֹמַת יְרוּשָׁלַיִם. רִבִּי שִׁמְעוֹן אוֹמֵר מִשָּׁעַת דְּחִיָּיתוֹ לַצּוּק:

Mishnah 6: What did he do? He split the shiny strip[92]; half of it he bound on the rock and half of it he bound between its horns. Then he pushed it[93] backwards, it rolled descending. It did not reach half of the declivity before it dissolved into limbs. He goes and sits under the last hut[94] until nightfall. From when on does he make garments impure[95]? From when he exits the wall of Jerusalem; Rebbi Simeon says, from when he pushes on the crag.

92 Which was tied to the scapegoat's horns, Mishnah 4:2. It was expected to turn white as a sign of divine forgiveness, *Is.* 1:18.
93 The scapegoat.
94 Since he left his Sabbath domain by biblical commandment, he was permitted to return the 4'000 cubits to the first hut where he could rest for the remainder of the day and found food to break the fast at nightfall.
95 *Lev.* 16:26.

(43d line 25) **הלכה ה:** [בָּרִאשׁוֹנָה הָיוּ קוֹשְׁרִין אוֹתוֹ בַּחֲלוֹנוֹתֵיהֶם. וְיֵשׁ מֵהֶן שֶׁהָיָה מַלְבִּין וְיֵשׁ מֵהֶם שֶׁהָיָה מַאֲדִים. וְהָיוּ מִתְבַּיְּישִׁין אֵלּוּ מֵאֵלּוּ. חָזְרוּ וְקָשְׁרוּ אוֹתוֹ בְּפִתְחוֹ שֶׁל הֵיכָל. וְיֵשׁ שָׁנִים שֶׁהָיָה מַלְבִּין וְיֵשׁ שָׁנִים שֶׁהָיָה מַאֲדִים. חָזְרוּ וְקָשְׁרוּ אוֹתוֹ בַּסֶּלַע.

כְּתִיב לְכוּ־נָא וְנִוָּכְחָה וגו'. תַּנֵּי. רִבִּי אֶלְעָזָר אוֹמֵר. אִם־יִֽהְיוּ חֲטָאֵיכֶם כַּשָּׁנִים שֶׁבֵּין שָׁמַיִם וָאָרֶץ כַּשֶּׁלֶג יַלְבִּינוּ. יָתֵר מִיכָּן כַּאֲמַר יְהִי׃ רִבִּי יְהוֹשֻׁעַ אוֹמֵר. אִם־יִֽהְיוּ חֲטָאֵיכֶם כַּשָּׁנִים. כִּשְׁנֵי אָבוֹת הָרִאשׁוֹנִים. כַּשֶּׁלֶג יַלְבִּינוּ. וְאִם יַאְדִּימוּ כַתּוֹלָע כַּאֲמַר יְהִי׃ אָמַר רִבִּי יוּדָא בַּר פָּזִי. אִם־יִֽהְיוּ חֲטָאֵיכֶם כַּשָּׁנִי כַּשֶּׁלֶג יַלְבִּינוּ. בָּרִאשׁוֹן. אִם יַאְדִּימוּ כַתּוֹלָע כַּאֲמַר יְהִי׃ בַּשֵּׁנִי. וְרַבָּנִין אָמְרֵי. בִּזְמַן שֶׁעֲוֹנוֹתָיו שֶׁל אָדָם כְּפִי שָׁנָיו. כַּאֲמַר יְהִי׃]

[96][Originally they were tying it to their windows; some of them were turning white and some turning red; these were ashamed in front of the others. They changed and tied it to the door of the Sanctuary. Some years it was turning white, in others turning red. They changed and tied it to the rock.

It is written[97], *let us go and argue,* etc. It was stated, Rebbi Eliezer said, *If your sins were like years*[98], etc., like the years from Heaven to Earth, *they will be snow white*; more than that, *they shall be like wool.* Rebbi Joshua said, *if your sins were like years*, like the years of the patriarchs, *they will be snow white*; more than that, *they shall be like wool.* Rebbi Yuda bar Pazi said, *if your sins were like years they will be snow white*, the first time, *if they were like purple they shall be like wool,* the second time. But the rabbis said, If the sins of a person are like his years, *they will be snow white.*]

96 Corrector's addition from *Šabbat* 9, Notes 119-121, not in the original text. Cf. Babli 67a, *Roš Haššanah* 31b.
97 *Is.* 1:18.
98 Reading שָׁנִים as "years", not "purple wool". Both the distance of Heaven from Earth and the combined lifetime of the patriarchs were 500 years, cf. *Berakhot* 1:1, Note 83.

(fol. 43b) **משנה ז**: בָּא לוֹ אֵצֶל הַפָּר וְאֵצֶל הַשָּׂעִיר הַנִּשְׂרָפִין. קְרָעָן וְהוֹצִיא אֶת אֵמוּרֵיהֶן נְתָנָן בַּמָּגָס וְהִקְטִירָן עַל גַּבֵּי הַמִּזְבֵּחַ. קְלָעָן בַּמַּקְלוֹת וְהוֹצִיאָן לְבֵית הַשְּׂרֵיפָה. מֵאֵימָתַי מְטַמִּין בְּגָדִים מִשֶּׁיֵצְאוּ חוֹמַת הָעֲזָרָה. רִבִּי שִׁמְעוֹן אוֹמֵר מִשֶּׁיִצַּת הָאוּר בְּרוּבָּן:

Mishnah 7: He[97*] comes to the bull and the he-goat to be burned, cut them open and removed the inner parts[98*], put then into a basin and burned them on the altar. He bound them to bars and took them out to the place of burning. When do they make garments impure[99]? From the moment they leave the wall of the Temple courtyard; Rebbi Simeon says, from when the fire ignites most of them.

משנה ח: אָמְרוּ לוֹ לְכֹהֵן גָּדוֹל הִגִּיעַ שָׂעִיר לַמִּדְבָּר. וּמִנַּיִין הָיוּ יוֹדְעִין שֶׁהִגִּיעַ שָׂעִיר לַמִּדְבָּר. דִּידְכָאוֹת הָיוּ עוֹשִׂין וּמְנִיפִין בַּסּוּדָרִין וְיוֹדְעִין שֶׁהִגִּיעַ שָׂעִיר לַמִּדְבָּר.

Mishnah 8: They told the High Priest that the he-goat arrived in the desert. And from where did they know that the he-goat arrived in the desert? They had overseers[100] posted who waved sheets and they knew that the he-goat had arrived in the desert.

משנה ט: אָמַר רִבִּי יְהוּדָה וַהֲלֹא סִימָן גָּדוֹל הָיָה לָהֶם שְׁלֹשֶׁת מִילִין מִירוּשָׁלַיִם וְעַד בֵּית חוֹרוֹן. הוֹלְכִין מִיל וְחוֹזְרִין מִיל וְשׁוֹהִין כְּדֵי מִיל וְיוֹדְעִין שֶׁהִגִּיעַ שָׂעִיר לַמִּדְבָּר. רִבִּי יִשְׁמָעֵאל אוֹמֵר וַהֲלֹא סִימָן אַחֵר הָיָה לָהֶם לָשׁוֹן שֶׁל זְהוֹרִית הָיָה קָשׁוּר עַל פִּתְחוֹ שֶׁל הֵיכָל וּכְשֶׁהִגִּיעַ שָׂעִיר לַמִּדְבָּר הָיָה הַלָּשׁוֹן מַלְבִּין שֶׁנֶּאֱמַר אִם יִהְיוּ חֲטָאֵיכֶם כַּשָּׁנִים כַּשֶּׁלֶג יַלְבִּינוּ:

Mishnah 9: Rebbi Jehudah said, did they not have an important sign? There are three *mil* from Jerusalem to Bet Horon[101]; they were walking one *mil*, returning one *mil*, and waiting for another *mil*; then they knew that the he-goat had arrived in the desert. Rebbi Ismael said, did they not have another sign? A shiny strip was tied to the door of the Temple hall; when the he-goat arrived in the desert it turned white[102], as it is said[95], *if your sins were like crimson they will be white like snow*.

97* The High Priest.
98* Greek μηρία, τά, "thigh bones", the parts of a sacrifice which have to be burned on the altar.
99 Lev. 16:28. It is implied that other priests transport the carcasses to be burned.
100 Greek διάδοχοι, οἱ.
101 Even though this text is confirmed by Maimonides's autograph Mishnah, it seems impossible since Bet Horon is NE of Jerusalem in inhabited territory. The Babli's reading, *Bet Hidud* seems more appropriate; it may designate *Wadi al-Hod*. R. Jehudah does not require the he-goat to be on the crag, only outside agricultural land.
102 He disputes the fact that the strip was no longer tied to the Temple door.

(43d line 38) [בָּא לוֹ אֵצֶל פָּרוֹ וכו'.] אֲנַן תַּנִּינָן. בָּא לוֹ אֵצֶל הַפָּר וְאֵצֶל שָׂעִיר הַנִּשְׂרָפִין. אִית תַּנָּיֵי תַנֵּי. בָּא לוֹ כֹּהֵן גָּדוֹל לִקְרוֹת. אָמַר רִבִּי חֲנַנְיָה. קְרָא מְסַייֵעַ לְמַתְנִיתִין. וְהַמְשַׁלֵּחַ אֶת־הַשָּׂעִיר לַעֲזָאזֵל יְכַבֵּס בְּגָדָיו. מַה כְּתִיב בַּתְרֵיהּ. וְאֵת פַּר הַחַטָּאת וְאֵת שְׂעִיר הַחַטָּאת. אָמַר רִבִּי מָנָא. [וַאֲפִילוּ] כָּאהֵן דְּתַנִּינָן תַּנָּיָא בָּרָיָא אַתְיָא הִיא. כְּאֵינָשׁ דִּסְלַק מִטִּיבֶּרְיָא לְצִיפּוֹרִין. עַד דְּהוּא בְטִיבֶּרְיָא אֲמָרִין. בְּצִיפּוֹרִין הוּא יָתִיב.

[He comes to his bull, etc.][103] We have stated: "He comes to the bull and the he-goat to be burned." There are Tannaim who state, the High Priest comes to read[104]. Rebbi Hananiah said, the verse supports our Mishnah: *He who sends the he-goat to Azazel shall wash his garments*[105]. What is written next? *And the purification bull and the purification he-goat*[106]. Rebbi Mana said, it may be interpreted even following the Tanna of the *baraita*. If a person moves from Tiberias to Sepphoris, while he still is in Tiberias do people say, he dwells in Sepphoris[107].

103 Addition by the corrector, slightly misquoted (Mishnah 3:9 instead of 6:7).
104 The public Torah reading which according to Mishnah 7:1 follows the completion of the service of purification.
105 *Lev.* 16:26.
106 *Lev.* 16:27. The sacrifices have to be burned outside the sacred domain.
107 All the verse indicates is that the he-goat has to be sent away before the purification sacrifices are removed from the sacred precinct; no exact time frame is given in view of the fact that the Torah reading is not biblically prescribed at this point.

(43d line 44) רִבִּי זְרִיקָן אָמַר רִבִּי זְעִירָה שָׁאַל. פָּרִים הַנִּשְׂרָפִין וּשְׂעִירִין הַנִּשְׂרָפִין שֶׁנִּיטְמְאוּ מָהוּ שֶׁיִּשָּׂרְפוּ כְמִצְוָותָן. מַה צְרִיכָה לֵיהּ. בְּשֶׁנִּיטְמְאוּ לִפְנֵי זְרִיקָה. אֲבָל אִם נִיטְמוּ אַחַר זְרִיקָה קוֹרֵא אֲנִי עָלָיו בְּמוֹעֲדוֹ. אַף בַּשַׁבָּת. בְּמוֹעֲדוֹ. אַף בְּטוּמְאָה. [אָמַר רִבִּי יוֹסֵי. וְעֵדָה שֶׁכָּתַב בּוֹ בְמוֹעֲדוֹ לֵית שְׁמַע מִינָּהּ כְּלוּם.] אָמַר רִבִּי מָנָא. לֹא מִיתְמְנַע רִבִּי יוֹסֵי קַיָּים הָכָא. וַאֲמַר לֵיהּ. קַיָּים בְּפַר מָשִׁיחַ וְעֵדָה. וְאָמַר לֵיהּ.

רִבִּי בּוּן בַּר חִייָה אָמַר רִבִּי לְעָזָר שָׁאַל. פָּרִים הַנִּשְׂרָפִין וּשְׂעִירִים הַנִּשְׂרָפִין שֶׁיָּצָא רוֹב הָאֵבֶר הַמַּשְׁלִים לָרוֹב. מִילְתֵיהּ אֲמְרָה. בְּרוּבּוֹ הַדָּבָר תָּלוּי. פְּשִׁיטָא הָדָא מִילְתָא. יָצָא רוּבּוֹ וְאַחַר כָּךְ יָצָא רוֹב הָאֵבֶר הַמַּשְׁלִים לָרוֹב. [לֹא צוֹרְכָא דְלֹא יָצָא אֵבֶר אֵבֶר וְאַחַר כָּךְ יָצָא רוֹב הָאֵבֶר הַמַּשְׁלִים לָרוֹב.]

Rebbi Zeriqan said that Rebbi Ze`ira asked: If bulls and he-goats to be burned became impure, may they be burned according to their rules[108]? What is his problem? If they became impure before the blood was poured, but if they became impure after the blood was poured[109] I am applying to it, *at its appointed time*[110], even on the Sabbath, *at its appointed time,* even in impurity. [Rebbi Yose said, there where it is written *at its appointed time*; you do not infer anything from it[111].][112] Rebbi Mana said, does not Rebbi Yose refrain from applying it here? He applies it to the bull of the Anointed and the Congregation[113] {he said to him}[114].

Rebbi Abun bar Ḥiyya said, Rebbi Eleazar asked: If of bulls and he-goats to be burned a limb left which completes a majority[115]? His question implies that the matter depends on a majority. The following is obvious: If most of it left and after this a limb left which completes a majority. [This must be: It left limb by limb and after this a limb left which completes a majority[116]..][117]

108 If the carcasses are pure, then they have to be burned on the Day of Atonement by biblical decree, *Lev.* 16:27, and by practice of the Temple service at a place different from that where disabled sacrifices are usually burned (Mishnah *Zevahim* 12:5).

If in impurity they follow the rules of disabled sacrifices, they can be burned only in the following night and at a different place.

109 Then the sacrifice is valid and does not have to be repeated even if some subsequent action would have been required which now becomes impossible.

110 *Num.* 9,2 28:2. *Sifry Num.* 65,142; *Mekhilta Ba* 5 (ed. Horovitz-Rabin p. 17), Tosephta *Pisha* 4:14; *Pesahim* 6:1 Notes 9,10, Babli *Pesahim* 66a.

111 Since in *Lev.* 16 neither the expression "at its appointed time" nor an equivalent is mentioned, the argument simply does not apply in our case.

112 Addition of the corrector, in good Yerushalmi language. The addition is necessary to understand R. Mana's remark and must have been taken from a manuscript source.

113 *Lev.* 4:1-21. Since these sacrifices can only be brought on a weekday, the only problem is that of the place of burning as given in Mishnah *Zevahim* 12:5. He will accept that they not be burned on the appointed place only if they become invalid by a cause other than impurity.

114 It seems that this has to be deleted.

115 Babli *Zevahim* 104b. Since it was stated in Mishnah 7 that the carcasses become a source of severe impurity once they are brought outside the enclosure of the Temple courtyards, the question is the determination of the exact point in time when this happens. As stated in the next sentence, it is agreed that a majority of the carcass must have left. The question remains whether the majority is counted atom by atom, which would be impossible to determine exactly, or limb by limb. Since the only practical solution is to count limb by limb, must the limb which completes the majority be totally outside or possibly only partially.

116 The preceding sentence in fact makes no sense.

117 Addition of the corrector, in good Yerushalmi language. They must have been taken from a manuscript source.

(43d line 54) רִבִּי חִיָּיה בַּר בָּא אָמַר רִבִּי לָעְזֶר שָׁאַל. פָּרִים הַנִּשְׂרָפִין וּשְׂעִירִים הַנִּשְׂרָפִין שֶׁיָּצְאוּ וְחָזְרוּ. פְּשִׁיטָא דֶּרֶךְ חֲזִירָה אֵינוֹ מְטַמֵּא בְגָדִים. לָא צוֹרְכָא דְלָא מִכֵּיוָן שֶׁהִתְחִילוּ לָצֵאת מַהוּ שֶׁיְּטַמּוּ בְגָדִים. הָתִיב רִבִּי בָּא. וְהָא תַנִּינָן. הָיוּ סוֹבְלִין אוֹתָן בְּמוֹטוֹת. יָצְאוּ הָרִאשׁוֹנִים חוּץ לְחוֹמַת עֲזָרָה הָאַחֲרוֹנִים לֹא יָצְאוּ. הָרִאשׁוֹנִים מְטַמְּאִין בְּגָדִים. הָאַחֲרוֹנִים אֵינָן מְטַמְּאִים בְּגָדִים עַד שֶׁיֵּצְאוּ. יָצְאוּ אֵלּוּ וְאֵלּוּ [מְטַמְּאִין בְּגָדִים]. אָמַר רִבִּי יוּדָן דְּרִבִּי מַתַּנְיָה. שַׁנְיָא הִיא דִּכְתִיב וְהוֹצִיא. עַד שֶׁיּוֹצִיא רְשׁוּת כָּל־הַמּוֹצִיא.

רִבִּי יִרְמְיָה אָמַר רִבִּי לָעְזֶר שָׁאַל. פָּרִים הַנִּשְׂרָפִין וּשְׂעִירִין הַנִּשְׂרָפִין שֶׁנִּטְמוּ מָהוּ שֶׁיִּיפָּסְלוּ מִשֵּׁם יוֹצֵא. מַה צְּרִיכָה לֵיהּ. כְּרִבִּי שִׁמְעוֹן בֶּן לָקִישׁ. בְּרַם כְּרִבִּי יוֹחָנָן פְּשִׁיטָא לֵיהּ. דְּאִיתְפַּלְגוֹן הַשּׁוֹחֵט תּוֹדָה בִּפְנִים וְלַחְמָהּ חוּץ לַחוֹמָה. לֹא קָדַשׁ הַלֶּחֶם. רִבִּי יוֹחָנָן אָמַר. חוּץ לְחוֹמַת יְרוּשָׁלַם. רִבִּי שִׁמְעוֹן בֶּן לָקִישׁ אָמַר. חוּץ לְחוֹמַת הָעֲזָרָה. רִבִּי שִׁמְעוֹן בֶּן לָקִישׁ כְּדַעְתֵּיהּ. דְּאָמַר רִבִּי אַמִּי בְּשֵׁם רִבִּי שִׁמְעוֹן בֶּן לָקִישׁ. בְּשַׂר שְׁלָמִים שֶׁיָּצָא כָּךְ נִכְנַס וְאַחַר כָּךְ נִזְרַק עָלָיו מִן הַדָּם

כְּבָר נִפְסַל מִשָּׁם יוֹצֵא. אָמַר רִבִּי יוֹסֵה. וַאֲפִילוּ כְּרִבִּי יוֹחָנָן צְרִיכָה לֵיהּ. יְרוּשָׁלַם אַף עַל פִּי שֶׁאֵינָהּ מְחִיצָה לְקָדְשֵׁי קָדָשִׁים מְחִיצָה לְקָדָשִׁים קַלִּים. חוּץ לְחוֹמַת יְרוּשָׁלַם אֵינָהּ מְחִיצָה לֹא לְקָדְשֵׁי קָדָשִׁים וְלֹא לְקָדָשִׁים קַלִּין. אָמַר רִבִּי מָנָא. אֵינָהּ מְחִיצָה לָהֶן.

Rebbi Hiyya bar Abba said, Rebbi Eleazar asked: If bulls and he-goats to be burned were taken out and brought back[118]? It is obvious for us that in returning they do not make garments impure[119]. What our problem is, do they make garments impure from the moment they started to be brought out[120]? Rebbi Abba objected, did we not state[121]: "They were carrying them on yokes. If the front carriers left the walls of the Temple courtyard while the back carriers did not yet leave, the front carriers make garments impure while the back carriers do not make garments impure until they also leave. After they left, these and those make garments impure." Rebbi Yudan, Rebbi Mattaniah's father, said, there is a difference, for it is written, *then he shall take out*[122], until he completely leave the domain from which it is taken out[123].

[124]Rebbi Jeremiah said, Rebbi Eleazar asked: If bulls and he-goats to be burned became impure, may they still become disqualified for being taken out[125]? What is his problem? Following Rebbi Simeon ben Laqish; but following Rebbi Johanan it is obvious for him. For they disagreed: [126]"If somebody slaughters a thanksgiving sacrifice inside while its bread[127] is outside the walls, the bread was not sanctified." Rebbi Johanan said, outside the walls of Jerusalem[128]; Rebbi Simeon ben Laqish said, outside the walls of the Temple court.[129] Rebbi Simeon ben Laqish is consequent in his opinion since Rebbi Simeon ben Laqish said, meat of well-being offerings which was taken out and then returned, if the blood is poured for it already it is disqualified because of removal[130]. Rebbi Yose said, he questions even according to Rebbi Johanan. While Jerusalem is not an enclosure for most holy sacrifices, it is an enclosure for simple sacrifice. Outside the walls of Jerusalem[131] it is an enclosure neither for most holy sacrifices nor for simple sacrifices. Rebbi Mana said, it is not an enclosure for them[132].

118 Since it was established in the previous paragraph that the carcasses are the cause of severe impurity by biblical decree once the majority of the limbs was removed from the Temple precinct, the question necessarily refers to single limbs which do not constitute a majority of the carcass. The question is different in the Babli, *Zevahim*

105a.

119 A limb even partially taken out of the sacred precinct becomes disqualified. Even if a person other than the carrier who touches a limb while it is taken back may become impure in his person, the impurity does not extend to his clothing since the biblical conditions for this are not satisfied.

120 As will be seen, the question is about people other than the carriers of the carcass or its limbs. If the carcass was partially taken out but then returned, and a third party touched the body, do his garments become impure?

121 Mishnah *Zevahim* 12:6.

122 *Lev.* 4:12, about the purification sacrifice of the anointed priest.

123 The carriers become impure the moment they are completely outside the wall of the Temple courtyard, but the carcass becomes a source of severe impurity for any who touch it only after it was completely taken out of the sacred domain. The carriers become impure even if they never come in contact with the carcass. The wooden bars on which the carcass is carried do not transmit impurity by touch; the impurity of the carriers is induced by the motion of the carcass, not by contact.

124 Babli *Zevahim* 104a.

125 If the carcasses become impure inside the sacred precinct they automatically are disqualified. Once disqualified they cannot become more disqualified by being taken out. Either with the classical commentaries one has to delete the words "became impure" and (with the Babli) ask whether bulls and he-goats to be burned, for which being taken outside is a biblical commandment at a later stage, can become disqualified by being taken out in a earlier stage, or one restricts the question to the sacrifices of the Day of Atonement which as public sacrifices may be offered in impurity if most of Israel are impure.

126 Mishnah *Menahot* 7:3.

127 A thanksgiving offering has to be brought *on* loaves of leavened bread (*Lev.* 7:13). This is interpreted to mean that the loaves have to be nearby. The question is the definition of "nearby".

128 Since the thanksgiving sacrifice as a family celebration may be consumed anywhere within the walls of Jerusalem (which takes the place of the camp of the Israelites in the desert), one only requires that the bread be at a place where it may be consumed.

129 He requires that the bread be inside the sacred precinct since the presentation of the sacrifice is possible only there.

130 Well-being sacrifices in general may be eaten in the entire city of Jerusalem (Mishnah *Zevahim* 5:7). Nevertheless, meat taken out of the sacred precinct into the city before its time (i. e., before pouring the blood on the altar walls) disqualifies the entire sacrifice. The same argument can be applied to the case under discussion.

131 Where the bulls and he-goats to be burned have to be brought.

132 R. Johanan qualifies the thanksgiving offering if all parts are in the place of their final destination at all times. If this argument is applied to bulls and he-goats to be burned, the walls of Jerusalem become irrelevant.

(43d line 72) רִבִּי לְעָזָר שָׁאַל. פָּרִים הַנִּשְׂרָפִין וּשְׂעִירִים הַנִּשְׂרָפִין מָהוּ שֶׁיִּטַמּוּ בְגָדִים בְּלֹא הֶכְשֵׁר בְּלֹא טוּמְאָה מִפְּנֵי שֶׁסּוֹפָן לְטַמּוֹת טוּמְאָה חֲמוּרָה. הֵתִיב שְׁמוּאֵל קַפּוֹדְקָיָא. מֵעַתָּה יִטַמּוּ אֶת אֵימוֹרֵיהֶן. אֶלָּא כְשֶׁפֵּירְשׁוּ. וַאֲפִילוּ תֵימַר. לֹא פִירְשׁוּ. כְּהָדָא. אֵין מֵי חַטָּאת מְטַמְּאִין דָּבָר לַחֲזוֹר וּלְטַמּוֹת מִמֶּנּוּ. הֵתִיב רִבִּי יִרְמְיָה. הֲרֵי נִבְלַת עוֹף הַטָּהוֹר הֲרֵי הוּא מְטַמֵּא טוּמְאַת אוֹכְלִין בְּלֹא הֶכְשֵׁר בְּלֹא טוּמְאָה מִפְּנֵי שֶׁסּוֹפָן לִיטַמּוֹת טוּמְאָה חֲמוּרָה. אָמַר רִבִּי יוֹסֵה. נִבְלַת עוֹף הַטָּהוֹר אֵין לָהּ מְחִיצָה. אֵילּוּ יֵשׁ לָהֶן מְחִיצָה. אָמַר רִבִּי מָנָא. נִבְלַת עוֹף הַטָּהוֹר יֵשׁ לָהּ מְחִיצָה. אָדָם הוּא מְחִיצָתָהּ. דְּאִי לֹא כֵן אִילּוּ הֵבִיא כֶלֶב וְהִלְבִּישׁוֹ בְגָדִים וְהֶאֱכִילוֹ נִבְלַת עוֹף הַטָּהוֹר. שֶׁמָּא אֵינוֹ מְטַמֵּא בְגָדִים בְּבֵית הַבְּלִיעָה. אָמַר רִבִּי לְעָזָר דְּרוֹמַיָּא. נִבְלַת עוֹף הַטָּהוֹר מְחִצָתָהּ בְּכָל־מָקוֹם. אֵילּוּ מְחִיצָתָן חוּץ לִירוּשָׁלַֽם.

Rebbi Eleazar asked, do bulls and he-goats to be burned cause impurity of garments[133] without preparation[134] and without impurity[135] since at the end they become sources of severe impurity? Samuel from Cappadocia objected, then they should make their parts[136] impure. So only after they were taken away. And even if you are saying before they were taken away, parallel to the following: purifying water does not make anything impure to make itself impure in return[137]. Rebbi Jeremiah objected, does not a carcass of a pure bird make food impure without preparation, without impurity, since at the end it becomes a source of severe impurity[138]? Rebbi Yose said, the carcass of a pure bird has no enclosure[139]; these have an enclosure. Rebbi Mana said, the carcass of a pure bird has an enclosure; the human is its enclosure[140]. If it were not so, if he brought a dog, clothed it, and fed it the carcass of a pure bird, would it not make the garments impure in its palate[141]? Rebbi Eleazar the Southerner said, the enclosure of the carcass of a pure bird is everywhere; the enclosure of those is outside of Jerusalem[142].

133 One has to delete this and replace it with "of foodstuffs". Garments become impure only from sources of severe impurity, but foodstuffs become impure even from impurity which is not transmissible tu human bodies or garments. Since the question is asked whether the carcasses cause impurity even before they are taken out, there cannot be any question of severe impurity at this point in time. Babli *Zevahim* 105a.

134 Foodstuffs in general can become impure only after "preparation" by contact with water; cf. *Terumot* 1:1 Note 7. Since the basis of this rule is *Lev.* 11:38 referring to grain which cannot become severely impure, it is concluded that severe impurity makes foodstuffs impure even without preparation.

135 The carcasses of bulls and he-goats to

be burned, as well as the carcass of the Red Cow, cause severe impurity to the people occupied with it but they themselves are pure; Mishnah *Parah* 8:3, Babli *Zebahim* 105a..

136 The inner parts (of the bulls of the Anointed Priest and the Congregation) which have to be burned on the altar; cf. Chapter 5 Note 155.

137 The person who purifies another by sprinkling him with water containing ashes of the Red Cow becomes impure (*Num.* 19:21) but the water itself remains pure in his hands, while in general an impure person makes water which he touches impure in the first degree.

138 .Mishnah *Tahorot* 1:1; *Sifra Ahare Pereq* 11(5-6). It is inferred that *Lev.* 17:15 must refer to meat that only is forbidden because it is carcass meat, and that the verse cannot refer to four-legged animals since they are impure from the start, and it cannot refer to non-kosher animals or birds since for them the reference to torn meat would be irrelevant. The only meat which causes impurity only if taken into the mouth to be eaten is that of pure birds not correctly slaughtered. Babli *Zevahim* 105a, *Hulin* 121a.

139 It is forbidden to be eaten anywhere, whereas *sancta* may be treated only in the sacred precinct.

140 Only the human mouth causes impurity from carcass meat of pure birds.

141 But since a living animal cannot become impure, textiles worn by a dog eating the carcass of a pure bird remain pure.

141 Since the place of burning is biblically prescribed, *Lev.* 4:12, it is as if that place were enclosed.

(44a line 9) אָמַר רִבִּי לְעָזָר. פָּרִים הַנִּשְׂרָפִין וּשְׂעִירִין הַנִּשְׂרָפִין שֶׁשְּׁחָטָן לִזְרוֹק אֶת דָּמָן לְמָחָר פִּיגֵּל. לְהַקְטִיר אֵימוֹרִין לְמָחָר פִּיגֵּל. לְשָׂרוֹף אֶת בְּשָׂרוֹ לְמָחָר לֹא פִיגֵּל. שֶׁלֹּא חִישֵּׁב לֹא לַאֲכִילַת אָדָם וְלֹא לַאֲכִילַת מִזְבֵּחַ.

רִבִּי שַׁמַּי בָּעֵי. אֲבָדוּ הָאֵימוֹרִין. מַהוּ לִזְרוֹק אֶת הַדָּם עַל הַבָּשָׂר. וְלָא שְׁמִיעַ דַּאֲמַר רִבִּי לְעָזָר. שֶׁלֹּא חִישֵּׁב לֹא לַאֲכִילַת אָדָם וְלֹא לַאֲכִילַת מִזְבֵּחַ. תַּנָּא רִבִּי זַכַּיי. [זָר] שֶׁשָּׂרַף מְטַמֵּא בְגָדִים. לֹא צוֹרְכָה דְּלֹא מָהוּ שֶׁיְּהוּ כְשֵׁירִים בַּלַּיְלָה. קַל וָחוֹמֶר. מַה אִם הֶקְטֵר אֵימוֹרִין שֶׁאֵינָן כְּשֵׁירִין בְּזָר כְּשֵׁירִין בַּלַּיְלָה. אֵילּוּ שֶׁהֵן כְּשֵׁירִין בְּזָר אֵינוֹ דִין שֶׁיְּהוּ כְשֵׁירִים בַּלַּיְלָה.

Rebbi Eleazar said, bulls and he-goats to be burned which he slaughtered with the intent to pour the blood the next day, he made *piggul*[142]. To burn the parts on the next day he made *piggul*[143]. To burn the meat the next day he did not make *piggul* since he neither intended it as food for humans nor as food for the altar[144].

Rebbi Shammai asked, if the parts were lost, may one pour the blood for the meat? He had not heard what Rebbi Eleazar had said, since he neither intended as food for humans nor as food for the altar[145]. Rebbi Zakkai stated:

A non-Cohen who burned makes garments impure[146]. One only has to ask, is it qualified during nighttime[147]? It is an argument *de minore ad majus*. Since burning of the parts which is not qualified for a non-Cohen may be done in the night, for these[148] which are qualified for a non-Cohen it is logical that it should be qualified during nighttime.

142 Cf. *Pesahim* 5, Note 67. Pouring the blood on the altar is qualified as "eating by the altar." Cf. Babli *Zevahim* 104b.

143 Parts burned on the altar are "eaten" by the altar.

144 Since the carcass has to be burned outside the sacred precinct and outside of Jerusalem, the places were the parts and the meat of well-being offerings would have to be consumed, the rules of *piggul* cannot apply.

145 While for other sacrifices one may pour the blood to permit the meat to be eaten by the owners (for family sacrifices), or by the Cohanim (for purification and reparation sacrifices), or by the altar (for elevation sacrifices), in the case of bulls and he-goats to be burned there is nothing to be permitted and therefore the blood may not be poured.

146 While the carcasses must be carried out by Cohanim since non-Cohanim cannot enter the inner courtyard where the ceremonies take place, there is nothing in the verses (*Lev.* 4:12,21; 16:28) to indicate that the burning outside the camp needs Cohanim.

147 It is clear from the verses quoted that the carcasses have to be taken out of the camp (Jerusalem) on the day of the sacrifice; but there are no indications that the burning has to be finished on the same day.

148 Bulls and he-goats to be burned.

(44a line 18) וְהַשׂוֹרֵף. לֹא הַמַּצִּית אֶת הָאוּר וְלֹא הַמְסַדֵּר אֶת הַמַּעֲרָכָה. אֵי זֶהוּ [הַשּׂוֹרֵף. זָהוּ] הַמְסַיֵּיעַ בִּשְׁעַת הַשְּׂרִיפָה. [אָמַר רִבִּי יוֹסֵי. הָדָא אָמְרָה. מְסַיֵּיעַ בִּשְׁעַת שְׂרִיפָה] מְטַמֵּא בְגָדִים. רִבִּי אִמִּי בְשֵׁם רִבִּי אֶלְעָזָר. הַמְהַפֵּךְ בִּכְזַיִת מְטַמֵּא בְגָדִים. לֹא צוֹרְכָה אֶלָּא הָיָה עוֹמֵד בִּפְנִים וּבְיָדוֹ קוֹרָה וּמְהַפֵּךְ בִּכְזַיִת [מָהוּ]. נִישְׁמְעִינָהּ מִן הָדָא. וְהוֹצִיא וְשָׂרָף. מָה הַמּוֹצִיא עַד שֶׁיּוֹצִיא לַחוּץ. אַף הַשּׂוֹרֵף עַד שֶׁיִּשְׂרוֹף בַּחוּץ. תַּמָּן אָמַר לִזְקִיָּה. וְטָמֵא עַד־הָעָרֶב׃ לְרַבּוֹת אֶת הַשּׂוֹרֵף. אוֹף הָכָא כֵן.

[148]*And he who burns*[149]. Not the one who starts the fire, and not the one who prepares the stake. Who is *he who burns*? That is the one who helps during the burning. [Rebbi Yose said, this implies that the one who helps during the burning][150] makes his garments impure. Rebbi Immi in the name of Rebbi Eleazar: One who turns over an olive-sized piece[151] makes his garments impure. The problem is only one who stands inside[152] and in his hand is a beam with which he turns over an olive-sized piece, [what is the

rule]¹⁵³? Let us hear from the following: *And he shall take out, and he shall burn*¹⁵⁴. Since one who takes out, only after he took to the outside, also he who burns only if he burns outside¹⁵⁵. There¹⁵⁶ Ḥizqiah said, *he shall be impure until the evening*¹⁵⁷; to include him who burns¹⁵⁸. Here it is the same¹⁵⁹.

148 Babli 68b, *Sifra Aḥare Parashah* 5(8).
149 *Lev.* 16:28.
150 Corrector's addition.
151 Less than this amount is not considered "consumed".
152 The Temple domain, or possibly the city of Jerusalem.
153 Unnecessary corrector's addition.
154 *Lev.* 4:12, about the Anointed Priest's bull.

155 Since the two expressions are written in the same verse.
156 About burning the carcass of the Red Cow.
157 *Num.* 19:7.
158 Even though the verse speaks only of the Cohen who directs the ceremony, all his helpers are included.
159 About bulls and he-goats to be burned; *Sifry Num.* 124.

(44a line 20) מָהוּ דְּיָדָכָיוֹת. קָבְלָן.

What are διάδοχοι? Ones opposite one another¹⁶⁰.

160 They were stationed so that each one could see the preceding and the following ones.

בא לו כהן גדול פרק שביעי

(fol.44a) **משנה א**: בָּא לוֹ כֹהֵן גָּדוֹל לִקְרוֹת. אִם רוֹצֶה לִקְרוֹת בְּבִגְדֵי בוּץ קוֹרֵא וְאִם לָאו בְּאִיסְטְלִית לָבָן מִשֶּׁלּוֹ. חַזַּן הַכְּנֶסֶת נוֹטֵל סֵפֶר תּוֹרָה וְנוֹתְנוֹ לְרֹאשׁ הַכְּנֶסֶת וְרֹאשׁ הַכְּנֶסֶת נוֹתְנוֹ לַסְּגָן וְהַסְּגָן נוֹתְנוֹ לְכֹהֵן גָּדוֹל וְכֹהֵן גָּדוֹל עוֹמֵד וּמְקַבֵּל וְקוֹרֵא וְעוֹמֵד וְקוֹרֵא אַחֲרֵי מוֹת וְאַךְ בֶּעָשׂוֹר וְגוֹלֵל אֶת הַתּוֹרָה וּמַנִּיחָהּ בְּחֵיקוֹ וְאוֹמֵר יוֹתֵר מִמַּה שֶׁקָּרִיתִי לִפְנֵיכֶם כָּתוּב כָּאן וּבֶעָשׂוֹר שֶׁבְּחוּמַשׁ הַפְּקוּדִים קוֹרֵא עַל פֶּה וּמְבָרֵךְ עָלֶיהָ שְׁמוֹנֶה בְּרָכוֹת עַל הַתּוֹרָה וְעַל הָעֲבוֹדָה וְעַל הַהוֹדָיָיה וְעַל מְחִילַת הֶעָוֹן וְעַל הַמִּקְדָּשׁ וְעַל יִשְׂרָאֵל וְעַל הַכֹּהֲנִים וְעַל שְׁאָר הַתְּפִילָה:

Mishnah 1: The High Priest comes to read. If he wants to read in the byssus garments[1] he may read; otherwise in his own while stole[2]. The beadle of the synagogue[3] takes the Torah scroll and hands it to the president of the synagogue, the president of the synagogue hands it to the executive officer of the Temple, the executive officer of the Temple hands it to the High Priest. The High Priest receives it standing, and reads standing. He reads *after the death*[4] and *but on the tenth day*[5], rolls up the Torah, keeps it in his bosom, and says: More than what I read before you is written here. *On the tenth day* in Numbers[6] he recites[7] by heart, and pronounces eight benedictions[8]: For the Torah, for the Service, for thanksgiving, for the remission of sin, for the Temple, for Israel, for the priests, and general prayer.

משנה ב: הָרוֹאֶה כֹהֵן גָּדוֹל שֶׁהוּא קוֹרֵא אֵינוֹ רוֹאֶה פַּר וְשָׂעִיר הַנִּשְׂרָפִים הָרוֹאֶה פַּר וְשָׂעִיר הַנִּשְׂרָפִין אֵינוֹ רוֹאֶה כֹהֵן גָּדוֹל כְּשֶׁהוּא קוֹרֵא. לֹא מִפְּנֵי שֶׁאֵינוֹ רַשַּׁאי אֶלָּא שֶׁהָיְתָה דֶרֶךְ רְחוֹקָה וּמְלֶאכֶת שְׁנֵיהֶן הָיְתָה נַעֲשִׂית כְּאַחַת:

Mishnah 2: He who sees the High Priest reading does not see the burning of the bull and the ram; he who sees the burning of the bull and the ram does not see the High Priest reading. Not because he would not be entitled to it but because the distance was large and the actions happened simultaneously.

1   The white garment which he wore for the ceremonies in the Temple building.
2   Greek στολή, ἡ.
3   The synagogue on the Temple Mount, outside the Temple precinct. The president of the Synagogue had to carry the scroll into the Temple courtyard. This clearly is a Pharisaic institution.

4	Lev. 16:1-34.	7	קורא always means to recite with the correct masoretic accents.
5	Lev. 23:26-32.		
6	Num. 19:7-11.	8	These will be detailed in the Halakhah.

(44a line 61) בָּא לוֹ כֹהֵן גָּדוֹל כול'. מְנַיְין לִקְרִיאַת הַפָּרָשָׁה. רִבִּי אִידִי בְשֵׁם רִבִּי יִצְחָק. וַיַּעַשׂ מַה תַלְמוּד לוֹמַר כַּאֲשֶׁר צִוָּה יְי אֶת־מֹשֶׁה׃ מִיכָּן לִקְרִיאַת הַפָּרָשָׁה.

"The High Priest comes," etc. From where the reading of the Chapter[9]? Rebbi Idi in the name of Rebbi Isaac[10]: *And he executed*, what does the verse say? *As the Eternal had commanded Moses*[11], from here the reading of the Chapter[12].

9	But there is no claim that reading of any text other than *Lev.* 16 is a biblical commandment.	11	Lev. 16:34.
10	The two Medieval quotes of this passage, *Tosaphot Yeshenim* and Ritba, read R. Joḥanan. This was the scribe's original text corrected by himself to: R. Isaac.	12	Since the commandment to Moses was verbal, so the execution had to be verbal. The Babli 5b has a similar argument concerning the initiation rites of the Cohanim.

(44a line 63) רִבִּי אִמִּי בְשֵׁם רִבִּי יוֹחָנָן. שְׁיָרֵי עֲבוֹדוֹת עוֹבְדִין בְּבִגְדֵי לָבָן. אָמַר רִבִּי מַתָּנָא. מַתְנִיתָה אֲמָרָה כֵן. וְאִם לָאו בְּאִיסְטְלִית לָבָן מִשֶּׁלּוֹ. רִבִּי יוֹסֵה בָעֵי. לָמָּה. שֶׁהֵן בַּחוּץ. הֲרֵי שְׁחִיטָה הֲרֵי אֵינָהּ אֶלָא בַחוּץ. וְהוּא עוֹבְדָהּ בְּבִגְדֵי זָהָב. רִבִּי יַסָא בְשֵׁם רִבִּי יוֹחָנָן. רָצָה עוֹבְדָהּ בְּבִגְדֵי זָהָב. רָצָה עוֹבְדָהּ בְּבִגְדֵי לָבָן. מָצִינוּ שְׁחִיטָה. רָצָה עוֹבְדָהּ בְּבִגְדֵי זָהָב. רָצָה עוֹבְדָהּ בְּבִגְדֵי לָבָן.

Rebbi Immi in the name of Rebbi Joḥanan: Ancillary services[13] are performed in white garments[14]. Rebbi Mattanah said, the Mishnah implies this: "otherwise in his own white stole." Rebbi Yose asked: Why? Even though they are outside? Is not slaughter only outside and is performed in golden garments[15]? Rebbi Yasa in the name of Rebbi Joḥanan: If he wants, he performs in golden garments, if he wants, he performs in white garments. We find that slaughter[16], if he wants, he performs in golden garments, if he wants, he performs in white garments.

13 Actions either such as reading the Torah which is not absolutely necessary, in that its omission does not invalidate the	service, or necessary actions which may be performed by a non-Cohen, such as slaughter of sacrifices.

14 But not necessarily in linen garments as prescribed in *Lev.* 16:4 for all service performed inside the sanctuary.

15 The Mishnah (3:5, 7:3,6) prescribes that the daily and holiday sacrifices are offered by the High Priest in his golden garments in which he serves all other days of the year.

16 While the High Priest must wear his everyday garments (Mishnah 7:7) for all priestly actions required for daily and holiday sacrifices, this is not directly prescribed for slaughter which is not a priestly duty.

(44a line 69) בְּכָל־אֲתָר אַתְּ אָמַר. הוֹלְכִין אַחַר הַתּוֹרָה. וְהָכָא אַתְּ אָמַר. מוֹלִיכִין אֶת הַתּוֹרָה אֶצְלָן. אֶלָּא עַל יְדֵי שֶׁהֵן בְּנֵי אָדָם גְּדוֹלִים הַתּוֹרָה מִתְעַלָּה בָהֶן. וְהָא תַמָּן מְיַיבְּלִין אוֹרְיָיתָא גַּבֵּי רֵישׁ גָּלוּתָא. אָמַר רִבִּי יוֹסֵה בֵירִבִּי בּוּן. תַּמָּן עַל יְדֵי שֶׁזַרְעוֹ שֶׁלְדָוִד מְשׁוּקָּע שָׁם אִינּוּן עָבְדִין לוֹ כְּמִנְהַג אֲבַהַתְהוֹן.

2 אורייתא | ס את התורה

[17]Everywhere you are saying, one goes to the Torah. But here you are saying, one brings the Torah to them. Only since they are important personalities, the Torah is honored by them[18]. Does one not bring there the Torah to the Head of the Diaspora[20]? Rebbi Yose ben Rebbi Abun said, there since the seed of David is absorbed in them[21], they follow the usage of their forefathers.

17 From here to the end of the Halakhah the text is also in *Sotah* 7:6, Notes 190-211, ס..

18 In the Babli 69a, the Torah scroll is brought by a chain of increasingly important people to stress the exalted position of the High Priest. Cf. Note 190.

19 The hereditary head of the Jewish communities in Mesopotamia.

20 The claim of the Heads of the Diaspora to Davidic descent may be questionable, but since it is accepted by the people, the Head of the Diaspora may claim Davidic prerogatives.

(44a line 73) תַּמָּן תַּנִּינָן. מְדַלְּגִין בַּנָּבִיא. וְאֵין מְדַלְּגִין בַּתּוֹרָה. מְדַלְּגִין בַּתּוֹרָה. וְאֵין מְדַלְּגִין מִנָּבִיא לְנָבִיא. וּבִנְבִיא שֶׁלִּשְׁנֵים עָשָׂר מוּתָּר. אֵין מְדַלְּגִין בַּתּוֹרָה. רִבִּי יִרְמְיָה בְשֵׁם רִבִּי שִׁמְעוֹן בֶּן לָקִישׁ. שֶׁאֵין גּוֹלְלִין סֵפֶר תּוֹרָה בָרַבִּים. רִבִּי יוֹסֵה בָעֵי. הַגַּע עַצְמָךְ שֶׁהָיְתָה פָרָשָׁה קְטַנָּה. אֶלָּא כְּדֵי שֶׁיִּשְׁמְעוּ יִשְׂרָאֵל תּוֹרָה עַל סֵדֶר. וְהָא תַנֵּינָן. קוֹרֵא אַחֲרֵי מוֹת וְאַךְ בֶּעָשׂוֹ. שַׁנְיָיא הִיא. שֶׁהִיא סִדְרוֹ שֶׁל יוֹם. דְּאָמַר רִבִּי שִׁמְעוֹן בֶּן לָקִישׁ. בְּכָל־מָקוֹם אֵינוֹ קוֹרֵא עַל פֶּה. וְהָכָא קוֹרֵא. רִבִּי יוֹסֵה מְפַקֵּד לְבַר עוּלָּא חַזָּנָא דִכְנִישְׁתָּא דְּבַבְלָאֵי. כַּד דְּהִיא חֲדָא אוֹרְיָה תְּהֵא גָּייֵל לָהּ לַהֲדֵי פָרוֹכְתָּא. כַּד אִינּוּן תַּרְתֵּיי תֵּי מְיַיבֵּל חֲדָא וּמַייְתֵי חֲדָא.

1 תמן תנינן | ל - 2 אין | ס ואין 3 גלין | ל גולים ס גוללין יוסה | ס יוסי 4 אלא | ל אמ' ליה. ישראל | ל את ישראל תורה | ל התורה ס - קורא | ס וקורא 5 שהיא | ל שהוא דומ' | ס דמר 6 והכא | ס וכא

קורא | **לס** קורא על פה   יוסה | **ס** יוסי   דבבלאי | **ל** שבבלייא   אוריא | **ל** אורייא   כד דהיא חדא אורייא | **ס**
כדי חזרה אורייתא   7 תהא | **ל** תהוי **ס** -   גייל לה | **ל** גוילא   להדי | **ל** אחורי **ס** לחורי   אינון | **ל** דאינונן תי | **ס** תו

²¹There²², we have stated: "One skips in prophets; one does not skip in the Torah.²³" "One skips in prophets," but one does not skip from one prophet to another, except that one is permitted to skip between the Twelve Prophets²⁴. "One does not skip in the Torah." Rebbi Jeremiah in the name of Rebbi Simeon ben Laqish: Because one does not scroll the book of the Torah in public. Rebbi Yose asked, think of it, if it was a small paragraph²⁵? But so that Israel should hear the Torah in due order. But did we not state: "he reads *after the death*⁴ and *but on the tenth day*"⁵? There is a difference since this is the order of the day. You should know this, as Rebbi Simeon ben Laqish said, one never recites from memory but here he recites²⁶. Rebbi Yose ordered Bar Ulla, the beadle of the synagogue of the Babylonians: If there is one Torah²⁷, scroll it behind a curtain. If there are two, take away one and bring the other²⁸.

21 This paragraph is also in *Megillah* 4:5 (75b l. 52), ל. Quoted in *Tosaphot Yeshenim* 70a.
22 Mishnah *Megillah* 4:5.
23 Public readings of the Torah must present a continuous text. Readings from the Prophets may be pieced together, such as in the Ashkenazic Haftara to Yitro, *Is.* 6:1-7:6, 9:5-6.
24 The 12 minor prophets are considered one book. The Ashkenazic Haftara for the Sabbath between New Year's day and Yom Kippur is composed of *Hos.* 14:2-10 and either *Joel* 2:15-27 or *Micah* 7:18-20.
25 If one continues on the same page after an interruption, nothing has to be scrolled.
26 The sacrifices detailed in *Num.* 19:7-11 (offered by the High Priest in his year-round "golden" garments) are completely different from those required by *Lev.* 16, for whose service white linen garments are prescribed. Therefore mention of the text in *Num.* 19 is essential, but scrolling such a large distance would be an interruption of the public service.
27 On a day which requires reading two different sections, such as a New Moon celebrated on a Sabbath, or a holiday. Then the Torah has to be scrolled, but this should not be done in public.
28 This is current Sephardic practice, in contrast to current Ashkenazic procedure where the second Torah is brought before the first is lifted.

(44a line 7) וּמְבָרֵךְ עָלֶיהָ שְׁמוֹנֶה בְּרָכוֹת. עַל הַתּוֹרָה הַבּוֹחֵר בַּתּוֹרָה. עַל הָעֲבוֹדָה שֶׁאוֹתְךָ נִירָא וְנַעֲבוֹד. עַל הַהוֹדָיָה הַטּוֹב לְךָ לְהוֹדוֹת. עַל מְחִילַת הֶעָוֹן מוֹחֵל עֲווֹנוֹת עַמּוֹ יִשְׂרָאֵל בְּרַחֲמִים.

עַל הַמִּקְדָּשׁ הַבּוֹחֵר בַּמִּקְדָּשׁ. וְאָמַר רִבִּי אִידִי. הַשּׁוֹכֵן בְּצִיּוֹן. עַל יִשְׂרָאֵל הַבּוֹחֵר בְּיִשְׂרָאֵל. עַל הַכֹּהֲנִים הַבּוֹחֵר בַּכֹּהֲנִים עַל שְׁאָר הַתְּפִילָה וּתְחִינָה וּבַקָּשָׁה. שֶׁעַמְּךָ יִשְׂרָאֵל צְרִיכִין לְהִיוָּשַׁע לְפָנֶיךָ. בָּרוּךְ אַתָּה יי שׁוֹמֵעַ תְּפִילָה.

1 נירא ונעבוד | **ס** לבדך ביראה נעבוד   2 ההודייה | **ס** ההודיה   3 על | **ס** ועל (2)   4 ותחינה | **ס** תחימה

"And pronounces eight benedictions[8]: For the Torah", He Who chooses the Torah[29]. "For the Service," for You we fear and serve[30]. "For thanksgiving," it is good to give thanks to You[31], "for the remission of sin," He who remits the sins of His people Israel.[32] "For the Temple," He Who chooses the Temple. Rebbi Idi said, He Who dwells in Zion[33]. "For Israel," He Who chooses Israel[34]. "for the priests." "And general prayer.", entreaty and begging, for Your people Israel need to be helped before You. Praise to You, Eternal, Who hears prayer[35].

29   In the Babli 70a and Tosephta 3:18, "in the way one recites the benediction for the Torah in the synagogue." This is understood also here for this and the following benedictions, in the Galilean versions.

30   The Galilean version of the 16th benediction of the *Amidah*.

31   The 17th benediction.

32   The final paragraph of the middle benediction in the *Amidah* for the Day of Atonement.

33   The full text of this benediction is unknown. Since R. Idi is quoted as commenting, not disagreeing, one has to assume that he quotes the beginning of the relevant prayer text.

34   In the opinion of I. Elbogen this refers to the benediction immediately preceding the recitation of *Shema`*.

35   This is the only prayer text which is unique to the High Priest's reading.

(fol. 44a)   **משנה ג:** וְאִם בְּבִגְדֵי בוּץ קָרָא קִדֵּשׁ יָדָיו וְרַגְלָיו וּפָשַׁט יָרַד וְטָבַל עָלָה וְנִסְתַּפָּג. הֵבִיאוּ לוֹ בִגְדֵי זָהָב וְלָבַשׁ וְקִדֵּשׁ יָדָיו וְרַגְלָיו.

Mishnah 3: If he read in his byssus garments, he sanctified hands and legs,[36] and undressed, stepped down, and immersed himself, came up, and dried himself with a towel. They brought him the golden garments[37], he dressed and sanctified hands and legs.

משנה ד: יָצָא וְעָשָׂה אֶת אֵילוֹ וְאֶת אֵיל הָעָם וְאֶת שִׁבְעַת כְּבָשִׂים תְּמִימִים דִּבְרֵי רִבִּי אֱלִיעֶזֶר. רִבִּי עֲקִיבָה אוֹמֵר עִם תָּמִיד שֶׁל שַׁחַר הָיוּ קְרֵבִין וּפַר הָעוֹלָה וְשָׂעִיר הַנַּעֲשֶׂה בַחוּץ

הָיוּ קְרֵבִין עִם תָּמִיד שֶׁל בֵּין הָעַרְבַּיִם: קִדֵּשׁ יָדָיו וְרַגְלָיו וּפָשַׁט יָרַד וְטָבַל עָלָה וְנִסְתַּפָּג. הֵבִיאוּ לוֹ בִגְדֵי לָבָן וְלָבַשׁ וְקִדֵּשׁ יָדָיו וְרַגְלָיו.

Mishnah 4: He went out and sacrificed his ram, and the people's ram[38], and the seven unblemished sheep[39], the words of Rebbi Eliezer. Rebbi Aqiba says, they[40] had been brought with the daily morning offering; the bull of elevation offering and the he-goat offered outside were brought with the daily afternoon sacrifice[41]. He sanctified hands and legs and undressed, stepped down, and immersed himself, came up and dried himself with a towel. They brought him the white garments[42], he dressed and sanctified hands and legs.

משנה ה: נִכְנַס לְהוֹצִיא אֶת הַכַּף וְאֶת הַמַּחְתָּה. קִדֵּשׁ יָדָיו וְרַגְלָיו וּפָשַׁט יָרַד וְטָבַל עָלָה וְנִסְתַּפָּג. הֵבִיאוּ לוֹ בִגְדֵי זָהָב וְלָבַשׁ קִדֵּשׁ יָדָיו וְרַגְלָיו.

Mishnah 5: He entered to remove the cup and the pan[43]. He sanctified hands and legs and undressed, stepped down, and immersed himself, came up and dried himself with a towel. They brought him the golden garments, he dressed and sanctified hands and legs.

משנה ו: נִכְנַס וְהִקְטִיר אֶת הַקְּטוֹרֶת וְהֵטִיב אֶת הַנֵּרוֹת. קִדֵּשׁ יָדָיו וְרַגְלָיו וּפָשַׁט יָרַד וְטָבַל עָלָה וְנִסְתַּפָּג... הֵבִיאוּ לוֹ בִגְדֵי עַצְמוֹ וְלָבַשׁ. מְלַוִּין אוֹתוֹ עַד בֵּיתוֹ וְיוֹם טוֹב הָיָה עוֹשֶׂה לְאוֹהֲבָיו בְּשָׁעָה שֶׁיָּצָא בְשָׁלוֹם.

Mishnah 6: He entered, burned the incense, and prepared the lights. He sanctified hands and legs, and undressed, stepped down, and immersed himself, came up and dried himself with a towel.. They brought him his own garments in which he dressed. One accompanies him to his house. He made a festivity for his friends when he exited in peace[44].

36 But if he read in his own stole he already had to wash hands and feet when he took off his white garments (Chapter 3, Note 98). Dressing and undressing profane garments does not necessitate washing hands and feet.

37 The High Priest's garments for service all year long. These are worn for all parts of the service of the Day of Atonement which do not involve entering the Holiest of Holies.

38 As prescribed by *Lev.* 16:24. The biblical expression "did" is read to imply that the entire work involved, slaughter, dismembering, cleaning, transporting to the altar, and burning the elevation sacrifices, had to be performed by the unaided High Priest.

39 As prescribed by *Num.* 29:8.

40 The animals enumerated by R. Eliezer were brought before the High Priest wore the white garments for the first time.

41 This statement is the common opinion of R. Eliezer and R. Aqiba. These sacrifices are *musaf* sacrifices prescribed in *Num.* 29:8

42 ..To re-enter the Holiest of Holies.

43 Which were left in the Holiest of Holies. Chapter 3, Mishnah 1.

44 He exited the Holiest of Holies, which is most dangerous; cf. Chapter 1, Notes 220-222.

(44b line 13) **הלכה ב**: אָמַר רִבִּי יוֹחָנָן. זוֹ דִבְרֵי רִבִּי אֱלִיעֶזֶר וְרִבִּי עֲקִיבָה. אֲבָל דִבְרֵי חֲכָמִים. כּוּלְהוֹן הָיוּ קְרֵיבִין עִם תָּמִיד שֶׁלְּבֵין הָעַרְבַּיִם. רִבִּי חוּנָה בְשֵׁם רַב יוֹסֵף. אַתְיָא דְּרִבִּי לִיעֶזֶר כְּבֵית שַׁמַּי. כְּמָה דְבֵית שַׁמַּי אֲמְרֵי. תָּדִיר מְקוּדָּשׁ מְקוּדָּשׁ קוֹדֵם. כֵּן רִבִּי לִיעֶזֶר אוֹמֵר. תָּדִיר מְקוּדָּשׁ מְקוּדָּשׁ קוֹדֵם. הֵיךְ עֲבִידָה. עֲבוֹדַת הַיּוֹם מְקוּדֶּשֶׁת וּמוּסְפֵי הַיּוֹם תְּדִירִין. עֲבוֹדַת הַיּוֹם קוֹדֶמֶת לְמוּסְפֵי הַיּוֹם.

פַּר וָאַיִל וְשִׁבְעַת כְּבָשִׂים תְּמִימִים הָיוּ קְרֵיבִין עִם תָּמִיד שֶׁלְּשַׁחַר. וְהַשְׁאָר הָיוּ קְרֵיבִין עִם תָּמִיד שֶׁלְּבֵין הָעַרְבַּיִם. רִבִּי שִׁמְעוֹן בֶּן לָקִישׁ אָמַר. טַעֲמָא דָהֵן תַּנָּייָא. כְּדֵי לִסְמוֹךְ חַטָּאת לְחַטָּאת וְעוֹלָה לְעוֹלָה. וְאִית דְּבָעֵי מֵימַר. הַפַּר וְהָאַיִל וְאֵילוֹ וְאֵיל הָעָם וְשִׁבְעַת כְּבָשִׂים תְּמִימִים הָיוּ קְרֵיבִין עִם תָּמִיד שֶׁלְּשַׁחַר. וְהַשְׁאָר הָיוּ קְרֵיבִין עִם תָּמִיד שֶׁלְּבֵין הָעַרְבַּיִם. וְהָדֵין תַּנָּייָא. תּוֹלֶה עֲבוֹדוֹת. מַה טַעַם. וְיָצָא וְעָשָׂה אֶת־עוֹלָתוֹ וְאֶת־עוֹלַת הָעָם. כָּאָמוּר בָּעִנְייָן. מָה אָמוּר בָּעִנְייָן. אֵילוֹ וְאֵיל הָעָם. אָמַר רִבִּי בּוּן בַּר חִייָה וְשָׂעִיר מַה טַעַם. מִדָּם חַטָּאת הַכִּפּוּרִים. כְּבָר קֵדְמָה חַטַּאת הַכִּפּוּרִים.

Halakhah 2: Rebbi Joḥanan said, these are the words of Rebbi Eliezer and Rebbi Aqiba. But the words of the Sages, all of them were brought with the daily morning offering[45]. Rebbi Huna in the name of Rav Joseph: Rebbi Eliezer follows the House of Shammai. Just as the House of Shammai say, frequent and holy, holy has precedence[46], so Rebbi Eliezer says, frequent and holy, holy has precedence. How is this? The service of the Day is holier and the day's *musaf* sacrifices are more frequent; the service of the Day has precedence over the day's *musaf* sacrifices.

The bull, the ram, and the seven unblemished sheep were brought with the daily morning offering; the remainder were brought with the daily afternoon offering[47]. Rebbi Simeon ben Laqish said, the reason of this Tanna is to join purification sacrifice to purification sacrifice and elevation sacrifice to elevation sacrifice[48]. But some want to say, the bull, the ram, the people's ram, and the seven unblemished sheep were brought with the daily morning offering; the remainder were brought with the daily afternoon offering. This Tanna distributes the services. What is the reason? *He leaves and brings his elevation sacrifice and the people's elevation sacrifice*[49]. As mentioned in the matter. What is mentioned in the matter? His ram and the people's ram[50]. Rebbi Abun bar Ḥiyya said, what is the reason for the he-goat? *Of the blood of the atoning purification sacrifice*[51]. The atoning purification sacrifice already preceded.

45 Since the same *musaf* offering is prescribed in *Num.* 29 for New Year's day, the Day of Atonement, and the Eighth Day of the Fall Festival, they are offered more frequently than the special offerings of the day of Atonement detailed in *Lev.* 16. Since the House of Hillel strictly follow the rule that the more frequent has precedence (cf. *Berakhot* 8:1), all of the more common sacrifices must be processed first. Cf. Tosephta 2:19.

46 *Nazir* 7:1 Note 54; Babli *Zevahim* 69a.

47 This is the rule of R. Aqiba.

48 Even though the he-goat as purification sacrifice is prescribed for all holidays and therefore is most frequent, as noted later in *Num.* 29:11 it is required that this sacrifice follow that of the he-goat whose blood was brought into the Temple, and be followed by the elevation sacrifice which is the evening daily offering. Therefore it makes sense to require the elevation offerings required by *Lev.* 16:3,24 to be brought after the atonement service and before the daily evening service.

49 *Lev.* 16: 24.

50 16:3,5.

51 This is misquoting *Ex.* 30:10 when it should be *Num.* 29:11: *A he-goat as purification offering* in addition to *the atoning purification offering.* Babli 70b.

(44b line 27) וּבָא אַהֲרֹן אֶל־אֹהֶל מוֹעֵד. מֵאֵיכָן בָּא. מִקְרִיַת הַפָּרָשָׁה. וּלְהֵיכָן הוּא הוֹלֵךְ. לְהוֹצִיא כַף וּמַחְתָּה. כָּתוּב וְיָצָא וְעָשָׂה אֶת־עֹלָתוֹ וְאֶת־עֹלַת הָעָם. וְאַתְּ אָמַר הָכֵין. וְלֹא כֵן אָמַר רִבִּי יוֹחָנָן. הַכֹּל מוֹדִין בְּהוֹצָאַת כַּף וּמַחְתָּה שֶׁהוּא לְאַחַר תָּמִיד שֶׁלְבֵּין הָעַרְבָּיִם. אָמַר רִבִּי יוֹסֵה בֶן חֲנִינָה. כָּל־הַפָּרָשָׁה כְּתוּבָה עַל סֶדֶר חוּץ מִזוֹ. אָמַר רִבִּי יוֹסֵה. עוֹד הִיא אֲמוּרָה עַל סֵדֶר. וּבָא אַהֲרֹן אֶל־אֹהֶל מוֹעֵד. מֵאֵיכָן בָּא. מִקִּידּוּשׁ הָרִאשׁוֹן שֶׁהָיָה בְּיָדוֹ. וּלְאַיִן הוּא הוֹלֵךְ. לְקִידּוּשׁ הָאַחֲרוֹן. אָמַר רִבִּי מָנָא קוֹמֵי רִבִּי יוֹסֵה. לָמָּה לִי נָן אָמְרִין. חוּץ מִקִּידּוּשׁ הָאַחֲרוֹן. אָמַר לֵיהּ. שְׁנִייָא הִיא. דִּכְתִיב וּבָא. וְיָצָא וּפָשַׁט אֶת־בִּגְדֵי הַבָּד. שֶׁאֵין תַּלְמוּד לוֹמַר. אֲשֶׁר לָבַשׁ. וְכִי עָלַת עַל דַעְתֵּינוּ כְּלוּם הוּא פוֹשֵׁט אֶלָּא מַה שֶׁהוּא לוֹבֵשׁ. אִם כֵּן לָמָּה נֶאֱמַר אֲשֶׁר לָבַשׁ. הִקִּישׁ פְּשִׁיטָה לִלְבִישָׁה. מַה לְבִישָׁה בְּקִידּוּשׁ יָדַיִם וְרַגְלַיִם. אַף פְּשִׁיטָה בְּקִידּוּשׁ יָדַיִם וְרַגְלַיִם. אָמַר רִבִּי אֶלְעָזָר. יֵשׁ לָךְ עֲבוֹדָה אַחֶרֶת שֶׁהוּא עוֹבְדָהּ בְּבִגְדֵי לָבָן. וְאֵי זוֹ זוֹ. זוֹ הוֹצָאַת כַּף וּמַחְתָּה. אָמַר רִבִּי יוֹחָנָן. הַכֹּל מוֹדִין בְּהוֹצָאַת כַּף וּמַחְתָּה שֶׁהוּא לְאַחַר תָּמִיד שֶׁלְבֵּין הָעַרְבָּיִם.

Aaron comes to the tent of Meeting[52]. From where does he come? From reading the Chapter. Where does he go to? To remove the cup and the pan[53]. It is written: *He leaves and brings his elevation sacrifice and the people's elevation sacrifice*[49], and you are saying so? Did not Rebbi Johanan say, everybody agrees that the removal of cup and pan follows after the daily evening offering[54]? Rebbi Yose ben Ḥanina said, the entire Chapter is written in order except for this verse[55]. Rebbi Yose said, even this is written in order. *Aaron comes to the tent of Meeting.* From where does he come? From the first sanctification which he encounters. Where does he go to? To the last sanctification[56]. Rebbi Mana said before Rebbi Yose: Why do we not say, except the last sanctification[57]? He answered him, there is a difference since it is written *he comes, (he leaves)*[58], *he takes off the linen garments.* [59]Why does the verse say, *which he wore*? Could we ever think that he could undress what he was not wearing? Then why is it written, *which he wore*? It brackets undressing and dressing. Since dressing requires sanctification of hands and legs, also undressing requires sanctification of hands and legs. Rebbi Eleazar said, there is another service for which he officiates in white garments. What is it? It is removal of cup and pan[53]. Rebbi Johanan says, everybody agrees that the removal of cup and pan follows after the daily evening offering[60].

52 *Lev.* 16:23.
53 For this he has to enter the Holiest of Holies, which only is permitted in white garments.
54 The last action of the High Priest is mentioned in v. 24, the offering of the remaining sacrifices of the day, which includes the daily evening offering. How can one understand R. Johanan's statement since v. 23, which has to be interpreted as referring to removal of cup and pan, precedes v. 24?
55 Babli 70b, as Tannaitic statement.
56 The verse only states that the High Priest has no pause in the day's service, from the first immersion to the last washing of hands and feet.
57 Since *Lev.* 16:23 mentions undressing the white garments but does not mention washing of any kind, whereas in vv. 4,24 it is stated that dressing requires immersion in water, would it not be logical to require washing only for dressing,. not undressing. Then R. Yose's interpretation becomes impossible.
58 Since the other two quotes are from *Lev.* 16:23., this quote from v. 24 has to be deleted.
59 Chapter 3:7, Note 98.
60 Since in vv. 21-22 Aaron is still wearing the white garments which he put on in the morning, and in v. 24 is wearing his

golden garments, there would be no reason in v. 23 to have him dress in white garments a second time. Therefore the second wearing has to be after the completion of the daily service in golden garments. The interpretation of R. Yose ben Hanina is the only possible one; it is compatible with the explanation which R. Yose gave to R. Mana.

(fol. 44a) **משנה ז:** כֹּהֵן גָּדוֹל מְשַׁמֵּשׁ בִּשְׁמוֹנָה כֵלִים וְהַהֶדְיוֹט בְּאַרְבָּעָה. בְּכֻתֹּנֶת וּמִכְנָסַיִם מִצְנֶפֶת וְאַבְנֵט. מוֹסִיף עָלָיו כֹּהֵן גָּדוֹל חֹשֶׁן וְאֵפוֹד וּמְעִיל וָצִיץ. בְּאֵלוּ נִשְׁאָלִין בְּאוּרִים וְתוּמִּים וְאֵין נִשְׁאָלִין בָּהֵן לְהֶדְיוֹט אֶלָּא לַמֶּלֶךְ וּלְבֵית דִּין וּלְמִי שֶׁצוֹרֶךְ הַצִּיבּוּר בּוֹ:

Mishnah 7: The High Priest officiates in eight garments and the common priest[61] in four, in shirt, trousers, turban, and belt[62]. The High Priest in addition wears breastplate, vest, coat, and diadem[63]. In these one asks Urim and Tummim, but one does not ask for common people, only for a king, or the Court, or one on whom rest the needs of the public.

61 Greek ἰδιώτης, ὁ. 63 *Ex.* 28:4,36,42.
62 *Ex.* 28:40,42.

(44b line 43) **הלכה ג:** וְלָמָּה בְּבִגְדֵי לָבָן. אָמַר רִבִּי חִיָּיה בַּר בָּא. כְּשֵׁירוּת שֶׁל מַעֲלָן כָּךְ שֵׁירוּת שֶׁל מַטָּן. מַה לְמַעֲלָן אִישׁ אֶחָד בְּתוֹכָם לָבוּשׁ בַּדִּים. אַף לְמַטָּן כְּתוֹנֶת בַּד קוֹדֶשׁ יִלְבָּשׁ.

Halakhah 3: Why in white clothing? Rebbi Hiyya bar Abba said, like the service up high so is the service down below. As up high, *a man in their midst clothed in linen*[64], so down below *a holy linen shirt he shall wear*[65].

64 *Ez.* 9:2. 65 *Lev.* 16:4.

(44b line 45) מִפְּנֵי מַה כֹּהֵן גָּדוֹל מְשַׁמֵּשׁ בִּשְׁמוֹנָה כֵלִים. רִבִּי חֲנַנְיָה חֲבֵרוֹן דְּרַבָּנָן אָמַר. כְּנֶגֶד הַמִּילָה שֶׁהִיא לִשְׁמוֹנָה יָמִים. עַל שֵׁם בְּרִיתִי | הָיְתָה אִתּוֹ. מִפְּנֵי מַה אֵינוֹ מְשַׁמֵּשׁ בְּבִגְדֵי זָהָב. מִפְּנֵי הַגַּאֲוָה. אָמַר רִבִּי סִימוֹן. אַל שֵׁם אַל־תִּתְהַדַּר לִפְנֵי־מֶלֶךְ. אָמַר רִבִּי לֵוִי. שֶׁאֵין קַטִּיגוֹר נַעֲשֶׂה סַנֵּיגוֹר. אֶתְמוֹל כָּתוּב בָּהֶם וַיַּעֲשׂוּ לָהֶם אֱלֹהֵי זָהָב: וְעַכְשָׁיו הוּא עוֹמֵד וּמְשַׁמֵּשׁ בְּבִגְדֵי זָהָב.

Why does the High Priest serve in eight vestments? Rebbi Hanania the colleague of the rabbis said, corresponding to circumcision, which takes place on the eighth day. Because of *My covenant was with him*[66]. Why does he not serve in the golden vestments? Because of haughtiness. Rebbi Simon said, because of *do not inflate yourself in front of the king*[67]. Rebbi Levi said, because an accuser[68] does not become a defense attorney[69]. Yesterday it was written about them, *they made golden gods for themselves*[70], and today he would officiate in golden vestments?

66 *Mal.* 2:5. In rabbinic usage, the common meaning of "covenant" is "circumcision".
67 *Prov.* 25:6.
68 Greek κατήγωρ, κατήγορος, ὁ.
69 Greek συνήγορος, ὁ.
70 *Ex.* 32:31. Babli *Rosh Hashanah* 26a, in the name of Rav Hisda.

(44b line 51) תַּנֵּי רִבִּי חִיָּיה. וּלְבֵשָׁם: וּבָלוּ שָׁם. שָׁם הָיוּ גְנוּזִין. שָׁם הָיוּ מַרְקִיבִין וְלֹא הָיוּ כְשֵׁירִים לְיוֹם הַכִּיפּוּרִים הַבָּא. [תַּנֵּי. רִבִּי דוֹסָא אוֹמֵר. כְּשֵׁרִים הֵם לְכֹהֵן הֶדְיוֹט.] תַּנֵּי. רִבִּי אוֹמֵר. שְׁתֵּי תְשׁוּבוֹת בַּדָּבָר. אַחַת בְּבִגְדֵי כֹהֵן גָּדוֹל. וְאַחַת בְּבִגְדֵי כֹהֵן הֶדְיוֹט. תַּנֵּי. לֹא נֶחְלְקוּ רִבִּי וְרִבִּי אֶלְעָזָר בֵּירִבִּי שִׁמְעוֹן עַל אַבְנֵיטוֹ שֶׁלְכֹּהֵן גָּדוֹל בְּיוֹם הַכִּיפּוּרִים שֶׁהוּא שֶׁלְבּוּץ וְעַל שְׁאָר יְמוֹת הַשָּׁנָה שֶׁיֵּשׁ בּוֹ כִּלְאַיִם. וְעַל מַה נֶחְלְקוּ. עַל אַבְנֵיטוֹ שֶׁלְכֹּהֵן הֶדְיוֹט. שֶׁרִבִּי אוֹמֵר. יֵשׁ בּוֹ כִּלְאַיִם. וְרִבִּי אֶלְעָזָר בֵּירִבִּי שִׁמְעוֹן אוֹמֵר. אֵין בּוֹ כִּלְאַיִם. רִבִּי יַעֲקֹב בַּר אָחָא רִבִּי אַבָּהוּ בְשֵׁם רִבִּי יוֹחָנָן. טַעֲמֵיהּ דְרִבִּי. וְעָשִׂיתָ לְאַהֲרֹן וּלְבָנָיו כָּכָה כְּכֹל אֲשֶׁר־צִוִּיתִי אֹתָכָה. מַה בְּגְדֵי אַהֲרֹן יֵשׁ בּוֹ כִּלְאַיִם. אַף בִּגְדֵי בָנָיו יֵשׁ בָּהֶן כִּלְאַיִם. מָה עָבַד לָהּ רִבִּי אֶלְעָזָר בֵּירִבִּי שִׁמְעוֹן. מַה אַהֲרֹן בְּרָאוּי לוֹ. אַף בָּנָיו בְּרָאוּי לָהֶן.

Rebbi Hiyya stated: *And he shall wear them*[71], they shall be worn out there, there they were hidden, there they were rotting, and were not qualified for the next Day of Atonement[72]. [It was stated: Rebbi Dosa says, they were qualified for a common priest.][73] It was stated[74]: Rebbi said, there are two answers in the matter; one for clothing of the High Priest, and one for clothing of the common priest. It was stated[74]: Rebbi and Rebbi Eleazar ben Rebbi Simeon did not disagree about the belt of the High Priest on the Day of Atonement that it was of byssus, and on all other days of the year that it contained *kilaim*[75], about what did they disagree? About the belt of the common priest, where Rebbi says, it contained *kilaim*, but Rebbi Eleazar ben Rebbi Simeon says, it did not contain *kilaim*. Rebbi Jacob bar Aha, Rebbi Abbahu in the name of Rebbi Johanan: The reason of Rebbi, *you shall do to Aaron and his sons so, all that I had commanded you*[76]. Since the garments of Aaron contain *kilaim*, so also the garments of his sons contain *kilaim*. How does Rebbi Eleazar ben Rebbi Simeon explain the verse? Aaron with what is appropriate for him, and his sons with what is appropriate for them.

71 *Lev.* 16:4, based on a metathesis לבשם -בל שם.
72 The Babli 12b and *Sifra Ahare Pereq* 6(7) have another argument based on *Lev.* 16:23.
73 Addition of the corrector, possibly from the Babli 12b or *Sifra Saw Pereq* 2(1). A common priest has to wear linen shirt and trousers for the removal of ashes from the altar; *Lev.* 6:3. In addition, there is the opinion, stated later in this paragraph, that the common priest's belt also was simply linen.
74 Babli 12b and *Sifra Saw Pereq* 2(1).
75 A linen belt for the Day of Atonement is prescribed in *Lev.* 16:4, while for the golden garments the belt is made from gold thread, blue, crimson, and purple wool, and linen (*Ex.* 28:5,39). The belt of common priests is mentioned as necessary in *Ex.* 28:40, but its materials are not specified.
76 *Ex.* 29:35.

(44b line 62) **הלכה ה**: אָמַר רִבִּי סִימוֹן. כְּשֵׁם שֶׁהַקָּרְבָּנוֹת מְכַפְּרִין כָּךְ הַבְּגָדִים מְכַפְּרִין. בְּכֻתּוֹנֶת וּמִכְנָסַיִם מִצְנֶפֶת וְאַבְנֵט. כֻּתּוֹנֶת הָיְתָה מְכַפֶּרֶת [לוֹבְשֵׁי כִלְאַיִם. אִית דְּבָעֵי מֵימַר.] עַל שׁוֹפְכֵי דָמִים. כְּמָה דְאַתְּ אָמַר וַיִּטְבְּלוּ אֶת־הַכֻּתּוֹנֶת בַּדָּם: מִכְנָסַיִים הָיָה מְכַפֵּר עַל גִּילּוּי עֲרָיוֹת. כְּמָה דְאַתְּ אָמַר וַעֲשֵׂה לָהֶם מִכְנְסֵי־בָד לְכַסּוֹת בְּשַׂר עֶרְוָה. מִצְנֶפֶת הָיְתָה מְכַפֶּרֶת עַל גַּסֵּי הָרוּחַ. כְּמָה דְאַתְּ אָמַר וַיָּשֶׂם אֶת־הַמִּצְנֶפֶת עַל־רֹאשׁוֹ. אַבְנֵט הָיָה מְכַפֵּר עַל [הַגַּנָּבִים. וְאִית דְּבָעֵי מֵימַר עַל] הָעוֹקְמָנִים. אָמַר רִבִּי לֵוִי. שְׁלֹשִׁים וּשְׁתַּיִם אַמָּה הָיָה בוֹ וְהָיָה מְעַקְּמוֹ לְכָאן וּלְכָאן. חוֹשֶׁן הָיָה מְכַפֵּר עַל מַטֵּי הַדִּין. כְּמָה דְאַתְּ אָמַר וְעָשִׂיתָ חֹשֶׁן מִשְׁפָּט. אֵפוֹד הָיָה מְכַפֵּר עַל עוֹבְדֵי עֲבוֹדָה זָרָה. כְּמָה דְאַתְּ אָמַר וְאֵין אֵפוֹד וּתְרָפִים: מְעִיל. רִבִּי סִימוֹן בְּשֵׁם רִבִּי יוֹנָתָן דְּבֵית גּוּבְרִין. שְׁנֵי דְבָרִים לֹא הָיְתָה בָהֶן כַּפָּרָה. וְקָבְעָה לָהֶן הַתּוֹרָה כַפָּרָה. וְאֵילּוּ הֵן. הָאוֹמֵר לְשׁוֹן הָרַע. וְהַהוֹרֵג נֶפֶשׁ בִּשְׁגָגָה. הָאוֹמֵר לְשׁוֹן הָרַע לֹא הָיְתָה לוֹ כַפָּרָה וְקָבְעָה לוֹ הַתּוֹרָה כַפָּרָה זוּגֵי הַמְּעִיל. וְהָיָה עַל־אַהֲרֹן לְשָׁרֵת וְנִשְׁמַע קֹולוֹ. יָבֹא קוֹל וִיכַפֵּר עַל קוֹל. הַהוֹרֵג נֶפֶשׁ בִּשְׁגָגָה לֹא הָיְתָה לוֹ כַפָּרָה. וְקָבְעָה לוֹ הַתּוֹרָה כַפָּרָה מִיתַת כֹּהֵן גָּדוֹל. וְיָשַׁב בָּהּ עַד־מוֹת הַכֹּהֵן הַגָּדֹל.

Halakhah 5: [77]Rebbi Simon said, just as sacrifices atone, so the garments[78] atone, shirt, trousers, turban, and vest. The shirt was atoning for [wearers of *kilaim*[79]. There are those who want to say,][80] for spillers of blood, as you are saying,[81] *they dipped the shirt in blood.* The trousers were atoning for uncovering nakedness[82], as you are saying[83], *make for them linen trousers to cover the flesh*[84] *of nakedness.* The turban was atoning for haughtiness, as you are saying,[85] *he put the turban on his head.* The belt was atoning for [thieves; but some are saying, for][80] the crooked ones. Rebbi Levi said, it was

32 cubits and he wound it around on both sides. The breast plate was atoning for those who bend the law, as you are saying[86], *you shall make a breast-plate of judgment.* The vest was atoning for idol worshippers, as you are saying[87], *without vest and household-gods.* The coat. Rebbi Simon in the name of Rebbi Jonathan of Bet-Guvrin: For two things there was no atonement[88] but the Torah established atonement for them. These are those: one who spreads slander, and the involuntary homicide. For him who spreads slander there was no atonement, but the Torah fixed atonement for them, the bells of the coat: *it shall be on Aaron in service, and its sound be heard*[89]. The sound may come to atone for the sound. For the involuntary manslaughter there was no atonement but the Torah established atonement for them, the death of the High Priest[90]. *He shall dwell there until the High Priest's death.*

77 A parallel (except for the corrector's additions) is found in the Babli, *Zevahim* 88b, *Arakhin* 16a, in the name of R. Anani bar Sason.

78 The High Priest's.

79 While most of the High Priest's garments contained *kilaim*, only the shirt was worn directly on the body. It seems that the tradent here interprets the argument at the start of *Kilaim* 9:1 to mean that biblically only *kilaim* which gives immediate protection to the body is forbidden.

80 Corrector's addition (from a different source, not in the parallel in the Babli.)

81 Gen. 37:31.

82 The technical term for incest and adultery.

83 Ex. 28:42.

84 "Flesh" as a limb always denotes the penis, the only boneless limb.

85 Lev. 8:9. This is a pun on the expression "thick of head" for "haughty".

86 Ex. 28.15.

87 Hos. 3:5.

88 They do qualify for any obligatory sacrifice.

89 Ex. 28:35.

90 Num. 35:25.

(44c line 4) תַּנֵּי. רִבִּי אֱלִיעֶזֶר בֶּן יַעֲקֹב אוֹמֵר. נֶאֶמְרָה כַפָּרָה בִּפְנִים וְנֶאֶמְרָה כַפָּרָה בַּחוּץ. מַה כַּפָּרָה הָאֲמוּרָה בִּפְנִים בֶּן בָּקָר מְכַפֵּר עַל שׁוֹפְכֵי דָמִים. אַף כַּפָּרָה אֲמוּרָה בַּחוּץ בֶּן בָּקָר מְכַפֵּר עַל שׁוֹפְכֵי דָמִים. כָּאן בְּשׁוֹגֵג. כָּאן בְּמֵזִיד. שְׁנִייָא הִיא עֶגְלָה עֲרוּפָה בֵּין שׁוֹגֵג בֵּין מֵזִיד. אָמַר רִבִּי יוֹסֵה. כָּאן עַל חֵט יָדוּעַ. וּבָאן עַל חֵט שֶׁאֵינוֹ יָדוּעַ.

צִיץ. אִית דְּבָעֵי מֵימַר. עַל הַגּוֹדְפָנִים. אִית דְּבָעֵי מֵימַר. עַל עַזֵּי פָנִים. מָאן דְּאָמַר. עַל הַגּוֹדְפָנִים. נִיחָא. דִּכְתִיב וַתִּטְבַּע הָאֶבֶן בְּמִצְחוֹ. וּכְתִיב וְהָיָה עַל־מִצְחוֹ תָּמִיד. מָאן דְּאָמַר. עַל עַזֵּי פָנִים. וּמֵצַח אִשָּׁה זוֹנָה הָיָה לָךְ.

It was stated: Rebbi Eliezer ben Jacob says, atonement is mentioned inside and atonement is mentioned outside[91]. Since in atonement mentioned inside cattle atones for spillers of blood,[92] also in atonement mentioned outside cattle atones for spillers of blood. Here unintentional, there intentional[93]. There is a difference for the calf whose neck is broken, whether unintentional or intentional[94]. Rebbi Yose said, here for known offense, there for unknown offense[95].

The diadem. Some want to say, about blasphemers[96]. Some want to say, about insolent ones. He who says about blasphemers is understandable, since it is written[97] *the stone sank in his forehead*, and it is written[98], *it shall be on his forehead permanently*. He who says about insolent ones, *you had the forehead of a whoring woman*[99].

91 Atonement is mentioned explicitly for the Temple sacrifices of the Day of Atonement, and atonement is mentioned explicitly in the ceremony of the calf whose neck is broken far away from the Temple to atone for an unexplained homicide, *Deut.* 21:8.

92 Since for the calf whose neck is broken, atonement for spilled blood is mentioned explicitly, one has to switch the references to "inside" and "outside" in this sentence. The reference to an inside sacrifice is to one of the bulls sacrificed on the Day of Atonement; it is not specified which one is meant.

93 The tannaitic statement of R. Eliezer ben Jacob seems to contradict the late Amoraic statement of R. Simon that the atonement for unintentional homicide was the death of the High Priest, not any sacrifice. A first answer is that R. Eliezer ben Jacob refers to intentional homicide but R. Simon to unintentional.

94 The previous answer is rejected, since neither the murderer nor his motives are known.

95 The argument of R. Eliezer ben Jacob is rejected; only that of R. Simon is valid. It is impossible to compare the ceremony of the calf whose neck is broken to the Temple service, since in the first case it might be that the killer acted in justifiable self-defense and no sin at all was committed. But purification sacrifices are permitted only if both the fact of a sinful act and proof that it was unintentional are established.

96 This explanation is not in the Babli sources, Note 77.

97 *1Sam.* 17:49.

98 *Ex.* 28:38.

99 *Jer.* 3:3.

(44c line 13) וְלָמָּה נִקְרָא שְׁמָם אוּרִים. שֶׁהֵו מְאִירִין לְיִשְׂרָאֵל. וְתוּמִּים. שֶׁהֵן מְתִימִין לִפְנֵיהֶם אֶת הַדֶּרֶךְ. שֶׁבְּשָׁעָה שֶׁהָיוּ יִשְׂרָאֵל תְּמִימִין הָיוּ מְכַוְּנִין לָהֶן אֶת הַדֶּרֶךְ. שֶׁכֵּן מָצָאנוּ (שֶׁוּוֹדוּ)

[שֶׁבְּיָדוֹ]⁰¹⁰ לָהֶן בְּגֶבַע בִּנְיָמִן. אָמַר רִבִּי יְהוּדָה. חַס וְשָׁלוֹם לֹא (וודו) [בְּיָדוֹ]¹⁰⁰ לָהֶם בְּגֶבַע בִּנְיָמִן. שֶׁבָּרִאשׁוֹנָה אָמַר עֲלֵה וְלֹא אָמַר נְתַתִּיו. וּבַשְּׁנִייָה אָמַר עֲלֵה וְאָמַר נְתַתִּיו.

Why are they called "Urim"? Because they were enlightening Israel[101]. And "Tummin"? Because they were straightening out the way before them. As long as Israel were straight, they were showing them the correct way; as we find that they lied to them in Geva Benjamin. Rebbi Jehudah said, may God forbid, they did not lie to them in Geva Benjamin. For the first time it said, "attack" but did not say "I gave", and the second time it said, "attack" and said "I gave"[102].

וְאֵין נִשְׁאָלִין שְׁתֵּי שְׁאֵילוֹת כְּאַחַת. אִם נִשְׁאֲלוּ. אִית תַּנָּיֵי תַנֵּי. מְשִׁיבוֹ עַל הָרִאשׁוֹנָה וְאֵינוֹ מְשִׁיבוֹ עַל הַשְּׁנִייָה. וְאִית תַּנָּיֵי תַנֵּי. מְשִׁיבוֹ עַל הַשְּׁנִייָה וְאֵינוֹ מְשִׁיבוֹ עַל הָרִאשׁוֹנָה. וְאִית תַּנָּיֵי תַנֵּי. אֵינוֹ מְשִׁיבוֹ לֹא עַל הָרִאשׁוֹנָה וְלֹאו עַל הַשְּׁנִייָה. מָאן דָּאָמַר. מְשִׁיבוֹ עַל הָרִאשׁוֹנָה וְאֵינוֹ מְשִׁיבוֹ עַל הַשְּׁנִייָה. מִן הָדָא וַיֹּאמֶר דָּוִד יְיָ אֱלֹהֵי יִשְׂרָאֵל וגו'. הֲיַסְגִּרֻנִי בַעֲלֵי קְעִילָה בְיָדוֹ וגו'. וְהֲיֵרֵד שָׁאוּל. דָּוִד לֹא שָׁאַל כְּהוֹגֶן. לָא צוּרְכָא דְלָא. הֲיֵרֵד שָׁאוּל. וְאִם יֵרֵד יַסְגִּרֻנִי בַעֲלֵי קְעִילָה בְיָדוֹ.] מָאן דָּאָמַר. מְשִׁיבוֹ עַל הַשְּׁנִייָה. וְאֵינוֹ מְשִׁיבוֹ עַל הָרִאשׁוֹנָה. מִן הָדָא וַיֹּאמֶר דָּוִד הֲיַסְגִּרוּנִי בַעֲלֵי קְעִילָה אוֹתִי וגו'. מָאן דָּאָמַר. אֵינוֹ מְשִׁיבוֹ לֹא עַל הָרִאשׁוֹנָה וְלֹאו עַל הָאַחֲרוֹנָה. וַיִּשְׁאַל דָּוִד בַּיְיָ לֵאמֹר אֶרְדּוֹף אַחֲרֵי הַגְּדוּד־הַזֶּה הַאַשִּׂיגֶנּוּ. דָּוִד בִּיקֵּשׁ עָלֶיהָ רַחֲמִים. יְיָ אֱלֹהֵי יִשְׂרָאֵל הַגֶּד־נָא לְעַבְדֶּךָ. תֵּדַע לָךְ. שֶׁהֲרֵי שְׁתַּיִם שָׁאַל וְהֵשִׁיבוֹ שָׁלֹשׁ. וַיֹּאמֶר רְדוֹף כִּי־הַשֵּׂג תַּשִּׂיג וְהַצֵּל תַּצִּיל. אִית תַּנָּיֵי תַנֵּי. הַקּוֹל הָיָה שׁוֹמֵעַ. אִית תַּנָּיֵי תַנֵּי. הַכְּתָב בּוֹלֵט. מָאן דָּאָמַר. הַקּוֹל הָיָה שׁוֹמֵעַ. נִיחָא. דִּכְתִיב וַיִּשְׁמַע אֶת־הַקּוֹל. מָאן דָּאָמַר. הַכְּתָב הָיָה בּוֹלֵט. וְהָא לֵית חֵי"ת בַּשְּׁבָטִים וְלֹא צַדִּ"י [וְלֹא קוּ"ף] בַּשְּׁבָטִים. אַבְרָהָם יִצְחָק יַעֲקֹב כָּתוּב עֲלֵיהֶן. וְהָא לֵית טִי"ת בַּשְּׁבָטִים. כָּל־אֵלֶּה שִׁבְטֵי יִשְׂרָאֵל הָיָה חָקוּק עֲלֵיהֶן.

One does not ask two questions simultaneously[103]. If they were asked, there are Tannaim who state, He answers the first but does not answer the second; and there are Tannaim who state, He answers the second but does not answer the first; and there are Tannaim who state, He answers neither the first nor the second. He who says, He answers the first but does not answer the second; from the following: *David said, Eternal, God of Israel*, etc., *would the people of Qeʽilah surrender me into his hand*[104], etc.?]*Would Saul descend*, David asked incorrectly. Was it not necessary, *would Saul descend*, and if he descended, *would the people of Qeʽilah surrender me into his hand?*][105] He who said, He answers the second but does not answer the first; from the following: *David said, would the people of Qeʽilah surrender me*[106], etc. He who said, He answers neither the first nor the last, *David asked the Eternal as follows, shall I pursue this troop, shall I reach it*[107]? David asked for mercy in this case, *Eternal, God of Israel, please tell Your servant*[104]. You should know, since he asked two [questions] and He answered three [answers]: *He said, pursue, for catching you will catch and saving you will save*[107]. There are Tannaim who state, he was hearing the voice; there are Tannaim who state, the writing was protruding. He who said, he was hearing the voice is understandable since it is written, *he heard the voice*[108]. He who said, the writing[109] was protruding, but there is no ח for the tribes, and there is no צ [and no ק] for the tribes! Abraham, Isaac, Jacob was written on them. But there is no ט for the tribes! *All these are the tribes of Israel*[110] was engraved on them.

100 The scribe (text in parentheses) and the corrector [text in brackets] intend to write the same. The scribe's spelling is phonetic; under the influence of Greek ב only had the *v*-sound given by double *wav*. Intended is the the biblical root בדה "to be lying."

101 Babli 73b.

102 The references are to *Jud.* 20:23,28 but the quotes are incorrect, the correct expressions are עלו and אתננו.

103 Babli 73a.

104 *1Sam.* 23:11.

105 Corrector's addition. The question asked in 23:11 was illogical since the first question was relevant only if the answer to the second question was positive. Therefore it was necessary for David to ask the first question a second time, *1Sam.* 23:12. There is no reason to assume a corruption of the biblical text.

106 *1Sam.* 23:12..

107 *1Sam.* 30:8.

108 *Num.* 7:89.

109 Identifying *Urim and Tummim* with an oracle involving the breast plate of the High Priest on whose precious stones the names of the 12 tribes were engraved, *Ex.* 28:21. This seemed to be excluded since not the entire alphabet was occurring in these names.

110 *Gen.* 49:28.

יום הכיפורים פרק שמיני

(fol.44c) **משנה א**: יוֹם הַכִּפּוּרִים אָסוּר בַּאֲכִילָה וּבִשְׁתִיָּה וּבִרְחִיצָה וּבְסִיכָה וּבִנְעִילַת הַסַּנְדָּל וּבְתַשְׁמִישׁ הַמִּטָּה. הַמֶּלֶךְ וְהַכַּלָּה יִרְחֲצוּ אֶת פְּנֵיהֶם. וְהַחַיָה תִנְעוֹל אֶת הַסַּנְדָּל דִּבְרֵי רַבִּי אֱלִיעֶזֶר. וַחֲכָמִים אוֹסְרִין:

Mishnah 1: On the Day of Atonement eating, drinking, washing, anointing, wearing shoes[1], and sexual relations, are forbidden. The king and the bride[2] wash their heads, and the woman recovering after childbirth wears shoes, the words of Rebbi Eliezer, but the Sages forbid it.

1 Leather shoes.
2 The newlywed, who should appear beautiful in her husband's eyes, just as the king always should look handsome in public.

(44c line 76) יוֹם הַכִּפּוּרִים אָסוּר בַּאֲכִילָה וּבִשְׁתִיָּה כול'. עָנוּשׁ כָּרֵת. וְאַתְּ אָמַר הָכֵין. אָמַר רִבִּי הִילָא. לְפָחוֹת מִכְּשִׁיעוּרִין נִצְרְכָה.

"On the Day of Atonement eating, drinking, etc., are forbidden." They are punishable by extirpation and you are saying so[3]? Rebbi Hila said, it was needed for less than the minimal quantities[4].

3 In Mishnaic terminology, "forbidden" either means forbidden rabbinically or biblically with no specified punishment. The term for severe biblical prohibitions, subject to extirpation or execution is "liable" (for a purification sacrifice in the case of inadvertent transgression.)
4 If someone eats or drinks less than the quantities specified in Mishnah 2, the transgression is not liable for a purification sacrifice. Babli 73b.

(44d line 1) תְּעַנּוּ אֶת־נַפְשֹׁתֵיכֶם. יָכוֹל יֵשֵׁב לוֹ בַחַמָּה וּבְצִינָה כְּדֵי שֶׁיִּצְטַעֵר. תַּלְמוּד לוֹמַר כָּל־מְלָאכָה לֹא תַעֲשׂוּ. מְלָאכָה אָסַרְתִּי לָךְ בְּמָקוֹם אַחֵר. וְעִינּוּי אָסַרְתִּי לָךְ בְּמָקוֹם אַחֵר. מַה מְלָאכָה שֶׁאָסַרְתִּי לָךְ בְּמָקוֹם אַחֵר [מְלָאכָה] שֶׁחַיָּיבִין עָלֶיהָ כָּרֵת. אַף עִינּוּי שֶׁאָסַרְתִּי לָךְ בְּמָקוֹם אַחֵר שֶׁחַיָּיבִין עָלָיו כָּרֵת. וְאֵילוּ הֵן. אֵילוּ הַפִּיגוּלִין וְהַנּוֹתָרִין. מִנַּיִין לְרַבּוֹת אֶת הַטְּבָלִין. תַּלְמוּד לוֹמַר תְּעַנּוּ אֶת־נַפְשֹׁתֵיכֶם. רִיבָּה. [מַרְבֶּה אֲנִי אֶת הַטְּבָלִים שֶׁהֵן בְּמִיתָה. וְלֹא אַרְבֶּה אֶת הַנְּבֵלָה שֶׁאֵינָן בְּמִיתָה. תַּלְמוּד לוֹמַר תְּעַנּוּ אֶת־נַפְשֹׁתֵיכֶם. רִיבָּה.] אַרְבֶּה אֶת הַנְּבֵילוֹת שֶׁהֵן

בְּלֹא תַעֲשֶׂה וְלֹא אַרְבֶּה אֶת הַחוּלִין שֶׁאֵינָן בְּלֹא תַעֲשֶׂה. תַּלְמוּד לוֹמַר תְּעַנּוּ אֶת־נַפְשֹׁתֵיכֶם. רִיבָה. אַרְבֶּה אֶת הַחוּלִין שֶׁאֵינָן בַּעֲמוֹד וַאֲכוֹל. וְלֹא אַרְבֶּה אֶת הַתְּרוּמָה וּמַעֲשֵׂר שֵׁינִי שֶׁהֵן בַּעֲמוֹד אֱכוֹל. תַּלְמוּד לוֹמַר תְּעַנּוּ אֶת־נַפְשֹׁתֵיכֶם. רִיבָה. אַרְבֶּה אֶת הַתְּרוּמָה וְהַמַּעֲשֵׂר שֶׁאֵינָן בְּבַל תּוֹתִיר. וְלֹא אַרְבֶּה אֶת הַקֳדָשִׁים שֶׁהֵן בְּבַל תוֹתִיר. תַּלְמוּד לוֹמַר תְּעַנּוּ אֶת־נַפְשֹׁתֵיכֶם. רִיבָה. דָּבָר אַחֵר. תְּעַנּוּ אֶת־נַפְשֹׁתֵיכֶם. דָּבָר שֶׁהוּא עִינוּי אב בֵית נֶפֶשׁ. וְאֵי זוֹ זוֹ. זוֹ אֲכִילָה וּשְׁתִיָּיה. מִשֵׁם רִבִּי יִשְׁמָעֵאל אֲמְרוּ. נֶאֱמַר כָּאן תְּעַנּוּ אֶת־נַפְשֹׁתֵיכֶם. וְנֶאֱמַר לְהַלָּן וַיְעַנְּךָ וַיַּרְעִיבֶךָ. מַה עִינּוּי שֶׁנֶּאֱמַר לְהַלָּן עִינּוּי רָעָבוֹן. אַף עִינּוּי שֶׁנֶּאֱמַר כָּאן עִינּוּי רָעָבוֹן.

וְלָמָּה שִׁשָּׁה דְבָרִים. כְּנֶגֶד שִׁשָּׁה עִינּוּיִין הָאֲמוּרִין בַּפָּרָשָׁה. וְהָא לֵיתְנוֹן אֶלָּא חֲמִשָּׁה. אָמַר רִבִּי תַּמְחוּמָא. וְאֶחָד מוּסַף.

[5] "*You shall deprive yourselves*[6]. I could think that one should sit in the sun or in the cold to make himself feel badly, the verse says, *do not do any work*. The work which I forbade you elsewhere[7]. And the deprivation of what I forbade you elsewhere. Since the work which I forbade you elsewhere is work for which one would be liable to extirpation, so also deprivation which I forbade you elsewhere is deprivation from which one would be liable to extirpation, and the following are those: *piggul* and leftovers[8]. From where to add *tevel*[9]? The verse says, *you shall deprive yourselves*; it added. [I am adding *tevel* which is a deadly sin, but would not add carcass meat which is not a deadly sin; the verse says, *you shall deprive yourselves*; it added.][10] I am adding carcass meat which is prohibited, but would not add profane meat which is not prohibited; the verse says, *you shall deprive yourselves*; it added. I am adding profane meat which is not under a commandment to be eaten, but would not add heave and Second Tithe which is under a commandment to be eaten[11]; the verse says, *you shall deprive yourselves*; it added. I am adding heave and tithe of which leftovers are not prohibited, but would not add sacrificial meat for which leftovers are prohibited, the verse says, *you shall deprive yourselves*; it added. Another explanation: *You shall deprive yourselves*, something which is a deprivation (father house) {which diminishes}[12] the spirit/ What is this? Eating and drinking. In the name of Rebbi Ismael they said, it is said here *you shall deprive yourselves*, and it says there, *He deprived you and made you hungry*[13]. Since deprivation there is one of hunger, also deprivation here is one of hunger."

And why six kinds? Corresponding to the six quotes of "deprivation" in the Chapter. But there are only five? Rebbi Tanḥuma said, one is with *musaf*[14].

5 Babli 74b, *Sifra Ahare Pereq* 7(1-4).
6 Lev. 15:29.
7 All Sabbath prohibitions apply to the Day of Atonement.
8 For *piggul*, cf. Chapter 5 Note 154. Eating sacrificial meat after the allotted time is sinful, *Lev.* 19:7.
9 Produce from which heave and tithes have not been taken
10 Corrector's addition, necessary by the context.
11 Heave must be eaten by Cohanim in purity, and Second Tithe by the farmer's family in Jerusalem in purity. It is sinful to let pure heave and tithes go to waste. One could have thought that food for which there is a biblical commandment that it be eaten would be exempt from the prohibition.
12 The incomprehensible אב בית has been emended to עֲבֵידת (Qorban ha-Edah).
13 *Deut.* 8:3.
14 Deprivation is mentioned in *Lev.* 16:29,31 and 23:27,29,32. In addition it is mentioned in the paragraph on *musaf* sacrifices for the Day of Atonement, *Num.* 29:7.

(44d line 21) בִּרְחִיצָה. רִבִּי זְעוּרָה בַּר חָמָא [רִבִּי יוֹסֵי בֵּירִבִּי חֲנִינָא] בְּשֵׁם רִבִּי יְהוֹשֻׁעַ בֶּן לֵוִי. בְּתַעֲנִית צִיבּוּר מַרְחִיץ פָּנָיו יָדָיו וְרַגְלָיו כְּדַרְכּוֹ. בְּתִשְׁעָה בְּאָב מַרְחִיץ יָדָיו וּמַעֲבִירָן עַל פָּנָיו. בְּיוֹם הַכִּיפּוּרִים מַרְחִיץ יָדָיו וּמְקַנְּחָן בְּמַפָּה וּמַעֲבִיר אֶת הַמַּפָּה עַל פָּנָיו. רִבִּי יוֹנָה תָּרֵי מַרְטוּטָה וְיָהֵב לַהּ תּוּתֵי כַדָּהּ. וְהָא תַנֵּי. אֵין בֵּין תִּשְׁעָה בְּאָב לְתַעֲנִית צִיבּוּר אֶלָא אִיסּוּר מְלָאכָה בְּמָקוֹם שֶׁנָּהֲגוּ. הָיָה הוֹלֵךְ אֶצֶל רַבּוֹ אֶצֶל בִּתּוֹ וְעָבַר בַּיָּם אוֹ בַּנָּהָר אֵינוֹ חוֹשֵׁשׁ. נִיטַּנְפוּ רַגְלָיו מַטְבִּילָן בַּמַּיִם וְאֵינוֹ חוֹשֵׁשׁ. הוֹרֵי רִבִּי בָּא כָּהֵן תַּנָּייָא. הוֹרֵי רִבִּי אָחָא. בָּא מִן הַדֶּרֶךְ וְהָיוּ רַגְלָיו קִיהוֹת עָלָיו. שְׁמוּתָּר לְהַרְחִיצָם בַּמַּיִם. תַּנֵּי. אָבֵל וּמְנוּדֶּה שֶׁהָיוּ מְהַלְּכִין בַּדֶּרֶךְ מוּתָּרִין בִּנְעִילַת הַסַּנְדָּל. לִכְשֶׁיָּבוֹאוּ בָּעִיר יַחֲלוֹצוּ. וְכֵן בְּתִשְׁעָה בְּאָב וְכֵן בְּתַעֲנִית צִיבּוּר.

1 ר'| - [ר' יוסי ביר' חנינא] | ו יוסה בריה דר' יהושע בן לוי   4 תותי | ו תחות   6 כהן | ו כחדין   7 הסנדל | ו סנדל

[15]"Washing". Rebbi Ze`urah bar Ḥama, [Rebbi Yose ben Rebbi Ḥanina,] in the name of Rebbi Joshua ben Levi: On a public fast day[16] one washes as usual his face, hands, and feet. On the Ninth of Av[17] one washes his hands and moves them over his face. On the day of Atonement one washes his hands, dries them with a towel, and moves the towel over his face. Rebbi Jonah moistened a rag and put it under the water pitcher[18]. But did we not state that there is no difference between a public fast and the Ninth of Av except the prohibition of work at places where they were used to it[19]? If somebody was

going[20] to his teacher or to his daughter and crossed a lake or a river he does not worry[21]. If his feet were dirtied he immerses them in water and does not worry. Rebbi Abba instructed following this Tanna. Rebbi Aḥa instructed that one who comes from the road and his feet are dulled, he may wash them in water. It was stated: A mourner and one in the ban[22] on a trip are permitted leather shoes. When they come to the town they shall take them off. The same applies to a public fast and the Ninth of Av[23].

15 A parallel is in *Taaniot* 1:6 (64c line 37), ו. The *Taaniot* text is reproduced by Tosaphoti *Taanit* 13a, s. v. אמר.
16 A fast day called to pray for rain in a year of drought.
17 The fast instituted to mourn the destruction of the Temple.
18 He soaked the rag before the start of the Day of Atonement, squeezed it and let it dry somewhat during the night so that the next morning it should be somewhat moist but not dripping.
19 There were places where the community had adopted the rule that one did not work on the Ninth of Av. Nowhere was this extended to fast days in years of drought.
20 On a day where washing was rabbinically forbidden. Babli 77b; Tosephta 4:5,
21 No rabbinic prohibition was violated..
22 Any weekday of the year, the mourner and the person in the ban are forbidden to wear leather shoes. The person in the ban has to follow these rules if he ever wants to have the ban lifted. Babli *Mo`ed Qatan* 15b.
23 For everybody.

(44 d line 32) בְּסִיכָה. כְּהָדָא דְתַנֵּי. בַּשַּׁבָּת בֵּין סִיכָה שֶׁהִיא שֶׁלְתַּעֲנוּג בֵּין סִיכָה שֶׁאֵינָהּ שֶׁלְתַּעֲנוּג מוּתָּר. בְּיוֹם הַכִּיפּוּרִים בֵּין סִיכָה שֶׁהִיא שֶׁלְתַּעֲנוּג בֵּין סִיכָה שֶׁאֵינָהּ שֶׁלְתַּעֲנוּג אָסוּר. בְּתִשְׁעָה בְאָב וּבְתַעֲנִית צִיבּוּר סִיכָה שֶׁהִיא שֶׁלְתַּעֲנוּג אָסוּר. שֶׁאֵינָהּ שֶׁלְתַּעֲנוּג מוּתָּר. וְהָא תַנֵּי. שָׁוְות סִיכָה לִשְׁתִיָּה לְאִיסּוּר וּלְתַשְׁלוּמִין. אֲבָל לֹא לָעוֹנֶשׁ. בְּיוֹם הַכִּיפּוּרִים לְאִיסּוּר. אֲבָל לֹא לָעוֹנֶשׁ. וְהָא תַנֵּי. וְלֹא יְחַלְּלוּ. לְהָבִיא אֶת הַסָּךְ וְאֶת הַשּׁוֹתֶה. אָמַר רִבִּי יוֹחָנָן. לֵית כָּאן סָךְ. אָמַר רִבִּי אַבָּמָרִי. אִין לֵית כָּאן סָךְ. לֵית כָּאן שׁוֹתֶה. דְּלֹ כֵן דָּבָר שֶׁהוּא בָא מִשְׁנֵי לָוְיִן מִצְטָרֵף.

[24]"Anointing." As it was stated: On the Sabbath both anointing for pleasure and anointing not for pleasure are permitted. On the Day of Atonement, both anointing for pleasure and anointing not for pleasure are forbidden. On the Ninth of Av and public fasts, anointing for pleasure is forbidden but anointing not for pleasure is permitted. But it was stated: Anointing is equal to drinking regarding prohibition and reparation but not punishment[25]. On the Day of Atonement regarding prohibition but not

punishment[26] But was it not stated, *they shall not desecrate*[27], to include him who anoints or drinks? Rebbi Joḥanan said, there is no "anoints" there. Rebbi Abba Mari said, if there is no "anoints" there is no "drinks". For if it were not so, do matters combine which come from two different prohibitions[28]?

24 This text is shortened from *Ma`aser Šeni* 2:1 (Notes 28-35), *Šabbat* 9, Notes 122-127 and *Ta`anit* 1:6.

25 Referring to illegal use of heave and dedicated food by non-Cohanim and its replacement by 5/4 of the value taken.

26 The only biblical prohibitions on the Day of Atonement are eating, drinking, and working. The other two, anointing and sexual relations, are rabbinic and not subject to biblical punishment.

27 *Lev.* 22:15. The verse refers to the non-Cohen who "eats" holy food in error. Babli *Niddah* 32a.

28 If the verse in *Lev.* is needed to subsume drinking under eating, it is incomprehensible that for inadvertently eating and drinking together on the Day of Atonement one should be responsible only for one sacrifice since in that case, one infringes on two separate biblical prohibitions and should be liable for two separate sacrifices. Similarly, if one illegitimately ate and drank heave he should be liable for two separate fifths. Since in both cases the Mishnah treats eating and drinking together, the verse cannot express a separate status for drinking; the addition of anointing and drinking is rabbinic interpretation but not biblical law and there is no reason to exclude anointing.

(44d line 40) גָּרַשׁ עַד הַגּוּף הַקָּדוֹשׁ בְּשׁוֹכֵחַ.

One repeats up to "this holy body that he forgot"[29].

29 The body of the following is copied by the corrector who prepared the text for the Venice printer from *Taaniot* 1:6; parts of it are also quoted in other tractates.

[מִנַּיִין שֶׁהוּא מְחוּוָּר בַּעֲשֵׂה. אָמַר רִבִּי אֶלְעָזָר בְּשֵׁם רִבִּי סִימַיי. לֹא נָתַתִּי מִמֶּנּוּ לְמֵת. מָה נָן קַיָּימִין. אִם לְהָבִיא לוֹ אָרוֹן וְתַכְרִיכִין. לַחַי הוּא אָסוּר כָּל־שֶׁכֵּן לְמֵת. וְאֵיזֶה דָבָר שֶׁמּוּתָּר לַחַי וְאָסוּר לַמֵּת. הֱוֵי אוֹמֵר. זוֹ סִיכָה.

וּבִנְעִילַת הַסַּנְדָּל. תַּנֵּי. כָּל־אֵילּוּ שֶׁאָמְרוּ. אֲסוּרִין בִּנְעִילַת הַסַּנְדָּל. יָצָא לַדֶּרֶךְ נוֹעֵל. הִגִּיעַ לְכָרַךְ חוֹלֵץ. וְכֵן בְּאָבֵל וְכֵן בִּמְנוּדֶּה. אִית תַּנָּיֵי תַנֵּי. יוֹצְאִין בְּאַמְפִּלְיָא בְּיוֹם הַכִּיפּוּרִים. וְאִית תַּנָּיֵי תַנֵּי. אֵין יוֹצְאִין. אָמַר רַב חִסְדָּא. מָאן דָּמַר. יוֹצְאִין. בְּאַמְפִּלְיָא שֶׁל בֶּגֶד. וּמָאן דָּמַר. אֵין יוֹצְאִין. בְּאַמְפִּלְיָא שֶׁל עוֹר. רִבִּי יִצְחָק בַּר נַחְמָן סָלַק לְגַבֵּי רִבִּי יְהוֹשֻׁעַ בֶּן לֵוִי בְּלֵילֵי צוֹמָא רַבָּא.

נְפַק לְגַבֵּיהּ לְבוּשׁ סוֹלְיָסָה. אָמַר לֵיהּ. מָה הוּא דֵין. אָמַר לֵיהּ. אִיסְתְּנִיס אֲנָא. רִבִּי שְׁמוּאֵל בַּר נַחְמָן סָלַק לְגַבֵּיהּ רִבִּי יְהוֹשֻׁעַ בֶּן לֵוִי בְּלֵילֵי תַעֲנִיתָא. נְפַק לְגַבֵּהּ. לְבוּשׁ סוֹלְיָסָה. אָמַר לֵיהּ. מָה הוּא דֵין. אָמַר לֵיהּ. אִיסְתְּנִיס אָנִי. רִבִּי סִמַּיי חֲמוֹנָה נְפִיק בְּלֵילֵי תַעֲנִיתָא לְבוּשׁ סוֹלְיָסָה. חַד תַּלְמִיד מִן דְּרִבִּי מָנָא הוּרֵי לְחַד מִן קְרִיבוֹי דְּנָשִׂיָא לְמַלְבֵּשׁ סוֹלְיָסָה. אָמַר לֵיהּ. אַן מִן הָדָא. אָמַר לֵיהּ. מִן דְּרִבִּי יְהוֹשֻׁעַ בֶּן לֵוִי הוּא. אָמַר לֵיהּ. רִבִּי יְהוֹשֻׁעַ בֶּן לֵוִי אִיסְתְּנִיס הֲוָה.

וּבְתַשְׁמִישׁ הַמִּטָּה. אָתֵי חָמֵי. בִּרְחִיצָה הוּא אָסוּר. בְּתַשְׁמִישׁ הַמִּטָּה לֹא כָל־שֶׁכֵּן. תִּיפְתָּר בְּמָקוֹם שֶׁאֵין טוֹבְלִין. אוֹ קוֹדֶם שֶׁהִתְקִין עֶזְרָא טְבִילָה לְבַעֲלֵי קְרָיִין. רִבִּי יַעֲקֹב בַּר אָחָא רִבִּי יֵיסָא בְּשֵׁם רִבִּי יְהוֹשֻׁעַ בֶּן לֵוִי. אֵין קָאי אֶלָּא מִתַּשְׁמִישׁ הַמִּטָּה. רַב הוּנָא אָמַר. אֲפִילוּ רָאָה עַצְמוֹ נִיאוֹת תּוֹךְ חֲלוֹם. הֲוֵו בְעַיָין מֵימַר. וּבִלְבַד הָאִשָּׁה. רִבִּי יוֹנָה וְרִבִּי יוֹסֵי תְּרוֵיהוֹן אָמְרִין. אֲפִילוּ מִדָּבָר אַחֵר. וְהָא תַנִּינָן. יוֹם הַכִּיפּוּרִים אָסוּר בַּאֲכִילָה וּבִשְׁתִיָיה וּבִרְחִיצָה וּבְסִיכָה וּבִנְעִילַת הַסַּנְדָּל וּבְתַשְׁמִישׁ הַמִּטָּה. וְתַנֵּי עֲלָהּ. בַּעֲלֵי קְרָיִין טוֹבְלִין כְּדַרְכָּן בְּצִנְעָה בְּיוֹם הַכִּיפּוּרִים. לֵית הָדָא פְלִינָא עַל רִבִּי יְהוֹשֻׁעַ בֶּן לֵוִי. דְּרִבִּי יְהוֹשֻׁעַ בֶּן לֵוִי אָמַר. אֵין קְרִי אֶלָּא מִתַּשְׁמִישׁ הַמִּטָּה. פָּתַר לָהּ. בְּשֶׁשִּׁימֵּשׁ מִטָּתוֹ מִבְּעוֹד יוֹם וְשָׁכַח וְלֹא טָבַל. וְהָא תַנֵּי. מַעֲשֶׂה בְרִבִּי יוֹסֵי בַּר חֲלַפְתָּא בַר שֶׁרָאוּ אוֹתוֹ טוֹבֵל בְּצִנְעָה בְּיוֹם הַכִּיפּוּרִים. אִית לָךְ מֵימַר בְּאוֹתוֹ הַגּוּף הַקָּדוֹשׁ בְּשׁוֹכֵחַ.]

[From where that there is a clear commandment³⁰? Rebbi Eleazar in the name of Rebbi Simai: *I did not give from it to the dead*³¹. Where do we hold? If not to bring a casket or shrouds for him, this is forbidden for the living, therefore certainly for the dead. What is permitted for the living but prohibited for the dead?³² I am saying that this is anointing³³.

"Wearing shoes". It was stated: In all cases where they said that one may not wear shoes, when he departs on a trip he puts them on, when he arrives at a walled city he takes them off; this includes the mourner and the person in the ban³⁴. There are Tannaim who state, one goes in slippers³⁵ on the day of Atonement; and there are Tannaim who state, one does not. Rav Ḥisda said, he who said one goes, in textile slippers, and he who said one does not go, in leather slippers³⁶. Rebbi Isaac bar Naḥman visited Rebbi Joshua ben Levi in the night of the Great Fast³⁷; he came to him wearing laced shoes³⁸. He asked him, what is this? He answered, I am asthenic³⁹. Rebbi Samuel bar Naḥman visited Rebbi Joshua ben Levi in the night of a fast day⁴⁰; he came to him wearing laced shoes. He asked him, what is this? He answered, I am asthenic. They saw Rebbi Simai walking in the night of a fast day in laced shoes. A student of Rebbi Mana permitted to a relative of the Patriarch to wear laced shoes[41]. He asked him, from where this? He answered, from this of Rebbi Joshua ben Levi. He said to him, in the case of Rebbi Joshua ben Levi it was an asthenic.

"And sexual relations." Come and see, he is forbidden to wash, not so much more to have sexual relations[42]? Explain it that it was a place where one does not immerse oneself, or before Ezra instituted immersion for people having had an emission. [43]Rebbi Jacob bar Aḥa, Rebbi Yasa in the name of Rebbi Joshua ben Levi.: *Qeri* is only from sexual intercourse. Rav Huna said, even if he saw himself enjoying in his dream. They wanted to say, only from a woman. Rebbi Jonah and Rebbi Yose both say, even from something else. But did we not state: On the Day of Atonement eating, drinking, washing, anointing, wearing shoes, and sexual relations, are forbidden?. And it was stated in that respect: Men with *qeri* immerse themselves secretly in their normal way on the day of Atonement[44]. Does this not contradict Rebbi Joshua ben Levi, since Rebbi Joshua ben Levi said, *qeri* is only from sexual intercourse? Explain it if he had intercourse on the previous day and forgot and did not immerse himself. But it was stated: It happened that one saw Rebbi Yose bar Ḥalaphta immersing himself secretly on Yom Kippur. Can you say about that holy body that he forgot[45]?]

30 While illegitimate use of heave oil for anointing is prohibited, it is mentioned in the framework of the farmer's declaration in the Temple, which is a positive commandment. Overstepping the prohibition of anointing when it is forbidden legally is overstepping a positive commandment not under the scope of biblical penal law.

This paragraph is copied from the parallels (Note 24); there is no connection to the rules of the Day of Atonement.

31 *Deut.* 26:14.
32 Cf. *Sifry Deut.* 302.
33 Second Tithe must be consumed; no other use is authorized..

34 Babli *Mo'ed qatan* 15b. The Yerushalmi version is quoted by *Or zarua* §277.
35 Latin *impilia, -ium* (pl/) "felt slippers".
36 *Yebamot* 12:1, Notev 35, Babli *Yebamot* 102b.
37 The day of Atonement.
38 A leather sole with a textile upper part held together by laces.
39 Greek ἀσθενής. Since the rules of not wearing leather shoes are rabbinic, they are waved for health reasons.
40 A rabbinic fast day.
41 Without a medical condition which would justify waving the rules.

42 Since the Day of Atonement is a day of prayer and by an institution of Ezra prayer was forbidden after sexual relations before immersion in a *miqweh*, the prohibition of washing should imply the prohibition of sexual relations without the need to spell it out.

43 This text to the end of the paragraph is also from *Berakhot* 3:4 (Notes 167-168) which is the original source.

44 In Tosephta *Kippurim* 4:5 and Babli 88a the reading is: "Men with *qeri* (emission of semen) immerse themselves normally on Yom Kippur"; one speaks of a full immersion and "in secret" is not mentioned. The Tosephta is Babylonian formulation.

45 Hence, the interpretation of Rav Huna is incorrect and that of rabbis Yose (the Amora) and Jonah is correct.

(44d line 68) הַמֶּלֶךְ) עַל שֵׁם מֶלֶךְ בְּיוֹפְיוֹ תֶּחֱזֶינָה עֵינֶיךָ וְהַכַּלָּה מִפְּנֵי אֵיבָה.

וְהֶחָיָה תִנְעוֹל אֶת הַסַּנְדָּל. דִּבְרֵי רַבִּי אֱלִיעֶזֶר. הַוִינָן סָבְרִין מֵימַר עַל סוֹפָהּ. אֶשְׁכַּח תַּנֵּי עַל כּוּלְהוֹן.

"The king," because *your eyes shall see the king in his beauty*[46].

"The bride," because of bad feelings[47].

"And the woman recovering after childbirth wears shoes, the words of Rebbi Eliezer." We were thinking to say that this refers to the last statement; it was found stated referring to all of them[48].

46 *Is.* 33:17. Babli 78b, bottom.
47 That the husband should not feel bad about her. Babli 78b, bottom.
48 The entire sentence is R. Eliezer's.

(fol. 44c) משנה ב: הָאוֹכֵל בְּיוֹם הַכִּיפּוּרִים כְּכוֹתֶבֶת הַגַּסָּה כָּמוֹהָ וּכְגַרְעִינָתָהּ וְהַשׁוֹתֶה מְלֹא לוּגְמָיו חַיָּב. כָּל־הָאוֹכָלִין מִצְטָרְפִין לְכַכּוֹתֶבֶת וְכָל־הַמַּשְׁקִין מִצְטָרְפִין לִמְלֹא לוּגְמָיו. אֲבָל וְשָׁה אֵין מִצְטָרְפִין:

Mishnah 2: He who eats the volume of a big date with its pit or who drinks the volume of a full gulp[49] on the day of Atonement is liable[50]. All foods combine for the volume of a date, and all drinks combine for the mouthful. What he ate and drank does not combine.

49 Greek λυγμός, ό.
50 Since these are biblical prohibitions, if the infraction was intentional it is a deadly sin punishable by extirpation, if in error it

requires a purification sacrifice.

(44d line 70) **הלכה ב**: אָמַר רִבִּי יוֹסֵה. זאת אוֹמֶרֶת (שו) [שֶׁ]צָּרִיךְ לְמַעֵךְ אֶת חֲלָלוֹ. דְּל כֵן נִתְנֵי. כְּמוֹהָ וּכְנַלְעִינָתָהּ וּמְחָלָלָהּ. תַּנֵּי רִבִּי שִׁמְעוֹן בֶּן אֶלְעָזָר. כַּכּוֹתֶבֶת נִמְרִית.

Halakhah 2: Rebbi Yose said, this implies that (he) [one][51] has to squeeze its empty space[52] since otherwise one should have stated, "it, its pit, and its empty space." Rebbi Simeon ben Eleazar stated, a date from Nimrin[53].

51 The scribe wrote שו, which has to be read as שֶׁהוּא "that he". The corrector, who did not understand the Yerushalmi spelling, replaced it by prefix ש.

52 If the pit is loose in the date, the space between pit and flesh of the fruit is not counted in determining the volume which triggers liability.

53 In the printed version and one ms. of Tosephta 4:2 he disagrees with the anonymous Tanna there who restricts the dates considered to those growing West of the Jordan, and therefore increases the possible maximum volume of a date (Mishnah *Kelim* 17:7), but in the Yerushalmi version and 2 Tosephta mss. he restricts the dates allowed as standards to just those of Nimrin and therefore reduces the permitted size.

Nimrin is *Bet Nimrah* (*Jos.* 13:27) in the plain East of the Jordan.

(44d line 73) תַּנֵּי. מְלֹא לוּגְמָיו. מַה וּפְלִיג. מְלֹא לוּגְמָיו. שֶׁהוּא נִיתָּן לְלוּגְמָא אַחַת. תַּנֵּי מִשֵּׁם בֵּית שַׁמַּי. מְלוֹא לוּגְמָיו כִּרְבִיעִית. רִבִּי חִייָה בַּר אָדָא בָּעֵי קוֹמֵי רִבִּי מָנָא. וְלָמָה לֹא תַנִּינָתָהּ מְקוּלֵּי בֵית שַׁמַּי וּמֵחוּמְרֵי בֵית הִלֵּל. אָמַר לֵיהּ. מִפְּנֵי לוּגְמוֹ שֶׁלְּבֶן אֲבַטִיחַ שֶׁהָיָה מַחֲזִיק יוֹתֵר מֵרְבִיעִית.

It was stated, "a full gulp." Does this disagree[54]? A full gulp, what is possible as one gulp[55]. It was stated in the name of the House of Shammai, a full gulp is equivalent to a *quartarius*[56]. Rebbi Hiyya bar Ada asked before Rebbi Mana, why was this not stated as one of the leniencies of the House of Shammai and restrictions of the House of Hillel[57]? He told him, because of the gulp of Ben Avatiah[58] which contained more than a *quartarius*.

54 In the Mishnah, the expression for solid food is "like (in the volume of) a date", implying that pieces of food eaten at different times are added together to determine liability. The expression for fluids is "a gulp", not "like (the volume of) a gulp", but the statement of the Mishnah that different fluids combine show that "like (the volume of) a gulp" is understood. Is this also the position of the Tanna of the *baraita* or does he deny that different sips can add to a large gulp?

55 The *baraita* also agrees with the Mishnah.
56 A quarter of a *log*, about 133 cm³.
57 A *quartarius* is the standard size of a cup whose contents normally are consumed in two gulps. Therefore the standard of the House of Shammai seems to be twice that of the House of Hillel.
58 He is mentioned in Mishnah *Kelim* 17:12 as largest Cohen on record.
In contrast to the House of Shammai who determine the volume for the Day of Atonement as a standard measure, the House of Hillel insist that they vary from person to person (Mishnah *Kelim* 17:11).

(fol. 44c) **משנה ג**: אָכַל וְשָׁתָה בְּהֶעְלֵם אֶחָד אֵינוֹ חַיָּב אֶלָּא חַטָּאת אַחַת. אָכַל וְשָׁתָה וְעָשָׂה מְלָאכָה חַיָּב שְׁתֵּי חַטָּאוֹת. אָכַל אוֹכָלִין שֶׁאֵינָן רְאוּיִין לַאֲכִילָה וְשָׁתָה מַשְׁקִין שֶׁאֵינָן רְאוּיִין לִשְׁתִיָּה שָׁתָה צִיר אוֹ מוּרְיָיס פָּטוּר:

תִּינוֹקוֹת אֵין מְעַנִּין אוֹתָן בְּיוֹם הַכִּפּוּרִים אֲבָל מְחַנְּכִין אוֹתָם קוֹדֶם שָׁנָה וְקוֹדֶם שְׁתַּיִם בִּשְׁבִיל שֶׁיְּהוּ רְגִילִין לַמִּצְוֹת:

Mishnah 3: If one ate and drank in one forgetting he is liable only for one purification sacrifice[59]. If he ate and drank, and worked, he is liable for two purification sacrifices[60]. If he ate foods which are not edible or drank drinks which are not drinkable, drank fish sauce[61] or *muries*[62], he is not liable.

One does not let children fast but one educates them one year of two in advance[63] so they should be used to commandments.

59 Since not eating and drinking are subsumed under fasting, only one biblical commandment was broken.
60 Since fasting is commanded in *Lev*, 23:27 but work is forbidden in 23:28, two distinct commandments were broken and two sacrifices are due.
61 Fluid squeezed out of raw fish.
62 A Latin word denoting fish sauce treated with salt, water, and sometimes wine, used to dip one's bread in but never used as a drink.
63 One lets girls aged 10 and boys aged 11 fast part of the day and at ages 11, respectively 12, a whole day, as education, not as biblical requirement.

(45a line 1) **הלכה ג**: לָמָּה. שְׁתִיָּה בִּכְלַל אֲכִילָה. אֵין אֲכִילָה בִּכְלַל שְׁתִיָּה. מִנַּיִין שֶׁהַשְּׁתִיָּה בִּכְלַל אֲכִילָה. רִבִּי יוֹנָה שָׁמַע לָהּ מִן הָדָא. עַל־כֵּן אָמַרְתִּי לִבְנֵי יִשְׂרָאֵל כָּל־נֶפֶשׁ מִכֶּם לֹא־תֹאכַל דָּם. מָה נָן קַיָּימִין. אִם בְּדָם שֶׁקָּרַשׁ. הָא תַנֵּי. דָּם שֶׁקָּרַשׁ אֵינוֹ לֹא אוֹכֵל וְלֹא מַשְׁקֶה. אֶלָּא כִי נָן קַיָּימִין. כְּמוֹת שֶׁהוּא. וְהַתּוֹרָה קָרְאַת אוֹתוֹ אֲכִילָה. וְהָתַנֵּי. הַמִּמְחָה הַחֵלֶב וּגְמָאוֹ. הִקְפָּה אֶת

הָדָם וַאֲכָלוֹ. [אִם יֵשׁ בּוֹ כְזַיִת] חַיָּב. מָה עָבַד לָהּ רִבִּי יוֹנָה. אֵינוּ אוֹכֵל לְטַמְאוֹ טוּמְאַת אוֹכְלִין וְלֹא מַשְׁקֶה לְטַמְּאוֹ טוּמְאַת מַשְׁקֶה. חָזַר רִבִּי יוֹנָה שָׁמַע לָהּ מִן הָדָא.. וְנָתַתָּה הַכֶּסֶף בְּכֹל אֲשֶׁר־תְּאַוֶּה נַפְשְׁךָ. מָה נָן קַיָּימִין. אִם בְּטוֹעֵם טַעַם יַיִן לְתוֹךְ הַתַּבְשִׁיל. וַהֲלֹא טַעַם יַיִן לִפְגָם הוּא. [אֶלָּא כֵן נָן קַיָּימִין כָּמוֹת שֶׁהוּא. וְהַתּוֹרָה קָרְאַת אוֹתוֹ אֲכִילָה.] רַבָּנָן דְּקֵיסָרִין אֲמְרֵי. תִּיפְתַּר בְּאִילֵין אוֹרְזָנַיָּיא וְגוֹמְנַנַּיָּא. כָּל־הַטָּפֵל לַאֲכִילָה כַּאֲכִילָה הִיא.

רִבִּי יוֹסָה שָׁמַע לָהּ מִן הָדָא. שְׁבוּעָה שֶׁלֹּא אוֹכַל. וְאָכַל וְשָׁתָה. אֵינוֹ חַיָּיב אֶלָּא אֶחָת. אָמְרוּן חֲבֵרַיָּיא קוֹמֵי רִבִּי יוֹסֵה. אָמוּר דְּבַתְרָהּ. שְׁבוּעָה שֶׁלֹּא אוֹכַל וְשֶׁלֹּא אֶשְׁתֶּה וְאָכַל וְשָׁתָה. חַיָּיב שְׁתַּיִם. אָמַר לוֹן רִבִּי יוֹסֵי. אִילוּ מִי שֶׁהָיוּ לְפָנָיו שְׁנֵי כִכָּרִים. וְאָמַר. שְׁבוּעָה שֶׁלֹּא אוֹכַל כִּכָּר זוֹ. וְחָזַר וַאֲכָלָן [שְׁנֵיהֶן] כְּאַחַת. שֶׁמָּא אֵינוּ חַיָּיב שְׁתַּיִם.

רִבִּי חֲנַנְיָה בְּשֵׁם רִבִּי פִּינְחָס שָׁמַע לָהּ מִן הָדָא. שְׁבוּעָה שֶׁלֹּא אוֹכַל. וְאָכַל אוֹכְלִין שֶׁאֵינָן רְאוּיִין לַאֲכִילָה. וְשָׁתָה מַשְׁקִין שֶׁאֵינָן רְאוּיִין לִשְׁתִיָּה. פָּטוּר. מִפְּנֵי שֶׁשָּׁתָה מַשְׁקִין שֶׁאֵינָן רְאוּיִין לִשְׁתִיָּה. אֲבָל אִם [אָכַל אוֹכְלִין שֶׁהֵן רְאוּיִין לַאֲכִילָה.] שָׁתָה מַשְׁקִין שֶׁהֵן רְאוּיִין לִשְׁתִיָּיה חַיָּיב. לֹא שְׁבוּעָה שֶׁלֹּא אוֹכַל אָמַר. נִיחָא כְּמַתְנִיתָן. דַּאֲנָן אֲמְרִין. שְׁבוּעָה שֶׁלֹּא אוֹכַל. כְּרִבִּי. דּוּ אָמַר. שְׁבוּעָה שֶׁלֹּא אוֹכַל וְשֶׁלֹּא אֶשְׁתֶּה.

רִבִּי חִינְנָה שָׁמַע לָהּ מִן הָדָא. [הָאוֹכֵל וְשׁוֹתֶה בְּהֶעְלֵם אַחַת אֵינוּ חַיָּיב אֶלָּא אַחַתַת.

רִבִּי אַבָּא מָרִי שָׁמַע לָהּ מִן הָדָא.] לֹא־אָכַלְתִּי בְאֹנִי. אֶלָּא שְׁתִיתִי. נִיחָא כְּמַאן דְּאָמַר. שְׁבוּעָה שֶׁלֹּא אוֹכַל. וְשָׁתָה. בְּרַם כְּמַאן דְּאָמַר. שְׁבוּעָה שֶׁלֹּא אֶשְׁתֶּה. וְאָכַל. שְׁתִיָּיה בִּכְלַל אֲכִילָה. אֵין אֲכִילָה בִּכְלַל שְׁתִיָּיה.

אִית דְּבָעֵי מִישְׁמְעִינָהּ מִן הָדָא. לֹא־תוּכַל לֶאֱכֹל בִּשְׁעָרֶיךָ וגו'. תִּירוֹשְׁךָ זֶה הַיַּיִן. יִצְהָרֶךָ זוֹ סִיכָה. וְהַתּוֹרָה קָרְאַת אוֹתוֹ אֲכִילָה. וְאֵינוֹ מְחוּוָּר. אִין תֵּימַר. מְחוּוָּר הוּא. יִלְקוּ עָלָיו חוּץ לַחוֹמָה. אָמַר רִבִּי יוֹסֵי בֶּן חֲנִינָה. אֵין לוֹקִין חוּץ לַחוֹמָה אֶלָּא עַל מַעֲשֵׂר שֵׁנִי טָהוֹר שֶׁנִּכְנַס לִירוּשָׁלֵם וְיָצָא. וּמִנַּיִין שֶׁאֵינוֹ מְחוּוָּר. כְּהָדָא דְּתַנֵּי. בַּשַּׁבָּת בֵּין סִיכָה שֶׁהִיא שֶׁלְּתַּעֲנוּג. גָּרַשׁ בְּהִילְכָתָא קַדְמַיָּיתָא.

מִנַּיִין שֶׁהִיא מְחוּוָּר בַּעֲשָׂרָה. רִבִּי לָעֶזֶר בְּשֵׁם רִבִּי סִימַאי. לֹא נָתַתִּי מִמֶּנּוּ לְמֵת. מָה נָן קַיָּימִין. אִם לְהָבִיא לוֹ אָרוֹן וְתַכְרִיכִין דָּבָר שֶׁהוּא אָסוּר לַחַי. לַחַי הוּא אָסוּר. לֹא כָל־שֶׁכֵּן לַמֵּת. אִי זֶהוּ דָבָר שֶׁהוּא מוּתָּר לַחַי וְאָסוּר לַמֵּת. הֱוֵי אוֹמֵר. זוֹ סִיכָה.

Halakhah 3: Why?. [64]Drinking is subsumed under eating but eating is not subsumed under drinking. From where that drinking is subsumed under eating? Rebbi Jonah understood if from the following:: *Therefore, I told the Children of Israel, none of you shall eat blood*[65]. Where do we hold? If about congealed blood, was it not stated that congealed blood is neither food nor drink? But we hold, as it is. And the Torah called it eating. And was it not stated: If one liquefied fat and drank it, or congealed blood and ate it, [if there is the volume of an olive] he is liable. What does Rebbi Jonah do with this?

It is not food to become impure in the impurity of food, or fluid to become impure in the impurity of fluids. Rebbi Jonah changed and understood if from the following:: *You shall spend the money for anything you desire*[66]. Where do we hold? If about one who gives the taste of wine into a cooked dish, is that not spoiling the taste of the wine? [But we hold as it is and the Torah called it "eating."] The rabbis of Caesarea said, explain if about *orzaraya* and *gomnanya*[67], since anything that is ancillary to food is like food.

Rebbi Yose understood all this from the following: "An oath that I shall not eat; when he ate and drank he is liable only once.[68]" The colleagues said before Rebbi Yose, but it is said following this, "an oath that I shall not eat nor drink, when he ate and drank he is liable for two"! Rebbi Yose told them, if somebody had two loaves in front of him said, an oath that I shall not eat this loaf[69], when he ate [both of them] together would he not be guilty on two counts?

Rebbi Hanania in the name of Rebbi Phineas understood it from the following: "An oath that I shall not eat; when he ate inedible food and drank undrinkable fluids, he is not liable.[70]" Because he ate inedible food and drank undrinkable fluids. Therefore if [he ate edible food,][71] drank drinkable fluids he is liable. Did he not say, an oath that I shall not eat? That is understandable following our Mishnah, where we are saying, "an oath that I shall not eat." But for Rebbi[72] who said, an oath that I shall not eat and shall not drink?

Rebbi Hinena understood it from the following[73]: ["If he ate and drank in one forgetting he is liable only once." Rebbi Abba Mari understood it from the following:] *I did not eat from it in my mourning,*[74] but I drank?

It is understandable for him who said, "{I swear} an oath that I shall not eat", and he drank. Drinking is subsumed under eating. But for him who said, "an oath that I shall not drink", and he ate? Is eating subsumed under drinking? Eating is not subsumed under drinking[75].

Some want to understand it from this: *You may not eat in your gates*[76] etc. *Your cider*, that is the wine. *And your shining oil* refers to anointing and the Torah called it 'eating'. But this is not clear. If you could say that it is clear one should be whipped because of it outside the walls[77]! Rebbi Yose ben

Hanina said, one is whipped outside the walls only for pure Second Tithe which entered Jerusalem and left. From where that it is not clear? From what was stated: "On the Sabbath, both anointing for pleasure", one reads this in Halakhah One[78].

From where that it is clear as a positive commandment[79]? Rebbi Eleazar in the name of Rebbi Simai: *Nor did I give from it to the dead*[74]. Where do we hold? If it were to bring a casket and shrouds for him, that were also forbidden for a living person[80]! If something is forbidden for the living, not so much more for the dead? What is something which is permitted for the living but prohibited for the dead? That is anointing!

64 This is a partial copy, in places completed by the corrector for the Venice edition and indicated by brackets, of a text in *Ma`aser Šeni* 2:1 (Notes 7-35), also partially reproduced in *Ševuot* 3:2 (Notes 26-36). It is clear that the original is in *Ma`aser Šeni* since the last paragraph has no connection with the rules of the Day of Atonement.

65 *Lev.* 17:12.

66 *Deut.* 14:26.

67 *Ma`aser Šeni* 2:1, Note 16. The first word may denote cedar resin (J. Levy) or a derivative of אֹרֶן "rice". The readings for the second word, גמרייה, גמזוזיניה, גומנייא show that the scribe did not know what to do with it; it may be a derivative of "gum" (*gummi*, κόμμι) (E. G.) used in the preparation of liquors.

68 Mishnah *Ševuot* 3:1.

69 Here a piece of text is missing, found in the other two sources: "and then he said, an oath that I shall not eat that one."

70 Mishnah *Ševuot* 3: 5.

71 Corrector's addition, added in error.

72 Obviously since Rebbi is the editor of the Mishnah, he cannot contradict his own text. With the text in *Ševuot* one has to read: "those rabbis who say, an oath that I shall not eat and I shall not drink." These rabbis are quoted in the Babli, *Ševuot* 23a.

73 Mishnah 3.

74 *Deut.* 26:14.

75 The preceding arguments show that drinking is subsumed under eating. Nobody holds that a mention of drink includes solid food. Babli *Ševuot* 23a.

76 *Deut.* 12:17.

77 If the verse were a formal identification of anointing and eating as far as Second Tithe is concerned, the use of impure heave oil for anointing should be a criminal offense.

128 While illegitimate use of heave oil for anointing is prohibited, it is mentioned in the framework of the farmer's declaration in the Temple, which is a positive commandment. Overstepping the prohibition of anointing when it is forbidden legally is overstepping a positive commandment not under the scope of biblical penal law.

78 Notes 24 ff.

79 While illegitimate use of Second Tithe oil for anointing is prohibited, it is

mentioned in the context of the farmer's declaration in the Temple, which is a positive commandment. Therefore overstepping the prohibition is violating a positive commandment not under the scope of criminal law.

80 Since only consuming Second Tithe is permitted.

(45a line 36) אַזְהָרָה לִמְלֶאכֶת הַיּוֹם כָּל־מְלָאכָה֙ לֹ֣א תַעֲשׂ֔וּ. עוֹנֶשׁ וְהַאֲבַדְתִּ֖י אֶת־הַנֶּ֥פֶשׁ הַהִֽיא. אַזְהָרָה לְעִינּוּי הַיּוֹם כִּ֤י כָל־הַנֶּ֨פֶשׁ֙ אֲשֶׁ֣ר לֹֽא־תְעֻנֶּ֔ה. עוֹנֶשׁ וְנִכְרְתָ֖ה הַנֶּ֥פֶשׁ הַהִֽוא. אַזְהָרָה לִמְלֶאכֶת הַלַּיְלָה לֵית כָּאן. עוֹנֶשׁ לֵית כָּאן. אַזְהָרָה וְעוֹנֶשׁ לְעִינּוּי הַלַּיְלָה לֵית כְּתִיב.

רִבִּי שִׁמְעוֹן בֶּן לָקִישׁ בָּעֵי. מָה הֲוָה לֵיהּ לְמֵימַר בֵּיהּ. לֹא־תְעוּנֶּה. אֶלָּא לֹא תֹאכַל. כָּל־אֲכִילוֹת שֶׁבַּתּוֹרָה כְּזַיִת. וְכָאן כְּכוֹתֶבֶת. אָמַר רַב הוֹשַׁעְיָה. הִשָּׁמֶר פֶּן וְלֹא תְעוּנֶּה. הָא תְלַת אַזְהָרָן. אָמַר רִבִּי חוּנָה. הִשָּׁמֶר בְּאוֹתָהּ הָאֲמִירָה שֶׁאֲמַרְתִּי לָךְ. הִשָּׁמֶר בְּנֶגַע־הַצָּרַעַת לִשְׁמֹר מְאֹד וְלַעֲשׂוֹת וגו'. תַּנֵּי רִבִּי חִיָּיה. [לֹא] יֵאָמֵר עוֹנֶשׁ בִּמְלָאכָה שֶׁאֵינוֹ צָרִיךְ. הָיִיתִי לָמֵד מִן הָעִינּוּי. [מַה אִם הָעִינּוּי] הַקַּל חַיָּיבִין כָּרֵת. מְלָאכָה הַחֲמוּרָה אֵינוֹ דִין שֶׁיְּהוּ חַיָּיבִין עָלֶיהָ כָּרֵת. הָא לֹא נֶאֱמַר עוֹנֶשׁ בִּמְלָאכָה אֶלָּא לִיתֵּן אַזְהָרָה לְפָנָיו. מָה עוֹנֶשׁ שֶׁנֶּאֱמַר בִּמְלָאכָה אַזְהָרָה לְפָנָיו. אַף עוֹנֶשׁ שֶׁנֶּאֱמַר בְּעִינּוּי אַזְהָרָה לְפָנָיו. אָמַר רִבִּי זְעוּרָה. הָדָא אָמְרָה. לְמֵידִין גְּזֵירָה שָׁוָה אֲפִילוּ מוּפְנֶה מִצַּד אֶחָד. אָמַר רִבִּי יוּדָן. וְלֹא דְרִבִּי עֲקִיבָה הִיא. דְּרִבִּי עֲקִיבָה אָמַר. לְמֵידִין גְּזֵירָה שָׁוָה אַף עַל פִּי שֶׁאֵינָהּ מוּפְנֶה.

תַּנֵּי. רִבִּי אֱלִיעֶזֶר בֶּן יַעֲקֹב אוֹמֵר. נֶאֱמַר בְּעֶצֶם הַיּוֹם הַזֶּה בִּמְלָאכָה. וְנֶאֱמַר בְּעֶצֶם הַיּוֹם הַזֶּה בְּעִינּוּי. מַה בְּעֶצֶם הַיּוֹם הַזֶּה שֶׁנֶּאֱמַר בִּמְלָאכָה לֹא חִלַּקְתָּה בּוֹ בֵּין יוֹם לַלַּיְלָה. בֵּין עוֹנֶשׁ לְאַזְהָרָה. אַף בְּעֶצֶם הַיּוֹם הַזֶּה שֶׁנֶּאֱמַר בְּעִינּוּי לֹא נַחֲלוֹק בּוֹ בֵּין יוֹם לַלַּיְלָה בֵּין עוֹנֶשׁ לְאַזְהָרָה. עַד כְּדוֹן כְּרִבִּי עֲקִיבָה.

כְּרִבִּי יִשְׁמָעֵאל. תַּנֵּי רִבִּי יִשְׁמָעֵאל. וְהָיְתָה לָכֶם לְחֻקַּת עוֹלָם בַּחֹדֶשׁ הַשְּׁבִיעִי. הִקִּישׁ מְלָאכָה לְעִינּוּי. מַה מְלָאכָה שֶׁאָסַרְתִּי לָךְ מְלָאכָה שֶׁחַיָּיבִין עָלֶיהָ כָּרֵת. אַף עִינּוּי שֶׁאָסַרְתִּי לָךְ עִינּוּי שֶׁחַיָּיבִין עָלֶיהָ כָּרֵת.

[81]"Warning about work on the day: *Any work you shall not do*[82]. Punishment, *and I shall destroy this person*[83]. Warning about deprivation on the day, *for any person who will not be deprived*[84]; punishment, *and this person will be extirpated*[84]." There is no warning about work in the night, there is no punishment. There is no warning nor punishment written for deprivation in the night[85].

Rebbi Simeon ben Laqish asked, what could He have said instead of *will not be deprived*? "Shall not eat"? All eating in the Torah is by the volume of an olive, but here by the volume of a date[86]. Rav Hoshaia said, "watch yourself, lest, not be deprived," would be three warnings[87]. Rebbi Huna said, watch yourself regarding the saying which I said to you, *watch yourself in matters of skin disease to be very careful and act*[88], etc. Rebbi Ḥiyya stated: Punishment could [not][89] have been said about work since it is unnecessary. I could have inferred it from deprivation. [Since for deprivation][90] which is minor one is liable to extirpation, for work which is major[91] it should be logical that one should be liable for extirpation. Therefore punishment was spelled out for work only to imply a warning preceding it[92]. Since the punishment indicated for work is preceded by a warning, also the punishment indicated for deprivation is preceded by a warning. Rebbi Ze'ira said, this implies that one may infer about an "equal cut" even if it is free only on one side[93]. Rebbi Yudan said, Is that not Rebbi Aqiba's? And Rebbi Aqiba said, one infers about an "equal cut" even if it is not free[94].

It was stated: Rebbi Eliezer ben Jacob says, it is said *on this very day* about work and it is said *on this very day* about deprivation. Since in regard of *on this very day* said about work you did not differentiate between day and night[95], between punishment and warning[96], so in regard of *on this very day* said about deprivation we shall not differentiate between day and night, between punishment and warning. So far following Rebbi Aqiba.

Following Rebbi Ismael? *It shall be for you an eternal law, in the Seventh Month*[97] He joined work and deprivation. Since the work which I forbade to you is work for which one is liable to extirpation, also deprivation which I forbade to you is deprivation for which one is liable to extirpation[98].

81 *Sifra Emor Pereq* 14(3). Babli 81a.
82 *Lev.* 16:29.
83 *Lev.* 23:30.
84 *Lev.* 23:29.
85 In both verses quoted from *Lev.* 23 it is stressed בְּעֶצֶם הַיּוֹם הַזֶּה which in general in interpreted "in full daylight" (*Mekhilta dR. Ismael Bo* 9.) Since the night is forbidden as is the day (*Lev.* 23:32), there is an obvious contradiction to be resolved.
86 Since it was established earlier that of the six kinds of deprivation required on the Day of Atonement only not fasting is biblically punishable, the question arises why instead of the generic expression "be deprived" the verse does not directly prescribe "do not eat." The answer is that in the latter case already eating the volume of an olive would be punishable.
87 This now addresses the problem from where could one infer that all prohibitions of the Day of Atonement also apply to the preceding night. He suggests that since there are several expressions biblically used

to indicate prohibitions, there could have been different expressions used for the warnings which would have been interpreted as applying to different times.

88 *Deut.* 24:8. This is a side remark noting that הֻשָּׁמֶר is used only in reference to rules spelled out on other occasions. In this particular case it is noted that the rules of the impurity of skin disease (*Lev.* 13-14) do not include prohibitions; the prohibition implied by *Deut.* 24:8 is interpreted (cf. Pseudo-Jonathan *ad loc.*) to mean that it is forbidden to eliminate the impurity of skin disease by surgically eliminating the diseased tissue.

89 Necessary addition by the corrector.

90 Corrector's addition which seems to be unnecessary.

91 "Major" means that prohibitions of work are frequent, applying to the Sabbath as capital crimes and to holidays as misdemeanors; deprivation is "minor" since it applies only to the day of Atonement.

92 The argument of Rav Hoshaia is essentially correct but has to be realized differently. Since the warning spelled out for work on the Day of Atonement is shown to be unnecessary, it has to be applied as if it were written twice; supplying the desired additional warning to be read as referring to the preceding night.

93 He reads the argument of R. Hiyya not as a conclusion *de minore ad majus* but as "equal cut" meaning that the expression בְּעֶצֶם הַיּוֹם הַזֶּה appearing in *Lev.* 23:29,30 implies that the rules indicated in both verses are the same. In general one requires that an expression used for "equal cut" not be used for any other inference; but here the entire v. 29 is needed both for warning and punishment (Note 84). There remains the problem that since now it is shown that בְּעֶצֶם הַיּוֹם הַזֶּה does not mean "during daylight only", the expression is not used for any other deduction and therefore the "equal cut" is between two identical expressions not other- wise needed and therefore valid according to everybody, even R. Ismael. One has to say that since the day is defined in *Lev.* 23:32 as from evening to evening, בְּעֶצֶם הַיּוֹם הַזֶּה means that while one has to start fasting and refraining from work somewhat earlier and finish sometime after nightfall the next day, the biblical penalties do not apply to these additional periods and therefore one mention of "on this very day" is needed for this legal implication.

Noted as opinion in dispute, Babli *Šabbat* 64a, *Niddah* 22b.

94 The Babli would reject the entire argument of R. Ze'ira since it permits the use of "equal cut" only based on an oral tradition. It still would recognize R. Hiyya's argument but it categorically rejects extending the scope of punishments by hermeneutical arguments.

95 As argued by R. Hiyya.

96 Which are written in one and the same verse.

97 *Lev.* 16:29.

98 As required by Rav Hoshaia.

(45a line 59) רִבִּי אַבָּהוּ בְשֵׁם רִבִּי יוֹחָנָן הָאוֹכֵל כִּלְאֵי הַכֶּרֶם לוֹקֶה. רִבִּי אַבָּהוּ בְשֵׁם רִבִּי יוֹחָנָן הַכּוֹסֵס חִיטֵי תְרוּמָה לוֹקֶה. רִבִּי אַבָּהוּ בְשֵׁם רִבִּי יוֹחָנָן. הַמְנַגֵּמָא⁹⁹ חוֹמֶץ שֶׁלִּתְרוּמָה לוֹקֶה.

הַמְגַמֵּעַ חוֹמֶץ שֶׁלִּתְרוּמָה מְשַׁלֵּם אֶת הַקֶּרֶן וְאֵינוּ מְשַׁלֵּם אֶת הַחוֹמֶשׁ. הַכּוֹסֵס חִטֵּי תְרוּמָה מְשַׁלֵּם אֶת הַקֶּרֶן וְאֵינוּ מְשַׁלֵּם אֶת הַחוֹמֶשׁ. רִבִּי אוֹמֵר. אוֹמֵר אֲנִי שֶׁהוּא מְשַׁלֵּם קֶרֶן וְחוֹמֶשׁ. רִבִּי יִרְמְיָה בְשֵׁם רִבִּי אִמִּי. מוֹדִין חֲכָמִים לְרִבִּי בִּמְגַמֵּעַ חוֹמֶץ שֶׁלִּתְרוּמָה לְאַחַר טִיבּוּלוֹ מְשַׁלֵּם קֶרֶן וְחוֹמֶשׁ. שֶׁהַחוֹמֶץ מֵשִׁיב אֶת הַנֶּפֶשׁ.

[100]Rebbi Abbahu in the name of Rebbi Johanan, he who eats of *kilàim* in a vineyard[101] is whipped[102]. Rebbi Abbahu in the name of Rebbi Johanan, he who chews wheat grain[103] of heave is whipped. Rebbi Abbahu in the name of Rebbi Johanan, he who sips vinegar of heave is whipped; he who sips vinegar of heave pays the principal but he does not pay the fifth[104]; he who chews wheat grain of heave pays the principal but he does not pay the fifth. Rebbi says, I am saying that he pays principal and fifth. Rebbi Jeremiah in the name of Rebbi Immi: The rabbis agree with Rebbi about one who sips heave vinegar from his dipping that he pays principal and fifth since vinegar refreshes[105].

99 Clearly a misspelling.

100 The main source of this paragraph are *Terumot* 6:1, Notes 16-19, *Šabbat* 14, Notes 83-89.. Babli *Yoma* 80b/81a.

101 Any non-vine produce in a vineyard is prohibited for usufruct.

102 If there are witnesses to the act, since he broke a biblical commandment. This corresponds to the term "is liable" used for Sabbath violations.

103 A pure Cohen who is entitled to eat heave may not spit out the grain after chewing.

104 The fifth computed from the top which is a quarter from the bottom, due for use of heave by people not entitled to its use.

105 Even though vinegar in itself is neither food nor drink, when it was absorbed by bread it becomes food and stays food. For heave it remains subject to the fine, on the Day of Atonement it remains forbidden drink, but on the Sabbath it may be used for a toothache.

(45a line 64) תִּינוֹקוֹת אֵין מְעַנִּין אוֹתָן בְּיוֹם הַכִּפּוּרִים. רַב חוּנָה פָתַר מַתְנִיתָהּ. תִּינוֹקוֹת אֵין מְעַנִּין אוֹתָן בְּיוֹם הַכִּפּוּרִים. וְלֹא מְחַנְּכִין אוֹתָן קוֹדֶם לְשָׁנָה. קוֹדֶם לִשְׁנָתַיִם מְחַנְּכִין. רִבִּי יוֹחָנָן פָּתַר מַתְנִיתָהּ. תִּינוֹקוֹת אֵין מְעַנִּין אוֹתָן בְּיוֹם הַכִּפּוּרִים. אֲבָל מְחַנְּכִין קוֹדֶם לְשָׁנָה. קוֹדֶם לִשְׁנָתַיִם מַשְׁלִימִין. עַד אֵיכָן. רִבִּי אָחָא רִבִּי חִינְנָה רִבִּי יַעֲקֹב בַּר אִידִי בְשֵׁם רִבִּי שִׁמְעוֹן בֶּן חֲלַפְתָּא. כְּבֶן תֵּשַׁע וּכְבֶן עֶשֶׂר.

"One does not let children fast on the Day of Atonement." Rav Huna explained the Mishnah: One does not let children fast on the Day of Atonement, and does not train them[106], but one or two years before one trains them¹⁰⁷. Rebbi Johanan explained the Mishnah: One does not let children fast on the Day of Atonement, but one does train them¹⁰⁸, and one or two years before they complete the fast. Until when? Rebbi Aha, Rebbi Hinena, Rebbi Jacob bar Idi in the name of Rebbi Simeon ben Halaphta: At age nine or age ten¹⁰⁹.

106 One tells them to fast part of the day.
107 One does not let minor children fast the entire day.
108 Younger than 10 for girls and 11 for boys.
109 According to the Babli 82a age nine refers to healthy children and age ten to sickly ones. Since the Yerushalmi gives no indication of this one might read this as 9 for girls, 10 for boys, in each case 3 years before they become obligated to fast as adults.

(fol. 44c) **משנה ד**: עוּבָּרָה שֶׁהֵרִיחָה מַאֲכִילִין אוֹתָהּ עַד שֶׁתָּשׁוּב נַפְשָׁהּ. חוֹלֶה מַאֲכִילִין אוֹתוֹ עַל פִּי בְקִיאִין. וְאִם אֵין שָׁם בְּקִיאִין מַאֲכִילִין אוֹתוֹ עַל פִּי עַצְמוֹ עַד שֶׁיֹּאמַר דַּיִּי:

Mishnah 4: A pregnant woman who smelled [food]¹¹⁰ one feeds until she is well again. A sick person one feeds according to experts¹¹¹; if there are no experts one feeds him on his own judgment until he says, enough¹¹².

110 She gets an urgent desire for the food and if she continues to fast there would be a danger of a miscarriage.
111 Medical personnel.
112 Even though fasting is a biblical commandment and breaking the fast is a deadly sin, biblical obligations never should endanger one's life (*Lev.* 18:5).

(45a line 70) **הלכה ד**: בַּתְּחִילָּה תּוֹחֲבָהּ בָּרוֹטָב. אִם שָׁבָה נַפְשָׁהּ הֲרֵי זֶה יָפֶה. וְאִם לָאו נוֹתְנִין לָהּ מִגּוּפוֹ שֶׁלְאִיסּוּר. שְׁתֵּי עוֹבָרוֹת בָּאוּ לִפְנֵי רִבִּי טַרְפוֹן. שָׁלַח לְגַבָּן תְּרֵין תַּלְמִידִים. אֲמַר לוֹן. אֲזָלוּן וְאַמְרוּן לוֹן. צוֹמָא רַבָּה הוּא. אֲמָרוֹן לְקַדְמִייָא וּשְׁדָךְ. וְקָרוּי עֲלוֹי מִבֶּטֶן אִמִּי אֵלִי אָתָּה: אֲמְרִין לִתִינְיָינָא וְלָא שְׁדָךְ. וְקָרוּן עֲלוֹי זָרוּ רְשָׁעִים מֵרָחֶם תָּעוּ מִבֶּטֶן דֹּבְרֵי כָזָב:

Halakhah 4: At first one dips it in sauce¹¹³. If she feels well again it is good. Otherwise one gives her of the body of forbidden food¹¹⁴. Two pregnant women came before Rebbi Tarphon. He sent two students to them and told them, go and tell them, it is the Great Fast-day. They said it to the first one and she quieted down. They said about him¹¹⁵, *from my mother's* womb You are my God[116]. They said it to the second, who did not quiet down. They said about him, *The wicked are perverts from the womb; they err from the belly, the speakers of lies*[117]!

113 One dips kosher bread in the non-kosher sauce which may be forbidden only rabbinically.
114 If the woman smells cooking on the day of Atonement, probably it is Gentile non-kosher food. But see the paragraph after the next.
115 Since it is the baby who craves the food, not his mother who simply is the provider. For similar stories Babli 82b/83a.
116 *Ps.* 22:11.
117 *Ps.* 58:4.

(45a line 75) חוֹלֶה אוֹמֵר. יָכוֹל אֲנִי. וְרוֹפֵא אוֹמֵר. אֵינוֹ יָכוֹל. שׁוֹמְעִין לָרוֹפֵא. רוֹפֵא אוֹמֵר. יָכוֹל הוּא. וְחוֹלֶה אוֹמֵר. אֵינוֹ יָכוֹל. שׁוֹמְעִין לַחוֹלֶה. לָא צוֹרְכָא (דְלָא) [אֶלָּא][118]. חוֹלֶה אוֹמֵר. יָכוֹל אֲנִי. וְרוֹפֵא אוֹמֵר. אֵינִי יוֹדֵעַ. רִבִּי אַבָּהוּ בְשֵׁם רִבִּי יוֹחָנָן. נַעֲשָׂה כְסָפֵק נְפָשׁוֹת. וְכָל־סְפֵק נְפָשׁוֹת דּוֹלְמָן אֶת הַשַּׁבָּת.

[119]The sick person says, I can[120], but the physician says, he cannot; one listens to the physician. The physician says, he can, but the sick person says, he cannot; one listens to the sick person[120]. The only question is if the sick person says, I can, and the physician says, I do not know. Rebbi Abbahu in the name of Rebbi Johanan: It is treated as an uncertainty of a danger to life, and any uncertainty of a danger to life pushes the Sabbath aside[121].

118 An unnecessary correction.
119 Babli 83a.
120 He can fast the entire day.
121 Since the principle is established for the Sabbath, the violation of which is a capital crime, it certainly holds for the day of Atonement, whose violation is a deadly sin.

(45b line 4) מְנַיִין שֶׁמַּאֲכִילִין אוֹתוֹ דְּבֵילָה וְצִימּוּקִין שֶׁלִּתְרוּמָה. מִן הָדָא יִתְּנוּ־לוֹ פֶּלַח דְּבֵילָה וּשְׁנֵי צִימּוּקִים. רִבִּי חוּנָה אוֹמֵר. עֶשְׂרִים וְאַרְבָּעָה עֶשְׂרוֹנוֹת שֶׁאָכַל דָּוִד בְּרַעֲבוֹן אֲכָלַן. רִבִּי יוֹחָנָן מְטוּתֵיהּ כֵּן וַאֲכַל מַה דְּאַשְׁכַּח קֳדָמוֹי. וְקָרוּן עֲלוֹי הַחַכְמָה תְּחַיֶּה בְעָלֶיהָ. תַּנֵּי. מַאֲכִילִין אוֹתוֹ אֶת הַכֹּל בְּקַל. נְבֵילָה וּתְרוּמָה מַאֲכִילִין אוֹתוֹ מִתְּרוּמָה. טֶבֶל וּשְׁבִיעִית מַאֲכִילִין אוֹתוֹ שְׁבִיעִית. חַלָּה וְעָרְלָה צְרִיכָה. אָמַר רִבִּי יוֹסֵה. קַשְׁיָתָהּ קוֹמֵי רִבִּי בָא. תְּרוּמָה בַּעֲוֹן מִיתָה. וּנְבֵילָה בְלֹא תַעֲשֶׂה. וְאַתְּ אָמַר הָכֵין. כְּמָאן דְּאָמַר. מֵאֵילֵיהֶן קִיבְּלוּ עֲלֵיהֶן אֶת הַמַּעְשְׂרוֹת.

[122]From where that one may feed him fig cake and raisins of heave? From this: *They gave him a slice of fig cake and two raisins*[123]. Rebbi Huna said, the twenty-four *esronot* which David ate, he ate in hunger[124]. This happened to

Rebbi Johanan[125] and he ate everything which happened to be before him. They quoted about him, *wisdom revives its possessor*[126]. It was stated: "One feeds him the least forbidden[127]. Carcass meat or heave, one feeds him heave. *Tevel* and sabbatical produce[128], one feeds him sabbatical produce." *Hallah* and `*orlah* is problematic[129]. Rebbi Yose said, I questioned before Rebbi Ba: Heave is a deadly sin, carcass meat a prohibition[130], and you are saying so? Following him who said, they accepted the tithes voluntarily[131]..

122 This paragraph should belong to the next Halakhah, discussion of Mishnah 5.

123 *1Sam.* 30:12. Since the verse reports that the Egyptian recovered from having been without food for 72 hours, this sugary food is proven antidote to boulimy and may be given even from prohibited food.

124 He implies that Ahimelekh gave to David all shew breads of the Tabernacle (*1Sam.* 21:7) and he ate all of them. There are 12 breads, each of them 2 *esronot* (*Lev.* 24:5). 24 *esronot* are 2.4 *epha*, or 7.2 *seah*, a volume of about 92 liter of flour. (Cf. S. Abramson, Sinai 63(1968), pp. 193-197.)

125 An attack of boulimy.

126 *Eccl.* 7:12.

127 If no kosher food is available at the moment. Babli 83a, Tosephta 4:4.

128 Eating *tevel*, produce from which heave was not taken, is a deadly sin for everybody. Eating sabbatical produce when there is nothing left for wild animals on the fields, is violating a positive commandment, not a criminal act.

129 *Hallah* as heave is a sanctum, forbidden to non-Cohanim. Its improper ingestion is a deadly sin. Usufruct of `*orlah* is forbidden to everybody as a simple prohibition.

130 Eating non-kosher meat is a simple prohibition punishable by 39 lashes.

131 In this opinion, tithes, heave, and Sabbatical produce are biblical obligations only if all 12 tribes are on their ancestral lands; today all these obligations were voluntarily accepted by the returnees from Babylon and have only rabbinic status.; *Ševi`it* 6:1, Notes 11-13. But non-kosher food is biblically forbidden.

(fol. 44c) **משנה ה:** מִי שֶׁאֲחָזוֹ בּוּלְמוֹס מַאֲכִילִין אוֹתוֹ אֲפִילוּ דְבָרִים טְמֵאִים עַד שֶׁיֵּאוֹרוּ עֵינָיו. מִי שֶׁנְּשָׁכוֹ כֶלֶב שׁוֹטֶה אֵין מַאֲכִילִין אוֹתוֹ מֵחֲצַר כָּבֵד שֶׁלּוֹ. רִבִּי מַתְיָה בֶן חָרָשׁ מַתִּיר. וְעוֹד אָמַר רִבִּי מַתְיָה בֶן חָרָשׁ הַחוֹשֵׁשׁ בִּגְרוֹנוֹ מַטִּילִין לוֹ סַם בְּתוֹכוֹ בַּשַּׁבָּת מִפְּנֵי שֶׁהוּא סְפֵק נְפָשׁוֹת וְכָל־סְפֵק נְפָשׁוֹת דּוֹחֶה אֶת הַשַּׁבָּת:

Mishnah 5: A person suffering from boulimy[132] one feeds even impure food until his eyes light up. One does not feed the cover of a rabid dog's liver to a person bitten by a rabid dog[133], but Rebbi Matthew ben Ḥarash permits it[134]. In addition, Rebbi Matthew ben Ḥarash said, if somebody suffers from throat ache, one pours him medicine into it since it is an uncertainty of a danger to life, since any uncertainty of a danger to life pushes the Sabbath aside.

משנה ו: מִי שֶׁנָּפְלָה עָלָיו מַפּוֹלֶת סָפֵק הוּא שָׁם סָפֵק אֵינוֹ שָׁם סָפֵק חַי סָפֵק מֵת סָפֵק נָכְרִי סָפֵק יִשְׂרָאֵל מְפַקְּחִין עָלָיו. מְצָאוּהוּ חַי מְפַקְּחִין עָלָיו וְאִם מֵת יַנִּיחוּהוּ:

Mishnah 6: If a wall collapsed over somebody[135], it is uncertain whether he is there or not, whether he is alive or dead, whether he is a Gentile or a Jew, one digs him out[136]. If one finds him alive, one digs him out, if dead one shall leave him[137].

132 Greek βουλιμία. ἡ. "ravenous hunger". It is presumed that the attack is life threatening.
133 Since this is not a recognized medical procedure.
134 For him it is proven medical practice.

135 On the Sabbath or the day of Atonement.
136 Even though this involves a Sabbath desecration.
137 Until after the end of Sabbath or holiday.

(45b line 12) הלכה ה: סִימָנֵי כֶּלֶב שׁוֹטֶה. פִּיו (סָתוּם) [פָּתוּחָה]. רִירוֹ יוֹרֵד. אָזְנָיו סְרוּחוֹת. זְנָבוֹ נָתוּן בֵּין שְׁנֵי יְרֵיכוֹתָיו. מְהַלֵּךְ לְצְדָדִין. וְהַכְּלָבִים נוֹבְחִין בּוֹ. וְיֵשׁ אוֹמְרִים. אַף הוּא נוֹבֵחַ וְאֵין קוֹלוֹ (הוֹלֵךְ) [נִשְׁמָע].

מַה עִיסְקֵיהּ דְּהָדֵין כֶּלֶב שׁוֹטֶה. רַב וּשְׁמוּאֵל. חַד אָמַר. רוּחַ תְּזָזִית עוֹלָה עָלָיו. וְחוֹרָנָה אָמַר. אִשָּׁה עוֹשָׂה כְשָׁפִים וּבוֹדֶקֶת בּוֹ. גַּרְמָנֵי עַבְדֵיהּ דְּרִבִּי יוּדָן נְשִׂיָּא נְשָׁכוֹ כֶּלֶב שׁוֹטֶה וְהֶאֱכִילוּ מֵחֲצַר כָּבֵד שֶׁלּוֹ. וְלֹא נִתְרַפֶּה מִמֶּנּוּ. אַל יֹאמַר לְךָ אָדָם שֶׁנְּשָׁכוֹ כֶּלֶב שׁוֹטֶה וְחָיָה. שֶׁעֲקָצוֹ חֲוַרְבָּר וְחָיָה. שֶׁבְּעַטָתוּ פִּרְדָה וְחָיָה. וּבִלְבַד פִּרְדָּה לְבָנָה.

Halakhah 5: The characteristics[138] of a rabid dog: His mouth is (closed) [open][139], his spittle drips, his ears are badly smelling, he tail is between his hips, he walks at an angle[140], the dogs bark at him, and some are saying, also he barks but his voice is not (carried) [heard][139].

What is the cause of a dog being rabid? Rav and Samuel. One is saying, a spirit of madness came over him. But the other one said, a woman uses him to try out witchcraft. German, the slave of Rebbi Yudan the Patriarch, was bitten by a rabid dog and he fed him the cover of its liver, but he never recovered. A person could never tell you that he was bitten by a rabid dog and survived, that he was stung by a brightly colored snake[141] and survived, that he was kicked by a mule and survived, but only by a white mule[142].

138 Greek σημεῖον, τό.
139 The text is brackets is the corrector's, corresponding to the text in the Babli, 83b.
140 His body makes a non-zero angle with the direction of his movement.
141 A sign of a poisonous reptile.
142 Babli *Hulin* 7b; Yerushalmi *Berakhot* 8:6, Notes 124-125.

(45b line 19) מְנַיִין שֶׁסְפֵק נְפָשׁוֹת דּוֹחֶה אֶת הַשַׁבָּת. רִבִּי אַבָּהוּ בְשֵׁם רִבִּי יוֹחָנָן. אַךְ אֶת־שַׁבְּתוֹתַי תִּשְׁמֹרוּ. מִיעוּט. אִית דְּבָעֵי מֵימַר. אָמְרָה תוֹרָה. חַלֵּל עָלָיו שַׁבָּת. והוא יוֹשֵׁב וּמְשַׁמֵּר שַׁבָּתוֹת הַרְבֵּה.

From where that any uncertainty of a danger to life pushes the Sabbath aside? Rebbi Abbahu in the name of Rebbi Johanan: *Only you shall keep My Sabbaths*;[143] a diminution. Some want to say, the Torah said, [144] desecrate the Sabbath for him, so he will dwell and keep many Sabbaths.

143 *Ex.* 31:12.
144 Since אַךְ everywhere is taken as sign of a diminution, but there is no indication of what is excluded from the observation of the Sabbath, the rabbinic authorities are empowered to determine the exclusion by an argument. Babli 85b, *Mekhilta dR. Ismael, Ki TIssa.*

(45b line 22) רִבִּי זְעוּרָה רִבִּי חִייָה בְשֵׁם רִבִּי יוֹחָנָן. מָבוֹי שֶׁכּוּלּוֹ גוֹיִם וְיִשְׂרָאֵל אֶחָד דָּר בְּתוֹכוֹ. וְנָפְלָה בּוֹ מַפּוֹלֶת. מְפַקְחִין עָלָיו בִּשְׁבִיל יִשְׂרָאֵל שֶׁלְּשָׁם. עַד אֵיכָן. תְּרֵין אֲמוֹרִין. חַד אָמַר. עַד חוֹטְמוֹ. וְחוֹרָנָה אָמַר. עַד טִיבּוּרוֹ. מָאן דְּאָמַר. עַד חוֹטְמוֹ. בָּהוּא דַּהֲוָה קַייָם. וּמָאן דְּאָמַר. עַד טִיבּוּרוֹ. בָּהוּא דַּהֲוָה רָבִין.

תַּנֵּי. (הַדַּיָּין מְשׁוּבָּח. וְהַנִּשְׁאָל מְעַתָּד.) [הַזָּרִיז מְשׁוּבָּח. וְהַנִּשְׁאָל מְגוּנֶּה] וְהַשּׁוֹאֵל הֲרֵי זֶה שׁוֹפֵךְ דָּמִים.

Rebbi Ze'ira, Rebbi Hiyya in the name of Rebbi Johanan: If a wall collapsed in a dead-end street populated by Gentiles, but where one Jew lived, one digs there because of the Jew[145]. How far[146]? Two Amoraim. One said, up to his nose; the other said, up to his navel. He who said, up to his nose, about one who was healthy; he who said up to his navel, about one who was intoxicated[147].

It was stated: (The one who decided is praiseworthy, one who is asked has to be ready,)[148] [the one who is quick is praiseworthy, the one who is asked is blameworthy,][149] and the one who asks is a spiller of blood.

145 Also quoted in *Ketubot* 1:10, Note 269.
146 Since in the Mishnah it is stated that a live person has to be dug out completely, the question is how much of a person has to be uncovered in order to determine his death.
147 Reading רוי for רבי.
148 The text in parentheses is the scribe's. It was not understood by the corrector who partially substituted the Babli text.

The original text states that the rabbi who decided in advance to instruct his congregation to act immediately in cases of danger to life is praiseworthy, the one who is asked anyhow has to have his instructions ready without hesitation, and the one who wastes time to ask is a murderer.
149 Corrector's text. The first statement is from the Babli, 84b (Tosephta *Šabbat* 15:11). The second clause is difficult to understand; what can a person do if he is asked? He is blameworthy if he does not cut the interrogator short and sends him to help others.

(45b line 27) תַּנֵּי. כָּל־דָּבָר שֶׁהוּא שֶׁל סַכָּנָה אֵין אוֹמְרִין. יַעֲשׂוּ דְבָרִים בַּגּוֹיִם וּבִקְטַנִּים. אֶלָּא אֲפִילוּ בִגְדוֹלִים בְּיִשְׂרָאֵל. מַעֲשֶׂה שֶׁנָּפְלָה דְלֵיקָה בַּחֲצֵירוֹ שֶׁלְיוֹסֵי בֶּן סִימַאי בְּשִׁיחִין. וְיָרְדוּ בְנֵי קַצְרָה שֶׁלְצִיפּוֹרִין לְכַבּוֹתוֹ וְלֹא הִנִּיחַ לָהֶן. אָמַר. הַנִּיחוּ לַגַּבַּאי שֶׁיִּגְבֶּה אֶת חוֹבוֹ. מִיַּד קָשַׁר עָלָיו הֶעָנָן וְכִיבָּהוּ. וּבְמוֹצָאֵי שַׁבָּת שָׁלַח לְכָל־אֶחָד וְאֶחָד מֵהֶן סֶלַע. וּלְאִיפַּרְכוֹס שֶׁלָּהֶן חֲמִשִּׁים דֵּינָר. אָמְרוּ חֲכָמִים. לֹא הָיָה צָרִיךְ לַעֲשׂוֹת כֵּן. חַד נַפְתַּיי הֲוָה מְגִירֵיהּ דְּרִבִּי יוֹנָה. נְפַלַת דְּלֵיקָתָא בִּמְגִירוּתֵיהּ דְּרִבִּי יוֹנָה. אֲזַל הַהוּא נַפְתָּיָא בְּעֵי מִטְפִּתָהּ. וְלָא שָׁבְקֵיהּ רִבִּי יוֹנָה. אָמַר לֵיהּ. בַּגְרָךְ מִדְלִי. אֲמַר לֵיהּ אִין. וְאִישְׁתְּזִיב כּוּלָהּ. רִבִּי יוּדָן דְּכָפַר אִמִּי פָּרַס גּוּלְתֵּיהּ עַל גַּדִּישָׁא דְנוּרָא. עֲרָקָא מִינֵּיהּ.

[150]It was stated: In any case of danger to life one does not say that the work be done by Gentiles or minors, but even by adult Jewish persons. "It happened that there was a fire in the courtyard of Yose ben Simai in Shihin, and the garrison of the barracks[151] of Sepphoris came to fight it but he did not let them fight it; he said, let the collector collect his due[152]. Immediately there formed a cloud which extinguished it. After the Sabbath he sent to each of them a tetradrachma and to their commander[153] 50 denarii." The Sages[134] said, there was no need for him to do that. A Nabatean was a neighbor of Rebbi

Jonah. There was a fire in Rebbi Jonah's neighborhood; the Nabatean wanted to fight it but Rebbi Jonah did not let him. He said to him, because of my property! He said, yes[135]. And everything was saved. Rebbi Jonah from Kefar-Immi spread his garment over the burning grain stack and the fire retreated from it.

150 This text also is in *Nedarim* 4:9 Notes 104-113. *Šabbat* 16, Notes 123-132; partially Tosephta *Šabbat* 15:15, Babli, *Yoma* 84b.
151 Latin *castra, -orum,* n. "military camp, barracks, fortress."
152 Since the fire was on a Sabbath, he took it as divine punishment.
153 Greek ἔπαρχος, ὁ, equivalent of Latin *praefectus (castrorum)*. Tosephta *Šabbat* 13:9 (ed. Liebermann).

154 In *Nedarim*: R. Hanina (the Chief Rabbi of Sepphoris in a later generation.) In the Babli *Šabbat* 121a, this is the opinion of the Sages, while Yose ben Simai wanted to encourage them to fight Sabbath fires at Sepphoris. The mention of the Sages here may be a contamination from the Babli.
155 R. Jonah agreed to be responsible for the Nabatean's loss if the fire reached his property.

(fol. 44c) **משנה ז:** חַטָּאת וְאָשָׁם וַדַּאי מְכַפְּרִין. מִיתָה וְיוֹם הַכִּפּוּרִים מְכַפְּרִין עִם הַתְּשׁוּבָה. הַתְּשׁוּבָה מְכַפֶּרֶת עַל עֲבֵירוֹת הַקַּלּוֹת עַל עֲשֵׂה וְעַל לֹא תַעֲשֶׂה. וְעַל הַחֲמוּרוֹת הִיא תוֹלָה עַד שֶׁיָּבוֹא יוֹם הַכִּפּוּרִים וִיכַפֵּר:

Mishnah 7: A purification sacrifice and a definitive reparation sacrifice[156] atone[157]. Death or the Day of Atonement atone if accompanied by repentance. Repentance atones for minor infractions, positive commandments, and prohibitions[158]. But for severe ones[159] it suspends until the next Day of Atonement arrives and atones.

156 Any reparation sacrifice (אָשָׁם) except the one for the suspicion of a sin which, if proven, would require a purification sacrifice; *Lev.* 5:17-19.
157 Since it is presumed that an impurity which requires a reparation sacrifice is divine punishment for some infraction, atonement applies also to these sacrifices.
158 Biblical prohibitions for which no punishment is indicated in the text.
159 Sins punishable by extirpation or the death penalty.

(45b line 37) **הלכה ו‎:** תַּמָּן תַּנֵּינָן. וְעַל זְדוֹן מִקְדָּשׁ וְקֳדָשָׁיו. שָׂעִיר הַנַּעֲשֶׂה בִפְנִים וְיוֹם הַכִּפּוּרִים מְכַפֵּר. וְעַל שְׁאָר עֲבֵירוֹת שֶׁבַּתּוֹרָה. קַלּוֹת וַחֲמוּרוֹת זְדוֹנוֹת וּשְׁגָגוֹת [הוֹדַע וְלֹא הוֹדַע עָשָׂה וְלֹא תַעֲשֶׂה כְּרִיתוֹת וּמִיתַת בֵּית דִּין. שָׂעִיר הַמִּשְׁתַּלֵּחַ מְכַפֵּר:]

Halakhah 6: There we stated: [160]Intentional [impurity][161] of the Sanctuary and its *sancta* is atoned by the ram whose blood is brought inside[162] and the Day of Atonement. The remainder of the transgressions mentioned in the Torah, minor or severe ones, intentional and unintentional, [known and unknown, positive commandments and prohibitions, extirpations and capital crimes, the scapegoat atones.][163]

160 Mishnah *Ševuot* 1:9.
161 Word missing in the quote.
162 On the Day of Atonement.

163 Corrector's completion from the Mishnah.

(45b line 40) לֹא הִיא קַלּוֹת עֲשֵׂה וְלֹא תַעֲשֶׂה. לֹא הִיא חֲמוּרוֹת כְּרִיתוֹת וּמִיתוֹת בֵּית דִּין. רִבִּי יוּדָה אוֹמֵר. כֵּינֵי מַתְנִיתָא. הַקַּלּוֹת וְהַחֲמוּרוֹת. אוֹתָן הַקַּלּוֹת בֵּין שֶׁעֲשָׂאָן בְּזָדוֹן בֵּין שֶׁלֹּא עֲשָׂאָן בְּזָדוֹן. אוֹתָן הַחֲמוּרוֹת בֵּין שֶׁנִּתְוַודַּע לוֹ בָהֶן בֵּין שֶׁלֹּא נִתְוַודַּע לוֹ בָהֶן. אֵילוּ הֵן קַלּוֹת. עֲשֵׂה וְלֹא תַעֲשֶׂה. אֵילוּ הֵן הַחֲמוּרוֹת. כְּרִיתוֹת וּמִיתוֹת בֵּית דִּין. כְּשֵׁם שֶׁהַשָּׂעִיר הַנַּעֲשֶׂה בִפְנִים מְכַפֵּר עַל הַזְּדוֹנוֹת וְתוֹלֶה עַל הַשְּׁגָגוֹת בְּדָבָר שֶׁיֵּשׁ בּוֹ חִיּוּב קָרְבָּן. אַף שָׂעִיר הַמִּשְׁתַּלֵּחַ כֵּן מְכַפֵּר..

[164]Are not minor sins positive commandments and prohibitions; are not serious ones extirpations and capital crimes? Rebbi[165] Jehudah said, so is the Mishnah: "Minor or serious ones. Those minor ones, whether he committed them intentionally or did not commit them intentionally[166]. Those severe ones, whether he obtained knowledge of them or did not obtain knowledge of them[167]. The following are minor sins: positive commandments and prohibitions[158]. Severe ones, extirpations and capital crimes. Just as the ram whose blood is brought inside atones for intentional infractions and suspends for the unintentional ones in cases where a sacrifice is required, also the scapegoat atones in the same way[168]."

164 The text of the Halakhah is from *Ševuot* 1:9, Notes 183-210. The present paragraph also in the Babli *Ševuot* 12b.
165 With the *Ševuot* text, read "Rav".
186 This must refer either to infractions for which the penalty is not spelled out (Note 158) or to cases where guilt cannot be ascertained. The standard example is that of a person who ate one of two pieces of meat, one of which was kosher, the other one severely forbidden either as forbidden fat or as sacrificial meat which became impure

(Rashi). If it is not possible to ascertain which of the two he ate, then a suspended reparation sacrifice is due; but the obligation to bring a suspended reparation sacrifice is cancelled by the Day of Atonement, as determined in the next paragraph (and *Ševuot* Halakhah 1:2, Note 69, *Horaiot* 1:1 Note 18).

167 This refers to the situation described in the previous Note. If he intended to eat one of the two, knowing that one was severely forbidden, he either committed no sin or he committed a serious crime for which no personal sacrifice can atone.

168 Which carries away "all their iniquities", *Lev.* 16:22). This last statement is missing in the Babli *Ševuot;* it is discussed in *Keritut* 25b.

(45b line 47) נִיחָא לֹא הוֹדַע. הוֹדַע. לֹא כֵן תַּנִּינָן. חַיָּיבֵי חַטָּאוֹת וַאֲשָׁמוֹת וַדָּאִין וְעָבַר עֲלֵיהֶן יוֹם הַכִּיפּוּרִים חַיָּיבִין. וְחַיָּיבֵי אֲשָׁמוֹת תְּלוּיִין פְּטוּרִין. אָמַר רִבִּי בּוּן בַּר חִיָּיה. בֵּין שֶׁנִּתְוַדַּע לוֹ בָּהֶן בֵּין שֶׁלֹּא נִתְוַדַּע לוֹ בָּהֶן. [וְלָמָּה לֹא אָמַר בְּשֶׁלֹּא נִתְוַדַּע לוֹ בָּהֶן.] מִילְּתֵיהּ אֲמָרָה. וַאֲפִילוּ לֹא נִתְוַדַּע לוֹ בָּהֶן יוֹם הַכִּיפּוּרִים מְכַפֵּר.

תַּמָּן תַּנִּינָן. עַל אֵלּוּ חַיָּיבִין עַל זְדוֹנָן כָּרֵת וְעַל שִׁגְגָתָן חַטָּאת וְעַל לֹא הוֹדַע שֶׁלָּהֶם אָשָׁם תָּלוּי. וְלֹא כְבָר כִּיפֵּר יוֹם הַכִּיפּוּרִים. רִבִּי שִׁמְעוֹן בְּשֵׁם לֵוִי סוֹכַיָּיה. בְּמוֹרֵד בְּיוֹם הַכִּיפּוּרִים הִיא מַתְנִיתָהּ.

It is understandable if it did not come to his knowledge[169]. If it did come to his knowledge[170]? Was it not stated:[171] "From where that those liable for purification sacrifices and certain reparation sacrifices for whom the Day of Atonement had passed, remain liable, but those liable for suspended reparation offerings are no longer liable?" Rebbi Abun bar Ḥiyya said, whether it was known to him on it, or not known to him on it[172]. [Why did he not say, if it was not known to him]. His words imply that even if it was not known to him on the Day of Atonement, the Day of Atonement atones.

There[173], we have stated: "For these[174] one is liable for extirpation in case of intentional transgression, or a purification sacrifice for unintentional transgression, and for what was not certainly known in their cases a suspended sacrifice." But did not the day of Atonement already atone[175]? Rebbi Simeon in the name of Rebbi Levi from Sokho: The Mishnah refers to one who rebels on the Day of Atonement.

169 Then no private sacrifice is due and the public sacrifice must atone for the damage done to the sanctuary.
170 Did we not imply that the public offering does not relieve the individual of his obligation to bring a sacrifice?
171 Parts of Mishnah *Keritut* 6:4. Purification sacrifices must be brought even

after the Day of Atonement but obligations of suspended reparation sacrifices are eliminated.

172 The text from *Ševuot* is copied here very incompletely, only partially completed by the corrector's addition [in brackets]. By the omission the text has become unintelligible; cf. *Ševuot* 1:9, Notes 194-196.

173 Mishnah *Keritut* 1:2.

174 The transgressions punishable by extirpation enumerated in Mishnah *Keritut* 1:1.

175 Does the Day of Atonement not eliminate the possibility of a suspended reparation offering for the possibility of a sin committed before this day?

(45b line 54) עָשָׂה אַף עַל פִּי שֶׁלֹּא עָשָׂה תְשׁוּבָה. לֹא תַעֲשֶׂה. רִבִּי שְׁמוּאֵל בְּשֵׁם רִבִּי זְעוּרָא. וְהוּא שֶׁעָשָׂה תְשׁוּבָה. הָאוֹמֵר. אֵין עוֹלָה מְכַפֶּרֶת. אֵין עוֹלָה מְכַפֶּרֶת עָלַי. מְבַפֶּרֶת הִיא. אִי אֵיפְשִׁי שֶׁתְּכַפֵּר לִי. אֵינָהּ מְכַפֶּרֶת לוֹ עַל כָּרְחוֹ. אֵין יוֹם הַכִּיפּוּרִים מְכַפֵּר. מְבַפֶּרֶת הִיא. [אִי] אֶפְשִׁי שֶׁיְּכַפֵּר לִי. מְכַפֵּר הוּא לוֹ עַל כּוֹרְחוֹ. אָמַר רִבִּי חֲנַנְיָה בְּרֵיהּ דְּרִבִּי הִלֵּל. לָא כּוֹלָא מִן בַּר נָשָׁא מֵימַר לְמַלְכָּא. דְּלֵית אַתְּ מֶלֶךְ.

A positive commandment, even if he did not repent. A prohibition? Rebbi Samuel in the name of Rebbi Ze`ira, only if he repented[176]. If one said, "the elevation offering does not atone,[177]" does the elevation offering not atone? It atones even against his will. But if he said, "it is impossible that the elevation offering atone for me," it does not atone against his will[178]1. If one said, "the Day of Atonement does not atone," It atones. "I cannot accept[179] that it atone for me," it atones against his will[180]. Rebbi Hanina ben Rebbi Hillel said, it is not up to a person to tell the King, "you are no king."

176 While the Mishnah in Rav Jehudah's interpretation treats positive commandments and simple prohibitions in parallel, there is a difference between the two kinds of sins. The non-performance of a positive commandment is atoned for even without repentance while the atoning for breaching simple prohibitions requires repentance.

177 The biblical text does not indicate for which kind of sin an elevation offering does atone but *Lev.* 1:4 indicates that it atones. The next paragraph will investigate for which sins it is atoning.

178 In the prior formulation, it was simply a false statement. But if somebody said, I am opting out, the atoning power of sacrifices shall not be valid for me, what he offers would be profane. If there is no offering, there cannot be atonement.

179 The scribe wrote איפשי, "it is impossible for me", which Galilean form the corrector did not recognize (and which the scribe himself in the preceding sentence exchanged for the Babylonian form), and added אי, for Babylonian אי אָפְשִׁי, meaning the same.

180 Since he brings the offering on his own initiative, if it is not brought for atoning it does not atone. But the Day of Atonement is given by God; it is not up to man to say what it can or cannot do. Babli, *Keritut* 7a.

(45b line 59) וְהָעוֹלָה מְכַפֶּרֶת עַל הִירְהוּר הַלֵּב. מַה טַעַם. וְהָעוֹלָה עַל־רוּחֲכֶם הָיֹה לֹא תִהְיֶה. אָמַר רִבִּי לֵוִי. וְהָעוֹלָה עַל־רוּחֲכֶם הָיֹה לֹא תִהְיֶה. וְכֵן אִיוֹב אוֹמֵר. וְהִשְׁכִּים בַּבֹּקֶר וְהֶעֱלָה עוֹלוֹת מִסְפַּר כֻּלָּם וגו'. [הָדָא אֲמָרָה שֶׁעוֹלָה מְכַפֶּרֶת עַל הִירְהוּר הַלֵּב.]

[181]The elevation offering atones for thoughts. What is the reason? *What rises in your spirits will not be*[182]. Rebbi Levi said, *What rises in your spirits will not be*[183]. And so *Job* says, *he got up early in the morning and brought elevation offerings in the number of all of them, etc.*[184] [This implies that the elevation offering atones for thoughts.[185]]

181 In *Lev. rabba* 7(3) the paragraph is reproduced and the doctrine is attributed to R. Simeon ben Iohai.
182 *Ez.* 20:32.
183 This quote is incorrect and makes no sense. The original is in *Ševuot* 1:9 Note 205.
184 *Job* 1:5. Job offered elevation offerings since he was afraid that his children might have had impious thoughts.
185 Corrector's addition from *Ševuot*.

(45b line 63) רִבִּי אוֹמֵר. עַל כָּל־עֲבֵירוֹת שֶׁבַּתּוֹרָה יוֹם הַכִּיפּוּרִים מְכַפֵּר חוּץ מִן הַפּוֹרֵק עוֹל וְהַמֵּיפֵר בְּרִית וְהַמְגַלֶּה פָנִים בַּתּוֹרָה. אִם עָשָׂה תְשׁוּבָה מִתְכַּפֵּר לוֹ. וְאִם לָאו אֵינוֹ מִתְכַּפֵּר לוֹ. רִבִּי זְבִידָא אָמַר. רִבִּי יָסָא מַקְשֵׁה. מִיסְבּוֹר סָבַר רִבִּי שֶׁיּוֹם הַכִּיפּוּרִים מְכַפֵּר בְּלֹא תְשׁוּבָה. רִבִּי אָשִׁיָין רִבִּי יוֹנָה רִבִּי בָּא רִבִּי חִייָה בְשֵׁם רִבִּי יוֹחָנָן. מוֹדֶה רִבִּי שֶׁאֵין יוֹם הַכִּיפּוּרִים מְכַפֵּר אֶלָּא בִתְשׁוּבָה. הָא מִיתָה מְכַפֶּרֶת בְּלֹא תְשׁוּבָה. תַּנֵּי. יוֹם מִיתָה כְיוֹם תְּשׁוּבָה. מָאן תַּנִּינְתָהּ. רִבִּי. הֲוֵי הָדָא הִיא דְתַנִּינָן. מִיתָה וְיוֹם הַכִּפּוּרִים מְכַפְּרִין עִם הַתְּשׁוּבָה. דְּלֹא כְרִבִּי.

[186]Rebbi says, the Day of Atonement atones for all sins against the Torah except for him who tears away the yoke, or who breaks the Covenant, or who finds aspects in the Torah[187], where it atones if he repented but does not atone otherwise. Rebbi Zevida said that Rebbi Yasa asked: Does Rebbi think that the Day of Atonement atones without repentance? Rebbi Ashian, Rebbi Jonah, Rebbi Abba, Rebbi Ḥiyya in the name of Rebbi Joḥanan: Rebbi agrees that the Day of Atonement only atones with repentance; therefore death cleanses without repentance[188]. We have stated thus: The day of death equals

the day of repentance. Who stated this? Rebbi! Then what we stated, "death and the Day of Atonement atone with repentance," does not follow Rebbi[189].

186 Babli *Ševuot* 13a, *Yoma* 85b, *Keritut* 7a. The parallel in *Ševuot* at the end reports the opposite of the tradition here.

187 This was explained in *Peah* 1:1 Notes 199-213; cf. also *Sanhedrin* 10:1, Note 8. One who tears away the yoke is he who recognizes the authority of the Torah but decides to break its laws; one who breaks the covenant is he who tries to reconstruct a prepuce and does not circumcise his sons; one who finds aspects in the Torah is he who denies the divine origin of the Torah.

188 This is a non-sequitur, but it fits well with the text in *Ševuot* which has to be considered as the original. The Babli supports the statement there about the Day of Atonement; it has no statement of Rebbi about the power of Death.

189 Since the Mishnah requires repentance also on the Day of Atonement. Rebbi formulated an anonymous Mishnah, i. e., authoritative doctrine, following the majority against his own opinion.

(fol. 44c) **משנה ח**: הָאוֹמֵר אֶחֱטָא וְאָשׁוּב אֶחֱטָא וְאָשׁוּב אֵין מַסְפִּיקִין בְּיָדוֹ לַעֲשׂוֹת תְּשׁוּבָה. אֶחֱטָא וְיוֹם הַכִּפּוּרִים מְכַפֵּר אֵין יוֹם הַכִּפּוּרִים מְכַפֵּר. עֲבֵירוֹת שֶׁבֵּין אָדָם לַמָּקוֹם יוֹם הַכִּפּוּרִים מְכַפֵּר וְשֶׁבֵּינוֹ לְבֵין חֲבֵירוֹ אֵין יוֹם הַכִּפּוּרִים מְכַפֵּר עַד שֶׁיְּרַצֶּה אֶת חֲבֵירוֹ.

Mishnah 8: If somebody say, "I shall sin and repent, I shall sin and repent,[190]" one[191] does not let him achieve to repent. "I shall sin and the day of Atonement will atone," the Day of Atonement does not atone. Transgressions between a person and the Omnipresent the Day of Atonement atones; but those between him and his neighbor the Day of Atonement does not atone unless he placated his neighbor.

190 Repeatedly.   191 Heaven.

(45b line 70) **הלכה ח**: שָׁאַל רִבִּי מַתְיָה בֶּן חָרָשׁ אֶת רִבִּי אֶלְעָזָר בֶּן עֲזַרְיָה בִּישִׁיבָה. אָמַר לוֹ. שָׁמַעְתָּ אַרְבָּעָה חֲלוּקֵי כַפָּרָה שֶׁהָיָה רִבִּי יִשְׁמָעֵאל דּוֹרֵשׁ. אָמַר לוֹ. שְׁלֹשָׁה הֵם חוּץ מִן הַתְּשׁוּבָה. כָּתוּב אֶחָד אוֹמֵר שׁוּבוּ בָּנִים שׁוֹבָבִים. וְכָתוּב אַחֵר אוֹמֵר כִּי־בַיּוֹם הַזֶּה יְכַפֵּר עֲלֵיכֶם. וְכָתוּב אַחֵר אוֹמֵר וּפָקַדְתִּי בְשֵׁבֶט פִּשְׁעָם וגו'. וְכָתוּב אַחֵר אוֹמֵר אִם יְכוּפַּר הֶעָוֹן הַזֶּה לָכֶם עַד־תְּמוּתוּן. הָא כֵיצַד. עָבַר עַל מִצְוַת עֲשֵׂה וְשָׁב מִיָּד. אֵינוֹ זָז מִמְּקוֹמוֹ עַד שֶׁיִּמְחוֹל לוֹ. עָלָיו הַכָּתוּב אוֹמֵר שׁוּבוּ בָּנִים שׁוֹבָבִים. הָעוֹבֵר עַל מִצְוָה בְלֹא תַעֲשֶׂה וְשָׁב מִיָּד. הַתְּשׁוּבָה תּוֹלָה וְיוֹם

הַכִּיפּוּרִים מְכַפֵּר. עָלָיו הַכָּתוּב אוֹמֵר כִּי־בַיּוֹם הַזֶּה יְכַפֵּר עֲלֵיכֶם. הָעוֹבֵר עַל כְּרִיתוֹת וּמִיתוֹת בֵּית דִּין בְּמֵזִיד הַתְּשׁוּבָה וְיוֹם הַכִּיפּוּרִים מְכַפְּרִין מֶחֱצָה. וְהַיִּיסּוּרִין בִּשְׁאָר יְמוֹת הַשָּׁנָה מְכַפְּרִין מֶחֱצָה. עָלָיו הַכָּתוּב אוֹמֵר וּפָקַדְתִּי בְשֵׁבֶט פִּשְׁעָם וּבִנְגָעִים עֲוֹנָם. אֲבָל מִי שֶׁנִּתְחַלֵּל בּוֹ שֵׁם שָׁמַיִם אֵין כֹּחַ לֹא לִתְשׁוּבָה לִתְלוֹת וְלֹא בְיוֹם הַכִּיפּוּרִים לְכַפֵּר וְלֹא בַּיִּיסּוּרִין לְמָרֵק. אֶלָּא תְשׁוּבָה וְיוֹם הַכִּיפּוּרִים מְכַפְּרִין שְׁלִישׁ וְהַיִּיסּוּרִין מְכַפְּרִין שְׁלִישׁ. וְהַמִּיתָה מְמָרֶקֶת בַּיִּיסּוּרִין. עָלָיו הַכָּתוּב אוֹמֵר אִם־יְכֻפַּר הֶעָוֹן הַזֶּה לָכֶם עַד־תְּמוּתוּן. הָא לָמַדְנוּ שֶׁהַמִּיתָה מְמָרֶקֶת.

Halakhah 8: [192]Rebbi Matthew ben Ḥarash asked Rebbi Eleazar ben Azariah in the Academy[183]. He said to him, did you hear the four types of Atonement which Rebbi Ismael explained? He answered him, there are three in addition to repentance. One verse says, *return, naughty children*[194]. But another verse says, *for on that day He shall atone for you*[195]. And another verse says, *I shall visit their crime with the rod*[196], etc. And another verse says, *the iniquity of this people shall not be atoned for until you die*[197]. How is this? If somebody violates a positive commandment and repents, before he moves from there it will be forgiven to him. About this one it says, *return, naughty children*. If one transgresses a prohibition and immediately repents, repentance suspends judgment, and the Day of Atonement atones. About this one it says, *for on that day, He shall atone for you*. If one intentionally transgressed {sins punishable by} extirpations or death penalties, repentance and the Day of Atonement atone half, and sufferings during the other days of the year atone half. About this one it says, *I shall visit their crime with the rod, and their iniquities with plagues*. But by whom the Name of Heaven was desecrated, there is no power in repentance to suspend judgment, nor in the Day of Atonement to pardon, nor in sufferings to scour; but repentance and the Day of Atonement atone one third, sufferings atone a third, and death scours with sufferings. About this one it says, *the iniquity of this people shall not be atoned for until you die*. From this we learn that death scours.

192 From here to the end of the Halakhah, the text is not only in *Ševuot* but also in *Sanhedrin* 10:1, Notes 23-37, 14-22 (and in the Babli *Yoma* 86b). For part of the text there exists a Geniza fragment (G) edited by L. Ginzberg in his *Yerushalmi Fragments* (1909) p. 267.

193 He asks for an answer on the record.

194 *Jer.* 3:22.

195 *Lev.* 16:20.

196 *Ps.* 89:33.

197 *Is.* 22:14.

(45c line 12) אָמַר רִבִּי יוֹחָנָן. זוֹ דִּבְרֵי רִבִּי לְעָזָר בֶּן עֲזַרְיָה וְרִבִּי יִשְׁמָעֵאל וְרִבִּי עֲקִיבָה. אֲבָל דִּבְרֵי חֲכָמִים. שָׂעִיר הַמִּשְׁתַּלֵּחַ מְכַפֵּר. אִם אֵין שָׂעִיר. הַיּוֹם מְכַפֵּר. כֵּיצַד הוּא מְכַפֵּר. רִבִּי זְעוּרָה אָמַר. כָּל־שֶׁהוּא. רִבִּי חֲנַנְיָה אוֹמֵר. בַּסּוֹף. מַה מַפְקָא מִבֵּינֵיהוֹן. מֵת. מָרַד. עַל דַּעְתֵּיהּ דְּרִבִּי זְעוּרָה כְּבָר כִּיפֵּר. עַל דַּעְתֵּיהּ דְּרִבִּי חֲנַנְיָה לֹא כִּיפֵּר. אָמַר רִבִּי זְעוּרָה. וּמַתְנִיתָהּ מְסַיְּיעָא לְרִבִּי חֲנַנְיָה. חוֹמֶר בַּשָּׂעִיר מַה שֶׁאֵין בְּיוֹם הַכִּיפּוּרִים. וּבְיוֹם הַכִּיפּוּרִים מַה שֶׁאֵין בַּשָּׂעִיר. שֶׁיּוֹם הַכִּיפּוּרִים מְכַפֵּר בְּלֹא שָׂעִיר. וְהַשָּׂעִיר אֵינוֹ מְכַפֵּר בְּלֹא יוֹם הַכִּיפּוּרִים. חוֹמֶר בַּשָּׂעִיר. שֶׁהַשָּׂעִיר מְכַפֵּר מִיָּד. וְיוֹם הַכִּיפּוּרִים מְכַפֵּר מִשֶּׁתֶּחְשָׁךְ. אָמַר רִבִּי חוּנָה. אִיתְּתָבַת קוֹמֵי רִבִּי יִרְמְיָה וְאָמַר. תִּיפְתָּר שֶׁהָיָה בְדַעְתָּן לְהָבִיא שָׂעִיר אַחֵר וְלֹא הֵבִיאוּ. רִבִּי יוֹסֵי בֵּירִבִּי בּוּן בָּעֵי. וְאֵין הַקָּדוֹשׁ בָּרוּךְ הוּא רוֹאֶה אֶת הַנּוֹלָד וִיכַפֵּר מִיָּד.

Rebbi Johanan said, these are the words of Rebbi Eleazar ben Azariah, Rebbi Ismael, and Rebbi Aqiba. But the Sages say that the scapegoat atones. How does it atone? Rebbi Ze`ira said, in small pieces. Rebbi Hanania said, at the end. What is the difference between them? If somebody died in-between. In the opinion of Rebbi Ze`ira, he already was pardoned. In the opinion of Rebbi Hanina, he was not pardoned. Rebbi Ze`ira said, a *baraita* supports Rebbi Hanina: "There is strength in the ram which is not in the Day of Atonement, and in the Day of Atonement which is not in the ram: The Day of Atonement pardons without a ram, but the ram does not atone without the Day of Atonement. There is strength in the ram since the ram atones immediately but the Day of Atonement only atones at nightfall.[198]" Rebbi Huna said, the question was raised before Rebbi Jeremiah and he said, explain it if they intended to bring another he-goat but they did not bring it. Rebbi Yose ben Rebbi Abun asked, does the Holy One, praise to Him, not see into the future? Then He should pardon immediately

198   Tosephta 4:16.

(fol. 44c) **משנה ט**: אֶת זוֹ דָּרַשׁ רִבִּי אֶלְעָזָר בֶּן עֲזַרְיָה מִכֹּל חַטֹּאתֵיכֶם לִפְנֵי יְיָ תִּטְהָרוּ, עֲבֵרוֹת שֶׁבֵּין אָדָם לַמָּקוֹם יוֹם הַכִּיפּוּרִים מְכַפֵּר. וְשֶׁבֵּינוֹ לְבֵין חֲבֵרוֹ אֵין יוֹם הַכִּפּוּרִים מְכַפֵּר, עַד שֶׁיְּרַצֶּה אֶת חֲבֵרוֹ.

Mishnah 9: The following did Rebbi Eleazar ben Azariah explain: *Of all your unintentional sins before the Eternal you shall be cleansed*[199]. Transgressions between a person and the Omnipresent the Day of Atonement atones; but those between him and his neighbor the Day of Atonement does not atone unless he placated his neighbor.

משנה י׃ אָמַר רִבִּי עֲקִיבָה אַשְׁרֵיכֶם יִשְׂרָאֵל לִפְנֵי מִי אַתֶּם מִטַּהֲרִין וּמִי מְטַהֵר אֶתְכֶם אֲבִיכֶם שֶׁבַּשָּׁמַיִם, שֶׁנֶּאֱמַר וְזָרַקְתִּי עֲלֵיכֶם מַיִם טְהוֹרִים וגו׳. וְאוֹמֵר מִקְוֵה יִשְׂרָאֵל יְיָ מַה מִּקְוֶה מְטַהֵר אֶת הַטְּמֵאִים אַף הַקָּדוֹשׁ בָּרוּךְ הוּא מְטַהֵר אֶת יִשְׂרָאֵל׃

Mishnah 10: Rebbi Aqiba said, blessed are you, Israel. Before whom do you cleanse yourselves, and who cleanses you? Your Father Who is in Heaven, as it is said[200], *I shall sprinkle on you pure water, so you shall be pure*. And it is said[201] *Israel's hope is the Eternal*, since a *miqweh* purifies the impure people[202], so the Holy One, praise to Him, cleanses Israel.

199 *Lev.* 16:30. The sentence is not parsed as *from all your iniquities, before the Eternal you will be cleansed*, but as *from all your iniquities before the Eternal, you will be cleansed*. *Sifra Ahare Pereq* 8:1.

200 *Ez.* 36:25.

201 *Jer.* 17:13.

202 Identifying מקוה "hope" or "ritual bath; pond".

(45c line 24) **הלכה ט**׃ שְׁמוּאֵל אָמַר. הָהֵן דְּחָטָא עַל חַבְרֵיהּ צָרִיךְ מֵימַר לֵיהּ. סָרַחִית עֲלָךְ. וְאִין קַבְּלֵיהּ הָא טָבָאוּת. וְאִין לָא. מַיְיתֵי בְּנֵי נַשׁ וּמְפַיֵּיס לֵיהּ קוּמֵיהוֹן. הָדָא הוּא דִכְתִיב יָשֹׁר עַל־אֲנָשִׁים. יַעֲשֶׂה שׁוּרָה שֶׁלַאֲנָשִׁים. וַיֹּאמֶר חָטָאתִי וְיָשָׁר הֶעֱוֵיתִי וְלֹא־שָׁוָה לִי׃ אִם עוֹשֶׂה כֵן. עָלָיו הַכָּתוּב אוֹמֵר פָּדָה נַפְשׁוֹ מֵעֲבָר בַּשָּׁחַת וְחַיָּתוֹ בָּאוֹר תִּרְאֶה׃ מִית. צָרִיךְ מְפַיְּיסָתֵיהּ עַל קִיבְרֵיהּ וּמֵימַר. סָרַחִית עֲלָךְ.

Halakhah 9: [203]Samuel said, a person who sinned against his neighbor has to tell him, I offended you. If he accepts it, it is good. Otherwise he brings people and appeases him in their presence. That is what is written[204], *being straight with men*, he shall form a row of men, *and say, I sinned, and straightforward I acted criminally, and I was careless*. If he acts in this manner, the verse says about him[205], *He delivered his soul from perdition, and his life enjoys light*. If he died, one has to appease him on his grave and say, I offended you.

203 Cf. Babli 87a. 205 *Job* 33:28.
204 *Job* 33:27.

(‎45c line 31) תַּנֵּי. עֲבֵירוֹת שֶׁנִּתְוַדָּה עֲלֵיהֶן בַּיּוֹם הַכִּיפּוּרִים שֶׁעָבַר אֵינוֹ צָרִיךְ לְהִתְוַדּוֹת עֲלֵיהֶן יוֹם הַכִּיפּוּרִים הַבָּא. אִם עָשָׂה כֵן עָלָיו הַכָּתוּב אוֹמֵר כְּכֶלֶב שָׁב עַל־קֵיאוֹ כְּסִיל שׁוֹנֶה בְאִוַּלְתּוֹ׃ תַּנֵּי. רִבִּי לִיעֶזֶר אוֹמֵר. הֲרֵי זֶה זָרִיז וְנִשְׂכָּר. מַה טַעֲמֵיהּ דְּרִבִּי לִיעֶזֶר. וְחַטָּאתִי נֶגְדִּי תָמִיד׃ מַה מְקַיְּימִין רִבִּי לִיעֶזֶר טַעֲמוֹן דְּרַבָּנָן. כְּכֶלֶב שָׁב עַל־קֵיאוֹ כְּסִיל שׁוֹנֶה בְאִוַּלְתּוֹ׃ בְּשׁוֹנֶה בְאוֹתָהּ הָעֲבֵירָה. מַה מְקַיְּימִין רַבָּנָן טַעֲמֵיהּ דְּרִבִּי לִיעֶזֶר. וְחַטָּאתִי נֶגְדִּי תָמִיד׃ שֶׁלֹּא יְהוּ בְעֵינָיו כְּאִילוּ לֹא עֲשָׂאָן. אֶלָּא כָעֲשָׂאָן וְנִמְחַל לוֹ.

[206]It was stated: "Sins which he confessed the past Day of Atonement he does not have to confess the next day of Atonement; if he would do this, the verse says about him, *like a dog returning to his vomit, so is the silly repeating his foolishness*[207]. It was stated, Rebbi Eliezer[208] says, he would be clever and be rewarded. What is Rebbi Eliezer's reason? *But my sin is always before me*[209]." How does Rebbi Eliezer interpret the rabbis' reason, *like a dog returning to his vomit, so is the silly repeating his foolishness*? If he repeats the same sin. How do the rabbis interpret Rebbi Eliezer's reason, *but my sin is always before me*? It should not be in his eyes as if he never did it, but that he did it and he was forgiven.

206 Babli 86b; Tosephta 4:15.   Jacob.
207 *Prov.* 26:11.   209 *Ps.* 51:5.
208 In Babli and Tosephta: R. Eliezer ben

(45c line 39) מִצְוַת הַוִּידּוּי עֶרֶב יוֹם הַכִּיפּוּרִים עִם חֲשֵׁיכָה עַד שֶׁלֹּא נִשְׁתַּקַּע בְּמַאֲכָל וּבְמִשְׁתֶּה. אַף עַל פִּי שֶׁנִּתְוַדָּה בְּעַרְבִית צָרִיךְ לְהִתְוַדּוֹת בְּשַׁחֲרִית. אַף עַל פִּי שֶׁנִּתְוַדָּה בְּשַׁחֲרִית צָרִיךְ לְהִתְוַדּוֹת בְּמוּסָף. אַף עַל פִּי שֶׁנִּתְוַדָּה בְּמוּסָף צָרִיךְ לְהִתְוַדּוֹת בְּמִנְחָה. אַף עַל פִּי שֶׁנִּתְוַדָּה בְּמִנְחָה צָרִיךְ לְהִתְוַדּוֹת בִּנְעִילָה. שֶׁכָּל־הַיּוֹם כָּשֵׁר לְוִידּוּי. כֵּיצַד הוּא מִתְוַדֶּה. רִבִּי בֶּרֶכְיָה בְשֵׁם רִבִּי בָּא בַּר בִּינָה. רִבּוֹנִי. חָטָאתִי וּמוֹרַע עָשִׂיתִי. וּבְדַעַת רָעָה הָיִיתִי עוֹמֵד. וּבְדֶרֶךְ רְחוֹקָה הָיִיתִי מְהַלֵּךְ. וּכְשֵׁם שֶׁעָשִׂיתִי אֵינִי עוֹשֶׂה. יְהִי רָצוֹן מִלְּפָנֶיךָ יי אֱלֹהַי [שֶׁתְּכַפֵּר לִי עַל כָּל־פְּשָׁעַי] שֶׁתִּמְחוֹל לִי עַל כָּל־עֲוֹנוֹתַי. וְתִסְלַח וְתִמְחוֹל לִי עַל כָּל־חַטֹּאותַי.

תַּנֵּי. צָרִיךְ לִפְרוֹט אֶת מַעֲשָׂיו. דִּבְרֵי רִבִּי יְהוּדָה בֶּן בְּתֵירָה. רִבִּי עֲקִיבָה אוֹמֵר. אֵינוֹ צָרִיךְ לִפְרוֹט אֶת מַעֲשָׂיו. מַה טַעֲמֵיהּ דְּרִבִּי יְהוּדָה. אָנָּא חָטָא הָעָם הַזֶּה חֲטָאָה גְדוֹלָה וַיַּעֲשׂוּ לָהֶם

אֱלֹהֵי זָהָב: מַה עָבַד לָהּ רִבִּי עֲקִיבָה. מִי גָרַם לָהֶם. אֲנִי. שֶׁהִרְבֵּיתִי לָהֶם כֶּסֶף וְזָהָב. לָמָּה. שֶׁאֵין חֲמוֹר (נוֹקֵק) [נוֹהֵק] מִתּוֹךְ כְּפִיפָה שֶׁלְחָרוּבִין.

[210]"It is an obligation to confess on the eve of the Day of Atonement when it gets dark, before he immerses himself in eating and drinking[211]. Even though he confessed in the evening, he has to confess in the morning; though he confessed in the morning, he has to confess at *musaf*[212]; though he confessed at *musaf*, he has to confess in the afternoon; though he confessed in the afternoon, he has to confess at *ne`ilah*[213], for the entire day is qualified for confession." How does he confess? [214]Rebbi Berekhiah in the name of Rebbi Abba bar Binah: My Master, I sinned and did evil, and I was involved in bad thoughts, and acting in aberrant ways. But as I acted I shall not act. May it please You, Eternal, my God, [that You will atone for all my crimes][215], forgive me for all my sins, and pardon (and forgive)[216] all my transgressions.

It was stated[217]: It is necessary to detail one's actions, the words of Rebbi Jehudah ben Bathyra. Rebbi Aqiba says, one does not have to detail his actions. What is Rebbi Jehudah's reason? *Please, this people committed a grave sin, they made themselves golden idols*[218]. How does Rebbi Aqiba treat this? Who caused it to them? I, for I gave them much silver and gold. Why? For a donkey is not braying[219] out of a basket of carob fruit[220].

210 Tosephta 4:14, Babli 87b.

211 The text is elliptic; it is understandable only in the Babylonian sources. Since confession is one of the obligations of the day of Atonement, one has to confess immediately after nightfall in the evening prayers (as presupposed in the following sentence.) But as a precaution there is a rabbinic obligation to confess in the preceding afternoon, during afternoon prayers, before taking the big meal before the fast, in case one would be incapacitated during the fast-day because of overeating.

212 The additional holiday prayers, parallel to the additional sacrifices required on such days. It is spelled out in the Babylonian sources that all confessions are appended to the prayers of the day.

213 The additional prayers on fast days (Mishnah *Ta`aniot* 4:1), shortly before the end of the fast.

214 *Lev. rabba* 3(3), ascribed to another author.

215 Corrector's addition from *Lev. rabba*.

216 Text of the scribe, deleted by the corrector. Since with this word and with the prior addition by the corrector one also has three requests for forgiveness, the original text of the scribe looks genuine.

217 Tosephta 4:14, Babli 86b, Yerushalmi *Nedarim* 5:4, Note 60.

218 *Ex.* 32:31.

219 The corrector's spelling נהק is biblical (*Job* 6:5, 30:7), but the scribe's spelling נקק may be the Aramaic form of Accadic *nagāgum*.. While in *Job* the verb describes the shout of the hungry, here it is used for the noise of the overbearing; cf. *Sifry Deut.* 308

220 In the Babli, *Berakhot* 32a, the argument is that a lion will shout eating a box of meat.

(45c line 53) כָּתוּב מִקְוֵה יִשְׂרָאֵל יְיָ. מַה הַמִּקְוֶה מְטַהֵר אֶת הַטְּמֵאִים. אַף הַקָּדוֹשׁ בָּרוּךְ הוּא מְטַהֵר אֶת יִשְׂרָאֵל. וְכֵן הוּא אוֹמֵר וְזָרַקְתִּי עֲלֵיכֶם מַיִם טְהוֹרִים וּטְהַרְתֶּם מִכָּל טוּמְאוֹתֵיכֶם וּמִכָּל־גִּלּוּלֵיכֶם אֲטַהֵר אֶתְכֶם:

It is written, *Israel's miqweh is the Eternal.* Just as a *miqweh*[202] purifies the impure, so the Holy One, praise to Him, purifies Israel. And so He says, *I shall sprinkle on you pure water and you will be pure; from all your impurities and your abominations I shall purify you*[221].

221 *Ez.* 36:25

Addenda and Corrigenda to prior volumes.

Peah Chapter 1, Note 136. According to a Gaonic responsum edited by S. Asaf, the meaning of the sentence is: Prevent the congregation from praying until they deal with his complaint.

5:1, p.. 198 line 3. For *Johanan* read *Jonathan*.

5:1, p. 199. Note 10 (missing): Tosephta *Sanhedrin* 1:2, Babli *Sanhedrin* 12a, Yerushalmi *Sanhedrin* 1:2 (Note 207), *Nedarim* 6:3 (Note 83).

Demay 2:1, p. 421. The expression יחמי לי is discussed in detail by Y. Sussman in *Mehqerei Talmud*, vol. 3, Jerusalem 2005, pp. 219-224.

Kilaim 5:1, pp. 176-177, figures 5-3, 5-5. For *a* read α.

6:2, Mishnah 2. For *cubit* read *hand-breadth*.

8:1, p. 259, Note 20. To the list of parallels add *Sanhedrin* 7:5.

Ševi'it 1:2, p. 343, line 5: For *Rebbi Yose ben Abun* read *Rebbi Yose ben Rebbi Abun*.

6:1, p.497, line 4 from bottom. For מסתנך read מסתמך.

9:1, p. 603, Note 37: To the list of parallels add *Pesiqta dRav Cahana* ויהי בשלח, ed. S. Buber p. 886.

9:2, p. 608, Note 57. Nelson Glueck (AASOR xxv-xxviii, 1945-1948) identifies *Tan`ala* with *Deir `Alla*.

Orlah 2:6, p. 486, line 6. For ומיכן read מיכן.

line 9: For אין read ואין.

3:1, p. 506, Note 11: Add: The name appears in the Munich ms. of the Babli.

p. 511, line 3 from bottom. For *Lev.* read *Deut.*

Sotah 7:6, p. 296. Nelson Glueck (l. c.) identifies *Saretan* as *Ṣa`idīyah*.

p. 302, line 2. For בירעה read ביראה.

Ketubot 3:10, p. 173, line 4. To *by a court* add: *by witnesses*.
    4:4, p. 197, line 7: For *atre* read *are*.
    4:11, p. 228, line 14; For *Aḥai* read *Haggai*.

Niddah 4:1, p. 714, line 13. For *of* read *or*.

Gittin 8:12, p.358, line 3. For *Rashi* read *Rashbam*.
    9:7, p. 387, line 5 from bottom. Delete *and*.

Sanhedrin 7:5, p. 230. Hebrew text line 5. For יוחמן read יוחנן.

Ševu'ot, Mishnah 2:4. A sentence has fallen out from the Hebrew text, וְהִשְׁתַּחֲוָה אוֹ שֶׁשָּׁהָה בִּכְדֵי הִשְׁתַּחֲוָיָה.

Avodah zarah 2:2, p. 300, Hebrew text line 1. For משפיחות read משפיכות.

Indices

Sigla

Parallel Texts from Yerushalmi Tractates

Roš Haššanah	א	Orlah	ע
Berakhot	ב	Peah	פ
Ginze Schechter	ג	Beṣah	צ
Horaiot	ה	Moed qatan	ק
Taaniot	ו	Eruvin	ר
Hallah	ח	Šeqalim	ש
Ševuot	י	Šeqalim Babli	שׁ
Sukkah	כ	Terumot	ת
Megillah	ל	Maaser Šeni	ם
Moed qatan	n	Chapter 6	6
Taaniot	נ	Chapter 10	10
Sotah	ס		

Other sources

Corrector	C	Munich ms. Šeqalim	M
Genizah, ed. Ginzberg	G	Qonteros Aharon	Q
Genizah, Moed qatan	g	Original Scribe	S
Genizah, Kaufmann	K		

Index of biblical quotations

Gen.		47 ;6	89	12:4	178 179	12:14	22
2:12	501	49.28	591		250 314 316	12:15	4 17
6:11	7			12:5	211		22 61 63 84 100
6:19	342	Ex. 1:6	89		342 348		253
8:22	7	3:14	474	12:6	161 162	12:16	22 109
18:9	336	4:16	585	12:7	296	12:17	4
19.15	450	6:7	359	12:8	242 287	12:18	73 84
32;33	53	6:8	356	12:9	218 239	12:19	13 17
35:11	261	9:9	195		246 284		23 50 62
37.21	508	12:3	196 305	12:9	93	12:20	84 100
40:11	354		340	12:11	340		101

12:22	340		583	6:12	399	16:6	380 468
	342 384	30:19	274	6:15	402		509
12:26	369	30:20	505	6:18	170	16:7	557
12:39	370	30:21	462	6:23	55	16:8	469 456
12:41	372	30:36	504 515	6:33	282		490 493 553
12:44	274	30:38	513	7:12		16:9	485 557
12:46	88 296	31.12	613		86	16:10	532
12:46	247	32:31	626 586	7:13	28	16:11	406
12:48	274	34:7	472	7:17	285	16:12	418 493
13:3	51 57 342	40:24	519	7:19	340		497 504 507
13:4	68			7:19	251	16:13	415 418
13:7	17 64 110	Lev. 1:2	342	7:20	62	16:14	495 514
13:8	369 370	1:4	618	7:23	53 56		526
13:14	389	1:7	424 428 444	8:5	388	16:15	381 471
14:11	121		445 446	8:6	389		493 526
16:28	218	1:10	177	8:9	588	16:16	529
20:27	168	1:12	445	8:34	381 392	16:17	417 522
21:28	55	1:15	384 517		394	16:18	524 529
22:30	52 57	1:16	436	8:35	390 392		530 535 536
23:18	185	2:2	515	9:2	384	16:19	436 530
	192 214	2:3	409	9:4	390		537 538 542
24:16	385	2:5	515	9:7	381	16:20	539 547
25:13	511	2:7	515	9:23	390		557 621
25:30	392	2:11	187	10:18	281 282	16:21	473 584
26:33	511 518	3:5	204	11:27	552	16:22	584 617
27:2	166	3:6	176	11:32	34	16:23	461 462
27:21	438 459	3:11	204	11:42	53		467 584
27:38	553	3:15	204	12:2	340	16:24	461 492
27:40	464	4:2	529 569	13:1	61		581 583
28:4	587	4:7	538	13:2	61	16:26	558 565
28:15	588	4:12	571 573	13:24	245		568
28:35	587 588		575	13:27	245	16:27	548 568
28:36	255	4:14	261	13:28	245	16:28	567 575
28:37	252	4:25	533	13:37	211	16:29	460 542
28:38	589	4:30	533	14:4	553		606 607
28:40	585	4:33	168 170	14:19	166 170	16:30	623
28:42	388 585		533	14:49	535	16:32	404 469
	588	5:16	77	14:21	167	16:34	477
28:43	274	5:17-19	615	15:16	456	17:1	168 202
29:1	388	6:2	420 423	15:24	395	17:10	202
29:9	389	6:3	423 424 428	15:25	445	17:11	544
29:18	441		436 437	15:29	594	17:12	604
29:30	02 407	6:4	424 436	16:1	385 386	17:14	544
29:37	394	6:5	425 458		418	19:7	61 171 594
29:38	161 411		506	16:2	416 518	19:9	62
29:39	161 458	6:6	506	16:3	385 468	21:2	273
30:7	435 436	6:7	440		497 583	21:10	412
	438 458	6:8	515	16:4	460 462	22:2	274
30:8	459	6:10	427		585 587	22:7	29
30:10	530 546	6:11	34	16:5	553 583	22:15	596

22:21	48	19:15	34	17:10	261	10:9	501
22:22	342	19:18	106 471	19:7	553	17:13	623
22:26	491	19:20	198	21:1-2	433	23:15	359
22:28	112	19:22	34	22:9	55	28:16	525
23:4	`251	20:1	386	23:22	214	35:2	501
23:9	152	28:2	207	24:8	607	33:17	599
23:14	53	21:1	387	24:17	553	43:7	483
23:19	250	24:11	501	26:5	368	46:20	457
23:20	606 607	26:56	489	26:14	274 598	51:7	359
23:27	601	28:3	553	23:11	442		
23:28	601	28:4	184 458			Ez. 1:10	417
23:29	606 607	28:15	222				522
23:32	606 607	29:8	581	Jos. 3:10	328	9:2	585
23:40	384	29:11	497 583	18:10	487	20:12	619
23:44	251	29:39	251	18:27	130	36:25	623 626
24:4	262	31:6	402			43:8	342
24:5	384	31:19	326	Jud. 3:26	449	44:9	274
24:8	384	33:38	387	5:2	374		
24:9	249 409	35:25	588	9:38	220	Hos. 3:5	588
25:2	154						
27:10	344 512	Deut. 4:2	110	1S. 17:49	589	Mi. 7:8	451
	513	6:4	152	23:11	591		
		6:9	396	23:12	591	Nah. 1:4	501
Num. 2:17	509	6:16	414	30:8	591		
4:13	509	6:20	369			Zeph. 1.12	5
5:1-4	509	8:3	594	2S. 7:18	452		
5:2	293 338	10:6	387			Zach 11:1	560
5:22	300	11:14	126	1K 6:17	519	14.20	122
6:9	266	12:9	240	6:22	501		
6:15	8	12:16	53 57	6:50	242	Mal. 2:5	586
7:1	394	12:17	198 604	7:2	501		
7:89	591	12:24	48	7:50	501		
8:19	127	13:1	110	8:47	473	Ps. 11:3	129
9:2	207 223 251	14:1	133	8:65	265	11:6	359
9:9	13 329 335	14:21	52 57	10:10	501	16:5	359
9:10	330	14:22	315	10:12	611	22:11	610
9:11	338	14:24	84 604	21:7	611	23:5	359
9:12	338	14:26	301			50:1-2	525
9:13	222 330	15:16	265	2K. 16:20	332	51:5	624
	338	16:1	168			55:15	446
10:2	553	16:2	80 211	Is. 3:26	322	58:4	610
10:8	404	16:3	23 68 101	16:16	562	71:4	560
10:10	27 196	16:4	17	19:8	322	72:6	387
15:19	79 80	16:5	320	22:8	399	75:9	359
15:26	261	16:6	125 165	22:14	621	89:33	621
15:20	79		335	30:29	331	106:6	473
18:7	424	16:7	125			113:1	196
18:17	198 258	16:16	126 372	Jer. 2:3	589	116:1	198
19:3	471	17:3	305	3:22	621	116:13	360
19:7	575	17:6	553	6:4	161	127:1	414

632 INDICES

135:7	199	Job 1:5	619	9:28	133	3:8	519	
136:25	199	33:27-28	624			4:6	477	
137:7	399			Neh. 8:15	62	9:15	501	
144:8	319	Thr. 2:8	293			9:20	402	
				Dan. 9:5	473	26:23	387	
Pr. 10:3	480	Eccl. 7:12	611	10:5	201	28:19	277	
16:4	481	8:1	362			28:27	332	
10:27	397			1Chr. 16:17	247	29:17	332	
16:4	213	Esth. 2:21	451	27:1	125	29:28	127	
20:27	5	6:11-12	451	29:4	501	35:11	198	
23:31	362	7:8	356			30:18	331	
26:11	624	8:15-16	451	2 Chr. 1:13	520			
30:19	332							

Index of Talmudical quotations

Babylonian Talmud

Berakhot 9a			67	35b	75	64a	192	
	165	6b	65	36a	94	64b	191	
10b	332	7a	65	36b	87	65a	199 201	
19a	243	7b	5 6	37a	88		202	
32a	626	8a	4 5 10	38a	84	66a	207 569	
38a	101	9a	19	39a	84 88	67a	293	
38b	101	10b	16 18	40a	95	70a	226	
		12b	23 24 63	40b	93	70b	211	
Šabbat 14b	32	13a	15 25 118	41a	94 101	72a	228	
	35	13b	27	41b	247	73b	237 278	
15b	32	14a	27 31	42b	98 99	74a	240	
31b	460	15a	31	45b	65 103 104		243 246	
63b	488	16a	141	50a	430 474	75a	248 507	
64a	607	16b	32 255	51a	130	76a	245	
94a	141	20b	41 43	52a	135	78b	253 316	
94b	218	21a	43 50	53a	243 244	79a	262	
100b	271	21b	52	53b	143	80a	261 264	
111a	187	22a	53 57	54b	146	80b	269	
114b	145	22b	53	55a	147 148	81a	226	
123a	202	23a	53	55b	150	81b	266 270	
142a	101	24b	54	56a	152 332		271 277	
148b	314	26b	58	56b	153	82a	277 278	
		27b	61	57a	417	83a	282	
Eruvin 40b	372	28a	68	58a	161 164	84b	284 288	
79a	270	28b	51 68	59a	165 166	85a	290 291	
		33a	100	58a	166	86a	293 296	
Pesahim 4a	67	34a	46	61a	179 180	88b	257 309	
4b	22	34b	278	62b	181	89a	312	
6a	12 13 18 65	35a	80 81	63b	187	89b	306 312	

	315	25b	441	70a	580	71a	319
91a	305 319	26a	439 442	70b	583 584	102b	598
	320	27a	445	72b	40		
91b	305	28a	447	73a	591	Sotah 27b	301
93a	334	30a	455	73b	591 592	40b	452
93b	329 330	32b	457	74b	594	41b	452
	331 450	34a	440	78b	599	47a	487
94a	450	34b	460	80b	608		
95a	246	36b	472	81a	608	Nedarim	
95b	338	37a	477 488	82a	609	36a	301
97a	237 348		529	83a	610 611		
97b	347	37b	478	84b	614 615	Gittin 10a	13
98a	344	38a	479 481	85b	613 620		
99a	316 320		482	86b	621 624	Nazir 62b	270
99b	356	39a	560		626		
100a	356	39b	474 490	87a	624	Qiddušin	
107b	356		522 560	87b	625	76a	13
108a	358	40a	493	88a	599	78b	452
109a	358	42b	471				
114B	367	43b	496	Sukkah 5a	488	Bava batra	
116A	367	44b	499 501	11b	384	122a	486
117A	374	45a	425 504	48b	417		
117b	112	45b	506			Sanhedrin	
118a	199	47a	515	Roš Haššanah		5a	445
119b	87 375	47b	401	3a	387	47a	332
		49a	497 515	26a	586	101b	465
Yoma 2a	382	49b	497	31b	566	108b	7
2b	277	51b	519	32a	503		
3b	383	52a	518 338			Makkot 17a 101	
4a	385 394		541	Besah 23a	243		
5b	388	53a	418 503	37a	112	Ševuit 11b	533
7a	255	53b	522 523			12b	244 507
8b	397	54b	523 525	Megillah 4a	13	13a	620
9a	397 399	55a	406 528	17a	445	21a	101
9b	399	57b	530 533				
10a	396	58a	530	Taanit 16b	208	Avodah zarah	
11a	396	59a	536 538	24b	521	5b	342
11b	396		544			14b	136
12b	400 464	59b	529	Mo'ed qatan		16a	139
	587	60a	546	10b	149	34a	389
13a	406	60b	539 546	12a	149		
15a	437	61a	493 592	13b	131	Horaiot 5b 261	
17b	409	61b	248	15b	595 598		
19b 415 419 420		63a	492			Zevahim	
21b	501	63b	491	Hagigah 7b 226		7b	168
23a	433	66b	559			8a	170
24a	424	67a	563 566	Yebamot		9a	170 171
24b 424 425 435		68b	575	13b	133	11a	194
25a	204 433	69a	576	17b	328	18b	464
	452	69b	452	33b	300	19b	462

20b	452	109a	504	Kerotut		Me'ilah 7a	180
20a	431			6a	418 503 513	11a	544
21b	421	Menahot		7a	619 620	12a	436
22a	255	4a	101	6b	504	17b	488
22b	274	11a	515	22a	201	18a	101
29a	543	15a	261	25b	473 617	17b	291
32a	427	19a	246	28a	417		
34b	201 533	24b	437			Arakhin	
36b	198	26a	426	Hulin 4a	13	16a	588
52b	542	26b	425 426	7b	613	21a	157
58b	538		430 457	39a	171		
60b	509	52a	94	101a	75	Temurah	
69a	583	57a	187	121a	573	16a	346
82a	282	63b	213	129a	65	20a	347
88b	588	71a	152			30b	312
95a	534	88b	437	Bekhorot			
100b	320 323	95a	509	2b	139	Niddah 22b	607
101b	281	98a	191	33b	46	32a	596
104a	571	109b	522 561	35b	48	44b	291
104b	569 474		562	39b	204		
105a	571 572 573	111a	537	43b	445		

Jerusalem Talmud

Berakhot		8:5	518	3:3	400	4:8	416
1:1	450	9:12	452				
1:2	216			Šabbat		Roš Haššanah	
3:4	599	Ševiit		2	284	1:1	214
3:6	456	6:1	611	8	362	2:1	447
4:1	163			9	596		
6:1	91	Terumot		12	212	Besah	
8:1	363	8:8	39 45	14	608	1:1	190
8:6	613	6:1	608	16	562 615	1:7	108
				17	202	2:7	243
Peah		Maaser Šeni		19	209 224 233	3:5	112
1:1	620	2:1	596 604			5:2	313
6:1	71	3:2	350	Eruvin			
7:8	153			10	200 216	Megillah	
		Hallah				1:1	488
Demay		1:1	79	Šeqalim		1:8	22
2:3	32	4:12	305	2:4	176	1:12	399 400
				4:15	513	3:1	465
Kilaim		Orlah		5:2	481 482	4:5	579
2:5	220	3:1	51	8:5	31	4:12	396
6:2	44						
6:3	10	Bikkurim		Sukkah		Taaniot	
8:1	55	1:5	23	5:5	27	1:6	129 595 596

INDICES

Taaniot		5:2	34	4:5	307	8:2	286
2:1	208	5:6	374	Nazir		10:1	621
3:14	199	7:6	578	2:5	301		
4:2	126	7:7	452	3:4	220	Ševuot	
		9:5	341	6:13	331	1:3	473
Moed Qatan				7:1	583	1:9	618
1:5	325	Ketubot		8:1	327 328	1:10	557
2:5	131	1:1	407	9:2	266	4:1	552
3:1	243	1:10	614				
		3:1	77	Qiddušin		Avodah Zarah	
Hagigah		7:7	11	1:1	24 67	3:12	246
1:7	120	7:11	476	1:7	301		
2:4	125	8:11	32			Horaiot	
				Bava Meṣia		1:2	265
Yebamot		Nedarim		8:11	157	3:2	322
11:7	191	4:9	615			3:3	399
12:1	598	5:4	626	Sanhedrin			
				1:2	331	Niddah	
Sotah		Gittin		2:1	322	4:1	9 38
2:1	300	3:3	271	3:10	552		
2:3	478	4:4	72	5:3	22		

Mishnah

Breakhot		1:14	350	3:9	435		
2:7	123	1:15	215 350	4:3	434	Ševuot	
3:6	455	3:2	362	6:1	435	1:9	616
6:2	376	8:10	362			2:4	454 518
8:1	363	18:1	362	Hagigah		3:1	604
9:8	293	19:4	230	3:3	321	3:5	604
		21:10	111				
Peah				Nedarim		Avodah zarah	
7:8	153	Eruvin		4:3	312	3:14	58
		10:11	106				
Ševiit				Nazir		Idiut	
2:3	395	Šeqalim		7:4	327	5:6	405
9:4	135	4:5	504	8:1	327		
		4:6	513	9:2	269	Avot	
Terumot		5:7	437			3:11	220
8:7	38 39 40			Gittin			
8:8	42	Sukkah		3:3	406	Zevahim	
10:2	81	4:8	417			1:1	181 346
				Qiddušin		1:4	182
Maaser Šeni		Roš Haššanah		1:7	305	2:1	201 273
3:11	84	1:11	507			2:2	281
				Sanhedrin		2:3	548
Šabbat		Taanit		11:2	308	2:5	183

3:1	427 471	7:3	571	Temurah		Negaim	
3:2	517 530	8:5	467	3:3	556	12:5	43
3:6	281	11:5	242	4:1	237 346 556		
5:1	483 542	11:7	145 392	6:4	312	Tahorot	
5:7	571	12:4	410	7:6	62	1:1	573
5:8	375					4:5	32
6:6	476	Hulin		Tamid		7:1	67
8:8	434	9:2	286	1:1	293		
8:10	110			5:5	497	Parah	
8:12	281	Keritut		7:2	196	2:3	210
12:8	571	1:2	618			3:7	382
		5:1	201	Middot		3:11	382
Menahot		6:4	617	2:3	439	8:3	573
1:13	431			3:1	197 469	11:4	218
2:2	262	Bekhorot		3:5	501		
3:4	253 258 426	1:1	140	4:7	477 518	Nddah	
4:2	384	5:2	45 47			6:13	38
4:3	251			Kelim			
6:1	213	Meilah		17:11-12	601		
6:4	384	3:4	436 545				

Tosephta

Berakhot		2:14	64 66	7:3	306	Yoma	
5:1-2	356	2:17	87	7:7	316	1:2	396
		2:19	88	7:9	315	1:4	400
Peah 3:15	154	2:20	87	8:1	330	1:5	409
		2:21	87	8:2	330	1:6	412
Demay 1:29	503	3:5	94	8:5	332	1:8	415
		3:11	277	8:9	340	1:9	420 431
Terumot		3:16	143	8:10	305	1:12	433
7:18	41	3:19	152	8:11	342	1:13	435 440
		3:20	159	8:21	68	1:16	452
Orlah 7	58	3:22	153	9:12	347	2:4	479
		4:2	180	9:16	344	2:5	481
Šabbat		4:3	185	9:19	349	2:6	482
8:34	141	4:5	194	9:20	349	2;7	482
13:9	615	4:10	213	10:9	372	2:12	519
14:3	10	4:12	201	10:13	376	2:14	525 529
15:15	615	4:14	569			3:1	536
		5:3	226	Šeqalim		3:2	538
Pisha 1:1	5 6	5:4	214	3:3	406	3:4	546
1:3	10	5:8	240			3:13	564
1:4	12	6:1	256	Yom Yov		3:14	559
1:5	41	6:2	261 264	1:14	108	3:18	580
1:6	32	6:6	278	2:15	243	3:19	583
2:3	13	6:11	296	3:2	112	4:2	600

4:4	611	Gittin 7:4	406			2:9	270 271
4:5	599			Bekhorot		Parah	
4:14	625 626	Ševuot 1:4	433	2:3	139	3:1	382
4:16	622					3:8	416
		Zevahim		Ahilut			
Sukkah		6:9	544	10:5	14	Tahorot	
3:16	417			15:5	270	3:5	19
		Menahot		16:3	19	8:1	67
Sotah 13:6	559	10:33	553	18.7	44		
13:8	522	12:7-8	410	Zavim			

Midrashim and Related Texts

Mekhilta dR. Ismael 22 51 55 57 68 80 84 87 94 100 161 179 180 195 211 226 245 247 274 284 294 296 305 316 342 369 374 387 596 606 613

Mekhilta dR. Simeon ben Iohai 22 61 67 68 84 100 162 187 274 296 305 316 374

Sifra 53 56 58 61 77 145 152 161 166 170 189 204 211 245 266 280 281 291 339 342 381 384 390 393 394 404 406 409 416 424 425 428 436 444 458 462 464 466 472 488 491 507 509 515 528 529 530 533 536 538 541 542 548 557 573 575 587 606

Sifry Num . 13 80 166 293 326 330 331 338 382 398 408 433 487 560 569

Sifry zuta   164 184

Sifry Deut. 23 48 53 87 165 211 212 305 320 368 396 598 626

Seder Olam 280 393 402 445

Megillat Ta`anit   125

Semahot   322 323

Avot dR. Natan 332 401

Gen. rabba   7 129 450 476 487

Lev. rabba 386 398 401 521 619 625

Num. rabba 301 393 401 501

Cant. rabba 136 481 501

Eccl. rabba   136

Esther rabba   159

Tanhuma   57 296 401

Pesiqta dRav Cahana 397 398 401

Midrash Tehillim 195 370

Targum Onkelos 560

Targum pseudo-Jonathan 55 330 359 607

Dead Sea Scroll 4Q394 417

Rabbinic and Modern Authors

Abramson, S.	611	Rabbinovicz)	49		387 413 507 509 621
Adani, S.	146 348	Epstein, J. N.	8 358	Grätz, H.	401
Allon, N.	397	Geonic Respomsa Lyck		Ibn Ezra, Abtaham	179
Asaph, S.	627		8	Ibn Ghiat, Isaac	10
Diqduqe Sopherim (R.		Ginzberg, L.	210 335	Glueck, N.	627

Kahle, P. 478	Milham, M. E. (Apicius)	Raviah 19 64
Liebermann, S. 7 36 67	106	Rosenthak, E. S. 98
98 105 106 157 161 166	Rav Nissim 8 163	Sefer Ha`ittur 67
222 305 344 354 401	Or zarua 8 241 367	Shulhan Arukh 226 357
503 615	Pene Mosheh (M.	Sperber. D. 501
Löw, I. 81	Margolis) 61 164	Stern, S.E. 96
Loewinger. S. 170	Qorban heEdah ((D.	Sussman, J. 627
Luria, B. Z. 136	Fraenkel) 396	Tosaphot Yeshenim 577
Maharil 62	Ritba 577	579
Maimonides 78 89 309	Rashi 39 78 208 243 280	Tur 10
567	387 617	Yalqut Shimony 336
Meiri 11 208 310	Ravad 58	R. Yeruham 19
Midrash Haggadol 87	Ravan 65	

Greek, Latin, Arabic, and Hebrew Words

ἀγκύλη	202	κόλλα	97	τρώξιμον	159
ἀσθενής	357 457 598	κόλλιξ	88	τρώξιμα	89
βουλευταί	397	κοχλίας	433	τύπος	88
βουλή	409	κώθων	498	ὑποθήκη	72
βουλιμία.	612	λαμπάς, -άδος,	478	φερνή	159
δήλωμα	197 451	λιμήν	479	χλῆδος	98
διάδοχοι	567 575	λοξόν	536	ψῆφος	519
διπλόν ποτήριον	359	λυγμός	599	ψυκτήρ	497
δισάκκιον	25	μαγίς	513		
ἔπαρχος	*615*	μάλαγμα	92	castra	615
ἐπικάρσιον	325	μηρία	567	cortices	130
ἐπικώμιον	375	αἰ μοῖραι	168	cothon	498
ἐπὶ κῶμον	369	ναρθήκιον	499	Impilia	598
ἐπίτροπος	299	πάρεδρος	380	missicus	19
ἐσχάρα	244	πλατεῖα (sc., ὁδός)	70	mulus	396
ζῦθος	97	πόλεμος	536	muries	362 601
ζύμη	97	πομπή	435	numerus	157
θέρμος	91	προϊεραθέντες	397	pars	498
ἰδιώτης	148	προλήνια	106	pompa	435
καθέδριον	489	πύξινον	476	quasso	98
καῖρος	211	σημεῖον	613	splenium	54
καλολογέω	325	σπληνίον	54	suetum	399
κάλπη	469	στολή	576	tractum	106
καλῶς	325 459	στρατήγιον	409		
καταφερές	95	στρατιώτης	328		
κατήγωρ, κατήγορος,		συμβόλαια	315	استمرّ	245
	586	συνήγορος	586	جمـيـز	154
κεντρόω	209	τάραξιν	518	خسّ	89
κεφαλωτόν	159	τεταρτεύς	362	ضرف	102
κιβωτός	106	τράγημα	356		
κόγχη	478	τρακτόν	106		

فرط	462	كبوتر (Farsi)	419	מצביע	422
فشى	423	ملوة	448	נקק	626
مذى	102			צוצל	562
قنر	503	גומנייא	604	רדף	303
				שו	600

Subject Index

Accidental menstruation	395
Altars, private	85
Amidah prayer	580
Animal, creeping	208
Animals, as *muqseh*	112
Anointed for war	401 403
Asherah wood	58
Azazel	485
Baking *mazzah*	114
Beauty treatment	99
Beer, Median	101
Bet happeras	52 327
Bone materials	284
Bran	91
Calendar computation	507
Canaan, biblical boundaries	132
Carcass meat, usufruct	55
Charity chest	355
Commandments specific for the Land	611
Confessing, multiple times	625
Cup (measure)	363
Daily flour offering	446
Date, volume of	600
Day of Atonement readings	577
Day of Atonement, praparing food	145
Debt, minimal	77
Dedicated animal, offspring	237
Deep mourner, mourning	281 323
Denar, Gordian	501
Disqualification by intent	281
"Do" as strict command	388
Elevation offering, atoning	541 618
Elimination by declaration	65 119
Emergency, acting in an	614
Equal cut, conditions	607
Equal expressions	207
Equalization payments	486
Far-away place	222
Fast, Monday and Thursday	129
Feeding forbidden food	58
Fence around the Law	23
Festival offering	225
First Fruits	84
Flesh, as limb	588
Follow-holiday	302
Food, in synagogue	8
Forbidden and liable	592
Foreskin, of fruit	55
Gates of Jerusalem	293
Gift to Heaven	341
Global cooling	98
Gold	500
Grain, object of worship	75
Grave of the abyss	268 270 274
Hallah	75
Hallah, obligation of	108
Hallah, on Passover	107
Hallah. as *muqseh*	111
Hallel, Egyptian	195 336 371
Hallel, great	198
Haroset	93 365
Heads of Diaspora	578
Heating iron bars	460
Heave, guarded	46
Heave, leavened	74
Heave, possibly impure	35
Heave, stolen	75
Hermeneutical rule 12	170
Hermeneutical rule 3	330

High Priest, daily offering	384
High Priest, Head of Commonwealth	397
High Priest, monogamous	381
High Priest's breastplate	464
High Priest's diadem	411 489
Hippos	448
Holiday, second day	191
Holiest of Holies	493
Hours, counting	20
House of Eutinoos	414
Immersion, ineffective	456
Immersion, precautionary	455
Impure, exile of	293 509
Impurity, after birth	61 317
Impurity, biblical	32
Impurity, by motion	571
Impurity, by purifying	408
Impurity, derivative	31
Impurity, emanating from own body	271 274 300
Impurity, menstrual	9 10 38
Impurity, non-menstrual	38
Impurity, of garments	572
Impurity, of Gentile land	32 44
Impurity, of Gentile	326
Impurity, of gonorrhea	264 317
Impurity, of hands	32
Impurity, of metal	34
Impurity, preparation for	53
Impurity, squeezed	270
Impurity, tent	270
Incense, payment for	513
Incest and adultery	399
Inflated prices	66
Inflation	312
Issaron	410
Kutah yogurt	25 96
Leavened matter	78
Leavened matter, Temple's	70
Leavening, abandoned	70
Leavening, Gentile's	18 49 64
Leavening, liability for	190
Lettuce	89
Levels of sanctity	400
Life blood	201
Lifting heave	42
Linen cloth, quality of	467
Lupines	91
Majority	101
Man's house	301
Marriage, preliminary	24
Meaning of הִשָּׁמֶר	617
Medical procedures on holiday	149
Mem privative	176
Mina, maneh	503
Minor Prophets	579
Minors, fasting	609
Miqweh, invalidated	460
Modius	159
Money horns	406
Moses as High Priest	389
Muqseh, biblical	157
Nazir's bread	84
Ne`ilah prayer	625
Nest	406
Oil to be burned	249
Omer	213 258 553
Ox, goring	54
Parhedrin lodge	380
Parsing a verse	56
Patriarchate	210
Pesah and feast of *mazzot*	35
Pesah	36
Pesah, as public offering	166
Pesah, for slaves	306
Pesah, for women	305
Pesah, freeloaders	315
Pesah, in impurity	333 338
Pesah, intermingled	353
Pesah, lost and found	194 347
Pesah, of convert	309 319
Pesah, subscription to	311
Pesah, too old	194
Pesah, using a calf	236
Pesah,, Second	329
Phineas's priesthood	281
Piggul	61 171 534 548
Plural, unspecified	424 444
Pollinating date palms	151
Preparing food for non-holiday	145
Priest in charge of Red Cow	381
Priest, invested	405
Prohibition in passive voice	61

Property, abandoned	71	Synagogue on Temple Mount	576
Proselyte's estate	71		
Public readings	579	Tearing away the yoke	620
Pumpkin, used as vessel	105	Temple domain, sitting in	204 274
Pure tithe, redemption of	84	Temple lottery	422
Purification sacrifice, lost and found	346	Temple Mount, stoa	26
		Temple service, musical	127
Qab	495	Temple timekeeping	26
Quantity, insignificant	104	Temple trees	153
Quartarius	601	Temple, as Lebanon	501 560
		Temple, donations to	155
Raising sheep and goats	136	Temple, executive officer	29
Rape, statutory	300	*Tevul-yom*	29
Reciting "Shema'"	152	Text, abbreviated	478
Religious observance, additional	131	Thanksgiving bread	26 63 78 86
Religious observance, local	133	The Name	468
Repartition of taxes	409	"Time" benediction	372
		Tithe, animal	226
Sabbath of Jewish animals	138	Translation rules, hermeneutical	52 53
Sabbath rest	218		
Sabbatical produce	134	Urim and Tummin oracle	591
Sacrifice, intent	170 171 180	Usha decrees	32
Sacrifice, of uncircumcised	170		
Sacrifice, suspended	62 617	Vessels, dedication of	465
Sacrifice, ungarded	375 376	Vow and voluntary offering	411
Sadducee rules	416	Vow of usufruct	155
Selling weapons	141	Vulgar	33
Sheqel	494		
Shew Bread	145	Wages of sin	312
Sins against neighbor	623	Washing hands and feet	421 430 431
Sins atoned	615	Watches, priestly	469
Sins, categories of	469	Water offering	417
Slaughter, minimal	456	Wheat kernels	92
Stadion	563	Witness, single	447
Status quo, permanence of	271	Women's obligations	101
Substitute sacrifice	343 344		
Substitution of sancta	555	*Zin*	494
Sycamore wood	153		